Encyclopedia of Cremation

Encyclopedia of Cremation

Edited by

DOUGLAS J. DAVIES
with
LEWIS H. MATES

ASHGATE

Published by
Ashgate Publishing Limited
Gower House
Croft Road
Aldershot
Hants GU11 3HR
England

Ashgate Publishing Company
Suite 420
101 Cherry Street
Burlington, VT 05401-4405
USA

Ashgate website: http://www.ashgate.com

British Library Cataloguing in Publication Data
Encyclopedia of cremation
   1. Cremation – Encyclopedias
   I. Davies, Douglas James   II. Mates, Lewis H.
   393.2'03

Library of Congress Cataloging-in-Publication Data
Encyclopedia of cremation / editor, Douglas J. Davies with Lewis H. Mates.
        p. cm.
   Includes bibliographical references.
   ISBN 0-7546-3773-5 (alk. paper)
   1. Cremation–Encyclopedias. I. Davies, Douglas James. II. Mates, Lewis H.

   GT3330.E53 2005
   393'.2'03–dc22

                                                                                2004027893
ISBN 0 7546 3773 5

Typeset by Bournemouth Colour Press, Parkstone, Poole.
Printed in Great Britain by TJ International Ltd, Padstow.

Contents

Illustrations

Abbreviations

Abbreviations

AAC	*Asociación Argentina de Cremación* (Argentine Cremation Association)
CAA	Cremation Association of America
CANA	Cremation Association of North America
CDD	Council for the Disposal of the Dead
CSA	Cremation Society Archive, University library, University of Durham. This abbreviation when used in the References following an encyclopedia entry indicates that a substantial amount of information for that entry has been derived from this archival material. A detailed description of this archive is given in 'Cremation Society Archive Sources' at p. 474.
CSGB	Cremation Society of Great Britain
FBCA	Federation of British Cremation Authorities
ICF	International Cremation Federation
LAPC	*Liga Argentina Pro Cremación* (Argentine pro-Cremation League)
LCC	London Cremation Company

Acknowledgements

Very many people have been involved in producing this volume. It began as a conversation between myself and Roger Arber, then Secretary of the Cremation Society of Great Britain, and Secretary-General of the International Cremation Federation. That was at a conference in Adelaide in 1996. Two significant things flowed from that and subsequent meetings. First, the Cremation Society of Great Britain decided to offer its considerable archive on permanent loan to the University of Durham and, second, the Golders Green Foundation made a series of generous grants to the University of Durham that not only enabled the removal, cataloguing and conservation of the archive but also the funding of a series of research assistants to work with me on an encyclopedia. These included Marilyn Marks and Simon Oram to whom I am grateful for the work done in establishing the archive at Durham and beginning the work of contacting contributors.

The longest-serving of these research assistants has been Dr Lewis Mates without whose steadfast commitment to liaising with contributors the publication of this volume would have been severely delayed. More than that, he has also demonstrated his competence as a modern historian in the extensive research he has pursued within the archive, and in the numerous articles written for this book. I warmly thank him, too, for his personal support and encouragement on this project, especially when I have, inevitably, been engaged in other tasks of research, teaching and university administration.

I thank Dr John Hall, University Librarian, for accepting the Archive of the British Cremation Society, and also the special archives librarian Elizabeth Rainey for a great deal of practical work in its removal to and establishment at Durham. Another benefit of the Golders Green Foundation support was that Lisa Kazmier, then at Rutgers University, New York, was able to come to Durham for a year as a Visiting Fellow to work on the archive. She has also contributed to this volume and I thank her for her work here. Numerous undergraduate and graduate students at Durham have also undertaken items of research on the archive, and some of these are reflected in particular entries; others have also helped with administrative duties. Together I would thank, Jenny Arkell, Rachel Bird, Tom Richardson and Martha Middlemiss. Stephen Ahrnke, Jamie Alvarez, Andrew Boardman, Artyom Chernikin, Marco Conti, Lucy Grimshaw, Eddie Huilbens and Ana Ludovico have assisted in translation work, while Helen Mobey and Ian Paterson have helped with tabulating statistics. I also thank Joseph Paddison for detailed assistance in proof-reading. Thanks to all of them.

We also thank all our contributors – the bedrock of this *Encyclopedia* – for their work; many of them have produced material that is published here for the first time. We are particularly appreciative of work done by Anna Salice, Cyril Schafer, Chris Molyneaux and, especially, Robert Nicol. Lewis Mates particularly expresses thanks to the following for information that might otherwise have been difficult or impossible to access: Carlos Roberto Belloso, Pedro Fernandez Benet, Osvaldo Chernitsky, Alejandra Forestier, César Augusto, Jaramillo Gomez, Guillermo Herrera, Eduardo Alvarado Lewis, Peter Mates, Pilar Nunez, Augusto Vargas, Liliana Castillo, Eduardo Dalesson, Hugo Estrella, Ricardo J. Fernandez, Alberto Gerardo Ferretty, Oscar Fidanza, Carlos Jure, Alberto Karmona, Gustavo Labriola, Beatriz Laufer, Sonja Leferink, Monica A. Lifieri, Emilio Alfonso Priede, John A. Kinahan, Pierre Vidallet, Sui sum Leung, Choy-hung Chong, Cristian Alvarez, Diego Casanova, Daniel de Michele, Juan Martín, Marcela Miozzo, Sergio E. Visacovsky, Aloyse Schmitz and Eric Spencer.

We are grateful to the Walker Gallery, Liverpool, for permission to use Poussin's *The Ashes of Phocion*, and Fournier's *The Funeral of Shelley* as illustrations. We also thank Pontypridd Museum, South Wales, for the painting of Dr William Price, John Murray, publisher, for permission to use John Betjeman's poem 'Aldershot Crematorium' and to Blackthorne Records for the use of Ewan McColl's 'The Joy of Living'.

The Cremation Society of Great Britain office has always been available as has Roger Arber: I thank him and his staff – in particular, Sue Jackson and Gillian Payne – for their ongoing helpfulness. Personally, I also thank the Society's president, Earl Grey, for his encouragement over the years and, through his capacity in connection with the Golders Green Foundation, for the financial support without which the work behind this volume could not have been undertaken. Lady Grey, too, cannot be forgotten as a welcome voice at the Society's gatherings.

Finally, I am more than grateful to Sarah Lloyd of Ashgate Publishers for her advice and sustained interest in this endeavour. She knew, best of all, just what such a volume entailed and was not dismayed when one requested, 'just a week or so more'.

Douglas J. Davies
Durham University

List of Contributors

GENERAL EDITOR

Douglas J. Davies. Professor in the Study of Religion at Durham University with extensive publications in the anthropology and sociology of religion. He holds a PhD from Nottingham University and a D.Litt. from Oxford University, and has received an Honorary Dr Theol. from the University of Uppsala. xvii–xxvi, 4, 8, 47–56, 57–60, 95–6, 106–7, 116, 125, 131, 143–6, 152–3, 165–7, 186–95, 197, 206–7, 210–11, 220, 232, 248, 259–60, 301–5, 310–11, 315–17, 320, 333, 335, 359–63, 373–4.

EDITORIAL ASSISTANT

Lewis H. Mates. Research Assistant at the University of Durham. A modern historian holding BA, MA and PhD degrees from the University of Newcastle. 28–36, 37–47, 83–9, 103–6, 148–51, 158–9, 179–80, 197–206, 231–2, 233, 242–7, 251–6, 262–71, 292–8, 299, 300–301, 305–10, 311–14, 318–19, 334–5, 338–42, 364–6, 416–22, 424–8, 431–74.

CONTRIBUTORS

Hei Jean Ahn. Student, University of Durham, England. 336.

Jenny Arkell. History graduate, University of Durham. Now works for the University of Southampton, England. 262.

Paul Badham. Professor of Theology and Religious Studies and Director of the MA Programme in 'Death and Immortality' at the University of Wales, Lampeter. 376–7.

Paul T. Barber. Research Associate at the Fowler Museum of Cultural History, UCLA. 410–12.

Anastasios Barkas. Priest in the Greek Orthodox Church of Thyateira and Great Britain. 226–7.

Jo Bath. Historical researcher, based in north-east England. 170–71, 175–8.

Andrew Bernstein. Assistant Professor of History at Lewis and Clark College, England. 279–81.

Christopher Binns. Formerly Lecturer in Russian and East European Politics at the European Institute, London School of Economic and Political Science, England. 370–71.

Jan Bondeson. Senior Lecturer at the University of Wales College of Medicine. 348–9.

Panagiotis J. Boumis. Professor Emeritus, University of Athens, Greece. 225–6.

Mariana Caixeiro. Honorary Researcher, Department of Anthropology, University Complutense of Madrid, Spain. 234–8, 371–2.

Maria Canella. Researcher, Department of Social Science and Historical Documentation, University of Milan, Italy. 21–8.

Wesley Carr. Dean of Westminster Abbey, London. 423.

Clive Chamberlain. Formerly Lecturer in Fuel and Combustion science at the University of Leeds, Managing Director of Evans Universal Ltd and Vice-President of Evans and Tabo Universal organization (now Facultatieve Technologies Ltd). Currently running his own company, Combustion Technology Consultancy Ltd. 132–3, 146–8.

Juan Luis Chulilla. Lecturer in Social Sciences, Philosophy and Methodology, Director of the Research Department at Universidad Pontificia de Salamanca en Madrid, Spain. 382–5.

Alice Collett. Doctoral Researcher in Sanskrit and Buddhism at Cardiff University, Wales. 96–100.

Peter Collins. Lecturer in Anthropology at the University of Durham, England. 351–2.

Fulvio Conti. Professor in Modern History at the University of Florence, Italy. 273–5.

Kate Crosby. Lecturer in Pali and Theravada Buddhism at the School of Oriental Studies, London, England. 96–100.

Colin Crowder. Lecturer, Department of Theology and Religion, University of Durham, England. 181–4.

Curt Dahlgren. Professor in the Sociology of Religion and Religious Studies, University of Lund, Sweden. 60–64.

Magdalini Dargentas. Doctoral Researcher in Social Psychology, Ecole des Hautes Etudes en Sciences Sociales, Paris, France. 223–5.

Christie Davies. Emeritus Professor of Sociology, University of Reading, England. 249–51.

Oliver T.P.K. Dickinson. Reader, Department of Classics and Ancient History, University of Durham, England. 6–7.

Liu Fengming. Engineer, Shanghai Research Institute of Cremation Technology, People's Republic of China. 120–23, 133–5, 151–2.

Shirley Firth. Freelance lecturer and writer. 238–40.

Claes Foghmoes. Chairperson, Association of Danish Crematoria, Denmark. 164–5.

Ute Georgeacopol-Winischhofer. Associate Professor in History of Architecture and Industrial Archaeology at the Vienna University of Technology, Austria. 70–77.

Xavier Godart. Member of the Belgian Cremation Society. 89–91.

Phil Gore. Funeral Director, Margate, England, and Doctoral Student, Brunel University, England. 94, 195–6, 261.

Dmitri Gorokhov. Graduate, University of Durham, England. Lives in St Petersburg. 369–70.

Hilary J. Grainger. Professor and Associate Dean, University of Wolverhampton, England. 15–17, 19–21, 65, 126–7, 128–9, 211–12, 212–15, 220–23, 343, 389–91, 401.

Arin Greenwood. Writer and lawyer, Saipan island near Guam. 175.

Daniel Grolin. Executive Board Member, Association for Bahá'í Studies English-speaking Europe. 80

Göran Gustafsson. Professor Emeritus, Sociology of Religion, Lund University, Sweden. 393–4.

Robert W. Habenstein. Formerly Professor of Sociology, University of Missouri, USA. 401–7.

Børge Hansen. Member of the Danish Cremation Association, Denmark. 162–4.

Graham Harvey. Lecturer in Religious Studies at the Open University, England. 4–5.

C.T.R. Hayward. Professor of Hebrew, University of Durham, England. 64–5.

Elfi Heider. Research Student on Japanese and German funerals. 66, 217–18.

Jan Hermanson. Assistant Professor in Psychology of Religion, Lund University, Sweden. 60–64.

Marianne Herold. Engineer, Director of Funeral Services Zurich, Switzerland. 287, 395–6.

Nils G. Holm. Professor of Comparative Religion at Åbo Akademi University, Finland. 184–6.

Zhang Hongchang. Administrator (section chief) Funeral Affairs, Department of Social Welfare and Social Affairs of the Ministry of Civil Affairs of the People's Republic of China. 121–3, 123–5, 261.

Leo Howe. Senior Lecturer in Social Anthropology, University of Cambridge, England. 81–3.

Li Jian. Assistant Research Fellow and project official, Department of Social Welfare and Social Affairs, Ministry of Civil Affairs, People's Republic of China. Also Administrator, funeral affairs, Central Government, People's Republic of China. 56–7, 121–3, 123–5, 261.

Zhu Jinlong. Director of the Shanghai Funeral and Interment Centre, Vice-President of the Shanghai Funeral and Interment Society, Chairman of the Cemetery Committee of China Funeral Society, People's Republic of China. 56–7, 121–3, 127, 400–401.

Katherine Johnson. Student, University of Durham, England. 227–8.

Peter Jupp. Minister of Westgate United Reformed Church, Peterborough, founding Editor of *Mortality*, Visiting Fellow in Sociology, University of Bristol, Director of the London Cremation Company plc, Chairman of the Council of The Cremation Society of Great Britain. 113–16, 135–42, 353–8.

Lisa Kazmier. Doctoral graduate, Rutgers University, New Brunswick, USA. Previously Golders Green Research Fellow University of Durham, England. 101–2, 129–30, 216, 398.

J.M.H.J. Keizer. President and Chief Executive Officer, 'Facultatieve Group', Holland and Board member of various international organizations. From 2003, Secretary-General of the International Cremation Federation. xxvi–xxvii, 165, 168, 170, 286–7, 292, 326, 352, 376, 409–10, 412.

Elizabeth Kent. Graduate Student, University of Durham, England. xxvi–xxvii.

Angelika Kretschmer. Librarian at the University of Erlangen-Nürnberg, Germany and doctoral graduate on Japanese religion. 279–83.

Ulf Lagerström. Managing Director, Swedish Federation of Cemeteries and Crematoria and President of the International Cremation Federation. 392–3.

Sonja Leferink. Researcher in Cultural Anthropology, Utrecht University, Netherlands. 36–7.

Pamela N. Lindell. Assistant Professor of Anthropology, Sacramento City College, USA. 93–4.

Eric T.L. Love. Teacher of History, University of Colorado, Boulder, USA. 8–9, 131, 299–300, 317–18, 358–9.

Ana Ludovico. Graduate, Universities of Durham and Kent at Canterbury, England. 1–4.

Bernard McHale. Former manager cemeteries and crematoria. Now Secretary of the Federation of British Cremation Authorities. 174–5, 181.

Jaqueline I. McKinley. Archaeologist, osteoarchaeologist, Senior Project Officer of Wessex Archaeology, England. 9–14.

Bruno Maldoner. Architect and sculptor, Councillor in the Austrian Federal Office for Historic Monuments (Bundesdenkmalamt), Austria. 15, 18–19, 91, 180, 241, 372.

Emma Mana. Doctoral graduate, Researcher in Contemporary History, University of Turin, Italy. 178–9.

Richard Marshall. Managing Director of F.G. Marshall Ltd, Memorial Studios, England, ecclesiastical craftsman. 92–3.

Martin A. Mills. Lecturer in the Anthropology of Religion, University of Aberdeen. 398–9.

Chris J. Molyneux. Former President of the NFDA South Africa, former Executive Director of the HT Group [Pty] Ltd. Doctoral graduate, funeral choice in South Africa. 378–82.

Karen Morrow. Senior Lecturer in Law, University of Leeds, England. 343.

Stanislav Motycka. Secretary-General, Czech Cremation Association, Czechoslovakia. 157–8.

John Newton. Doctoral student, history of ghosts – apparitions, University of Durham, England. 107–9, 112.

Robert Nicol. Australian historian and researcher. 67–70.

Marco Novarino. General Secretary, 'Fabretti Foundation'. 207–10, 337–8.

David Noy. Lecturer in Classics, Lampeter, University of Wales. 366–9.

Charles Owiredu. Lecturer in Biblical Studies, Central University College, Ghana. 219–20, 287–9.

Judith Okely. Professor of Social Anthropology, University of Hull, England. 228–9.

Börje Olsson. Technical Director, Stockholm Cemeteries Administration, Sweden. 65, 300, 394–5.

Christopher Pancheri. An administrator for Celestis, Inc., Houston, Texas, USA. 117–18.

Chang-Won Park. Doctoral student in theology and religion, University of Durham, England. 289–91.

Brian Parsons. Doctoral graduate, University of Westminster, London, England. Active in funeral service education. 399–400.

Stephen Prothero. 396–7, 407–9.

Timothy Pursell. Professor of History at the University of Alaska Fairbanks, USA. 168–9, 218–19, 284–6, 323–4, 373.

Francisco Queiroz. Lecturer in History of Architecture and Urban Planning in the Escola Superior Artística do Porto, Oporto, Portugal. 344–7.

Thorsteinn Ragnarsson. Manager, Funeral Services, Fossvogur, Reykjavik, Iceland. 196–7, 256–9.

Erling Rikheim. Former Director of the Association of Norwegian Insurance Companies and Former Board Member of the Norwegian Cremation Society. 329–32.

Julie Rugg. Cemetery Research Group, University of York, England. 118

Anna Salice. Researcher in Civil Law, University of Camerino, Italy. 111, 277–9.

Cyril Schafer. Doctoral student in anthropology, University of Otago, New Zealand. 326–9.

Alan Schofield. Masters graduate in Comparative Religion, former funeral director. 428–9.

Bruno Segre. Lawyer and journalist, editor of the magazines *L'Ara* (Italian Cremation Federation-IFC), *L'Incontro* (politics-culture monthly), and *Libero Pensiero* (Association of the Free-Thinker 'Giordano Bruno'). Former Chairman of the IFC and Vice-President of the Cremation Society of Turin. 276–7.

Bal Krishna Sharma. Lecturer in Religions, Nepal. Doctoral Student, University of Wales. 325–6.

Berit Sigvallius. Osteologist, National Heritage Board, Archaeological Excavations Dept., Stockholm, Sweden. 412–15.

David Smale. Extensive experience in crematorium management. Editor of Davies' *Law of Burial, Cremation and Exhumation*. 159–60, 160–62.

Rolf Solheim. Counsellor of the Norwegian Humanist Association and a Humanist Funeral Officiant. 249.

Marina Sozzi. Scientific Director of the Fabretti Foundation, Torino, Italy. 179, 314–15.

Eric Spencer. Former Chief Executive of the Great Southern Group. Now Organist and Master of the Choristers of the Anglican Cathedral at Port Elizabeth, South Africa. 101.

Giorgio Spina. Professor of English Literature at the University of Genoa, Editor of *La Scelta*, magazine of the Cremation Society of Genoa. 158, 216–17.

Jack M. Springer. Executive Director of the Cremation Association of America since 1982. 102–3.

Christian Stadelmann. Historian of civilization in Vienna. 77–9, 375–6, 412–13, 423–4.

Walter Tucci. Author of biographical dictionary of those cremated in Turin, edited by the 'Ariodante Fabretti' Foundation. 127–8, 283–4.

Colin Turner. Lecturer in Islamic Studies at the University of Durham, England. 271–3.

Yon van der Pijl. Assistant Professor in Cultural Anthropology, Utrecht University, Netherlands. 391–2.

Anthony J. Watkins. Control Horticulturist, City of Windhoek's Parks, Recreation and Cemeteries Division, South Africa. 175, 320–3.

Ken West MBE. Extensive experience in cemeteries and crematorium management. Awarded the MBE in 2002 for services to burial and cremation in Great Britain. 172–4.

Stephen White. Formerly Senior Lecturer at Cardiff Law School, Wales. Member of the Council of the Cremation Society of Great Britain. 94–5, 119, 131–2, 154–6, 162, 167–8, 230, 333, 336, 348, 349–51, 374–5, 385–9, 397–8.

Zuo Yongren. Administrator (assistant inspector) in funeral affairs, Department of Social Welfare and Social Affairs, Ministry of Civil Affairs, People's Republic of China. 121–3, 123–5, 261.

Gao Yueling. Investigator for the Department of Social Welfare and Social Affairs, Ministry of Civil Affairs, People's Republic of China. Also Administrator in Funeral Affairs of the Central Government of the People's Republic of China. 56–7, 121–3, 123–5, 261.

Introduction

Cremation is one of the elementary forms of human behaviour, uniting, as it does, fire and death, two of the most fundamental features of existence. In cremation, fire combines with death not simply as some mechanical technique of corpse combustion, even though at certain times and in certain cultures that industrial image may predominate, but also as a value-laden and socially grounded means of coping with death and reflecting upon the meaning of life. This social frame elevates the process beyond mere combustion to a higher domain of action – one rooted in beliefs drawn from myths and religious doctrines and ritually expressed in symbolic ways that give meaning to life and significance to human destiny. The mid-nineteenth century witnessed the intellectual birth of modern cremation and the later twentieth its real implementation and growth. As the twenty-first century begins, the significantly high levels of cremation in many parts of northern and western Europe stand as a backdrop for a rapid increase of acceptance of cremation in many other parts of the world.

This *Encyclopedia of Cremation* seeks a broad account of the nature of cremation across the ages and within many different societies. It is the first single volume devoted to such an extensive task. To achieve its goal it has sought contributors from the academic, as well as from the practical, world of cremation management. The differences of interest present in those worlds are represented in the many articles produced through the generous participation of authors. Often, it has been necessary to generate information from primary resources precisely because cremation has seldom attracted widespread intellectual attention. Although it would be easy to view the *Encyclopedia*'s entries as so many distinct and separate items, any sustained reading will show how the practice of cremation serves as one potentially fruitful means of access to a culture and its view of the world. It will soon become apparent how cremation has served as a means of expressing key cultural values. Indeed, cremation has served, at different times and places, as both a fundamental means of religious symbolism and a crucial form of religious and political protest.

This Introduction indicates key aspects of these social expressions of value and also highlights the interdisciplinary nature of this *Encyclopedia* with its sociological, psychological, historical, legal, philosophical, theological and religious dimensions as well as its scientific, medical and engineering aspects of human endeavour. Attention is also drawn to architecture and art surrounding the emergence of cremation whilst not forgetting the economic and political dimensions of the practice. Throughout this volume, too, some literary and poetic responses to cremation are also described.

Even though it attempts a representative expression of material on cremation, this volume lays no claim to an exhaustive coverage. It is but a first step in the process of providing material both for specialists and for those engaged in the practice of cremation. Some entries are full and detailed, whilst others are very short. The longer articles provide information on little-known topics, drawing on primary resources, often those of the Archive of the British Cremation Society housed at the University of Durham, England. Sometimes the length depends entirely on the availability, or lack, of information on the subject. It has not always, for example, proved possible to find individuals with appropriate knowledge or expertise. The editors have allowed each author to engage with the subject as they will and, although a degree of uniformity has been sought, it was decided to allow some entries to take the form of longer essays whilst others were permitted to remain more note-like in character. The differing styles of authors have been respected, given that some write from specific and very diverse academic traditions and others from a practical engagement with cremation and death services.

Because some of the entries are, necessarily, brief and easily isolate cremation from its social context and the rich associations and networks that naturally occur in cultural life, in this Introduction we outline ten contextual themes that surround cremation and furnish its cultural rationale. Other entries that complement this Introduction in a significant way include **ashes**, **literary cremation** and **ritual and symbolism**. The great majority of topics mentioned in the remainder of this Introduction have entries of their own. In addition to consulting these, the reader will find cross-references after appropriate entries and will also find the final Index of considerable value. It should be noted that there is no separate entry for Great Britain because of the large number of separate, specialist contributions related to that country, as the Index will make clear.

CONTEXTUAL THEMES

Tradition

Cremation has long been established as the prime funeral rite in many cultures of the world, where it frames life and helps to explain its nature and destiny. For some prehistoric, ancient and classical societies and civilizations, evidence of cremation lies in urn-burials, mounds and the literary creations of classical texts. Accounts of cremation and the interment of cremated remains are found in Homer's *Iliad* with its description of the funerals of the heroes Achilles and Patroclus and their wine-washed cremated remains that are, subsequently, buried. Likewise, in the eighth-century BCE *Odyssey*, Elpenor's body and armour are burned while comrades 'with the tears streaming down [their] cheeks' perform the funeral rites for him, and build a barrow above his remains marked by a stone and an oar from their ship (Homer, *Odyssey*, 12:10–15). Something of the classical world is reflected in Poussin's *Ashes of Phocion*, illustrated in this book and described in the entry, on **art**.

After the establishment of Christian religion in Europe from the fifth century, cremation was increasingly abandoned, and the symbolism of earth burial came to be identified with the burial of Christ and with the final resurrection of the body. The Emperor Charlemagne criminalized cremation in the Christian West in 789 AD and, except for its use on battlefields to save the dead from the ravages of the enemy and as an emergency measure during plagues, as in the Black Death of the seventeenth century, burial has been deemed the normal Christian funeral rite within the overall scheme of the Christian sacraments. Apart from the unusual seventeenth-century treatise of Sir Thomas Browne on urn burial, *Hydriotaphia* (1658), prompted by archaeological discoveries of his day, and the brief French revolutionary attempt to foster cremation in antagonism to Christian burial in the 1790s, it was not until the nineteenth century that any serious interest in cremation developed. And in that most creative of centuries, with its dramatic complement of scientific discovery, expansion in engineering and the rapid energy of the Industrial Revolution, cremation emerged as a topic of debate in medical and philosophical circles. Even so, academic interest in these themes remained minimal. Even Ariès' magisterial work on European death largely ignores cremation, and, when it emerges, analysis is negligible (1981: 577–78, 600). Here, this *Encyclopedia* has its part to play in drawing attention not only to crucial social and historical issues, but also to contemporary authors who have made, and are making, considerable contributions to an understanding of cremation, both in traditional contexts and in the modern world.

In those traditional contexts cremation is familiar in the case of India and the Indian-influenced cultures of Buddhism and Sikhism. Basic to Hinduism is the belief that the lifeforce underlying human existence is not restricted to one lifetime but undergoes very many transmigrations. This, inevitably, means that the 'self' is not simply and inevitably linked to any one bodily person. In symbolic terms cremation is an extremely appropriate form or vehicle for expressing this idea of the ongoing existence of a lifeforce whether in terms of reincarnation or, as in classical Greek, ideas of the soul fleeing the prison-house of the body to return to its realm of true being.

It is in its traditional Hindu version that cremation may be seen as an extensive scheme that frames and interprets the nature of human destiny as, for example, in Jonathan Parry's (1994) study. He describes how, in symbolic terms, the human embryo resulted from the combination of male seed making bones and female blood providing flesh. The spirit came to the foetus in the womb, entering through the cranial suture of the skull, with the growing embryo in a metaphorical sense being 'cooked' by the 'heat' of the womb. At the end of life a similar symbolic reversal sees the heat of the funeral pyre separating flesh from bones and the rite of skull cracking frees the spirit for its samsara journey influenced by the karma or merit accrued during life. The fire becomes the medium of offering the body as a kind of last sacrifice to deity while the remains should be placed in the sacred river Ganges. Thus, cremation in Banaras, on the very banks of the Ganges, is a desired end. Hindus living away from India also practise cremation and either place cremated remains in local rivers, thereby maintaining part of the tradition, or else send the remains to be placed in the Ganges. Although rites are also performed for set periods after cremation there is no monument for the dead whose ultimate destiny lies in the future and not in some past event.

In Buddhism, too, cremation is the preferred funeral rite, reinforced by the fact that the Buddha was, himself, cremated. According to tradition, his funeral pyre self-ignited, but only after many followers had come to pay respects to his body. When the flames ceased, only bones were left, and no other ash. As described elsewhere, his remains were divided into portions, and his cremation furnishes a good example of how cremation makes possible a greater variety of memorializing the dead than is usually the case with buried bodies. Although many contemporary Buddhist societies do employ cremation they may also use burial.

When Hindus or Buddhists move to other parts of the world an ability to continue the practice of cremation makes their settlement easier than it would be were cremation not permitted by a host society. At the same time, some degree of change is often demanded as a consequence of compromises that need to be made between traditional practice and what is practically feasible or acceptable in a new context. This is the case with the use of modern crematoria by Indians in Europe, America and Australasia. Even within India some aspects of innovation may be problematic as, for example, with the introduction of electric cremation in Banaras in place of wooden-pyre cremation.

Over time, even an innovation can, itself, become part of a tradition, as with the emergence of cremation as the dominant funeral rite in England from the mid-1960s or permission for the private use of cremated remains dating largely from the 1970s. Something similar happened with the Zoroastrian Parsees whose traditional form of exposing dead bodies in Towers of Silence in India gave way to cremation in other countries. However, there are periods when societies undergo major changes as a result of internal developments as happened in numerous European- and European-influenced societies in the late nineteenth century. This period of marked scientific and technological advance, following the Industrial Revolution, witnessed the modernization of many tradition-focused societies.

Modernization

From the later eighteenth century, ideas of cremation emerged as part of social change and political revolution in France, as the entry on **materialism and enlightenment** shows. But it was from the mid- and later nineteenth century that major changes in both thought and practice over funerals really engaged with Western societies. Frequently spearheaded by strongly motivated individuals who often formed small pressure groups ideologically committed to seeing the establishment of cremation as a legal and publicly acceptable form of treatment of the dead, formal associations or societies for cremation were established in many influential cities including London and The Hague in 1874, Washington in 1876 and New York in 1882. Central to these interest groups were influential individuals such as Sir Henry Thompson, surgeon to Queen Victoria, whose highly influential book on cremation, *The Treatment of the Body After Death*, was published in 1874, followed shortly by William Eassie's *Cremation of the Dead* of 1875. Italy was even more seminally influential in the renaissance of cremation; Brunetti's model cremator and display of cremated remains at the Vienna Exhibition of 1873 are credited with having prompted Sir Henry Thompson's interest. There was also a congress on cremation in Milan in 1874. Sometimes ancient history and the present were linked through the imaginative reflection of an individual such as the Swiss Wegmann-Ercolani who, as is documented in the **Switzerland** entry, was in part stimulated by the sight of the preserved columbaria of Pompei.

Together, such freethinking people provided both the intellectual motivation for, and the technical competence to advocate, various kinds of social reform, not least cremation. As the entries on cremation societies and influential individuals in different countries will show, many leading figures were medical doctors, scientists and engineers. These, along with town planners and civic leaders devoted to sanitary reform, saw in cremation a major potential contribution to social welfare and human well-being. Occasionally, medals were even struck to celebrate the establishment of crematoria, as with Stuttgart in 1907, or to commemorate the leadership of cremation reformers as with Burkhard

Reber – archaeologist and pharmacist – whose 25 years as founding leader of the Cremation Society of Geneva was celebrated in 1912 (Weber, 1918: 575–6). Similar medallions, as at the Welsh Folk Museum of St Fagan's, were produced to mark Dr William Price's influential instigation of cremation in Britain.

Cremation became identified as one very specific vehicle for social change. Groups often existed for years before they achieved the goal of cremation as a legal and established practice. In the Netherlands, for example, the 1874 group did not actually open a crematorium until 1914. Often there were objections from a variety of Christian churches, sometimes for theological reasons on the grounds that cremation would interfere with the resurrection of the body, or that cremation turned away from the example of the 'burial' of Jesus, and sometimes for more political reasons. Catholics in Italy, for example, found cremation unacceptable because it was favoured and advocated by freemasons as antipathetic to the Church. Indeed, it was not until 1963–64 that the Roman Catholic Church accepted cremation as an appropriate form of funeral for its members. In technological terms many European nations were caught up in ever-increasing industrialization in which innovation in dealing with new problems was prized, not least when thinking about death. In this industrial and pre-Holocaust age it was relatively easy to contemplate building what would be ovens for the combustion of human bodies as well as architectural features to house them. Later developments, such as machines like the cremulator, for grinding larger bone fragments into dust, were similarly industrial in nature.

Cultural changes fostering the acceptance of cremation also included the world wars with their attendant loss and burial of millions of soldiers away from their homelands. Slowly but steadily, cremation began to be incorporated into social welfare provisions in numerous countries and, just as the mid- and late nineteenth century had occasioned the establishment of large cemeteries in European cities, following urban growth, so the later twentieth century was marked by the growth of crematoria. Cremation was not only a response to massive urbanization and the drive for social hygiene but also matched changes in other patterns of dealing with the dead.

Factors underlying modernization came from a series of interlinked forces, including science and technology, politics and economics, and philosophy and theology. Many of these were combined, through the Industrial Revolution from the late eighteenth century, in a movement that can never be underestimated in terms of its impact on European life. At the practical level huge numbers of people abandoned a rural way of life and migrated to the dense centres of population in industrial towns where the illnesses and accidents of work, coupled with periodic epidemics, including cholera, led to the overfilling of burial grounds. More theoretically, the relatively rapid developments in biological and medical knowledge, along with the increasing use of engineering technology and the socially-focused use of architecture, posed new solutions for issues of public health and town planning.

Theology and ideology

Although we have already discussed aspects of cremation within traditional societies, it is also important to focus specifically on aspects of philosophical and theological thought that have engaged critically with modern debates on cremation. The entry on **materialism and enlightenment** provides one interesting backcloth for this discussion and leads into the later nineteenth and early twentieth centuries when significant strides were being taken in rethinking established ideas, including new perspectives on the Bible and traditional Christianity. During this period many thinkers were open to new developments in their assessment of the human condition and of social responsibility for the world. Within religious circles this was not an easy period – for example, some Catholic scholars who came to be called modernists were condemned by Pope Pius X in 1907. A similar British Anglican movement – The Churchmen's Union – continues to this day, despite changes in name. However, not all Catholic thought was negative towards cremation, as the entry on **Influential individuals**, under **Austria**, makes clear.

Nevertheless, one of the most enduring features of the relationship between cremation and society in Western societies concerns the influence of Catholic, Protestant and Orthodox traditions, and, at the beginning of the twenty-first century, Greek and Russian Orthodoxy stand in firm, formal, opposition to cremation and are involved in considerable political-religious debate in Greece. In the former USSR and in eastern European countries during periods of communist control, cremation was often advocated on ideological grounds, provoking opposition from Christian traditions of all sorts. The interaction of political ideology and Christian belief has also added to the complexity of the relationship between cremation and burial as in the case of freemasonry and Catholicism. It has only been in the post-communist era, with its greater degree of freedom that Christian opinions have been able to be formed without the need to react excessively to impinging ideologies.

In Europe the major distinction between countries, so far as cremation rates are concerned, lies in their Catholic, Protestant or Orthodox traditions. The entry on **Switzerland** with its diverse cantons makes this point very clearly. The broad reasons for this are complex, but include the significant fact that Catholicism's theological interest in the dead is extensive and relates to the liturgy of the dying and the dead – in last rites and requiem masses – not least because of the doctrine of purgatory as a state in and through which the sinful believer needs to pass and be transformed before gaining the full presence of God. Another reason is the Catholic Church's long-established interest in the tombs and relics of the saints, involving pilgrimages and prayer. Both these concerns place significance on the physical body of the dead. One feature of the Protestant Reformation was a shift away from rites for, and of, the dead; indeed, prayers for the dead, let alone prayers to dead saints, were strongly condemned. During the Reformation both Reformers and Catholics agreed in their belief in a soul that departed after death but disagreed over what assistance it might gain from the living. For the Protestants, generally speaking, once an individual had died it was God alone who dealt with the soul and who would furnish a suitable resurrection 'body' on the Last Day: the individual's life decisions and the inscrutable will of God would underlie human destiny, and the ongoing prayers of the living could not affect that. Such differences in attitudes towards the dead affected attitudes to the human body at and after death. For Protestantism, as a religious culture, the sharp divide between life and death in respect of eternal destiny provided a pre-adaptation for the kind of sharp divide between possessing a bond with the buried relative and having that removed through cremation. The absence of investment in the remains of the dead as a focus for the identity and destiny of the deceased made it easier for Protestants to accept cremation. I have already mentioned hostility towards the Catholic Church harboured by some freethinkers and freemasons, especially in Italy, as a significant element in Catholicism's earlier opposition to cremation.

The outcome of the historical background was that, by the close of the twentieth century, the northern countries, with strong Lutheran or Anglican backgrounds, tended to have a much higher cremation rate on the whole than the southern Catholic countries: by 1999, for example, Great Britain and Denmark cremated approximately 71 per cent and Sweden 68 per cent of their dead. Finland, by contrast, which notably possesses both an established Lutheran Church and an established Orthodox Church, along with a Catholic presence, cremated only 25 per cent. In Greece cremation is non-existent as a result of strenuous opposition by the Greek Orthodox Church. The Netherlands, lacking the Orthodox influence but divided between Protestant and Catholic traditions, stood at about 48 per cent. The Catholic influence is more evident in Hungary's 30 per cent, Austria's 21 per cent, and even more so in France's 16 per cent, Spain's 13 per cent, and in Italy and the Republic of Ireland which each have a cremation rate in the region of 5 per cent. Given that the Catholic Church has permitted cremation since the mid-1960s, those low rates in many countries reflect also the time it takes for social customs to change. The USA's overall cremation rate of approximately 25 per cent may seem unusually low, but it conceals a wide diversity involving local differences of religious tradition as well as tremendous differences in rural and urban practices. Washington, Nevada and Oregon, for example, had the highest cremation rates of approximately 57 per cent, while Alabama, Mississippi and West Virginia stood at approximately 5 per cent.

Human societies are, of course, forever changing, and the late nineteenth-century ideas of urban sanitary reform had become transformed, by the late twentieth century, into the wider ecological concerns of global and atmospheric protection. Here, again, cremation stands as a test case of social concern with, for example, new laws passed in several countries relating to the gaseous output of cremation exhaust processes. Ironically, those environmental considerations that once propelled cremation into favour have now called it into question, at least in some Westernized and urban contexts in which environmental issues have begun to become established. Accordingly, in Britain, for example, some minority groups have fostered the idea of woodland or 'green' burials in which individuals are buried without elaborate coffins or caskets and in full recognition that their bodies would soon return to the earth in a form of earth-friendly decay.

Professionalism and medicalization

One distinctive feature of modernization lay in the increased levels of professionalization within society as increased control was exerted by managing bodies over the practitioners of particular skills and this, notably, was true so far as medicine was concerned. In many urban centres of population this has led to what has been described as the 'medicalization of death'. The dying were moved to hospitals and no longer died in their homes; their bodies were collected by funeral directors and might be kept in specially designated and purpose-built premises. Indeed, the concept of a 'funeral home', as a place where bodies could be kept and 'visited' by their bereaved family, developed speedily. This was accompanied by the emergence of funeral directors as a distinctive occupation, although whether or not they can be classed as a profession remains open to doubt. In many respects, they serve more as an intermediate form of service agency performing a particularly important role in mediating not only between the established professions of medicine and the church on the one hand and their clients on the other, but also with crematorium officials.

The commercialism that inevitably and properly underpins funeral management also came, increasingly, to mirror a growing individualism and degree of personal choice over the form of funeral as the option of cremation entered into competition with traditional burial. For much of the twentieth century, science and technology came to underlie aspects of consumerism and the availability of new products fostered an ethos of efficiency and a popular 'scientific' mindset and, to a certain extent, cremation was one example of this.

Individualism and choice

Modern cremation, then, is significant in that it provides options about funerals, not simply in the choice between burial or cremation – the only real options in most developed societies – but also in what may happen to the ultimate cremated remains of the dead. Though largely unanticipated when cremation was introduced in the nineteenth century and largely unexplored until the later twentieth century, a momentous unintended consequence of cremation is that cremated remains offer a convenient, portable, form of the dead. Various traditions, albeit of a private form, have evolved as family members or friends have developed ways of placing the remains of individuals in specially chosen locations. This custom seems to have developed most rapidly in Great Britain, as not all countries permit such freedom with cremated remains as the various country entries make clear. It is, however, probably only a matter of time before legal reform increases this freedom of action in most cremation-focused societies.

Although many countries with Protestant and Catholic backgrounds would still, in the early twenty-first century, see a close bond between traditional religion and burial, that link is less strong with cremation. Now that cremation has come into existence some, albeit relatively few, people and organizations are now offering non-religious or secular rites, thereby further extending the range of funeral options available to the public as a whole.

The fact that, in most countries though not all, crematoria are owned and managed not by churches but by civic authorities or private companies gives further freedom of choice with regard to the content of funeral rites. The fact that traditional religious services often use music and some form of eulogy on the dead, as well as some sermon on the place of death in life, has made it relatively easy for non-religious and secular forms of rite also to employ music and reflections on the deceased person but with wider options in terms of content. Playing the dead person's favourite music instead of singing hymns or using an appropriate reading from a favourite author or poet rather than sacred scriptures changes, and personalizes, the content while maintaining the continuity of cultural form.

In and through these options the personal identity of the dead and the nature of their relationship with the living can be given a breadth of expression that is more difficult to achieve through strictly religious liturgical forms. This reflects the process of individualization that has accompanied the rise in standards of living in some contemporary societies in which individualism is offered a medium of expression through consumerism. Increased levels of income available to significant numbers of people in developed societies have paralleled the enormous growth not only in the variety of basic goods needed in life, but also in the supply of non-essential goods and in an entire culture of advertising that seeks to turn all goods into perceived necessities. So far as death is concerned, at the beginning of the twenty-first century, cremation is the key area through which lifestyles may be reflected in what are, in effect, deathstyles.

Psychology and gender

Whilst it may seem strange to speak of options for funerals in the context of ordinary consumerism, in which choice operates over such things as luxury goods or mundane provisions, it is important to do so because of the deeply personal, existential and more psychologically rooted issues that motivate choice over matters of death rites. One factor of importance in these matters of choice is that of gender and, in close association with it, the issue of fear in relation to burial and cremation.

Until cremation became available, the fear of burial, of being buried alive or of the sense of decay – themes touching the domain of despair – all had to be ignored, repressed or merely alluded to in folk-tales. Well-known European horror stories of being buried alive were, in some respects, the tip of emotional icebergs that, otherwise, were only manifest in special holding mortuaries or curiosities such as coffins and graves with alarm systems that any unfortunate person might activate if awakening in the grave (all discussed in the entry on **premature burial**).

One of my own studies addressed such fears and produced some evidence of a potential gender difference underlying attitudes to death that might favour cremation over burial. That study of some 1600 Britons conducted in 1995, showed that women tended to think more negatively of burial in terms of disliking the idea of rotting, being eaten by worms or being buried alive, than did men (Davies and Shaw, 1995). Approximately 20 per cent of the respondents had some personal fears and anxieties over forms of funeral. Of the total sample some 6 per cent of men and 14 per cent of women feared being buried alive, while 4 per cent of men and 8 per cent of women feared being burnt alive: in addition, nearly half of all those studied felt that religious ideas would be more influential on those choosing burial than on those choosing cremation (Davies and Shaw, 1995: 21, 24, 27, 29). This suggests that, at least in Britain towards the close of the twentieth century, if the constraints of religion are low and cremation easily available, then cremation offers a means of avoiding one area of potential anxiety, especially perhaps for women. At a more general level there remains the question of human attitudes towards the dead in which psychological dynamics overlap with social convention, and these are dealt with in the entry on **hope and fear**.

Secularization

One significant, but not entirely unintended, consequence of the emergence of modern cremation involves secularization. Understood as a process in which established religious influences cease to be formally effective in the public life of a society, secularization has been clearly evident amongst some cremation groups. This was especially true, for example, in Italy in the nineteenth century when some freethinking groups sought to remove death ritual from the control of the Catholic Church, and elicited a corresponding negative response from the Church. Several communist regimes of the early and mid-twentieth century also introduced cremation in an attempt to persuade people to abandon traditional forms of Christian burial. Where cremation emerged in competition with Catholic practice, the Catholic Church prohibited its use amongst the faithful. This was especially the case when cremation was seen as a direct expression of freemasonry, as it was in some Catholic, but not in most Protestant, countries. However, even when Protestant churches came to accept cremation, they very largely framed the ritual with the words of the traditional burial services and did not engage in any serious theological and ritual creativity: they did not invent a new tradition but, rather, existed in a tension between tradition and innovation.

Yet, in one sense, Christianity had laid the foundation for aspects of secularization in that, after it achieved religious dominance in Europe in its first millennium and firmly established itself geographically in the second, it fostered much formal theology and ritual concerning death. Catholic Christianity's funerary rites included preparation of the dying for their eternal journey and masses and prayers to advantage their migrant souls. Cemeteries were closely aligned with churches and, overall, death rites were under ecclesiastical control. Some have even regarded the simplifying of funerals that took place at the Reformation to have been 'the beginning of the decline' in the ritual provision for death (Thomas, 1971: 722). Certainly, in the nineteenth century many new cemeteries were built under local authority control but the rites taking place in them remained largely religious.

With the advent of cremation there arose a new possibility of engaging in death rites separate from ecclesiastical control. Nevertheless, for much of the late nineteenth and the first two-thirds of the twentieth century the great majority of cremation rites were set within a religious ritual framework in that Protestant clergy participated by conducting the formal rite. Catholic priests were also freed to do so from the mid-1960s. However, slowly at first, but with increasing frequency towards the later twentieth century, others might also be involved or might even replace members of the clergy. This became most obviously apparent, and was spearheaded, in Britain in connection with cremated remains. The technology of cremation had produced two fundamental differences between cremation and burial: first, the fact that it resulted in a product that could be utilized in quite different ways from a corpse or a skeleton; and, second, that it made possible a second ritual. Traditional burial was conducted under the control of a Christian church and, although remains might later have been removed to a charnel house, it was an unceremonial affair. In some places burials could also be conducted without church rites but it was with modern cremation that the possibility of a secular conductor became acceptable. Often the emphasis of what came to be called 'life-centred' funerals was celebratory, with a focus on the past life of the deceased and not, as in traditional Christian rites, on the future hope of resurrection. For some people and societies this is likely to express secularization for some and privatization for others. Churches that adopted cremation as a funeral practice were very slow to develop theological interpretations of cremation. This might have been partly due to fire's ambiguous association with both purification and destruction.

At the beginning of the twenty-first century, however, the secularization that is evident in many parts of Europe and Australasia and, to a limited extent in North America, is not so evident in many parts of both South America and Africa. In these latter contexts, numerous forms of Protestant religion, especially of Pentecostal forms of religious enthusiasm, have considerable force and tend to be associated with attitudes that perceive burial as the more directly biblical form of funeral. Just as in contemporary Europe cremation practice tends to mirror the historical divide between Catholic and Protestant so, in these developing parts of the world, it is likely that cremation will reflect those of a more secular attitude and burial the attitude of the more traditional religious believers – whether Protestant or Catholic.

Politics and economics

Ideological factors of political, as well as of religious, forms have also played a significant historical role in cremation; these have sometimes been related to, or couched in, economic arguments. The entry on **Austria** provides clear examples of how cremation may become a direct vehicle of political social protest. The degree of social control possessed by a state or by the individual over the dead body and its means of disposal is a major index of the nature of a society. This is exemplified in the entries on both **Russia and the USSR** and contemporary **China**, where a strongly-focused desire to shift popular practice from burial to cremation expressed the political wish to change public attitudes towards prior beliefs and customs and, in some cases, to conserve land and to avoid excessive expenditure on burial rites. At the start of the twenty-first century just such an encounter is evident, albeit on a different scale and with a different motivation, in contemporary Greece between the Orthodox Church and those wishing to see cremation as an option for the people.

Even cremated remains have been able to embody and serve political ends as when political leaders, such as China's Zhou Enlai in 1976 and Deng Xiaoping in 1997, had their ashes scattered throughout the country. A similar phenomenon had occurred earlier in India with Mahatma Gandhi's ashes. The entries on both **Japan** and **Korea** show, on a larger scale, how cremation could be used as a vehicle of national identity and conquest. To emphasize the deep significance of such political issues in respect of cremation we have a dedicated entry on **Politics** that emphasizes, in particular, some European contexts and examples. Other cases, such as that of the individual Andries de **Rosa** and his activity in the Netherlands, highlight the complex interplay of political and economic elements within the drive for the social well-being of people and communities. Similar cases are found in entries on Spain and Portugal. More divisively, political and economic factors have also influenced cremation practice at the local level as, for example, in Bali where contested claims for social prestige are expressed in funerary display, or in Vienna where Catholic tradition opposed cremation as a means of defending a religious–political establishment.

Pluralism

As the twentieth century progressed, the crematorium came to be a ritual arena open to a great variety of religious, secular or mixed forms of expression of beliefs and values. In fact, crematoria came to be among the major social innovations so far as funeral sites were concerned and, indeed, so far as new forms of purpose-built constructions were concerned. Since, in urban societies, buildings play an enormously significant role in public and private consciousness, the development of the crematorium provided an opportunity for architects not only to reflect on, but also to influence, cultural values of death. Here, there is evidence of a period in which traditions of ecclesiastical architecture enter into tension with new ideas in which a sense of the rational control of life and death processes interfuses with aesthetics that seek to express the depth and meaningfulness of human life, relationships and destiny. The entries on **architecture** and individual architects such as **Schumacher** are particularly important in revealing the degrees to which religious and secular forces are, or have been, opposed or aligned in different countries.

One distinctive feature of modern cremation that should not be ignored, for some countries, concerns that aspect of religious pluralism deriving from the shared use of crematoria. In those societies where crematoria are owned by local authorities or private companies they are in fact used by groups belonging to many religious denominations or to none. At the beginning of the twenty-first century in England, for example, it would not be impossible for a crematorium to host rites of Catholics, Protestants, Sikhs, Hindus, Buddhists and certain Jewish groups as well as a Humanist and a non-religious or non-ideological ceremony. Also, the very large crematorium in Seoul, Korea, possesses a whole range of ceremony halls within which different religions conduct their basic rites. The very fact that a single building can be a site for such mixed activity is remarkable and highlights the importance of architecture and building management in relation to a mixed religious and ideological economy.

Globalization

This adaptability of cremation and crematoria also facilitated their use in a wide range of societies. The single process of burning the dead could be framed by an extremely wide variety of interpretations of the process itself. Here, individualism does not contradict a process of globalization of cremation. Though often used in relation to multinational companies and their products that are exported and established across the world, globalization can also apply to particular processes, especially those that affect people as consumers of goods, services and ideas. In these terms, the close of the twentieth and opening of the twenty-first centuries has been a period of the globalization of cremation. Cremation has been exported to, or developed within, what were hitherto traditional burial societies. On the one hand, this has been due to developments within civic, secular or religious provisions for funerals in a general sense of options becoming available, sometimes, as business concerns have sought expansion of their trade. But, on the other hand, cremation has also been established by political authority as a formal funeral preference as in the People's Republic of China and the former USSR.

One important aspect of the globalization of cremation lies in the birth and influence of the International Cremation Federation (ICF). This organization has done more than any other to raise the profile of cremation as both a historical and contemporary practice. Because its influence is evident in many subsequent entries it is appropriate that this Introduction should provide a brief account both of the ICF's initial rationale and of its subsequent changing emphases. It is also highly appropriate that the strongly collegial nature of this encyclopedia be marked at the outset and, with that in mind, I now include material from one of my students, Elizabeth Kent, and also from Henry Keizer, the current Secretary General of the International Cremation Federation, in the following and final introductory section. **Douglas J. Davies**

INTERNATIONAL CREMATION FEDERATION

The International Cremation Federation was formed when a constitution was approved by delegates at the International Cremation Congress held in London between 24th September and 2nd October 1937. It developed from a history of international cooperation. Even as early as 1910 there had been an attempt at collaboration, but meetings in Brussels (1910) and Dresden (1911) had failed as international gatherings through a relative lack of purpose and structure. However, a turning point came in 1936 when delegates from Great Britain, Denmark, France, The Netherlands, Yugoslavia, Germany, Austria, Romania, Sweden, Switzerland and Czechoslovakia met in Prague and agreed that a 'New Congress' should meet in London the following year with the aim of establishing an International Cremation Federation. A committee was assembled to plan the event with Fr Mencl (Czechoslovakia) as President, and Vice-Presidents. Prof. Dr H. Zeiss (Germany) and M. Henri Ferre (France). The Secretary-General was P. Herbert Jones (Great Britain). They achieved their purpose and, at the 1937 meeting in London, the new body formally came into existence with Dr P.H. van Roojen elected as the first President of the ICF. He was also the President of the 'Royal Dutch Cremation Society, The Facultatieve' and had for many years been a strong supporter of the forming of an international federation.

At its inception the ICF's objectives were eightfold and reflected both ideological and practical concerns. In abbreviated form they sought (i) to spread knowledge of cremation as superior over burial as far as hygienic, ethical, economical and aesthetic factors were concerned. (ii) To seek the removal of hindrances in customs restrictions over the transport of cremated remains from country to country. (iii) To share experience of good practice in cremation techniques. (iv) To bring about international agreements between members of the Federation to ameliorate troubles caused to survivors by the death of a relative when abroad. (v) To assist all members, whether individuals or organizations, with advice and information on matters concerning cremation. (vii) To publish periodicals and other literature on the subject of cremation. (viii) To organise international cremation congresses, to publish reports on them, to maintain an international secretariat, and to foster the wider spread of the practice of cremation throughout the world. Later emendations, as in 1954 and 1967, reflected various degrees of success of the ICF. It would, for example, speak of the 'merits' of cremation rather than of its 'superiority', indicating a softening of the initial campaigning zeal of the movement, and would replace such clauses as the 'removal of restrictions' with reference to 'having cremation placed on an equal footing with interment', not least 'in ecclesiastical circles'. The original goals are obvious expressions of some of the concerns evident, for example, in papers given at the germinal 1936 Prague Conference. 'The transportation of ashes from one country to another.' 'The demand for a crematorium at Monaco.' 'The removal of cremation restrictions.' 'The standardisation of dimensions of official urns.' 'Cremation legislation in various countries.' 'Administrative cremation.' 'Methods of propaganda.' 'Practical co-operation of cremation societies in various countries.' 'International reciprocity.' 'Interchange of cremation facilities for members of cremation societies.' A year later the obvious business of the 1937 London Congress, which included delegates from all member countries, was to establish the objectives, rules and structures of the ICF. By December 31st 1938, the cremation organisations of some 18 countries were paying membership to the ICF, viz., Australia, Austria, Belgium, Canada, Czechoslovakia, Denmark, Finland, France (2 societies), Germany, Great Britain (5 organisations), The Netherlands (2 societies), Japan, Latvia, Luxembourg, Romania, Sweden, Switzerland and Yugoslavia (3 societies). No sooner had these ideals begun to be addressed and implemented than the Second World War broke out and significantly affected the work of the ICF some of whose constituent countries were now formal antagonists. Some social attitudes to cremation, especially, in Europe, would also be deeply affected by the War and its actions.

After the War, as the ICF Annual Report of 1951 shows, the total membership amounted to 17 countries, comprising of those listed above plus the expanded membership of USA, Iceland, Italy, Malaya, and Norway, but without Canada, Germany, Japan, Latvia, Romania, and Yugoslavia. The ICF, with its three official languages of English, French and German, now sought to establish a pattern of meeting every three years in different countries. After London in 1937 and the severe hindrance of the war the 1948 Congress at The Hague was followed, for example, by Copenhagen 1951, Oslo 1954,

Zurich 1957 and Stockholm in 1960, with subsequent regular meetings in member countries. The early Congress topics were marked by the optimism and campaigning zeal of its founders then, after the Second World War, attention turned more to the attitude of the churches toward cremation, especially in challenging the Roman Catholic Church's ban on cremation. After the lifting of the ban in 1967 and the increasing acceptance of cremation, the focus and purpose of the ICF appears to have foundered somewhat and in 1978 and 1981 papers were given raising the need for the ICF to look again at its function and aims. Soon the developing concern with ecological and ethical issues increasingly came to exert an influence. At the 1978 Congress, for example, papers included the issues of, 'The disposal of cremated remains', by J.M. Evans; 'Ecologie et crémation', by Jaques Godard, and 'Aims and future problems of ICF', by Richard Ozmec. By the 1981 Congress the environmental and ecological aspect has increased as evident in papers on, 'Cremation, comparison with interment from an environmental point of view', by Hendrik Adam; 'Caskets made of wood – how much longer?' by Heiko Hansen, and 'Cremation, environment, energy', by W. van Horssen. With the closing decades of the twentieth and the opening years of the twenty-first century ethical issues only intensified as matters of bereavement and grief also attracted popular attention, at the very time when death studies were making their presence felt in many modern societies. Many of these issues have been covered in conference papers published in *Pharos*, the journal of the British Cremation Society that had been in existence prior to the establishing of the ICF but which, at the ICF Congress in Copenhagen in 1951, was adopted as its official publication. This has served as a basic public forum and, from the 1990s, came to be an increasingly well-produced journal embracing diverse and international material.

The structure of the ICF itself has also developed over time. Initially it consisted of an Executive Committee, a General Council and a Congress. The Executive Committee was comprised of the President, two Vice-Presidents, Honorary Treasurer, and Secretary-General. The Secretary-General was a permanent position, the others holding office until the following Congress. Changes in the structure of the Executive Committee were made at the Vienna Congress in 1966 when the number of Vice-Presidents was increased from two to three. The General Council consisted of one member from each organisation in the ICF and met every three years. The General Council, which met in 1966, amended its voting procedures as it was difficult to work 'one country one vote' where a country had more than one national cremation society. Each country was given as many votes as the country with the highest number of national societies who were members of the ICF. Among later developments in the ICF was its inclusion, in 1996, in the United Nations 'Roster' list of recognised bodies that are accorded consultative status. By the time of the 2003 Congress in Barcelona it was recognised that a review of the ICF structure and organization was due in the light of changing circumstances and responsibilities. By 2005 the executive was planning a world division for regional organization aligning North and South America in one group, Europe and Africa in another, and Asia and Australia-New Zealand in yet another. Doubtless, the ICF will change still further in its organization and purpose as attitudes towards cremation change and as it pursues partnerships between areas of the world that are strongly committed to cremation and those that are, as the twenty-first century begins, far less committed.

Many of the entries that follow provide detailed accounts of historical aspects of these commitments whilst also indicating possible future trends, certainly, the global nature of cremation organization is evident in many of them. While detailed references are provided, when appropriate, for individual entries there is also a final Bibliography covering material cited in this Introduction and also including texts appearing in more than one entry. **Douglas Davies, Elizabeth Kent, Henry Keizer**.

A

ADVERTISING: THE RHETORIC OF CREMATORIA

Because crematoria are businesses offering services to bereaved people who are in a delicate emotional and psychological condition the way in which they advertise their services needs to convey respect, support and sympathy for their prospective clients' pain. Nevertheless, their major interest is, like that of any business, an economic one. It is noteworthy that many crematorium advertisements worldwide share a common structure in that they begin by attempting to deal with people's fears and suspicions, perhaps by answering common questions people might raise concerning cremation, such as whether it goes against their religious tradition, especially in the case of Christianity and Judaism. Throughout an advertisement it is important to note not only what is said but also, and perhaps more significantly, how it is said. Indeed, it can be argued that the whole rhetoric of an advertisement works for marketing purposes and is specially targeted, as will be seen, at a postmodern mentality.

Fears and suspicions

Whereas in the UK the majority of people choose to be cremated, in other countries, such as the USA and Portugal, most people still express their suspicions – grounded in fears of one sort or another – about the practice of cremation. Crematoria, especially those established in countries where they serve a minority of the population, are aware of people's wariness towards cremation and one of their major efforts is to inform potential clients of the positive side of their services. To this end, it is common for crematoria in the USA, for example, to provide potential clients with brochures, both at their offices and on their webpages. These describe every step of the cremation process, the professionalism of the staff, the quality of the technology used and all the 'extra' services the company has to offer. In addition, the brochures aim to reassure people that choosing cremation does not imply a denial of traditional beliefs and practices, and that, contrary to what might be thought, it is a respectful and dignifying means of dealing with the body of a loved one. People are usually concerned about tradition, the future of the cremated remains, environmental issues and the costs of cremation, and it is precisely these issues that crematoria address.

Clients are assured that the licensed cremation director supervises the entire process of cremation. The 'highly trained professional staff' are presented as those whose purpose is to guide the bereaved through one of the most difficult times of their lives, and who will, at no cost or obligation, be available to review the 'program' with their clients and answer any questions concerning their services. People are welcome to visit crematoria or to call in order to discuss any issues. Frequently the crematoria have support available from psychologists and even have brochures advising on how to explain cremation to a child and how the bereaved should deal with the cremated remains so as to avoid future psychological damage.

In countries marked by Christian traditions people may fear that their salvation is jeopardized if they are cremated instead of buried. This springs from the notion that the Bible favours burial of the body of the believer; it is tied in with the Christian doctrine of the resurrection of the body, the concept of cremation as a pagan practice, and the idea that God reserves the flame for those who deserve punishment. The sentence 'you are dust, and to dust you shall return' (Genesis 3:19), curiously, is used both by those who oppose cremation and by those who favour it, as it does indeed seem to fit both contexts. In the context of cremation this expression is taken more literally, as the cremated remains are seen as the 'dust' to be returned to 'dust'. In this way, crematoria borrow legitimacy from the Bible. On the Internet there are some 'discussion rooms' where these issues are debated, and which are often supported by the companies that offer cremation services. To those who put forward the doctrine of resurrection of the body as an obstacle to cremation practices, the reply is that just as God can resurrect a decomposed buried body, so can He resurrect a body from its cremated remains. Those who doubt this doubt God's omnipotence. Cremation, it is argued, need not to be looked upon as being a break in family or religious traditions. The choice of cremation does not imply absence of a traditional funeral. In fact, a funeral service usually takes place before cremation, and it need be no different to a funeral followed by an interment. Memorial services held before cremation can have the body present, or the service may occur after cremation with the cremated remains present.

Some people question whether their ashes may end up being mixed with those of someone else or with other materials resulting from the cremation process, such as wood. To this, crematoria reply that only one person is cremated at a time and that the equipment is carefully cleaned before the next cremation. Further, they claim that, as their technology has improved cremated remains are easily separable from other materials. Environmental issues may also be raised. Cremation is seen as a positive way to respond the shortage of land available for burial, for one urn takes much less space than a coffin. Those who want their ashes to be scattered in the sea sometimes express concern that because ashes do not sink, they may end up on the shore. To this crematoria reply that there are companies that take the cremated remains to the seabed, thus circumventing this problem. Some crematoria, however, advise the bereaved to put the ashes in a place that may serve as a memorial or a focus of grief, such as a garden, since psychologists claim that this facilitates the grieving process. Through such advice crematoria express their concern for their clients, demonstrating that they care for, and support, them in times of pain. Indeed, they attempt to convey the message that they *provide* a service; they do, not impersonally and coldly *sell* it.

Crematoria often advertise cremation as a cheaper alternative to burial. Moreover, taking account of the fact that nowadays families tend to be more scattered, they remind people that cremation is the best option if the family lives far away for, otherwise, 'who would tend their grave?' Cremation is thus presented as offering more freedom of choice in disposing of the remains of the deceased. The practice of cremation, as it is advertised, is imbued with the idea that, if pursued with respect and dignity, it will help to deal with grief, achieve emotional stability, peace of mind and even alleviate guilt (see Cremation Association, 2003).

Strategic wording

Interestingly, when advertising cremation, words such as 'death', 'fire' and 'burn' are usually avoided, and the process of grinding the

cremated remains – especially bones and calcium deposits milled down to finer particles in a cremulator – is frequently downplayed or omitted. In an attempt to acknowledge the importance of the body, some advertisements explicitly or implicitly convey the message that a dead body feels no pain and that the cremation process is gentle, respectful and dignifying. This theme is frequently repeated throughout advertisements, along with the message that the practice is increasing in popularity worldwide and is becoming more and more accepted as the 'taboos' of the past are progressively overcome. Cremation is also described as a fashionable option since many well-known personalities, such as statesman, prominent military persons and people from the worlds of sports and entertainment, have chosen to be cremated. Cremation advertisements, while adopting a tone of sympathy for the pain of the bereaved, often emphasize, too, the opportunity to celebrate the life of the deceased and to therefore introduce a tone of joy in the midst of grief.

Between the first and last paragraphs of an advertisement there is frequently a change in the type of vocabulary. The initial paragraphs may include words such as 'shock', 'confusion', 'tremendous grief', 'pain' and 'suffering'. In this way the advertisement shows to potential clients that the company in question understands the emotional and psychological dilemmas the bereaved are experiencing. The following paragraphs may then take on a more positive tone, intending to convince the bereaved that the company has 'solutions' to the problems in question. This more positive vocabulary includes words such as 'warm atmosphere', 'beautiful rooms' (with reference to the place where the memorial service can be conducted), 'supportive', 'caring', 'respectful', 'dignifying' and 'best technology'. This 'positive' part of the advertisement is charactized by the constant use of euphemisms, such as 'time of need' when referring to 'death' and 'applied high temperatures' rather than 'burn' which connotes physical pain. The same type of discourse is evident also in advertisements for pet cremation since owners tend to search for a caring way to deal with the body of a beloved pet in order to better deal with their own grief.

The rhetoric of crematoria aims to persuade – to engage both the public's intellectual and emotional responses. Aristotle distinguished between *logos* (the logical content of a speech) and *lexis* (its style and delivery), although, this division is an artificial one since ideas and their verbal expressions are so intimately connected that they form a continuum. As Burton (2003) suggests, the overlapping nature of *logos* and *lexis* can be understood through the word 'ornament', which has its roots in the Latin verb *ornare* – 'to equip': 'The ornaments of war, for example, are weapons and soldiers. The ornaments of rhetoric are not extraneous; they are the equipment required to achieve the intended meaning or effect'. Thus, cremation advertisements are rich in figures of speech such as metaphors, repetitions and euphemisms – rhetorical ornaments that emphasize the ideas the author intends to inculcate in the readers' minds, touching their intellect and emotions in an effort of persuasion.

The postmodern mentality

Nowadays, crematoria advertisements focus on individuality and diversity, appealing both to people who are religious and wish for a traditional funerary ritual and to those who are not religious and therefore prefer a different type of ritual. Crematoria inform their clients that funeral services can be traditional or non-traditional, elaborate or simple, and they can be set in accordance to different religious traditions, such as Christianity, Buddhism or Hinduism. Emphasis is placed on individual choice, and funerary services are therefore organized strictly according to the client's preferences, convenience and instructions. By informing the client of the flexibility of ritual that cremation permits, crematoria appeal to a postmodern mentality, characterized by an increased acknowledgement, acceptance and celebration of individual idiosyncrasies. The advertisements make it clear that, contrary to what might be thought, cremation does not limit choice but, rather, increases options in the process of 'memorialization'. Some brochures distributed by crematoria to potential clients include quoted personal recommendations from people who favour cremation. These accounts often implicitly suggest that, as times change, perspectives and opinions change, often in a tone that may be interpreted as defying tradition. For example, in a rebellious tone, writing in favour of cremation, Jackie O'Neil (2003) states, 'I'll set a new trend, tradition be damned.'

Some companies nowadays offer a 'pre-paid bereavement plan' in which individuals may choose the type of funerary service they prefer and pay in advance for all expenses. Naturally, in order to prevent clients from feeling that the fact of 'prearranging' their funerals might imply that their death is imminent, when advertising such schemes' funerary companies use expressions such as 'before the need arises, often years before'; they imply that clients are 'moving toward peace of mind for them and their families' (Flynn Funeral & Cremation Memorial Centres).

Great flexibility is offered in making this kind of arrangement: the client may visit the company's office, a member of the company can visit the client's home or office, arrangements may be completed directly over the Internet, and there are several payment options. Prearranging one's cremation is sold as a way of guaranteeing that one's wishes are known at *time of need*, and advertisements emphasize the fact that the client is protected from inflation. As Flynn Funeral & Cremation Memorial Centres state on their webpage:

'You and your family will have the security of knowing final needs are taken care of as you wish.

- You have relieved your family and loved ones of burdens during a time of emotional stress.
- Your wishes and desires have been established.
- You have made a wise financial decision by pre-funding for funeral expenses.'

Conclusion

The communication of ideas and beliefs about cremation is shaped by rhetorical elements that intend to induce people to adopt a certain ethos and world-view. The rhetorical elements employed by crematoria in their discourses aim to affect people's thoughts, imagination, associations of ideas and judgements. One persuasive way of convincing potential clients is to invest cremation with emotional and intellectual meaning. Further, like any other business, crematoria have to deal with competition – namely, other crematoria and funerary companies that organize interments. When competing with other crematoria advertisements often emphasize the company's technological superiority and the professionalism of their staff. When competing with companies that promote interments crematoria try to assure people that choosing cremation does not imply a break with tradition as a traditional funeral may still be performed. **Ana Ludovico**

References

Burton, G.O. (2003), *Silva Rhetoricae,* available at: http://humanities.byu.edu/rhetoric/silva.htm (accessed 12 April 2003).

Flynn Funeral & Cremation Memorial Centres at: http://www.cremationmemorialcenters.com/plan /index.html (accessed 20 May 2003).

Jackie O'Neil (2003), *Peace of Mind,* available at: http://www.forpeaceofmind.com.au/considerin gcremation.cfm (accessed 20 May 2003).

Cremation Association at: http://www.cremation association.org/docs/end.pdf (accessed 20 May 2003).

AIDS/HIV

The emergence of HIV/AIDS as an infection and illness in the latter half of the twentieth century has carried various consequences for cremation. When individuals who had died of AIDS were first cremated there was some concern over whether the cremation process might in any way involve elements of contagion. These issues, and some popular fears associated with them, were largely resolved in and through a redoubled concern with normal and proper processes of hygiene in connection with cremation. It remains to be seen whether, for example, cremation will come to be accepted in relatively non-cremation societies, such as Africa, in contexts of very high death rates due to the terminal effect of the virus. **Douglas J. Davies**

See also Islam (in the content of Islamic burial tradition); South Africa; Zimbabwe.

ALTERNATIVE SPIRITUALITIES

Stephen Prothero has argued that cremation in the USA indicates confidence that the 'true self is spiritual rather than material' (2001: 5). If so, this might suggest that those who identify themselves as New Agers or as members of spiritualist, esoteric or transcendentalist movements could be expected to prefer cremation to burial. It might also suggest that pagans (members of a growing nature-centred spirituality, see Harvey, 1997) and many indigenous peoples could be expected to prefer to bury their dead rather than cremate them. In addition to these more specific implications of Prothero's thesis, cremation might be tested for its utility as an indicator of religious and cultural positions with regard to spirituality versus materiality, transcendence versus immanence or inner selfhood (perhaps 'soul') versus embodied selfhood. That is, cremation may be far more than a choice between modes of disposal and serve, rather, to indicate significant cultural constructions of personhood, identity and culture.

However, matters are more complex than this. While Prothero notes that some, at least, of the first exponents of cremation among white North Americans were members of esoteric movements such as the Theosophical Society, he is also clear that their motivations were not primarily religious. Understandings of cremation as 'more modern', 'scientific' and 'hygienic' were reiterated more frequently than notions about the immortality of the soul or reincarnation. It seems likely, then, that the first US cremationists found that their notions of spirituality and materiality supported developments in wider cultural notions about modernity.

When applied to contemporary alternative spiritualities Prothero's argument also requires refinement. It seems fairly straightforward to map some prominent movements according to the degree to which they celebrate or dismiss the body as religiously meaningful. Similarly, these groups could be mapped according to the degree to which they understand the 'true self' to be spiritual, interior, and/or transcendent rather than thoroughly embodied. Two examples may usefully represent contrasting positions with regard to the significance of spirituality and materiality – namely, paganism and esoteric movements. Most pagans not only describe their religion as nature-respecting, but also consider embodiment and materiality to be a prime location for encounters with the divine and other sources of value. Conversely, some esoteric movements and some new religions evolving within a Hindu context consider the body to be a shell inhabited temporarily by a 'soul', or the person's true self, during its continuing quest for enlightenment that will curtail further incarnation. However, while it is true that Hindu-derived groups prefer cremation as a means of disposal, the situation for pagans and for many avowed esotericists is much more ambiguous. It may be that the choice between burial and cremation is not decided with reference to the material/spiritual dichotomy but by reference to taken-for-granted and established cultural usage or to pragmatic considerations of cost and availability. Some more detail may illustrate this situation.

When a Druid, William Price, cremated his son, named in Welsh Iesu Grist (Jesus Christ) in 1884 (White, 2002), he was among the first revivers of cremation in Britain. Druids of various kinds have followed his example ever since. Some of these Druids have been part of a Welsh cultural movement centred on competitive performances of bardic poetry and rooted in non-conformist Christianity, but others have been avowedly pagan. Far from negating the body or trying to liberate some putative soul, spiritual essence or 'true self' from its material confines, these pagan Druids celebrate embodiment. Their reasons for cremating include knowledge of ancient traditions, drawing on literary and archaeological evidence, the ease with which crematoria permit highly personalized (or do-it-yourself) ceremonies, cost and availability. In other words, practical motivations blend with specifically religious ones. However, a brief survey of pagan contacts reveals that pagans are as likely to bury as to cremate, and to wish to be buried as to be cremated. Individuals may express preferences, but both can be justified by reference to similar motivations, including respect for nature and embodiment.

Similarly, adherents of New Age – a contemporary form of European esoteric tradition centred on the development of the inner self (see Hanegraaff 1996) – are now also as likely to bury as they are to cremate. About 20 years ago matters were more as Prothero's argument would suggest: the notion that the 'true self' transcends individual embodiment (and sometimes even individual identity) led New Agers to prefer cremation to burial. However, an increasing stress on the 'goodness of the Earth' and embodiment of the inner self has led to significant evolutions in the movement. New Agers are now as likely to engage in 'body work', physical fitness and therapeutic programmes, as those whose traditions are specifically centred on celebrating 'nature'.

Although this trend alone might have affected New Agers' choices between cremation and burial, another trend has intervened that makes a considerable difference within the parameters of Prothero's dynamic tension. With the rise of 'green burial' in woodland or meadow sites in which not only ecological concerns but also the personalization of ceremonies is stressed, many of the spiritual concerns of both pagans and New Agers can be met. Thus, human remains can be disposed of in ways that seem more 'natural' than some previous systems that seem determined to deny death, mortality and even the necessity of decay. It is also, of course, possible to inter the ashes resulting from cremation in such burial plots.

Thus the current situation among members of alternative religious movements indicates a fairly equal choice between popularly available modes of disposal. It seems likely that cremation will continue to be popular not only to those with strong notions of transcendence but also to those wishing for more control over the ceremonial context of the disposal of their dead. Burial, meanwhile, will continue to maintain its popularity where 'green burial' is an option. **Graham Harvey**

References

Hanegraaff, Wouter (1996), *New Age Religion and Western Culture*, Leiden: Brill.

Harvey, Graham (1997), *Listening People, Speaking Earth: Contemporary Paganism*, London: Hurst.

Prothero, Stephen (2001), *Purified by Fire, A History of Cremation in America*, Berkeley: University of California Press.

White, S. (2002), 'A Burial Ahead of its Time? The Crookenden Burial Case and the Sanctioning of Cremation in England and Wales', *Mortality*, 7(2): 171–90.

ANCESTORS

In some societies, especially in Africa and allied areas, cremation is rejected because of beliefs in the ancestors and in the commitment to burial as a medium that permits an ongoing sense of contact with the dead. In others, as in China and Japan, cremation has come to exist alongside ancestral rites. **Douglas J. Davies**

See China; Japan; Kenya; South Africa; Suriname.

ANCIENT GREECE

Although the history of cremation in ancient Greece is extremely complex, certain underlying patterns can be identified. First, even though there are examples where the cremation pyre has been covered over with the remains still on it, it is much more usual for ashes and bone-remains to be gathered from the pyre and placed within a pot of some kind, which is itself put within a tomb cut in the earth or soft rock or built of stone. It was quite common for goods to be burnt with the body on the pyre, but they might also be placed, unburnt, within the grave. Cremations were normally single, but the remains of two individuals can sometimes be found in the same container (Musgrave, 1990: 285).

Second, in the early stages, cremations were frequently found in multiple-burial tombs or in cemeteries of single burials, alongside inhumations, with the preferences for various sites changing markedly over time and those fluctuations being particularly notable at Athens. These features hardly suggest that the adoption of cremation entailed any marked change in beliefs about death and the afterlife, for in either case it was the living users of these tombs who would have organized the burials, so any ideological element involved must have been acceptable to them. Sometimes particular families or groups within a community might continue to cremate when the rest had gone over to inhumation – another indication that no deep change in mentality was involved. Thus, the famous remarks of the ghost of Odysseus's mother in *Odyssey* 11.218–22 cannot reflect some after-death effect attributable *specifically* to cremation as opposed to inhumation.

It may be suspected that cremation was often associated with attempts to assert status and may have been chosen because it offered greater potential for a flamboyant funeral. But although there are clear examples of high-status cremations, inhumations of apparently equal status – if one can judge by the range of grave-goods – can be found contemporaneously with cremations, even at sites where cremation is the more prevalent rite – for example, in the Lefkandi 'Heroön' (see below). That considerations of social position were involved is indicated by the fact that, even in communities that showed a preference for cremation, small children were usually inhumed and not cremated, although cremated children and even infants have been identified in Early Iron Age cemeteries (Musgrave, 1990: 284).

With the exception of some Neolithic examples, which include ash-urn cemeteries, only one exceptional, perhaps primary, example dating before approximately 1400 BCE is reported, from Argos. But examples dating from the fourteenth and thirteenth centuries occur in the cemetery at Müsgebi in Caria within an otherwise fairly typical Mycenaean-style cemetery of rock-cut chamber tombs; there are others on Rhodes and Cos and in eastern Crete, and a double female cremation is reported from Tholos 2 at Tragana in Messenia. The heavy bias of the distribution to the east Aegean suggests that cremation was introduced from Anatolia (Asia Minor), where it was widely practised in the Late Bronze Age. These cremations were clearly secondary, as is commonly the case in Anatolia.

Cremation became more common after *c*.1200 BCE, in the Postpalatial period that followed the collapse of the most advanced Aegean societies, when many innovations were spreading. It occurred always as a minority rite, practised by the same communities that practised inhumation, and so usually involved the deposition of the remains alongside inhumed burials in the traditional types of multiple-burial tomb. The rite seems to have spread through the Aegean from its eastern side, but rare examples occur as far away as the western Peloponnese (Snodgrass, 1971:189; Dickinson, 1994: 231) and Thasos. The placing of an ash-urn in the tomb was typical, but in at least one case, in Achaea, the ashes were placed directly on the tomb floor. It is noteworthy that at Perati in eastern Attica the majority of examples seem to be adult males (Musgrave, 1990: 284), and most were found in the richer tombs – another indication of a tendency to reserve the rite for leading personalities.

With the onset of the Early Iron Age, around 1050 BCE, there is evidence that some communities adopted cremation as a common, though still not universal, rite. This is particularly clear at Athens, Lefkandi, Medeon, Knossos and other central Cretan sites, as well as at Torone (Chalcidice), which appears to be a 'Greek' settlement in a previously 'non-Greek' region. Occasional examples occur elsewhere, particularly in other parts of Crete and in Caria (which may reflect continuing influence from the native Anatolian tradition), and rarely at the great tumulus cemetery of Vergina (ancient Aigai) in Macedonia (which may reflect a response to contacts with communities further south). The rite was also taken in the eighth century to some of the first colonies in the western Mediterranean. However, the majority of the Greek Early Iron Age communities consistently inhumed their dead, and inhumation continued to be practised at most sites where cremation was common, even for high-status burials. In Crete, cremations were commonly secondary, and the ashes were placed in various forms of vase (and, later, sometimes in bronze vessels) within multiple burial tombs of the traditional types, but elsewhere in the Aegean each burial was normally in a separate grave.

There is thus a striking contrast with the evidence of the Homeric poems that are now widely agreed to reflect the practices and culture of the Early Iron Age in so far as they relate to anything real. In these poems cremation is the only burial custom clearly described, and it always seems to take the form of burning on a pyre, the collection of the ashes in a receptacle, and their deposition, with grave-goods, in a pit; in the most detailed descriptions this is covered by a mound on which a marker is erected. Apart from the Lefkandi 'Heroön' burial, this kind of burial is best paralleled in eighth-century cemeteries in Asia Minor: although there are other examples of cremations under mounds, these were commonly used for multiple burials rather than just one.

It is quite common to find different forms of cremation at the same Early Iron Age sites. At Athens, inurned cremation is most common, but the provision of a hole to contain the ash-urn within the basic pit was not a universal feature, and some cremains are placed loose within pits, whether brought in from the pyre or burnt on site. Such uncontained cremations have been identified at other sites; at Medeon the pyre was constructed to fall into a pit, the remains then being covered with earth. Nevertheless, inurned cremations are most common although they are found only very rarely at Lefkandi, where in some cases burials were left on the pyre and in others a token amount of the cremated bones was put in a pit or cist, with unburnt grave-goods. In the most elaborate example, a male's ashes and unburned items of clothing were placed in an antique bronze amphora,

accompanied by weapons and a richly arrayed female inhumation, in a pit within the massive 'Heroön' structure (c.1000–950 BC), while horse sacrifices were placed in an adjoining pit. This represents the nearest that reality is likely to come to the burial of Patroclus described in the *Iliad*, Book 23.

The history of cremation in Greece after approximately 700 BCE shows that many of the communities that had practised it more or less throughout the Early Iron Age continued to do so; but it did not spread to new regions, although it appeared in some colonies, and practice continued to vary. At Athens, many seventh- and sixth-century cremations were primary, taking place over or in the pit where the remains were left, and a mound would be heaped over this, perhaps as a deliberate echo of Homeric practice. Similar primary burials can be found on Rhodes, but it was more common there to place ash-urns in graves. Often, as on Crete and Thera, these were rock-cut tombs intended to hold several burials. Like their Early Iron Age predecessors, these ash-urns were often of very high quality with elaborate decoration, even bronze vessels or, on Thera, stone boxes, which suggests that the rite continued to have associations with high social status. By the end of the Archaic period (technically 480 BCE) inhumation had become dominant throughout Greece, and cremation was used principally to deal with deaths away from home and mass burials after battle (and also for victims of the late fifth-century 'plague' in Athens). However, there is evidence that individual families might have continued the practice, cremations and inhumations continued to be found together, and the continuing use of cremation for elite burials is exemplified at Vergina in the burial in Tomb II, widely identified as that of Philip II. **O.T.P.K. Dickinson**

References

Dickinson, O. (1994), *The Aegean Bronze Age*, Cambridge: Cambridge University Press.

Kurtz, D.C. and Boardman, J. (1971), *Greek Burial Customs*, London: Thames and Hudson.

Musgrave, J.H. (1990), 'Dust and Damn'd Oblivion: A Study of Cremation in Ancient Greece', *Annual of the British School at Athens*, 85: 271–99.

Stampolidis, N.C. (ed.) (2001), *Καύσεις στην εποχή του Χαλκού και την πρωιμή εποχή του Σιδήρου*

Athens: University of Crete and Mesogeiaki Archaeological Society.

Snodgrass, A.M. (1971), *The Dark Age of Greece*, Edinburgh: Edinburgh University Press. Reprinted 2000.

ANIMALS

Animal remains have been revealed amongst the human remains in various archaeological investigations of human cremation sites. This is the case, for example, in Sweden where Viking sites have revealed the remains of many species, including periods when dogs were the dominant species found and in Britain prior to the Middle Ages. In this sense it seems proper to use 'cremation' for animals rather than incineration or burning. Also, in some South American traditional tribal cultures, some cherished pets are known to have been cremated, especially prized hunting dogs, their bone remains being buried (Chagnon, 1992: 116).

Quite separate would be the burning of animals as part of animal sacrifices known in several religious contexts, most notably that of ancient Israel. Indeed, the entry on Isaac demonstrates perhaps the closest of symbolic relationships between a human and an animal, expressed through the symbolism of ashes, that the history of religions can furnish. **Douglas J. Davies**

See also archaeology of Britain; ashes of Isaac; Viking Sweden.

Reference

Chagnon, N.A. (1992), *Yanomamo*, New York: Harcourt Brace.

APPARENT DEATH

One of the advantages of cremation is that it avoids the possibility of someone being placed in a grave and buried when only apparently dead. In the phenomenon of apparent death the body's vital functions diminish so dramatically as to give the appearance of death when actual death has not occurred. Mistaken diagnoses confusing apparent death for actual death have been associated with cases of unintended vivisection and premature burial.

Science has long understood that physical death does not occur in a single instant but is a process that may continue for several hours after the major vital functions associated with life, including heartbeat, respiration and brainwave activity, have ceased. In general, in most Western medical practice, death is said to have occurred once resuscitation is no longer feasible or desirable.

In cultural terms, apparent death occupies a perilous region between what is obviously 'living' and what is absolutely dead. People have a deep human concern and a primal fear about being mistakenly declared dead and having their body disposed of in a manner that will carry with it tragic, unintended pain and suffering and certain death. For hundreds of years physicians relied on their own imperfect senses, methods, equipment and training to distinguish the living from the dead. Andreas Vesalius (1514–64), author of *De humanis corporis fabrica* (1543), based his atlas of human anatomy on dissecting human cadavers, a controversial and (in the era of the Spanish Inquisition) dangerous practice, and is said to have mistakenly pronounced dead one unfortunate nobleman whose heart was still beating when Vesalius opened his patient's chest cavity to perform the autopsy.

History offers countless stories of misdiagnoses – of catalepsy, 'trances', comas, exposure to extreme cold, or other conditions that severely depress the vital functions – accompanied by either 'miraculous' or tragic endings. Incidents where apparent death could be confused for real death probably occurred with above average frequency in times of social panic, such as wars or periods marked by plague, epidemics or famine. Efforts to detect apparent death have taken many forms – some practical and others extreme – but these should be seen primarily as a measure of the intense fears that were attached to premature burial.

Until the very recent past, physical decomposition of the body was the only absolute method of ruling out apparent death: this is certainly still the case in many parts of the world where advanced technology has not been put to work to confirm that actual death has taken place. Otherwise, elaborate methods have been employed to guard against the most horrible consequences of an apparent death. Some were intended to detect signs of life, – for example, placing mirrors or lit candles by the nostrils in order to detect breathing, irritating the flesh in some extreme manner, perhaps with fire, to excite a pain reflex – while others aimed to prove death – for example, placing the body in a warm room and watching it closely for decomposition to occur. To guard against premature burial elaborate mechanisms were invented, such as linking coffins to the surface to allow the victim to signal to the living. The most extreme methods undertaken to guard against the worst consequences of apparent death involved guaranteeing death: severing veins and arteries, draining the body of blood or, perhaps, severing the head.

Far more numerous and infamous are accounts that associate apparent death with premature burial that appear in scientific and medical records, folklore and literature. In his poem, 'The Premature Burial' (1844) Poe wrote what remains the most famous meditation on the phenomenon of apparent death: 'The boundaries which divide Life from Death, are at best shadowy and vague. Who shall say where one ends, and where the other begins?' That Poe's hero survives to tell the story of his ordeal provides the reader with a measure of relief and comfort absent from Wolfgang von Goethe's 'Apparent Death' (c. 1769).

> Weep, maiden, weep here o'er the tomb of Love;
> He died of nothing – by mere chance was slain.
> But is he really dead? – oh, that I cannot prove;
> A nothing, a mere chance, oft gives him life again.

Goethe punctuates two fears: first, the primal, universal apprehension of being the victim of a living inhumation; and, second, the fear arising from the uncertainty of the living that they may have been fooled by apparent death into wrongly burying a loved one.

A more obscure understanding of apparent death may be attached to the Christian doctrine of the resurrection of the literal body. In this context, while the physical body is dead in every earthly sense, Christianity interprets it to be in a temporary state of repose, waiting for divine reanimation on the Day of Judgement described in the book of Revelation. **Eric Love**

See also premature burial.

ARCHAEOLOGY OF BRITAIN

ANTIQUITY

The mortuary rite of cremation was practised in Britain throughout much of prehistory from the Early Neolithic (4000–3000 BC) to the early (pagan) Saxon period (410–650 AD), with a few examples of Norse cremations from the eighth to tenth centuries AD (Richards *et al.*, 1995). Cremation formed the predominant rite for disposal of the dead within the early–Middle Bronze Age (2300–1100 BC), the early Roman period (43–150 AD) and in parts of the northern frontier zones, adjacent to Hadrian's Wall, in the late Roman period (250–410 AD), and the early Saxon period in the northern and eastern areas of Saxon occupation – for example, in Yorkshire, Lincolnshire and East Anglia. Whilst some inferences about the attendant rites and rituals may be gained from textual and pictorial references – for example the late Bronze Age cremations described in Homer's *Iliad* and *Odyssey*, Roman rites referenced by contemporary scholars (see **Romans**), the cremation of the Saxon hero Beowulf (Bradley, 1982), and the tenth-century account of a Nordic cremation by the Islamic trader Ibn Fadlan (Brøndsted, 1965) – most of our knowledge about ancient cremation in Britain is based on archaeological evidence. Archaeological manifestations of cremation include the remains of the pyre site, the burial and deposits of pyre debris; study of the distribution of the various archaeological components within these deposits and the materials themselves informs on the formation processes from the laying-out of the body for cremation, to the burial and clearing-up processes. There were many similarities within the rite across the temporal range, with procedural variations only in minor details and cultural associations. The theme of fire as a cleansing/purification process and one of release with 'immediate' transformation appears to run throughout, as recited within the Old English poem, *Beowulf*:

> And so the warriors proceeded to kindle upon the hill-top a most mighty funeral pyre. Smoke from the wood climbed up ...until, when the swirling of the turbulent air dies down, the fire had by then destroyed his [Beowulf's] bone-framed body ...Heaven swallowed up the smoke (XLIII 3136–3156).

Most pyre sites – of which relatively few survive archaeologically – indicate that the pyre was constructed directly on the ground surface, rendering the ephemeral remains susceptible to destruction by subsequent activity. The under-pyre scoops associated with some late Iron Age pyres were probably dug to aid draught (McKinley, 2000). Some larger under-pyre pits – approximately 1.0 x 0.70m x 0.50m deep – known as *busta* have been found in Roman cemeteries, predominantly within the northern frontier zones but occasionally in the larger towns. These supposedly represent the remains of pyre sites that also served as graves, but the majority of those in Britain appear to represent only the pyre site, most of the cremated bone clearly having been removed (McKinley, 2000). Wood generally formed the fuel for cremation, doubling as support for the body and associated pyre goods, using the robust rectangular pyre construction described and depicted in art and texts stretching from Classical Greece to the present day. Logs, predominantly of oak – or pine where it formed the main species, as in parts of Scotland – were used for the main structure with other species as brushwood. Re-used timber was also sometimes employed. Peat also seems to have been used in the west and north of Scotland, including the islands, at least in the Bronze Age, and experiments have shown this to be a very efficient fuel for the purpose, although some wood would be necessary to construct a pyre platform. There is limited evidence from York for the use of coal as a pyre fuel in the Roman period.

The deceased was commonly accompanied on the pyre by a variety of objects, including personal items associated with the mode of dress or personal adornment, 'pet' animals and food offerings. The pyre goods evident from archaeological remains represent only a minimum of what would have been present, since most organic materials – items of wood, cloth, leather, food, drink or plants – would generally have been destroyed during cremation. Many of the items found would have related to the clothing in which the deceased was laid out; worked bone pins would have served to fasten clothing and are the most common artefacts recovered from the Bronze Age burials; brooches have been found in burials from the Iron Age to the Saxon periods, as have belt attachments, with hobnails indicating the presence of boots on

some Roman pyres. Items of jewellery are another common find; these include bracelets and rings from the Iron Age and Roman periods, earrings from Roman burials, and necklaces of coloured glass beads in Roman and – particular – Saxon burials. Personal items such as knives – for domestic use – are common from the Iron Age through to the Saxon period and were probably attached to the person by a belt. Other items such as toilet sets (tweezers, ear-scoops, shears and razors), worked bone combs and bone playing pieces are all common items in the Saxon period and would generally have been carried in a bag attached to the waist, as illustrated by the frequent recovery of ivory bag-rings (forming the opening to the bag and to which the organic fabric of the bag would have been attached). Fragments of spindle whorls and flint tools reflect another side of life carried over into death. Fragments of various types of container – bowls and buckets of copper-alloy and wood, ceramic and glass vessels – from Roman and Saxon burials suggest that the deceased was also accompanied on the pyre by food and drink. Fragments of intricate worked bone inlay from Roman deposits represent the remains of decorated boxes, with large quantities of such items – mostly from fourth-century burials in the northern frontier zone – representing the decoration from funeral couches. The inclusion of items of weaponry on the pyre such as implied in some textual references (for example, Beowulf's pyre was … 'hung about with helmets, with battle-shields, with bright mail-coats…') is not reflected in the archaeological evidence, such material being only very rarely recovered from Saxon sites. It is, of course, possible that the remains of such items were collected from the pyre site after cremation and disposed of elsewhere or the metal re-used, the requirement being their inclusion in the cremation process rather than in the burial.

Throughout the use of the cremation rite, the inclusion of whole or partial animal carcasses on the pyre was a common trait. The frequency of occurrence, quantity of animal bone and number of species tends to increase over time (McKinley, 1997). The quantities of animal bone found in Neolithic and Bronze Age burials are generally small, including immature sheep/goat and bird bone in the later period. The most popular species in the late Iron Age and Roman periods were pig and domestic fowl. In all these cases, the animals appear to represent the remains of food offerings, and only part of the animal was placed on the pyre. The Saxon period saw a dramatic change with almost half the burials found in areas where the rite predominated containing animal bone – most commonly horse – the animal being cremated whole. Multiple species are also found, apparently representing different types of offering: horse and dog represent 'status' animals or 'pets'; sheep, cattle, pig and probably bird, fish and deer represent food offerings; with fox, bear (claws), beaver and raptor claws having amuletic or more 'decorative' qualities.

The efficiency of cremation was generally high, with open pyres achieving temperatures commensurate with those of modern crematoria at 800–1000°C, and consequenty, most of the bone from the majority of burials from all periods is fully oxidized. Consistently less well oxidized bone has been observed in the Roman period, particularly amongst the poorer burials in some of the town cemeteries, which are also the locations where the only evidence of partial cremation has been found. Unlike in earlier and subsequent periods, and in the rural Roman cemeteries where the cremation was probably organized and carried out by relatives or designated individuals within the community, cremation in the towns is likely to have been undertaken by professionals (see **Romans**). Consequently, some of the poor may not have been able to afford as much fuel for their pyres as others, and failed attempts at cremation (for example, due to adverse weather) may have been less likely to have been followed by a a second attempt. The human bone remaining at the end of cremation was very rarely, if ever, all collected for burial (McKinley, 1993); from a multi-period sample of >4000 undisturbed adult cremation burials a wide range of between 57 and 2200 grams was recorded (McKinley, 1994) and an average of around 40–60 per cent of the expected bone weight (commensurate with weights from modern crematoria) found. There is no evidence that the bone was deliberately fragmented prior to burial; the size of bone fragments from many of the relatively few known Neolithic burials tends to be small, but this is due to the mode of burial in communal chambered tombs where the bone (cremated and inhumed) from earlier burials was 'curated' and moved about after the initial deposition.

Bone was generally buried in some form of container – organic or inorganic. The latter predominantly comprised ceramic vessels, though glass was also occasionally used in the Roman and Saxon periods. The form of the organic containers is largely unknown – their presence being indicated by the compact concentration of bone in these burials – but is likely to have included skin/leather, fabric and basket. Unenclosed burials, with the bone deposited in a spread or heap on the base of the grave, seem to have been relatively rare, with examples from the Neolithic, Bronze Age and possibly the Iron Age where the bone was deposited with ceramic vessels (see below) but not within them. Urned burials were common in the Early–Middle Bronze Age and Roman period, and represented the almost exclusive form of burial in the Saxon period. Unurned, but contained burials were most frequently seen in the Late Bronze Age and Roman periods. Grave-goods – items that had not been on the pyre – became part of the rite during the Late Iron Age and Roman periods, generally in the form of ceramic vessels, sometimes amounting to entire dinner services. Other items might include food offerings and clothing, with these and other organic items occasionally contained in wooden boxes or caskets; in the Roman period, the latter sometimes also acted as the container or secondary container to the cremated bone.

In most periods (Bronze Age to Saxon) around 5 per cent of burials include the remains of two individuals, with more in a very small proportion of cases. In most instances the evidence suggests that these are the remains of individuals cremated together on the same pyre. They most commonly include a sub-adult (aged over 13 years) or adult (aged over 18 years), of either sex, with an immature individual (aged under 12 years), particularly infants (aged under five years). The implication is these individuals, placed together in death, were closely related in life.

Most known Neolithic burials have been recovered from chambered or passage tombs where potentially large numbers of individuals may be buried together over many years. Bronze Age burials are also commonly associated with earthworks, often being made in association with barrows that may occur in groups and sometimes have associated 'flat cemeteries' extending between them, and they too were often used over an extensive timeframe. Burials may be found singly in isolated locations or in cemeteries of up to around 150. The few known Iron Age cemeteries are relatively large with 100 plus burials and appear to have served small communities. Roman cemeteries range from around five to ten burials in some rural locations to almost 1000 in some of the larger towns that may have supported more than one cemetery on the outskirts of the settlement. The largest cremation cemeteries are those of the Saxons, Spong Hill in Norfolk containing almost 3000 burials, some of which are made in what appear to have been communal grave pits. There is evidence to suggest that these large (essentially rural) Saxon cemeteries served the surrounding area rather than one immediately neighbouring settlement.

In all but the Saxon (and possibly the Neolithic) period the vicinity of the cemetery also appears to have functioned as the crematorium. Pyre sites were frequently cleared of debris, often to facilitate re-use, and consequently redeposited pyre debris – mainly fuel ash incorporating cremated bone and pyre goods not collected for burial – is routinely found in all except the Saxon cemeteries of the north and east. Sometimes the deposition appears to have been a simple 'cleaning-up' operation, as with the large quantities of debris found in some Bronze Age barrow ditches (McKinley, 1997) and the surface spread of debris (from a minimum 19 cremations) from the Roman cemetery of east London (McKinley, 2000), but elsewhere the deposition was clearly part of the mortuary rite. Pyre debris would be deposited within the grave (below or above the burial itself), over the backfilled grave as if to 'seal' it, or in specifically excavated features almost forming a burial of itself. This latter type of deposit may sometimes be linked with features which may carry all the attributes of a grave – being of commensurate size and shape and containing grave goods – but no bone; the cenotaph as a mortuary feature is referred to in Roman texts (Toynbee, 1996: 54), but archaeological evidence may be seen in the Bronze Age, Iron Age and Roman period. In some cases, the body may have been unavailable for cremation, but in others it appears that the bone was sent or taken elsewhere for burial.

Jacqueline I. McKinley

See also Romans.

References

Bradley, S.A.J. (1982), *Anglo-Saxon Poetry*, London: Dent.

Brøndstead, J. (1965), *The Vikings*, Harmondsworth: Penguin.

McKinley, J.I. (1993), 'Bone Fragment Size and Weights of Bone from Modern British Cremations and its Implications for the Interpretation of Archaeological Cremations', *International Journal Osteoarchaeology*, 3: 283–87.

McKinley, J.I. (1994), 'Bone Fragment Size in British Cremation Burials and its Implications for Pyre Technology and Ritual', *Journal Archaeological Science*, 21: 339–42.

McKinley, J.I. (1997), 'Bronze Age "Barrows" and the Funerary Rites and Rituals of Cremation', *Proceedings Prehistoric Society*, 63: 129–45.

McKinley, J.I. (2000), 'Phoenix Rising: Aspects of Cremation in Roman Britain', in M. Millett, J. Pearce, and M. Struck (eds), *Burial, Society and Context in the Roman World*, Oxford: Oxbow Books, 38–44.

Richards, J.D., Jecock, M., Richmond, L. and Tuck, C. (1995), 'The Viking Barrow Cemetery at Heath Wood, Ingleby, Derbyshire', *Medieval Archaeology*, 34: 51–69.

Toynbee, J.M.C. (1996), *Death and Burial in the Roman World*, London: Johns Hopkins University Press (paperback edn).

BRONZE AGE

Cremation was a way of disposing of the dead throughout the Bronze Age in Britain (2300–700 BC), occurring contemporaneously with inhumation burials in the early phase (2300–1500 BC), predominating in the middle phase (1500–1100 BC) and practised to a lesser extent in the late phase (1100–700 BC). The rite represents a continuum in practice from the preceding Neolithic period. Our knowledge of cremation in Britain throughout the period is based on archaeological evidence which may take one of three principal forms – the pyre site, the burial and redeposited pyre debris – and each may occur alone or in combination with one or both of the others, the burial being the most frequently encountered. All these forms of evidence are commonly linked with round barrows (*tumuli* or 'burial mounds' of various sizes and forms (Grinsell, 1941; fig. 1) – though not all of these are associated with burials. They may be found sealed below barrow mounds, incorporated within the ring-ditches associated with them or within the barrow construction – the barrows themselves often being built episodically over time rather than on a single occasion (Woodward, 2000) – as insertions into the mound (grave cuts), or as deposits placed adjacent to them. Individual barrows or groups of barrows were often used over many years; some barrows that commenced in the Neolithic and Early Bronze Age were still in use in the Middle Bronze Age, centuries after their initial construction. Flat cemeteries may extend between the barrow groups or around an individual barrow. In the Middle Bronze Age, some single or small groups of burials were also made in new open sites (Woodward, 2000). The rite was not exclusive to one or other sex, or to certain age groups; the remains of neonates through to elderly adults have been recovered from burials and pyre debris.

Pyre sites – indicated by an 'appropriately sized' area of on-site burning with or without associated pyre debris – are by nature ephemeral features. A large proportion of those currently known of in Britain date from the Bronze Age, largely because they have been protected from subsequent disturbance by the barrow mound. Evidence suggests that the deceased was most commonly laid in an extended position, but bodies will have varied in size and the inclusion of pyre goods or dual cremations may have necessitated extending the size of the pyre. Homer's description of Patroclus' pyre in the *Iliad* (later Bronze Age Greece) as 100-foot square, and holding the carcasses of many sheep and cattle, plus four horses and two dogs arranged around the corpse of their former owner (Book XXII, 124–37) may partly be poetic licence, but does give some indication of what may have been considered appropriate pyre goods.

Since all recoverable bone was very rarely, if ever, included in the burial as a deliberate policy (McKinley, 1993, 1997) some of the cremated bone and pyre goods remained with the other pyre debris (predominantly fuel ash). Analysis of the distribution of cremated remains on uncleared or partially cleared pyre sites suggests that the surface ashes were raked over at the end of the cremation, breaking up any remaining charred soft tissues and encouraging further oxidation. Such raking may also have served to draw the bone together into a heap to facilitate recovery for burial. It is evident, however, that many pyre sites were cleared of debris immediately or shortly after cremation, possibly to allow re-use of the site, so little or no debris may remain. Where no trace of a pyre site remains – generally as a result of subsequent disturbance – its presence may be inferred from the recovery of redeposited pyre debris as, for example, at Twyford Down, Hampshire (Walker and Farwell, 2000) where large spreads of debris from the ring-ditch of the barrow clearly indicated that the pyres had been built within its confines – that is, below the mound. Redeposited pyre debris has also been found in the backfills of cremation graves (deposited below, around or above the burial itself), deposited over cremation graves, dumped into pre-existent features (see above) as spreads – for example, as at Linga Fold, Orkney (Downes, 1995) – or deposited in apparently deliberately excavated features. In some cases the deposition of this debris appears to form merely a 'clearing-up' process, but there is also clear evidence for its being a deliberate part of the mortuary rite. Where directly associated with a burial, the bone in the pyre debris generally gives no indication of having originated from other than the same cremation as that in the burial. It is also clear in many cases that a proportion of bone from the cremation was not included in either of the two related deposits, but must have been disposed of in a third location (or even in multiple locations) perhaps distributed as mementos, as in nineteenth-century Aboriginal Australia (Hiatt, 1969), or used as votive offerings, or scattered.

The efficiency of cremation was generally high, with full oxidation of the bone in the vast majority of cases. There is no evidence to suggest either deliberate fragmentation of bone prior to burial or of the selection of any specific skeletal elements for burial. As is common to the rite in all periods, the weight of bone recovered from individual adult burials is highly variable with no obvious reasons why this should be so. To date, the only apparent pattern is in relation to primary or central Bronze Age barrow burials (see below), which consistently produce high weights of bone (*c.* 900–2800g) with an average of 1525.7g (McKinley, 1997). Many Bronze Age cremation cemeteries have one or two burials with over 1000g, but the average weights of bone are much lower, in the region of 327–466g. As with other aspects of the rite it may be that the time expended on collecting bone for burial and/or the number of individuals involved in the collection reflected the status of the deceased.

Pyre goods, such as worked bone or antler pins for fastening clothing, copper-alloy objects and worked flint tools, are commonly recovered from amongst the cremated human bone. Animal offerings were also cremated on the pyre with the deceased; approximately 16 per cent of British burials have been found to contain small quantities of one or two species of animal, most commonly immature sheep/goats and birds.

Barrow burials are generally referred to as 'primary' or 'central', 'satellite' and 'secondary' burials, depending on their position. Often several burials were made before any barrow construction commenced, and the form of the barrow could be altered over time, sometimes in association with successive mortuary activity (Woodward, 2000). In the Early and Middle Bronze Age burials were frequently made in ceramic vessels – beakers (Late Neolithic/Early Bronze Age), collared urns (Early Bronze Age) and Deverel Rimbury vessels (middle Bronze Age) – deposited upright or sometimes inverted. Unurned burials were also made; in the majority of cases the bone appears to have been placed within some form of organic container, made of skin, cloth or basket, leaving the bone in a confined concentration within the grave fill. In a few instances, the bone was spread across the base of the grave. Most graves were simple pits, but stone-lined cist graves were also constructed. Cemeteries tended to be relatively small – averaging around thirteen burials (Woodward 2000) – but where larger groups have been found (c. 150), the burials appear to form clusters of some 10–30 graves. As in other periods in which the rite was practised, approximately 5 per cent of cremation burials include the remains of two individuals, with more in a very small proportion of cases. These generally appear to represent the remains of a 'dual' cremation – that is, two individuals cremated on the same pyre – and most commonly comprise an adult (predominantly female) with an immature individual (mostly young infants, including neonates). There is some evidence for successive deposits of bone – presumably from different cremations – being made in the same urn (McKinley, 2000). The retention of bone collected for burial from one cremation until that

from a second could be included prior to burial is supported by a passage in Homer's *Iliad* where Patroclus' spirit speaks to Achilles …'Do not let them bury my bones apart from yours, Achilles. Let them lie together, just as you and I grew up together in your house…. So let one urn …hold our bones' (Book XXIII: 83–91). That his instructions were followed is confirmed by a passage from Homer's *Odyssey* in which the spirit of Agamemnon addresses that of Achilles: 'In this [golden amphora] your white bones lie, my lord Achilles, and mingled with them the bones of Menoetius' son Patroclus, dead before you, and separately those of Antilochus, who was your closest friend after Patroclus' death' (Book XXIV: 73–76). The implication is that Achilles' and Patroclus' bones were mixed ('mingled') and those of Antilochus added separately.

Individual graves – generally the central/primary grave – may have been reopened several times for new burials to be made. These most commonly included inhumation burials or mixed rites (inhumation and cremation) with about three or four burial episodes. One late Neolithic/Early Bronze Age cist grave in Cornwall, however, contained the cremated remains of a minimum of 19 individuals made as successive deposits, the remains from the previous burial being pushed to the back of the cist each time. **Jacqueline I. McKinley**

References

Downes, J. (1995), 'Linga Fold, Sandwick, Orkney; Excavation of a Bronze Age Barrow Cemetery 1994', *GUARD*, 59(2) (Glasgow University).

Grinsell, L.V. (1941), 'The Bronze Age Round Barrows of Wessex', *Proceedings Prehistoric Society*, 7(3): 73–113.

Hiatt, B. (1969), 'Cremation in Aboriginal Australia', *Mankind*, 7(2): 104–15.

Homer (1950), *The Iliad*, trans. E.V. Rien, Harmondsworth: Penguin.

Homer (1972), *The Odyssey*, trans. E.V. Rieu, Harmondsworth: Penguin.

McKinley, J.I. (1993), 'Bone Fragment Size and Weights of Bone from Modern British Cremations and its Implications for the Interpretation of Archaeological Cremations', *International Journal Osteoarchaeology*, 3: 283–87.

McKinley, J.I. (1997), 'Bronze Age "Barrows" and the Funerary Rites and Rituals of Cremation', *Proceedings Prehistoric Society*, 63: 129–145.

McKinley, J.I. (2000), 'Human Bone and Funerary Deposits' in K.E. Walker and D.F. Farwell (eds), *Twyford Down, Hampshire. Archaeological Investigations the M3 Motorway from Bar End to Compton, 1990–93*, Hampshire Field Club Monograph 9: 85–119.

Walker, K.E. and Farwell, D.F. (eds) (2000), *Twyford Down, Hampshire. Archaeological Investigations the M3 Motorway from Bar End to Compton, 1990–93*, Hampshire Field Club Monograph 9.

Woodward, A. (2000), *British Barrows; A Matter of Life and Death*, Stroud: Tempus.

ARCHITECTS

Architects have played a dominant role in the emergence and development of modern cremation. Gunnar Asplund (Sweden), Erich Boltenstern (Austria), W.M. Dudok (Netherlands), Stefan Fayans (Poland), Edwin Maxwell Fry (UK) and Sigurd Lewerentz (Sweden) are the most important architects in this field, and each has been allocated a separate entry.

The following articles discuss the role of architects in the context of cremation in Austria and Britain. **Douglas J. Davies**

See also architecture; Asplund; Boltenstern; Dudok; Fayans; Fry; Holzmeister; Lewerentz; Schumacher.

AUSTRIA

From the 1890s onwards the issue of cremation increasingly interested Austrian architects, with a leading role being played by students and professors at the Technische Hochschule in Wien (currently the Vienna University of Technology). It was here that draft projects for cremation facilities were drawn up and internal competitions held on this topic. The building and operation of crematoria was first made possible following the establishment of the Austrian Republic in November, 1918. The architect, Max Freiherr von Ferstel (1853–1936), a professor at the Technische Hochschule, made a name for himself through drawings of this new type of building and subsequently awakened interest in a number of his students including Clemens Holzmeister, Erich Boltenstern and Julius Schulte. He submitted entries for the architectural competitions for the crematoria in Graz in 1903–1904 and Vienna in 1921. A

significant contribution to the architectural development of crematoria in the German-speaking world was made by the architect Stefan Fayans in scientific publications, as his separate entry shows.

At the beginning of the twenty-first century in Austria there are 11 crematoria in operation: Wien-Simmering by Clemens Holzmeister (1922); Steyr (Upper Austria) by Franz Koppelhuber (1927); Linz (Upper Austria) by Julius Schulte (1929); Salzburg by Eduard Wiedenmann (1931); Graz (Styria) by Erich Boltenstern with Ludwig Dawidoff (1932); Villach (Carinthia) by Erich Boltenstern (1953); Wien-Stammersdorf by Erich Boltenstern with Josef Strelec (1966); Knittelfeld (Styria) by Wolfgang Lukas (1975); St Pölten (Lower Austria) by Erich Boltenstern with Paul Pfaffenbichler (1975); Hohenems (Vorarlberg) by Gerhard Brunner (1988); and Innsbruck (Tirol) by Eleonore Bidwell (1998–99). Preparations have already been completed for the construction of an additional crematorium at Linz-Urfahr by Klaus Kada. All crematoria built prior to the Second World War have been expanded since 1963 when cremation was finally accepted by the Roman Catholic Church.

The design of crematoria demands, in addition to specialized knowledge regarding organizational contexts, a gift for empathizing with the emotional life-situation of people. The architects Clemens Holzmeister, Julius Schulte and Erich Boltenstern, whose biographies reveal various points of contact, conceived of buildings currently regarded as classic. Architects of the younger generation are Eleonore Bidwell, Gerhard Brunner, Klaus Kada and Wolfgang Lukas. **Bruno Maldoner**

See also Bolterstern; Fayans, Holzmeister; Schulte.

Reference

Fayans, S. (1907), *Bestattungsanlagen* (Handbuch der Architektur, IV, Volume 8, Halbband, Heft 3, Stuttgart: Alfred Kröner Verlag. Reviewed in *Der Bautechniker. Zentralorgan für das österreichische Bauwesen*, 27: 847.

BRITAIN

In 1904 the architect Albert Chambers Freeman (c. 1874–1938), published what would appear to be the first British text dealing with the architecture and planning of crematoria, entitled *Crematoria in Great Britain and Abroad*. It illustrated an extraordinary and heterogeneous collection of buildings drawn from Italy, France, Germany, Sweden, Britain, America and Canada. The book took the form of a short history of cremation followed by a discussion of the design of crematoria and columbaria, an account of systems of incineration and individual accounts of crematoria. It provided not only an invaluable insight into the development of crematoria to date, but also an international context into which to place the 13 operational British crematoria built by 1904. Although Freeman purported to discuss 'design', which one might expect to embrace 'architectural style', his deliberations are largely confined to issues of planning and the more technical aspects of cremation. One-sixth of the text is devoted to a consideration of systems of incineration. Individual accounts, while mentioning the style adopted, make no attempt to discuss the associative values which might attach to particular styles. In 1906 Freeman addressed the Society of Architects in London on the planning of crematoria and columbaria, opening with the rather surprising admission that, as architects, they were to discuss 'a subject upon which the architectural profession at present possesses little information'. Freeman's book included one of his own designs for a columbarium (1904), in the form of a Renaissance dome. When his ecclesiastical design for a 'proposed new crematoria for a London Borough' (1931), is compared with his geometric, quasi-modern Islington Crematorium, East Finchley (1937), it is clear that the question of style was still wide open. To date, Freeman's text remains the only dedicated book examining British crematorium architecture.

Sir Ernest George, (1839–1922) was the first architect of national repute to be involved with the design of a crematorium. One of the most prolific and successful of late Victorian domestic architects, he was best known for his town houses in Harrington and Collingham Gardens, Kensington, London (1880–88), dubbed by Osbert Lancaster as 'Pont Street Dutch', and for his many country houses, built over a period of 50 years. George was recommended by his friend William Robinson to the Board of the London Cremation Company to design Golders Green Crematorium in 1901. It was announced to

shareholders that the directors 'felt sure that Mr. George would command the confidence of the public'. Although George's involvement in crematorium architecture was confined to Golders Green, his choice of Lombard Romanesque, his bold manipulation of masses and 'more abstract elements of Design', together with sensitivity to the special building type (which led him to include porte-cochere cloisters and what is believed to be the first purpose-built columbarium), established Golders Green as arguably the finest British example of the building type. Other architects of national reputation involved with crematorium architecture included Sir E. Guy Dawber, (1861–1938), Sir Edwin Cooper (1873–1942), Sir Robert Lorimer (1864–1929) and H.S. Goodhart-Rendel (1887–1959).

One of the most important publications to give a lead to architects came not from the profession, but from the Cremation Society of Great Britain. *Cremation in Britain* (Jones and Noble, 1909) ran to three editions (1909, 1931 and 1945 (Jones, 1945)). All contained essays on 'The Ideal Crematorium' written respectively by A.C. Freeman, H.T. Herring, (honorary secretary of the Cremation Society) and J. Seaton Dahl, architect of Barham, Ruislip and Maidstone crematoria. All three authors addressed issues of planning of the site, choice of fuels, the interior of the chapels, architectural plan, disposal of the ashes, memorials and 'other requirements', contending that 'No rules can be laid down as to the external features of a crematorium' (Dahl, 1945: 114). Crematoria architecture remained something of a Cinderella subject. Despite some signs of interest on the part of the architectural profession as whole in the years immediately preceding the Second World War, there was little in the way of formal preparation for the sudden call for burgeoning numbers of purpose-built establishments in the 1950s. It fell to the Cremation Society to provide a lead. Architect Harold W.R. Orr, based in Bletchley and responsible for the design of crematoria at Oxford (1935), Torquay (1956), Barnstaple (1966) and Slough (1963), addressed the Society's Conference in 1950 with the missionary zeal of a modernist. His designs reflect his admiration of modern Scandinavian work and he encouraged colleagues to design 'neither with sentimentality, nor sensationalism' (Orr, 1950: 2).

The internationally renowned architect,

Edwin Maxwell Fry (1899–1987) made a significant contribution to the discussion of crematoria in Britain and is discussed in his own dedicated entry. In 1967, architect Peter Bernard Bond published an influential article in the *Architectural Review*, 'The Celebration of Death: Some Thoughts on the Design of Crematoria'. Bond, an associate partner of Maxwell Fry, took up Fry's argument about the devaluing of the ceremonial and personal aspects of the experience of the mourners. Bond believed that architects had lost sight of the purpose of the crematorium, by concentrating on the dead at the expense of the living. He argued that the architect's responsibility was to 'provide a context in which the living can experience to the full the reality of death and perhaps, from this, the privilege of life' (Bond, 1970: 87). He accused the Church, 'which has been throughout history our tutor in matters of meaning and purpose of existence', of acquiescence in respect of the liturgical arrangements of crematoria (Bond, 1970: 90). The challenge was taken up by Mr Gilbert Cope, deputy director of the Institute for the Study of Worship and Religious Architecture in the University of Birmingham. Cope was in Anglican Orders and applauded Bond's somewhat controversial suggestion of separating the chapel from what happens afterwards, allowing the opportunity of direct access to the committal chamber, which it was felt would benefit a variety of faiths. Cope organized a conference at Birmingham University, 'The Last Enemy', intended to 'bring into conjunction the many aspects of Dying, Death and Disposal which are normally considered in isolation from one another'. He was invited to speak and, in so doing, drew architecture into this new interdisciplinary nexus. The conference revealed that the dissatisfaction with cremation as anonymous and resembling a conveyor-belt resulted from a combination of wide-ranging factors. It vindicated architecture to an extent, since, to date, it was the crematorium building which had been held responsible, with its planning centred around the perceived philosophy of 'one in, one out' (Davies, 1995: 37). Bond emerges as one of the most influential architectural theorists on the architecture of post-war crematoria.

Other architects who have addressed the Cremation Society on matters of architecture and design included A. Douglas Robinson, who discussed 'The Architectural Approach' in 1957 and Christopher Robinson, partner in Sir Guy Dawber, Fox & Robinson and architect of the Mid-Warwickshire Crematorium, Leamington Spa (1971). Robinson presented a paper, 'Economy in Crematorium Design' in 1977. Since the majority of British crematoria were designed in between 1952 and 1962, it is hardly surprising that the theoretical discussions were concentrated in the post-war period. Since the 1970s there has been a relative slowdown in crematorium construction, the majority having been being built by the private sector since 1980, but professional architectural publications, including the *Architectural Review* and *Architects Journal* have taken a greater interest in the crematorium as a building type. Articles now include appraisals in addition to providing merely technical details and in so doing they have endorsed the importance of the crematorium in a modern society. **Hilary Grainger**

See also Fry.

References

Bond, Peter B. (1967), 'The Celebration of Death: Some Thoughts on the Design of Crematoria', *Pharos*, 33(3): 62–66.

Bond, Peter B. (1970), 'Architecture for Mourning', in G. Cope (ed.), *Dying, Death and Disposal*, London: SPCK, 85–98.

Dahl, J.L. Seaton (1945), 'The Ideal Crematorium', in P.M. Jones (ed.), *Cremation in Britain*, London: Pharos Press.

Davies, D. (1995), *British Crematoria in Public Profile*, Maidstone: The Cremation Society of Great Britain.

Freeman, A.C. (1904), *Crematoria in Great Britain and Abroad*, London: St Bride's Press.

Jones, P.H. and Noble, G.A. (eds) (1909), *Cremation in Britain*, London: The Cremation Society. Second edition 1931.

Jones, P.H. (ed.) (1945), *Cremation in Britain*, London: Pharos Press.

Orr, H.R.W. (1950), 'Crematorium Architecture', *Pharos*, 16(4): 2–5.

Robinson, A. Douglas (1957), 'The Architectural Approach', *Pharos*, 23(4): 15–19.

Robinson, C. (1977), 'Economy in Crematorium Design', *Report of Proceedings – Annual Cremation Conference, Brighton, 12–14 July, 1977*, Maidstone: The Cremation Society of Great Britain, 27–33.

ARCHITECTURE

AUSTRIA

The first crematorium in Austria was built within the remains of a walled, Renaissance garden, across from the Zentralfriedhof, a communal cemetery in Wien-Simmering. The subsequent crematoria (Salzburg, Villach, Innsbruck, Wien-Stammersdorf, St Pölten, Knittelfeld) have also been located within, or near, communal cemeteries. Where cemeteries were denominationally administered, crematoria with urn cemeteries could only be erected outside of, or near, the cemetery proper, as was the case with Graz and Steyr. A separate area for a crematorium with an urn grove has been chosen for the new crematorium in Linz-Urfahr, which is situated in the Stadtwäldchen (municipal woods), and a second installation is planned for a neighbouring area. Most crematorium buildings also feature a centrally located columbarium.

The design of Austrian crematoria extends significantly beyond the utilitarian since the architecture and surroundings both have a considerable effect on the mourner's experience. In this respect, the first structures of this type remain unsurpassed since their architects placed great importance on the design of impressive edifices. Before entering the ceremonial halls, the mourners traverse architecturally fashioned courtyards, similar to those found in classic forecourts of temples, thereby preparing them for the forthcoming ceremony. Nearly all crematoria erected up to 1933 were conceived in the form of a tower, incorporating the chimneys into the structure so that they were not recognizable as such from the outside. The first Austrian crematorium erected in Wien-Simmering could well have functioned as the ideal. Only with the crematorium in Graz, constructed in 1932, did the chimney appear as a technical element, while crematoria built after the Second World War show the chimney shaft as just such a technical element, the only exception being the crematorium in Knittelfeld which has the chimney integrated into the belfry.

The ceremonial halls of the smaller crematoria built between the two World Wars were originally either non-existent or were only roofed with glazing added later. Since the Second World War, ceremonial halls have occasionally been conceived for the dual purpose of cremation and burial as at Villach, Knittelfeld and St Pölten. Whenever individual viewing rooms were available they were also situated on the main level. These rooms were part of the original design in the installations in Villach and Graz, but were added later in Salzburg and Linz. In nearly all Austrian crematoria the operational areas and catafalques are on the same level as the ceremonial halls, but they can also be arranged like a stage slightly above the level of the hall. At the end of the ceremony, sliding gates separate the coffin from the mourners. Artistically noteworthy gates are found in Salzburg, Graz and Steyr. However, the crematoria in Wien-Simmering and Linz are organized differently, with their operational areas being located directly below the ceremonial hall. In both these crematoria the coffin is placed on a platform that can be lowered into the operational area after the leave-taking ceremony has been completed thus imitating a traditional burial.

When considering their artistic decor – windows, ornamental statues, paintings, artistically constructed equipment and tapestries – crematoria need not fear comparison with churches built at the same time. Of particular importance is the artistic decor in the Wien-Simmering, Linz and Villach crematoria. The building methods employed were, as with other buildings, dependent on the financial circumstances of the commissioning organization at the time. The most modern construction technology of its time is found, for example, with the crematorium in Wien-Simmering where the reinforced concrete shell is modelled after a project by the structural engineer Rudolf Saliger. The crematorium built shortly afterwards in Steyr and erected in part by volunteer labour, has brick walls and wooden roofs.

The cremators, constructed on the principles of the regenerative process, were originally fuelled by coke, coal, wood or gas. The crematorium at Wien-Simmering opened in 1923, has a cremator that was constructed by Wiener Gaswerksbau- und Maschinen-Fabrik AG Franz Manoschek and was licensed by Klingenstierna-Beck. This installation was later replaced, and it currently runs on electricity in order to meet modern-day environmental protection directives.

Although crematoria are usually managed municipally, in some cases the building was financed by a private organization such as the Arbeiter-Feuerbestattungsverein 'Die Flamme' and its branches, whose goal was to promote the practice of cremation. Cremation is up to 40 per cent less expensive than a traditional burial, and the percentage of cremations compared to interments in Austria has greatly increased. **Bruno Maldoner**

Reference

Fayans, S. (1907), *Bestattungsanlagen*, Handbuch der Architektur, Volume 8, Halbband, Heft 3, Stuttgart: Alfred Kröner Verlag. Reviewed in *Der Bautechniker. Zentralorgan für das Osterreichische Bauwesen*, 27: 847.

BRITAIN

The choice of an architectural style appropriate for crematoria was to tax the skill and ingenuity of architects throughout the twentieth century, since this type of building possessed no architectural precedent. In this sense, crematoria were analogous to the early railway stations of the nineteenth century. The style also had to be appropriate for a movement seeking official and public approval in the face of continuing public opposition. While the function of a crematorium is singular, the form the building takes remains a matter of taste.

The British crematorium must be unique in the history of building types with 140, representing more than half of all British crematoria, built between 1950 and 1967. The majority of early examples echoed, albeit lamely, traditional ecclesiastical Gothic, presumably with the intention of providing reassurance through a visual connection with the Church and traditional burial. This, of course, had been necessitated by the need to convert existing cemetery chapels. Woking (1879), Glasgow (1895), Liverpool (1896) and Kingston-upon-Hull (1901), the first municipal crematorium, all followed ecclesiastical precedents. The early exception was Manchester (1892), where local architects Steinthal and Solomons chose northern Italian Lombard-Romanesque. They drew on the designs of the great vaulted churches decorated on the outside with bands and arcades, with their detached bell towers and elaborately carved facades, exemplified at Como, Milan and Verona. Similar in style to the churches of Lombardy and Venice, the exterior of the Manchester chapel was finished in a golden buff-coloured terracotta, which, together with slate

used for the roof, gave a warm appearance. Entrance to the crematorium was through a lofty arched porch with steps on either side connecting the colonnade and columbarium.

Nine years later the architects of Darlington were content to adopt a cottage-like form with a Gothic entrance and a disconcertingly homely looking chimney. The design of Nottingham Crematorium resulted from a competition held in 1899 and assessed by Aston Webb, one of the leading Victorian architects. The winning design by Birmingham architects Arthur E. McKewan and Alfred J. Dunn showed a bold employment of a late Gothic style, more in keeping with contemporary architectural fashion. Sadly, Nottingham's ambitions to become the first municipal crematorium were thwarted. The plans were shelved and the honour fell to Kingston-upon-Hull in 1901. Built in red brick, with ashlar stone dressings and slate roofs, Nottingham was early perpendicular Gothic in style, freely treated. Leicester Crematorium (1902), erected in the Gilroes Cemetery and designed by local architects Goddard & Company, comprised two lofty chapels, one intended for burial services, the other for cremations. These two buildings were divided by a carriageway, above which stood a tower. The group presents a coherent and dignified composition. The massing is impressive, and Goddard interpreted late Gothic convincingly, using warm red brick and stone banding and detailing. The use of materials made a passing reference to William Butterfield's Keble College, Cambridge, (1867–83), although a more likely source is Bentley's Westminster Cathedral, nearing completion in 1902. Birmingham and Ilford crematoria followed in 1903. The former provided a chapel described as being 'of an ecclesiastical character in brick and red stone'. The 80-foot furnace shaft was contained within a lofty ornamental tower. Walter Samuel Braithwaite's design for Headingly Crematorium (1903) at Lawnswood Cemetery, Leeds, is ecclesiastical in appearance with a disproportionately high belltower housing the furnace shaft. Bradford Crematorium (1905) by the City architect, F.E.P. Edwards revealed a more compact solution, with a rather squat tower.

There can be little doubt that the commissioning of Sir Ernest George (1839–1922) for the design of Golders Green Crematorium was to be of great significance. George was one of the most prolific and successful of late Victorian architects and he provided a magnificent composition in Lombard-Romanesque, acknowledged by the architectural press as forming 'a complete contrast to the dead kind of official architecture often found in erections of this class built for public authorities' (*The Builder*, 1901). The 45 crematoria designed between 1915 and 1943 continued the pattern established in the pre-war period – that of a lack of commitment to a singular architectural treatment. Those built between 1915 and 1939 – West Norwood (1915), Hendon Park (1922), Pontypridd (1924), Bristol (1928), Ipswich (1928), Guernsey (1929) and Edinburgh (1929) – all involved the necessity for 'architectural good manners', having to harmonize with existing cemetery buildings.

The reception of the modernist style in Britain in the 1930s had been mixed. It tended to be adopted only by avant-garde clients and, for the most part, architects and clients preferred traditional forms. However, the designs for Lodge Hill, Birmingham (1938), Stoke-on-Trent (1940) and South Yardley, Birmingham (1936) reveal a possible influence of the Dutch architect Willem Dudok whose work offered a more acceptable brand of modernism, being executed largely in brick. Stylistic pluralism continued throughout the 1930s and 1940s, albeit infused with contemporary fashions and preferences. Overt modernism was rejected, presumably on the grounds that cremation in a building which resembled an Odeon cinema or the home of a 'vegetarian bacteriologist' might be deemed distasteful. Instead, styles included Gothic, interpreted in a 'modern' way in the cases of Rochdale (1938) and Coventry (1943) and in a more traditional way as at Newcastle-upon-Tyne (1934), Harrogate (1936) and Bournemouth (1938). Variations of Romanesque can be found at Leeds, Cottingley (1938), Weymouth (1939) and Brighton (1941). Reading (1932) and Northampton (1939) both follow a Renaissance style.

The 1930s had witnessed a growth in architectural departments under the state and public authorities. Every county council had an architectural staff of its own, designing schools, housing schemes and other public buildings. As a natural consequence, many of the designs for crematoria emanated from council offices and were by local authority architects or by engineers or surveyors, rather than architects of national standing. There were some notable exceptions such as Sir E. Guy Dawber, (1861–1938) and Sir Edwin Cooper (1873–1942), although both were at the end of their careers. As plans for the reconstruction of post-war Britain gathered momentum, it became clear that nascent new towns, hospitals, schools and all manner of social amenities, would be prodigal in their use of land, therefore placing an ever-increasing strain on resources. The cremationists, aware of a growing acceptance of cremation on the part of the public, were quick to broker a position for crematoria in the post-war nexus of town and country planning, architecture and social purpose.

However, facilities to cope with the increased demand simply did not exist. Following The Cremation Act of 1952, the rapidity with which the building programme was implemented was breathtaking. The steady rate of growth between 1952 and 1959 accelerated into a period of rapid expansion from 1960 onwards. In 1961 and 1962 alone, 30 new crematoria were opened, and 1968 witnessed the opening of the 200th, in Worthing. However, speed of response and economic stringency, coupled with a degree of contemporary architectural austerity, accounts for a building type in which practical and planning imperatives were allowed to overshadow architectural language.

The crematoria of the 1950s and 1960s assume many of the stylistic characteristics of the period. They were designed in a well-mannered, humane and decent English style, with strong nuances of contemporary Scandinavian work. Nevertheless they attracted widespread criticism and were considered by many to be banal and anonymous (Curl, 2001: 193). Indeed, many remain almost indistinguishable from contemporary church halls and school buildings. While a hint of austerity of style might well have contributed to their widespread reputation as being dull and uninspiring, it was more likely to have been a consequence of the stereotypical planning, dictated by economy. The dominant planning feature which formed the core of the new purpose-built designs was the idea of one route through the building. This resulted in their reputation as being rather like a conveyor-belt – 'one in, one out' (Davies, 1995: 37).

Architects known to have designed more than one post-war British crematorium include: J.

Seaton Dahl and Cadman; J. Percival Chaplin; Critchell, Harrington & Partners Ltd, Sir Guy Dawber, Fox & Robinson; Fry, Drew &: Partners; E.A. Heppenstall; Harold W. Orr, James Ralph & Partners; Sanger and Rothwell; Hatfield Oatley Associates; Hugh Thomas; and F.G. Williamson & Associates. During the late 1960s attitudes began to change and it was felt by some that architectural style *per se* was not as significant as the power of architectural language (Bond, 1968: 85–87). Architecture could provide a process of communion between spatial arrangements and an inner condition. Crematoria must, in Ruskin's words, 'propose an effect on the human mind, not merely a service to the human frame' (Ruskin, 1883). The examples of West Suffolk (1989) and Telford (2000) bear witness to the fact that the British crematorium had finally come of age as a building type. Although different in terms of style, both examples involve a carefully negotiated relationship between architecture and landscape and give a valuable pointer to British crematorium architecture of the twenty-first century. **Hilary Grainger**

See also Fry; Golders Green Crematorium.

References

Curl, J. Stevens (2001), *The Victorian Celebration of Death*, Stroud: Sutton.

Davies, D. (1995), *British Crematoria in Public Profile*, Maidstone: The Cremation Society of Great Britain.

Fry, E. Maxwell (1964), 'The Design of Modern Crematoria', *Report of Proceedings – Annual Cremation Conference, Bournemouth, 23–25 June 1964*, Maidstone: The Cremation Society, 39–44.

Grainger, H.J. (2000), '"Distressingly Banal": The Architecture of early British Crematoria', *Pharos*, 66(1): 42–48.

Grainger, H.J. (2001), '"The Removal of Mournful Suggestions. ... A Fresh Start"'. The Architecture of British Interwar Crematoria', *Pharos*, 67(1): 3–11.

Ruskin, John (1883), *The Seven Lamps of Architecture*, 4th edn, Orpington: George Unwin.

EUROPE

European crematoria: classical cases

Any consideration of crematorium architecture needs, at the outset, to relate it to the architecture of civic buildings in general. This involves both a chronological and, partly, geographical distinction. There was an initial period which can be defined as 'heroic' that produced the historical architecture of cremation which relates to most crematoria constructed between 1876 and the First World War in Italy, France, England and Switzerland. The first and second post-war periods then produced the modern architecture of cremation and relate to crematoria of Scandinavia and central Europe. In relation to these spatial–temporal factors one also needs to consider popular attitudes to cremation itself and the fact that, although idealistic pioneers of cremation in Latin countries founded cremation associations and built crematoria, cremation still remains relatively unpopular there. In northern European countries, by contrast, cremation has generally come to appeal to a majority of the population.

The first architecture of cremation emerged in northern Italy in the 1870s and to grasp something of the fundamental phases involved in that construction is to gain a perspective on the subsequent configuration of crematoria in the rest of Europe. Once the heroic phase of the struggle in favour of cremation was overcome and shifted from Italy to England, France and Switzerland, with the construction of crematoria in great urban centres such as London, Paris, Strasbourg, Zurich and Lugano, the practice of corpse incineration spread rapidly and comprehensively in central and northern European countries. Modern crematoria were obviously constructed very differently from the first Italian cremation examples due to the technological developments of the ovens and to the technical progress of architecture. The stylistic traditions of each nation were also brought to bear upon the architectural language in each national context rendering any single typological and formal strategy in designing cremation buildings redundant. Nevertheless, it is possible to identify some common features in this architecture, not least that crematoria were not generally considered to be a symbolic expression of the struggle for cremation against civil and religious authorities as they were in

Italy. On the contrary, in the buildings of northern and central Europe, one can feel the strong civic character of the function they fulfil. They are also devoid of the rhetoric and gloomy symbolism of architecture connected with death. The simplicity of the architectonic form, the elasticity of use of the internal spaces and their constant use over a century make crematoria built after the 1920s important examples of the functional tradition. According to the analysis of James M. Richards, these combined characteristics have made this the best period in European architecture. In his volume *The Functional Tradition in Early Industrial Buildings* (1958), Richards recalls how the adjective 'functional', has, more than any other, been associated with modern architecture in which a building begins with an accurate analysis of the needs it must meet, the materials available for construction and the economic constraints under which it has to be built. Obviously, the functional element is always present in architecture, in the sense that buildings have a practical function to which they have to respond; yet some architecture, especially that of crematoria, is 'functional' in a most direct fashion. Even so, the architecture of cremation in its different national contexts has provided a life of exceptional beauty without creating a model that is repetitively imposed but, instead, has blended historical tradition, national language and contemporary influence in original works of strong symbolic impact and great enjoyment for the public.

In describing individual buildings we begin with the most significant English, French and Swiss examples belonging to the historical architecture of cremation. In England, Woking crematorium, where Paolo Gorini was commissioned to make the cremator, was built in 1879 by the engineer Turner. At the time of construction it was noted how this building responded well to its purpose, despite its original, rather rudimentary facilities. Although its objective was to carefully avoid the brusque transition from flesh to ash, it was still criticized for the immediate proximity of the chapel and the ceremony room, on the one hand, and the cremator on the other. Nevertheless, there was praise for the positive habit that prevailed in Great Britain of providing the building with a ceremony room where, during the cremation, the mourners could attend a religious service

accompanied by sacred music played by the organ, situated in the room itself. The non-monumental and strongly functional tendency of the Italian tradition was well received in England because of the domestic nature of English funerary architecture as a whole and because, in England, crematoria did not have to function as symbolic expressions of cremation ideology. In all countries of Nordic Protestantism and Anglican religion, cremation was rapidly and easily accepted, first by the cultured and higher classes and, later, at a popular level.

In France, the Paris crematorium was built in the Père-Lachaise cemetery by the architect Jean Camille Formigé in 1889 and completed with the surrounding columbarium in subsequent years. This is probably the most complex and imposing example of the historical phase of cremation building. A compact square shape with narrow arched windows, a central dome and three posterior apses, it appears more reminiscent of oriental or Romanic funerary architecture (for example, the fifth-century Mausoleo di Galla Placidia in Ravenna) than neo-Egyptian or neo-Greek styles. The interior is planned particularly efficiently. At ground level is the ceremony room in which the coffin vanishes under a catafalque, there is a surrounding passageway and, at the end, in the three apses, are three cremators, initially of the Gorini system and later replaced by Toisoul-Fradet and Fichet systems. Nevertheless, this Parisian example was criticized with regard to its functioning, highlighting the fact that experimentation in cremation was still in its initial phases.

The modern-day Strasbourg crematorium, however, is one of the most successful examples of the architecture of cremation. The complex, built in the 1990s, represents the safest interpretation of the idea of a funerary centre for cremation conceived as a secular and civil institution, distanced from revivalist, consolatory influence.

The first Swiss crematorium, built in Zurich by the engineer E. Bourry in 1889, was of a rigorous neo-classical style with only one large room serving the dual functions of ceremony and cremation. The cremator was in the centre, hidden by a simulation of a sarcophagus. The room also acts as a columbarium. At the back are two small rooms for the management and the workers. It should be noted that the Zurich crematorium was located at the summit of the site of the small cemetery designed by the architect Geiser. It is worth comparing this crematorium with that of Lugano of 1916 and noting the differences due to date, local architectural traditions and, above all, to different religious conceptions and therefore to different conceptions of cremation. Protestant Zurich sees cremation as the norm for treating corpses, with burial as an exception; Catholic Lugano, on the contrary, resists cremation, as do many other Italian cities.

The modern phase of European cremation architecture began in northern and central Europe and produced buildings of quite different characteristics. These differences are mainly due, in the Nordic countries, to the Protestant acceptance of cremation from a moral and legal perspective and to the comprehensive diffusion of such practice and its related structures. In Catholic central European countries, the differences are due to the delay of diffusion of the idea of cremation and consequently the ability to benefit from an already established architectural tradition in this sector.

As for Scandinavia, the first crematorium in Stockholm was the project of architect Valfrid Karlsons in 1886–87: it still had a strongly eclectic design in terms of the materials used and its imposing symbolism. Although the temporary crematorium of Hagalund of 1887, built by Magnus Isaeus, was constructed at the same time as Stockholm's, its conception was of a diametrically opposed nature. Here, perhaps because of the temporary character of the building, the radiant domesticity of Swedish architecture is revived with an extremely pleasing outcome, devoid of the gloomy monumentality of much funerary architecture. On the other hand, the crematorium of Gothenburg, designed by Hans Hedlund and built in 1889, heralded the revival of classical Roman architecture that was common to all Nordic and central European architecture (one only has to think of the design of Giovan Battista Piranesi). The architect Gustav Lindgre, however, found inspiration in the Norra crematorium of 1909, with its neo-classical Palladian style. In 1914, during the Baltic Exposition of Malmö, a beautiful cremation room was created in liberty style; this symbolized the triumph of cremation in Sweden.

However, the first real example of indigenous cremation architecture in Sweden was the beautiful crematorium of Hälsingborg, built in 1926 by the architect Ragnar Östberg and illustrating a real fusion of more original Swedish design and irresistible Roman funerary architecture. The structure is of brick and the interior is plastered with lime. The ceremony room has the shape of a perfect circle with 12 columns in grey-blue marble. The interior comprises the rotunda; basement rooms for the reception of the body; the technical area with cremation ovens, archives, the keeper's room; the clergy's room with a library; and a patio where the urn is placed. The crematorium of Luleå (1930) by Erik Lundgren is once again reminiscent of Swedish domestic buildings, but with influences from the archaeological model of the Mausoleo di Galla Placidia in Ravenna. In the 1930s the crematorium of Eskilstuna by Otar L. Hökerberg opened up the modern phase of the architecture of cremation, marked by a strong rationalist influence. The design was pure and linear with references neither to the classical tradition nor to the national architecture, but to the lessons of Italian, French and German rationalism. In contrast to the compact and almost inaccessible front, the rear of the building is completely covered in glass, which creates a very luminous interior.

In the 1930s the crematorium of Karlskoga by Åke Porne anticipated, with the cube in the foreground, all the monuments to the dead that were to be built after the Second World War, while the main building in the background, with orange-coloured tiled roof and pale grey plastered walls, seems to anticipate, more than half a century in advance, postmodern architecture. The crematorium of Norrköping by Kurt V. Schmalensee, a white construction with a black slate base, follows a rationalistic style resulting in a sacred, almost monastic, architecture. Malmö saw the restoration of the crematorium of the great architect Sigurd Lewerentz who added two chapels. The chapel of S. Knuts in particular and the beautiful relief in sandstone by Bror Marklund give clear testimony to the relaxed attitude towards cremation in northern Europe. Finally, in Stockholm, the enlargement of the cremation temple built in 1931 by Gunnar Asplund and Sigurd Lewerentz took place between 1935 and 1940. This space became completely integrated in the surrounding countryside and yet conveying a sense of transcending it, almost as a metaphysical painting, with which it has often been compared.

In Norway the Hamar Crematorium was built by Rolf Prag in 1937–38. The structure is of reinforced concrete and brick; externally it is covered with a special granulated plaster and has a base of green slate. Inside, there is a balcony with an organ and a catafalque glazed in green, and all the machinery and services are located in the basement. In Denmark the crematorium of Söndermark (Copenhagen) was designed by architect Schlegele Thomsen. The structure is of dark red brick, and the skirting board, cornice, panels and the sculpture above the main door are all of granite. It is important to emphasize that the base is an almost exact reproduction of two of the most popular images of the funerary architecture of the Roman period: the columbarium of liberty of Cesare and the columbarium of liberty of Livia on the Via Appia.

In Holland, Velsen Crematorium, designed by Marius Poelzaal in 1914, is an extraordinarily interesting complex on account of the successful fusion of roman funerary architecture and the influences of the Viennese secession. In contrast, the crematorium of Dieren designed by architect Dieter Nuyten and built in the 1930s, is characterized by a very marked rationalistic style. Austria's Vienna Crematorium was built in 1922 by Clemens Holzmeister on the site of a sixteenth-century castle, and preserves the boundary walls and the main existing features, making it the only example of an extraordinary restoration for the use of cremation. The construction is situated in the centre of a square-shaped garden, surrounded by the arches of the interior face of the boundary walls, which serve as the cells for the urns.

The gigantic site of the crematorium of Prague in the Czech Republic, built between 1929 and 1931 by Alois Mezera, is of purely rationalist characteristics. The most outstanding elements are the quasi-industrial appearance of the south-eastern façade, the small courtyard entrance with the arches of the columbaria and the basilica-like room of ceremonies. The crematorium of Brno designed by Ernst Wiesner in the 1930s offers clear proof of the exceptional originality and creativity invested in the construction of crematoria. The building, reminiscent of a castle, possesses an inner courtyard where ceremonies may take place in the open air, while an inner room is illuminated by a glass ceiling.

This account of the more representative examples of cremation architecture in Europe concludes with the work of architect Fritz Schumacher in two extremely interesting German crematoria. In the Dresden crematorium of 1907 he sought to avoid the traditional reference to the church model through an original type of construction. Although the crematorium could not avoid presenting itself as a religious building, he nevertheless developed its functions at two levels: at the technical level of a machine in which bodies dissolve, and at the symbolic level as a monument in which the architectural and decorative elements expressed the social and ritual function of transition. At that symbolic level it invokes the non-temporal space of myth. With this building, Schumacher wanted to express 'the monumentality of feelings' that 'have a strong formal effect on the style'. After analysing the transformation of the image of death from medieval to contemporary times, Schumacher supported the necessity of 'creating a great architectural language for our cemeteries, monuments, chapels and crematoria' (quoted in Venier, 1983). In this sense, the crematorium of Dresden represents, in all its parts, the perfect success of Schumacher's programme. The same judgement is equally valid for Schumacher's second crematorium, built in Hamburg. Here, the search for an isolated and symbolic monumentality was fulfilled through large stained glass windows of diverse colours – violet, blue and green at the catafalque, yellow and brown at the exit – windows that also fill the gigantic interior arches with a warm exterior light. **Maria Canella**

See also Asplund (for Sweden); Boltenstern (for Austria); Dudok (for the Netherlands); Fayans (for Poland); Schumacher (for Germany).

References

Richards, James M. (1958), *The Functional Tradition in Early Industrial Buildings*, with photographs by Eric de Maré. London: Architectural Press.

Venier Arnalda (1983), 'Technological Death: Fritz Schumacher's Dresden Crematorium', in Lotus International Heft II, *Funerary Lotus: The Architectue of Crematoria and Cemeteries*: 121–24.

ITALY: CLASSICAL CASES

The architecture of cremation in Italy originated as a response to the demands of the rising crementationist movement. The first crematoria were built in the largest urban centres of northern Italy from the 1870s. The history of this civic architecture is complicated in the sense that it involves analysing the invention of a new kind of building – not a traditional model, but one that had a completely unprecedented function in Western history. To fully understand the configuration of the architecture of cremation, it is necessary to follow some fundamental phases in the building of these 'cremation temples' or *templi crematori*.

As is the case for many public buildings, it is important to account for the relationship between the sponsor and the municipal authority for, in the case of cremation, this relationship may be particularly complex. This was due, in the first place, to the absence of a law that regulated the practice of cremation itself; second, the legalizing of cremation in 1888 gave cremation temples a strong symbolic value in cultural, social and philosophical terms. The long and fierce debate over cremation, the strong cohesion of the cremation societies which were formed by high-profile exponents from the local community, as well as a certain emulation by smaller towns of larger urban administrations equipping themselves with this symbol of civil progress, encouraged numerous municipalities to accept the construction of crematoria. They even shared the costs and provided building land, sometimes allowing a building inside the municipal cemetery. While they sometimes provided part of the cost, the larger part was carried by the cremation societies and the donations of its members in their wills.

In this sense it is important to emphasize that, even though the crementationist battle arose in open contrast to cemeteries and burial, the construction of temples and crematoria necessarily took place in the cemetery itself. In consequence, this weakened the symbolic message of the buildings connected with cremation and imposed restrictions both in relation to the urban location and the architectural and stylistic value. When considering the strong technical constraints on this architecture, it is important to remember that cremation temples emerged to satisfy the completely new function in modern and contemporary Europe – the cremation of corpses. Such novelty involved, above all, accelerated technological research, to create and update

crematorium apparatus to the highest standards. This helped deal with the problems associated with the early cremations by the pioneers of the sector (Gorini, Polli, Clericetti, Venini), often dramatically described in publications focusing on unpleasant smoke, smells and horrifying sights. More efficient apparatus reduced opposition from the anti-crementationists on these grounds and offered the architects better machines located underground, leaving uncluttered space. In contrast, the early crematoria built in Italy had always had to locate the cremation area in the central room, which remained exposed to the public and created numerous technical and architectural problems.

These fundamental aspects surrounding the emergence of crematoria at the end of the nineteenth and beginning of the twentieth centuries in Italy involved civil society, the scientific world, freemasonry – which provided many pro-cremation texts – and the Church as the main opponent of the crementationist project. The cremation societies pursued their own battle of ideals not only through a conspicuous array of pamphlets and documents aimed at popularization but also through the use of the cremation temples themselves. These in fact turned out to be the true light that illuminated the conscience of those who contemplated that sad world of death represented in the cemetery. Taking into account all the contingent factors that conditioned the choices of working methods in the construction of cremation temples, the trend reflected in the north Italian cremation temples – largely constructed between 1870 and the First World War – was eclectic. This eclectic style was driven both by the design of the cemeteries as host sites of the emerging crematoria and, in more general terms, by the public and private building styles of the day.

These constraints and trends yielded a new typology that can be briefly summarized in terms of the following essential rooms, one set addressing the public funerary ceremonies and the other devoted to cremation itself along with the relevant staff rooms:

1 an entrance peristyle and passage to the cremation room and to the columbarium with walls that could be used to hold urns or inscriptions to particular persons;
2 a room for the last inspection of the body and for its deposition on the trolley that will carry it to the cremation altar;

3 a main hall for the performance of the final ritual honours to the body;
4 a room for the technical function of cremation that might variously be called the 'cremation altar' or 'combustion camera', with other annex rooms for the collection of ashes, placing the urn and so on;
5 rooms for the management and staff and, in some crematoria, accommodation for the caretaker.

There was some controversy about the position of the cremation altar in the temple: in the early crematoria the altar was located next to the ceremony room or in the ceremony room itself so one could be present during the whole rite. In modern crematoria, by contrast, the technical part of cremation takes place in separate rooms and is closed to the sight of mourners. The position of the chimney – necessary for the combustion and elimination of fumes – was also controversial, since it recalled the image of industrial buildings. In contrast, some commentators defended the more prosaic aspect of cremation temples, even proposing the separation of the civil architecture of cremation from the empathetic architecture of the cemeteries by means of external access doors and separate avenues, just as in Protestant, Jewish and non-Catholic cemeteries. The main objective, however, was to invest the act and the ceremony of cremation with the sacredness that it was feared would be lost in the mere incineration of corpses. To achieve this, a suitable space was needed, with decoration, sacred music and funeral prayers during the processes of body preparation and cremation.

Looking at the most important examples of crematoria that have been built in Italy in the last quarter of the nineteenth century, we inevitably start with the case of Milan, where in 1876 the first modern cremation temple was erected, due to the legacy of Alberto Keller. The temple was inaugurated with a solemn ceremony of the cremation of the mortal remains of the dead donor, prominently reported in the press. Milan thus became the model and starting point of the cremationist project, rapidly followed by other Italian and European cities. The designer of the temple, Carlo Maciacchini, designer of the whole Monumentale Cemetery project, adopted a significantly Doric style to reconnect with the classical traditions and recover the dignity of the ancient rituals of purification: the result was a building with much character, but of a certain gloomy heaviness, especially if one thinks of the beautiful design Maciacchini had conceived for the Monumentale a few years before. It is probable that, in this case, the lack of a typological tradition, the difficulty of the subject due to its ideological sensitivity or, possibly, pressure from the sponsors may all have been influential.

The present building constitutes the outcome of many enlargements that have taken place over the years. The original part of Maciacchini constitutes the central body, a square base preceded by a double-hemicircle vestibule. Here, in the space surrounding the columns, the first cremations took place in the stone altar where the invisible gas flames burst out. In 1896, the cremation system was much improved thanks to the work of the doctor-scientist Paolo Gorini. The architect Augusto Guidini enlarged the building, adding to the rear a new room with four ovens within suitable divisions. The apparatus, with a Gorini system for ordinary cremation, was supported by a second one with a Venini system for the cremation of the corpses of those who died of infectious diseases or who came from other regions or from abroad. There was also a service room and space to contain funerary remembrances. The front part, therefore, was used as a vestibule for the funerary ceremonies, while on the sides two columbaria were built with 200 niches in each.

If Milan possessed the title of the pioneer city of cremation, Lodi was the laboratory city, for it hosted and supported the work of Paolo Gorini, inventor of the first modern cremation oven. Gorini had Lodigiano Crematorium named after him; it was inaugurated in the Riolo cemetery in 1877, with the full support of the communal authority which made him into a real and proper civic institution.

The cremation temple of Cremona was built in 1883 with the cooperation of the local cremation society and with the support of the communal council, which offered the free concession of land, as well as important funding towards building expenses. It was completed by the engineer Francesco Podestà, and comprises two small classical-style buildings – one housing the Gorini system cremation apparatus and the other functioning as the mortuary room – connected by a 10-metre-long metallic roof. In the middle of the two small buildings, the large

32-metre-high column-shaped chimney emerges with two statues at the base.

The differences between the Milan and Cremona temples are evident: the former was built in the monumental tradition while the latter provided – at the same time as Lodi – the first example of the modern conception of an architecture conceived in terms of its function. Podestà, despite the influence of the recent Milanese example, opted for a clear neo-classical style, inspired by the secular architecture of the Enlightenment; maybe even drawing slight inspiration from masonic lodges. He neither relied on the Catholic funerary tradition nor on the heaviness of the neo-Greek or the neo-Egyptian styles that characterized the architecture of cremation.

The construction of the cremation temple of Rome encountered tough opposition due to the resonance of the welcome given to cremation in Verano and to its location: in the capital and a few kilometres away from the Vatican. The somewhat lesser involvement in central Italy also had an influence. The year 1883 saw the inauguration of the temple designed by engineer Salvatore Rosa. Marked by a very strong neo-Egyptian influence in its form, its sculptured symbols also recalled the iconographic tradition of masonry. Located in Perugia, the front of the cremation temple represented a fusion between neo-classical purity and the neo-Egyptian influences possibly the most successful example of this blend of styles amongst Italian crematoria.

The cremation temple of Varese, designed by architect Augusto Guidini, was constructed in 1883, thanks to a private donation and the joint participation of the local and the municipal cremation society. Its form, formal conclusion and architectonic style fitted harmoniously with the hosting necropolis. The temple itself is square-shaped with a central cremation altar. An original portico extends out in front of the entrance and a monumental chimney dominates the building. At the sides are two columbaria, which complete the formal structure of the building. The crematorium of Brescia was also built as a result of a donation, but, unlike other northern Italian venues, it encountered strong resistance from the communal council. Inaugurated in July 1883 it was built on the principles of minimal expense and maximum simplicity, providing only for the strict necessities of cremation practice. The building is rectangular, with the cremation altar with Venini apparatus. The principal façade is constituted by pillars, which create three openings in the central part. These provide access to the interior by means of a short flight of steps. The other sides are all provided with windows. The building is crowned by a simple frame with a triangular frontispiece in the middle.

The battle in favour of cremation started early in Turin, going back to the 1850s; however, it was only in 1882 that the communal council decided to concede the land to build the cremation temple in the cemetery of Turin and subsidize its construction. The first project, carried out by the architect Pompeo Marini in 1888, corresponded with the current entrance and comprised the rooms for the funerary ceremonies, the cremation altar with Gorini apparatus, rooms for the management, some for the staff and two rooms for the columbaria. The temple occupied a prestigious location, to the right of the cemetery's main entrance. The interior is decorated with numerous sculptures, among which are two statues by Pietro Della Vedova, positioned at the entrance of the crematorium, and representing a winged genius and the pietà. In 1895 the architect Daniele Donghi designed an enlargement of the temple. This comprised a new columbarium and portico, separated from Novara Street only by wrought-iron railings. The cremation temple of Turin, enlarged again in 1950, represents, due to the complexity of its structure, its successive enlargements and the degree of its current activity, the most important centre for cremation in Italy, and the only one comparable to the northern and central European cremation temples.

In conclusion we recall four temples that were successively built in the *periodo eroico*: the monumental invention of the neo-classic temple of Livorno at the end of the nineteenth century; the eclectic invention of the temple of Genova in the first years of the twentieth century; the functional rigour of the small temple of Savona in 1913; and the pleasing neo-liberty influence of the new temple of Mantova in 1930.

The architecture of cremation in Italy has no monograph or periodical publication devoted to it. The only texts which it is possible to rely on are Gaetano Pini's book, *La crémation en Italie et à l'étranger de 1774 jusqu'à nos jours (Cremation in Italy and Abroad From 1774 to the Present Day)* published in Milan in 1884, and the chapter dedicated to cremation temples in the second volume of the Manuale dell'architetto (Architect's Manual) by Daniele Donghi, published in Turin in 1925: the former was among the most important ideologues of cremation, and the latter was responsible for the enlargement of Turin's cremation temple. **Maria Canella**

See also Keller.

ARGENTINA

The following articles on Argentina complement each other in presenting an account of the complex social, political and religious history of the country, whilst retaining the integrity of each contribution.

THE DEVELOPMENT OF CREMATION IN ARGENTINA

Uncertain beginnings and false dawns, 1879–1922

Argentina witnessed rudimentary cremation during Colonel Charlone's campaign against the indigenous population at Bahía Blanca in the late 1850s and later in the Paraguayan War, 1865–70. In 1867 a few victims of a cholera epidemic in Pergamino, Buenos Aires Province, were cremated. However, the cremation movement had its true origins in a conference organized by the Argentine Scientific Society *Sociedad Científica Argentina* under the hygienist Dr Pedro Mallo. Earlier, freemason Juan A. Kelly (1847–1924) had written a thesis (*La Cremación*, 1876) and Bartolomé Novaro a book (*Breves Apuntes Sobre la Cremación*, 1877) on the topic. Mallo, in a dissertation published in the Argentine Scientific Society's *Anales*, argued that cremation was the best means of body disposal and urged the society to be first to ask the Buenos Aires authorities for a crematorium. At its conference on 5 September 1879 the Society obliged, passing a resolution supporting cremation and proposing a competition with prizes for those propounding the best cremation methods. Mallo also proposed establishing a cremation society but nothing concrete came of these early initiatives. In the early 1880s, Pedro N. Castro (1883), P.C. Payró (1884) and Dr Samuel Gache (1884) all produced pro-cremation texts. Hygienist Gache's

suggestion that the Argentine Medical Circle *Círculo Médico Argentino* form a cremation association received a degree of support in 1885. In the same year, Celedonio Pereda produced a book on cremation in Buenos Aires and Dr Eduardo Wilde dedicated a chapter to cremation in a more general work on public hygiene.

It is likely that little more would have happened had a national emergency not occurred. The first cremation in modern Argentina, on 26 December 1884, was the result of a case of yellow fever that was diagnosed by two eminent cremationist doctors, Dr José María Ramos Mejía (director of Public Assistance) and Dr José Penna (director of the *Casa de Aislamiento*, literally 'House of Isolation' and founded because of the epidemic). Ramos Mejía ordered the cremation and Don Torcuato de Alvear (the municipal administrator of Buenos Aires) approved it. The infected body, of French citizen Pedro Doime, was cremated in an improvised oven in the *Casa de Aislamiento* apparently without public protest. This was done, according to cremationists, because the process destroyed the contagion and the experience of previous epidemics in 1858–70, and especially that of 1871, had had their effect. Dr Penna, supported by Ramos Mejía, took the initiative and agitated for cremation until the Buenos Aires authorities began to respond (Baca, 1923a; Mendoza, 1923: 68; FDR 1928: 91–92).

In April 1886, during municipal discussions on the reorganization of the Buenos Aires cemetery system, councillors Dr Benjamín Dupont and freemason Manuel Blancas (1823–1906), on behalf of Ramos Mejía and Penna, proposed a by-law (to come into effect on 1 July 1887). It proposed the obligatory cremation of all epidemic victims without exception, of body parts from hospitals and medical schools and for those requesting cremation. The bill had not yet been passed when, in autumn 1886, cholera claimed over 20 000 victims. When, on 5 November 1886, Penna received the first victim's body, Ramos Mejía immediately acceded to Penna's request to perform a cremation and recommended that all epidemic victims be cremated. After overcoming many obstacles, Penna conducted the cremation with an improvised apparatus on the same day. The proposed cremation by-law was then modified to include the construction of a purpose-built crematorium in December 1886.

The fear of contagion again outweighed religious opposition, and cremation ovens were built in the *Casa de Aislamiento*, in the *lazaretos* (quarantines) of Martín García and Richuelo, at La Ensenada, La Boca and La Plata cemetery. Accordingly, cremation played its part in controlling the epidemic. Buenos Aires became the first city anywhere to have compulsory cremation for certain types of corpse (unclaimed in hospitals and epidemic victims). This did not provoke public protest as it was, according to Eduardo Baca, widely accepted as part of good municipal administration.

Encouraged by these developments, a group composed largely of doctors held a meeting on 17 January 1887 in Buenos Aires with the objective of establishing the first Argentine cremation society. As with countries like Italy, many early Argentine cremationists were freemasons: at least 14 according to Lappas (2000). These cremationists took the Milanese Cremation Society as their model, but also studied the Paris society. However, the first Argentine cremation society lasted only months before falling victim to public indifference. Ideas about cremation were still embryonic, and much opposition remained. Indeed, once the cholera epidemic had passed in mid-1887, all the cremators were closed except those at the *Casa de Aislamiento* and in the Martín García *lazareto*, which continued until 31 December 1903. By then, the municipality had properly complied with the December 1886 by-law and built a crematorium opposite the main gateway of the Cemetery of the West *Cementerio del Oeste,* also known as 'Chacarita') in Buenos Aires. There had been a total of 13 181 cremations between 1886 and 1903, but these included all cremations (voluntary, mandatory and of body parts) and no comparison is possible with figures after 1903, when they were finally properly categorized.

The new crematorium began operation on 13 November 1903, and Penna oversaw cremations there. A new by-law in 1903, far from making cremation more accessible and easier, complicated the process by requiring that each body have an autopsy before cremation. The number of cremations now actually declined with only 16 voluntary cremations in the eight years following 1903. An article in *La Vanguardia* in 1919 identified problems encountered after 1903, including bad management of the cremators, lack of experience in using them, the apathy of certain officials and deliberate obstruction by others, as well as the immense antagonism of the Catholic Church. Accordingly, the crematorium was used almost exclusively by so-called 'dissidents', including atheists, freethinkers, socialists, communists and anarchists (Oscar Fidanza, personal communication).

In October 1909 the municipality financed renovation to the crematorium, and in January 1911 Penna (now director of Public Assistance) closed the crematorium whilst installing 'Baker system' cremators. This work was completed on 28 October 1913 but their operation was suspended again for a short time. However, new cremators and a new by-law in 1910, which partly modified some of the 1903 articles, were insufficient to end the stagnation, and the number of voluntary cremations remained very low: there were only 64 between 1914 and 1923. In 1917 municipal administrator Dr Joaquin Llambías tried to remedy the situation with a partly pro-cremation report to the Department of Public Assistance. Despite this and Victor Delfino's pro-cremation *La Cremación Cadáverica* in 1917, the situation remained unchanged. Three years later, the ex-councillor and freemason Carlos R. Gallardo (1856–1938), proposed the construction of a columbarium. Though sanctioned on 23 December 1920, it, too, failed to be implemented.

Yet 1918 saw the 'conversion' of Eduardo Baca, a doctor who become a cremationist after a study of hygiene and cemeteries. Highly regarded, he had, from 1912, published a substantial body of work on animal parasites, medical chemistry, medical hygiene, health initiatives in Buenos Aires, brain diseases, tuberculosis, alcoholism, the domestic fly and Louis Pasteur. Aided by Joaquín M. Montaña, Baca promoted cremation in correspondence with his friend, councillor Don Remigio Iriondo. Baca attributed most of the problems of the Argentine cremation movement to the cremation by-law which, he argued, repelled many potential supporters due to the large number of pointless compulsory procedures and the costs they incurred. Whilst Baca acknowledged the oppositional role played by religion and custom, he also identified, along with the by-law, the low status of the crematorium itself – it being more an 'annex of the cemetery', rather than a 'dignified monument' – and a lack of competent civil servants prepared to advocate cremation as the main problems. This analysis allowed for action and Baca wrote a new by-law (Baca, 1923a; 1923b; 1928: 5, 8–9, 11–12; 1934: 4; FDR, 1928: 92–93; Mendoza, 1923: 18–19).

Years of hope, the new by-law and the AAC, 1922–1928

Baca's by-law was passed unanimously and unmodified by the Buenos Aires municipality on 28 December 1922. The old by-law's nine procedural stages were replaced with only one. On 7 September 1922 Baca also spoke on cremation at the Second National Medical Congress. After Baca had received the public support of his friend, Dr Felipe A. Justo, the conference voted unanimously in favour of the resolution that cremation was the best method of disposal of the dead, and called on the authorities to promote and implement it. On 4 November 1922 Baca was invited by the Argentine Scientific Society to hold a tribunal on cremation. He then helped to establish the Argentine Cremation Association *Associación Argentina de Cremación* (AAC) in the same year. The new by-law came into force on 10 March 1923, and Baca and José Perez Mendoza, the AAC president, were initially optimistic that it would help overcome 'illogical' opposition based on custom. In 1924 the AAC bulletin reported that there had been a large increase in cremations in Buenos Aires – about 1000 per month with 20 voluntary cremations in six months, compared to only two in the whole of 1922. The fact that in 1924 there were more voluntary cremations than in the previous 14 years put together suggested to Dr Nicolás Lozano and others that it was merely a question of time before the practice of cremation became established (Baca, 1922: 21–24; 1928: 6,10; Mendoza, 1923: 19–20,30).

The continued growth in cremations throughout the 1920s sustained the AAC's hope. In July 1926 the AAC bulletin pointed out that, in 1923 there were only 28 voluntary cremations and now the figure had increased to 125. The slow but apparently inexorable growth of AAC membership (to 324 members by summer 1926) also fed this positive attitude, although the bulletin made it clear that the AAC had been established by people who knew that they would not triumph immediately and that there was much to do, especially in the provinces. Baca liked to quote a saying to the effect that a dream

in the morning becomes a reality the following day. By 1928 he proudly announced that the number of cremations had increased so much in Buenos Aires that the city now cremated more bodies than any other crematorium in the world. In 1927 alone, it performed a total of 18 949 cremations – more than Britain's Golders Green crematorium had managed in 25 years. Between 1923 and 1927 the crematorium performed 72 212 cremations. Had there had been some epidemics during the 1920s, Baca pointed out, these figures could have been even larger.

However, the fact that there were several categories that demanded compulsory cremations – something of which Baca was proud – diminished the importance of the figures quoted. Baca did not ignore the issue of voluntary cremations: he noted that, in 1928, there were 287 voluntary cremations, over ten times as many as 1923. Baca saw these figures as evidence that the 1923 by-law had changed things fundamentally. Yet, regardless of whether Baca was truly satisfied with these figures, cremations still accounted for a minuscule proportion of total deaths in Argentina in 1928 (0.2 per cent). Moreover, Argentinians constituted only 36 per cent of all voluntary cremations between 1923 and 1927. Thus, only around 0.07 per cent of Argentinian deaths ended in cremations. Baca's 1923 by-law and the AAC's activities had made some positive impact in the 1920s, but there remained a very long way to travel (Baca, 1928).

Years of obscurity, 1929–1956

After 1928, the AAC appeared to fall into decline, but this did not halt development of Buenos Aires Crematorium, which was extended in 1930. In 1936 Dr Andres Sein took over as director of the crematorium and, doubtless keen to make an international mark, became the first Argentinian to contact the British Cremation Society since 1928. This communication with the British Society was as far as Argentine international cooperation went during this period (Sein, 1936a: 1; 1936b).

Despite an active cremation society, the progress made in Argentina in the inter-war period was distinctly limited. The society itself suffered from lack of finances and members, inactive members and internal factional fighting. Still, it was struggling in a very difficult context. The main barrier to progress was the Catholic Church through the pulpit, press and devotees in the administration. Other factors also help explain cremation's slow development.

Theoretically, the cheapness of cremation should have been an advantage; certainly this factor was stressed by many, and the AAC depicted itself as an altruistic organization promoting cheap cremations that helped relieve the plight of the poor. Indeed, cremation was advertised on the back page of the AAC's bulletin almost solely on its 'economic advantages'. The experience of successful European countries appeared to support the idea that 'economy' was important for success. The director of the German Cremation Society, for example, told the AAC that the success of cremation in his country was due its low cost.

Yet the cheapness of cremation might, paradoxically, have created some obstacles. An article in *La Acción* in March 1926 claimed that Argentina was the most expensive country in the world in which to bury one's dead and that funeral companies were making a great deal of money. Moreover, cremationists, like Sara Justo, claimed that Argentinians were exploited by the cost of burial and contrasted this with cremation's cheapness. Cremation, therefore, represented a serious threat to the profits of Argentine funeral directors and must have been strongly opposed by many of them.

There was a second, cultural aspect that also acted to cremation's detriment. The *La Acción* article implied that the lavish expense required for funerals was a peculiarity of Argentine culture – a culture in which cremation was unlikely to have much of an appeal. Another aspect of this question was highlighted at the 1936 Prague Cremation Congress. In a talk on 'administrative cremations' Mencl, a Czech delegate, pointed out that '[i]t is a well-known fact that people always look with mistrust on anything that is supplied gratis'. Of particular concern for Mencl was the practice of 'administrative cremation' when the authorities used cremation to dispose of body parts from hospitals and the corpses of those who had no means and no families to bury them. This he regarded as 'injurious' rather then helpful to the advocacy of cremation. Mencl highlighted the fact that in many of the cities where administrative cremation was employed, normal cremation rates were very low. This clearly applied to Buenos Aires. The practice, though useful to municipalities which could dispose of 'waste' easily and cheaply, meant that cremation

'is to a certain extent degraded to being a sort of incinerating establishment for debris'. The possible effect on the attitudes of the general public was 'very unpleasant', as cremation might be seen as only fit for a 'pauper's funeral'. Mencl suggested that administrative cremations should not be introduced and, where the practice already existed, cremationists should try and limit them as much as possible and ultimately eliminate them altogether.

A separate explanatory factor in cremation's slow development was mentioned at the 1937 London International Cremation Congress where it was noted that, in Britain, the density of the population placed a great deal of pressure for a solution to the heavy land requirements for burial. Argentina, a far less densely populated country, did not experience these same pressures. French cremationist Robert Hazemann talked of the problems of 'Latin' countries that remained more rural, with people maintaining a closer relationship with the soil and a consequently stronger inclination to bury rather than cremate (Hazemann, 1972:1–6). Although these considerations partly explain the limited advance of cremation in Argentina during this period, they were surely of only minor significance compared with to the powerful influence of the Catholic Church.

The outbreak of world war in 1939 did not help matters. Indeed, later cremationists lamented the fact that the Argentine situation regressed in respect of the promotion of cremation during the war years (LAPC, 1959:10). This was despite the fact that cremation continued to be employed where there was a danger of disease spreading. For example, in February 1944, at least 4000 victims of the San Juan earthquake were cremated, and it was felt that the danger of an epidemic had been forestalled by this action. Still despite the AAC's decline and eventual death, cremation figures reveal some slow progress. The figure of voluntary cremations hovered around the 400–450 mark between 1933 and 1936 and stood at 510 in 1938, which was almost double the 1928 figure.

The Argentine Pro-Cremation League and the dirty war period, 1956–1986

After a decade or more without an Argentine cremation society, 1956 witnessed the founding of the Argentine Pro-Cremation League (*Liga Argentina Pro Cremación* (LAPC)), which heralded another period of slow development. In 1956 there were 543 cremations in Argentina. In 1959 the LAPC president Dr Miguel Servera lamented the fact that, in the previous 15 years, the annual number of voluntary cremations had remained stationary at 500–600, despite the fact that the Buenos Aires population was growing rapidly. Nevertheless, Servera believed that the LAPC would achieve its aim, where all previous Argentine cremationists had failed (LAPC, 1959: 11–12). In terms of crematoria, the LAPC period did see some positive developments, although there were also some false starts. In 1965 *Pharos* reported, for the first time, that there was a proposal to build a second Argentine crematorium in the seaside town of Mar del Plata (in Buenos Aires province). However, the plan must have been shelved as this piece of information had disappeared by 1970. The year 1974 was good for cremationists as Argentina finally got its second crematorium, in Mendoza (Mendoza province). In October that same year a garden of remembrance was inaugurated in the Florenco Varela cemetery, thanks to support in the locality and municipality. However, it took another decade before Mar del Plata finally got its crematorium – the third in Argentina – in 1984. (This does not include crematoria such as that at San Vicente cemetery, Córdoba, which was built in 1977 and was probably only used to incinerate exhumed remains and not the recently dead (Sonja Leferink, personal communication)). Despite these developments, early LAPC optimism was not borne out by results. After a little more than 20 years propagandizing, there were still just 2210 voluntary cremations in Argentina in 1978. Although this was over four times the 1956 figure it still only represented less than 1 per cent of all deaths in Argentina. Thus, though the LAPC saw Argentina get its second and third crematoria, there was still a very long way to go.

The conditions for the growth of cremation came under conflicting influences in the late 1970s and early 1980s. While recurrent economic crises lent themselves to the growth of cremation as a cheaper funeral option, cremation had also taken on sinister connotations as a weapon in the 'dirty war' of the military junta against its left-wing opponents (Oscar Fidanza, personal communication). In May 1983 allegations were made by Jack Anderson, one of the United States' most influential political columnists, that

Argentine military rulers had tried to buy cremators to eliminate 'the traces of thousands of murdered political opponents'. Some Argentine officials had apparently tried to strike a deal with a Florida-based company to build a £9 million crematorium in Buenos Aires, claiming that they required a modern crematorium to replace that at Chacarita. It was further claimed that they also ordered a device designed to open caskets and dump them on a conveyor-belt feeding a furnace. Suspicious, too, was the allegation that the proposed crematorium would be able to cope with 400 bodies per day – 'a remarkable figure in a Catholic nation where cremations are rare' (Connew, 1983). A Brazilian airforce document in the Rio de Janeiro public archive later confirmed that the bodies of prisoners of the Argentine military dictatorship were incinerated in the 'crematoria of state hospitals'. Cremation was to replace the earlier practice of throwing the mutilated bodies into the Rio de la Plata as they were causing problems when they appeared on Uruguayan beaches.

Furthermore, these activities were not confined solely to the capital and its immediate environs. In Córdoba, for example, there was a clandestine crematorium in the former municipal palace also used to incinerate the bodies of *desaparecidos* (disappeared people) (Sonja Leferink, personal communication). Still, the precise role of cremation remains unclear. Adolfo Francisco Scilingo, a naval captain involved in two 'flights of death', said that cremation was used on occasion to destroy victims' bodies. According to Oscar Fidanza, the military dictatorship did not employ cremation as a method of disposal to any great extent, and Sonja Leferink did not believe that many corpses were incinerated in Córdoba, 'because the smell would have aroused suspicion'. Regardless of the extent to which cremation was employed by the dictatorship, the common perception that linked its activities with cremation meant that the practice gained a bad reputation amongst the population.

Cremation takes off, 1987–1990s

In 1987 Lindberg Argentina SA, an Argentine-owned company operating from 1958 under licence from an American company to manufacture heat-treating equipment, formalized an exclusive agreement to manufacture cremators locally. The company was selected as the sole supplier for a new six-unit cremator installation in Buenos Aires City Crematorium costing approximately $1 million. The same year, Neuquén municipality (in west central Argentina) ordered a cremator in order to relieve demand for cemetery space (Eduardo Dalesson, personal communication). These were the first signs that cremation was finally about to take off in Argentina.

More indications came in the early 1990s. In 1991 and 1992 Lindberg installed cremators in four new crematoria – Villa Allende (Córdoba province) and Boulogne, Lanus and Moron (all in Buenos Aires province, two of which were private) – which made a new total of eight crematoria for the entire country. By 1994 it was clear that Argentina was now merely one example of a sub-continent-wide phenomenon – that of Catholic countries which had been traditionally resistant to cremation but were now beginning to embrace it. Traditionally a primarily municipal concern in Argentina, by 1994 cremation was coming under the control of private businesses – again a phenomenon occurring in many Latin American countries (Sousa, 1994:51–55). In 1997 new crematoria opened in Rio Gallegos in Santa Cruz province, in the far south of the country and Bahía Blanca in Buenos Aires province. By 1998 Argentina had 12 crematoria. There were two more, in Concordia (Entre Rios province) and Despamparados (San Juan province) in 1999. By winter 2000 Buenos Aires and Córdoba both had six crematoria each. There was another new crematorium in the far-flung San Salvador de Jujuy, making a total of 21 crematoria for the whole country. In 2000, several Argentine cities were cremating around a quarter of their dead. Buenos Aires had the highest percentage, 26.6 per cent (7716 cremations). Close behind was Rosario with a 25.1 per cent cremation rate (1057 cremations) followed by Mendoza with a 22.8 per cent rate (1320 cremations) (Alberto Gerardo Ferretty and Beatriz Laufer, personal communication). Two years later the number of crematoria had doubled to 42 with Buenos Aires province boasting 24 crematoria, Entre Rios province five, Jujuy and San Juan provinces two each, as well as new crematoria in Santa Fe and Chaco provinces. That year there were 16 632 cremations out of 220 884 deaths, making a cremation rate of 7.53 per cent-over 2 per cent higher than the previous year.

Two case studies illustrate this phenomenon.

The first is that of the Crematorio Mesopotámico, in the city of Concordia, Entre Rios province. The crematorium began to function on 1 June 1999 and was the first in 'Argentine Mesopotamia' (an area between the rivers of Uruguay and Paraná, comprising three north-eastern provinces), which gave the crematorium its name. The idea to build this crematorium came from Emilio Alfonso Priede, the director of a funeral service firm since 1976. The firm also formed part of a society in charge of the management of the Concordia municipal cemetery between 1992 and 1994. Whilst performing this task, Priede noticed an increasing trend for people not to visit the tombs of their dead relatives. This attitude extended even to young members of his own family. For Priede, cremation was an obvious solution. With cremation, people did not have to visit cemeteries in order to be close to their dead loved ones, and they could also maintain a more intimate contact with their ancestors by keeping their remains in their own homes, if they so desired. The cheapness of cremation was also regarded as advantageous.

When Priede attempted to advance his idea, he encountered reticence and rejection on the part of political organizations due, above all, to ignorance about the topic (especially among civil servants) and the lack of existent cremation regulations, as well as the strength of the custom of burial prevalent throughout the society. His task was therefore to attempt to win over these sceptics and 'create the social necessity for cremation'. Although the by-law permitting cremation in Concordia was passed on 5 June 1988, this did not automatically open the way for the crematorium project. 'Administrative obstacles' impeded the actual operation of the by-law, and it took more than five years of struggle after the conception of the idea before the project could finally go ahead.

The experience of Crematorio Mesopotámico suggests that the cheapness of cremation has, on the whole, yet to attract the poorer sections of society. Cremation services tend to be requested by 'people of good and stable resources'. The poor (those supported or part-supported by the state, 'an important number' in the region), are buried at the expense of the municipality, partly because this is free and partly because the poor largely remain 'culturally traditionalist'. The municipality does not have a policy of paying for cremations for these people; therefore if they desired cremation they would have to pay the bill, cheap though it is. In contrast, Buenos Aires municipality, which has its own crematorium, does cremate the poor free of charge.

With regard to local ritual, cremation follows after the vigil service held in a purpose-built room. It takes place after the entourage has left, as people are not 'accustomed to cremation in a direct form'. Crematorio Mesopotámico is fitted with a Lindberg natural gas-fired cremator, giving a cremation of time of between 90 and 120 minutes. With regard to the storage of ashes, the crematorium is developing a practice of offering a wooden cremation urn in the form of a book. This allows it to be stored in the family library as a reminder of the family's genealogical tree. The crematorium is also taking steps to develop a parcel of land for those who wish to bury ashes in urns and then plant a tree on top of the grave to remind them of their ancestors.

The second case study is that of the private crematorium in the Jardín de Los Ceibos, Matanza (Buenos Aires province), which began operating on 20 March 2001. The idea of constructing a crematorium in the cemetery only came at the turn of the century, as the cemetery's owners did not want to lose out in the growing cremation market. The company, after studying the situation, agreed that an unsatisfied demand for cremation existed in the zone. Around 70 per cent of crematoria are built in cemeteries in Argentina, as those built outside cemeteries often 'have problems with their neighbours'. Moreover, it is beneficial for the business, as those attending cremation ceremonies become acquainted with, and ideally purchase, other cemetery products such as parcels of land to bury ashes, or urn storage niches. In its first two years, 2000 corpses were cremated at the Jardín de Los Ceibos – generally three or four per day, using the cremator for an average of about 12 hours per day. The Jardín de Los Ceibos also has a natural-gas fired Lindberg cremator. As Argentina is a producer of gas, it is cheap and abundant (the gas is piped from its extraction point in Patagonia, more than 2000 kilometres away) (Oscar Fidanza, personal communication).

The history of the development of cremation in Argentina certainly has its ironies. The country had a cremation society of one sort or another for approximately half of the twentieth century. This made it the vanguard country in Latin America for cremation, and it cremated small numbers from late in the nineteenth century, before anywhere else on the sub-continent. Yet, when cremation really began to take hold in Argentina, in the 1990s, it did not have a cremation society. Moreover, it was also no longer in the vanguard, as countries such as Mexico had become the new trendsetters in the sub-continent (Sousa, 1994: 52–53). Mexico had a cremation society only for a brief period in the early 1990s. Most other Latin American countries where the practice of cremation was expanding did not have, nor had they ever had, a cremation society. Arguably, therefore, the efforts of two earlier generations of Argentine cremationists had had almost no effect on the overall development of cremation in their country and in Latin America as a whole. But perhaps the two Argentine cremation societies can be excused. An ICF report in 1988 noted that, where cremation was 'exclusively a municipal task', there was left 'virtually no scope for the influence of cremation societies' and this certainly applied to Argentina until the late 1980s.

The present day

In 1975 the Argentine cremationist Mauro Naselli said that cremation was going to 'impose itself' in Argentina by the year 2000. If Naselli had intended 'imposing itself' to mean a majority cremation rate (that is, of 50 per cent or more), clearly he was too optimistic. However, a wider interpretation of his prediction lends it a degree of prescience. The years after 1975, and particularly after 1987, have seen the practice of cremation develop rapidly in the country, and it appears to be maintaining a steep upward trajectory. In 2002 there were 34 320 cremations representing a cremation rate of 13.73 per cent. In the larger cities the cremation rates start at around 20 per cent, with some reaching as high as 45 per cent of deaths (Oscar Fidanza, personal communication). However, as Beatriz Laufer explains, cremation is still very new: 'people are seeing it more as a possibility; before they not only ignored it, but they also rejected it'. Monica Lifieri supports this assessment, explaining growth in cremation as 'people's mentality has changed'. This meant that the bereaved increasingly 'want to simplify the destiny of their loved relatives', with 'economics' particularly influencing the decision. Eduardo Dalesson also notes that the increasing popularity of cremation 'illuminates a cultural change as well as an economic one'. Many cremation experts in

Argentina, such as Oscar Fidanza, regard the 'economic reason' as of prime importance in explaining the increasing popularity of cremation. At the outset of the twenty-first century the cost of a cremation in Argentina is substantially less than that of a mausoleum or vault in a traditional municipal cemetery or a parcel of land in a cemetery park. It also costs less than the rent for a five-year period of an interment niche in a municipal cemetery. (This is the normal period for which niches are rented: 25 years is the maximum time for which it is possible to keep a body in such a location. After this, there is the further problem of finding another place for the remains.) Thus, due to the cheapness of cremation when compared with the other options, the custom is now being established (Gustavo Labriola and Emilio Priede, personal communication).

The recent economic problems in Argentina have certainly enhanced cremation's 'economical' status, as well as having complex effects on the business side. For the cremator-manufacturing company Lindberg Argentina SA, the situation turned '180 degrees', and by summer 2003 it was taking more orders than it could manage: many more cremators were being both exported and sold locally (Osvaldo Chernitsky, personal communication). Hygiene remains an important motive. The health risks of overcrowded inner-city cemeteries, where the dead are located above ground in tombs and unable to properly decompose, are deplored by the authorities and much of the middle class (Sonja Leferink, personal communication).

Of course, there are still impediments to the development of cremation in Argentina. For Osvaldo Chernitsky, the main obstacles relate to the municipality's problems in obtaining the necessary permits and the populace's general lack of knowledge about cremation. Other difficulties surround the practicalities of actually achieving the requisites demanded by law. For example, some cremations do not occur due to the cause of death (there being a possibility of murder). Sometimes the family do not like the choice of cremation made by their dead relative and oppose it. A lack of documentation demonstrating the family link with the deceased is a further problem (Monica Lifieri, personal communication). A cremation can only go ahead after the following documents have been provided: a document relating the identity of the deceased, with two witnesses; a marriage or birth certificate to show

the relationship; and, up to a decade after the death, a death certificate. The cremation can be self-authorized (if the deceased has left evidence that they desired cremation) or authorized by a marriage partner or by parents for their children. If there is no direct family, then the closest relative can authorize a cremation; in this case, two witnesses are also required.

The status of cremation, or rather the lack of its status as a political issue, is also problematic. None of the political parties has an official position on the topic, and this reticence is reflected in the ignorance that remains about cremation as well as the lack of regulation linked with this (Gustavo Labriola and Emilio Priede, personal communication). This means that there is no likelihood of a national law being brought in to encourage and properly regulate cremation. At present, the legislation required is passed by city municipal councils; it is not even considered a matter for individual provinces to act on. However, this is not to say that those at provincial level have no influence. For example, in the Province of San Luis cremation remains prohibited. In order to cremate a body, it is necessary to transport it to another province with the cost and complications that this entails (Hugo Estrella, personal communication).

Then there remain longer-term obstacles. As Beatriz Laufer explains, 'It's very difficult, or, better expressed, it takes a fair amount of time for people to change their way of thinking in respect of a theme that is as delicate as death and customs so rooted as burying loved ones'. Although the larger cities are moving ahead, smaller cities and rural areas are still largely impervious to cremation. The inhabitants of the remote northern province of Jujuy, for example, have not particularly taken to cremation yet due to their 'idiosyncrasies' (Carlos Jure, personal communication). Sonja Leferink shows in the next article that cremation is far from popular amongst the Argentine working classes. Although there is usually no law explicitly banning cremation, the Catholic Church still sometimes lobbies to prevent the installation of crematoria. According to Hugo Estrella, 'It's a tough situation, they [the Church] don't usually confront, but take advantage of the politicians' weaknesses or fears, same as everywhere, I guess'.

The final irony regarding the development of cremation in Argentina is that it is precisely now, as the twenty-first century opens, that a cremation society would be able to do useful work in helping the growth of this new phenomenon. Now that cremation is more a private than a municipal concern, an Argentine cremation society would have far more scope to make an impact. For a start, it could systematically collect figures for cremations at all crematoria, both private and municipal – a task that no organization presently performs. As laws concerning the disposal of the dead are a municipal matter, there is no central information and the national statistics department does not collect cremation statistics. Yet it seems that now, when the objective conditions for a cremation society are far more favourable than they ever have been in Argentina – conditions which would allow a cremation society to perform a useful task – there is no sign that one will be formed. **Lewis H. Mates**

Acknowledgements

I am grateful for information to:
Liliana Castillo (Argentine Centre for Statistical Services).
Osvaldo Chernitsky (managing director of Lindberg Argentina SA).
Eduardo Dalesson (Neuquén Municipal Cemetery).
Hugo Estrella (vice-president of *Logia* 431, Córdoba).
Ricardo J. Fernandez (*Chacarita* crematorium, Buenos Aires).
Alberto Gerardo Ferretty (*Chacarita* Crematorium, Buenos Aires).
Oscar Fidanza (general director of the Jardín de Los Ceibos).
Carlos Jure (Servicios Sociales Futuro SA, San Salvador de Jujuy)
Alberto Karmona (Argentine Ministry of Health).
Gustavo Labriola (administrator of DRI PRESTACIONES SRL, the company running *Crematorio Mesopotámico*).
Beatriz Laufer (of CACEPRI – *Camara Argentina de Cementerios Privados*).
Sonja Leferink (academic researcher).
Monica A. Lifieri (secretary of *Obras y Servicios Publicos*, Chacarita crematorium, Buenos Aires).
Emilio Alfonso Priede (director of *Crematorio Mesopotámico*).

See also Argentine cremation societies; Argentine cremationists.

References

Baca, Eduardo J. (1922), *Proyectos de ordenanza reglamentando la cremación de cadéveres y ordenando la construcción de un nuevo Templo Crematorio en la ciudad de Buenos Aires*, Buenos Aires: Guidi Buffarini, CRE/F/AG/3.

Baca, Eduardo J. (1923a), 'Breve Historia de la Cremación Cadáverica en la Ciudad de Buenos Aires, 1879–1923' (part one). *Boletín de la Asociación Argentina de Cremación*, 1: 10–19.

Baca, Eduardo J. (1923b), 'Breve Historia de la Cremación Cadáverica en la Ciudad de Buenos Aires, 1879–1923' (part two). *Boletín de la Asociación Argentina de Cremación*, 4&5: 1–6.

Baca, Eduardo J. (1928), *Estatística de la Cremación de Cadáveres Humanos en la Ciudad de Buenos Aires, 1884–1927*, Buenos Aires: Ferrari Hnos., CRE/C/AG/1928/1.

Baca, Eduardo J. (1934), *Breve Reseña del Crematorio de Buenos Aires*, Buenos Aires: Alma Libre Cuerpo Vano, CRE/F/AG/4.

Connew, Paul (1983), article in *Daily Mirror*, 5 April, reproduced in *Pharos*, 49(2): 75.

FDR (1928), 'Para la Historia de la Cremación en la Republica Argentina, La Primera Sociedad Argentina de Cremación', *Boletín de la Asociación Argentina de Cremación*, 12: 91–93.

Hazemann, R.H. (1972), 'The Social and Cultural Aspect of Cremation', paper presented at the ICF Congress, Grenoble, CRE/D4/1972/10.

LAPC (Liga Argentina pro Cremación) (1959), *Memoria: Ejercicio Mayo 1958 a Mayo 1959*, Buenos Aires: Liga Argentina pro Cremación, CRE/C/AG/1959/1.

Lappas, Alcibíades (2000), *La Masonería Argentina a Través de sus Hombres* (3rd edn), Buenos Aires: Alcibíades Lappas.

Mendoza, José Perez (1923), *Sobre Cremación*, Buenos Aires: Ferrari Hnos., CRE/C/AG/1923/2.

Sein, Dr Andres S. (1936a), *Crematorio de Buenos Aires – Ordenanzas y Decretos Reglamentarios Sobre la Incineración de Cadaveres Humanos, Vigentes en la Capital Federal cuyo Cumplimento se Observa en el Crematorio de Buenos Aires*, Buenos Aires: Eduardo Ghio, CRE/F/AG/2.

Sein, Dr Andres S. (1936b), *Crematorio y Cienca*, Buenos Aires: Guidi Buffarini, CRE/F/AG/5.

Sousa, Terry (1994), 'A Cremation Overview', *Pharos*, 60(2): 51–55.

Popular Class Perceptions and Cremation Practices

In Argentina, more specifically the city of Córdoba, one has to make a clear distinction when discussing perceptions and practices concerning cremation, especially between the direct incineration of a deceased person and the cremation of the remains exhumed from graves after burial rights have expired. The latter practice is common and widely accepted, with the cremated remains being scattered or placed in a columbarium or the grave of a relative. Until approximately the 1980s, however, direct cremation was virtually taboo in Argentine society, which was still overwhelmingly Catholic in orientation. Cremation was thought to inhibit the resurrection of the body on the day of the Last Judgement and thus to interfere with God's divine plan. The burning of corpses was retained for the case of mortal sinners, heretics and traitors, with this defiling profanation of the body constituting part of or an additional element of punishment.

The association of cremation with punishment is still traceable in popular class perceptions, as this anecdote from a Cordobese slum illustrates. A neighbourhood youngster was caught stealing and was killed by the police in the shooting that followed. The mother was so embarrassed that she had her son cremated without granting him the traditional death wake. She scattered his ashes in the river, instead of conserving them in a special place. In the slums, where the death, wake and burial of a neighbour are collective ritual events and where the continuing relationship with the deceased, focused on the resting place of the remains, are important cultural characteristics, the mother's act was a powerful symbolic statement.

Another element provoking aversion towards cremation is the bad reputation of the municipal crematory in Córdoba. Informants in the slums have accused the crematorium personnel of cremating various bodies at the same time and being sloppy about identification. According to these informants there is a high probability that the ashes of various bodies get mixed or that the bereaved receive the ashes of another person, – an idea that horrifies them.

However, since the 1990s the attitude towards cremation has slowly been changing. One factor in that process is the more liberal stance of the Catholic Church which now agrees with cremation so long as it is not an act of defiance of God's will. Another factor is the municipality's recent decree that the bereaved can dispose of the ashes as they prefer, and that includes taking them home. Taking the remains of a loved one

home is an idea that appeals strongly to the popular classes. Their ongoing emotional relation with the deceased, focused on the material remains and needs of the dead person, is an important feature of popular death culture. A third factor is an economic motive: cremation is cheaper than burial. By 2002 some 15 per cent of the Argentinian population were opting for direct cremation. The popular classes, however, continue to have an ambivalent attitude towards direct cremation, as is illustrated by the words of *doña* Margarita, a 30-year-old woman living in one of Córdoba's many slums: 'My wish regarding my mother is to cremate her when she dies. To cremate her and to take her [ashes] home. But sometimes I think, if I do that, I do not let her rest in peace.' 'Resting in peace' implies a body that lies in a place where it cannot be disturbed. 'By reducing the body to ashes, cremation preludes the possibility of this kind of existence,' writes Badone (1991: 225). Margarita's ambivalence is also expressed in her wishes considering her own final resting place: she wants to be buried. **Sonja Leferink**

Reference

Badone, E. (1991), 'Memories of Marie-Thérèse,' in D. Counts and D. Counts (eds), *Coping with the Final Tragedy: Cultural Variation in Dying and Grieving*, Amityville: Baywood Publications Inc., 213–30.

ARGENTINE CREMATION SOCIETIES
ARGENTINE CREMATION ASSOCIATION

The Argentine Cremation Association (*Asociación Argentina de Cremación* – AAC) was established on 4 December 1922. Eduardo Baca, author of the 1922 Buenos Aires cremation by-law, became its secretary until his appointment as director of Buenos Aires Crematorium in 1923 forced him to relinquish the post. José Perez Mendoza was the first president. He was converted to cremation in 1880 having had to organize the exhumation and cremation of the body of a family friend, due to a lack of cemetery space. The unpleasantness of seeing someone in an advanced state of decomposition convinced him that cremation was a far more dignified, as well as hygienic, means of disposal. As president of the Argentina Society for the Protection of Animals and an advocate both for the blind and the game of chess, Mendoza was a relatively well-known personality. These roles brought him the respect of other cremationists and his tenacity made him a worthy figurehead for the AAC.

Membership figures and occupations

The AAC had 128 active members in January 1923, three of whom were paid-up life members. Another 32 were 'adhering members' with a further 189 having written in agreement with the AAC's aims. Impressive increases in early membership, which reached 425 by June 1925, could not be maintained and the two years before July 1927 saw only an 8 per cent increase in membership. As with earlier Argentine cremationists, a large proportion of AAC activists were doctors. In 1923, both vice-presidents, both secretaries, the directors of AAC's library and museum and several other important members were all doctors. In fact, of the main officials, only Mendoza was not involved in the medical profession.

The foreign influence

Foreign influence was reflected by the fact that some of the most important AAC members were born in Europe or possessed strong familial ties there. AAC founder member Teodoro Alemann (1862–1925), for example, was Swiss-born. A journalist, Alemann had published many articles in both the new and old worlds. Of German origins, Hans Bôche regularly contributed articles to the AAC bulletin on, for example, 'The German Protestant Church and Cremation', and also corresponded with German newspapers. The European origins of some senior AAC members allowed the society to maintain good contact with developments in Europe and, through correspondence with European cremation societies, inspiration was drawn from successes in countries such as Germany, Switzerland and Denmark.

The importance of a large British (as well as German) presence in wider Argentine society was revealed by the existence of both British and German cemeteries in Buenos Aires. However, there were few recognizably British surnames in AAC membership lists, whereas over half were of Italian or German origin. German influence manifested itself outside the AAC too, as German organizations in Argentina also actively agitated for cremation. In 1923, for example, the German Scientific Society organized its own cremation conference in Buenos Aires. Although more Argentines were cremated in the 1920s than any other nationality, in terms of percentages of the population, Germans were by far the keenest. Of the total voluntary cremations between 1923 and 1927, Germans constituted 18 per cent (half the number of Argentines), followed by 15 per cent Italians, 10 per cent Spaniards and 4 per cent French. The British only constituted 2 per cent of cremations.

Freemasons?

Although very many pre-AAC cremationists were freemasons, they were less easy to identify in the AAC. In fact, only five can be positively identified as freemasons (Lappas, 2000). AAC literature seldom mentioned freemasonry and, when it did, it was normally to deny that cremation was an exclusively masonic practice. Indeed, a cremation opponent observed that not all Argentine freemasons supported cremation, but did not elaborate. Due to the secretive nature of masonic activities it is not certain that Argentine freemasons were more reluctant to involve themselves in cremation advocacy in the 1920s than they were before that time.

Influence of the left

There was certainly extensive involvement in the AAC from those on the political left. Significant in this context was Dr José Ingenieros (1877–1925), a socialist, eminent doctor, noted psychologist, professor in Buenos Aires University and also a freemason. His socialist comrade Dr Angel M. Giménez was another active cremationist, as was Dr Juan Bautista Justo (1865–1928), a founder and leader of the Argentine Socialist Party. Another eminent doctor, Bautista, was a sociologist, professor in Buenos Aires University, national deputy and senator who was cremated in January 1928.

Articles in the AAC bulletin suggest that some cremationists were inspired by egalitarian, 'socialistic' motives. The sixth bulletin, for example, carried an unattributed quote that cremation was the 'purifying fire' that 'vanishes the abominable privileges of class'. In 1927 freemason Eliseo Cantón called for more cremation propaganda in all social classes, and especially within the poorer elements of society who would benefit most from the cheapness of cremation. He, too, argued that 'in the incinerator oven, we are all equal'. Baca emphasized the egalitarianism in the operation of cremation in Buenos Aires, its crematorium being owned and run by its citizens through the municipality. For that reason, all who wanted to be cremated could afford it, and there were no 'odious privileges' for the dead (Baca, 1928: 4).

Although Baca argued that cremation practice in Buenos Aires conformed to Christ's teachings of equality for all, even atheist 'socialist' cremationists received positive treatment. Thus Soviet Russia was praised for its attempts to implement cremation, and particularly for its 1924 cremation exhibition in Moscow, despite its modest success. According to Bôche, Russia was a land of extremes and progress there was not marching, but galloping. In 1928 the fact that cremation was still a minority practice in Russia was attributed to religious beliefs and the 'backwardness' of the populace. Two years earlier, a Soviet representative had visited Buenos Aires Crematorium. Other revolutionaries who favoured cremation also received supportive coverage. These included the 'sublime martyr' Joe Hill (a revolutionary trade unionist) and Bartolome Sacco and Nicolas Vanzetti, two anarchists and 'supposed' murderers who had been executed after an 'intense protest movement' worldwide. Yet, despite early suggestions that the AAC should operate in workers' and mutualist organizations, it appears that this did not occur to any significant extent (Mendoza, 1923: 69).

Propagandizing activities

AAC members saw their task as one of propagandizing for cremation. Curiously, at least two cremationists publicly ruled out the use of violence to achieve their ends. Cantón deemed violence counterproductive: if Nero had not persecuted Christians so much, he argued, perhaps Christianity would not have spread so far in the world. Thus the AAC concentrated on the distribution of written propaganda and it succeeded in producing some quality pamphlets. The organization also produced and distributed a considerable numbers of leaflets. In October 1926, for example, it sent out 40 000 leaflets requesting participation in the society and calling for money.

The AAC also produced a bulletin. First appearing in January 1923, it was well produced, with some colour, photographs and abundant information. It was, perhaps, over ambitious, for while initially intended as a bi-monthly, only the first edition (for January and February 1923), achieved this aim. Subsequent bulletins emerged further apart in time and, by the eleventh, the bulletin appeared to be little more than an annual report that lacked much of the material of earlier issues. Other propagandizing activities included the organizing of conferences on cremation, some of which appear to have had a positive effect. For example, Dr Sara Justo's cremation conference and fiesta in June 1926 received praise on account of the many women among the audience of over 1000. Occasionally, other media were also employed. In July 1923, for example, Baca spoke about cremation on the national radio station. All this activity kept AAC officials busy. During the year ending June 1926 the AAC sent out 643 bulletins, 1627 circulars and 428 invitations to a conference, totalling 3723 pieces in all. Another important area of activity was lobbying, with some success, the Buenos Aires municipal authorities on the provision of crematoria and columbaria and modification of the cremation by-law. The AAC also lobbied other Argentine authorities, such as La Plata municipality in 1923 to build crematoria – an ultimately fruitless task.

Pan-Americanism and internationalism

Argentine cremationists were aware that cremation was less advanced in the rest of Latin America, and they regarded it as their duty to advocate cremation throughout the continent. In December 1924 Buenos Aires Crematorium produced a film of the whole cremation process to be shown at the Third Pan-American Scientific Congress in Lima, Peru. On the invitation of the University of Chile, the University of La Plata sent a professor to Santiago to speak on cremation in 1928, and the talk provoked a good deal of interest. Yet only small numbers of Latin Americans were cremated in Buenos Aires during the 1920s. The largest proportion was of Uruguayans (2 per cent, 15 individuals) with smaller numbers of Bolivians, Brazilians (three each), Chileans (two), Venezuelans and Puerto Ricans (one each).

Beyond the AAC's pan-Americanism lay its internationalism. In 1922 Mendoza went on a world tour of crematoria, which included the USA, Europe, India and Japan. While the extent to which countries in the Far East cremated surprised Mendoza he also realized that Argentina compared poorly with most of the 'civilised world' that was firmly set on the path to cremation (Mendoza, 1923: 19). AAC publications regularly dealt with the development of cremation around the world in a detailed and well-informed manner, no doubt due to the aforementioned involvement of many members who had familial and cultural links to Europe.

Opposition from the Catholic Church

The AAC identified the Catholic Church's antagonism as one of the most important obstacles to cremation in Argentina and Latin America as a whole. Those who opposed Mendoza's cremationist 'call to arms' in his 1922 pamphlet did so on the grounds of their Catholicism. L.C. Maglione, for example, though an early cremationist (from 1876), later changed his mind after properly taking his Catholicism into account (Mendoza, 1923: 39–41). With educated middle-class individuals adopting such attitudes, the AAC evidently had an extremely difficult task ahead of it. Clearly it was necessary to change the Church's mind, and Mendoza, himself a Catholic, visited the Vatican in April 1922 with this aim. The AAC then sent the Vatican two letters on cremation in 1923, appealing to the Church's desire for funds by arguing that urns containing ashes could be buried in churches. This would augment income by bringing increased visits from relatives of the deceased. The Church's attitude naturally occupied a prominent place in AAC propaganda. A main cremationist argument was that there was nothing in Christian doctrine that outlawed cremation, and priests throughout the centuries were quoted to this effect. Curiously enough, the AAC frequently quoted from, a Catholic anti-cremationist work by Luis Duprat (*Cremación*, 1886), to the effect that cremation did not oppose any Roman Catholic dogma. Catholic opposition to cremation was instead attributed to the distaste of unbelievers, freethinkers and freemasons who the Church regarded as the principal advocates of cremation. The objection that cremation was a pagan practice was countered by Eliseo Cantón who pointed out that it was also employed in 'civilized' ancient Greece, and, besides, not everything pagans did was abominable. Francisco Abba even suggested that, if the Church needed relics, it would be better served by ashes than by flesh-stained bones that had not been 'purified' by cremation. Catholic cremationists received extensive coverage in the AAC's bulletin, and the AAC even sent a letter on the topic to cremation societies throughout the world.

In March 1924 the AAC asked representatives of different denominations in Argentina for their opinion on cremation. The cardinal of Buenos Aires's response was predictable, quoting several saints and papal decrees that had pronounced against cremation. This obvious obduracy provoked a more barbed approach to the Church as the AAC's bulletin began to highlight Catholic hypocrisy. In 1924, for example, it pointed out that a Catholic Buenos Aires newspaper, *El Pueblo*, though ostensibly anti-cremation, did not oppose cremation for corpses that had not been taken out of the vaults they were occupying on time. This was followed by a catalogue of examples of Catholic 'hypocrisy' in subsequent years, such as the cremation performed by the Church of the corpses of 11 monks and nuns in Buenos Aires in October 1925. Cremationists differed considerably on the likelihood of change in Church's attitude. Hans Bôche was optimistic, taking solace from Germany, where the Protestant Church changed its attitude to cremation in the face of its increasing popularity. Others cited the failed Argentine divorce law as an example of the extent of the Church's power to destroy what it did not approve of, and the signs regarding cremation were not encouraging. Indeed, the very formation of the AAC appeared to stimulate latent Catholic opposition into action. Between 1922 and 1924 three Catholic anti-cremation works were published: before 1922 there had only been Duprat's book which, by then, was impossible to get hold of.

Attitude of the press

As Lord Horder pointed out at the London Cremation Congress in 1937, 'propaganda and unrestricted publicity are the lifeblood of any progressive movement' (Report, 1937: 8). 'Unrestricted publicity' in the Argentine press was a pipe-dream for cremationists, and it appeared that certain newspapers did not wish to report on cremation at all. *La Nación* for example, reported that the famous socialist and cremationist Juan Justo had been buried, when he had in fact been cremated. According to the AAC, this happened because newspapers only said what their owners wanted the populace to hear and because *La Nación* wanted to avoid offending its Catholic readership. Negative publicity was another problem: a spoof article on cremation in *La Nación* in April 1926 provoked an angry response from the AAC.

In contrast, *La Prensa* seemed the best AAC press ally. It detailed Justo's cremation, published the text of the new cremation by-law in December 1922 and several other stories that the AAC reproduced in its bulletin. Occasional positive cremation stories also appeared in several other newspapers, including *El Progreso* of Mar del Plata, *El Telegrapho*, *La Razón* and *La Voz de Chaco* and these few, small propaganda victories were published in the AAC bulletin 'without comment'. Ultimately, though, the AAC had to rely for consistent good publicity on its own bulletin, with its small circulation and declining size and quality.

Attitudes of administrators

Despite the Catholic Church's pervasive influence and press hostility or indifference, councillors in Buenos Aires municipality seemed fairly supportive of cremation. They passed the new cremation by-law unanimously and unmodified in December 1922 and decided that, from April 1924, unclaimed corpses in hospitals and the like would be compulsorily cremated after 36 hours. The AAC proposal to construct a columbarium and a monument to cremation pioneer José Penna was also passed unanimously. In 1928 the municipality was again unanimous in voting to allow the deposit of ashes in churches, a rare example of where the Catholic Church's will did not prevail. The municipality helped the AAC in other ways – for example, by putting up its posters throughout the city free of charge.

Cremationists such Eduardo Baca, director of Buenos Aires Crematorium, certainly appreciated the municipality's actions. However, Baca's negative comments about bureaucrats and 'anonymous calumnies' against him (such as the untrue claim that he was paid for his AAC work) suggested that some municipality workers attempted to obstruct cremation by making Baca's job difficult (Baca, 1928: 4–11). Stories in the AAC bulletin also revealed that some municipal workers used their positions to frustrate cremation. For example, in 1923 an unspecified municipal authority 'maliciously and falsely' informed the family of a dead cremationist that they would have to wait three months before he could be cremated.

The closing of a chapter

By 1928 it was clear that the AAC was in serious trouble. The back page of the 1928 bulletin carried an item consisting of two columns under the headings 'how to make the association prosper' and 'how to destroy it'. Presumably the latter highlighted the problems that the AAC faced, including members' inactivity, intriguing, not paying dues and generally failing to contribute to the vitality of the society. It is likely that the AAC's bulletin ended in 1928. The AAC itself was still operating to some degree in December 1939 when its president Dr Andres Sein contacted *Pharos*, but it must have expired soon after. Post-war Argentine cremationists, who formed a new cremation society a decade or more later, thought that the AAC had died because of the indifference and hostility of the atmosphere in which it operated (LAPC, 1959: 10). Still, they remained impressed and inspired by what they deemed the 'most serious' previous attempt at cremation advocacy in Argentina. These post-war cremationists remained convinced of the validity of the project and that they could succeed where their illustrious predecessors had failed. **Lewis H. Mates**

See also Argentine cremationists.

References

Baca, Eduardo, J. (1928), *Estadística de la Cremación de Cadáveres Humanos en la Cuidad de Buenos Aires, 1884–1927*, Buenos Aires: Ferrari Hnos., CRE/C/AG/1928/1.

Boletín e la Asociación de Cremación, nos 1–7, 9–12, CRE/A/AG.

LAPC (Liga Argentina pro Cremación) (1959), *Memoria: Ejercicio Mayo 1958 a Mayo 1959*, Buenos Aires: Liga Argentina pro Cremación, CRE/C/AG/1959/1.

Lappas, Alcibíades (2000), *La Masonería Argentina a Través de sus Hombres* (3rd edn), Buenos Aires: Alcibíades Lappas.

Mendoza, José Perez (1923), *Sobre Cremación*, Buenos Aires: Ferrari Hnos., CRE/C/AG/1923/2.

Report of the London International Cremation Congress (1937), CRE/D4/1937/1.

ARGENTINE PRO-CREMATION LEAGUE

The Liga Argentina Pro Cremación (LAPC – Argentine Pro-Cremation League) was established by 27 individuals in 1956. As with the earlier Argentine Cremation Association (AAC), doctors were essential to the organization. The key figure in its establishment was a doctor, Miguel Servera of Buenos Aires, and other doctors, such as Dr Arturo A. Tigier, also performed important roles. The LAPC founders were also freemasons, holding their meetings at a Buenos Aires address which also served as the base for several masonic lodges. At least one LAPC founder, Samuel Kramer, had been involved in the earlier AAC.

Again like the AAC, some LAPC members were prominent members of the Socialist Party. This included José Antonelli, who was also a freemason. There was another parallel with 1920s Argentine cremationists, and that was the reference in LAPC propaganda to left-wing revolutionaries. The first edition of the LAPC bulletin, *Cremación*, carried an article on the fiftieth anniversary of the execution of the Spanish anarchist and educationalist Francisco Ferrer Guardia. Possessing, according to the cremationists a 'sturdy and tranquil character', Ferrer had been 'legally assassinated'. A few hours before his execution he had made clear his wish to be cremated.

In 1959 the LAPC president Dr Miguel Servera said that their 194-strong membership was 'very poor' for a capital of Buenos Aires' importance (LAPC 1959: 9). Still, 194 was a considerable improvement on the original 27 members just three years previously. Apart from one membership decline in 1962, the trend in LAPC membership was always upwards, with some years recording very impressive increases (see the table below). By the 1980s membership appeared to be levelling out, as there was only a 6 per cent increase between 1980 and 1986. Although the LAPC peaked with a membership 11 times that of the AAC's peak (457 in July 1927), it remained a small figure for a city of Buenos Aires' size.

LAPC Membership Figures, 1956–1986

Year	Membership	% Change
1956	27	n/a
–	–	–
1958	121	+ 348
1959	194	+ 60
1960	247	+ 27
–	–	–
1962	240	– 3
–	–	–
1964	450	+ 88
1965	503	+ 12
1966	631	+ 25
–	–	–
1968	1117	+ 77
1969	1330	+ 19
1970	1627	+ 22
1971	1984	+ 22
1972	2257	+ 14
1973	2548	+ 13
1974	2878	+ 13
1975	3212	+ 12
–	–	–
1978	4200	+ 31
–	–	–
1980	5103	+ 22
–	–	–
1986	5400	+ 6

Like its predecessor, the LAPC was a propaganda-based organization and thus held conferences on cremation. Again echoing the AAC, the LAPC also organized a competition in 1960 with a 10 000 peso prize offered for the best pamphlet on the advantages of cremation over inhumation. The LAPC's journal *Cremación* was launched on 15 June 1960. It was, however, a lower-quality publication than the AAC bulletin; although it had larger-sized pages, they were of a lower-quality print and far fewer in number. Moreover, *Cremación* was only ever an annual publication. The front page of the first edition announced that the LAPC was hoping that an increase in membership (and therefore finance) would allow them to convert the bulletin into a proper magazine. This never happened. Indeed, by 1973 *Cremación* was only four pages, half the size of the first edition. Apart from that difference, it was largely the same as the first edition and therefore did not reveal much evidence of having improved over time. The 1975 edition (no. 16) was slightly smaller in size and had a more basic, less professional layout, although it was eight pages long. By 1975 the bulletin was little more than an annual report on the state of the LAPC and contained very little pro-cremation propaganda or news. In 1973 and 1974 *Cremación* had an annual circulation of 3500. In 1975 the circulation was down to only 3000 per issue. In the late 1970s and early 1980s *Cremación*'s circulation figure stagnated at between 3000 and 4000.

Lobbying the municipal authorities was an important aspect of LAPC activity. Recognizing that the only crematorium in the country was now antiquated and inefficient, the LAPC, in 1959, identified areas for its improvement. The four Baker-system cremators had specific operating problems. One of the most serious was the inevitably 'disagreeable spectacle' that occurred when the cremators were opened at regular intervals during operation in order to manipulate the corpse to ensure complete combustion (LAPC, 1959: 6). Suggestions for improvements were made to the crematorium's director. At its AGM of that year the LAPC voted to ask the municipality to replace or modernize the over 50-year-old cremators, including switching fuel from diesel to gas. A cremulator was also required, as were gardens of remembrance. The municipality was also requested to build a garden for urns. Servera argued that the implementation of these initiatives would bring a big step forward for cremation in the country.

The LAPC appeared to have a degree of support in the municipal parliament. Some important LAPC members, like Erwin Kaunitz, had themselves been members of the municipal council. In 1959 Servera expressed hope that the society would have 'more luck' with Buenos Aires councillors, although the author of another article in the same publication was more pessimistic, expecting little action from the authorities on the increasingly urgent question of declining cemetery space. Despite this, the LAPC did receive some concessions from the municipality. In November 1959, for example, it gained 'judicial power', which meant that it was better equipped to help people who wanted to be cremated with the legal process.

As in the 1920s, the newspaper *La Prensa* continued to deal with cremation questions, although the evidence suggests that it had become, if anything, less supportive. A *La Prensa* editorial in 1959 highlighted the problems facing Buenos Aires cemeteries, which were rapidly filling up. The LAPC wrote to the newspaper suggesting that cremation was the solution, but *La Prensa* did not even print their letter. The tactic of sending letters in response to press articles was employed in subsequent years, with the LAPC, for example, responding to an article on cremation in a magazine called *Esqui-Color* in January 1973. As with the AAC, the LAPC identified Catholic Church opposition to cremation as the crucial obstacle to overcome. In the first edition of *Cremación*, an article on the

attitude of the Church expressed the hope that the new pope would alter the Church's stance. Only three years later the Vatican did alter its position, but this did not have an instant effect on the attitudes of Argentine Catholic clergy. For example, in response to a magazine article published in December 1972 by an individual wanting to be cremated in order to save his family money, a Buenos Aires bishop pronounced that inhumation should remain the choice of the majority, with cremation being employed only in 'exceptional circumstances'.

Internationalism played an important part in the LAPC's outlook. In place of inter-war Germany for pre-war Argentine cremationists, it was post-war England that now provided the best example of success. *Cremación* pointed out in June 1960 that, in less than 20 years, England had gone from cremating 4 per cent to 31 per cent of its dead. Thus England, recognized as being at the head of the world cremation movement, provided the inspiration for most of the innovations that the LAPC wanted to see implemented in Argentina in the early 1960s, such as the use of gas as the cremator fuel and gardens of remembrance. In 1959–60 Servera corresponded with the British Cremation Society regarding the types of cremator employed there, advice on the best fuel to use and other topics. The fact that cremation existed in 'most developed countries' acted as a spur, as did Argentina's position at the bottom of a list of cremating countries that appeared in *Pharos* in August 1959. The final (number seven) in the list of the LAPC's aims was to establish relations with similar societies in other countries. It was thus a natural step for the LAPC to join the International Cremation Federation (ICF). In fact, Servera had been in touch with the ICF for three years before establishing the LAPC. At the 1957 ICF Congress in Zurich, a Swiss delegate who was in touch with the Argentines agreed to be their observer. Severa paid a visit to the ICF offices soon after the LAPC was established, and the LAPC formally joined in January 1959. Argentina became the twenty-third country to affiliate to the ICF.

The benefits of the ICF were obvious to Servera. Membership would give the LAPC 'an international personality' and its publications were vital due to the lack of an indigenous body of cremation material. So acute was this lack that it had hitherto proved impossible for cremationists to find a single book on cremation in any language in any of the most important libraries in Buenos Aires, which was particularly surprising given that several Argentines had produced works on the subject from the 1880s to the 1930s. As the 'pioneer propaganda organization' of the South America Republics, the LAPC was obviously important to the ICF, which had guided it in its formation and promised to support it in its 'difficult task'.

Though unable to take up an invitation to attend an ICF executive meeting in 1960, an Argentine delegate was present at that year's ICF triennial international congress in Stockholm. However, this was the peak of direct involvement in the ICF for Argentine cremationists. There was no LAPC delegate at the 1963 ICF Congress nor were there LAPC representatives at ICF general council meetings during the 1960s. This was due to a lack of finance, which remained an acute problem and seriously limited LAPC involvement in the ICF in the 1970s. In 1975 a list of donors and their donations was printed in the LAPC bulletin. These were thanked, as they had solved the immediate economic difficulties the society was experiencing. However, although there was enough capital to remain a member of the ICF, there was still not enough to send a LAPC delegate to the triennial congress in Helsinki in 1975. It was the same story in subsequent years. No Argentines were ICF officials and there was no LAPC representation in ICF congresses (although *Pharos* was listed as circulating in Argentina). This isolation was reflected in other ways. There seemed to be a lack of communication between the ICF and LAPC in the early 1960s, reflected in the lack of up-to-date information on Argentina in *Pharos*. Like the AAC before it, it is difficult to determine precisely when the LAPC expired. The last cremation statistics that the LAPC supplied to *Pharos* came in 1978. The same information on Argentina was then repeated annually in *Pharos* until 1985, when the opening of a new Argentine crematorium was announced. Even then, there was no update on cremation statistics. The following year, *Pharos* gave a new LAPC membership figure but none of the other information was updated. This was the last time information came from the LAPC. The next time *Pharos* carried new information on Argentina, it had been supplied, in 1992, by a new contact who was not obviously linked with the LAPC.

The painfully slow progress cremation was making in Argentina was presumably one of the reasons for the death of the LAPC. The cause was hindered considerably when cremation became associated with the disposal of left-wing dissidents by the military regime in the early 1980s. The Catholic Church, too, as in Ireland, seemed stubbornly opposed to cremation, despite the Vatican's change of attitude in 1963. Like the AAC before it, the LAPC was dogged by a lack of funds. The LAPC always gave the impression of just about keeping its head above water, despite its relatively rapidly growing membership. Although it was much larger and longer-lived than its predecessor, it seemed, oddly, a more sickly creature than the AAC. It was ironic, not to mention unlucky, that it ceased to exist some time between 1986 and 1992, just as cremation was about to become considerably more popular in Argentina. It must have laid some of the groundwork, but its precise contribution to the subsequent development of cremation should not be overestimated. **Lewis H. Mates**

See also Argentine cremationists

References

Cremación, Boletin de la Liga Argentina Pro-Cremación, 1 (June 1960), 15 (June 1973), 17 (October 1973), CRE/AO/AG.

LAPC (Liga Argentina pro Cremación) (1959), *Memoria: Ejercicio a Mayo 1959*, Buenos Aires: Alcibíades Lappas.

ARGENTINE CREMATIONISTS
EARLY CREMATIONISTS

The first and second generations of modern advocates of cremation in Argentina were all born between 1835 and 1861 and died between 1899 and 1937. Though from all over Argentina (Wenceslao Tello, for example, was born in the far-flung Andean province of Jujuy) and further afield (Eduardo Wilde was from Tupiza in Bolivia), they all shared the common characteristics of being freemasons and doctors. The earliest to become a mason was José Baca in 1858; the last was Eliseo Cantón in 1905. All eight became doctors after studying in Buenos Aires University.

Several of them had the experience of completing or furthering their knowledge abroad, which must also have influenced their thinking on cremation. After graduating, Eduardo Wilde (1844–1913) opened a consultancy, but quickly obtained a provincial government scholarship that, in 1873, paid for his studies in Europe. He lived in Paris and there attended courses run by some of the most renowned specialist surgeons of the time. He also came into contact with famous scientists such as Louis Pasteur and Claudio Bernard. Similarly, Telémaco Susini (1856–1936) studied with both Pasteur and Koch in Europe before returning to organize a campaign against rabies. José Teodoro Baca (1835–1914) went north to study philosophy in San Francisco and later made several medically focused trips to Europe. Wenceslao Tello (1851–1934) was another Argentine cremationist who completed his studies in Europe. However, José Penna, the 'father of Argentine cremation', did not study abroad.

At least four had military experience of some kind. The son of an army colonel, Wilde was a surgeon in the Paraguayan War of 1865–70 during which some rudimentary cremation had occurred. Similarly, in 1861, Baca joined the army and participated as a surgeon in the Battle of Pavón, 1861. He became a naval doctor and then, in 1868, a police doctor. Pedro Mallo (1838–1899) reached high rank in the navy, and was also professor in the Navy Military School and editor of its annals. As a student, Tello also served in the army.

Many of these cremationists became outstanding in the field of medicine. Baca achieved the directorship of the 'Hospital de Clínicas' and later worked in the Hospital Rawson, where he developed an extensive field of experimentation for his students. Samuel Gache (1850–1907) worked in the same hospital, where he created and organized an effective maternity ward, bringing him many acolytes. He also founded the nursing school and was secretary of the National Committee of Lazaretos (quarantines) by 1884. Gache later became president of the Círculo Médico Argentino (Argentine Medical Circle) and director of the *Anales*, the only Argentine medical magazine of the time. He also dedicated himself to the fight against tuberculosis and, to this end, formed the Liga Argentina Contra la Tuberculosis (Argentine League Against Tuberculosis) in May 1901. This organization, of which he became president, involved some of the most prominent doctors of the period, including fellow cremationist Emilio R. Coni and later cremationist Eliseo Cantón. As

soon as Cantón (1861–1937) became a doctor he went to the rural interior of Argentina to help treat epidemic victims and there established several isolation hospital centres.

As masons and doctors, it was to be expected that many cremationists would work together closely on areas outside of cremation. In 1880 Mallo helped establish the Masonic Body of Aid to the Injured *Cuerpo Masonico de Ayuda a los Heridos*, designed to help the victims of contagious diseases. Wilde and Baca became involved in this organization and others established by masons to help victims of the cholera and yellow fever epidemics of the 1880s. Many masons were also involved in the Argentine Red Cross, which, in 1880, Gache helped establish. He then became its first, and long-standing, secretary. Later, Cantón was its director for several years and Susini was also notably involved.

Academic excellence also characterized the careers of many of the cremationists, who all worked in Buenos Aires University Faculty of Medical Sciences. Susini, a university professor, was director of the Biological Institute and founder of the Pathological Institute. A member of the Academy of Sciences, in 1882 he took part in the International Pedagogic Congress, speaking on hygiene topics. Baca became university vice-dean and was professor of General Pathology and History of Medicine from 1876. In 1906 Gache won, by competition, the post of Professor of Obstetrics, whilst Mallo was professor of Public Hygiene. As well as teaching in the university, Tello was a member of the Argentine Scientific Society. Samuel Gache excelled at university. In 1879, while still a student, he won an Argentine Medical Circle first prize for a thesis on insanity. Cantón, by contrast, became a professor of Medical Zoology. A great hygienist and researcher, he won many prizes for works of science from Argentine, Latin and northern American and European scientific organizations. Along with José María Ramos Mejía (1849–1914), Susini and others, Cantón was a member of the Academia Nacional de Medicina (National Academy of Medicine). In fact, he was several times its president and only the third person to be designated its honorary president. Cantón developed a procedure for suppressing pain during birth and gained plaudits for his refusal to exploit the procedure commercially.

Several cremationists produced important scientific and academic writings contributing to many areas of knowledge. One of the wider-ranging individuals was Ramos Mejía, an initiator of psychiatric studies in Argentina and an important thinker who was heavily influenced as a student by the historian Vicente F. López. Master of numerous disciplines, Ramos Mejía wished to establish a study of the history of Argentine society that combined psychological and medical with sociological and historical knowledge. As well as collaborating in almost all medical publications of the period, Ramos Mejía went on to produce numerous high-quality works on psychological, historical and sociological themes. Gache's first book on tuberculosis was well received in scientific circles and was recognized as one of the most important on the topic. In his final years he concentrated on his clinical expertise, obstetrics, including publications on Caesarean operations and abdominal tumours. Mallo published *La Historia de la Medicina en el Rio de la Plata* (*History of Medicine in Rio de la Plata*) whilst, in a similar vein, Cantón produced *Geografía Médica de la Republica Argentina* (*Medical Geography of the Argentine Republic*) and other scientific works. Gache collaborated in many published works on public health. Others concentrated their efforts more on journalism rather than scientific writings. Wilde, noted for his literary disposition at an early age, became a journalist and a fine writer, adeptly using irony to make his case. Similarly, Gache was a regular contributor to newspapers and magazines and Susini also wrote a good deal of journalism, especially for scientific journals.

Some of these cremationist doctors made their impact on medical issues and public health through more political activity. Probably the most important cremationist in this area, apart from José Penna himself, was Ramos Mejía who, from 1880, occupied various posts in public administration. A national deputy at various times, by 1882 he was vice-president of the Municipal Commission of Buenos Aires from where he promoted the creation of a Department of Public Assistance. The following year he became the first director of Public Assistance and oversaw the first cremation in 1884 and its subsequent general implementation in 1886.

Ramos Mejía continued his sanitary work as president of the National Department of Hygiene, 1893–99, where he promoted measures against yellow fever which was then endemic in Brazil. He built a floating hospital and the Martín Garcia Lazareto and also created the post of port sanitary inspector, water-cleaning services and the Bacteriological Institute. In addition, he waged a campaign against smallpox, took effective measures against leprosy and secured the regulation of medicinal and pharmaceutical practice by ordering the creation of a medical code. In 1908 he was invited to become president of the National Council of Education, charged with the task of establishing new schools and developing the 'national character' of teaching.

Others also had a significant impact. Wilde became a provincial legislator, national deputy and president of the Department of National Hygiene. As Minister of Justice, Culture and Public Instruction and later from within the Department of the Interior, he masterminded the defence, before the national assembly, of the government's bill providing for secular, free and obligatory education and the civil marriage bill, among others. Lappas attributed the success of these bills to Wilde, who was also an Argentine diplomat and represented his country in various international congresses. From 1874 Baca became a deputy in the provincial legislature, using his position to promote public health initiatives, such as the first projects of draining waterlogged and contaminated lands. He acted in the Councils of Hygiene and Health helping to initiate the purification of running waters. Likewise, Gache was Secretary of Public Assistance between 1893 and 1896, helping to create institutions aimed at promoting public health. Susini, a director in the same department, created the Laboratory of Public Assistance. In 1881 he helped establish the *Club Liberal*. Another activist in liberal politics was Cantón, who was several times member of the national chamber of deputies and its president between 1908 and 1911. Author of a progressive marriage law, Tello specialized in infectious diseases and worked in the port sanitation department and later in the national Department of Hygiene. Many of these cremationists were also involved in other cultural institutions including Susini as President of the Liga Helénica de la Argentina (Helenic League of Argentina). **Lewis H. Mates**

ARGENTINE PRO-CREMATION LEAGUE CREMATIONISTS

Three important cremationists of the Argentine Pro-Cremation League (*Liga Argentina Pro*

Cremación (LAPC)) were Miguel Servera (Sancho) (1892–1961), Samuel Kramer (1890–1960) and Virgilio Atilio Lasca (1894–1958), who were all born and died within a few years of each other. Two others, Arturo A. Tigier (1900–72) and José Antonelli, died in the early 1970s. At least two had some form of foreign influence in their backgrounds. Originally from Spain, Servera travelled to Puerto Rico in 1911 before moving again to Argentina in 1921. Kramer was the son of a German who had emigrated to Argentina. Three were involved in politics: Servera was a Spanish Socialist Party (PSOE) activist forced to leave Spain for political reasons. Antonelli was 'outstanding' in the Argentine Democratic Socialist Party (*Partido Socialista Democratico*). In contrast, Lasca became involved in liberal politics. Originally a member of the Radical Party, he left to join the Progressive Democratic Party, in which he became a metropolitan, national committee and Buenos Aires executive representative.

In strong contrast to the first generation of Argentine cremationists, only one was a medical doctor. Tigier, who became a doctor of medicine in 1928, had an eminent and outstanding professional career. Initially qualifying in 1948, he worked in many different hospitals including Hospital Penna, named after the 'father' of Argentine cremation. Publishing his work in *Cuadernos de la Libertad* (*Notebooks of Freedom*), Tigier founded the Medical Association of Artistic Culture (*Asociación Médica de Cultura Artistica*) (Medical Association of Artistic Culture) and a pan-American university exchange. Lasca did complete a doctorate, but it was in jurisprudence rather than medicine. Whereas Lasca began practising as a lawyer in Buenos Aires, Kramer and Servera were businessmen. Servera started his commercial activities in Puerto Rico, continuing his textile business when he moved to Argentina. Following in his father's footsteps, Kramer began commercial activity in farming and importation in the southern regions of Patagonia and Tierra del Fuego. Antonelli became an 'outstanding sports journalist'. Like the first generation of Argentine cremationists, at least four (and perhaps all five) were freemasons (only Tigier was not noted as being a freemason) All were active in many of the same institutions. For examples, Servera, Lasca and Antonelli were all involved in the Argentine League of Lay Culture (*Liga Argentina de Cultura Laica*). Servera was several times its president and Antonelli its secretary. Servera and Lasca also operated together in the Spanish Republican Centre (*Centro Republicano Español*) – Lasca being its secretary for several years and also its legal adviser – and the Argentine Liberal Group, (*Ateneo Liberal Argentino*) and both collaborated in a masonic magazine. Servera also contributed to the magazine *Liberalis*. Kramer, whose father had been one of the founders of the Argentine Red Cross, was involved in similar philanthropic, liberal and democratic institutions. Regarding cremation, only one, Kramer, revealed evidence of having been a cremationist for any length of time. He was listed as a supporter of the Argentine Cremation Association (AAC), though not as an 'active member', in 1923. Although he maintained a low profile during the AAC's lifetime, he became the first treasurer of the LAPC in 1956. However, the single most important person in the establishment of the LAPC and its first president, Servera, was not an AAC member in the 1920s. In 1959, the year of his death, Lasca was a 'collaborator' in the LAPC. Another collaborator that year was Tigier. Antonelli did not have an official position within the LAPC. **Lewis H. Mates**

See also politics.

ART

Art expresses human imagination, not least when it engages with humanity's destiny. Historically speaking, perhaps the single most important painting relating to cremation, and predating modern cremation, is that of Nicholas Poussin. Mirroring classical antiquity, his *Landscape with the Ashes of Phocion* (1648) portrayed Plutarch's account of a human tragedy and stands as one of the great paintings of the world, a testimony to the place of human relationships expressed through cremated remains (see Plate 1). It depicts the Roman rite of ossilegium, collecting the bones and remains of cremation, as discussed in the entry on Romans, which also alludes to the picturing of cremation on coins. Poussin focuses on a faithful wife collecting the ashes of her husband who has been politically shamed and unceremoniously cremated. The background against which she stoops to collect the remains is one in which the beauty of nature and the powerful architecture of a proud society frames

1 *Landscape with the Ashes of Phocion*, Nicolas Poussin (1648)

2   *The Funeral of Shelley*, Edouard Fournier (1889)

3 *Dr William Price,* Unknown artist, after a photograph by Thomas Forest

4   Stockholm Crematorium. Interior: fresco *Life-Death-Life* by Sven Erixson

5   Stockholm Crematorium. Courtyard Sculpture, *The Resurrection*, Joel Lundqvist (wide view)

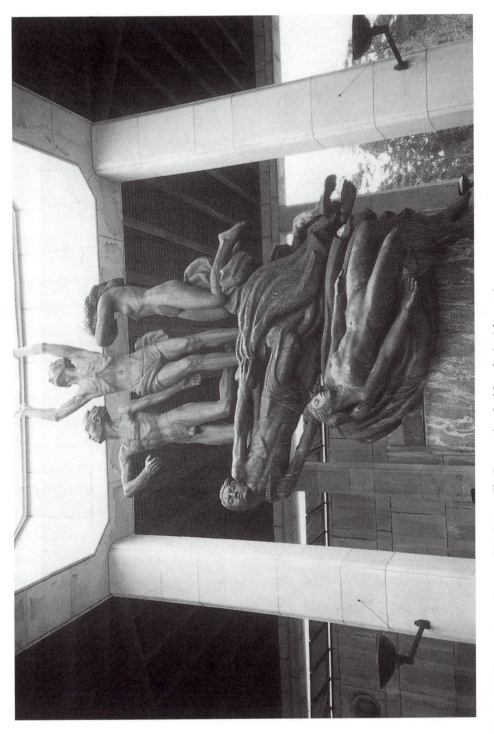

6 Stockholm Crematorium. Courtyard Sculpture, *The Resurrection,* Joel Lundqvist (close-up)

7   Bordeaux Crematorium. Interior: minimalist

Bordeaux Crematorium. Interior: with Christian symbols

the ongoing activities of those uninvolved in her grief. Quite different was the spectacle of the cremation of Roman emperors that even involved a rite in which an eagle was released from above the cremation pyre symbolizing the emperor's deification and the passing of the emperor-god's spirit.

Nearly 250 years later Edouard Fournier's 1889 painting, *The Funeral of Shelly* (Plate 2) takes up a sense of pathos, but now reflected in the Romantic ideal of the poet himself and, in fact, painted a generation after Shelley's death and cremation in 1822. Shelley's friends, author Trelawney, the pre-Raphaelite painter Leigh Hunt and fellow-poet Lord Byron are depicted as standing around the funeral pyre. The day is depicted as cold and inhospitable but, apparently, it had actually been a hot August day. One of the ironies of the painting, being located at the sea-edge as it was, is its echo of Mary Shelley's fantasy on the final cremation of her monster, as told in the entry on **Frankenstein**.

The heroes and legends of cremation come to their sharpest and most personal focus, perhaps, in Dr William **Price** of South Wales, as his entry indicates and as is portrayed in the painting of him at the Pontypridd Museum reproduced here (Plate 3). The firebrand in his hand is the direct symbol of his contribution to the history and development of cremation in Britain.

Certainly, the emergence of modern cremation proved a challenge and opportunity for architects and artists as they sought to meet the aesthetic and religious demands of this new context for human values and emotion. Every crematorium possesses its distinctive features, and many are mentioned in their appropriate entries. Here we draw attention to the illustrations provided of the interior of Asplund's Woodland Crematorium in Stockholm (Plate 4). The main Chapel of the Holy Cross displays Sven Erixson's fresco 'Life-Death-Life' that surrounds the altar. It also frames the central catafalque with its coffin, a focal point which is emphasized by the fact that the entire floor slopes downward towards it. This provides an overwhelming unity of symbolic purpose with the depth of the positioning of the coffin, its centrality, and yet with the artistic context of *Life-Death-Life* reflecting something of the death-conquest motif explored in the entry on **rites of passage**. Picking up that motif, just outside that chapel stands Joel Lundqvist's sculpture, *The Resurrection*. This is reproduced here (Plates 5 and 6) to illustrate both its courtyard context, and its detail of the figures that reach heavenwards and move from death to life.

By sharp contrast to these full symbolic spaces we also illustrate the extreme minimalism of the later twentieth-century Bordeaux Crematorium. In Plate 7 it is shown with a bare catafalque, with one curtained wall and with a structure that might, under appropriate circumstances, serve as an altar, but which need not assume that sacred role. The bare walls speak a minimalism of extreme utility. Plate 8 adds a crucifix and candles, additional symbols that can be used when the rite follows an explicitly Christian form, and demonstrating the breadth of value and belief to which modern cremation has responded.

A great deal more could be illustrated, indeed, the art of cremation is a field hardly yet born. Still, each context speaks for itself as, for example, the distinctive tile art depicting ancient cremation and described in the entry on **Portugal** and the role of art in the aesthetic phase of approach to cremation in the **USA** entry. **Douglas J. Davies**

See also Frankenstein; Portugal; Price; rites of passage; Romans; Shelley, P.B., Stockholm Woodland Crematorium; Sweden – Skogskyrkogården (Woodland Cemetery); USA.

ASHES

CHINA

At present, the cremated remains of almost 4 million people per year in China – the largest volume in the world – are mainly consigned in cities to special halls, walls, porches or towers or buried in public cemeteries or burial grounds. In rural areas they are mainly kept in special halls built by local villagers. Funeral rooms, too, usually possess facilities for storing cremains. At the Jing'an Temple Cemetery in Shanghai, for example, the storage facility takes the form of a marble structure with more than 400 cases divided into 17 regions. At the crematorium of Western Baoxing Road, there is a hall of Tang-Dynasty style: on one side of the hall is a cremation chamber in the same style and, behind the chamber, a room for cremains in the shape of an octagonal pavilion.

Increasing demand for the burial of cremains

has led to more cemeteries. For example, since 1984, the Shanghai branches of the Civil Affairs Department have, in succession, set up the Zhuanqiao, Binhai, Dianshanhu, Weijiajiao and Xujing cemeteries, in order to satisfy the citizens' demand for burying cremated remains. During this period, many cemeteries were built in large and medium-sized cities throughout the country. According to statistics from the national Civil Affairs Department, in 2000 the number of cemeteries in China had reached 692. Consistent with the spread of cremation in urban areas in China, these cemeteries are generally intended for the burial of cremated remains. With the deepening of funeral and interment reform, governments at all levels now encourage disposal rather than retention of cremains. In response to government appeals, more and more people are choosing to have cremains scattered at sea, buried under trees or buried deeply with no grave marker.

The desire to return to nature has prompted the new funeral custom of sea-burial advocated by some people in Chinese coastal cities such as Shanghai and Guangzhou. In recent years the trend towards sea-burial of cremated remains has also spread to other cities in China. The first sea-burial of cremated remains took place on 19 March 1991 in Shanghai. The sponsor rented a large passenger ship, had several hoppers deployed on the stern and the cabins decorated with flowers. A ceremony was held in the main cabin en route to the site. A local official gave a speech, and several representatives of the relatives of the deceased expressed their sorrow. Arriving at the appointed spot, the participants went to the stern in turn, slowly scattering the cremains, mixed with petals, into the sea.

Over the last ten years the popularity of sea-burials has rapidly increased throughout China; particularly in Shanghai, Guangzhou, Beijing and some other places. Taking Shanghai as an example, by the end of 2002, 50 sea-burials had taken place, with the cremains scattered into the sea in an area between the Changxing and Hengsha islands. Advocated and supported by government at various levels, this method attracts customers on account of its low price and grander ceremonies. People regard it an honour to take part in this kind of activity because their choices help protect the environment by saving land. Participants include intellectuals, senior officials and overseas residents. Following the suggestions of those using sea-burial, the Cremation Sea-Burial Company in Shanghai also holds memorial ceremonies for descendants at sea and at appropriate times of the year. It also sponsors an online cemetery website (at http://fis.88547.com). On this website relatives who have participated in a sea-burial can create homepages for their deceased next-of-kin and hold online memorial ceremonies. **Zhu Jinlong, Gao Yueling and Li Jian**

REMAINS

'Ashes' is one popular and basic description of the form of human remains resulting from the process of modern cremation. As the separate entry on **cremulation** indicates, this process regularly involves rendering all remains into a uniform form of 'ashes', and has not always found approval. 'Cremains' is another name for 'ashes' and is discussed separately. It is important to note that many 'remains', especially from archaeological sources and, indeed, from traditional Eastern forms of cremation include larger pieces of burnt bone and are not simply 'ashes'. For that reason it is important to observe the precise context in which 'ashes' or 'remains' are used so as to be sure of the meaning ascribed to them. Sometimes in this book they appear as interchangeable terms. In this entry, however, 'ashes' and 'remains' are used with care to maintain something of the distinction between traditional and modern forms of cremation. Particular attention is drawn to 'ashes' as the result of the full cremation–cremulation process and to the symbolic significance resulting from it.

Important archaeological and classical accounts of remains are provided in the entries on **Ancient Greece**, the **Romans**, and **the archaeology of Britain**, as well as on contemporary **Spain**. Relevant material is also covered on the containers for remains in those and in the entries on **cineraria**, **columbaria**, and **urns**. Ashes have also been used to express symbolic messages, as in the former USSR where leaders' ashes are placed in the Kremlin's wall (see **Russia and the USSR**). Sometimes they have been accorded a very pragmatic status as the **Luxembourg** entry shows in respect of the value added tax imposed on ashes received back into the country after cremation abroad because they are regarded as 'material processed by a foreign firm'. By sharp contrast the entry on the **ashes of Isaac** demonstrates the closest and deepest of religious interpretations in which human and animal remains are symbolically aligned and invoked for particular purposes. Changes in style over the use and means of final disposing of ashes and remains have varied a great deal over time and in different countries (see Davies and Guest 1999, for Britain).

Symbolic ashes

Cremation introduces an important dimension into the symbolism of human remains, and this is especially true in developed forms of modern cremation in which even the larger bone remains are specially ground to granular ashes. Here I consider two different cases to exemplify this point. First, in forms of both ancient and modern cremation in some eastern and south-east Asian Buddhist cultures, cremation is relatively incomplete, thereby allowing skeletal remains to be removed from the cremator and the family to gather round and use special chopsticks to extract from the cremated remains certain bone fragments. These are placed in special containers and will be the basis for future commemorative rites. Over time, those who were personally known to the living pass into the status of more distant ancestors and, for this, there is a degree of appropriateness in ash-bone remains. The remains are remains of kin, but there may well be no intimate knowledge of them as distinct individuals. The same could also happen to the skeletal remains of those who have been buried or placed in family tombs.

In most Western forms of cremation, however, there is none of this intimate link between skeletal remains and the living kin. The bone-remains, crushed as the **cremulator** entry shows, result in an ash of relatively uniform consistency. This is easily viewed as a processing of remains in a fairly industrial sense. Once placed in a largely functional, rather than artistic, container the ashes are ready for their next destination. This can be burial, scattering or placement at a site of special and personal interest.

But what kind of symbol is this batch of finely ground cremated remains? It is a symbol that is far more detached from the living person from which it is derived than is the corpse. It is a less personal symbol. It is not a skull that can be located on an ancestral shelf. In offering this possibility of a certain distance, cremated remains provide a canvas on which the images of memory of the survivor may be painted. This may be the reason why, where the freedom of action is possible – as in Britain – ashes have become a very mobile means of a survivor taking them and using them as a means of expressing their own view of the dead person. The urn used for long-term use can, itself, be of artistic design and reflect something of the character of the deceased person whose ashes it contains.

It is as though ashes become a very distinctive type of symbol – one that is relatively open-ended as far as its precise meaning is concerned and yet is highly charged with emotional significance. In other words, such ashes are full of potential; they are charged with an energy that can be directed in a variety of ways, depending on the wishes of the living. One way of developing this theme is through the philosopher Martin Buber's distinction between an I–Thou and an I–It relationship (Buber, 1958). The I–Thou relationship is one in which people view each other as equal partners possessing a degree of respect and concern for each other; indeed, Buber employed the older English usage of 'thou' to stress this familiarity between equals. In an I–It relationship, by contrast, one person treats another person more as a 'thing' than as a person. It implies a degree of disregard, disrespect and depersonalizing of the other. If we take this distinction and think of a continuum from I–Thou to I–It and apply it to death, some interesting features emerge. In doing this we employ the sociological concept of the ideal-type, a form of description that brings together the essential features of a situation in a kind of a cameo or shorthand version of events.

Take the case of someone dying in hospital with a loving relative alongside. Here we have a strong I–Thou context in which a lifetime's relationship frames a tender and deeply concerned moment. At death, and for a period afterwards, the living may still regard the dead person in an I–Thou relationship and may even talk to them. This is possible if the body still 'looks like' the once-living individual but, sooner or later, they are likely to say that the other person has 'gone', and it is only the body that remains. The wife may, for example, say it is 'no longer' her husband. They may believe that the real self has departed as a soul. Indeed, many are struck immediately by the sharp difference between even a very sick person and the utterly still form of the dead but, certainly, as time progresses still further, and the body shows increased signs of being dead, the living may come to relate to the corpse more in terms of an I–It than an I–Thou relationship. This kind of situation is reflected in what some people say about their own future death, observing that they do not mind what happens to their body since they 'will not be there' or since their body is 'only a shell'.

What, then, of ashes? Certainly, they will elicit a great variety of attitudes, and the very fact that there is no physical body to which to relate, no familiar features to trigger a response, makes cremated remains an ambiguous symbol capable of prompting two extreme responses. First is the case of an ongoing form of I–Thou relationship by those who retain the ashes of their dead partners, keeping them at home and talking to them as though they are speaking to the actual living person. At one level this allows the survivor's imagination to operate powerfully in terms of relatively restricted memory. The dead person is 'kept alive' within the ongoing forms of relationship that had previously existed. The very fact that, in some countries but certainly not in all, ashes may be kept at home may foster an attitude that hinders what many would regard as a necessary detachment of the living from the dead. Corpses, by contrast, are at least detached from the living space of survivors, even though people regularly keep photographs or other mementos of the deceased person.

The second type is reflected by the larger number of people for whom cremated remains are likely to lie further towards the 'It' pole of the Thou–It continuum. For these people, ashes present a much wider opportunity for the individual imagination to range over a variety of options. Memory may become a more personal expression of how a survivor or a family thought of the deceased person. Here the reflexive element of a relationship comes to prominence. An individual is working out their own thoughts of the relationship and, although this is intensely personal, it is not so intensely interpersonal. The very form of ashes offers a kind of neutral substance or an almost blank canvas on which the mourner may paint a memorial picture. This is one way of interpreting the behaviour of individuals who deposit ashes in places whose significance derives from significant moments or periods in the life of the dead person. More especially, these places reflect the images the living have of the dead, not least their own image of their relationship with them. In what is almost a form of irony it is the possibility of an I–It relationship with cremated remains that facilitates a deep I–Thou relationship – but it is an I–Thou relationship grounded in the memory and, indeed, in the identity of the living partner.

In societies where religious convention or civil regulation firmly prescribe what will happen to ashes or cremated remains, these kinds of personal option do not come into play. For example, cremated remains in India, or ashes in many other places where people of Indian origin may be cremated, are placed in flowing water as symbolic of the sacred river Ganges, according to Indian tradition. Here, individual thoughts are framed by strong religious ideas on the destiny both of the soul and of the body. The entry on **Spain** offers one case of an extremely strong traditional society, in which, for centuries, cremation was almost unimaginable, changing into one in which the practice became adopted and in which ashes rapidly came to be taken and used in such private deposition.

Symbolic power

A powerful religious symbol attracts the faithful because of a deep affinity between it and the idea it expresses as, for example, in the case of the Christian use of wine as a symbol of the sacrificial blood of Christ. Within that tradition it does not take any excessive stretch of the imagination to make this connection. When the imagination has to be stretched too far, it is likely that a symbol will rupture and cease to be useful. Symbols often possess a distinctive appropriateness; there is a degree of fit, a kind of affinity, between the symbol and what it symbolizes. This is well expressed in the idea that a symbol participates in what it represents. This contrasts, for example, with 'signs' which bear a much more arbitrary relationship to what they represent.

How, then, does this relate to ashes? What is the affinity between ashes and the dead? What might be the attraction that makes them a symbol of the dead? This is a complex question and, while it is likely that any answer will need to take careful account of the local social, religious and historical context, the following issues are likely to be relevant. Ashes are the product of fire and, because of that, some of the strongest layers of significance derive more from fire and its activity than from the ashes themselves, as we consider in the entry on **fire**, and on **fire – particularly – Christianity**, which explores both its positive and negative dynamics as presented in both religious and secular forms of thought. The following article on ashes in Sweden is important in this regard and demonstrates the variety of attitudes present in that country towards the dead. Finally, in the entry on identity, we also see how ashes reflect memory and existence. **Douglas J. Davies**

See also Ancient Greece; archaeology of Britain; cineraria; columbaria; cremains; cremulator; fire; identity; Luxeumbourg; Romans; Russia and the USSR; Spain; urns

References

Buber, Martin (1958), *I and Thou* (2nd rev. edn), trans. Ronald Gregor Smith, Edinburgh: T&T Clark.

Davies, Douglas J. and Guest, Matthew (1999), 'Disposal of Cremated Remains', *Pharos*, Spring: 26–30.

SWEDEN

Changing customs in the late 1990s

In the late 1990s in Sweden a growing number of people chose to scatter the ashes of their cremated relatives in places other than public or private burial grounds. The option of scattering was, itself, made possible in 1957, and is strictly regulated. An application to the country administration is demanded, and the place of scattering approved. A further condition requires respectful handling of the ashes. Relatives who have scattered ashes must also make a report to the county administration that they have done so.

Most of those cremated are either buried in an urn-grave or spread on a memorial grave. The use of urns is more than 100 years old in Sweden and is the most common way of burying the ashes. The custom of spreading the ashes in a memorial grove started in the beginning of the 1960s, when the first memorial groves were constructed (Wall, 2000: 24). Available statistics indicate that

in 1980, 422 (17 per cent) of the 2569 Church of Sweden parishes (which cover the whole of Sweden) reported they had a memorial grove. By 1995 this had risen to 32 per cent (Lund University Archive for Church History: Questionnaires 19, 23), and is likely to have increased beyond that with time. Although it is difficult to get a total picture of changes in the use of memorial groves for placing the ashes, some image is possible.

In 2000 the cremated remains 869 deceased people were scattered, of a total out of 93 285 (0.94 per cent) and in 2001 some 940 out of 93 752 (1.1 per cent) (*Kyrkogården*, 2003: 15). In 2002, in the cities possessing a crematorium, an average of 48 per cent of cremated remains were scattered in the memorial groves (*Kyrkogården*, 2004: 13), with the rest buried in an urn, transported abroad or spread on places other than a graveyard.

Theoretical issues

The suggestion that death rituals reflect changes in a secularized and late modern society leads us to consider the motives behind the scattering of ashes, and to pose two question. First, does the increasing trend for scattering in places other than public or private burial grounds lead to the formulation of special rites? Second, if so, what do these special rites mean to those using them?

We assume that death rites in a late modern society are the product of a personalized experience of loss, with self-selected images and symbols making the experience meaningful and helping the surviving individual cope with loss. Regional differences may be influencial, as may other aspects of social change.

According to a law of 1957, in force by January 1958, the scattering of cremated remains must be preceded by an application for permission made by relatives to the county administrative board in the county where the ashes are to be scattered (SFS, 1957: 640). In Sweden the principle of public access to official records facilitates data collection on this topic.

The Religious Liberty Act of 1951 (in force from January 1952) brought the question of scattering ashes to the fore again. The Minister of Justice commissioned an official report (completed in 1955) which suggested that no reform to permit scattering of ashes was necessary. However, the Minister of Justice was sympathetic towards the custom of scattering ashes and, after a lively parliamentary debate in 1957, the governmental bill was accepted and the custom was permitted. As a result, in 1958, the first year the law was in force, there were no ashes buried or spread in a memorial grove; in 1959 17 ashes were buried and none spread; in 1960 60 ashes were buried, and none spread; in 1961 63 ashes were buried and eight spread; 1962 80 were buried and 38 spread. Durng this period Sweden only had seven memorial groves (Enström, 1964: 379–88).

The applications for permission contain much varied and valuable information. Besides naming relatives who apply, the motives for the application are sometimes expressed as well as wishes for a certain locality for the scattering. Some applications are rejected due to lack of consensus among relatives over scattering. Others are rejected if the place for the scattering is, for various reasons, not considered suitable as, for example, on an Iron Age archaeological site. According to the county administration, the reasons for rejecting permission for scattering on such a site might be that

1   The place is visited by many people who will most probably walk on the ashes of the cremated person which, in turn, means that the ashes are not handled with piety – a condition demanded by the law.
2   The site is pre-Christian, and the persons buried there had another religion. Since they, too, were also cremated, we have no idea as to whether they would prefer to have their ashes mixed with the ashes of Christians.
3   It would be difficult for future archaeologists to differentiate the pagan ashes from the Christian.

We have worked with applications archived at the county of Jönköping and the county of Skåne. The number of applications is much fewer in Jönköping than in Skåne, probably because parts of Jönköping lie in the Swedish Bible belt whereas Skåne is one of the most secularized parts of Sweden. This, perhaps, is also reflected in the much higher rate of cremation in Skåne than in Jönköping. Also the number of inhabitants is about 3.5 times higher in Skåne (1 150 000) than in Jönköping (329 000). The rate of cremation is approximately 60 per cent in Jököping and 90 per cent in the Skåne. Below, we present findings only from the Skåne applications. These total 1154 applications covering the period of 1958–2003 (with the exception of 1998 and 2000).

During this period, approximately 4.7 per cent of the applications were rejected and 94.1 per cent were approved; the rest were withdrawn. One application sought permission to bury the urn at 'a quiet and beautiful place'. This was refused, as this way of handling the ashes is forbidden by law. Instead, the relatives spread the ashes without asking for permission. Of the remaining rejections, one reason was that living persons were not allowed to apply for permission to spread their own ashes. Other applications were rejected because they were incomplete or because they were sent to the wrong county administration board. Excluding such cases, 1092 applications remain for study. Of these 98 per cent were approved, 1.7 per cent were rejected, and no information was available for three applications.

Some 87.1 per cent of the applications concerned scattering the ashes in the sea, 7.7 per cent applied for permission to scatter the ashes on private ground, 2.7 per cent on public ground, and 1.3 per cent in lakes. In 55.2 per cent of the applications the location requested for the scattering was very close to the place where the dead person lived; 26.3 per cent of the applications related to people living within the county of Skåne but not close to the place for scattering; 10.5 per cent came from people who were not county residents but still lived in Sweden – for example, in Stockholm but with a summer house in Skåne; 1 per cent of the applications came from people who had lived and died abroad; and in 6.9 per cent of the applications it was impossible to code the distance.

Interestingly, 65.1 per cent of the applications were for men and 34.2 per cent for women; a few names remained unidentifiable. For most people (45 per cent) the desire for spreading the ashes was expressed by the individual before their death and in 5 per cent the desire was that of relatives. For the remainder (some 49 per cent), lack of information in the applications made it impossible to decide on whose part the application was made.

Although the remains related, generally, to older people we found applications for 22 children aged under 3. The next two youngest persons were 14 years old and the oldest was 98. Some 50 per cent of the applications concerned people of 69 years of age or older, and this way of handling ashes was most frequent for persons who were 75 years old at time of death.

Interviews

To obtain a more detailed picture of issues associated with the choice and meaning of the locality for the scattering, the relationship between the deceased and the locality, the relationship between other ceremonies and the scattering, and the comprehension of the ceremony, we interviewed people who had engaged in ash scattering. Here we present some of the main findings, expressing the motives and meanings from the relatives' point of view.

From the 96 applications found for the period of 1979–96 in Skåne; 25 were finally selected and contacted and, of these, 12 people agreed to a telephone interview. Accordingly, we interviewed ten of these: nine women and one man. Seven of the ten investigated were widows who talked about their husbands and one was a husband who spoke about his dead wife. In a further case a mother spoke of her son and in one, final, case a daughter spoke of her father's remains. The oldest of the deceased was born in 1917, and the youngest in 1964. The interviews were semi-structured, and, within a framework of questions, the respondents were encouraged to talk freely about their experiences as suggested by the questions. (The interviews were transcribed and analysed with help of the computer software, NUDIST and NVivo.)

Death, ceremonies at the time of death and the funeral

Even in this small group, death occured in various places. While the most common place was in hospital, one was murdered, another died while hunting, and one person died in South America. When asked about any ceremonies for the deceased person – for example, in hospitals – the majority of interviewees reported that there were none. In one case, however, the respondent was reluctant:

Q: Did you have a ceremony at the ...
A: No, actually not. After they took care of the body we took a farewell.
Q: So nobody was reciting or lit a candle or ...
A: Yes, there were candles and there was a Bible. I do not remember if we read a 'Peace of Mind' prayer or something ... I think we did that.

Apparently, in most cases relatives do not regard the moment at the deathbed as a ceremony; instead, they consider it as a way of saying a plain farewell to the deceased. Indeed, this fact raises questions about how people define a ceremony. A deathbed situation is, of course, upsetting for relatives, and it is most likely that no one is thinking in terms of ceremonies. But it is worth asking whether the lack of a minister or pastor is a pivotal component in explaining the act at the hospital as 'non-ceremonial'. In all our cases, funeral services were held later for the deceased in churches or chapels.

Choice of location

The decision to scatter the ashes originated in most cases from the deceased person. In seven cases it was evident that a discussion had taken place; indeed, in three of these cases the wives had apparently discussed the matter with their husband over a long period. In one case, however, the widow took the decision herself, motivated by her husband's dislike of burial grounds, and decided to scatter the ashes in the sea close to his home where the widow continued to live. Some locations were described in detail; others less so. Where ashes were scattered over water the locality was sometimes described as just 'the sea', while in other cases the locality was picked out in detail. Several of the deceased who had expressed a prior wish for a scattering over water had connections with the sea. These included fishermen and sailors but also people who had lived by the sea or those whose hobby had been sailing. In one case the motive lay in the honeymoon once spent at a certain spot on the coast. Other motivations, which in some cases were combined with an attachment to the sea, involved a dislike for funeral grounds and an unwillingness to place a responsibility for looking after the grave on the children. More symbolically, the sea was also regarded as something eternal and omnipresent. Even if people move, the sea remains the sea – both very beautiful and a little terrifying. Locations for scattering on the ground were, in most cases, given in detail. In fact maps were enclosed with the applications. In one case the scattering took place on private ground.

The ceremony of scattering

Relatives and friends attended the event and, in

cases where ashes were scattered in the sea and relatives did not have a boat, crew were present. Sometimes funeral directors attended the scattering and in one case a minister was present. The responsibility for the scattering varied. In some cases the funeral director dispersed the ashes; in other cases the task was carried out by relatives (a father, a daughter, a son). In one case several relatives did it together and in another case the minister scattered the ashes.

Where ashes were scattered on the sea flowers (a single rose or a bouquet) followed them. In some other cases the widow brought a large bouquet with flowers similar to those in the wedding bouquet and relatives threw an armful of flowers in the sea as well. In one case a widow let 'little angels of gold' (plastic) follow the ashes into the sea. Sometimes relatives or the funeral director recited a poem. At the occasion attended by the minister, he said a prayer but the widow could not remember which prayer. No speeches were made. Hymn singing occurred, but secular music (often well-known Swedish ballads) also had its place. One grandchild who stayed on the beach played a hymn on the trumpet for her grandfather.

When asked about the experience of the ceremony six of the interviewees expressed positive reactions. The ceremony was 'solemn', 'very solemn' or 'in any case it was fine'. Three of the relatives also indicated that the scattering was the terminal point in a long process beginning with the death at the hospital. Essentially speaking, there are many endings. Partly there is an ending in the hospital, and then there is some kind of farewell in the church. There are, perhaps, many endings ... 'but this was of course the very end because ... when you scatter the ashes ... it becomes the last thing [you do]'. We asked relatives about thoughts on their death and what would become of their remains. Five of them expressed a wish to be cremated and scattered, as had been done for their relatives. These respondents also shared the same motivation for cremation as their deceased relatives: they disliked burial grounds either because they looked like 'true forests' or they were unwilling to force the responsibility for attending to the grave on their children. However, although the relatives had no grave to visit, the location of the scattering was also a place of commemoration. Those who scattered

ashes in the sea tried to come as close as possible to the place of the scattering, but at the same time any sea or the sea in general had the function of a place for commemorating the dead. As one respondent expressed it:

> My wife died on New Year's Eve [and her ashes are scattered in the sea below the X estate] ... and on ... New Year's Eve we go to X and we put a rose on the stone. In case of good weather we stay for a while ... and we have stayed at the X estate for a cup of coffee ... my parents, my sister and her husband have joined me, and my grandmother as well ... it has become a sort of a family trip.

Although ceremonies seem to be more related to graves in burial grounds than to the scattering of ashes at some anonymous place, one family, who had scattered the ashes over the ground, had other ceremonies:

> We scattered the ashes on a meadow which we own ... from the bathroom window we can look at the place and we have placed flowers there ... every Friday night we lit a candle there during the dark season ... we have planted flowers ... he would have been forty [years] in March. Then we put some extra flowers there. It is a kind of feeling one has. Before I go to bed in the evenings I go to the bathroom and I look down [on the meadow] and say: 'Good night L-G'.

Some reflections

We found that relatives were deeply engaged in the scattering and that they found the ceremony solemn – definitely a non-everyday experience. However, we know less about the ideology behind the ceremony. Theoretically speaking, does a rite create meaning? Ronald Grimes suggests that one of the functions of the rite is to preserve personal control at events such as birth and death. According to him, 'a rite of passage is a set of symbol-laden actions by means of which one passes through a dangerous zone, negotiating it safely and memorably' (Grimes, 2000: 6). Such control is made possible by the rite (which can be designed very individually), and from this process meaning is created. Grimes also calls attention to the retelling of the rite that might function as a recurrence of the rite, which further reinforces its meaning (2000: 10). Perhaps our conversation with the respondents had his function. Nevertheless, the scattering of the cremated remains is not formalized, neither as an ideology nor as an act. The relatives create the act, possibly supported by the deceased's wishes. According to Grimes, the motives for the scattering of the remains from a dead relative belong to a group of motives that he calls 'releasing, integrating, embracing death's finality' (2000: 220). The dead person is obviously delivered to the soil or to the water as a symbolic act of liberation. The act also symbolically helps the relatives come to terms with the finality of death.

Traditional cultural symbolic configurations are missing at the scattering of remains. This is a distinct observation, for the symbols used at the scattering come from, or are related to, the dead person. Mostly, the symbols are connected to water or to places of great importance both for the deceased and the survivors. Instead of traditional, transcendent, timeless symbols immanent symbols are employed. From a phenomenological point of view, it is possible to perceive water as something that exists everywhere and is in continuous circulation. Most likely, Tony Walter is correct when he states that the point of reference in both death and life 'is no longer God but man; death is seen as the end of the person's life rather than the beginning of a life in heaven' (Walter, 1997: 166).

Using this point of departure it is possible to see the private deposition of the ashes as a postmodern way of relating to the rites of death. The purposes of these acts are to handle and structure a process, an event, an important value, or to create a meaning-shaping situation, which involves a considering of the will and intention of the deceased. According to Jenny Hockey, postmodern anthropologists claim that individuals can – and should – personalize their experience of loss, making it meaningful through self-selected images and practices, which help them manage their loss as they see fit (Hockey, 2001: 207).

In Sweden the homogeneity of funeral behaviour is dissolving. According to a reanalysis of data from an investigation done by Göran Gustafsson in 1997, 60 per cent of the clergy in the Church of Sweden (Gustafsson, 2001) are ignorant of what will happen with the ashes. These figures indicate that the final rite for a dead person is not a traditional ceremony in the Church of Sweden or other congregations.

Rather, the rite at this end-point is created by the funeral director, by one of the staff at the ceremony, or by the relatives themse.ves. **Curt Dahlgren and Jan Hermanson**

References

Enström, B. (1964), *Kyrkan och eldbegängelserörelsen 1882–1962* (*The Church and the Cremation Movement 1882–1962*), Lund: Gleerups Förlag.

Grimes, R.L. (2000), *Deeply into the Bone. Reinventing Rites of Passage*, Berkeley: University of California Press.

Gustafsson, G. (2001), *Begravningssed på 1990-talet. Materialredovisning och resultatöversikt* (*Funeral Customs in the 1990s. Report on Sources and Overview of Results*), Lund: Lunds Universitets Kyrkohistoriska Arkiv.

Hockey, J. (2001), 'Changing Death Rituals', in Jenny Hockey, Jeanne Katz and Neil Small (eds), *Grief, Mourning and Death Ritual* Buckingham: Open University Press.

Kyrkogården (*The Churchyard*), March 2004.

SFS (Swedish Code of Statutes), 1957.

Wall, B. (2000), *Gravskick i förändring; tradition och visioner* (*Changing Funeral Customs: Traditions and Visions*), Stockholm: Svenska Kyrkans Församlingsförbund.

Walter, T. (1997), 'Secularization', in Collin Murray Parkes, Pittu Laungani and Bill Young (eds), *Death and Bereavement across Cultures*, London and New York: Routledge.

ASHES OF ISAAC

Genesis 22 records Abraham's agreement to offer Isaac his son as a sacrifice on Mount Moriah, a site already identified by the Bible (2 Chronicles 3:1) as the Jerusalem Temple. A ram was sacrificed in place of Isaac; and many rabbis of the period after the fall of the temple in 70 CE came to speak of this ram's ashes as 'the ashes of Isaac'. Thus R. Eleazar ben Pedath in *Midrash Ha-Gadol* on Genesis 22:19 remarks: 'Although Isaac did not die, Scripture holds it as if he had died, and that his ashes lay on the top of the altar.' In some accounts, Isaac's ash is raised to life by the 'dew of the resurrection'. Indeed, the Babylonian Talmud *Zebahim* 62a tells how Jews returning from exile in Babylon in the sixth century BCE recognized the place of the temple because they saw Isaac's ashes heaped up on the site. The two ram-lambs offered daily in the temple service perpetually commemorated Isaac's offering. While two Aramaic translations (known as Targumim) of Genesis 22:14 made Abraham understand God's command to sacrifice Isaac as meaning that his son should be reduced to 'dust and ashes', other rabbinic texts went as far as they could in suggesting that Isaac was burned in sacrifice, even though his life was spared. These 'ashes of Isaac' possessed great symbolic power, and were recalled in times of drought, when it was customary for communities to fast, for the leaders of the community to sprinkle wood ash on their heads, and for the Ark from the synagogue containing the Torah Scrolls to be brought into the public square and sprinkled with wood ash. This wood ash specifically recalled Isaac's offering and was sprinkled so that God should remember the ashes of Isaac and show mercy now just as he had showed mercy to Abraham by sparing Isaac (Babylonian Talmud Ta`anit 16a). **C.T.R. Hayward**

References

Spiegel, S. (1967), *The Last Trial: On the Legends and Lore of the Command to Abraham to Offer Isaac as a Sacrifice*, New York: Pantheon Books.

Vermes, G. (1973), 'Redemption and Genesis xxii', in *Scripture and Tradition in Judaism* (2nd edn), Leiden: Brill, 193–227.

Grossfeld, B. (1977), 'The Targum to Lamentations 2:10', *Journal of Jewish Studies*, 28: 60–64.

Hayward, C.T.R. (1990), 'The Sacrifice of Isaac and Jewish Polemic against Christianity', *Catholic Biblical Quarterly*, 52: 293–306.

Silberman, L.H. (1997) '`Aqedah" in (eds), *The Oxford Dictionary of the Jewish Religion*, ed. R.J.Z. Werblowsky and G. Wigoder, Oxford: Oxford University Press, 58–59.

ASPLUND, ERIK GUNNAR

Erik Gunnar Asplund (1885–1940) holds an important place in the history of modern architecture, not least for his work on Stockholm's Woodland Crematorium. For more than 20 years he was one of the dominant personalities of Scandinavian architecture, influencing architects much further afield. Emerging from the national romanticism of the 1910s he became one of the most admired representatives of the neo-classicism of the 1920s known as Swedish Grace. Nowhere was this fusion of romanticism and neo-classicism more apparent than in his design for the Stockholm City Library (1920–28) where the high circular reading room rose as a drum above the rest of the composition, invoking the ageless theme of the merging of the cube and cylinder.

Modern European architecture, formulated in the early twentieth century, was derived from the processes and products of the machine and was designed to capture the spirit of the age. In addition, the designation of modernism was infused with social and political ideology and was believed to be a catalyst in the transformation of society. Scandinavian countries occupied a singular position in Europe. Since their own native tradition had not been debased by industrialization in the nineteenth century, they felt no need to respond to the revolutionary impetus of the new architectural movement. Nevertheless, the Stockholm Exhibition, organized by the Scandinavians in 1930, aroused a great deal of public interest in modern architecture across Europe. As principal architect for the Exhibition, Asplund embraced European modernism by combining thin structural members and great expanses of glass to create functionalist forms of graceful translucency.

Although regarded as the leading light of functionalism, before long Asplund indicated a way from stereotyped modernism to a more traditionally-based architectural form. By the time he came to design the Stockholm Woodland Crematorium, it is evident that Asplund was combining modernism and tradition effortlessly to create a confluence which resonated with cultural, religious and mythical references.

Throughout all these various periods Asplund's architecture is characterized by an uncommon richness, springing from profound empathy and a search for architectural types. His architecture is timeless in the best sense of the word. Indeed, the changes by which architecture has been overtaken in recent years have returned Asplund to the focal point of international debate. **Börje Olsson and Hilary Grainger**

See also Stockholm Woodland Crematorium.

AUSCHWITZ

The history of the twentieth century has assigned a special role to the crematorium in the logistical development of the mass extermination of the Jews by the National Socialists. Auschwitz-Birkenau is a symbol for the systematic extermination of the European Jews and the killing of innumerable innocent people by poison gas. Long before the purposeful mass murder, the high death rate within the concentration camps led to consideration of establishing efficient crematoria in the camps themselves. Besides many political opponents, uncountable numbers of 'unacceptable' civilians, as well as mentally and physically handicapped people, were condemned to extermination, especially after war had broken out. The burying of corpses in mass graves involved the risk of contaminating the groundwater, and the burning of corpses on piles of wood with oil or methanol additives irritated the surrounding population with its unbearable stench and the nightly glow of fire.

Up until the end of the 1930s, the cremator consisted of one chamber or sleeve for the coffin; a generator, heated with gas, oil or coke for the requisite temperature and a recuperator, which heated the fresh air on its way to the sleeve by means of a connected circulation system of ventilation and used air. This system reduced the amount of fuel needed, but it was still a very expensive and complex technical installation requiring a great deal of space.

As a result, a new oven model was developed in the mid-1930s. Instead of heating the fresh air in the recuperator, warm compressed air was blown into the sleeve. With permanent heating, the amount of fuel needed could once more be considerably reduced because now the cremating procedure could continue by adding heated air. Two companies, Heinrich Kori Ltd from Berlin and J.A. Topf and Sons from Erfurt, were both successful in the competition to build cremation ovens for the concentration camps. Kori was still building single-sleeve ovens, while Kurt Prüfer, an engineer of the company Topf, had already constructed and delivered double-sleeve ovens with oil heating, compressed air and a draught enhancer to the camps of Dachau and Buchenwald. Beginning with the war in France in 1940, when liquid fuel was no longer available, Prüfer merely modified this simple but highly efficient and easily maintained oven model. For Auschwitz-Birkenau he designed a solid cremating oven with two isolated-sleeve ovens, two coke generators and a chimney with a draught vacuum to shorten the cremating time. Following this 'Auschwitz' model, Prüfer first developed a crematorium plant with five three-sleeve ovens. This made it possible to cremate 60 corpses per hour – 1440 corpses per day. In 1943 he combined two double-sleeve ovens with four kilns each and built two further plants, each with an eight-sleeve oven. By 1943 there were, altogether, five big crematorium plants, constructed by the Topf company, functioning in Auschwitz-Birkenau concentration camp.

Under the order of Heinrich Himmler, Auschwitz-Birkenau was extended into a centre for the systematic and bureaucratically-ordered deportation of the Jews. In the end, this concentration camp played a central role in the 'Final Solution'. Besides the good geographic location and the already existing rail network, the decisive factor was the very efficiently working crematorium. The technique of mass murder, however, reached a sad climax in combination with cremation. The first killings with the highly effective delousing poison Zyclon B had already taken place in Auschwitz in December 1941. A year later, in 1942, in the outer camp of Birkenau, two former farmsteads (the later so-called bunkers I and II) were transformed into gas chambers. In 1943 the extension and modification of the ventilation system of the former mortuary of the concentration camp was finished by the Topf company. A cynical contempt for humankind had already been quite early expressed in the SS's rentability calculations for the economical use of prisoners in the concentration camps. But now this contempt mounted in considerations of optimizing the procedure of killing and cremation: from the undressing room to the gas chambers disguised as shower cells, from the mortuary basement, using the hoist, to the sluice of the hall with the cremating ovens. In the autumn of 1944 the killings with poison gas were stopped by the order of Heinrich Himmler, and the deconstruction of the crematoria began. By the end of January 1945 the remaining pieces of the crematorium plants were hastily blown up in the face of the approaching Red Army. **Elfi Heider**

See also Nazi cremation.

References

Czech, D. (1992), *Kalendarz wydarzen w KL Auschwitz*, Oswiecim: Wydawn. Panstwowego Muzeum w Oswiecimiu-Brzezince.

Piper, F. (1993), *Die Zahl der Opfer von Auschwitz aufgrund der Quellen und der Erträge der Forschung 1945 bis 1990*, Staatl: Museum Oswiecim.

Pressac, J-C., (1993), *Les Crématoires d'Auschwitz*, Paris: CNRS Edition.

AUSTRALIA

In the last quarter of the twentieth century, cremation became the disposal method of choice for the majority of Australians, with over 60 per cent of funeral processes ending at the crematorium furnace. This figure reached as high as 70 per cent in the major, highly urbanized population centres where cremation facilities are well developed. One hundred years earlier, the most enthusiastic cremationists were certainly predicting that level of success, but few in the broader community would have put money on such an outcome. Before Federation in 1901, the English cremation model was closely followed in the Australian colonies, although there was also a keen awareness of developments on the Continent and in the USA among the small band of Australian cremation proponents and some of their efforts pre-dated the work of Sir Henry Thompson. At the forefront of the Australian movement were leading British trained medical practitioners and academics, prominent social reformers, and influential business and political figures. They were attracted not only by the sanitary and hygiene arguments in favour of cremation but also by its supposed social and economic benefits. The cremation cause also began with strong links to the funeral reform movement, which experienced a brief period of prominence in several colonies in the 1870s and 1880s. Other significant support came from members of the contemporaneous theosophical societies, which were well established in several of the Australian colonies by the end of the nineteenth century, the various colonial Royal societies and mechanics' institutes, the Unitarian Church, and the Liberal Catholic Church, as well as the temperance, spiritualist and fledgling feminist movements. In cities such as Adelaide, Melbourne and Sydney, prominent Theosophists, spiritualists and Unitarians were frequently to be found organizing pro-cremation meetings and supporting fund-raising projects to enable a formal crematorium to be built. They included controversial Theosophist and Liberal Catholic bishop Charles Webster Leadbetter and Unitarian clergyman Revd George Walters. In Sydney, the prominent and well-connected feminist campaigner Rose Scott was among the most influential advocates of cremation. The earliest documented campaigning was in November 1863 when Dr John Le Gay Brereton addressed 'a fashionable audience, numbering about four hundred' at the Sydney Mechanics' School of Arts. Brereton, an advocate of homoeopathy, the value of the Turkish bath and rational clothing, strongly supported the merits of cremation on aesthetic, public health and religious grounds as well as arguing that it would facilitate funeral reform. An active Swedenborgian, his emphasis was on the soul rather than the flesh. Some community interest followed in the pages of the newspapers, but little of a practical nature.

Campaigning switched from Sydney to its arch-rival Melbourne. There, in 1873, Dr James Neild, a lecturer in forensic medicine at the University of Melbourne, a medical profession organizer, a leading newspaper theatre critic and a colleague and friend of Dr Brereton, presented to the Royal Society of Victoria a paper 'On the Advantages of Burning the Dead'. Neild and another prominent Victorian cremationist Henry Keylock Rusden also promoted the cause through the Australian Health Society, founded in 1875. A new champion emerged in New South Wales in the person of John Mildred Creed, a medical practitioner and member of the NSW parliament. In 1886 he introduced to the NSW Upper House, the Legislative Council, a bill to regulate cremation. His parliamentary arguments were publicized in the *Australasian Medical Gazette* and aroused considerable interest throughout the colonies. His Cremation Bill was passed by the Upper House in 1886 and again in 1887, but each time failed to achieve consideration by the Lower House. One vigorous parliamentary opponent, William Piddington, labelled it 'a vile and atheistic bill'. It was based on the English common law notion that burning a corpse was not a crime and on a belief that cremation should be regulated. After the failure of his bill, Creed carried the cause to the other colonies, presenting addresses and distributing printed material on cremation, much of it sourced from the English cremation movement. In 1890 he helped form the short-lived New South Wales Cremation Society, which did manage to produce two issues of its journal, the *New South Wales Cremation Funeral and Sanitary Reform Review*. In Victoria, the Royal Society, spurred on by Dr Neild's continuing enthusiasm and by support from Henry Keylock Rusden, established its own committee to investigate cremation. Its report was published in 1892 and came out strongly in support. In October 1892 the Cremation Society of Victoria was formed. One of its founders, William Kernot, professor of Engineering at the University of Melbourne, publicly advocated low-cost cremations for £1 and the construction of a formal crematorium at a proposed new cemetery at Frankston. There were unsuccessful attempts by Frederick Grimwade to push a Cremation Bill through the Victorian Parliament in 1895, 1898 and 1899–1900, but it was not finally passed until 1903. By then, both New South Wales and Victoria were lagging behind South Australia in the provision of formal cremation facilities.

There were numerous links between Sir Henry Thompson and the Australian cremation movements. John Creed was sometime secretary and president of the NSW branch of the British Medical Association and long-term editor of the *Australasian Medical Gazette*. As a medical student he had acted as a clinical clerk to Thompson, and he corresponded with Thompson and other leading English cremationists during the debates over his bill, as did South Australian cremationist Dr Robert Wylde. Thompson's *Contemporary Review* article was reprinted in the colonial press and distributed in pamphlet form soon after it was first published. In August 1874, as part of the ongoing debate over the need for a new public cemetery in Adelaide, the South Australian Minister of Justice, William Bundey, read an extract in parliament. Throughout the 1870s and 1880s there was regular coverage of the pros and cons of cremation, some of it exhibiting an impressive familiarity with contemporary international developments, as well as locally written pro-cremation pamphlets such as 'Cremation Not Opposed to the Scriptural Doctrine of the Resurrection. A Tract For the Times' by 'Resurgam' (1875) and J. Fife

Atkinson's 'What Shall We Do With Our Dead? Discussed as a Sanitary Question' (1878). *The Illustrated Sydney News* claimed that 'scarcely a journal in the country but had its chapter on the subject of 'Cremation', when that fashionable idea of disposing of defunct humanity was broached'. In September 1887 Creed presented an address on cremation to the first Intercolonial Medical Congress meeting in Adelaide, basing his arguments largely on Thompson's work and calling for the formation of cremation societies in all the Australian colonies. It would be their duty to promote the suitability of cremation, to provide appropriate cremating apparatus and to advocate laws that would allow proper regulation. In October 1890 a local Adelaide doctor, Robert Wylde, took up the cause, delivering an address at a meeting chaired by South Australian Chief Justice Sir Samuel Way, and calling for the founding of a cremation society. The new Cremation Society of South Australia set about gathering social and business support and then turned to parliament, where a petition calling for an Act to make cremation legal was presented to the Lower House, the House of Assembly. J. Langdon Parsons, a former Minister of Education and ardent funeral reformer, introduced a Cremation Bill in December 1890. Its overriding principle was that cremation should be permissive and that the right to please themselves on the matter should be conceded to the public. The bill passed successfully through both houses in 1891, becoming Australia's first cremation legislation.

Despite this success, the cremation cause in South Australia languished as Wylde and his supporters tried to raise the necessary funds in the face of government refusal to provide financial assistance. Delays everywhere allowed opposition to grow. In Victoria, parliamentarian George Ievers put the opposition case succinctly. There had been no expression of opinion on the part of the general public in favour of cremation. It was not a Christian, but a pagan, practice. He had seen a cremation in Milan, and it was not a pleasing sight and not one he would care to see happening in Victoria. In complete contrast, Dr Gregory Sprott, the health officer for Hobart, told a meeting of the Royal Society of Tasmania in 1897 that cremation would inevitably replace earth burial on sanitary grounds and that there was nothing un-Christian or heathenish about it. Events seemed now on the side of the cremationists, but ironically helped promote the idea that cremation was disrespectful to the dead.

A number of cremations did take place in the Australian colonies for public health reasons, the threat of infectious disease often proving a fillip to the cause. In 1890 and 1892 there was some publicity surrounding the cremation of two Chinese lepers at Point Nepean quarantine station in Victoria – in the open and with little ceremony. In 1897 a 19-year-old Indian typhoid victim was cremated in a paddock belonging to the West Australian Gun Club near Perth. Press reports painted a scene of chaos with the coffin bursting and exposing part of the body. Between 1901 and 1906 a number of bubonic plague victims were cremated at Perth's Woodman Point quarantine station, and their ashes were buried in the small station graveyard. In 1895 there were three cremations using log pyres on the beach at Sandringham near Melbourne. Two were of Indians in traditional ceremonies, but one marked the first cremation of a European, Elizabeth Hennicker, an 83-year-old Theosophist and spiritualist piano teacher, apparently carried out on philosophical grounds and according to her wishes. In the Victorian parliament this was described as 'a scandalous and horrible occurrence', although some press reports were quite favourable.

In 1900 Sydney Theosophist Frederick Farrant Cox was cremated in the open at Botany Bay using a small transportable oven that he had commissioned from a local foundry a few months before his death. Open-air cremations, mostly associated with Eastern cultural ceremonies, continued to be conducted around the country well into the twentieth century. But if cremation was to achieve general community acceptance, modern formal facilities were required rather than primitive open-air pyres which many Europeans dismissed as a sign of barbarism. The South Australian cremationists were by now the best placed. After tortuous negotiations, a suitable site was donated by the colonial government adjacent to Adelaide's main public cemetery, West Terrace. Local architect A. Barham Black drew up plans for a crematorium based on the City of London Burial Board Crematorium and a cremating furnace was imported from Henry Simon and Company of Manchester, made possible by a £1000 donation from the colony's wealthiest businessman, Robert Barr Smith. On completion of the new facility, the Cremation Society handed over control to the South Australian government. The first cremation was that of a local Sikh, Bishin Singh, on 4 May 1903. It was the first human cremation in a purpose-built modern crematorium in Australia.

Developments in the other Australian states followed a wearisome path. In Victoria a Cremation Bill was finally passed in 1903, but the first cremation under the new Act did not take place until April 1905 and, even then, the crematorium consisted of nothing more than a hole dug in the lawn at the Springvale Necropolis and surmounted by a primitive pyre. In 1906 this was lined with brick, and iron girders and plates were used to separate the human remains from the fire residue. Various upgrades followed in ensuing years but did little to assuage public suspicion of cremation. A new Cremation Society of Victoria was established in 1924 to lobby for the construction of better facilities. In Tasmania the first specific legislation was the Cremation Act 1905. In the same year, two open-air cremations were carried out. In 1912 the Cremation Society of Tasmania was formed in Launceston to lobby for the cause. Also in that year a formal campaign was launched in Queensland and a Brisbane Cremation Association was established in 1915.

New South Wales took the lead in developing the second generation of cremation facilities. The Cremation Society of New South Wales was founded in October 1908, with that redoubtable old campaigner John M. Creed as its first president, and heavily influenced by Rose Scott and Revd George Walters. The new society assiduously spread the word about cremation. In its first year, it sponsored 18 public lectures, sent out 4243 letters and circulars to the medical profession, dentists, clergymen and parliamentarians, as well as debating, professional and community groups. The society had printed 5500 pamphlets on cremation and 4500 leaflets and 2000 booklets containing Creed's lecture on cremation. It was rewarded with a membership of 344 but, despite persistent lobbying, was unable to gain government support for the construction of a crematorium. In 1923 New South Wales cremationists reorganized and formed the Cremation Society of Australia, with Creed as president and, linked to the New South Wales Cremation Company, registered in 1922 with Creed as one of its directors.

The injection of private enterprise proved the catalyst. In 1925 a modern crematorium was built in Rookwood Cemetery by the private company on land supplied by the state government and leased to the society. It was immediately successful, with 122 cremations in its first year. In 1927 a modern crematorium for Melbourne was built at Fawkner Cemetery. Springvale Necropolis followed with modern facilities in 1936 and expensive chapels added in 1939 and 1940. Brisbane achieved its first crematorium in 1934, Hobart and Newcastle in 1936, Perth in 1937 and Launceston in 1939. Only Northern Suburbs and Brisbane met the pioneer cremationists' ambition of crematoria being constructed separate from cemeteries.

The level of public acceptance of cremation was directly linked to the quality of the facilities provided. In New South Wales, for example, when well-planned modern crematoria were built in the 1930s, the practice of cremation spread rapidly, resulting in the construction of Northern Suburbs Crematorium (1933), Woronora Crematorium (1934), Beresfield Crematorium at Newcastle (1936), and Eastern Suburbs Crematorium at Botany Cemetery (1938). The second-generation crematoria were all substantial undertakings exhibiting a common desire to make cremation a more readily acceptable and attractive alternative to earth burial. They were built and operated by local government, by existing cemetery boards or by private companies, and they slowly but steadily began to change the character of human remains disposal in Australia. Their design was heavily influenced by American and European technological advances and by non-religious architectural fashion rather than the ecclesiastical heritage which had determined the design of the Adelaide Crematorium. Crematorium design was an area of increasing interest for a number of prominent Australian architects in the 1930s. Among them were Charles and Frank Heath (Fawkner and Brisbane), Louis Robertson (Woronora, Eastern Suburbs and Beresfield), Eric Hazel Round (Hobart), William L. Clennett (Launceston), Reginald Summerhayes (Perth) and Frank I'Anson Bloomfield (Rookwood and Northern Suburbs).

Despite all this apparent success, within the general Australian community cremation remained a minority choice until after the Second World War. In the 1950s levels of acceptance steadily increased and in the 1960s and 1970s there was a period of consolidation and then expansion. The quality of facilities continued to improve as incomes grew and public expectations increased. As the rate of cremations climbed and then overtook earth burials, pressure mounted in all states for the development of additional regional crematoria. Most of the new crematoria were built and operated by public trusts, but in the 1990s there was also an influx of private capital from multinational corporations, which led to several of the pioneering 1930s crematoria being taken over. Increasingly, purpose-built chapels and reception rooms associated with the crematoria competed with the church and home as the central part of the funeral process, often overtaking them in popular usage. The 1990s witnessed an increased use of 'backdoor' facilities where there was no service and the body was simply delivered to the crematorium for processing. Cremation furnaces were made more community- and environment-friendly. Smoke and odour emissions remained a perceived, if not always real, problem, but gone were the days when thick black smoke and descending ash was a familiar part of the cremation process.

Another change worth noting arose from the popular practice of scattering ashes in some favourite haunt of the deceased or their retention in a suitable container in the home, at least for a generation. An often unacknowledged consequence is that many of Australia's dead now go unmemorialized. **Robert Nicol**

References

Nicol, Robert (2003), *The Grave or Burning Question. A Centenary History of Cremation in Australia*, Adelaide: Adelaide Cemeteries Authority.

AUSTRIA

The Austrian context of cremation presents an instructive example of the complex relationships between a funeral practice and political, economic and religious issues. It brings to sharp focus social class relationships with formal state authorities, as well as matters of political alliance and war. In particular, this Austrian material demonstrates the way in which cremation as a potentially simple funerary activity can become the vehicle of and for intergroup relationship, communication, protest and the display of authority. First, Ute Georgeacopol-Winischofer sets the historical background before describing some key leaders involved in these numerous activities. Austrian architects are dealt with separately under **architects**, as are Austrian cremation societies. **Douglas J. Davies**

BACKGROUND (AUSTRIA-HUNGARY)

Since the eighteenth-century Enlightenment the burial system in Austria has been regulated on a uniform basis by a number of statutes, regulations and decrees, covering burial in burial chambers, cemeteries, graves and regulating the transport of the dead and exhumation. The General Civil Code, the General Penal Code and the Code of Civil Procedure were imperial statutes and could not be amended by individual regulations of the provinces and the districts. The construction of a crematorium was therefore in conflict not only with applicable canon law but also and above all with state legislation, which only provided for burial 'in the ground'.

The frequent cholera epidemics, diseases and contagious illnesses, mainly in the urban centres of population, made special measures necessary and, in such cases, it was permissible, and indeed a requirement, to burn 'infectious corpses' and the war dead. Moreover, the burial of the dead was handled by private enterprises as an unrestricted trade and was only subjected to a licence from 1885. The growing number of licensed burial and carrier enterprises entitled to charge burial fees at their own discretion led to the development of an unacceptable system of agents and commissions that was the cause of frequent complaints by the population and ultimately resulted in the burial of the dead being taken over by the public administration. The Gemeinde Wien-Städtische Leichenbestattung was founded on 1 July 1907. It gradually took over the operations of the then 80 private enterprises in Vienna and, in 1922, constructed the first crematorium in what is today Austria. It was only in 1951 that the undertaking trade in Vienna was completely integrated into local government administration. Interment is still, at the outset of the twenty-first century, handled in a variety of ways in the other provincial capitals, with both private and local government enterprises providing the services.

The beginning of the effort to introduce cremation in what was Austria-Hungary at the time was the construction of the Vienna Central Cemetery, commenced on 7 December 1866 as a result of a city council resolution and opened on 1 November 1874. At the same time, the old district cemeteries in the suburbs of St Marx, Auf der Schmelz, Matzleinsdorf, Währing and Hundsturm were abandoned. Ever since the Vienna World's Fair of 1873 the issue of cremation as an alternative to burial had increasingly been a topic of discussion – a discussion that became particularly acute as a result of a cholera epidemic that occurred in Vienna in the same year. Nevertheless, a motion for the introduction of optional cremation proposed to the Vienna City Council in 1874 was rejected.

Subsequently, it was realized that, as a basic condition for a broader acceptance of cremation, a technically refined cremator, permitting cremation without smell or smoke, would have to be constructed. As early as 1867, at the International Technological (World) Exposition in Paris, a special award was given to the invention of a regenerative gas burner designed by Friedrich Siemens. During the 1873 Vienna World's Fair the technically interested public was able to view a cremator according to the system of the Italian Professor Brunetti, which was subsequently followed by numerous other inventions. Finally, the first European Congress for Cremation held in Dresden in 1876 saw the first formulation of the general conditions that were to be made of a modern *Feuerbestattungsapparat* (cremation apparatus) in aesthetic, ethical and economic terms.

In May 1874, a first cremation society (*Verein für Leichen-Verbrennung*) was founded in the Mariahilf district of Vienna with the aim of constructing a hall of ceremonies. It was unsuccessful. When, in spring 1885, the Siemens company presented the model of the Friedrich Siemens regenerative gas furnace to an interested specialist public at its Vienna sales branch, Oskar Siedek was sufficiently encouraged by the new technology to found the Austrian Cremation Society 'Die Flamme' (*Verein der Freunde der Feuerbestattung 'Die Flamme' in Wien*) together with a number of kindred spirits. Contacts were made with all the European specialist associations and there was considerable advertising activity. In 1886 Oskar Siedek played an advisory role in the foundation of the

Federation of German-Language Cremation Societies for the Reform of the Burial System and Optional Cremation (*Verband der Feuerbestattungsvereine deutscher Sprache für Reform des Bestattungswesens und facultative Feuerbestattung*) in Gotha. The third Federation conference was held in Vienna as early as September 1888, followed by two more in 1902 and 1912. The sixth Federation conference and a large international crematory exhibition were held in Budapest in 1894, simultaneously with the Eighth International Congress for Hygiene and Demography, the exhibition being presented in Vienna two weeks later. Crematory exhibitions in Austria-Hungary up to the end of the monarchy were also held in Brno in 1895, Vienna again in 1898 and in Linz for the first time in 1909.

The incorporation of the suburbs around Vienna between 1890 and 1892 also brought 23 cemeteries into the city territory. In 1891, in the context of the measures to be taken, the Lower Austrian provincial health councillor expressly emphasized the need for cremation to be legalized. However, the Vienna city council, with its then conservative majority, failed to take up the corresponding recommendation by the Imperial and Royal Governorship. Although the official bodies in the Austrian-Hungarian monarchy maintained a deliberate distance, the idea of cremation was also disseminated in schools. In 1892 the *Zeitschrift zur Förderung der Erziehung und des Unterrichtes (Journal for the Promotion of Education and Teaching)*, published in Vienna, ran a five-page article in the section on *Gesundheitspflege* (Healthcare) about '*Die Cremations-Bestattung*' (Cremation-Burial). This stated that the members of the Cremation Society, as 'the intelligent sector of the population', wanted the introduction of cremation-burial as an option. And in the society's journal, *Phoenix*, an appeal was addressed in 1894 'To the women!' and their efforts at emancipation, calling on them to become interested in, and to apply their efforts in favour of, cremation.

The close links between the Catholic Church in Austria and the emperor as 'Apostolic Majesty' were the greatest obstacle to the legalization of cremation up to the collapse following the end of the First World War. In a treatise published in 1874 concerning the legal situation of cremation in Austria, the Viennese lawyer Dr Leopold Adler pointed out that the function of the burial of the dead was a church and state institution, and that the social feasibility of the burial reform aimed at depended on the position of the state and the churches. The theologians of the various religions would not be able to avoid issuing a verdict on this 'burning' question.

The beginning of the twentieth century saw the Vienna 'Die Flamme' society intensify its efforts towards the construction of a crematorium in Austria, and by 1904 public competitions had produced concrete plans for Budapest, Prague and Graz. The only crematorium constructed in the Monarchy in 1914–15 despite all the resistance, in Reichenberg, Bohemia, only commenced operations following the end of the First World War. On the occasion of the start of operations at the Vienna Crematorium in 1922, the archbishop of Vienna, Friedrich Gustav Cardinal Piffl, addressed the question of cremation in detail in a Pastoral Letter dated 21 January 1923. In an Instruction from the Holy Office dated 19 June 1926 it was admitted for the first time that cremation, of itself, was not wrong, nor in conflict with any dogma; it was therefore permitted 'if it should prove to be necessary in order, for instance, to prevent the spread of the plague', but Catholics were still not allowed to be members of a cremation society or be associated with freemasonry. If a Catholic ordered the cremation of his own body or that of another, he was not to be given the last sacraments and he was to be denied the blessing of the Church. The Old Catholic Church did not share these reservations.

In November 1961 the Director of the Labour Cremation Society 'Die Flamme' (*Arbeiter-Feuerbestattungsverein 'Die Flamme'*), Dr Franz Michelfeit, addressed a request to Pope John XXIII for the repeal of the ban on behalf of the International Federation for Cremation. Finally, the Church withdrew its ban (Instruction from the Holy Office dated 5 July 1963) and the official visit to the Simmering Crematorium by the archbishop of Vienna Cardinal Dr Franz König in 1966 became a symbol of the relaxation of the provisions of canon law concerning cremation and its acceptance by the Church. A church burial was only to be refused 'if it is found that cremation is being used as an expression of a denial of Christian dogmas, for sectarian reasons or out of hate for the Catholic religion and church'. Nevertheless, burial was given preference for theological reasons.

Four stages can thus be distinguished in accordance with the reasons for the acceptance of cremation in Austria. The building and operation of crematoria was first made possible after the institution of the federal constitution following the establishment of the Austrian Republic in November, 1918.

1   Cremation in the First Republic was one of the weapons used by the workers against subordination and repression by the state and the Church. The first crematorium in the Simmering district of Vienna was built in the initial period from 1920 to 1933 and, following 1945, that was marked by philosophical and political motivation. In defiance of express instructions from the (Christian-Social) Minister for Social Affairs, Richard Schmitz, the Simmering Crematorium was ceremonially opened by the (Social Democrat) Mayor Jakob Reumann on 17 December 1922. Soon cremation facilities were constructed in Steyr (1927), Linz (1929), Salzburg (1931) and – after replanning – in Graz (1932).

2   Following the Second World War, stage 1 was concluded with the construction of the very individualistic crematorium in Villach (1953).

3   Three facilities represent the spread of the movement following the acceptance of cremation by the Catholic Church: the second Vienna Crematorium in Stammersdorf (1966) and the two crematoria of Knittelfeld and St Pölten both built in 1975.

4   Since then there has been an interesting development in the conservative Austrian provinces of Tyrol (Innsbruck Crematorium 1998–99) and Vorarlberg (Hohenems Crematorium 1998). In these provinces, it is the positive effects on the environment that are appreciated, with the 'ethical and environment movement' in cremation arguing that urn-burial saves space and that the ashes after cremation are germ-free and environmentally neutral. In addition, the process involves a reduction of costs.

In recent decades, numerous local districts in the Rhine Valley in Vorarlberg, Austria's most westerly province, have faced the question of whether to extend existing cemeteries or construct new ones far outside the towns. Thanks to the increasing acceptance of cremation in the villages (also outside the towns) the extensions to the cemeteries required proved to be much smaller than had been usual only a few decades previously. In the village parish churches (both Catholic and Protestant), a dignified church service, last farewell and interment have become usual irrespective of the form of burial. Cremation is also being increasingly used for people belonging to no religious confession. Interment is in collective graves, or urns are buried in the ground. In recent years, cremation has overcome all the philosophical and political barriers in Austria, it is now accepted that it also involves dignity and piety. **Ute Georgeacopol-Winischhofer**

See also Austrian cremation societies.

References

Adler, L. (1874), *Die Leichenverbrennung. Mit besonderer Rücksicht auf die österreichische Gesetzgebung*, Vienna: Verlag der G.J. Manz'schen Buchhandlung.

Hacker, E. and Sederl, J. (1881), *Statuten des Vereins für Leichen-Verbrennung in Wien*, Vienna: Selbstverlag des Vereins.

Hawelka, F. (1904), *Studien zum österreichischen Friedhofsrecht*, Vienna-Leipzig: Franz Deuticke.

Jordan, E. (ed.) (1892), 'Gesundheitspflege: Die Cremations-Bestattung', *Elternzeitung Schule und Haus. Zeitschrift zur Förderung der Erziehung und des Unterrichtes*, Vienna, 9: 329–33.

Verein der Freunde der Feuerbestattung 'Die Flamme' in Wien (ed.) (1894), *Catalog der Crematistischen Ausstellung des VIII. Internationalen Congresses für Hygiene und Demographie in Budapest, 1.-9. September 1894*, Vienna: Selbstverlag des Vereines der Freunde der Feuerbestattung 'Die Flamme' in Wien.

INFLUENTIAL INDIVIDUALS

Champions of cremation in Austria have included doctors, lawyers, engineers and scientists who have argued in favour of cremation for hygienic and economic reasons. The frequency of cholera and other epidemics in the urban centres and the lack of local burial places gave rise to the new science of bacteriology. Scientific discoveries were discussed at international conferences and were presented to the Austrian public in the form of lectures and popular publications aimed at overcoming both social prejudices and ecclesiastical prohibitions.

The physician Dr Eligius Hacker was a founder member and chairman of the first Verein für Leichen-Verbrennung (Society for Cremation) in Mariahilf, Vienna, his deputy being the stonemason Josef Sederl. As early as 1874, Dr Hacker proposed a motion to the Vienna city council for the introduction of optional cremation; the Society was unsuccessful, and folded after only a brief existence. The first president of the Austrian Cremation Society (*Verein der Freunde der Feuerbestattung 'Die Flamme' in Wien*), founded in 1885, was Dr Josef Scholz, likewise a Viennese physician, who was succeeded in 1893 by the engineer and railway expert Karl Freiherr von Engerth. After the latter's death in 1903, the post was occupied by the most untiring of the champions of cremation in Austria, the bank clerk Oskar Siedek (1853–1934). For more than 30 years, Siedek fought for the acceptance of the idea in the Monarchy and in the First Republic. His efforts met with an initial success in 1914 with the construction of a crematorium in Reichenberg, Bohemia, despite huge resistance in Austria-Hungary: however, it was only able to start operations following the collapse of the Monarchy. The construction of the Vienna Crematorium was also the result of his preparatory work, but was initially frustrated by the First World War. Siedek played a decisive role in the international cremation movement, through public lectures, publications, petitions, questions to politicians and his participation in all the association congresses, conferences and exhibitions throughout central Europe. He was also a co-founder of the *Verband der Feuerbestattungsvereine deutscher Sprache für Reform des Bestattungswesens und facutative Feuerbestattung* (Federation of German-Language Cremation Societies for the Reform of the Burial System and Optional Cremation) in 1886. When he died in 1934, it was the bishop of the Old Catholic Church, Robert Tüchler, who gave the final blessing to his mortal remains.

The many members and supporters in Austria and abroad included the Viennese physician Leopold Schrötter von Kristelli (1837–1908), the professor of archaeology Carl Lützow (1832–97), the author and politician Josef Freiherr von Doblhoff (1844–1928), founder of the Scientific Club, and the architect Max Freiherr von Ferstel (1853–1936), professor at the Technische Hochschule in Wien (Vienna University of Technology) and winner of the second prize in the 1921 architecture competition for the Vienna Crematorium. The architectural development of cremation facilities in the German-speaking world was decisively influenced by the academic publications of the architect Stefan Fayans (1879–1942).

The Cremation Society regarded themselves as 'cultural pioneers' and, for this reason, the new journal *Phoenix* published articles by doctors, academics and prominent individuals campaigning in favour of the idea. Under the title 'Champion of Contemporary Culture', for instance, the Nobel Peace Prize winner Bertha Freifrau von Suttner (1843–1914) wrote in 1911 that, having cremated her husband in the Gotha Crematorium in 1902, she wished to be 'lowered into the grave of flames' at the same place.

The political acceptance of cremation in Austria was mainly due to the first Social Democrat mayor of the City of Vienna, Jakob Reumann (1853–1925) who had taken part in the first major demonstration by the workers of Vienna in front of the parliament building as early as 1869. Following the foundation of the Social Democratic Party he became First Secretary in 1898 and was elected district councillor in 1900. As a representative of the working-class district of Favoriten in the Imperial Diet, he was involved in the introduction of the general franchise in 1907. After he was elected mayor on 22 May 1919 Reumann allocated funds for preliminary studies on the construction of a crematorium by the city of Vienna at the Vienna Central Cemetery, and supported the competition to design a crematorium for the Vienna district of Simmering. Despite all resistance and in defiance of express instructions from the Minister for Social Affairs, Richard Schmitz, the Simmering Crematorium was ceremonially opened by Mayor Jakob Reumann on 17 December 1922. The ceremony was also attended by the then chairman of the Social Democratic Party and future mayor, Karl Seitz (1869–1950), deputy mayor Georg Emmerling (1870–1948) and the Social Democratic city councillors and district councillors in office.

This historical background meant that the legalization of cremation in the First Republic became one of the weapons used by the workers against subordination and repression by state and church, with less attention being paid to aesthetic and economic aspects. To begin with, the Roman Catholic Church tolerated the efforts made from the eighteenth century onwards in favour of cremation. When, during the nineteenth century, resistance against Christianity, the Catholic Church and the pope began to increase, and because the dispute also involved the issue of cremation, the Church reacted by adopting a position of unbending disapproval. In the last two decades of the nineteenth century and during the first half of the twentieth century, the cremation issue was regarded increasingly passionately by both sides (by its supporters and by the dignitaries of the churches) as an expression of hostility to Christianity and the Church. For this reason, Rome banned Catholics from being cremated (Holy Office, 19 May 1886). Various bodies were heard over the following decades, but the ban was renewed on several occasions. The supporters of the cremation movement were faced with vehement opponents from within the Christian-Social camp. These included the lawyer and economist Dr Richard Schmitz (1885–1954), a Vienna district councillor from 1918, member of the national parliament from 1920 and Minister for Social Administration under the Christian-Social government from 1922. He was the minister who banned the start of operations at the new crematorium in the Vienna district of Simmering. During the conflict, an action was filed against Mayor Reumann before the Constitutional Court following a resolution of the Council of Ministers, since the mayor had refused to comply with a legal order issued by the government. It was only one year later that the case was decided in favour of the city of Vienna. In its decision of 21 January 1924, the Constitutional Court, following a second examination of the issue, confirmed the lawfulness of cremation in Austria.

On the occasion of the start of operations at the Vienna Crematorium, the archbishop of Vienna Friedrich Gustav Cardinal Piffl (1864–1932) addressed the question of cremation in detail in a Pastoral Letter dated 21 January 1923, emphasizing the fact that the Catholic Church agreed 'with devout Protestants and Jews' on this issue. It was only after the fundamental differences had been settled by

several decades of dialogue that it was gradually realized that the desire to be cremated was not as a matter of principle to be regarded as hostility to the Church and religion. The Catholic Church withdrew its ban, and decreed that sound reasons might argue in favour of cremation in individual cases (Instruction from the Holy Office, 5 July 1963). Finally, the official visit to the Simmering Crematorium by the archbishop of Vienna, Cardinal Dr Franz König (b. 1905) in 1966 became a symbol of the Catholic Church's acceptance of the cremation of devout Catholics.
Ute Georgeacopol-Winischhofer

See also architects; Boltenstern; Fayans; Siedek.

References

Czeike, F. (1974), *Wien und seine Bürgermeister*, Vienna and Munich: Jugend und Volk.

Engerth, K. Freiherr von, (offprint, 1893), 'Über Feuer-Bestattung und ihre sanitären Vortheile', *Mittheilungen der Oesterr. Gesellschaft für Gesundheitspflege*, 2, Vienna: self-published, 3–15.

Fayans, S. (1907), 'Bestattungsanlagen', *Handbuch der Architektur*, IV. Vol. I, 8. Halbband, Heft 3, Stuttgart: Alfred Kröner Verlag.

Höfert, V. (1934), 'Der Abschied von Oskar Siedek', *'Phoenix' Blätter für wahlfreie Feuerbestattung und verwandte Gebiete*, 47: 87–90

AUSTRIAN CREMATION SOCIETIES

The variety of societies and groups related to cremation is more extensive in Austria than in most other regions. This section comprises two separate articles on the Austrian Cremation Society followed by articles by Christian Stadelman on the more politically developed Labour Cremation Society that developed from it and the ideologically problematic Vienna Society.
Douglas J. Davies

THE AUSTRIAN CREMATION SOCIETY 'DIE FLAMME' (1)

On 10 April 1885 the Austrian Cremation Society, literally the Vienna Society of Friends of Cremation 'Die Flamme' (*Verein der Freunde der Feuerbestattung 'Die Flamme' in Wien*) held its founding assembly in the festival hall of the Scientific Club. On the initiative of the bank clerk, Oskar Siedek, a number of academics and intellectuals, writers and artists formed a committee chaired by the Viennese physician Dr Josef Scholz seeking the legalization and equal status of cremation as an alternative to earth burial. According to its rules, the society was charitable, non-political and interdenominational. It would, however, toil for many years to eliminate the old habits and prejudices amongst the population and to overcome political and religious resistance. In 1904 the society moved to its own premises at Siebensterngasse 16a, in the Neubau district. This address was the headquarters for the society's work, the editing of the journal *Phoenix*, the archives, the library and the Assembly Hall. In 1887 the Federation of German-Language Societies for the Reform of the Burial System and Optional Cremation (*Verband der Vereine deutscher Sprache für Reform des Bestattungswesens und facultative Feuerbestattung*) resolved to publish its own monthly journal under the name *Phoenix, Blätter für facultative Feuerbestattung und verwandte Gebiete*. To begin with, the journal was published in Darmstadt under the direction of the physician Dr Ernst Vix but, in 1891, the editorial offices were moved to Vienna, with Oskar Siedek as editor (See also Siedek, 1901). The journal was intended to disseminate information about facts or events within the flourishing movement for the reform of the burial system. Until after the First World War, the journal was published by the Austrian Cremation Society 'Die Flamme' with the assistance of the societies in Baden-Baden, Chemnitz, Frankfurt am Main, Hamburg, Heidelberg, Heilbronn, Lahr, Leipzig, Mannheim-Ludwigshafen, Munich, Stuttgart and Wiesbaden but from around 1920, the Austrian 'Die Flamme' society was the sole publisher. February 1939 witnessed what was provisionally the last edition of *Phoenix*, although the journal reappeared under the same name in July 1947.

A number of famous personalities from the liberal and enlightened bourgeoisie joined the society. The supporters of cremation were active in all fields of advertising, using brochures, journals, press articles, advertisements and the like yet, despite untiring work, the Austrian 'Die Flamme' society initially only managed to recruit a small number of new members: in 1895, ten years after it was founded, it listed 461 members, while in 1905 there were still only 583. Two decisive factors against new forms of funeral were

conservative and Catholic Austria reservations, and the expensive transfer of the deceased abroad for cremation. The society guaranteed advice and legal protection to its members, a subscription to the magazine *Phoenix* from 1887 and, depending on membership status, either free cremation for regular members or the arrangement and handling of cremation at the survivors' expense at reduced rates for supporting members. All the costs for the transport, city hall fees, laying out and the burial ceremony with lighting and music were included, although the costs for church services, death notices, the grave and special wishes were not included. Impoverished deceased members could also be cremated without costs to the survivors with the assistance of a 'Cremation Fund'.

On 29 March 1904, at the initiative of Anton Widlar, a small group of Social Democrats founded the Labour Cremation Society 'Die Flamme' based in the first Viennese workers' home built in 1902 at Laxenburgerstrasse 8–10 in Favoriten. Despite continuing financial difficulties and the small number of members, the working class soon constituted the largest group within the cremation movement. In October 1922 the branch society, with its 4236 members, broke away from the parent association, adopting the name of Labour Cremation Society 'Die Flamme' (*Arbeiter Feuerbestattungsverein 'Die Flamme'*). The public discussion on the start of operations of the Vienna Crematorium led to the new society more than doubling its membership within a few months. In 1923 membership stood at 12 637, rising to 31 823 in 1924, 120 677 in 1928 and to over 160 000 in 1931. When in 1929, in conjunction with domestic political changes, a uniform Burial Act was adopted for the whole of the Austrian federal territory, the officials of the Labour Cremation Society successfully joined together in a major protest demonstrating against the legislation. In 1930 the society moved to the newly adapted society premises at Ungargasse 39–41 in the third district of Vienna.

Before the Monarchy collapsed, branch societies of the Austrian Cremation Society 'Die Flamme' were founded in the Crown territories at Reichenberg (Liberec) (1903), Teplitz-Schönau (Telplice-Sanov) (1907) and Olmütz (Olomouc) (1911). Within the territory of today's Republic of Austria, other branch societies were established, as well as a number of independent societies in Graz, Innsbruck, Salzburg, Steyr and Vienna. In 1925 the Austrian People's Cremation Society (*Volks-Feuerbestattungsverein in Österreich*) was founded – the first society established on an insurance basis. In order to cover the cremation costs, its members were insured at the society's expense with the 'Phönix in Vienna' life insurance company.

The beginning of the twentieth century witnessed an increase in the efforts of the Austrian Cremation Society 'Die Flamme' in Vienna for the construction of a cremation hall in Austria. A number of towns in the Monarchy applied for permission to build a crematorium, the aim being to obtain an official statement by the Austrian government on the question of cremation. By 1904 prize-winning competition designs by famous architects had been prepared for Budapest, Prague and Graz, but were not implemented. Following the Administrative Court's rejection of the construction of the Graz Crematorium in 1909, the Austrian Cremation Society 'Die Flamme' concluded an agreement with the municipal council of Reichenberg/Liberec in Bohemia according to which the society would advance the construction costs for a crematorium on local authority land – to be refunded after entry into final effect of the official operating licence. The building, constructed between 1914 and 1915, could not be prevented by legal measures, but the cremation facility only started operations after the end of the Monarchy, and was thus lost to the Republic of Austria.

In January 1923 the senior society 'Die Flamme' was finally able to commence operations in the first Austrian crematorium in the Simmering district of Vienna. In the working-class strongholds of Styria and Upper Austria, the branches of the Labour Cremation Society 'Die Flamme' were particularly successful: 1929 witnessed the construction of the crematorium in Linz, followed by Salzburg in 1931 and Graz in 1932. The Linz and Salzburg crematoria were owned by the Labour Cremation Society, while the Graz crematorium was jointly owned by this society and the non-political Austrian Cremation Society 'Die Flamme'.

Following the change in domestic political conditions, the Labour Cremation Society was dissolved in 1934 and its assets confiscated. It was replaced by the newly founded Vorsorge Society for burial costs. The *Ostmärkische Feuerbestattung Versicherungsverein auf Gegenseitigkeit* (Eastern March Mutual Insurance Society), the successor to the Vorsorge society in 1938, was created under the leadership of the *Wiener Städtischen Versicherungsanstalt* (Vienna Municipal Insurance Company), and in 1942 was finally renamed as the *Wiener Verein, Lebens- und Bestattungsversicherung* (Vienna Society, Life and Burial Insurance), which is still in existence today. This society is the only burial cost insurance undertaking in Austria, and leaves the choice of type of interment entirely to the persons concerned. **Ute Georgeacopol-Winischhofer**

References

Arbeiter-Feuerbestattungsverein 'Die Flamme' in Wien (ed.) (1929), *25 Jahre Arbeiter-Feuerbestattung in Österreich. Gedenkschrift anläßlich der Feier des 25 jährigen Bestandes des Arbeiter-Feuerbestattungsvereines 'Die Flamme' in Wien*, Vienna: Verlag des Vereines.

Kronfeld, A. (ed.) (1892–1949), *Phoenix. Blätter für facultative Feuerbestattung und verwandte Gebiete. Organ des Verbandes des Vereins deutscher Sprache für Reform des Bestattungswesens und facultative Feuerbestattung*, 5–62.

Pallester, P. and Brunner v. Wattenwyl, K. (1904), *Statuten des 'Arbeiter-Zweigvereines, Wien'*, Vienna: Verlag des Vereines der Freunde der Feuerbestattung 'Die Flamme' in Wien.

Siedek, O. (1901), *Die Verbandstage der Feuerbestattungsvereine deutscher Sprache in der Zeit von 1886 bis 1900 nach authentischen Quellen geschildert* (2nd edn), Vienna: Verlag des Verbandes der Feuerbestattungsvereine deutscher Sprache.

Verein für Geschichte der Arbeiterbewegung (ed.) (1993), *Arbeiter-Feuerbestattungsverein 'Die Flamme'*, Vienna: Verein für Geschichte der Arbeiterbewegung.

THE AUSTRIAN CREMATION SOCIETY (2)

The Austrian Cremation Society (*Verein der Freunde der Feuerbestattung, 'Die Flamme'*) was inaugurated in Vienna on 10 April 1885. Compared with other European countries this was rather late. Its initiator, Oskar Siedek, worked as a bank official in Vienna and, as the story goes, was so fascinated by a cremation furnace (part of the Siemens enterprise), that he was inspired to found the Cremation Society. Its proponents were very keen to spread the idea of cremation, and one of the most important media available to them was the magazine *Phoenix, Blätter für facultative Feuerbestattung* which was published in cooperation with German cremation societies. It appeared monthly from 1887 until 1939. The political stance of the Austrian Cremation Society was liberal and interdenominational. For a long time its major concern was to prepare the ground for the acceptance of the idea of cremation that, at the time, contradicted prevailing Catholic–conservative attitudes in Austria. Although a model cremation furnace had been exhibited at The Vienna World's Fair of 1873, and despite the fact that in the following years crematoria came into operation in Austria's neighbouring countries of Germany and Italy, the idea of cremation could not gain acceptance in the Austro-Hungarian Monarchy. An earlier attempt to found a cremation society, enabling people to be cremated in their own country, had failed. Indeed, until 1918 anyone wishing cremation had to be taken to Zittau in East Germany, far away from home: in the territory of the Austro-Hungarian Monarchy cremation remained prohibited and the construction of a crematorium was opposed by all available means. Although, for example, the town government of Liberec (in the Czech Republic, which then belonged to the Austro-Hungarian Monarchy and was called Reichenberg) had decided to build a crematorium in 1898, the Bohemian administration managed to prevent its realization until 1915. And even after its completion, no cremation was permitted until October 1918, right after the decline of the Austro-Hungarian Monarchy. Even then, the act of cremation remained controversial in the newly founded Republic of Austria. It was against intense political and clerical opposition that the crematorium of Vienna – Feuerhalle der Stadt Wien – was built in 1922 and put into service the following year, and then it took until 1924 for the constitutional court to accept the legality of cremation in Austria. Subsequently the number of members of the Austrian Cremation Society of 'Die Flamme' continuously rose. Between 1927 and 1932 crematoria were built in four further Austrian towns: Steyr (1927), Linz (1929), Salzburg (1931), Graz (1932) and, after the

Second World War, Villach (1953) and Hohenems (1998). Although the idea of cremation spread rapidly, it still remained a controversial topic inciting considerable cultural conflict within the Republic of Austria.

In comparison with the Labour Cremation Society, which itself had emerged from the Austrian Cremation Society, the Austrian Cremation Society aimed more at spreading the idea of cremation by stressing the aspect of hygiene and urban economy and did not dwell so much on religious motivations and on the pope's prohibition of cremation dating back to 1886. When, in 1934, an authoritarian regime with a clerical–conservative political programme was established in Austria, the Austrian Cremation Society was not, by contrast with the Labour Cremation Society, immediately dissolved. But in 1938 the National Socialist dictat integrated the society into the Ostmärkische Feuerbestattung, an organization that controlled all aspects of cremation in Austria. In 1942 the name of this organisation was changed to *Wiener Verein Lebens-und Bestattungsversicherung auf Gegenseitigkeit* (Vienna Society). After the Second World War, the Austrian Cremation Society 'Die Flamme' was re-established with the aim of fulfilling the idealistic concerns of Wiener Verein. **Christian Stadelmann**

Reference

Hauf, Heidelinde Helene (1996), 'Die Feuerbestattung in Wien', Phil. thesis, Vienna.

LABOUR CREMATION SOCIETY 'DIE FLAMME'

The Labour Cremation Society (*Arbeiter Feuerbestattungsverein 'Die Flamme'*) was founded on 19 April 1904 as a section of the Austrian Cremation Society 'Die Flamme'. Its first assembly was convened by Anton Widlar, an employee of the *Arbeiter-Zeitung*, a working-class newspaper. It followed more pronounced political aims than its parent society. Not only did its members consider cremation as a modern, socially appropriate alternative to burial, they simultaneously declared their fundamental social-democratic view of life – particularly as the Catholic Church in Austria opposed cremation as an un-Christian act. A major problem for the

Labour Cremation Society was that, for the time being, it did not have sufficient funds to bear its members' cremation costs: costs for the transportation of bodies to the nearest crematoria in Zittau (East Germany) or Liberec (Czech Republic) by far exceeded the sum raised from its membership fees. As a result, the membership of this section of the Cremation Society increased only slowly from 40 (1904) to 216 (1913) during the first ten years of its existence. This abruptly changed when the Vienna – Feuerhalle der Stadt Wien – Crematorium opened in 1922; at this point the society achieved a total of of 4236 members. This meant that it had become larger than its parent association, and it consequently broke away as an independent organization. Now that cremation had become a realistic alternative to burial the society prospered enormously. By the beginning of the 1930s it had achieved a membership of about 160 000.

With the establishment of an authoritarian conservative government in Austria after the civil war in 1934, when democratic structures were destroyed, the Labour Cremation Society 'Die Flamme' was dissolved and turned into a general society for funeral costs, *Vorsorge*. This new organization propagated a general death provision and, at the same time, favoured burial over cremation, causing 15 per cent of the former members to leave the new society. Under the National-Socialist scheme 'cremation-insurance' was newly and uniformly settled for all interested persons. In 1945 the Austrian Cremation 'Die Flamme' was re-established with the aim of idealistically supporting the actual insurance society Wiener Verein. **Christian Stadelmann**

References

Ebner, Paulus (1989), 'Der Streit um die Feuerbestattung zwischen katholischer Kirche und Sozialdemokratie. Eine Studie zum Kulturkampf in der Ersten Republik', Phil. thesis, Vienna.

Arbeiter-Feuerbestattungsverein 'Die Flamme', Verein für Geschichte der Arbeiterbewegung, Dokumentation 3, 1993.

Grandl, Robert (1998), 'Die Geschichte der Arbeiter-Feuerbestattungsbewegung "Die Flamme" – Vorbedingungen, ideologischer Hintergrund, Nachgeschichte', Phil. thesis, Vienna.

Michelfeit, Franz (1954), *50 Jahre Arbeiterfeuerbestattung in Österreich*, Vienna: Vereinder Freunde der Feuerbestattung 'Die Flamme'.

THE VIENNA SOCIETY

The Vienna Society or Wiener Verein is the successor organization to the first cremation societies in Austria, its name being the brainchild of National Socialism. Initially, in 1938, after the 'association' of Austria with the Third Reich, all cremation concerns were newly organized under the name of Ostmärkische Feuerbestattung. Soon, the name Ostmark was removed from the National Socialist nomenclature because it was too reminiscent of the Austrian Republic. Then, for the administration of cremation (which was centrally organized in Vienna), in 1942 the general name Wiener Verein was chosen, which actually did not mention the nature of its task. Consequently the name seemed ideologically neutral by the end of the Second World War.

The new organization had also changed in substance into a more 'neutral' institution, consciously eschewing the attitudes of class warfare and anticlericalism that had characterized the Labour Cremation Society 'Die Flamme' during the inter-war period. Likewise, the exclusiveness with which cremation had previously been supported was no longer stressed because it was considered that a socio-political stance could now be dispensed with, particularly as the Catholic Church in Austria was now showing some accommodation to the idea of cremation. Consequently, the Wiener Verein was changed into a limited liability company in 1991 and was incorporated into an Austrian insurance company, the Wiener Städtische Versicherung. At that time about 450 000 people could claim an insurance benefit. Despite all these changes, the traditions of the Austrian Cremation Society 'Die Flamme' and the Labour Cremation Society 'Die Flamme', the forerunners of the Wiener Verein had not been forgotten. Sensitive to the historical tradition of cremation in Austria and its development into a socially accepted alternative to burial, its history was documented in an exhibition from 1997 to 2003. **Christian Stadelmann**

B

BAHÁ'ÍS

The Bahá'í faith has its origin in the Bábí-religion, that emerged in Iran with the Messianic claims of Siyyid Ali Muhammad (1819–50), known as the Báb. After the execution of the Báb, a period of turmoil ensued where the Bábí community (the followers of the Báb) relented under severe persecution. The majority of the Bábís, however, soon came to recognize Mirza Husayn Ali (1817–92), entitled Bahá'u'lláh, as the messianic figure predicted by the Báb, and thus emerged the Bahá'í religion.

Bahá'í practices regarding burial and cremation have their roots in Iranian culture, where cremation has not been practised, except in pre-Zoroastrian times (second millennium BCE). It is therefore not surprising that neither the Báb nor Bahá'u'lláh addresses the issue of cremation directly. Instead Bahá'u'lláh turns to address features of Zoroastrian and Islamic funeral practices. In the *Kitáb-i-Aqdas* Bahá'u'lláh prescribed the use of coffins made of either 'crystal, of hard, resistant stone, or of wood that is both fine and durable' (Section 128), clearly indicating that the body of the deceased should be preserved as well as possible. Presumably referring to the not uncommon practice amongst Persian Muslims to send the body of their deceased to the shrine cities (resting places of the holy descendants of Muhammad), such as Qum, Mashad or the 'atabat in Iraq, Bahá'u'lláh enjoined that the deceased should be buried no more than an hour from the city in which the death occurred.

The first direct treatment of cremation appears in a letter from Bahá'u'lláh's son, Abbas Effendi, entitled 'Abdu'l-Bahá (1844–1921). In response to an American Bahá'í, he set out in brief why, despite Western science's advocacy of cremation, burial was still to be preferred:

> The whole creation is like a chain in which everything is ever in a state of being formed or growing or in the state of decomposition or dispersal. Thus, as the body is allowed to grow gradually, so it should be allowed to decompose gradually. Cremation transfers the body from the plane of human existence directly to the mineral plane. As a result the chain of creation slackens and impairs creation as a whole.

Thus 'Abdu'l-Bahá's first argument is essentially an ecological one.

In the midst of reviewing the various funeral practices of the Zoroastrians, Egyptians and Hindus, 'Abdu'l-Bahá explains another reason for preferring burial. It is human nature, 'Abdu'l-Bahá states, that, despite the fact that the soul has left the body, friends will remain attached to physical remains and will not wish to see it instantly come to nothing. This is a rationalistic argument based on an emotional response. The Hindu practice therefore is deemed to be a religious response, rather than 'natural'. In an appended note, 'Abdu'l-Bahá adds that the principle, applicable to most aspects of Bahá'í law, requires that medical exigencies override the practice of burial. Thus, in the case of plague or cholera, where cremation will ensure the arrest of contagion, it should be practised at the discretion of medical authorities. The concern reflected in this appended note is presumably also that lying at the heart of the commandment not to bury the body further than an hour's travel from the place of death.

Shoghi Effendi (1897–1957), the grandson of 'Abdu'l-Bahá, later responding to a question about donating one's body to science, states that this is up to the conscience of the individual so long as it is ensured that the body is not cremated or carried further than an hour from the city in which the death occurred. He likewise specified that it was not permissible to embalm the body of the deceased. **Daniel Grolin**

Note

Bahá'u'lláh (1992), *Kitáb-i-Aqdas* Haifa: Bahá'í World Centre, and 'Abdu'l-Bahá's 'Tablet of Cremation' exists in two translations: the earlier one translated by Ali Kuli Khan in [no editor] (1919), *Tablets of 'Abdu'l-Bahá* Abbas Chicago: Bahá'í Publishing Society; the later translated by the Research Department of the Universal House of Justice, in Gail, Marzieh (1987), *Summon up Remembrance*, Oxford: George Ronald. Other texts exist in the Research Department of the Universal House of Justice (1990), *Compilation of Compilations*, Haifa:Bahá'í World Centre.

References

Smith, Peter (2000), 'Burial', in *A Concise Encyclopaedia of the Bahá'í Faith*, Oxford: Oneworld Publications.
Vahid, Rafati (1990), 'In Bahai Communities', *Encyclopædia Iranica*, ed. Ehsan Yarshater, London: Routledge & Kegan Paul.

BALI

Although Indonesia is the most populous Muslim state in the world, Balinese religion, though undergoing rapid change, still preserves links with Indian practices and beliefs that were adopted over 1000 years ago. These include cremation with *brahmana* priests using a Shivaite liturgy, the preparation of purifying holy water and, until the Dutch banned it in the nineteenth century, high-caste widow-burning (*masatia*). As in other parts of south-east Asia, death in Bali involves the double obsequies to which Robert Hertz drew attention nearly a century ago. On death the body is washed and quickly buried in a sombre ceremony with minimal offerings. Some time later – maybe years later – the remains are disinterred and cremated in what is a vastly more expensive and exuberant ritual involving the whole community, priestly services and very large amounts of offerings.

These two events and the long intermediary period that connects them signify different processes. Initial burial is mostly an affair for the immediate family, neighbours and friends, distraught at the loss of a valued family and community member whose social roles must now be reallocated to those still living. The emphasis is on mourning, bereavement and social rearrangement, so expressions of sadness and strong emotion are, within limits, permitted and expected. Ideally, the body should then remain buried long enough for the flesh to decompose fully so that only the bones are cremated. For, whereas the transcendent 'soul', symbolized by the indestructibility of the bones, comes from the gods above (purified ancestors), the material body is created and sustained by the earth and the products (rice) which grow in it, and each must be returned to its origin. Moreover, the intermediary period provides the time for both the living and the deceased to relinquish their ties to each other, the transition from complete body to bones signifying the

gradual distancing of the former from the latter. Cremation finally converts a polluted soul (which while buried must be cared for lest it turn dangerous) into a purified ancestor who can be prayed to in the family temple. It should, however, be pointed out that priests of any description, many wealthy and high-ranking Balinese and various others are not buried as it is considered too polluting to be placed under the ground; such people are cremated shortly after death.

Although cremation is perhaps the most important ceremony concerning death, it is still only one amongst several others that are performed days, months and even years later. Only at the end of the sequence, and after getting confirmation from a spirit medium, can a family feel assured that the deceased has reached a final resting place. Death in Bali is therefore a process, not an event. Furthermore, death ceremonies comprise only one set in an even larger cycle of ceremonies that connect death with life. The newborn (often said to be *nu déwa*, 'still gods') are the reincarnations of deceased lineal ascendants. In the ideal case great-grandparents reincarnate into their great-grandchildren. The kinship term for both is *kumpi*, showing their identity and equality. Birth is followed by many rites of passage in the first few years and later by teeth-filing and marriage, culminating in cremation. To an important extent the focus in cremation, therefore, is on life and fertility, not death. It is both a celebration of an individual life entailing much fun, noise and display (the opposite of initial burial), and in which the whole local community must participate, and it is also an expectation that new life flows from this death. The obligation for carrying out all these ceremonies is divided between parents and children. There is a parental duty to perform for their children all the ceremonies from birth to marriage, after which it becomes the duty of the children to perform the death rites for their parents. People who die childless, in which case the link between life and death is severed, suffer terrible torments in a Balinese purgatory, a theme often depicted in paintings.

If all this provides the basic cultural logic with which to understand Balinese cremation, it tells us little about the political connotations of such rituals, the way in which cremation is a prime site of status competition, or the kinds of changes that have occurred in both the practices and beliefs surrounding death over the course of the twentieth century. Bali is a hierarchical society whose population is divided into groups not dissimilar to Indian castes, although there is no pronounced division of labour. Approximately 8 per cent of Balinese are high caste (*anak jero*, or 'insiders') with prestigious titles and many ritual prerogatives. The rest are *anak jaba* ('outsiders'). Status competition between and within these groups can be intense, especially in the context of offerings and the paraphernalia of major life-crisis rituals – in particular, cremation. Two of the most status-sensitive pieces of equipment used at cremation are the *badé* and the *patulangan*. The former is a pagoda-like, multi-roofed tower that is used to carry the body (or its remains) to the cremation ground. Once there the body is transferred to the *patulangan* which is a structure taking the form of an animal, real or mythical. Both of these are then burned. The number of roofs (always odd) provides an indication of relative status; the highest-ranking groups have *badé* with 11 roofs, the lower-ranking *jero* may have nine or seven depending on their title, while *jaba* usually have a single-roofed tower. The *patulangan* are also ranked. Families attempting to assert a higher status than the one they currently enjoy, or to enhance their prestige, may increase the number of roofs on the cremation tower or use a *patulangan* usually reserved for groups of superior status. Whether such attempts succeed depends on many factors that cannot be discussed here, although, clearly, issues of group size, power, wealth and influence are all extremely important. Resistance to aggressive status assertion can also be very violent. If the local community feels that the deceased was unusually negligent in the performance of their customary duties during life, or their family is attempting an unjustified assertion of higher status, the village community may destroy the cremation tower and even desecrate the body by pulling it apart. However, in those areas of Bali where tourism forms, a major part of the economy, such violence is relatively rare. Cremations are a major tourist attraction and the presence of large numbers of tourists effectively prevents violence occurring as it works against Bali's reputation as a paradise of peace, harmony and beauty.

That this competition takes place at every level of Balinese society, and in relation to a great many aspects of life, is perhaps surprising given that, since about 1920, there have been many attempts to reform cremation practices. These reforms were introduced partly with a view to dampening status conflict and partly to reduce the enormous costs of cremation, especially for poorer families who had to borrow money or sell land to meet the very onerous expenses. In the early part of the twentieth century in northern Bali, urban-based, low-caste intellectuals (teachers, government administrators and so on), with some Dutch education, began to argue that what really mattered so far as the fate of the soul in the afterlife was concerned was how the deceased behaved during life, rather than how much money was spent on the cremation or what offerings and equipment were used. In short, they began to criticize a hierarchical caste system based on ascriptive criteria by advancing a meritocratic ideology based on wisdom, achievement, and actions in life – an argument derived partly from European ideas and partly from neo-Hindu reform movements in India. During the colonial period, the Second World War, the revolution and post-independence economic and political turbulence, status competition was dampened since there were few available resources to cremate at all, let alone in extravagant fashion. By the late 1960s, however, the economy began to expand, fuelled by the discovery of oil and the boom in tourism. Since then much new wealth has been channelled into sumptuous religious activity and status competition has been reignited.

In tandem with these changes and developments reformers agitated for new cremation practices that would alleviate the heavy financial burden on poorer people. One such reform was the introduction of collective cremation ceremonies (*ngaben ngiring*) in which a group of families coordinate their activities and share the services of a priest and certain offerings. For example, all the bodies, or remains, are carried to the cremation ground in the same cremation tower, rather than each having its own tower. Once there, the bodies are then transferred to their individual *patulangan* to be burned. This does pose the problem of how to arrange the bodies in the tower since physical separation on the vertical axis is a very significant sign of status difference. Before a community adopts such a practice it needs to agree on an acceptable system of body arrangement. However, partly because collective cremations may give the impression of flattening status distinctions, those who can afford to cremate individually may opt to do this. The introduction of reformed, collective ceremonies may ironically provide new opportunities to express differences. Because of their expense and their problematic nature in modern Bali it has frequently been predicted that the great cremations of kings and high-ranking and powerful people will become a thing of the past. Whether or not this becomes true only time will tell. However, below this level, many cremations are, if anything, becoming more elaborate, more expensive and more status-sensitive than ever. **Leo Howe**

See also Sati.

References

Bloch, M. and Parry, J. (eds) (1982), *Death and the Regeneration of Life*, Cambridge: Cambridge University Press.

Connor, L. (1996), 'Contestation and Transformation of Balinese Ritual: The Case of Ngaben Ngirit', in A. Vickers (ed.), *Being Modern in Bali: Image and Change*, New Haven, CT: Yale University Southeast Asia Studies.

Geertz, C. (1980), *Negara, the Theatre State in Nineteenth-Century Bali*, Princeton, NJ: Princeton University Press.

Hertz, R. (1960), *Death and the Right Hand*, trans. Rodney and Claudia Needham, London: Cohen & West. First published 1907.

Howe, L. (2001), *Hinduism and Hierarchy in Bali*, Oxford: James Currey.

Warren, C. (1993), *Adat and Dinas: Balinese Communities in the Indonesia State*, Kuala Lumpur: Oxford University Press.

BALKAN STATES (FORMER YUGOSLAVIA)

A doctor, famous poet and 'great Serbian writer', Dr Jovan Jovanović-Zmaj (1833–1904), brought the idea of cremation to Serbia from England in 1875, publishing a long article on the subject in his popular magazine *Orao-Eagle*. In 1887 he returned to the subject, writing on the contemporary European cremation movement in his weekly literary publication, *Javor-Maple*. Some of the most famous verses of his poetry were about fire and, on his wife's death, he wrote the cremationist poem 'Djuli ée-uveoke' ('Withered Roses') (Kujundžic, 1936: 51). However, an early brake on the advancement of cremation, remarked on by a Serbian delegate to the 1936 International Cremation Congress, was that the region was at this time 'not entirely liberated from the Turkish yoke'.

In 1902 Dr Vojislav Kujundžic (1872–1946), a young physician practising in Belgrade, went on a study tour of Europe, visiting all the major cities. He became particularly interested in cremation, visiting the crematoria in Paris, Zurich, St Gallen and Gotha. In Vienna he met the important Austrian cremationist Oskar Siedek who promised to help Serbia cremationists. On his return, Kujundžic, who was a freemason, wrote a long report on his experiences in Europe for Belgrade municipality, and his proposal that it should build a crematorium was supported by the mayor, Socialist Party leader Dragi Lapéevié. The following year, Kujundžic and a group of progressives established the Oganj (Ignis) ('The Fire') Cremation Society, to propagandize for cremation and ultimately establish a crematorium in Belgrade. In 1904 the society's statutes were approved and Kujundžic became general secretary of Oganj, a post he held until 1924. He was then president until 1934, and life president after that.

The Oganj Society soon began propagandizing, producing and distributing leaflets and annual reports and holding numerous lectures on cremation. In 1904 Kujundžic's earlier trip to Europe paid dividends when Siedek sent a model of a complete crematorium to Belgrade for the city's first cremation exhibition. The society also sent petitions and appeals to the municipality and the Minister of the Interior, but these efforts were not immediately successful. One illustration of the lack of contemporary understanding in official circles occurred when a petition requesting optional cremation was sent to a national minister. On receiving the petition, the minister sent it to the municipality as he mistakenly thought that it was the institution competent to judge the matter.

The Balkan Wars (1912–13) and the First World War (1914–18) disrupted the Oganj Society's work, but, according to Kujundžic, many 'saw the necessity of a mobile war-crematorium. If there had existed crematoria at the time of the war, one would not be able to find the bones of our soldiers lying about on the Kajmak and Gu and in the Boranja Mountains, as is the case now.' When the hostilities ended the society resumed its pre-war activities, providing a constant stream of petitions to the Ministry of Public Health and Belgrade municipality. This time, the society was more fortunate, for Belgrade's chief medical officer, Dr Joksimovié, was an enthusiastic cremationist. In 1928 Joksimovié managed to get Belgrade municipality to petition the ministry for permission to construct a crematorium. On 27 December 1928 the minister Ceda Michailovié, a physician himself, issued order number 57775, which allowed the municipality to build its crematorium. Michailovié himself later chose cremation, after falling ill in Paris. He was cremated in Père-Lachaise, and the urn containing his ashes was buried in Belgrade on 23 July 1933.

However, controversy soon followed the 1928 decision, when the Oganj Society published – to coincide with the first anniversary of the cremation order – a 'Declaration' arguing that the implementation of cremation would not affect the Church. Simultaneously, the society sent a petition to the patriarch of the Serbian Orthodox Church requesting the Church's blessing for the crematorium project and extracts of both texts appeared in Belgrade and Zagreb newspapers. The Holy Synod responded by announcing that it would not support cremation, and, in spring 1930, a controversy erupted in the press. The anti-cremationists were headed by a professor in the University Theology faculty and a Roman Catholic priest. The cremation society was ably supported by a priest of the Old Catholic Church. Feeling that they had emerged victorious, Serbian cremationists were pleased with the outcome of the debate as it 'showed the cremation question in a clearer light' (Kujundžic, 1936: 53).

Refusing to allow themselves to be distracted, the Oganj Society sent another petition, along with plans and estimates, to the municipality requesting that it provide a suitable site for the crematorium. On 22 April 1932 the petition was presented to a Belgrade city council plenary meeting. The meeting unanimously passed a motion to allocate a 2500 m² plot in some recently purchased land on a hillside outside Belgrade to the Oganj Society for the construction of the crematorium. A further boost

came when, in early 1934, a Mihael Pavlovié-Ponin bequeathed 1 million dinars (£4500 at the time) in his will for the construction of a crematorium in Belgrade. In 1936 the society began producing a periodical, *Oganj*, which it soon found to be a 'very effective means of propaganda' (Kujundžic, 1936: 53). An eight-page monthly, *Oganj* contained, as well as news from Yugoslavia, translated articles from many European countries.

However, significant problems remained. Belgrade's new lord mayor, Petrovié, as 'a son of the church', acted to prevent the city council from carrying out its motion, saying that there would be no crematorium in Serbia as long as he lived. The Oganj Society had to take Petrovié to the presidential Court of the Royal Government for refusing to carry out the council's clearly expressed desire. In his defence, Petrovié claimed that, although there were many reasons why he could not carry out the resolution, the main one was 'clerical'. Thus, no progress was made while Petrovié remained mayor. Then the Serbian Orthodox Church also joined the active opposition to the cremation plan, showing its disapproval by forbidding, for the first time, the attendance of one of its priests at the cremation society's annual *slava* (birthday ceremony). Of course, the Oganj Society denied allegations that it was an atheist organization and, frustrated by the situation in Belgrade, began concerted efforts to promote cremation elsewhere. It presented petitions to Pan and Stara Pazova municipalities, both close to Belgrade, and achieved some success when both councils passed motions supporting the principle of building crematoria in their districts. The society then ventured further into the provinces, targeting the larger towns and establishing several new branches in them.

The 1930s saw development in other areas of Yugoslavia, as it was then. In 1931 the Slovenian town of Maribor saw the establishment of a second Yugoslavian cremation society, Ogenj. A cremation society had been founded in Ljubljana in 1926, but this appears to have been short-lived (Mitrovic, 1960: 48). The inhabitants of the region had been familiar with cremation since before 1914 when some had chosen cremation in Gotha, but this new society still represented a significant move forward. Initially, the new society was intended merely to be a branch of the Belgrade society (Oganj). However, it was eventually decided that it should be autonomous from Belgrade as this allowed for better relations with cremationists in the neighbouring Austrian town of Graz which was in the process of building a crematorium. The statutes of the Maribor Cremation Society were approved on 15 July 1931. Good relations with the Austrians meant that, initially, Maribor Cremation Society members had the option of being cremated in Graz. The cremations were carried out by society representatives who would accompany the corpse to the Austrian border where it was met by a Graz Crematorium motor-hearse. The Graz authorities would then take charge of the corpse and oversee its cremation. The Maribor Cremation Society could also arrange the cremation of non-members, but this cost from 8000 to 10 000 dinars.

As in Belgrade, there was conflict with the clergy in Slovenia. This peaked when the Maribor Cremation Society arranged an elaborate and very public ceremony for the funerals of two of its members. There was a large attendance at the ceremony, although, of course, the Roman Catholic Church was not represented. However, the Roman Catholic attitude to cremation did not operate completely independently of worldly considerations. Dr August Reisman (president of the Maribor Cremation Society) noted that the Catholic Church opposed cremation 'with the greatest severity, it is true, only where it is to its financial advantage'. A case that 'attracted great attention' revealed that the opposite also held: that where it stood to gain financially, the Roman Catholic Church seemed able to suspend its opposition to cremation. In 1932 a Dr Kunej of Slovengradec bequeathed 15 000 dinars in his will to build a hospital chapel in his town. However, he added a condition: that the town's Roman Catholic priest should perform his funeral ceremony, which was to be a cremation. The deacon, unsure how to react, asked the archbishop for guidance. He allowed the priest to perform the ceremony, after which Kunej's corpse was carried in procession to the Graz crematorium motor-hearse on the Austrian border. Yet this did not stop Catholic clergy from preaching strongly against cremation immediately afterwards. In 1936 the Maribor Cremation Society planned to build its own crematorium, with a special 36 000 dinar-fund for the purpose. However, the demand for cremation did not seem great: only 16 had been

performed by the society in Graz in five years (Kujundžic, 1936: 53).

In Croatia, Professor Fran Gundrum Oreoviëanin advocated cremation amongst his circle in the Croatian town of Kri contemporaneously with Jovanovié in Serbia, in the 1870s and 1880s. However, in contrast to Serbia, no one took up the idea in the early twentieth century and cremation was forgotten for several decades. Then, on 26 November 1930, a branch of the Oganj Society was established in Zagreb. It had the same statutes as the Belgrade society as this was the quickest and easiest way to establish a cremation society. However, the society rapidly expired and in 1932 a new cremation society named Plamen ('the Flame') was established, although its statutes were not legally agreed until 30 March 1934. Like the Belgrade society, it aimed to build a crematorium but, like its counterpart in Maribor, it also began to arrange collective insurance to be able to cremate members at Graz Crematorium. Headed by Dr Duan Jurinac MD, the society established *Plamen* as its propaganda paper, and Zagreb cremationists addressed many conferences of journalists, Rotarians and others during the 1930s.

By 1936 there were three cremation societies in the most important parts of Yugoslavia, which, despite their formal separation, mutually supported each other. For example, in early 1936, the Croatian Dr Boris Zarnik (professor of biology at the University of Zagreb), lectured on 'Biological opinions in regard to the disposal of the dead', under the auspices of the Belgrade society both in Belgrade and in other Serbian provincial towns. Cooperation began to solidify when, at a joint congress on 20 July 1936, the three cremation societies decided 'to work together hand in hand' (Kujundžic, 1936: 53). Another step towards formal organizational unity was made at the Belgrade society's annual meeting on 17 April 1938, when it decided to cooperate with the Zagreb society to form a federation of Yugoslav cremation societies. In 1939 the Zagreb Cremation Society's AGM unanimously supported the formation of a Yugoslav cremation federation, with members also pressing for a vigorous propaganda campaign.

The year 1936 also saw Yugoslav delegates playing an important role in the re-establishment of formal international relations between cremationists at the Prague International Cremation Congress. They also hoped that this development would help them. Indeed, Kundžic, when asking for support for cremationists working in difficult conditions, said that he spoke for all countries that did not have cremation. He also talked of the 'brotherly feelings' between Yugoslavs and Czechs (who were hosting the congress) and acknowledged that the Yugoslav cremation movement had already been helped by the Czechs. When the International Cremation Federation (ICF) was formed the following year, all three Yugoslav cremation societies joined it, and this facilitated the hoped-for support of foreign societies, particularly from the British. For example, in December 1937, Dr Viktor Ruzic, a member of the Zagreb municipality on a private visit to London, was met by the ICF secretary-general who showed him round local crematoria and urged him to support pleas for a crematorium in Zagreb. Ruzic apparently agreed that, if a crematorium was proposed in a constitutional way, then he would not oppose it. Zagreb cremationists had also availed themselves of British propaganda, using, for example, the British cremation film *The Great Purifier* in their conferences.

Still, this new-found international support could not immediately deliver the prize, despite Kujundžic's optimism at the election of the industrialist Vladalli as mayor of Belgrade in early 1935. Vladalli was determined that the council's resolution to build a crematorium should be carried out as soon as possible and he had, after liaising with the technical experts, fixed a definite site for it. An optimistic report also appeared in *Pharos*, claiming that Belgrade Crematorium would be completed by September 1936. Work had, apparently, already begun and it was expected that the crematorium would not only serve Yugoslavia, but Bulgaria and Greece as well. Over a year later, *Pharos* reported Yugoslav cremationist claims that, after doing a great deal of propaganda work, there would soon be a crematorium in their country, although no date was now given for completion. If work *had* actually begun on Belgrade Crematorium, it was certainly not ready to open before the outbreak of the Second World War. When plans were again mooted for a crematorium in Belgrade in the post-war years, there was no mention of any building work already completed, suggesting that

either none or very little had been done, or that it had been destroyed in the war. The lack of progress on this project before 1939 was attributed, 30 years later, to the 'unceasing opposition from the church on the one hand and the prejudices of some of the political factions on the other' (*Report*, 1969: 15).

As with most of continental Europe, the Second World War completely disrupted Yugoslav cremationists' activities. The cremation societies were forbidden from operating, their property was confiscated by occupying forces, and their offices and records were largely destroyed. Like some French cremationists, individual cremationist leaders suffered. The president of the Maribor Cremation Society, Dr Reisman, was deported to Serbia, although he was able to return at the end of hostilities. A worse fate befell the secretary of the Zagreb Cremation Society, Mr Saulik, who was executed during the occupation. After 1945 the Belgrade and Zagreb societies were allowed to resume their existence. However, it was not long before the Belgrade society was again indicted and all its property confiscated by the municipality. Yugoslav cremationists suffered a further blow as Dr Kujundžic, a founding father of the cremation movement and president of the Yugoslav Cremation Federation, died in March 1946. His remains were finally cremated in 1968 at the expense of the Belgrade Cremation Society. The Maribor Cremation Society did not even manage to resume activities after 1945 at all and by 1950 only the Zagreb Cremation Society was operating, although its activities were also severely curtailed, partly due to the death of its president, Dr Jurinac, in May 1947. However, despite this, Zagreb city council had decided to build a crematorium and was holding a competition to design it. It had already been decided that the crematorium would use an electric furnace, and a Swiss firm had offered to install it. However, Zagreb cremationists were also interested in receiving bids for the work from British companies. Though confident that Zagreb, rather than Belgrade, would become the first town in the Balkans to have a crematorium, Zlatko Turkovic, secretary of the Zagreb Cremation Society, remained convinced that there would be a great deal of Roman Catholic opposition to overcome and, for this reason, he asked for international help and advice about propaganda. The information supplied by

Turkovic in 1950 was the first received by the international movement on developments in the country since 1939. It had become clear in 1948 that Yugoslav cremationists were 'unable' to resume their association with the ICF. Eight years later, it appeared that the Zagreb plans had gone the same way as the prospects for a Belgrade crematorium before 1939. However, by 1954, the Belgrade society (Oganj) had reconstituted itself once more and, by 1956, it was again an ICF member. The 1957 ICF Congress at Zurich heard that the Yugoslavs had been in contact by means of a long letter in German from Dr Mitrovic of Belgrade. The Yugoslavs sent their greetings, but said that they could not attend the congress for reasons that the ICF president could not fathom. However, they did request help regarding their propaganda campaigns. By 1958 the Belgrade Cremation Society was in the process of collecting information for a crematorium that was once again proposed for Belgrade and many in the ICF had already offered their advice. Even more encouraging was the news that funds had been granted and plans were being prepared for a crematorium in Ljubljana, Slovenia. A doctor from the University of Ljubljana had met ICF representatives at the London headquarters, been shown round a crematorium and received all the requisite information. Yugoslavia would soon, *Pharos* confidently predicted, be among the cremationist countries of Europe.

This new hope also heralded the reintegration of Yugoslav cremationists into the international movement, 'prevailing post-war conditions' having made this 'impossible' earlier. At the Stockholm ICF Congress in May 1960, Dr Branka Mitrovic reported on Yugoslavia. Her address was upbeat, claiming that, finally, Yugoslav cremationists had 'real grounds' for hoping that their first crematorium would be open within a year. Moreover, Yugoslavia again had three cremation societies, in Belgrade, Ljubljana and Zagreb. They had been in close contact – on their own initiative and with the help of former ICF secretary-general Herbert Jones – with many national cremation societies that had provided information and advice, particularly regarding the practice of scattering cremated remains.

The plan for Belgrade was to build a new park cemetery outside the city and to install a crematorium in this. Belgrade cremationists thought this a bad idea as 'even the vicinity of a crematorium can in itself serve as good propaganda', so they asked the municipality instead to build it in the existing cemetery, which was close to the city centre (Mitrovic, 1960: 48). The municipality agreed to this solution as a temporary experiment, and work on converting a chapel at the cemetery's entrance into a crematorium was due to begin soon. The idea was for the temporary crematorium to furnish the authorities with experience of cremation and to gauge the demand for it, thereby determining the size of the permanent crematorium. The central cemetery itself was also to be converted into a park, thereby making a crematorium in the grounds even better placed. Another factor that made the old central cemetery a superior site was that there were still some years to wait before the new cemetery was due to be operational. It remained unclear, however, if it would be possible to build the permanent crematorium in the city centre cemetery or not. Mitrovic seemed sufficiently satisfied that the entire project would be carried out by the municipality as it lent its strong support 'to all progressive endeavour in the field of municipal policy'.

Outside Belgrade, although there were hopes of establishing crematoria in both Zagreb and Ljubljana, no definite decisions had been made. Yet Mitrovic was hopeful that this would soon change 'as the introduction of cremation is quite in line with the public policy of realising all projects calculated to enhance the dignity of human life' (Mitrovic, 1960: 48). A year later, Belgrade Cremation Society reported to *Pharos* that the crematorium plan was going ahead that year. A ceremony hall was to be provided and a Stuttgart company was to supply the cremator. A larger space for the scattering of ashes was also being planned, which was predicted to encourage the future development of cremation. Belgrade Crematorium was built in 1963 and opened the following year. Installed with one modern electric cremator, it performed very few cremations in its early years. However, the numbers cremated did increase, and by the end of 1968 it was cremating about 10 per cent of the Belgrade dead annually. Colonel Jarvic of Belgrade regarded this as 'incontestable evidence that the cremation movement is growing considerably in Yugoslavia'. This was due to 'both objective and subjective conditions' being 'propitious' for the movement: for example, the fact that cremation cost almost a third of a 'modest' traditional burial (*Report*, 1969: 16). The cremation rate continued to grow and, by 1974, the 881 cremations comprised just over 18 per cent of Belgrade deaths.

In 1965, the Belgrade Cremation Society had 600 members, rising rapidly to 3300 by 1969. Of this membership, more than 400 were from 70 different places dotted around most of the country. This was because, by 1969, there had been an amalgamation of forces and Yugoslavia now only had one cremation society (also called Oganj). Thus the new Yugoslav Cremation Society now organized cremationists in Slovenia, Bosnia, Macedonia and Croatia, as well as in Serbia. In March 1969 the Yugoslav Cremation Society, at a meeting to discuss its new statutes, reorganized itself by establishing an administrative commission and an executive committee composed of three sections: 'publicity and foreign relations', 'organization and technical matters' and 'finance'. Its growth continued and by 1974 it had 8000 members. In 1969 Jarvic predicted that within five to ten years, there would be two crematoria in Belgrade, as well as others in Ljubljana, Sarajevo, Skopje and Zagreb.

With regard to the religious opposition, Jarvic noted that the Catholic Church had altered its perspective, and, although atheists were in the majority in the Yugoslav Cremation Society, it also contained churchgoers. The Serbian Orthodox Church remained the only Christian church in Yugoslavia that still opposed cremation, and yet even some of its practitioners were cremation society members. In fact, cremationist hopes that the Orthodox Church's position on cremation would soften were increasing, and this was anticipated to boost the cremation movement.

Addressing the same ICF triennial congress in 1969, Janko Vidovic, an observer from the Yugoslav Chamber of Commerce, reported on positive developments in Ljubljana, which was reorganizing its cemetery facilities and, due to the increasing interest, planned to build a crematorium as part of this. Serious consultation on this was underway by January 1967. Those wishing to be cremated had been using the crematorium in Villach, Austria, as it was closer than Belgrade. Vidovic felt thankful that the Yugoslav authorities supported cremation, which made conditions more favourable than in some other countries. However, there were still problems in raising the necessary finances for these projects, and this had prevented their quicker development. Despite this, Vidovic predicted that a crematorium in Ljubljana would be operational in 1973 or 1974. Good cremation propaganda and the higher costs of burial were expected to help the new crematorium, and there was the new requirement to provide facilities for tourists who were visiting the country in increasing numbers.

By autumn 1984 it was clear that developments in Yugoslavia had taken longer and been less dramatic than predicted in 1969. The new Belgrade Crematorium only opened in 1983 and had not been an instant success. In its first year it did not cremate significantly more than the earlier 'temporary' crematorium. However, the total cremated in Yugoslavia had almost doubled with the opening of the crematorium in Ljubljana in December 1978 – some five years later than planned. It cremated almost 30 per cent of the city's dead in its first full year. This startling percentage even surpassed the results of a market survey carried out prior to construction that predicted it would take a decade before 30–40 per cent of Ljubljana's dead were cremated.

More positive, too, was the good health of the Yugoslav Cremation Society. It had around 10 000 members, in addition to a considerable number of supporters, and these numbers were still rising. Publication of the newspaper *Oganj*, which had been sent free to members, had ceased in 1983. In 1984 it was replaced by *Informator*, a less financially burdensome publication. In addition, there was a plan to build what would be the third crematorium in Yugoslavia, in Zagreb. Required largely because of a lack of new space for burials, it was due to open in 1985. Other important towns in Yugoslavia, including Split, Rijeka, Novi Sad, Sarajevo, Skopje and Ni, were also interested in building crematoria. Yet, due to a plethora of problems, the main one being the perennial lack of finance, there was no indication about when any were likely to be able to start construction work.

Like many before it, the crematorium in Zagreb did not materialize. Yet, the Balkan states' second crematorium, in Ljubljana, continued to grow in popularity. After only a decade of operating it was cremating around 70 per cent of the city's dead. In 1995 this figure was a little over 70 per cent, with the entire country of Slovenia cremating around a third of its dead.

The crematorium in Ljubljana took on more importance when, on 25 June 1991, Slovenia attained independence and the city became the nascent republic's capital. By 1995 Ljubljana and its environs had a population of 300 000, out of a total Slovenian population of 2 million. The crematorium was run by the public company Zale, which had been established by the city council. As the funeral authority, it was responsible for managing ten cemeteries in the city. In 1998 Slovenia got its second crematorium, in Maribor. By 2002, at least 48 per cent of the deceased in Slovenia were cremated (the figures in *Pharos* did not include the new Maribor Crematorium). **Lewis H. Mates**

See CSA.

References

CSA.

Kujundžic, Dr Vojislav (1936), 'Report on the Cremation Movement in Yugoslavia', in *Report on the International Cremation Congress, Prague*, CRE/D4/1936/2, 51–54.

Mitrovic, Dr Branka (1960), 'A Report From Yugoslavia', in *Report of the ICF Congress at Stockholm*, CRE/D4/1960/1, 48–49.

Oganj, paper of the Oganj Cremation Society of Belgrade, CRE/AO/AU.

Veselinovic, M. (1985), 'Cremation in Yugoslavia', *Pharos*, 51(1): 2.

Report of the ICF Congress at London (1969), Working Session, 29 May, typescript, CRE/D4/1969/9.

BARRIER, GUSTAV

When the Paris Cremation Society was established in 1880, Gustav Barrier (1853–1945), then aged 27, was one of the 109 founding members. Barrier became an important authority in the world of medicine, becoming president of the French Academy of Medicine. A doyen of the French cremation movement, it was Barrier's initiative and 'great authority' that led to the formation of the Fédération Française de Cremation ('French Cremation Federation') in 1930. Naturally, Barrier became the Federation's first president, serving until 1938. Unfortunately, his age prevented him from playing a full part in the international developments in the cremation movement in the 1930s: he was unable, for example, to attend the International Cremation Congress in Prague in 1936. In June 1938 Barrier was replaced as president of the French Cremation Federation and was elected its honorary president in recognition of his years of service.

On his death, the wartime lack of fuel did not prevent Barrier's cremation as his Paris colleagues managed to secure special dispensation to conduct the operation in February 1945. A decade earlier, fellow cremationist Dr Ichok wrote that Barrier, who had 'remained in the fight', was owed by the French cremation movement 'a debt it can never repay'. **Lewis H. Mates**

See also France.

References

Ichok, Dr G. (1935), 'The Development of the Cremation Movement in France, Part Two', *Pharos* 1(3): 24–25.

ICF Committee for Propaganda (1963), 'The World Problems of the Disposal of the Dead', paper Presented at the ICF Congress, Berlin, CRE/D4/1963/3.

BELGIUM

Ideas of cremation in Belgium belong to the later nineteenth century when it was supported by freethinking people as a means of opposing the quasi-monopoly on funerals held by the Catholic Church. In 1874 the Commune of Brussels discussed the purchase of land for the Cimetière d'Evere with the intention of setting a portion apart for cremation, an idea revisited in 1876. However, this early discussion did not set the pace of the cremation movement. Even the Belgium Cremation Society (*La Société Belge de Crémation*), founded in February 1882, had short-lived success, and discussions for building a crematorium in the St Gilles cemetery outside Brussels came to nothing. Again, in July 1882 a Brussels alderman decreed that the cremation issue needed to be discussed by a higher body but when the Minister of Interior declared cremation illegal, on the grounds that there were no laws to regulate it and that it destroyed potential evidence in murder cases, the cremation movement ground to a halt. Later, in March 1906, the Belgian Society for the Propagation of Cremation (*Société Belge pour la Propagation de la*

Crémation) was established, and its journal, *La Crémation*, began publication. This society was the direct predecessor of the current Belgian Cremation Society.

Finally, in 1930, through the Cooperative Cremation Society a crematorium was constructed at Uccle, south of Brussels. Despite the fact that cremation was, at that time, neither authorized nor permitted, the justice system reacted immediately and positively by passing a law on 21 March 1932 concerning the incineration of human corpses and entrusting cremation only to public authorities. As a result, 12 Brussels Communes created a mutual society to purchase appropriate installations and inaugurate the crematorium; the first Belgian cremation took place 15 months later. This made Belgium one of the last Western European countries to legalize cremation. At this time, the ashes had to be interred.

Subsequent dates of significance include the 1963 Catholic authorization of cremation for the faithful, and a 1971 law abolishing the obligation to possess written authorization from the deceased in order to undertake a cremation: ashes could also now be spread on a cemetery's lawns, interred, or put in a columbarium. In 1977 a further law obliged each *commune* to have a lawn for ash-spreading and a columbarium in its cemetery. By the beginning of the twenty-first century Belgium possessed ten crematoria – five private and five publicly owned. New legislation in 1989 permitted anyone to make their wishes regarding their funeral arrangements known in writing in their local registry office, and in 1990 a regulation permitting disposal of ashes at sea, within territorial waters, was enacted. Subsequent legislation of 1999 stipulated that a soluble urn must be used for sea-burials of ashes.

In 2001 a new law liberalized the potential destination for ashes, allowing them to be preserved, scattered or interred in a location other than a cemetery or in territorial waters. This clause is subordinated to any pre-existing expression of preference on behalf of the deceased concerning the method and place of burial and designating a responsible executor. By 2001 cremation represented 35.17 per cent of total burials. Since 2000 people have been able to be more precise concerning their preferred place of burial when writing their final wishes in the register and, in August 2001, a law defined clearly the eight possibilities concerning choice of burial

and produced a form designed to ratify this expression of preference.

In 1992 a Commission was set up by Louis Tobback, the Home Secretary, culminating in the creation of a new law in 1998 whose most important change was to entrust again the establishment and use of any crematorium to public control. Privately owned crematoria had to conform to this by November 2003. In September 2001 another law dealt with the establishment and control of crematoria, as well as the ethical considerations of cremation. In this regard the managements of public crematoria have been very busy contributing to the installation of computerized systems for controlling the handling of mortal remains at crematoria. Likewise, the consideration of ethics – usually a vague subject – has made its entry into legal documents, with the aim of guaranteeing respect for Belgian citizens' mortal remains, as deceased human beings, until the end of the funeral process. In November 2001 a further law dealt with the composition of the cremation coffin. On this subject, the Belgian crematoria came to agreement with funeral directors' associations over rules concerning the quality of coffins, shrouds, dressing of the coffins and even the appearance of the deceased. These organizations have each, in turn, echoed these agreements, notably with their partners in the coffin manufacturing industry.

With regard to environmental legislation, the country is divided into three, largely relatively autonomous, regions, and this is certainly reflected in the setting of regulations concerning the quality of smoke emitted at cremation. As the twenty-first century begins, Flanders, in the north, enforces very strict criteria, called the VLAREM 11 regulations, over the obligatory installation of smoke treatment equipment. Since 1995, in the Bruxelles-Capitale region, the Brussels Institute for the Management of the Environment has imposed parameters that do not oblige the use of filters, whereas Wallonia, in the south, has no regulations, but makes continuous efforts to improve the burning process. The tendency is towards a harmonization of regulations, making the installation of smoke treatment equipment mandatory.

As to ceremonial factors, the crematorium has become the location of an increasing personalization of rites as expressed in the employment of an infinite variety of music, texts, speeches and poems, whether by priests, pastors, lay ministers or other officiants. Commemorative ceremonies are also regularly organized. Many crematoria decorate their buildings with works of art to give the best setting possible for the sad occasion of the funeral of a parent or a friend. Cultural events are also organized at crematoria aimed at removing their mystique. Those managing crematoria have a role as a public service and the obliged to provide information to the population on cremation services offered, whether by means of the Internet or interally produced publications. A large number of crematoria have opened restaurants for the convenience of families when they gather, for example, for the placing of ashes, reflecting the country's tradition of meeting for a meal, a drink or a coffee at important moments in life. **Xavier Godart**

Note

This entry is based largely upon Xavier Godart's 'Cremation in Belgium', a paper delivered at the 2003 ICF Conference, Barcelona, translated by Andrew Boardman, with additional historical contributions by Jennifer Arkell.

Reference

'L'incinération des Cadavres Humains en Belgique' (1970), in *La Cremation*, December, Belgian Cremation Society Publication, CRE/C/BE/ 1934/20.

BOLTENSTERN, ERICH

Born in Vienna on 21 June 1896 and dying there on 2 June 1991, Boltenstern pursued architectural studies between 1918 and 1922 at Vienna's Technische Hochschule. He secured an internship under A. Ahrends and Professor Hans Poelzig in Berlin, then studied in Barcelona, in Vienna again under Professor Siegfried Theiss and Hans Jaksch, and in Linz under Professor Julius Schulte. He owned his own firm by 1930. His academic career in Vienna lay under Professor Oskar Strnad at the Kunstgewerbeschule and Professor Clemens Holzmeister at the Akademie der bildenden Künste. From 1936 to 1938 he taught the Master Class of Professor Peter Behrens at the Akademie but during 1938–45 was forbidden to teach for political reasons. Throughout 1945–54 he taught the Master Class of Professor Holzmeister and from 1946 to 1967 was, himself, professor at Vienna's Technische Hochschule.

His numerous structures made Boltenstern one of the most important twentieth-century architects of funerary culture in Austria, and he engaged with the building of crematoria as soon as this became possible after the establishment of the Austrian Republic in 1918. His first project was with the Julius Schulte firm that designed the crematorium at Linz-Urfahr although whether this was his first contact with the cremation movement is unsure. The timelessness of his works well suits the architectural task, offering those confronted with death a safe, secure environment: a testimony to his way of thinking, stamped by humanitarian ideals. His buildings are distinguished by their great stillness and calm but complete lack of pathos. Their style is marked by a reduction to geometric simplicity, uniform measuredness with clear lines, and quiet elegance. The building shapes and interiors exhibit impressive proportions with forms devoid of any decoration. The function and the construction of simple details are clearly connected with contemporary technology. As such, his unpretentious buildings are irreplaceable witnesses of the spirit of the 1950s.

After the Second World War, Boltenstern not only contributed to the physical post-war reconstruction after the dark times of dictatorship, but more importantly to the spiritual resurrection of the Austrian Republic. His principal funerary works in Austria are the crematorium buildings at Graz (1930–1932 with Ludwig Dawidoff); Villach-Waldfriedhof (1952–53); Wien-Stammersdorf (1966, with Josef Strelec); St Pölten (1975, with Paul Pfaffenbichler); the cemetery buildings at Schwechat, Mürzzuschlag, Deutschlandsberg, Trofaiach, Leoben and Großenzersdorf (over the period 1965–1984) and the renovation of buildings (for lying in state) in Wien-Zentralfriedhof. Non-funerary work included the Kahlenbergrestaurant and the competition for transformation of the Kahlenberg, Vienna, 1933–34; the rebuilding of the Wiener Staatsoper, Vienna, 1948–55; renovation of the Tiroler Landestheater, Innsbruck, 1963–68 and the hall for the Technische Hochschule Vienna, 1967–74. He was, at times, in partnerships with Clemens Holzmeister, Eugen Wachberger, Robert Weinlich and Kurt Schlauss. **Bruno Maldoner**

See also architects.

References

Anon. (1954), 'Krematorium in Villach', *Der Bau*, 9: 264–65.

Boltenstern, E. (1935), *Wiener Möbel in Lichtbildern und maßstäblichen Rissen*, Stuttgart: Julius Hoffmann.

Boltenstern, E. (1955), 'Vom Wiederaufbau der Staatsoper', *Der Aufbau*, 10: 425–33.

Schmidt, W. (1955), 'Verabschiedungshalle im Waldfriedhof Villachlkärnten', *Das Münster*, 8: 76–77.

Sequenz, H. (ed.) (1965), 'Bauten und Institute: Lehrer und Studenten', *150 Jahre Technische Hochschule in Wien 1815–1965*, Vienna: Technische Hochschule, 496–97.

Stein, S. (1998), 'Architekt Professor Dipl.-Ing. Erich Boltenstern', *Österreichische Ingenieur- und Architekten-Zeitschrift (ÖIAZ)*, 143: 21–22.

BOOK OF REMEMBRANCE

The book of remembrance, in its present form, was the result of the foresight and skills of Frederick George Marshall (1899–1971) who introduced the book to the cremation movement in 1932. However, it was not until 1938 that the first book of remembrance was installed at England at the Woking Crematorium in Surrey. Cremation at that time was growing but memorialization was just an adaptation of burial practices with the gravestone miniaturized and fixed to a wall and with mausoleums having become columbaria, all sold in perpetuity. Marshall realized that a new form of commemoration was needed if crematoria were not to become encumbered with miles of walls and niches which, when filled, would generate no more income but would nevertheless still incur expense in their maintenance. The new memorial system had to be permanent with a high capacity and low maintenance costs. The solution that George Marshall arrived at was to create a lavishly bound, inscribed and illustrated book with calendar date titling so that the entries would be displayed on a specific date. The medieval monasteries had produced large bindings that had already been proved to outlast most stone memorials (except granite) but their techniques had largely been lost after the dissolution of the monasteries under Henry VIII.

However, with the aid of Thomas Harrison OBE, Marshall was able to unravel the secrets of their construction, and these methods are now used again in the production of these Marshall books. Using materials such as calf vellum, sheepskin parchment and leather, they are constructed by hand, using the traditional methods of the medieval monastic binderies. It is anticipated that books made following this format, and housed under correct conditions, will last for many centuries.

The name 'book of remembrance' was taken from the biblical Book of Malachi (3.16). Although the books are produced in many variations of size and format, the most commonly used in crematoria measure approximately 20.5 x 15.25 ins when closed, and have a capacity of 36 500 two-line entries. Smaller versions are used by churches, hospices and many other organizations. Each individual volume represents a quarter of the year, (for example, January, February March) so that four volumes make up one complete book. This system enables volumes to be updated while not on display. In the book, each page or opening represents one day of the calendar year and it is displayed, opened on the relevant page, in specially designed cabinets, generally housed in specially dedicated chapels of remembrance.

Memorial entries are inscribed under the date of death, wedding anniversary or any other anniversary of significance to the family. Viewing of a memorial entry is generally restricted to the specific date of the entry, although many crematoria will arrange viewing on other dates under special circumstances. Entries are inscribed by hand using a traditional round hand style and calligraphic ink, most books employ a standard format of two, five or eight lines. Memorial entries can be decorated with small hand-painted emblems, decorative gold capital letters or gold-blocked capital letters. The emblems can represent family crests and coats of arms, membership of the armed services or associations, hobbies, birds, animals or flowers – in fact, any subject deemed suitable by the local crematorium authority. Most crematoria offer personal copies of memorial entries, hand-inscribed on cards or in miniature books as an additional option.

To take the book of remembrance into the twenty-first century, it can now be recorded after each updating as a digital image, which can be

viewed on a computer screen. This innovation, developed by F.G. Marshall Ltd in 1997 and known as the 'visual reference system', allows families access to their memorial entries on any day of the year via a touch-screen facility, usually housed with the book in the chapel of remembrance. Crematoria staff can also access the books via their office computers, allowing them to answer queries regarding an entry without referring to the book itself, which may be some distance away or in another building. Widely acknowledged throughout the UK, USA, Australia and the Netherlands, the book of remembrance now represents one of the most popular forms of family memorialization.
Richard Marshall

See also Economics; South Africa; Zimbabwe.

BORNEO/SARAWAK

The Bidayuh (Dayak)

The Bidayuh are an indigenous, or 'Dayak', group living in Sarawak, Malaysian Borneo and adjacent areas of West Kalimantan, Indonesia. They are the only Dayak group in Sarawak known to have practised cremation. In the past, some scholars argued that Bidayuh cremation originated from Indic influences, but it is now considered to have originated independently. Cremation was one of three mortuary rites practised by the Bidayuh in the past. The bodies of children less than eight days old were abandoned in baskets in the cremation ground because it was thought that they did not yet have a soul and that cremation was therefore unnecessary. In the 1800s and early 1900s, some Europeans reported that some Bidayuh buried their dead or buried some and cremated others, but this may have been a result of Christian missionary activity. Cremation, however, is thought to have been the primary means of traditional mortuary treatment. Due to widespread adoption of Christianity, only a few remaining villages practise cremation, as discussed below.

Cultural variation exists to some extent between Bidayuh subgroups, but cremation practices appear to have been generally similar. Upon a death in the village, the *peninuh*, a man who specialized in death rites, was summoned by the deceased's household. The body was rolled in a mat or tree bark and placed in the corner of the room with the deceased's belongings. The cremation took place on the day after death. The *peninuh* led a funeral procession to the cremation ground (*tinungan*), in which he or another male would carry the wrapped corpse on his back. On arrival at the *tinungan*, which lay downstream of the village, the corpse was placed on a stack of firewood and burnt, together with the deceased's possessions. It was believed that if the possessions were not burnt or otherwise destroyed, the ghost of the dead would return for them. During the ceremony, male religious specialists recited prayers for the dead, and women sang mournful 'crying dirges' called *muas*, in which they lamented the death of the loved one and urged his or her spirit to make a swift and straight journey to the afterworld, rather than lingering to haunt the living. If the smoke from the burning body rose straight up, it was thought that the deceased's spirit was making a prompt departure. If the smoke swirled near the ground, it was interpreted as meaning that the spirit was lingering in this world. The ashes of the deceased were left in place at the cremation ground.

Although the cremation was thought to have released the spirit of the dead person from this world, there were additional rites that marked the separation between the dead person and his or her immediate surviving family. Following the death, the deceased's family observed a four-day proscription against work. On the fourth day, the *peninuh* performed a ceremony called *bitotak wee*, in which he held one end of a length of rattan while the family held the other end. The *peninuh* then cut the rattan in half, symbolizing the separation of the family and the deceased, in the hope that the ghost of the dead person would not return to visit them.

As the tasks of the *peninuh* were thought to be very polluting, it was often difficult to find anybody willing to take in this role, and those who did were often socially marginal. It is not surprising, therefore, that this was one of the first traditional ritual roles to be abandoned when the Bidayuh began converting to Christianity. Those villages that still practise cremation are those that have a *peninuh*. In other villages, practitioners of the old religion are buried.

The Bidayuh: Christian conversion

The Bidayuh began to abandon cremation upon large-scale conversion to Christianity. In the

Singai villages, for example, the last cremation was held in the 1970s. However, there are remnants of earlier rituals in modern funerary practices. In Singai, both Christians and practitioners of the old religion (*bigawia*) bury their dead, but the possessions of the deceased are often burned. Whereas Christians only burn items that can no longer be used, bigawia believe that none of the deceased's property should be kept because the spirit may return for it. As to why they cremated their dead in the first place, the Bidayuh tend to explain this in terms of suppression by the Malays, with whom they have long experienced ethnic conflict. One informant's account states that, long ago, the Bidayuh abandoned corpses in the tops of trees. Malays, complaining of the stench, thought that the Bidayuh should bury their dead but, because they did not trust the Bidayuh to dig a deep enough grave for the bodies, they told them to burn the bodies instead. Another account states that the Bidayuh used to bury their dead in shallow graves near riverbanks. Malays, finding themselves stepping on bodies that had been uncovered by the water, told the Bidayuh to cremate their dead.

Now rarely performed, cremation is one of many older Bidayuh practices that have almost or totally been abandoned due to conversion to Christianity. While some Bidayuh Christians attempt to revive parts of 'traditional' culture, such efforts are only aimed at practices that can be removed from their customary religious contexts. This excludes cremation, which is deemed to be at odds with Christian practice. Such older rituals, which also include the agricultural rites that petition the spirits for bountiful harvests, are rapidly vanishing.
Pamela N. Lindell

BRITISH FUNERARY COMPANIES

Until the 1930s cremation was a little unusual, and local churchyard or cemetery burial dominated disposal processes in Great Britain. In comparison with the hundreds of churchyards and cemeteries that operated in the past, crematoria are comparatively few in number. Since, with greater urbanizaton and population growth more funerals are organized through fewer 'outlets'. The rise in popularity of cremation has also led to the almost complete loss of the craft-based skills of coffin-making. In contrast to the inherited Victorian custom of elaborate and expensive coffins, simpler choices are available that reflect the logic of simple cremation.

Compared to the more casual churchyard undertakings of the past, Cremation is also a significant factor in the concentration of funeral firms which, in the past, used to be casual or part-time and based near churchyards and cemeteries. This development has further magnified what can be described as three 'concentrating issues'. First, in comparison with churchyard burial, the official paperwork required for cremation necessitates formal office arrangements and not the ad hoc working of casually organized companies who once combined funerals with other occupations such as building or timberwork. Second, due to high levels of demand at crematoria, the time between death and the funeral has become longer to enable everything to be organized and to get an appropriate time acceptable to the family. This has therefore increased the custodial demand on funeral firms and contributed to the growth of the practice of embalming. Third, because crematoria are often located a fair distance from the deceased's home, funeral companies need reliable vehicles to work within this market.

The need to invest in office, mortuary procedures and rolling stock has gradually removed the informal and part-time element of the funeral industry. These issues have favoured the organized and effective companies at the expense of the casually-oriented firms which undertook funerals as a useful diversion from other work. Moreover, as the predictable nature of crematoriaum services allows funerals to be scheduled closer together, effective firms have been able to grow larger and larger. These complex changes have had a remarkable impact on the funeral directing industry and have contributed towards its concentration. Before the Second World War there were perhaps 6–7000 small, part-time undertakers. Now, in the early twenty-first century, there are approximately half as many more or less full-time funeral directors.
Phillip Gore

BRODRICK COMMITTEE

The Brodrick Committee, chaired by Norman Brodrick QC, was appointed by the British Home Secretary in 1965 to 'review (a) the law and practice relating to the issue of medical certificates of the cause of death, and for the disposal of dead bodies and (b) the law relating to coroners and coroner's courts, the reporting of deaths to the coroner, and related matters'. The Committee was appointed as a consequence of concerns about inadequacies in the law and practice of death registration and coroners, many of which were marshalled in a report published in 1964 by the British Medical Association, *Deaths in the Community*. One of these concerns in particular – namely, the occurrence of undetected homicide – had been the subject of a learned monograph, *The Detection of Secret Homicide* (1960) by Dr J.D.J. Havard.

The Committee presented its report in 1971 and, amongst other things, recommended an improved procedure for ascertaining and certifying the causes of deaths. Two of the report's chapters were devoted to the operation of the Cremation Act and Regulations. The Committee argued that, with the improved procedure for registering deaths that it was proposing, there would be no need for the special protections against undetected homicide required by the Act and Regulations. It recommended, accordingly, that the statutory provisions relating to Forms A – D, (E, presumably), F and H, and to the office of medical referee, should be revoked. Only Form G, the register of cremations, would be retained.

None of the Committee's recommendations relating to cremation was acted on, but the issues addressed by the Committee have been recently reviewed by two inquiries established in response to the discovery of the serial murders committed by Dr Harold Shipman. Although they do not agree on the details, both inquiries have recommended, as the Committee did, a uniform system of death registration and certification for the disposal of dead bodies, whether by burial or cremation, and the government has accepted this in principle. **Stephen White**

References

British Medical Association Private Practice Committee (1963), 'Medico-Legal Investigation of Deaths in the Community (England and Wales)', *British Medical Journal Supplement*, 11 May: 220–27.

British Medical Association (1964), *Deaths in the Community*. London: British Medical Association, London: BMA. Revised and reissued in 1986.

Brodrick, N. (chairman) (1971), *Report of the Committee on Death Certification and Coroners*, Cmnd 4810, London: HMSO.

Havard, J.D.J. (1960), *The Detection of Secret Homicide: A Study of the Medico-legal System of Investigation of Sudden and Unexpected Deaths*, Cambridge Studies in Criminology Vol. XI, London: Macmillan and Company.

Home Office (2004), *Reforming the Coroner and Death Certification Service: A Position Paper*, Cm. 6159, London: The Stationery Office.

Luce, Tom (chairman) (2003), *Death Certification and Investigation in England, Wales and Northern Ireland: The Report of a Fundamental Review*, Cm. 5831, London: The Stationery Office.

Smith, Janet (2003), *The Shipman Inquiry Third Report: Death Certification and Investigation of Death by Coroners*, Cm. 5854, London: The Stationery Office.

BROWNE, SIR THOMAS

Sir Thomas Browne (1605–1682) wrote one of the earliest comprehensive European reflections on the place of cremation amongst the other funeral customs of the world. After his early days at Oxford and extensive travel, Thomas Browne trained as a medical doctor at Holland's famed University of Leyden and became a Doctor of Medicine at Oxford University in 1637. He was knighted by King Charles II in 1671. His book of 1658, *Hydriotaphia*, had its theme and topic fully described in its subtitle, *Urne-Buriall. Or, A Brief Discourse of the Sepulchrall Urnes Lately Found in Norfolk*. Browne thought that these funerary urns contained Roman remains, although later scholars regard them as Saxon, and this prompted him to ponder the nature of death and of funeral rites. As Sir John Evans observes in his introduction to the 1893 edition, the style of Sir Thomas is strongly classical, more like a translation from Latin than a direct English composition. His title too, *Hydriotaphia*, represents a new word in which he links the Greek word for a funeral urn or bucket ('Υδριά) with a variation of the Greek for a burial place (ταφη).

Although, in the piety of his day, Browne sees burial as the original form of funeral represented in the Bible with the death of Abraham, he notes that 'the practice of Burning' is extensively present in the classical authors of Greece and Rome. He is also familiar with 'the Indian Brachmans' as 'great friends unto fire', as well as with the reverence towards fire that led the Persian Magi and the Parsees (the Zoroastrians as we might now identify them) to avoid cremation and favour the exposure of corpses. He also deals with the Egyptians and Chinese, with Islam and the Jews and with Druids, noting reasons for and against cremation.

Browne often adds his own comment to his more objective descriptive accounts as when he likens funeral urns to the womb. Their circular body and narrow neck reflect the 'Urnes of our Nativity', the 'inward vault of our Microcosm' and, by likening our death to our birth, they make 'our last bed like our first' (Browne, 1958: 23). From today's perspective we might see in this an echo of the Hindu comparison of the funeral pyre with the womb, the one undoing by literal heat what the other did, metaphorically, with the 'heat' of the mother in maturing the foetus. Browne also sees the significance of cremation in producing ashes that, in classical cultures, allowed the ashes of partners and friends to be buried together: 'The ashes of Domitian were mingled with those of Julia, of Achilles with those of Patroclus: All Urnes contained not single Ashes; Without confused burnings they affectionately compounded their bones; passionately endeavouring to continue their living Unions' (Browne, 1958: 27). In other, Roman, contexts he refers to the desire to keep ashes separate from other matter by using 'sheets made with a texture of Asbestos'. And he notes how babies were not cremated 'until their teeth appeared' lest their 'gristly bones would scarcely leave separable reliques after the pyrall combustion' (Browne, 1958: 37).

Browne sees advantage in cremation in that no extensive bone remains 'to be gnaw'd out of our graves' and turned into objects for enemies to use and thus become 'Tragicall abominations'. Similarly, no bodies are left 'in fear of worms': yet, he notes the Christian preference for burial of the body and for its emphasis on a resurrection rather than devolving all hope 'upon the sufficiency of soul existence' (Browne, 1958: 32, 35).

So far as the best memorial is concerned he expresses, in a short note, what many have held to be the case: namely that 'Our Fathers find their graves in our short memories, and sadly tell us how we may be buried in our Survivors'. Indeed, his final chapter rises to poetic heights as he dwells upon life and death and the hope for immortality. Even the ancient Egyptians are to be pitied in their pyramids for even 'Mummie is become Merchandise', as 'Pharaoh is sold for balsams' (Browne, 1958: 48). For Sir Thomas Browne 'there is nothing strictly immortall, but immortality'. For him 'the sufficiency of Christian Immortality frustrates all earthly glory'. Nevertheless, underlying his text is the semi-mystical attitude of one possessing an 'admixture of scepticism and credulity,... whose belief in witchcraft was firmly fixed, who still retained some faith in judicial astrology' (Evans in Browne, 1893: xiii). So Browne concludes that 'Life is a pure flame, and we live by an invisible Sun within us'. To effect 'prodigall blazes' in our funeral pyre is, ultimately a folly, and wise funeral laws should, by contrast, produce 'sober obsequies, wherein few could be so mean as not to provide wood, pitch, a mourner, and an Urne' (Browne, 1958: 49). **Douglas J. Davies**

References

Browne, Sir Thomas (1958), *Urne Buriall and The Garden of Cyrus*, Cambridge: Cambridge University Press.

Browne, Sir Thomas (1893), *Hydriotaphia: Urn Burial; with an account of some urns found at Brampton in Norfolk, By Sir Thomas Brown*, with Introduction and Notes by Sir John Evans, London: Charles Whittingham and Co. at the Chiswick Press.

BUDDHISM

Buddhism teaches that the individual is made up of a stream of ever-changing, continually replaced psychophysical constituents that continue on through an unending series of deaths and rebirths. This round of rebirth is called samsara. Only an individual who has achieved the highest goal of Buddhism, namely Enlightenment or Awakening (nirvana or *bodhi*) is free from rebirth: Enlightenment is regarded as a rare, if not impossible, achievement in this current age of corruption. In Tibetan traditions, it is believed that some spiritually advanced beings can choose not to return, but do so to assist others on the spiritual path. Such individuals, of whom the Dalai Lama is the most famous example, choose their re-embodiment and can then be identified as such through special tests.

People in general are unaware of the details of their past or future rebirths. They will be reborn in one of a range of heavens or hells, or as an animal, as a 'hungry ghost' in a kind of purgatory or as a human again. What determines their future fate is their previous actions, karma, in both their most recent and other previous lives. Good or meritorious actions lead to benefits to the individual in this or a future life, whereas bad actions create demerit and result in misfortune. Buddhist doctrine states that it is intentional actions that cause these results. Bad intentions are those based in greed, hatred or delusion, while good intentions derive from the opposite virtues. Our immediate rebirth after this is also determined by our state of mind at death. If death is expected, a calm and collected mind is desirable. Means of engendering an appropriate state of mind include meditation, for example on the qualities of the Buddha, one's own previous meritorious actions, one's personal Buddha or Bodhisattva from tantric practices, or one's teacher. Alternatively, monks or priests may give sermons, recite sacred texts or whisper mantras – sacred symbolic phrases – into the ear of the dying person. In some Buddhist traditions, particularly 'Pure Land' Buddhism of east Asia, there is a belief that one may go to a special heaven and become enlightened listening to the teaching of the Buddha of that heaven, usually Amitabha (Amida in Japanese). Preparation for this involves devotion to that Buddha – for example, by reciting his name repeatedly.

Although Buddhist teachings emphasize the impermanence of all things and the inevitability of death for all, this does not mean that all of the 500 million or so Buddhists in the world are 'at ease' with death, as is often suggested. The fear of death and grief for one lost are as reasonable to anticipate among Buddhists as among adherents of any other faith. Also, although Buddhist doctrine denies the existence of an enduring soul and different philosophical traditions developed complex explanations of the transition from one life to the next in the absence of it, standard Buddhist language and practice relating to funerals may refer to such an entity in a way very much akin to the use of the term 'spirit' or 'soul' by Christians. Furthermore, while the doctrine of karma emphasizes personal responsibility for one's future rebirth, many actions and rituals performed or sponsored by relatives as part of the funerary rites are designed to ensure or enhance the good rebirth of the deceased. The merit of such activities is transferred to the deceased. The dedication is often formalized by the pouring of water or coconut juice onto the ground, an act that traditionally accompanies the making of a gift. In most Buddhist traditions, people may prepare for death not only when terminally ill or very old, but also while still in good health. A filial duty in traditional China is to buy the funerary dress and coffin for one's parents. In the Newar Buddhism of Nepal there are rituals preparatory for death, which include gifts of appropriate paintings or sculptures to ageing parents.

The role of monks

The role of ordained monks and lay priests at funerals is fairly universal in different traditions. As the most meritorious objects of giving, they receive donations. They perform rituals, and they advise on the funerary rites, such as the appropriate period of mourning or the location of the cremation or burial. They, or specialist astrologers, may consult the deceased's astrological chart and the configurations of the constellations at the time of death in deciding these matters. While Buddhist monks may be excluded from life-focused life-cycle rituals such as weddings in some traditions, they are the death ritual experts throughout the Buddhist world. Funerals are the occasion for sermons by monks on the subject of impermanence and the inevitability of death, one of the key tenets of Buddhism.

Means of disposal

The disposal of the body may take place within a day of death or after as much as an entire year, depending on the arrival of relatives and the status of the deceased. The higher the status, the longer is the intervening period. Cremation is the main, but not universal, means of disposal of the dead in Buddhism. In Newar Buddhism, if the person's body cannot be recovered, their horoscope is cremated. Other forms of disposal include dismemberment and leaving the body for vultures to consume, known from Tibet, where corpses might also be buried, cremated or thrown into a river. A rare practice still found in mainland south-east Asia, even in the twentieth century, was for the individual to bequeath their corpse to the local monastery so that it could act as the focus of meditation. The body would be placed in a cage to protect it from carrion and monks would watch it in its different stages of decomposition. This form of Buddhist meditation goes back to the beginnings of the religion around the fifth–sixth centuries BCE, at which stage it was apparently common practice to dispose of corpses by exposing them in special charnel grounds. The meditation instils in the practitioner a deeper understanding of impermanence and dispels lust and greed. In contrast to the above practices, Chinese funerals are based on Confucian beliefs. Even if they incorporate Buddhist elements, they usually involve burial. Burial also became increasingly common in Burma during the colonial period.

Death rituals are often elaborate. They vary according to region. They may even incorporate practices from other local religious traditions, in part because Buddhism did not on the whole seek to monopolize social religious practices outside matters that deal strictly with salvation. This leaves room for the participation of non-Buddhist ritual specialists. Within individual traditions death rituals vary according to the status and relative wealth of the deceased, including whether male or female, monk or layperson. Royal funerals can involve extensive ritual and commemorative practices. Rites include practicalities such as washing, oiling and dressing the body. The colour of death and mourning in most Buddhist traditions is white, and this is often the colour of the shroud as well as of the clothes of mourners. In Tibet, ritual preparations include transferring consciousness out of the body, while in Laos a special offering to the deceased individual informs them of their own death, so that they know not to linger among the living.

A key Buddhist practice at funerals is the reciting of sacred texts by monks or priests. The texts recited vary according to tradition. In Chinese funerals Buddhist monks may recite sutras, texts containing sermons of the Buddha. In Tibet, Perfection of Wisdom sutras are commonly used. In the Theravada of mainland south-east Asia, Abhidhamma texts, the scholastic philosophical texts of the canon, are recited, while in Sri Lankan Theravada, important funerary texts include the *Satipatthanasutta*, a text on meditation. Verses relating to themes of impermanence and *paritta*,

protection texts in the Pali language, are also recited in all Theravada countries and the merit dedicated to the deceased. Similarly in Nepal, apotropaic texts may be recited, such as the 'five protections'. These are sacred formulae in Sanskrit that embody protective deities and offer assistance in a range of dangerous situations. The 'Tibetan Book of the Dead', famous in the West because of its relatively early translation and the subsequent interpretations given to it by Leary and Jung, is just one of a number of funerary texts used in Tibetan traditions to guide the departed through the intermediate realm to the next life. This intermediate state is called *bar do*, and may last up to 49 days, this being the duration of intense mourning and activities to assist the dead. In Buddhism, periods of mourning range from a few days to three years, depending on status and tradition. It is usual to hold further rites to mark the anniversary of the death, especially after the first year. Other meritorious acts performed on behalf of the deceased include offerings to the Buddha and gods at the local temple, gifts to the poor, the feeding of friends and relatives and, especially important, feeding monks and offering them gifts, such as new monastic robes.

In addition to transferring merit to the deceased, it is quite common to make gifts to the corpse. Some gifts provide for the needs of the deceased in the afterlife; these are often similar to the needs in this earthly life, such as food and water, often continuing to provide the meals that the individual would have taken in life throughout the mourning period. Some gifts enable the deceased to make offerings and acquire merit, while others pay off or divert the attention of potentially malevolent spirits. Gifts may be placed alongside or near the corpse, or they may be burnt, such as the widespread practice of burning money and 'passports' for the deceased in China and mainland south-east Asia. Special funerary money can be purchased for this purpose. In Laos, the deceased may be fed after cremation by an offering placed at the base of the *bo* tree in the temple – the sacred tree descended from that under which the Buddha gained Enlightenment. Gifts or payment for malevolent spirits may be placed on the body or scattered on the ground during the funeral procession. A common practice is to seal a coin into the mouth to pay the ferryman over the river of death, reminiscent of Charon of Western classical mythology. The corpse may also be given offerings to be presented to the Buddha, such as incense and flowers. Also, the deceased gains the merit of the great act of generosity to monks, when those officiating remove robes placed on the bier.

Funerary gifts are often interpreted as symbolizing aspects of Buddhist teaching, as are all other aspects of the funeral. Thus the number of monks invited, the offerings made, the coffin, the direction of the cortege, and the layout of the funeral ground have a symbolism that relates to Buddhist doctrine, to beliefs about ancestors and beneficial or harmful spirits, or family hierarchy. This symbolism often extends to the smallest details. For example, in Thailand the string bound round the hands of the corpse three times to hold them in the respectful position of greeting and prayer symbolizes the bonds of greed, hatred and delusion and is severed just before the cremation. The symbolism of the funeral itself as the occasion of great merit-making and rebirth for the deceased has been harnessed in Cambodia until quite recently. A person still living or their representative could undertake a rebirth ritual based on the funeral in order, for example, to overcome a serious illness.

To some extent all death is seen as inauspicious, and rites purifying the participants or the deceased's property are common. However, violent or premature deaths are regarded as particularly inauspicious in Buddhism and always require special handling. These include death in childbirth, a stillbirth or even death under adverse astrological constellations. The nature of the adaptation of rites varies. For example, in northern Thailand the body may not be cremated or given proper funeral rites straight away. Rather, it is buried for a few months or even years, until the danger is considered past, then exhumed and given full cremation and funeral rites. In contrast, in central Thailand the corpse may be cremated as soon as possible to prevent the spirit causing problems for the living.

Cremation is often partial, rather than full, as the remnants of teeth and bones and the coin, particularly those of important people, can have ritual, commemorative and protective significance. The use of the physical remnants from cremations goes back to the funeral of the Buddha himself. His funeral is described in a text called the *Mahaparinirvanasutra*. The remains of his cremation were divided up among different peoples who built funerary mounds (stupas) over them. Legend has it that in the third century BCE the Indian emperor Asoka had the relics re-excavated and divided into 84 000 portions over which new stupas were built. All countries in which Buddhism has been the dominant religion have myths relating to how relics of the Buddha or other holy personages ended up in that country and sites where they are housed. The stupa, in its various forms, dominates the sacred landscape of Buddhism. Buddha relics are believed to have magical protective powers. This belief in the power of relics extends to highly venerated monks and to royalty. Thus the ashes from the pyres of renowned monks in mainland south-east Asia are one of the sacred ingredients for making protective amulets. The relics of Thai kings have become the focus of royal cults, while King Chulalongkorn of Thailand, in an act that combined ancient and modern means of commemoration, used the timbers from the cremation of three of his children in 1888 to begin the construction of Thailand's first hospital.

In general, the remains of the cremation undergo a second phase of funerary rites. They may be kept on the family shrine, buried under a small stupa in the temple precincts, or placed in a pot and buried near the temple, usually to the west of the city or village. The burial grounds were a traditional place for the wandering forest monks of northern Thailand to meditate, and their presence was believed to benefit the deceased interred there. In China, deceased ancestors may be housed on the family shrine in a wooden spirit tablet. In northern Thailand, relatives may shape the ashes into the figure of a person first pointing west, the direction of death, then turned around to face east, enacting the rebirth of the individual.

Like the Buddha's remains, those of ordinary mortals may be dug up and given fresh funerary rites at a later stage, perhaps when their son is in a position to given his parents a more elaborate send-off. In China sometimes a 'lucky burial' is performed after some years. The bones are exhumed, washed and dried, then stored in a large urn and eventually reburied in an auspicious spot.

Participation in funerals is seen as an act of great merit in itself. The entire community may participate. Funerals therefore serve the additional role of reinforcing social ties and binding the community. Throughout mainland south-east Asia death rituals have traditionally been noisy and festive periods with monks invited from other villages and many people provided with lavish hospitality. It is a time for music and other entertainment, such as dances and plays, drinking, gambling and symbolic tugs-of-war. However, reforms to Buddhism, especially since the nineteenth century, have severely reduced some of these activities, particularly in urban areas. Royal funerals have often involved ostentatious displays of pomp, with elaborate biers and cremation platforms, and huge military processions. Such funeral rites re-emphasize the power of the lineage and demand a renewed demonstration of loyalties to the royal family. Both aspects contribute to a stable transition of power between the late king and the new king at a potentially precarious juncture.

Western Buddhism

Although there are many schools of Buddhism practising in the West, on the whole they tend to converge in both their attitudes to death and dying, and their approach to death ritual. In attitude, there is an adherence to the traditional Buddhist view of death as an inevitable fact of human existence, as outlined above. It is widely held that there is a need to acknowledge death both spiritually and ritually. Manifestations of this reflect a fusion of Western secular beliefs with traditional Buddhist views. Rituals performed by Western Buddhists for the dying and recently deceased are, on the whole, based on traditional Buddhist funerary rites, but have developed away from some aspects of tradition for both pragmatic and doctrinal reasons. First, on purely pragmatic grounds, it is illegal in the UK, for example, to burn a corpse on an open-air fire. This means that cremations must take place in the crematorium, with its attendant restrictions on space and allocated time. This is likewise increasingly common in the urban centres of traditionally Buddhist countries. Second, to appeal to Western audiences Eastern Buddhist teachers have needed to adapt elaborate traditional rites of passage. These have been modified to accord with the more low-key Western rites and thus syntheses of Western and traditional Buddhist practices have emerged. Western Buddhist communities often perform sessions of communal meditation, chanting or

ritual for members who are terminally ill. Sometimes this is done simply in order to bear the person in mind or send them positive thoughts. At other times such practices are motivated by a belief that this process will help the departed consciousness of the individual. After death, a body is often taken to a Buddhist centre or communal building where people can come and perform rituals such as *puja* (devotion to the Buddhas), chanting, meditations for the departed consciousness, or reading aloud from sacred texts. Whether a body is cremated or buried is largely personal choice. While there is an awareness of the Buddhist significance of cremation, a Western Buddhist may also be concerned with modern ethical issues, such as whether to donate one's bodily organs to others in current need, or one's whole body for medical research to benefit others in the future. **Kate Crosby and Alice Collett**

See also Tibet.

BUSINESS

Cremation has often been conducted by people who have made a living or a professional business out of the task. As the **Hinduism** entry shows, this often involved specific caste groups. In modern cremation both funeral directors and companies managing crematoria have developed businesses out of the social need to cope with the dead by cremation (Howarth, 1996). Entries on **Argentina**, **New Zealand**, **Sweden**, **undertakers** and the **USA** make this particularly clear. The following case of Great Britain offers one fuller account that could be repeated for many other countries. **Douglas J. Davies**

See also Argentina; British funerary companies; India; New Zealand; Sweden; undertakers; and early cremations; USA.

Reference

Howarth, Glennys (1996), *Last Rites: The Work of the Modern Funeral Director*, Amityville, NY: Baywood Publishing Co., Inc.

GREAT BRITAIN: COMPANIES FOSTERING CREMATION

The Victorian pioneers of cremation in the late nineteenth century realized that the essential prerequisite for fostering cremation was to provide suitable buildings for both the religious and practical aspects of cremation. Hence, the predominance of private organizations such as the Cremation Society and locally incorporated companies in the construction of the first crematoria – indeed most of the first ten, built between 1885 and 1904 – were established by such entrepreneurs. From that era remain the London Cremation Company plc (Woking, Golders Green), Manchester Crematorium Limited (Chorltun-cum-Hardy), Glasgow (Maryhill) and Birmingham (Perry Bar) which was later acquired by the Great Southern Group. In the first half of the twentieth century, other locally-based private companies such as Kent County Crematorium (Charing and Barham), Brighton (the Downs), Norwich (St Faith's) and Edinburgh (Warriston and Leith), contributed to the growth of facilities in their areas. But by the 1950s it had become normal for new crematoria to be a local authority service, and this numerical predominance remains today.

However one company, The Great Southern Cemetery & Crematorium Company Limited (Great Southern Group) which in 1937 had built the South London Crematorium (Streatham), became active at a national level during the period of major growth from 1950 to 1970. In these 20 years cremations more than doubled to 65 per cent of deaths and numbers of crematoria almost doubled to 206. Although local authorities were responsible for the construction of most of these new crematoria, Great Southern Group built Surrey and Sussex (Crawley), Exeter and Chichester crematoria and acquired Oxford and Birmingham (Perry Bar). In the 1970s and 1980s it became the first company to privatize municipally-owned crematoria (Lancaster, Leatherhead and Loughborough) and by 1994, when it was acquired by Service Corporation International, Great Southern had built or acquired 14 crematoria and had long been the largest single cremation authority in the UK.

As well as fostering cremation by actually building crematoria, companies such as Great Southern Group, London Cremation Company, Kent County Crematorium and many others were active in expanding the demand for cremation through through local initiatives as well as through their membership of organizations such as the Proprietary Crematoria Association and by supporting the work of bodies such as the Cremation Society. These companies were dependent on their own efforts to become and remain viable enterprises, with no recourse to public funds. So in addition to providing attractive facilities for the bereaved, they often led the way in the provision of services such as memorialization, 24-hour availability for funeral directors arranging services, annual services of remembrance for bereaved relatives and other services that were not necessarily viewed as essential by local authorities. Experience proved that people desired more than a mere disposal service for their loved ones and most local authorities have since followed the early initiatives of the private sector which became adept at making cremation the most attractive option for those who were not necessarily influenced by ideological reasons. In the 1980s and 1990s long-established companies, such as the London Cremation Company and Great Southern Group as well as newly formed private companies, have been much more involved in the building of new crematoria again. Without an active private sector it is doubtful whether cremation would have prospered so successfully in the UK. **Eric Spencer**

C

CAMERON, SIR CHARLES

Sir Charles Cameron, Bart (1841–1924) served from 1904–21 as the second president of the Cremation Society of England (later the Cremation Society of Great Britain), following the death of the group's founder, Sir Henry Thompson. He had not joined the Cremation Society on its initial formation and, according to an 1875 survey compiled by the Massachusetts Board of Health in which he was quoted, Cameron was inclined to believe that earth burial, with proper management, could be safely practised. Yet he saw cremation as superior to badly maintained cemeteries and later raised an alarm over burials that took place, especially in Scotland, without any certification at all. Cameron later reconsidered his position, perhaps in light of serving as a journalist for the *Daily Mail*, as medical officer of health in Dublin or as president of the public medicine section of the British Medical Association.

Cameron was concerned about diseases such as cholera and was impressed with Louis Pasteur's research on the ability of germs from dead animals to remain in the soil and poison other livestock. By the mid-1880s, he had become an ardent devotee of cremation and, immediately after Justice Fitzjames Stephen declared cremation legal in 1884, Cameron, a Radical member of parliament representing Glasgow, sponsored the Disposal of the Dead Bill along with Scottish MPs Sir Lyon Playfair and Dr. Robert Farquharson. Although this legislation would have recognized and regulated cremation, with neither major political party supporting the bill, it failed on its second reading. Nevertheless, it had gained sufficient public and parliamentary support to check any effort by the Home Office to ban cremation.

Cameron also served as a chief witness and committee member with Cremation Society members Sir Walter Foster (later Lord Ilkeston) and Dr Robert Farquharson on the 1893 Select Committee on Death Certification (Cameron became a baronet the same year). After the passage of the Cremation Act of 1902, Cameron hoped his movement would enjoy a growth spurt that did not in fact materialize until after the First World War. The Cremation Society commemorated Cameron and Thompson with a stained glass window at Woking – Cameron was cremated there. His son and heir, Sir John Cameron, also became an advocate of cremation and ultimately also served as the society's president from 1960–68. **Lisa Kazmier**

See also Cremation Society of Great Britain; Thompson.

References

Obituary in the *Times*, 28 February 1924.

Erichsen, Hugo (1887), *The Cremation of the Dead Considered from an Aesthetic, Sanitary, Religious, Historical, Medico-legal, and Economic Standpoint*, Detroit: D.O. Haynes & Company.

Cameron, Charles (1887), 'The Modern Cremation Movement', *The Scottish Review*, 10:1–38.

Stenton, Michael (1978), *Who's Who of British Members of Parliament: A Biographical Dictionary of the House of Commons, Vol. 2: 1886–1918*, Hassocks: Harvester Press, 54–55.

CANA

In 1913 Dr Hugo Erichson started the Cremation Association of America (CAA) which changed its name to the Cremation Association of North America (CANA) in 1975. At the time of its inception there were approximately 52 crematoria in the United States and in that year 10 119 cremations took place. Dr Erichson served as CAA president until his death in 1942 and devoted his time and energy to this association that he had founded as an instrument of social and sanitary reform. Cremation in the United States and Canada was slow to gain acceptance; it was 1973 before the US cremation rate reached 5 per cent. Canada reached 5 per cent six years earlier. It took another eight years for the percentage of cremations in the US to reach double figures. Canada registered 10 per cent in 1974. Since 1981 the US rate of cremations as a percentage of deaths has increased an average 0.75 per cent per year reaching 26 per cent in 2000 (625 000 cremations). Canada surpassed 40 per cent in 1997. If the current US trend continues, it is estimated that the cremation rate in the US will reach 44 per cent by 2025 with an estimated 1.4 million cremations.

When CANA was formed, members had to have a crematorium. Since crematoria were, at that time, all located in cemeteries, the membership consisted entirely of cemeterians. Membership was also offered to any cemetery that offered disposition for cremated remains. It was not until the mid-1970s that membership was available to firms, mainly funeral homes, that operated a crematorium without being a part of a cemetery. In the late 1980s an associated membership was offered to organizations that arranged cremations and/or memorialization thus opening membership to funeral directors and cremation societies that did not operate their own crematorium. In 2000 regular membership was opened to all firms engaged in some aspect of cremation and/or cremation memorialization. In 1982 CANA appointed Smith, Bucklin & Associates, Inc., the world's largest professional association management firm to manage CANA. Prior to that time Paul Bryan, of Pasadena, California, had been the association's secretary and was responsible for day-to-day operations.

Jack Springer was appointed CANA's first executive director and has continued in that position. While membership in 1982 was a little under 400, by 2003 it stood at slightly over 1400.

CANA is a very proactive organization having drawn up a model cremation law in 1985 for states considering cremation legislation, co-sponsoring emission stack testing in 1999 with the US Environmental Protection Agency (EPA), and conducting crematorium operators certification programmes, which are becoming mandatory in several states. Most recently CANA is offering Advanced Cremation Arrangers Seminars for Cremation Providers. In 1998 CANA's website, www.cremationassociation.org, was launched and is now the primary source for North American cremation statistics and cremation facts and articles for both the general public and cremation professionals. CANA members are dedicated to the statement that 'cremation is preparation for Memorialization'.
Jack M. Springer

See also Canada; USA.

CANADA

Modern cremation in Canada began in Montreal, with the Mount Royal Cemetery Company in 1901. Formerly known as the Montreal Cemetery Company, it had been in existence since 1847, when the city's older burial grounds had become exhausted and a new cemetery was required. Accordingly, the cemetery trustees purchased land on the mountainous northern slopes of the city of Montreal, Mount Royal, to provide a rural backdrop for a cemetery to serve the city for many decades. The farmland there soon became one of the most beautiful and well-designed traditional cemeteries in North America (Roy, 1981: 85).

In the 1880s the idea of constructing a crematorium in Mount Royal Cemetery, supported by an anonymous financial backer, was put to the cemetery's trustees for the first time. However, the trustees did not support the idea, and it was forgotten for some years. Then, in 1897, John Henry Robinson Molson, a Montreal brewer and philanthropist, was cremated in nearby Boston (USA). Unable to be cremated in his home city, he left funds in his will to Mount Royal Cemetery for the building of a crematorium there. The trustees' main preoccupation was to ensure that the cemetery's funds, a good proportion of which were already allocated, were not wasted on what could well be a high-risk venture. As the Molson bequest was, by itself, far from sufficient to build and maintain a crematorium, they decided to accept the donation in trust for the future, presumably in the belief that there would eventually be a demand for cremation.

However, the situation soon changed. Possibly inspired by Molson's enthusiasm for cremation, a former friend of his, Sir William Christopher Macdonald, a Montreal entrepreneur and philanthropist, approached the trustees in June 1900 with a formal proposal to build a crematorium. He offered to finance the building of this crematorium entirely from his own funds, thereby assuming all the legal and financial risks. The trustees naturally accepted, and Macdonald immediately started work, charging his architect, Sir Andrew Taylor, with the responsibility of designing the building. As part of the planning process a study group was sent to investigate the operation of cremation in the United States and Britain. As cremation was not provided for in the cemetery's original charter, the trustees had to have an amended charter approved by the Quebec parliament which was, unfortunately, largely Roman Catholic. Predictably, it initially raised strong objections but, eventually, approved the legislation subject to heavy restrictions on the crematorium. However, this delay had not prevented Macdonald from beginning to construct the crematorium before the legislation had been passed.

Macdonald also successfully overcame one of the main restrictions imposed by the Quebec parliament – that of limiting cremation to Protestants – by getting the Canadian federal government in Ottawa to incorporate the crematorium separately from the cemetery thereby making it non-sectarian. When this occurred, in 1903, its 1901 name, 'Mount Royal Crematorium', was changed to 'The Crematorium Limited'. The building, which began working on 18 April 1902, was originally installed with two cremators, situated on one of the chapel walls. In 1981 Donald Roy thought that the cremators' 'very presence, readily available to view, undoubtedly must have left a fearful reminder in people's minds of the cremation about to take place and possibly contributed little, by their ghoulish appearance, to promote the cremation movement' (Roy, 1981: 87). However, he was more complimentary about a substantial and 'impeccably maintained conservatory and greenhouses' containing a selection of flowering plants, which was built to greet mourners on their way into the chapel and 'offered a welcome diversion to the bereaved'.

Although, by the time Canada got its first crematorium there were already 26 operating in the United States, its opening did not appear to tap instantly into a latent market. Six bodies were cremated in its first full year (1903); thereafter numbers rose steadily to 97 in 1910 and then fluctuated between 62 and 77 until 1918 when the 100 mark was broken for the first time (109). A steady upward trend began in 1922 (141 cremations) and ended in 1929 (with 354). After 1930, although the upward trend remained, cremations did not always increase year-on-year: the pre-war peak year was 1937 with 450 cremations. Given the relatively low cremation figures in these early years, it is no surprise that the establishment of Canada's first crematorium did not immediately stimulate similar projects. The second Canadian crematorium did not open until 1913 in Vancouver, British Columbia and it was another 20 years before the third was built, in Toronto, Ontario, in 1933. By then, an 'urgent demand' for cremation had led the trustees to decide that the expense for a crematorium and columbarium was justified. Its first cremation was performed on 21 November 1933 and it had cremated 16 corpses by February 1934.

There seems to have been little involvement of Canadian cremationists in the Cremation Association of North America (CANA), apart from W. Ormiston Roy, a cemetery superintendent in Mount Royal Cemetery, Montreal who was CANA president between 1920 and 1922. Many CANA conventions in the inter-war period did not have a single Canadian delegate, CANA's main activities seeming to be centred around California. Of Canada's two (and, after 1933, three) crematoria at the time, only Montreal was mentioned as being in existence in CANA inter-war annual convention reports, implying a degree of ignorance of what was happening north of the border. However, CANA's focus is understandable given that it had 109 crematoria to Canada's two in 1931. And some US cremationists did have a good grasp of the situation in Canada. For example, in 1934 Hugo

Erichsen, noting that Canada had only three crematoria, asserted that the country needed more and an 'aggressive' type of pro-cremation propaganda.

The 1930s saw the greatest advances so far for cremation in Canada. Fred D. Clark of Toronto Crematorium became the second Canadian vice-presiden of CANA and, in the same year Ormiston Roy represented the country at an international level, as a delegate at the London International Cremation Congress. Roy announced that cremation figures were rising, that cremation was 'growing fast' and that a 'quiet propaganda' was being conducted, which had eliminated many prejudices. By that year, Canada had gained two more crematoria both in British Colombia (one in Barnaby near Vancouver and one in Victoria). Two years later, in 1939, Canada had another two new crematoria, in Calgary, Alberta and St John, New Brunswick, taking the total to seven private crematoria. These developments were reflected in the cremation statistics. During the five year period 1934–38, Canada cremated 36 per cent more bodies than between 1929 and 1933. This was the fifth largest increase in CANA during that period (CANA divided its US states into ten geographical groups, including Canada, Panama and Hawaii).

During the Second World War, James Draper, a funeral director, built New Denver Crematorium in 1943 for the use of Japanese evacuees from the coastal areas of British Columbia. Between 1943 and 1948 it carried out about 300 cremations, almost none of which were of Caucasians. Although the war had no apparent adverse effect on the number of cremations – for example, the Montreal, Victoria and Toronto crematoria all saw steady increases in cremations during the war years – some of the momentum built up in the late 1930s did seem to have dissipated. The ninth Canadian crematorium was Toronto's second, and opened on 21 January 1948. Despite the lack of new crematoria in the later 1940s, the cremation rates still grew.

There were few developments in the Canadian cremation movement in the 1950s, which 'remained fairly inactive' throughout the decade (Roy, 1981: 88). One occurrence was the refurbishment of the first Canadian crematorium in Montreal. Due to their high maintenance costs, the conservatory and greenhouses were demolished and three new oil-fired, 'forced-air ventilation' cremators were installed out-of-sight of mourners. By 1959 Canada cremated just over 3 per cent of its dead, slightly less than the United States' 3.6 per cent.

In the late 1960s and 1970s, the growth of cremation in Canada was, according to Roy, 'phenomenal' (Roy, 1981: 87). By 1963, Canada had a total of 11 crematoria (compared to 247 in the United States), 13 a year later and 17 by 1967. By December 1975 there were 'at least' 31 crematoria throughout Canada, with most provinces having at least one. Ontario, with 16, had the most, including five in Toronto and two each in Ottawa and London. By 1974 there had been over 6000 cremations in Ontario, more than 65 per cent of which had been performed in Toronto's crematoria. Next was Quebec with five crematoria – three in Montreal and two in Quebec City. British Colombia had three crematoria, one each in New Denver, Victoria and Vancouver and Alberta had two (in Calgary and Edmonton). Four other provinces, New Brunswick, Nova Scotia, Manitoba and Saskatchewan, had one crematorium each (in St John, Halifax, Winnipeg and Regina respectively). That year 20 694 cremations were performed in Canada, representing 12 per cent of deaths. By 1976 there were 39 crematoria, 42 by 1977, 47 by 1978 and 54 by 1979. The cremation rate was 14 per cent in 1977 and nearly 17 per cent a year later.

Roy attributed this rapid growth partly to the Roman Catholic Church's change in attitude in 1963. The lifting of the ban gave cremation in Canada 'a healthy impetus', particularly in areas like the Province of Quebec (Roy 1981: 87–88). For example, two cemeteries in Montreal's largest Catholic parishes built crematoria to meet the increased demand in the 1970s. In less than a decade after 1970 the Province of Quebec gained 13 new crematoria; previously it had only had the single crematorium in Montreal.

Yet the picture was not quite as simple as this. In 1971 Nunzio Defoe, executive director of a cemetery in Surrey, British Colombia, conducted a survey of 12 Catholic dioceses in Canada and discovered that none of those responding had issued instructions to their priests on cremation in the eight years since the Vatican had changed its attitude. Moreover, none had a written policy on cremation available either, indicating a resistance to, and discouragement of, cremation on the part of the Catholic Church in Canada. Defoe claimed that the 12 per cent Catholic population of British Colombia, regardless of their age, barely knew about the decrees of their Church (Macdonald, 1975: 4).

Another indication of this resistance outlined by Defoe was the problems that planners encountered when trying to obtain land to build a crematorium. Although there was a great deal of undeveloped land in British Columbia, the only place where planners could build a crematorium was 30 miles from the centre of the metropolitan area, and the 1.5 million plus population within that 30 mile radius was concentrated in the centre. Thus only 10 per cent of this population lived within a 12-mile radius of the proposed crematorium. However, commensurate with Roy's claims, Defoe also noted that, in British Colombia, the number of Catholics cremated had jumped by 1000 per cent in the period 1966–71. Thus, despite the lack of encouragement from their Church, and despite their ignorance of the Church's revised attitude, individual Catholics were still adopting cremation relatively rapidly (Macdonald, 1975: 7,12). In 1972 the six crematoria in British Colombia accounted for over 50 per cent of the cremations in Canada as a whole, and this included around three-quarters of all Roman Catholics cremated in the country.

Another factor aiding the growth of cremation was the increasing availability of the 'package-type pre-manufactured cremation unit', which originated in the United States (Roy, 1981: 87–88). In 1972 Montreal Crematorium, finding that the capacity of its 1950s cremators was too limited and that they did not comply with new air purification laws, bought three 'package-type' units in the United States, transporting them as fully-constructed cremators. All they required on arrival in Montreal was to be connected to gas and electric supplies and the stacks to be put up, making them rapidly operable. The cheapness, availability and relative lack of technical knowledge required to install these units opened up the cremation market to smaller operators and thus allowed cremation to spread more rapidly in both Canada and the United States. Unsurprisingly, most cremators installed in Canada in the 1970s were of this 'package-type'.

By 1981, however, the popularity of 'package-type' cremators was on the wane and Canadian-designed cremators, generally of the 'on-site construction' type were coming into favour.By that year there were a total of 65 crematoria in Canada, most of which were located in the more populated regions. However, the west coast, like the west coast of the United States, carried out the highest proportion of cremations in Canada, a little over 50 per cent, and this was regardless of population density. According to Roy, some groups in more heavily populated areas did not favour cremation. Most notable were those of Italian origin, especially in Montreal and Toronto, who tended to favour burial in a mausoleum rather than cremation despite the extra expense this incurred.

The most popular way of disposing of cremains in 1981 was earth burial in a cemetery. Most cemeteries provided a garden for this purpose, as well as normal graves. Alternatively, there were niches for urns provided in columbaria or walls, which were becoming more numerous. A third, and increasingly common, option was to deposit remains in niches in some of the newer mausoleums. The scattering of ashes, however, remained prohibited, although the depositing of ashes in a common grave provided an alternative (Roy, 1981: 88).

The strong progress made by cremation in Canada from the late 1960s was sustained in the final two decades of the twentieth century. In 1981 approximately 71 crematoria cremated just over 20 per cent of Canada's dead. Again indicative of new trends, in 1987 the Mount Royal Crematorium, Montreal, ordered fully computerized Newton cremators. Two of its American cremators were removed and a third was repositioned to allow for increased capacity. In that year there were 100 crematoria in Canada, and the cremation rate was 27 per cent.

Growth continued throughout the 1990s and, by 2001, Canada had 155 crematoria: 98 in eastern Canada (the provinces of New Brunswick, Newfoundland, Nova Scotia, Ontario, Prince Edward Island and Quebec) and the remaining 57 in western Canada (the provinces of Alberta, British Columbia, Manitoba, North West Territory, Saskatchewan and Yukon Territory). The cremation rate was almost 49 per cent. Once relatively 'backward' in terms of the development of cremation when compared to the United States, Canada's cremation rate is now almost double that of its larger neighbour to the south. **Lewis H. Mates**

References

'ALL' Crematory Co. website at: www.allcrem.com.

Canadian Funeral Service (1964–66), CRE/AO/CA.

'Fernhill Cemetery and Crematorium' (nd), brochure, CRE/F/CA.

Laux, Edward C. (1991), 'Evolution of Cremation in North America', *Pharos*, 57(2): 50–53.

Macdonald, Revd John F. (1975), 'A Decade of Cremation in the Roman Catholic Church', paper presented at the Helsinki ICF Congress, CRE/D4/1975/5.

Roy, Donald, K. (1981), 'Eighty Years of Cremation in Canada', address to the ICF Congress at Berlin, CRE/D4/1981/10, reproduced in *Pharos*, 48(2) 1982: 85–88.

Roy, Donald K. (1991), 'The Past, Present and Future of the International Cremation Federation', *Pharos*, 57(3): 110–111, 115.

'The Toronto Crematorium' (nd, 1934?), brochure, CRE/F/CA.

CANNIBALISM

Cremation has made possible one form of cannibalism, namely the mixing of some cremated remains with a soup for consumption by living kin. The anthropologist Napolean Chagnon's well-known account of the Yanomamo, who live in the forest areas of Brazil and Venezuela, describes their traditional custom of endocannibalism – that is, eating remains of their own people – as opposed to exocannibalism – eating people from outside one's group.

First, a body is cremated in the village clearing. Taking care to put at a distance anything that may be adversely affected by the cremation smoke: it is deemed better, for example, for the children and the sick to leave the village during the cremation. After the cremation the ashes are 'solemnly sifted', and the unburned bones and teeth are collected and placed in a special log in which they are pulverized with a stick. The remains are then transferred into gourds, but the dusty interior of the log is washed out with plantain soup that is then 'solemnly drunk' while the company 'mourn loudly and frantically, rending their hair with their hands and weeping profusely' (Chagnon, 1992: 115). According to Chagnon, the ashes in the gourds are then kept for a future ceremony when more relatives can gather and when more soup is, similarly, drunk. Children's ashes tend to amount to but a small volume and are drunk by the parents only. But, in the case of really important adults, all the ashes are drunk and by many people. Special attention is paid to the remains of an adult killed in warfare. Their remains may be kept for several, or indeed many, years until it is felt that revenge has been achieved over the killers. Only women drink these ashes and may do so, for example, on the night before a revenge killing party sets out to avenge the cremated man. **Douglas J. Davies**

Reference

Chagnon, N.A. (1992), *Yanomamo*, New York: Harcourt Brace College Publishers.

CATHOLIC CHURCH

The Catholic Church, or Roman Catholic Church as it is sometimes designated, has been profoundly significant in the history of cremation. This is especially the case from the later nineteenth century when anti-clerical aspects of ideology, often aligned with freemasonry, most especially in Italy, provoked a strong reaction against, and antipathy towards, cremation at the heart of Catholic doctrine and politics in the Vatican itself. Within that context cremation came to serve as a vehicle of, and for, issues of Church identity, not least because it was not simply a matter of ideology but of a ritual practice that touched the heart of Catholic theology – that of death, and its framing and transcendence. As can be seen from the entry on **France** it was the political aspects of the Revolution in relation to cremation that became a political issue.

Cremation also came to serve as a boundary marker between not only the Catholic Church and other churches but also with secularism. A very similar process of identity marking and boundary maintenance is also evident at the beginning of the twenty-first century in the context of the Greek Orthodox Church in relation to the Greek state and to what it views as the tendency towards secularization in wider social contexts: this is illustrated well by the entry on **Greece**. Although the history of Catholic opposition to cremation, especially from 1886 until its formal acceptance in 1963, emerges in numerous entries, this section focuses on this issue in complementary ways:

1   a broad historical theology of Catholic doctrine relating to death and cremation;
2   the 1886 Declaration on the propriety of cremation;
3   an account of the Italian historical context;
4   a description of the more accommodating Catholic Church in North America;
5   an account of the Catholic Church in Great Britain alongside an account of the Anglican Church of England. **Douglas J. Davies**

See also Argentina; Cremation Society of Great Britain; France; freemasonry in Italy; Greece; Hazeman; Ireland; Monaco.

CREMATION, DEATH AND ROMAN CATHOLICISM

The physical body is important in Roman Catholic thought, for God not only created it and regarded it as good, but Himself took a body when 'the Word became flesh' and so sanctified the human form. Even after death, the body of the individual Christian still possesses a certain dignity. No matter how imperfectly it may have been manifested in the life of the deceased the individual Christian was another Christ, joined to Him in baptism and incorporated into His mystical body: the individual's own body was a temple wherein the Holy Spirit dwelt. It was the body that received the waters of baptism, was anointed with the chrism of confirmation and which physically received the unleavened bread of the Eucharist, which in Catholic belief is very really the body and blood, soul and divinity of Christ. Closely linked with this view of the body is belief in the resurrection of the dead, which was part of the Jewish inheritance of the faith. It is believed that the dead will rise again, albeit transfigured and transformed into a glorious and immortal form. Indeed, by the fifth century the Church commemorated the Assumption, or Dormition, of Mary – the belief that at the end of her life she was privileged to uniquely share in the resurrection when she was taken into heavenly glory body and soul.

Following Jewish practice, early Christians buried the bodies of their dead. However burial was not always accorded to them, and during the early persecutions the Roman authorities would consign the bodies of martyrs to the flames, believing that this would ensure that the body would not rise again at the resurrection of the dead. This was refuted by the apologist Minucius

Felix in the third century, in his dialogue, *Octavius*, where he rejects the idea that cremation made resurrection an impossibility, stating that while they continued the older and better custom of burial, the way in which the corpse was disposed did not affect God's ability to raise the individual concerned back to life.

The canons of various local Church Councils either implicitly or explicitly reaffirmed the normative status of the body being buried: at Braga in 563; various meetings held at Nantes between the seventh and ninth centuries; at Mainz, in 847; and at Tribur, in 865. Throughout the medieval period burial remained the normative practice, with no consideration of any other mortuary practice being raised. The body of the deceased was to remain whole after death, and to this end, in 1300, Pope Boniface VIII announced the *ipso facto* excommunication of anyone who boiled a corpse to separate the flesh from the bones in order to transport them to the individual's place of birth for burial.

It was only in the nineteenth century that the Church began to encounter cremation again. In 1884 a case arose in India, when the bodies of two newly baptized Christians had been cremated according to the local custom, although their parents testified that no pagan ceremonies had been performed in conjunction with the burning of the bodies. This prompted the vicar apostolic of Vizagapatam (the region concerned) to raise the following questions with the Sacred Congregation of Propaganda: If a pagan seeks baptism at the hour of death, should the missionary grant it, even if he believes that the pagan parents of the individual seeking baptism will probably cremate them according to the local custom? In such cases should missionaries object to what is considered a privilege of caste, or may the current practice regarding baptism continue? The answer, which came on 27 September of that year, was: 'Do not approve of cremation, but be passive in the matter and always confer baptism.'

In Europe at the time there was also a growing movement promoting the cremation of the body, and various societies dedicated to promoting the practice began to spring up, which in many cases were associated with masonic lodges. This led to Leo XIII declaring in 1886 that to choose to be cremated was not consistent with the Catholic faith. A decree issued that year forbade Catholics to join cremation societies and declared that it

was unlawful either to demand cremation for one's own body or that of another. Another decree was issued on 15 December, restating this position. On 27 July 1892 the archbishop of Freiburg, in Switzerland, enquired of the Vatican whether it was lawful to cooperate in the cremation of bodies either by command or counsel, or to take part as doctor, official or labourer working in the crematorium. The reply came that it is never allowed, either by command or counsel, to cooperate in the act of cremation. However in the case of 'material cooperation' – that is, aiding only in the physical act – the Church decreed that there was nothing in it which amounted to a rejection of Catholic doctrine. Material cooperation was tolerated so long as it was clear that those involved were not rejecting the teaching of the Church, nor seeking to promote distinctly masonic practices.

Following this line of thought William Devlin's entry for 'Cremation' in *The Catholic Encyclopaedia* of 1913 noted that 'cremation in the majority of cases today is knit up with circumstances that make of it a public profession of irreligion and materialism'. He also noted that, in most cases, it was freemasons who had been involved in securing official approval of this practice from the governments of various countries. However, significantly, he concluded that:

> … there is nothing directly opposed to any dogma of the Church in the practice of cremation, and that, if ever the leaders of this sinister movement so far control the governments of the world as to make this custom universal [referring to the influence of freemasonry], it would not be a lapse in the faith confided to her were she obliged to conform.

The 1917 Code of Canon Law (1203) restated that burial of the body was the norm. Although cremation was not prohibited, it was only allowed in exceptional circumstances, such as large numbers of deaths caused by plague or some other serious disease, when grave public necessity required the bodies to be rapidly disposed of. In individual cases it was still not permitted as it was regarded as a sign of denial of the Christian faith. While the Church continued to state its preference for the burial of the corpse there were subtle shifts in the Church's attitude in the 1960s allowing cremation under certain circumstances. In 1963 an instruction from the Holy Office (Congregation for the Doctrine of the Faith) *Piam et constantem* lifted the penalties that had formerly been attached to the practice, while reiterating the Church's traditional position, stating that:

> Cremation does not affect the soul nor prevent God's omnipotence from restoring the body; neither then, does it in itself include an objective denial of ... dogma. The issue is not therefore an intrinsically evil act, opposed per se to the Christian religion.

This line of thinking was enshrined in *Ordo Exsequiarum* of 1969 (the new funeral rites produced by the post-conciliar liturgy committee after the Second Vatican Council), which made provision for the committal rite to take place either at the graveside or at a crematorium. The requiem mass itself was celebrated in the presence of the body with cremation occurring afterwards. This is still generally the case, although an indult excepting North America was issued in 1997 allowing the requiem mass for the deceased to be performed in the presence of the cremated remains as discussed below in the entry on **North America**.

This subtle shift in the Church's attitude towards cremation was reflected in the 1983 Code of Canon Law which states: 'The Church earnestly recommends that the pious custom of burial be retained; but it does not forbid cremation, unless this is chosen for reasons which are contrary to Christian teaching' (1176§3). This echoes the directive in *Ordo Exsequiarum* that 'Funeral rites are to be granted to those who have chosen cremation, unless there is evidence that their choice was dictated by anti-Christian motives'. The Code prohibits Christian burials, or any other form of prayer, for the departed for 'those who for anti-Christian motives chose that their bodies be cremated', unless they show some sign of repentance before their death. (1184 §1). The Catechism produced in 1994 elucidates the reasons that the Church regards as contrary to the faith when it states that cremation is permitted 'provided that it does not demonstrate a denial of faith in the resurrection of the body' (Catechism 2301).

Although the practice of cremation is now generally allowed in the Church, despite its stated preference for burial, there are certain regulations in force governing cremation in a Christian context. This includes the instruction that a 'worthy vessel' must be used to contain the ashes, and that due care and respect must be ensured in the manner in which the remains are carried and transported, and that the final resting place of the remains should be a worthy one (*Order of Christian Funerals* 416). The scattering of ashes is discouraged, although the bishop has the authority to grant a dispensation if he believes that it will 'contribute to the spiritual good of the faithful' (Canon 87). It is advised that the cremated remains of the body should either be buried or else entombed in a mausoleum or columbarium, where the relatives of the departed will be able to visit. **John Newton**

References

Catholic Church (1969), *Ordo Exsequiarum*.
Catholic Church (1983), *Code of Canon Law*, Canons 1176§3; 1184 §1.
Catholic Church (1997), *Catechism of the Catholic Church*, Paragraph 2301.
Catholic Church (1998), *Order of Christian Funerals*, Appendix 2.
Devlin, W. (1908), 'Cremation', *The Catholic Encyclopaedia* at: http://www.newadvent.org/cathen/04481c.htm.
Thurston, H. (1908), 'Burial, Christian', *The Catholic Encyclopaedia* at: http://www.newadvent.org/cathen/03071a.htm.

THE DECLARATION OF 1886

Here we furnish the Latin original and a broad translation by Dr Marco Conti of a decree of the Congregation of the Inquisition, later called the Holy Office and now the Congregation of the Doctrine of the Faith. (For a wider list of pre-Vatican II rulings on cremation and allied issues see Denziger, 1967). This indicates the problems faced by the Church, not least from freemasons, in the later nineteenth century and its categorical response. **Douglas J. Davies**

DECLARATIO

EDITA A SANCTA ROMANA ET
UNIVERSALI INQUISITIONE
FERIA IV DIE XIX MAII MDCCCLXXXVI
DE HUMANA CORPORA CREMANDI

Non pauci sacrorum Antistites cordatique

christifideles animadvertentes, ab hominibus vel dubiae fidei, vel massonicae sectae addictis magno nisu hodie contendi, ut etnicorum usus de humanis cadaveribus comburendis instauretur; atque in hunc finem speciales etiam societates ab iisdem institui: veriti, ne eorum artibus et cavillationibus fidelium mentes capiantur, et sensim in eis imminuatur et existimatio et reverentia erga christianam constantem et solemnibus ritibus ab Ecclesia consecratam consuetudinem fidelium corpora humandi; ut aliqua certa norma iisdem fidelibus praesto sit, qua sibi a memoratis insidiis caveant; a Suprema S. Rom. et Univ. Inquisitionis Congregatione declarari postularunt:

1.° An licitum sit nomen dare societatibus, quibus propositum est promovere usum comburendi hominum cadavera?

2.° An licitum sit mandare, ut sua aliorumve cadavera comburantur?

Eminentissimi ac Reverendissimi Patres Cardinales in rebus fidei Generales Inquisitores, supra scriptis dubiis serio ac mature perpensis, praehabitoque DD. Consultorum voto, respondendum censuerunt:

Ad I.m Negative; et si agatur de societatibus massonicae sectae filialibus, incurri poenas contra hanc latas.

Ad 2.m Negative.

Factaque de his Sanctissimo Domino Nostro Leoni Papae XIII relatione, Sanctitas Sua resolutiones Eminentissimorum Patrum adprobavit et confirmavit ut opportune instruendos curent christfideles circa detestabilem abusum human corpora cremandi, utque ab eo gregem sibi concreditum totis viribus deterreant.

Ios. Mancini S. R. et Univ. Inquis. Notarius.

(*Leonis XIII Pontificis Maximi Acta*, Vol. VI, Romae, Ex typographia Vaticana, 1887, pp. 72–73.)

DECLARATION

PUBLISHED BY THE HOLY ROMAN AND UNIVERSAL INQUISITION ON THE FOURTH HOLY DAY THE 19TH OF MAY 1886 CONCERNING THE CREMATION OF HUMAN BODIES

Many wise Doctors in sacred matters, who take care of the Christian faithful, have in these days been eagerly pressed with arguments by men of dubious faith, or belonging to Masonic groups, in order that the pagan custom of cremating human corpses might be restored; and also that special societies might be established for this purpose: since they have been afraid lest the minds of the faithful might be enticed by the artifices and sophistries of such individuals, and in them the esteem and respect for the constant Christian use, consecrated by the Church through solemn rituals, of burying the bodies of the faithful might be significantly diminished; in order that the faithful might have at hand a certain precept, through which they are enabled to guard against the dangers mentioned above; they have demanded the Supreme and Holy and Universal Congregation of the Inquisition to declare:

1. Whether it is licit to give a name to societies, whose purpose is to promote the custom of cremating the corpses of men?

2. Whether it is licit to consign one's own or others' corpses to be burned?

The very Distinguished and very Reverend Fathers Cardinals, General Inquisitors in matters concerning the faith, after seriously and opportunely examining the questions described above, and after the vote of the DD. Advisors was given, decided to answer:

First Question: Negative; and if it is a matter of societies affiliated to a masonic group, one will also incur the penalties brought against such a group.

Second Question: Negative.

After a report concerning these questions was presented to the very Holy Pope Leo

XIII, Our Lord, His Holiness approved the decisions of the very Distinguished Fathers and confirmed that they should take care of instructing the faithful in Christ about the detestable impious custom of cremating human bodies, so that they might deter the flock assigned to them with all their strength (from practising such a custom).

Iosephus Mancini (Giuseppe Mancini) S.(anctissimus) R.(everendissimus) and Secretary of the Universal Inquisition.

ITALY

In Italy the Catholic Church, strong in its position of absolute religious predominance, not only exerted notable moral influence on the practices and customs of the Italian population, but also inserted itself in political, juridical and social life. Although, in Europe, the distinction between civil society and religious community began to emerge in the wake of the French Revolution, during the late eighteenth and nineteenth centuries the secularization of Italian society started in earnest in 1861 with the birth of a unified Italian kingdom. The new Italy founded its unity no longer on faith but on civil and state laws. The Catholic Church battled against this, interpreting this territorial and political renewal as a detachment of religion from the civil life of the nation. With the secularization of the civil society, doctors, scientists, politicians and freemasons began to disseminate the concept of cremation.

The Catholic Church was firm in its opposition to the cremation of corpses. It neither refuted the socio-political argument based on health and hygiene, nor the limitations of the urbanization of cemeteries, but pointed out: first the choice of cremation was instigated by freemasonry and had assumed a connotation of an anti-clerical and anti-religious position; second, cremation, even though not expressly prohibited by sacred scripture, was interpreted as a negation of the dogma of the resurrection of the body and the immortality of the soul; and, third, cremation constituted an attack on its monopoly of religious funerals.

Accordingly, on 19 May 1886, in the decree *Quod cadaverum cremationes*, the Catholic Church defended itself against associations that were promoting the right to cremation. The Church, fully realizing that not all of the cremation associations were anticlerical, preferred not to make distinctions and cautioned its congregation to conserve the ancient practice of the solemn rite of the burial. Even when cremation was introduced as freedom of choice in the civil health law no. 5849 of 1988, the Catholic Church continued to resist, assuming an even firmer stance. Its rigid position, based on a subjective presumption of anti-religiosity in the choice of cremation, was officially further emphasized in the Canon Law 1917 (Title XII *De sepultura ecclesiastica*), which ordered the sanction of a deprivation of an ecclesiastical funeral for those who chose cremation. This sanction was applied not only to those who had their bodies or those of others cremated, but also to those who joined cremation associations. So, over the nineteenth and twentieth centuries, in a highly religious Italian society, cremation did not become as widely practised as in other European countries.

In the later twentieth century the Church moderated its position, which was expressed in the instruction *De cadaverum crematione* of 1963 and then reiterated in the new Canon Code of Law 1983. Above all, it advised burial because it more faithfully reflects the mystery and the hope of the resurrection. Cremation is not prohibited, but the prohibition and sanction of the Code of Canon Law 1917 remains for whoever chooses cremation in an anti-religious function or as a rejection of the dogma tied to death. Therefore, even though cremation became interpreted as not contrary to the Christian religion, there is still no encouragement for believers to choose this form of disposal. However, the open position of the Catholic Church today permits reconciling the choice of cremation with a religious funeral. Notwithstanding the expansion of cremation, at the beginning of the twenty-first century the Italian national average of 5 per cent remains low compared to the rest of Europe, and in some places, where religious sentiment is still very strong, the figure is close to 0 per cent. **Anna Salice**

See also Italy.

Reference

Denzinger, Heinrich (ed.) (1967), *Enchiridion symbolorum definitionum et declarationum de rebus fidei et morum*, quod primum edidit Henrich Denzinger; et quod funditus retractavit auxit not ulis ornavit Adolfus Schonmetzer, Editio 34 emendata, Freiburg; Herder.

NORTH AMERICA

The Catholic Church in North America has probably become far more permissive in its attitude towards cremation than in any other part of the world. In 1984 the Canadian Conference of Catholic Bishops petitioned the Congregation for the Doctrine of the Faith and the Congregation for Divine Worship at the Vatican for an indult (that is, an exception to the current Canon Law of the Church) to allow requiem masses to be held in the presence of cremated remains: this was granted on 11 March 1985. Subsequently, a number of bishops in the United States successfully applied for indults for their dioceses, beginning with Bishop Ferrario of Honolulu in 1986. On 6 August 1996 the US National Conference of Catholic Bishops, noting the increasingly frequent practice of cremation, asked the Vatican for 'an indult to permit the diocesan bishop to allow the presence of the cremated remains of a body at the Funeral Liturgy in dioceses of the United States'. The reply from the Congregation for Divine Worship and the Discipline of the Sacraments came on 21 March 1997. It reiterated the provisions of canon law to stress that 'it is greatly to be preferred that the funeral liturgy take place in the presence of the body of the deceased prior to its cremation'. However, permission was granted for funeral liturgies, including the requiem mass, to take place in the presence of cremated remains instead of the natural body. Bishops were authorized to permit such celebrations on a case-by-case basis. In practice this is not always the case. In some dioceses, such as the archdiocese of Newark, the archbishop has delegated the authority to grant permission to the local priest.

The Congregation for Divine Worship called for adaptations of texts in existing liturgical books to be adapted for such situations, rather than developing a whole alternative rite for cremation. New texts were required to be submitted to them for approval and confirmation. They particularly wanted to ensure that the liturgical books 'provide adequately for the possibility of liturgical rites at the place of cremation which are analogous to the traditional rites of burial at the graveside'. Such texts were submitted and duly approved on the Feast of Saint Francis of Assisi (4 October) 1997. These texts now form an appendix to the *Order of Christian Funerals* as published in America.

Finally, the Congregation echoed the bishops' concerns that 'the remains, even cremated, be accorded proper respect as befits the dignity of the human person and of baptised Christians'. To this end, the guidelines of the cemeteries of the archdiocese of Chicago discourage the use of the term 'cremains' to refer to the cremated remains: 'We encourage people to show due respect by always using the term the "cremated remains of the body" or the "cremated remains". In this way, even our words show respect.' It should be noted that the indult applies only to the Latin rite and that the various Eastern rites of the Church, which follow their own liturgical traditions, still do not permit the cremated remains to be present at either the *parastas* (funeral liturgy) or any liturgy held in memorial of the deceased individual.

Although the scattering of ashes is still generally prohibited, bishops may permit this practice when it is thought to be pastorally appropriate. Following the deaths of John F. Kennedy, Jr, Carolyn Bessette Kennedy and Lauren Bessette in a plane crash, their families were granted permission to scatter their ashes on the sea. The scattering was later followed by a memorial mass 'to celebrate' their lives at which no remains were present. Given that the scattering of ashes is still generally prohibited, a common practice is the entombment of the cremated remains in a columbarium. The term comes from the Latin word for 'dovecote' which is seen as appropriate since the dove is the symbol of God's spirit and peace. For example, the Eastern rite Catholic Pro-Cathedral of St Stephen's in Phoenix, Arizona has built a columbarium next to the church, and many Catholic dioceses, such as Chicago, are now making provision for entombment or burial of ashes, denoting the acceptance of pastoral reality of cremation. **John Newton**

References

Catholic Cemeteries of the Archdiocese of Chicago (Catholics and Cremations) at: http://www. cathcemchgo.org/cremation.htm.

Helner, Fran (1997), 'Cremation: New Options for

Catholics', *St Anthony Messenger Catholic Update*, October.

St Stephen's Byzantine Pro-Cathedral (Columbarium) at: http://www. ststephen byzantine.org/Columbarium.htm.

United States Conference of Catholic Bishops Committee on the Liturgy (Appendix to the *Order of Christian Funerals* for Cremation) at: http://www.nccbuscc.org/liturgy/innews/897.htm.

THE UK: CATHOLIC AND ANGLICAN CHURCHES

Until the nineteenth century the Christian tradition favoured burial because its founder, Jesus Christ, was buried in a cave-tomb and his empty tomb underlay the Christian conviction of His resurrection from the dead. Accordingly, burial–resurrection beliefs and motifs became central to Christianity, especially in the Eucharist and in baptisms and funerals while the expectation of bodily resurrection became attached to Christian burial sites which increased in number following Roman Emperor Constantine's conversion to Christianity in 313 AD.

Although earlier opposition to Christianity was expressed, for example, in the burning of the bodies of martyrs, leaders such as Augustine argued that mode of disposal would not affect their prospects of resurrection; on the other hand, in later centuries, Christian churches did sanction the burning of witches and heretics to symbolize social reprobation and the victims' dismal prospects in the afterlife

For 1500 years following the conversion of the Roman Empire, the only challenge to the Christian tradition of burial came from Viking customs of cremation. Heart burial was occasionally permitted during the period of the Crusades. The Reformation of the sixteenth century, whilst it fractured attitudes about the purposes of funerals and the efficacy of rituals on behalf of the dead, did not basically affect attitudes to burial.

From the later eighteenth century, cremation offered itself as a weapon to secularists, anti-Catholics and French revolutionaries. In the UK, during the 1840 cholera epidemic, cremation was suggested on public health grounds. In Germany in the 1850s and in Italy from 1867 anti-Catholic elements promoted cremation in order to challenge the Church's authority. These often included masonic groups, particularly in Italy and the Netherlands. In many European countries, during the 1870s cremation societies and associations were formed, promoting cremation as an alternative to burial on grounds of sanitation and public health. The scandal and growing impracticality of urban burial grounds, made salient by the cholera epidemics, helped bring the cremation alternative to the fore. The first crematoria were built in Italy and England.

Catholic opinion

In 1886 the Catholic Church responded to the anti-Catholic cremationist challenge by forbidding cremation for Catholics: 'The bodies of the faithful must be buried, their cremation is forbidden' (Canon 1203: 1) and 'anyone who has requested that his body should be cremated shall be deprived of ecclesiastical burial unless he has shown signs of repentance before death' (Canon 1240: 1). The Catholic position at this time is well described in *The Dublin Review* of 1890. Only 70 years later the Catholic position was reconsidered and reversed. In the meantime, it could be said that, as cremation became legal in an increasing number of countries, cremationists and Protestant leaders made some common cause. A specific case was Czechoslovakia, one of the new nation states carved out of the break-up of the Catholic Austro-Hungarian Empire after 1918. Catholics were a minority in the new state, and Protestants steadily promoted and adopted cremation as an alternative to the Catholic tradition of burial.

In Prague, the Czechoslovak capital, the International Cremation Federation (ICF) was specifically proposed in 1936 to work for a change of Catholic attitudes. In the changed world situation after the Second World War, the ICF made successive attempts to persuade the Catholic authorities. This culminated in a fresh initiative in 1960 when Pope John XXIII called for a revision of the Code of Canon Law and summoned the Second Vatican Council (Vatican II). The ICF sent letters to 270 Catholic bishops urging them to place the removal of the ban on cremation on the Council's agenda. In May 1964 it was announced that, on 6 July 1963, Pope Paul VI had removed the Vatican ban on cremation; 'the burning of the body, after all, has no effect on the soul, nor does it inhibit Almighty God from re-establishing the body again'. This announcement came as something of a surprise, but its delay will have been due to the death and funeral of Pope John XXIII in June 1963.

Yet while the theological argument for cremation was thus being advanced, the traditional pastoral and political positions were largely retained. The Catholic Church continued to discourage cremation: 'the greatest care must be taken to see that the custom of burying the bodies of the faithful must be preserved intact. Therefore the bishops should see to it that ... Christian people should maintain the present custom of burial and not abandon it unless driven by necessity' (Instruction', 1965: 15–16).

This discouragement was underlined by an instruction that 'the rite of Christian burial and the accompanying public prayers may never be held at the crematorium itself, nor may the cortege be accompanied even without ceremony' ('Instruction', 1965: 15–16). The practical implications of the latter instruction were immediately apparent in England where Monsignor John McDonald had been encouraged by Cardinal Heenan, the archbishop of Westminster, to monitor the development of cremation in England after Vatican II. By 1966 McDonald had persuaded the cardinal to waive this instruction for England, and Catholic clergy were permitted to accompany Catholic funerals to crematoria and conduct Catholic rites there.

Catholic adoption of cremation has not yet been wholehearted worldwide, Japan being among the exceptions. Studies have revealed much official discouragement for Catholics seeking to choose cremation for at least the first 20 years after 1964. In a country like the Netherlands with a mixed population of Protestants and Catholics, the effect of Vatican II's permission was to break the political stalemate and break the burial monopoly. Elsewhere, the rapid advance of secularization has meant that countries once predominantly Catholic but with negligible Protestant minorities, which might otherwise have already ushered in cremation, saw a growth in the practice of cremation during the 1990s. This has particularly been the case with Spain and France.

From 1972 Catholic liturgies developed to provide a range of suitable rites in response to the changing situation. *The Order of Christian Funerals* (1991–) has continued the development. Within England, the moderating stance of Catholics towards cremation was signalled by the

acceptance of Cardinal Cormac Murphy O'Connor, Archbishop of Westminster, to become an honorary vice-president of the Cremation Society of Great Britain in 2002.

Anglican attitudes

The development of Anglican attitudes to cremation may best be indicated in four stages. First, from the Protestant Reformation until *c*.1800 the Church of England, established by law was the dominant Church in England and Wales. The Church owned nearly all burial grounds save for the small number owned by certain Free Church groups such as the Baptists and the Quakers. Anglican clergy presided at all funerals in parish churchyards.

Second, the balance was suddenly altered when the inclusion of Ireland in the British parliament increased the Catholic proportion of the British population to 25 per cent. This meant that between 1800 and 1850 the authority of the Church of England and its traditional responsibilities in both location, liturgy and leadership in disposal were increasingly challenged. Catholics were allowed their own burial grounds in 1829. Private cemetery companies, often promoted by Protestant Dissenters, were successfully established in many of the growing cities. The inadequacy of existing Anglican churchyards to cater for the burial of the dead in an era of rapid urbanization, alongside the new concern for public health stimulated by the cholera epidemics, led to the Burial Acts of the 1850s. These Acts established cemeteries owned by (secular) local government authorities as a charge on the public purse, providing competition to churchyards – a competition which, within a few decades, had successfully provided a secular alternative to the Church's former monopoly.

Third, the traditional mode of disposal by burial was successfully challenged in 1874 when the Cremation Society of Great Britain was founded by Sir Henry Thompson to promote cremation. Anglican opinion was divided from the outset. The bishop of Manchester favoured cremation as an alternative to burial on the grounds of the shortage of land and greater convenience to the poor. The bishop of London, on the contrary, interpreted cremation as a danger to society: it would 'undermine the faith of mankind in the doctrine of the resurrection of the body, and so bring about a most disastrous social revolution' (Wordsworth, 1874). His concern was implicitly about the secularization of death. The Church's traditions and authority in matters of death and funerals would clearly be challenged if crematoria were established outside the Church's control and a mode of disposal were adopted that was unrelated to any Christian tradition or theology.

In 1879 the Cremation Society asked the bishop of Rochester to permit the building of a crematorium on consecrated ground in the privately owned cemetery at New Southgate, north London. Permission was denied. Five years later, the judgment in *Regina* v. *Price* ruled that cremation was not illegal The first legal cremation was carried out in the Cremation Society's crematorium at Woking in 1885.

The Church of England thus had to adapt to this new legislation. The relative merits of burial and cremation were frequently debated at Church Congresses. This debate was facilitated by the rival campaign to Sir Henry's by Francis Seymour Haden and his earth-to-earth burial proposals. Meanwhile, the powers of local authorities had been increased by the Local Government Act 1886. Metropolitan local authorities turned to consider cremation as an economical way of discharging their responsibilities for burial, which had been passed to them in the 1850s legislation. A number of local authorities pressed for crematoria in Private Acts but it was London pressure which led to the passing of the Cremation Act 1902 which formalized the legalisation of cremation in the UK. In face of widespread Anglican opposition to cremation, the British House of Commons agreed that the incumbent of a parish was not obliged to preside at a burial service before, at or after a cremation.

The First World War (1914–18) indirectly stimulated public acceptance of cremation in that it accelerated great changes in popular attitudes to death, bereavement and funerals. After 1918 the public preference for simpler funeral customs, together with both the increasing shortage of land as city suburbs were developed and the increasingly necessary subsidy of burial by public funds all put pressure on local governments to facilitate a shift to cremation. By 1939 nearly 4 per cent of funerals included cremation.

The growing shift in public attitudes to cremation put pressure on the Church to provide official liturgies for cremation services. Attitudes were still divided for, although many bishops had expressed support for cremation, many parish clergy were still suspicious. In 1937 the dean of Westminster drew attention to the absence of any official Anglican liturgies for cremation. This led to a series of debates in the Convocation of Canterbury between 1942 and 1944. Commencing with the need for cremation liturgies, the debates centred on the disposal of cremated remains. For the parish clergy cremation was acceptable only as a prelude to the burial of ashes in consecrated ground. The bishops, on the other hand, accepted cremation as an alternative to burial. They were content to let the service in a crematorium chapel provide the last ritual word and to let ashes be buried or scattered at the crematorium, where the ground had not usually been consecrated. They were reluctant to encourage a second ceremony for the disposal of the ashes on another day.

The bishops' case was accepted. Their 1944 pronouncement included the words, 'For the avoiding of all scruple and doubtfulness it is declared ... that the practice of cremation has no theological significance'. This response thrilled cremationists. They received even greater encouragement when, four weeks after this verdict, the archbishop of Canterbury, Dr William Temple, who had died unexpectedly, was cremated at Charing Crematorium after a service at Canterbury Cathedral. No more powerful symbol of Anglican approval was needed.

The fourth stage commenced with this official Anglican approval. With the popularization of cremation in England and Wales (50 per cent by 1967, and just over 70 per cent by 2004) Anglican clergy have been happy to adapt to the practice of cremation. Today, clergy are reluctant to extend existing churchyards even where, as in the countryside, these are still open, and, it must be said, conducting cremation services has proved more convenient for clergy in a funeral process now dominated by funeral directors and the motor-driven cortege to out-of-town crematoria. Unlike the Lutheran Church in Sweden, the Church of England has shown little enthusiasm for purchasing or operating its own crematoria. With the decline of belief in the resurrection of the body there are few theological reasons sufficiently strongly held to discourage cremation. Douglas Davies (1990) has argued that as the implicit message of cremation is that, after death, the body has no use or future, the popularity of cremation may have contributed to the decline of belief in the resurrection of the body. With hindsight, the Church of England adopted cremation as a practical measure without an adequate formulation of a theology either of cremation, or of the disposal of ashes or of postmortem identity. Only in recent years have scholars revived concern for articulating a theology of cremation, among whom Davies is at the forefront. **Peter Jupp**

See also Argentina; Austria; Cremation Society of Great Britain; Luxembourg; Monaco.

References

Augustine, St (n.d.), *How to Help the Dead*, trans. M. Allies, London: Burns and Oates.

Brown, Peter (1981), *The Cult of the Saints*. London: SCM.

Catholic Church (1991–), *Order of Christian Funerals*.

Daniell, Christopher (1997), *Death and Burial in Medieval England 1066–1550*. London: Routledge.

Davies, Douglas (1990), *Cremation Today and Tomorrow*, Nottingham: Grove Books

The Dublin Review, 1890.

'Instruction on Cremation for Catholics' (1965) (translation from *Acta Apostolica Sedis, Official Commentary*, 24 October 1964, Sr. III, Vol. 5, no. 133), *Pharos*, February: 15–16.

Jupp, Peter (1993), 'The Development of Cremation in England, 1820-1990: A Sociological account', unpublished London PhD thesis.

Jupp, Peter (2005), *From Dust to Ashes: The Growth of Cremation in England*, Basingstoke: Palgrave-Macmillan.

Jupp, Peter and Gittings, Clare (1999), *Death in England: An Illustrated History*, Manchester: Manchester University Press.

Jupp, Peter and Rogers, Tony (eds) (1997), *Interpreting Death: Christian Theology and Pastoral Practice*, London: Cassell.

Parsons, Bryan (2004), *Committed to the Cleansing Flame*, Stroud: Sutton.

Rugg, Julie (1999), 'Nonconformity and the Development of Early Cemeteries in England 1820–1850', *The Journal of the United Reformed Church History Society*, 6(5): 309–21.

Wordsworth, Christopher (1874), 'On the Burning of the Body and on Burial'. A Sermon Preached in Westminster Abbey on Sunday July 5th 1874, London: James Williamson. (As paraphrased in *The Times*, 6 July 1874.)

CELEBRITY

Social change is an intriguing process in many societies. One of the ways through which new ideas are accepted is through well-known or famous people adopting and implementing them for themselves. Practice often brings to abstract debates a reality that becomes undeniable or at least highly persuasive. One feature of the development of modern cremation as a new form of funeral rite has been precisely that of its acceptance by people respected by the public at large. This serves to focus social attitudes and provide a forum for the public to ponder the issue for themselves. Numerous entries refer to cases for many countries. Here we highlight a varied sample of people drawn from different walks of life, countries and times.

An early example was the noted industrialist Alberto Keller who was cremated in Milan in 1878, and the literary Swiss figure Gottfried Keller in Zurich in 1890. In Denmark, in 1901, the poet Sophus Schandorph was cremated followed by the politician Viggo Hørup in 1902, the latter having had a funeral procession through crowd-lined streets. In Britain, around the beginning of the twentieth century the Duchess of Connaught, wife of Albert, the third son of Queen Victoria, was cremated in 1917. Nearly a century later, in 2002, Her Royal Highness The Princess Margaret was cremated in 2002 – a notable event since burial has always been the standard practice of the British Royal Family. More significant in the mid-century was the cremation of William Temple, archbishop of Canterbury, who died unexpectedly in 1944 and whose death followed very shortly after the Church of England's acknowledgement of cremation as a proper practice, even though no distinctive doctrinal meaning was given to it. At the turn of the twenty-first century the very well-known actor Tony Doyle and the tenor Josef Locke were cremated in Ireland, where Catholic tradition had long predominated against cremation. In China political leaders such as Mr Zhou Enlai in 1976 and Mr Deng Xiaoping in 1997 set examples in implementing the government's new policy on cremation. **Douglas J. Davies**

CELESTIS

Celestis, a company that provides for the deposition of cremated remains in space, was incorporated in May 1994. The founders reviewed the earlier (1984) attempt by the Celestis Group, Melbourne, FL to enter the market in conjunction with Space Services Inc. and concluded that conditions were favourable for initiating the Celestis, Inc. venture. With the permission of the remaining founders of the Celestis Group, the company sought and succeeded in trademarking the Celestis name. Celestis was founded by R. Chan Tysor Jr, the current president and chief executive officer. Mr Tysor coordinated the formation of Celestis, Inc., including: assembling the Celestis team; obtaining necessary permits from regulatory agencies including the Department of Banking, the Funeral Service Commission, and the Federal Trade Commission; and securing start-up capital. Since 1994, he has been responsible for the successful implementation of initial phases of financial and business operations of the company.

Charles M. Chafer, co-founder of Celestis, 'is a pioneer on the cutting edge of a new era' wrote the industry-standard publication, *Space News*, in September 1999. Mr Chafer directs marketing, media relations, and strategic partnering for the company. Previously, from 1981–88, Mr Chafer was a vice-president of Space Services Inc. of America (SSI), the company founded by David Hannah Jr and headed by former astronaut Donald K. 'Deke' Slayton that successfully conducted the first privately financed launch into space (Conestoga, 1982). SSI pioneered the space burial concept in 1984 with the Celestis Group, Melbourne, FL. Celestis carefully analysed the US regulatory environment and has taken all necessary measures to comply with relevant provisions. This included obtaining and maintaining a permit from the Texas Department of Banking to sell prepaid funeral service contracts. A variety of other state and federal agencies were contacted during the formation of Celestis, and written responses were obtained from these agencies stating compliance or non-relevance. There are varieties of funeral regulations unique to individual foreign countries, local compliance is required for all Celestis distributors. Distributor agreements require distributor certification of compliance with applicable funeral regulations, and Celestis has engaged the service of experienced legal experts in the funeral industry for instruction on the form and content of these agreements. Currently, Celestis offers four space memorial services. Cremated remains can be launched into space to orbit around the Earth, to fly to the moon, to travel infinitely in deep space, or personal messages can be digitized and transmitted to deep space through a radio astronomy transmission facility. At the time of writing, services offered include the following.

Earthview Service I (Price : US$995)

Introduced in 2002, this places a one-gram sample of the cremated remains into earth orbit. The Celestis memorial satellite eventually re-enters earth's atmosphere and harmlessly vaporizes, blazing like a shooting star in final tribute.

This service provides: (i) launch of a one gram symbolic portion of the cremated remains into earth orbit; (ii) flight capsule imprinted with personal message; (iii) invitation to the launch event; (iv) personalized video of the launch event and memorial ceremony; (v) dedicated virtual memorial of the deceased on the Celestis website; (vi) contribution to the Celestis Foundation; (vii) performance assurance.

Earthview Service II (Price: US$5300)

The Earthview™ Service II launches a symbolic portion of cremated remains (approximately seven grams) into earth orbit and includes the following features: (i) an individual flight capsule imprinted with a 24-character message; (ii) personalized video of the launch event and memorial ceremony; (iii) contribution to the Celestis Foundation; (iv) invitation to a family tour and launch events; (v) performance assurance.

The first Earthview Service launch – the Founders Flight – took place on 21 April 1997 over an Atlantic Ocean site near the Canary Islands. Celestis 01 included the remains of 'Star Trek' creator Gene Roddenberry, 1960s pop icon Timothy Leary and 22 others. Celestis 02 – the Ad Astra Flight – was launched on 10 February 1998 at Vandenberg airforce base, California. On board were the remains of 30 individuals, including some from Japan and the Netherlands. Celestis 03 – the Millennial Flight – was launched on 20 December 1999 from Vandenberg airforce base,

California and included the remains of 36 individuals from several nations, notably the United States, Japan, Germany, China and the Netherlands.

Lunar Service (Price: US$12500)

Celestis lunar missions orbit and/or land on the moon. Celestis pioneered its Lunar Service with the successful launch of NASA's Lunar Prospector mission on 6 January 1998. This mission included a Celestis flight capsule containing the cremains of noted planetary geologist Dr Eugene Shoemaker. When this spacecraft impacted on the moon's surface on 31 July 1999, Dr Shoemaker became the first person 'buried' on the moon.

Voyager Service (Price: US$12500)

Voyager service missions are deep-space missions that provide a virtually infinite journey through space. Celestis's first Voyager mission is scheduled for launch in the fourth quarter of 2005, as a secondary payload aboard an interplanetary spacecraft.

Ad Astra Service (Price: US$299)

The Ad Astra Service proposes to name a star for a loved one and beam a digital memorial message towards that star through a deep-space radio telescope. Messages may include photos, biographies and tributes from family and friends. Customers receive a Certificate of Star Registry and Verification of Transmission accompanying a star map identifying the location of the newly named star. **Christopher Pancheri**

CEMETERIES AND CREMATORIA

To a degree, the relationship between crematoria and cemeteries varies between different societies. Here we consider only the UK, where there is a close relationship between cemeteries and crematoria: indeed, around half of all crematoria are physically located within cemeteries that were often well established before the crematorium was built at the same site. This trend has seen some change over time. Before 1960 most crematoria were built within existing cemeteries. Although local authorities were quick to respond to the demand for cremation facilities – particularly after the Second World War – planning and economic considerations had the potential to restrict development. Building crematoria within cemeteries was a pragmatic

solution: planning requirements had already been fulfilled, and existing landscapes could be adapted as gardens of rest. After 1960 crematoria were far less likely to be established in existing cemeteries: infact, around two-thirds built after that time were laid out as independent sites. This move has reflected the growing interest of private sector concerns in crematoria development. Cemeteries tend not to be profit-making enterprises over the long term because stringent legislation prohibits the re-use of graves, and so income from cemetery land is finite. Consequently, the private sector has seen little advantage in laying out 'joint-purpose' sites.

Recent trends have begun to blur the distinction between cemeteries and crematoria. The cremation movement was promoted, in part, as a modern development that opposed the land wastage involved in full-body burial. Crematoria landscapes were initially envisaged as gardens of remembrance dominated by well-ordered natural features that contrasted with the heavy stone monumentation of cemeteries. Indeed, striking differences remain evident in many of the older cemetery-crematoria. However, concern to maximize income and so offset the losses inherent in cemetery management has led to a diversification in the types of memorial available following full-body burial. Nowadays, local authorities are as likely to offer the option of dedicating a natural feature – such as a tree or a bush – as permit a traditional kerb set and headstone. As at the beginning of the twenty-first century in Britain, some 4 per cent of cemeteries offer the option of woodland burial – a proportion that is likely to increase with time.

However, while cemetery landscapes are becoming more 'naturalized', crematoria landscapes are showing signs of a growing desire to formalize the rituals attached to the disposal of cremated remains. There is an increasing demand for the supply of cremated remains plots, fashioned from stone and with some sort of built marker. Although, in principle these plots are leased, in practice the interment is 'in perpetuity' since once cremated remains are buried, their disturbance requires a special licence from the Home Office. It has been estimated that, in some sites, up to 30 per cent of cremations are interred in a plot of this nature. Over time, if demand for these plots continues to rise, crematoria may encounter land supply problems similar to those facing cemetery managers. **Julie Rugg**

CERTIFICATES AND MEDICAL FORMS (UK)

Before a person can be lawfully buried in England and Wales, their death must be properly registered and a certificate of disposal obtained from the registrar or an order for burial obtained from a coroner. The cause of death also has to have been certified either by a doctor who attended the individual during their final illness (who need not have seen them after their death) or a coroner.

The Cremation Act 1902 and the Cremation Regulations 1930 impose further requirements before a body or part of a body can be cremated. These requirements all converge on the medical referee of a cremation authority, who must be medically qualified, granting an authorization for a cremation to proceed. The Regulations prescribe the contents of the required forms and certificates. Since February 2000, when the Regulations were amended to accommodate the cremation of parts removed from a body during a postmortem examination and not reunited with its host before its host's cremation, there have been parallel forms and certificates for bodies and body parts. In either case, the cremation must be applied for (Form A (body) or Form AA (body parts)) by the executor or nearest surviving relative of the deceased, and if someone other than these the fact that neither of these is applying, this must be explained. Unless an inquest has been opened on the body and the coroner has issued the appropriate certificate (Form E) or the body was donated for anatomical examination under the Anatomy Act 1984 and the anatomist has issued the appropriate certificate (Form H), an application for the cremation of a body must be supported by a either one or two medical certificates. Only one (Form D) is required when a postmortem examination has been performed on the body by a pathologist appointed by the cremation authority. Only one is required (Form B) if the deceased died in a hospital while an inpatient and the doctor providing the certificate was aware of the results of a postmortem examination carried out by a doctor who was neither a relative of the deceased nor a relative or partner of the doctor providing the certificate. In any other case a Form B certificate must be supported by a further certificate (Form C) either from the medical referee or from another doctor who is neither related to the deceased nor a relative or partner of the doctor providing the Form B certificate. Whether or not a Form C certificate is required, the doctor completing a Form B certificate must have both attended the deceased during their final illness and seen their body after their death; and the doctor must not issue such a certificate unless he or she can certify definitely as to the cause of death (a doctor issuing a certificate of the cause of death for the purpose of the registration of a death need certify the cause of death only to the best of his or her knowledge or belief). The doctor who issues a Form C certificate must also have seen the body after death and must have certified a cause of death and that he or she has no reasonable cause to suspect that either the mode or circumstances of the death are such as to require the holding of an inquest into it. An application for the cremation of body parts (Form AA) should usually be supported by a certificate (Form DD) from the hospital or other authority holding the parts that were removed during the postmortem examination. If no such certificate is forthcoming, the medical referee may still permit the cremation to go ahead so long as he or she is satisfied that the parts were removed from the body of a person during a postmortem examination. The medical referee's authorization is given either in Form F (body) or FF (body parts), and details of all cremations must be kept by the cremation authority in a register (Form G (body) or GG (body parts)).

Similar certificates are prescribed for use in Scotland and Northern Ireland by separate regulations. Under government proposals in response to *Death Certification and Investigation in England, Wales and Northern Ireland: The Report of a Fundamental Review* (2003) and the third report of the Shipman Inquiry, *Death Certification and the Investigation of Death by Coroners* (2003), the position of medical referee would disappear, all deaths would be subject to the same three-stage process of investigation and certification, and no further or extra procedures or certificates would be required before a body could be cremated. Such changes cannot be introduced, however, without primary legislation. **Stephen White**

References

Cremation Act 1902.
Cremation Regulations 1930.

The original texts of all Cremation Acts and Regulations relating to the United Kingdom and texts of the Act and Regulations as amended at any time are available on the Web site of the Cremation Society of Great Britain (http://www.cremation.org.uk)

James, D.S. (1995), 'An Examination of the Medical Aspects of Cremation Certification: Are the Medical Certificates Required under the Cremation Act Effective or Necessary?', *Medical Law International*, 2: 51–70.

White, Stephen (2000), 'Body Parts: Cremation Regulations Amended', *New Law Journal*, 150: 654–655, 709.

CHINA

ANCIENT CREMATION PRACTICE

In China, cremation can be dated from the New Stone Age, 8000–10 000 years ago. In 1945 archaeologists found three large, grey gallipots in a tomb in the prehistoric Siwa relics in Gansu province, one of which contained the bone ashes of cremated human bodies. On 24 July 1987 the remains of burned human bones, gallipots and stone spinning wheels that had been buried together were found in the Shipeng tombs of Shuangfang, Xinjin County, eastern Liaoning Province. These are the earliest known cases of cremation in China. According to the Book of Mo-tse, 'there exists a state known as Yiqu in the west of the Qin Kingdom, where people collect firewood to cremate their family members after their deaths'. Yiqu was situated around today's Qinghai and Gansu provinces in China.

For centuries the Chinese people were influenced by the ancient tradition of ancestor worship, honouring their ancestors as part of their religion, showing filial piety in behaviour and through funeral ceremonies. Confucius also paid much attention to the role of filial piety in funeral and interment practices; as the *Analects* express it, 'Handling funerals carefully and mourning the dead will cultivate virtue in the people'. Extravagant funerals that also indicated the deceased's social position became customary with the Han people, living in middle China. They valued inhumation and regarded cremation as a heresy. However, by the Tang Dynasty (618–907 AD), the cremation customs that had existed among some minorities were adopted by Han people in remote areas such as Dunhuang, then an important fort on the Silk Road. At the same time, with the spread of Buddhism, ancient Indian Buddhist cremation funeral practices, in which bodies were burned on a firewood pyre, also became widely accepted amongst Buddhists in middle China. One fundamental Buddhist idea argues that living implies death, and death embodies living.

During the periods of the Liao and Kin and Song Dynasties (960–1279 AD) this kind of cremation funeral, as opposed to Confucian interment ceremonies, peaked, especially in Bianjing, the capital of the North Song Dynasty, and in the Hedong region. During the South Song Dynasty, the custom of cremation rapidly spread from middle China to the south, becoming predominant there. Cremation became traditional, especially in south-eastern China. During the Song Dynasty, places for burning corpses were built in many areas in southern China: they were the country's earliest crematoria. During the Yuan Dynasty (1279–1368 AD), the custom that '[t]he corpses of the deceased are burnt up' remained. According to Marco Polo, the famous Italian traveller, cremation was in vogue throughout a large area, including Ningxia, Sichuan, Shandong, Jiangsu, Zhejiang, Hubei, Anhui and Fujian. Dadu, the capital of the Yuan Dynasty, was among the areas where cremation was most widely accepted.

At the beginning the Ming Dynasty (1368–1644 AD), the Song and Yuan Dynasties' tradition of cremation still remained. However, in the third year of the Hongwu regime, the emperor Zhu Yuanzhang released an edict stating that each prefecture and county had to define burial grounds, and cremations and water burials were now illegal. This was because Ming rulers believed that the dead could only achieve quiet rest by being buried. The Ming Dynasty's 'Rules of Ceremonies' laws meant that those obeying the desire of the deceased to be cremated or thrown into waters were subject to a 100-blow stick beating. This prohibition of cremation was continued by the Qing Dynasty (1644–1911 AD) whose Ceremonial Rules stipulated that cremations were not suitable for subjects belonging to the 'Eight Banners', with the exception of those who were poor and living far away and who therefore could not be brought home after their deaths. Those who broke the rule were punished accordingly. Because of this vigorous prohibition by the rulers, the tradition of cremation was discontinued. Due to a shortage of farmland, however, cremation remained popular in some economically developed areas, such as that around Suzhou. Although the authorities repeatedly gave orders to forbid cremations, they were ignored. **Liu Fengming**

DEVELOPMENTS IN THE TWENTIETH CENTURY

Because of the dominance of burial, with cremation restricted to only a few foreign nationals, Buddhists and some with a distinctive vision, modern cremation advanced only when Western people came to China. At the beginning of the twentieth century, a cemetery for Japanese nationals at the Western Baoxing Road, Shanghai added a cremation facility at the western part of the cemetery that was, later, taken over by the local government and renamed the Western Baoxing Road Cemetery. During the same period, a charity set up a crematorium in Beixin especially for corpses found in the streets. Cremators were also installed in the Fazang Temple in the Southern Road 1 of Zhongshan Roads, with one urn-shaped cremator decorated with a water lily seat and another in which coffins could be cremated together with corpses. This facility mainly served Buddhists. Americans opened the first funeral room in 1925 and the first coal-fired crematorium in Jing'an Temple in Shanghai in 1927. The first crematorium in Dalian was set up by Japanese in the same year. Crematoria also became available to serve foreigners in Beijing in the same period. In Shanghai, cremation businesses were concentrated at the Jing'an Temple and focused on 'individual cremation', as opposed to the 'collective cremation' of the unidentified dead found in public places and collected by charities.

Cremation in a real sense only came after the founding of the People's Republic of China in 1949. With the establishment of 'New China', the Communist Party of China and the People's Governments launched a nationwide campaign challenging traditions in an attempt to change popular custom. This was prompted by China's large population, inadequate availability of farmland for burial and strong popular beliefs. In 1950 the Haihui Temple Crematorium was set up, with governmental approval, in Haihui Temple, Shanghai. The Datong and Hudong Cemeteries were incorporated into a Datong Crematorium Company Limited in 1951, and

two cremators were installed in the Longhua Cemetery for the specific disposal of corpses found in streets. A greater impetus came at a working conference of the Central Committee of the Communist Party on 27 April 1956, when a secretary presented a 'proposal for cremations' to Chairman Mao Zedong. It read:

> It is natural for the mortal to die. The major interment measures in China and other nations of the world are inhumation and cremation, with the former more popular. But inhumation consumes farmlands and woods, without mentioning that luxurious funeral ceremonies held by the ruling classes of dynasties in China too often caused family bankruptcies when they chose interments. Cremations, needing no farmlands nor abundant wood for coffins, can save expenditure without hindering the mourning of the dead … . Therefore, we suggest that some people, especially leaders in national institutions, set an example by choosing cremation of their own will as their funeral after their death … .

Chairman Mao pronounced his agreement with this suggestion and signed his name on the proposal. Then, more than 160 people, including Zhu De, Peng Dehuai, Liu Shaoqi, Zhou Enlai, Pen Zhen, Dong Biwu and Deng Xiaoping, signed the proposal paper. On hearing this news, those who were absent also expressed their support for cremation. This marked the real initiation of the reform of funerals and interments against a 1000-year long tradition; for China, this was the first 'revolutionary' transformation. From the 1950s, the Communist Party set an example in its advocacy of cremation in an endeavour to spread the practice throughout the whole society. Mr Zhou Enlai, the first premier of New China, was not only cremated after his death in 1976, but also had his ashes scattered throughout the country. In 1997 the second-generation leader of the Communist Party of China, Mr Deng Xiaoping, died. He set an example by being cremated and also had his ashes scattered throughout the motherland he deeply loved.

To facilitate the change from inhumation to cremation, new crematoria needed to be constructed. The Beijing Babaoshan crematorium was built in 1957 and opened the following year in the Shijingshan District of the capital under the jurisdiction of the Beijing Bureau of Civil Affairs. It became well known throughout the country because it undertook the cremation and storage of the remains of the Communist Party's national leaders and social celebrities. The Dongjiao Crematorium was established soon after, also in Beijing. Cremation was promoted mainly in large and medium-sized cities and nearly 100 crematoria were established between 1956 and 1965. In Shanghai, for example, several promotional campaigns for cremation were launched and, from the mid-1960s, crematoria were set up in succession in its suburban areas (such as Nanhui, Songjiang, Baoshan, Chongming, Jinshan, Qingpu and Fengxian). The Longhua and the Western Baoxing Road Crematoria were also expanded. The number of these kinds of crematorium greatly increased in the late 1960s and throughout the 1970s: by 1978, there were 1100 crematoria, with cremation and funeral services also spreading into rural areas. However, restricted by economic conditions, practical techniques and lack of social development, the first modern crematoria in China were poor, crude and inconvenient to use. By the end of 1980 there were 1183 crematoria and 2508 cremators in the whole country. Most of the presently existing funeral rooms were constructed at that time – a time of hardship for China's funeral industry.

With reforms leading to an opening towards the outside world, increasing attention began to be paid to environmental protection and land resources, with the idea of 'sustainable development' becoming more profoundly understood. In February 1985 the State Council produced 'The Provisional Regulations on the Management of Funerals and Interments', as the first administrative regulation regarding funerals and interments implemented by the People's Republic of China. It declared that 'cremations should be spread designedly and actively, and inhumations should be reformed so as to reject superstitious funeral customs and advocate frugal and reasonable ones'. This regulation specified the matter and goal for funerals and interments.

The 'Administrative Rules of Funerals and Interments' of July 1997 stated that cremation should be practised by preference over inhumation to save farmland, to discontinue undesirable customs concerning funerals and interments, and to advocate frugal and dignified funerals. To effect these reforms, the whole country speeded up construction of the funeral service establishment. For example, between 1997 and 2002, the Beijing municipal authority invested 70 million yuan in developing the Babaoshan funeral facilities with the construction of a main ceremonial building and a large parking place, the expansion of the cremation shop and the purchase of new cremators. This scheme operates a dozen business sections, more than 200 morticians, 50 hearses and 15 cremators, annually cremating an average of 18 000 corpses. Its services include the reception of corpses, funeral dressing, mourning sites and services for relatives, cremation and facilities for keeping cremated remains and the sale of funereal utensils such as boxes for remains and wreaths.

In Shanghai, early cremators were mostly coal-fired, gas and diesel oil being employed later. With the development of a cremation industry in China and the improvement of equipment, advanced cremation facilities have become available. At the Yishan funeral room, for example, there are 24 cremators including two automatic trolley ones (since 1985 all crematoria have been renamed 'funeral rooms'). The advanced control systems of these cremators ensure cremation quality and satisfy the state's demand for environmental protection. At present, there are a total of 15 funeral rooms in Shanghai, among which the Yishan funeral room performs the largest number of cremations. Some 12 of these funeral rooms are located in suburban areas. In addition to cremation facilities, the funeral rooms in Shanghai also have halls for the relatives of the dead to hold mourning and funeral ceremonies. Funeral rooms also have the capacity to handle corpses and supply a variety of goods.

Thanks to the suggestions, policies and activities of governments at all levels, the rate of cremation is soaring, reaching almost 100 per cent in the large and medium-sized cities along the coasts, especially the economically developed areas along the north-eastern coast. Now, cremation has spread to eight provinces and municipalities directly under the jurisdiction of the central government, and in other large cities cremation has become the people's choice. By the beginning of the twenty-first century there were some 1500 funeral rooms, 4300 sets of cremating facilities, more than 3000 urban and township public cemeteries and 40 000 morticians supported by a new special service industry. In 2002, 4.152 million bodies were cremated throughout China – a cremation rate of almost 51 per cent. **Zhu Jinlong, Liu Fengming, Zuo Yongren, Gao Yueling, Zhang Hongchang and Li Jian**

MODERN ADMINISTRATION OF FUNERALS AND INTERMENTS

The administration on funerals and interments is undertaken by the government's Ministry of Civil Affairs of the State Council. Civil Affairs branches of local government – above county level – take responsibility for the administration of their jurisdiction. Their main task is to advocate and implement the reform of funerals and interments, and to manage funeral and interment facilities, the disposal of bodies, funeral activities and appliances. This is achieved through various funeral service establishments, especially funeral parlours, crematoria, cremains halls, public burial grounds and mortuary parlours.

The goal of funeral reform has been to foster the practice of cremation, including both the cremation of bodies and arrangements for remains. Since 1956, when the central government began to advocate cremation, local governments have undertaken effective measures to progress the spread of cremation, with the result that cremation rates have been increasing year-by-year. In comparison with traditional inhumation, cremation preserves farm and woodland and helps boost economic development. The advocacy of frugal and dignified funerals helps reduce people's expenditure, and the reform of funeral customs is increasingly welcomed. The 'Administrative Rules of Funerals and Interments', issued and enforced in July 1997, included directions for the partition of areas for cremation and inhumation, stipulating that cremation should be carried out in areas of greater population where there is less farmland and more convenient transportation. Inhumation is allowed wherever cremation is inconvenient: these areas are determined by provincial governments and municipalities and reported by the Civil Affairs branches to the Ministry of Civil Affairs of the State Council for documentation.

Ethnic minorities

As China is a country of multiple ethnic groups, manners and customs of funerals and interments vary. In the regulations of funerals and interments the government provides that the customs of minorities should be respected. This is particularly manifest in the guarantee of their freedom to keep or reform their funeral customs without external intervention. For instance, it is particularly stipulated that the inhumation tradition of the ten minorities of the Hui, the Uygur, the Kazak, the Kirgiz, the Ozbek, the Tajik, the Tatar, the Salar, the Dongxiang and the Baoan should be respected, and that those willing to practise cremation shall not receive outside interference from anyone.

Cremation morticians

In 1989 'cremation morticians', the technical workers engaged in the operation and control of cremation equipment, became an independent type of work included in the national technical grading standards for workers. They are graded in three levels: the primary, the medium and the superior. Each technical grading has a specific standard both of theoretical knowledge and of skills, and requires a period of learning and practice, each grade change taking over two years. Others included in technical grading were funeral carriers, dressers, antisepsis workers, ceremonial attendants and burial ground attendants. Through the establishment of types of funeral work, the personnel quality, management level and service of funereal service institutions have been obviously enhanced, their social profiles effectively improved, and the social statuses of funeral workers dignified.

The cremation of corpses

The cremation of corpses in China follows strict requirements in terms of administration and operations. First, the cremators used have to meet the technical standards regulated by the state, and the polluting discharges must not exceed set limits. Cremation facilities have to be sufficient to cope with the number of dead requiring cremation at peak times. The use of industrial conveyer belts or hanging chains for carrying corpses is rigorously prohibited. Second, operating morticians have to be technically qualified above the primary level and possess a 'professional morality', strictly following the 'Rules of Morticians' and working rigidly according to operational specifications. Third, certificates of death and cancellation of registered permanent residences must be carefully checked to ensure the correct identification of corpses, and should carry signatures of the relatives of the deceased. Cremation without certificates is rigorously prohibited so as to prevent the cremation of the wrong bodies. Fourth, time limits for cremations must be strictly followed. Generally, corpses should be cremated within 72 hours and those who died from infectious diseases within 24 hours. Even in some special cases, corpses should not kept longer than 90 days. The principle of cremating a single corpse at a time, thus ensuring that the cremains of different corpses do not mix, must be strictly followed. No mixture of the cremains of different corpses is allowed. The quality of cremations should be ensured, and the problem of poor-quality cremains, perhaps caused by inadequate combustion due to a lack of fuel, be prevented.

Cremation discharge standards

Since the very beginning of the development of modern cremation, the Chinese government has paid much attention to its polluting effects, especially those of dust and smell which affect both the natural environment and people's psychological condition. To overcome the pollution from cremation discharges, the authorities have strengthened research on the one hand and adopted new techniques and new materials to produce new cremating facilities on the other. In terms of fuel, the cremating equipment can be classified into three types: coal-, oil- and gas-fired. Oil-fired cremators are the most numerous and most widely used. In order to strengthen the administration of the production and uses of oil cremators, the Ministry of Civil Affairs issued the 'Common Technical Terms for Oil Cremators' in 1985, providing limits for pollution discharges and prohibiting the production of cremators that exceed these limits. With the improvement of cremators, China imposed higher national standards on discharges from crematoria in a document entitled 'Limitations and Testing Measures of Pollution Discharges from Oil Cremators' in 1992. These standards list the limits for a variety of pollution discharges from oil cremators, defining the limits of pollution in cremating 'shops' and the total pollution

discharge limits from chimneys, as well as a set of specific three-level standards for the density limits of smoke from chimneys. They also specified the limits both of noise intensities generated by cremators and of odour indexes in 'cremating shops'. The limits are now all based on the highest peaks of pollution, rather than on averages as in the past. This provides a strict control on both the intensities and total volumes of pollution discharges.

Principles in handling bodies

In China the handling of bodies is also subject to regulation. Those bodies that need to be transported have to receive the technical treatment necessary to assure sanitation and prevent pollution. Apart from some special cases, the transportation of bodies has to be undertaken by funeral rooms; transportation by others is subject to special permission. Bodies should be transported by means of special hearses. For those who die distant from their home town, their bodies should be, in principle, dealt with as soon as possible and at the nearest practical place. In special cases where bodies have to be transported to other places, relatives have to make applications to funereal administration institutions above county level. The funeral administration institutions then go through corpse transportation procedures in line with the Death and Funereal Certificate of Residents issued by health-care and public security institutions. Then the bodies are transported with special hearses and cremated and buried in accordance with the relevant local regulations for funerals and interments. The corpses of people who have died from serious infectious diseases are quarantined. Relatives must be supervised and urged to report to funeral administration institutions within 24 hours to arrange disposal. Those who attempt to transport a corpse without a death certificate from a hospital will be refused transportation by sections of the railway, communications or airlines. Equally, public security institutions have the right to prohibit the transportation of corpses if those involved cancel certificates of registered permanent residence issued by public security institutions or certificates of corpse transportation issued by funeral administration institutions.

Before cremation, death certificates are issued by medical institutions appointed by public security institutions or health-care administrative institutions. All cremations are conducted in crematories or funeral rooms possessing cremating facilities. In areas for inhumation, no burials or tombs are allowed in any places outside urban cemeteries or rural public burial grounds. **Zhang Hongchang, Li Jian, Zuo Yongren and Gao Yueling**

See also ashes – China.

OPERATING AND ARCHITECTURAL STANDARDS

From the 1980s to the late 1990s, the Chinese funeral industry entered into a period of steady progress with economic and social development and the speeding up of reform and openness. In 1990 the Civil Affairs Department of the People's Republic of China issued 'Grading Standards of Funeral Homes' aimed at boosting the construction and reconstruction of funeral homes to meet the demands for funeral services. These standards specified the goals of relieving sorrow among relatives of the deceased, aiding the expression of emotions and consoling their minds. The standards set out strict requirements for the natural and social environments, communication and transport conditions and general layout of the site. Other points cover the forestation and beautification of the settings for funeral homes and the cremating facilities such as hearses, video and audio facilities, supervision, fire facilities and other funeral services.

The 'Criteria for the Architectural Design of Funeral Homes', implemented at the beginning of 2000, brought in still more rigorous requirements for the architecture of funeral homes, directing the construction of crematoria to develop to a new, higher, level and implementing the basic scientific and technological developments. Changes included architectural designs for the construction, reconstruction and expansion of funeral homes in cities and towns. The implementation of these criteria marked the first time that named functions of each aspect of funeral facilities in China have been specified, including the architectural type and orientation of funeral homes. This involved a specialized combination of civil services and industrial process, including issues of ceremony, cremation, cremains, water supply and drainage, heating, air-conditioning, ventilation, communications, electricity,

lighting, sanitary protection and technical guarantees against kinds of pollution. The protection and preservation of cremated remains is accorded special importance. **Gao Yueling and Zuo Yongren**

CHOLERA AND TYPHOID

Cholera and typhoid fever were two devastating illnesses that prompted numerous societies to consider cremation, in association with issues of quarantine and public health, often prior to the institution of modern cremation and, often, quite regardless of popular attitudes towards cremation. Numerous entries deal with these conditions. **Douglas J. Davies**

See Argentina; Cameron; Denmark; Germany; Shelley; Switzerland.

CHURCH OF ENGLAND

See Catholic Church – The UK: Catholic and Anglican Churches.

CINERARIA

A cinerarium is a container for cremated remains and its Latin name derives from their widespread use in Roman times. Urns and pots have been used as containers for such remains since the British Bronze Age to modern times. In some countries, such as Spain, ancient versions took a strong artistic form and, in the twenty-first century too, this long-standing custom persists, with a great variety of containers for ashes being marketed in artistic or even custom-made designs that reflect something of the character of the individual concerned. In the USA some cineraria are available that have provision for the inclusion of a photograph of the dead. **Douglas J. Davies**

See also archaeology of Britain; Italy; Spain; urns; USA.

CLASS

The issue of social class and caste is important in association with cremation at several levels. In numerous entries on the history of cremation movements it is apparent that professional people and intellectuals were much involved with advocating cremation in the nineteenth and early twentieth centuries. Only later did working-class groups become involved with the practice. Social class differences were sometimes important in the development of cremation movements aligned with labour or union groups, as in Austria, but class issues were also evident in Portugal and Norway as well as in Russia where the custom of burial has been revived amongst the post-communist new-rich but cremation remains an economic necessity for many others. The economic aspect of class is also evident in Spain as one element in the extraordinarily speedy adoption of cremation in that country.

Historically, lower-class and lower-caste groups have often been allocated the task of dealing with the dead and in the conducting of traditional cremations or the burning of those deemed anti-social or dangerous as the entry on **vampires** shows. The sati tradition of (the burning of widows) in India also shows a clear caste element. **Douglas J. Davies**

See also Austrian cremation societies; Norway; Portugal; Russia and the USSR; Sati; Spain; vampires; Widlar.

CLOISTERS

Planned originally as quadrangles surrounded by roofed or vaulted passages, cloisters connected the monastic church with the domestic parts of a monastery. They have now however become an essential feature of crematoria, either leading to, or including, the columbarium, which accommodates the urns for the ashes. During the course of the twentieth century, as columbaria gave way to the broadcast scattering of ashes, so, additionally or alternatively, cloisters began to provide space for plaques or memorials bearing the names of the dead, and cloisters are often divided into bays for this purpose. However, it was soon recognized that the popularity of this form of memorialization might result in interminable extensions of cloisters at the expense of land reserved for gardens of remembrance. The installation of recordia, normally constructed from marble with a suitable text and inscription and room beneath for small removable pieces of stone or marble on which names and dates may be inscribed, have often prevented this problem from arising.

Architect Ernest George made a special study of cloisters in Italy before designing a range at Golders Green Crematorium in 1901 (completed in 1913). He was influenced by the Campo Santo, the medieval cloister built on the site of a Roman graveyard, which, together with the cathedral and baptistery, lay at the heart of the city of Pisa. It was here, in the Campo Santo, that the deaths of the citizens of Pisa were commemorated. The symmetrical placing of glazed *della Robbia*-inspired tablets at the top of each bay at Golders Green created a Renaissance feeling to the whole.

Cloisters came to form an important feature of many inter-war British crematoria, accommodating the display of floral tributes in addition to more permanent memorials, notable examples being Leeds, Cottingley (1938), which was designed in a Romanesque style, and the Italianate Mortlake Crematorium (1939), with its well-judged groupings and beautiful cloisters with discrete brick detailing. A more modern interpretation appears at Oxford (1935), designed by Harold R.W. Orr. Sir Guy Dawber designed Enfield (1936) with a main group of buildings consisting of two chapels, the cloister (which is also the main entrance) and two wings. Those planning and building crematoria in Britain after the Second World War were advised by architect J. Seaton Dahl that, in general, cloisters were best placed to form three sides of a square on the south side of the chapel, often around a formal garden, with possibly a lily pond or some other central feature. The fourth side should overlook the garden of remembrance on which the ashes are scattered (Dahl, 1945: 114).

Access from the cloisters is generally obtained either directly from the chapel or possibly from the corridor leading to the waiting room from the entrance vestibule. Many crematoria follow this arrangement, whether classical or modern in style. In 1964 architect Maxwell Fry, in his paper to the Cremation Society of Great Britain, proposed that cloisters might play a more direct role in memorializing the dead in the heart of the post-war British new towns. He argued for something that might correspond to the Campo Santo in Pisa. Such a cloister, decorated with carving, paintings and sculpture, could be a beautiful construction – a reminder of death near the market places of our cities (Fry, 1964: 42–43). However, this idea was never adopted.

In addition, cloisters afford visitors shade

from the sun and protection from the wind and rain. Linn Park Crematorium in Glasgow (1962), was designed with dramatic cantilevered walkways to ensure the comfort of mourners in the most adverse weather conditions, providing, arguably, one of the most modern interpretations of cloisters. Together with columbaria and pergolas, cloisters play an important part in linking crematorium buildings with gardens of remembrance and the wider landscape beyond. **Hilary Grainger**

See also architecture; Fry; Golders Green Crematorium.

References

Dahl, J.L. Seaton (1945), 'The Ideal Crematorium', in P.M. Jones (ed.), *Cremation in Britain*, London: Pharos.

Fry, E. Maxwell (1964), 'The Design of Modern Crematoria', *Report of the Proceedings – Annual Cremation Conference, Bournemouth, 23–25 June 1964*, London: The Cremation Society, 39–44.

Grainger, H.J. (2000), '"Distressingly Banal": The Architecture of Early British Crematoria', *Pharos*, 66(1): 42–48.

Grainger, H.J. (2001), '"The Removal of Mournful Suggestions … A Fresh Start". The Architecture of British Interwar Crematoria', *Pharos*, 67(1): 3–11.

COFFINS

The use of coffins in relation to cremation has varied in several ways, especially in terms of their composition in relation to exhaust gases. Here a detailed example is drawn from China. **Douglas J. Davies**

See also ecology; Norway.

CHINA: CREMATING COFFINS

To improve the sanitary standards of cremations and to show respect to the deceased, a new measure to cremate bodies in coffins has been implemented in many cities and rural areas in China. This is a change from the mid-1990s when the practice was to feed exposed corpses with no coffin. (Inhumation in wooden coffins had been the traditional form of funeral in China, and had resulted in a high consumption of timber.) Nowadays, to save resources, most coffins used in cremations are made from regenerated or fast-growing materials, such as composite boards of bamboo, Paulownia or, in most cases, paper materials. Corrugated paper or honeycomb paper made from paper pulp have a certain density and can bear the weight required. Honeycomb paper, in particular, both saves materials and is light in weight because of its novel structure. To prevent harmful smoke generated by paper coffins coagulating within the cremator, the bonding used in honeycomb paper has been improved to the desired effect.

The shapes of these coffins follow customers' wishes, with traditional Chinese coffins having bigger and thicker heads and smaller ends. Western-style coffins are more hexagonal or cubed with handles. Although made of the same ecological materials, these coffins – known as environmental coffins – have the same attractive appearance as wooden coffins due to elaborate design and processing. They are economical to produce and are harmless in the cremation process. **Zhu Jinlong**

COLETTI, FERDINANDO

Dr Ferdinando Coletti first opened the debate on cremation in Italy. A moderate liberal and an active patriot in the 1848 Veneto rising, he was the most important exponent of the Italian medical–hygienist movement, as well as being Professor of pharmacology and rector of the University of Padua. Born in Tai di Cadore (Belluno) on 17 August 1819, he graduated in medicine and surgery at the University of Padua in 1845 and, until 1848, was a voluntary assistant in the Department of General Pathology, headed by Professor Stéer. In 1849 he refused the post of head of Department of Pathology in protest against the Austrian government and pursued a private medical practice while, concurrently, engaging in scientific research in collaboration with the Brescian pathologist Giacomini, building upon the work of the pathologist Biaggi. In 1858 Coletti founded and directed the *Gazzetta Medica Italiana delle Province Venete* (*Italian Medical Gazette for the Province of Veneto*). From 1866 to 1880 he was a member of the Communal Council of Padua (*Consiglio Comunale di Padova*), and leader of the Veneto Liberal Union (*Unione Liberale Veneta*), advocating the protection of workers' conditions in the context of burgeoning industrialization. In 1875 he was nominated president of the commission inquiring into 'the industrial work of children and women', supporting the need to improve conditions in the factories, raising salaries and reducing working hours.

Among many posts held between 1866 and 1880 were the presidencies of the Padova Academy of Science, Letters and Art (*Accademia di Scienze Lettere ed Arti di Padova*), of the Italian Medical Academy (*Accademia Medica Italiana*) and of the Padovan Comittee for Marine Hospices (*Comitato Padovano per gli Ospizi Marini*). As rector of the University of Padua he served on the sanitary commissions in the province and city of Padua. As professor of medicine and therapeutics in the University of Padua from 1866, he concentrated his research on the areas of pharmacology (*Previous Lessons of the Pharmacological Course; New Military Pharmacopoeia*) and toxicology (*About Arsenic; The Effects of Salt in Chemistry; The Beneficial Cure According to the Toxicological School*). We should also recall his hygienist study in De l'Hygiène Publique en Italie (*About Public Hygiene in Italy*) and a work on the professional ethics of doctors and the behaviour of patients.

Ferdinando Coletti is considered to be a pioneer in cremation as he was the first to open the debate in Italy with an important conference on the topic in 1857. His ideas – underscored by four principles of hygiene, morality, religion and economics – were evident in the following decades in debates on all aspects of the subject. Moreover, Coletti argued that cremation should belong to public institutions – that each municipality or town should build its own crematorium. After his death on 27 February 1881, Coletti's body was cremated in the Cremation Temple of Milan and the ashes were deposited in the Cimitero Maggiore di Padova. He gave his name to the Cremation Society that was constituted in Padua on 31 August 1881. **Walter Tucci**

See also Italy.

References

Cimegotto, C. (1941), *Ferdinando Coletti. Patriotta e scienziato*, Feltre: Stabilimento grafico 'Panfilo Castaldi'.

Conti, F. (1998), *Aspetti culturali e dimensione associativa*, in *La morte laica*. Vol. I. *Storia della cremazione in Italia (1880–1920)*, Torino: Paravia Scriptorium, 3–6.

Gazzetta Medica Italiana. Province Venete, 9, 1866.

Pogliano, C. (1984), 'L'Utopia Igienista (1870–1920)', in *Storia d'Italia. Annali 7: Malattia e Medicina*, a cura di F. Della Peruta, Torino: Einaudi.

Premuda, L. (1982), 'Ferdinando Coletti', in *Dizionario Biografico degli Italiani*, Vol. 26, Roma: Istituto della Enciclopedia Italiana, 731–34.

COLUMBARIA

Originating from Roman times, a columbarium was a subterranean sepulchre with walls containing niches to accommodate cinerary urns. William Robinson was an early advocate of columbaria, singling out 'the marvellously well preserved columbaria on the Vigna Codini and Via Aurelia' as particularly fine examples. He argued that '[t]he design of these columbaria or tomb-temples would be worthy of the best efforts of the architect, and their formation in the most lasting and noble form would not be so costly as the system of deep burial of the body' (Robinson, 1889:12).

Robinson, a director of The London Cremation Company, encouraged his architect friend, Ernest George, to include a columbarium in his plans for Golders Green Crematorium (1901). The West Columbarium, acknowledged as the first purpose-built example in Britain, was originally designed to be octagonal with a domed roof. George, however, substituted a design resembling an Italian brick baptistery. Square in plan, with a pyramidal roof, the centre was open to full height and the four storeys and galleries were approached from the polygonal turret stair tower. The Italianate feel was enhanced by the bold simplicity of the brick elevations articulated by brick piers and the other openings with their mouldings of tiles or smaller bricks. A second, East Columbarium followed in 1912. The Ernest George Columbarium, (1922–28), a three-sided building, grouped around a central lawn and lily pond was designed by George's partner Alfred B. Yeates, and described as 'the most beautiful and expensive building of its kind ever made' (Berridge, 2001: 209).

Architecturally, columbaria may form part of a crematorium's chapel buildings or may be separate and linked to them by a colonnade. Urns are generally stored in purpose-built recesses in the walls, allowing for enlargement or the provision of an additional building. The recesses, necessarily of varying sizes, are often enclosed with glass or metal and are rarely placed higher than seven feet (or just over two metres), so that inscriptions can be read. Architecturally, columbaria vary enormously but are generally designed to be in keeping with the architectural style of the crematorium, often serving, together with cloisters and pergolas, to link the crematorium with the gardens of remembrance. In England, one of the most unusual is at Hull (1899); here, the columbarium takes the form of a central avenue with irregular masses of tufa, brick and concrete, mostly rendered to resemble natural rock formations. Designed by local architect James Rhind (1894–97), the columbarium at Liverpool Crematorium was housed below the chapel, in three well-lit corridors with a series of 486 niches to accommodate urns, some in groups of four or five.

Research has shown that, in Great Britain, columbaria were much more popular in the earlier years of crematorium building. 'Of the twenty-four crematoria ... built before 1938, the great majority – seventy percent or seventeen – had columbaria. By contrast, of the 101 crematoria built between 1952–1990 only eight (eight percent) possessed a columbarium' (Davies, 1995: 12). Anfield, Liverpool is an example of a columbarium built in response to the lack of accommodation in the crematorium building for the storage of urns. Designed in 1953 by city architect Ronald Bradbury, it took the form of a memorial colonnade containing a further 1200 niches, effectively linking the lodge and offices to the crematorium chapel. Interestingly, in the UK, the Department of the Environment document on *The Siting and Planning of Crematoria*, published in 1978 (Arber, 2001: 83–86), offered no advice on the planning of columbaria, in sharp contrast to the attention afforded to such provision in the three editions of *Cremation in Britain*, published by The Cremation Society in 1909, 1932 and 1945.

The current demise of the columbarium results from the rising popularity of scattering ashes. **Hilary Grainger**

References

Arber, R.N. (ed.) (2001), *Directory of Crematoria*, Maidstone: The Cremation Society.

Berridge, K. (2001), *Vigor Mortis: The End of the Death Taboo*, London: Profile Books.

Cremation in Britain (1909), Maidstone: The Cremation Society. Republished 1932 and 1945.

Davies, D. (1995), *British Crematoria in Public Profile*, Maidstone: Cremation Society of Great Britain.

Grainger, H.J. (2000), '"Distressingly Banal": The Architecture of Early British Crematoria', *Pharos* 66(1): 42–48.

Jones, P.H. (1945), Cremation in Great Britain (3rd edn), London: Pharos Press, 113–14.

Robinson, W. (1889), *Cremation and Urn Burial – or The Cemeteries of the Future*, London.

CONNAUGHT, DUCHESS OF

The context for royal cremations in Britain was set by Princess Louise Margaret of Prussia, born in 1860, who became the Duchess of Connaught on her marriage to Prince Arthur, the third son of Queen Victoria. On her death in London on 14 March 1917, her body was transported to Golders Green for cremation prior to her funeral, held on 19 March at St George's Chapel, Windsor.

The duchess's cremation marked a definite departure from royal rituals; no member of Britain's royal family had ever before been cremated. Although King George V ordered four weeks of mourning dress, and the funeral included military guards of honour, the duchess's funeral possibly anticipated post-war habits of simpler funerals and requests to forego floral tributes. The *Times* of London published a request by the Duke of Connaught that, owing to the war, no flowers be sent, and the newspaper described the funeral service as very simple. The duchess's ashes probably remained in the chapel until the royal burial ground at Frogmore was consecrated in 1928, and her ashes now share a grave with her husband, who died in 1942. Her cremation might, perhaps, have also inspired HRH Princess Margaret's decision to be cremated without ceremony at Slough Crematorium on 15 February 2002, although Princess Margaret wished to remain in St George's Chapel, thereby avoiding a grave at Frogmore – a place she found gloomy. The last royal cremation had taken place in 1939, when Princess Louise, daughter of Queen Victoria, was cremated at Golders Green and was eventually interred at Frogmore. **Lisa Kazmier**

References

Packard, Jerrold M. (1999), *Victoria's Daughters*, London: Griffin.

Times, London, 15, 16, 17 and 19 March, 1917.

Biographical information at: www.regiments.org/ milhist/biography/royals/1860marC.htm and at: mypage.uniserve.ca/~canyon/frogmore.html.

CONVEYOR-BELT

As mentioned in the Introduction to this volume, the image and idea of a conveyor-belt became associated with a negative view of cremation as more of an industrial process than a personal treatment of an individual human being, particularly in Britain from the 1960s. This image became established despite the fact that the great majority of British crematoria had never made use of conveyor-belts as part of the cremation ceremony. It may be that the image served as an appropriate expression of the feeling, noted by many, of being 'processed' as participants in cremation ceremonies. This impression was largely fostered by the way in which mourners entered the crematorium by one door and made an exit through another in a kind of flow that is best expressed as 'one door in and another door out' (Davies, 1990). This was an innovation when compared with long-established church-based ritual in which both entry to, and exit from, the ritual space was by a single door.

In fact, the double-door scheme partly served to speed up the cremation service at a time when cremation was rising in popularity in Britain and the building of crematoria was not entirely keeping pace with demand. It allowed one funeral party to leave and engage in another innovative rite, that of 'looking at the flowers' while another arrived for their service. This was made possible by laying out the floral tributes on racks or in special areas opposite, or out of sight of, the main entrance to the crematorium building. **Douglas J. Davies**

See also architects–British.

Reference

Davies, Douglas J. (1990), *Cremation Today and Tomorrow*, Nottingham: Alcuin/GROW BOOKS.

CORPSE SYMBOLISM

In general terms, the human corpse is a powerful and yet strange symbol of the person who was once alive. The dead body participates in the person of the once living individual in the sense that it is the body in and through which the living individual once acted. At death, and for varying periods afterwards, it may closely resemble the person it once was, except for its stillness; yet that very stillness is amongst the first and most profound aspects of the corpse, since the living person is always moving, if only by breathing when asleep.

Soon, however, the body begins to change and, depending on local and personal circumstances, may rapidly show signs of decay (Mims, 1998). The further that process continues the greater becomes the distance between the corpse and the person it once was: the corpse begins to move from being a symbol of the person and begins to symbolize another 'reality' – that of decay. It shifts from being a symbol of the living to a symbol not of the dead 'person' but of death itself. That is why some Buddhist traditions have been known to use a corpse as an object of meditation for pondering the transience of life or possibly, in the absence of a corpse, for a symbolic object such as a written horoscope to take its place.

If the corpse is medically and cosmetically treated, as in developed forms of dealing with the dead in parts of the USA, especially from the second half of the twentieth century, it may continue to resemble the dead and to 'be' the deceased person. If, by sharp contrast, it is specially disjointed and prepared to be eaten by wild animals as is traditional in parts of Tibet, it rapidly loses its 'sense of identity'. These two stark contrasts reflect their respective underlying ideologies: a Western idealization of the self that is now at rest in its protective casket in a reinforced concrete grave, and an Eastern conception of the self as separated from its body as it moves on its spiritual path of transmigration and possible reincarnation.

Cremation now opens up many possibilities for the remains of the corpse, now transformed into ashes, to be used in a great number of symbolic ways, from being buried as a body to being used as commemorative jewellery. **Douglas J. Davies**

See also Buddhism; Tibet.

Reference

Mims, Cedric (1998), *When We Die*, London: Robinson.

CREMAINS

AS MATERIAL

The term 'cremains' is an abbreviated expression and euphemism referring to 'cremated remains', a neologism believed to have been invented by American funeral directors. In the modern cremation process the body is placed in a combustible container – typically either a conventional casket or some other receptacle – that is then placed inside the cremation device. The temperature generated in the cremation chamber ranges between 1400 and 2100°F (between 760 and 1148.8°C) which is sufficient to consume both the container and the body's soft tissue and reduce the skeleton to fragments and particles. The remaining substance, the cremains, may be processed further by mechanically breaking the larger particles down, producing a consistent mixture of grain and powder, to be scattered or stored in an urn as part of the funeral rites. **Eric Love**

See also ashes; remains.

AS SYMBOLIC

This American English word is retained throughout this book when used by the author concerned. This is the case, for example, with several of the entries from China. The invention of a new word inevitably involves the expression of new values and brings contradictory values into opposition. So, for example, it should be noted that some Catholic Church authorities have positively wished to avoid 'cremains' as the entry on the **Catholic Church – North America** describes. The **Canada** entry also shows how Catholic intentions have sought earth burial for remains rather than scattering or the like. These cautions reflect the way in which many words carry symbolic significance and overtones of particular values that some appreciate and others dislike.

As a neologism, 'cremains' expresses the innovatory nature of modern cremation and of the fact that it involves a processing of human remains. 'Ashes', by contrast, even though they, too, are the result of a process, retain something of the echo of the traditional burial and biblical phrase of 'ashes to ashes' that so closely partnered 'earth to earth' and 'dust to dust'. 'Cremains' marks something of a cultural discontinuity in burial practice. One interesting US literary expression of this change, and a degree of uncertainty over it, occurs in Dave Eggers' novel, *A Heartbreaking Work of Staggering Genius*, itself one of the ten best books of the year in the *New York Times Book Review*. In a conversation on the death of his parents, whose bodies went for medical research, and were cremated, the text runs: '"So you don't have the remains?" Right. Actually, it's kind of funny – they don't call them *remains*; they call them "cremains". But we still think the ashes might be coming.' (Eggers, 2000: 223). **Douglas J. Davies**

See also Canada; Catholic Church – North America.

Reference

Eggers, Dave (2000), *A Heartbreaking Work of Staggering Genius*, New York: Simon & Schuster.

CREMATION ACTS AND REGULATIONS (UK)

The first UK Act of Parliament concerning cremation was the Cardiff Corporation Act 1894. Section 71 of this Act empowered the Corporation to establish a crematorium in its cemetery. Between 1894 and 1902, at least 11 similar local Acts were passed. In 1902, Parliament passed the Cremation Act, the first general Cremation Act, which repealed all the previously passed local Acts. Since then, Parliament has passed one other Cremation Act, in 1952. Both general Acts are still in force, although they have been amended.

Since 1902 Parliament has also passed several local Cremation (or Crematorium) Acts, as well as approving a set of Cremation Regulations, made under section 7 of the Cremation Act 1902. The first set was the Cremation Regulations 1903. These were replaced by a new set of Cremation Regulations in 1920, which in turn were replaced by another set of Regulations in 1930. By that time, a separate set of Cremation Regulations had been approved (in 1928) for Scotland. The 1930 Regulations, as subsequently amended, are still in force in England and Wales. The Scottish Regulations were replaced by a new set in 1935. The 1935 Regulations, as subsequently amended, are still in force in Scotland. The Cremation Act 1902 did not apply to Northern Ireland until 1948, when the Belfast Corporation (General Powers) Act 1948 empowered Belfast Corporation to provide and maintain a crematorium and applied the Cremation Act to any crematorium provided under the 1948 Act. Since 1985, councils in Northern Ireland have been empowered to establish crematoria. **Stephen White**

References

Cremation Act 1902, as amended.
Cremation Regulations 1930, as amended.
The original texts of all Cremation Acts and Regulations and texts of the Act and Regulations as amended at any time are available on the Cremation Society of Great Britain website at: http://www.cremation.org.uk.

CREMATION PROCESS

The actual process of cremation varies, to a degree, depending upon the type and era of technology employed. Several entries offer differing kinds of description as with, for example, **cremators**. The following contributions offer complementary examples of contemporary cremation processes. The first, from Britain, describes the broad process while the second, from China, is more technical in its analysis. **Douglas J. Davies**

See also cremators.

BRITAIN

The development of large urban communities has strongly influenced the way in which cremations are carried out and, in most cultures, the open cremations of early history have been replaced by cremation in closed equipment to provide a high throughput of cremations, whilst preserving the dignity of disposal of human remains. The minimization of the environmental impact of crematoria has, increasingly, become important, as described here for the beginning of the twenty-first century.

For most cremations, but not all, the body is contained within a coffin, and cremation takes place one cadaver at a time. Both the coffin and the body burn in a chamber shaped so as to be a little larger than the coffin itself. The process involves a number of steps, which repeat for each cremation, and results in cremated remains, or ashes, which can be recovered individually and, after cooling, presented to the family or other final destination according to local custom or wish.

The sequence begins with ignition of the external surface of the coffin. At the outset, the interior of the cremation chamber lies in the range 700–850°C. Air for combustion is admitted to the chamber along its length so as to establish burning along the whole of the coffin. Since the human body comprises up to 75 per cent of water, much of this must be dried out before burning proper can take place. This drying dominates the cremation process with most modern cremators requiring from 60 to 90 minutes for completion from insertion of the coffin.

The sequence of cremation is:

1   ignition and burning of coffin and outer layers of the body;
2   drying of the 'wet' parts of the body followed by the burning of the contents of the thoracic, cranial and abdominal cavities;
3   completion of the burning of combustible parts;
4   calcination of bones;
5   cooling of the ash remains, and ash processing to produce a final ash of small particles.

The process needs to deliver well-calcined remains in an acceptable time and with a minimum environmental impact. From an engineering point of view, this is achieved only by close control of the temperatures, air admission and other parameters. The starting and finishing stages are supported by the provision of external energy in the form of small support fuel burners using any 'clean' fuel. Some specialist cremators use only electrical heating in the cremator rather than fuel-fired burners.

All cremators have a secondary combustion zone in which all the gases from the cremation are burned to completion to eliminate smoke, smell and pollution. The zone is maintained at a temperature of at least 850°C and this, too, is heated by support fuel burners. The temperature and the oxygen concentration in this chamber is maintained under close control in order to achieve the clean exhaust gases which are discharged from the chimney. **Clive Chamberlain**

CHINA

The cremation process phases

The time needed for the cremation of corpses of Chinese extraction averages 60 minutes. In line with this length of time, the process of cremation is generally divided into eight phases as illustrated in Figure 1 and Table 1.

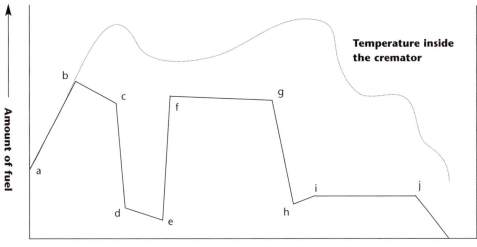

Figure 1 Phases of cremation combustion

Table 1 Combustion characteristics in each phase

Phases	Time (minutes)	Conditions	Phenomena
(1) a–b	0–2	Combustion begins.	The coffin is burning.
(2) b–c	2–6	The temperature inside the cremator is rising.	Moisture within the corpse is evaporating.
(3) c–d	6–7	The temperature inside the cremator is controlled.	The corpse begins to burn (dissolving due to heat).
(4) d–e	7–11	The corpse is burning.	Full-scale combustion.
(5) e–f	11–13	The corpse is burning.	Flammable parts have been burnt out.
(6) f–g	13–34	The corpse is burning.	The belly and loin parts are burning.
(7) g–h–i	34–38	The temperature is declining.	The belly and loin parts are burning.
(8) i–j	38–60	Heat preservation.	The corpse is burnt out.

During the process of cremation, between five and 20 minutes after a corpse is put into the cremator (the 'b–e phase' in Figure 1), deflagration can easily occur. The characteristics of deflagration are:

1 too rapid an increase of temperature inside the hearth (above 1100°C);
2 a sudden increase of pressure inside the cremator (from negative pressure to positive pressure);
3 a great deal of smoke generated inside the hearth, accompanied by sounds of small explosions;
4 an odour blowing from the apertures such as the hatch of the hearth, the operational opening or exit for the cremains;
5 the chimney discharging extremely thick black smoke and odour.

Deflagration occurs when a burner ignites the corpse, coffin and burial utensils and keeps supplying more heat. The coffin and utensils begin to burn rapidly and the temperatures inside the hearth rapidly rise up to about 800°C. The body fat, amounting to between 10 and 20 per cent of total body weight, is the principal fuel for the cremation. When the coffin and burial utensils are burnt out, the corpse is exposed to the high temperature, so that the epidermis and subcutaneous fat becomes evaporated, gasified, fissioned and dissolved, discharging plenty of inflammable materials and stench. When mixed with combustion-supporting air, the inflammable materials generate a large amount of heat, which rapidly increases the temperature inside the hearth. This higher temperature generates more inflammable materials and hence more combustion-supporting air will be needed. After several limited cycles of dissolve–combustion temperature increase, the combustion inside the hearth becomes more furious, the supply of combustion-supporting air and discharge of smoke configured by the cremator turn out to be inadequate, thus causing deflagration. There is no sufficient measure for controlling deflagration once it occurs. Prevention is the key: that is, to estimate the amount of fat in a body and to control the speed of the rising temperature so that the dissolving speed of fat is under control.

The human body and cremation

A human body is an intricate organism, mainly consisting of protein, fat, sugars, water and mineral salts. The contents of the human body are shown in Table 2.

Table 2 The main chemical substances in the human body (weighing 60 kg)

Body component	Weight (kg)	Percentage of body
Protein	9.18	15.3
Fat	8.40	14.0
Sugars	0.30	0.5
Water	38.40	64.0
Mineral Salts	3.00	5.0
Others	0.72	1.2

Protein is composed of amino acid molecules, amino acid is composed of amidogen, and amidogen is composed of of nitrogen atoms. This means that a human body contains many nitrogen atoms. Fat amounts to between 10 and 20 per cent of human body weight. Sugars are also known as carbohydrate. These two kinds of substance easily ignite and generate plenty of heat in the course of cremation. Water, basically consisting of cytochylema, endochyme and plasma, makes up most of the human body, accounting for around 64 per cent of the whole. The younger the individual, the higher the percentage of water. In fact, water accounts for a greater percentage than is usually assumed because physical drinking and therapy (transfusion) supply extra water, which usually happens shortly before death. Water in corpses is the main decalescent substance in the course of cremation, and the water vapour in smoke coagulates and takes up acid gases which erode metal equipment.

Clothing, coffins and burial utensils for corpses are generally composed of natural macromolecule compounds, such as cotton, wool and silk, or synthesized macromolecule compounds, such as nylon, acrylic fibres and rubber. The calculations for cremation mentioned above can only work as a broad reference when a cremator is designed, with other factors also being important. These include the changes in both the moisture and weight of corpses and the presence of burial utensils. According to our research, the size, weight and gender of corpses and the cause of death (such as natural deaths, accidents or diseases) all affect the projections of cremators.

The contaminants generated when corpses are cremated are shown in Table 3. Figure 2 illustrates, in graphical form, the odour generated during the cremation process.

Table 3 Contamination levels after the cremation of a corpse, coffin and burial utensils

Contaminants	Discharges (kg)
Powder dusts	5.0
C_3H_3	8.0
Ammonia	0.005
Trimethylamine	0.001
Organic Acids	1.7
Oxysulphide	0.7
Nitrogen Oxide	4.0
Moisture	52.0

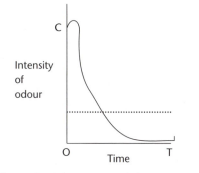

Figure 2 Odour generated during corpse cremation

Within the first 11 minutes of the course of a cremation, coffins and burial utensils easily generate floating dusts, while substances not burnt up are easily decomposed into carbon granules. The first dust peak thus occurs. As combustion approaches its end, the corpse needs to be turned over, sometimes to speed up the process, which causes the second dust peak. The second peak is much smaller than the first, however (see Figure 3).

No precise theory has been formed from the research into cremation mechanisms, and many questions remain to be answered. These include the effects of the causes of death on cremations; the relationship of the generation of cremation contaminants to both hearth structure and hearth temperature; and the generation and

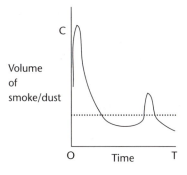

Figure 3 Smoke and dust generated during corpse cremation

decomposition mechanisms of carcinogenic substances such as dioxaanthracene, benzopyrene and benzanthracene. **Liu Fengming**

CREMATION SOCIETY OF GREAT BRITAIN

The Cremation Society of Great Britain (CSGB) was founded in 1874. Originally titled the Cremation Society of England, it was the first of a number of national and local voluntary cremation societies founded specifically during the last quarter of the nineteenth century in western Europe, North America and Australia to promote cremation as a radical alternative to burial. Modern communication accelerated their establishment, although not all of them have survived to the present day. Their major priority was to change existing legislation so as to permit cremation. The CSGB was the first cremation society to be founded, followed by the (now Royal) Dutch Cremation Society three months later. The narrative of how cremation came to be established in the UK as an acceptable alternative to burial is, to a very large measure, the story of the CSGB for its first 60 years.

The formative years of the society

The founder of the CSGB was Sir Henry Thompson, a famous lithotriptist who had become surgeon to Queen Victoria and was a society figure. Following his visit to the Vienna World's Fair of 1873, where he had been impressed by the cremation equipment developed by Brunetti, he published a paper, in January 1874, promoting cremation in the *Contemporary Review*. On 13 January he assembled a group of friends supportive of the idea at his London home where a declaration was signed:

> We, the undersigned, disapprove the present custom of burying the dead, and we desire to substitute some mode which shall rapidly resolve the body into its component elements, by a process which cannot offend the living, and shall render the remains perfectly innocuous. Until some better method is devised, we desire to adopt that usually known as cremation.

The list of his early provisional council members and subscribers (White, 1999, 2003b) draws particularly upon friends in the medical and literary professions, especially a contingent from the magazine *Punch*.

The next major task was to raise funds to build a crematorium. An acre of land was sought from the privately-owned Great Northern Cemetery at New Southgate, north London, and Sir Henry agreed to build a Siemen's furnace at his own expense. The society then sought permission from the bishop of Rochester who, in a now-famous letter, refused permission on the grounds that the land was consecrated (Parsons, 2005). Later, the society successfully bought land at Woking, but the disappointment at New Southgate forced it to go on to the offensive to seek changes in the law to permit cremation, with the intention of putting cremation on an equal legal footing with burial. The construction of a Gorini furnace on land bought in 1878 at Woking caused sufficient controversy amongst local inhabitants as to provoke the Home Secretary of the day to refuse cremation until authorization by parliament. Although, at the time, the society had insufficient funds to promote a private bill, the opening of crematoria in regions of Germany, for example, where cremation was not illegal, encouraged the society to persist.

The Home Office's opposition to cremation was partly based on its concern that forensic evidence in cases of suspicious deaths, especially by poison, might be destroyed by the cremation process (Leaney, 1989). For this reason, the Home Office was involved in cremation matters for over 120 years, and in the later 1990s burial matters also became its responsibility. In 1882, however, the Home Office refrained from taking action when a certain Captain Hanham cremated two

dead members of his family in a crematorium built on his own land (Hanham's adopted son, J. C. Swinburne-Hanham, later became the secretary of the Cremation society). The Society's council had initially given Hanham permission to use Woking, perhaps intending to use the cremations as a test case, but Sir Henry's threatened resignation over the issue forced it to retract its offer; hence Hanham's lone action.

Encouraged by the Home Office's lack of intervention, the society decided to draw up a scheme of regulations governing cremations, with the particular aim of ensuring that unnatural deaths would not go undetected (Leaney, 1989). At this time, it was not entirely clear whether or not cremations could be lawfully performed, so there were no regulations for its processes, but the society wanted to prepare for the day when the Home Office would be forced to change its mind. It prepared three forms: the first certified that the deceased had not objected to cremation; the second and third were for medical practitioners to certify that the circumstances of the death had been explored and that there would be no necessity for a future exhumation. These provided the basis for the dual medical certification, later strengthened in the 1903 Cremation Regulations, which slowed the procedures for cremation and was regarded by the movement as a deterrent to cremation choice from the mid-twentieth century. Dual certification also survived the Interdepartmental Committee on Cremation (1947–51) and the Brodrick Report (1967–71). It may prove to have been finally superseded when the British government acts on the Shipman and Coroners and Death Registration Reports of 2003 (Leadbeater and White, 2004). It should be noted that, among early Society members, men such as Sir Henry Thompson, Charles Cameron and Ernest Hart were also campaigners against infanticide (Rose, 1986). Reformed death certification was vital in each cause. Infanticide was to prove a protracted campaign: the Births and Deaths Registration Act 1926 not only required the registration of stillbirths but, by insisting on the registration of deaths *before* burial, helped to put burial and cremation on a more equal footing.

Meanwhile, as its lobbying of the government continued, the CSGB exploited fascinated media interest. The most well-known case was that of the English cricket team's defeat by Australia in

1882. A journalist quipped that the body of English cricket was to be cremated and the ashes sent to Australia; 'the Ashes' have been the trophy of matches between the two countries ever since (White, 1990).

Cremation is legalized

Two years later, the Cremation Society was handed an unexpected, early victory. In January 1884, Dr William Price was sent for trial for the attempted cremation of his dead baby son, Iesu Grist. The celebrated judgement by Mr Justice Stephen at the Cardiff Assizes in April was that cremation was not illegal so long as no public nuisance was caused (White, 2003a). On 30 April Dr Charles Cameron MP seized this opportunity to introduce a Private Member's Bill in the House of Commons to enable the regulation of cremation. He was defeated, by 149 votes to 79. Undeterred and with the opportune Price verdict behind it, the society proceeded to prepare its Woking crematorium for legal use. Arrangements were made with the London funeral directors, Garstins, to encourage and facilitate funerals at Woking (Parsons, 2005). On 26 March 1885 the society's first cremation took place – that of Mrs Jeanette Pickersgill (Parsons, 2005). Cremation was expensive, however, and the CSGB found that funds were hard to come by. Its fortunes changed, however, when in 1888 the Duke of Bedford made the first of two generous gifts: at Woking he provided for a chapel to be attached to the crematorium as well as a further piece of land and, later, provided a chapel at Golders Green Crematorium.

The Woking Crematorium was run by the Cremation Society. In 1890 the society first considered either turning itself into a limited company or establishing a limited company of its own – an idea that seems to have originated from council member Martin Ridley Smith. Eventually, the London Cremation Company (LCC) was formed in 1900. The Cremation Society held shares in the company, its secretary, George Nobel, became the company's secretary and Swinburne-Hanham became the managing director. The LCC opened its first crematorium in 1902 at Golders Green (Jupp and Grainger, 2002). In 1933 the society transferred Woking Crematorium to the company.

The Local Government Act 1888 gave new powers to local authorities. The realization that cremation was lawful, following the Price edict, offered local authorities opportunities to reduce the amount of land required for burials, particularly in the metropolitan areas. In 1894 the Association of Municipal Corporations (AMA) submitted to the CSGB a draft bill to empower local authorities to erect crematoria. The society turned it down on the grounds that the forensic safeguards were inadequate. Meanwhile, other local authorities such as Cardiff, Leamington, Hull and Leicester, were seeking to include crematoria in local bills (White, 2003b). In 1899 London County Council drafted a bill which was passed by the House of Lords in 1901. At its third attempt the Cremation Act was passed in 1902, and the Cremation Regulations followed in 1903.

The passing of the 1902 Act had the dual effect of checking the development of privately-funded crematoria and promoting that of the publicly-funded. Before 1902, six of the eight crematoria then in existence had been privately funded, but now local authorities could provide crematoria on burial land they already owned, and the building of facilities for cremation in twentieth-century Britain was subsequently very largely undertaken by local government. Not until the Environmental Protection Act 1990, and the expense it entailed for the cremation process, was the private–public balance reversed.

Nevertheless, in the first decade of the twentieth century, cremation did not prove immediately popular. Only after the First World War, when attitudes to death and disposal changed significantly, and with the post-1918 massive requirements for new land for urban housing would local authorities accelerate their efforts to promote the economical choice of cremation.

The inter-war years, 1918–39

The CSGB had refrained from active promotion of its work during the war years but then returned to its campaign with vigour. In 1917 HRH the Duchess of Connaught, a daughter-in-law of Queen Victoria, had been cremated at Golders Green Crematorium. She was the first member of the royal family to be cremated, although one of her husband's servants had been the twelfth person to be cremated at Woking. This royal precedent lent weight to the arguments advanced for the wider adoption of cremation after the war. In the inter-war years the society's propaganda would make much of the statesmen, churchmen, intellectuals and other personalities who chose cremation.

In addition, there was an influx of new people on to the society's council. The Duke of Bedford succeeded Sir Charles Cameron as president. Sir Thomas Horder, the king's physician, joined the council in 1922 and became president in 1940. An *eminence grise* of the medical profession, he was very influential in promoting cremation during and after the Second World War. In the programmes of its annual conferences, the CSGB sought to attract leading proponents of cremation, Bishop Charles Gore of Oxford being particularly influential in 1924.

In 1921 the society had decided to expand its influence by organizing an annual conference of the (then 18) cremation authorities. The first was held at the London Guildhall in 1922. In 1924, at its third conference, the society decided to establish a daughter organization, the Federation of (later, British) Cremation Authorities (FCA). For a quarter of a century, the society and the FCA collaborated well. In 1932 the FCA joined with the National Association of Cemetery and Crematorium Superintendents (NACCS) for an annual series of conferences held jointly until 2002. One reason for the society's establishment of the FCA was to promote public confidence in the way in which cremation authorities ran their crematoria. From 1924 onwards, a specific target of both the CSGB and the FCA was to influence local authorities, for two principal reasons. First, in the 1920s, working Labour Party majorities were being elected in local councils and health and social issues were important for them, especially given the recent extension of the vote to women. Second, local government was tackling the problems and opportunities of new housing and the suburbanization of the larger towns and cities. Cremation offered an economic way of discharging the responsibilities for burial which it had shouldered in urban areas and increasingly in rural areas since the burials legislation of the 1850s.

In 1927 the FCA approached the Home Office about revising the 1903 Regulations in order to simplify cremation procedures and make a cremation a more attractive choice for bereaved families. Revised regulations were issued in 1930. These streamlined a number of procedures: for example, the number of doctors available to sign cremation certificates was increased and the coroner was permitted to do what, up until then,

he could only do for burial – namely, issue a cremation certificate after a postmortem and certification of cause of death but without an inquest. The adjournment of the inquest following the Sevenoaks rail disaster of 1927 had prevented the cremation of several of the victims despite the fact that they had left written instructions for cremation.

In 1930 there were only 21 crematoria and the cremation rate was 0.9 per cent of total deaths, but this decade saw a strong increase in preference for cremation: by 1939 58 crematoria were in existence and the cremation rate was 3.9 per cent. However, the rapid growth of local authority investment in crematoria after 1930 made the position of the Cremation Society as the parent body of the FCA and as a cremation authority in its own right somewhat difficult. As a result, in 1937 the FCA became autonomous with a new constitution as the Federation of British Cremation Authorities (FBCA).

In the 1930s the CSGB launched a number of new initiatives to promote cremation. In 1933 it formed the Council for the Disposal of the Dead (CDD), involving a number of interested parties, including the British Undertakers' Association. Lord Horder became its president. One of its objectives was the revision of the burial and cremation laws; another was the state registration of undertakers. However, the CDD found an implacable opponent in Sir Arnold Wilson MP, who had a background of 20 years of military and civilian administration in Mesopotamia. A radical Conservative, he was concerned with social insurance issues and published, with Herman Levy, two studies on *Industrial Insurance* (1937) and *Burial Reform and Funeral Costs* (1938). Calculating that state registration of funeral directors would benefit the larger firms as opposed to the smaller, Wilson gathered sufficient supporters in parliament to defeat Lord Horder's proposals in The House of Lords. Horder may have hoped that parliamentary approval for state registration would persuade the larger undertaking firms to throw their weight behind (less expensive) cremation and, burial laws being so complex, this was possibly the most practical way to secure parliamentary time for funeral reform. By 1951 he would have been proved correct in his judgement that only a combination of the interested parties would secure better facilities and more favourable attitudes towards cremation. In 1939, however, the CDD had to admit defeat, and it disbanded.

A far more effective and far-reaching innovation was the establishment, in 1937, of the International Cremation Federation. This was formed in London, with the CSGB a major contributor, providing both the first treasurer and the first secretary, P.H. Jones. This permanent international body was formed with three principal aims: to convince the Roman Catholic Church of the benefits of cremation; to develop better facilities for the cross-border transportation of the dead; and to establish standard systems of cremation law and regulations. Intended as a triennial conference, the second ICF was postponed with the outbreak of the Second World War: its successes in promoting cremation were entirely post-war.

Two other initiatives were the development of cremation insurance as a competitor to the wide-ranging schemes of burial insurance in 1933. Working-class families invested strongly in these schemes of so-called 'industrial assurance' and were little interested in cremation. Only with the election of a Labour government committed to a welfare state would the 'death grant' (from 1948) help alleviate funeral costs for the poorer families, and help to make redundant the existing schemes of 'industrial assurance', Sir Arnold Wilson's old target. The Cremation Society, meanwhile, continued to administer its Pharos scheme of cremation insurance until 2002.

Pharos was also the name of the journal launched by the CSGB in 1934. It continues to be published quarterly. Like its sister journals published by burial and cremation groups, it has continued to promote the cause of cremation with conference papers, views and information. In the 1990s it also became the quarterly journal of the ICF.

Cremation as a majority practice

For reasons not yet wholly understood, the cremation rate doubled during the war years (7.8 per cent in 1945). In 1939 the society's council asked the Home Office to ease cremation regulations in order to permit cremation following air-raids. The Home Office at first resisted, but then allowed emergency regulations which lasted for the duration of the war. Recent research has shown that despite these regulations local authorities preferred to encourage burial

(Rugg, 2004). This makes it all the more surprising that, by the war's end, over 200 local authorities were preparing applications to build crematoria.

With hindsight, it seems that the exigencies of wartime and the task of post-war reconstruction had direct effects on the popularization of cremation. The use of land for housing, recreation and agriculture was a major concern. The welfare state (welfare 'from the cradle to the grave') not only brought in a death grant as one of its policies for easing the costs of death and funerals for families, but also altered the context of death with the introduction of its national health service (1948) which served to distance death from families by replacing the home as the place of death with the institution (by 1958 over one half of deaths took place in institutions).

The economic burdens shouldered by local authorities after 1945 caused them to give serious attention to the economies offered by providing cremation facilities. The structure of the funeral directing industry was overhauled from within, facilitated by the use of the motor-hearse in place of the horse-drawn carriage and the greater use of refrigeration techniques. These all streamlined the funeral process and made the use of crematoria far more convenient for funeral directors. Finally, a major encouragement was given to cremationists by the new stance of the Church of England. From 1942 to 1944, the Convocation of Canterbury debated cremation issues as a pressing liturgical task, including the necessity of providing proper rituals for cremation services. Broadly, the bishops were more favourably disposed to cremation than the parish clergy but, in 1944, the Convocation published its report which included a statement that 'the practice of cremation has no theological significance'. In the opinion of the Cremation Society, this served to give a green light to families formerly hesitating to choose cremation, and the Church's statement was greeted with enthusiasm. Thus, by the end of the war, many of the key interest groups involved in funeral choice had, broadly, adopted a consensus favouring cremation.

Following the end of the war, the society made several adjustments to its policies, including the formulation of a new Code of Cremation Practice which was adopted by all creation authorities. Its secretary P.H. Jones, also took on the secretaryship of the FBCA. In 1946 the first post-war Cremation Society conference was addressed by Aneurin Bevan MP, the Minister for Health. His personal stance in favour of cremation and his public authority in government made him a key figure in promoting post-war facilities for cremation. On the Society's side, Lord Horder was a key figure. Local governments became the society's chosen target and its slogan 'Cemeteries or playing fields?', like its former slogan, 'Save the land for the living', underlined the theme of land use as a pressing reason for cremation. Jones, meanwhile, was convinced that the 'old-time system of joint conferences with the burial interests would be folly', and the society withdrew from collaboration organizations – a decision that Turner, a later FBCA leader, felt was a mistake. Whatever the rights and wrongs of this argument, the growth of post-war cremation was the consequence of local authority initiatives, on which the NACCS and the FBCA were allies, and it seems that the Cremation Society had surrendered part of its initiative in promoting cremation at this point.

This impending development did not impede a joint initiative in 1947 by the CSGB and the FBCA to adopt a new policy to enlist the support of Aneurin Bevan, Minister of Health, Housing and Local Government. As all post-war building projects had to compete with each other for restricted resources and funding, the CSGB and the FBCA chose 15 crematoria authorities with the most pressing claims for financial investment. When their request was refused, they reduced their list to six and resubmitted. Finally, in December 1948, permission was given to six local authorities to submit building proposals and a seventh was invited to convert an existing cemetery chapel into a crematorium. The log-jam was broken. Bevan's decision presaged a new government policy of encouraging local authorities to phase in cremation as an alternative to burial. After 1952 this would bear full fruit.

A vehicle for the changed direction of national and local government in favour of cremation was the Government's Interdepartmental Committee on Cremation which started work in 1947. By the time its investigation was completed in 1951, any concern that public money would be ill-advisedly invested in crematoria had been dispelled by the endorsement of the general public. In 1951 the UK cremation rate had reached 17.8 per cent.

Two of the reasons for the establishment of the Committee were the rise in the cremation rate during the 1940s and some public concern about malpractice at crematoria. If cremation was to be endorsed by the public, then its processes had to be regularized and publicized. The Cremation Council, which included the Cremation Society and the Federation of Cremation Authorities, played an active role in the Committee's discussions. The Committee considered the siting of, and planning permission for, crematoria; site inspections; coffin handling and security; staff quality; wishes of the deceased; doctors; and cremation certification. The latter caused the most difficulties on account of the clear division between medical and legal professions' groups, on the one hand, and cremation groups, together with local government authorities, on the other. The outcome was the retention of the second and confirming medical certificate that the cremation authorities were convinced deterred the public from choosing cremation and which the medical and legal groups were convinced assisted the detection of crime.

The recommendations of the Committee on Cremation were taken up by Joseph Reeves MP in a Private Members' Bill which was drafted in consultation with the Home Office in 1952 and enjoyed an easy passage through both parliamentary houses. Revised regulations followed the same summer. At the same time, arrangements were made with the British Medical Association (BMA) for the voluntary standardization of doctors' fees for cremation certificates. (The rising level of doctors' cremation fees has continuously proved an irritation in discussions about cremation.) With this parliamentary approval and increasingly favourable attitudes on the part of the general public (Jupp, 1993a), the number of new crematoria rose rapidly (from 59 in 1951 to 161 ten years later) and the cremation rate topped 50 per cent for England and Wales in 1967.

A fresh attempt by the cremation movement to remove the requirement for a second certificate was launched in 1958 and, as a result, the Home Office agreed to set up a governmental working party. This included the Cremation Society, the Federation of Cremation Authorities and the Institute of Burial and Cremation Administration (IBCA, formerly the NACCS). Once again, legal and medical groups with others argued, successfully, for its retention. However the working party successfully recommended that the decision to cremate was henceforth to be left entirely to the next-of-kin.

In 1964 the BMA published *Deaths in the Community* arguing for more accurate certification of the causes of death, and this led to the setting up of the Brodrick Committee which finally reported in 1971 that the system of a second certificate gave only the illusion of security against a totally non-existent threat and therefore recommended a simplification of the certification procedures and forms. The Cremation Society hoped that its long post-war campaign for the abolition of the second certificate would be victorious. In the event, the Brodrick Report was never even fully discussed in parliament for reasons that have never been formally explained.

In 1964, however, a far more significant event occurred. The ICF had been specifically founded to influence the Catholic Church in favour of cremation. After 1945 it began to press its case with the Vatican, but Pope Pius XII resisted the appeal of the 1948 ICF Congress. Some time later, P.H. Jones in his dual roles of secretary of the CSGB and of the ICF had approached the papal nuncio in Paris, Cardinal Roncalli. In 1958 Roncalli became Pope John XXIII and, the following year, announced a series of new initiatives – one for the revision of canon law and another the calling of the Second Vatican Council. Cremationists seized on these opportunities and, in the ICF Congress of 1960, agreed on a new approach to the Vatican, to be headed by the Austrian Cremation Society. This approach necessitated assuring the Vatican that cremation movements had no hostile attitudes towards any church. This was important because cremationists in the second half of the nineteenth century had included leaders with both anti-Catholic and pro-masonic stances – positions which had partly prompted the Vatican's declaration forbidding cremation in 1886 (*Dublin Review*, 1890). The ICF sent letters to 270 Catholic bishops asking them to place consideration of the removal of the Catholic ban on cremation both on the Vatican Council's agenda and on that of the canon law revision. On 2 May 1964 the British newspapers broke the story that, the previous year, Pope Paul VI had announced the relaxation of the Catholic ban on cremation in a confidential letter to bishops and had issued his Instruction on 5 July, 1963. The reason for the year's delay may be easily explained: on 3 June 1963, Pope John XXIII had died, with Pope Paul VI succeeding him on 21 June, and this was clearly not the appropriate moment for the Catholic Church to announce a radical change in its traditional funeral rites. However, Catholic acceptance of cremation was very slow. One of the reasons for this may be demonstrated in the clauses of the Instruction itself, one of which forbade the funeral rite to be held at the crematorium and the accompaniment of the cortege thither by the priest, even without ceremony.

In the UK, a change of heart and policy was effected by the devoted efforts of Monsignor John McDonald, whom Cardinal Heenan had sent as his representative to the 1965 Cremation Society conference. As a result, the CSGB's secretary, Kenneth Prevette, wrote to Cardinal Heenan requesting 'the Authorities of the Church ... to permit the presence of a priest in the crematorium chapel'. McDonald took the resolution to Cardinal Heenan who took it to the pope. Whatever other influences had also been at work, a new Instruction was announced in July 1966 whereby Catholic priests were told that 'at the request of the Hierarchy the Holy See has relaxed this [earlier] rule for England and Wales. You may attend the crematorium and conduct an appropriate ceremony.' Monsignor McDonald had by this time become a member of the Cremation Society council and continued to promote the cause of cremation among Catholics until his death in 1991. Nevertheless, tradition had the last word in his funeral rites: members of the society's council were invited to his funeral only to find that it was to be followed by burial. However, today Catholic cremations are estimated at about one-third of all Catholic deaths in some areas.

During the 1980s, with the cremation rate appearing to settle around 70 per cent, it might have seemed that the Cremation Soceity's work was completed. Then two government initiatives stimulated new issues within the burial and cremation movement. First, an Audit Commission report of 1989 argued for procedures and funding by local authorities which would make burial pay its own way, whereas it had hitherto been subsidized. Second, the Environmental Protection Act 1990 (the EPA) necessitated a revision of cremation procedures to ensure that emissions from crematoria did not harm the atmosphere. A new concentration on meeting government targets by 1998 and investment in enhanced technology stimulated all cremation organizations, including the Cremation Society. Environment and finance were neatly encapsulated in the government's instruction, BATNEEC: 'best available technology not entailing excessive cost'.

At the beginning of the 1990s the London Cremation Company (LCC) acquired only its third crematorium, when it purchased St Marylebone from the public sector. By now, the LCC's parent company was the Cremation Society. Back in 1958 the company had lost control of its Woking and Golders Green crematoria but had them restored in 1962 as a result of negotiations which eventually led to the Cremation Society becoming a major shareholder in the company. As White (2002) has described, the relationship between the society and the LCC, apart from this brief hiatus, had always been close. The Cremation Society's secretary had often also served as the managing director of the LCC (as with the current holder of both positions, Roger N. Arber) and members of the society's council had often sat on the LCC board, although nowadays the council must retain a majority of members who are not LCC directors. The LCC has built two more crematoria, at Banbury (1999) and Swale (2003). The Cremation Society, through its ownership of the company, seeks to set and operate the highest standards for cremation.

Meanwhile, the requirements of the EPA began to affect all sides of the cremation movement, as well as coffin suppliers and funeral directors. On one side, local authorities, which owned seven-eighths of the UK's 240 crematoria, did not welcome the extra investment involved. On another side, a series of realignments within the funeral directing industry had involved a number of takeovers, and the advantages had become more apparent to larger funeral directing groups. Moreover, the government's Private Finance Initiative of 1995 encouraged local authorities to consider selling or leasing their crematoria to private enterprise. In this climate the building of privately-owned crematoria resumed and local authority involvement reduced.

The Cremation Society, together with its sister organizations, monitored all these developments, seeking where the best interests of the cremation movement, of bereaved people and of the public at large lay. Environmental concerns began to take centre-stage across the new Europe. The British government had itself taken the lead in abating mercury emissions to which amalgam from dental fillings was a major contributor. This caused problems for crematoria. In 2000 the FBCA organized a survey of crematorium authorities whose results suggested that up to 23 per cent of crematoria might have to be closed because of insufficient space to accommodate the new cleansing equipment required for environmental protection. In 2001 the Cremation Society collaborated with the FBCA on a jointly funded project to independently test crematorium emission levels and presented these to the government's Department of Food, Environment and Rural Affairs (DEFRA). This joint project led to enhanced discussions with the government. In 2003 the society moved to adopt a policy of collaboration with the Government's policy on atmospheric emissions.

From the late 1980s there has been increasing media interest both in disasters and in the funeral industries. A series of government reports has investigated funeral directing, funeral directing takeovers, monopoly concerns, prepaid funeral plans, the registration of death, the reorganization of coroners' procedures and cemeteries. This is a new and particularly ethical context not only for the cremation world but also for the whole of the death-care industry. The Cremation Society has played a full part in discussing the implications of these reports. The inquiry into the Shipman case is of both particular and traditional importance as it concerned a GP who murdered at least 200 of his patients and used the cremation certificate procedures to conceal his crimes. This not only raises issues that date from the very start of the Cremation Society's life but provides an opportunity to revise the law and procedures of cremation in light of contemporary needs (Leadbeatter and White, 2004). As an independent charity, the Cremation Society remains well placed to analyse, communicate and contribute to new developments in a changing environment. **Peter Jupp**

See also Cameron; Catholic Church; Connaught; Declaration of 1874; Hanham cremations; law; mercury; Price; The Ashes; Thompson.

References

Arber, R.N. (2002), 'Contemporary Issues Facing the Cremation Movement', in P.C. Jupp and H.J. Grainger (eds), *Golders Green Crematorium 1902–2002: A London Centenary in Context*, London: The London Cremation Company plc; 93–100.

Dublin Review, The (1890).

Grainger, H.J. (2005), *Death Redesigned: The Architecture of British Crematoria*, NJ: Spire Books.

Jupp, P.C. (1993a), 'Cremation or Burial? Contemporary Choice in City and Village', in David Clark (ed.), *The Sociology of Death*, Oxford: Blackwell.

Jupp, P.C. (1993b) 'The development of cremation in England, 1820–1990: A Sociological Account,' unpublished PhD thesis, University of London.

Jupp, P.C. (1999) 'History of the Cremation Movement in Great Britain: The First 125 Years', *Pharos International*, 66(1): 18–25.

Jupp, P.C. (2005), *From Dust to Ashes: The Growth of Cremation in England, 1820–2000*, Basingstoke: Palgrave-Macmillan.

Jupp, P.C. and Grainger, H.J. (2002), *Golders Green Crematorium 1902–2002: A London Centenary in Context*, London: The London Cremation Company plc.

Leadbeater, S. and White, S.R.G. (2004), 'After Brodrick, Luce and Smith – What?' *Pharos International*, 70(2): 14–19.

Leaney, J. (1989), 'Ashes to Ashes: Cremation and the Celebration of Death in Nineteenth-century Britain', in R. Houlbrooke (ed.), *Death, Ritual and Bereavement*, London: Routledge, 118–35.

Parsons, B. (2005), *Committed to the Cleansing Flame*, Old Tappan, NJ: Spire Books.

Pharos (now *Pharos International*) (1934–), the journal of the Cremation Society of Great Britain.

Prevette, K.G.C. (1974), 'The First Hundred Years of the Cremation Society', in *Proceedings of the 'Centenary' Conference of the Cremation Society London, 1974*, Maidstone: The Cremation Society of Great Britain.

Rose, L. (1986), *The Massacre of the Innocents: Infanticide in Britain 1800–1939*, London: Routledge & Kegan Paul.

Rugg, J. (2004), 'Managing "Civilian Deaths due to War Operations": Yorkshire Experiences during World War II', A Hidden History', *Twentieth Century British History*, 15(2): 152–73.

White, S.R.G. (1990), 'Cricket and Cremation' *Pharos International*, 56(4): 134–35.

White, S.R.G. (1999), 'Founder Members of the Cremation Society', *Pharos International*, 66(1): 7–17.

White, S.R.G. (2002), 'The London Crematorium Company: Its Early Years', in P.C. Jupp and H.J. Grainger (eds), *Golders Green Crematorium, 1902–2002: A London Centenary in Context*, London: The London Cremation Company, pp. 11–16.

White, S.R.G. (2003a), 'A Burial Ahead of its Time? The Crookenden Burial Case and the Sanctioning of Cremation in England and Wales', *Mortality*, 7(2): 171–200.

White, S.R.G. (2003b), 'From Private to Local to General: The Cremation Act 1902', *Pharos International*, 69(1): 14–18.

CREMATIONIST

The word 'cremationist' is often used when people wish to refer to those who not only support the idea of cremation but also wish to foster its practice. It carries the connotation of an ideological position, often in opposition to burial. Sometimes, but not always, it implies a rejection of religious authorities when those authorities only encourage burial. It was a term that gained some currency in the late nineteenth and early twentieth centuries when individuals, groups and associations sought to establish cremation as a legal and socially acceptable option to burial. Since its use varies, it is important to read it in its context, as with many entries in this encyclopedia. **Douglas J. Davies**

CREMATORIUM

The term 'crematorium', with its plural 'crematoria', is the term generally used throughout this encyclopedia to refer to the overall set of buildings housing the actual cremator in which bodies are incinerated, along with a chapel or ceremonies room, waiting room and other facilities that may include, for example, a room for a book of remembrance. Other terms are preferred in different countries and these will be encountered, for example, in some references to 'crematory' in the USA, and in Chinese contexts where, since 1985 crematoria have been named 'funeral rooms'. Historically, there have even been portable crematoria as can be seen from the account of the 'Hygienic Wagon and Portable Furnace' mentioned in the **USA** entry. Mobile crematoria have also been developed in Tokyo for pet cremation (Davies, 2002: 186).

Fire and death

Whatever else a crematorium is, it is a place where fire and death meet. While it is certainly true that both fire and death have been fundamental phenomena in the long history of human societies it is also the case that in many contemporary, developed, Western societies both have become relatively invisible or marginal. The development of central heating systems has removed actual fire from the domestic context just as the emergence of professional undertakers has removed the dead from the home. Cremation, too, in such contexts is distant from the actual experience of many in the sense of any direct contact with the actual burning of bodies. Here we explore some of the implications of these changes.

Although Eastern and many other cultural traditions have employed open-air cremation for millennia, the modern crematorium entered Western cultural life only from the mid and later nineteenth century, to flourish in the twentieth. Its appearance was novel, for there was nothing else like it in terms of its specific function. Europeans who had lived in India and other parts of Asia would already have gained some familiarity with cremation conducted on open-air pyres, but the idea of an enclosed oven with a surrounding building presented architects and town planners with new challenges. It cannot be said that all of these challenges have been fully met, not even in the early twenty-first century, for aesthetic, moral, religious and environmental circumstances and popular demands are ever changing. Here I draw attention to some of the significant features of these changes, especially to issues related to paradoxical aspects of the crematorium as a background for the detailed examples found throughout this encyclopedia.

Relationships and places

The first of these issues concerns human relationships and places including the home's traditional hearth as a focus for domestic life. As such, the 'fireplace' or hearth defined a family, serving as a magnetic centre for its relationships. What of a crematorium? To suggest that the home surrounds the hearth as the crematorium surrounds the cremator would be radically inappropriate in that the crematorium brings the living together in order to part them from the deceased. In this, the crematorium is the symbolic opposite of the domestic hearth.

A second issue relates to one of the principal criticisms sometimes levelled against crematoria – namely, that they are 'impersonal' places. While an element of that criticism reflects the enforced parting of the living and the dead it is, much more frequently, due to the way in which crematoria are designed and organized in relation to the necessary functions they perform. The development of modern cremators, emerging at the high point of European industrialization, resulted in enclosed ovens with cremation being a largely automatic process. Coffins may be fed automatically into the cremator and the cremated remains withdrawn at the close of the process without any family or kin being, in any way, party to these events. The architectural design of crematoria regularly separates the main ceremony room from the cremators and, with rare exceptions, it is only crematorium operatives and managers who are found in the combustion areas. The major exception applies largely to those of Indian religious traditions who may be allowed to watch or even be party to the coffin entering the cremator. Within Hinduism this more personal association with the fact of fire in cremation is perfectly consonant with the use of fire as a central symbol in Hindu marriage rites as also in *arti*, or the use and offering of light in regular acts of *puja* or devotion whether in the home or at a temple.

Factory, church or theatre

However, for most other people, the fire reflects much more an industrial process. Indeed, the English word often used to describe the placing of the coffin into the cremator is 'to charge' the cremator – a verb taken from industrial language to describe the placing of things in a furnace. In ordinary life there would never be an occasion when family and friends would attend such an industrial setting. A much more likely kind of classification of crematoria is with a church or religious building and yet this, too, often appears paradoxical, especially for committed religious believers. For while many crematoria in countries of a strong Protestant cultural heritage do echo or reflect ecclesiastical schemes they were not churches in the accepted sense of regular places of worship. One of the best examples is in Debrecen in Hungary, where the Reformed Protestant influence set the pulpit, as the key-preaching place of God's Word, immediately and obviously above the catafalque. Many other crematoria possess structures that look like altars but are never, or very seldom, used for the holy communion or mass.

Indeed, the later in the twentieth century that the crematorium was built the less likely it is to resemble a church. This is also partly because traditional church design changed, resulting in the emergence of a kind of default building pattern for human association, coupled with the use of non-representational art and design, that was shared by various groups. In crematoria even religious symbols, such as a cross or items associated with churches such as candlesticks, are now likely to be removable. Some crematoria find themselves burdened with fixed stained-glass windows with strong religious motifs that, obviously, cannot be switched depending on whether any particular service is religious or not. Some crematoria even carry a stock of symbols so that they can be matched with the faith of a particular family. In this way, Catholic and Protestant Christians may be shown to differ from each other and from Sikh, Hindu or some Jewish groups.

Non-place or allurement

This very plasticity of form and arrangement aiming at personalizing what is, otherwise, a relatively symbolically neutral space can yield its own negative value. For such a place is simply not part of a long-standing and specific tradition. There is a sense in which time and tradition are not part of its dynamic significance. In this, a crematorium is more like a theatre in which many different plays may be performed and not like a religious building in which one set of doctrines and sacred stories are repeatedly rehearsed. The way in which some people spoke of crematoria in the mid- and later twentieth century suggested this kind of absence of enduring symbols. For such people, it would be perfectly possible to describe crematoria in terms of what one anthropologist called 'non-places' (Augé, 1995). Non-places are locations of transition – places that people pass through but

which carry no personal significance for those individuals. Airport lounges and bus stops would be typical examples. Although these are often very important places in the sense that we cannot do without them and they are necessary to contemporary life, they lack depth of meaning. For many, the crematorium has become just such a non-place. It is a necessity as part of someone's 'journey' but is devoid of particular significance. There is little opportunity for that process of 'allurement' to occur – a process Lindsay Jones associated with 'ritual-architectural events' in which someone brings their hopes, joys and sorrows into a ritual arena and is able to make various sorts of links between experience, this place and other similar places (Jones, 2000: 79).

And yet, for some, the crematorium – or at least its gardens and books of remembrance – can come to possess a degree of allurement, especially for those people who visit and revisit them as memorial sites. Some relatives even deem them sacred places: it is as they become suffused with memory and with the moods engendered by many visits, that this allurement develops (Davies, 1996). But here, too, numerous issues arise. It takes time for people to form relationships of memory with a place, and a single cremation ceremony is not likely to be sufficient, especially when the bereaved are in no state to take an active interest in their surroundings. Only if a single crematorium serves a neighbourhood and if a family or community resides there long enough for people to attend many cremations may such associations occur. The same may apply if the cremated remains of numerous family members are located on a single site. However, since the closing decades of the twentieth century increasing numbers of countries permit the removal of cremated remains that are subsequently located in places of individual or family significance. This diverts attention from the crematorium and reinforces its role as a transient place of utilitarian necessity.

Many architects have sought to invest their crematoria with significance and meaning by developing cultural ideas of life and death, as many cases in this encyclopedia show. But the provision of art, architecture, statuary and garden designs is one thing and acceptance of them is another – and that is where the experience of the mourner comes into play, as does the passage of time within a culture. Unlike churches that are likely to be arenas of experience embracing both sorrow and joy, the crematorium tends to be associated with a limited range of emotion, mostly at the sad end of the experiential spectrum. The managerial style associated with them is also one of efficiency which is rarely the cultural image associated with churches. The image of the conveyor-belt, – one that became a popular description of crematoria in Britain in the 1960s and 1970s – reflected both the industrial image and the ideal of efficiency. The very fact that cremation services were thought of as taking place very rapidly reflected this.

To a degree, crematoria came to possess a certain ambiguity. For some, they were obviously secular, even anti-Christian, locations; for others, they served Christian needs. Indeed, for approximately half of the twentieth century, cremation was one boundary marker between Protestantism on the one hand and Catholicism on the other as the entry on **Germany** shows. In Lutheran Sweden, for example, the Church came to own and manage crematoria, while in Anglican England local authorities or private companies did so. In Italy the thought of church-owned crematoria remains almost unthinkable. Still, in general terms, crematoria have benefited from the nature of their diverse social location in terms of 'ownership'. As other entries show, many architects – especially in historically Protestant parts of Europe – have taken up the challenge of designing crematoria and, in so doing, have brought distinctive cultural styles, each with their aesthetic and emotional ethos, to bear upon these buildings. This has allowed a broad band of cultural commitments to find expression in their own decade or stylistic period and, in so doing, to make some firm assertion on the nature of life and death in ways that have not been determined by the direct patronage of churches. **Douglas J. Davies**

See also fire; Germany; Hinduism; USA.

References

Augé, Marc (1995), *Non-places: An Introduction to an Anthropology of Super Modernity*, trans. John Howe, London: Verso.

Davies, Douglas J. (1996), 'The Sacred Crematorium', *Mortality*, 1(1): 83–94.

Davies, Douglas J. (2002), *Death, Ritual and Belief* (2nd rev. edn), London: Continuum.

CREMATORS

Modern cremation would be inconceivable without the technical advances that have been made in engineering and design. While many similar principles have come to apply across the world there are also some regional differences. Here we consider first some general aspects of cremator development in Western societies, then outline some historical design features in influential European systems before, finally, considering the case of China. **Douglas J. Davies**

EUROPEAN CREMATOR DEVELOPMENT

The earliest 'modern' cremators were developed from approximately 1850. Successful cremators were used in Germany, Italy and France, and the fuels available were coke or coal.

Coke-fired cremators

Until about 1930 most cremators were coke-fired, the coke being burned in a chamber 'back-to-back' with the cremation chamber. Hot gases from the coke furnace side entered the chamber holding the coffin and the whole apparatus relied on natural draught to draw the gases to the chimney and thence to the atmosphere. The objective was to operate the coke combustion as a gas producer – that is, with insufficient air to burn the coke completely. This resulted in a gas rich in carbon monoxide that burned in the cremation chamber and completed the cremation. While the coke-fired cremator was quite successful in realizing the primary objective of the disposal of human remains, there remained a number of unwelcome features. These included the need for prodigious quantities of coke, with some 500 kilograms required to get the cremator up to working temperature and 250 kilograms per cremation thereafter, as well as the fact that operating the cremator was very labour-intensive.

Development of the gas-fired cremator

In modern cremation, as in many industrial processes, developments took place using the materials and fuels available at the time. The gas industries were advancing rapidly, and their new techniques were applied to cremation: in fact, they were seeking new outlets for their manufactured gas. The first gas-fired cremators were installed in the early 1900s, with several more models following on over the next 20 years. The infant cremation industry was ready to welcome the advent of gas-fired cremators because of the operational advantages of cleanliness, lower cost and reduction in labour requirements. Developments in cremators came quickly, and both the furnace manufacturers and cremator operators contributed to the result. The cremator became a much smaller and simpler furnace once the coke-firing equipment was removed. The gas burners were of the Bunsen-burner type, and there were as many as 16 burners in one cremator – in the first such cremators, each one had to be ignited by hand.

Most of the furnace companies in Europe that eventually developed successful cremators had already achieved an impressive record in the gas-making and coke-making industries. The industrial research of the early years of the twentieth century was largely empirical, but the gas industries led the systematic development of a more technical product. Special attention was paid to the safety of operation. Gas supply undertakings of municipalities in most countries became national bodies during the 1950s and 1960s, and were given another major boost by the discovery and distribution of natural gas. Some countries did not have natural gas, or were not able to secure a nationwide distribution, and they continued to use light oil as the support fuel. Cremation was becoming ever more popular, and many new crematoria were established. By the end of, say, 1975 there existed a number of cremator types able to provide a clean and dignified cremation. Taking a general overview, it can be said that cremators, as developed and operated thus far, were capable of producing good-quality ashes and well-calcined remains. However, about this time, movements to improve air quality were gathering momentum, and cremators were brought progressively into the 'clean air' regime.

Electric cremators

At the same time as gas-fired cremators were being developed, several manufacturers produced a cremator heated only by electrical energy, with no burners being used. The furnace was, in effect, a heat storage device, which was kept warm during the night by electric heating elements. The cremation movement has always been attached to the concept of the disposal of human remains without any contact with other agents such as flames; indeed, the slogan 'Cremation in the sole element of air' was very attractive to cremationists. Even so, this rather elegant method of cremation has always been limited in its application because of the high furnace cost and the somewhat longer cremation times required.

Atmospheric emissions from cremators

The history of cremators from this point on is the relationship of the cremation process to the minimization of environmental impact. Improvement in environmental performance has been something of a moving target. As knowledge of the risks associated with different types of pollution grew so it was applied to cremators in layer after layer of regulation.

Perhaps the most serious concerns have focused on the emission of heavy metals, particularly mercury. Although mercury accumulates in the body during life, by far the biggest contributor to emissions is dental amalgam, so that at cremation there can be a few grams of mercury emitted with each cremation. It has become well understood that mercury emissions are toxic and enter the food chain via the marine and land routes. Mercury also persists in the environment, with no natural route by which it can be rendered harmless. As a result, those industries which use or process mercury have reduced their emissions to such an extent that crematoria are now one of the biggest contributors to mercury emission. Driven by such a serious environmental impact, the regulatory agencies demanded that effective abatement must be applied to crematoria.

Although the speed of improvement and of regulatory regime has differed in different countries, and there is no international standard for cremator environmental performance, a consensus has emerged such that, by the start of the twenty-first century, the concept of best available technique (BAT) for crematoria had become established. The application of computer-controlled technology has enabled the most modern techniques to be applied to cremators. Briefly, this entails the minimization of the emissions of dust, mercury and dioxins involving the use of abatement techniques such as dosing the gases with adsorbent reagents followed by filters: the final exhaust gas quality is recognized as 'best available technique'. The ultimate disposal of spent reagent, loaded with dust, mercury and so on, must follow the local requirements for controlled landfill as 'special waste' or recovery. **Clive Chamberlain**

See also mercury; pollution control (UK).

SIEMENS, SCHNEIDER AND KLINGENSTIERNA CREMATORS

The Siemens system

The design of the Siemens system, employing 'regenerative' chambers, provided the basis for most of the early modern Western cremators. Its originality lay in the fact that it did not use the heat directly produced by the burning fuel (coal) but took the gases from the original combustion and thoroughly mixed them together with oxygen from the air to yield a much higher temperature thus avoiding the potential heat loss of incomplete combustion. (Hoyos, 1922a). With careful regulation of the relative proportions of burning gases and air, diverse cremator temperatures could also be achieved. Two basic design variations emerged: cremators receiving air as a forced current and those receiving air at ordinary pressure through small gratings, as in the original Siemens design.

The Siemens cremator was composed of four basic parts: the generator, the incinerator chamber itself, the ash repository and the chimney. All the fuel burning takes place in the generator. Briefly outlined, air arrives through a grating and comes into contact with the lower layer of burning coal, at a high temperature. The formation of carbon dioxide and nitrogen shows that combustion is complete. The carbon dioxide passes to the upper layers of fuel where it takes on more carbon and becomes carbon monoxide, which is combustible. This high temperature forces the release of hydrocarbons, carbon monoxide and hydrogen, which are combustible, and also carbon dioxide and nitrogen. The composition and proportions are shown in Table 1.

Table 1 Proportions of gases in a Siemens cremator

Gas	In weight	In volume
Carbon monoxide	263	25
Carbon dioxide	83	5
Nitrogen	636	60
Hydrogen	6	8
Hydrocarbons	12	2
Totals	1000	100

A valve allows the combustible gases produced by the burning coal to pass through a channel to a second chamber where they encounter a current of atmospheric air drawn from outside. This mixture burns, the flames change colour, and the process intensifies to produce an extraordinarily high temperature. This intense combustion heats a wall. When the wall is incandescent, valves are closed so that neither gases nor flames can penetrate into the adjoining incineration chamber. As it is impossible for flames produced by the burning gases to come into contact with the corpse, a total cremation without smoke or odour is achieved. Air continues entering the second chamber, heating up when it comes into contact with the incandescent wall, which heats to a temperature of 1000°C. Carrying this temperature, the air enters into the adjoining incineration chamber, which has a floor formed by a grill of heat-resistant material. The air then passes through a channel and escapes via the chimney.

The coffin containing the corpse is carried on rails to the door of the cremator on an iron cart, then introduced into the incineration chamber and placed on the grill. The iron cart is then removed and the door closed. As the cremator has normally been preheated for three or four hours, the cremation process begins immediately, as the internal temperature is around 1000 degrees centigrade. Only a few minutes after being placed in the incinerator, the coffin will have disappeared. If it is made of zinc, it will combine with oxygen from the air and escape via the chimney as blue-white zinc oxide smoke. In less than two minutes inside the cremator the zinc is gone, as it melts at 440°C. A wooden coffin is also quickly reduced to ash.

Ashes from the burnt coffin, clothes, any flowers and so on are sucked out by the ventilation in the incinerator, which is determined by the chimney design. At such a high temperature, water in the corpse quickly evaporates, reducing its weight by over 50 per cent. The corpse is dry in around fifteen minutes. Then the cremation proper begins as the body carbonizes. The ashes produced are sieved through the grill into a receptor. The process is complete in between 60 and 90 minutes. The white ashes, which is all that remains of the corpse, are composed of mineral substances that the heat is not able to destroy, such as phosphates of calcium, calcium oxide, and calcium fluoride. Once cold, they are collected and placed in an urn. The Siemens cremator could be operated by one individual. The cost of the fuel depended on the number of cremations performed at one time: the more that were carried out consecutively, the less fuel each single cremation required.

The Schneider system

By 1922 the basic Siemens system was only employed in Gotha Crematorium, Germany, where engineer Richard Schneider had successfully modified the system following operational problems. The Schneider system was now in operation in 33 German crematoria (Hoyos, 1922b). The Schneider system differs from Siemens in that it does not have a 'regenerative' chamber. Instead, the heat is generated by the 'recuperative system' based on the principle of continuous air current. For this, the small coke-fired burner is not separate from the main oven, but instead forms part of a whole unit with it. As illustrated in Figure 1, The Schneider cremator is divided into the following main parts: the generator 'A', the incineration chamber 'B', the ash repository 'C' (in funnel form), and the channelling 'D' that carried the gases to the chimney 'E'. The effect of forcing the gases to pass through the network of tubes and ash repository was to completely remove all odour from the cremation process. To light the cremator, a fire of wood is built and lit on the grating of the generator. Gradually more fuel (generally coke) is added until, within 30–45 minutes, the generator is full. The entry of air into the generator is regulated by means of valve 'F'. A deposit of water located below the grill was designed to ensure the complete combustion of the coke burning on it. The heat produced by the burning coke evaporates the water and the resultant vapour penetrates the hot gases, thereby ensuring that they do not deteriorate too rapidly. The combustible gases arrive through a tube into the incineration chamber via the aperture 'G'. There, they combine completely with the red-hot atmospheric air. The flames produced by the combustion pass through the incineration chamber and then through the grill, downwards towards the ash repository. There they pass

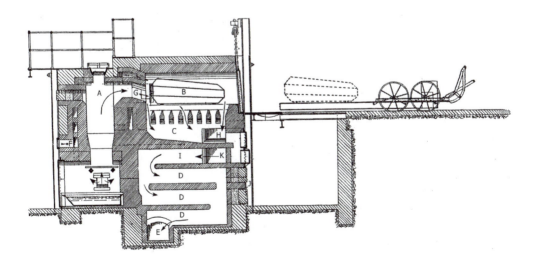

Figure 1   The Schneider system

Reproduced by permission of Durham University Library

through apertures 'H' towards area 'I' where they burn unincinerated parts that have fallen from the corpse above. This ensures that combustion is continuous and complete. Between four and five hours are required to heat the cremator and approximately a quarter of a ton of coke is required to reach this stage. Once the correct temperature is achieved, the air apertures 'F' are closed. This limits the production of gas until it extinguishes. Shortly before the introduction of the coffin, the chimney door is opened, thereby establishing the draught. Lowered from the chapel located above the cremator, the coffin can, if required, have flowers and other offerings and objects removed from it. Then it is carried by a cart, on rails, to the incineration chamber. The coffin is introduced into the incineration chamber and the door closed behind it – an operation that takes a trained operator around 15 seconds to perform. Placed directly onto a grill of heat-resistant bricks, the coffin is then surrounded by superheated air: it does not come into contact with the burning fuel or the flame produced by the fuel. After the introduction of the coffin, the air valves 'J' are opened, with the aim of allowing sufficient air to enter in order to raise the temperature to 1000°C. The ashes produced collect in the repository and the burning gases pass down through aperture 'K' without odour or smoke.

From outside the cremator, apart from the tremor in the air due to convection, nothing can be observed that reveal it is in operation. There is a small window that allows sight of the progress of the cremation as if through a veil. The whole operation lasts 90 minutes. Although the time taken for a cremation is similar to that using a Siemens system cremator, the Schneider design had the advantage of costing up to 25 per cent less to purchase.

The Klingenstierna system

Like the Siemens system before it, the Schneider system was also modified. A variation on Schneider's system, designed by Colonel Klingenstierna, was in use in the early 1920s in Offenbach and Heidelbert (in Germany), Gothenburg and Stockholm (Hoyos, 1922c). The key difference between Klingenstierna's system and Schneider's is that, in the former, the cart is left in the cremator for the entire cremation, acting simultaneously as the grill and the receptacle for ashes (see Figure 2). For this reason it merits attention. The wheels and frame of the cart 'L' are made of high-quality materials. The frame is double–walled, and between the two walls is sandwiched a heat-resistant substance. Heat-resistant bricks rest on the frame and support the grill. This is inclined towards the front from the head to the feet of the coffin. The

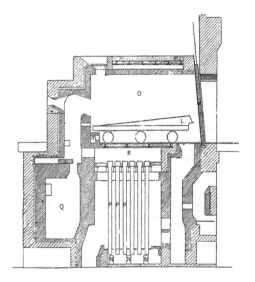

Figure 2 The Klingenstierna system

Reproduced by permission of Durham University Library

cart originally caused design problems due to the need for it to withstand the very high temperatures in the cremator without becoming deformed. In order to protect the cart's wheels, cold air is passed through aperture 'M' below it. This helps prevent the wheels from breaking and also precludes their expansion, which would make the cart difficult to extract from the cremator on its rails.

The cremator design permits atmospheric air to enter the chamber through apertures in the exterior wall 'N', which is separated from the interior wall by heat-resistant material. The air distributes itself throughout the apparatus in order to enter into the piping 'P' that is located in the hermetically-closed chamber in such a way as there is no other exit for it. Already heated to 400°C by a small fire, the atmospheric air is conducted by the system of 36 pipes located at the base of the cremator towards the incineration chamber 'O'. There are two heating rings in the generator 'Q', the larger for burning the fuel (coke in this system) that produces combustible gases, reaching a temperature of 200°C. The chemical process for the production of the combustible gases is almost the same as in the Schneider system. These gases rise to the incineration chamber where they meet with the heated atmospheric air. There they mix and burn, reaching 800°C, the necessary temperature for cremation to occur.

The oven must be heated for at least two hours before use (half the time of the Schneider system). When ready, the interior and exterior iron doors, covered with a heat-resistant material, are opened and the cart, with the coffin on it, is introduced. In this system, the haste required when performing this operation in a Schneider cremator is unnecessary. Once inside, the doors are closed and the gases entering the incinerator chamber uniformly bathe the coffin in intense heat. As the corpse is cremated, the ashes fall through the grill and collect in the ash repository 'R', under the cart.

Through adequate manipulation of the ventilation system, the entrance and exit of combustible gases and atmospheric air can be graduated to allow the maintenance of the correct temperature. In the walls close to the chimney, holes allowed observation of the interior, which would be fairly clear after the coffin itself had been incinerated. When the cremation is complete, the cart is removed and

the ashes collected from it. As with the other systems, combustion, at such a high temperature, is complete and produces no smoke or odour. A normal cremation in a Klingenstierna system cremator lasts two hours, some 30–45 minutes longer than with the Schneider system. However, an advantage of the Klingenstierna system over Schneider is that the chimney does not need to be as tall. A Schneider system chimney has to be at least 13 or 14 metres tall, whereas a Klingenstierna cremator can be much shorter – in fact, no greater than the height of the crematorium building, which allowed architects greater leeway in design. One final advantage was that Klingenstierna cremators were up to 25 per cent cheaper than their Schneider counterparts.
Lewis H. Mates

References

Hoyos, Dr Candido (1922a), 'Sociedad para la propaganda de la Incineración en Cuba. La tecnica de la Incineración', *Revista de Medicina Legal de Cuba*, 5: 25–27,31, CRE/A/CU1.

Hoyos, Dr Candido (1922b), 'Sociedad para la propaganda de la Incineración en Cuba. Tecnica de la Incineración II', *Revista de Medicina Legal de Cuba*, 6(22): 25–28, CRE/A/CU1.

Hoyos, Dr Candido (1922c), 'Sociedad para la propaganda de la Incineración en Cuba. Tecnica de la Incineración III', *Revista de Medicina Legal de Cuba*, 7: 21–22, 25–27, CRE/A/CU1.

THE PEOPLE'S REPUBLIC OF CHINA

The production of cremators in China began after the introduction of Czech models in 1958. Based on them, China developed '61'-, '62'-, '63'- and '64'-type Czech-like cremators, fuelled by coal and wood, a few of which are still in use. In 1968, with the onset of the Cultural Revolution, research and development of cremators was discontinued and it was not resumed until the reforms leading to the opening up to the outside world in the 1980s. In 1981 the Ministry of Civil Affairs established the Shenyang Cremator Research Institute, the first research institute for cremation facilities in China. In 1982 the Institute successfully developed '82B-1' cremators. With corpses cremated on stilts, cremators of this type offer rapid cremation, low energy consumption, no manual turnover, and low costs. Their defect, however, lies in the black smoke discharged ten minutes after a corpse is put into the cremator. At present, the '82B-1' cremators are widely employed in medium-sized cities, towns and rural areas in China. Subsequently, research and development on cremators in China has focused on the handling of smoke, but basically no new types are projected. In 1989 the 101 Research Institute under the National Civil Affairs Department was founded, and in 1992 this institute formulated and publicized national standards for cremators.

In 1989 the Shanghai Administration Section of Funerals and Interments organized experts from universities and research institutions to analyse the smoke produced during cremations. It took four years to conclude a 'Sensual Testing of Stench' which was adopted later by environmental protection institutions in large cities. However, the 'Innocuous Cremators' they developed failed because of possible secondary pollution caused by the 'Venturi' dust removal system. Based on this, the Shanghai Funeral Service Centre established the Shanghai Baolong Cremation Mechanical Research Institute in 1998. In 1999 this institute developed 'GC-H Green Cremators', which were granted a Certificate of National New Key Products, the highest certification level in China. Controlled by computers, these cremators operate quietly and with a low energy consumption. The indexes of smoke discharged are far below national standards.

Different from former cremators, the 'GC-H' system successfully combines with Chinese funeral customs thus expanding the use of crematoria. During the process of cremation, several ceremonies can be held:

1   a farewell ceremony, in which the relatives and friends make their last spiritual communications with the deceased;
2   a sending-off ceremony, when the relatives and friends salute with eyes to the deceased, seeing the latter slowly into the hearth;
3   a 'watch-soul' ceremony, watching the deceased be cremated in the hearth;
4   'Meeting the soul' and accepting the cremains, placing them into a utensil in accordance with established ceremony.

In 2001 the Baolong Cremation Mechanical Research Institute developed 'GC-W Green Cremators', including chamber cremators. The chamber cremators are installed in the world's largest crematory, Shanghai Yishan funeral room, which, under perfect working conditions, cremates 50 000 corpses or more per year. The automatic corpse conveyers developed at the same time are also installed in the Yishan funeral room, carrying 200 or more corpses per day. **Liu Fengming**

See also fuel.

CREMULATION

Cremulation describes the process of rendering burnt bone fragments and other remains into a granular form of 'ash' or 'cremains'. Various styles and types of cremulator machine have been, and are, used in modern cremation, with the process itself developing from previous and unrelated industrial procedures. Most involve some form of rotating chamber or grinding mechanism as, for example, the heavy metal balls used in early models. Remains taken from the cremator often include portions of larger bones and cremulation allows for all the remains to be presented in a uniform fashion. Cremulation is standard in most forms of modern cremation. Issues of health, hygiene and propriety have also led to cremulators being located in separate rooms at a crematorium, or to being surrounded by, or furnished with, air-extractor units to cope with any extremely fine dust that might accompany the grinding process. However, in several Eastern traditions, especially Buddhism, certain bones are removed from the remains of cremation for ritual purposes while other remains are not ground down but are placed in various kinds of containers. In traditional Indian cremation, as at Banaras, there is no cremulation of remains; instead, they are placed in the river Ganges.

The practice of grinding remains into ash has not always found approval. Stephen Prothero has documented the debates in the USA during the late nineteenth and early twentieth centuries between those objecting to ash-cremation, along with its implied consequence of scattering, and those favouring the placing of the remains as they come from the cremator into urns as an ongoing memorial (Prothero, 2001: 149–51). While some of the motives for this were economic, since funeral directors could sell urns and memorial spaces whereas scattering could be done at no cost, others expressed ideas of

desecration of the bodily outcome of cremation.
Douglas J. Davies

See also ashes – remains; ashes – China; Buddhism;
Hinduism.

Reference

Prothero, Stephen (2001), *Purified by Fire. A History
of Cremation in America*, Berkely: University of
California Press.

CRIME

Opponents of cremation have long argued that
cremation can be used to destroy evidence of
murder, and of murder by poisoning in
particular. When, in 1874, Sir Henry Thompson
published the article in the *Contemporary Review*
which led to the formation of the Cremation
Society of England, he was aware that this
objection would be advanced to his proposal.
Opponents would, and did, say that burial
preserved a dead body – at least to some extent –
so that it could be exhumed and evidence of
crime recovered from it. As a matter of public
policy, this objection became the biggest obstacle
to cremation's adoption and even now explains
why it is attended by stricter legal formalities
than burial in the UK. The objection was not,
however, a point addressed either by Thompson
in his first paper or one advanced by Philip
Henry Holland, the inspector of burials, in his
immediate critique of Thompson's proposal.
Thompson did, however, confront it in his
riposte to Holland. Thompson's answer was first
that were the incidence of undetected poisoning
to be what it would be if corpses were cremated,
the harm caused by it would be nowhere near as
great as that presently caused by the death and
disease attributable to earth burial. In case the
results of this straightforward felicific calculation
did not convince, Thompson argued further that
the so-called superiority of burial as a deterrent to
poisoning depended on the corpse being there to
be exhumed, and the fact that the corpse would
still be there was, conversely, partly responsible
for the lamentably inadequate system of
registration of deaths which failed to detect
poisoning before burial.

Whatever the method of corpse disposal,
what was needed was an improved system of
death registration. Thompson proposed the
adoption of the French and German system so
that the verification of death and of the absence
of suspicion of crime was taken out of the hands
of family doctors and entrusted to public
officials. Because the fear of undetected
poisoning was the ground on which the Home
Office formulated its final resistance to
permitting cremation and because it was
something in respect of which practical measures
could be taken, cremationists became foremost
amongst those campaigning for an improved
system of registering deaths. In 1891 the
Cremation Society amended its rules to add the
advocacy of what would now be known as a
medical examiner system to its objects, and
Thompson's contribution to a deputation to the
Home Secretary in January 1893 was largely
responsible for the establishment, later in the
year, of a House of Commons Select Committee
to inquire into the adequacy of the system of
registering deaths. Of the 11 committee
members, two, Drs Cameron and Farquharson,
were members of the Cremation Society's
council, and Cameron himself, as well as
Thompson and Sir Thomas Spencer Wells,
another council member, gave evidence to it. The
society's hopes of legislation, however, were
disappointed. Until 1926 it remained lawful to
bury the body of a person whose death had not
been registered and only then did it become
necessary in practice for a serious inquiry to be
made into the cause of a death before it could be
registered.

Thompson had also suggested that another
deterrent to poisoning could be provided – at less
expense than burial and with greater effect than
the possibility of exhumation after burial – by
preserving the stomach and some of the viscera
of corpses for a certain period, either in all cases
or in those where a doctor or relative of the
deceased thought it wise or desirable. In 1882 the
council of the Cremation Society decided that
cremations would not be permitted at the
society's crematorium at Woking except under
regulations which provided for the preservation
of such parts of the body as would preserve
evidence of poison. But, when the first
cremations were performed in the wake of the
acquittal of William Price, the published
conditions of the society made no mention of
this. Instead the society required two medical
certificates. The first medical certificate had to be
provided by a doctor who had attended the

deceased until their death. The doctor had to state the cause of death unhesitatingly and record when he or she had last seen the deceased. The doctor signing the second certificate, who had to be different from the first, had to attest that he or she had 'carefully and separately investigated the circumstances connected with the death' and had to declare that 'there are no circumstances connected with the death which could, in my opinion, make exhumation of the body hereafter necessary'. If no doctor had attended the deceased, the society required a postmortem examination to be performed by a doctor appointed by it, as it did if the certificates provided raised suspicions in Thompson's mind about the circumstances of the death: indeed, until 1899 he examined all the certificates himself. The society also reserved the right to refuse an application for cremation without giving any reason whatsoever. Although the published conditions did not mention that organs might be removed at a postmortem and preserved, this was occasionally done. Thompson told the House of Commons Select Committee on Death Certification in 1893 that the society had preserved parts of the kidney, liver, stomach and spleen of four or five of the 393 persons so far cremated at Woking and Thomas Herring, who took over Thompson's role in examining the certificates in 1899, told the Departmental Committee drafting the regulations under the Cremation Act of 1902 that relatives of the deceased knew when parts had been kept.

When Thompson gave evidence to the House of Commons Select Committee, he provided the Committee with copies of the certificates used by the Cremation Society. The copy of the first certificate he gave the Committee was an enlarged version of the certificate in use until that point. The enlargement consisted of the addition of a questionnaire of eight questions, and thereafter the society used the enlarged certificate. Private and local authority crematoria established between 1885 and the passage of the Cremation Act in 1902 adopted conditions and regulations almost identical to those of the Cremation Society. Statutory powers were required to allow local authorities to provide crematoria and the statutes which conferred them invariably required such regulations to be made and to be approved by the Home Office. Although there were only two crematoria in operation – at Woking and Manchester – when

the Select Committee reported in 1893, it recommended that the Society's rules should be mandated by statute. The Cremation Act, passed in 1902, required the Home Secretary to fashion regulations prescribing the conditions under which cremations were to be allowed to take place and a Departmental Committee was established to draft them. The Cremation Regulations, which came into effect in 1903, essentially elaborated on those of the Cremation Society, but formalized the role of the 'medical referee' as an independent agent whose authority was required before a cremation could take place and who could refuse to authorize a cremation without giving any reason. The Departmental Committee recognized that no rules could completely remove the risk of homicide going undetected, but, having regard to the fact that parliament had sanctioned cremation by passing The Cremation Act and had obliged the Home Secretary to make regulations laying down the conditions under which cremations could be performed, the Committee saw its role as being the framing of 'regulations, which, while avoiding the unnecessary restrictions such as might discourage cremation or involve undesirable delay in the disposal of the body, would reduce to a minimum the risk of cremation being used to destroy evidence of murder by violence or poison'. The Committee investigated 86 exhumations ordered either by coroners or the Home Secretary between 1893 and 1901, about which full information was available. Three had been followed by convictions of murder and one by a conviction for manslaughter. The Committee was satisfied that, had its draft regulations been in force, none of the victims would have been cremated and, indeed, that the detection of these crimes might have been expedited. Similarly, the Committee thought that the chances of conviction in other cases where crime was suspected but no prosecution brought or conviction obtained would have been increased by the regulations since they would have led to earlier postmortems and the collection of fresher evidence from witnesses. The Interdepartmental Committee which reviewed the Cremation Regulations in 1950 did not think it would be useful to carry out a similar analysis of exhumations since exhumations were running at only 2 per cent of (about 500 000) deaths. The Committee was informed of only two cases of murder since 1902 in which cremation had been involved. In one, the medical referee had referred the matter to the police when his suspicions had been raised by the application for cremation. In the other, police had had to abandon inquiries into the death of a doctor's third wife because she had been cremated.

The Committee established by the Home Office in 1965 under the chairmanship of Norman Brodrick QC to review the law relating to death certification, the disposal of dead bodies and the operations of coroners, had a similar review made of the results of exhumations. When it reported in 1971, its overall judgement, taking into account the results of this review, was that 'the risk of secret homicide occurring and remaining undiscovered as a direct consequence of the state of the current law on the certification of death has been much exaggerated, and that it has not been a significant danger at any time in the past fifty years'. The Committee was particularly critical of the evidence for the claims made by Dr John Havard and the British Medical Association that a worrying proportion of deaths from homicide were being registered as deaths from natural causes. As for the cremation certification procedure, the Committee 'found no evidence that the procedure had ever led to the exposure of a previously unsuspected crime' and thought it unlikely that it ever would or, indeed, could. It made proposals for improving the procedures for investigating, certifying and registering deaths in general and recommended that, once these were in place, the only part of the procedure for carrying out cremations that would need to be retained was the registration of cremations. This was very much in line with the view that the Cremation Society had advanced since its early years – namely, that the procedures for registering death should be uniformly rigorous so that no distinction need be drawn between subsequent procedures for burial and cremation.

Despite the primary concern of the Act and Regulations to protect against cremation being used to destroy evidence of crime, a lacuna was revealed in the drafting of the Act shortly after its passage. The Cremation Society's Disposal of the Dead Bill, which had been introduced into parliament in the immediate aftermath of William Price's acquittal, would have provided that it would be unlawful to 'burn ... the dead body of any person ... except in a place licensed for that purpose by the Secretary of State'. The Cremation Act empowered – indeed required – the Home Secretary to make regulations prescribing in what cases and under what conditions the 'burning of human remains' could take place. Regulation 3 stated that 'No cremations of human remains shall take place except in a crematorium' of whose opening the Secretary of State had been informed. The Act made it an offence to contravene the Regulations. A baby-farmer had attempted to dispose, on her kitchen grate, of the body of a baby who had died in her charge. At her trial for contravening the Regulations, the judge ruled that she had not done so because Regulation 3 applied only to 'cremations' of human remains and not to any 'burning' of human remains. Neither Act nor Regulations contained a definition of 'cremation', but the Act did define 'crematorium' as 'a building fitted with appliances for the purpose of burning of human remains'. The judge reasoned from this that a 'cremation' must be a burning which takes place in a crematorium and that Regulation 3 had no wider effect than to prohibit the use of a crematorium until its opening had been notified to the Secretary of State. Quite clearly, Jessie Byers's kitchen was not a crematorium, however many infants she might have incinerated on her kitchen grate. Had the terms of the Disposal of the Dead Bill been adopted – as the draft amended Cremation Regulations which have been in existence since 1989 have adopted them – she would clearly have been guilty. The Act and Regulations have never been amended in this respect and *R. v. Byers* has not yet been held to have been wrongly decided.

One of the legal mechanisms for detecting homicide is a coroner's inquest. In no circumstances, however, could a coroner hold an inquest once a body had been cremated. This was because, at least until the early years of the twentieth century, the coroner and jury had to view the body. They had, as the term was, to 'sit upon the body' and indeed, in earlier times, inquests were conducted in the presence of the decomposing corpse – often in inns and public houses. It was taken for granted that, after a cremation, there could be no 'body' to give a coroner jurisdiction. In his evidence to the Departmental Committee which drafted the Cremation Regulations, the coroner for Central London suggested that coroners should be given power to hold inquests after cremations, but the Committee took the view that such a provision, if included in the Regulations, would make the regulation-making power *ultra vires*.

After 1903 the Central London coroner's proposal was occasionally revived when amendments to the Coroners Act were being considered. It had been decided finally that no provision would be made for a power to order an inquest which it was anticipated would be very rarely used, when Herbert Armstrong, a solicitor in Hay-on-Wye, was convicted of poisoning his wife. A suggestion that if she had been cremated Armstrong's crime would never have been detected led to the proposal being revived. The result was section 18 of the Coroners Act 1926 (now section 15 of the 1988 Act). This allows a coroner, where a body has been destroyed by any means, including fire, or is lying in a place from which it cannot be recovered, to report the matter to the Home Secretary who may then direct an inquest.

Over the years, the circumstances in which this power should be exercised has been a matter of debate between the Home Office and the Registrar-General's department. The Home Office came under pressure to direct inquests almost as a matter of routine when registrars felt unable to register deaths because no informant was available who could confirm that death had taken place either from direct observation or from very compelling circumstantial evidence. Until the provision was invoked to allow the coroner for South Manchester to hold inquests on some of the victims of Dr Harold Shipman, the power had rarely, if ever, been used in cases of cremation. The Brodrick Committee's view was that 'the general risk of homicide going undetected is extremely small; and there is no reason – to put it at its lowest – to think that the risk of homicide by doctors is higher than for any other profession'. Establishing the truth of this view is complicated by the difficulties in ascertaining the extent to which euthanasia is being performed by doctors and in determining which mercy killings (if any are taking place) would be found to be murders by juries. The cremation certification procedures did not prevent the cremation of Lillian Boyes whom Dr Cox was convicted of attempting to murder in 1991. Had a postmortem examination been made of her body and established definitely that potassium chloride had caused her death, the charge against Dr Cox would probably have been murder rather than attempted murder. Nor did the cremation procedures prevent the cremation of George Liddell in 1997, although the fact that Dr George Moore was acquitted of murdering him might be taken as indicating that there was no reason why they should have prevented the cremation. A large number of the patients Shipman was convicted for, or suspected of, killing were cremated. Professor Richard Baker, who carried out an audit of Shipman's clinical practice, found that a relatively – although not significantly – greater proportion of his patients were cremated than in general, but he also told the Shipman Inquiry that he had found no evidence that Shipman exerted any influence on the patients' relatives to have their bodies cremated and counsel to the Inquiry revealed that, at that stage, no relative had reported any such pressure to the Inquiry. In fact, suspicions about Shipman's offences were partly aroused by the large number of cremation form Cs that his fellow and neighbouring practitioners were being asked to complete in respect of his patients, and a police investigation was begun.

Dame Janet Smith, who conducted the inquiry into the deaths of Shipman's patients, concluded that, if the police investigation had been conducted competently, Shipman's crimes would probably have been detected earlier and a small number of his murders forestalled. She also concluded that the cremation certification process, as then implemented, had lamentably failed to prevent the cremation of patients he had killed, partly because the forms and certificates were not wholly suited to their purposes; partly because doctors generally, including medical referees, were ignorant of, were given no training about and had never reflected on those purposes, and, in the case of some medical referees, were unsuited, through lack of relevant clinical experience, to be medical referees; and partly because of the shortcomings of individual doctors in particular circumstances. If her recommendations were to be implemented – and it would require primary legislation to implement them in full – the legal incidents of the system of death investigation and registration would no longer vary according to whether a dead body was to be buried or cremated; and the verification and certification of all deaths would become more rigorous under the overall control of a national Coroner service.

Stephen White

See also Cremation Society of Great Britain; Thompson.

References

Baker, Richard (2000), *Harold Shipman's Clinical Practice 1974–1998: A Clinical Audit Commissioned by the Chief Medical Officer*, London: Department of Health.

British Medical Association (1964), *Deaths in the Community*, London: BMA.

Havard, John (1960), *The Detection of Secret Homicide: A Study of the Medico-legal System of Investigation of Sudden and Unexplained Deaths*, London: Macmillan.

Holland, P.M. (1874), 'Burial or Cremation?', *Contemporary Review*, 23: 477–84.

Home Office (1903), *Report of the Departmental Committee appointed … to prepare a Draft of the Regulations to be made under the Cremation Act, 1902*, Cd 1452, London: HMSO.

Home Office (1950), *Cremation Committee: Report of the Interdepartmental Committee*, Cmd 8009, London: HMSO.

Home Office (1971), *Report of the Departmental Committee on Death Certification and Coroners*, Cmnd. 4810, London: HMSO.

House of Commons (1893), *First and Second Reports from the Select Committee on Death Certification*, C. 373 and 402, London: HMSO.

Smith, Dame Janet (2003), *The Shipman Inquiry Second Report: The Police Investigation of March 1998*, Cm 5853, London: The Stationery Office.

Smith, Dame Janet (2003), *The Shipman Inquiry Second Report: Death Certification and Investigation of Death by Coroners*, Cm. 5834, London: The Stationery Office.

Thompson, Henry (1874), 'The Treatment of the Body after Death', *Contemporary Review*, 23: 319–28.

Thompson, Henry (1874), 'Cremation: A Reply to Critics and an Exposition of the Process', *Contemporary Review*, 23: 553–71.

White, Stephen (1993), 'An End to D-I-Y Cremation?', *Medicine, Science and the Law*, 33(2): 151–59.

CZECH REPUBLIC

On 8 December 1899 the Association for Cremation was founded in what was, then, Austria-Hungary, and the Prague physicist and hygienist, Dr Jindrich Zahor (1845–1927), was the prime promoter of cremation in Czechoslovakia. Others included Dr Josef Schemer, later chairman of Sokol, an organization for physical education, the municipal engineer Ludvik Cizek, the poet J.V. Sladek, and the National Theatre director, Jaroslav Kvapil. The breakdown of the Hapsburg Monarchy in 1918 was accompanied by the removal of a psychological barrier that had categorically rejected cremation. Although the Monarchy had not prohibited cremation, it had not allowed it to take place in Austro-Hungarian lands. This was exemplified by a curious situation when the city of Liberec decided to build a crematorium and, although the Supreme Court allowed construction to go ahead, it was not possible to carry out cremations in the completed building. So, although the first Czechoslovak crematorium was built between 1915 and 1917, it was unable to start working until after October 1918 when the Cremation Association enforced the acceptance of cremation. Consequently, on the memorable day of 1 April 1919, the national parliament approved the cremation law and the first cremation was accordingly carried out on 31 October 1919 in Liberec.

Initially, the attitude of the Roman Catholic Church was hostile, but nowadays people have a free choice between cremation or burial, regardless of their religion. It is now common for Catholic priests to attend the service in a crematorium's ceremonial hall. The Cremation Association, too, has undergone many changes since 1909, including its name, but it has always remained active, regardless of wider political changes. It has also always embraced those in favour of cremation irrespective of their political attitude or religious affiliation and this trend is, at present, more important than ever before.

In religious terms an important feature of Czech culture was the foundation of an independent Church – the Czechoslovak Church – after 1918. After 1925, in their newly built chapels, suitable places were found for establishing columbaria to offer a dignified setting for cremated remains.

Cremation is more popular than burial in the Czech lands, currently comprising some 75 per cent of annual funerals. There were no changes in this rate registered after the political revolution in 1989, and this percentage seems quite constant. Accordingly, the Cremation Association now concentrates more on the treatment and location of cremated remains, which are disposed of in the following ways:

- urns placed in normal graves
- urns placed in special graves dedicated solely for urns
- urns placed under gravestones
- spreading cremains on cemetery meadows
- placing cremains into a special plot of ground dedicated to the scattering of ashes – a method that was the idea of Prague architect Svoboda and is often preferred because it removes the anonymity inherent in the classical way of scattering ashes and makes it possible to add the cremated remains of other relatives to the same plot
- urns placed in a columbarium as a separate building
- urns placed in columbarium walls in the cemetery
- urns taken away by the family to be placed where they decide – an option chosen only by a few.

The level of ceremony adopted in funeral halls depends on individual choice. Almost all halls are equipped with high technology and a wide choice of musical compositions. Mourners usually chose favourite compositions and songs of the deceased, but may also leave the choice to the person responsible for the ceremony. Most people prefer organs for the performance of live music. **Stanislav Motycka**

D

D'ALBERTIS, LUIGI MARIA

One of the illustrious founders of the Genoese Cremation Society in 1897, Luigi Maria D'Albertis was born in Genoa on 21 November 1841. In 1860 he took part in Garibaldi's military expedition to Sicily. Being an adventurous and intellectually curious person, he travelled to New Guinea and there undertook geographical explorations and studies of natural sciences as well as pursuing ethnographic subjects, as evidenced in his book, *To New Guinea*. He died in Sassari, Sardinia, in 1901 and, in accordance with his last will, his corpse was cremated in Genoa on 4 September 1902 in the Sanitary Station of Lucedio Dock, near the Lanterna, the lighthouse of the Port of Genoa. His considerable legacy

enabled the Genoese Cremation Society to build its crematorium. Located in the Cemetery of Staglieno, it was designed by Professor Demetrio Paernio and completed in 1903. A marble bust to D'Albertis' memory was erected there in 1905. **Giorgio Spina**

See also Genoese Cremation Society.

DAUBENFELD, DR ARTHUR

Dr Arthur Daubenfeld (1880–1950) became the founding father of cremation in Luxembourg, after reading an article on cremation in a German newspaper. Instantly struck by the obvious advantages of cremation, he wrote to the newspaper's editor requesting more information. After securing copies of a cremation journal, Daubenfeld familiarized himself with the arguments and then, in November 1906, advertised in a newspaper for support for a cremation society, of which he was secretary and, at that moment, the only member. He was aged 26. Immediately, he received 17 positive responses and called a general meeting, which agreed the constitution of the Société pour la Propagation de l'Incinération. From 1922 until his death in 1950, Daubenfeld was the president of the Luxembourg Cremation Society – a society that would, according to his obituary, have failed earlier had it not been for his energy and dedication. Daubenfeld was instrumental in everything that the cremation society did. After becoming editor of its new bi-monthly journal, *Flamma*, in 1932, he was the main protagonist in dealings with the government and the Catholic Church throughout the 1930s. The Second World War brought further trials as, in September 1942, the occupying German forces deported him, although he managed to escape from Germany in September 1944.

An honorary member of many foreign cremation societies, in 1948 he was elected vice-president of the ICF in recognition of his extensive work. Yet history seemed to prove him wrong to reject ICF approaches to the Catholic Church on cremation in 1948, as the tactic did, eventually, yield the desired results.

Employed by the railway, Daubenfeld eventually became a member of the administrative council of the railways and was also a burgermeister in his native Hollerich. He was educated at the University of Nancy and completed a doctorate in political science at Strasbourg University before later becoming president of a medical college. He received many awards and decorations.

Daubenfeld's death on 17 August 1950, aged 70, was a significant loss to the cremation movement, especially as he was apparently on the verge of persuading the Luxembourg authorities to build a crematorium. In the event, this did not happen for almost another half century. He had to be cremated where most other Luxembourg citizens had been cremated, in the French city of Strasbourg. Yet, by the time he died, the cremation society he founded 44 years earlier had 700 members and around 17 Luxembourg citizens were cremated in Strasbourg annually. **Lewis H. Mates**

See also Luxembourg.

References

Daubenfeld, Dr Arthur (1939), 'How Cremation Began in Luxembourg', *Pharos*, 5(4): 14–15.
'Historique du Mouvement crématiste en Luxembourg' (1968), *La Flamma January*, CRE/A/LU.

DAVIES' LAW OF CREMATION

In the first edition of *The Law of Burial, Cremation and Exhumation* published in 1956 Dr M.R. Russell Davies wrote: 'The principal purpose of this book is to give as clear and as comprehensive a statement as is reasonably possible of the important legal principles, provisions and cases underlying the bewildering complexities of the law relating to the disposal and disinterment of the dead'. Since, in the early years of the twenty-first century the number of deaths in Great Britain averages over half a million per year, the importance of the work of those responsible for the proper and sympathetic disposal of the dead really cannot be overemphasized. An important part of that process with regard to cremation, as also to burial, is the understanding of the law, in its many and various forms, by those who own or are responsible for the day-to-day management and operation of crematoria and cemeteries and matters relating to the disposal of the dead. The list in this respect includes funeral directors, registrars of births and deaths, medical practitioners, medical referees, coroners and, of course, registrars and other officers at crematoria and cemeteries.

M.R. Russell Davies continued to update the book for over 20 years. In 1993 David Smale, former superintendent and registrar of cemeteries, crematorium, mortuary and associated services at Brighton, a past president of the Institute of Burial and Cremation Administration (now registered as Institute of Cemetery and Crematorium Management, Inc.) and, at that time, editor of *Resurgam*, the quarterly journal of the Federation of British Cremation Authorities, became responsible for the sixth edition. 'Davies', as the book has become known within the professions associated with these most essential services, was revised and republished in 1994 and 1997. In December 2002 the seventh edition of this well-established comprehensive book of reference was published and updated all the legislation relating to cremation, burial, the registration of deaths and other associated subjects. This latest edition included details and comment about the Cremation (Amendment) Regulations 2000 which specifically deal with the cremation of body parts. The Cremation (Scotland) Amendment Regulations 2003 has also been published which – as in England and Wales under the 2000 Regulations – deals with: 'regulations to facilitate the cremation of parts of the body of a deceased person which were removed in the course of a post-mortem examination'; updates on previous legislation including the Data Protection Act 1998, the Deregulation (Still Birth and Death Registration) Order 1996, Access to Justice Act 1999, Registration of Death Abroad; and a review of the emotional factors associated with the respectful disposal of a non-viable foetus which is not provided for in cremation or burial legislation. There is also reference to the Home Office Review of Death Certification, the Review of the Coroner's Service, the Shipman Inquiry and the White Paper, *Civil Registration: Vital Change*, presented to parliament in January 2002.

In 1887, James Brook Little in his book *The Law of Burial* (the third edition published in 1902 did include reference to the Cremation Act, 1902) mentioned that there were over 120 Acts of Parliament dealing with the disposal of the dead. By 2003 there were at least as many Acts and Statutory Regulations and other legal requirements to be considered and observed when dealing with deceased persons, and regulations in respect of cremation and matters associated with such procedures, such as the Environmental Protection Act 1990 the Secretary of State's Guidance – Crematoria, form a significant part of that legislation. The need to consolidate all legislation regarding the care and disposal of the dead is long overdue but Davies' *Law of Burial, Cremation and Exhumation* does go a long way towards helping those involved with these sensitive and most essential services in ensuring that all Acts and Regulations are documented in an easily accessible format and adequate cross-references made to other statutory legislation related to the care and disposal of the dead. **David Smale**

Reference

Davies, M.R. (2002) *Davies' Law of Burial, Cremation and Exhumation* (7th edn), ed. David Smale, Crayford: Shaw & Sons.

DEATH REGISTRATION SERVICE

In all civilized countries the registration of deaths, as of births, is considered an essential part of the management of the life of the inhabitants providing, as it does, both important statistics and, in the case of deaths, a safeguard against suspicion of foul play. In the UK the first legislation for the registration of births and deaths was passed in 1836 with subsequent Acts in 1874, 1926 and 1953. Specific Statutory Regulations have also been made under the provisions of the various Acts. These prescribe procedures for registration of deaths (including stillbirths) and details of certificates required and issued by the registrar of births and deaths. Information about offences and fines is also provided. Since civil registration began in England and Wales in 1837 there have been substantial changes in society and life in general. In the 16 decades or so that have passed since the first legislation was enacted, the total number of deaths occurring every year in the UK has remained at a fairly constant level, although the population has increased. For example, in 1897 there were 541 487 deaths out of a population of just over 31 000 000 people and, in 1967, there were 542 516 deaths in a population of 48 390 000. The first crematorium in Britain opened in 1885 and by 1902 there were eight

operational crematoria carrying out 431 cremations – 0.08 per cent of all deaths. In 2000 there were 437 609 cremations, representing about 71.5 per cent of the total deaths registered (611 960), undertaken at 242 crematoria then in operation.

With the progressive increase in the practice of cremation it is, perhaps, surprising that the basic documentation associated with the application, medical certification and even the actual death registration process has barely changed since the implementation of the first Cremation Act 1902 and the first Cremation Regulations in 1930. As long ago as 1927, the date of the Registration (Births, Stillbirths, Deaths and Marriages) Consolidated Regulations relating to death certification, no notice was taken of a recommendation made by a Select Committee that, under the heading 'The Fact of Death', there should be a statutory requirement for the doctor to see the patient within eight days of the death. The Committee report highlighted the invidious position of the family doctor if he refused to issue a certificate or if he gave one that he knew or suspected to be false. At present, a registrar of births and deaths is required, under the provisions of The Registration of Births and Deaths Regulations 1987, to report to the coroner, on an approved form, the death of any person (a) where the deceased was not attended during his last illness by a registered medical practitioner; (b) where a certificate of cause of death indicates that the certifying medical practitioner had not seen the deceased either after death or within 14 days before death; or (c) where the cause of death is unknown and in a number of other circumstances detailed in the Regulations – for example, when a death appears to have occurred during an operation or before recovering from the effect of an anaesthetic, or a death which seems to the registrar, from the information supplied, to have been due to industrial disease or industrial poisoning.

The Brodrick Committee *Report ... on Death Certification and Coroners*, published in 1971 after six years of deliberation, observed that:

> ... it would be practicable, without causing appreciable hardship to doctors or to the relatives of the deceased, to impose quite a short time limit within which the certifying doctor must have attended the patient if he is to be qualified to give a certificate. We believe that a seven-day rule

is feasible and we therefore recommend that a doctor should be permitted to certify the cause of death only if he has attended the deceased person at least once during the seven days preceding death. If the 'seven-day rule' is imposed directly on the doctor in this way, there will certainly be no need to attempt the more difficult task of providing a statutory definition of attendance during the last illness, which term can, in fact, be abandoned. (Brodrick, para. 5.12)

In 1990 a White Paper, *Registration: Proposals for Change*, recommended a number of largely technical reforms in the registration service and in September 1999 a consultation document *Registration: Modernising a Vital Service* was published. In 2001 the Shipman Inquiry, arising from the criminal activities of Dr Harold Shipman, was opened under the provisions of the Tribunals of Inquiry (Evidence Act 1921) and this was superseded by the Laming Inquiry into the Shipman Case. Also in 2001 the Home Office published a *Report of the Home Office Review of Death Certification* and, consequent on an independent review of the coroner and inquest arrangements announced in January 2001 when the Redfern report on organ retention at Alder Hey Hospital was published, have also referred the main recommendation of the *Review of Death Certification* to the Home Office Fundamental Review of Coroners' Systems. A radical recommendation of the Home Office Report, mentioned in the previous paragraph, was for further consideration to be given to a system for the certification of all deaths by a 'medical examiner' whose duties and responsibilities would probably impinge directly on the current duties of registrars of births and deaths, medical referees and, to some extent, coroners. The introduction of such a procedure could well create a more focused and coherent system than currently exists with different procedures in place for cremations and burials. The Shipman Inquiry, an Independent Public Inquiry into the issues arising from the case of Harold Frederick Shipman, made a series of reports on such matters between 2002 and 2004.

In January 2002, under the terms of the Regulatory Reform Act 2001, a *Civil Registration: Vital Change* was presented to parliament. Under the 2001 Act, important reforms to regulatory regimes can be made without taking up the amount of parliamentary time required by a public bill. The framework described in the White Paper provides for new and improved registration services and enables the full use of technology. The White Paper proposals have been drawn from a wide-ranging consultation process and will simplify and modernize services by, for instance, enabling individuals to register births and deaths online, in person or by telephone and the same information will be recorded for men and women. However, much will depend on the outcome of any changes resulting in consequence of the Shipman Inquiry, the Review of Death Certification and the Review of the Coroners' Service. As of 2005, the implementation of the recommendation is still awaited.

As the Home Office report on death certification states, 'the existing arrangements for the certification of deaths suffer from lack of consistency and the absence of clear responsibility to account for the causes of all deaths' (Home Office, 2003: recommendation 4). That report recommended that 'more emphasis should be placed on the training of doctors in death certification procedures' and that 'although it is important for death certification processes to be uniform, it is also important that the processes are carried out sensitively and with due regard to the reasonable requirements of the deceased and their friends and families, whatever their cultural background' (Home Office, 2003: recommendation 8). Other proposals made in the report include reference to the unacceptability of 'old age' being recorded as a cause of death.

The report also noted that the Brodrick Committee had recommended that the certification of both the fact and cause of death should be carried out by a doctor who had attended the deceased person at least once during the seven days preceding death. However, it is mentioned that such a requirement may not be so practical following the development of general practitioner deputizing services and the fact that many deaths occur within care homes. The need to have both a reliable and responsible system of death certification and a procedure for the convenient and accurate registration of deaths is well documented, and the results of the various inquiries and reviews currently taking place may well set the pattern for the future registration of deaths and matters associated with the care and disposal of the dead. **David Smale**

See also Brodrick Committee.

References

Brodrick, N. (chairman) (1971), *Report of the Committee on Death Certification and Coroners*, London: The Stationery Office.

Department of Health and Social Security (1990), *Registration: Proposals for Change*, London: The Stationery Office.

Home Office (2001), *Report of the Home Office Review of Death Certification*, London: The Stationery Office.

Home Office (2003), *Death Certification and Investigation in England, Wales and Northern Ireland. The Report of a Fundamental Review 2003*, London: The Stationery Office.

Office of National Statistics, *Civil Registration: Vital Change*, London: The Stationery Office.

Registrar-General of England and Wales (1999), *Registration: Modernising a Vital Service*, London: The Stationery Office.

DECLARATION OF 1874

The 'Declaration of 1874' is the declaration signed initially by those who attended the meeting on 13 January 1874 at Sir Henry Thompson's house at 35 Wimpole Street, London, which led to the establishment of the Cremation Society of England (later of Great Britain). The subscribers to the Declaration declared that:

> We, the undersigned, disapprove of the present custom of burying the dead, and we desire to substitute some mode which shall rapidly resolve the body into its component elements, by a process which cannot offend the living, and shall render the remains perfectly innocuous. Until some better method is devised we desire to adopt that usually known as cremation.

Those at the meeting were: Revd Hugh Reginald Haweis, Shirley Brooks, Frederick Lehmann, Dr Charles Lord, Dr Ernest Hart, Rudolph Chambers Lehmann, Sir Henry Thompson, John Cordy Jeaffreson, and Revd Charles Voysey. The signatories included these as well as John Everett Millais, John Tenniel, Anthony Trollope, Sir

Thomas Spencer Wells, E.B. Gayer, Alexander Strahan, and Rose Mary Crawshay. Those at the meeting agreed to a proposal to form a society on the basis of the Declaration. The proposal was made by Shirley Brooks, the convivial editor of *Punch* and close friend of the Thompsons. Within a month he was dead, but his connection with the society may partly explain why the obituary of English cricket published in the *Sporting Times* in August 1882 recorded that 'the body will be cremated and the ashes taken to Australia'. The author of the obituary was Reginald Shirley Brooks, Shirley's dissolute son, who was editing the *Sporting Times*. The Declaration is in the possession of the Cremation Society. **Stephen White**

See also Cremation Society of Great Britain; Thompson.

Reference

White, Stephen (1999), 'Founder Members of the Cremation Society', *Pharos International*, 65(1): 7–17.

DENMARK

CREMATION ASSOCIATIONS

Although cremation had been the most common form of funeral in Denmark from about 800 BC, from the year 200 AD, Danes were influenced by developments in neighbouring countries and began to bury their dead. At that time Christianity was spreading across southern Europe and, according to Catholic doctrine, the dead first needed to be cleansed of their sins in purgatory before being allowed to enter paradise. This meant that cremation, which involves destroying the body, came to be seen as a punishment, which must not be practised on Christian people. Witches and criminals, on the other hand, were always to be burned. With the coming of Christianity to Denmark around 1000 AD, and as a consequence of the power the church achieved in the community, it was soon fixed by law that the cremation of common people was illegal. This prohibition remained even after the introduction of the Protestant Church in 1536.

In the 1850s (especially 1853 and 1854), Europe experienced major cholera epidemics and, because standards of hygiene were poor, many people died and the cemeteries could scarcely cope with the numbers of dead bodies. Something new was needed, and the possibility of cremation was put forward as a realistic alternative to burial. This discussion reached Denmark, where a few farsighted individuals decided to found the Association of Cremation in 1881 – mainly for reasons of hygiene – in order to seek a change in the law to permit cremation once more in Denmark. At the outset, although the association had to deal with strong opposition from the Church and politicians, it also found considerable support amongst Danes at large, so much so that, as early as 1886, they began to build the first crematorium in Nylandsvej in the municipality of Frederiksberg, Copenhagen. Once the crematorium had been built, it was necessary for the first cremation to take place as soon as possible, because one of the contributors had linked his subscription of 5000 Danish kroners to the condition that the crematorium should be operative by 16 September 1886. However, as cremation was still illegal – the police were expected to try to prevent the use of the crematorium – the association was in serious trouble. It had, however, managed to buy, through the University of Lund, the body of a Swedish convict, on the condition that the university received the ashes after the cremation. Because of the official prohibition, it was necessary to transport the corpse without notice, and the whole operation almost failed when the driver could not find the way to the crematorium. Finally, however, they arrived and the cremation took place to everyone's satisfaction on 13 September 1886 and the subscription of the 5000 Danish kroner was thereby secured. The authorities, however, immediately closed the crematorium down.

Despite the association's pro-cremation advertising and the building of the crematorium, the prohibition on cremation was maintained. A judgement in 1888 by the Royal and Municipal Court and another in 1891 by the Supreme Court confirmed this prohibition. Some 11 years passed from the association's foundation before cremation was publicly accepted through the first cremation law in 1892. This provided that a person should at least be over 18 in order to be cremated and that they should have notified their wish to a public notary in the form of a last will. The first legal cremations followed the

reopening of Nylandsvej Crematorium on 13 January 1893.

Although cremation was totally apolitical and religiously neutral, two single incidents had a significant influence on its development. In 1901 the poet Sophus Schandorph died. He had insisted on being cremated, and his funeral attracted so many people that Georg Brandes had to speak to them while standing on a staircase. Then, in 1902 Minister Viggo Hørup died and, according to his last wish, was cremated after his coffin was brought to the crematorium through heavily crowded streets. In 1908 the Association of Cremation built Bispebjerg Crematorium in Copenhagen and, at the same time, Denmark's first crematorium in Nylandsvej was closed down. In 1913 Bispebjerg Crematorium was sold to the municipality of Copenhagen, because the association's members did not think that it was their task to run crematoria. The original task of the idealistic founders of 1881 was very difficult on account of considerable resistance from politicians and the Church. They travelled all over the country making speeches and showing lantern slides, yet, despite everything they did to promote cremation, it was 1919 before 1 per cent of the deceased in Denmark were being cremated.

In 1975 a law was passed guaranteeing the individual the freedom to choose the manner of their body's disposal. By this time, the cremation rate had risen to 50 per cent. By 2002 Denmark's 32 crematoria was conducting 42 539 cremations per year, a cremation rate of 72.4 per cent. However, the cremation percentage is likely to remain unchanged in the near future and may even decrease a little due to increasing numbers of people taking up residence in Denmark, who do not practise cremation.

As mentioned earlier, influenced by contemporary debates and events in Europe, a group of idealistic individuals, including chief physician Dr Ferdinand Emanuel Levison, founded the Association of Cremation on 24 March 1881. Its purpose was to promote cremation and have it made into a legal option for those who might choose it. Despite the association's efforts in building the first Danish crematorium and performing the first cremation in modern Denmark in 1881, the prohibition of cremation was not repealed until 1892. The cremation of the poet Sophus Schandorph and Minister Viggo Hørup, in 1901 and 1902 helped popularize cremation among working people and craftsmen and led to the foundation of a second association, the National Cremation Association in 1902. As the Association of Cremation and the National Cremation Association were both working for the same purpose, they found it natural to merge, and did so in 1914 to form the Danish Cremation Association which, ever since 1914, has taken an active role in building crematoria all over the country by lending or donating money.

The Danish Cremation Association has also left its mark on cemetery culture. With the number of urn-graves increasing, the association began to work for the establishment of common urn-graves to reduce the number of neglected graves in cemeteries. The first common urn-graveyard was established in 1926, at the association's request, at Bispebjerg Cemetery in Copenhagen. The Danish Cremation Association's aim had been to make cremation both popular and legal. It did indeed achieve both these aims, even though it took until 1975 before cremation became as common as burial.

In 2001, having fully achieved its aims, the Danish Cremation Association decided on a new goal: 'To work for a dignified way of ending life'. Accordingly, it changed its name to the Danish Association *Life and Death*. Its main tasks for the future are:

1   to provide information on everything connected with death and funerals;
2   to help people have their last wishes fulfilled;
3   to help relatives in this difficult situation, both before and after death;
4   to support the establishment of hospices and other forms of help for the dying and their relatives;
5   to run an information centre;
6   to hold conferences and issue publications about, among other things, the ethical questions concerning life and death.

In an eighteenth-century house situated at Nikolaj Plads 27 in the heart of Copenhagen, the association established, in 1998, the *Funebariet* – an exhibition of information on cremation and burial that is open to the public each weekday free of charge. **Børge Hansen**

THE DEVELOPMENT OF DANISH CREMATORIA

A total of about 550 cremations took place in Nylandsvej Crematorium, Copenhagen, from January 1893 until its final closure in 1908. Shortly after this, the new Bispebjerg Crematorium was inaugurated in Copenhagen. This, the largest Danish crematorium, has been rebuilt many times and, in 2002, was replaced by a new one, with only the chapel facilities being retained for further use.

The following list gives the crematoria, together with their dates of establishment, that can now be found in Denmark: Aarhus (1923); Slagelse (1926); Rønne (1927); Frederiksberg (1929); Aalborg (1931); Nykøbing/Falster (1931); Sundby (1931); Svendborg (1932); Kolding (1933); Næstved (1933); Holbæk (1934); Odense (1934); Struer (1935); Helsingør (1935); Gentofte (1936); Esbjerg (1939); Horsens (1939); Nakskov (1941); Silkeborg (1945); Hjørring (1951); Aabenraa (1952); Randers (1954); Køge (1954); Glostrup (1960); Roskilde (1961); Gladsaxe (1964); Viborg (1965–87); Lyngby (1967); Hillerød (1967); Vejle (1967); Ballerup (1968); and Holstebro (1977). At nearly all of these crematoria, the cremators have, over time, been rebuilt or replaced by newer and more modern ones. Only Viborg Crematorium has been closed down completely.

About one-third of all Danish crematoria are owned and run by local municipalities, with all the others being owned and managed by the Danish National Church. This, however, causes many financial problems, as nearly all of the Danish crematoria are run at a financial loss: Danish law only permits crematoria to make a charge that covers the operating costs of cremation, and the local municipalities or the special Danish church tax has to cover any resulting shortfall. Because of this special arrangement, different rates may be asked for a cremation, depending on whether, for example, someone lives in the local municipality that owns the crematoria or whether they are a member of the Danish National Church (if the crematorium is owned by the church). From 2002 onwards all Danish crematoria became voluntary members of the Association of Danish Crematoria (*Danske Krematoriers Landsforening* – DKL).

The DKL was founded in 1983 to foster the

interests of Danish crematoria, representing and defending them in relation to public authorities, especially on technical, educational and environmental matters. It maintains consultants for techniques, environment and international relations, and provides basic courses for crematoria employees, offering 'theme-days' when crematoria managers and employees discuss practical topics and problems. The DKL is a member of both the Nordic Forum on Cemetery and Crematoria Subjects and the International Cremation Federation and is joint editor of the magazine *Kirkegården* (*The Cemetery*). **Claes Foghmoes**

de ROSA, ANDRIES

A board member of the General Netherlands Diamond Workers Union (*Algemene Nederlandse Diamantbewerkers Bond*) – one of the first trade unions, established in 1894 – Andries de Rosa, was extremely interested in the issue of cremation, having lived in Paris for many years and spoken at length with advocates of cremation. In the Netherlands he organized meetings and helped form a plan for cremation to assist labourers and other less wealthy persons who, otherwise, could not afford the expense of cremation. On 22 December 1919, the Labour Cremation Society (*Arbeiders Vereeniging voor Lijkverbranding* – AVVL) was established under de Rosa's chairmanship. It was regarded as a socialist movement. A fund was established from small contributions made by each member and representing a type of insurance premium. After a short while, de Rosa ensured that 'his' association became a member of the Association for Cremation 'die Facultatieve' (*Vereniging voor Lijkverbanding*). Six months later, all members of the AVVL were entitled to cremation in Velsen Crematorium, which was commissioned by the Association for Cremation 'die Facultatieve'. The year 1922 witnessed the development of the idea for a merger between the two societies. This failed due to the differences in ideologies and opinions regarding contributions. According to de Rosa, the merger was only theoretically possible because the practical approach of the AVVL conflicted with the idealistic character of the Association for Cremation 'die Facultatieve': the intended merger was eventually abandoned in 1924. **J.M.H.J. Keizer**

DIGNITY AND VIOLENCE

One theme seldom discussed in relation to cremation concerns what some might see as violence done to the dead body, although the entries on **Japan** relating to its Confucian heritage and **Kenya** concerning attitudes towards the ancestors are the exceptions. Here, the issue is raised in association with the notion of dignity as an attitude widely regarded as appropriate on the part of the living towards the corpse. The issue of dignity in relation to how a corpse is treated before burial, especially by funeral directors, has been astutely analysed by Glennys Howarth in her study, *Last Rites*, where she documents the basic realism of some funeral directors to the blatant indignity of a corpse as such, and also the attitudes these professionals adopt towards the dead in the process of cosmetic treatment and making it appear presentable for the family's gaze (Howarth, 1996: 152).

Another aspect of violence and dignity emerges when we compare cremation with many traditional forms of burial. Earth burial has often been associated with the concepts of sleep and of 'resting in peace'. Mourners can remember the dead 'as they were' and, in an imaginative way, can think of them as being in the grave. This is reflected in the widespread practice of visiting graves and speaking to the dead as though they are still involved in an active relationship. While cremation can be similar, in the sense that cremated remains can be buried and treated as a focus of the imagination of the living towards the dead, it can also be quite different. One major difference lies in the fact that cremation destroys the body. There can be no obvious 'resting in peace'. This poses the question of whether it is right and proper to burn a human body. Does not the very act of cremation perpetrate a kind of violence upon the corpse? The Western tradition of burning heretics and witches furnishes one cultural backcloth that seems to align the corpse and violence, as the entry on **Spain** indicates. Similarly, the burning of victims of epidemics involved a response to a desperate situation. The Nazi use of cremators to burn the dead as part of the 'Final Solution' of genocide of the Jews reinforces this negative use of cremation. What, then, of burning someone who is a loved relative? Here, the idea of the dignity of the dead reappears.

Dignity is a word that enshrines important cultural and legal aspects of dealing with the living and has been of real importance in medical ethics in many countries (see, for example, Chochinov, 2002; Parliament of Victoria, 1987; Ramsey, 1998). It has also been taken up in respect of the dead where 'dignity' reflects an attitude towards the dead that mirrors the attitude of respect held towards someone while still alive. The greater the respect paid in life the greater the dignity accorded in death. If the very dignity of the dead might be contravened by cremation how can that possibility be circumvented or reduced? One answer is to see nineteenth-century cremation as a respectful way of coping with corpses and saving them from potential indignity in the cemeteries of large conurbations, or from premature burial. The association of modern cremation with scientific, medical and engineering advances was to align the dead with positive social values. Nevertheless, there may be some for whom cremation does involve doing things with the dead that they would not contemplate if the processes involved were blatantly obvious. (Here we are only considering modern forms of cremation and not the Indian traditions that developed their own extensive explanations and theologies of the event.) In modern cremation, by contrast, there is very little 'explanation' of the event. Even Christian churches have devoted very little time indeed to the theological considerations of cremation.

One possible, though speculative, approach to the vague awareness of the problem of 'violence' in cremation may lie in the care taken by many societies to ensure that the body is placed in a coffin and is not removed from it for the cremation itself. The whole ritual event is surrounded by a sense of decorum, respect and propriety. The fact that cremation takes place in an enclosed furnace also helps the facts of burning to be ignored. Here the 'out of sight, out of mind' aspect of life becomes important. Indeed, the way in which even the sight of smoke rising from a cremator became objectionable is not without interest. Why should this be? In Indian traditions, the sight of smoke was an anticipated part of the symbolic process of the transformation of the corpse into its constituent elements as they took their way to the heavens. In modern cremation, by contrast, smoke as sight and as smell has been reduced as much as possible. In one sense this is easily interpreted as a matter of sensitivity and aesthetics. But we should not ignore the possibility that it prompts something akin to a sense of guilt in the mourner. Smoke is a clear symbol of what is being done to the dead and what the mourner consents to being done to the dead – namely, the destruction of their body. Smoke may be symbolic not only of burning but of the violence done to the body.

One related issue concerns the use of machines to render the bone that comes out of the cremator into ashes. Some nineteenth- and earlier twentieth-century opinion in the USA, for example, strongly discouraged the practice. Even in 1944 the Cremation Association of America could speak of having 'no right to crush, grind or pulverize human bone fragments' (Prothero, 2001: 150). Some might find that attitude quite appropriate, but others might find that it sits oddly alongside the view that one does have the right to burn the body and render it into its boney fragments.

Many issues underly these attitudes, and it is always potentially dangerous to interpret behaviour as some sort of unconscious or deeply implicit aspect of a people's understanding – and this may be so in these cases, too. This is one such speculation that is avoided here but explored in the entry on **Freud**. Nevertheless it is worth asking whether the many cautions and formal regulations placed around cremation are not one expression of an anxiety of the final removal of the corpse. Of course, many cremation authorities and societies pay great attention to proper form as part of social welfare and common humanity, and it must be recognized that such factors are dominant. It is, for example, easy to speak of violence in relation to death when dealing with murder and war. So, too, in terms of sacrifice where, for example, Walter Burkert in his influential study of sacrificial ritual and myth in ancient Greece reckoned that sacrifice was an encounter with death that had its origin in early human experience of hunting, in which the killing of animals was its own guarantee of food provision which, in turn, supported life (Burkert, 1983: 296). In this way, the sacrificial death of animals led to life in humans. He then suggested that the close union of death and life in hunting came to another kind of expression in the ritual of sacrifice. Sacrifice is thus a kind of hunting and a source of life and succour for humanity. This line of argument poses an interesting question for cremation. Accounts of traditional Indian cremation show cremation to be a type of sacrifice; it is the last sacrificial offering the deceased person makes – an offering of the self. Although modern, non-Indian, forms of cremation do not present themselves as sacrifices they might, perhaps, be viewed as part of the process that produces advantage for the living. By destroying the deceased, the living are making way for new generations and acknowledge their capacity to deal with the dead and turn again to life.

Still, the issue of violence remains and was, for example, pinpointed by the Catholic writer J.F. McDonald when he spoke of cremation as 'violently destroying the corpse by fire' (1966: 2). Since that issue is raised, dramatically, by cremation in a way that the issue of decay is not raised so immediately by burial, it requires some comment. One obvious response is to wonder whether ritual – say, in the funeral liturgies of churches – ought not to seek what I have called 'liturgical permission to destroy' (Davies, 1997: 80). Another approach might follow, for example, Maurice Bloch who saw violence within some ritual as the human attempt 'to create the transcendent in religion and politics' (1992: 7). Leaving politics aside, it is possible that the violence of bodily destruction, so much more apparent in cremation than in burial, is not a violence achieved by natural processes alone but is fostered by the human act of cremation. In this a certain degree of 'transcendence' may be achieved in the sense that humans have a hand in producing ash that can be put to further symbolic use. It can foster memory, relate to a fulfilling of the identity of the dead and foster hope. **Douglas J. Davies**

See also Freud; Japan; Kenya; Spain.

References

Bloch, Maurice (1992), *Prey into Hunter*, Cambridge: Cambridge University Press.

Burkert, Walker (1983), *Homo Necans, The Anthropology of Ancient Greek Sacrificial Ritual and Myth*, trans. Peter Bing, Berkeley: University of California Press.

Chochinov, H.M.C. (2002), 'Dignity-conserving Care – A New Model for Palliative Care'. *Journal of the American Medical Association*, 287: 2253–60.

Davies, Douglas J. (1997), 'Theologies of Disposal', in P.C. Jupp and T. Rogers (eds), *Interpreting Death: Christian Theology and Pastoral Practice*, Cassell: London.

Howarth, Glennys (1996), *Last Rites: The Work of the Modern Funeral Director*, Amityville, NY: Baywood Publishing Company, Inc.

McDonald, J.F. (1966), *Cremation*, London: Catholic Truth Society.

Parliament of Victoria (1987), *Inquiry into Options for Dying with Dignity*, Melbourne: Social Development Committee.

Prothero, Stephen (2001), *Purified by Fire: A History of Cremation in America*, Berkeley: University of California Press.

Ramsey, Paul (1998), 'The Indignity of "Death with Dignity"', in Stephen E. Lammers and Allen Verhey (eds), *On Moral Medicine*, Cambridge, UK: William B. Eerdmans. First published in 1974 in *Hastings Center Studies*, 2: 47–62.

DILKE, LADY KATHERINE

Katherine Mary Eliza Gore Sheil, first wife of Sir Charles Wentworth Dilke (1843–1911), was cremated at Dresden on 9 October 1874. Lady Dilke was 26 and had been married for only two years to Sir Charles Dilke, the Radical Liberal MP for Chelsea and proprietor of *The Athenaeum* and *Notes and Queries*, when, on 20 September 1874, she died, two days after giving birth to a son. Sir Charles Dilke was distraught and immediately took himself off to Paris, leaving the funeral arrangements for his wife to his younger brother, Ashton Wentworth Dilke.

Lady Dilke had wanted to be cremated: she had expressed her desire for this to be done as a 'scientific experiment'. Cremation being impossible in England at the time, Ashton Dilke asked the newly formed Cremation Society for assistance. Almost the only place in Europe where it was clear that a cremation could be carried out without legal obstruction was Dresden, but only if the scientific value of the particular cremation could be proven. Lady Dilke's body was embalmed by Garstens, and, armed with a letter of introduction to the military surgeon-general at Dresden from William Eassie, the Cremation Society's secretary, Ashton Dilke travelled with the coffin to Dresden, not at all certain that the cremation would be permitted. Eventually it was, and, almost two weeks after his arrival in Dresden, the cremation itself took place, witnessed by a large number of scientific observers. Once the coffin had ignited, the doors of the furnace, which been designed by Friedrich Siemens, were thrown open so that those present could observe the process. It took 75 minutes and left ashes weighing $3^1/_4$ lbs. It is, perhaps, an indication of popular feeling about cremation in 1917 that nothing is said about this notable cremation in the biography of Dilke begun by Stephen Gwynne and completed by Getrude Tuckwell. **Stephen White**

References

Gwynn, Stephen Lucius and Tuckwell, Gertrude (1917), *The Life of the Rt. Hon. Sir Charles Dilke*, London: John Murray.

Jenkins, Roy (1958), *Sir Charles Dilke: A Victorian Tragedy*, 89–91, London: Collins.

'The Burning of Lady Dilke's Body', *British Medical Journal*, 17 October 1876.

DOCTORS

Medical doctors were particularly influential in advocating cremation, especially in the nineteenth century and in relation to hygiene and sanitary health. **Douglas J. Davies**

See also Barrier (for France); Coletti (for Italy); Lien Teh (for Malaysia), Price (for Wales); Thompson (for England).

DOUWES DEKKER, EDUARD (MULTATULI)

Eduard Douwes Dekker was born in Amsterdam in 1820. He moved to the Dutch East Indies in 1838 and enjoyed a successful career as a civil servant, being appointed assistant commissioner of Ambon in 1851. That same year, he began to voice ideas about 'incineration of the deceased'. Given the interest in cremation within scientific circles in the first half of the nineteenth century, the discussion became topical. Douwes Dekker, who had since become well known as the author of *Max Havelaar* under the pseudonym Multatuli, was the first Dutch person to consciously choose cremation despite not being a member of the Association for Cremation 'the Facultatieve' (*Vereniging voor Lijkverbranding*), founded in 1874. Because he had gambled away his fortune by the

time he died in 1887, his widow Mimi asked an ophthalmist friend to lend her 1000 DM for a cremation in Gotha in Germany, cremation still being prohibited in the Netherlands. The ophthalmist did not have sufficient cash but, after considerable research, discovered the Association for Cremation 'the Facultatieve', which lent the money to Mimi, allowing Douwes Dekker to become the first Dutch person to be cremated.

The urn containing his ashes was, initially, stored at home by his wife but, in 1947, the Multatuli Fellowship (*Multatuli Genootschap*) asked the association if the ashes of both Douwes Dekker and his deceased wife could be interred at Velsen Crematorium. Permission was granted, and their urns were interred in the urn garden of the crematorium on 6 March 1948 'in commemoration of this great figure'. In the 1970s, doubts grew as to whether the ashes in the urn were truly those of Multatuli. The story was that the former manager of the crematorium used to take the urn home to protect it during the Second World War. Apparently his housekeeper used the urn as a flower vase, after having removed the contents. This story was researched in 1990 and found to be untrue; the ashes in the urn really are those of Eduard Douwes Dekker. **J.M.H.J. Keizer**

DRESDEN

For the history of cremation, Dresden offers two stories. First, in 1911 the Saxon capital inaugurated a crematorium complex at Dresden. Second, in February 1945 Dresden was hit with the heaviest single aerial bombardment in the Second World War, the celebrated and controversial incendiary bombardment of the city by Allied aircraft. These events highlight both the achievement of the cremationist movement in imperial Germany and the transformation of entire city streets into incinerators due to the firestorms caused by bombing raids. It is important to note here that, while the history of cremation in imperial Germany enjoys only a small amount of historical attention, Dresden's fire-bombing inspires impassioned and lively debate from a variety of perspectives, including those of Holocaust revisionists and deniers.

Dresden had been a centre for cremationist activity since the 1870s, and the kingdom of

Saxony had legalized cremation in 1906. When it opened in 1911, Dresden's crematorium was the world's most lavish crematorium and was hailed as a landmark of the growing social acceptance of cremation in Germany. In particular, Dresden Crematorium was praised for its natural setting and its functional design. After the triumph of the Bauhaus, we tend to think of functionalism in terms of industrial design, but in the 1910s functionalism meant transcending previous models in the search for a formal architectural vocabulary suited to new building types and drawn from essential components. Fritz Schumacher's design for Dresden Crematorium was one of the first to avoid using revivalist forms based on gothic and baroque churches or Greek temples. The heavy forms of the two distinct facades of Schumacher's design represented the culmination of a trend toward monumentality and simplified forms that was characteristic of architecture before the First World War.

It is ironic that a city with a major connection to the cremationist movement should also have become the site of a fire-bombing in the Second World War and even more ironic that this took place in the early hours of Ash Wednesday. On the night of 13–14 February 1945 the British and American airforces began an incendiary bombardment of Dresden. Dresden was targeted because, as German forces were collapsing on the eastern front, Dresden's rail depots were increasing in strategic importance. Allied goals also included 'de-housing' workers, disrupting war production and breaking the German people's will to continue fighting. The desire to avenge German terror bombing of London and Coventry earlier in the war also played its part.

Fire-bombing required dry weather conditions and skilled deployment of the bombs. The result would be a column of fire and superheated air with a powerful updraft. An entire city could be turned into a furnace. The mission succeeded beyond the expectations of the British bombers and central Dresden became a superheated blaze, burning away all oxygen at ground level and causing high winds in a fire column that replaced oxygen with deadly carbon monoxide and sucked people into the flames. Most of the deaths in the Dresden firestorm seem to have resulted from asphyxiation rather than burning although many corpses were subsequently charred beyond recognition. It has been argued that Dresden citizens were essentially 'gassed' and 'cremated' as a consequence of the fire-bombing of the city.

Although Allied intentions behind the bombing remain contested, the effects of the bombing are clear. The city was turned into an incinerator and further corpse disposal quickly passed beyond the capabilities of mass graves. Within 24 hours British fire-bombing was followed by American conventional bombing. Intended to destroy the rail depot, the bombing chiefly resulted in vast civilian casualties and the destruction of Dresden's historical landmarks. Some eight square miles of the city centre were laid to ruin, and fires continued to burn for a week. Total deaths are usually estimated at 35 000, with thousands more severely wounded and homeless. Many corpses were completely consumed by the blaze. Charred and boiled corpses filled the streets. After initial attempts to identify corpses, fear of disease made it necessary to construct huge pyres that were dispatched with flame-throwers. The city remained in ruins for many years, and survivors of the fire-bombing remain passionate in their descriptions of the horrors of the night. The American Kurt Vonnegut was a prisoner of war during the fire-bombing, and his experience in the city became a central metaphor in his novel, *Slaughterhouse Five*. After the Second World War, Dresden and Coventry became twinned cities in mutual recognition of the horrors of total war and civilian bombing. **Tim Pursell**

References

Fischer, Norbert (1996), *Vom Gottesacker zum Krematorium: Eine Sozialgeschichte der Friedhöfe in Deutschland seit dem 18. Jahrhundert*, Cologne: Böhlau.

Irving, David (1964), *The Destruction of Dresden*, New York: Holt, Rinehart and Winston. (A controversial work by the most infamous attacker of the Holocaust.)

McKee, Alexander (1984), *Dresden 1945: The Devil's Tinderbox*, New York: Dutton.

Verbrannt bis zur Unkenntlichkeit: Die Zerstörung Dresdens, 1945, Altenburg and Dresden: DZA-Verlag für Kultur und Wissenschaft, 1994.

Winter, Henning (2001), *Die Architektur der Krematorien im Deutschen Reich 1878–1918*, Dettelbach: Verlag J.H. Roell.

DUDOK, W.M.

When the Association for Cremation 'the Facultatieve' (*Vereniging voor Lijkverbranding*) decided to build a second columbarium in Velsen Crematorium, the choice fell upon W.M. Dudok, architect and director of public works in Hilversum, following a number of references from influential people and a recommendation by H.P. Berlage. The building work began on 24 August 1925, and the new columbarium was completed in the summer of 1926, which was certainly not too early, since the 'old' columbarium had been full for quite some time.

Dudok's design was very favourably received on account of the new columbarium being linked to the crematorium and being in keeping with the wooded dune landscape. The columbarium offered space for a maximum of 2600 urns in both open and closed niches. A 'model urn' of 4.5 litres was designed for the interment, in order to retain the aesthetic value of the columbarium design. The columbarium attracted some criticism in 1930 due to the lack of a space in which to commemorate loved ones. This resulted in the construction of an urn garden in 1933 following fact-finding visits to crematoria abroad.

In 1937 a decision was taken to build a new office at the crematorium. Once again, Dudok was the chosen architect. In 1941 he also completed the construction of director's housing and a reception room where next-of-kin could enjoy refreshments after a ceremony. The management of Westerveld cemetery, which was next door, was not pleased with these developments, as visitors had previously made use of their reception facilities. In 1952 Dudok designed and built the fifth columbarium at Velsen Crematorium. In 1977, the Association for Cremation 'the Facultatieve' finally put an end to the dispute between the cemetery and crematorium regarding the two reception rooms; the decision was taken to form facilities that could be jointly managed. The crematorium in particular was very pleased with this development because the cemetery reception room always attracted more visitors, thanks to its favourable location. Dudok's complex was sold.
J.M.H.J. Keizer

See also Netherlands.

E

EARLY MODERN WESTERN EUROPE: 1500–1750

Transcending status or circumstances, a strong concern for the decent treatment of the corpse ran throughout early modern western European society, by and large because of the belief in the resurrection as a corporeal phenomenon. Even criminals, beggars and plague victims, it was thought, deserved no less than a respectful funeral. This meant burial, and the idea of bodily disposal in fire would not have crossed the mind.

Early modern people did not strongly disassociate the soul from the body, even after death. The idea that the soul remained, in some sense, aware of what occurred to its physical body was partly encouraged by the continued popularity of Day of Judgement beliefs, in which the flesh was resurrected to stand before God for judgement at the Second Coming. Ecclesiastical writers stressed that God could restore destroyed bodies, just as he would restore all those who had died at sea as we see in the committal for funerals at sea, from the Church of England's 1662 *Book of Common Prayer*. Nonetheless, a popular, and somewhat heterodox, belief lingered that those who had not been properly buried would not rise again (Ariès, 1977: 31–32). Others thought that incomplete remains encouraged the spirit to remain and haunt the site, since it had no resting place.

A spectrum of beliefs existed concerning the placement of the soul and the timing of judgement, varying between different denominations and eras. The idea of waiting for ultimate judgement in a 'a place of refreshment, light and peace', as stated in the canon of the Catholic mass, was gradually supplanted by the notion of an oblivious sleep until Judgement Day. Despite debates over the mechanics of postmortem existence, the resurrection of the flesh remained a popular coinage, and 'iconography and funerary inscription continued to refer to it among Protestant and Catholic alike' (Ariès 1977: 106) – affecting attitudes to the body.

Indeed, where fire was applied to a body, it was in the context of punishment for the most heinous of crimes. Such punishment was rare, and had both symbolic and practical significance, most clearly visible in France. Here, it was intended as an action against the integrity of the body, but also was thought to involve the destruction of the soul, as there would no be no judgement or resurrection for the victim. The ashes would also be scattered to the winds, the intention being to destroy all memory of the individual, and leave nothing behind (Nicholls, 1988: 50). Such intentions could be highly targeted, as when the entrails of an Englishman receiving the most dramatic of punishments – hanging, drawing, and quartering – were burnt. One 1615 death sentence explained that this action was 'because in them he hatched the treason' (Gittings, 1984: 70).

The connection between corpse and soul allowed punishment to continue after death. In early modern France, at least, the corpse of a heretic might receive in death, at the hands of the people, the burning punishment it was believed had been deserved in life (Nicholls, 1988: 52). A similar emphasis on the fate of the body was responsible for the widespread horror elicited by the dissection of notorious English criminals. There could be no greater indignity – or, perhaps, peril to the soul – than to have bodily fat made into candles, as was rumoured in the late eighteenth century to be the fate of some such unfortunates (Richardson, 1987: 97). Thus despite orthodox doctrine, the belief that the integrity of the body was necessary for final judgement remained widespread, such that the act of cremation was viewed – when it was considered at all – as a negation of both the bodily and spiritual life of the individual. Indeed, this must have provided a useful tool for those devising the most deterrent of punishments. **Jo Bath**

References

Ariès, P. (1977), *The Hour of Our Death*, London: Penguin.

Gittings, C. (1984), *Death, Burial and the Individual*, London: Routledge.

Litten, J. (1991), *The English Way of Death. The Common Funeral Since 1450*, London: Robert Hale.

Nicholls, D. (1988), 'The Theatre of Martyrdom in the French Reformation, *Past and Present*, 121: 49–73.

Richardson, R. (1987), *Death, Dissection and the Destitute*, London: Routledge and Kegan Paul.

EASSIE, WILLIAM

The first secretary of the Cremation Society of England from 1874 to his death in 1888, William Eassie was born in Lochee in Forfar, Scotland, in 1832. Sometime between 1845 and 1849 his family moved to England and settled in Gloucester, where his father established himself as a railway contractor. Eassie became an assistant of Isambard Brunel. During the Crimean War the wooden huts, or 'pavillions' as they were called in the medical terminology of the day, which Brunel designed for the hospital at Renkioi in the Dardanelles were prefabricated at Eassie's father's works, and, in April 1855, Eassie went to the Crimea as John Brunton's assistant to superintend their erection. He appears to have had another role at Renkioi as superintendent of the sanitary arrangements. He worked under Edmund Parkes who is described by the *Dictionary of National Biography* as the 'founder of modern hygiene and famous throughout Europe in the field of military hygiene'.

It was at Renkioi that Eassie may have first met Thomas Spencer Wells, later to become a founder member of the Cremation Society. Spencer Wells had gone out to serve in the military hospital at Smyrna in February 1855 and moved to Renkioi as superintendent of its surgical division in October, remaining there until June the following year. When the Crimean War ended, Eassie led an expedition in search of the site of Troy and is reported in some obituaries to have discovered it: Heinrich Schliemann, the German merchant, is conventionally credited with having done so. *Romaic Beauties and Trojan Humbugs*, an impenetrable book published in 1858 under the pseudonym 'Rathbain', has been attributed to Eassie and could have been based on his experiences during and after the war.

On the death of his father in 1861, Eassie and his younger brother took over the business, which they continued to run until his brother's death in 1875, when it was sold. Eassie was elected to the membership of the Geological and Linnean Societies in 1864, being proposed for the latter by Joseph Paxton. In 1868 he produced a plan for transporting Cleopatra's Needle to Britain, the main features of which, it has been said, were adopted by Sir Erasmus Wilson when the Needle was transported and erected on the Thames Embankment ten years later. In the meantime Eassie had editorial responsibility for the dairy engineering pages of the *Milk Journal*. In 1872 he published *Healthy Houses* and in 1874 *Sanitary Arrangements for Dwellings*. In 1875 he published *Cremation of the Dead*, perhaps the most methodical British text about cremation. Together with Ernest Hart, the editor of the *British Medical Journal* and founder member of the Cremation Society, Eassie founded *The Sanitary Journal*. He was elected to the Royal Society of Arts in 1876 and was a founder member and member of the Council of the Sanitary Institute of Great Britain, which was established in the same year. **Stephen White**

References

'Death of Mr William Eassie, C.E.', *Gloucester Journal*, 25 August 1888: 5.

Eassie, William (1875), *Cremation of the Dead: Its History and Bearings upon Public Health*, London: Smith, Elder & Co.

Toppin, David (1981), 'The British Hospital at Renkioi 1855', *Arup Journal*, 16(2): 3–20.

ECOLOGY

In 1961, when I began work, the cremation movement in the UK was very different from what it is today. Cremators were unsophisticated, and smoke was a constant problem. In addition, coffins were constructed of wet elm and other pure wood that was often incompletely incinerated. A modified flour grinder was used to macerate the cremated remains and, because of charcoal dust, the unit had to be sealed in a cupboard. The strewing of cremated remains was often completed whilst holding one's breath, to reduce the possibility of swallowing unburned carbon dust from the enveloping cloud of particles glistening in the sunlight. At that time, poor combustion and charcoal were accepted as operational norms and were not recognized as environmental or 'green' issues. It was a period when everyone felt that cremation was the technological solution to the seemingly insoluble problems associated with burial. Poor resources over the preceding decades had led to unkempt cemeteries and unsafe memorials. A culture had developed in which it was believed that burial was archaic and outmoded. It was not unusual to hear both cemetery staff and councillors state that burial ought to be prohibited! The promotion of cremation for virtually all deaths was an overriding management objective, and was unchallenged.

Apart from the fact that this approach would potentially have denied people the choice of burial, it also expressed our ignorance. The environmental impact of cremation was not considered, even though smoke routinely poured out of the crematorium chimney. Our ignorance suited the need because, without cremation as the panacea for the disposal of the dead, there appeared to be no future. The Environmental Protection Act 1990 began to change this, as action on reducing emissions focused on the negative aspects of the process. This negativity was, around that time, fuelled by the introduction of green burial, and the opening of the first woodland burial site by myself at Carlisle, in the north-west of England. As woodland burial expanded, the Natural Death Centre took up the green burial mantle and this, in part, revitalized interest in the burial option in the UK. Further emphasis on burial arose with the proposal to re-use old graves in London, where diminishing burial space had become an acute problem. The grave re-use proposal, which allows for the infinite re-use of burial land, added weight to the environmental benefits of burial.

A small number of people now choose their form of disposal based on environmental impact, and thereby reject cremation. This is a reversal of the situation in the 1950s, when people chose cremation 'to save the land for the living'. Green burial options are now regularly contrasted to the negative aspects of cremation, especially the need for increasing use of finite fuel resources to provide for the higher temperatures and emission scrubbing, all seen as unsustainable factors. The use of finite fuel is perhaps not as threatening to cremation as the continuity of supply. As part of a risk management approach, it is difficult not to feel nervous about gas supplies that are increasingly drawn from countries in unstable parts of the world. It seems inevitable that supplies will be interrupted at some point in the next few decades. This will paralyse crematoria and throw the disposal of the dead into crises in the UK. Both urban and rural crematoria have progressively developed a service network across the country. Expanding cremation numbers have been matched by a similar reduction in burial capacity around each crematorium so that, if crematoria stop working, a civil emergency would quickly arise.

In the new millennium the professionals providing the service find themselves in a dilemma. They are now expected to consider and minimize the environmental impact of disposing of the dead. Within this remit, it might be considered that incineration as such wastes fuel, pollutes, is unsustainable and therefore unacceptable. Counterbalancing this is the social organization of the UK as a small country full of large urban concentrations. Burial space does not exist in many areas. Even if it did, using it for conventional burial simply creates huge expanses of stone memorials imported from India and China, and long-term maintenance liabilities. Neither of these aspects is sustainable.

The technology of cremation involves both financial and environmental costs. The cost of cremators tripled with the introduction of the Environmental Protection Act 1990: fuel use quadrupled and servicing costs increased. Added to this, there is the environmental impact of manufacturing the cremators, and the highly technical consumables, such as thermal probes. This impact apart, there is no way of assessing whether the metals, the refractories and other materials used are sustainable. In truth, the environmental impact is not calculated because, as costs rise to reflect the increasing technology necessary to control emissions, people continue to use the service. Market forces do not apply because there is no viable alternative. Nonetheless, there must be a point at which the environmental and financial costs exceed the benefits obtained. We have yet to reach that point, and cremation continues to expand, albeit more slowly. The customer clearly identifies in cremation a package of benefits. Environmental and financial costs clearly do not outweigh other attractions. Is it because cremation is clean and clinical, or that it 'saves the land for the living' by dispensing with the grave? Perhaps most people simply see burial, in whatever form, as outmoded. Woodland burial is, at least in rural areas, a solution to the emission problem. Emissions, though, are considered by only a small percentage of those choosing cremation. The perceived benefits of cremation, which might include indoor comfort, or avoiding biological (grave) decay, still carry the day. The fact is, cremation must continue until the social response to environmental issues reflects the impact of the process, or burial can be made more attractive. Even then, burial cannot replace cremation in densely populated areas where grave space does not exist. This then begs the question of whether cremation be made 'green'. The answer is that it can be, as the following considerations indicate:

1   *Batching cremations*: the UK has, traditionally, cremated the body on the same day that it is received. Often, this necessitates preheating a cremator for just one or two cremations, which is a great waste of gas. Some authorities now cremate over 24 hours by adopting the Guiding Principles Charter for the Bereaved. This, at least, often allows a cremator to be stood down for a period. In reality, all cremations should occur when a cremator can be operated over extended periods. This is proven to minimize both emissions and gas consumption.

2   *Recovering heat and power*: utilizing heat and power from the process has generally been shunned in the UK; yet it ought to be obligatory.

3   *'Green' coffins*: these are now available in the UK, made of cardboard, bamboo, wicker and pure wood from sustainable sources. They can be entirely free of plastics, resins and varnishes and therefore reduce harmful emissions. Being lighter, they also reduce the ash content. Many users also see them as avoiding the waste of resources used in the coffin. Using a green coffin is symbolic of environmental awareness, and suggests that information about the problems posed by the process is familiar to users.

4   *Re-usable coffins*: this is sometimes referred to as a coffin cover. It takes the form of an attractive wooded outer 'casket' into which an inexpensive green coffin is fitted. After the ceremony the cardboard coffin enclosing the body is removed and cremated, a new coffin inserted and the outer casket re-used for another funeral.

5   *Coffin contents*: hardly a crematorium in the UK does not get periodic smoke problems caused by rubber footwear, fishing rods, golf balls, alcohol and so on, placed with the body for symbolic reasons. Legislation to control this is essential.

6   *Wildlife-friendly grounds*: most crematorium grounds are intensively maintained, which adds to environmental damage. The benefits of a nature reserve situated around a crematorium could more than compensate

for the environmental damage caused by the process.

Each of these aspects offers positive promotional opportunities by which we can inform users and invite their support. Cremation must become greener, and this will rely on a mix of new legislation and public support. We cannot allow people to casually choose cremation in ignorance of the damage it occurs. Where large populations exist, the need for cremation is proven and paralleled by the need for the car. Unfortunately, both these solutions to a human need create environmental problems. Just as the 'green' car is gaining momentum, so too must 'green' disposal. The challenge for cremationists is to face reality and move cremation into this new arena. **Ken West**

ECONOMICS (UK)

'Save the Land for the Living' was once the motto used by the Cremation Society of Great Britain in promoting the practice of cremation. Although its meaning alluded to avoiding using large areas of land for burial purposes, integral to this objective was also the cost for the provision and maintenance of such land. While this is an issue of real importance to every country the case we make here relates, specifically, to the UK.

In the UK, land provided for burial will have a finite period of use and, allowing for roads, pathways and some horticultural embellishment, will provide approximately 750 graves per acre of ground. Once the land has been used to capacity burial income will cease, but the costs of ground maintenance and site safety continue for an indefinite period. By contrast, a crematorium does not have a maximum capacity in terms of its longevity and, providing the gardens of remembrance are utilized in a way that provides for their long-term future, they too should be available for an almost indefinite period.

The relatively short-term use of land for the siting of a cemetery when compared with the very long-term use of a crematorium sets a financial background which in turn influences the costs for burial and cremation. In the year 2000, the cost of cremation in Britain ranged from £100 to £335, with the average cremation fee being approximately £275. To this had to be added the £85 cost of certificates payable to the medical practitioners who completed the statutory forms necessary for cremation and a fee of £68 payable to an officiating minister, if required. The cost of purchasing and interring in a grave space has a far greater range in cost than for cremation but, for many burial authorities, the fees would be in the range of £600–£900, sometimes increased twofold or even threefold if the deceased person had not been a resident of the town or borough in which the chosen cemetery is situated.

The Cremation Act of 1902 empowered cremation authorities to make a charge for the cremation of human remains, provided that the table of fees are approved by the local government board. This latterly changed to approval from the Department of Housing and Local Government until 1974 at which time cremation authorities were empowered to set and approve their own tables of fees.

For the majority of bereaved families there will be a wish to create a memorial following a funeral. In the case of an interment this is invariably in the form of a headstone erected on the grave space. The cost of such a stone will depend on the type of material used – for example, granite, marble, slate – the size of the stone and the intricacy of any carving which may be required. A memorial following cremation could be similar to that used for burial particularly if the cremated remains have been interred but, more typically, would be an entry in a book of remembrance or a memorial rose bush, tree or shrub with an inscribed plaque in a crematorium garden of remembrance. The fee for an entry in a book of remembrance would be substantially less than for the purchase of a memorial stone, as would be the fee for a rose, shrub or tree memorial – although the latter are usually for a limited period, renewable upon expiry, if so desired.

During the twentieth century the cost of constructing a crematorium rose dramatically. At the turn of the century, the cost of provision for Anfield Crematorium, Liverpool, together with columbarium and garden of remembrance was £8800, an expensive project when compared with the cost of £3486 for the construction of Hull Crematorium, with a further £1034 expended on a columbarium and the grounds. By the close of the twentieth century new crematoria were costing upwards of £1 750 000.

The primary responsibility for the disposal of the dead falls upon the executors, who are accordingly entitled to recover from the deceased's estate their reasonable and proper funeral expenses. However, the Public Health (Control of Disease) Act 1984 contains appropriate powers for the burial or cremation, by public authorities, of bodies in the interests of public health and also makes it incumbent on those authorities to cause to be buried or cremated the body of any person who has died or been found in their area, where it appears to the authority that no other suitable arrangements are being made. In any of the above cases, the authority may recover the funeral costs from the estate of the deceased person.

By the end of 2001, there had been 18 210 028 cremations undertaken in British crematoria. On a basis of 750 graves per acre of ground and two burials per grave space, cremation will have contributed to a saving of well in excess of 12 000 acres of land. **Bernard McHale**

EPIDEMICS

See also cholera and typhoid; Malaysia; vampires.

ETERNAL REEFS

Eternal reefs are artificial coral reefs consisting of pollutant-free concrete and human cremains. The artificial reefs – called 'reef balls' – are enormous golfball-shaped structures deployed in parts of the ocean – so far, mostly in Florida – that need more fish habitats. The areas are all sanctioned for this deployment by relevant laws, and the reef balls are donated to the federal, state, local, or county governments. Reef balls are such good hosts for oceanic life that, within a year, they are covered with around 400 pounds of biomass. The biomass includes coral pupae that attach to, and then grow on, the reef balls, plants that grow around the reef balls, and fish that live in them.

Cremains can be located in a one-person reef ball, or else be part of a 'community reef' containing the remains of up to five people. One woman, for example, had the ashes of her first husband, her second husband, and her second husband's first wife all placed into one reef ball. Although the cremains become mixed together in the community reef balls, each person gets their own commemorative brass plaque, – a plaque that becomes a permanent part of the artificial reef.

Further commemorative activities include special deployment ceremonies during which relatives and friends of the person or people whose ashes are included in a particular reef ball take a boat out to the designated site and watch as the reef balls are sunk. The precursor to eternal reefs is the plain reef ball, an artificial reef without any human remains. Eternal reefs were created when the father of one of the reef ball company's founders asked whether his ashes could be included in one of the reef balls. The request was granted in 1998, when the father died. **Arin Greenwood**

ETHIOPIA: ADDIS ABABA

Cremations in Addis Ababa are performed according to Hindu customs. The structure where the funeral pyre is located is a corrugated iron structure with a stone or concrete floor (see Figure 1). A pit in the centre of the floor collects the remaining ashes. Eight beams rise vertically out of the pit in two rows of four each. These beams contain the logs used in the pyre's construction. A layer of logs is placed in the bottom between the beams, the linen-wrapped body is placed on this layer and further logs and wood are added around and on top of the body. The structure is enclosed on four sides to provide a degree of privacy. Openings around the base of the walls obviously allow for a free flow of air to the funeral pyre. **Anthony Watkins**

EXECUTION

Here we consider burning at the stake in early modern western Europe, 1500–1800, when the lethal and purifying power of fire was harnessed as a method of execution by many of the judicial systems of Europe. In general, burning was reserved for the most severe of crimes – those that, it seemed, called for not only the death but also the obliteration of the criminal. The exact parameters of these crimes varied between times and places, but frequently included actions considered in some way 'unnatural'. For instance, in Counter-Reformation Germany, those to be burnt were 'blasphemers, heretics, witches, coiners, poisoners and sodomites' (and their animal co-criminals!), as well as arsonists subject to the logic of a 'mirror punishment' (Evans, 1996: 30). France made similar rulings (Nicholls, 1988: 50). From 1401 in England, too,

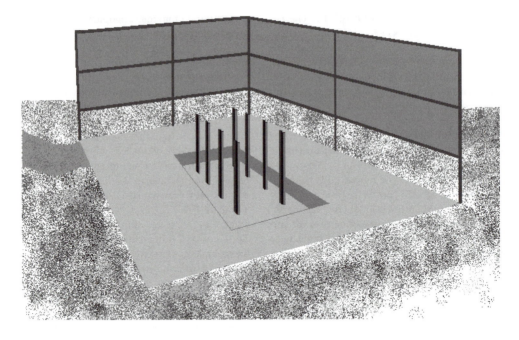

Figure 1 Pyre at Addis Ababa, Ethiopia.

burning was the punishment for heresy, culminating in the deaths by fire of over 300 Protestants during the reign of Mary I (Pettifer, 1992: 119). In subsequent years burning was reserved for women who had committed treason, which in practice usually meant the petty treason of coining or husband-murder, and very occasionally their male co-conspirators. It was an almost exclusively female punishment in deference to what Blackstone called 'the decency owing to their sex' – unlike the equivalent male punishment of hanging, drawing and quartering, the body was not intended to be exposed, although in practice it was noted that clothes often burned fastest (Gatrell, 1994: 264).

In the modern imagination, burning at the stake has become closely associated with the various inquisitions which operated in Catholic Europe. It is true that the Spanish Inquisition sent many 'stubborn and impenitent' heretics to the stake, and France saw massive numbers of burnings during the 1550s, in a last-ditch attempt to prevent Protestantism consolidating its grip on the country (Henningsen, 1980: 40; Nicholls, 1988: 69). Practices such as the 'dipping' of heretics into the fire before the final burning, ostensibly to encourage confession or recantation for the salvation of the condemned's soul, have understandably cast a long shadow

(Nicholls, 1988: 64). But the heyday of heretic-hunting was the late medieval period, and indeed it has been argued that most inquisitions, barring a few episodes of hysteria, acted with 'considerable restraint in inflicting the death penalty' (Peters, 1988: 94). A wide range of other penalties was at the disposal of the inquisition, and relaxation to the secular arm – who alone could pronounce a death sentence – was a last resort, which was almost always limited to the punishment of heretics who could not be persuaded to recant and who had value as examples to the masses. Languedoc, for instance, only burned 6 per cent of its suspected heretics in the period 1500 to 1562 (Nicholls, 1988: 50). There is evidence that, in some cases, a burning might be ordered and staged with the intention of frightening a peasant heretic into recanting, who would then be freed – and it is interesting to note the unusual choice of the Venice inquisition to hold all its executions in private (Haliczer, 1987: 80; Peters 1989: 118). Elsewhere, a burning was a public occasion, and seems to have attracted crowds at least as large as those that watched hangings. In Scotland, at Aberdeen in 1597, a special barrier of stakes had to be erected 'to withstand the press of all the pepill' – not surprising if the crowd was even a small fraction of the 20 000 said to have attended a burning in

London in 1786 (Larner, 1981: 113; Gatrell, 1994: 337). Authorities used such gatherings as an opportunity to preach moral lessons to the populace, and there is some evidence that many crowds watched in awed silence (Larner, 1981: 113; Henningsen, 1980: 194). French heretics would be burned in effigy if the intended subject could not be found, and particularly famous criminals could be burned in effigy several times in selected spots around the country (Nicholls, 1988: 54).

Depending on the wind conditions, and the products used – which could vary from Scotland's inefficient, slow-burning peat, to the German use of tar, sulphur and pitch in addition to straw and wood – a burning could be over very quickly, or last for several hours. It was also expensive; in Scotland, where rich relatives of the condemned could be made to pay for the execution, they might expect to pay £60–£80 (Larner, 1981: 115). This reflects a desire for profit on the part of the state – actual costs were perhaps a third of this – but also the costs of material to burn, the hiring of an executioner, and the construction of a frequently quite complex system of timbers, restraints and pulleys (Burford and Shulman, 1992: 44).

Most countries made the burning itself the finale to a formalized, theatrical, ritual. The journey of the condemned to the stake, their last prayers or words of warning, allowed the crowd to feel a part of the action – even if, in some cases, this meant showing their condemnation through the throwing of stones (Burford and Shulman, 1992: 44). This theatrical element to the execution might allow the condemned themselves to make certain symbolic choices – whether it be to 'put the rope around her neck with her own hand', or to wear their very best clothes – or might take choices from them in the interests of a better show, as with those Frenchmen forced to wear a fool's outfit for their final moments, for the amusement of the crowd (Nicholls, 1988: 56). Symbolic actions remained a part of the process right up to the disposal of the ashes, which in many areas were disposed of in a ritual fashion. In Germany they were ground to a powder, and either buried under the gallows or thrown into a river, so that, as the sentence put it, 'the memory of this shameful deed may be forever eradicated' (van Dülmen, 1990: 92). Across the border in France, ashes were scattered to the winds for similar reasons (Nicholls, 1998: 50).

It is certain that many people were alive when they burnt, and were, as the Prussian sentence had it, 'brought from life to death by fire' (Evans, 1996: 213). Partisan accounts suggest that some at least went to their deaths 'with calmness and dignity, rearranging the straw … that the flames might do their work more quickly' (Pettifer, 1992: 120) – and asphyxiation must have come as a relief to others in advance of the flames. But there can be little doubt that many more died in agony, 'heard to shriek out terribly' like the English woman whose death was recorded by diarist John Evelyn in 1652 (Burford and Shulman, 1992: 41). Even worse was the fate that befell a Scottish witch who came to consciousness during the burning, and 'half brunt, brak out of the fyre and was cast back into it again' (Larner, 1981: 115).

Such spectacles can only have fuelled an increasing tendency, unevenly expressed, to strangle or hang the criminal first, so that they were unconscious or, more often, dead before the burning took place. This was standard practice in England from the seventeenth century, the body often being left to hang for half an hour or more to be sure of death. In Scotland the method was enshrined in the sentence itself, that the condemned would be 'taken to the place of execution and there bound to a stake and strangled until she is dead, and thereafter her body burned until it is ashes'. Live burnings still occurred though, whether as with the last definite English live-burning, in 1726 through error on the part of the executioners, or because a harsh judge specifically ordered that the mercy or 'reward' of strangulation be withheld (Gatrell, 1994: 317; Pettifer, 1992: 120; Nicholls, 1988: 64). The burning of a dead body was thought to defeat at least some of the object lesson provided to the crowd, and indeed they might greatly resent it – in France they occasionally massed to try to prevent a strangling (Nicholls, 1988: 69). To avoid this, the Prussian practice from the 1740s was that the criminal should be 'strangled in a manner not visible to the spectators', special large cotton hoods being provided to aid in the deception (Evans, 1996: 213). Alternatively, a sachet of gunpowder might be placed at the condemned's neck, to discreetly speed the process (van Dülmen, 1990: 91).

Increasingly, however, the extremity and violence of burning was seen as unnecessarily cruel and its symbolism as irrational. In England, an Act of Parliament was passed in 1789, 'in the cause of humanity', abolishing the punishment (Gatrell, 1994: 317). In Germany, too, instances of burning, along with other punishments which relied on the purification powers of the elements, were very rare after 1800. It is impossible to say how many had already died in the flames – variable record survival means that it is rarely possible to assess numbers of burnings with accuracy. All that can be said is that many thousands of people did burn, some in isolated incidents, and some in great purges like the burning of 368 men and women for sorcery in Trier, 1587–93, before changing ideas about appropriate punishment removed the stake from the arsenal of justice (Evans, 1996: 39). **Jo Bath**

References

Burford, E. and Shulman, S. (1992), *Of Bridles and Burnings – The Punishment of Women*, London: Robert Hale.

Evans, R. (1996), *Rituals of Retribution: Capital Punishments in Germany 1600–1987*, Oxford: Oxford University Press.

Gatrell, V. (1994), *The Hanging Tree: Execution and the English People, 1770–1869*, Oxford: Oxford University Press.

Haliczer, S. (ed.) (1987), *Inquisition and Society in Early Modern Europe*, London: Croom Helm.

Henningsen, G. (1980), *The Witches Advocate*, Reno: University of Nevada Press.

Larner, C. (1981), *Enemies of God: The Witch-hunt in Scotland*, London: Chatto and Windsor.

Nicholls, D. (1988), 'The Theatre of Martyrdom in the French Reformation', *Past and Present*, 121: 49–73.

Peters, E. (1989), *Inquisition*, Berkeley: University of California Press.

Pettifer, E. (1992), *Punishments of Former Days*, Winchester: Waterside Press.

van Dülmen, R. (1990), *The Theatre of Horror: Crime and Punishment in Early Modern Germany*, Cambridge: Polity Press.

F

FABRETTI, ARIODANTE

For over 50 years of the nineteenth century in Italy, Ariodante Fabretti's importance was both political and cultural. In the *risorgimentali* events he played a role in the conspiracy as well as in the parliamentary assemblies; he wrote important works in historical and archaeological fields; he had a brotherly friendship with Giuseppe Mazzini, a republican insurrector; and he was a correspondent with many exponents of the Italian and European cultural and political scene.

Fabretti was born in Perugia on 1 October 1816, where he completed his main studies. Though most inclined to historical studies, along with early political interests, he nevertheless pursued veterinary medicine courses at Bologna to satisfy his father's wish. However, his historical, literary and political interest quickly took the upper hand and, once back in Perugia, Fabretti supported the Carboneria and subsequently the young Mazzinian organization of Italy, which represented a reference point for the liberal movement in the Umbrian urban centres which belonged politically to the pontifical state. Also after his return from Bologna, Fabretti began to support freemasonry. Archaeology also turned out to be one of his main subjects, first as a student, and then as a teacher in different parts of Italy. In January 1849 he was elected a representative of Perugia at the Roman Constituent Assembly and was nominated secretary at his first attendance. Overwhelmed by the experience of the Roman Republic, Fabretti was compelled to take the route of exile, leading him to Turin, which became his chosen fatherland. Here he continued his studies and dedicated himself to the compilation of a glossary of the entries of ancient italic languages, engraved in the epigraphs of the writers. In 1858 he was nominated assistant of the Egyptian and Antiquity Museum of Turin, of which he became director in 1872. He strongly influenced the museum, adding quality and quantity to its scientifically valuable collections. In 1860 he was invited to teach in the Archaeology Department in Turin's University; in 1874 he became the most influential member of the Piedmontese Society for Archaeology and Fine Arts.

Over time, Fabretti's political position did not undergo any substantial changes: he remained faithful to his democratic, secular and republican beliefs. Continuing in Turin, he was a candidate in the Umbrian schools for the national parliament several times, and he was finally elected in 1876. He did not attend the parliament very often at this point, preferring to focus on his studies and deepen his engagement in masonic activities. In the long run he became a venerable master of the *Loggia Dante Alighieri di Torino*, but also continued to follow the masonic life of his city of birth; in 1867 he became part of the assembly of the *Grande Oriente*.

In 1883 he was elected president of the newly constituted Turin Cremation Society (*Società per la Cremazione di Torino*), a post that he held until his death. This presidency acknowledged the role he played in freemasonry and its role in the creation of the society and was a homage to the venerable master, freethinker and prestigious academic and student who dedicated part of his interest to burial forms and funerary inscriptions. In 1887 he was also elected in the Turin Communal Council (*Consiglio comunale di Torino*) and, two years later, was nominated senator of the kingdom. In the years following 1860 Ariodante Fabretti received a long series of honours and recognition, both in Italy and abroad. In particular he was a member of the Academy of Lincei, and correspondent partner in the French Institution, the History Academy of Madrid and the Germanic Archaeological Institute. He died on 15 September 1894 in his village of Monteu da Po, near Turin. A solemn civil funeral ended with the cremation of his remains in the temple of the sub-alpine city, and his ashes were later transferred to his city of birth. **Emma Mana**

References

Furiozzi, G.B. (1997), *Ariodante Fabretti tra Mazzini e Garibaldi*. Perugia: Benucci editore, s.d. Id., *Ariodante Fabretti politico*, in 'Rassegna storica del Risorgimento', a. LXXXIV, fasc. 2, April–June.

Orsini, Cottini G. (1985), *Giuseppe Goffredo Ariodante Fabretti e i suoi tempi*. Roma: Tip. Veant.

Mana, E. (1998), 'Associarsi oltre la vita', in *La morte laica*, II, *Storia della Cremazione a Torino (1880–1920)*. Torino: Scriptorium Paravia, 3–85.

FABRETTI FOUNDATION

The Ariodante Fabretti Study Centre was created in 1992 on the initiative of the Turin Cremation Society with the aim of studying the origins and historical development of cremation in Italy, and in Turin in particular. It has pursued historical research both by considering the French Revolution with its discussion on the liberalization of cremation and by studying cremation during the Italian fascist period. On 30 June 1999 the Study Centre became a Foundation, whose founding members, in addition to the SOCREM (Society for Cremation), included the town council, the regional council and Turin University.

Its goal is to create a scientific point of reference for those who, in various disciplines, study death through its rituals, traditions, behaviour and wider discourse. It embraces historical and contemporary developments in the context of urban and industrial civilization and fosters a comparative perspective. Every two years, three two-year study grants are awarded and one international colloquium is organized. The Foundation also sets itself a teaching role by mounting public seminars and conferences in the hope of removing some of the taboo surrounding the discussion of death in society, and by offering educational resources in the areas of assistance to the dying, funeral details and support for people in mourning. The Foundation seeks to encourage degree-level study in the training of social and health personnel specializing in the management of funeral rites and mourning. The interest of the Foundation's local institutions is particularly linked to these latter issues, aiming to improve qualifications and practical standards within public services. **Marina Sozzi**

See also Fabretti.

FALBISANER, ROBERT OSCAR LÉON

From being a law student in his native Strasbourg, Robert Falbisaner (1889–1957) participated in the First World War in a role that involved much travel. He met and married a British woman in London in 1915. After the war, he toyed with embarking on a career in banking, but then joined an insurance company where he soon gained promotion. Falbisaner was active in the French cremationist movement by 1936, when he attended the Prague International Cremation Conference. Following the outbreak of the Second World War he joined the French Resistance in 1940 and was, from January 1941, part of Dr Bareis' organization. In March 1941 he went into the unoccupied zone to attend a cremation congress. There he met with other members of the Resistance and made plans for his future resistance activities. On returning to Strasbourg he began to gather information, which included making films of Nazi troop marches and meetings in order to inform the Allies about German activities and propaganda in the annexed countries. The films were smuggled into Switzerland and there received by the US authorities. In March 1942 the systematic internment of British citizens meant that Falbisaner and his wife had to escape Gestapo surveillance. They managed to get to Mulhouse by train where a police commissioner in the Resistance helped smuggle them to Switzerland. They later went to Lyon, but were still pursued by a Gestapo agent. This forced a brief period of hiding in an infirmary.

In December 1944 Falbisaner and his wife returned to Strasbourg and successfully re-established the insurance business. An attempt to enter politics in 1945 was, however, unsuccessful, although he did become president of the Strasbourg Cremation Society, representing it at many international congresses. Remaining president for many years, he was also vice-president of the French Federation of Cremation Societies. Highly respected, he received the following awards, medals and decorations: *Chevalier de la Légion d'honneur, Médaille de la Résistance, Croix du Combattant Volontaire, Médaille des Evadés, Chevalier du Mérite Agricole* and *Chevalier du Mérite Social*. **Lewis H. Mates**

References

Mouchard, M. (1957), 'La cérémonie funèbre pour notre Président O.L. Robert Falbisaner', *Crematorium*, 34: 2.

Obituary of Robert Oscar Léon Falbisaner (1993), in *Documents pour l'Histoire de la Cremation*, Strasbourg: L'Association Crématiste de Strasbourg, CRE/B/FR/4.

FAYANS, STEFAN

Stefan Fayans was born in Warsaw, Poland, on 15 June 1879 and died on 14 April 1942. From 1897 to 1902 he pursued architectural studies at the Imperial Academy for Civil Architects in St Petersburg, taking his doctoral degree in Technical Sciences from the Technische Hochschule in Vienna in 1904. Then followed an internship under Ludwig Baumann, chairman of the Board of Works, in Vienna in 1905 and under Alfred Messel in Berlin in 1906. From 1907 he was a freelance architect in a studio partnership with Fritz Bretschneider in Vienna, and by 1910 he headed his own firm. In 1910 he sought an academic career as a private university lecturer in interment design planning at the Technische Hochschule in Vienna, but this failed. In 1926 he was awarded Austrian citizenship.

The editors of the *Handbook of Architecture* in Darmstadt put Fayans in charge of revising the *Interment Design* volume in 1906. The attention of the architectural world had been attracted two years previously by his doctoral dissertation, *The Development of Modern Cemetery Design*, approved at the Technische Hochschule in Vienna and published in 1905, which included the ideal project for the planning of the main cemetery in Warsaw. Between 1902 and 1904, several journeys through Europe with the purpose of studying cemeteries turned the young architect into a specialist. In his project for Warsaw, Fayans took the geological disposition of the chosen area into special consideration, succeeding exceptionally well in the allocation of the grounds and arrangement of the various kinds of graves. In the centre of the cemetery is a church surrounded by arcades with columbarium graves. The entrance portal, flanked by the administrative buildings, is located at the beginning of the main axis of the cemetery while the crematorium with arcades for the ash columbariums is situated at the other end. Midway between the church and the crematorium are two huge halls designated for contagious and non-contagious corpses. The monumental architecture of the entire installation, with its rich neo-baroque-classic style, is reminiscent of the monument designs drawn up simultaneously by Otto Wagner in Vienna. However, although as an architect Fayans was much cited over questions of style and used lectures to propagate his views on cremation, he is largely remembered for his residential buildings rather than his crematorium projects. **Bruno Maldoner**

References

Fayans, S. (1905), *Die Entwicklung der modernen Friedhofsanlagen und der verschiedenen Bestattungsarten vom Standpunkte der Technik und Hygiene*, including appendix *Idealprojekt einer Friedhofs-Anlage für die Stadt Warschau*, Vienna: Anton Schroll & Co. (published doctoral dissertation at the Technische Hochschule in Vienna).

Fayans, S. (1907), *Bestattungsanlagen*, Handbuch der Architektur, IV. Teil, 8. Halbband, Heft 3, Stuttgart: Alfred Kröner Verlag. Reviewed in: *Der Bautechniker. Zentralorgan für das österreichische Bauwesen*, 27: 847.

Fayans, S. (1908), 'Kunst und Architektur im Dienste des Totenkults', *Zeitschrift des Österreichischen Ingenieur- und Architekten-Vereines*, 60: 593–98, 613–17.

Fayans, S. (1921), 'Feuilleton, Das Wiener Krematorium', *Neue Freie Presse*, 22 August: 1–2.

FEDERATION OF BRITISH CREMATION AUTHORITIES

The Federation of British Cremation Authorities (FBCA) was formed at a meeting held at the British Empire Exhibition, Wembley, on 1 August 1924. Its original rules were periodically amended and eventually entirely redrafted as the constitution, which was adopted at the fourteenth annual general meeting held at Edinburgh on 28 June 1938.

At the inauguration of the FBCA in 1924 there were 16 operational crematoria in Great Britain performing 2848 cremations representing 0.6 per cent of all deaths. Eighty years later there were 242 crematoria performing in excess of 420 000 cremations accounting for over 72 per cent of all deaths. Membership of the FBCA comprises of 95 per cent of the cremation authorities in Great Britain. Through its technical and executive committees, standards of performance have been devised and informative publications produced including *A Guide to Cremation and Crematoria*. However, the most important document has been the *Code of Cremation Practice* that clearly and precisely sets out the ethical standards to which member authorities are required to work. This Code, first published in 1945 and periodically updated and revised, is essential in the maintenance of standards at crematoria and observance of the Code is an obligation of FBCA membership

The FBCA's quarterly journal *Resurgam* was first published in 1958 and continues to have a wide circulation within the cremation movement both in Great Britain and overseas. The FBCA provides, for all its members, a comprehensive technical advisory service based on experience and knowledge accumulated over many years on all matters relating to the cremation service. It also has a policy of visiting member cremation authorities whereby the president and two technical officers will visit crematoria and subsequently submit a report on their findings. This contact has the additional advantage of enabling meetings with the elected members or directors of the cremation authority and also with crematorium managers. Experience has shown that the meetings and discussion with these personnel can be helpful to all concerned and can assist with determining future direction and policy for the organization.

On an annual basis, the FBCA co-sponsors a Joint Conference of Burial and Cremation Authorities at which experts in particular areas of burial and cremation disciplines are invited to give an address. Government departments consult the FBCA on matters affecting the law and practice of cremation. In recent years such consultation has increased, most particularly with the Home Office and the Department for the Environment. The FBCA's wish for a review of death and cremation certification has become a need in recent years, and its involvement with the Home Office in the course of the review has been much welcomed. The introduction of 'Process Guidance Notes' made under the Environmental Protection Act, 1990 and the need for a four-yearly review of the Notes, created a newly formed working relationship with the Department for Environment. When dealing with government departments the need to liaise with one authoritative voice in relation to cremation has become apparent. The FBCA has two classifications of membership-namely, members, who are operating cremation authorities, and associate members, comprising prospective cremation authorities. **Bernard McHale**

FILM

James Bond stirs, somewhat shaken, to find himself trapped in an extremely confined space which is beginning to fill with smoke: knocked unconscious, placed in a coffin, and deposited in a crematorium furnace, he is waking up just in time to realise that he is being cremated alive. A moment later, 007 is looking up at his unlikely rescuers – including Morton Slumber, the funeral director whose business has turned out to be a front for crime – and the plot moves on. This scene, in *Diamonds Are Forever* (Guy Hamilton, 1971), often comes up in discussions of the perception or representation of cremation, and its strange grip on the popular cultural memory may be connected with 'a cluster of emotional fears of cremation focused on claustrophobia and being burned alive' (Davies, 1996: 19). But given that so few mainstream British and American films feature cremations, as opposed to burials, the lack of competition could also be a significant factor.

It is not surprising that cremations were few and far between in the films of Hollywood's classical era, from the 1930s to the 1960s, given that cremations were still comparatively rare in most areas of the United States. Since then, however, cremation has become much more common, particularly in some of the western states, yet the inexorable rise in the national cremation rate over the past 30 years – which reached 25 per cent by the end of the 1990s (Prothero 2001: 10) – has left very little trace in popular cinema. This is not to deny that the sequence from *Diamonds Are Forever* is a memorable one; on the contrary, its portrayal of 'Slumber Inc.' (a portrayal which brings together 'the baroque wonderland' of the traditional funeral parlour [Mitford, 1963: 27] with a self-consciously modern preoccupation with technology) is, in effect, a striking satirical postscript to serious commentaries on 'the American way of death'. Nevertheless, it is ironic that the one cremation scene in the cinema which many of us are likely to remember is a cremation without so much as a corpse.

There is, of course, no shortage of deaths, particularly violent deaths, in the cinema; 'the pornography of death', identified by a pioneering sociologist of death nearly half a century ago (Gorer, 1960: 406), has been with us for a very long time. Relatively few of these deaths are succeeded, on screen, by rituals of disposal, but the funeral scene is not uncommon in Hollywood films, and some film-makers have made the most of its potential as a vehicle for exploring families and friendships. Funerals can open dramas, as in *The Big Chill* (Lawrence Kasdan, 1983), or conclude them, as in *The Deer Hunter* (Michael Cimino, 1978); in *The Godfather trilogy* (Francis Ford Coppola, 1972, 1974, 1990),

funerals are among the numerous rituals, both religious and secular, through which the saga of the Corleone family unfolds (Boswell and Loukides, 1999: 11–24). A few films, especially black comedies, like *The Loved One* (Tony Richardson, 1965) – an adaptation of Evelyn Waugh's 1948 novel – and *Harold and Maude* (Hal Ashby, 1971), put funerals, and the funeral business, in the foreground.

Significantly, most cinematic funerals reflect the 'ritual uniformity' of actual funerals, the general features of which (according to Richard Huntington and Peter Metcalf) include 'rapid removal of the corpse to a funeral parlour, embalming, institutionalised "viewing", and disposal by burial' (1979: 187). In any given film, some or perhaps all of these elements might only be implied, or one of the elements might appear in a variant form – the domestic wake, for example, standing in for an 'institutionalised "viewing"', particularly if the setting is Italian- or Irish-American. Since the late 1970s, however, the 'ritual uniformity' has been gradually eroded, as cremation, which provides considerable scope for customization, has become more common: 'the American way of cremation is not yet as routinized as the American way of burial' (Prothero, 2001: 3). A number of film-makers have portrayed the scattering of ashes by surviving friends or family, exploiting the dramatic, or, as in *The Big Lebowski* (Joel Coen, 1998), the comic possibilities of the material, but, in most cases, cinematic funerals continue to follow more traditional models.

Even in the classical era, however, Hollywood found space for cremation, of one kind or another, in some thoroughly mainstream entertainments. On screen, the spectacle of a body being ritually consumed by fire regularly featured in films based on the Viking sagas or the Arthurian legends; but the funeral rites of kings and other 'great men', far away and long ago, were so far removed from the experience of the cinemagoer that they might not have been recognized *as* cremations. Off screen, on the other hand, where cremation sometimes performed a very useful service as a plot device, it was implicitly acknowledged as a practice which was far from exotic, even if it remained unusual from the statistical point of view. The most interesting use of cremation as a plot device has perhaps been in films such as *Here Comes Mr Jordan* (Alexander Hall, 1941), later remade as

Heaven Can Wait (Warren Beatty and Buck Henry, 1978), which belong to what might be called 'the cinema of second chances': in these films, an error in the celestial bureaucracy leads to a soul being prematurely parted from its body, but given a second chance to live in a different, newly vacated body – the original having been cremated before the error could be rectified. (*Here Comes Mr Jordan* and several other 1940s films imagine an 'administrative beyond' which Roger Caillois, the sociologist, sought to explain in terms of 'the negation of the sacredness of death' in American society [Caillois, 1951: 12, 17]).

Film-makers working in other traditions have treated cremation in other ways, although rarely as controversially as in the film *Spalovač Mrtvol* (*The Cremator*), by the Slovakian director Juraj Herz (1968), which shows the operator of a crematorium descending into madness in the first stages of the Nazi occupation of Czechoslovakia, increasing his productivity in a terrible anticipation of the mass cremations which are to follow. In those European countries where cremation is much more common than it is in the United States, and even more so in Japan, for example, where cremation is normative, the fact that a character is cremated, rather than buried, need not carry any special significance; it is as natural for the Japanese family of *Ososhiki* (*The Funeral*) (Juzo Itami, 1984) to be making preparations for a cremation as it is for the American family of *The Funeral* (Abel Ferrara, 1996) to be making preparations for a burial. It might be argued, however, that we must look not only beyond Hollywood, but beyond fictional film as a whole, to find films which seriously engage with cremation rituals – that is, to ethnographic documentaries focusing on rituals in specific locations, such as Banaras, in *Forest of Bliss* (Robert Gardner, 1986), or Bali, in *Releasing the Spirits: A Village Cremation in Bali* (Linda Connor, Patsy Asch, Timothy Asch, 1981), although it is possible that the representation of the dead in fictional films and in documentaries produces very different responses in us, as is certainly the case with the representation of death itself (Sobchack, 1984: 293).

Back in the United States, it is not cinema, in fact, but television – in the form of the critically acclaimed drama series *Six Feet Under* (Alan Ball, 2001–), centring on a family-run funeral business in Los Angeles – which is now providing what is surely the most intelligent investigation of the American way of death to be found anywhere in contemporary popular culture. In spite of its title, *Six Feet Under* rarely stages the graveside scenes often presented in other dramas, but, rather, focuses on the viewings and services which take place in the funeral home, and on the cosmetic restoration of the body which precedes them. The distinctively American emphasis on embalming and subsequent viewing is not (as some have suggested) an implicit 'denial of death', a concept which, in so far as it confuses psychological processes and social practices, might not be especially useful in any case (Seale, 1998: 52–55, 70). More credibly, Philippe Ariès has argued that 'Americans are very willing to transform death, to put make-up on it, to sublimate it, but they do not want to make it disappear (1974: 100), and that the viewing is not a purely modern phenomenon, but the reappearance of 'the old romantic attitude, the death of the other, in modern dress' (1981: 596). It is to the great credit of *Six Feet Under* that it has succeeded in dramatizing these kinds of ideas – and yet, for all its sophistication, it seems that on those few occasions when it has portrayed a cremation, or even a request for one, it has usually been treated as a signal of some kind of failure within a family. The possibility of seeing things differently is one that might be suggested by a scene, near the end of *What's Eating Gilbert Grape?* (Lasse Hallström, 1993), which features what amounts to a cremation: when Gilbert's mother, a woman who weighs 500 pounds, and who, for fear of mockery, is unable to leave her home, eventually dies, Gilbert and his younger siblings do not call the local funeral director, but burn down the house around her – and this is, without any doubt, an act of love. **Colin Crowder**

References

Ariès, Philippe (1974), *Western Attitudes Toward Death: From the Middle Ages to the Present*, trans. Patricia Ranum, Baltimore, MD: Johns Hopkins University Press.

Boswell, P. and Loukides, P. (1999), *Reel Rituals: Ritual Occasions from Baptism to Funerals in Hollywood Films 1945–1995*, Bowling Green OH: Bowling Green State University Press.

Caillois, R. (1951), 'La Représentation de la Mort dans le Cinéma Américain', in *Quatre Essais de Sociologie*, Paris: Oliver Perrin, 11–23.

Davies, D.J. (1996), 'The Social Facts of Death', in G. Howarth and P.C. Jupp (eds), *Contemporary Issues in the Sociology of Death, Dying and Disposal*, London: Macmillan, 17–29.

Davies, D.J. (2002), 'Book, Film and Building', in *Death, Ritual and Belief: The Rhetoric of Funerary Rites* (2nd edn), London: Continuum, 196–210.

Gorer, G. (1960), 'The Pornography of Death', in M.R. Stein, A.J. Vidich and D.M. White (eds), *Identity and Anxiety: Survival of the Person in Mass Society*, New York: Free Press, 402–407. First published 1956.

Huntington, Richard and Metcalf, Peter (1979), *Celebrations of Death: The Anthropology of Mortuary Ritual*, Cambridge: Cambridge University Press.

Prothero, Stephen (2001), *Purified by Fire: A History of Cremation in America*, Berkeley: University of California Press.

Seale, Clive (1998), *Constructing Death: The Sociology of Dying and Bereavement*, Cambridge: Cambridge University Press.

Sobchack, V. (1984), 'Inscribing Ethical Space: Ten Propositions on Death, Representation, and Documentary', *Quarterly Review of Film Studies*, 9: 283–300.

FINLAND

For about 700 years Finland belonged to Sweden. After the 1808–1809 war Finland was taken over by Russia and became a grand duchy under Tsar Alexander I but managed to preserve its cultural ties with the West. This was confirmed by the tsar's personal guarantee that the form of government, constitution and the authority of the Lutheran Church would remain in force. Nevertheless, the first part of the nineteenth century remained a period of conservatism and stagnation in Finland. When Tsar Alexander II ascended to the throne in 1854, however, the strictly bureaucratic state machinery in Russia loosened its grip. Liberal ideas were allowed to emerge. Censorship became less oppressive, and associations once again dared to operate more openly. In this more positive intellectual climate, liberalism made its final breakthrough particularly among the Swedish-speaking educated class in Finland. The majority of Finnish daily newspapers also supported these freethinking ideas. By the middle of the 1880s, then, conditions began to become ripe in Finland for broader circles to show an interest in cremation, although this applied principally to the Swedish-speaking, educated part of Finland.

The concept of cremation reached Finland from Sweden, where the first crematorium had been built as early as 1887. The idea was first publicly presented in 1887 when Professor Anders Wilhelm Bolin gave a lecture on the subject. In March 1889 Bolin demanded openly that a cremation association should be formed in Finland. Apparently inspired by Bolin's article, a number of people in Helsinki who were interested in the issue decided to convene a meeting on 2 May 1889 to discuss the need for a cremation association. The meeting decided unanimously to found such an assocation, although the majority of those present nonetheless felt that public opinion was in need of further preparation before the authorities could be approached. Consequently, it was decided to form a preparatory committee, to which Bolin was elected chairman. Little progress was made, however, for at the 1890 annual meeting it was decided that the time was still not ripe for approaching the authorities, although a decision was taken to collect funds for the building of a crematorium. In 1891 Bolin began to appear more sceptical about the registration of the association – an attitude that probably reflected the threat against Finnish autonomy as the period of Russification started. From the beginning of the first period of real oppression in 1899, apparently because members were frightened of the authorities, meetings for the crematorium fund were only organized on an annual basis.

The year 1905, with its widespread popular movements in both Russia and Finland, produced a number of concessions with regard to Finland's position. The result was a significant liberalization of the general political climate. The activities of various societies began to flourish, and the Cremation Association also awoke from its slumbers. At the annual meeting of the crematorium fund in 1905, Dr A. Wallenskiöld suggested that the association should immediately apply to the Senate to become legally registered. Some people still felt, however, that the time was not ripe for such a move. Before the matter could be discussed by the Senate, the Act for Freedom of Speech, Assembly and Association came into force. This law guaranteed citizens of the autonomous Grand Duchy of Finland the right, without prior application, to form associations for purposes that were not contrary to the law or public morality. The Senate therefore considered that no permission was required for the registration of the Cremation Association, but it did not approve, its statues. The Cremation Association, at its annual meeting on 25 October 1907, felt that after 18 years of existence it could approve its own statutes and legally constitute itself. However, the legal status of the association remained unclear. The second period of oppression, together with new attempts at Russification, began in 1907. These efforts were more determined than before, and, during the following years, the association was forced to struggle for its right to exist. The chief opposition came from conservative Christians, who allied themselves with the Old Fennomans and the Russian authorities to prevent the introduction of cremation. The following years were difficult for the association. The First World War brought such an enormous increase in the cost of raw materials that it became impossible for the association to begin building a crematorium, despite large donations. Then, in aftermath of the war, there was such sharp inflation that the association now only possessed a fraction of the capital required to build a crematorium.

In 1917 independence and freedom finally became a reality in Finland, and the association now felt that it could operate within fear of future obstacles. The Helsinki city council granted the association a loan of 1 million marks and the construction work began. At the end of 1925 the crematorium was ready. On 24 March 1926 the first cremation in Finland in modern times was carried out, after 37 years of struggle. In the autumn of 1927 it was decided to arrange a formal inauguration of the crematorium. In accordance with the Swedish model, the chapel had been provided with Christian symbols and it was hoped that the Church would celebrate the inauguration of the chapel. But the bishops who were approached to conduct the inauguration ceremony declined the honour. Relations between the Church and the Cremation Association had once again proved inflammatory.

Although the Cremation Association had individual supporters all over the country, there was no organization for building crematoria in other places. The introduction of cremation in Helsinki had proved extremely useful in terms of saving cemetery space. An understanding of cremation on the part of the Church now emerged in Helsinki and in Turku (Swedish: Åbo), where congregations planned the building of a crematorium at the end of the 1930s. However, the Second World War intervened and the project never materialized.

The end of the war brought important political, cultural and spiritual transformations, together with a rapid increase in the process of urbanization. In simple terms, it might be claimed that, after the war, agrarian-Christian Finland took the step into the modern world. The fact that the war ended in a less than honourable fashion also dealt a blow to the ideology of 'Home, Church and Fatherland'. The reassessment of Finland's position in world politics swung the internal balance of power in favour of the left so that the Church was forced to reconsider its social commitments with a new emphasis on its social and ethical responsibility, in addition to its purely spiritual message. A powerful tendency towards secularization had begun. Nevertheless, the new crematoria were long in coming. During the post-war years of reconstruction such building projects were too expensive, even though in the 1950s the idea of crematoria was popular. Crematorium projects were planned in several places but the process still needed to be approved. Finally, it was the congregation of Karjaa (Swedish: Karis) which approached the Porvoo Diocesan Council, which in turn turned to the Bishops' Council in 1960 to hear the bishops' opinion as to whether the building of crematoria was the business of the Church. The Bishops' Council shared the positive attitude of the Church Council. It was therefore in Karjaa that Finland's second crematorium entered service in 1964. In the same year Espoo (Swedish: Esbo) crematorium began to function; this project, too, was entirely in the hands of the congregation. In the 1960s a total of six crematoria were built. Now, at the beginning of the twenty-first century, there are some 20 crematoria functioning in Finland. They do not cover the whole country – they are lacking in the northern and eastern parts of Finland – but there are plans for new crematoria in due course.

The attitude of the Church towards cremation has changed completely. Having long opposed and obstructed this kind of activity, it has begun to take the initiative. Of course, this does not mean that Christian opposition towards cremation has completely ceased. There are few converts to cremation in Finland: in 2000 the cremation rate was bout 25 per cent in total, although in the south and in the greater Helsinki area it is about 75 per cent. A survey conducted by the Department of Comparative Religion at Åbo Akademi University in the 1980s showed that there is a large degree of openness in Finnish attitudes towards cremation. In light of this study, it is possible that cremation will gradually become as popular as it is in the rest of the Nordic countries.

In 1989 the cremation movement in Finland celebrated its centenary. The future of cremation seems to be promising, thanks to new and modern legislation, and cremation could be said to have become just as valid as ground burial in the larger cities. The Orthodox Church in Finland (with 50 000 members – that is, about 1 per cent of the population), which has the same status as a national church as the Lutheran Church, nevertheless still has reservations about the process. **Nils G. Holm**

References

Holm, Nils G. and Lahtinen, Tuomo (1985), *Jordbegravning eller kremering? En studie of gravskicket i Finland*, Åbo: Åbo Akademi.

Lahtinen, Tuomo (1989), *Kremering i Finland: Idéhistoria och utveckling*, Åbo: Åbo Akademi.

FIRE

CHAOS AND COSMOS

Fire is a universal symbol capable of expressing a wide variety of meanings from the negativity of chaos to the positive cosmos often symbolized by the sun. Cremation, in its uniting of fire with death is, also, a kind of foundational phenomenon open to expressing a society's own sense of significance. The constant human capacity to construct meaningful accounts of life fosters the diversity of significance given to such phenomena as fire and death and, inevitably, to their combination in cremation. In considering some of the meanings that fire carries in different cultures, we emphasize not only fire's dual attributes of creativity and destruction, but also its sacred and profane potential. A particularly close relationship between fire, death and life was drawn in A.M. Hocart's anthropological essay, 'Baptism by Fire' which brought together a series of activities as examples of 'life-giving by means of fire', including cremation, burning heretics, burnt offerings and fire-walking (1973: 157). Here we highlight some general features of both the sacred and profane aspects of fire in the mythical and religious traditions of selected, but diverse, human societies.

The two natures of fire

Through their myths, many societies have reflected on the origin and nature of fire, knowing its power to influence life for both good and ill (Frazer, 1930; Campbell 1959: 276–81). For earliest peoples, as for many in the world today, fire fostered survival, serving as a focal point for family and community gathering after dark as well as a defence against wild animals. Its social focus developed with the rise of more permanent housing as the hearth, the permanent site of domestic fire and the point of welcome for family members and guests, an issue to which we return at the close of this entry on fire (Raglan, 1964: 75). Over time, it was found that fire would also turn mud into bricks, the literal building blocks of villages, towns and cities. But, equally, in many towns, especially in medieval Europe, fire was a major hazard of life even, at times, competing with the plague as 'the greatest threat to security' (Thomas, 1973: 17). Here we can contrast the Great Fire of London with the devastation of Dresden. London's Great Fire of 1666, started accidentally and destroying a large part of the old city, became the occasion for a great deal of new building and architectural development, whereas the destruction of the German city of Dresden during the Second World War by the British was completely intentional with fire being used as a weapon. Nevertheless, fire is also capable of highly positive outcomes. It helped the supply of edible materials as people developed cooking as a means of converting natural and raw products into food – and, by so doing, they also expressed their difference from other animals. To cook was to be human, and in that very basic sense fire became intrinsically symbolic as it helped foster a sense of humanity.

René Girard evocatively describes how a fire provides a focus for such a human experience of togetherness using the biblical example of Peter who, having denied Jesus with whom he really belonged, tried to warm himself by a fire amidst people with whom he did not belong (1986: 150). In that case, the context of the fire was

Peter's undoing, for it made others identify him as a 'misplaced person'.

This example shows something of the dual potentiality of fire for, as with many aspects of human life and culture, its positive property is partnered by a negative. With fire this involves its very literal capacity to destroy. Fire can render crops and food stores, houses and cities like Dresden useless. In some societies complex associations of ideas exist between fire, life, death and cooking. Some South American myths tell how human beings lost immortality because they were curious to find the origin of the sound of bird-calls. Leaving the safety of living with their ancestors they climbed through a hole and discovered the earth but also the power of death. Yet, in the further paradox of myth, even the death of trees could yield the wood that furnished the basis of cooking. Indeed, the very use of fire to destroy trees as part of their slash-and-burn form of agriculture has been seen, partly, as a kind of killing and 'cannibalism' of the trees. It has been argued that 'there is an intrinsic link between the theme of man's loss of immortality and the obtaining of fire for cooking purposes' (Lévi-Strauss, 1970: 152). This is but one example of the way in which, in fire, humanity found its friend and enemy. Fire demanded control, and this sometimes extended from the practical control of flames to a more mystical control. Such 'a mastery of fire' is a feature of forms of religion in which a sense of power, generated through various disciplines, underlies a person's religious status and identity, as with many traditional shamans. This is expressed through walking over burning coals, or handling or even licking red-hot metal. To be able to do this is to demonstrate the power of the spirit – indeed, it is to demonstrate the body's conquest of the spirit (Eliade, 1960: 95).

South American myth

The mythological tradition of South America's Aztecs is particularly interesting for it accounts not only for the role of fire underlying the existence of sun, moon and stars, but also of the practice of human sacrifice as a means of perpetuating the ongoing life of the universe. A dispute arose amongst the gods as to who should be responsible for illuminating the world. This was no easy task for it involved leaping into the great cosmic hearth and the fire raging in it. Ultimately this was accomplished and light was

brought to the world. This myth also accounts for the ultimate death of these heroic gods and shows how central fire is to all life and all destiny (Girard, 1986: 57–60). Their act of sacrifice, with the help of the wind god *Ehecatl*, also brought about movement in both the sun and the moon which had, before that, been stationary. These epic events were recalled and celebrated during one of the 18 divisions, each of 20 days, that together comprised the ancient Aztec calendar: it included major sacrifices made to fire and to the fire god *Xiuhtecuhtli* (*Aztecs*, 2002: 205).

Middle-Eastern and Mediterranean myths

Within the wider history of religions the importance of fire is also evident in studies of Indo-European language, mythology and religion, and some would also argue for the even earlier Proto-Indo-European world of approximately 5000 BCE (Lincoln, 1991: 1–10). Later, in the ancient Zoroastrian religion of Persia, fire was the seventh aspect of creation of *Ahura Mazda*, coming immediately after mankind. This tradition honoured fire, having a fire-altar at the centre of its devotion and avoiding cremation in the belief that dead bodies would negatively influence the sacred flame. Fire will also remain powerful at the end of the world when a great battle between good and evil will see the evil destroyed in an immense conflagration prior to a new creation in an eternal realm of divine good will (Nigosian, 1993: 95).

The ancient Greek world also made a contribution to the symbolism of fire in the Eleusinian mysteries. From 500–600 BCE until approximately 400 CE, when Christianity rendered it redundant across the expanse of the Roman Empire, candidates were initiated into a group of devotees charged never to disclose what they were taught. Indeed, a paucity of teaching has come from these sources, but there are archaeological remains of the ritual buildings used. Central to these is the Telesterion, the main chamber, and the Anaktoron, a side-room from which the initiate encountered a 'great light' in the form of a fire. Indeed, scorch marks have been found in excavated examples. It is extremely likely that the fire carried sacrificial and purificatory significance (Burkert, 1983: 277). Many early Christians knew of these mysteries and even spoke against them, while others even used the word 'mysteries' to refer to their own rites of baptism and Eucharist.

Northern European traditions

Fire has held a notable place within religious traditions of northern Europe, especially in Scandinavia, as Viking fire-funerals demonstrate. In Celtic religion, too, the seasonal ritual associated with the coming of summer involved the building and ignition of a Beltane fire. This fire (*tan*) honoured the sun-god *Bâl* (or *Belanos*) and was associated with the idea of the death of the old year and the birth of the new. This occurred on the night that brings in May Day. It seems that these fires were used to purify the cattle as they set out for the summer pastures. There is some record from classical antiquity concerning the Druids, as the prime movers in Celtic culture, also being leaders in sacrifice, including human sacrifice (Lincoln, 1991: 176–87). This may have involved victims, perhaps criminals, being built into figures constructed out of interwoven branches and then being burnt: the film *The Straw Man* is a contemporary and fictional reflection of those traditions. In association with the growth of religious groups identifying themselves as pagan in the late twentieth and early twenty-first century there has been a resurgence of the Beltane fire ritual, albeit devoid of any such literal sacrifice. Sometimes this event can have a relatively high social profile as, for example, in the lighting of such a fire in Edinburgh in 2004. The rite has even been recognized in music, in the *The Beltane Fire* by contemporary composer Sir Peter Maxwell Davies. The lighting of the 'new fire' employed in this ritual is very similar to the kindling of the new fire in the Christian ritual of the Easter Vigil.

Hinduism and Buddhism

In Indian scriptures the Vedas tell of the god Agni as a fire-deity, born in the sky but who may, for example, still descend to earth as lightning or be seen in the divine play of flames (Eliade, 1979: 208–209). Most important for cremation is the belief that this act is, in effect, the last sacrifice a person may offer to a deity: cremation is a self-offering through fire. This view of fire is, however, far from simple, for it exists within an extensively complex set of Indian ideas that extend from the place of the domestic fire through to the fact that 'fire can be reduced to

heat, and that heat can be seen as the final property of life' (Knipe, 1975: 37). This perspective qualifies our earlier generalization that fire is one of the irreducible elements of life, and focuses on the essence of fire – its heat. Interestingly, this very issue of how fire and heat are related to human existence was a theme discussed by the pre-Christian Roman thinker Cicero in his book *The Nature of the Gods* (1972: 206–207). In ancient India and in later developments of the association between fire and 'heat' or *tapas*, fire can become interiorized, with such inward fire playing its part in the process of transcendence which, itself, may involve pain and anguish. But, it is the outward fire that is our major concern for, '[t]he cremation fire is the translator of the deceased from this world to heaven' (Knipe, 1975: 132). Cremation in its Indian traditions, then, gains its significance from, just as it imparts ideas to, many other aspects of life and the universe.

Buddhist tradition developed the idea of fire, using it as a symbol that describes inner transformations of the self, most especially of the Lord Buddha. Cremation, as the process by which fire may achieve its goal, came to be an important ritual expression of these important inner changes. According to tradition, the Buddha's body was cremated, but a dispute took place over the ashes. It was decided to divide them into eight portions so that the quarrelling rulers might each have some for their own kingdoms. Later, a miracle caused the separated remains to gather at Rajagrha and be placed in a secret chamber until the powerful Indian king, Asoka, had them taken and placed throughout his kingdom in some 84 000 places. Such remains were located in a structure called a stupa, which has an extensive symbolic nature. These solid domed or spired structures are not simply architectural memorials of a great man but are thought to come alive through the cremated remains. The ashes act as a form of seed that animates the structure, transforming it into something of power and extensive significance for devotees. A portion of ashes, or of other objects associated with the earthly Buddha, placed within a stupa is also an expression of the Buddha's teaching or dharma, and that dharma is, itself, the dynamic means by which devotees may themselves be spiritually transformed.

The idea of spiritual transformation is also expressed through fire. The process of enlightenment, involving meditative, educative and ethical factors, is likened to cremation with one domain – that of ignorance or the 'body' – removed. The act of burning the Buddha is said to have occurred after he had already undergone that inner transformation of 'burning' away of ignorance to achieve enlightenment. The fire sacrifice of Shingon Buddhism expresses this; sticks are burned while the monk seeks to undergo an inner 'burning' and removal of desire through the 'fire of knowledge' (Snodgrass, 1992: 353–56). The Budhha becomes 'a flame' and is sometimes depicted as surrounded by fire and with a flame emanating from the crown of his head. Indeed, at his cremation, he was both a fire himself and was cremated by a fire. In Hindu terms he becomes 'the humanized type of Agni' (Snodgrass, 1992: 356).

Jewish, Christian and Islamic traditions

Although in Jewish and Christian religious traditions fire also carries some deep significance, it does not exist in anything like such a complex ideology, mythology and ritual practice as in Buddhism. Nevertheless, these traditions are important because of the way in which cremation has emerged within Christianity despite its strong tradition of burial. In the Qu'ran, too, Islam echoes many Jewish and Christian themes, including the punishing quality of fire and with terms that reflect the Jewish Gehenna (Qu'ran, xxxii: 13). Although Islam does not accept cremation, these allusions to fire and punishment are retained specifically for moral guidance and warning as to the next life and continue to play a part in fostering the good life in some parts of contemporary Islam. Given the avoidance of cremation no special attention will be paid to fire in Islamic thought. The negative aspect of fire in these religious traditions all relate to punishment due to the wicked or to a purgative process that is ultimately of benefit to them

Hebrew religion

Jewish traditions used fire as a symbol open to both creative and destructive energies. In the Hebrew Bible fire and flames are associated with the divine being and with moments of divine revelation, as when an angel of God appears to Moses in a flame of fire in the burning bush or when the Lord descended in fire upon Mount Sinai (Exodus 3: 2, 19: 18). Fire was also central to

Israel's temple worship, being used to consume sacrifices offered to God. Indeed, a fire was always to be kept burning upon the altar and should never be allowed to go out (Leviticus, 6: 13). Acknowledging that some of Israel's neighbours used fire for child-sacrifice the Bible is keen to warn against such practice, and even to issue a command against it (Deuteronomy, 12: 31, 18: 10; Levenson, 1993). Some Canaanite religion seemed to offer both sons and daughters in fire-offerings to the deity Molech, a practice detested by the Jewish prophets (Jeremiah, 32: 35). By contrast, certain crimes were, ideally, punishable by fire – for example, when a man has sex with his wife and mother-in-law, 'they shall be burnt with fire' (Leviticus, 20: 14). Certainly the wicked at large might be burnt with fire (Ezekiel, 28: 18). While fire was also used on enemies, whether property or crops, it could also exert a purifying influence (Numbers, 31: 23). The **ashes of Isaac** entry also adds quite another dimension to ancient Jewish ideas. All these examples show how fire is a symbol that is able to express quite different meanings.

So far as cremation was concerned, the tradition of tomb burial makes cremation highly unusual within the Jewish scriptures and, when it occurs, it marks some distinctive event as in the burning of the body of King Saul after he had been beheaded and desecrated by his enemies (1 Samuel 31: 12–13). Even so, his cremation was not complete in the sense that it did not destroy his bones, for these were buried and in that sense they, too, follow the pattern of the double burial of bodies that was, centuries later, established as the normal mode of funeral by the time of Jesus Christ. Double burial refers to a practice in which one rite applies to the corpse and another to the subsequent dry bones of that corpse. Jews traditionally allowed the corpse to decay, often in a tomb, before placing the bones in an ossuary, a special box that often carried the name or mark of identity of the deceased individual. **Douglas J. Davies**

See also ashes of Isaac; Buddhism; fire – Christianity; Hinduism; Islam; Judaism; Viking Sweden.

References

Aztecs (2002), London: Royal Academy of Art.
Burkert, Walter (1983), *Homo Necans, The*

Anthropology of Ancient Greek Sacrificial Ritual and Myth, trans. Peter Bing, Berkeley: University of California Press.

Campbell, Joseph (1959), *The Masks of God, Primitive Mythology*, London: Souvenir Press.

Cicero (1972), *The Nature of the Gods*, trans. Horace C.P. McGregor, with an introduction by J.M. Ross, Harmondsworth: Penguin.

Eliade, Mircea (1960), *Myths, Deaths and Mysteries*, London: Collins, Fontana Library.

Eliade, Mircea (1979), *A History of Religious Ideas*, Vol. 1, London: Collins.

Frazer, James G. (1930), *Myths of the Origin of Fire*, London: Macmillan.

Girard, René (1986), *The Scapegoat*, Baltimore, MD: John Hopkins University Press.

Hocart, A.M. (1973), *The Life-Giving Myth and Other Essays*, intro. Rodney Needham. London: Tavistock Publications with Methuen and Co. Ltd. First published 1952.

Knipe, David M. (1975), *In the Image of Fire, Vedic Experiences of Heat*, Delhi: Motilal Banarsidass.

Levenson, J.D. (1993), *The Death and Resurrection of the Beloved Son: The Transformation of Child Sacrifice in Judaism and Christianity*, New Haven, CT: Yale University Press.

Lévi-Strauss, Claude (1970), *The Raw and the Cooked*, London: Jonathan Cape.

Lincoln, Bruce (1991), *Death, War and Sacrifice: Studies in Ideology and Practice*, Chicago: Chicago University Press.

Nigosian, S.A. (1993), *The Zoroastrian Faith*, Montreal and Kingston: McGill/Queen's University Press.

Raglan, Lord (1964), *The Temple and the House*, London: Routledge and Kegan Paul.

Snodgrass, Adrian (1992), *The Symbolism of the Stupa*, Delhi: Motilal Banarsidass.

Thomas, K. (1973), *Religion and the Decline of Magic*, Harmondsworth: Penguin.

CHRISTIANITY

Early Christianity

The New Testament scriptures produced by early Christians continue some of the themes of punishing and purging fires present in Hebrew religion. Gospel references to a place of burning punishment for the unrighteous (Matthew 10: 28. Mark 9: 43) combined ideas of a rubbish heap with sites where impure sacrifices had been made. This site of Gehenna is, primarily a fire (Matthew 5: 22) and in the Book of Revelation (19: 20) this place becomes the 'lake of fire' and the ultimate destination of all that is evil. This trend of seeing fire as punishment for sin is developed as it echoes down the ages from early Christianity. Some writings of the second Christian century that are not included in the Bible also give a dramatic role to fire at the time of divine judgement of the earth. In but one case, that of the Apocalypse of Peter, 'Floods of fire shall be let loose ... and the waters shall be changed and turn into coals of fire, and all that is in them shall burn, and the sea shall become fire....The spirits also of the dead bodies shall .... Become fire at the commandment of God'. Indeed some of the images are as dramatically terrifying as anything imagined in the medieval world, a thousand years later. For example, the angel of wrath, Ezrael, carries around half-burning bodies, while breast-milk flows, congeals and give rise to monsters. Eyes are also tormented with red-hot irons. (James, 1953: 513, 515).

St Augustine, in the fifth century, could even mount an argument that wicked angels could suffer the torment of fire: 'For one fire shall torment both men and devils. Christ has spoken it' (1945: 333). So far as actual fire was concerned Augustine was quite untroubled as to its potential effect on human bodies. Such was his belief in the resurrection that, even if bodies were cremated, God's power could 're-collect and unite every atom of the body, were it burnt, or torn by beasts or fallen to dust, or dissolved into moisture' (1945: 386).

Even so, early Christianity largely set itself against burning individuals as a punishment, although the later Catholic Church did extend this notion of hell, furnishing it with further lurid descriptions of punishments, not least as a warning to the living. This was especially important with the flourishing of the idea of purgatory in the twelfth century (LeGoff, 1984). Dante's fourteenth-century *Divine Comedy* offered an extended poetic description of the concepts of hell, purgatory and heaven for his fourteenth-century readers, and fire played its punishing but, more positively still, purifying role. As Dante's guide to the inferno explained, 'There are souls concealed within these moving fires, each one swathed in his burning punishment' (Dante, 1955, Canto XXVI: 48). Fire also appears as a kind of falling snowflake, and those being punished are caught up in a 'rhythmic dance of wretched hands ... this side, that side, brushing away the freshly fallen flames' (Canto XIV: 42). Having said that, it is important to note that Dante also knows joy and possesses a hope of an ultimate positive eternal outcome of these trials. Indeed, care is needed in the way purgation and fire are viewed by Dante as, indeed, by other Christian writers. Protestant perspectives opposed and downplayed the very idea of purgatory, irrespective of other processes of spiritual development after death that might prepare the believer for the full presence of God, tending to favour salvation as a dramatic and rapid change in the believer.

Christian heretics, witches and criminals

Against that kind of background it is not surprising that burning was accepted by churches when exerting discipline against both witches and heretics. One of the most famous is the trial and death of Joan of Arc (1412–31) whose heavenly voices brought her great fame through her service to King Charles VII of France. Capture led to her trial and to an ultimate conviction, her visions were declared spurious, and she was burned on 30 May 1431 at Rouen. Some 20 years later this conviction was reversed by Pope Callistus III and, centuries later, in 1920 she was canonized, becoming St Joan of Arc.

During the religious disputes of the Reformation both Protestants and Catholics burned those they regarded as heretics. Just a generation after Joan, across the Channel in England, one of the most famous of all British churchmen, Archbishop Thomas Cranmer (1489–1556), who had helped King Henry VIII establish the Church of England as it broke free from Catholicism, was himself burned as a heretic in Oxford on 21 March 1556. This was a year after Bishops Latimer and Ridley had also been condemned and burned at Oxford as part of church and state politics and doctrinal debate. Cranmer had also been influential in composing *The Book of Common Prayer* whose burial service underpinned the history of British funeral rights until other forms were added to it in the late twentieth century. The hand that had written so much memorable liturgy had also signed his recantation. This so disturbed him that he famously held his hand in the pyre's flames, crying 'This has offended!', finally standing by what he had really believed all along.

In addition to such eminent persons, many ordinary folk, often of limited resources and social significance, were charged with heresy and with doing harm to their neighbours. These so-called witches tended to be burnt in Catholic countries, although also in Protestant Scotland where the last witch was burned in 1727. England preferred to hang witches but, heretics, who denied a church's doctrine and imperilled their own souls, were burnt, as with Cranmer (Thomas, 1971: 521).

Centuries later, this powerful symbolism of burning at the stake returned with tremendous poignancy – for example, in Abel Gance's film *J'accuse*, a fictional reflection on the First World War in which the hero, Jean Diaz, calls the spirits of the dead to return to earth to bring a sense of realism to human society to stop it falling into warfare. But, before that goal is achieved he is in fact killed, and burned at the stake, 'appropriately at the foot of a war memorial – by the ignorant masses who failed to see that war must never happen again' (Winter, 1995: 17). Here the symbolism of being burned at the stake as a 'heretic' casts into relief the very notion of those in authority not being sensible to what is, in fact, the truth. To equate the cremation-stake with the war memorial is to highlight aspects of human folly.

One English folk element emerging from Catholic and Protestant opposition involving fire, though not regarded as a cremation, is the burning of an effigy of Guy Fawkes on 5 November each year. In 1606 Fawkes took part in a Catholic plot – the Gunpowder Plot – to blow up the essentially Protestant Houses of Parliament. In today's context very few are probably aware of the historical, political and religious background of what is an occasion for bonfire and firework parties located halfway between the summer and Christmas holiday seasons.

Evil cremation

Of quite a different order was the fire of cremation used by the Nazis during the Second World War as a means of eliminating Jews, Gypsies, some mentally ill people and homosexuals as part of the goal of establishing a pure culture of genetically worthy individuals in Hitler's Third Reich. This Nazi extermination of Jews between 1933 and 1945 came to be called the Holocaust – a word that had been used in the Hebrew Bible to describe sacrificial offerings entirely consumed by fire. In this context, however, it was people and not animals that were subject to the destruction that took place at concentration camps such as Auschwitz-Birkenau, and that has come to symbolize the utter inhumanity of killing men, women and children and cremating them. In that context, cremation was nothing less than an industrial process of destruction. Devoid of ceremony, dealing as it was with dehumanized bodies and not people in the proper sense of that word, this was an attempt to achieve Hitler's 'Final Solution' to the Jewish 'problem', a 'problem' which some interpret as having been established through Christian anti-Semitism. This case shows how possible it is for a process such as cremation to be open to absolutely different interpretations. The entry on **Argentina** raises a similar issue in relation to the possible use of cremation to eliminate bodies as part of political programmes of assassination. The blasphemy, whether against God or humanity, inherent in such elimination-cremation stands starkly contrasted with the traditional Hindu cremation as a final self-sacrifice to a deity. Many Jews, though not all, have objected to any form of ordinary cremation since that period because of these associations and, to a degree, something of a similar shadow came to be thrown over cremation in Germany and even in parts of Poland that neighbour Auschwitz.

Creative fire

Fire, then, has been profoundly ambiguous in Christian history with even its positive connotation as a purifying agent being overshadowed by its negative capacity as a form of punishment. This is clearly expressed in the Book of Malachi, part of which was popularized in Handel's Messiah, and the idea of the messenger of the Lord coming as a refiner's fire (Malachi 3: 2). The same Book, however, also speaks of the day of the Lord as one that will 'burn as an oven' with the wicked burning like stubble (Malachi 4: 1). Both those motifs combine in Luke's Gospel where John the Baptist describes the coming messenger of God as one who will baptize 'with the Holy Spirit and with fire' but who will also burn 'the chaff…with unquenchable fire' (Luke 3: 17). This is an important reference because it displays the strong potential of a double meaning. Amongst some early church thinkers, such as Origen in the second century, fire could be viewed positively so that even God's vengeance could take the form of a healing fire. Similarly, later generations of Christian mystics such as Catherine of Genoa, for whom love is a driving force in the growing knowledge of God, can speak of the divine 'fiery love' that works a metamorphosis on the soul (Catherine of Genoa, 1979: 79).

The analogy of the divine servant as a refiner's fire is taken further, with both an added visual symbolic component and a distinctly positive significance, in the form of the Holy Spirit described as descending upon the disciples of Jesus as 'tongues as of fire' framed by the sound of rushing mighty wind (Acts 2: 3). This symbolic association of Holy Spirit and fire was developed in various ways in subsequent traditions. Gregory of Nyssa in the fourth century, for example, took the idea of fire, especially in the more focused symbol of 'flame', as a means of expressing both the descent of divine love into the human heart and the subsequent upward leap of that heart, now freed, from its sinful, earthy gravity (Nygren, 1982: 431, 445). Christian piety has reflected such ideas in the hymns that became popular in the nineteenth and twentieth century; these are clearly exemplified in Bianco da Siena's original Italian words:

> Come down O Love Divine,
> Seek Thou this soul of mine,
> And visit it with Thine own ardour glowing;
> O Comforter draw near,
> Within my heart appear,
> And kindle it, Thy holy flame bestowing.

The hymn then asks not only that this holy flame might 'freely burn,/Till earthly passions turn,/To dust and ashes in its heat consuming', but also that the 'glorious light' of the divine Spirit might 'Shine ever on my sight,/And clothe me round, the while my path illuming'. Here the power of the double feature of the fire of the Spirit is invoked for both the transformation and direction of life.

These elements of fiery purification and illumination are manifest in numerous hymns on the Spirit. One verse of S. Longfellow's hymn 'Holy Spirit, Truth Divine', prays: 'Holy Spirit, Love divine,/Glow within this heart of mine;/Kindle every high desire; /Perish self in Thy pure fire'. But, perhaps, the most widely used expression of these themes lies in 'Come Holy Ghost our souls inspire'. This famous translation of a profoundly simple ninth-century hymn by the seventeenth-century Bishop of Durham, John Cosin, became part of the ordination service in the Church of England from 1662. Its dual stress on the 'celestial fire' of the Spirit falls both on its power to enlighten and foster love:

Thy blessed unction from above
Is comfort, life, and fire of love;
Enable with perpetual light
The dullness of our blinded sight.

These hymns of spirit-fire are often associated with the Feast of Pentecost, the day that celebrates the Acts of the Apostles account of the Holy Spirit coming to the disciples and energizing them to form the early church (Acts 2). In some popular, though not official, interpretations the mitre or hat that came to be worn by bishops in western Christianity from about the eleventh century is interpreted as representing these tongues of flame.

Liturgical fire

The best example of the use of fire in Christian liturgy was developed not from the biblical images of the descending Spirit but of Christ as the light of the world and of his resurrection from the dead. As part of today's Easter vigil rites in some churches a new fire is kindled outside the church and is used to light the Paschal Candle that symbolizes the resurrected Christ. This is carried into the church when priest and people acclaim 'The Light of Christ'. Carl Jung wished to set this tradition, which he identifies as existing from at least the eighth century in France, within the broad tradition of Hermetic literature that had its origin in the second Christian century. Hermetic material came to be aligned with aspects of alchemy with its extensive symbolism and commitment to discovering a way of transforming materials into higher-order realities, including the transformation of human nature. The stone from which the new fire is struck is variously identified with Christ as the 'cornerstone' or with the rock-tomb or the rock door of the tomb from which Christ sprung in resurrection, perhaps even after having visited the fires of hell. Another depiction of fire in association with Christ can be found iconographically as the wounds of the crucifixion are framed in fire as in some fourteenth-century Christian art (Jung 1993: 352–55, 122). That was at a time when Franciscan

spirituality had developed the strong theme of St Francis receiving the stigmata – the wounds symbolic of Christ's passion and crucifixion. In some art, fire frames these as glorious wounds. Equally powerful, though much less well known, were alchemical texts that seemed to link ideas of an alchemist's cremation furnace with the miracle of the Christian mass, both being contexts of transformation (Jung, 1993: 350).

Despite the powerful currency of even the more mainstream of these symbols of divine love, purification, illumination and transformation of life through the Spirit and through Christ, Christian churches made little attempt to utilize them in relation to cremation funerals. One reason for this lies in the long tradition of burial in Christianity. From the tomb or cave burials of the time of Christ, which often involved a secondary collection and relocation of the bones, the emphasis on earth burial of the corpse developed in many parts of expanding Christendom, especially in Europe. Interment as a ritual practice possesses a powerful affinity with doctrinal ideas of resurrection and might even be regarded as depicting God's judgement upon humanity: 'In the sweat of your face you shall eat bread till you return to the ground, for out of it you were taken; you are dust, and to dust you shall return' (Genesis 3: 19).

To bury someone in a grave, to throw soil on them and to pronounce the words, 'earth to earth, ashes to ashes, dust to dust', makes an integrated rite in which biblical words, theological ideas and practical knowledge of life combine in a symbolic pattern. In some periods of history it is also likely that the complementary belief in a resurrection from the dead also gained power as the hoped-for transformation of the buried corpse. It may be, however, that in parts of Europe in the late nineteenth and twentieth centuries, a dual shift in beliefs occurred with, on the one hand, increasing numbers ceasing to believe in any sort of afterlife and, on the other, those who did believe in it working on the assumption of some kind of ongoing soul rather than a resurrecting body. For both groups the fire of cremation brought a positive advantage. Indeed, it is probably unusual for a single phenomenon – in this case cremation fire – to be of positive advantage to people of quite different views.

Fire and identity

For those seeing death as the end, cremation makes a clear symbolic expression of their belief. Fire removes the human body allowing mourners to express their varied memories of the deceased through rites performed with the cremated remains. Where the law allows it, secularists or humanists can dispose of them in ways that enhance the memory or to express the personality and life of the deceased. For them, there is what might be called a retrospective fulfilment of identity. A good example is provided in the entry on the folk-singer Ewan **MacColl**.

By sharp contrast, traditional Christianity, for much of its history, saw human fulfilment lying in the eternal future. On gaining heaven, on experiencing the beatific vision, this was when people would really become themselves. Such events belonged to the 'last things' of this existence; they were eschatological. Accordingly, we might speak of them as bringing about an eschatological fulfilment of identity. That kind of vision could, itself, be enhanced by cremation which removed the body so that the soul could pass on into its eternal destiny. Yet, in most traditions, the language of burial, of earth and of resurrection remained, even when, as in Catholic funeral rites, the journey of the soul was also given a firm place.

The ambiguity inherent in fire within the Christian tradition, alongside the explicit burial language of scripture, combined to prevent the emergence of liturgies and theologies of fire. This is not to say that occasional individuals did not see the power of the symbolism of fire in general. One outstanding example is that of Teilhard de Chardin (1881–1955). This Catholic priest and scientist speaks in his religious writings, published only after his death, of the original divine presence at the creation of the world as fire – 'in the beginning was the fire' – just as that presence now becomes a blazing Spirit (Chardin, 1970: 21, 22). 'Fire' comes to flood everything; it is the metaphor by which earthly things become divine. Then, in terms of prayer that expresses his own spiritual dynamics he prays: 'Lord, lock me up in the deepest depths of your heart: and then, holding me there, burn me, purify me, set me on fire, sublimate me, till I become utterly what you would have me be, the utter annihilation of my ego.' Death, too, can participate in this blaze of glory: 'Lord Christ, it

is you who must set me ablaze and transmute me into fire that we may be welded together and be made one' (Chardin, 1970: 31, 95).

Perspectives like these could fairly easily be taken and developed for use in Christian funeral rites, but there seems to have been a resistance to so doing. The poetic grasp of language, so poignant in mystical thought, has often been less influential than more pragmatic expressions of doctrine in the development of much Catholic and Protestant liturgy. William Watson's brief lines on 'Birth and Death' capture something of the poetic possibility, (1909: 12):

'Twas in another's pangs I hither came;
'Tis in mine own that I anon depart.
O Birth, though doorway hung with swords of flame,
How like to Death thou art!

Some possibilities for liturgical use have been suggested that are rooted in developing motifs of light, spirit and fire (Davies, 1990, 1997).

Religious ambivalence

This element of freedom is the positive outcome of a final element of paradox associated with crematoria, relating to matters of religion and ideology and to the fact that for much of the late nineteenth and very early twentieth centuries most denominations of the Christian religion either objected to, or were ambivalent in their views of, cremation. For example, several entries show how freemasonry, especially in Italy and some other strongly Catholic societies, promoted cremation and the building of crematoria not only as a consequence of their freethinking philosophical and scientific ideals, but also as a form of clear opposition to the Catholic Church. The very use of the term 'cremation temple' in Italy partly signalled that, for example, the main ceremonies room of Turin's first crematorium, with its pillars and a symbolic pyramid, echoes ancient Egypt more than any Christian era. The fact that Catholicism did not, doctrinally and officially, accept cremation until 1963–64, and that many Catholic areas only began to adopt the practice to any significant degree nearly 30 or 40 years later, meant that relatively little architectural input from a Catholic perspective could be expected. The same could be said of the continuing hostility of Greek Orthodoxy at the beginning of the twenty-first century. Where churches did come to accept crematoria as part of their active pastoral and liturgical engagement, as in Anglicanism, Lutheranism, and Protestantism in general, a degree of overlap between ecclesiastical ideas and the design of crematoria became possible. Still, crematoria have attracted very little theological interest. Even Harold Turner's important study of places of worship, published as late as 1979, could entirely ignore the crematorium, despite its treatment of the earliest Christian buildings, the *martyria*, which were built over tombs and used for memorial gatherings in honour of the dead (Turner, 1979: 164). Other authors, too, can focus on Christian ideas of place and, while acknowledging the significance of ancient martyrs and their burial sites and also emphasizing the sacred nature of contemporary places of worship and pilgrimage, almost always ignore the location of today's dead, let alone see it fit to ponder the place of crematoria (Inge, 2003).

This very ambivalence of Christianity towards cremation may yet, however, prove valuable for the crematorium itself during the twenty-first century. Given the mixed background of cremation, prompted by freethinkers, medical reformists and town-planners as well as its mixed reception by Christianity, it is not duty-bound to any particular constituency. It is likely that cremation will maintain the dominance it has achieved in many societies while expanding in areas currently focused on burial. It may be, for example, that parts of the world where epidemics of various sorts wipe out large numbers of the population may employ cremation to avoid the pressure on land use. In other countries, where secularization will make its presence felt, the crematorium is a useful place of relatively neutral significance for people to congregate and bid farewell to their dead. Whether or not ecological concerns will cause crematoria to be viewed in a negative light remains to be seen.
Douglas J. Davies

See also Argentina; freemasonry in Italy; Italy; MacColl.

References

Augustine (1945), *The City of God*, Vol. 2, ed. R.V.G. Tasker, London: J.M. Dent and Son.

Catherine of Genoa, Saint (1979), *Purgatism and Purgatory: The Spiritual Dialogue*, trans. Serge Hughes, London: SPCK.

Chardin, Teilhard de (1970), *Hymn of the Universe*, London: Collins/Fontana.

Dante, Alighieri (1955), *The Divine Comedy – 2 Purgatory*, trans. Dorothy L. Sayers, London: Penguin Books.

Davies, Douglas J. (1990), *Cremation Today and Tomorrow*, Nottingham: Alcuin/GROW Books.

Davies, Douglas J. (1997), 'Theologies of Disposal', in P.C. Jupp and T. Rogers (eds), *Interpreting Death: Christian Theology and Pastoral Practice*, Cassell: London.

Inge, John (2003), *A Christian Theology of Place*, Aldershot: Ashgate.

James, M.R. (1953), *The Apocryphal New Testament*, Oxford: Clarendon Press.

Jung, C.G. (1993), *Psychology and Alchemy* (2nd edn), trans. R.F.C. Hull, London: Routledge. First published 1944.

LeGoff, Jacques (1984), *The Birth of Purgatory*, Chicago: University of Chicago Press.

Nygren, Anders (1982), *Agape and Eros*, trans. Philip S. Watson, London: SPCK.

Thomas, K. (1971), *Religion and the Decline of Magic*, Harmondsworth: Penguin Books.

Turner, Harold W. (1979), *From Temple to Meeting House: The Phenomenology and Theology of Places of Worship*, The Hague: Mouton.

Watson, William (1909), *New Poems*, London: John Lane, The Bodley Head.

Winter, J. (1995), *Sites of Memory Sites of Mourning*, Cambridge: Cambridge University Press.

FOETUS

Since the changes in British cremation-related legal processes in the early 1990s, the procedures for the cremation of tiny, non-viable foetuses have become well established in certain areas of the country. The paperwork is not dissimilar to that necessary for stillborn cremations, but no certificate from the registrar is necessary, merely a declaration from the midwife or physician and appropriate 'self-generated' crematoria forms that the sympathetic crematorium registrar might deem necessary. In practice, this constitutes a modification of the usual cremation forms.

After consideration by hospital chaplains or other clergy, a brief but meaningful service can be fairly easily procured. This may be attended by only the parents, or a much wider family and social group. As with the funeral of any child, the procedures prior to the service at the cremation can be as simple or complex as requested. Some parents wish to view their tiny children, others may wish to sit with the closed casket, and parents often supply a small toy to accompany their child. Any resulting ashes are necessarily of small volume, but these remains are frequently treasured by the families concerned.

It is puzzling that not all crematoria participate in this emerging, but significant process, due, I understand, to differing interpretations of the legal requirements. Apparently the 'way around' the apparent legal impediment is to officially class the foetus as 'the product of the mother', as the foetus has no legal existence separate from its mother. Foetal cremations are recorded separately from those of others, so as not to distort annual returns.
Phillip Gore

FOSSVOGUR CHURCH, REYKJAVIK

Opened in 1948 as a special funeral church, seating 350, and with an emphasis on cremation, Fossvogur Church's interior was renovated in 1989 with designs created by the brother architects Árni and Sigbjörn Kjartansson. Well lit, it has fine acoustics with a 14-stop organ manufactured by the Danish firm, Starup. The sculptor Helgi Gíslason designed the altarpiece representing the Holy Trinity, along with other works of art in the choir, made of bronze, glass and basalt.

Annexed to the church is a chapel, a house of prayer, mortuary, crematorium and office. Designed by the architects Ólafur Sigurðsson and Guðmundur Kr. Guðmundsson, the chapel was dedicated in 1983, seats 90 and is used for prayer services when bodies are laid in the casket, as well as for funerals. A corner stained-glass window adds warmth to the atmosphere. This piece of art is by the famous artist Leifur Breiðfjörð and is named *The Passion* (*Píslargangan*). The chapel organ, which has eight stops, is from the Danish firm Bruno Christensen & Sönner. Dedicated in 1980, the house of prayer seats 50 and is used almost exclusively for prayer services as bodies are laid in the casket. Again, stained-glass windows by Leifur Breiðfjörð glorify the building, along with a beautiful five-stop organ built by Björgvin Tómasson. An important annex to the church is the mortuary which, after considerable renovation in 1995, can accommodate 70 bodies. A special section of the building is reserved for preparing each corpse and for reception of those close to the deceased.

Monuments and memory

Outside the door of the church stands an impressive statue of Christ by Bertel Thorvaldsen. This bronze replica of Thorvaldsen's original created in Rome in 1821 for the choir of Vor Frue Kirke, a church in Copenhagen was commissioned by the Society for Cremation (*Bálfararfélag Íslands*) and unveiled on 27 September, 1962.

The plaza in front of the church also contains a monument commemorating aborted foetuses and stillborn babies by the artist Borghildur Óskarsdóttir. Composed of an arched wall with a side view of an angel, it is formed of concrete and ceramic with shining glass symbols partly conceived as an idea derived from a book by the former president of Iceland, Kristján Eldjárn, concerning the 1954 excavations at the ancient bishopric of Skálholt. Its inscription comes from part of Psalm 139:15: 'Thy eyes beheld my unformed substance' (*Revised Standard Version*; in Icelandic: '*Augu þín sáu mig, er ég enn var ómyndað efni*'). Mourners wishing to place flowers or candles can do so on the specially shaped foot of the monument, which was dedicated in 1994. There has, in fact, been a special area for the remains of any cremated person, whether child or adult, available since 1950, shortly after the dedication of the church. These memorials and areas for cremated remains are part of the wider area also available for the burial of uncremated bodies.

Next to the 'Monument to an Unknown Sailor,' for example, is a memorial called, 'Waves of Remembrance for Sailors' Day', commemorating those lost at sea. Constructed in 1996 by those responsible for organising Sailors' Day in Reykjavík and Hafnarfjörður its smooth basalt rock surfaces – symbolizing four ocean waves – bear the names of drowned seamen who have neither been located nor brought to consecrated ground. A freestanding rock by the waves presents a verse from the Old Testament, in Isaiah 43: 1: 'But now thus says the Lord, he who created you, O Jacob, he who formed you, O Israel: "Fear not, for I have redeemed you; I have called you by name, you are mine."' (Icelandic: '*Nú segir Drottinn svo, sá er skóp þig: "Óttast þú eigi, því að ég frelsa þig með nafni, þú ert minn."*').

Friends, relatives and shipowners may ask for the names of seamen to be carved on to the monument. This addition to the cemetery clearly answered a deep yearning of all concerned to pay their respect to loved ones lost at sea. In passing, it may be noted that between 1938 and 2000 a total of 1330 Icelandic sailors had drowned at sea, with 400 of these never found.

In addition to this strong biblical element in Icelandic Lutheran traditions, reference can also be made to the Icelandic folk tradition and to Gunnar Hinriksson, a weaver, the first to be buried at Fossvogur Church on 2 September 1932, and who counts as 'guardian' of the cemetery and whose body, according to folk beliefs, will not rot but serve to watch over those arriving later. **Thorsteinn Ragnarsson**

See also Iceland.

FOUNTAIN DISPERSAL – BUDAPEST

One of the most creative systems developed in the later twentieth century for coping with large numbers of cremated remains is that of artificial fountains established at Budapest's large civic cemetery. The system comprises several water fountains each capable of operating quite separately from the others. The key design feature of this system lies in three elements: a centrifuge located at the top of a central pillar; a surrounding circle of water jets; and a means of draining away the water and remains. The wider area also contains an open-air structure that could serve as a focal point for a religious ceremony. In effect it is an altar.

At an appropriate point in the ceremony a special urn can be carried, formally and ceremonially, from the site of the religious or secular service to one of the pillars and fixed on to an underlying motor. The person performing that act then retires from the immediate area to rejoin any other participants there and, at an appropriate moment the water jets are switched on. This has the effect of projecting many jets of water inwards towards the base of the pillar. As the water pressure increases, these jets rise up the pillar until they reach above it, forming an encircling canopy of water. During this process the centrifuge is started up and this spins the ash-urn at some speed. The holes in the urn, operating in a pepperpot fashion, allow the remains to be thrown out into the air and to be caught up in the water spray. The visual effect is that of a cloud forming amidst the fountain. For those familiar with certain religious rituals, the appearance is not unlike that of a cloud of incense. As the water falls to the ground so it carries the ash back to earth. A series of channels set within the lawned area allows the water and ash to drain away into a specially prepared soak area beneath the soil.

This system, although highly technical in its centrifuge, fountains and drainage channels, still conveys a deep sense of a natural process. Set amidst trees and with well-kept lawns the cremated remains seem to return to 'nature'. **Douglas J. Davies**

FRANCE

Early advocates

The first advocate of cremation in early modern France, according to Pierre Vidallet, was Theophraste Renaudot (1586–1653), an eminent doctor and journalist, who held a conference on the decay of the human body in Paris in 1642, and concluded by making a strong case for cremation (Vidallet, 1991:143). The social and political upheaval that heralded the French Revolution from 1789 did witness the practice implemented in modern Europe, although only a handful of corpses were in fact cremated, and the practice's legal status was not confirmed due to opposition discussed elsewhere (see **materialism and enlightenment**).

With the establishment of the French military dictatorship, 'Cremation, with Liberty, foundered' (Ichok, 1935b: 25). In 1804 Napoleon imposed the Saint Cloud Edict, which dealt with the problems of burial without reference to cremation. In Luxembourg this edict became a legal hindrance to cremation, although in France itself, due to a different interpretation of the law, it did not. Curiously, by the time of his death Napoleon favoured cremation, at least for himself. On 14 December 1816, in exile on St Helen's island, he told his Irish surgeon that 'at my death I want to be burned; this is the best way not to trouble anybody'. The British, however, did not respect his wish.

Cremation issues emerged sporadically throughout the nineteenth century, due to epidemics, especially those of 1814, 1870 and 1871. At other times, too, cremation was considered: for example, in October 1867 Dr

Jules Guerin published a pro-cremation article in *La Gazette Médicale de Paris*. Rationalists began to advocate cremation in the later nineteenth century, using two basic arguments: that cremation would 'save the earth for the living' and that it promoted 'hygiene' – the physical 'hygiene' of unpolluted soil and the 'psychological hygiene' aided by the speed of bodily combustion (Vidallet, 1991: 143–44). Yet concrete action was not taken until 1874, when the parlous state of Paris's three overcrowded cemeteries containing around 1.5 million corpses demanded attention. Castigating the policy of 'courting pestilence', Maxine du Camp called for action in the *Revue des Deux Mondes* and Parisian Dr Gratiouet began to perform experiments in cremation. On receiving a proposal to bury the Parisian dead in a cemetery outside the capital, Paris Municipal Council urged the Assembly to legalize cremation in the capital. Although there appeared to be unanimity amongst commentators that something had to be done, there was little support for cremation due to sentimentalism and strong Catholic opposition. A parliamentary bill predictably failed, largely due to the opposition of medico-jurists, who argued that cremation would help murderers escape detection (Ichok, 1935b: 25).

Three years later, the first modern cremator, tested in Milan, prompted French cremationists to attempt to produce their own version and, in 1877, Paris Municipal Council, on the proposal of M. Cadet, held a competition with three cash prizes to find the best system for disposing of the dead by incineration. The plans had to guarantee a smokeless combustion of organic matter that was economical and allowed for religious rites. Ultimately the competition failed to produce a worthy winner. The same year saw another failure, this time of a certain Monsieur Morin's attempt to establish a *'Société de Crémation Pratique'*.

The French Cremation Society and Père-Lachaise

Italy remained influential: three Frenchmen – Georges Salomon, a mining engineer, Alfred Koechlin-Schwartz, a Paris burgermeister, and Dr Lacassagne, professor of legal medicine in Lyon – attended the 1880 International Hygiene Congress in Turin, which observed a demonstration on cremation. On 6 September 1880 at the Congress, Dr Lacassagne signed a motion supporting cremation. Already convinced cremationists, Salomon and Koechlin-Schwartz returned to France, determined to act. On 20 October 1880 Salomon advertised a meeting on cremation in *Le XIX Siècle (The Nineteenth Century)* which drew support from 109 individuals. The Society for the Propagation of Cremation (*Société pour la Propagation de la Crémation*) was founded a month later in Paris, with Lacassagne a founder member, Koechlin-Schwartz as president and Salomon as secretary.

At its general assembly in December 1881 the society boasted 420 members (including 36 women) who were 'an elite of scientists, writers and politicians': these included Alfred Nobel, then a Paris resident; politicians Léon Gambetta, Edouard Herriot, Casimir Perier and Paul Bert; poet Maurice Bouchor; pioneering chemist Marcellin Berthelot; astronomer Camille Flamarion; and Ferdinand de Lesseps (planner of the Suez and Panama canals and another founder member). This middle-class, professional society seemed well placed to influence the authorities and the public at large (Servoz-Gavin, 1975: 1, 8; Simond, 1972: 1, 4; Ichok, 1935b: 25). The society planned to cremate corpses in Milan until a French crematorium was built. It was committed to the difficult task of establishing cremation's legality: in May 1881, M. Constans, the Minister of the Interior, refused a request from the Paris Municipal Council to legalize cremation, and another private motion failed in 1882. A cholera epidemic in Egypt provided another opportunity. Arguing that cremation prevented contagion, Salomon moved a pro-cremation petition in parliament in 1883. He attacked the Council of Health and Hygiene (*Conseil d'Hygiène et de la Salubrité*) practice of incinerating corpses used for anatomical study purposes, which tainted the public's attitude to cremation and, in August 1883, the Council agreed that cremators which did not produce foul odours could be used. Then, on 25 July 1885, the Council of Hygiene of the Department of the Seine gave permission to construct a crematorium in Père-Lachaise cemetery. Mm. Barrett and Formice produced plans for an ornate, neo-classical crematorium with a large portico in front of a domed main building. Four Corini-system cremators, also in use in Rome and Milan, were installed. Siemens cremators were rejected as the heat produced was too intense and they cost over ten times more per cremation.

The cremation bill

Initially the crematorium, costing 245 875 francs, was solely intended to dispose of unclaimed corpses from hospitals. However, the authorities could hardly cremate those who had not requested it but refuse cremation to those desiring it and, on 30 March 1886, Dr Blatin presented a bill to eliminate this anomaly by legalizing it for those expressing the wish to be cremated in their wills. The bill passed its first reading by 371 to 174 votes in the Chamber of Deputies, France's second chamber.

Catholic Bishop Freppel of Angers, a veteran opponent of cremation, provided the main opposition to the bill. He argued that burial posed a minimal danger to public health and emphasized the potential for cremation to allow murderers to escape undetected. Disingenuously, he claimed that the bill would help make cremation obligatory, although the bill in fact stressed freedom of choice for the deceased and their family. A further claim was that republicans supported cremation because it was a way of attacking Catholics, most of who were royalist and favoured burial. Cremation was 'an act of savagery', a return to 'materialistic paganism ... a real decay in civilisation'. Frédéric Passy, who later won the Nobel Peace Prize in 1901, responded by saying that he was a 'spiritualist and profoundly believe[d] in the immortality of the soul', but that he rejected the 'corruption' of decomposition and preferred 'mortal remains to be purified by the flame'. The Senate ratified the law on 15 November 1887, and it came into effect in April 1889. The cremation society was satisfied with the law's terms (Ichok, 1935b: 25; Simond, 1972: 2–3).

However, the first experimental cremations in 1887 were disappointingly slow and smoky, and the cremators were replaced in August 1889. On 30 January 1889 the first cremation of a whole body, that of the 11-year-old son of one Dr Jacoby, was performed in Père-Lachaise. This was followed by 48 further voluntary cremations in the same year, as well as the incineration of 749 unclaimed hospital corpses and embryos. Between 1889 and 1934 Père-Lachaise performed 219 337 cremations, but of these only about 10 per cent (21 687) were voluntary – that is, a response to a request by either the deceased or their relatives. The other 90 per cent were cremations of corpses and body parts from hospitals and universities. It was not until 1911

that the number of voluntary cremations in a year exceeded 500, and it took another 17 years for this figure to reach 1000.

Pre-1918 successes and failures

These figures show that the social elite of French cremationists could build crematoria, but could not make them popular. They had drastically underestimated the Catholic Church's influence on the populace – an influence that endured into the twentieth century. At least 14 other municipalities had abortive plans to build crematoria between 1891 and 1914. Only four other cities successfully followed Paris's example during this period: Rouen (1899); Reims (1903); Marseille (1907); and Lyon (1914) (Ichok, 1935b: 25; Simond, 1972: 2–4, 6; Servoz-Gavin, 1975: 7).

Despite the Paris society's efforts at nationwide recruitment it still only had 1000 members by 1913, and many of these were lost during the First World War, which itself hampered plans for crematorium construction in Dijon. In 1916 Le Mans municipality received a donation for the construction of a crematorium, but this was rendered almost worthless by a devaluation of the franc. However, the war's effects were not all negative as a new cremation society was founded in Lyon with 346 members. More significantly, the subsequent Versailles Treaty ceded the 'eastern provinces' to France, thus bringing the influential Strasbourg Cremation Society with its 2500-strong membership into the French cremation movement. The numerically strong Strasbourg society was helped by the strength of pro-cremation Germanic influence in the region. Although, in 1922, Strasbourg gave France a new crematorium, Strasbourg's unusual status did bring some problems, for its cremation advocates remained reluctant to become fully integrated into the French cremation movement.

Inter-war obstacles and failures

By 1929 it was clear that cremation had not taken hold as France's six crematoria only performed 1118 cremations, which was only around 0.2 per cent of total deaths. A year later, Professor Barrier published an analysis in the *Annales d'Hygiène* of the different types and causes of resistance to cremation in his country. First, was 'popular resistance', defined by 'ignorance and fetishism of the cadaver', brilliantly illustrated by the German academic Dr Joseph Schnitzer, in *Traité*

Psycho-Religieux de l'Incinération. Second, there were the 'religious objections' of the Catholic Church that regarded cremation as a weapon wielded against it by atheistic, materialistic and, most importantly, anti-clerical freemasons (Riquet, 1972: 5). And certainly, before 1945 many French cremationists were freemasons and freethinkers: but, although they were characterized by anti-clericalism, they outwardly emphasized respect for all religions and advocated support for cremation solely for reasons of hygiene. However, this did not convince the Church, which continued to exert its powerful influence against cremation. Indeed, in France this influence was arguably stronger than anywhere else: during the Middle Ages the country was deemed 'the eldest child of the Church'. Worse, this influence may even have grown in the twentieth century. Robert Hazemann (1972) asserted that during the Second World War the Church 'took a step forward' into the political arena, whereas before 1914 France had been a 'neutral' country, with the state acting as a 'lay force' and Catholic priests staying 'in their churches'. This development was, according to Hazemann, exacerbated by the Second World War.

Cremationists argued that the French Catholic Church had a particular historic reason to oppose cremation for, during the French Revolution, cremation had prospered at a time when the Church had suffered and it subsequently regarded the practice as intrinsically linked with everything that it opposed. French Catholics remained 'disciplined' and eschewed cremation, so only the non-Catholics and the anti-religious joined the movement, which only served to accentuate the Church's suspicions. A third objection was 'juridical': some forensic pathologists were, for legal reasons about determining the cause of death, strongly opposed. Fourth was the 'inertia of public servants': fear of death and everything linked with it meant that body disposal was a low priority in administrative circles – an especially serious factor in France where cremation was solely a municipal responsibility. Barrier's analysis provided a template for explaining France's lack of development regarding cremation, although Henri Ferre also partly blamed French cremationists' own inactivity (Vidallet, 1991: 144; Simond, 1972: 6; Servoz-Gavin, 1975: 7).

Legal standing

A further problem was the legal standing of cremation – paradoxically, because the 1887 law treated it as equal to burial. Bureaucrats took legal 'equality' to absurd lengths, insisting, for example, that cinerary urns be transported in special lorries or in an entire train 'baggage car', precisely the same legal requirement as for a corpse in a coffin. In 1933 three cremationist politicians found the minister of public works sympathetic to their case but unable to make the rail authorities yield on the issue of urn transportation by rail. Cremationists could do nothing but resolve to continue propaganda on the issue and investigate the transportation of urns in cars and aircraft.

Catholics also successfully challenged the law. In the mid-1930s, Catholics who wanted to bury a deceased relative whose will expressed a desire to be cremated, and who had not written anything refuting this, took their case to the Appeal Court. They argued that the deceased had received Catholic sacraments before death and would not have been granted them if intending to be cremated: therefore, the deceased must have renounced cremation. The Catholic relatives emerged victorious and buried their cremation-supporting relative. The French cremationists could not go to the highest court, as they could only appeal on the grounds of formal mistakes in legal procedure. As Dr Ichok pointed out, legal recognition was insufficient by itself: it was vital to tackle anti-cremation prejudices.

Hazemann explained France's problems in the wider context of 'Latin' countries that were late to industrialize. It was no surprise that cremation was strong in England, as it was the first country to industrialize. The urbanization accompanying industrialisation also furthered cremation. In 1972 England had a population density of 226 per square kilometre; France, in contrast, had less than 91 per square kilometre. As more 'Latin' peoples experienced life in agricultural communities, so they had closer relations with the soil and were consequently more inclined to bury than cremate (Hazemann, 1972: 1–6).

Reasons for optimism

Despite these difficulties, there were reasons to be optimistic. In 1930 the cremation societies of Paris – whose membership had haemorrhaged to less than half their pre-war level – and of

Strasbourg and Lyon established the French Cremation Federation (*Fédération Française de Crémation*). By 1936 the Federation's membership had increased from 2863 to 3797 and there were new cremation societies in Annecy, Chambéry, Marseille, Nantes, Rennes, and Toulouse, with another being formed in Nice. In 1939 there were discussions about building a crematorium in Nice, and another new cremation society was being formed in Toulon, signifying new interest in the south of France.

Another development the French recognized as aiding their cause was the creation of a strong international movement: their delegation at the 1936 Prague International Cremation Congress was the largest. Indeed, a French delegate was one of only four on a committee established in Prague to plan what became the International Cremation Federation (ICF), and French cremationists were subsequently much involved. By January 1938 both the French Federation and Strasbourg societies were affiliated, although this also revealed the historic division between them (a division which, incidentally, still existed in the ICF as late as 1976). The French got the ICF to place pressure on the Prince of Monaco to open an existing crematorium in his territory, although he refused to yield.

Effects of the Second World War

The Second World War brought the partial Nazi occupation of France and many new problems. Cremationists in the 'free zone' were totally cut off from those in the occupied zone and the Federation could not operate. Although Strasbourg Cremation Society's headquarters was bombed, at least the crematoria themselves remained intact. However, due to a lack of fuel, all the crematoria closed down either for the whole war or for the last two years of it. By January 1946 only Paris was operating. The war also halted plans for new crematoria such as at Chambéry. A 150 000 franc donation which Chambéry municipality had been planing to use for this purpose lost much of its value in a war-induced devaluation. Some important cremationists were victims of the Nazis: the president of Nice Cremation Society was shot in late 1943 and the secretary of Nantes Society was deported in 1942. Among those imprisoned were the secretary and president of the Rennes Cremation Society, along with their son and daughter respectively, and M. Schneider of Strasbourg. The Gestapo put a figure of 2 million francs on the head of Robert Falbisaner, president of the Strasbourg Cremation Society, as he was a prominent leader of the French wartime resistance. He eventually died peacefully in 1956.

All this disruption led to the disbanding of the Nantes and Rennes cremation societies and a consequent decline in the French Cremation Federation's membership (its 1419 membership in 1948 was less than half the 1936 figure), but at least it still existed. Although there were many problems getting the crematoria operational again, hope was manifest in a national cremation congress in June 1946, seven years after the last. Six cremation societies attended and heard that there were proposals for new crematoria at Chambéry, Grenoble, Nice and Toulon, with good prospects at Lille, too. The following year the Federation established its journal, *La Flamme*.

Post-war hope

At the 1948 national congress, president Robert Hazemann presented a plan to construct a crematorium serving every city with a population of more than 100 000. Although the Supreme Council of Hygiene approved, the Association of French Mayors did not even acknowledge having received news of it from the French Federation. The 1948 Federation annual congress was less upbeat, despite an increase of 210 members on the previous year. The newly elected Grenoble city council revoked a 1947 decision to use 1 million francs for building a crematorium, and there was now no immediate prospect of any new crematoria in France (Simond, 1972: 5; Servoz-Gavin 1975: 7–8).

Re-involvement in the ICF provided a boost. At the 1948 ICF Congress, French cremationists argued forcefully for an ICF approach to the Vatican over cremation, which, if it had no immediate effect, would be beneficial in the long term. So long as it did not feel under attack, the Church apparently knew how to 'stretch out its hand to men of goodwill'. French cremationists had already requested an audience with Catholic authorities and been told by a prelate to persevere. At the same conference there was strong criticism of the 'antiquated' French cremation law, which was depicted as the main obstacle to cremation in the country. A French delegate commented that the Catholic Church, rather than French legislation (whose stipulations for those desiring a cremation required little time to fulfil), was the greatest obstacle to cremation in France.

Developments in the 1950s included French involvement in the ICF reaching new heights when Hazemann was elected president in 1951. He remained in the post for six years, unprecedented at the time. The French Federation won further sympathy for cremation in scientific and medical circles by encouraging its members to donate their bodies to medical science prior to their cremation. Aware of marble workers' hostility, due to the potential threat that cremation posed to their livelihoods, Lyon cremationists organized a competition for suitable monuments in the crematorium's newly inaugurated urn garden, which had the desired effect of generating a degree of goodwill. Other pressures also seemed to be working in cremation's favour as, by 1960, lack of burial space had forced severe restrictions on the amount of time that a corpse could be left in the ground. There were plans for a new crematorium in Nice, with another in Mulhouse.

Changing Catholic attitudes

However, the Catholic Church remained obstructive, having used all its powers to ensure that ex-French president and lifelong cremationist Edouard Herriot was buried. The French press was also unsupportive. For example, in November 1959, the funeral of John Edwards (president of the Consultative Assembly for the Council of Europe) received extensive coverage in the French press, but no mention was made of the fact that he was cremated. French cremationists failed to get press confirmation of what was, for them, an important omission. For René Hofmann, this was evidence of the Catholic Church's influence over those who were otherwise 'free in their thoughts'. Even the liberal press was not pro-cremation, sometimes even refusing to publish cremation adverts.

Then, in 1963, the Vatican changed its attitude to cremation, apparently vindicating the French advocacy of ICF approaches to it. Yet Hazemann attributed the decision to a letter he and Reverend Michel Riquet had written to Pope Pius XII on behalf of the French Federation in June 1953. The letter assured the Church of cremationists' 'perfect ideological independence' and posited arguments 'which were primarily of an urbanistic order: "to reserve the earth to living people"' (Hazemann, 1972: 1). Riquet, by 1972 a doctor of theology and lecturer at Notre Dame in Paris, was also in no doubt of the importance of the letter (Riquet, 1972: 5, 7). Later, Jean Simond also claimed that this letter, which 'contained telling arguments for cremation in relation to town planning' had 'contributed much to the changed attitude of the Roman Catholic Church' (Simond. 1972: 4). Although the letter may well have contributed, the extensive ICF lobbying of the Catholic Church immediately prior to its decision must have had the most impact. Still, recognizing that the successful development of cremation was dependent on the Church, French cremationists announced themselves pleased with the change in attitude and hoped that French Catholics would no longer oppose crematoria.

The late 1960s appeared to reflect the Vatican's changed attitude as, by 1967, there were plans for five new crematoria. The ICF showed that it was taking the country seriously by establishing a committee to organize a touring exhibition to visit France, as well as Belgium and Luxembourg. An increase of almost 35 per cent in the numbers cremated between 1961 and 1966 was regarded as good progress but the 1307 cremations in 1966 still only amounted to 0.25 per cent of all French deaths. And the French Federation remained weak. In 1969 Jean Simond remarked that, although the Federation had many sections, most had very few members and were therefore dependent on a handful of individuals.

Progress in the 1970s

Further progress came in the 1970s. France's seventh crematorium, at Toulouse, opened in July 1971. It was the first new crematorium in France for half a century. By 1972 at least six other towns were planning to build crematoria and new cemeteries were reserving areas for crematorium construction. Between 1972 and 1974 the French Federation gained nine new societies and 2000 new members in only two years. This was due, in part, to the 1972 ICF Congress being held in Grenoble. Throughout France, cremationists were pleased at proof of the ICF's confidence in them. In the region of Grenoble itself the effect was more direct, as membership doubled to 600 between 1970 and 1974. The Federation's 34 separate societies with a total membership of more than 7000 compared very well with 1960, when it had only 14 societies with 3000 members. The circulation of *La Flamme* rose from 2165 in 1969 to 5000 in 1975. The composition of the cremation movement had also changed, becoming more socially inclusive with female membership also increasing faster than the male. Although the cremation societies were not wealthy (they were not insurance societies), several were able to contribute towards the cremations of their deceased members. This was due to the dedication of their officials, most of whom were unpaid pensioners.

In 1975 Paul Servoz-Gavin noted that French cremationists had discovered that the existence of columbaria could exercise a positive influence on public opinion, and progress had been made in this area. For example, in 1970 a woman cremationist secured the construction of a columbarium in a small Savoyian village (of only 1600 inhabitants) in which she lived. The columbarium was quickly used and ten villagers became cremationists. Columbaria numbers had increased from seven in 1965 to 26 by 1974. Although the cremation rate had not increased proportionately, Servoz-Gavin thought this 'only normal' and hoped that the increase would be more rapid in the future. Simond recognized that the French cremation figures, though 'modest' when compared to Protestant countries, provided hope as they 'put France in the first ranks of Catholic countries' and revealed 'an irreversible increase'. What was clear to Servoz-Gavin was that 'wherever a crematorium is in operation the number of cremations is on the increase as the public cannot ignore such an opportunity'. Moreover, given the rapid processes of industrialization and urbanization in France, and the consequent concentration of the population in the large cities, there would soon be nowhere to build new cemeteries. This was when cremation would come into its own (Simond, 1972: 5–6; Servoz-Gavin, 1975: 4–5, 8–11).

However, some serious problems and obstacles remained. Servoz-Gavin echoed Hazemann's comments regarding Latin countries being characterized by a strong agrarian tradition where inhumation remained a 'deeply-rooted' custom. He even saw this attitude reflected amongst many cremation supporters who wanted their ashes to be scattered in 'free nature'. Thus, the desire to entrust human remains to the soil was the same; the only difference was

whether the remains were the body in its entirety or simply its ashes. Widespread ignorance of the Vatican's new attitude was also problematic, although Servoz-Gavin recognized that only a little time had passed since 1963 and, as France was a 'traditional' country, change occurred slowly. Inhumation was well established, with solid structures and the livelihoods of many depending on it. Both Simond and Servoz-Gavin complained of 'indifference' to cremation – Simond citing press indifference. Another problem was the still small number of crematoria combined with their 'unfavourable geographical distribution' (there were none in western France) and the consequential relatively high cost of cremation. Servoz-Gavin claimed that this was the result of 'archaic' cremation legislation.

Whilst national government appeared indifferent to these calls, municipalities also provided obstacles. Approaches to municipalities were often 'only heard with half an ear' and remained unsupported. Alternatively, municipalities, under serious financial constraints, contended that constructing a crematorium was uneconomic, due to the low cremation rate. However, this did not prevent municipalities from periodically spending sums greater than would be required for a crematorium on building new cemeteries. This generally occurred without any consultation, so the case for the money being spent on a crematorium instead, which, in the long run, would better serve the area, was not heard. Unfortunately, only rarely were influential cremationists available in these municipalities to put the case for cremation. Due to the difficult economic and financial circumstances, the state was unlikely to take the initiative in building crematoria, and neither state nor local authorities were concerned with informing the public on cremation. Servoz-Gavin complained that the bureaucracy 'seems to take pleasure to complicate rather than simplify the formalities'.

French cremationists' two immediate demands to improve this situation were for the scattering of ashes to be permitted and for an extension of the distance that a corpse in a pine coffin with plastic wrapping could be transported, from 200 to 600 kilometres. They supported allowing any funeral service of any denomination desired in crematoria, thereby making them interdenominational, as cemeteries already were. Ultimately, the movement was advocating the building of many 'decent, simple and unpretentious' crematoria, in order to provide France with the requisite infrastructure. Although such crematoria, Servoz-Gavin argued, could be easily and relatively inexpensively built, cremationists did not want construction to be undertaken by private enterprise (Simond, 1972: 5–6; Servoz-Gavin, 1975: 2–6, 9–11).

In 1975 Servoz-Gavin, though acknowledging the 'quite modest' progress, took solace from the 'constant progress made during the last few years' and looked 'with confidence' to the future. Subsequent developments appeared, at least partly, to justify this optimism. Two years after Toulouse, Amiens got the eighth French crematorium. In another two years there was a crematorium at Joncherolles, on the outskirts of Paris. (It was now the eighth functioning French crematorium, as Reims had ceased operating.) The first 'truly modern' crematorium appeared in Mulhouse in 1978, the year that Pierre Vidallet regarded as marking the beginning of 'modern cremation' in France (Vidallet, 1991:145; 2003: 3). It had been planned since at least 1960. A new French burial law, necessitated by the rising cost of land around cities, was to make cremation easier. It even envisaged dispensing with the cemetery altogether.

The 1980s watershed

By 1980 France still had only ten crematoria (one per 54 000 of annual deaths) and the cremation rate had just reached 1 per cent. Encouragement came, however, from a 1979 survey into attitudes towards death in which 20 per cent of respondents said they would prefer to be cremated and only 53 per cent actually expressed a preference for burial (27 per cent 'didn't know'). Overall, the survey appeared to show that a large percentage of French people wanted simpler funerals and many of them would prefer cremation, which was the obvious answer to their requirements (Spencer, 1981: 74–76). Further encouragement could be drawn from the trend for new crematoria, which increased slightly in the 1980s. There were 14 crematoria by 1984, 16 by 1985 and 21 by 1987. The real explosion in crematoria numbers came in the late 1980s and 1990s (some 38 by 1989, 46 by 1990, 54 by 1991, 69 by 1995, 78 by 1999, and 98 by 2001).

There was a 'watershed' in cremation in France in the 1980s. In 1981 Eric Spencer cited France as an example of the problems that arise when building crematoria is a solely municipal responsibility, as municipal authorities 'were bound by the laws and traditions of the country to observe the status quo'. In addition, crematoria could only be built in cemeteries, all of which were municipally owned. Thus, no crematorium was likely to be built, even if legally permissible, as municipalities were inclined to spend their funds in other ways (Spencer, 1981: 74–6). However, this situation soon changed. The first experimental 'delegated management' of a crematorium came in 1982 when the monopoly funeral company, Pompes Funèbres Générales (PFG), began to promote crematoria (located in cemeteries). It soon faced competition from other privately-financed or privately financed and operated crematoria, often built on private land outside of cemeteries. Private funeral directors also began to build crematoria, either in cemeteries (in which case they had to return the building, free of charge, to the community after 30 years), or on their own land. Municipalities were keen to employ the new services offered by private funeral companies for total or partial construction of crematoria as well as their management – so much so, in fact, that by 1990, only 40 per cent of crematoria were publicly operated, with 60 per cent privately managed. At this time, management of the 60 per cent of the privately run crematoria was divided as follows: the PFG group managed the majority (64 per cent of private crematoria), other private companies controlled 25 per cent and cremation societies ran the remaining 11 per cent. Nevertheless, of the total number of cremations in 1990 (33 710), publicly run crematoria were responsible for 51 per cent. A further 33 per cent were performed by PFG-owned crematoria, 8 per cent by other private investors and another 8 per cent by the cremation societies (Vidallet, 1991: 145–48; Moreaux, 1994: 82–85).

The 60 per cent of privately-owned crematoria was predicted to increase further due to the alternatives available: a private company could either run the whole project or it could finance a project whereby it had the monopoly for organizing and managing the crematorium, but the building itself remained public. All this had occurred despite the French Federation's stance in support of public ownership and against private management and investment due to a continuing feeling that profit should not be made out of cremation. Of course, this new, more flexible approach did not preclude all difficulties. An increasing problem lay in disputes between different parts of the cremation business. For example, in Annecy, the PFG was granted ministerial authorization to convert a cemetery building into a crematorium. Displeased at the fact that the PFG was in control of the whole project, the Cremation Society decided to also open a crematorium only 10 kilometres from Annecy. Consequently, both were performing around the same number of cremations annually.

Although the explosion in crematoria numbers had a significant impact, it was not perhaps as great as might be expected. In 1991, although the overall cremation rate remained low, in some urban centres it was far higher. In the city of Mulhouse the rate was 40 per cent; in Lille, opened in 1982, 30 per cent; and in Lens, the rate after only two years was 12 per cent. In 2001, 98 French crematoria cremated a total of 100 238 dead – around 19 per cent of total deaths. In the same period (1988–2001) that crematoria had increased in number from 21 to 98, cremations had only increased, on average, by under 12 per cent per year. Over more or less the same length of time, before the expansion in crematoria (1975–87), cremation numbers experienced an average annual increase of almost 20 per cent – almost double. So, not only did the rate of growth not increase after 1988, it actually *decreased*. This is not, of course, to claim that increasing numbers of crematoria *decrease* the demand for cremation, but it does suggest that the present need for cremation in France is being fairly well met, and that there is no simple, direct relationship between numbers of crematoria and cremation rates.

Pierre Vidallet pointed out that there were positives and negatives arising from the fact that France was a late developer regarding cremation. Positively, all but one crematorium was fitted out with modern equipment, and the new European environmental laws did not require French crematoria to undertake expensive upgrading with its consequent new costs for the consumer. Negatively, there was little education of cremation personnel, sometimes leading to 'very poor' behaviour in crematoria. France had also had little time to develop suitable cremation rituals, although some 'individual initiatives' inventing rituals depending on the type of ceremony and mourners present, were 'very, very

interesting'. Two years later, Pascal Moreaux, director of Père-Lachaise Crematorium, was more upbeat on this point, claiming that ceremonies had been 'sensitively modified' and that new 'ceremonial forms' were already 'appearing to bestow on the ceremonies all the dignity that the families need to find peace and comfort'.

Concluding remarks

Custom and burial tradition still weigh against the development of cremation in France. A 1994 survey revealed that, although two-thirds of French people questioned described themselves as Catholic (down from 81 per cent in 1986), only 7 per cent attended mass every Sunday and 25 per cent had no religion. Yet, death still seemed to bring out 'religious' sentiment, as 70 per cent continued to want a religious funeral. This suggested that the decline in regular church attendance did not necessarily indicate a rejection of all belief. Stark regional disparity also remains: in 1999 the average cremation rate was 13 per cent. In regions like Alsace it was as high as 26 per cent, whereas other rural areas had rates under 10 per cent and even as low as 6 per cent. A more specific problem for French cremationists has been the development of another solution to the problems of overcrowded cemeteries: 'multi-storey cemeteries', such as that in Marseille, where concrete tombs are stacked on top of each other. In 1984 the French cremationist Godard went as far as to condemn them in a press interview: 'It is disgusting what goes on inside .... In these supposedly air-tight caskets the bodies exude ... . There is no respect for the dead'. (*Le Monde*, 1984).

However, in the 1990s, cremation appeared to be becoming fashionable in municipal circles. A leading French undertaker commented in 1994:'A few years ago, what every mayor wanted was a swimming pool for his town ... Then it was pedestrian precincts, and now it's crematoria. Every town has to have one!' (*The Guardian*, 1994). Municipal interest in cremation endured in the later 1990s. In 1999 a feature of the previous 18 months had been the large number of requests for crematoria from municipalities, the vast majority opting for delegated private management. Many explained the increasing popularity of cremation by its cheapness in comparison with burial. In 1997 a reasonable cremation cost around £500, whereas merely the lease of a six-foot burial plot cost £2 650, and this before the cost of the tomb itself. The recent economic crisis has merely exacerbated this situation. Other explanations for the increasing popularity of cremation in France were: its simplicity; the growing number of civil ceremonies; the break-up of the family unit which leads to graves being abandoned; and philosophical reasons often linked with ecological motives.

In 2003 the national cremation rate was close to 20 per cent with cities like Paris and Mulhouse reaching rates of around 50 per cent and the French Riviera (the south coast) approximating 30 per cent. As a result of the 1993 cremation law, 75 per cent of crematoria were owned by the municipalities and privately managed, and this percentage was predicted to increase. French cremationists also predicted that, in a decade, France would have a cremation rate of 35 per cent. France still has no law concerning ashes, however (although there has been a new law on hospital remains that have to be cremated), and Pierre Vidallet noted that there was very little in terms of memorialization at present. There had also been a 'lack of concern' for rituals and ceremonies themselves, although this topic was receiving more attention. Although Vidallet thought that France would definitely establish memorialization parks, the law required alteration before that could occur (Vidallet, 2003: 3–6). Yet, with the long overdue upgrading of Père-Lachaise, France's oldest and grandest crematorium, in 2000, the country appears well placed to deal with the increasing demand on cremation services in the twenty-first century.
Lewis H. Mates

See also Barrier; Hazemann; materialism and enlightenment; Monaco.

References

Boone, P.C., Heuer, A. and Raild, N.J. (1960), 'The Sociological Aspects of Cremation', paper given at the ICF Congress in Stockholm, CRE/D4/1960/6.

ICF Committee for Propaganda (1963), 'The World Problems of the Disposal of the Dead', paper presented at the ICF Congress, Berlin, CRE/D4/1963/3.

Hazemann, R.H. (1972), 'The Social and Cultural Aspect of Cremation', paper presented at the ICF Congress, Grenoble, CRE/D4/1972/10.

Ichok, Dr G. (1935a), 'The Development of the Cremation Movement in France, Part One', *Pharos*, 1(2): 27.

Ichok, Dr G. (1935b), 'The Development of the Cremation Movement in France: Part Two', *Pharos*, 1(3): 24–25.

Le Monde (1984), Interview with Dr Godard, 19–20 February, reproduced in *Pharos*, 50(2), 1984: 71.

Moreaux, Pascal (1994), 'Cremation in France in 1992', *Pharos*, 60(2): 82–85.

Noth, Ernest (1969), 'Cremation One Hundred Years Ago', paper presented at the ICF Congress, London.

Riquet, Michel (1972), 'The Catholic Church and the Cremation of Corpses', paper presented at the ICF Congress, Grenoble.

Servoz-Gavin, Paul (1975), 'From Inhumation to Cremation', paper presented at the Helsinki ICF Congress, CRE/D4/1975/7.

Simond, Jean (1972), 'Cremation in France', paper presented at the ICF Congress, Grenoble.

Spencer, Eric (1981), 'Where Do We Come From; What Are We; Where are We Going?', address to the ICF Congress, Berlin, CRE/D4/1981/12 also reproduced in *Pharos*, 48(2), 1982: 73–77.

The Guardian (1994), article, 13 December, reproduced in *Pharos*, 61(1), 1995: 30.

Vidallet, Pierre (1991), 'Cremation in France', *Pharos*, 57(4): 143–48.

Vidallet, Pierre (2003), 'Cremation in France', *Pharos*, 69(4): 3–6.

FRANKENSTEIN

The famous tale of Frankenstein ends with an evocation of cremation long before the topic was part of public interest, being published in 1818. Its authoress, Mary Wollstonecroft Shelley (1797–1851), wife of the poet, imagines a creative young scientist – Victor Frankenstein – who discovers how to bring 'the principle of life' to inanimate matter. While the 'man' he constructs from anatomical pieces comes to be a complex being, seeking love and affection, he ends by killing people. The entire story moves upon deep currents of death and the desire to conquer it. The experiments to 'bestow animation upon lifeless matter' might enable him to 'renew life where death had apparently devoted the body to corruption' (Shelley, 1945: 48).

Mary Shelley's own mother had died days after her birth, and it is difficult not to see aspects of her personal reflections on death reflected in the story. At one crucial point Frankenstein tells how his mother died of scarlet fever, caught while tending her adopted daughter. The text describes her calm death, the affection visible on her face after death and the period of grief that followed. Within its single paragraph it sketches quite incisively what, a century and a half later, would become a much more clinical concern with processes of grief. In the first days of bereavement ties are rent, the bereaved sense a void in their life, experience a despair that is visible on the face, and they come to know the dead really has gone. It is then with 'the lapse of time' that 'the actual bitterness of grief commences'. But the author notes that, since all know this experience, there is no need for her to rehearse it. Still, she notes that grief can become an indulgence and turns her mind to the fact that a day comes when 'the smile that plays upon the lips, although it may be deemed a sacrilege, is not banished' (Shelley, 1945: 35). Life must go on.

However, the book ends in the death of this 'monster', a creature invested with much power of self-analysis and self-reflection. He speaks, finally, to the captain of the ship on which they are icebound in northern seas, and vows that he will now quit the vessel, seek the 'northern extremity of the globe' and, he continues,

> I shall collect my funeral pile and consume to ashes this miserable frame ... polluted by crimes and torn by the bitterest remorse, where can I find rest but in death? Soon these burning miseries will be extinct. I shall ascend my funeral pile triumphantly, and exult in the agony of the torturing flames. The light of the conflagration will fade away; my ashes will be swept into the sea by the winds. (Shelley, 1945: 241–42)

The monster that had been animated by means of electricity in a story that emerged from discussions involving scientific ideas, including very early views of Darwin, is to be destroyed by fire. There is a sense that the torturing flames are an appropriate medium for this anguished mind, just as the windswept ashes will find their proper dispersal in the sea. A mere grave with slow decay would not balance the creature's mode of origin and would not frame his demise in as necessarily powerful a way as the pyre.

Moving from fiction to biography it is profoundly ironic that Mary's husband Percy Bysshe Shelley, initially buried on the beach after a shipwreck in Italy, was exhumed a month later and cremated with his ashes being interred in Rome – and this in 1822, only four years after Frankenstein's publication. **Douglas J. Davies**

Reference

Shelley, Mary W. (1945), *Frankenstein*, London: J.M. Dent & Sons. First published 1818.

FREEMASONRY

The role of freemasons in the history of cremation is particularly important and is represented in numerous entries. Here we focus on the masonic contribution to the cremationist movement in Italy where freemasonry had a substantial influence. **Douglas J. Davies**

See also Argentina; France; Hanham cremations; Italy; Politics; USA.

FREEMASONRY IN ITALY

The masonic contribution to the development of the cremationist movement in Italy was articulated both through the individual engagement of freemasons and the direct and official intervention in economic and logistical terms of the lodges and highest ranks of the Grand Lodge of Italy (*Grande Oriente d'Italia*). Three main factors determined this close relationship between cremation and freemasonry.

The first lay in the ideological aim to increasingly secularize civil society, seeking to establish the knowledge of natural reality behind each religious–metaphysical reference; this was led by the freemasons of Latin countries. The second factor, also approached through this scientific–positivist perspective, concerned the medical–sanitary aspects of cremation. This was encouraged through the medical doctors belonging to masonic lodges and the leading role they played in the development of cremation societies. The third factor concerns the role, and in certain cases the promotional usage, that cremation assumed in the conflict between freemasonry and the Catholic Church, which was strong at the time that the cremationist project was developing in Italy.

The crematianist debate, which preceded the establishment of cremation societies, originated more or less with the birth of the Italian Unitarian state. The basic pillars of the project, born and bred in a period dominated by positivism, were doctors and liberals, Milanese thinkers and freemasons. At the end of the 1860s the debate established itself in international medical conventions and in parliament, thanks to the member of parliament, freethinker and freemason, Salvatore Morelli, famous for his pacifist, feminist and pro-divorce struggles. The periodicals *Il libero pensiero* (*Free-thought*, founded by Luigi Stefanoni) and *Il libero pensatore* (*Freethinker*, born out of an editorial schism within the former journal and directed by Giovanni Battista Demora), became the crematianist 'voice' in the secular and masonic world during the period that preceded the creation of cremation societies.

After 1874 the task of promoting cremation was handed over from the circles of 'liberal thought' to freemasonry which, in the Grand Lodge of Italy constituent assembly of May 1874, committed itself to the greater promotion of cremation in the municipalities. From this moment onwards, cremation associations began to spread throughout the entire Italian peninsula, due, mainly, to the influence of the Milanese masonic lodges and, in particular, the masonic doctor Gaetano Pini. He was considered the main creator, not only of the Milanese Society for Cremation, but of the whole organized crematianist movement. Pini's medical activities, his position of dignity within masonry and his involvement in many philanthropic associations, made him the embodiment of the hygienist–masonic–philanthropic complex that gave birth to the Society for Cremation (Socrem).

The contacts and relationships fostered within masonic lodges – ritual bodies particularly engaged in social endeavours, and characterized by a strong politicization and anti-clericalism – were fundamental to the development of the crematianist project. Until the revival, triggered by the establishment of the 'Ausonia' lodge of Turin in 1859, Italian freemasonry was divided into two main rites: the Ancient Accepted Scottish Rite (AASR – *Rito Scozzese Antico ed Accettato*) and Italian Symbolic Rite (*Rito Simbolico Italiano* – RSI). After some marked divisions, schism and reunification, the lodges adhered to the Great Council of Italian

Freemasonry of Symbolic Rite (*Gran Consiglio della Massoneria Italiana al Rito Simbolico*) reunited with the Grand Lodge of Italy. This union took place within a united masonic organization (the Grand Lodge of Italy) with completely different hierarchical structures and rites. After the fusion, the isolated Italian Symbolic Rite lodges found themselves in a great minority compared to the AASR. This unfavourable situation produced such a profound crisis that it was feared that the symbolic lodges would gradually disappear. In 1874 Pini participated in the Grand Lodge of Italy's assembly, where, under the principle of the so-called *Libertà di Riti e unità di governo* (freedom of rites and government unity), the constitutional regulations for the co-existence of lodges of different rites were established. It also served to establish precise rules of how to adjudicate the government posts in the main Italian masonic *Obbedienza* (Obedience).

Pini, who was the recognized moral leader in the Symbolic Rite lodges, started the campaign in favour of cremation through the masonic lodges and other Milanese associations of democratic–positivist tendency. These played a fundamental part, contributing both in terms of men and means, in the creation of the Milanese Cremation Society in 1875. Not by chance, the first report in favour of cremation appearing in the masonic press was in the *Almanacco del Libero Muratore* (*Freemason's Almanac*), of the Ambrosian lodge 'La Cisalpina', in 1873. On 22 January 1876 the body of Alberto Keller was cremated in Milan – the first cremation authorized by the Italian state. Keller's cremation proved fundamental both to the creation of a specific organ that disseminated and managed cremation in Italy and to the passing of legislation to regulate the process. With regard to the passing of legislation, it is worth recalling that the authorization to cremate Keller was conceded by the Minister of the Interior, the freemason Nicotera, who visited the Milanese lodges in 1876, complimented them on the task they were carrying out and donated a substantial sum to support their activities.

The *Rivista della massoneria italiana* (*Magazine of Italian Freemasonry*), conscious of the historical importance of Keller's cremation, dedicated much space to the event, publishing the prayer of Gaetano Pini and a detailed description of the cremation oven and the costs of a cremation.

Almost certainly, this event marked the beginning of an irreversible process which, following the example of the Milanese 'La Ragione', would have involved the major lodges of the whole territory, encouraged by the circular written by the Grand Master Giuseppe Mazzoni, who urged 'all the lodges and all the masonic bodies to energetically engage in this major issue, as nobody could avoid its extraordinary importance'. In the circular, Mazzoni, in addition to encouraging the lodges to become active in the creation of cremationist associations and crematoriums, stressed that the greatest effort should be made in converting public opinion, and that cremation was 'a new step towards the route of civil progress'. The Grand Master's plea had positive effects in all the lodges of the Italian peninsula. For example, the Roman lodge 'Tito Vezio' and the Napolitan 'Perfetta Unione' and 'Losanna' appointed commissions to form cremation societies and construct cremation temples, following the example of the Milanese lodges.

On 18 January 1882 the 'Dante Alighieri' and the 'Pietro Micca – Ausonia' met in Turin. The temporary committee which they formed for the promotion of a crematorium in Turin consisted entirely of freemasons. The *Rivista della massoneria italiana* continuously followed the evolution of the cremation movement, publishing 40 items between 1876 and 1914. Among these there were articles, circulars, essays about opening of cremation temples, as well as detailed descriptions of funerals and the cremations of senior freemasonic dignitaries, including Giuseppe Mazzoni (Grand Master, 1871–80), Giuseppe Petroni (Grand Master, 1880–85), Luigi Pianciani (Honorary Grand Master 'for life'), Luigi Castellazzo (Grand Secretary), Amerigo Borgiotti, Mauro Macchi, Agostino Bertani, Enrico Chambion, Gian Battista Prandina, Gaetano Pini, Antonio Meucci, Raffaele Jovi, Ariodante Fabretti, Timoteo Riboli and Silvano Lemmi.

The masonic magazine also aroused national interest in the cremationist association movement as, with the closing down of Milan's *Bollettino della Società per la Cremazione dei Cadaveri*, the cremationist movement was left without its own press organ. The articles in the *Rivista della massoneria italiana* not only offer important information about the organizational structure and development of the cremationist movement but also about the important connections between the cremation world and masonic institutions. For example, in the report of the Second Congress of the Italian Cremation Societies held in Florence in 1885, there was a shock when Adriano Lemmi, Grand Master of the *Grand Lodge of Italy*, was elected on to the central committee together with the freemasons Pini, De Cristoforis, Cantoni, Bertani and Pagliani, and when, on the same occasion, Lemmi's son Silvano, also a high-ranking masonic dignitary, proposed a significant motion requesting the intervention of the state in support of the construction of new cremation temples.

After the cremation of Alberto Keller another fundamental stage in the dissemination of the cremationist message was represented by the death, on 2 June 1882, of Giuseppe Garibaldi, formerly Grand Master of the Grand Lodge of Italy, whose last wish was to be cremated. However, despite his repeated insistence in his will, the desire of the 'hero of two worlds' was not respected by his family who were able to count on the support of the government on this delicate matter. This rejection angered the League of the Italian Societies of Cremation and of Freemasonry. At meetings held on 15 May and 2 June 1883, the Council of the Association of the Grand Lodge of Italy voted that the general's corpse be cremated as he had desired, and invited its lodges to protest in order to ensure that his last wishes were carried out. The solid pro-cremationist campaign encountered fierce opposition from the clerical establishment and the press, which stirred up a violent protest, supported by the hierarchy of the Catholic Church, which finally culminated in the excommunication – from the Sant'Uffizio Congregation in 1886 – of those who belonged to cremation societies.

Although the anti-clerical controversy was normally represented in a very bland way in cremationist essays in the masonic press, in 1886 controversy broke out strongly in reaction to the publication of the papal decree *De cadaverum crematione*. In this decree the Supreme Congregation of Santa Romana and Universal Inquisition (*Suprema Congregazione di Santa Romana e Universale Inquisizione*) raised the following questions. First, is it lawful to subscribe to societies whose objective is to promote the scorching of men's corpses? Second, is it lawful to order the scorching of one's own or somebody else's body? It responded negatively, emphasizing the response to the first question: 'if it is a matter of societies affiliated to a masonic group, one will also incur the penalties brought against such a group'. The embracing of this official position by the Catholic Church made the cremation issue a fundamental element of the Masonic anti-clerical programme after 1886. This can be seen in the programme of tasks of the commission that was created in 1888 for the relaunch of masonic activities. Giovanni Bovio, in the listing of these tasks, supported, in the electoral field, the need to 'take away the ballot-box from the priest's dominion and purify it'; in the educational field to 'secularize schools', and in the funerary field – aiming to deal with the appointed commission concerned with the issues of burial and cremation – 'to remove the priest from life and from death'.

In the same way, the commission passed the following acts: 'La Ragione' and 'La Cisalpina' of Milan, to 'combat every effort which involved the revival of clericalism', and in the eighth point supported 'diffusion of cremation everywhere'. It is interesting to note that these two Acts, at the time of constitution of this anti-clerical commission (August 1886), were already on bad terms with the high-ranking positions of the Grand Lodge of Italy, and in particular with the policy of the Grand Master Adriano Lemmi. This disagreement led to the schism headed by Malachia De Cristoforis. These events are fundamental to understanding the issue of cremation, not only in terms of the patrimony of the Grand Lodge of Italy, but also of all the components of the masonic world at that time.

The anti-masonic controversy was exacerbated after 1884 and reached its crisis point at the time of the anti-masonic Congress of 1896 and the subsequent publication of the *Rivista antimassonica* (*Anti-Masonic magazine*). This magazine frequently reported news under headings such as 'famous and nauseating human barbecue', and asserted that freemasonry wanted to introduce cremation to 'destroy a Christian custom and substitute it with a pagan custom', in the sense that freemasonry, 'like Satan, is only rewarded and satisfied by the loss of souls, the opposite of the church that only seeks salvation'. Between 1900 and 1925 pro-cremationist texts notably decreased in the masonic press. Likewise, masonic dignitaries became less significant in the leadership of the cremation movement. Supporters of cremation tried to encourage

greater masonic autonomy and abandoned any policy that suggested marked anti-clericalism in recognition that this had been an obstacle to the mass diffusion of cremation. **Marco Novarino**

References

Conti, F., Isastia, A.M. and Tarozzi, F. (1998), *La morte laica. I. Storia della cremazione in Italia (1880–1920)*, Torino: Scriptorium Paravia.

Comba, A., Mana, E. and Nonnis Vigilante, S. (1998), *La morte laica. II. Storia della cremazione a Torino (1880–1920)*, Torino: Scriptorium Paravia.

Novarino, M. (1999), 'El papel de la masonería en el nacimiento del movimiento crematorio europeo a fines del siglo XIX', in Ferrer Benimeli José Antonio (coordinador), *La Masonería española y la crisis colonial del 98*, Zaragoza, CEHME, 93–111.

Novarino, M. (2000), 'Gaetano Pini: medico, filantropo e cremazionista', Hiram, 2: 65–68.

Suchecki, Z. (1995), *La cremazione nel diritto canonico e civile*, Città del Vaticano: Editrice Vaticana.

FREUD, SIGMUND

Although it is unusual to discuss Freud in association with cremation, it is discussed here in connection with the theme of violence, death and cremation as already intimated in connection with ritual and symbolism in the Introduction. Central to the discussion is Freud's key psychoanalytic idea of the death instinct and of what he saw as two major forces, 'two basic instincts', underlying the whole of existence – namely, the death instinct (which he called *thanatos*, the Greek word for death), and the life instinct (which he called *eros*, the Greek for love or desire). Freud not only accepted that human beings had evolved from inorganic into organic forms of life, as evolutionary theory ably demonstrated, but also that there was a force 'which sought to do away with life once more and re-establish the inorganic state' (Freud, 1973: 140). This was the death instinct. Although Freud was not the first to speak of a death instinct, his development of it, and the way in which he relates it to violence, are significant (Clark, 1982: 432). Life and existence was to be interpreted as a conflict or interaction between *eros* as the positive force driving life and *thanatos* as its opponent. For Freud, the death instinct can be directed against the self or against others, but it always exists in relation to the drive for life.

Very few, even of Freud's followers, have accepted these views (Jones, 1961: 407). Nevertheless, if there is any substance in this theory it would be potentially applicable to cremation in three ways. First, it can be argued that the death instinct achieves its goal in as rapid a fashion as possible by reducing the body to its inorganic base through cremation. Cremated remains would, thus, be a dramatically clear symbolic outcome of the death instinct. Second, the process of cremation could also be viewed as an act in which the violent aspect of the *thanatos* principle is displayed by what is done to the corpse in destroying it. Third, cremation allows for a clear apprehension of *thanatos* and *eros* as distinctive dynamics of human existence. The act of cremation separates the living from the dead in a speedy fashion and permits *eros* to affirm life just as *thanatos* completes its work of reduction of life to basic elements.

Although no direct evidence in Freud substantiates these speculations, one of his case studies does prompt a comment, especially if one is allowed to apply to Freud some of the unconscious processes he readily ascribes to others. The case – one to which Freud returns several times in his *Interpretation of Dreams* – consists of a dream told to Freud by one of his patients: a father who awakes from a dream in which his daughter, who was actually lying dead in the next room surrounded by candles, comes to him and tells him that she is burning (Freud, 1976: 652–55). The father wakes to find that a candle has fallen on the corpse that is, in fact, burning. Freud interprets the dream by focusing on the double desire of the exhausted father to sleep a moment longer and to wish that his child was still alive. The element of burning is removed from any 'interpretation', being simply taken as the pragmatic cause of the dream since the father 'must have' been aware of light and flames that aroused him from sleep.

Initially, this interpretation seems entirely logical and consistent with his theory that dreams express wish fulfilments. But it is not entirely consistent with that part of his theory of dreams described as 'condensation' – the process by which different ideas become associated, and compressed into, each other. By his unusual

literalism in interpreting this case Freud completely avoids any suggestion of negative or destructive wishes the father might have held towards his dying child or to any prior thoughts the father might have had over the kind of funeral that awaited his dying daughter. Since Freud often extends his interpretations, allowing several meanings to interplay within the symbolism of a dream, it is noteworthy that this does not occur in this case. There is no mention of any potential burning of a body in cremation. This may be perfectly appropriate, and yet one wonders about it because of the indirect fact that Freud's *Interpretation of Dreams* was published in 1900, a time when many intellectuals, not least medical doctors, and especially in Freud's home city of Vienna, were actively debating cremation. Moreover, when Freud finally died, years later and while in exile in London in 1939, he was, in fact, cremated and his ashes placed in an antique Greek urn that remains in the columbarium of Golders Green Crematorium to this day. **Douglas J. Davies**

References

Clark, Ronald W. (1982), *Freud, The Man and the Cause*, London: Granada Publishing.

Freud, Sigmund (1973), *New Introductory Lectures on Psychoanalysis*, Harmondsworth: Pelican Books. First published 1932.

Freud, Sigmund (1976), *The Interpretation of Dreams*, Harmondsworth: Pelican Books. First published 1900.

Jones, Ernest (1961), *The Life and Work of Sigmund Freud*, London: The Hogarth Press.

FRY, EDWIN MAXWELL

Maxwell Fry (1899–1987), an architect of international reputation, a pioneer of modernism in Great Britain and one-time partner of the outstanding European architect, Walter Gropius (1883–1969), addressed the British Cremation Society's conference in 1967, advancing arguments about crematoria design away from a pragmatic base towards a consideration of the psychological impact of the buildings. In doing so he raised the stakes by asking the question 'What part do crematoria play in the structure of modern society … and what significance the celebration of the fact of death has in a modern society; in a modern world of science with the whole of this vast rational system which is in itself the foster child of science?' It was his belief that the widespread confusion over the design of crematoria resulted from the fact that they were built by a secular power, 'the cremation authority – and serves indifferently for several religions. The sense of belonging is absent' (Fry, 1964: 42). Crematoria lacked a conceptual basis and this presented untold problems for architects. Fry argued that, when it came to the design of technical buildings such as schools, architects were very much at home. 'What is required is understood clearly by both parties and is appreciated by both, and as a result the expression that goes into our buildings is clear and unequivocal. But when it comes to a thing like a crematorium, we find this confusion' (Fry, 1964: 41).

Fry and his second wife, Jane Drew, designed Bridgend Crematorium (1970), a second chapel at Ruislip and Mid-Glamorgan, (1969) and Breakspear, Northwood, London, (1975), and all of these take account of his concern to accommodate the reinstatement of meaningful ceremony. **Hilary Grainger**

Reference

Fry, E. Maxwell (1964), 'The Design of Modern Crematoria', *Report of the Proceedings – Annual Cremation Conference, Bournemouth, 23-25 June 1964*, London: The Cremation Society, 39–44.

FUEL

The fuel used for cremation has varied from a variety of wood in traditional Indian cremation to oil, gas and electricity in modern cremation. The use of these materials is related to availability and cost, as well as to ecological and environmental factors. Issues related to fuel are included in entries on: **Argentina**, **cremators – development**, **China**, **ecology**, **India**, **Romans** (for papyrus and incense), **vampires** (for pitch and animal fat used as accelerants and for oxygen) and **Zimbabwe**. Nowhere is the issue of fuel quite as important as for Zoroastrianism for, as that entry shows, the sacred nature of fire needs to be protected from the ritually impure corpse, and the use of electricity becomes crucial as a source of heat rather than gas or oil as a source of flame. **Douglas J. Davies**

See also Argentina; cremators – development; China; ecology; India; Romans; vampires; Zimbabwe; Zoroastrianism.

FURNACE SHAFT ARCHITECTURE

A perennial difficulty facing architects designing crematoria is the necessary furnace shaft which demands thoughtful design so as to avoid the innate psychological revulsion associated with chimneys, smoke and burning bodies. By the same token, extravagant towers concealing comparatively small flues have to be avoided. Historically, chimneys did not group happily with either the Greek temples, Renaissance domes or Gothic chapels chosen as the models for early crematoria. In the majority of cases chimneys tended to be concealed within belltowers – a course hardly to be commended on the grounds of truth. A good example of this is Headingley Crematorium in Leeds (1903), designed in a Gothic style by local architect Walter Samuel Braithwaite, with what appears to be a disproportionately high belltower, and the louvres that should have emitted 'joyful peals often belched black smoke' (Curl, 1993: 310). The Americans seem to have been less restrictive and the Earl Crematorium at Troy, New York, in Richardsonian Romanesque style, and the Old Fellows' Crematorium, San Francisco, in indifferent Renaissance style, both had uncompromising chimney shafts.

In 1906 architect A.C. Freeman recommended that the chimney shaft be constructed with a minimum internal measurement, at the base, of two square feet and be carried up to a height of 60 feet. Chimneys at Hull (1901) and Ilford (1903) were 70 feet and at Birmingham (1903) 80 feet. Freeman contended that when operating, the dampers were rarely withdrawn to their full extent and argued that they were excessively high. The differentials between the volume of the flue and height pull always have to be considered carefully. A successful early solution was at Golders Green (1901) where architect Ernest George (1839–1922) designed flues to rise from the four furnaces within a Lombard Romanesque tower acting as a campanile to the chapel. Being entirely in accordance with architectural precedent, it was unobtrusive. Bells added a further note of authenticity. A small upper furnace in the tower, contrived to consume smoke and gas, ensured that no smoke could be seen rising from the tower.

Most British crematoria were designed between 1950 and 1967. In 1950 architect Harold W. Orr argued that it should be possible to design a beautiful chimney, invoking Norman Shaw, the late nineteenth-century domestic architect with a reputation for designing 'this utilitarian feature which graces so many of the stately old homes of England' (Orr, 1950: 4). Stylistically, however, crematoria of the 1950s and 1960s assumed many of the characteristics of the period, being built in a well-mannered, humane and decent English style, with strong nuances of contemporary Scandinavian work. Chimney shafts did become more domestic in scale and were invariably built out of brick, for reasons of economy. Many architects shared A. Douglas Robinson's view that the crematorium stack should fall into line with the general masses of the buildings and be expressed with honesty and truthfulness, relying for effect on scale, choice of materials, subtle use of entasis and final treatment at the top, and should convey a sense of compactness and purpose. Architects often chose to use the chimney to give vertical balance to the general horizontal massing and volume of the buildings (Robinson, 1957: 17).

British examples from the 1970s reveal a preference for low-lying buildings which negotiate a relationship with the landscape. The prominence of the chimney stack, however, could not be avoided. At Llwydcoed, Wales (1971), the chimney rises with roof apex for visual dominance, confronting the central purpose of the crematorium directly, and highlighting the ambiguity of contemporary attitudes towards death. Crematoria sited in woodland have the advantage of the scale of the chimney being offset by surrounding trees, a notable example being Mid-Warwickshire (1971), designed by Christopher Robinson amidst tall, dark pine trees. **Hilary Grainger**

See also architecture – British.

References

Curl, J.S. (1993), *A Celebration of Death. An Introduction to Some of the Buildings, Monuments and Settings of Funerary Architecture in the Western European Tradition*, London: Batsford.

Freeman, A.C. (1906), *Crematoria in Great Britain and Abroad*, London: St Bride's Press.

Grainger, H.J. (2000), '"Distressingly Banal": The Architecture of Early British Crematoria', *Pharos*, 66(1): 42–48.

Grainger, H.J. (2001), '"The Removal of Mournful Suggestions … A Fresh Start". The Architecture of British Interwar Crematoria', *Pharos*, 67(1): 3–11.

Orr, Harold R.W. (1950), 'Cremation Architecture', *Pharos*: 4.

Robinson, A. Douglas (1957), 'The Architectural Approach', *Report of Proceedings – Annual Cremation Conference, Folkestone, 25–27 June 1957*, The Cremation Society, 15–19.

G

GARDENS OF REMEMBRANCE (UK)

Cremation not only introduced a new way of dealing with human remains, but also a new way of commemoration. The scattering of ashes on special gardens of rest or remembrance was officially recognized in the UK during the 1920s, and the growing popularity in this practice led to a decline in the need for columbaria as new forms of memorialization developed within the landscape of crematoria.

From the outset, cremationists rejected mournful Victorian cemeteries and called for the abolition of grounds strewn with an endless sea of derelict graves and withered flowers. The jostling ranks of competitive memorials and emblems of those long forgotten, were considered dreary, depressing and redolent of decay. A fresh start was to be made involving the creation of a 'carefully managed landscape of mourning, suggesting that the dead had "only passed over"' (Herring, 1931: 9). Many early British crematoria, particularly those built in the late nineteenth century, were denied the opportunity of landscaping, by being placed within, or adjoining, existing cemeteries. Examples include Leicester (1902), erected in the Gilroes Cemetery and Headingley Crematorium (1903), in Lawnswood Cemetery, Leeds. While comforting to some, such established surroundings tended to reinforce established preconceptions about burial and decay.

However, just as there were no architectural precedents for early crematoria, so there were none for gardens of remembrance. However, a love of nature and an appreciation of landscape and gardening were deep-rooted in the English psyche. In 1904 the German architectural commentator, Herman Muthesius talked of 'a people for whom a fresh breath of country air blowing across the fields is worth more than the refinements of an artificial city life' (Muthesius, 1979: 8). Gardens of remembrance tapped this rich vein of associative values, creating symbolic and sacred places in which a balance might be struck between individual commemoration and a more collective response to the shared human experiences of loss and memory.

The role of William Robinson (1838–1935), in conceiving such places cannot be overestimated. In 1880 he published the first edition of *God's Acre Beautiful or The Cemeteries of the Future*, in which he envisaged landscaped 'garden-cemeteries', in which urns would be buried and into which 'no body in a state of decay should ever enter'. Robinson, a gardening writer and horticulturist, introduced the dimension of aesthetics into the discourse on cremation in the same way that J.C. London had written about cemeteries in the 1830s and 1840s. In Robinson's words it was 'a question of art': cemeteries would become a 'new field for artistic effort'. Robinson's prophesies were to shape future attitudes about the importance of the landscaping of crematoria. It was he who placed the garden at the heart of the issue:

> By the common consent of mankind 'God's Acre Beautiful' is most fittingly arranged as a garden, and as the place for urn burials need not occupy more than a fourth of the space of a large cemetery the whole central or main part would be free for gardens and groves of trees. ... The cemetery of the future must not only be a garden in the best sense of the word, but the most beautiful and best cared for of all gardens'. (Robinson, 1889: 5).

Not surprisingly, since Robinson was an original director of the London Cremation Company, its Golders Green Crematorium is acknowledged as being 'England's first purpose-designed crematorium landscape'. Robinson oversaw the planning, but despite his advocacy of urn-burial, urns were accommodated in three purpose-built columbaria. Henceforth, the consensus that the garden, 'perpetually renewed and revived by nature's hand' would provide a model, remained essentially unchallenged in Britain, and Robinson's ideas formed the basis for gardens of remembrance from the 1920s onwards (Herring, 1931: 10).

Gardens of remembrance, rapidly acknowledged as essential to the success of new crematoria, began to command the attention of contemporary landscape architects and gardeners of repute. One of the most eminent, Edward White, (*c*.1873–1952), president of the Institute of Landscape Architects (1931–33) and director of Milner, White and Son, designed an informal woodland garden as an extension to the south garden at Golders Green in 1938. Interrupted by the war, his plans were implemented as the Horder Garden and Copse in 1955. White was also responsible for the garden of remembrance at Kensal Green Crematorium in 1938, comprising:

> [a] rectilinear garden in an Arts-and-Crafts style, with a terrace and a quadrangular sunken panel with stone retaining walls, flower-boxes, and flower-beds with kerbs. His plan envisaged a central canal and banks of clipped yews: this was amended to a central path and grass verges. (Elliott, 2001: 295).

White appears to have published the first guidance on the layout of crematorium gardens, in an essay 'Crematorium Gardens' published in *Cremation in Great Britain*, (White, 1945: 124–26). Illustrations included White's designs for the Stoke Poges Memorial Gardens in Buckinghamshire, an axial arrangement of small formal gardens, surrounded by hedges and culminating in a large parterre, and also his work at Kensal Green. White argued that, while the general rules for the laying out of parks and gardens 'are much the same', the 'Garden of Rest or Remembrance ... is in a category of its own, and special modifications are therefore necessary' (White, 1945: 124). He claimed that it was 'a kind of public park ... and as an idealistic affair' it was deserving of the best artistic treatment, involving, as it did, delicate psychological problems. One of these psychological problems was that not all visitors might want to see the crematorium buildings; hence the adoption, by most architects, of the principle that the crematorium be masked by trees from the exterior of the site and, conversely, from the interior of the crematorium, buildings outside the site also be screened from view.

White pointed out that, in a country where

there was a good standard of garden art, resulting from the best gardens being open to the public, expectations were high. Although interpretations varied – mirroring wider contemporary gardening debates – the layout of inter-war gardens tended towards an English tradition, with the columbarium, cloisters or pergolas and rose gardens forming a satisfactory architectural and visual link with the gardens beyond. Fine examples include St Marylebone (1937), Putney Vale (1938) and Mortlake (1939). Others felt that gardens should not be of the 'set or institutional type, but rather approach the wild beauty of nature, planted with trees, flowering shrubs and perennials, with broad stretches of grass unadorned by the mason's emblems of the dead and with pleasant views' (Herring, 1931: 10). At Lawnswood, Leeds, the gardens were intended as:

> ... resting places similar to those scenes beloved by all – the moorlands of the north of England with their large bluffs of rocks and heather; the more intimate rockeries of many of our larger gardens, with dwarf alpine plants creeping over them; the flowering trees of our suburbs, under the shade of which many in their old age sit quietly reminiscing; and of the meadows of the countryside, wherein countless lovely wild flowers bloom practically the whole year through. (*The Gardens of Remembrance*, Lawnswood, 1959–60: 10).

White, in referring to the 200 new crematoria planned for the post-war period, emphasized the important contribution that gardens could make to the 'general desire for worthy and beautiful resting places for the dead'.

Furthermore, in 1953 cremation and gardens of remembrance were advocated in the context of land preservation, of paramount importance in the post-war years when 'New Towns' were consuming some 60 000 acres per year. Cemeteries, it was argued, were 'outstripping food, our vital heritage' and, as a result, many town planners favoured crematoria (Sudell, 1953: 18). In terms of design, architects were responsible for the general layout of gardens and landscaping, indicating the most propitious orientation of the crematorium and ancillary buildings and harnessing any special landmarks, natural vistas and contours. Wherever possible, existing trees were retained, as at Pardon Wood,

Harlow (1951) and Exeter and Devon (1964). Principles commonly adopted included balance and relation of the formal to the informal, study of contours, boundaries and roads, details of the formal garden section, tree plan and grass areas, planting plans for shrubs, and herbaceous borders, path construction and provision for weeding (Robinson, 1957: 18).

In 1955 R.C. McMillan proposed the adoption of lawns, flower, rose and heather gardens, rockeries, trees, shrubs, hedges, walks, seats and water gardens as desirable elements. While some or all of these components feature in gardens of remembrance to a greater or lesser degree, according to the geography, climate and topography of the site, one consistent feature is the introduction of water, the sight and sound of which is universally agreed to foster tranquillity and solace. Many gardens of remembrance include ponds – either formal, as at Solihull, Warwickshire (1958) or natural and informal, as at Sutton Coldfield, West Midlands (1960). Of equal importance is planting. For thousands of years, plants have been symbols of complex ideas. Nature, with its annual renewal of growth, is profoundly symbolic of the hoped-for resurrection and since many trees, plants and shrubs serve as memorials, every care is taken to ensure that they flower throughout the year.
Hilary Grainger

See also Golders Green Crematorium; Robinson.

References

Elliott, B. (2001), 'The Landscape of Kensal Green Cemetery', in J. Stevens Curl (ed.), *Kensal Green Cemetery of All Souls, Kensal Green, London, 1824–2001*, Chichester: Phillimore, 287–96.

Herring, H.T. (1931), 'The Ideal Crematorium', in P.H. Jones and G.A. Noble (eds), *Cremation in Britain*, London: The Cremation Society of Great Britain, 9–12.

McMillan, R.C. (1955), 'The Garden of Remembrance', *Report of Proceedings – Annual Cremation Conference, Ayr, 28–30 June 1955*, London: The Cremation Society of Great Britain, 15–19.

Muthesius, H. (1979), *The English House*, ed. D. Sharp, trans. J. Seligman, London: St Martin's Press. First published 1904.

Robinson, A. Douglas (1957), 'The Architectural Approach', *Report of Proceedings – Annual*

Cremation Conference, Folkestone, 25–27 June, 1957, London: The Cremation Society of Great Britain, 15–19.

Robinson, W. (1889), God's Acre Beautiful – or the Cemeteries of the Future, London: John Murray.

Sudell, R. (1953), 'Planning the Garden of Remembrance', Report of Proceedings – Annual Cremation Conference, Llandudno, 29 June–1 July 1953, London: The Cremation Society of Great Britain, 17–20.

White, E. (1945), 'Crematorium Gardens', in P.H. Jones (ed.), Cremation in Britain, London: The Cremation Society of Great Britain, 124–26.

GENDER

Research in the 1990s intensified in uncovering the relationship of gender to attitudes about death, including the choice of cremation. Well-known society women who opted for cremation in the nineteenth century became talking points for early propagandists who looked to Lady Dilke's cremation at Dresden or Mrs Jeannette Pickersgill's Woking incineration to argue that faith or delicate sensibilities need not find the crematorium offensive. These ladies frequently appeared in the Cremation Society of Great Britain's lists of worthies cremated at Woking and Golders Green, but because the group concerned itself with demonstrating that people from all career fields elected cremation, the society dame only loomed large in one category of the list. Yet by the inter-war period, although the leadership of the Cremation Society was dominated heavily by men, examination of the rank-and-file membership began to reveal that women made up about 60 per cent. This prominence may reflect either the group's belief that it had changed its advocacy to emphasize the aesthetics of cremation, or its decision to attempt this may have been prompted by a need to satisfy the influx of female members. Irrespective of whether the belief changed before or after the influx of women, the appeal of a peaceful, floral garden has become a mainstay of cremation's success in Britain. Perhaps the variety of memorial landscape elements and designs cremation engendered in Britain serve as symbolic treatments marking this space as nurturing and emotive – as essentially feminine.

Sociological research, also, has suggested that women are more likely to specifically mention cremation in their final bequests, which can be interpreted as their greater ease with reconciling themselves to death and the loss of their bodies. Some may view this as a gesture of sacrifice, with women more likely not to want distant families to face a burdensome responsibility in tending a grave. This concept also has a parallel in the Indian practice of sati in that, if the widow has voluntarily destroyed herself, Hindus believe that she has made a sacrifice to ensure the couple's future heavenly happiness. Of course, pride also may affect both sati and women's greater propensity to direct their families to cremate their corpses. In the latter case, women may be reducing or eliminating the potential for their bodies to be viewed after their death.

In sum, the relationship of gender and cremation may be subject to significant differences according to race, social class and cultural context: it is in its early stages of serious scholarly interest as a topic of investigation as also intimated in the Introduction's comment on gender. **Liza Kazmier**

See also Cremation Society of Great Britain; Dilke; sati.

Reference

Kazmier, Lisa (2001), 'Her Final Performance: British Culture, Mourning and the Memorialization of Ellen Terry', Mortality, 6(2): 167–90.

GENOESE CREMATION SOCIETY

In the closing decades of the nineteenth century one Italian group that provided occasion for discussing cremation and for establishing a society for cremation was the Popular Circle of Giuseppe Mazzini, itself a brilliant focus of cultural interests and intellectual impulse in the Mazzinian and liberal tradition. Constituted by professional men, tradesmen, craftsmen, intellectuals and modest townspeople, its intention was to tackle the sanitary problems inherent in traditional funerary customs to which physicians and sociologists were then drawing attention. Accordingly, the Genoese Cremation Society was established on 4 April 1897 and become a charity by the Royal Act of 13 April 1902 that sanctioned its articles of Association. On 14 November 1971 the general meeting of members established a regulation, updated on 30 May 1999, stipulating, among other things, the preservation of relationships with similar institutions in Italy and other countries.

Thanks to the considerable legacy of one of its members, Luigi Maria D'Albertis, the society gained a crematorium in 1903. This underwent various developments and expansion and, by the beginning of the twenty-first century, possesses three stories with an area of more than 4000 square metres, with floors and walls covered with high-quality marble and with sculptures, amphorae and burial niches. Electric light was introduced in 1927 to replace the small, traditional, votive lights. The society pays close attention to the relatives of the deceased by providing a dignified and comfortable room for those attending funerals. Technically, the crematorium is equipped with three modern Shelton incinerators that are able to meet the increasing demand.

The society has received distinguished support from such people as the poet Ceccardo Roccatagliata Ceccardi, the doctor Domenico Di Negro, a descendant of an ancient dogal line who was the third president of the society (elected in 1900), and the lawyer Giuseppe Macaggi. Living members of the Genoese Cremation Soceity now number more than 15 000 (63 per cent men, 37 per cent women) while cremations have increased from 380 in 1985 to 1938 in 1995. To celebrate its centenary, the society published the book *Ritorno* (*Return*) in which developments such as the widening of the crematorium and the new areas acquired in various suburban cemeteries for the reception of the latest cinerary urns are described. Since l998 the society has been publishing two periodicals, *Il Notiziario* (*The Newsletter*) and *La Scelta* (*The Choice*) with the aim of keeping its members informed on activities and the researches of its study centre. **Giorgio Spina**

See also D'Albertis.

GERMANY

These two accounts focus, respectively, on the historical development of cremation and on movements and individuals influential on German cremation. The entry on the **USA** is also useful on the place of German-Americans in fostering cremation assurance societies. **Douglas J. Davies**

See also USA

HISTORICAL DIMENSIONS

In pre-Christian Europe cremating the dead on open wood pyres was as customary as burying them. Christianity's expansion restricted and finally suppressed cremation because of its heathen origin and because it was believed to contradict both the concept of resurrection of the body and of the cult of relics which had begun with the martyrs. Only in the eighteenth century did the weight of thought of the Enlightenment give new impetus to the idea of cremation. Beginning in medical discourse on matters of hygiene, issues concerning the human body gained increasing importance, with graves, in particular, being called into question.

In Prussia the *Bestimmungen des Allgemeinen Landrechts* (Regulations on the General Law of the Land) of 1794 required the construction of funeral sites outside residential areas. At the same time, it restricted the former influence of the churches by installing an authority to issue directives and measures of control over funeral matters. Instead of indiscriminate burying in joint graves, the use of single graves with appropriate periods of non-disturbance was demanded. In the nineteenth century, Jakob Grimm, the well-known researcher, gave the formation of a cremation movement a new impetus through his speech '*Über das Verbrennen von Leichen*' ('On Cremating Corpses'), which emphasized the limited space required by urn-graves as well as their hygienic benefit. As early as 1855 the Prussian regimental doctor Johann Peter Trusen pleaded for obligatory cremation after having repeatedly experienced how the inadequate burial of soldiers during war helped cause disease. Furthermore, he demanded the introduction of legitimate postmortem examination as well as public mortuaries and the handing over of the funeral matters from the church to the state. He thus countered society's reservations towards cremation through forensic arguments.

The most important opposition to cremation came from the churches which criticized the mechanistic–materialistic image of the human body as mere body parts that seemed to be involved with cremation. They also stressed the break with the Christian funeral tradition of burial. Protestant opinion varied geographically:

while the old Prussian union did not allow pastors to officiate at cremation ceremonies, the churches of Baden, Hamburg and Würtemberg soon came to tolerate clerical involvement. The strict rejection of cremation by the Catholic Church not only prohibited church officers taking part in cremation ceremonies but also denied the last sacraments to Catholics wishing to be cremated or those who were members of a cremation organization. Despite this ban, cremation organizations were founded from the mid-1870s with events, speeches, brochures and magazines supporting their cause. Advocates and representatives of this movement, especially in big cities, came from doctors, architects and engineers as well as merchants and civil servants. The first crematorium in Germany was established in 1878 in Gotha. In 1886 various local groups amalgamated to form the *Verband der Vereine deutscher Sprache für die Reform des Bestattungswesens und facultative Feuerbestattung* (Association of German-speaking Organizations to Reform Funeral Matters and Cremation). This helped strengthen their self-confidence. Further crematoria were established in Heidelberg (1891) and Hamburg (1892), and by 1910 some 20 crematoria were functioning.

Being an expression of the pragmatic–rational attitude towards death, the architecture of crematoria adapted ancient models to contemporary taste. The stark technical aspects of cremation were skilfully hidden, often in the basement, out of consideration for personal sensitivity while chimneys and ventilation tubes were covered by architectural features. The polemical way in which public discussions were held reveals just how difficult some of these architectural problems were to solve. The installing of the urn in its resting place was modelled on ancient examples, with the ashes placed in an urn and interred in a special grave site or in the wall of a columbarium.

Despite official authorization in Prussia and Bavaria and the building of further crematoria at the beginning of the twentieth century, cremation was still not generally accepted before the First World War. It was only the death and cremation of August Bebel, a social-democratic politician in 1913 that prompted many among the working class to give up their reservations and speed cremation on its road to success. By 1930 some 102 crematoria were in existence. A cremation law for all German states came into effect in 1934 and various regional regulations were repealed as cremation and burial were given equal status. This law and the cremation of Bebel explain why Germany had, despite the negative attitude of both the Protestant and Catholic Churches, the highest cremation rate in Europe until 1945. The dark chapter of cremation in German history – namely, the cremation in the National Socialists' concentration camps is dealt with separately under **Nazi cremation**.

Immediately after 1945 the influence of the churches' disapproval meant that the cremation rate stagnated in Germany, whereas in England it grew rapidly, being aided by the cremation of the remains of Prince Arthur, the son of Queen Victoria in 1941 and William Temple, archbishop of Canterbury, in 1944. However, intensive measures to promote cremation were then taken in the German Democratic Republic, and the trend towards cremation continues until today. Nevertheless, differences still exist between regions, city and countryside with continuing lower rates of cremation in largely Catholic areas. For example, the cremation rate in 1995 was 71 per cent in Protestant Braunschweig compared to 26 per cent in Catholic Augsburg, and 64 per cent in protestant Konstanz compared with 30 per cent in Catholic Regensburg. A high acceptance in the new, mainly Protestant, states, especially in Thüringen, is evident in the 1995 statistics for Gera (95 per cent cremations), Jena (90 per cent), and Gotha (90 per cent). **Elfi Heider**

See also D'Albertis; Nazi cremation.

INDIVIDUALS AND ORGANIZATIONS

As in most countries, cremationism in Germany was the work of both driven individuals and activist interest groups. Whether acting as individuals or groups, cremationists typically included physicians, local officials, minor bureaucrats, architects and engineers. A few women, such as the Nuremberg-based Else Dorn, also played a major role in the movement, particularly as public speakers and contributors to the cremationist press. Numerous public health authorities and doctors expressed concern about overcrowded cemeteries and the comparative advantages of cremation. Carl Reclam, a Leipzig physician, became one the leading cremationist proponents until his death in 1887. The authors Gottfried Kinkel and Gottfried Keller used their intellectual standing to describe the adoption of cremation as an inevitable sign of human moral progress, scientific advance, and enlightenment. Friedrich Siemens, an important inventor and industrialist, became interested in cremation and developed a cremation apparatus based on superheated air that enjoyed considerable publicity despite its expense. His models were displayed in 1876 at a hygiene exhibition in Dresden that was seminal for the propagation of cremationist enthusiasm in Germany.

The German penchant for joining clubs and organizations translated into considerable activity by cremation societies (*Feuerbestattungsvereine*). The first cremation societies were founded in Gotha, Dresden, Berlin, Hamburg, and Frankfurt in the 1870s. Their propaganda efforts reached beyond the borders of their respective regions. The Berlin-based journal *Die Flamme* (*The Flame*) the Viennese *Phoenix* and a short-lived Krefeld paper *Feuerbestattungs-Zeitung* (*Cremation Newspaper*) became the leading organs of the movement. From 1886 the various societies were part of an umbrella organization, the League of German-Speaking Cremation Societies (*Verband der Feuerbestattungsvereine deutscher Sprache*). Although Berlin was highly influential in the cremation movement, it was in Germany's lesser cities that the first crematoria were constructed. Due to the sympathy of the local prince, the tiny state of Saxe-Coburg-Gotha became the first state in Germany to permit cremation. Within the kingdom of Prussia, cremationists, such as Eduard Müller from the small industrial city of Hagen, became leading proponents of cremation at both local and international levels. Müller succeeded in getting a local art patron to underwrite part of the construction costs of Hagen's crematorium, although he was less enthusiastic about allowing Osthaus to select a modernist, Peter Behrens, as the architect.

A number of public figures expressed opinions on cremation. Robert Koch, one of the originators of germ theory, was a prominent advocate of cremation as was Rudolf Virchow, one of the fathers of modern anthropology. A number of intellectuals and writers used their literary talents to advocate cremation as a voluntary form of burial, including the feminist Lily Braun and the socialist August Bebel. Bebel's massive funeral in 1913, followed by his cremation, is generally considered a watershed in the history for German cremation. Although the

avid anti-clerical sentiments of some individuals attracted considerable press attention and have caused some studies of German cremation to see the movement as an atheistic phenomenon, the bulk of German cremationist publications affirmed how perfectly cremation could fit with religiosity. **Tim Pursell**

References

Fischer, Norbert (1996), *Vom Gottesacker zum Krematorium: Eine Sozialgeschichte der Friedhöfe in Deutschland seit dem 18. Jahrhundert*, Cologne: Böhlau.

Fischer, Norbert (2001), *Geschichte des Todes in der Neuzeit*, Erfurt: Sutton Verlag.

Pursell, Timothy (2001), 'The Burial of the Future and the Architecture of the Future: Hagen's Crematorium', in 'Art on the Edges, Hagen 1890–1922: Art and Society in a German Industrial Town', PhD thesis, Indiana University, Bloomington: 224–74.

Thalmann, Rolf (1978), *Urne oder Sarg? Auseinandersetzungen um die Einführung der Feuerbestattung im 19. Jahrhundert*, Frankfurt-am-Main: Peter Lang.

GHANA

In the second half of the twentieth century cremation became an alternative to the practice of burial in Ghana – particularly in the major population centres of the country – with four open-air pyres located in four regional capitals. It is on record that the first crematorium was established in the year 1950 in Cape Coast. This was followed by Takoradi in the 1960s, Accra (1977) and Kumasi (1993). In 1986 the Ghana Cremation Society was formed, and these various crematoria operate under this society which has a membership of some 1500. The most active wing in the society operates under the registered name of Ridge Cremation & Funeral Service in Accra. From 1999 to 2001, an average of about 2 per cent of the dead were cremated in Ghana as shown by Table 1:

Year	No. of cremations	Total deaths	Percentage of deaths
1999	250	15 000	1.67
2000	300	17 000	1.76
2001	335	18 500	1.82

This figure would be quite significant in a country where burial is the main mode of corpse disposal were it not for the fact that many of those cremated are non-Ghanaians. Nevertheless, Ghana stands out in the practice of cremation in West Africa for there appears to be very little interest in cremation in other West African countries. Consequently, corpses prepared for cremation are brought into Accra via Ghanaian embassies on the West Coast of Africa. It is interesting to note that the statistics for annual recorded cremations in Ghana from January 2002 to 30 August 2002, for example, reveal that out of a total of 14 cremations only three were females, 13 were foreign nationals and only one was a Ghanaian. Foreign nationals cremated included two from France and single individuals from Sri Lanka, China, the Czech Republic, Germany, India, Italy, the USA and Switzerland.

The long preserved tradition of earth burial as a sign of respect for the dead and the prominence of Christian beliefs about the resurrection in relation to the body account for the low public acceptance of cremation. An opinion poll conducted by the Revd E.A. Quagraine in 2002 among Christian leaders in Accra, revealed an almost 100 per cent aversion to cremation. Most of these Christians argued that Jesus Christ, the Chief Shepherd of the Church, was buried and therefore left his followers no better example of corpse disposal than that which he himself experienced. **Charles Owiredu**

GILGAMESH

One of the earliest references to cremation and the identity of the dead is found in the ancient Babylonian poem *The Epic of Gilgamesh*. This is one of the oldest myths, dating back to approximately 2000 BCE, and concerns grief, the human fear of death and ideas of survival after death. Although it talks about a shadowy afterlife in an underworld, that existence is reckoned to be far less desirable than life in this world. It was important to enter the afterlife as an entire and complete body and those who suffered some loss of limb or serious bodily affliction would retain that disadvantage in the underworld, with the exception of stillborn babies who seemed to have a very positive existence there. The one category of individual not found in the afterlife, however, was that of an individual who burnt to death. It is said that the ghost of such a person was not

there because the smoke of such individuals had gone into the air. This reflects the dislike of cremation amongst the ancient Babylonians and their strong emphasis on burial and the power of memorial monuments as places where people's names could be remembered. **Douglas J. Davies**

Reference

George, Andrew (1999), *The Epic of Gilgamesh*, New York: Barnes and Noble.

GOLDERS GREEN CREMATORIUM

The seventh crematorium to be built in Britain, Golders Green holds a unique position in the history of cremation, being London's first crematorium and England's first purpose-designed crematorium landscape. It opened in 1902, the year that the Cremation Act was passed by parliament, and was commissioned by the London Cremation Company. Designed by one of the most successful late Victorian architectural practices, Ernest George & Yeates, it occupies a 12-acre site adjacent to Hampstead Heath.

Its development was accretive, the building work extending from 1901 until 1939, with landscaping continuing into the 1950s. The crematorium buildings run west to east along the north boundary formed by Hoop Lane and are in a consistent Lombard-Romanesque style, in red brick with round arches and pantiled roofs. While Lombard-Romanesque marked a departure from the traditional Gothic style employed for early crematoria, Golders Green was nevertheless ecclesiastical in idiom and offered the practical advantage of a campanile, which mitigated the appearance of the furnace shaft which it contained.

The West Columbarium, (1902), West Chapel (1903), offices and staff houses form the nucleus of the original complex. The columbarium designed to house urns containing ashes was the first of its kind in Britain and George's design resembles a square Italian brick baptistery with a pyramidal roof. The West Chapel, the most prominent element of the picturesque grouping, has a rectangular nave and round-arched clerestory windows and entrance porch with porte-cochere to the west and campanile and furnace rooms to the east. Internally, it is oak-panelled to a height of five and a half feet, with red brick walls above an open timber roof.

The East Columbarium, (1912) and the cloisters linking the West Chapel and Columbaria (1913) were by George & Yeates as were the Crawshay memorial fountain (1909) and the small, single-storey rectangular Duke of Bedford Chapel (1911). The Ernest George Columbarium (1922–28), considered by many to be the most impressive building of its type, is symmetrical in plan with end towers, small northern apse and external diapered brickwork, and was designed by Alfred B. Yeates. The East Chapel, the Chapel and Hall of Memory and the adjacent columbarium at the eastern end of the complex, (1938–39) were by Mitchell & Bridgwater.

Golders Green Crematorium offers a new landscape of mourning in place of the Victorian graveyard. Its creator, William Robinson, the celebrated gardening writer and horticulturalist, was an early supporter of cremation and a director of the London Cremation Company. In his book *God's Acre Beautiful or the Cemeteries of the Future* (1880) Robinson argued that such spaces were most fittingly arranged as a garden. At Golders Green the open lawns and flowerbeds in front of the cloister give way to an informal woodland garden with pools, the latter designed by Milner, White & Son in the 1950s.

Memorialization is confined to the cloister where the symmetrical placing of glazed della Robbia-inspired tablets serve as a reminder of the influence of the Campo Santo at Pisa. Some individual memorials stand in the gardens, including the Philipson Mausoleum (1914–16), a circular domed cell, open to the sky, surrounded by a lattice stone wall, designed by Edwin Lutyens (1869–1944) in Portland stone to stand along the eastern edge of the garden. The Smith Mausoleum, by Paul Phipps (1880–1953) in 1903 closes the vista at the east end of the principal pathway. To its north is a garden with exedra, formerly with a pergola by Robinson (1907). Edward Maufe's War Graves Commission memorial, an Ionic temple with segmental pediment, consecrated in the early 1950s closes the western end of the vista. Architecture and landscape combine to make Golders Green one of the most successful crematoria in Britain.

The Landscaping of Golders Green Crematorium

The historical significance of Golders Green 'as London's first crematorium and England's first purpose-designed crematorium landscape' was confirmed in 2002 when English Heritage placed it on the Register of Parks and Gardens as a Grade II listed site. At Golders Green Crematorium the mournful associations of the Victorian cemetery, with its Gothic romanticism and heterogeneous assortment of individual memorials, were rejected in favour of a new aesthetic. The new landscape, based on an elegiac interpretation of the garden, encouraged a more collective response to the shared human experiences of loss and memory. The status and success of Golders Green Crematorium can be attributed to the collaboration between William Robinson (1838–1935) and Ernest George (1839–1922) who, by 1902, were each eminent in their respective fields of horticulture and architecture. They brought to the scheme, not only their individual expertise, but also a shared feeling for art and a belief in the importance of the relationship between architecture and landscape.

The London Cremation Company was fortunate to count William Robinson as one of its original directors, when it was formed in 1900. Robinson was well established as an indefatigable and outspoken gardening writer and horticulturist. A great friend of the leading landscape gardeners of the day, including Gertrude Jekyll and Harold A. Peto, Robinson was also an early campaigner for cremation. It is hardly surprising therefore, that he was to play an instrumental role in the formation of Golders Green Crematorium. The six crematoria built in Britain before Golders Green had either been denied the opportunity of landscaping, by being placed in existing cemeteries, or had underestimated the potential of their surroundings. At Golders Green, Robinson ensured that landscaping was integral to the project from the outset. Indeed the board is reported to have proceeded with planting and fencing, so that the trees might be growing while they were 'thinking out plans for building', (London Cremation Company Outletter Book, 1900). In 1880 Robinson published *God's Acre Beautiful or The Cemeteries of the Future*, in which he envisaged 'garden-cemeteries', where urns would be buried and 'no body in a state of decay should ever enter'. Robinson introduced another dimension to the discourse on cremation, that of aesthetics. This was 'a question of art' – cemeteries would become a 'new field for artistic effort'. Indeed, his prophesies about the importance of the landscaping of crematoria would find physical expression at Golders Green.

Robinson's early plans remain unaltered. The grounds, 12 acres in extent, are surrounded by a belt of sheltering trees, 2000 of which were planted in the first 12 years, in addition to those already growing on the site. Robinson's belief that '[t]he lawn is the heart of the garden, and the happiest thing that is in it' certainly holds true at Golders Green. The crocus planting, such a feature of the landscape, is reminiscent of Alfred Parsons' illustration in the 1881 edition of Robinson's *The Wild Garden*, showing drifts of bulbs in naturalized woodland. At Golders Green the lawn is flanked by the Western and Eastern Paths, which join at the southern end. Lined with flowering trees and shrubs and surrounded by flower borders, they are backed by a belt of trees around the perimeter. The wooded slopes of Golders Hill Park and Hampstead Heath form a picturesque background to the arrangement, the main portion of which was to remain as a garden. Today, the extant planting remains extensive and varied, with formal beds of standard roses along the main path, beds of informal shrubs and roses around the other paths, flowering trees and mature broadleaves and conifers.

The first of a number of formal elements was introduced in 1926, when architect Alfred B. Yeates was commissioned to design a Memorial Court for tablets, behind the West Columbarium. His plans included a lily pond. Other developments during the late 1920s and early 1930s were confined to maintenance and planting. In 1938, three years after Robinson's death, his mantle was assumed by Edward White, a director of Milner, White & Sons, another distinguished landscape architect, who was a former president of the Institute of Landscape Architects. At the suggestion of H.T. Herring, then honorary secretary of the London Cremation Company, White was invited to prepare a survey of the gardens and a scheme for replanting the western boundary with memorial trees. He produced a plan, together with a list of trees and shrubs suitable for planting in each month. Replanting was completed in 1938. In 1939 White's plan for developing the southern end of the company's property were approved and Mr Braithwaite was informed that his lease on the tennis court at the southernmost tip of the site would be terminated. Here, White designed an informal woodland garden, lying beyond the Cedar Lawn, which had formed part of Robinson's original layout. A path surrounded by scattered trees, rose and shrub beds crosses the Cedar Lawn which now divides the dispersal lawn to the north from White's Southern Garden. White's plan was halted by the Second World War and was not implemented until 1955.

The Cloister Garden or Exedral Cloister, was planned in 1940 to the north of the Martin Smith Mausoleum, in the north-east corner of the gardens and to the east end of the range of buildings. Milner, White & Son were again involved in the planning. This garden is now backed by the red brick boundary wall which curves around at this point to form an exedra, incorporating part of a pergola, originally planned by Robinson in 1906, but never fully executed.

Few changes were made to the gardens during the Second World War, although records show that they were well maintained, despite a shortage of labour. In October 1944 Walter Slocock, from the firm of Slocock of Knapp Hill, and a landscape gardener, 'Mr. Lever', submitted plans for the planting of additional memorial trees to the west of the lawn. Unfortunately, no contractor could be found. Despite help from soldiers in digging over and tidying up 'the newly prepared beds', planting was not completed until April 1946. Lever subsequently planned new beds on the east side of the garden which were completed in January 1947.

In 1955, Milner, White & Son implemented Edward White's 1939 plan for the Southern Garden. Now planned as the Horder Garden and Copse in memory of Lord Horder, president of the Cremation Society since 1940. A contemporary drawing shows an almost Japanese arrangement of willow trees planned around two ponds, crossed by a path leading over a bridge. The Horder Alpine Garden at the southern end of the garden was laid out in 1999. The Children's Garden, between the Western Path and the west boundary wall, dates from the late twentieth century.

Although some individual mausolea were introduced gradually into the gardens, there are no graves, only plaques and commemorative tablets on the boundary walls, in the columbaria or by memorial planting. A balance between spacious lawns and more intimate, enclosed spaces with garden furniture and sculpture has been carefully maintained. Individual memorials include the Smith Mausoleum, designed in 1904–05, by Paul Phipps (1880–1953). Erected by Martin-Ridley Smith, the first chairperson of the London Cremation Company in memory of his son Nigel Martin Smith, it is executed in brick with Portland stone dressings in a late Victorian version of the Baroque style. The Philipson Mausoleum (1914–16), by Sir Edwin Lutyens (1869–1944), was erected on the eastern side of the garden to house the remains of the Philipson family. Arguably considered to be the finest mausoleum of the twentieth century, it was executed in Portland stone and invokes the Pantheon in Rome and Lutyens's own design for the Durber Hall in the Viceroy's House in New Delhi, dating from 1912.

One of the finest pieces of sculpture at Golders Green can be found further to the south, in the belt of trees bordering the eastern side of the gardens. Dated 1924, 'Into the Silent Land' was the work of the sculptor Henry Pegram RA. It depicts a shrouded figure raising a girl above a sea of souls and was a gift presented to Golders Green by the Royal Academy of Arts in 1937, the year of Pegram's death. Just off the Western Path, on the edge of the central lawn, is a standing bronze statue of Ghanshyarn da Biria (1894–1983), a supporter of Gandhi. At the western end of George's range of buildings lies the War Memorial, a stone Ionic porticoed temple with a low segmental pediment, erected by the War Graves Commission in 1949 to the designs of the Commission's chief architect, Edward Maufe, (1883–1974).

Golders Green presented not only the first opportunity to 'landscape' the grounds of a crematorium, but also allowed Robinson to make the leap from theory into practice. With its amphitheatre of grass, and commemorative roses, bordered by well-chosen trees with many weeping willows and wall-borne plaques on the eastern side, it recalled the 'sylvan charms' of 'God's Acre Beautiful' and afforded Robinson the opportunity to realize at least some aspects of his ideal elegiac natural garden, namely 'undisturbed lawns, stately and beautiful trees in many forms . . a background of surrounding groves' and the avoidance of 'hideous vistas of crowded stones' (Robinson, 1889). Furthermore, the contiguous elements of the composition are important in contriving to give an area of 12 acres a feeling of increased spaciousness, reminiscent of larger country house gardens. The recessional perspective of the cloister continues as a wall running off as a boundary with the trees then taking over, leaving one to imagine that they continue into infinity. Golders Green is a uniquely affecting place, in which the choice of architectural style and the landscaping of the gardens have combined to create an atmosphere of serenity and comfort. **Hilary Grainger**

See also cloisters; columbaria; gardens of remembrance; George; Robinson; White.

References

Grainger, H.J. (2000), 'Golders Green Crematorium and the Architectural Expression of Cremation', *Mortality*, 5(1): 53–73.

Grainger, H.J. (2002), 'The Development of the Gardens at Golders Green Crematorium', in P.C. Jupp and H.J. Grainger (eds), *Golders Green Crematorium 1902–2002: A London Centenary in Context*, London: The London Cremation Company, 39–48.

Jupp, Peter J. and Grainger, Hilary J. (eds) (2002), *Golders Green Crematorium 1902-2002: A London Centenary in Context*, London: The London Cremation Company.

GREECE

Greece offers a complex picture of cremation involving, at the commencement of the twenty-first century, both a call for legal cremation for those requesting it and a firm opposition by many on the part of the Greek Orthodox Church. Issues of secularization and modernization compete with ideas of patriotism and tradition. To illustrate this complexity this section presents three contributions. The first offers a broad and general account, the second a view from a theological Church perspective and the third a brief descriptive account of some members of the Greek Orthodox Church in Great Britain. **Douglas J. Davies**

CREMATION AND MODERN GREECE

Although Greece is the only country in the European Union where cremation is at present (2005) forbidden by law, it is an idea coming under discussion for practical reasons. This is a novelty for Greece which is dominated by strong rituals and beliefs of the Greek Orthodox Church which not only opposes cremation but also demonstrates an awkward unwillingness to discuss such matters. Those wishing to be cremated for ideological, religious, personal or other reasons, have to be sent abroad, to European countries such as Poland, Italy, Germany, Belgium or Bulgaria, which proves to be very expensive for families (*Ta Nea*, 1996, 1997).

Since the fourth century, the traditional and only manner of dealing with dead bodies in Greece has been burial, followed by numerous rituals well regulated in space and time and which symbolically express communication between living and dead people (Pharos, 1989). Today, because of lack of space, dead bodies are generally exhumed after three years, especially when they are in rented graves, and the bones placed in boxes stored above ground. This scheme causes numerous problems with incompletely decayed bodies with consequences in terms of hygiene as well as trauma for the bereaved.

The first ever debate on cremation in Greece took place in 1912; it was not discussed again until 1941 when the medical profession spoke in favour of cremation but, in 1943, the first legal ban was issued. An association defending cremation was created in 1946 but broke up some years later (*Ena*, 1992). Moreover, two synods of the Greek Orthodox Church condemned the practice in 1960 and in 1972 (*Eleytherotypia*, 1997).

The debate on cremation resurfaced following a strong heatwave during the summer of 1987 when a high mortality rate and severe problems linked to the lack of burial space prompted the media and some politicians to refer to cremation as a possible solution (*To Vima*, 1987). Since then, cremation has been at the centre of a debate involving numerous people including those drawn from the law, from an association defending cremation, the 'Association of Cremation's Friends', from local authorities, politics, the press and the Orthodox Church, as well as anonymous and eminent people from society at large (Dargentas, 2002). However, this debate has not yet led to institutional acceptance of this practice. Initial discussions focused on the the legitimacy of the association defending cremation, as its creation had initially been refused by the court as 'contrary to public order and to customs' (*Ta Nea*, 1992; Giotopoulou-Maragopoulou, 2000). Subsequent discussion was dominated by the demands made by this association and by the local administrative authorities in the Athens area, which were the most affected by space problems. These demands were addressed to the state and requested the institutionalization of cremation (*Ta Nea*, 1996). However, these were ignored until 1998, when the first bill raising the possibility of cremation for non-Orthodox people was drafted by parliament. This bill was contested by the Communist Party, which proposed to widen this possibility to Orthodox people. These amendments were then adopted by the parliament (*Ta Nea*, 1998), but the bill was shelved due to strong protests coming from the Orthodox Church (*Eleytherotypia*, 1999). This debate created inner conflicts within the Orthodox Church and provided an opportunity to explore other polemical matters concerning links between the state and the Church, such as the new identity cards that do not mention the bearer's religion, and also civil funerals that are currently non-existent in Greece (*Kathimerini*, 1998). It was only in 2002 that the issue of cremation was discussed once again, after a break in the debate and in the media publications on the topic (*Ta Nea*, 2002; *Ethnos*, 2003). It should be stressed that the Orthodox religious institution has played an important role in this debate, and the political viewpoint conforms with the Orthodox Church (Dargentas, 2003).

Among the reasons given in support of cremation by the Association of Cremation's Friends and other supporters are: the problem of space; hygiene; advantages linked to the management of mourning for the bereaved; the need to provide an option to suit different religious positions and practices; as well as human rights issues, such as the democratic freedom of choice. There is also the fact that some well-known Greeks have opted for cremation, including the opera singer Maria Callas and the conductor Dimitri Mitropoulos. There is also support from Ancient Greek practice. Among the arguments given by the Orthodox Church and opponents of the practice are religious matters linked to institutional, ritual and dogmatic issues, to Greek and or Orthodox identity which is deemed incompatible with cremation, as well as to the importance of burial for the bereaved. There is, also, the representation of cremation as being too final – an ultimate death (Dargentas, 2002, 2003).

Furthermore, according to a survey examining religious belonging (Orthodox versus Catholic) and church attendance (high versus low), it was found that arguments associated with identity and used to oppose cremation are mainly invoked by Orthodox people and by regular churchgoers (Dargentas, 2002). The main obstacle for cremation is that, for part of the Greek population, it is seen as a practice which is detrimental to the individual because it completely obliterates the deceased and as a threat to society because it eliminates Greek identity: according to a priest, 'with cremation, the society is also signing its own end, its own nihilism' (*Kathimerini*, 1999). Given both the novel character of cremation in Greece and its inevitable future institutionalization in the light of international conventions regarding human rights (Giotopoulou-Maragopoulou, 2000), one should expect distinctive attitudes to evolve around this whole matter. **Magdalini Dargentas**

References

Dargentas, M. (2002), 'Mémoire sociale et enjeux identitaires: à propos de la représentation sociale de la pratique d'incinération en Grèce', in S. Laurens and N. Roussiau (eds), *La mémoire sociale, identités et représentations sociales*, Rennes: Presses Universitaires de Rennes.

Dargentas, M. (2003), 'Discourses, Social Representations and Political Decisions about Cremation in Greece: Analysis of a Press Data Corpus', paper for the first PhD Symposium on Modern Greece at the London School of Economics, Hellenic Observatory, 21 June 2003 available on the LSE website, Hellenic Observatory (e-paper).

Eleytherotypia (1997), 'Burning the Dead and Human Rights', 6 December.

Eleytherotypia (1999), 'A War Has Broken Out Regarding Cremation', 11 March.

Ena, (1992), 'Going Out by Fire: A Social Dilemma' 23 September.

Ethnos, (2003), 'Amendments in the Bill: They are burning the ban regarding cremation'.

Giotopoulou-Maragopoulou, A. (2000), 'Proposal of the National Committee for Human Rights Regarding Cremation', Text Number 6 in The National Committee for Human Rights (NCHR), *Report 2000*, Athens: Hellenic Republic, National Press.

Kathimerini, (1998), 'After Cremation Theoklitos Proposes also Civil Funerals' 19 December.

Kathimerini, (1999), 'Cremation: Definitive Oblivion or Eternal Memory?'.

Pharos, P. (1989), *Το πένθος* (*The Bereaving*), Athens: Akritas.

Ta Nea (1992), 'Constitutionally-Permitted Cremation', 5 November.

Ta Nea (1996), 'They Ask for Cremation', 12 January.

Ta Nea (1997), 'Abroad for Cremation', 24 November.

Ta Nea (1998), 'Paving the Way for Cremation: It is Becoming Legal for Greek Citizens Who are not Orthodox', 16 December.

Ta Nea (2002), 'Cremation on the Doorstep', 15 November.

To Vima (1987), 'Is Cremation to be Sanctioned?', 9 August.

GREEK ORTHODOXY

Neither the authentic tradition of the Orthodox Church, nor the inspired Holy Bible, nor the infallible decisions of the oecumenical Councils, doctrinal definitions (όροι) and sacred canons give us a straight answer on the question of whether cremation is either prohibited or necessary, or even allowed. Even if we have no canonical decisions or biblical commandments, this does not mean that there are not natural laws given by God or very ancient human customs based on natural laws. After the Fall, the Creator utters prophetic and binding words saying: 'you are dust, and to dust you shall return' (Genesis 3:19). The natural end of a dead body is burial. Likewise, there are testimonies in the Old Testament according to which the cremation of bodies is regarded as punishment, and degradation followed this as in Leviticus 20:14 which says that 'if a man takes a wife and her mother also, it is wickedness; they shall be burnt with fire, both he and they that there may be no wickedness among you' (see also Genesis 38:24 and Leviticus 21:9). Burial was, then, customary in Israelite tradition. The fourth Gospel gives us similar information, testifying that 'they took the body of Jesus, and bound it in linen cloths with the spices, as is the burial custom of the Jews'. Nor did Jesus go against that custom.

In addition, this natural law was followed by the Greeks, who interpreted it the same way.

It is known from history and archaeology (domed tombs) that the ancient Greeks believed in the afterlife and therefore buried their dead. Burial of the dead was likewise the prevailing custom among the Romans (Cicero, *De Legibus* 11, 22, 26; *Plinius*, 1,VII,44). It should be noted that it was only during times of war that cremation was employed as a necessity in order to prevent the bodies of dead soldiers from being dishonoured by the enemy, and to protect the population from diseases created by decomposing bodies.

It was natural for the early Christian Church, especially the Orthodox Church, to adopt and maintain the traditional way of dealing with dead bodies – that of decomposition (2 Timothy 4:6). It did this because the Lord himself indirectly indicated his preference for the burial of his body by saying to Judas 'Let her alone, let her keep it for the day of my burial' (John 12:7). Saint Simeon, archbishop of Thessalonica, in relation to the Orthodox Church's use of burial wrote: 'and we place the corpse in the grave and give it to the earth with prayers, fulfilling the divine commandment "you are dust, and to dust you shall return" and thus we proclaim the resurrection.'

Another reason why the Church adopted the practice of burying the dead is because it proclaims and foretells the resurrection of the dead. Burial is a symbol, proof and confession of faith and hope in the immortality of the soul and in the resurrection (See 1 Corinthians 15:42–44). That is why, in Greek, death is called repose (ανάπαυσις) or sleep (κοίμησι), and the cemeteries (κοιμητήρια are places of those who sleep, see 1.Thessalonians 4:13). In addition, graves mark a place as a motherland and are one of the strongest motives for patriotism [Translator's note: although this point is irrelevant to the main subject, it expresses the strong relationship that exists between the Greek Orthodox Church, national identity and religion.] Moreover, it is declared in the Holy Bible that 'Do you not know that your bodies are members of Christ? ... Do you not know that your body is a temple of the Holy Spirit within you, which you have from God? You are not your own; you were bought with a price. So glorify God in your body' (1 Corinthians 6:15–20). The importance and seriousness of St Paul's words is more obvious when God pours his grace into a relic or the dead body of a saint and makes it a cause of miracles and consequently of faith in the existence and providence of God. In fact often, if not always, Orthodox Christians hope to benefit from the grace which streams from the uncorrupted relics of the saints, which often produce myrrh and work various miracles. Thus, although the burial of the dead is neither command, nor canon, nor church law and therefore cannot be imposed on Christians, it is nevertheless suggested strongly and persistently by Holy Scripture, by the natural and canonical order and by the apostolic and liturgical practice. It is suggested and prescribed because it is natural law and Christian tradition and custom.

However, no one should think that anyone who is cremated will not be raised from the dead and will escape the judgement of the second coming of the Lord. Again, let no one think that those burnt in the furnaces of the German concentration camps ceased to exist. Even more let no one think that Christian martyrs who have been burnt will not inherit the kingdom of God. The Holy Bible assures us that everyone, without exception, will continue into everlasting life (1 Corinthians 15:51–52). **Panagiotis J. Boumis, translated by Revd Anastasios Barkas**

Biblical texts are from the Holy Bible, Revised Standard Version, Collins, 1973.

GREEK ORTHODOXY IN GREAT BRITAIN

The Orthodox Church, inspired by affection towards her departed children, has, since early times adopted the custom of burying her dead (as is evidenced from the catacombs and from the graves of the martyrs and of the saints). Cremation therefore is contrary to the tradition of our church and forbidden for Orthodox Christians. In cases where relatives cannot go against the expressed last wishes of their departed loved ones the funeral service may take place in the church, and at the end of the service the remains will be handed over to the relatives.

This text, found in the annual (2004) church calendar of the Greek Orthodox Archdiocese of Thyateira and Great Britain, is the only instruction issued for priests and laypeople on the matter of cremation. Making an opaque reference to the love of the church towards its flock, it prohibits cremation on the grounds of tradition. This ban on cremation can be lifted if cremation is the last will of the deceased and, in such cases, cremation will have no other theological, ecclesiastical or liturgical consequences than the fact that the funeral service will be conducted in the church. It will not be conducted in the crematorium. No further instructions are given to the priests.

The results of an informal survey conducted among parishes of the Greek Orthodox Archdiocese of Britain in 2003 indicated that only 0.5–1.0 per cent of people opted for cremation. Of course, there is the possibility that many who decide to be cremated do not want a church service and therefore no information about them is available. While this might apply to a few, the main reasons given by parish priests for people opting for cremation are the lack of religious commitment and the relatively higher cost of burial. Some may have expressed a desire to receive an Orthodox funeral service but did not express their wishes over burial or cremation, leaving the relatives to decide according to their own personal feelings and beliefs. Others may have had strong feelings against religion, not wanting burial or a funeral service, but their relatives still decided to hold a church service and pray for the deceased's soul. Still others, with religious but non-Orthodox relatives, may have opted for cremation on financial grounds. Religious, but non-Orthodox, relatives may not understand burial as a necessity and make their decision based on a variety of criteria. Many parishes answered that mixed weddings and the rapid 'anglisation' (*sic*) of the diaspora are responsible for the choice of cremation.

Since cremations are infrequent, the archdiocese has not created an action plan to advise and support burial, such as a central fund for those who cannot bear its cost, leaflets or a visiting counselling committee for bereaved relatives. Parish priests vary in their attitudes towards cremation: some may insist on burying the dead; others may modify the funeral service that takes place, particularly by omitting words or psalms referring to the earth, burial and so on.
Revd Anastasios Barkas

GUY FAWKES NIGHT

The burning of an effigy of an historical figure occurs each year on 5 November in England on what is called Guy Fawkes' Night. This very popular custom focuses on the building of pyres both by families and local community groups and the letting off of fireworks. Now devoid of active political and religious significance and merely an occasion for festivity and parties, this event has its roots in the action of Guy Fawkes, who was born in 1570 in York, the child of Protestant parents whose mother later remarried a recusant. Fawkes himself later converted to Catholicism, and joined the Spanish army.

Prior to the reign of James I, persecution of Catholics had been rife in England. This was witnessed through various acts of parliament, such as the second Act of Supremacy in 1563, which required an oath, on pain of death, from all subjects acknowledging the monarch as the head of the Church. Although James pardoned a number of recusants, hopes that he would further ameliorate the situation of Catholics were largely unrealized. Fawkes, along with a group of conspirators, planned to depose the king and parliament through an attack on the palace of Westminster. The organizer of the plot was Robert Catesby. The plot having been leaked, Fawkes was apprehended on the night of 4 November 1605 in the grounds of the Palace; the night before the opening of parliament. Fawkes and the other conspirators were executed for treason.

So it was that Guy Fawkes and the 'Gunpowder Plot' are remembered every year in the celebration of bonfire night. It is suggested that the tradition began on the night of the attempt, when citizens realized that the conspirators had been apprehended and lit fires to celebrate. Effigies of Fawkes are placed on to the fires. The effigy may be carried around town at the start of the ritual, with his escorts requesting 'a penny for the guy'. Children are entertained by making their own 'Guy' – a word that has come to stand for the effigy itself. It is often made from old clothes stuffed with paper or similar and a mask is drawn for its face.

It is not unknown for effigies of the pope to also be placed on the fire. The town of Lewes in the south of England is renowned for its celebration of Guy Fawkes Night. Here, the papal effigy is Paul V, pope during the reign of Queen Mary I (1553–1558). During her reign, 17 Protestant martyrs were burned at the stake. Similar events occurred elsewhere in England. The Lewes celebrations on 5 November involve a procession carrying 17 burning crosses to commemorate the martyrs. This well-known poem is recited during the celebrations:

> Remember, remember the fifth of November
> Gunpowder, treason and plot.
> I see no reason why gunpowder treason
> Should ever be forgot.
> Guy Fawkes, Guy Fawkes
> 'Twas his intent
> To blow up the King and the Parliament
> Three score barrels of powder below
> Poor old England to overthrow
> By God's providence he was catched
> With a dark lantern and burning match.
> Holloa boys, holloa boys,
> Ring the bells ring
> Holloa boys, holloa boys,
> God save the King!
> Hip hip hooray
> Hip hip horray.
> A penny loaf to feed ol' Pope
> A farthing cheese to choke him
> A pint of beer to rinse it down
> A faggot of sticks to burn him.
> Burn him in a tub of tar
> Burn him like a blazing star
> Burn his body from his head
> Then we'll say old Pope is dead.
> Hip hip hooray
> Hip hip hooray

Katherine Johnson

References

Ainsworth, W. (c.1890), *Guy Fawkes: or, The gunpowder treason: An historical romance*, London: Routledge.

Blyth, J. (1991), *Guy Fawkes*, London: Ginn.

Deary, T. (1996), *The Truth about Guy Fawkes? A Stuart Mystery*, London: Watts.

GYPSIES

According to research in Britain, Eire, France, Italy, Hungary, Scandinavia, Poland and parts of central Asia, there are, it seems, no examples of Gypsies or Roma selecting cremation over burial. This fact, ironically, runs counter to the Gypsy folklorist obsession with their mythical Indian origins, for, in Hinduism at least, there is a significant cultural emphasis on the funereal pyre. By contrast, the Gypsies, Travellers, Manus or Roma elect to bury their dead in graves or large family tombs.

Okely (1983) describes how the elaborate mortuary rites conducted by English Gypsy Travellers reflect beliefs in the transformation of the body and the risk of pollution at the death of an individual Gypsy. Non-Gypsies or *gorgios* are brought in to deal with the pollution of death: ideally, a person should die in hospital. Suggestions of the extraction of organs for transplant into others are considered deeply threatening. *Gorgios* lay out the body which is brought back to the camp for open display over several days while fellow-Travellers congregate to pay their respects. Since the dominant non-travelling society monopolizes graveyards, the Gypsies go through a church funeral in order to gain access to graves. When Okely attended funerals, the events were seen as important rituals and as a final farewell attended by relatives of the deceased and many other Gypsies, but, because the groups were largely non-literate, the hymns and other details of the church service were largely talked through.

Ideally, deceased Gypsies are buried alongside relatives. The graves, marked by the final names of the dead, are places to visit regularly. The ghost of the dead, the *mulo*, may be threatening if the right ceremony has not been held. Cremation, for example, would be felt to effect the uncertain displacement and dispersal of the dead who may take on characteristics of the gorgio and, for example, become unpredictable, menacing and polluted. If a gypsy dies in his or her trailer caravan, it is regarded as being especially polluted and is either burned or otherwise disposed of. Moreover, the last camp occupied by the deceased must be abandoned by the close kin.

There seems to be no afterlife for English, if not other, Gypsies, so the dead are not buried in anticipation of any Christian hope. Rather, the body must be pinned down in space; the deceased has ceased to, and must cease from, travelling. Similar emphasis on burial is found among the Manus in France (Williams, 1993). The tombs are described as perhaps the only permanent and visible signs of Gypsies in *gorgio* space and are regularly visited and regarded as important places for silent remembrance and respect for the dead. Trinkets and decorations linked to the deceased are often visible.

In Eastern and Central Europe, Elena Marushiakova has recorded elaborate tombs (personal correspondence). In 2002 she was shown a large tomb in which the personal laptop computer of the wealthy and prestigious Rom had been placed. Evidence concerning Gypsies in western and eastern Europe reveals the practice of either the destruction or concealment of the property of the dead. Although the body must never be burned and cremated, ideally, their property should be burned or otherwise disposed of. Relatives of Manus Gypsies in France may retain a few items, but these are regarded as private and special and usually to be kept from public gaze (Williams, 1993).

The Vlach Roma in Hungary also bury their dead in tombs and, although they have little respect for the priests who conduct the burial service, they see such *gajes* (non-Gypsies), as in the English case, as vital for gaining access to burial space. At death the soul and the body have to be separated so that the body can be secretly placed in the ground. Then the dead Rom will not return as a restless ghost (*mulo*) (Stewart, 1997: 218).

The Slovenka Roma in Italy have large tombs with statues and mosaics. As with the English Gypsies, the body must remain intact. In life, parts of the body must not undergo modifications. At death, to burn a body would be equivalent to burning a *mulo* (Piasere, personal correspondence). Although some researchers, (for example, Marushiakova, personal correspondence) assert that, in some Roma groups, there are no bodily pollution beliefs and practices, there nonetheless is the same rejection of cremation and of the scattering of the bodily remains. Tombs are the right place for the dead, and further research might throw light on the bodily meaning of such burial places. Nevertheless, among many Roma and Gypsies, there is a widespread philosophy of the body, which is subject to regulation in life through beliefs about pollution that emphasize the boundary between non-Gypsy and Gypsy. At death, the body is regarded as polluted and the ghost of the deceased as potentially threatening. For this reason, cremation and the implicit scattering of the polluted body are rejected.
Judith Okely

References

Okely, J. (1983), *The Traveller-Gypsies*, Cambridge: Cambridge University Press.

Piasere, L. (1984), *Mare Roma: Categories humaines e structure social: Une contribution a l`ethnologie Tsigane*, Paris: Etudes et documents balkaniques, no.6.

Stewart, M. (1997), *The Time of the Gypsies*, Boulder, CO: Westview Press.

Williams, P. (1993), *Nous, on n´en parle pas: les vivants et les morts chez les Manouches*, Paris: Editions de la Maison des Sciences de l'Homme.

H

HADEN, SIR FRANCIS SEYMOUR

Francis Seymour Haden (1818–1910) began his career as a surgeon and member and then fellow of the Royal College of Surgeons, but gained greater fame as an etcher and as an opponent of cremation. Haden's fame regarding the latter stemmed from his 1875 letters to *The Times* proposing what came to be known as the 'Earth to Earth' system. Haden believed that the earth possessed vast capacities as a purifying agent and was the 'natural' receptacle for decaying corpses. Considering himself a burial reformer, he argued that if people were buried soon after death (also reducing the funeral ceremony) in perishable containers, the earth would require little assistance and graves could consequently be re-used many times.

While never stating it outright, Haden felt a great revulsion toward cremation, revealing to *The Times* that he devised his system only to answer the cremationists, although he ironically continued to see cremation as merely an elitist fad. His prime motivation being antipathy towards cremation perhaps explains his failure to organize a successful 'Earth to Earth Society', although he also won little praise for insisting that parliament outlaw any method of disposal other than his. Haden did get the London Necropolis Company interested enough to produce a perishable coffin, but London municipal officials found that his coffins were too expensive for pauper graves. He also cooperated with the Church of England's burial reform group but became angered when that body became infiltrated by those sympathetic to cremation. By the time he testified before the Select Committee on Death Certification in 1893, sanitary science did not share the same faith in the earth's purifying power, and he focused more on denouncing cremation as 'an incentive to crime'. Haden also appeared before the Home Office committee looking into regulating cremation after the passage of the Cremation Act of 1902, but he could only plead again that the task was impossible and thus cremation should be declared illegal. His ideal of a 25-year turnover of burial grounds, however, remains largely unpopular, although some cremation memorials have shorter rental periods than this. **Liza Kazmier**

References

Cremation: Regulations under S.7 Cremation Act, 1902 (1903–08), London: Public Records Office, HO/10249/B38626.

Haden, Francis Seymour (1875), *Earth to Earth: A Plea for a More Rational Observation of the Conditions Essential to the Proper Burial of the Dead*, London: Earth to Earth Society. British Library (7404.a.51).

Haden, Francis Seymour (1892), *Cremation, An Incentive to Crime: A Plea for Legislation*, a paper read at the Society of Arts, 23 November 1892 (2nd edn), London: Edward Stanford.

Jalland, Pat (1996), *Death in the Victorian Family*, Oxford: Oxford University Press (especially Chapter 9 'Funeral Reform and the Cremation Debate').

Jalland, Pat (1999), 'Victorian Death and its Decline: 1850–1918', in Peter C. Jupp and Clare Gittings (eds), *Death in England: An Illustrated History*, Manchester: Manchester University Press.

Select Committee on Death Certification (1893), *First and Second Reports from the Select Committee on Death Certification; together with the Proceedings of the Committee, Minutes of Evidence, appendix, and index*, London: HMSO: 190-96. (Haden was examined on 2 June 1893.)

The Times, 2 June 1910.

HANHAM CREMATIONS

The Hanham cremations comprise three English cremations that took place in a purpose-built crematorium at Manston House, near Sturminster Newton, Dorset, on 8 and 9 October 1882 and 5 December 1883. Manston House was the home of Captain Thomas Barnabas Hanham, JP, chairman of the Sturminster Board of Guardians, and a very active freemason. The cremation on 8 October was of his third wife (who was also his deceased first wife's sister); that on 9 October of his mother. Since their deaths in 1876 and 1877 respectively, their bodies had rested in a small mausoleum at Manston House. Both had desired to be cremated.

At a meeting from which Sir Henry Thompson was absent, the council of the Cremation Society agreed to the use of the society's crematorium at Woking for these cremations. But when Thompson learned of this, he resigned from the council. Other members of the Council who had previously been unaware of Thompson's opposition also resigned. They withdrew their resignations, however, and were readmitted to the Council when it was agreed that the crematorium at Woking would not be used until assurance was received from the Home Secretary that those involved would not be prosecuted. This assurance was never forthcoming. Despite this, one member of the council, William Robinson, the horticulturalist, did assist Hanham with the cremations.

When Hanham himself died on 27 November 1883, another crematorium was constructed, incorporating improvements suggested by the former cremations. At the time of Hanham's death the freemasons' *Book of Constitutions* was being revised. One particular amendment was intended to put an end to the use of masonic rituals and display at funerals. Hanham was opposed to this change. On the day before the meeting of the Grand Lodge which approved the change, a full masonic funeral was conducted at Manston. After the funeral Hanham's body was placed in the mausoleum. In the evening, after most of those who had attended the funeral had departed, his body was removed and cremated. Despite the Home Office's threat made to the Cremation Society that anyone involved in cremating a body at the society's crematorium at Woking would be prosecuted, no one involved in any of the Hanham cremations was prosecuted.

Hanham had adopted the two sons of his third wife by a former marriage. One of these, John Castleman Swinburne-Hanham became secretary of the Cremation Society in 1888 on the death of William Eassie and, shortly afterwards, married the daughter of Sir Thomas Spencer Wells, one of the signatories of the Declaration of 1874. **Stephen White**

See also Cremation Society of Great Britain; Robinson; Thompson.

References

Ashby, Bro. J.F. (1995), 'Death and the Freemason', *Transactions of the Quatuor Coronati Lodge*, 108: 11–47.

Comyns Leach, J. (1884), *Cremation: A Lecture*, London: Balloon Society of Great Britain.

'Crematorium Recently Built and Used at Manston Dorsetshire, December 1883', *Building News*, 21 December 1883, 56.

'Grand Masonic Funeral. Cremation of the First Modern English Cremationist', *Western Gazette*, 7 December 1884.

Robinson, William (1889), *Cremation and Urn-Burial; or The Cemeteries of the Future*, London: Cassell & Company, 113–30.

HAWEIS, HUGH REGINALD

The Revd H.R. Haweis (1838–1901) served as one of the first members of the Cremation Society of England, joining 15 others in signing Sir Henry Thompson's original declaration in favour of cremation on 13 January, 1874. Haweis served as a Church of England minister in London, being the incumbent of St James, Marylebone where he was popular for his preaching. A published author, he was also a violinist and an authority on music.

As a cremation advocate, he is best known for his throwing a thin guise of fiction on his treatise, which he called *Ashes to Ashes: A Cremation Prelude*, which first appeared in 1874 and was reprinted in 1875. In his didactic novel, the hero, Francis Le Normand, a doctor and cremation advocate, convinces his female love and a new friend, a cleric, of cremation's virtues. Yet he dies after catching a patient's fever, and his body endures a humiliating, tastelessly showy, but hypocritical burial as arranged by his estranged family, who forbid the fiancée from attending any of the services. The display includes all the stereotypical Victorian touches: ostrich feathers, hat bands, kid leather gloves and a deep grave where the bearers, after dropping the coffin, lower it until the mourners hear a splash of water. When the friend returns to the grave, he finds it empty, and realizes that Le Normand has been turned out of his coffin and abused, thanks to 'graveyard management'.

Haweis argued that disenchanting the world with its false sentiments surrounding burial was the first step toward making people adopt cremation, a belief that the first generation of cremationists generally endorsed. Haweis' wife, Mary, also an accomplished author, was cremated in 1898 according to her own wish. **Liza Kazmier**

See also Cremation Society of Great Britain.

References.

The Concise Dictionary of National Biography: From Earliest Times to 1985, Vol. 2, Oxford: Oxford University Press, 1992, 1354.

Haweis, Hugh Reginald (1875), *Ashes to Ashes, A Cremation Prelude*, London: Daldy, Ibister & Co.

The Times, 30 January 1901.

Transactions of the Cremation Society.

HAZEMANN, DR ROBERT HENRI

Having studied in Paris and the USA, Robert Hazemann (1897–1976) became a medical practitioner, then general health inspector (*inspecteur général de la santé*) and, in 1936, a cabinet member of the French Ministry of Health (*chef de Cabinet du Ministre de la Santé*). A member of both the Superior Council of Hygiene (*Conseil Supérieur de l'Hygiène*) and the Department of Hygiene of the League of Nations, he was also a consultant for the World Health Organization. He was also an energetic writer of articles on various aspects of town planning and health.

Hazemann's involvement in the French cremation movement began when he joined the Paris Cremation Society in 1935, becoming, in 1943, its general secretary and then its president five years later. Holding this position until 1972, he was also president of the French Cremation Federation for a similar period (1948–1973). As a versatile linguist of high standing in international health service circles, he was a natural choice for the post of president of the International Cremation Federation. Elected in 1951, he held the position until 1957. This was the first time in the history of the ICF that one person had been president for two terms and was an indication of his importance within the international cremation movement. He was an honorary member of the ICF from 1960.

When able to influence public policy, he took a great interest in all matters concerning cremation, including the transportation of urns and corpses and the disposal of ashes. Perhaps his most significant single achievement was his letter on cremation, written with the priest Fr Riquet, to the pope in 1953: many, himself included, claimed that the letter, which used mainly practical arguments, went a long way towards convincing the Vatican, albeit a decade later, that cremation posed no type of threat whatsoever to the Catholic Church. Ill-health forced him to curtail his cremationist activities in 1973. **Lewis H. Mates**

See also France.

References

Hazemann, R.H. (1972), 'The Social and Cultural Aspect of Cremation', paper presented at the ICF Congress, Grenoble, CRE/D4/1972/10.

'Interview with Robert Hazemann' in *Le Monde*, reproduced in *Pharos*, 38(4), 1972: 123.

Obituary of Robert Hazemann, in *Pharos*, 43(1), 1977: 42–43.

Simond, Jean (1972), 'Cremation in France', paper presented at the ICF Congress, Grenoble.

HERETICS

See also Introduction; Early Modern Western Europe.

HERTZ, ROBERT

Hertz (1881–1915) was a French sociologist/anthropologist whose theoretical contribution to an understanding of cremation is particularly important because of the distinction he drew between primary and secondary aspects of funerary rites. His important study of 1907, 'Contribution to the Study of the Collective Representation of Death', did not become widely known until its English publication in 1960 (Davies, 2000). For Hertz, each individual was a kind of symbol of society itself, which meant that the individual's death posed a kind of problem for society. He argued that funeral rites involve a change in a person's status from possessing an identity as a living member of society to being, for example, an ancestor, or one of the 'dead' members of society. The main value of his work lay in his contention that funeral rites often involved two major phases that brought this change about. The first he described as the 'wet' phase involving the decay of the corpse which might occur through temporary burial, and the second he termed the 'dry' phase involving separate rites for the dry

bones. The wet/decay phase involved a change in the identity of the dead as they relinquished their status as a member of the living community. The dry/bones phase witnessed a new identity, as the dead became part of the afterlife realm as in the case of ancestors. More importantly, he applied this double schematic to cremation, claiming that the wet phase applied to the rapid process of cremation itself whereas the dry phase related to the rites conducted with the cremated remains. He was insistent on the fact that cremation by itself was never sufficient as a funeral rite: it always demanded a second rite. All of this was based on the cultural life of tribal peoples in south-east Asia and not on Europe where, at the time, cremation was a novelty.

Closely related to this double process affecting the dead person was the ongoing process of adapting to bereavement on the part of the living. Hertz conceived of grief as the way in which the survivor comes to terms not only with parting from the pre-existing relationship with the dead person but also with a new kind of relationship with the transformed 'dead' person. For Hertz, both sociological and psychological ideas merge into each other. He was, for example, very alert to the 'internal partings' experienced in bereavement. Yet, he maintained, life has to go on because society itself always goes on, irrespective to what happens to its individual members. But it is in and through individuals that ongoing life is achieved. This is reflected, for example, both in a sense of revulsion that the living might, initially, feel for the dead and then in a sense of 'reverent courage' that takes its place. Hertz is also very conscious of the sense of transition and change underlying all these sociological and psychological elements. **Douglas J. Davies**

References

Davies, Douglas J. (2000), 'Robert Hertz: The Social Triumph over Death', *Mortality*, 5(1): 97–102.

Hertz, Robert (1960) 'A Contribution to the Study of the Collective Representation of Death', in Rodney and Claudia Needham (eds), *Death and the Right Hand*, New York: Free Press. Originally published as 'Contribution à une étude sur la representation collective de la mort', in *Année Sociologique*, 10, 1907: 48–137.

Parkin, Robert (1996), *The Dark Side of Humanity, The Work of Robert Hertz and its Legacy*, Netherlands: Harwood Academic Publishers.

HILL, JOE

Joe Hill was born as Joel Hagglund (and was also known as Joseph Hillstrom) in Gavle, a Swedish town north of Stockholm, on 7 October 1879. In 1902 he emigrated to New York City. Becoming an itinerant labourer, he worked in the mines and lumber industry, moving to Cleveland, Ohio, and then to San Francisco. Around 1910, while working on the docks in San Pedro, California, Hill joined the Industrial Workers of the World (IWW or 'Wobblies') a revolutionary trade union. He soon became highly active within the IWW, travelling widely agitating and organizing workers. He began writing songs about the life of the working man, such as 'Rebel Girl' and 'Casey Jones'. Published in the IWW's *Little Red Song Book*, many of these songs became world-famous. In 'The Preacher and the Slave', a parody of the hymn 'In the Sweet Bye and Bye', Hill coined the phrase 'pie in the sky': 'You will eat, bye and bye/ In that glorious land above the sky/ Work and pray/ Live on hay/ You'll get pie in the sky when you die.'

In 1913 Joe Hill went to Utah and began working in the Park City mines. The following year, and in the context of bitter struggles over free speech in the state, he was accused of the murder of a Salt Lake City store owner. Hill's supporters regarded the interests of capitalists, especially those of the Utah copper industry, as guilty of conspiring to have him eliminated. While direct evidence of this allegation did not surface, there was clear and extensive hostility towards the IWW, and Joe Hill from the ruling class and the flimsy circumstantial evidence presented by the prosecution at Hill's trial should never had led to his execution. Despite interventions from President Woodrow Wilson, deaf and blind humanitarian Helen Keller and an international solidarity campaign by working-class organisations to save him, Hill was executed by firing squad on 19 November 1915. His body was taken to Chicago where over 30 000 people attended his funeral procession and eulogies were read in nine languages. He was then cremated. As Hill had said to fellow IWW activist 'Big Bill' Haywood that he 'didn't want to be caught dead in Utah', his ashes were sent to IWW groups in every other American state.

Written just before he was executed Joe Hill's will, as well as being a reflection of his political outlook, shows his support for cremation:

My will is easy to decide,
For there is nothing to divide,
My kin don't need to fuss and moan –
'Moss does not cling to a rolling stone'.
My body? Ah, If I could choose,
I would to ashes it reduce,
And let the merry breezes blow
My dust to where some flowers grow.
Perhaps some fading flower then
Would come to life and bloom again.
This is my last and final will,
Good luck to all of you, Joe Hill.

Lewis H. Mates

References

Foner, Philip S. (ed.) (1965), *The Letters of Joe Hill*, New York: Oak.

Foner, Philip S. (1965) *The Case of Joe Hill*, New York: International Publishers.

'Joe Hill' in 'Wikipedia, the free encyclopaedia', at: http://en.wikipedia.org/wiki/ Joe_Hill (accessed August 2004).

'Red Robin's Red Channels, Left Links, and Proletarian Places' at: http://members. tripod.com/~RedRobin2/index-42.html (accessed August 2004).

Sillitoe, Linda (nd), 'Joe Hill and the IWW', at: http://historytogo. utah.gov/joehilliww.html (accessed August 2004).

Smith, Gibbs M. (1969), *Joe Hill*, Salt Lake City: University of Utah.

Smith, Gibbs M., (2004), 'A Brief Biography of Joe Hill', at: http://www.newyouth. com/archives/music/joehillbio.asp (accessed August 2004).

HINDUISM

Hinduism is of considerable importance for cremation as it has one of the longest and most complex traditions of this mode of treating the dead and of relating them to an overarching theory of life and death. Accordingly, included here are four contributions: three focused on traditional and modern aspects of Hindu cremation centred on the archetypical site of Benares, and one exploring aspects of traditional rites as developed within a contemporary British context. **Douglas J. Davies**

ANTIESTHI: TRADITIONAL HINDU CREMATION

To speak of cremation in Hinduism entails engaging with the philosophical and mystical dimensions of death. Indeed, cremation is more than a social funerary practice, for Hinduism perceives cremation as a fire-sacrifice and as a self-sacrifice and often calls it *dah sanskar*, the sacrament of fire or *antim-sanskar*, the last transforming ritual of the life cycle. Learned Hindus often call it *antiesthi*, literally 'the last sacrifice'. In the ritual literature of Hinduism, it is a sacrificial offering of the self to the gods. Sacrifice is a ritual tearing of life out of death, themselves two facets of a single, never-ending cycle. Through it, both the world and the sacrificer are reborn.

Cremation is an act of creation and, consequently, is a source of fecundity. The model of sacrifice structures not only the rituals that Hindus perform, but also much of their thinking about death and, in particular, about a good death (Parry, 1994: 189). Because Hindus believe in the rebirth and reincarnation of souls, death is not a great calamity, not an end of all, but a natural process in the existence of the soul as a separate entity; in death, the soul reassembles its sources, adjusts its course and returns again to the earth to continue its journey. In Hinduism, death is a temporary cessation of physical activity, a necessary means of recycling resources and energy, and an opportunity for the *jiva* (the incarnating part) to review its programmes and policies. The person is never entirely new when born, and never entirely gone when dead.

The Brahamanical sacrifice itself is a fire-sacrifice, and the sacrificer's last oblation to the fire is his own body (Aiyangar, 1913: 14). When a person expires, the corpse must be washed, anointed with ghee (clarified butter), wrapped in a white cloth, perfumed and decked with garlands. A piece of gold should be placed into the mouth and in both nostrils as a means through which the body may be worshipped. This worship of the deceased is what it is called *shava pujan* in Banaras, where being cremated is believed to end the cycle of incarnation. Like the sacrificial victim, the corpse is itself treated as a being of great sacredness, even as a deity (Parry, 1994:179). It is purified and ornamented before being placed on the altar, the pyre itself. Cremations are, then, symbolically constructed

as a sacrificial offering of the self to the gods. The site of cremation is prepared as a place for fire-sacrifice and is purified by its consecration with holy water. Cremation is not only the last sacrifice, but is an act of self-sacrifice. Through it, as presented in the sacred text, Satapatha Brahmana, Prajapati, primal man, created the cosmos by the sacrificial dismembering of his own body. His reconstruction was achieved through rituals performed by the gods. So the son reconstructs a bodily substance for the soul of his deceased parent.

The offering is itself the act of creation, and therefore generates life-energy. The Doms (formerly described as the 'untouchables', who make their living from their work in the cremation grounds of Banaras), besides being funerary workers, also act as mediators of the process of tearing life out of death. They attend patients suffering from fatal illnesses such as leukaemia and cancer. On the very top of the corpses that are being cremated, the Doms cook bread prepared by the patients, then give it back to them. They believe that the bread has absorbed the life-energy liberated by the corpse during the process of cremation. The assimilation of this energy through the digestion of the bread regenerates the body, liberating it from the dead energy that created the mortal illness. Gold (1988: 201) reports that Rajasthani pilgrims to Hardwar make a point of taking Ganges water from the very spot at which they immerse the ashes they bring. The water is then carried home, where it is drunk by the bereaved group which thereby 'reincorporates the life-substance of the death' contained in the water as it is contained in the bread. In Hindu culture, man is what he eats. This notion is intimately associated with death and food, which is transformed by digestion in the blood, the substance of life. Cremation is seen as a process of transformation, like cooking.

In Hindu law, the one who inherits is charged with the duty of performing the obsequies for the deceased. Indeed, in a case of disputed inheritance, courts favour the claimant who has performed the mortuary rituals and there are chief mourners who have a photographer record these rituals, as proof of their role. The day after cremation, the chief mourner begins a ritual that takes ten days, symbolizing the ten lunar months of gestation. The parent who has nurtured the child will be nurtured by his child who liberates the deceased from his ghostly condition and ensures that he attains a 'good state' after death. In this ten-day ceremony, colloquially called *pindadana*, the mourner-son offers *pindas*, balls made of rice. These represent the bodily substance of the departed. Each *pinda* constitutes a different part of the new body. The *Preta Manjari*, a death-ritual prescription manual followed by the ritual priests of north India, says that the head is made on the first day; the eyes, nose and ears on the second; the neck, arms and chest on the third; sexual organs on the fourth; legs and feet on the fifth; the vital organs on the sixth; veins on the seventh; nails, teeth and hair on the eighth; semen on the ninth; and hunger and thirst on the tenth. By the reconstruction of his father's body, the son repays his debt to his father by giving him birth in a new and higher dimension, that of the ancestors. This newly created ancestor in turn confers fertility and material prosperity. Although *pindadana* should, theoretically, be performed in ten days, such are the demands of modern life that, in fact, it is generally performed all at once, on the tenth day, for 'practical reasons'. Nevertheless, there are still a significant number of people, mainly in rural areas, who perform it daily, early in the morning before going to work.

This ritual ends the period of greatest pollution and the most dangerous period that follows death in that, before being integrated into the ancestors' world, the deceased's soul can be a threat to the living relatives, as it is difficult for it to detach itself from this world. Besides the sacred entity that is self-donated to the fire-sacrifice, there is also the 'sacrificer's profane and mortal being' that is dispatched by the fire, conferring a pollution characteristic to cremation. According to a somewhat esoteric level of Hinduism, death occurs not at the cessation of physiological functioning but during cremation. The vital breath is released by the heat of the pyre and climbs into the cosmos. The smoke of the pyre floating towards the sky is seen by Hindus as a metaphor of that release and integration. It is considered a 'good death'. For some of those well versed in texts, death pollution begins when the vital breath is released; therefore, it is cremation that spreads pollution and not the body. But, for others, pollution begins at the moment of physiological demise. The former see the corpse as a purified oblation to the gods; for the latter, the body is merely an impure carcass. Nevertheless, in Hindu social life, death pollution, and its associated natural and supernatural danger, begins at the moment of physiological decease. However, it is clear that cremation is also considered to impart pollution, since participants in the funeral ceremony must undergo rites of purification when they return to their homes from the cremation ground. In India, cremation grounds are marked off from the town. **Mariana Caixeiro**

References

Aiyangar, B.N. (1913), 'Funeral Ceremonies', *Quarterly Journal of the Mythic Society*, 4: 13–25.

Biardeau, M. and Malamoud, C. (1976), *Le sacrifice dans l'Inde ancienne*, Paris: Presses Universitaires de France.

Gold, Anne G. (1988), *Fruitful Journeys: The Ways of Rajasthani Pilgrims*, Berkeley: University of California Press.

Pret Manjari (2032 according to the Hindu calendar Samvat), compiled by Sudama Misr Shastri and revised by Mannala Abhimanyu.

The Garuda Purana (nd/1980), Ancient Indian Tradition and Mythology Series, 12(e. 14), New Delhi: Motilal Banarsidass.

BANARAS AND THE GANGES

Banaras, a city where energy is transformed into culture and holiness, is one of the most sacred places of Hinduism where thousands of pilgrims arrive daily from all over India. They come to worship divinities and bathe in the Ganges, or to take a relative's ashes and perform rituals for the dead or for the ancestors. The most pious come to die in the city, as they believe that, through Shiva's grace, they can be liberated from the cycle of reincarnations. From its front along the River Ganges, Banaras has witnessed the history of Indian civilization as it evolved in north India, and has always been a seat of learning and religious authority. It has attracted disciples, philosophers, pilgrims and sages for more than two-and-a-half millennia. Throughout the centuries, disciples have encountered, in its monasteries, eminent founders of important religious and philosophic movements, such as Buddha, Mahavira (the founder of Jainism), Guru Nanak (the founder of Sikhism), Shankara and Pantanjali.

Like a loved one, the sacred city is called by

many names that express its various powers and attributes and reveal the dimensions of its sacred authority. As a *thirta* – or sacred place of Hindu travel meaning 'ford' or 'crossing places' – the city is known as Kashi, the most ancient name, used nearly 3000 years ago to refer to the capital of the kingdom of the same name. There, according to Hindus, one's prayers are heard more quickly, one's petitions more readily fulfilled and one's rituals more likely to bring manifold blessings. Kashi, in Hindu imagination, is a place that gathers together the whole of India. All the gods and sacred places are represented there, although Shiva is its main deity.

Varanasi is another ancient name, found in both Buddhist and Hindu stories about the city. It sits between the Varuna, which flows into the Ganges in the north, and the Asi, which joins the Ganges in the south. Independent India adopted this name, although the citizens continue to call themselves Banarsis. In both British and Muslim India, the city was known as Benares, a corruption of the Pali name, Baranasi, and this is what it continues to be called by Westerners today. Banaras is also the *Mahasamashana*, 'the great cremation ground'. It is at Manikarnika *ghat*, the most important cremation ground, that the genesis of the universe occurred at the beginning of time, and it is also the place where the corpse of creation will burn at time's end (Parry, 1994: 14).

It is the interrelationship of Kashi, Lord Shiva and the River Ganges that makes the magnitude of Banaras. Every morning as the sun is rising, men and women move down through the ghats, the 'landing place along the river', to bathe in the Ganges. They crowd into temples with their hands full of flowers and sweets destined for a divine image. The Ganges is the River of Heaven, and its water is holy. It is *amrit*, 'the nectar of immortality'. It purifies and sacralizes the corpses that are bathed in the river before being placed on the pyre. The river is revered as goddess and mother – Banarsis call it Gangaji. All along the river, Hindus bathe in her and take up her water cupped in their hands and pour it back as an offering to ancestors and to the gods. They present to the river, as to a deity, offerings of flowers and small, clay oil-lamps. On festival occasions, they go in boats, leaving behind garlands of flowers to adorn the goddess river, they sip her water and when they return to their homes, they take with them brass vessels of her water. **Mariana Caixeiro**

References

Eck, D. (1978), *Banaras: City of Light*, London: Routledge and Kegan Paul.

Kane, P.V. (1941–74), *History of Dharmashastra*, Poona: Bhandakar Oriental Research Institute.

Kashi Kanda (nd), compiled and provided in Hindi by Baikunthnath Upadhyay, Varanasi, Shri Bhragu Prakashan.

Parry, J.P. (1994), *Death in Banaras*, Cambridge: Cambridge University Press.

THE ELECTRIC CREMATORIUM (*VIDYUT SHAV DAHH GRIHA*) OF BANARAS (*VARANASI*)

Varanasi is the holy city of Hinduism, better known in the West as Benares, and among its citizens as Banaras. The pious Hindus call it Kashi, the city of light, the abode of Shiva. It is one of the most ancient cities in the world. Famous for its rewards to whoever dies there, Banaras has as its motto 'Death in Kashi is liberation', the religious assertion that the sacred specialists make when they negotiate their services with the pilgrims. Kashi is also considered a microcosm of India. To go on a pilgrimage to Kashi is equal to going on a pilgrimage to all the *tirtha*s or places of pilgrimage in India. With all these charms, facilities and benefits it is not difficult to imagine the population of the city fluctuating periodically due to the daily influx of pilgrims that come from all over India. They come in simple pilgrimage, or to cremate their relatives, or to perform rituals to their ancestors. Hindus believe that, if they die or are cremated in Kashi, they are liberated from the cycle of reincarnation. The main income of the city comes from commercial activities directly or indirectly concerned with death, rituals and the goods that pilgrims take back home.

At the end of the 1970s, negotiations took place between the central government of India and the local authorities of Banaras to establish conditions for the building of an electric crematorium in this traditional cremation centre, following similar projects in other urban centres of the country within the Ganga Action Plan (a governmental organization to control the pollution of the river Ganges). The construction of an electric crematorium was aimed at stimulating ecological awareness in terms of decreasing the pollution of the River Ganges by corpses, and reducing deforestation, as well as introducing new social models common to industrialized societies, such as saving time and money, as cremation was expected to last 25 minutes from the moment the corpse entered the cremator until the relative receives the ashes.

From the first negotiations until the start of construction at Harishchandra Ghat in 1988, there was strong political, social and religious opposition to the scheme. The principal opponents were the leader of the Doms (who, in caste terms, had formerly been called the 'untouchables' and who are believed to have an important role in death rituals because they hold the sacred fire to set light to the pyre without which liberation is not possible) and the wealthy and influential president of the Kashi Tirth Purohit Sabha (the association of pilgrim-priests). Although they cited traditional reasons as the basis for their opposition, there was also the issue of financial disturbance to their businesses, leading them to organize protests against the construction of the crematorium, originally planned for the Manikarnika Ghat, the main cremation ground. The principal argument of the president of the pilgrim-priests' association was the technical impossibility of stopping the cremation to perform the ritual of *kapalakrya*, which, for him, was the most important in the Hindu tradition. This ritual consists of breaking the skull with a stick towards the end of cremation. However, although the ritual is described in the ritual literature, it is not usually performed nowadays, having been replaced by another that takes the same name and consists of throwing on a catalytic substance that increases the power of the fire and makes the skull burst. But as the president was not concerned with social reality, and did not usually go to the cremation ground, he was not unaware of such changes, and based his argument on the literature. In the end, he was persuaded by the argument that the electric crematorium was for poor people who, because of lack of money, used to throw the bodies into river Ganges, and for unclaimed corpses. In both these cases, it was impossible to perform the *kapalakrya* ritual anyway.

The crematorium was finally inaugurated in January 1989, but was in operation only until November, as neighbouring residents complained of the smoke. The chimneys were extended from five metres (15 feet) to 11 metres (35 feet), and the crematorium reopened, although the same complaints continued. The building, in reinforced concrete, has two floors. If the electric power is run at the full 240V, one complete cremation takes only 25 minutes, but this never happens, because the voltage is always lower, so cremation takes more than one hour. The temperature of the furnaces should be 630°C, but it never goes beyond 400°C. The cost of the cremation was 100 rupees in the first five years, with an increase of 20 rupees in 1995. This was against nearly 1000 rupees or even more for a traditional cremation, depending on the individuals' bargaining skills.

The crematorium works 24 hours per day in three shifts, each with six workers. In total, there are 21 employees: an electrical engineer, three electricians, four operators, three watchmen, four orderlies and six sweepers. During its first ten years of existence, the crematorium never worked at full capacity, because the maintenance budget was insufficient. The crematorium or *bidjli-vala* (literally, 'the electric one') as it is known among the service castes who work on the cremation grounds, has year-round functioning problems related to low voltage, or power cuts, or lack of replacement refractory bricks. This situation causes long queues of bodies waiting to be cremated. Sometimes the crematorium spends all day idle because of electrical power cuts, and for most of the year it works with only one furnace.

The crematorium tries to continue the Hindu traditional death rituals by being located on the banks of the River Ganges, and although its construction was intended to introduce new environmental ideas and new social models, tradition demanded changes to the initial project, such as orienting the furnaces north–south to allow for the practice of placing the body with its feet to the south. In the same way, the division of labour followed tradition, with a visible differentiation between the employees, even though the workers all belonged to the modern social category described in the Mandal Report (an officially inventoried category of people consisting of around 30 per cent of the Indian population on whom is conferred a special status in a variety of contexts), as 'backward classes' and 'other scheduled castes and tribes'. The Doms clean the place, push the trolley bearing the corpse into the furnaces and hand over the ashes at the end of the cremation, while the other employees refuse any kind of work that involves close contact with the body. The orderly, the electrician, the operator and the watchman maintain a much closer and more preferential relationship between themselves. A *mahapatra* (a category of ritualistic priests, in the lowest rank of the Brahman hierarchy that officiates from the moment of death until the ritual of *sapindakarana*, when the soul of the deceased becomes part of the world of ancestors) is also employed to perform the necessary death rituals.

The Hindus who use the electric crematorium come mainly from the villages outside Banaras and even outside the district. They say that they prefer it because it is cheaper and faster than the traditional method, but, in fact, they often have had to go back home without even seeing their relatives cremated. During the monsoons, and especially during very hot weather, the death-rate increases, and if both furnaces are not working, or if the voltage is quite low, it triples the time needed for cremation, and long queues of corpses form. Taking advantage of this situation, contractors then appear. They negotiate with relatives a price for the corpse to be cremated in the traditional way that is lower than if this method had been chosen straight away, even though it is twice that of electric cremation. The contract includes all the services: wood for the pyre and its building, fire from the Doms and their work. In this situation, a considerable number of bodies are given to contractors and are cremated together. The quantity of wood used to cremate the corpses under contract is often insufficient for complete cremation. As a result, they are thrown into the River Ganges half-cremated, negating one of the crematorium's principal aims: to avoid corpses in the river.

Less than 15 per cent of crematorium users are from the city, as initially the crematorium was advertised as being for the use of unclaimed corpses and the poor. Those who use it are socially stigmatized, since death is always an opportunity to demonstrate to others one's social status. Even so, although electric cremation is not costly, tradition is strong, and the corpses of children and *sadus* continue to be thrown into the 'holy waters' of the River Ganges.

The ashes remaining at the end of the day are collected and sieved in the river to recover any kind of metal that could have accompanied the deceased to the cremation, such as gold from earrings or teeth or other metal prostheses. It is believed that to keep a tiny amount of gold near the body, on the ear or nose, is auspicious, because it purifies. **Mariana Caixeiro**

HINDU CREMATIONS IN BRITAIN

Hindu cremation has to be viewed as part of a process that not only disposes of the body, but also ensures the progression of the soul to the next world or to rebirth in this one. However, in the diaspora, the time, place and structure of this process has had to change radically because of bureaucracy, legal requirements and problems in arranging rapid cremations. Traditionally, death for Hindus is a process lasting at least 12 days. The process in India can be seen in terms of nine stages:

1 preparation for death;
2 moment of death;
3 preparation of the body;
4 *pinda-dana* (offerings of rice balls) and procession to the cremation ground;
5 cremation;
6 collection of bones and ashes;
7 *shraddha*, the tenth- to twelfth-day rituals;
8 generation of *sapindi-karana*;
9 the annual rituals.

(These nine stages are a development of Evison's (1989) six stages.)

The rituals are an interesting illustration of Van Gennep's (1960) model of rites of passage. There is a seamless flow of ritual activity from before the death up to the cremation (rites of separation), followed by ten days in which a new body is ritually created for the disembodied ghost, *preta*. This is a liminal or transitional period of great impurity for the family, who withdraw socially. On the twelfth day (a symbolic year), a new ancestor is generated (*sapindi-karana*), followed by a ceremony legitimating the new heir. This represents Van Gennep's third stage, incorporation, when the new ancestor is incorporated into the world of ancestors, and the family is reincorporated in society. The family are in charge, with the assistance of qualified priests who direct the rituals, with strict gender divisions of activity.

Although this structure provides a socially acceptable framework for grieving and helping to make sense of death, its pattern is ruptured in Britain, where professionals take control of the dying and dead out of the family's hands. Changes in timing, location and form of funerals alter the structure of the mourning period, which now begins before the rites of separation are complete, instead of afterwards. Experienced Brahmin priests may be unavailable. Some rituals disappear and others are reinvented and condensed. Without the familiar ritual framework there is less certainty, with beliefs no longer making sense outside their original context. The twelve-day period, for example, is difficult to maintain against work obligations, but the final rites of reincorporation (*shraddha*) are still considered essential.

Rites before death have virtually disappeared. These involve preparing for death and often fasting, making specific gifts, arranging marriages of daughters/granddaughters, an act of penance, and often a ritual involving the Vaitarani cow which enables the soul to cross the terrible river of death. At death, which ideally should be at home, the dying person should be placed on the prepared floor and given Ganges water, a Tulasi leaf in the mouth, as well as a coin to pay the ferryman. In Britain most deaths occur in hospital and pandits rarely attend. A few hospitals allow the patient on to a mattress on the floor; others refuse on grounds of health and safety. Relatives may be refused an opportunity to give Ganges water, which is regarded as the most essential element, and there may be no opportunity to say prayers, chant hymns or say goodbye.

In India, the corpse is bathed and dressed, according to caste traditions, immediately after death by same-sex relatives. Purifying substances are placed on the body to prepare it as the last sacrifice (*antim sanskar*) to fire, *agni*. It is then carried on a stretcher by male relatives to the cremation ground. During the ritual procession the chief mourner – the eldest son or nearest male relative – offers balls of wheat, barley or rice (*pindas*) at strategic locations to protect the soul and the corpse from dangerous spirits (Firth, 1997: 74–76; Parry, 1994: 175–76). The cremation, which usually occurs on the same day or within 24 hours of death, is attended by some women amongst Punjabi communities but not by Gujarati women, because it is considered to be too upsetting.

In Britain the body is removed to the undertakers and bathed just before the cremation, often one week later, although in cities with a large Hindu population Asian undertakers may manage to arrange an earlier cremation. Timing depends on the space available in the crematorium and also on the availability of a registrar of deaths, especially at weekends or holidays. Laying out a refrigerated body by same-sex relatives in the impersonal surroundings of funeral director's premises creates great distress. Some families leave this to the undertaker, and simply sprinkle the body with Ganges water and say a few mantras themselves before the corpse is placed in a coffin and taken to the family home by hearse. The ritual procession has vanished, to be replaced by a hearse and sometimes a double-decker bus full of mourners going to the crematorium, after the domestic ritual. The rice-balls, if offered at all, are offered at home and placed in the coffin. The delay before the funeral raises questions about the fate of the soul, although some pandits have commented that it would not suffer if the rituals are performed with faith (Firth, 1997: 193).

Funeral rites

After the body is placed on the pyre in India, the pandit recites Sanskrit texts as the chief mourner circumambulates the body with water and then with a firebrand before lighting the pyre. In many parts of India, he may break the skull (*kapala-kriya*), halfway through the cremation, to release the soul (Firth, 1991: 70–71; 1997: 78–79; Parry, 1994: 177). Afterwards the mourners bathe and return home. The women purify the house, bathe and change. Food, prepared by relatives, is eaten for the first time since the death. At this point, mourning proper begins.

In Britain, if no pandit is available, a senior family or community member presides over rituals in the home and at the crematorium, reciting Sanskrit verses. Priests are evolving their own rituals, negotiating with each family within the constraints of time and the family tradition. There can be prolonged arguments with senior members of the community, particularly the women (Firth, 1991: 54–55; 1997: 193; Menski, 1991: 48–49). At home, the ritual contains condensed elements from the preparation of the body, the ritual procession and the pyre. As Vedic verses are recited, the coffin is opened and the mourners, led by the widow, circumambulate it with flowers, butter and herbs, placing them on the body. Incense sticks may be used as a substitute for the firebrand, but some pandits refuse to allow this on the grounds that it is an inadequate substitute (Firth, 1991: 73–74; 1997: 81–87). *Pindas* are then placed in the coffin. Viewing the body gives *darshan*, and the entire family, including children, participate. After further circumambulations, the coffin is closed and taken by hearse to the crematorium.

Gujarati women are discouraged from going to the crematorium, although younger ones increasingly do so. Panjabi women attend the service, sitting separately from the men. The service is modelled on the Western pattern, containing a few prayers and readings, and a homily intended to enlighten and comfort the mourners (Firth, 1997: 87ff.). The National Council of Hindu Temples has produced a standardized service, which is criticized by some pandits as being for the consolation of the mourners instead of the progress of the deceased.

It is impossible to circumambulate the body in most crematoria, although several new ones have Hindu and Sikh needs in mind. The chief mourner and male relatives go below and press a button, or push the coffin into the cremator. Returning home, relatives bathe and change, often at a friend's house. Other mourners sprinkle themselves with water from a bowl outside the house, and then sit with the bereaved, the men and women often in separate rooms.

In India the bones and ashes are collected on the third day and either disposed of immediately in a sacred river, or kept outside the house hanging in a pot or bag from the roof or a tree until a pilgrimage can be made to the river. This may be done before the ritual on the tenth day (below). If they can afford it, many British Hindus wish to take the ashes back to the Ganges or a sacred river. The remains may even be posted there. However, others prefer to dispose of the ashes in a river in the UK. Londoners may take a boat down to the Thames Estuary. Lord Montague of Beaulieu has allowed a stretch of his river bank to be used by members of the Swami Narayan sect.

Reincorporation

Complex rites incorporate the deceased as an ancestor and reincorporate the mourners into society. A new ethereal body is ritually formed over ten days, although the ten days are often condensed into a single ritual on the tenth day. There may be further rituals on the eleventh day, before the climactic ritual on the twelfth day, *sapindikarana*, which creates a new ancestor (Knipe, 1977; Firth, 1997: 93ff.). Arya Samajis complete their mourning in India on the fourth day with the Vedic fire ritual, *havan*. In Britain this follows cremation. The chief mourner is then given a turban by his wife's or mother's family acknowledging his new role as heir and head of the family, and the widow embarks on her new marginalized role in society.

The ancestors, now ritually located in *pitr-loka*, the abode of the ancestors, are thought of as being in heaven with God or reborn, often within the family (Firth, 1997: 40ff., 93ff.). They are in a symbiotic relationship with their descendants, giving progeny, protection and safety in return for offerings. They can be demanding and capricious. Dreams of the deceased indicate that they are unsatisfied, and relatives hasten to make offerings to pacify them. Those who have had premature or bad deaths can create great mischief. Anger against parents is taboo and it would not be appropriate to express negative feelings after death; only the best things are remembered and discussed in an effort to view the death as a good one. Further offerings are made at monthly, three- and six-monthly intervals and on the lunar year after the death, as well as during the *Pitr Paksha*, the feast of ancestors.

In Britain there is a combined, condensed ritual on the twelfth day. Its significance as an act of regeneration seems to be disappearing, and it is often seen as 'giving a send-off'. However, it remains fundamentally important and may be done instead, or in addition, in India, by proxy or when the family take the ashes back to India. Brahmins, as surrogates for the deceased, are given gifts of money, food and clothing, although some families prefer to give to charity. A number of pandits allow daughters to act as chief mourners, citing evidence in some ancient texts that this is appropriate, although this can create dissension in the community. As in India, there are further rituals for the first year, and then annually. The mourning period is abbreviated because of the need to go back to work, but also to allow auspicious rituals to take place. **Shirley Firth**

References

Evison, Gillian (1989), 'Indian Death Rituals: The Enactment of Ambivalence', unpublished DPhil thesis, University of Oxford.

Firth, Shirley (1991), 'Changing Patterns of Hindu Death Rituals in Britain' in Dermot Killingley, Werner Menski and Shirley Firth, *Hindu Ritual and Society*, Newcastle-upon Tyne: S.Y. Killingley, 52–84.

Firth, Shirley (1997), *Dying, Death and Bereavement in a British Hindu Community*, Leuven: Peeters.

Knipe, D.M. (1977), '*Sapindikarana*: The Hindu Rite of Entry into Heaven', in E. Reynolds and E.H. Waugh (eds), *Religious Encounters with Death: Insights from the History and Anthropology of Religions*, University Park and London: Pennsylvania State University, 112–24.

Menski, Werner (1991), 'Change and Continuity in Hindu Marriage Rituals', in Dermot Killingley, Werner Menski and Shirley Firth, *Hindu Ritual and Society*, Newcastle-upon Tyne: S.Y. Killingley, 32–51.

Parry, J.P. (1994), *Death in Banaras*, Cambridge University Press.

Van Gennep, Arnold (1960), *The Rites of Passage*, London: Routledge & Kegan Paul.

HOLZMEISTER, CLEMENS

This Austrian architect was born at Fulpmes, Tirol, 27 March 1886 and died at Hallein bei Salzburg, 12 June 1983. He studied architecture at Vienna's Technische Hochschule with Professors Max Ferstel, Karl König and Leopold Simony from 1906 to 1913. Influential architects and artists of the time included Otto Wagner, Josef Hoffmann, Josef Plecnik, Josef Olbrich, Gustav Klimt and the sculptor Ivan Mestrovic. Between 1919 and 1924 he taught architecture at the engineering school in Innsbruck having submitted his doctoral dissertation in 1919 at the Technische Hochschule on the virtual reconstruction of the Romanesque scheme of the abbey of Stams (Tirol). He was, subsequently, professor of architecture in Vienna, Düsseldorf (Germany) and Istanbul (Turkey).

Holzmeister's building style was greatly influenced by his Tyrolean background. The first crematorium in Austria was built at Wien-Simmering between 1921 and 1923 after the fall of the Hapsburg Monarchy and the declaration of the Austrian Republic. It was built according to Holzmeister's plans, and has served as a model for many others. Located in the remains of the walled Renaissance garden of the former Neugebäde palace, the design makes use of the windowless and crenellated outer walls of the former palace and the centuries-old garden walls and towers. Although the project is not without pathos, it is also influenced by romantic and historical ideas.

Romantically inclined, Holzmeister always placed his buildings very imaginatively in their surrounding city-landscapes and personally his design details developed in conjunction with skilled labourers and artists with a view to creating a complete work of art – indeed, he believed that architecture was still the mother of the arts. Nevertheless he also included classic principles of composition in his works. The design for a world shrine, the Cosmogral, on a ledge overlooking the St Katherine Cloister on Mount Sinai is considered to be his legacy.

Clemens Holzmeister is counted among the most influential Austrian architects of the twentieth century. His empathetic capacity combined with his understanding of theatrical productions, religious rites and celebrations has made him a renowned architect of churches, monuments, festival theatres, stage scenery and government buildings. His principal works include the State House and other buildings in Ankara (Turkey), a number of churches in Germany and Austria, cathedrals in Brazil, festival halls for the Festival of Salzburg as well as the crematorium building in Wien-Simmering. Sometimes he worked in partnership with Erich Boltenstern. **Bruno Maldoner**

See also Architects – Austrian; Boltenstern; Vienna Crematorium.

References

Gregor, J. (1953), *Clemens Holzmeister: Werke für das Theater*, Vienna: Österreichische Staatsdruckerei.

Holzmeister, C. (1927), *Entwürfe und Zeichnungen*, Vienna: Officina Vindobonensis – E. Hübsch.

Holzmeister, C. (1937), *Bauten, Entwürfe und Handzeichnungen*, Salzburg and Leipzig: Anton Pustet.

Holzmeister, C. (1951), *Kirchenbau ewig neu*, Innsbruck: Tyrolia.

Holzmeister, C. and Fahrner, R. (1955), *Bilder aus Anatolien*, Vienna: Österreichische Staatsdruckerei.

HONG KONG

Ancient cremation

As with the rest of China, the influence of Buddhism encouraged the practice of cremation in what would become Hong Kong. University of Hong Kong excavations at Chak Lap Kok and Lam Ma Island have found evidence that cremation was performed during the Tang Dynasty (618–907 AD). However, the wealthy classes, being more influenced by Confucianism tended to opt for burial, and cremation was largely rejected during the Ming Dynasty (1368–1644 AD). Consequently, by the twentieth century, burial was the majority practice. The attempted reintroduction of cremation to modern Hong Kong was initially opposed, with some citing the teachings of Confucius that, for example, the skin and hair of human beings, inherited from their parents, should not be damaged or destroyed. This philosophical tradition regarded cremation as an 'act of cruelty' (Lee, 1988a: 57; 1988b: 89).

Modern influences

Although there was no formal society to advocate cremation, there was sufficient Western influence to necessitate a crematorium for Europeans in the British colony. Built in 1899, by 1932 it had conducted some 1179 cremations of Caucasians. Other religious communities represented in twentieth-century Hong Kong were also favourable to cremation and, unsurprisingly, advances also came from these quarters. By the time the Hindu community opened its first formal crematorium, on Mount Caroline, on 9 October 1937, a private crematorium attached to a Buddhist monastery was already in operation. That year, 1937, also witnessed the Japanese community open a crematorium, very close to the Hindu site. Japanese influence was even more overt when, during the Second World War, the occupying Japanese army built a crematorium in Boundary Street, Kowloon, to treat their war dead.

Early post-war changes: Cape Collinson Crematorium

After 1945 the government requisitioned the crematoria built by the defeated Japanese, and the 1937 Japanese crematorium on Hong Kong Island was demolished. By contrast, the Kowloon crematorium was rebuilt and operated between November 1948 and September 1950 before being demolished in order to build a housing estate. Its Japanese-designed cremators were kept and, in July 1951, these were installed in a smaller crematorium in Diamond Hill cemetery but, due to its low-quality facilities, this crematorium was not popular. Its Japanese cremators gained the unfortunate reputation of being 'frying pans'. Each cremator could only perform two cremations per day, making the service inefficient. They also produced problematic levels of smoke and odour. On the positive side, the cremators were cheap to operate and required little maintenance, and they were kept in service until 1979 (Lee, 1988a: 57–58).

The immediate post-war years saw dramatic changes in Hong Kong's fortunes. The colony's population of 600 000 in 1945 had, only five years later, risen to 2.3 million; these were largely immigrants escaping political upheaval in mainland China. This tremendous and rapid change posed many serious problems, not least the need to dispose of far larger numbers of dead efficiently in a densely populated area of only 1067 square kilometres. These developments acted as a spur to cremation, and the first 'full-sized' public crematorium was opened at Sai Wan (later known as Cape Collinson) on 12 November 1962. Due to the shortage of building land, the crematorium was sited on a steep gradient and was cut into a mountainside. Its design had to accommodate the only approach road, to the east, and the shoulder of the hill to the west. The architectural design process had been informed by close consultation between the Public Works Department and representatives of the colony's various religions. The crematorium had to provide facilities for the three main groups of religions that would use it – namely, Christian, Hindu and Chinese – with each facility being independent with separate vehicular entrances. At the same time, none could overlook another, nor could any one have prominence over the others. The solution was to split the crematorium into three levels, each supporting a separate service hall centred around the cremator room.

The Christian chapel on the first level was kept simple so that it could be easily used by the various denominations. As the cremators were installed on a lower floor, a catafalque hoist allowed coffins to be lowered to them. A 27-ton rock supported a covered entrance and dominated the approach. The interior was pastel-coloured and the furniture and fittings completed in teak. The Hindu temple was on the second level and, in response to the Hindu community's request, it had its own cremator and was completely separate from the rest of the crematorium. Its interior was decorated by inscribed marble plaques set into the walls. Once the new Cape Collinson Hindu facilities were operational the earlier Hindu crematorium was demolished (FEHD, 2002a: 4). The third level was a 'farewell pavilion', specially designed to cater for Chinese customs. This was divided into two to allow for the transferral, after a farewell ceremony, of the coffin to a family farewell room immediately prior to cremation. In the external garden there was a six-foot diameter bronze joss-bowl and two carved stone lions standing guard at the pavilion's entrance. Chinese influence was also present in the slightly 'lipped' style of the roof, along with red and gold colouring of the exterior, which was chosen by the Buddhist community. In addition, there was a 30-foot high anodized aluminium flèche rising from the roof, as well as a 367-niche columbarium and a four-acre garden of remembrance overlooking the crematorium.

Cape Collinson crematorium took 18 months to build and cost £113 750. It was fitted with the latest technology including five 'Lawnswood' Dowson & Mason cremators, which had been specially adapted to deal with the traditional large-board Chinese coffins that weighed three or four times more than an average British coffin. This was the first time that Hong Kong had used British cremation technology, and the new links were retained. Dowson & Mason, recognizing the importance of the project, used their involvement to mark their place in the world of cremation. Two more cremators were added in 1978. An 'Award of Distinction' from the Hong Kong Architects' Society was made to a government architect for the innovative design of the crematorium.

Another design demand at Cape Collinson had been that the flue stack should be concealed as much as possible. The solution to this, which won plaudits in 1962, ironically turned out to be a design fault later on. The crematorium chimney was placed on a slope 100 metres away from the building and out of sight of its visitors. To achieve this, ducting had been cut through 100 feet of rock. However, after two more

cremators were added in 1978, the chimney could not properly disperse the extra smoke quickly enough. Maintenance of the chimney also proved difficult as it was built underground and the considerable distance smoke had to travel before reaching the air also proved problematic. If the prevailing wind was blowing down the hill, a 'down-wash effect' pushed the smoke back into the cremator. Nevertheless, these problems were not insurmountable, and modifications dealt with them. Although the crematorium had a slow start, only performing 27 private cremations in its first year, these figures soon grew, from 342 in 1963 to 555 in 1965 (approximately 17 per cent of the total of 3339 cremations in Hong Kong that year).

Six years after the establishment of Cape Collinson, a smaller crematorium for the disposal of exhumed human remains was built in Wo Hop Shek Public Cemetery (the largest public cemetery in Hong Kong by 1988). These remains were the result of the compulsory exhumation, after six years, of all burials in public cemeteries – a measure introduced in order to conserve land. The remains could either be cremated or reburied in urns. By 1988 Wo Hop Shek Crematorium had performed 267 155 cremations, consisting of 214 164 'government' cremations and 52 991 private cremations (Lee, 1988a: 57–58).

Cremation and new crematoria: 1960s–1970s

By the mid-1960s cremation was becoming more popular. Land scarcity had begun to send the cost of traditional Chinese burial soaring. Those who could still afford to bury often had to have the bodies of their loved ones stored in refrigeration units while they queued for weeks waiting for a good burial place. By 1973 two Hong Kong cemeteries had been recently closed down as they were full, and many others were reaching bursting point. Another development which compounded this problem was the fact that many Chinese in Hong Kong had been forced to almost completely end their previous practice of burying their relatives in China due to the increasing number of bureaucratic obstacles raised by the mainland Chinese administration. In 1966 the fact that cremation was subsidized by the Hong Kong government and therefore cost about a quarter or less than burial, was recognized as a contributory factor to its increase in popularity. The poorer classes, especially, were increasingly adopting the practice. Government investment in new cremators and its aim to quickly provide 2800 more columbarium niches were both intended to alleviate the cemetery space shortage by supporting cremation.

By the mid-1970s it was clear that Hong Kong's two public crematoria could not keep up with the demand for cremation. The government responded by launching a 'crash programme' to build two more crematoria – Diamond Hill and Kwai Chung. Inspired by a visit to British crematoria, they were identical in design. Diamond Hill was commissioned on 5 August 1979 to replace the outmoded facilities based on the remains of the Japanese wartime crematorium. Built on part of a former urn cemetery, it was located close to a high-rise housing estate and thus subject to many constraints. Only low-rise columbaria could be built, totalling 4588 niches after the completion of the first phase of construction, with a further 2024 niches added after a second phase of building in 1983. An eight-storey columbarium, with 36 000 niches, was added in 1987. In 1985 two more Dowson & Mason cremators were installed at Diamond Hill and, by the end of that year, the crematoria on that site (both the original and its replacement) had performed a total of 45 623 cremations since July 1951 (Lee, 1988a: 58–59).

Construction work on a 1.7-hectare site in Kwai Chung was completed in 1979 at a total cost of HK$8.3 million. It was designated to cremate exhumed remains and as a training facility for all Hong Kong crematorium operators. Fitted with two Dowson & Mason reflux twin cremators, it was designed to take two more cremators if required in the future. It also had two air-conditioned service halls – one for Chinese services and the other for Christians – as well as 'encoffining' rooms, a mortuary and offices. In addition, a columbarium with 3508 niches was constructed and it, too, had the capacity to be expanded by a further 3000 niches. Kwai Chung was the first large crematorium in the 'non-urban' part of the colony and, as such, was immediately working at capacity: in slightly over six years it performed 18 896 cremations.

The fifth public crematorium in Hong Kong, commissioned on 21 January 1985, was at Fu Shan. The Scottish architect who designed it blended elements of Chinese architecture with modern British concepts. The building's roof was in a 'contemporary Gothic style' with 'golden glazed colour tiles', a characteristic of many Chinese temples and palaces. The four 'Phyros' cremators were controlled by a microcomputer system. Like the 1979 Hong Kong crematoria, it had two halls, Christian and non-Christian, as well as a seven-storey columbarium. Unfortunately, on 31 July 1983 Fu Shan suffered a fire which damaged the cremators, and a year later, a thunderstorm damaged the microprocessor system. Despite these setbacks, however, it became operational and was designed to have an annual capacity of 4000 cremations that could, after a successful trial period, be increased to 5,280. It cost a total of HK$20 million (£1.8 million). A good proportion of this investment (HK$8.4 million) was recouped in the first year from the sale of columbarium niches, and the entire cost was recovered shortly after (Lee, 1988a: 59–62).

The position in 1988

In addition to these five public crematoria by 1988, there were a further five private crematoria in Hong Kong. These small and primitive crematoria, fuelled by firewood and attached to Buddhist monasteries were, for historical and religious reasons, authorized in 1983 to cremate members of Buddhist religious houses and Buddhist monks and nuns. They only conducted a very small number of cremations – there were 22 in 1985, for example. Before 1994 a sixth private crematorium was opened at Kwun Yam Temple

In 1988 pressure on the land of Hong Kong was very great, despite the fact that reclamation programmes had added 1725 hectares to the colony's landmass. The population that year was 5.3 million, and overall population density per square kilometre was 5012. In the urban area the density was 28 479 per square kilometre, and in the most densely populated places this rose to 165 445 people per square kilometre. Lee calculated that, if all those who died in Hong Kong in 1985 (25 325 people) had desired burial, 28.13 hectares (28 full-sized football pitches) would have been required. Thus land conservation had been a governmental priority for some time. As stated earlier, all burials in public cemeteries were exhumed after six years, the remains then being reburied in an urn area of a cemetery or cremated and placed in a columbarium. This policy of compulsory exhumation was unique to Hong Kong and, as the process had to be carried out under health-inspector supervision and was disagreeable, to say the least, cremation seemed more desirable. Moreover, although burying urns containing uncremated remains was more land-efficient than full, permanent, burial, a hectare of land was still required for every one hectare for 2 470 urn-burials, making it more wasteful of land than full cremation.

Government action and new 1990s factors

Recognizing these considerations, the government expressed the aim of reaching a 65 per cent cremation rate by 1985. This was to be facilitated by the continuation of the six-year exhumation cycle in public cemeteries and a refusal to allow the building of new private cemeteries on either public or private land. The government also planned to provide small local public crematoria and columbaria in non-urban areas (new towns and outlying islands) and to improve the facilities in existing public crematoria. To this end, the government provided 50 per cent subsidies for crematoria and withdrew subsidies for land burial. By 1988 a building programme of five new crematoria was at an advanced stage of planning with its completion anticipated by 1995 at the latest. Regarding the siting of columbaria, a good 'feng shui' (literally 'wind water') site was a prerequisite, as this would benefit the deceased and make the service more attractive to those with these beliefs.

The government also sought to rationalize its departments by organizing joint offices for all services linked to cremation. The legal process was also streamlined to make cremation even more simple and quick to arrange. This approach was augmented by the 'marketing job' done on cremation by the Regional Services Department (created to implement the government's policy objectives), which allocated some of its senior management to the task. Part of this task was to provide information, and, to this end, 'question-and-answer' format brochures on cremation, based on material produced by the Federation of British Cremation Authorities, were produced. Further British influence was also evidenced by the translation of the British Code of Practice into Chinese in 1979, which was subsequently closely followed in all matters relating to cremation. Crematorium attendants were trained to a high standard, with a manual on funeral rites written for all crematoria workers. Research and development was also of importance, and Hong Kong officials were sent to Britain, Holland, Australia, Japan and other south-east Asian countries to observe cremation methods and gather information in order to improve service standards. As more crematoria were built, waiting lists declined and this also helped cremation gain in popularity. Almost a decade after the governmental plan first came into operation, Hong Kong reached the desired 65 per cent cremation rate. In 1985 Lee pointed out, if the cremations of exhumed remains were included in the figures, then Hong Kong had a cremation rate of more than 90 per cent, which made it second only to Japan in the world. Cape Collinson was the most popular crematorium as it was the only public crematorium on Hong Kong Island (in the urban area). Annually cremating to capacity (6 800 cremations) it was due to have new cremators installed after over 25 years of service: by the end of 1985 it had performed 138 951 cremations.

Government policies had helped make cremation economically more attractive as burials remained expensive. The average cost of a funeral in 1988 was around £636 (HK$7000) plus an extra £72 for burial fees in a public cemetery. This did not take into account the expense of the exhumation and second (urn) burial, which took the total cost to around £1353. The wealthy, desirous of establishing their status in death as well as life, could pay over ten times as much for a permanent burial plot. In contrast, the only expense for a cremation was the fee of HK$250 (£22) for an adult, and half of this for children under 12.

In 1988 Lee recognized that cremation would lose momentum if there were no plans for future development. This perspective was shared by the administration which planned to continue many of the developments already initiated, such as improving crematoria by replacing older cremators with the most modern technology. The building of new columbaria was also regarded as important, especially in existing cemeteries and in open spaces near settlements as this would make cremation more acceptable and meet with the Chinese social custom of visiting cemeteries, especially during the Ching Ming and Chung Yeu Festivals. The possibility of using crematoria as funeral homes to facilitate the Chinese custom of maintaining a 'waking vigil' before a funeral was also explored. In 1988 around 98 per cent of the Hong Kong population were of Chinese origin. Finally, it was deemed necessary to provide more incentives to funeral parlours run by voluntary organizations or non-profit-making groups to provide concessional rates for cremation funerals. On the basis of the cremation trends, and with these plans in mind, the administration helped to achieve a 75 per cent body cremation rate (that is, initial cremations rather than cremation of exhumed remains) by the early 1990s.

In the early 1990s, new factors came into play that further boosted cremation. As Hong Kong was due to be returned to China in 1997, many were planning on emigrating. In 1990, 60 000 people were expected to emigrate. This helped boost the number of cremations as about 90 per cent of those leaving the colony chose to cremate their dead so that they could take the ashes with them when they went. In contrast to the situation in the early 1970s, by 1994 cheap burial pits were available on the Chinese mainland. This, however, had not dented the 'booming' demand for cremation in Hong Kong, which had risen, in only a few years, to 85–95 per cent of funerals by 1994. There was also an increasing demand for funeral services such as the spreading of ashes at sea. Two new public crematoria built in this period facilitated matters. Wo Hop Sek crematorium, opened in 1990, had four cremators, whilst, the following year, another crematorium, with two cremators, was opened at Cheung Chau (Choy-hung Chong, personal communication).

Profits and beliefs

An interesting case illustrating the money that was involved in the Hong Kong cremation business and the opposition that could arise came when, in 1989, developer Ben Fung paid $40 million for an unfinished columbarium at Po Fook Hill, on a hillside above the small village of Pau Tai. The plan was to build 48 memorial halls and a five-tiered pagoda inside the walls of an 18 000 square metre site to house the cremated remains of 43 000 people. Three giant Buddhas and a Chinese garden, including a turtle pond, were to decorate it, and it was to be served by a Swiss-built cable car. The main attraction of the site for Ben Fung was that it had commanding views over the Hong Kong suburbs and hills bordering the South China Sea. This made the building attractive to potential users and the projected profitability of the enterprise was high. Each of the approximately 0.3 cubic metre niches cost between HK$1300 and almost HK$12 000 for the most luxurious – a silk-lined, rosewood-covered box niche with a magnificent view of the valley. With some investors buying entire rows of niches for families or to sell on at a later date, by November 1992 20 per cent of the niches had already been sold. Sales were hoped to reach HK$20 million per year, which included accounting for profits lost when a Buddhist restaurant was shut down to build more niches. However, in accordance with Chinese beliefs, the 'feng shui' had to be right. Po Fook Hill columbarium, according to Ben Fung, was 'one of the famous spots in all feng shui'.

Still, this did not prevent opposition to the development as wrongly performed 'feng shui' fails to negate the bad spirits said to dwell around columbaria. Popular opposition based around bad 'feng shui' could be fatal. In 1991, for example, the Hong Kong government refused permission for developers of another columbarium site to go ahead as it supported a claim of bad 'feng shui' made by villagers near the proposed site. The Po Fook Hill development had its opponents, too. In 1989 it was embroiled in a dispute with Buddhists, who, citing the project's emphasis on profitability, argued that the columbarium had no claim to be a temple. There was also a good deal of misgiving within the local village community, centred around fears that the columbarium would bring ghosts. To overcome this the developers gave almost HK$100 000 of what Fung deemed 'direct charity' to the Pau Tai villagers, although many said that they had received nothing. Fung claimed that the extra tourists attracted by the site could bring even more money into the local community. This had not happened to any great degree by late 1992, and many villagers still felt the need to burn incense to ward off evil spirits.

Recent developments and the current situation

Naturally, the handing-back of the colony to China has brought changes. In 2000 the Food and Environmental Hygiene Department (FEHD) was established to take over the administration of cremation services from the former Urban

Services Department and Regional Services Department of the Hong Kong government (Sui sum Leung, personal communication). However, the upward trend in the cremation rate has not been affected by these changes. In 1992 Hong Kong's 12 crematoria disposed of 21 511 out of 29 257 deaths, a cremation rate of over 73 per cent. In 1996, the year before the colony's handover, there were 24 240 cremations out of 32 049 deaths, an almost 76 per cent cremation rate. Five years later, Hong Kong's 12 crematoria performed 26 933 cremations out of a total of 33 305 deaths, a cremation rate of almost 81 per cent, 96 per cent of which were carried out by the six government crematoria (Choy-hung Chong, personal communication).

The still increasing demand for the cremation service has placed a heavier burden on crematoria in recent times and has necessitated more frequent maintenance and servicing of cremators as well as more timeslots available for cremation. At present, the FEHD operates about 23 cremators, with each providing three daily 'sessions'. Demand is particularly high from January to March, the months preceding and after the Lunar New Year. The FEHD is aiming to provide an efficient and dignified service, which will meet public demand. It is attempting to ensure that a cremation session is available for booking within 15 days from the date of application and that ashes are ready for collection within four days of the cremation. During a period of public consultation, some expressed strong objections to cremation on environmental grounds. As a consequence, the FEHD has begun investigating new, more environmentally-friendly and efficient technology for use when replacing or refurbishing its cremators.

In order to secure a cremation in Hong Kong, a visit must be made to the Immigration Department, which has two joint offices with the Department of Health. Here, an applicant can obtain a death certificate, a cremation permit and a booking for a cremation. The documents required for cremation are: a certificate of registration of death (Form Twelve) from the Deaths Registry of the Immigration Department; a medical certificate of the cause of death (Form Eighteen) from the doctor who attended the deceased; a medical certificate (cremation) (Form Two) from the doctor who attended the deceased; and a cremation permit (MD Form

Three) from the Port Health Office of the Department of Health.

In Hong Kong there are several ways of disposing of the ashes: storage in monasteries, nunneries or temples; interment in the urn section or a niche in the columbarium of a private cemetery; and scattering in the crematorium's garden of remembrance (perhaps followed by the planting of a commemorative tree in the garden of remembrance or by a commemorative tablet fixed on the columbarium wall); storage at home; and storage in a niche in a government columbarium (niches are of two sizes, with a storage capacity of two or four urns). These disposal methods can only take place if the ashes are those of someone in one of the following categories: (a) a resident of Hong Kong at the time of death and whose remains were cremated in a government crematorium within three months of death; (b) a resident of Hong Kong for at least ten years during a preceding 20-year period and whose remains were cremated outside Hong Kong; (c) a person whose remains were lawfully exhumed and cremated at a government crematorium; or (d) for those niches in the columbaria or gardens of remembrance in the outlying islands, in addition to the above rules, on the production of a certificate from the respective rural committee to certify that the deceased is a local resident. **Lewis H. Mates**

Acknowledgements

Thanks to Sui sum Leung (director) and Choy-hung Chong of the Food and Environmental Hygiene Department (FEHD) for information they provided.

References

CSA.

FEHD (2002a), *Brief Notes on Cremation Service in Hong Kong*, leaflet.

FEHD (2002b), *What to do When Someone Dies*, leaflet.

Lee, John Sheung-yee (1986a), 'An Overview of Coffin Technology – Part I', *Pharos*, 52(3): 82–84.

Lee, John Sheung-yee (1986b), 'An Overview of Coffin Technology – Part II', *Pharos*, 52(4): 123–24.

Lee, John Sheung-yee (1988a), 'Cremation in Hong Kong – Part I', *Pharos*, 54(2): 56–59.

Lee, John Sheung-yee (1988b), 'Cremation in Hong Kong – Part II', *Pharos*, 54(3): 88–92.

HOPE AND FEAR

Cremation cannot be separated from emotions associated with death and with the dead, most especially hope and fear – elements that may even combine in an attitude of violence (discussed in a separate entry). Numerous thinkers have pondered the complex human ambivalence towards the dead, as well as the ambiguity of status of the deceased. The influential early twentieth-century anthropologist Bronislaw Malinowski pinpointed key features of this situation in what he called the 'two-fold contradictory tendency' in the attitude of the living to the dead (Malinowski, 1974: 49). On the one hand there is a desire to preserve the dead body, keep it intact, or retain parts of it while, on the other, there is a strong sense of needing to 'put it out of the way, to annihilate it completely'. He points out that these two tendencies meet their ideal expression in mummification on the one hand and cremation on the other. He did not regard such practices as any 'accident of belief' or of historical context but as expressing 'the fundamental attitude of mind of the surviving relative, friend or lover', it is the same double attitude of 'longing for the remains of the dead person' and 'disgust and fear of the dreadful transformation wrought by death'.

Although Malinowski is renowned for his detailed study of tribal societies he was also prepared to make general statements about humanity. One of the most important of these was his conviction that funeral rites had become, over the course of human development, a key means of focusing and expressing the 'deepest emotional fact of human nature, the desire for life'. Their effectiveness was such that human beings were saved from 'the fear of annihilation' and of 'surrender to death and destruction' (Malinowski, 1974: 51). From the more literary world of mythological thought, René Girard also focused on the 'curious mixture of terror and hope' in those who mourn (Girard, 1977: 255). Some other early social scientists, influenced by the notion of the evolution of ideas, also saw positive adaptive significance in the values expressed through funeral rites and stressed the nature and role of hope in human life. Oxford's R.R. Marett, for example, saw in hope a key religious idea affording 'survival-value for the human race' (1933: 225). A very similar line was pursued by A.M. Hocart whose anthropological essays saw in funeral ritual the task of 'securing life' (1973: 51), a theme that is pursued in the **fire** entry. From the psychological and therapeutic domain and well known within death studies, Elisabeth Kübler-Ross's work also stressed the power of hope in human survival (1970:123).

In general terms, modern cremation can be seen to offer at least two forms of hope. One removes the fear of premature burial; the other stresses the life of the soul. As the entry on **premature burial** shows, there were many, especially in the nineteenth century, who feared being buried alive. Cremation offered a potential resolution in that; even if one awoke in the cremator the suffering would be very short-lived compared with awakening in the dark of the grave. As for the soul, the hope offered by cremation is more complex, grounded in the fact that because cremation destroys the body it offers a clearer focus on the soul or the life-force that has left the body for its onward destiny. **Douglas J. Davies**

See also dignity and violence; fire-chaos and cosmos; premature burial.

References

Girard, René (1986), *The Scapegoat*, Baltimore; John Hopkins University Press.

Hocart, A.M. (1973), *The Life-Giving Myth and Other Essays*, intro. Rodney Needham, London: Tavistock Publications with Methuen and Co. Ltd. First published 1952.

Kübler-Ross, Elisabeth (1970), *On Death and Dying*, London: Tavistock.

Malinowski, Bronislaw (1974), *Magic, Science and Religion and Other Essays*, London: Souvenir Press. First published 1948.

Marett, R.R. (1933), *Sacraments of Simple Folk*, Oxford: Clarendon Press.

HUMANISM

The history and development of cremation has involved people with humanist or other designated ideological views quite distinct from those of established religious traditions, and often in opposition to them. Modern cremation provided one very sharply focused opportunity for the expression of non-religious life-values and beliefs grounded in the practical action of ceremony or ritual. Precisely because major religions have, for millennia, possessed an almost exclusive claim over death rites, the new rites furnished an opportunity for a claim to independence and autonomy by those of a humanist commitment. This single case, taken from Norway, serves as one example but could be repeated for many other countries. **Douglas J. Davies**

NORWAY

As the twenty-first century begins, some 30 per cent of all funerals in Norway are cremations; this rate has not increased since the 1980s. Officiants of the Norwegian Humanist Association conduct a total of 350 funeral ceremonies every year – less than 1 per cent of the total number – but approximately 90 per cent of these humanist funerals are cremations. A large proportion of the deceased in these cases, some 40 per cent, are not members of the association. The ceremonies are always planned according to the wishes of the bereaved, provided that they actually request a humanist, secular, ceremony. The rather individual formats of these ceremonies when followed by cremation do not, in general, differ from those followed by burials. In many crematoria the coffin can be lowered at the end of the ceremony – a procedure now encouraged by humanist officiants as well as by clergy because of its appropriate symbolic significance.

Legal regulations allow for crematoria to charge a fee for cremations, and in most cases they do, while burials, by law, are free. The Norwegian Humanist Association has argued that this fee system is unjust since municipal authorities have to pay for the staff involved in burials just as for crematorium staff. Most importantly, ash-urns take up less space when buried than do coffins. Indeed, coffin-burial takes up so much ground that it has become a major challenge to local planning. New regulations effective from 1997 allow for the spreading of ashes and, increasingly, on application, this spreading will be allowed in solitary places in nature and at sea. The rite of spreading is conducted by the family, and occasionally by humanist officiants. It cannot take place at the graveyards. The most frequent questions from Humanist Association members deal either with the spreading of ashes or with the option of burial of ash-urns anonymously at the graveyard 'urn-fields'. Some think that an identifiable grave may serve the mourning process, whereas, to others, the lack of it may be problematic. While anonymous burial and the spreading of ashes will often be in accordance with the life-stance or even the lifestyle of many Norwegian humanists, the organization does not actively encourage any particular arrangement.

Because Norway has had a cremation-promoting society for 100 years the Norwegian Humanist Association has not, generally, had to campaign for cremation. Occasionally, however, a new crematorium in the international functional style is inaugurated, as occurred in the Norwegian town of Bodoe in 2002. There, humanists cooperated with the local church administration to ensure that the ceremony room was appropriate for all ceremonies and displayed no distinctive religious symbols. **Rolf Solheim**

HUMOUR

There are far fewer jokes or other forms of humour about cremation than about burials partly because it has only recently become common in Europe and, in America, is still the choice of a relatively small minority. There is nothing to compare with the long tradition of grave humour about burials, corpses, graveyards, ghosts or skeletons. It is difficult to imagine Hamlet's jocular gravedigger as a crematorium attendant for, although one may address an unearthed skull mockingly or ironically as if its owner were still present how might one speak to a handful of dust that has lost all sign of its human let alone personal origin? Indeed, jokes about cremation tend to play on this anonymous nature of the remnant left behind after a particular known person has been reduced to ash. In the jokes the ash is treated with carelessness or derision by the surviving relatives. Consider the following:

A husband had had his wife cremated and kept her ashes in an urn on the mantelpiece. In the months that followed he would from time to time absentmindedly tap off the ash from the cigarette he was smoking into the urn. On the anniversary of his wife's death a friend called round and commented that the wife was still above the fireplace. 'Yes,' said the widower. 'Funnily enough she's been putting on weight.'

Winston had been a shiftless husband, and his wife had had to support the family. When he died she had him cremated and put his ashes in an hourglass which she kept in the kitchen. When a neighbour asked her about it, she said, 'When he runs out, I know it's time to take the meat out of the oven. I've got him working at last.'

These cynical jests about the married state (marry and then burn) are made possible by the dual status of the ashes from the crematorium. They are the sacred remains of a particular human individual yet they are also a mere formless heap of particles. Dust to dust. Ashes to ashes.

Paralleling these jokes are urban legends about crematoria or the transport of ashes in which something unseemly, horrendous and ludicrous actually happened to someone known to a 'friend of a friend'. Keizer's reference to misplaced ashes in his entry on **Douwes Decker** offers one example. Or take the following 'story':

Every year cousin Megan in Australia would send her relatives in Wales a parcel of dried fruit mixture with which to make their Christmas cake. Last year the parcel arrived on time but without the usual accompanying card. 'Funny,' they thought. The cake, though, was a great success. Then, in the New Year they got an official-looking letter from Australia. It said, 'We regret the delay in informing you that Megan Hughes was killed in a motor accident last November. Her will left instructions that she was to be cremated and the ashes sent to her next of kin in Wales.

These unlikely stories are similar to jokes but are always told as if they really happened. Whether they are humorous or macabre is a question for teller and listener to decide.

The most repellent humour about cremation relates to the compulsory cremation of those murdered by totalitarian governments to hide the evidence. Hitler's government transported the handicapped and the mentally ill to Hadamar where they were murdered and cremated. Most people in the town knew this, and the old people in the town were fearful lest they too be classified as 'useless eaters' and end up in the crematorium. The children of Hadamar joked about the smoke from the buildings and would tell one another 'tomorrow it will be your turn to go *durch den kamin* [up the chimney]'. The children of the town were creating humour by breaking two restrictions on how people were allowed to speak. First, in theory the killings were kept secret from the public; they were not to be spoken about. Second, it was a disrespectful way of speaking about death and cremation. In time, the humour was succeeded by the jokes about cremation and the Holocaust that first appeared in Germany in the 1960s and were later told in Ivrit (modern Hebrew) by secondary school pupils in Israel. In either case it followed on from when teaching about the Holocaust was made compulsory. Whenever people are told that they must only speak about something in one particular way, they inevitably invent jokes that evade the prohibition. For example:

How many Jews can you get in a Volkswagen?
Fifty-five. Two in the front, three in the back and fifty in the ashtrays.

These are grim jests in bad taste about a vile phenomenon but today such jokes inevitably follow any death by fire and disaster as happened after the twin towers disaster in New York on 11 September 2001:

Why are fire officers called New York's finest?
Because you can run them through a sieve.

These jokes are no different from other humour about people who die by accident or violence whether in motor accidents (Diana, Princess of Wales), death on the barbed wire in 'no man's land' in the First World War or death at the hands of a serial killer. By social convention and popular sentiment these events call for grief, respect and reverence, yet precisely for this reason they are all the subject of humour. Cremation hides, sanitizes, speeds up and renders dry the inevitable decay of the body after death. As such, any humour about it is the opposite of the humour of vivid visual dismemberment that follows death by accident or violence. Nonetheless, the humour occurs under the same circumstances and takes the same form. By referring to the disposal of ashes in a frivolous way the jokers break the rules laid down about how we should talk about the dead. *De mortuis nisi bonum. Quid rides?* **Christie Davies**

See also Hill; literary cremation.

References

Davies, Christie (1989), 'The Ethics of Certain Death: Suicide, Execution and Euthanasia', in Arthur Berger *et al.* (eds), *Perspectives on Death and Dying: Cross Cultural and Multi-Disciplinary Views*, Philadelphia, PA: Charles Press, 149–62.

Davies, Christie (1990 and 1997), *Ethnic Humor around the World: A Comparative Analysis*, Bloomington, IN: Indiana, University Press. Second edition 1997.

Davies, Christie (2002), *The Mirth of Nations*, New Brunswick NJ: Transaction.

Davies, Christie (2003), 'Jokes about Mass Mediated Disasters in a Global Electronic Age', in Peter Narvaez (ed.), *Of Corpse, Death and Humor in Folklore and Popular Culture*, Logan, UT: Utah State University Press.

Dundes, Alan and Hauschild, Thomas (1983), 'Auschwitz Jokes', *Western Folklore*, 42(4): 249–60.

Smith, Paul (1983), *The Book of Nasty Legends*, London: Routledge and Kegan Paul.

Smith, Paul (1986), *The Book of Nastier Legends*, London: Routledge and Kegan Paul.

HUNGARY

As part of an empire

As part of the Habsburg Monarchy before 1918, Hungary was in a position to be influenced by Austrians who had established a cremation society in the other most important part of the empire. Indeed, in 1894 Budapest was the venue for the eighth International Congress on Hygiene at which Austrians organized an exposition on cremation. At the same time, the city was the venue for an important meeting of the Federation of German-Language Cremation Societies, bringing many leading European figures to Budapest. Naturally, cremation did have some Hungarian supporters, manifest in a competition to design a crematorium for Budapest held by the Institute of Engineers and Architects in 1903. Nothing came of this, and it soon became clear that ideas of introducing

cremation would be frustrated by government authorities and the Catholic Church.

However, the position of cremation amongst Hungarians was weaker than with their Austrian counterparts, who at least had formed a cremation society. Count Keglevich asked the Hungarian House of Magnates (the upper chamber) to allow the formation of a Hungarian cremation society in March 1904. Strong opposition came from the Catholic party, represented by Count Zichy whose intervention helped convince the government that a cremation society might offend popular religious feelings: it therefore refused to approve the society's statutes. Yet this lack of legal status did not completely prevent cremation advocacy in Hungary. For a decade from 1905, Dr William Frigyes edited the periodical *Hamvasztás* which supported the cause.

Debrecen Crematorium and Protestant influence

In 1910 Hungary's second city, Debrecen, looked as though it would surpass Budapest in cremation development. Located 20 miles from the Romanian border and around 80 from the Ukraine, Debrecen contrasted with the rest of mostly Catholic Hungary having become 'almost uniformly' Protestant in the sixteenth century and having remained the capital of a 'strongly radical and Protestant region' in the twentieth century (Sápi, 1980: 317; Spencer, 1992: 115–17). Debrecen's Mayor Josef Kovacs helped formulate a plan to provide more burial grounds in the region by building a new cemetery. Costing 1 million crowns, the budget included a 100 000 crown provision for a crematorium. To encourage fund-raising, Kovacs bequeathed 5000 crowns to the crematorium project and beckoned others to follow his example. Funding was not instantly forthcoming, however, and there were no immediate moves to begin construction of the crematorium. Meanwhile, in 1911, authorities in the town of Arad drew up plans to build a crematorium near the site of an ancient fortress where 12 rebellious Hungarian generals had been executed in 1849, although this, again, came to nothing. More funds were made available when, in 1914, Dr Desider Kemény, who was later cremated at Dresden, left a legacy of 150 000 crowns to build a crematorium in Budapest or any other town. But, in the end, it took over a decade of independence for a far smaller

Hungary (post-1918 the country was a third of its pre-1914 size) before cremation made any real progress. Curiously, the same was true of Austria.

Given its strong Protestant tradition, is was not surprising that the first crematorium in Hungary was built in Debrecen which was, by the inter-war years, one of the most important cities in Hungary and growing rapidly. On 25 June 1930, Debrecen city council unanimously demanded the provision of cremation facilities, and a crematorium was built the following year on a good site in a forest on the city's outskirts. A municipal project, it included a columbarium and was sponsored by the mayor, Dr Istvan Vasary. Support was also forthcoming from clerical representatives of some of the five different churches represented in the city. These included the Evangelical bishop of Debrecen, Balthasar who, according to Czech cremationist Mencl, deserved the greatest thanks in fostering the crematorium, as well as Bishop Laslo Ronas of the Baptist Church, clergy of the Old Catholic Church and Dr Lajos Simonides of the Budapest 'Martin Luther' Society. Both crematorium and columbarium were designed by the best city architect, Jôzsef Borsos, in a 'Hungarian national style'. The building, which received some foreign funding, was constructed of brick and high-quality materials including hand-made glazed tiles and a vast amount of stained glass. The cremators were Viennese and the entire project cost 600 000 pengó (Mencl, 1937: 1; Spencer, 1992: 115–17). A distinctive feature of the chapel is the large pulpit structure immediately before and under which is the catafalque that brings the coffin – often open – up from a lower floor on a lift. This later descends to take the body away. The distinctiveness of this ritual space lies precisely in the pulpit – an indication of the strong Protestant influence on the architectural organization of what is, essentially, a chapel.

However, when Debrecen Crematorium was completed, the Minister of the Interior, despite having initially approved the project, refused to allow it to open. The local Catholic bishop had already expressed his opposition as had the Catholic Women's Union and the Catholic National League, so, when the Catholic Archbishop Justinian Szeredi added his authoritative voice to this opposition, the federal government acted. This was despite the fact that the minister's stance did not appear to be backed by law: the part of the 1876 Public Health Act

regulating the disposal of the dead in Hungary did not explicitly rule out cremation or, indeed, any other method of disposal. Yet, despite the strength of Protestantism in the immediate vicinity, initial attempts spearheaded by cremationist Dr Gyorgy Fésus to establish a cremation society that could help secure the opening of Debrecen crematorium failed, again due to the Roman Catholic Church's 'dogmatic opposition'. This left those wishing to be cremated having to be transported all the way to Vienna Crematorium, which had itself only been open since 1922.

ICF support

The re-establishment of international relations between cremationists on a more formal basis in 1936 provided another arena of support for Hungarian cremationists. Thus Czech delegate Fr Mencl's proposal that the Prague Cremation Congress of that year ask the Hungarian government to open Debrecen Crematorium was passed unanimously. Unfortunately, the following year Mencl had to explain at the London Cremation Congress why he had not written to the Hungarian government about this matter. Instead, the issue was passed onto the new ICF executive to deal with, along with an analogous situation in Monaco. Nothing happened until August 1938 when Fésus asked the ICF executive committee to send a memorandum on the topic to the Hungarian prime minister, Dr Imredy, requesting that he allow the opening of Debrecen Crematorium. By the end of December 1938 there had been no reply to the ICF letter: the executive remarked that it was 'perhaps unfortunate' that the current Hungarian prime minister was an 'ardent Roman Catholic' and that the Eucharist Congress was currently being held in Budapest. By May 1939, as there had still been no answer from the Hungarian government, the ICF executive decided to approach the Hungarian consulate in London in the hope of making progress there. This course of action had been advocated by Mencl two years earlier, as Britain was a 'highly estimated country among Hungarian politicians'.

The ICF could do nothing during the Second World War, but contact was re-established when it was over. In August 1945 the mayor of Debrecen requested permission to open the town's crematorium. As before, the government refused the application. However, at least the government was now well aware of the need to remedy the hiatus in the legislation and had begun working on the topic. In this task, the Minister of Social Affairs and Health looked to English law for guidance. In April 1947 Fésus attempted once more to get the Ministry of the Interior to permit the opening of the crematorium. By November 1947 the minister had secured information on the costs of cremation, and was considering the matter. In summer 1948 Fésus received a request from the ministry for a report on the cremation movement, to help further inform their deliberations. Possibly sensing victory, the ICF Congress of that year passed a unanimous resolution urging the opening of the crematorium. Only three years later, in April 1951, the necessary legislation was in place and Debrecen Crematorium, a 'major work of architecture', was finally opened for business. Happily, Debrecen crematorium's architect, Borsos, lived just long enough to see his design perform the first cremation in Hungary, although he himself was not cremated but instead buried very close by (Spencer, 1992: 115–17).

Catholic changes and Budapest Crematorium

The 1960s witnessed more developments. A Hungarian Catholic Episcopacy conference in May 1967, in light of their Church's change in attitude to cremation in 1963, officially accepted that the last rites could be performed prior to and after cremation. Soon after, a crematorium opened in Budapest's massive 'New Public Cemetery' (*Budapest Ujköztemetô*) on 2 May 1968 (the cemetery was apparently one of the largest in Europe). Previously, all cremations had taken place in Debrecen, and in 1967 of the approximately 22 000 deaths in Budapest, 4000 had been cremated in Debrecen, which had had a new cremator recently added (Spencer, 1992: 115). Budapest Crematorium was of a triangular-shaped design and fitted with three gas-fired cremators. With a 120-metre chimney faced with Russian marble slabs, it was built at a cost of around 8 million Austrian schillings. No committal room or chapel was built, however, and ceremonies were performed at one of the city's cemeteries, with the bodies being taken to the crematorium afterwards. The crematorium did have a mortuary with a capacity of 12 corpses as well as three storage refrigerators each also

with a capacity of 12 corpses. It was forecast that the new crematorium would deal with about 6000 cremations in its first year, with a cremation costing 1000 Austrian schillings. Long-standing relations between Vienna and Budapest municipalities' funeral services helped the service develop.

After a low point in the late 1950s, Hungary became increasingly involved in the ICF. In 1968 ICF president Dr Michelfeit attended Budapest Crematorium's opening ceremony. Hungarian cremationists were also invited as observers to the London ICF Congress in 1969, but, as there was still no cremation society in the country, there was a little uncertainty as to whom the invitation be addressed. In 1972 Hungarian representatives invited to the ICF Congress in Grenoble were unable to attend 'for one reason or another'. Those involved in cremation in Hungary did communicate occasionally with the ICF, but the information they provided was not always strictly accurate. For example, in 1975 a certain Mr Ortutay reported that 'in the past years', 32 per cent of funerals were cremations, which was a far higher figure than the reality at the time (under 13 per cent).

'Levelling off': the late 1970s and 1980s

In January 1977 the one-hundred-thousandth cremation took place in Hungary. Budapest Crematorium had, less than a decade after it opened, undergone extensive reconstruction. New buildings designed by János Pomsár included extra refrigeration chambers and, in August 1976, two Swedish cremators were installed. The crematorium had experienced a difficult period, however, due to an influenza epidemic. As reported by Papp Rezsö, 'almost superhuman efforts' were required to deal with the increased demand. Rezsö was pleased that the crematorium staff had received awards and commendations and that the cremation rate had increased from 11.4 per cent to 12.7 per cent in only two years (Rezsö, 1977). Only three years later, in February 1980, the next landmark was reached as Budapest Crematorium performed the two-hundred-thousandth cremation. In the early 1980s, the crematorium was again fitted with new equipment, including another new refrigeration room.

By 1981 there were plans to build a third Hungarian crematorium, in Szeged. A columbarium had also been opened in

Rákospalota. More generally, the funeral authorities had published a large book on good practice, in order to educate employees and, in Debrecen, a reference book on secular funeral rites was published for those carrying out these kinds of service. International links had improved; a professional delegation from West Germany had visited and was impressed by what it saw. Papp Rezsö noted that there had been positive reporting of Hungarian efforts 'to achieve progress in arranging up-to-date burials' of a 'high cultural standard' in Italian, French, Czechoslovak, West German, Finnish, Austrian and English journals.

During this period, Dutch cremationist J.J. Visman bracketed Hungary in a top group with Czechoslovakia and Belgium as countries that had 'strikingly high numbers of cremations per crematorium'. However, with regard to actual cremation percentage rates Hungary, unlike Belgium and Czechoslovakia, was relegated to an intermediate group of countries with cremation rates that were increasing at a slower speed than those of the top group. Visman noted that Hungary showed a marked increase in cremations in the 1970s, but that this 'levelled off' in the late 1970s and early 1980s. Between 1978 and 1983 the cremation rate had fluctuated between around 13–15 per cent. Cremation figures took a decisive step upwards again the year *before* the opening of Hungary's third crematorium, at Szeged in November 1985. Thus, in 1984 the cremation rate was over 16 per cent, and this percentage – if not always the actual number of cremations – increased year on year during the late 1980s. By 1989 the 30 409 cremations in Hungary indicated a cremation rate of almost 22 per cent.

The end of Soviet government

In the late 1980s the end of 'Soviet communism' engendered massive political, social and economic change throughout eastern Europe, presenting new opportunities and challenges to the development of cremation. In 1992 Hungary had a population of 10.5 million of whom around 2 million lived in Budapest. There were 147 214 deaths that year, with 34 306 cremations performed in three crematoria. Of these, Budapest Crematorium performed 24 000 cremations annually (16 000 from the city itself and the remainder from the large region that the crematorium served around the capital). The two other crematoria, Szeged and Debrecen, split the remainder between them. In Budapest, bodies were cremated on a 24-hour, three-shift system with a maximum of 72 cremations a day. In 1992 the crematorium had five cremators, which were each coping with up to 15 corpses every day, and, because demand was remaining high, a new building with five more locally designed cremators was being built. On a visit to Hungary, British cremationist Eric Spencer was impressed by the provisions for the crematorium staff who had to handle corpses in unsealed coffins. A total change of clothing at the beginning and end of their shifts was compulsory, and they were provided with showering facilities. He also thought that the cremated remains there 'appeared to be handled as ethically as possible despite the pressures under which they work'.

The cremation facilities had suffered from underfunding in the communist period. This lack of resources had demanded sacrifices and the crematorium's director, Jeno Ladanyi, had been forced, for example, to remove the marble cladding on the crematorium chimneys in order to pay for much needed repairs and improvements. Indeed, he even offered to sell to Eric Spencer's delegation the fittings to the old Communist Party members' urn mausoleum! (Spencer, 1992: 117). Some of the other remnants of the communist/regime were of more use, however. Beneath the mausoleum was a columbarium that was only partially filled with the remains of former Party members. In 1992, the large amount of remaining space was being offered to anyone interested. In addition, the communists had had an exclusive funeral home in the main cemetery, which, too, was made available to all who wanted to use it – although few did.

Another predicted problem for cremation in Hungary was that the state subsidy, totalling £40 for each cremation (compared with a basic death grant of around £15), was to be withdrawn. According to Eric Spencer, 'everyone' expected the cremation rate to decrease once this occurred. Elsewhere, there were other difficulties. By 1992 Debrecen was the centre of a region of about 300 000 people and its crematorium, by then equipped with modern 'Tabo' cremators, was carrying out around 3000 cremations annually. The building had also become, 60 years after it was built, an official monument and tourist attraction. Its problems stemmed from a regional fuel shortage that had seen the implementation of a three-day week, which had already been in operation for some time by 1992 (Spencer, 1992: 117).

However, in Budapest the pressures were not all in one direction, and modern problems that face all large cities worldwide were, as elsewhere, a spur to cremation. Of the 14 Budapest cemeteries there was a 'desperate shortage of space' in all but three, and even they were expected to be full within a few years. In 1995 a national minister reported that 140–150 000 corpses had to be disposed of annually and that, despite the extension of several cemeteries, the lack of burial space remained a problem. Expansion of cremation was regarded as at least part of a potential solution to the problem, and the trends were seen as encouraging. In 1994 the Hungarian cremation rate reached almost 25 per cent and Budapest had recently cremated its five-hundred-thousandth corpse. Notwithstanding this, and although there had been some relatively recent investment in the crematorium, there appeared to be little chance of Budapest city council building any new crematoria in the near future (Rezsö, 1995).

The private sector, however, was not so cash-strapped, and a new private crematorium was under construction near Lake Balaton, Hungary's main holiday and retirement region.

With the transition from communism in 1990 the state-owned regional funeral companies (or 'institutes'), run by local authorities, lost their previous total monopoly over the provision of funeral services and it became possible for private enterprise to provide aspects of these services, although the 'institutes' retained control over the cemeteries and crematoria. One of the major problems of the communist period was that cremationists 'had no opportunity to compare themselves, or their service, with anything outside the Soviet Bloc' (Spencer, 1992: 115).

Arranging a cremation

The formalities for arranging a cremation in early post-communist Hungary were as follows:

1 The deceased had to be collected from their place of death and taken to one of the Institute's mortuaries.
2 The relative(s) of the deceased had to attend one of the institute's eight offices (five of which were situated in the main cemeteries) for an arrangement interview.

3 The relative(s) must then pay the entire funeral bill (minus any grants, which were due to be phased out).
4 The body, in a coffin, was then placed in one of the 42 service chapels at whichever one of the cemeteries the family had been told to attend – usually that nearest where they lived (although there was no body embalming in 1992, by mid-1995 it was possible to have a body embalmed, and death masks could also be commissioned).
5 In Budapest, the cremation service, like the burial services, was held in one of these chapels, but, unlike burials, the family left the deceased in the chapel after the ceremony and there was no service at the crematorium itself.
6 After the ceremony the body was returned to the refrigeration centre (as the chapels were not attached to the crematorium).
7 The body was then taken to be cremated (although sometimes, if a ceremony had been chosen, it could take place when the body had already been cremated, as there was a heavy demand for chapels). In Budapest, relatives were not allowed to attend the cremation itself as there was normally a three-day waiting period during which bodies were stored in one of the many refrigerators located both inside and outside the crematorium building. Individual bodies for cremation were identified by means of non-combustible metal tags.
8 The cremated remains could either be interred in family graves or in urn-cemeteries dotted throughout the Budapest suburbs. In 1986 it was made possible to sprinkle ashes on 'plot number fifty-three' of Budapest Cemetery. An innovative method of ash disposal was also developed and is discussed separately under **fountain dispersal**. Urns could also be placed in numerous churches. In fact, the deposition of 'secular' urns in cathedrals was also permitted by this time, although the area allocated to them was kept separate from the ashes of servants of the Church. These cemeteries often also had a chapel for the associated ceremonies. Eric Spencer expressed surprise that these 'much more attractive' facilities were seldom used: he suspected that this was because 'everything is geared to the high volume centralised cremation system'. In 1994 there

were 2177 ash-scattering ceremonies, carried out in Pest, Buda and Szeged cemeteries (Buda and Pest being two cities, on either side of the Danube). There were also a further 2198 cases of relatives requesting the cremains in order to take them home (Spencer, 1992: 115–17; Rezsö, 1995).

Concluding remarks

Since 1992, and particularly since 1998, the number of crematoria in Hungary has grown appreciably. The fourth Hungarian crematorium was inaugurated in Siófok in 1991. Before its opening, the crematorium received the blessing of the bishop of Veszprém diocese, illustrating how much the Catholic Church's attitude had changed. The fifth crematorium was built in Szolnok in 1998. Two more were built in both 1999 and 2000, at Pécs and Tatabánya and Magyarszecs and Gesztely respectively, and a tenth in Csanádpalota opened in 2001. In 1991 the cremation percentage dropped for the first time since 1983. Presumably Siófok Crematorium helped put it back on an upward trajectory in 1992. Although the percentage dropped again in 1998 (from 27.8 per cent in 1997 to 26.6 per cent), the increase after was the speediest yet, reaching 33.7 per cent in 2001. Like many Catholic majority countries throughout the world, cremation has only really developed quickly in recent years, but this progress has been quite dramatic. It is clear, though, that the potential problems and obstacles of the early 1990s have not had a major negative effect on the development of cremation, which, as with many other Catholic countries worldwide, is likely to continue apace. **Lewis H. Mates**

See also fountain dispersal.

References

CSA.

Mencl, Fr. (1937), 'The Crematorium of Debrecen in Hungary', typescript, CRE/F/HU.

Rezsö, Papp (1977), 'The Hundred Thousandth', typescript, CRE/F/HU.

Rezsö, Papp (1995), 'Hungary: May Catholics Choose Cremation?', article in *Christian Life*, 29 October, reproduced in *Pharos*, 62(1), 1996: 2.

Sápi, Lajos (1980), 'Old Cemeteries in Debrecen', in *Temetőművészete*, Debrecen: Hajdú-bihar, 317.

Spencer, Eric N. (1992), 'Cremation Today in Czechoslovakia and Hungary', *Pharos*, 58(3): 112–7.

Visman, J.J. (1983), 'Twenty-five Years of Cremation in Europe', *Pharos*, 49(1): 36–38.

I

ICELAND

During the first decades of the twentieth-century, physicians in Iceland argued for cremation, stressing reasons of public hygiene and maintaining that the dead were often inadequately handled due to lack of money or care. In 1915 the Icelandic parliament, or *Alþingi*, passed a law on cremation in Iceland, on the recommendation of Sveinn Björnsson, later Iceland's president. A committee to formulate suggestions for a crematorium and its location was selected by the city government of Reykjavík in 1930. Reykjavik's mayor appointed an engineer to prepare drawings and a budget, but little occurred until 1934 when the Society for Cremation was founded. Its first officers were: Gunnlaugur Claessen, a medical doctor; Benedikt Gröndal, an engineer; Ágúst Jósefsson, a health inspector; Björn Ólafsson, a wholesaler; and Gunnar Einarsson, a printing office executive. In 1935 society officials discussed the economics of purchasing cremation services in Copenhagen using the Icelandic shipping company, Eimskip Ltd to transport bodies to that destination until such time as a crematorium could be constructed in Reykjavík. The media turned the cremation affair into a heated issue and, although proponents sought to inform the public on the subject, they drew a generally negative response and were even ridiculed in various magazines and newspapers.

In 1945 the business committee of the Society for Cremation approved the purchase of two electrically fired incinerators from Iföverken AB in Sweden, but their main goal was not achieved until 1948 when a complete crematorium was built at Fossvogur Church, just outside Reykjavik. Two progressive leaders, governmental minister Jónas Jónsson and Reykjavik's mayor Knud Zimsen, were responsible for this idea of a 'funeral church'. Various delays included an attempt in 1943 by the city government to take over the management of cemeteries from the church organization. The Ministry for Church

Affairs, however, declined to permit this. Accordingly, sensing their opportunity, officers of the Cemetery Board hired the architects, Sigurður Guðmundsson and Eiríkur Eiríksson, to design Fossvogur Church. On 25 April 1946, the 'first day of summer' holiday in Iceland, the country's president, Sveinn Björnsson, set its cornerstone. Before the church was finally completed Gunnlaugur Claessen, who had been president of the Society for Cremation died. Many wished to fulfil his desire to be cremated and, accordingly, on 31 July 1948 his became the first modern cremation in Iceland. It was only later, on 12 December 1948 that Fossvogur was dedicated by a church leader. The former mayor, Zimsen, emphasized how the new facilities should help ensure simpler and cheaper funerals: 'We can wish that this innovation and the work here ... a quarter of a century in preparation, will receive the blessing of God and serve the community well, helping rid it of the discomforts and even some of the cost that archaic traditions have led to.' Still, at the outset of the twenty-first century, Fossvogur Church remains the only crematorium in Iceland. The initial emphasis on the health and sanitation benefits of cremation became transformed, over time, to a focus on economics and efficiency. Facilities have been updated to ensure that all pollution and environmental requirements are being met in contemporary cremation.

The twenty-first century

In Iceland, cremation services are in no way different from other funerals, except of course that the coffin is not carried to the grave. Other details, such as the distinctive practice and ritual accompanying the placing of the dead person into the coffin and the ceremonies at church, take place in the traditional manner. Relatives or friends are informed of the date for cremation, which makes it easy to decide a burial time for the ashes. A certificate of death, confirmation that the sheriff has been notified and documentation from the chief of police that there is no objection to cremating are all required. Funeral parlours help collect the necessary papers. Following incineration the ashes are stored in an urn, and relatives of the deceased decide when to inter them in cooperation with funeral officials, the only stipulation being that it takes place within a year of cremation. A pastor is often called upon to officiate at the burial, delivering prayers and a benediction by the grave.

The main cemetery at Fossvogur contains a special section for cremation urns covering some 5500 square metres; others also exist. Options are thus available for setting urns in any grave plot, subject to official permission, or for placing them in areas reserved for urns marked by horizontal gravestones positioned to incline towards visitors. In front of the church there is a monument commemorating life, composed of an arched wall with a side view of an angel. Consecrated in 1994 its inscription reads, 'Thy eyes beheld my unformed substance' (Psalm 139:15). Interestingly, no columbarium has ever been constructed in Iceland and there has never been any demand for one. So far as miscarried and stillborn children are concerned, the usual custom is cremation, and the cemetery at Fossvogur possesses a special plot for such burials, consecrated in 1994.

The site of Fossvogur Church consists of the main sanctuary, a chapel, a house of prayer, a mortuary, cremation facilities and offices for administration. The staff of three make reservations as requested by pastors or funeral companies, meet and direct funeral guests, as well as seeing to the mortuary and crematorium. They cooperate closely with the staff of funeral companies, both when receiving bodies into the mortuary and at services. This church belongs to no specific parish but, as a facility of the wider church organization, it is equipped like a congregational church so that all parish functions can be performed there. During 2000, for example, there were 388 funerals at Fossvogur, averaging two for every workday, along with one memorial service and two farewell services.

In 2000, there were also 1018 services at the church to mark the laying of the body into the casket. As already noted, this is a distinctive rite in Iceland at which a priest and the family say special prayers, and the house of prayer, dedicated in 1980 and seating 50, is used almost exclusively for this purpose. Stained-glass windows by Leifur Breiðfjörð adorn the building, along with a fine five-stop organ built by Björgvin Tómasson. There is also a mortuary annexed to the church, with room for 70 bodies, and part of this building is reserved for preparing each corpse and for reception of those close to the deceased. By the year 2000, over 100 000 people were using all these facilities at Fossvogur, not counting the many who visit the cemetery not least on 23 December, *Þorláksmessa*, and 24 December, Christmas Eve, when some light graves with illuminated crosses. All Saints' Day, in November, also attracts many family members.

The growing popularity of cremation in Iceland.

Cremation gradually grew in popularity in Iceland and by 2000 represented 19 per cent of all funerals in the capital city area, or over 13 per cent of funerals in the country as a whole. Now that transportation has improved, there is no reason for residents outside the capital area not to choose cremation. The office of Capital Area Cemeteries (CAC) provides full information on these matters, including the most convenient mode of transport. The goal is that there should be no difference at all – or at least very little difference – in the cost of opting for cremation, regardless of where the individual concerned has resided.

Laws and economics

In Iceland, laws on cremation stipulate that '[c]remation may not be performed anywhere other than at institutions formally approved by the Ministry of Justice and Church Affairs', and that: 'Ashes are to be placed in properly prepared urns which must be deposited in a church cemetery or registered burial plot. Urns may be buried in plots reserved for them or in graves belonging to families. Graves for urns shall be one metre in depth. Cemetery officers may determine to have a particular plot for urns; in it the size of each grave should generally be equal, or about half a square metre.' Again, 'The names of those resting in gravesites with urns are to be entered in a register, and each grave is to be numbered ... It is impermissible to keep urns with human ashes elsewhere than in cemeteries or publicly registered gravesites.' So far as economic factors are concerned, a law of 1993 (Law 36, para. 39) states that 'each month, the national treasury shall pay part of the total income tax to the country's cemeteries. The exact sum is to be calculated ... for each individual 16 years or older by the end of the next year previous to that of payment.'

Because normal graves occupy six times the surface area as those for urns, cremation is very efficient from the perspective of land use and upkeep. The grave need not be as deep, nor are conditions regarding groundwater and drainage as strict, making urn plots less expensive than those for coffins. If a considerable proportion of the populace chooses cremation it even becomes possible to use old graves in cemeteries that are otherwise full. Old family grave plots can be accessed again and used for years to come. Indeed, it is common to deposit urns in occupied graves subject to the agreement of relatives. Older cemeteries are often the most beautiful and peaceful sites in a city, and their beauty is more likely to be preserved if they stay in regular use.

The national church has made no declarations against cremation, this type of funeral is only another form of handling the body after death, with no implications for Christian creed or doctrine. Although cremation deviates from traditional church practice, the habits and customs of the church have by no means remained steady and unchanged throughout history. In 1997 CAC published a booklet, distributed to schools, libraries and churches, which provided information on cremation and associated funeral services to help people consider the options of burial and cremation. Subsequently, a website has also been provided.

Future cremation in Iceland

In the year 2000 there were 212 cremations amounting to over 13 per cent of all deaths in the country or 18 per cent of the total in the capital city area. It is anticipated that the cremation rate will rise to approximately 25 per cent of all funerals in Iceland by 2020. Approximately 60 per cent of the nation resided in the capital area in 2000, and this figure is predicted to increase to 68 per cent by 2010 and to 73 per cent by 2020. The age distribution of the nation is changing considerably, and those in the older age groups are constantly on the increase. Icelanders over 60 years of age will increase from 15 per cent to 17 per cent of the total population by 2010, to 21 per cent by 2020 and to 25 per cent by 2030 – a rate of increase approximating to that in other Western countries.

Business and religious organisation

It is important to note how some key religious bodies are linked to cremation in Iceland. For example, the independent organization, Capital

Area Cemeteries (CAC), belongs to the various evangelical Lutheran congregations in the Icelandic capital, Reykjavik, and two nearby towns. Because of the concentration of population in these areas this organization handled approximately 50 per cent of the entire operations of Icelandic cemeteries in 2000. Its board of directors is composed of representatives from local groups of the national church, along with a representative from the evangelical Lutheran congregation that is not state-affiliated. This board, in turn, selects a managing group of three who work closely with the director of the cemeteries in his day-to-day administration.

Attitudes to cremation

Surveys on Icelanders' attitudes to cremation were conducted in 1998 and 2000, the object being to explore the views of people aged 18–75. The results have been analysed according to age, gender, residence, income and occupation. There are two residential categories: one comprises individuals who live in the capital area and the other comprises individuals who live outside it.

The following three questions were posed:

1 How well or badly informed about cremation do you feel you are?
   Although nearly 14 per cent of respondents felt well informed about cremation some 83 per cent felt poorly informed.
2 Would you like to know more about cremation?
   Just over half the respondents said that they would like to know more about cremation and, of those wanting to know more, the proportion of women was higher than that of men.
3 How positive or negative is your attitude towards this kind of funeral?
   The majority, more than 60 per cent, was generally positive towards this kind of funeral. Over 25 per cent were neither positive nor negative, and just over 15 per cent considered themselves as having a negative attitude towards cremation.

The results of this survey illustrate that the attitude to cremation in Iceland is generally positive and that cremation rates are likely to increase substantially. Nevertheless, the public needs more information about cremation and regular discussion of the subject in the press and other media. A few people expressed a desire to reactivate the Society for Cremation. Backed by a strong society, more people would have the opportunity to express their ideas and promote cremation as a social practice. **Thorsteinn Ragnarsson**

See also Fossvogur Church.

IDENTITY

Cremation is an important process in relation to human identity and to changes brought to it by death and through funerary rites. Identity, itself, is important in any consideration of the meaningfulness of life and exists at numerous levels, from that of various formal social status and personal relationships to our inner sense of who we are and of what we are doing in and through our life. For many, identity has historically been framed, worldwide, by the wider sense of eternity, including postmortem states. For an increasing minority in the contemporary world, but especially within northern and western Europe, such a belief in an afterlife is decreasing, matched by a corresponding increased emphasis on this earthly world. In such groups, personal identity is as likely to be related to the world and its ecology as to any ultimate deity and afterlife. The entry on **ecology** draws attention to the way some people – in Britain at least – are coming to prefer woodland burial to cremation. Given the increased attention to issues of chemical pollution associated with cremation, along with a growing awareness of ecological ethics and ecologically-related lifestyles, cremation may begin to lose its attraction. In the later nineteenth century, by contrast, a sense of identity that included a commitment to scientific development and social welfare could relate fairly directly with the practice of cremation. As the twenty-first century begins, that very sense of cremation as modern and advantageous might give way to a rejection of it in some societies where it has reached a position of dominance and where some potential negative effects are brought to public attention.

Cremation can also affect the more personal realm of how people view others as explored in the entry on **ashes (remains)** with regard to how people view the ashes of their kin. The North American novelist and funeral director Thomas Lynch neatly caught the sense of this issue when describing how people collected such ashes from him as the funeral director. He called such ashes 'their tiny dead' and spoke, for example, of a woman calling for the ashes of her dead sister – a task left to her since the deceased's adult children seemed unbothered about it:

> She carried her sister's ashes to the car. Opened the trunk but closed it up again. Opened the back door of her blue sedan but closed that too. Then she walked around to the front passenger seat, placed the parcel carefully there, paused momentarily, then put the seat belt around before getting in and driving away. (Lynch, 1997: 103)

In contrast to the significant sense of mutual identity evident in this account he tells of many others who did not even bother to collect the ashes at all. Such an attitude would seldom be possible towards a corpse, whose identity is still, to some degree, evident in the body.

In any context, then, ashes reflect something of the identity that underlies mutual human relationships or even the status of a high-profile politician whose ashes, like those of Mahatma Gandhi in India, might be distributed throughout the land he loved. **Douglas J. Davies**

See also ashes – remains; ecology.

Reference

Lynch, Thomas (1997), *The Undertaking*, London: Jonathan Cape.

IMPURITY AND PURITY

The idea of ritual purity and of contexts or events that may render an individual ritually impure has been widely important in many cultures in association with death and cremation. The basic notion of ritual purity is that individuals are in a fit state to perform specific duties or meet particular obligations expected of them as part of the normal functioning of society. These may be associated with ceremonial or religious ritual or with social formalities. Sometimes this refers to many members of a society and sometimes to special individuals – often priests. At the heart of these actions lie the key values and prime beliefs of a culture – ideas that underpin the ongoing meaningfulness of life. Ritual impurity results

from a variety of life events and circumstances, whether inevitable, as in menstruation, or accidental, as in an unforeseen encounter with a corpse as in some traditional forms of Orthodox Judaism. **Hinduism** offers a complex picture of pollution, with some attributing impurity to the body at the time of physiological death and others to the actual cremation of the corpse once the spiritual life-force has departed.

In general terms, when rendered ritually impure, a person is unable to engage in those obligatory activities until they undergo a purification rite: this may be quite simple and take the form of washing, or it might be quite complex and involve sacrifices or prayer. These complex rules help identify and focus respect on prime social values. Dead bodies are often the source of rendering the living ritually impure. This may be because the body is, when alive, the very symbol of life, and life itself is a prized possession. Once dead, the corpse becomes a confused and confusing agent: it contradicts the life-principle, and, accordingly, contact with it brings the living into a dangerous state – one that contradicts life. Traditional Indian cremation rites were conducted by hereditary castes of priests who were regarded as sources of such impurity (Parry, 1994), so, too, in the case of cremation attendants as in **Japan**. In **Zoroastrianism**, the corpse must be prevented from bringing ritual impurity to fire – itself a sacred element of that religion. In many Western cultural settings modern cremation has tended to be identified with a process that purifies the dead body. Negative ideas of decay and corruption within the grave have given way to the cleansing capacity of fire. **Douglas J. Davies**

See also Hinduism; Japan; Zoroastrianism.

Reference

Parry, J.P. (1994), *Death in Banaras*, Cambridge: Cambridge University Press.

INDIA

Cremation in India is described in several ways under **Hinduism**, and also with related cultural effects in, for example, **Bali** and **Suriname**. Related elements also occur in **Zoroastrianism**. **Douglas J. Davies**

INTERNATIONAL CREMATION FEDERATION (ICF) (*See* Introduction: Globalization)

INTERNATIONAL MOVEMENT OF REMAINS

Cremation has made the transportation of human remains easier than is the case with corpses. Here we present two different accounts of such movement, first for England and Wales and, second, for the People's Republic of China. Other countries, too, possess distinctive rules not specifically covered in this book. **Douglas J. Davies**

England and Wales

With Britons travelling to ever more distant holiday destinations and buying second, overseas, residences, the requirement to bring back deceased nationals to their home country is common and is a necessary skill for any funeral director to acquire. Funeral companies at the 'foreign' end will need to do whatever is required by the British consul present, as well as complying with shipping regulations and the local legal issues of the country concerned.

At the UK end, any death abroad will need to be brought to the coroner's attention as a formality and any violent, sudden or unexpected death will be dealt with through the usual coroner's channels, ultimately producing a coroner's 'Form E' for cremation. By contrast, an unproblematic foreign death will require from the English registrar, a certificate confirming no liability to register in the usual way as well as a licence from the Home Office permitting cremation, which enables cremation to take place without much of the usual British paperwork. These additional documents are not difficult to acquire, and any competent funeral director will know the procedure, which involves taking the completed British cremation forms to the Home Office together with all the foreign documents. The Home Office can usually translate most documents to enable the licence to be generated, provided that a clear and appropriate cause of death is reported in the foreign certificates.

The timings involved do, however, necessitate some care before scheduling cremation. It is also a good idea to remove the usual zinc lining from the coffin or casket before cremating, or at the very least to puncture it, as this may otherwise interfere with the cremation process. **Phillip Gore**

THE PEOPLE'S REPUBLIC OF CHINA

The Chinese government has specific policies regulating the transportation of corpses of Chinese and foreign nationals in and out of China. The Several Regulations for the Administration of Corpse Transportation was co-issued in 1993 by the Ministry of Civil Affairs, the Ministry of Public Security, the Ministry of Foreign Affairs, the Ministry of the Railway, the Ministry of Communications, the Ministry of Public Health, the Chinese Customs Service and the General Administration of Civil Aviation of China. These regulations require that all corpse transportation or other funeral activities in or out of China be undertaken and supervised by the International Corpse Transport Networking Service Centre of the Chinese Funeral Association and funeral rooms throughout the country. No other sections shall undertake this kind of business without permission.

With regard to foreign nationals in China or overseas Chinese (or Chinese in Macao and Taiwan) who wish to have their bodies or cremains transported into or out of China, an application should be made by their relatives, their affiliating embassy or consulate in China or their recipient organizations. The transportation of corpses and cremains is carried out by the International Corpse Transport Networking Service Centre of the Chinese Funeral Association or its local branches in the country. In line with the aforementioned regulations, the common process in handling a foreign national's death in China involves:

1 ascertaining the death;
2 giving notice to the relative's embassy or consulate in China;
3 postmortem of the corpse;
4 completion of documentation by the relatives of the deceased;
5 discussing and agreeing with the relatives how to handle the corpse;
6 checking and handling the remains of the deceased;
7 organizing the outward transportation of the corpse or cremains;
8 compiling the Report on the Settlement of Death. **Zhang Hongchang, Li Jian, Zuo Yongren and Gao Yueling**

INTERNET

Cremation has a sizeable presence on the internet. By July 2003, even a quick search on the Internet for 'cremation', depending on the search engine used, can produce up to 2 million suggested websites whose content ranges from the practical to the humorous, from the delicate to the macabre. It is possible to look at the specification of cremators, buy urns, read the history of cremation, discuss the religious implications of cremation and locate the nearest funeral directors. Many cremation societies throughout the world have their own websites, providing factual information for interested 'surfers' and details of conferences, publications and news for members. New legislation relating to cremation is available from governmental websites, and information about the codes of practice for industry workers is open for scrutiny.

In practice, this means that anyone can find out for themselves about aspects of the cremation industry which were previously not necessarily in the public domain. In the future, it is likely that the Internet will be used for new, more practical uses – perhaps families who cannot attend ceremonies will be able to watch their loved one's funeral via a live webcam, or workers in the funeral industry will be able to liaise directly with their local crematorium through Internet technology. **Jennifer Arkell**

IRELAND (EIRE)

This account of cremation in Eire, along with some material on Northern Ireland, is given in some detail to exemplify the complex local deliberations amongst politicians, Church representatives and service providers that have often occurred in many places concerning the introduction of cremation. Social factors interweave with economic and political issues, with land availability and, in this case, also with strong religious traditions maintained locally even when the international mind of a Church has changed.

Problems of burial arose in Eire before the Second World War. In March 1939, for example, a local government department inquiry into the parlous state of several burial sites where human remains had been found above ground recommended they be closed down. Due to the Catholic Church's attitude however, cremation

was not suggested as an alternative. Yet even Northern Ireland, which is two-thirds Protestant, remained underdeveloped in terms of cremation in relation to mainland Britain. The British 1902 Cremation Act did not apply to Northern Ireland until as late as 1948, when the Belfast Corporation was empowered to provide a crematorium. Even then, it took 12 more years before the first crematorium on the island was eventually opened, in Belfast on 10 May 1961. In the first three years of operating, 705 cremations were performed (Fenner, 1964: 76–77).

In Eire, Denis Gallagher, manager of Dublin cemeteries, earmarked a site in Prospect Cemetery for a crematorium in 1966. Nine years later, the lack of burial space in Dublin was becoming problematic, particularly as it was needed in the new suburbs, exactly where land was most scarce and costly. There was a general acknowledgement of the need for long-term burial planning, which, in Eire, had 'religious and social significance beyond that accorded it in other countries'. Although crisis point was being reached, cremation was still regarded as a 'less than acceptable' solution. The registrar, Pascal Brennan, admitted that the authorities had been discussing cremation, but thought it a 'big step to take' (*Dublin Evening Herald*, 1975). Instead, Dublin Corporation began to buy land outside the city for new cemeteries.

In December 1975 supporters of cremation in Dublin seemed optimistic, reporting that the government and the Dublin Corporation had no theoretical objections to cremation, although finance could be problematic. In order to determine the likely demand in Eire and how long it would take to recoup building expenses they sought advice from the British Cremation Society. At the time only about 60 bodies per year were taken from Eire for cremation in Belfast, although demand might rise given a local facility were available. Some at Dublin also reported that Catholic clergy 'contacts' would not oppose a crematorium.

This optimism appeared at least partly justified when a delegation of Dean's Grange Joint Burial Board went on a tour of British crematoria in January 1976, although a change in Irish law was apparently necessary before a crematorium could be built. Of the 'big three' Dublin cemeteries, the 60-acre Dean's Grange was closest to the end of its useful life. On the delegation's return, the board voted by five votes to four to set aside space in its new graveyard for a possible future crematorium. But the board remained tentative and, in late February 1976, changed its mind. Claiming that £300 000 and ten acres of land were required to build the crematorium, Councillor Fred Faulkner mentioned that less than 2 per cent of the 933 cremated in Belfast in 1973 were Catholic. A new crematorium was therefore unlikely to perform the 4000 annual cremations that Faulkner reckoned necessary for the venture to break even. Faulkner also argued that Belfast Crematorium demonstrated that cremation was not much cheaper than burial and this convinced the board, which revoked its earlier support by six votes to four. Dublin Corporation subsequently announced that it had no plans to build a crematorium.

It seemed paradoxical that the effect of Belfast Crematorium during this period was to act against cremation in Eire, yet Faulkner's arguments were strong. Establishing a Dublin crematorium would cost an estimated £600–£700 000 and, if similar to its Belfast counterpart, would run at a loss, making the project unattractive to investors until traditional attitudes towards burial had changed. Another argument was that, as it was running under capacity, better use should be made of Belfast Crematorium, with cheaper transport and permission to perform Catholic funeral rites there. The problem was that this would necessitate an advancement in cross-border trade that would not be achieved during the turmoil of 'the troubles'. Indeed, the political situation meant that Eire funeral directors were not even permitted to rent their funeral cars in Northern Ireland.

Regardless of the strength of these arguments, the purported failures of Belfast Crematorium clearly helped defeat plans for crematoria outside of Dublin, too. In May 1976, at a meeting of Cork Corporation, the city manager argued that the unimpressive Belfast Crematorium figures showed that cremation in Cork city was not economically viable. But the idea of cremation did not go away. A month later, Councillor Jim Kenny suggested that Limerick city needed a crematorium to save land and money wasted in sending corpses to Belfast. In July 1976 Councillor Norman Morgan proposed a crematorium for County Galway, as its cemeteries were 'bursting at the seams'. Neither of these proposals, however, was taken seriously.

The Irish Roman Catholic Church's attitude

continued to frustrate cremation. In early 1977, *Pharos* commented on its 'puzzling' stance given the existence of the Catholic order of service book for cremation: it offered to send anyone, and especially Catholic priests, a copy. Popular understanding of the Catholic Church's attitude also remained confused, with the *Farmer's Journal*, for example, reporting in September 1980 that the Church 'still officially frowns' on cremation. Church influence might also have been present in some Irish newspapers that carried a surprisingly extensive volume of items dealing with unfortunate mistakes made regarding cremation in Britain.

Despite opposition, the issue re-emerged in March 1977 when Cork County Council commissioned a regional burial survey. Midleton Councillor Noel Collins, who had proposed a crematorium in 1974 again advocated the move, arguing that cremation would remove class distinctions from funerals and that there was a growing demand, especially as the Church now recognized the practice. He emphasized that he had no 'anti-Church motives'. However, the deputy county engineer claimed that there was no case for a crematorium in Cork, which would cost at least £250 000 per year to run, an assessment supported by three Cork bishops. Another councillor argued for the retention of the 'old custom of Christian burial': Collins' proposal was not even seconded.

The same month (March 1977) saw renewed moves to secure a crematorium in the capital. Dublin County Councillor C.J. Smythe saw cremation as 'something inevitable' within five to ten years, basing his case on the increasing 'cost of dying'. Dublin funerals were the most expensive in the country and many, especially the elderly, could not afford it. A cremation costing approximately £200 was affordable. However, nothing came of Smythe's call for a council-sponsored survey. Two months later, Mayo joined the cremation debate when Kilmeena township could not find suitable land (free of sand and rocks and having a stable subsoil structure with no groundwater to a depth of ten feet) for a desperately needed new cemetery.

The cremation option was again avoided, though, and a 'land swap' was suggested to solve the problem.

More frustrated calls for a crematorium in Dublin soon followed. Dun Laoghaire Borough Council controlled Dean's Grange Cemetery, which was to be closed for new burials from 1978. A council meeting in August 1977 passed a motion by eight votes to two calling for a municipal crematorium, again based on the relative costs of cremation and burial. Ned Brennan pointed out that burial space was so scarce that Eire would have to employ cremation eventually. However, Dublin Corporation, after having completed extensive studies on cremation in the British Isles (including Northern Ireland), remained unconvinced that there would be sufficient demand for the service. Undeterred, Dun Laoghaire called for the building of crematoria in both Dublin and Cork at the Association of Municipal Authorities of Ireland's annual conference in September 1977. Their respective positions on the issue led to a degree of friction between Dun Laoghaire Council and Dublin Corporation.

When there finally came an application for planning permission to build a crematorium, in October 1977, it was not for Dean's Grange. Instead, the Dublin Cemeteries Committee (a charitable, non-profit-making organization with autonomous statutory status that operated several Dublin graveyards) was planning a crematorium costing an estimated £100 000 for a secluded part of Dublin's Glasnevin Cemetery (along with Dean's Grange, another of the 'big three' Dublin cemeteries). Submitted to Dublin Corporation, the plan was considered by the city council planning committee. The choice of site seemed obvious: Glasnevin Cemetery was the largest in Eire, with approximately 1.2 million people interred there (Glasnevin Crematorium, 2003). The plan was carefully researched to avoid some obvious objections. The site was, for example, in the approximate centre of a 250-acre-plus wooded space (the cemetery itself was over 100 acres, and, to its north and east was the 70-acre National Botanic Gardens whilst to its west were the 80-acre grounds of a convent). The crematorium would thus be located further from inhabited areas than even British standards demanded. Despite this seclusion (the crematorium would not be visible from any building other than those associated with it), Glasnevin was still situated in the middle of a highly populated area (it was only one-and-a-half miles from Dublin city centre) and was easily accessible with good public transport links. This set of fortuitous circumstances made the site unique within the boundaries of Dublin city. The

Dublin area itself was the most obvious choice for a crematorium as it dealt with around a third of the approximately 38 000 annual deaths in Eire. Eight acres of Glasnevin Cemetery were allocated for the disposal of ashes and there was also provision for placing plaques in a nearby wall, and a third option of interring ashes in existing family burial plots.

Another positive aspect was the cost of the project, which, at £100 000, was between a third and a seventh of the earlier predicted costs, generally cited as a reason for not proceeding with such a project. Indeed, the estimated cost was put at only £50 000 in a subsequent press report (although it had risen to £60 000 by 1979). The pre-October 1977 cost estimates were accurate, though, as it was noted that if a crematorium were to be built anywhere other than Glasnevin, it would have cost between £300 000 and £500 000. Glasnevin was cheaper as it already had all the auxiliary services required for the crematorium. These included offices, a chapel that could accommodate 200, waiting rooms, public toilets and large car-parking areas (Gallagher, 1984: 108).

The Glasnevin plan included a proposal to conduct a survey on public attitudes if the idea was approved. Anticipating a large demand for the service, Denis Gallagher (manager of Dublin Cemeteries) predicted that a cremation would cost about a third of the price of a burial as there would be no burial plot to buy and a combustible coffin was far cheaper. Anecdotal evidence, as well as the surveys Dublin cemeteries had already conducted, suggested that there was a 'substantial groundswell' for a crematorium. Denis Gallagher claimed that increasing numbers of bereaved relatives supported a crematorium, which would save them the long walk to graves 'where you would arrive soaked and mud-spattered on a wet day' (*Irish Independent*, 1978). There had also been a growing number of enquiries about cremation from younger people.

Yet Dublin Corporation still remained unconvinced. A spokesperson, though admitting that securing land for cemeteries was problematic, maintained that the experience of Belfast suggested that there was simply no demand for a crematorium. Curiously, those supporting cremation had cited Belfast as an example of the demand *for* cremation: the statistics were open to the interpretations of both sides. Cremation supporters argued that cremation was clearly increasing in popularity in Belfast whereas opponents pointed out that Belfast Crematorium was still operating only at two-thirds capacity, at a little over 1000 cremations annually.

Claims about Catholic attitudes also conflicted. Opponents claimed that there was no evidence of the increasing popularity of cremation among Catholics as, in 1976, only 16 Catholics were cremated in Belfast, and only 33 in total were cremated from Eire (around half of those being Dubliners). By contrast, supporters estimated that 'several hundred' from the Republic were cremated annually in Belfast, and that this would be more but for the long journey from places like Cork and Kerry. A report in the *Irish Sunday Press* in June 1981 lent credence to cremation supporters' claims: Belfast Crematorium was apparently 'growing in popularity', which had much to do with those from Eire using the service. In fact, some corpses were transported by sea from Galway for cremation in Belfast and one undertaker, at least, was convinced that business from Eire was keeping Belfast Crematorium going.

In November 1977 Dublin's lord mayor, Michael Collins, announced that Eire's first crematorium would be operational in Glasnevin by 1979. This air of inevitability that suddenly appeared to surround cremation was reflected in January 1978 in an *Irish Independent* article that discussed cremation in Bronze Age Eire and remarked that cremation would 'in time' once again be the norm in the country. This optimism seemed justified as Dublin Corporation duly approved outline plans for the crematorium. Now it remained for the results of the nationwide survey to be secured.

Elsewhere, however, cremation did not advance. Westmeath County Council gave full support to its general council's unanimous resolution rejecting cremation in favour of 'traditional' burial in a new lawn cemetery. Chairperson of the general council, Jimmy O'Brien, commented: 'It's a poor day for rural Ireland if the people can't get enough land to bury their dead' (*Westmeath Independent*, 1979). Yet the nationwide survey provided the requisite results: 40 per cent of respondents, irrespective of age or religion, favoured cremation, and this despite the population being 94 per cent Catholic. The Dublin Cemeteries Committee, after receiving detailed planning permission in

February 1980, announced that it hoped to have Glasnevin Crematorium operating within a 'few years'. The planning process, begun in October 1977, had been 'efficiently dealt with' by Dublin Corporation planning officers, Eastern Health Board officials of the Dublin region health authority and the Department of the Environment (Gallagher, 1984:109).

However, Glasnevin's success did not spread. In May 1980 the Association of Municipal Authorities refused to support another call from Dean's Grange Joint Burial Board for a crematorium on its site. A new argument was employed by opponents when Frank O'Neill claimed that a crematorium would incur the loss of around 6000 jobs nationwide, including those of 1500 quarrymen, 1500–2000 undertakers, 2000 gravediggers, 200 lorry drivers and monumental sculptors. Another member of the association, T. Wade, claimed that the organization did not have the responsibility to decide whether the country should have another crematorium.

Despite this opposition, Dean's Grange Joint Burial Board persisted, referring an idea to build a crematorium to serve Dublin City and County and Dun Laoghaire to the joint committee of the councils of the three boroughs in November 1980. At the joint committee meeting debating the idea in February 1981, Jackie Loughran argued that an 'alternative' to burial should be provided. He employed the now-standard argument that the Catholic Church had changed its view and that many British Catholics were cremated. Ned Brennan supported the call by claiming that there had been no opposition to the Glasnevin project. There were, however, specific arguments against placing a crematorium on the south side of Dublin: Tony Finnucane said funerals would have to travel daily through many built-up areas of Dublin. In addition came the standard opposition claims that cremation would be no cheaper than burial. The Catholic opposition was voiced by Frank Sherwin, who thought that cremation was not acceptable 'because we are too religious' (at which point someone heckled 'We are when we are dead!'). A more specific problem was that people would not like taking home ashes as, 'They try to forget death'. The discussion ended with a decision to see how significant the demand was for Glasnevin Crematorium before deciding on a second.

Glasnevin Crematorium opened at Finglas Road, Dublin in March 1982. A year earlier it had been scheduled to be open by autumn 1981. At £160 000, it had also cost a little more than predicted. However, its cost remained low, due partly to the aforementioned site advantages and also because of the employment of 'direct labour': the work would have cost twice as much had it been had been carried out by contract workers. Imaginative use of the existing buildings also helped save money. For example, a watch-tower (several of which had been built in the cemetery to deal with the common mid-nineteenth-century problem of body-snatching) was incorporated into the crematorium as its chimney stack (Gallagher, 1984:108). Without these mitigating factors, the crematorium could have cost between £1.5 million and £2 million. The opening ceremony was accompanied by an ecumenical blessing and dedication of the crematorium. Representatives of the Church of Ireland, the Methodist and Presbyterian Churches and even of the Catholic Church were present (John Kinahan, personal communication). The Catholic Press Office issued a clear statement that Irish Catholics could freely choose cremation for themselves or members of their family.

At this point, the main problem was the lack of specific cremation legislation. All that existed was legislation based on a law of 1846, albeit updated in 1970 to allow for the disposal of corpses by means other than burial. This uncertainty worried the medical community, especially the possibility that murderers might avoid detection. Indeed, the state pathologist, Dr J.F.A. Harbison, aired this view publicly in October 1980, and even called for the introduction of proper legal safeguards before cremation be allowed to proceed. In October 1981 another intervention from Harbison helped the cause; he called for an end to the practice of burying corpses at sea, after that of a woman buried at sea was washed up two months later. Those desiring a sea burial should first be cremated, he argued. Cremationists asked the Department of Justice to draft the necessary cremation legislation but, six months later, the department told the secretary of Glasnevin Crematorium, Brendan Quinn, that it had never received this initial request.

Instead, the legal problem was referred to the Department of the Environment, which suggested that Glasnevin Cemetery Committee open the crematorium under its own statutes. The Dublin Cemeteries Committee, which was also the crematorium authority, itself contained several individuals well qualified to deal with the situation including lawyers, solicitors, barristers and a senior councillor. After consultation with the city coroner Professor Patrick Bofin, Harbison, the police chief commissioner, and the heads of all the main religious denominations (including Catholic archbishop Dermot Ryan), the Department of the Environment approved the by-law amendments. These regulations required that the doctor dealing with the body of the person who desired cremation must view the body after death before filling out the medical certificate. In this certificate the doctor had to state:

1 the hour, date and place of death;
2 who, if anyone, was present at the time of death;
3 how soon after death they had viewed the body and the extent of this examination;
4 whether they were the deceased's regular doctor;
5 for how long they had attended the deceased during their final illness;
6 whether any relationship had existed between themselves and the deceased;
7 whether they had any monetary interest in the individual's death;
8 whether they thought there was any doubt over the cause of death.

One advantage of this system was that only one medical certificate was required, unlike, for example, Scottish law, which demanded two medical certificates. Those dealing with the legal situation in Eire had been 'anxious to make cremation as simple as possible within moderate legal limits' and therefore 'eliminated the second doctor' (Gallagher, 1984:109). Initially, there was no fee for doctors completing the cremation medical form (called form 'C'), but this was changed and a doctor's fee was implemented.

By mid-June 1982, only a few weeks after it had opened, Glasnevin Crematorium had already cremated 61 corpses, 35 of which were those of Catholics. Brendan Quinn was very pleased with these unexpectedly good figures, attributing them to the cheapness of cremation. The costs of a cremation that included the disposal of ashes ranged from £65 to £110. This figure comprised the basic cost of cremation, which was under £50 sterling, with a further £60 to have the ashes placed in the 2000-niche columbarium with a marble memorial tablet. Alternatively, ashes could be interred in the garden of remembrance for £15, and a further £12 bought an inscribed limestone tablet. By contrast, burial cost between £350–£500 at the least. It cost £100 to have a grave dug and the burial carried out. If the plot had to be bought, the minimum price in Glasnevin Cemetery was £100, and this figure could be as much as £600 (land on the outskirts of Dublin, for example, averaged around £40 000 per acre, making burial plots increasingly expensive). The least expensive burial monument cost £150–£200. Thus cremation was between a fifth and a quarter of the cost of burial. The percentages cremated were about the same a year later. In summer 1983, 51 per cent of the 425 cremations performed in Dublin were of Catholics (Gallagher, 1984:109–10). By late 1985 the upper cost of buying a plot was around £800. It was predicted that, within the next ten years, cremation would become increasingly popular as land prices escalated with the ending of the recession. This, of course, would make urban burial, which already cost up to twice as much burial in a rural area, even more expensive.

With the apparent early success of Glasnevin, cremation once more became a live issue elsewhere in Eire. After failures in 1976–77, Cork Corporation again debated building a crematorium in March 1984. Councillor Vincent O'Connell supported the idea, highlighting the large sum being spent on graveyards: the council had approved a programme that allowed for spending £237 500 on the maintenance and provision of burial grounds. Claiming that land used for burial was wasted, O'Connell requested £5000 to finance the requisite initial studies for a crematorium. In response, the city manager T.J. McHugh suggested that the council obtain an up-to-date report on Dublin Crematorium. O'Connell accepted a suggestion that the council make a token grant of £5 while it investigated the situation, but even this sum was too much for Councillor Brian Sloane, who asserted that there was only a 'minimal' demand for cremation. O'Connell agreed to a suggestion that the matter be discussed in committee, but even the token £5 was not granted.

At the same time there were renewed discussions in Limerick. Jim Kenny, who had advocated cremation in 1976, organized a visit of Limerick city councillors to Glasnevin Crematorium, which he thought was working very satisfactorily. He also noted the high cost of burial that especially affected the poor. Kenny had even earmarked a site: the church in Mount Saint Lawrence burial grounds. As it was disused and vandalised, Kenny thought that there could be no objection to siting a crematorium there, and he was supported by Councillor Jack Bourke, who highlighted the increasing problem of securing land for burial. Councillor Clem Casey, also underlining cremation's inexpensiveness, thought that a crematorium should be constructed in one of Limerick's graveyards. Casey emphasized that he was not advocating cremation, but thought that it should be an alternative for individuals to decide on. Support also came from some in the Limerick funeral industry. For example, Gerard Griffin of Griffin's Funeral Home thought that cremation was 'the mode of disposal of the future' (*Limerick Consumer*, 1985). However, with only around 50 people from Limerick having been cremated in 1984, the authorities saw the demand as insufficient to warrant a crematorium. The argument that more would surely have chosen cremation had there been a local crematorium clearly did not swing the decision.

By the time of its seventh anniversary, in March 1989, Glasnevin had completed 3403 cremations. For the first time since it opened, the cost of a cremation was to increase by a small amount. Despite this, Dublin Cemeteries Committee maintained that cremation could still cost one-fifth of the cost of burial and it remained very optimistic about the crematorium's future, expecting a sharp rise in demand. Cremation again appeared to be in vogue, as, in May 1989, a Dublin firm applied for planning permission to build a crematorium and garden of remembrance costing around £500 000 near the town of Dundalk.

In October 1989 there came another application for a crematorium, this time from the General Cemetery Company of Dublin, which submitted a £250 000 plan for its Mount Jerome Cemetery (the third of the 'big three' Dublin cemeteries). The plan, including a rose garden and columbarium, was part of a wider attempt to upgrade the 154-year-old cemetery, which the company had bought in 1984, and make it into a viable business. The architect, John Batt, made much of the crematorium's advanced design, based on the newest Dutch and British crematoria. However, the application aroused strong and increasing local opposition, with residents' associations lodging various official objections, mostly relating to the traffic congestion and environmental problems that the crematorium might bring. Thus, in July 1990, and on the behest of the applicant, Dublin Corporation postponed its decision on granting planning permission as the applicants tried to placate the opposition.

Nevertheless yet another plan for a crematorium in Dublin was proposed. This proposal was different, though, as it was for what would be the first publicly-owned crematorium in Eire. Councillor Owen Hammond called on Dean's Grange Joint Burial Board to plan a crematorium for a site already earmarked for the purpose in the newly opened Shanaganh Cemetery in Shankill, County Dublin. Hammond claimed that a publicly-owned crematorium would not need to make a profit and could therefore cut the cost of a cremation by two-thirds. Councillor Barbara Culleton seconded his motion. Arguing for choice, she admitted that the estimated £1.2 million cost was considerable, but defended it as an 'investment' and added that the British Cremation Authority was willing to help. This argument did not convince the opposition. Jimmy Murphy thought the proposal 'highly irresponsible' as the crematorium would only provide a return of £35 000 for the high expenditure. The crematorium would cost £245 000 annually, based on the £35 000 income subtracted from a £280 000 annual debt repayment. Murphy's attitude also appeared partly based on antagonism to British influence as he asked: 'Must we always blindly follow everything they do in Britain? ... Have we no traditions of our own?' (*Irish Evening Press*, 1991).

The publicity surrounding the thirtieth anniversary of Belfast Crematorium did cremation no favours in Eire. After three decades of operating, the cremation rate in Northern Ireland was still only 10 per cent – very low when compared with mainland Britain (although in Belfast itself the rate was 30 per cent). Belfast Crematorium was only operating at 55 per cent capacity and running at an annual loss of £18 000. A major problem remained Catholic

reluctance. In 1990, for example, only 2 per cent of the 1591 cremated in Belfast were Catholics.

Still, some indefatigable veterans of cremation advocacy maintained their efforts. In January 1992 Councillor Collins once again tried to get a crematorium in Cork, employing the usual arguments: that the Vatican now agreed with cremation and it was a 'very Christian way of burial'; that it was cheaper; and that neither local authorities nor national government were able or willing to maintain deteriorating burial grounds. But despite Collins' almost 20 years of agitation on the issue and the fact that cremation was, albeit slowly, taking hold in Dublin, this latest attempt was even more of a failure than previous ones: in 1974 and 1987 Collins had seconders for his unsuccessful crematorium proposals; in 1992 he did not. Worse, he even received several poison pen letters, some accusing him of atheism. Refusing to be deterred Collins said: 'Roast in hell or roast in a crematorium, I will leave that to the one Judge'. (*Cork Examiner*, 1992).

Curiously, only three years later a firm proposal to build Eire's second crematorium in County Cork did emerge. A plan by two businessmen to convert the former Protestant church of St Mary's at Athowen Cemetery, Carrigane into a £750 000 crematorium received planning permission from Cork County Council on 26 July 1995. Not surprisingly, the proposal was subject to intense opposition and, fearing a possible health risk, local residents demanded an environmental impact study. Another unfortunate problem was that the proposed crematorium site was in the village of Ovens. As Dr Hugh O'Neill, chairperson of the village community group, articulated, 'We are proud of the name Ovens. Are future generations going to think it is named after a crematorium?' (*Walsall Express and Star*, 1995). The centuries-old name was, apparently, related to the Gaelic word for caves. Four hundred people soon signed objections to the development and an appeal was lodged with An Bord Pleanála (the planning appeals board) in an effort to block it. A second objection was lodged against the granting of an air pollution licence for the proposed crematorium – vital for its operation. In December the objectors were victorious, as An Bord Pleanála overturned Cork County Council's decision by upholding local objectors' appeals. The board ruled that the proposed alterations would seriously damage the character of the church, a protected building. Its ruling that the visual impact of the proposed alterations and the building's change of use would seriously damage residential amenities in the area, and that the proposal would also be prejudicial to public health, served to finish the proposal off.

Eire's second crematorium finally came not in Cork, but in Dublin. Advised by the British Cremation Society, the planners had learned from past mistakes. The 'tasteful conversion' of the cemetery chapel at Mount Jerome Cemetery on Dublin's south side opened in February 2000. The crematorium was needed as the 50-acre Victorian cemetery on the site had only a very limited amount of burial space left. In February 2000 the government minister responsible for the maintenance of graveyards expressed his hope that the income generated by the new Mount Jerome crematorium would be used 'to restore the cemetery, which is an important heritage centre because of some of the people who are buried there' (Dail Debates, 2000). In addition, there was a need for a crematorium on Dublin's south side. Building a new crematorium when cremation was not especially popular in Eire was seen as advantageous by cremationists as the facility had an 'opportunity to become well established before cremation becomes more popular' (Massey, 2000: 15). No planning objections were lodged against the project, which surprised its sponsors given the 'considerable' opposition when the plan was first mooted only a few years before. This was because the earlier proposal placed the cremator behind the cemetery chapel, which put it within 100 yards of the nearest neighbours (Mount Jerome is a residential area two-and-a-half miles from Dublin city centre). The later, successful, plan had the cremator some distance from the cemetery chapel, making it 200 yards from the nearest boundary. Remains are transported by hearse from the chapel to the cremator building after the bereaved have left the graveyard.

As there was still no Irish cremation law, the project's sponsors adopted British law and environmental standards. So thorough was the planning proposal that that Dublin Corporation itself admitted that it 'was one of the best applications it had ever received', although project sponsor Alan Massey thought there were 'very few hurdles to overcome' (Massey, 2000: 6). Another positive aspect of the plan was that most

of the infrastructure was already in place, as was the case with Glasnevin. Thus, use was made of the existing cemetery chapel which was completely refurbished with most of the features of a standard modern English crematorium. Designed to be the crematorium's 'main selling feature', the chapel ably performed this role when the facility opened. The only new building required was that housing the cremator and the laying of a gas and electricity pipe. The cremator and ancillary equipment were assembled on site. A single-unit cremator was chosen as it was anticipated that the facility would perform about 400–500 cremations annually in the first years. The entire project was completed in 18 months, of which six months comprised the building work itself. A 'hands-on approach' also helped keep the cost of the project down to around IR€ 300 000 (much less than the cost of a typical English crematorium). However, the building and refurbishment period did bring numerous small problems: for example, as the Irish economy was at full capacity at the time, contractors were difficult to coordinate. Although sharing some similarities with Glasnevin, Mount Jerome had more advanced facilities, and it was hoped that it would capitalize on the cemetery's central location and the goodwill of around 350 000 annual visitors. In its first six months Mount Jerome Crematorium performed 300 cremations (Massey, 2000: 5–7).

On 15 June 2001 Eire's third crematorium, at Newlands Cross Cemetery in Tallaght, Dublin, was officially opened. Costing £1 million, it was installed with Eire's first viewing room to allow for those whose religion (Sikhs, Hindus and Buddhists) requires more direct observation of the cremation process. The rationale behind this third crematorium was that Glasnevin and Palmerstown Cemeteries were both almost full. Moreover, the dramatic growth in cremations at Glasnevin meant that it was becoming a victim of its own success: traffic restrictions were increasingly problematic. The solution was to develop a greenfield site between the Dublin suburbs of Tallaght and Clondaikin to provide both burial space and a new crematorium. As planning laws forbade the building of cemeteries on greenbelt land, the landowner, South Dublin County Council, refused permission for a full cemetery. It did, however, allow the development of a lawn cemetery with full development of the rest of the site, which included a public recreational park, an amenity park, restoration of Ballymount Castle and the creation of two lakes. The initial application was for a cemetery only, in order to allow the easy passage of the plan. After receiving initial local authority approval, the crematorium idea was advanced, and the authority made it clear that crematorium buildings could not be intrusive. Based on the experience of Glasnevin and elsewhere, the crematorium building was situated some way from the temple or assembly area, with remains being moved by hearse. The crematorium's architect, a Pole called Andrzej Wejchert, was given a remit of designing a utilitarian building that would not be obtrusive in the landscape. Its main structure is of reinforced concrete with an offset wigwam roof to hide the flues, so they cannot be seen from the public park. As the offset overhangs the building's walls, only the roof of the building can be seen from the outside (McCullough, 2001: 37–39).

Curiously, Dublin could have had three new crematoria in three years, as there was a renewed effort to build one at Shanganagh Cemetery. A feasibility study of the proposal, funded by the Public Private Partnership (PPP) Unit of the Department of Environment and Local Government, was considered by Dun Laoghaire Area Committee in May 2001. The committee then reported this to the county council meeting in February 2002. However, the study's conclusions were negative. The estimated cost of the crematorium was IR€1.57 million (£1.237 million) and the facility was projected to perform approximately 400 cremations in its first year (predicted to increase to over 500 cremations by 2011 and to 700 by 2031). These figures meant that the crematorium could be run to yield a small surplus only if it was built with 'free' capital. The low rate of return on capital invested in its first five years meant that private investors could not be attracted and no substantial level of debt could be serviced. A PPP could only be viable if it were based on the council funding the capital cost of the project, an option for which the council did not have the funds (although, as the report noted, there was more of a chance of securing private investment if the proposed PPP were to include the entire cemetery and not solely the crematorium). For the same reason, the council could not afford to build a crematorium at Shanganagh by itself. And, even if the council

had had the finance, the project had other problems. If the entire 11-acre site allocated for the project was used by the crematorium, Shanganagh's burial capacity would be significantly reduced – so much so, in fact, that the cemetery would be forced to close around five years earlier, incurring a loss of around IR€2.857 million (£2.25 million) in income. Moreover, the crematorium was predicted to have little impact on reducing the numbers of burials at Dean's Grange Cemetery. In the end the county council had little option. It could not build a crematorium either by a PPP or by itself, so instead it decided to establish 'attractive memorial facilities' (a rose garden, memorial trees and columbaria) which would 'provide a valuable service, but on an economic basis' (Dun Laoghaire Minutes, 2002).

Similar problems beset yet another attempt to establish a crematorium in Limerick. A feasibility study carried out for Limerick County Council estimated that a crematorium based in Mount St Oliver Cemetery would cost IR€1.4 million and, due to the lack of demand (an appropriate site in the Limerick area would only handle about 275 cremations in its first year), it would not be commercially viable. The idea had been to have a crematorium operating by 2004, but the study claimed that a crematorium in Limerick might not be viable until at least 2025. The projected site had more specific problems: there was insufficient room for the requisite ancillary facilities to be built around the chapel of St Laurence in Mount St Oliver and there was residential housing in close proximity. The council, retaining some hope, anticipated an increase in demand for cremation and decided to review the situation in 2005.

At the beginning of the twenty-first century, cremation is still in its infancy in Eire, although its growth since the opening of Glasnevin Crematorium has been marked. In 1999 Glasnevin performed 850 per cent more cremations (1700) than it had in its opening year of 1982. The cause has also been boosted by Irish celebrities such as the actor Tony Doyle and the tenor Josef Locke opting for cremation. The Dublin Cemeteries Committee believe that cremation is becoming more common due to the increasing secularism and multidenominational nature of Eire society, in addition to the cost factor. Curiously, given the initial emphasis placed by cremationists on cost, this aspect is now not stressed by service providers. Several cremation-linked websites remark that:

> It is difficult to compare the costs of cremation and burial. The undertakers' charges are usually the same. In the case of burial there is the cost of a grave and headstone as well as other charges. Only a fee is involved for cremation. The bereaved may also choose to purchase a memorial plaque which is maintained free of charge in perpetuity. (Glasnevin Crematorium, 2003; Grey's, 2003; Thompson Funerals, 2003).

Given the relative size of Dublin and the fact that all of Eire's crematoria are there, it is no surprise that it has experienced the greatest leap in cremation rate. In 2001 Dublin had a cremation rate of around 10 per cent. This figure was nearer to 15 per cent by late 2003. However, Eire as a whole cremates only 5 per cent of its dead – a low rate even amongst Catholic countries. This figure is likely to increase significantly, but cremation in Eire might well benefit from the propaganda work of an active cremation society – something it has never had. **Lewis H. Mates**

Acknowledgment

Thanks to John A. Kinahan for his comments on an earlier version of this article.

References

Much of the information for this piece is based on newspaper articles reproduced in the following editions of *Pharos*: 5(3) 1939: 9; 41(4) 1975: 204; 42(1) 1976: 12, 44,105; 42(3) 1976: 162; 42(4) 1976: 193–94; 43(2) 1977: 99, 101; 43(3) 1977: 114, 179, 196, 201, 203; 44(1) 1978: 29, 36; 44(2) 1978: 101; 45(1) 1979: 41; 45(2) 1979: 71; 46(1) 1980: 28; 46(2) 1980: 85; 46(3) 1980:125; 47(1) 1981: 15, 17–18, 35–36; 47(2) 1981: 76; 47(4) 1981: 143; 48(1) 1982: 40; 48(2) 1982: 91, 102; 48(3) 1982: 115, 143; 50(1) 1984: 36–37; 50(2) 1984: 73; 51(1) 1985: 26–27; 51(4) 1985: 157; 55(2) 1989: 76; 55(3) 1989: 127; 56(1) 1990: 39; 56(4) 1990: 157; 57(1) 1991: 19; 57(3) 1991: 129; 58(1) 1992: 18; 61(3) 1995: 124; 61(4) 1995: 141; 62(1) 1996: 13; 67(3) 2001: 16.

Cork Examiner (1992), article, 7 January, reprinted in *Pharos*, 58(1): 18.

Cremation Society of Great Britain (2000), 'Annual Report for Year ended 31 March 2000': http://www.srgw.demon.co.uk/CremSoc/Constitution/AnnualReports/ Rep99-00.html#eire (accessed January 2004).

Dail Debates website: http://www.gov.ie/debates-00/1march/sect13.htm (accessed January 2004).

Dublin Evening Herald (1975), article, 14 November, reprinted in *Pharos*, 41(1), 1975: 204.

Dun Laoghaire Rathdown County Council (2002), 'Minutes of Meeting' 10 June, at: http://www.dlrcoco.ie/meetings/2002/CoCo/minjun02.htm#c200 (accessed December 2003).

Fanagans Funeral Service at: http://www.fanagans.ie/general_crematoria.html (accessed December 2003).

Fenner, Bryan (1964), 'Cremation in Ulster', *Pharos*, 30(4): 76–77.

Gallagher, Denis F. (1984), 'Cremation in the Republic of Ireland', address given to the 1983 British Cremation Society Conference, reproduced in *Pharos*, 50(3) 1984: 108–10.

Glasnevin Crematorium website at: http://www.glasnevin-cemetery.ie/html/crematorium.html (accessed December 2003).

Grey's Funeral Home, Templemore, County Tipperary, website at: http://www.ejgrey.com/cremat. html (accessed December 2003).

Irish Evening Press (1991), article, 30 January, reprinted in *Pharos*, 57(1), 1991: 19.

Irish Independent (1978), article, 7 January, reprinted in Pharos, 44(1), 1978: 36.

Irish World (2002), article, 22 Novmeber, available at: http://www.theirishworld. com/pdf/2002/824%20-%2022.11.2002/6%20.pdf (accessed December 2003).

Limerick Consumer (1985), article, 25 October, reprinted in *Pharos*, 51(4), 1985: 157.

Massey, Alan (2000), 'Mount Jerome Crematorium', *Pharos*, 66(3): 5–7.

McCullough, George (2001), 'The New West Dublin Crematorium', *Pharos*, 67(2): 34–9.

Thomspon Funerals website at: http://www.thompsonfunerals.ie/cremation.htm (accessed December 2003).

Walsall Express and Star (1995), article, 17 August, reprinted in *Pharos*, 61(3), 1995: 124.

Westmeath Independent (1979), article, 19 January, reprinted in *Pharos*, 45(1), 1979: 41.

ISLAM

For the overwhelming majority of jurisconsults who comprise the unofficial Islamic scholarly hierarchy or 'ulama, the perceived consubstantiality of religion and politics has as its inevitable corollary the axiom that Islam, or more precisely Islamic law or shari'a, legislates for every aspect of human life – and death. There exists in Islamic jurisprudence a considerably large corpus of ethical directives regarding the disposal of the dead, the funeral and its attendant rites, and the etiquette of mourning. These directives are derived almost exclusively from the Sunna or exemplary practice of Muhammad as enshrined in the ahadith – the recorded acts and sayings of the Prophet – collected in the Sihah Sitta, the six authentic Books of Tradition. The Sunna, variously translated as 'custom', 'code' or 'usage', means whatever Muhammad, by positive example or implicit approval, demonstrated as the ideal behaviour for a Muslim to follow, and therefore complements the Qur'an as a source of legal and ethical guidance.

The normal practice in Muhammad's time was to bury the dead, and Muslims everywhere still follow the Prophetic code, albeit with minor regional and cultural variations. Muslims around the world bury their dead as quickly as possible, preferably before sunset on the day of death. The corpse is cleaned by a person preferably of the same sex as the deceased and is given a ritual ablution, the ghusl. The ghusl is performed an even number of times and may be followed by another ablution known as a wudu. The bodily orifices are stopped with cotton and wool. The body is typically shrouded in a winding cloth or kafan. However, martyrs are buried as they died, in their clothes, unwashed, for their wounds supposedly bear testimony to their martyrdom.

A funeral prayer is performed for the recently dead by the mourners and by anyone present in the mosque at the time. Funeral prayers are performed in mosques as a matter of course after the canonical daily prayers. The corpse may or may not be present. As the mourners carry the corpse through the streets to a mosque for prayers or to its resting place, the shahada, or profession of faith, is recited. Piety calls upon those whom the procession passes to rise, join in the chanting and help carry the bier for a short distance. Lying on the right side with the face towards Mecca, the body is buried in a grave. There are no injunctions against the use of coffins, but burials with the body only in a wrapping are typical. For several days after death, it is common to recite litanies in remembrance of the deceased. The third, seventh and fortieth days after death are also commemorated, often with a complete communal reading of the Qur'an and the performance of special supererogatory prayers.

The Qur'an and Sunna are silent on the question of cremation, which, although not strictly forbidden by Islamic law, is generally viewed by Muslims with abhorrence. The philosophical basis of this attitude remains unclear. Nowhere in classical Islamic theology is it stated, for instance, that an intact body is required at the time of resurrection. Moreover it is unlikely that the abhorrence – which Orthodox Jews share – arose out of a desire to differentiate Islamic practices from those of other 'people of the Book' (that is, Jews and Christians). This attitude towards dead bodies has had practical consequences, particularly in relation to medical education. For example, it is almost impossible to carry out postmortem examinations in many Islamic countries. Medical students in Saudi Arabia, for example, practise anatomy on corpses imported from non-Islamic countries. They learn pathology only from textbooks; many complete their medical training never having seen a real brain destroyed by a real cerebral haemorrhage. The possibilities afforded by the growth and popularity of the Internet in recent years have led to a proliferation of websites offering advice not only on grey areas of Islamic orthopraxy but also on contemporary issues – in vitro fertilization, organ transplants and gene therapy, to name but a few – that are not covered by existing shari'a law.

While cremation does not figure prominently among the questions submitted to this new breed of 'cyber-imams', concerns regarding the permissibility of cremation appear to be on the increase, particularly among Western converts to Islam and, to a lesser degree, second-generation Muslims living in the West. Paradoxically, converts appear to be more cognisant of traditional teachings on death and burial than their 'birth-Muslim' co-religionists, and rarely broach the issue of the validity of cremation for themselves as Muslims; their enquiries focus almost exclusively on the crisis of conscience that inevitably occurs when a non-Muslim parent or dependent dies, having specified either verbally or in a formal will that the body be cremated. In cases such as these, the majority of jurists show deference to the religion of the deceased and advise that the body be disposed of in accordance with his or her wishes; in the absence of a will or prior verbal agreement, converts are advised to bury their non-Muslim dead, albeit either in accordance with the rites and traditions of the religion of the deceased or in a secular ceremony.

The impression given by the general tenor of questions submitted to these jurisprudential websites by second-generation Muslims, however, is of a generation concerned not so much with the simple question of permissibility or impermissibility, as with the reasoning which underpins the rulings given. The growth in recent years of the intellectual trend known as 'liberal Islam', a movement which has evolved from the thoughts and writings of certain Muslim academics and polemicists who are committed to Islam on the one hand, but who consider traditional Islam to be misrepresentative of the Qur'anic ideal, has led to vigorous debate on a whole range of controversial and, in some cases, hitherto taboo subjects. The Qur'anic ideal, they argue, not only adumbrates a liberal interpretation, but also actively commands man to follow liberal positions on all matters Islamic. Thus, supporters of 'liberal Islam' champion issues such as free speech, the freedom to choose one's religion and not be coerced into following Islamic law if one is not a true believer, and the right to practise *ijtihad* – all of which, they claim, is upheld by the Qur'an. Other concerns they discuss include the question of democracy, the separation of Church and state, the real meaning and role of secularism, the issue of gender and the rights of women, the position of religious minorities, and environmentalism and the notion of human progress. At the heart of the liberal Islamic discourse is the vexed question of *shari'a* reform, which itself hinges on the issue of the authority, authenticity and validity of secondary sources of law such as the Sunna and juristic consensus or *ijma'*.

Given the more pressing problems faced by the global Muslim community at the start of the twenty-first century, it is not surprising that the issue of cremation is not on anyone's list of priorities. However, with the rise of problems in the Third World caused by the spread of HIV/AIDS, urbanization and the risks associated with crowded cemeteries, Muslim authorities may be forced by exigency to reconsider the popular taboo on cremation. Under the provisions of *ijtihad*, and with the revitalization of defunct sources of law, such as *maslaha* or public interest, there is nothing to prevent reform-oriented jurists from sanctioning the use of cremation in Muslim societies, either as a solution to health and environmental problems or as a principle of personal preference. **Colin Turner**

ITALY

Italy is particularly important in the history of modern cremation, not only because of creative individuals relating to the process itself, but also because of ideological and political factors that led to cremation becoming the hostile focus of relationship between secular and religious groupings that helped forge the Catholic Church's 80-year opposition to cremation. Italy's importance is also due to the paradox of the very early introduction and practice of modern cremation in that country and yet the extremely slow adoption of the practice at the popular level. Given this importance, we first present two overlapping, but complementary, background accounts of the development and history of cremation in Italy, before relating an important parliamentary Act and moving to a final reflection on secularization. **Douglas J. Davies**

DEVELOPMENT OF CREMATION

The idea of cremation started to spread in Italy in the second half of the nineteenth century and was closely related to the 'hygiene issue' – the ruling class's growing consciousness of the terrible conditions that existed in the country in terms of public health. Doctors and scientists argued that one of the main causes of this degradation was cemeteries. Increasingly concentrated in urban areas, these produced fetid and toxic emissions, polluted drinking water and aided the spread of terrible diseases such as cholera. The first person to argue for the need to substitute burial with cremation was the head of the Department of Pharmacy of the University of Padua, Ferdinando Coletti, in January 1857. He proposed that cremation should become exclusively the practice of public institutions and that it should be carried out by the municipalities under the surveillance of the Ministry of Religion. He believed that there was, in fact, no ethical or religious objection to cremation. Nor was there, he argued, an obstacle to cremation on the basis that it made judicial investigations of a medical–legal nature difficult: an accurate examination of dead bodies would eliminate any doubt about the cause of death.

After the birth of the Kingdom of Italy in 1861 the cremationist movement found a favourable cultural context – one that was not only strongly conditioned by positivism and secular ideology, but also possessed an important reference point in the re-establishment of masonic lodges. In 1867 MP Salvatore Morelli proposed the abolition of cemeteries and their substitution with a series of cremation 'temples' located outside the city. His plan did not meet with support but, in 1869 – coinciding with an international medical congress at Florence – a document arguing for the legal recognition of cremation and its need to supersede the current burial system, 'in the interest of hygiene laws' was unanimously approved.

In 1873, the year after some scientists (Giovanni Polli, Celeste Clericetti and Paolo Gorini) had completed the first experiments on methods of cremation, the sanitary–hygienic reasons for cremation were once again supported in parliament by Senator Maggiorani during the discussion about the sanitary code project. Yet, not even this request was successful, because, at the time, the government and parliament did not seem inclined to institute laws to regulate this field. The decisive turning point for the Italian cremationist movement came in January 1876 with the cremation in Milan of Alberto Keller, a rich industrialist of Swiss origin. On the same day, in the Lombard city, the first Italian Society for Cremation was constituted, and it immediately found many followers within the urban middle class. Cremation then experienced rapid growth: from eight cremations in 1877 to some 66 per year in the 1890s. In the association, which carried out an intense popularizing campaign throughout Italy, freemasons were a very strong influence: both the president, Dr Malachia De Cristoforis, and the secretary, Gaetano Pini, another doctor who was a promoter of the campaign against rickets, were masons.

The proselytizing work of the Milanese cremationists yielded good results. While in Lodi it was the municipality itself that took the initiative of constructing a cremation temple,

new societies were constituted in Cremona in 1878, in Udine and in Rome in 1879 and in numerous other locations in the following years. The results were so good that, in 1882, it was possible to organize a congress attended by nearly all of the 24 existing societies, boasting 6000 members and located – due to reasons connected with the historical backwardness of the Mezzogiorno (south) – mainly in the centre–north regions. The congress, which took place in Modena, approved the statute of a league whose main aim, besides the coordination of efforts to obtain full legislative recognition of cremation, was to establish an important reciprocal principle among the member societies. Each of the members, having paid membership fees to the society, had the right to be cremated free of charge in any place where the proper means existed.

During this period the cremationist movement consolidated its own territorial presence and its own social base. By 1886 there were 36 constituted associations and 14 crematoria in which 668 bodies had already been incinerated. At that time, the Catholic Church's anti-cremationist campaign had acquired growing strength because, according to the Church, cremation offended the sacredness of death and was contrary to the values of Christian religion. The apex was reached with the decree from S. Uffizio on 19 May 1886 (*Quod cadaverum cremationes*), that sanctioned the official and definitive viewpoint of the Catholic Church on cremationist practices. Nevertheless, in 1888, the Italian parliament approved the new sanitary code that explicitly legislated for cremation and ordered the municipalities to 'freely concede the necessary cemetery space for the construction of cremation sites'.

This much-anticipated legal recognition marked the culminating moment of the phase of affirmation and consolidation of the Italian cremationist movement of the late nineteenth century. In the years immediately following, while on the one hand there was still some success in enlarging the number of associations, on the other, the initial thrust was weakening and, gradually, motivation and participation decreased, which was one of the essential components of the projected goals. In 1906 a new unitary structure was constituted, the Italian Federation for Cremation, which, from 1909, was presided over by Luigi Pagliani, with a head office in Turin. It decided to include among the federated bodies those municipal councils that already had the task of managing the cremation service autonomously. In 1909 this happened in 15 cities, a testimony to the fact that, in these municipalities, the cremation of corpses was recognized at the same level as burial and considered to be one of the essential services that the local government should offer its citizens. Nevertheless, in 1909 there were 31 cremation plants working in Italy and there had been a total of 6404 cremations since 1876. In 37 out of 69 provinces, cremationist principles were completely unknown. These provinces were all those of the Mezzogiorno (south) and the islands, with the exception of Naples; at the other end of the country, however, in the centre–north, the diffusion was quite widespread.

In the first two decades of the twentieth century cremations increased, albeit unsteadily, until they peaked in 1920. There was a quantitative variation throughout the 1920s which affected women to a lesser extent, and implied the relative increase of the percentage of female cremations (more or less 500 to 600 per year at the time). In 1929 the total number of cremations reached almost 11 000. During the fascist period the cremationist movement encountered many difficulties as a consequence of the restrictions on freedom imposed by the dictatorship and of the continuing opposition of the Catholic Church – an opposition that had become more powerful after the signing of the Agreement (*Concordato*) of 1929. The associations and municipalities equipped with cremation plants still carried out their activities, and in October 1936 the Italian Federation for Cremation succeeded in organizing its national congress in Turin.

The proselytizing and popularizing activities were restarted with renewed energy after the Second World War and achieved important successes both from the normative point of view and in countering the attitudes of the Catholic hierarchy. In 1963 the Catholic Church definitively abolished the prohibition on Catholics choosing cremation, and successive modifications of the mortuary police regulations have simplified the procedure of cremating a corpse. The regulation of 1990 has established, that, besides the testamentary disposition of the deceased or of his declaration of wanting to be cremated that was undersigned when he or she became a member of a cremation society, it is now legal for the spouse or next-of-kin of the deceased to request their cremation. Yet it was only after the passing of a 1987 law that cremation was made equal to burial and became a free public service paid for by the municipality.

The delay in providing this service has made cremation a minority practice for many years. The mean number of cremations in Italy each year was between 500 and 600 in the 1950s, and 700 and 800 in the 1960s; it surpassed the 1000 threshold for the first time in 1970 and the 3000 threshold in 1986. In that year the cities which had the greatest number of cremations were, respectively, Milan, Turin, Genoa – the most industrialized city in the country – followed by Livorno, Bologna, Savona and Florence. In the pope's city, however, only 82 cremations took place. The approval of the law of 1987 subsequently added impetus to the cremationist movement, although its geographical popularity remains almost exclusively in central–north Italy – in 1998 the only active societies in the south were those of Matera, Catania, Torre del Greco and Cagliari, the only place that also has a crematorium. The total number of cremations carried out in Italy each year increased from 3650 in 1988 to 23 613 in 1998, which equals 4.3 per cent of the total deaths, as opposed to 0.7 per cent ten years earlier. In the same period, the number of subscriptions to cremation societies nearly doubled (from 86 000 in 1988 to 160 000 in 1998), and the number of operational crematoria in 1998 was 37. **Fulvio Conti**.

See also freemasonry in Italy; Pini.

References

Conti, Fulvio, Isastia, Anna Maria and Tarozzi, Fiorenza (1998), *La morte laica*, I, *Storia della cremazione in Italia (1880–1920)*, Torino: Paravia-Scriptorium.

Maccone, Luigi (1932), *Storia documentata della cremazione presso i popoli antichi ed i moderni con speciale riferimento alla igiene*, Bergamo: Istituto Italiano d'Arti Grafiche.

Suchecki, Zbigniew (1995), *La cremazione nel diritto canonico e civile*, Città del Vaticano: Libreria Editrice Vaticana.

HISTORY OF CREMATION

The first modern cremation in Italy took place in 1822 when the corpse of the poet Percy Bysshe Shelley, who drowned in the Gulf of La Spezzia, was cremated. His body was burned on the beach of Viareggio on a pyre on the wish of his friend Lord Byron. In those years at the beginning of the 1800s a host of thinkers, those fostering notions of hygiene and politicians promoted the idea of cremation. One of these was the Dutch professor, Moleschott, who taught philosophy at the Universities of Rome and Turin. Another was Ferdinando Coletti (1819–81), professor of pharmacology at the University of Padua, patriot of the Risorgimento and founder and director of the *Gazzetta Medica Italiana delle Province Veneto* for 23 years, who read a memoir on the incineration of corpses, *Memoria sulla incinerazione dei cadaveri*, in a historical session of the Academy of Sciences, Letters and Arts at Padua on 11 January 1857.

This encounter produced the first apostles of the reform: Dr Vincenzo Giro (who in 1866 published his *Osservazioni sulla incinerazione dei cadaveri (Observations on the Incineration of Corpses)* in the *Gazzetta Medica Italiana*, Professor Giovanni Du Jardin who supported the principle of cremation on the basis of hygiene and economy in the Genoese newspaper *La Salute* of September 1867 and the patriot Salvatore Morelli. In Paris in 1867 during the international congress on soldiers wounded in the war, Dr Piero Castiglione and the honourable Dr Agostino Bertani gave eloquent speeches on cremation. In Florence in October 1869, on the occasion of the second International Congress of Medical Sciences, Drs Castiglioni and Coletti spoke on incineration as a method for replacing the burial of corpses. This congress voted on a motion requesting that 'all possible means be used to have a law passed, in the interest of hygiene, to substitute the burial of corpses with incineration'. This motion was realized with the cremation, on a wooden pyre, of Rajah Maharaja of Kelapur, an Indian prince who died in Florence, in December 1870. After burning for about seven hours, the corpse was finally incinerated, and Indian priests scattered the residues of the cremation in the wind. During those years there were numerous publications, speeches, conferences and memoirs, involving academies and governments, in favour of the rite

of incineration. Experiments were also conducted on various methods for destroying corpses with Professors Polli and Clericetti using gas in 1872, Professor Gorini using liquids in 1872, and with Professor Brunetti's reverberatory furnaces of 1873. Brunetti exhibited this furnace and also cinerary urns at the Vienna World's Fair.

In January 1874 Alberto Keller, a rich industrialist from Milan known for his philanthropic works, died and in his will asked that his corpse be put to the flames. To this end he named Professor Polli the executor of his will and left a large sum of money for studies and tests on cremation. Although there was no law in Italy that permitted cremation, Polli, in agreement with Clericetti, had a crematory temple built. This was made possible by the financial generosity of the Keller family and a land grant from the City of Milan in its Monumental Cemetery. This was the first crematory temple ever built in the world, inaugurated in 1876 to cremate Keller's corpse.

In 1875 the Milanese Cremation Society was founded. Among its promoters were Senator Malachia De Cristoforis (a Garibaldian veteran), Dr Gaetano Pini (later Secretary of the freemasons), Professor Giovanni Polli, Celeste Clericetti, Osvaldo Lazzati, Giovanni Sacchi, Giulio Mylius, and Giuseppe Pozzi. Later cremation societies (SO.CREM) were founded in Lodi (1877), Cremona (1878), Udine, Rome (1879), Brescia (1883), Padua, Varese, Novara, Florence, Leghorn, Pisa (1884), Como (1886), Asti, Sanremo, Turin (1887), Mantua, Verona (1888), Bologna (1889), Modena (1890), Venice (1892), Spoleto (1894), Perugia (1895), Genoa (1897), Pistoia (1901), Bergamo (1902), Monza (1903), Bra (1904), Savona (1911). Still others were established in Arezzo, Codogno, Ferrara, Pallanza, Piacenza and La Spezia. Over the years, the total number of cities with crematory furnaces reached 36. Then, due to the alliance of the fascist regime with the Catholic Church, there was a decline and only 20 cremation societies remained. The Milanese Cremation Society actively propagandized in Italy and abroad by means of bulletins, articles in political and medical journals, conferences, public meetings and technical publications.

The International Hygiene Congress at Turin in 1880 held a special session in Milan on 12 September to witness cremation tests and to set up an International Commission which, in agreement with the Milanese Cremation Society, waged a battle for new reform in the subsequent years and won: importantly, the congress used the word 'cremation' instead of 'incineration'. The delegates of the 14 nations represented Italy, France, Belgium, Germany, Russia, England, Switzerland, Spain, Portugal, Austria-Hungary, Holland, Romania, Greece and Egypt, and they proposed a motion which requested: (a) that the various countries readily pass special laws to practise the optional cremation of corpses; (b) that the governments which accepted the Sanitary Convention of Geneva add an article according to which armies be equipped with special portable apparatuses to cremate their dead on the battlefields.

In 1882 the first Congress of Italian Cremation Societies was held in Modena. The 24 societies attending approved the institution and by-laws of the League of Italian Cremation Societies whose presidents were Senator Professor Giovanni Cantoni and Senator Dr. Malachia De Cristoforis. In the meantime the Catholic Church, considering cremation anti-religious because it was upheld by members of Freemasonry and socialism, took a stand with a document of the Holy Office in 1886, in which it denied funeral rites to whomever asked to be cremated. In July 1888 the Law on Public Health and Hygiene of the Kingdom – the so-called Crispi Act – was passed, article 59 of which stated:

> The cremation of human corpses must be done in crematories approved by the provincial doctor. Municipalities must always grant the land needed for the construction of crematories in the cemeteries. The cinerary urns, containing the residues of the complete cremation, can be placed in the cemeteries or in chapels or temples belonging to moral associations recognised by the state or in private funeral niches with a stable destination and in such a way as to be protected from any sort of profanation.

Article 59 later became article 198 of the Consolidation Act of the Health Laws (1 August 1907). Since then, the activities of cremationists have been aimed fervently at calling national and international congresses to resolve problems of a technical and socio-legislative nature, and to fight against religious and conservative prejudices.

Cremation Societies held congresses in Milan (1890), Genoa (1905), Novara (1906) and Turin (1919). International congresses were held in Dresden (1874), Berlin (1890), Budapest (1894), Brussels (1910), Dresden (1911), Turin (1911, during the International Exposition of Industry and Labour), Milan (1914), Gotha (1916) and Lugano (1925). After the Second World War the various cremation societies resumed their activity despite finding difficulties. In 1963 the Catholic Church removed its canonical ban on cremation after insistent requests from the International Cremation Federation. The Congregation of the Holy Office sent the bishops a circular letter to inform them that the Holy See had decided to modify regulations regarding those who had decided to have their body cremated. Cremation in Italy continued to develop largely due to the initiative of city governments and, by 2002, more than 160 000 people were registered in over 40 cremation societies belonging to the Italian Federation. Cremation is relatively well practised in northern Italy, accounting for 30 per cent of deaths in Milan and Turin, but is little practised in southern Italy. The 2002 national cremation rate was approximately 7 per cent. **Bruno Segre**

See also Catholic Church; Coletti; journals (Italian).

PARLIAMENTARY ACT

Until 1946 Italy was a monarchy. With the advent of the Republic, the legislative authority became assigned principally to the parliament and to the government of the Republic as the executive branch of the state. Parliamentary and governmental laws constitute the 'basic foundation' of Italian law. Additionally, rules provide 'the secondary source' needed to apply the law in detailed contexts. Under Italian law, cremation is cited for the first time in Law No. 5849 of 22 December 1888 for the protection of hygiene and public health. This law is regulated by only one article (article 59) which is organizational in nature. It is only through the secondary source of the Special Regulation of the Mortuary Police, approved by Royal Decree No. 448 of 25 July 1892, that cremation received detailed regulations. The wish to be cremated has to be the result of a testament by the deceased or declaration by the dead person's relatives. The authorization of the public authority is always necessary and, in the case of a suspicious death, the authorization of the judicial authority is also required. A medical doctor must confirm the absence of a suspicious death caused by a criminal act. A cremation without a coffin is possible.

In 1907, Royal Decree No. 636 (1 August), published the 'sole text of the sanitary laws', which reiterated the disposition contained in the preceding Law No. 5849 of 1888. The same organizational nature is in article 343 of Royal Decree No.1265 (27 July 1934), in the new 'sole text of the sanitary laws'. With Royal Decree No. 1880 of 21 December 1942, a new 'Regulation of the Mortuary Police' was issued. With the preceding regulation of 1892 rescinded, cremation was now possible only with the expressed testament of the deceased, relatives no longer had the option of requesting it, and cremation had to include the entire coffin. In a Decree of the President of the Republic No. 794 (8 May 1968), the Special Regulation of the Mortuary Police (1892) was modified so that, in addition to the testament, the written desire to be cremated expressed by the deceased in a cremation note recognized by the public authority would now be considered valid. It is necessary that the deceased remained 'associated' with the said note up until the time of death. A new regulation of the mortuary authority was issued with Decree No.803 (21 October 1975), but nothing new was introduced with respect to the preceding norms.

In order to encourage cremation, the process became sanctioned, without charge, with Decree No. 359 (31 August 1987), article 12, parag. 4. This benefit, with Decree No. 392 (27 December 2000), was limited in favour of impoverished individuals only. The actual (April 2002) existing Regulation of the Mortuary Police refers to the Decree of the President of Republic No. 285 (10 September 1990). The only new element concerns the recognition of the spouse and relatives to arrange the cremation of the deceased. Finally Law No.130 (30 March 2001), entitled 'Regulations in the Matter of Cremation and Dispersal of the Ashes' recognizes, if only by the expressed will of the deceased, the possibility of dispersing the ashes, which had, up to this point, been considered a penal crime punishable by inprisonment. In addition, it was made incumbent upon the public authority and doctors to disseminate information to citizens and relatives of the deceased regarding all of the

funeral practices and different options for the disposal of the body. **Anna Salice**

SECULARIZATION

The French Revolution and the political, juridical, social and economic reforms in eighteenth- and nineteenth-century Europe were the cause of remarkable social change. The French Declaration of Human and Civil Rights, the privatization of lands, aristocracy's decadence, the industrialization of work and the birth of the proletariat, along with the expropriation of ecclesiastical property and the new organization of public life, constituted the principal events that began the secularization of society. Religion lost influence over civil society and was no longer the bond of people's unity. As the interface between religion and civil society began to break up, the movement from confessional society to lay society began. In this context, burial was the only type of funeral in Europe; cremation was absent. In Italy, thanks to the total identification between the state and religion, the Catholic Church was in firm possession of the monopoly of burial, which took place within the churches, in churchyards and in ecclesiastical grounds. This dominion began to decrease when, as a result of the military occupation of France and Austria, the principles of the Saint Cloud's Edict, emanating from Napolean Bonaparte in 1804, became effective in Italy. These located burial places outside inhabited centres, and insisted that they were properly enclosed. Following the principles of equality expressed in the French Revolution, the location of, and inscriptions on, tombstones were regulated. The edict originated because of concern over public health, since interments were often hurried with unhygienic consequences and, moreover, expanding towns had come to include cemetery areas. It was in the wake of the secular needs of the modern states and of the progress of civilization that the concept of cremation began to assert itself. It followed that the Catholic Church disapproved of cremation, viewing it as an underlying reason for the dissociation between religion and civil society. Moreover, cremation was also opposed at the political level, not only in respect of the habits of the citizens, but also for legal reasons, because it could be an obstacle to justice if a postmortem examination became necessary after the funeral.

However, in Italy, as in other European

countries, cremation has not been expressed through the secularization of burial, but has come to exist side-by-side with it. It has, rather, become the expression of the progress of a civil society careful over hygiene and urban planning. It has become a choice that goes beyond ideological and religious convictions. Nevertheless, the spread of cremation in Italy has been negatively affected by the strong influence of the Catholic Church. Only in 1963 did it take note of non-religious reasons for cremation and remove its prohibition with the sanction of excommunication, thereby allowing an ecclesiastical funeral to be followed by the cremation of the deceased. This adaptation to social and civil reality has not meant that the Catholic Church supports or approves of cremation, but that it has recognized that the Catholic faithful are also citizens with the right of acting according to their inner conviction, especially when the choices offered by civil society do not contradict the dogmas of religion.
Anna Salice

J

JAPAN

Following the major account of the history and development of cremation in Japan are descriptions of modern-day cremation rituals and of the distinctive practice of object cremation.

HISTORY AND DEVELOPMENT

Although cremation is now taken for granted throughout Japan, where the nationwide cremation rate is nearly 100 per cent, this broad acceptance is relatively recent, full-body burial having been the preference for most Japanese until the twentieth century. It was not until the 1930s that the majority of the dead in Japan were burned instead of buried, and in some regions, cremation did not predominate until the late 1970s. In fact, from the early seventeenth to the late nineteenth centuries, cremation was the object of intense controversy, which peaked during an official ban on the practice in the early 1870s. These were the years just following the Meiji Restoration of 1868, executed by an alliance of disgruntled samurai who overthrew

the ruling Tokugawa shogunate (in power since 1603) in the name of the imperial family, which had lacked real political power for centuries. In its zeal to reform Japan from top to bottom, the new Meiji state sought to abolish what it considered to be 'evil customs of the past', one of these being cremation, a long-standing practice in urban areas and in many rural communities as well. When cremation was outlawed in 1873 it was understood to be a uniquely Buddhist mode of handling the dead, making it a natural target for virulently anti-Buddhist Confucian scholars and Shinto nativists who were in favour with the new government. During the first few years after the revolution, Buddhist temples were subject to land seizures, destruction of property and outright closures, while thousands of monks and nuns were forced to return to lay life. By 1873 the worst attacks against the Buddhist establishment had passed, but the cremation ban was one more blow against what enemies labelled a heretical and foreign teaching – 'foreign' despite the fact that Buddhism had entered Japan via the Korean peninsula as early as the sixth century, making an incalculable impact on the development of Japanese civilization.

Perhaps the most important and enduring way in which Buddhism infiltrated the lives of the Japanese was through death. From the seventh century, Buddhist rituals were integrated into funerals for the elite, eventually making their way into the death rites of commoners. By the start of the Tokugawa period (1603–1868), Buddhist priests were entrenched as funerary specialists, a role reinforced by the shogunate's rule that all families officially register with a Buddhist temple. The Buddhist hegemony over death does not mean that funeral and memorial rites were uniform across Japan. There was a wide variety of form and content, especially with regard to the disposal and memorialization of remains. The Buddhist canon recognizes four different ways of disposing of a corpse: earth burial (*dosô*), water burial (*suisô*), cremation (*kasô*), and exposure in the wild (*fusô*, or 'wind burial'). Until the twentieth century, most communities in Japan opted for earth burial, while some abandoned corpses in the mountains. Yet Shâkyamuni Buddha was himself cremated, so after Buddhism was introduced to Japan, aristocrats and then many commoners adopted cremation, a practice that they believed to be particularly meritorious – a means to 'becoming a buddha' (jôbutsu) after death. According to an eighth-century history (*Shoku nihongi*), cremation was introduced to Japan by the Buddhist priest Dôshô (629–700), who was burned on a funeral pyre by his disciples in 700. The cremation of Empress Jitô (645–703) followed several years later, establishing a precedent among the aristocracy.

Recent archaeological evidence, however, shows that cremation was practised in Japan well before Dôshô's time, and the written record suggests that not all cremations in the centuries immediately following Dôshô's funeral were motivated by Buddhist beliefs. By the end of the Heian period (794–1185), however, cremation had become closely tied to Buddhist belief and ritual. The relics of Shâkyamuni were enshrined in stupas; likewise, the cremated remains of those aspiring to buddhahood (or, at least, a Buddhist paradise) were interred under stupas at Mt Kôya and other sanctified locations. There was also a commonly held belief that the flames of the cremation fire helped to liberate the soul of the deceased and send it on its way. From a more philosophical perspective, the sight of burning bodies clearly manifested the Buddhist teaching that all things are impermanent. Cremation became especially popular among adherents of the Jôdô Shinshû (True Pure Land) school of Buddhism, whose founder, Shinran (1173–1262), was cremated and interred in Kyoto. To this day, believers send cremated remains to Kyoto for interment alongside Shinran and other patriarchs.

Over the course of the medieval period, communities developed different conventions to manage cremation. In some areas, it was common for relatives to burn their own dead, with neighbours providing the necessary wood. In others, particularly in western Japan, the task was committed to a professional class of cremators and graveyard caretakers called *onbô*. Depending on the characters used to write it, this term can refer to a Buddhist monk and his residence or can be roughly translated as 'shadowy death'. This dual meaning is appropriate for a group of people who were viewed as quasi-religious figures but also shunned as outcasts contaminated by their regular contact with death. Whether performed by family members or outcast professionals, cremation had become prevalent throughout Japan (especially urban Japan) by the

seventeenth century, when it came under attack from Confucian scholars inspired by anti-cremation tracts from Song-period China (960–1279). 'Song studies' (*Sogaku*) captured the imagination of much of the intellectual elite in Tokugawa Japan, and one of its main premises was that Buddhism, a creed that encouraged people to leave their families to become monks and nuns, was unfilial and inhumane. The Buddhist practice of cremation, which in many instances required children to burn the flesh of their parents, was particularly reviled by Chinese Confucians and their Japanese counterparts. In the words of one Song magistrate, casting one's parents into fire 'is the very highest pitch of cruelty; there is in such deeds nothing that tallies with the natural feelings of man' (De Groot, 1967: 1403). The famous Japanese scholar Kaibara Ekken (1630–1714) wrote that the filial child 'loves the flesh of his parent' and, 'even though the parent has died, treats [the parent] as if still living'. Therefore, cremating a parent was even more reprehensible to Kaibara than 'abandoning the body in the fields and making it food for the foxes and badgers'. Confucian scholars actively propagated their anti-cremation stance among the Tokugawa-period elite; and even the imperial court, which had burned its dead for centuries, abandoned the practice in 1654, when Emperor Gokômyô (1633–54) was buried whole. The feudal lords of several domains also tried to ban cremation among commoners, but the range of these bans was limited, and it is not clear to what extent they were actually enforced.

With the founding in 1868 of an imperial government hostile to the Buddhist establishment and bent on turning Japan into a centralized nation-state, anti-cremation forces saw their chance to extinguish the practice once and for all. Perhaps because they had more pressing matters to attend to, Meiji leaders took no action for several years, despite public calls to do so. In May 1873, however, the Tokyo police proposed to move crematoria from densely populated neighbourhoods in the capital to outlying areas, setting in motion a chain of events that culminated in an all-out ban on cremation the following month. The Tokyo police were concerned that smoke from cremation grounds – consisting of little more than fire pits topped with roofs to keep out the rain – was injuring the health of those who lived nearby. But when the department suggested that cremation be removed from the city centre, officials in the central government baulked, since approving this plan would be tantamount to state recognition of a practice loathed by many in the Meiji elite. In response, therefore, the ruling Council of State prohibited cremation throughout Japan. The council's action provoked an outcry among cremation supporters, who included not only *onbô* and Buddhist priests but also ordinary Japanese and even sympathetic government officials. Through letters to the editor and petitions to the state, they waged a vigorous campaign that led to the prohibition's repeal in May of 1875, less than two years after it was enacted. Meiji officials justified the ban on two grounds: first, throwing bodies into fire was disrespectful to the dead and therefore damaging to public morality; second, the foul smoke produced by burning corpses was dangerous to public health. Opponents of the ban accepted these terms of engagement and turned them to their advantage, arguing that cremation actually contributed to the physical and moral health of the nation by producing compact, portable and hygienic remains for use in ancestor worship. It was better to gather the bones of family members in one spot than to bury their rotting bodies in different locations, they argued, pointing out that the ban was particularly onerous for urban dwellers who depended on cremation to maintain family gravesites in cramped temple cemeteries. To bolster their case, opponents of the ban also trumpeted the fact that medical professionals in Europe and America, the models for Japan's modernization, had begun promoting cremation as an alternative to full-body burial (Shiroshi, 1976: 232).

Ironically, the ban in fact stimulated a public discourse on cremation, resulting in a widely accepted rationale for burning the dead. Pressured by campaigners and a lack of space for burial, the Meiji government lifted the ban in 1875, and working within legal guidelines, coalitions of businessmen, Buddhist priests and local governments began building modern crematoria. Complete with ventilation systems and smokestacks, their design and efficiency impressed European cremation promotors, who looked to them as models (Bermingham, 1881: 45–48). In a remarkable about-face, Meiji bureaucrats began to actively promote cremation, no longer seen as a strictly Buddhist

practice, but now viewed as a means of conserving space and protecting public health. Some anti-Buddhist ideologues continued to speak out against the practice, but their voices were muffled and soon smothered by the pro-cremation consensus that spread among policy-makers and the educated elite. As Japan underwent rapid industrialization and urbanization in the decades that followed, civic authorities banned full-body burial in one city centre after another and promoted the building of modern crematoria. This trend spread to rural areas as well, until, by the end of the twentieth century, cremation had become the fate of nearly every Japanese. **Andrew Bernstein**

References

Bermingham, Edward J. (1881), *The Disposal of the Dead: A Plea for Cremation*, New York: Bermingham and Co.

Bernstein, Andrew (1999), 'The Modernization of Death in Imperial Japan', PhD dissertation, Columbia University.

Bernstein, Andrew (2000), 'Fire and Earth: The Forging of Modern Cremation in Meiji Japan', *Japanese Journal of Religious Studies*, 27(3–4): 297–334.

De Groot, J.J.M. (1967), *The Religious System of China*, Vol. 3, book 1. Taipei: Ch'eng-wen Publishing Co.

Saito Tadashi (1987), *Higashi Ajia sô, bosei no kenkyū*, Tokyo: Daiichi Shobo.

Shiroshi, Sakatani (1976), *Meiroku zasshi: Journal of the Japanese Enlightenment*, trans. William Braisted, Tokyo: University of Tokyo Press.

MODERN DAY CREMATION RITUALS

Cremation in Japan requires the active participation of family members and close friends of the deceased. Normally, cremation follows the funeral ceremony, in which the body is placed in a coffin flanked by an elaborate, multi-tiered altar. A wide circle of acquaintances attends the funeral, during which guests typically approach the altar to offer incense and pay respects to the mourning family. However, only relatives and close friends follow the corpse to the cremator, where mourners witness the body being placed in the furnace, usually accompanied by the chanting of Buddhist scriptures. They then retire for approximately one hour to a waiting room where they can drink and have refreshments. It is common to bring a picture of the deceased to preside over the gathering.

After the cremation is finished, the mourners assemble once more in front of the furnace to collect the remains. The body is not reduced completely to ash but to small bones that are heaped on a metal tray. It is the task of family and friends to approach these remains in pairs, together lifting the bones with chopsticks and placing them in a ceramic urn. Different explanations are given for why the bones are collected two-by-two and not by one person at a time. One is that it helps to dilute the dangerous pollution associated with death. Another is more mundane: it ensures that the bones are not accidentally dropped. In many instances, the mourners will place only a portion of the remains in the urn, with the rest handled by the crematorium staff. The last bone to be placed in the urn is called the *nodobotoke*, or the 'throat Buddha'. Popularly thought to come from the throat, this bone is actually a portion of the upper spine. It is placed on top of other bones in the urn because its shape suggests a Buddha seated in meditation.

Once the urn is sealed, it is placed in a box wrapped in white cloth, which is then usually brought back to the site of the funeral – whether a temple, a home, or a funeral parlour – for a second ceremony to help the dead person on their way in the afterlife. Formerly, this ceremony took place on the seventh day after death, but it is now performed on the day of the funeral itself in order to save time. This compression of the ritual calendar was facilitated in the early twentieth century by the introduction of oil-powered crematoria, which drastically reduced the time it took to incinerate a corpse. Instead of having to bring the body to a crematorium one day and retrieve the remains the next, since the 1930s mourners have been able to pick up the bones after only an hour has elapsed. Once the 'seventh-day' ceremony is finished, the cremated remains are generally placed on an altar at the mourning family's home for a little over a month, after which they are interred in a family grave, the site of periodic memorial services.

OBJECT CREMATION

Fire is an important element in a number of religious rites in Japan. While its function may vary widely, depending on context, there are celebrations during which a ceremonial cremation of objects takes place as part of a rite of separation in which people bid farewell to objects that have played an important part in their lives but are now old, broken or beyond use. After a religious ceremony, objects are disposed of in a ritual manner either by cremation or by being interred. Cremation is the more common both because fire is thought to cleanse any adhering impurities and because cremation is the normal way of dealing with human bodies. Practically speaking, cremation also leaves behind fewer final remnants that would demand further attention.

These rites of ritual farewell and disposal are usually known by the name *kuyô*, an essentially Buddhist term used today mainly for Buddhist ancestral rites – a series of religious ceremonies set in progress upon human death. By using the word *kuyô*, rituals performed on behalf of objects are directly linked to human funerary rites. But *kuyô* rites for objects are not limited to a Buddhist context since the ceremonial farewell of object cremation can also be a Shintô ritual. Besides the word *kuyô*, with its Buddhist connotations, these rites are also sometimes called *kanshasai* which can be translated as 'thanksgiving festival'. Underlying religious concepts for these ceremonies can be found both in animistic beliefs and in Buddhist teaching, which ascribes the Buddha-nature not only to humans but also to animals, plants and objects.

Such rites are not performed on behalf of every object but only for objects to which an individual has formed a particularly strong attachment. Some items – such as needles and writing brushes – have received ritual attention for centuries; others – such as shoes and hairdressers' scissors – have only attracted ritual attention in the second half of the twentieth century. The usual explanation for attending the ceremony is that worshippers wish to express their gratitude on the occasion of parting with an item that has played an important part in their lives. Tools used to perform the traditional Japanese arts are frequently among cremated items but, as the cases of hats and semiconductors show, any object can receive ritual attention if there is a group of people willing to organize and sponsor such an event. These festivities are often organized by professional associations that also use the occasion as a means for fostering public relations and furthering social contacts.

Kuyô rites for objects are generally annual events held at Buddhist temples or Shintô shrines. One example of an item usually cremated are wooden chopsticks, which are cremated during an annual ceremony sponsored by the chopsticks-producing industry. The ceremony is performed on 4 August, which has been designated 'Chopsticks Commemoration Day'. Other items to be mentioned are writing brushes, bamboo whisks used in the tea ceremony and paper umbrellas. Clocks, watches and dolls are cremated if they are combustible. There are cases in which cremation is performed in an incinerator, others in which it is carried out in a basin or on a funeral pyre and – rarely – even on a very unspectacular site resembling one where household waste is burnt. **Angelika Kretschmer**

References

Abe, Masaji (1993), *Hashi no hanashi – hashi to shoku no bunkashi* (*A Talk about Chopsticks – A Cultural History of Chopsticks and Food*), Tokyo: Horupu shuppan.

Kobayashi, Minoru (1987), 'Tokei kuyô' ('Kuyô Rites for Clocks'), *Minzoku*, 126: 3–4.

Kretschmer, Angelika (2000), *Kuyô in Contemporary Japan: Religious Rites in the Lives of Laypeople*, Göttingen: Cuvillier.

Matsuzaki, Kenzô (1996), 'Kibutsu no kuyô kenkyû josetsu: kutsu no kuyô o chûshin ni' ('An Introduction into the Research on Kuyô Rites for Utensils, with a Focus on Kuyô Rites for Shoes'), *Mingu kenkyû*, 112: 23–32.

Ôsaki, Tomoko (1995), 'Ueno Kaneiji Kiyomizu Kannondô no ningyô kuyô' ('Kuyô Rites for Dolls in the Kaneiji Kiyomizu Kannondô Temple Hall in Ueno'), *Nihon minzokugaku*, 201: 109–19.

Tanaka, Senichi (1987), 'Dôgu no kuyô – fuyô dôgu no shobunhô ni miru mingukan' ('Kuyô Rites for Utensils – Aspects of Folk Objects to be Observed in the Way of Disposal of Useless Objects'), *Mingu Monthly*, 20(5): 1 (3854)–9 (3862).

JOURNALS (ITALIAN)

The Italian cremationist movement did not, during its emergent stage, have any official information sources; rather, there was a proliferation of articles in medical–scientific and freemason magazines and journals. In addition, there were reports in the local press in the cities where the movement was strongest, due to the popularizing work of positivist scientists and doctors. A first popularizing attempt, closely connected with the masonic world, emerged in 1876 in Milan, when the *Bollettino della Società per la Cremazione dei Cadaveri di Milano* (*Bulletin of the Society for the Cremation of Corpses in Milan*) was published. This was the result of an idea of Gaetano Pini, one of the most important exponents of the movement. The *Bollettino* was published irregularly until the beginning of the 1890s and became an efficient popularizing and reflective instrument, which gave information on the progress of the Milanese association, cremation in Italy and in the rest of the world. From 1890 the periodical adopted the title of *Bollettino della Cremazione. Organo della Lega Italiana e della Società di Milano per la Cremazione* (*Cremation Bulletin. Organ of the Italian League and the Society of Milan for Cremation*). The year 1886 saw the publication of an issue of the newsletter *La Cremazione* (*Cremation*). Edited and printed by the printer Giovanni Testera in Alessandria (Piemonte), it claimed to be the national voice for cremation ideas. Despite this, for decades the *Bollettino* continued to be the only attempt by the cremationist movement to use a periodical that was able to promote cremation.

To find other periodicals – except the only issue of *La Cremazione* printed in 1901 by the Cremation Society of Pistoia (Toscana) – we need to go to the late 1930s, when, after many attempts during more than a decade of fascist dictatorship, the Italian Federation for Cremation (*Federazione Italiana per la Cremazione*) decided to print its own annual information organ for the confederated associations. The result was *La Circolare*, a bulletin of but few pages which was published between 1937 and 1941. From the beginning of the twentieth century until the Second World War, it is impossible to trace newsletters or periodicals directly related to cremationist associations. Nevertheless, this lack of formal published information did not seem to stop the circulation of information to members, for there was much lively activity in publishing monographs, reports, statutes and commemorations – a strategy widely consolidated in the previous decades.

The recovery of the activities of the *Federazione* after 1945 was marked by a higher sensitivity towards information. This led to the publication of a national periodical, the *Bollettino della Federazione Italiana per la Cremazione* (*Bulletin of the Italian Federation for Cremation*), published between 1954 and 1957. This was followed – after an isolated issue in 1958 entitled *La Cremazione* – by the periodical *L'Ara*, organ of the confederated society, which was published continuously from 1959 until 1998. In the second half of the 1990s one observes a sea change in attitudes, by which many of the individual associations (Bologna, Genoa, Livorno, Pavia, Reggio Emilia, Turin, Varese) established a more direct contact with their members and sympathizers through the publication of newsletters. Noteworthy is the experience of the Turin Cremation Society, which, since 1993, has continued to print its own newsletter, *Socrem News*, alongside another periodical which has been published since 1994: *Confini. Temi e Voci dal Mondo della Cremazione* (*Borders. Themes and Concepts of the World of Cremation*), in cooperation with the scientific activity of the Ariodante Fabretti Foundation of Turin. This embraces many views and reflections connected to the rite of cremation, processes of mourning, the formation of funerary operators and the many problems associated with death in contemporary society, making *Confini* a national reference point for all those who are involved with cremation and death. The cremationist periodicals cited here are at present preserved – in original and copied versions – in the Fondazione Ariodante Fabretti di Torino (www.arpnet.it/fabretti), which possesses a rich collection of national and international cremation journals.

Walter Tucci

See also Fabretti Foundation; freemasonry in Italy; Pini.

References

Conti, F., Isastia, A.M. and Tarozzi, F. (1998), *La morte laica. Vol. I: Storia della cremazione in Italia (1880–1920)*, Torino: Paravia Scriptorium.

Comba, A., Mana, E. and Nonnis Vigilante, S. (1998), *La morte laica. Vol. II: Storia della cremazione a Torino (1880–1920)*, Torino: Paravia Scriptorium.

Filippa, M. (2001), *La morte contesa. Cremazione e riti funebri nell'Italia fascista*, Torino: Paravia Scriptorium.

JUDAISM

The National Socialist use of cremation to dispose of millions of murdered victims during the Holocaust complicates Jewish conceptions of cremation in a way that is unique in the Western religious world. However, from the 1870s to the 1930s, long before the Nazis began a policy best termed as corpse incineration, most Jewish opinion-makers argued that cremation was basically incompatible with traditional Jewish burial. In this, Judaism was no different from many Christian denominations. However, the reasons for rejection differed. Although a significant number of secular and Reform Jews have elected to be cremated, Conservative and Orthodox opinions utterly reject the practice.

As noted above, Judaism's response to modern cremation is complicated by the Nazi use of crematoria to dispose of the corpses of Jews murdered during the Holocaust; whereas few non-Jews think about the Holocaust when considering cremation, virtually all Jews do so. For some Jews, the choice of cremation is often tantamount to apostasy as Professor Neil Gillman of New York's Jewish Theological Seminary noted, '[a]fter the Holocaust, any Jew who opts for cremation is obscene' (Woodward and Underwood, 1997). In ancient times Jews of all statuses tended to prefer earth graves and tomb burials, even during periods of Hellenization. Indeed, Tacitus considered Jewish preference for burial rather than pyres to be one of their cultural distinctions.

Beginning in the second century the evolving rabbinic tradition described how corpses should be washed, attended and prepared for burial, and the elaborate rituals of the Jewish burial society (*chevra khadisha*) always assume an earth burial. Many biblical passages have been cited to justify the preference for earth burial including the description of Adam's eventual return to dust (Genesis 3:19) and spiritual rebirth through burial (Ecclesiastes 12:7). The legal injunction to bury the dead (Deuteronomy 21:23) became the most important starting point for rabbinic commentary. The Hebrew phrase, *Kavor tikberenu* ('thou shalt surely bury him'), gained the character of a biblical commandment and was so treated by distinguished shapers of the rabbinic tradition such as Maimonides and Joseph Caro. Interpretation of this biblical passage has been key in Jewish discussions of burial law and cremation. Although the passage specifically discusses the corpse of a hanged man, in rabbinic exegesis, extrapolation from specific meanings is necessary to draw lessons applicable for contemporary situations not explicitly addressed in scripture. Hence, the admonition to bury a hanged man has a broader meaning for Talmudic discussion because it is the main commandment dealing with burial.

By contrast, biblical discussions of burning refer either to the destruction of something evil or impure or to the burning of offerings as 'odours pleasing to God'. Cremation and funeral pyres fall outside these orbits in traditional exegesis since the dead are neither evil nor an offering to God. In most cases, corpse burning was reserved as a severe punishment or was inflicted by enemies. Biblical passages in the prophetic books posit a clear connection between pyres and human sacrifice. Passages referring to objectionable rites of 'the nations' (for example, the Phoenicians) note that the burning of children was particularly abhorrent (Deuteronomy 12: 31; II Chronicles 28: 3; Jeremiah 7: 30–32), and even describe the act of burning bodies as so offensive that God would exact divine wrath and turn the place of burning into a place where vast numbers would be buried 'until there is no room'. Slim evidence for some ancient Israelite use of pyres is provided in 1 Samuel 21:12, which describes how Saul and his sons were burned by Israelite rescuers after their bodies were cut down from the walls of Beth Shan where they had been executed by the Philistines. This passage excited great interest among Jewish supporters of cremation in the early 1900s. Yet, even in this case, the biblical passage goes on to describe that, after burning, the bones were buried.

Jewish discussion of modern cremation was generally shaped in Germany and the United States. Hence, Jewish opinion on cremation developed in areas with highly assimilated Jewish populations and in societies with significant cremationist activity. By contrast, Jews in the Russian Empire were much less concerned with the issue, even as cremationist movements there were much smaller. The three major denominations within Judaism disagree on many issues including cremation. On many issues,

Conservative and Reformed views have accommodated modernity by adapting and changing Jewish customs to varying degrees. Orthodox Judaism emphasizes the distinctiveness of traditional Jewish practices as fully compatible with modernity. Since cremation has no place in Jewish tradition it would be unconscionable for Orthodox observance to include cremation. Conservative views tend to share with Orthodoxy the idea that cremation represented a denial of Jewish culture, but Conservative views tend to make reference to the role of history and the trauma of the Holocaust more directly.

European interest in modern cremation developed during the Enlightenment, a period which also saw a new German Jewish movement interested in reforming Judaism and Jewish rituals. Leading Reform responses to questions about cremation's compatibility with Judaism note that enough variety of opinion exists even within the Orthodox tradition to show that the matter was never fully resolved. In 1894 the Central Conference of American Rabbis decided that no ritual associated with burial should be withheld in the case of cremation, and that ashes could unquestionably be buried in Jewish cemeteries. However, the general sense even within Reform Judaism was that cremation was best not chosen as a burial option.

In 1904 Rabbi Meir Lerner, an Orthodox authority from Hamburg, issued a widely cited denunciation of cremation that remains a cornerstone of Orthodox discussions. In this Orthodox interpretation, 'burial' can only mean interment in the ground, and burial in the ground is a scriptural imperative and not merely a custom. The injunction 'thou shalt surely bury' is at the centre of such arguments. The distinction is important because, whereas rabbinic interpretation permits changes in customs, rabbinic tradition considers deviation from scriptural imperatives (divine laws) to be sinful. One Orthodox authority even draws a connection between the rise of cremation and the decline of Jewish cultural strength: 'the widespread practice of cremating Jewish bodies is a tragic commentary on the erosion of Jewish norms and values. Cremation is a gentile practice ... It nullifies the atoning process of the body's underground disintegration' (Weiss, 1991: 80).

Orthodox arguments often see the wish to be cremated as constituting a final denial of

Judaism. Indeed, the Orthodox view includes an obligation for observant Jews to ignore the wishes of an otherwise pious Jew who desires cremation. The need to fulfil biblical commandments takes precedence over the deceased's instructions. One who has been cremated should be denied all further burial rituals. In Orthodox Judaism burial is more than something to be done to a corpse; the actual process of lengthy decomposition is part of the atonement for earthly sins. Decomposition becomes a ritual act. Fear of incorrectly performing a ritual is a central feature of Orthodox religiosity. Appreciation of this aspect of the religious life is essential to understanding why cremation becomes not merely unacceptable but sinful. Many Orthodox opinions further hold that (excepting victims of terror, discussed below) cremated ashes may not be buried in a Jewish cemetery, although this view has been challenged within the Orthodox community.

It is in the opinions of Conservative rabbis on cremation that the clearest distinctions of Jewish opinions vis-à-vis Christian opinions on cremation may be seen. By a direct comparison with other middle-of-the road religious movements in the West, such as Methodism or Presbyterianism, one might expect the Conservative Jewish movement to have gradually tolerated cremation. However, the great historical trauma of the Holocaust with the gross violation of Jewish corpses utterly changed the conditions of consideration. The result is that, in order to affirm the continued existence of Jewish traditions and embrace a Jewish cultural identity, burial becomes a more central issue and 'cremation' is linked with the Nazi gassing of Jews. Whereas cremation gradually moved from a radical space in Christian culture to a reformist space in a general secular culture, it became incompatible with renewed Jewish cultural identity in the wake of the Holocaust and especially troubling for Conservative Jews. Awareness of the Holocaust informs even the most sympathetic Jewish discussions of cremation.

In Jewish discussions from whatever denomination, crematoria themselves are frequently linked with the Nazi killing process. At killing centres like Auschwitz-Birkenau, the crematorium and gas chambers were in the same building. Hence, memories of the camps or rabbinic discussion of the implications of whether or not someone was murdered hinge on whether or not someone was seen entering 'the crematorium for de-lousing' or had been at a camp 'where there was a crematorium' (Zimmels, 1977: 145) In this way, rabbinic discourse on the subject confirms the notion that cremation is inextricably linked with an attack on Judaism rather than being a voluntary form of burial. Given the trauma inflicted by the Holocaust, such a rejection of cremation in official discussions is fully understandable, although in many ways it merely underscores Jewish objections to cremation which existed prior to the Holocaust. **Tim Pursell**

See also Nazi cremation.

References

Freehof, R. and Solomon, B. (1971), *Modern Reform Responsa*, Cincinnati: Hebrew Union College Press.

Freehof, R. and Solomon, B. (1980), *New Reform Responsa*, Cincinnati: Hebrew Union College Press.

Lamm, Maurice (1969), *The Jewish Way in Death and Mourning*, New York: Jonathan David Publishers.

Lerner, R. Meir (1905), *Chaye Olam (Eternal Life)*, Berlin: Defus T.H. Ittskovski.

Weiss, R. Abner (1991), *Death and Bereavement: A Halakhic Guide*, New York: Ktav.

Woodward, Kenneth L. and Underwood, Anne (1997), 'The Ritual Solution,' *Newsweek*, 22 September: 62.

Zimmels, H.J. (1977), *The Echo of the Nazi Holocaust in Rabbinic Literature*, New York: Ktav.

K

KAN, J.M.

J.M. Kan was a civil servant within the Netherlands' Ministry of Home Affairs responsible for preparation of a bill covering the legality of cremation, formulated in 1938 and passed in 1940. On 13 April 1949, a committee of nine members, representing the varied opinions of the day, was established under Kan's leadership to enable the general public to make a free choice over cremation, which would affect the building of new crematoria.

The second Kan committee was established in 1954. Its task was to fundamentally revise the Funeral Act (*Begrafeniswet*) of 1868. On 23 September 1959, the Burial and Cremation Act (*Wet op de Lijkbezorging*) of 1955 was amended following publication of a report by the committee. Persons considered unable to give informed consent could be cremated, following judgement by a district court. Municipalities were also obliged to make ground available for construction of a church cemetery.

Concern that cremation was discriminated against in favour of burial in the existing *Wet op Lijkbezorging* law prompted the Ministry for Home Affairs to request advice from J.M. Kan for the third time. There was concern that cremation was discriminated against in favour of burial in the existing Burial and Cremation Act. Accordingly, the third Kan committee published its report in 1965, proposing that cremation be made equal to burial in principle. This allowed local authorities to build their own crematoria. A number of years later, the law was amended on the basis of this report. A bill for a new Burial and Cremation Act was drafted in 1991, once again based on the advice of the third Kan committee, in which cremation and burial were finally rendered equal on all aspects. **J.M.H.J. Keizer**

KELLER GOTTFRIED

The Swiss, Gottfried Keller, was born at the 'Haus zum goldenen Winkel' at Neumarkt 27 in Zurich, on 19 July 1819, the son of a wood-turner. Having begun at industrial school in 1833 he was expelled a year later for disciplinary reasons and studied painting only to abandon this in 1843 in favour of writing. He then lived in Germany from 1848 to 1855, returning to his mother and sister in Zurich after an unhappy love affair. He was elected as the city's first secretary in 1861 and the first public debates about cremation took place during his period of office, which ended in 1875. He then devoted himself entirely to novel writing and poetry. His creative talent, which gave unmistakeable local colour to mundane human conflicts, put Swiss literature on the world map for the first time ever. Keller died on 16 July 1890 and was the first well-known personality to be cremated in the newly opened crematorium. His honorary grave may be visited at the Sihlfeld A cemetery in Zurich. **Marianne Herold**

KENYA

There is no wide acceptance of cremation in African culture; the majority of Africans choose burial over cremation. Most Africans believe that to dispose of a dead body by burning it and reducing it to ashes is a sign of disbelief in the immortality of the soul, as well as an act of disrespect for the body. Cremation is also repugnant to many African Christians because of the belief in the resurrection of the body.

In Kenya cremation is very rarely practised, except by Hindus. Perhaps the most well-known crematorium is located at the Kariokor Cemetery, Nairobi. The former cabinet minister, Peter Okondo who died in August 1996, was among the few high-ranking Kenyans to have been cremated. His cremation offended his clan members. But Father Denis O'Connor, arguing in 1996 in support of cremation, said the rite is 'cheap and hygienic' (Onyango and Ochieng, 2002).

In 2002, the cremation of the body of Mary Nyambura Kuria, aged 75, triggered a major controversy in Kenya. She was the wife of Archbishop Manasses Kuria, a former head of the Anglican Church in Kenya. Her body was cremated on Monday 8 July 2002, at Langata, Nairobi. Although the decision was reached by her family members, it was greeted with violent opposition from many Kenyans. However, the head of the Anglican Church in Kenya at the time, Archbishop David Gitari, lent his support to her cremation, by saying that this method of disposal of human remains would help reduce funeral costs. Archbishop Kuria himself said, 'We do it because it is Christian.' Some Kenyan clerics sided with him in his support for cremation. One of them, Revd Benson Kimuru said, 'Burying or burning, the Christian issue is the condition of the soul. The Christian faith in life eternal with God in heaven is what counts' (Onyango and Ochieng, 2002).

However, some church leaders thought cremation unbiblical, arguing that such great figures as Abraham, Sarah, Jacob, Joseph, David and even Jesus Christ were buried. One Christian lady expressed her utter disappointment in the words: 'Mrs Kuria was an honourable lady and head of Mothers Union, and she needed an honourable burial.... Whether it's biblical or not, she deserved a burial' (Kagure, 2002). Samson Obwa, a Kenyan pastor of the African Inland

Church believes that the honourable way of treating the dead is to bury them. On the other hand, Archbishop Gitari argued for cremation, saying that it is common in England, the home of the Anglican Church. Pastor P. Chelule of the Deliverance Church agrees with Obwa, noting that the cremation rite is not African.

In the same year, 2002, Revd Errol A. Quagraine, general overseer of the Family Bible Church conducted research on Ghanaian pastors' response to cremation. An analysis of his findings reveals that the reasons for the rejection of cremation as an alternative to burial among Christians in the Independent churches were the same as those put forward by the East African Christians in Kenya: it is unbiblical because there is no precedent for it (all the scriptures' great figures were buried). What is more, Jesus' resurrection followed his burial and not a cremation. Besides, humans must return to the dust of which they were made. Conversely, some Christians in both Ghana and Kenya have argued that cremation in no way interferes with God's ability to resurrect the dead.

The reasons suggested for the strong argument that burning the dead is not African have to do with African beliefs regarding the relationship between the living and the dead and between the corpse and the earth. Traditional Africans conduct their lives and perform their rituals within the framework of the belief that the ancestors govern the social and religious lives of their living relatives. The ancestors, who are the dead forebears of the family, are always held in deep reverence, both the dead and the living being part of one family. The living retain sentimental and emotional ties with the dead and depend on them for their well-being. The spirit of the deceased is believed to continue to influence the lives of their living relatives with blessings or curses, depending on how he was treated by the living. It is therefore incumbent upon surviving families to properly send off the relative who is joining the ancestors. The departed one is honoured through being given a decent burial, which is a way of preserving the memory of the dead. It is believed that the dead have the same desires as the living, such as money, food, drink, and clothing, so all of these are placed in the coffin or beside the grave. In the case of a tribal chief, weapons and servants are necessary to accompany him. Cremation has no place for such burial goods. Like the Akan of West

Africa, most Africans bury their dead because of the significant place of the earth in their concept of life and death. We note that in most Akan prayers, Mother Earth (*Asase Yaa* or *Asase Efua*) is mentioned next to the Supreme Being, *Onyankopon*. *Asase Yaa* is personalized in the sense that she is like a mother; human beings depend on her for their sustenance. It is she who provides food for man, and when death comes she makes available a resting place. An Akan maxim observes that 'the earth does not hate a corpse' (*Asase nkyiri funu*). Burial takes the body intact back to the earth where it came from, whereas cremation reduces the body to ashes thereby desecrating it. In his response to the controversy regarding cremation in Kenya in 2002, one lecturer at the University of Nairobi stated:

> We cannot do it. The dead would not simply accept it … . Destroying the body could destroy the human spirit. We bury our dead several feet underground and that is where they should remain. It is a taboo for a black man to be cremated. We believe in spiritual and physical lives and, if we cremate, resurrection of the dead would be affected.

The words of this Institute of African Studies lecturer sum up what can be said to represent what most Africans think of cremation.

The fact that the body of a loved one lies lifeless does not diminish the family's respect for it. To respect the body means to respect the person. As a matter of fact, in traditional African thought, when a person dies, it is the whole person in an invisible form that is said to have gone to be with others in the world of the dead. It is not said that only the soul or part of the person exists in the spirit-world. Of the Bantu death belief, P. Tempel notes that '[w]hat lives on after death is not called by the Bantu by a term indicating part of the man. I have always heard their elders speak of "the man himself"' (1969: 55). It is therefore difficult to convince such people that the body does not matter after death and therefore could be cremated. The rationale behind the African traditional objection to cremation is one of respect for the body of the departed loved one. The great extent to which most Africans celebrate funerals has led to such maxims as the popular Akan saying, '*Abusua do funu*' ('The Family loves the dead body'). The care for the body, the filing around it when it is laid in state, accompanied by comments regarding how good or bad it looks indicate the mourners' respect for the body. Relatives of the deceased would not like to mutilate the body of their departed loved one in any form. The death and loss of the body of the deceased relative brings double agony to the surviving relatives.

Thus, the argument that cremation must be an alternative to burial because it is a cheaper or more hygienic method of corpse disposal is not convincing to the African, for even in the midst of poverty, it is common to have expensive burials. Most African families, whether poor or rich, will do everything within their power to raise sufficient funds to give their deceased relative an honourable burial to preserve family reputation. As the Ghanaian (Akan) proverb says, 'Everyone helps to carry the burden of a funeral'. Africans will continue to find the idea of burning dead bodies very outrageous. Any attempt to sell the cremation rite to various black Africans countries is likely to trigger the same mixed reactions as in what might be described as 'the Kuria Controversy' in Kenya. Perhaps, the rite will appeal more to the elite population, a minority on the African continent influenced by modern Western world-views or Eastern religions. Most traditionalists, Christian and Muslim, will continue to frown on the rite.
Charles Owiredu

References

Kimaru, Benson (2002), 'Cremation is not Unchristian', *Daily Nation*, 11 July.

Mbiti, John S. (1992), *Introduction to African Religion*, Nairob: East African Educational Publishers.

Namunane, Bernard (2002), 'Former ACK Head's Wife Cremated', *Daily Nation*, 9 July.

Onyango, Dennis and Ochieng, Moses (2002), 'Cremation: The Death of Burials?', *Daily Nation* 10 July at: http://www.nationaudio.com/News/DailyNation/10072002/News/News_Spotlight34.html.

Quagraine, Errol A. (2002), 'Ghanaian Christian Objection to Cremation', *Family News*, Accra, July–September.

Soper, Edmund Davidson (1938), *Religions of Mankind*, Cokesbury: Abingdon Press.

Tempels, Placide (1969), *Bantu Philosophy*, Paris: Presence Africaine.

KOREA

The turn of the twenty-first century witnessed a dramatic change in funeral culture in South Korea, with a significant increase in cremation against the background of traditional burial customs. Cremation had largely been practised among very poor people in urban areas and employed in the case of exceptionally bad deaths, such as suicide. From the mid-1990s, however, the social perception of cremation increasingly shifted with the nationwide cremation rate doubling within less than ten years. Exceeding 40 per cent nationwide and reaching 60 per cent in major cities by 2002, the cremation rates in South Korea are expected to continue increasing.

History of cremation in Korea

Korea has deep-rooted traditions of Buddhism, Confucianism, Daoism, and shamanism extending over one and a half millennia, as well as the new and strong influence of Christianity since the late eighteenth century. All these traditions affected concepts and rites surrounding death but, historically speaking, the most influential were Buddhism and Confucianism, at least as far as the method of body disposal was concerned. While Buddhists cremated their dead in the hope that they would reach paradise without delay, Confucians practised burial to keep their dead ancestors in the ground as secure as possible: a well-preserved grave was not only an expression of filial piety, a core Confucian value, but also a guarantee for the well-being of both the dead and the living (Deuchler, 1992: 197).

Although modern cremation began in Korea in the early twentieth century, the practice of Buddhist cremation dates back to as early as the Three Kingdoms period, during which Buddhism was introduced to the Korean peninsula via China in the late fourth century CE. Buddhism soon prevailed and cremation became popular during the Unified Silla period (676–935) and the Goryeo Dynasty (918–1392) when Buddhism was the state religion. During the Unified Silla period, eight out of 27 kings were cremated and archaeological evidence – including unearthed urns – suggests that the popularity of Buddhist cremation reached its peak at this time. During the Goryeo Dynasty, funeral rituals were profoundly affected by Buddhist traditions although Confucianism was also influential as the main political ideology. The Goryeo people frequently awaited death at the Buddhist temple and cremation was widespread as a Buddhist rite among aristocrats and ordinary people alike. However, with the introduction of the Confucian 'Family Rites of Zhu Xi' from China in the late Goryeo Dynasty and the establishment of the Confucian state of the Joseon Dynasty (1392–1910), cremation was gradually abandoned in favour of burial. Although Buddhist cremation was still popular among ordinary people in the early Joseon Dynasty, continuous strict prohibition by the Confucian regime resulted in the disappearance of cremation. Burial, along with beliefs in geomancy for choosing auspicious sites for graves, remained prevalent until the twentieth century.

It was during the Japanese colonial period (1910–45) that the system of public cemeteries and the modern form of cremation were introduced. After the construction of a crematorium in Seoul in 1930, the Japanese imperialist government began to build crematoria to promote cremation as a medium of its colonial policy of obliterating traditional Korean customs. However, the Korean people were reluctant to cremate because of their strong national rejection of the Japanese coercive policy of cremation as well as their desire to maintain traditional burial customs. Since 1945, soon after liberation from the Japanese rule and as a result of the Cold War, the Korean peninsula has been divided into the democratic South Korea and communist North Korea. The Korean War (1950–53) did not change the prevalent funeral customs based on Confucian burial.

Cremation since 1953

In South Korea, the period following the Korean War can be generally divided into two so far as the social significance of cremation is concerned. From the 1950s to the mid-1990s the social perception of cremation was very negative. Although traditional funerary rites had been modified and simplified in parallel with the swift industrialization and urbanization since the 1960s, cremation remained a taboo because the Korean people had observed burial customs based on Confucian values for more than six centuries. The national sentiment of reluctance to cremate was also reinforced by memories of

Japanese imperialist rule. Furthermore, the age and poor quality of crematoria added a further negative impression. As a result, cremation was largely practised among very poor people in urban areas and was limited to the cases of death of children, unmarried people, and other exceptionally bad deaths such as suicide. Cremation was not popular even among the Buddhist population despite the strong influence of Buddhism in modern Korean society. Accordingly the national rate of cremation remained at less than 20 per cent until the mid-1990s: 1955 (6 per cent); 1970 (11 per cent); 1981 (14 per cent); 1991 (18 per cent).

From the early 1990s, however, a fundamental reform of funeral culture has become a major national issue. This is mainly because of problems raised by the encroachment on land by graveyards all over the country. By 1998 graveyards (totalling 998 km²) occupied approximately 1 per cent of the gross area of South Korea (99 434 km²) an area that is bigger than that of Seoul metropolitan city (605 km²). About nine square kilometres of land was passing into graveyard every year. Moreover, the landscape was seriously deteriorating with rampant private gravesites and uncared-for tombs across the country. In addition, there was the absolute shortage of burial sites in the case of Seoul and other major cities. To ameliorate these problems, the South Korean government launched a funeral policy promoting cremation and restraining burial, while also modernizing crematoria, charnel houses and other related facilities. The mass media have actively supported government policy, and many citizen groups have emerged to promote cremation-based funeral culture. Although there had been a moderate increase in the cremation rate since the early 1990s, it was from 1998 that the social perception of cremation changed with the cremation rate dramatically increasing, due in part to the cremation of some leading figures causing a sensation and matching a full-scale supportive campaign by citizen groups. Revised legislation on funeral policy in 2001 also spurred the shift of funeral culture towards cremation, placing stricter controls on the size of graveyards and restricting the period for holding tombs to a maximum of 60 years.

The nationwide rate of cremation doubled in less than ten years from the mid-1990s and showed an even more speedy increase with the turn of the new millennium. The reasons for choosing cremation include concerns about limited land resources and the difficulty of visiting and maintaining traditional graves. The nationwide cremation rate first reached 20 per cent in 1994; it attained 30 per cent in 1999 and, by 2002, it stood at 42 per cent with 104 000 cremated out of 247 000 deaths. The cremation rate of major cities was already well over 50 per cent in 2002: Busan (66 per cent); Seoul (59 per cent); Incheon (55 per cent); Ulsan (53 per cent). In addition, the number and capacity of charnel houses for holding cremated remains was also hugely increased: for example, the 54 charnel houses of 1995 had increased to 100 by 2001. As of 2002 there were 45 crematoria and 126 charnel houses in South Korea. As for the disposition of cremated remains, both placing in charnel houses (*Napgol*) and scattering in appropriate places (*Sangol*) have generally been practised, with the former becoming increasingly popular in parallel with the increased availability of charnel houses. In the case of Seoul in 2001, for example, 67 per cent of cremated remains were laid in the charnel houses, 24 per cent were scattered, and about 3 per cent were interred (Kim, 2001: 22). However, the Seoul metropolitan government has now begun to encourage the practice of scattering with the introduction of the new type of memorial park dedicated to this activity, and people have responded positively to this.

Generally speaking, modern South Korea is a mono-ethnic yet multi-religious society. Christians and Buddhists constitute the majority of the religious population (around half the total population), while Confucianism and Shamanism are deeply ingrained in the mindset of the Korean people and in their everyday life. This religious diversity is also observed at crematoria, where many different religious rituals are practised. Some crematoria have, for instance, separate service rooms for Buddhists, Christians and non-believers. Major religions such as Buddhism, Protestant Christianity and Catholic Christianity have campaigned to support a new funeral culture based on cremation.

By contrast, communist North Korea has a considerably different stance on funeral customs, as with other rites of passage. On seizing power in 1945, the communist regime in North Korea proclaimed that all traditional customs surrounding birth, marriage, funerals and memorial services must be abolished because they were the remnants of the old age and, therefore, must be changed in accordance with socialist norms of life. Cremation has been recommended by the government because of the shortage of land for cemeteries, although the majority of North Korean people still prefer to practise burial. All burials take place in public cemeteries allotted to each administrative unit, and there are so many that sites for graveyards are running out, just as in South Korea.

As the twenty-first century begins, South Korea, with its population of 48 million, is now in the transitional period from a burial-based to a cremation-based funeral culture. Although some have worried over such a sudden and unilateral shift to cremation, the nationwide cremation rate, exceeding 40 per cent, is likely to rise further. Major cities will reach even higher rates: for example, Seoul, with a population of 10 million, is expected to reach a cremation rate of 80 per cent by 2010 (Kim, 2001: 49). It seems to be generally agreed that a most urgent task is to reframe funeral culture in ways appropriate to contemporary and future Korean society, whether cremation or burial. **Chang-Won Park**

References

Deuchler, Martina (1992), *The Confucian Transformation of Korea: A Study of Society and Ideology*, Cambridge, MA: Harvard University Press.

Horlyck, Charlotte (2002), 'Tracking Chronological Change in Korean Burials of the Koryo Period', *Journal of East Asian Archaeology*, 3: 199–218.

Kim, Hong-Eun (1990), ' 한국의 화장제도에 관한 연구 (Historical Review on Cremation System in Korea),'농업과학연구, *Journal of Agricultural Science*, 8: 196–208.

Kim, Kyung-Hye (2001), 장묘시설 수급 및 정책방향 연구 (*Demand-Supply Projection of Funeral Facilities and Proposed Policy Guidelines*), Seoul: Seoul Development Institute.

Lee, Hyun-Song (1996), 'Change in Funeral Customs in Contemporary Korea', *Korea Journal*, 36: 49–60.

National Folk Museum (1990), 영원한 만남: 한국 상장례 (*Eternal Beauty: Korean Funeral Customs*), Seoul: Mijinsa.

KÜCHENMEISTER, FRIEDRICH

In 1874, the first cremation of a dead body took place in a Siemens cremator. This was done in Dresden, and Friedrich Küchenmeister, doctor and member of the Medical Council, was partly responsible for it. Küchenmeister introduced a number of areas of attention for subsequent cremations. An autopsy was required upon death, for example, in order to detect murder, and the sides and lid of the coffin needed to be removed to facilitate the incineration process. Family members also needed to stay far away from the cremator in order to ensure that they would not hear or smell anything distressing.

It was also Küchenmeister who introduced the idea of a columbarium. In 1872 he proposed facultative cremation in his handbook for combating cholera. He believed that just as there was freedom of religion, there also needed to be freedom in the choice of cremation or burial. His ideas became widely adopted, and he came to be seen as an important figure in the process of positive developments regarding cremation. In 1883 Küchenmeister was appointed an honorary member of the Cremation Association 'the Facultatieve'. **J.M.H.J. Keizer**

L

LATIN (CENTRAL AND SOUTH) AMERICA

The dominance of Roman Catholicism in Latin America made the subcontinent a difficult ground for cremation to take root. Nevertheless, although they all share this key characteristic, there were, and still are, differences in how various Latin American countries reacted to modern cremation, with Argentina some way ahead of anywhere else in Latin America. By the 1920s the only evidence of cremation regularly occurring anywhere else in Latin America was at the publicly-owned 'American Crematory', at Ancon, in the Panamanian Canal Zone. There was also a crematorium on the Isla de Flores in Uruguay, but this was only seldom used (Mendoza, 1923: 28). In 1923, it was possible to be cremated in Peru, although this only appeared to happen in exceptional circumstances. The *Boletin de la Asociación Argentina de Cremación* mentioned the case of a Japanese man living in

Lima whose body was exhumed and cremated so that his ashes could be returned to Japan. Elsewhere, there was certainly interest in Paraguay, where Señor Alfaro, mayor of the capital, Asunción, saw his plan to build a crematorium receive initial approval from the municipal executive in May 1927. However, the plan did not appear to advance further. A contemporary Cuban cremationist, Dr Candido Hoyos, claimed that there was at least one 'Schneider system' cremator installed in Mexico, which was capable of cremating five bodies at once, but he was unsure whether it was actually in use.

Hoyos was an important member of the Cuban Society for the Propagation of Cremation (*Sociedad Para la Propagación de la Incineración*). An official of the Cuban Urban Society of Legal Medicine, he published (as the Cuban cremation society's president) at least three articles on aspects of cremation in the first year of the medical society's monthly journal (1922). In 1925 the American cremationist Hugo Erichsen praised Hoyos's 'able articles' on cremation, which had 'attracted great attention in the medical press' (CANA, 1925: 43). Apart from Argentina, Cuba was the only other country in the entire subcontinent mentioned by Erichsen in his report on the world cremation movement, suggesting the very limited extent of cremation societies there. However, it seems that the Cuban cremation society was short-lived, as it did not feature in any more of Erichsen's reports on the state of the international cremation movement that he regularly delivered to conventions of North American cremationists.

The 1930s saw some Latin American developments for cremation was certainly legal and practised in Mexico by 1934 with approximately 1600 cremations in Mexico City between 1934 and 1939. These, however, were for those who could not afford a burial, as 'indigent' people comprised around 95 per cent of those cremated. In the Panamanian Canal Zone, cremation continued in what was then called the Gorgos Hospital, although the numbers were not great. Between 1929 and 1933, 655 were cremated and this figure decreased by 24 per cent to 525 in the following five-year period (1934–38). In Uruguay, too, the Isla de Flores crematorium was still occasionally operated by the Ministry of Public Health. In the 1930s there were single cremations there in 1933 and 1934 and three in 1938, but none in other years.

Cremation was made legal in many central and southern American countries in 1936, although this did not lead to the immediate establishment of more crematoria. There certainly appeared to be little interest in becoming involved in the international cremation movement, which was beginning to reactivate. There were no delegates from, nor reports on, any Latin American country at the 1936 International Cremation Congress in Prague. The only evidence of interest was from the Paraguayan consulate, which sent its 'greetings' to the congress. Yet, by the late 1930s, there was interest in cremation in Brazil. By February 1938 the Brazilian Red Cross was attempting to get permission to establish a crematorium and columbarium. Cremationists recognized that the Catholic clergy wielded great power in government circles, but thought that they could count on the support of foreign elements, most notably North Americans and Europeans.

However, a report on the development of global cremation for the International Cremation Federation (ICF) in 1948 revealed that little had changed in Latin America since the outbreak of the Second World War. In fact, there was now no functioning cremation society in the entire area. The Brazilian Red Cross's earlier efforts had failed, as the country still had no law relating to cremation and no crematorium. Five countries had crematoria that were utilized: Argentina, Mexico (though there were no statistics available), Uruguay (very occasionally, as before 1939), Panama and Peru. There, Lima's Cementerio General had a cremation chamber. No statistics are available, but numbers of cremations in Peru would have been small, for 'religious reasons'. It appeared that significant advancement only came in Panama, which had, by 1946, a second crematorium. Also government-owned, it was located outside of the Canal Zone in the Hospital Amador Guerrero Colon. The crematorium in the Canal Zone performed 703 cremations between 1939 and 1943 – an increase of 34 per cent on the previous five years. In the following five-year period (1944–48), this figure again improved, by 14 per cent.

Bolivia, though it had no crematorium, apparently allowed cremation to be carried out in occasional 'special cases'. However, here, too, cremation remained 'contrary to custom'. Although cremation became accepted in Venezuelan law that year, this did not stimulate the development of a cremation society or crematorium (Guillermo Herrera, personal communication). In countries such as Chile and Cuba, cremation was legal in 1948 but there were no crematoria. In El Salvador cremation's legal status was indeterminate: it was neither explicitly legal nor illegal. In Guatemala, Colombia and Nicaragua conditions were more hostile as cremation was actually illegal. In Paraguay, the ICF report stated merely that no cremation was practised.

Little changed in the subsequent 20 years, despite the Cremation Society of Great Britain having cremationist contacts in at least two Latin American countries in the 1950s. In 1955 a contact in British Guyana informed the society of plans to build a crematorium there and asked for its advice. There followed an exchange of letters but, apparently, no concrete result was achieved. Dr Marcus Vergara Letelier was a Chilean, based in Santiago, who had met British cremationist Herbert Jones in 1951. Letelier was in touch with the British for at least a decade, but was not forthcoming with news of progress in Chile until 1962, when he asked the British for advice on the possibility of establishing a crematorium in Santiago. The Cremation Society asked Dowson and Mason (a company specializing in cremators) to send Letelier the technical information he required, although, again, it appears that the project ultimately came to nothing.

In the late 1960s there was a development in Guatemala where Dr Jules Bonge, a Belgian cremationist, began propagandizing for cremation. Using information from *Pharos*, Bonge published articles in several journals, initiating a debate on cremation among some of the higher echelons of society. He drew up a draft constitution for a proposed cremation society and the Guatemalan National Cremationist Association (*Associación Crematista Nacional de Guatemala*) was eventually launched in 1967. Bonge had been agitating for some time before this, but, because of the oppositional influence of Catholic priests, he had not had a sufficiently favourable reaction to allow further progress. By 1969 the society had 80 members and Bonge, now its president, had plans for a crematorium to be built on land reserved for it by the Ministry of

Health, although he still awaited full approval. In the early 1970s the Guatemalan National Cremationist Association kept in touch with the international movement by sending its *Boletin Informativo*, which had a circulation of 700, to *Pharos*.

There was progress elsewhere, too. In 1967 São Paulo city council, in Brazil, voted to build a crematorium in the city's cemetery. Legally, cremation could only take place when the deceased left written instructions for it, witnessed by three people. Hugh Murdoch, a British national, had been in correspondence with the Cremation Society of Great Britain in 1960 over the best kinds of cremator to use in Brazil, although it is unclear whether he played any role in São Paulo city council's decision. The plan was to equip the crematorium with two liquid petroleum gas cremators, supplied by Dowson and Mason, which would deal with ten corpses and 20 exhumations daily. Unfortunately, communication between both Brazil and Guatemala and the international movement then broke down as the information *Pharos* carried on them was not updated throughout the 1970s and 1980s.

The 1970s witnessed developments elsewhere on the subcontinent. According to César Jaramillo, interest in cremation in Colombia began in 1975, when he was director of the sales department of the company Casa Médica Ltd in the city of Cali. That year his company established contact with a large American industrial furnace company, and the two companies appointed Jaramillo as their exclusive representative. He began visiting all the major Colombian cities, promoting cremation to the municipal directors who were responsible for supplying such services. The concept of cremation was novel, and there were doubts that it would be accepted in communities with large Catholic majorities, which were highly conservative. 'Attached to the tradition of inhumation and vault burial', Jaramillo explained, 'they were doubtful if cremation was the appropriate final fate for human remains and wondered if it would affect in some way the resurrection of their bodies at the end of time' (personal communication). In late 1979, after four years, César Jaramillo finally succeeded in making his first sale – that of two cremators to the city of Bucaramanga. This was not quite the first cremator in Colombia as a locally

constructed unit was installed in a Bogotá cemetery park in 1978, but it did not begin functioning until 1982. In Panama, cremation continued at a low level, with Gorgas Mortuary in the Canal Zone cremating some of its residents (and those of the Republic of Panama by special request) at a rate of around 60 per year. In 1979 it appeared that there had been further progress as, for the first time, *Pharos* carried the address of the Panama Cremation Society. Interest in Mexico was revealed by enquiries received from that country by Dowson and Mason in 1976.

In the early 1980s the pace of change began to quicken. By 1983 São Paulo finally had its crematorium, and there were plans for a second crematorium in Rio de Janeiro in the near future, although it still had not materialized by 1989. In Mexico pressure was increasing to expand the cremation facilities in Mexico City. With a population of 17 million living and 20 million dead, the city was running short of burial space. In 1984, stating that cremation was the solution, the municipal authorities outlined plans to build 12 crematoria the following year and issued a decree forbidding the further use of the 109 municipal cemeteries in the capital. However, in line with Mexico's policy of encouraging the private sector, the wealthy would continue to have the option of burial in the city's private graveyards. By 1988 Mexico City's population had grown to over 20 million, making it the world's largest city, and the cremators were in the process of being installed.

In Peru cremation continued to operate on the same small scale as it had for the previous half-century. There was still only one crematorium in the country, in Lima's Cementerio Britanico, founded in 1835. In 1983, of the 112 deaths that the cemetery dealt with, only six were cremations. However, the figures did increase. In 1986 and 1987 there were 117 and 114 cremations, respectively, giving cemetery cremation rates of 43 and 31 per cent. In Colombia there was little further advancement for cremation until 1989.

The beginnings of real change occurred in the late 1980s. Between 1987 and 1994 one major American cremator company secured around 70 separate orders from Latin American countries. By 1994 there was at least one crematorium being installed somewhere in Latin America every month, making the subcontinent probably 'the fastest growing area for cremation in the world' at that time (Sousa 1994: 51). The change resulted from the fact that the authorities had realized the economic necessity of cremation and its utility in dealing with the large numbers of 'indigenous' deaths. In addition, many of these countries had growing economies, and entrepreneurs had begun to become aware of cremation's profit-making potential.

Mexico was the prime example of this phenomenon. After receiving enquiries about cremation, a representative of an American cremator company visited Mexico City to inform private businessmen and funeral directors of the serious and extensive nature of this public interest. There he was met with indifference, as it was widely thought that cremation would never happen in a country that was 99 per cent Catholic. But Mexico City municipality did show an interest as it had recognized the demand for cremation. Thus, by 1994 Mexico City municipality owned all three crematoria in the city and was responsible for the construction of more, legally excluding private funeral directors from cremation in the city (Sousa, 1994: 52–53).

Private capital was not, however, legally excluded elsewhere in Mexico in the early 1990s, where cremation was also developing. By 1992 there were already 24 Mexican crematoria. Only a year later there were 79 operating in 66 cities and the federal district (Mexico City), cremating an estimated 5000 corpses annually, a figure that was expected to double by the year 2000. The first-ever national meeting of private Mexican crematorium owners was held in October 1993 in Cuernavaca and was organized by Sergio Ruiz. He was deemed the 'father of cremation in Mexico' as he had been 'laying the groundwork' for cremation since the 1970s and was, by 1993, the managing director of a private crematorium. Over 309 owners from 20 cities and the federal district attended the meeting, which decided, as cremation was still in its infancy, to form the National Association of Cremationists (*Asociación Nacional de Cremacionistas*) dedicated to improving cremation practices. With Ruiz elected as its first president, the association planned to hold annual meetings throughout the country and applied to join the ICF. Unfortunately, the association was short-lived. In 1994 there were only 20 Mexican crematoria involved in it, and only 22 a year later. In the later 1990s *Pharos* failed to receive updated cremation figures from Mexico, suggesting that the only organization

competent to do so, the cremation association, had ceased to function properly.

A similar development process was occurring throughout much of Latin America. In Brazil, which was 90 per cent Catholic, cremation was generally deemed unacceptable in the mid-1970s, yet by 1994 it had been established there as well. Although Brazil still only had two municipally-operated crematoria (in São Paulo and Rio, which opened in 1991) there were several new cremation installations planned. By 1995 São Paulo Crematorium disposed of 2846 corpses, a cremation rate of almost 4 per cent for the city (Sousa, 1994: 53,55).

Colombia had only two crematoria in the mid-1980s. In 1989 there was a renewed initiative in the country to promote cremation – this time directed at private cemeteries or cemetery parks, as they then began to be called. By 1992 the number of Colombian crematoria had doubled to four, located in Bogotá, as well as in Medellín and Bucaramanga. Three years later there were 13 crematoria in Colombia, with new installations in Manizales, Barranquilla, Cúcuta, Cali, Villavicencio and Pereira. Medellín and Bogotá now both had four crematoria each. Cremation was making a rapid impact, too. In 1993 the 42 490 cremations in the country represented almost 17 per cent of deaths. In two years, cremations rose to 48 812, a rate of almost 29 per cent. In 1997 there were another seven new crematoria, in Cali, Neiva, Medellín and Bogotá (César Jaramillo, personal communication; Sousa, 1994: 55).

The early 1990s saw cremation introduced into other Latin American countries. By 1992 Puerto Rico had three crematoria and Suriname two, and there were single crematoria in Costa Rica and Grenada. By 1994 Chile was clearly cremating at some level, as exiled East German communist leader Erich Honecker was cremated there. In 1996 Chileans bought a pyrolitic cremator from an Argentine cremator company (Lindberg Company, 2002; All Crematory Corp., 2003). The first Venezuelan crematoria began operating in 1995. Important in this process was Guillermo Herrera of Crematorios La Venezolana CA, Charallave, who advertised the cremation service in the press and on television. A second pioneer was the late Alejandro Kaufman of the Cementerio del Este in Caracas, and its crematoria began to operate almost simultaneously (Guillermo Herrera, personal communication). In Guatemala, cremation began on 31 May 1996. The law required that those choosing cremation record this in their wills, and Guatemala's first crematorium, owned by Corporación Reforma, only completed six cremations in its first year (Pilar Nunez, personal communication).

By 1998 Peru had three crematoria: in Lima, Trujillo and a new installation which opened that year in Cuzco. The Cementerio General in Lima cremated 362 corpses that year, a cremation rate of almost 75 per cent of the corpses disposed of at its facilities. These subcontinent-wide developments were soon recognized by the ICF, which began to employ Spanish as a language for communication as a replacement in 'great part' for German. In 2000 Ecuador became the latest Latin American country on the burgeoning list of those that cremated, by building crematoria in the capital, Quito, and in Cuenca, the second largest city (All Crematory Corp., 2003). By 2002 Cuba had at least one crematorium, in Havana, which, with 89 cremations in 2001, was responsible for disposing of 0.5 per cent of deaths for that year.

This rapid advance naturally brought with it certain problems. Difficulties arose because 'cremation is a new phenomenon in these countries and their experience is in some instances non-existent' (Sousa, 1994: 53). Some of the more extreme examples of the consequences of this lack of experience included plans for a crematorium that did not include a door on the administrative building and another impressive crematorium, the first in an unnamed South American city, that did not have a gas or electricity supply. This was particularly important as problems in operating crematoria properly in Latin America could potentially set back cremation worldwide. There seemed to be a great need for cremation societies in these countries to promote guidelines, establish and maintain high standards and provide advice on good cremation practices (Sousa, 1994: 53–55). However, in the 1990s there was only the short-lived Mexican cremation society. Nevertheless the growth in cremation continues unabated. Like other countries on the subcontinent, cremation is growing in Colombia due to the scarcity of land for burial, the scarcity of water for the irrigation of cemeteries, the contamination of air, land and water that cemeteries cause and the increasingly high cost of burials. In some

Colombian cities cremation is now very popular. In the city of Medellín, for example, the cremation rate is close to 56 per cent. Although this rate is exceptionally high for the country as a whole, it is clear that cremation has begun to be accepted. César Jaramillo reports that cremation 'is no longer taboo. In fact, much of the population has adopted a positive view of cremation.'

Though not as advanced as Colombia, cremation is progressing in Brazil. In 2001 two cremators bought from the Argentine company Lindberg were installed in Rio de Janeiro and São Paulo (Lindberg Company, 2002). In less than a decade Brazil has doubled the number of its crematoria to four, located in Brasilia and Rio with another two in São Paulo. In Guatemala, the numbers of cremations have increased as a result of advertising and the dissemination of information on the process. The ease of transporting ashes abroad and of transporting cinerary urns, the little space they require and their ease of conservation all help make cremation more popular. The Catholic Church has allowed cremation to go ahead, and Guatemalan cremationists have had no problems nor encountered any significant obstacles. According to the statistics, cremation in Guatemala has been 'well accepted'; there were 76 cremations in 2003 at the only crematorium – ten times more than during the first year of operation (Pilar Nunez, personal communication).

It was not until the year 2000 that more crematoria began operating in Venezuela – in Maracaibo, the country's second largest city, with a 1.2 million population. Since then, several more crematoria have been built (Guillermo Herrera, personal communication). Now there are eight crematoria in the country, located in Caracas, Guarenas, Guatire, Charallave, Valencia, Puerto Ordaz, Maracaibo and San Cristobal. All of them are privately run, in private cemeteries: current legislation only allows the installation of crematoria in cemeteries (Pedro Fernandez, personal communication). Legally speaking, the requisites for a cremation are the authorization of next-of-kin, to leave 24 hours to pass after death before cremation is performed, and to carry it out only if the death is not being investigated by the authorities. Nowadays, between 3600 and 3800 cremations are performed annually in Venezuela, representing

3–4 per cent of total deaths. Pedro Fernandez points out that, if this figure is low compared to other countries, the growth is fairly rapid, especially given how recently cremation began. The crematorium he owns and operates in Valencia has doubled its number of cremations in only three years. Fernandez also notes that, due to the relatively high cost of a cremation, it has been considered 'elitist' but, with the installation of more crematoria, the cost has dropped and made the service more accessible to more people. The Internet, 'globalization', television and other modern media have allowed more people to access information on subjects like cremation and this has helped eliminate fear of it. Indeed, this process of popular education has led to an increasing acceptance of cremation as an alternative means of corpse disposal. Guillermo Herrera comments that, in addition to the 'economical' aspects of cremation, cultural and religious factors have helped it grow. Although the Catholic Church had been traditionally opposed to the practice, one of the factors that encouraged people like Guillermo Herrera to proceed with their cremationist projects was the fact that many Catholic priests commented in the press, and on the radio and television, about the advantages of cremation and made it clear that it had not been prohibited by the church since 1964.

Panama was exceptional in that cremation was not novel there in the early 1990s. Nevertheless, advances continued, and by 1992 it had five crematoria. In 1994 Comercial de Administradora Internacional de Cementerios, SA founded its own crematorium company (called Incresa), after having been involved in another crematorium project from 1984 and observing how the practice was increasing in popularity. In 2000, market research conducted by the company found that around 20 per cent of families chose cremation. This figure had risen to 23 per cent by 2003. The majority of Panamanians who choose cremation are of the middle and higher socio-economic classes: those of the lower socio-economic classes generally continue to bury their dead (Eduardo Alvarado, personal communication).

In some Latin American countries, although cremation occurs, it does not currently seem to be expanding in the same way. Rodolfo Forestier had been convinced for some years that Uruguay would be affected by the worldwide trend towards increasing cremation levels. The country had a crematorium, located in the Cementerio del Norte in the capital city, Montevideo, where more than half the total population lives. Municipally-operated, the crematorium service was run at a 'fairly rudimentary' level. Noting the number of people using the crematorium's service and tired of hearing poor reports about it, Forestier proposed a reform of the running of the crematorium that would involve private companies. After some delays, the municipality declared its interest in the project and asked for details in 2001, although the situation was complicated by the sudden involvement of another company that had 'stolen' the idea. Then the Argentine economic crisis intervened, which had serious repercussions for the small, neighbouring country of Uruguay. Planned in dollars, the proposal became 'economic madness'. The municipal crematorium continues to operate; it performed 650 cremations in 1997, rising to 786 in 1999, a cremation rate of 2.4 per cent (Alejandra Forestier, personal communication).

Likewise, in Bolivia, cremation has only developed to a very limited extent. At the crematorium in the Cementerio General, La Paz, only exhumed remains are cremated. There is a second crematorium in the Cementerio General in Cochabamba where both exhumed remains and the recently deceased are cremated. A third crematorium is operated in Santa Cruz de la Sierra by Inmobiliaria Kantutani, which, with four cemetery parks and funeral parlours in the three most important cities in the country, is the largest funeral business group in Bolivia. Inmobiliaria Kantutani has another crematorium in construction in La Paz, and its Santa Cruz installation performed 37 cremations in 2003 (Augusto Vargas, personal communication). In El Salvador there are two crematoria, the first of which started operation in 1994. They perform around 30 cremations per year. Carlos Roberto Belloso reports that cremation is definitely not increasing; in fact, it has hardly begun and one of the crematoria is 'almost closed'. The main obstacle is religion, even though cremation is no longer prohibited by the Catholic Church. Custom and tradition keeps the demand for burial at a very high level. One factor that should not be ignored, however, is the marked development of Protestant religiosity since the late 1960s. Indeed, some sociologists even speak of the 'explosion of Protestantism in Latin America' over the closing decades of the twentieth century (Martin, 1990). It remains to be seen exactly how this might echo the Protestant bias towards cremation so evident in Europe in the twentieth century.

It will be clear from the above that reliable statistics for annual cremations in Latin American countries are difficult to obtain. Presumably the case of Colombia is representative of why this is the case. In the course of my research, César Jaramillo kindly agreed to attempt to provide me with reliable annual statistics for cremations in Colombia. He wrote to the central government asking about this and was informed that the present system for collecting national statistics in Colombia cannot deal with collecting cremation statistics. The Colombian National Office of Statistics is presently looking into the possibility of collecting cremation statistics but has not made any firm decisions as yet. Pedro Fernandez could not provide exact cremation statistics for Venezuela due to the fact that private crematoria remained 'jealous' of the supply of the numbers of cremations they performed. Cremation societies could theoretically perform this function, assuming they could overcome private companies' reluctance to share information, as well as regulating cremation and supporting good practice. However, it does not seem likely, at present, that cremation societies are on the agenda of cremationists in any Latin American countries, despite the fact that they have formed a small part of the history of Argentina, Cuba, Guatemala, Panama and Mexico for differing lengths of time in different periods of the twentieth century.

Notwithstanding a lack of reliable statistical data, it seems clear that great changes have taken place in Latin America during the closing decades of the twentieth century, and especially in the 1990s. The development of cremation clearly varies considerably between the countries of the subcontinent, as well as, of course, within each country, with urban areas, generally better served by crematoria, consequently being those where cremation is most popular. The rapid expansion of cremation is most evident in Mexico, Colombia and Argentina. Although most, if not all, the other countries in the region now possess at least one crematorium, in places such as Suriname (as discussed elsewhere in this

Encyclopedia), there are many significant obstacles to cremation's further development. Notwithstanding this, cremation seems likely to continue advancing at variable rates throughout the subcontinent, as the social, economic and political factors that have brought it thus far take it further. **Lewis H. Mates**

Acknowledgements

I am grateful for information to:

Carlos Roberto Belloso (of Parques y Jardines de Cuscatlan SA de CV, El Salvador).

Pedro Fernandez Benet (of Crematorios del Centro CA, Venezuela).

Osvaldo Chernitsky (managing director of Lindberg Argentina SA).

Alejandra Forestier (of Forestier Pose SA, Uruguay)

César Augusto Jaramillo Gomez (general manager of Representaciones Jaramillo Ltda, Colombia).

Guillermo Herrera (of Cementerio Parque Valles del Tuy, Venezuela).

Eduardo Alvarado Lewis (director of Comercial de Administradora Internacional de Cementerios, SA Panama).

Pilar Nunez (assistant manager of Corporación Reforma, Guatemala).

Augusto Vargas (general director of Inmobiliaria Kantutani, Bolivia).

See also Argentina; Suriname.

References

All Crematory Corporation website, at: http://www.allcrem.com/ (accessed August 2003 and May 2004).

CANA (1924–54), Reports of CANA Annual Conventions, CRE/A/US4.

CSA.

Lindberg Company (2002), List of Units Built, 1988–15 May 2002.

Martin, David (1990), *Tongues of Fire, The Explosion of Protestantism in Latin America*, Oxford: Blackwell.

Mendoza, José Perez (1923), *Sobre Cremación*, Ferrari Hnos: Buenos Aires, CRE/C/AG/1923/2.

Revista de Medicina Legal de Cuba (Magazine of Cuban Legal Medicine), CRE/A/CU1.

Roy, Donald K. (1991), 'The Past, Present and Future of the International Cremation Federation', *Pharos*, 57(3): 110–11, 115.

Sousa, Terry (1994), 'A Cremation Overview', *Pharos*, 60(2): 51–55.

LAW

As the important entry on **crime** makes clear for one national focus, laws relating to cremation have been of absolute importance in the emergence of modern cremation practice. Many of the entries for specific countries note the distinctive features of their own history in the various Cremation Acts that have been passed by their respective governments. A major factor in many of these has been a concern that death should be certified in as appropriate and thorough a way as possible given the potential for the destruction of evidence of criminal acts that might have served as the cause of death, and the destruction of that evidence in the cremation of the corpse. **Douglas J. Davies**

See especially Argentina; Brodrick Committee; certificates and medical forms (UK); cremation Acts and Regulations (UK); death registration service; Kan (for the Netherlands); international movement of remains; medicine; pollution control (UK); postmortem examination.

LEGRAIN, PAUL-MAURICE

An active cremationist, Paul-Maurice Legrain (1860–1939) was vice-president of the French Cremation Federation and the Paris Cremation Society and he attended and held many successful conferences on the topic. He is one of the many medical doctors who played crucial roles in the emergence of cremation movements in their respective countries. A brief biography indicates the wide network of influence held by such an advocate of cremation in its early decades.

Born in Paris, Legrain, after medical training, became doctor-in-chief of a lunatic asylum for 45 years. He also founded an asylum for alcoholics in Ville-Evrard and directed that for 20 years. A member of the High Council of Public Assistance for 40 years, he represented the council as an expert on a project to develop the law on convalescent lunatic and alcoholic asylums, being awarded the 'Medal of Public Assistance' for his work. During the First World War he volunteered for five years, becoming an honorary medical colonel and an expert on the War Council. He received many awards including 'Officer of the Legion of Honour'; 'Officer of Public Instruction', 'Laureate of the Academy of Medicine' and 'Laureate of the French Institute' (Academy of Sciences). He also won the Montyon prize for his work on alcoholism.

Legrain became president of many prestigious organizations, including the Society of Medical Psychology, the Clinical Society of Mental Health Medicine, and the Society of Pathology and the Abolitionist League. A professor and teacher at the College of Social Sciences, a judge on the pension tribunal, one of the founders of French popular universities, ex-president of the Paris Society of the League of Public Morality, Legrain was also a founder of 'social welfare'. In academic study and teaching his work dealt with social degeneration and hereditary alcoholism, applied mental health medicine and the law, the treatment of alcoholism, social drugs and the degenerate and psychological causes of alcoholism. He also produced many publications on pathology and neurology. **Lewis H. Mates**

References

Bulletin of Clichy Cremation Society, 1939: 5–6, CRE/A/FR1.

Flacâra Sacra, 6(9) 1939 (September), CRE/AO/RO.

LeMOYNE, FRANCIS JULIUS

LeMoyne was born on 4 September 1798 and died on 14 October 1879 at Washington, Pennsylvania, USA. He was a physician, an abolitionist and a pioneer in the cremationist movement in the United States and the son of a French physician, Dr John Julius LeMoyne. Accompanied by other emigrants, his father had left Paris after the Revolution and formed a modest French community in Gallipolis, Ohio and, in 1797 married Nancy McCully, an immigrant from Ireland. Soon after, the couple moved to Washington, Pennsylvania, where Francis Julius was born in 1798. The younger LeMoyne graduated from Washington College in 1815 then studied medicine, first with his father and then at the Jefferson Medical College in Philadelphia. While travelling in the winter of 1822 LeMoyne was caught in a violent snowstorm. The severe exposure he suffered left him permanently debilitated with chronic rheumatism which would eventually cut short his medical career. In May 1823 he married Madeline Romaine Bureau. The couple went on to have five daughters and three sons.

During much of the 1820s LeMoyne was occupied with the task of restoring the family's wealth following his father's bankruptcy. In the mid-1830s he joined the anti-slavery movement, where he became an opponent of the American Colonization Society. LeMoyne believed that the organization's agenda – colonizing free blacks to Africa – was designed to strengthen the institution of human slavery in America, not emancipate the slave. His political activism drew the attention of the anti-slavery Liberty Party, which nominated him for the vice presidency of the United States in 1840. In 1841, 1844, and again in 1847 he was the Liberty Party candidate for the Pennsylvania governorship. LeMoyne's anti-slavery labours culminated with his work for the Underground Railroad – the network of guides and sympathizers who assisted runaway slaves in reaching freedom in the northern United States and Canada before the Civil War – making his home into a safe 'station' on the escape route.

At the age of 55, LeMoyne's disabilities forced him to retire from practising medicine. He turned his energies to scientific farming, animal husbandry, public service, education, and reform. He became a trustee of his alma mater, Washington College (which became Washington and Jefferson College in 1865) and the Washington Female Seminary. A gift to the American Missionary Association led directly to the founding of the LeMoyne Normal Institute for Colored People. He continued to be a generous benefactor to education until the end of his life.

LeMoyne's obituary in the *New York Times* (15 October 1879) described the doctor as 'an eccentric man with many queer ways, but it was not until late in life that he began to show a liking for cremation'. In 1875 he began to study cremation, made himself a minor expert on the subject, and mastered its technical aspects. The following year, he built a crematory furnace and began experimenting with it, the first subject being a sheep, whose ashes he kept in a glass jar, displayed on the counter of his drug store. The first human cremation was the body of a Bavarian nobleman, Baron Joseph Henri Louis de Palm. The success of this operation was overshadowed by a hostile response from the local community and the newspaper press. Public opinion was so opposed to LeMoyne's work that the furnace was shut down until 1878. Four days

after his own death at the age of 81, LeMoyne was cremated and his ashes buried. At the time, his was the only operable cremation furnace in the United States. **Eric Love**

LEWERENTZ, SIGURD

Sigurd Lewerentz (1885–1975) was the most purposeful and sophisticated personality in twentieth-century Swedish architecture. He pursued his own insights, and chose radical architectonic forms often devising straightforward solutions that exhibited signs of genius. As young architects, Gunnar Asplund and Sigurd Lewerentz won the competition to design the Woodland Cemetery (*Skogskyrkogården*) outside Stockholm in 1915. For many years they worked together on this project, Lewerentz mainly devoting himself to the site plan. The most subtle work of Swedish neo-classical revival is the Chapel of the Resurrection at the Woodland Cemetery, designed by Lewerentz in 1925.

Lewerentz's field of activities covered workers' dwellings, magnificent villas, industrial buildings, churches, wallpaper, furniture, advertising design, and so on. For some time, he was a manufacturer and inventor. With time, his radicalism intensified and, when he died in 1975, at 90 years of age, he had become world-famous for his timeless design of churches such as St Mark's outside Stockholm, and his last great work, the Petri Church in Klippan in the south of Sweden. **Börje Olsson**

See also Asplund; Stockholm Woodland Crematorium; Sweden.

LIEN-TEH, DR WU

In January 1911, the coldest month of the year, Dr Wu Lien-Teh was the young chief medical officer of the Chinese city of Harbin, Manchuria where the modern form of the 'Black Death' – the Pneumonic Plague – had already killed 2200 people. Their corpses lay 'unburied on the frozen ground' and problems over providing medical care for the sick and the dying were enormous (Lien-Teh, 1949: 9). Of 25 000 people some 7000 had fled the city or died and it was impossible to find gravediggers. As the doctor in charge, Cambridge-educated Lien-Teh 'decided upon a radical course' and appealed to the imperial government in Peking for permission to use cremation. A young, low-ranking doctor suggesting 'such an unusual procedure' was 'unheard of', but 'the times were unusual, and, as in a war crisis, needed radical measures'. Three days later the emperor gave his permission, and Lien-Teh's staff immediately set about their task in what was his 'first direct connection with cremation affairs'. Bodies were collected, whether in coffins or not, piled in 22 groups of 100 corpses, drenched with kerosene and simultaneously set alight. Within three days all the corpses had been cleared from the fields and disposed of, and the plague began to decline in Harbin. The heat from the cremations also helped thaw the ground sufficiently to allow for the digging of proper mass burial trenches that served as collection points for new corpses, which were regularly cremated in them. Within two months of the first cremations, the plague had been eradicated (Lien-Teh, 1949: 9).

In 1937 an article Lien-Teh had written on cremation in China was published in *Oganj*, the newspaper of the Belgrade Cremation Society. Writing from Ipoh, the capital of the northern Perak State of Malaya in 1940, where he now lived, he reported to the British Cremation Society that cremation in Malaya was 'gathering momentum' and that he intended to raise funds to build a municipal crematorium. He had wanted to be present at an International Cremation Federation (ICF) meeting but was prevented by the war situation in the Far East. Seven years later, after the war, Lien-Teh was still seeking to build a crematorium in Ipoh. He was instrumental in establishing the Cremation Society of Perak, itself the direct outcome of a meeting at the Ipoh Buddhist Association he addressed on 27 March 1949. As the society's first president, he advised cremationists in Singapore to establish their own cremation society to capitalize on the new interest in cremation in the Singaporean municipality (Lien-Teh, 1949: 11).

That same year, in Britain, he addressed the British Cremation Society on 'Cremation Among the Chinese – Past and Present', praising it for the 'wonderful progress' made in Britain. Clearly preferring the Western model, he was critical of cremation practices in the East:

> Out in the East, the methods of cremation so far adopted are not yet sufficiently advanced. You are no doubt aware of the primitive way in which bodies have for

centuries been and are still being cremated in the sacred cities of India. (Lien-Teh 1949:11).

Lien-Teh's visit to Britain enabled him to seek advice from experienced cremationists on the building of the crematorium in Perak: his 'model crematorium' opened in May 1950. Lien-Teh had visited Japan, studied cremation there and published a subsequent article in *Pharos* (1949). In June 1953 Lien-Teh again visited Britain and the ICF's office, to report on progress in Malaya. In 1954, though absent, Lien-Teh expressed his ongoing support in a message to the Oslo ICF Congress remarking on the present and future need for land. In 1956 Lien-Teh was, again, due to address the British Cremation Society's annual conference on the situation in Malaya. Unfortunately, his wife became ill and, though in London, he could not attend. Likewise, though unable to attend the 1957 ICF Congress in Zurich, he sent a message thanking the ICF for helping him foster cremation in Malaya. Now an old man, Lien-Teh's powers were failing. *Pharos* did not receive any updated information on the situation in Malaya after 1956 and the Perak Cremation Society stopped paying its dues to the ICF in 1961. This was presumably linked to the death of Lien-Teh, and shows just how essential he was to the organized work of cremation in Malaya. **Lewis H. Mates**

Reference

Lien-Teh, Dr Wu (1949), 'Cremation Among the Chinese – Past and Present', *Pharos*, 15(2): 9–11.

LITERARY CREMATION

From a discussion of Mary Shelley's interesting use of ideas of cremation discussed in the entry on **Frankenstein**, itself belonging to a period before the major debates on the topic in Europe, we move to literary contexts in which modern cremation began to make its presence felt. Here I focus most specifically on Britain, but with one comparative element from the USA, as we witness cremation beginning to move from its major nineteenth-century place as a topic of medical, philosophical and religious concern into the qualitatively different realm of fiction (although, as the entry on H.R. **Haweis** indicates, the later nineteenth century did in fact own a strongly ideological novel on cremation).

In the first case dealt with here we, similarly, encounter a strong ideological overtone. In the others we consider, however, we see a move into cremation as an existing, though unfamiliar, practice, and then into the kind of familiarity that even allows for humour. Although I discuss, in a separate entry on **MacColl**, that songwriter's important reflection on cremation and cremated remains I mention it now, in passing, because of its own literary merit as a folk-song.

One of the earliest, and starkest appearances of cremation in fiction is in Aldous Huxley's *Brave New World* first published in 1932 as a tract against depersonalization and, indeed, dehumanization itself. Its reference is to 'Slough Crematorium' from which a busload of boys and girls are returning, young citizens of the 'brave new world' where, we are told, 'death-conditioning begins at eighteen months' with every small child spending 'two mornings a week in a Hospital for the Dying'. Obviously, they also have visits to the crematorium built into their programme when somewhat older so that 'they learn to take dying as a matter of course ... Like any other physiological process' (Huxley, 2004: 142). Slough, as a real-life town, belongs to that category of location that prompts a sense of profound ordinariness, a place devoid of depth or interest, a kind of geographical banality. In that sense, Huxley chose well the location of his brave new crematorium.

A contemporary of Huxley, the redoubtable G.K. Chesterton, turned his mind to cremation but in a quite opposite, and whimsical, fashion in his poem 'The Song of the Strange Ascetic' where he – genial Catholic hedonist that he was – imagines himself a heathen and contrasts himself with 'Higgins', the strange ascetic (Freed, 1933: 216).

> If I had been a Heathen,
> I'd have piled my pyre on high,
> And in a great red whirlwind
> Gone roaring to the sky.
> But Higgins is a Heathen,
> And a richer man than I;
> And they put him in an oven,
> Just as if he were a pie.

A different kind of contemporary Catholic – one born in 1904 and converting to the faith as a young adult – the novelist Graham Greene adopts quite a different stance from both Chesterton and, especially, Huxley. In the 'real'

emergent new world of the 1960s, Greene, who had spent most of his life aware of the Catholic ban on cremation begins his novel, *Travels With My Aunt* with a chapter on a funeral at an unnamed but 'famous crematorium' in London, which was very probably modelled on Golders Green Crematorium. Published in 1969, six years after the lifting of the Catholic prohibition on cremation, the book provides a rather full account of distinctive features of this newly emerging cultural convention. He describes the crematorium funeral including 'that slight stirring of excited expectation which is never experienced at a graveside'. People wonder 'Will the oven doors open? Will the coffin stick on the way to the flames?' Here, he echoes Britain in its early popular engagement with cremation. Even the clergyman uses a prayer that 'he must have composed himself', for the key character – Henry – has never heard it before at the many funerals he has attended. Still, the funeral 'goes without a hitch': the flowers are 'economically' taken from the coffin which 'at the touch of a button slid away from us out of sight' (Greene, 1971: 797). Efficiency is the order of the day.

Then, outside, he meets relatives and, pondering his behaviour, he 'understands' that he has to 'wait for the ashes'. As he does so, 'the chimney of the crematorium gently smoked overhead'. The tone is one of uncertain convention over ashes while the inevitable smoking chimney firmly demarcates this new territory. He then takes a walk in the crematorium gardens (Golders Green was noted for its landscaped gardens) and muses that such a place 'resembles a real garden about as much as a golf links resembles a genuine landscape. The lawns are too well cultivated and the trees too stiffly on parade: the urns resemble the little boxes containing sand where one tees up' (1971: 797). And he should know, because he is a keen gardener; he cultivates dahlias.

Then the ashes are ready in 'a very classical urn in black steel', but they are presented to him 'with a package very neatly done up in brown paper with red paper seals' that remind him of 'a Christmas gift' (1971: 11). He is slightly disconcerted because, somehow or other, he would have liked to have seen the urn to make sure of his purchase. His indefatigable aunt Augusta, with whom he walks in the garden and who is about to take him with her on her remarkable travels, asks him what he is going to do with the ashes and he replies that he has plans to place them on a plinth amongst his dahlias, his actual words being 'I thought of making a little throne for it among my dahlias' (1971: 12). Nevertheless he has to acknowledge that perhaps he will have to bring the urn in for the winter, much as, we are to assume, he would do with his dahlia tubers, to save them from the frost. In fact, the remains are to become part of the adventure of his travels with his aunt. What is interesting is this reference to taking away remains and using them in a private fashion – a practice still in its relative infancy at the time he wrote the novel. Like his aunt, Henry is somewhat eccentric amidst his utterly conventional lifestyle as an early retired and bachelor bank manager.

Of much the same generation as Graham Greene was John Betjeman. Although Greene was a youthful convert to Catholicism, he was as entirely Catholic-English in outlook as Betjeman was Anglican-English. Betjeman was one of the greatest English poets reflecting on life in twentieth-century England – one for whom verse seemed to be 'the shortest way/Of saying what one has to say'. Indeed, verse was 'A memorable way of dealing/With mood or person, place of feeling' (Betjeman, 2003: 235). Betjeman addressed himself to the subject in his poem 'Aldershot Crematorium' (2003: 302).

> Between the swimming-pool and cricket-ground
> How straight the crematorium driveway lies!
> And little puffs of smoke without a sound
> Show what we loved dissolving in the skies,
> Dear hands and feet and laughter-lighted face
> And silk that hinted at the body's grace.
> But no-one seems to know quite what to say
> (Friends are so altered by the passing years):
> 'Well, anyhow, it's not so cold today' –
> And thus we try to dissipate our fears.
> *'I am the Resurrection and the Life'*:
> Strong deep and painful, doubt inserts the knife.

His description of the crematorium's location is telling: 'Between the swimming-pool and cricket ground/How straight the crematorium driveway lies!' The partner sporting and leisure institutions, and the very fact that there is a straight driveway hints at an 'out-of-town' location and contrasts with his many homely descriptions of urbanely nestled and welcoming churches redolent of hope. Indeed, Betjeman's Aldershot compares extremely well with Huxley's Slough, as similarly unremarkable towns. From the setting he moves directly to the symbol of the place's function:

> And little puffs of smoke without a sound
> Show what we loved dissolving in the skies.

Interestingly, Betjeman, does not focus on, nor even mentions, ashes. For him, it is not the cremated remains but the 'little puffs of smoke without a sound' that catch the attention. This is understandable, for in mid-twentieth-century Britain, just as cremation was gaining popularity, the smoke and not the ashes would have been the more familiar reality. Besides, his intention does not lie with the residual remains of a person but with the transience, the ephemeral presence in smoke that soon passes and is gone.

Of particular interest in this poem is the framing of belief that it presents. In fact it is an extremely stark framework, for the apparently innocent 'little puffs of smoke' that are seen 'dissolving in the skies' can be contrasted with the idea of a soul passing to heaven. Indeed, the very use of the plural 'skies' is recognizably unusual and marks as secular a note as would 'the heavens' as opposed to 'heaven'. Such an interpretation might be deemed fanciful were it not for the second and final stanza in which not only do those present not seem 'to know quite what to say', but turn to talk about the weather – 'it's not so cold today' – and do so to hide their fear: 'thus we try to dissipate our fears'. That fear is summarized starkly in the final two lines, the first taking the biblical quote of Jesus that was the traditional opening utterance of the Anglican funeral service – 'I am the Resurrection and the Life' – and the second: 'Strong, deep and painful, doubt inserts the knife.'

Words that so often describe faith – 'strong' and 'deep' – are now used for 'doubt'. In this short poem, the 'little puffs of smoke' seem to symbolize not only the person that is gone, with their 'Dear hands and feet and laughter-lighted face', but also the one watching. Is belief also 'dissolving in the skies'? Certainly 'the body's grace' is ended – a grace that was 'hinted at' by the 'silk' that the person wore. Here, then, we have a poem that serves as a possible cultural marker of a practice that brought to critical observation the ultimate destiny of humanity. From the all-too-straight driveway, 'Between the swimming-pool and cricket ground', we find ourselves seeking to hide life-fear as the sight of smoke brings doubt to insert the knife. It seems that, for Betjeman at least, the experience of a cremation prompted a reflection of some considerable degree as the process itself reconfigured symbols in deeply challenging ways.

Two generations after Huxley and a generation after Betjeman and Greene, in the 1980–1990s rather than the 1930s and 1950–1970s we encounter Iain Banks. Cremation is now a much more accepted part of British life and this well-known Scottish novelist begins his novel *The Crow Road* with the highly memorable first line: 'It was the day my grandmother exploded. I sat in the crematorium, listening to my Uncle Hamish quietly snoring in harmony to Bach's Mass in B Minor' (Banks, 1992: 3). In this novel the crematorium is an accepted part of modern life, as given as the jeans, trainers, personal stereos and male earrings, all mentioned in the account of the event. There is no particular drama as the coffin 'slid away into the wall' or as a 'little purple curtain lowers itself over the doorway'. It is interesting to see, perhaps for the first time in an English novel, attention drawn to the 'obviously important and formal business of Leaving the Chapel', supervised by the undertakers. There is an odd reference to the crematorium in the story normally waiting until night to burn the bodies 'to avoid the possibility of resulting smoke-plumes sending overwrought relations into unsightly paroxysms of grief', but that is for effect, and told rather as an urban myth. The point of it all is to frame the event of his grandmother 'exploding' or, rather, her heart pacemaker exploding in the cremator – her doctor having forgotten to get it removed. Although, with dramatic licence, this local doctor dies of heart failure as he runs to try to stop the cremation before she explodes.

As an American complement, also published in 1992, and describing a black American context, is Darryl Pinckney's *High Cotton*, it is interesting because its Aunt Clara, not unlike Graham Greene's Aunt Augusta, is a woman of firm, but eccentric, opinion. Living in Alabama

where cremation, 'if not illegal ... was not done', she, nevertheless, wanted to be cremated. 'She couldn't bear the thought of worms and bacteria eating away at her. ... She wanted to be compact' (Pinckney, 1992: 39). She also liked the idea of cremation because it was something 'no one else had. It was newfangled, like an item in a catalogue she was the first in town to receive.' What is more, she fancied having her ashes placed in a 'hollowed out' decorative flamingo' or 'discreetly' scattered 'in the aisles of Rich's Department Store'. The problem was she rather wanted to be with her deceased husband, but he was buried, albeit 'on the wrong side of town'. Obviously, cremation responded to her sense of identity as an innovative and upwardly mobile lady

Death itself occupies a significant place in contemporary literature and, in British society at least, cremation and its associated motifs are now, very largely, a normal part of the stories told. Television plays are, as the twenty-first century begins, more likely to employ a crematorium than a cemetery if dealing with contemporary life. Even so, certain motifs still retain an element of uneasiness about them as with the fear of premature burial picked up, for example, in Tracy Chevalier's *Falling Angels* where the rather mischievous gravedigger's son even rehearses a limerick on the topic. This popular American novelist, in her writing on Britain and about some very British characters, has them spend a great deal of time and energy on and in cemeteries in this novel, which is set earlier in the twentieth century as cremation began to be an option. The columbarium, in particular, looms large in the earlier part of her book. The comment on one Mrs Coleman, who was keen to see it, was that it probably 'appeals to her sense of tidiness and economy', and this despite the fact that 'it would never be appropriate for Christians' (Chevalier, 2001: 81).

Set amidst an earlier generation, this novel is notable for raising the issue of cremation and burial as funeral options during times of social change. This is partly enshrined in the issue of memorial statues – angels – that fall with time, and with those who, though buried, really had wished to be cremated. When pondering the wishes of a third party for cremation one character questions where the remains might go – '"What, and placed in the columbarium?" "No", replies another, "she wanted her ashes scattered where flowers grow. That's what she said. But daddy wouldn't do it"' (2001: 383). Then, in a deeply sympathetic but highly illegal move on the part of the gravedigger and cemetery manager, the dead woman's remains are exhumed, burned, and the story ends: '"Afterwards as the sun's coming up we get some buckets and half fill 'em with sand. We mix the ashes into it and we sprinkle it all over the meadow. Mr Jackson has plans to let wildflowers grow there, like she wanted. That'll make a change from all them flowerbeds and raked paths".' Still, even that is not enough and the final sentences of the novel tells how the remainder of the ash-sand mixture is taken '"to our Granpa's rosebush.... That way I'll be sure of where some of her is ... 'Sides, bone meal's good for roses"' (2001: 401). So it is that burial amidst paradoxically falling memorials and overly organized pathways is set against free-flowering nature just as social conventions stand against personal wishes. The compromise is one that only cremated remains could fulfil, with part scattered in the meadow, lost to record, and part placed on 'Granpa's' rosebush. The rosebush ends the book – the symbol of a very English-located individualism. **Douglas J. Davies**

References

Banks, Iain (1992), *The Crow Road*, London: Abacus.

Betjeman, John (2003), *Collected Poems*, London: John Murray.

Chevalier, Tracy (2001), *Falling Angels*, London: Harper-Collins.

Freed, Peter James (1933), *The Collected Poems of G.K. Chesterton*, London: Methuen.

Greene, Graham (1969), *Travels With My Aunt*, London: Penguin.

Huxley, Aldous (2004), *Brave New World*, London: Vintage. First published 1932.

Pinckney, Darryl (1992), *High Cotton*, London: Faber and Faber.

LUXEMBOURG

The advocacy of cremation began in Luxembourg in November 1906 with Dr Arthur Daubenfeld founding the Society for the Propagation of Cremation (*Société pour la Propagation de l'Incinération*). An early coup came when Daubenfeld persuaded Dr Fonck, president of Luxembourg's prestigious College of Physicians, to become its president. Fonck, unfortunately, had to resign for reasons of ill-health a year later. Catholic opposition made it difficult for the new society to make an impact in its early years, but it still organized exhibitions and conferences, and distributed pamphlets. In 1909 Daubenfeld bought, on behalf of the society, a 2.5-acre plot within the city boundaries. Earmarked as the site for a crematorium, this was a shrewd move as, by 1935, the as yet undeveloped plot was of 'considerable value'. A landmark was reached in 1912 with the first cremation of a society member in Mayence (Germany). Three years later Daubenfeld took advantage of a modification in the law and founded the Cremation Joint Stock Company with a view to constructing a crematorium. Thus, from 1916 there were two Luxembourg cremation societies: one to raise funds for the proposed crematorium, the other to propagandize and make cremation abroad possible for its members.

The 1920s saw wrangling over the position of cremation in Luxembourg law. In 1920 a government adviser who was, curiously, a Catholic, advised Esch City Corporation that it was entitled to buy shares in the Cremation Joint Stock Company because cremation was not illegal. However, six years later, problems arose when the Cremation Joint Stock Company and the city of Luxembourg decided to form a company with the purpose of building a crematorium in the city's main cemetery. The joint stock company was set to agree to establish the crematorium and to guarantee the city council against any losses that might result from its operation. Yet the government's attitude was contradictory and confused. A government councillor of liberal outlook opined that cremation was not illegal, and that therefore the articles of partnership could be approved. However, the Liberal minister was unhappy with this and asked the state council to consider the problem. Then, another Liberal councillor argued that cremation was forbidden by a decree of 1804, so the articles of partnership could not be ratified. In the end, the government sided with this latter opinion and refused to ratify the contract, arguing that, as the decree of 1804 did not provide for cremation, but only mentioned inhumation, it was not legal (Daubenfeld, 1939: 14–15).

Cremationists challenged the government's

stance that all methods for the disposal of the dead other than inhumation were prohibited, and that cremation could only become legal through new parliamentary legislation. They argued that the 1804 decree did not actually forbid cremation, but merely omitted to regulate it. Therefore, the government could issue regulations on cremation without referring to parliament. To this end Mr Blum, a deputy and cremation society member, placed a bill before parliament in 1933 to annul the 1804 decree and allow governmental regulation of disposal of the dead.

Alarmed at these developments, the Catholic Church mobilized action against cremation. The bishop of Luxembourg sent two pastoral letters on 1 April and 1 June 1935 to be read out in all churches, reminding Catholics that those choosing cremation would incur severe ecclesiastical penalties. Asserting that cremation societies were used by freemasons to ensure that people lost their faith, the letters promised damnation for any Catholics who joined cremation societies. The cremation society responded by stating that it had members who continued to receive the sacraments, thereby proving that they were not anti-religion. Moreover, the society argued, two important German Catholics had been recently cremated, and freemasonry did not take an especial interest in cremation. France was cited as evidence for this: there, Catholics thought that freemasonry was 'almighty', yet the cremation movement was in its infancy. However, this refutation was printed only in cremationist publications, and was therefore unlikely to have been read by Catholics, who, in any case, had recently been reminded that contact with cremation societies would end in damnation.

Catholic opposition did not initially prevent events overtaking Blum's cremation bill as, in 1936, Luxembourg City Council made two 250 000-franc grants: one to help the enlargement of a Catholic Church and another towards the cost of a crematorium. The government approved both grants. Asking the aldermen to give their permission for the crematorium's construction, the government was clear that the question of cremation should not thereby be prejudiced. This was hailed as a 'great victory' in *Pharos*, which even speculated that the cause of cremation might be won in Luxembourg even though the legal question remained

unsettled. The cremationists hoped to begin constructing the crematorium and settle the legal question later, thereby presenting the state with a *fait accompli*. However, the Catholic Church mobilized again, this time more energetically. After 15 months more of intensive Catholic lobbying against the crematorium, the city council lost its enthusiasm for the project and refused permission for it to go ahead. Daubenfeld found this 'ridiculous state of affairs' amusing, especially the fact that, this time, the Committee of Jurists found that cremation was illegal not by the decree of 1804, but by an article of 1803! Continuing the struggle against the 'best Jesuitical methods' of the Catholic Church, Daubenfeld appealed to the state council, which responded that cremation was not illegal but, in the absence of cremation regulations, the building of the crematorium could not be continued. The cremation society responded by submitting plans for a columbarium, and asked the government to make the necessary regulations. The Second World War then intervened.

Despite these setbacks the cremation society had made advances during the 1930s. In 1932 it decided to advance its propaganda activities by establishing its own bi-monthly journal, *Flamma*, with Daubenfeld as editor. By 1939 the cremation society had 900 members and between 20 and 24 cremations were being carried out annually in Mayence or Strasbourg (France). Daubenfeld was proud of the fact that the percentage of dead cremated in Luxembourg was higher than that of either Belgium or France, although in both countries, in contrast to Luxembourg, cremation was legal and crematoria existed. In 1933, for example, some 0.56 per cent of the dead in Luxembourg were cremated, whereas in France the figure was 0.19 per cent. In 1939 Daubenfeld thought that 'in spite of the Catholic machinations and the failures of those who ought to be our friends, we are fully convinced that one day we will succeed because reason in the long run always triumphs over stupidity'. (Daubenfeld 1939: 15).

Like the cremation movement in occupied France, the Luxembourg Cremation Society suffered during the Second World War. In May 1940 the country was occupied by Germany, and the occupying administration appointed a special commissioner to bring all societies into line with Nazi aims. Many diverse societies were dissolved and had their property confiscated. Others, including the cremation society, had to pay large amounts of money in order to remain in existence. However, the joint stock company for the construction of a crematorium was not so fortunate. Dissolved by the German commissioner, its assets were handed to the City of Luxembourg, along with a requirement to construct a crematorium. It was not to be resurrected after the war. Although the cremation society tried to continue its activities, its membership dropped from 822 in 1940 to 653 in 1944, and, naturally, its income also declined. *Flamma* ceased publication in February 1941 in order to avoid having to carry German propaganda and advertisements for German companies. Worse still, the society lost its president when, in September 1942, the Germans deported Daubenfeld – although he escaped from Germany in September 1944. Despite all this, however, the numbers of cremations maintained pre-war levels: there were 20 in 1940, 21 in each of the next two years and 19 in 1944. Only in 1943 did they decrease to ten.

The immediate post-war years did not bring respite; the cremation society continued to suffer and, despite 'great efforts' to restore the society to its pre-war level, by 1948 membership had decreased again, to 572, which was below its 1944 level. *Flamma* was still not back in circulation either, and Luxembourg remained in the rearguard of the cremation cause in Europe, ranking alongside Hungary and Yugoslavia as countries that had no laws relating to cremation but did not object to their citizens being cremated in other countries. A new approach was needed, and it was, perhaps, the International Cremation Federation (ICF) that offered it. Before the war, Luxembourg cremationists had been lukewarm towards the ICF. In 1937 Daubenfeld expressed the opinion that the ICF could do little to help alter the situation in Luxembourg, although he was happy to be proved wrong. In the post-war years, his attitude altered. At the 1948 ICF Congress at The Hague, Daubenfeld, remarking on the legal situation in Luxembourg, called for ICF support for a resolution he intended to move, urging the UNO Commission of Human Rights to pronounce in favour of the right of every person to decide on the form of disposal of his or her own body. Daubenfeld dismissed the French argument that an approach to the Catholic Church would yield results as ultimately it knew

how to listen to reason. Maintaining that the Catholic Church always opposed progress, he argued that approaching it was a waste of time. Instead, he once again spoke up for his proposal to get the right to the disposal of one's own body in the UNO charter: the church would then have its hand forced as it would 'ill become' it to oppose a UNO decision. Daubenfeld's death in August 1950 appeared to be a severe blow. Ernest Noth of France claimed that, shortly before his death, Daubenfeld had almost persuaded the Luxembourg authorities to build a crematorium. With his death the project was indefinitely postponed. The 1954 ICF congress sent its moral support to Luxembourg via a letter of encouragement. However, it is unclear if it acted on a proposal, based on the cremation society's financial weakness since its only income was an annual subscription of 200 francs from its members, to provide more help to Luxembourg.

If the ICF had infact acted it had been ineffective as very little appeared to change, and this despite the distribution by mail of 91 000 cremation prospectuses in 1954 (Boone, 1960: 38). In 1961 cremationist Charles Knaf wrote that his country 'appears before the civilised world as the most backward and intolerant among the countries of Western Europe' (Knaf, 1961: 13). Only Luxembourg, Portugal and Spain officially rejected the construction of crematoria, and this was due, according to Knaf, to the influence of Catholicism. Although Luxembourg's population was over 97 per cent Roman Catholic in 1961, Knaf asserted that only half of these were 'really and sincerely' Catholics. Despite this, the Catholic Church, eager 'to conquer the temporal power', took advantage of those who did not care that it 'governed or influenced' their 'private lives and public activities' and maintained its 'sway over the state by putting in every important place people devoted to the church or dependent on it'. According to Knaf, the Church also hindered members of the cremation society in their attempts to attain certain elevated positions. This, for Knaf, meant that the Catholic Church's political power in Luxembourg was far greater than its cultural importance. For the previous half-century no government had held office without being supported, or at least tolerated, by the Catholic Party, such was the all-pervading political influence of the Catholic clergy. No legislation could be enacted if the Catholic Party opposed it. And it was for this reason that the Luxembourg authorities had consistently refused permission to build a crematorium or even a columbarium. However, the cremation movement's problems were not all about the power of the Church, but also the weakness of the laity. Knaf thought that many administrators lacked 'strength of character' and he lamented that 'so many among my country men are too respectful, immoderately respectful of tradition and they lack initiative and independence of spirit even in more general matters' (Knaf, 1961: 11).

The legal arguments of the inter-war period had not altered. The government maintained that the 1804 decree had to be amended, but, due to fear of the Catholic Church, it still refused to produce the necessary legislation. Seeing this position as merely an excuse for inaction, cremationists still argued that there was no need for special legislation as anything that was not prohibited by law should be lawful. They also pointed out that there was inconsistency as other parts of the 1804 decree were being violated continually – for example, allowing the burial of dignitaries in churches which had been prohibited in 1804 for reasons of hygiene. This suggested that the 1804 decree had fallen into abeyance and that an overhaul of the regulations on the disposal of the dead was very necessary.

Another thing galled Luxembourg cremationists. The 1804 decree had been promulgated in France but, though still in force, no specific legislation had been deemed necessary to legalize cremation there. The 1887 French law guaranteeing individuals choice in how their dead body was to be disposed of was all that was required. The difference clearly lay in the attitudes of the authorities and had led to Knaf's contemptuous attitude towards the Luxembourg legislators. Convinced that the authorities would find legal arguments to support cremation if the Vatican changed its attitude, Knaf appealed to the ICF for support and to continue its efforts to persuade the Vatican to alter its stance – a change in emphasis from his predecessor, Daubenfeld. Knaf was clear that the Luxembourg Cremation Society did not need more finance nor more propaganda, but a change in the Vatican's attitude, which he regarded as the 'final hope for Catholic countries'. However, he recognized that previous ICF approaches to the 'highly intolerant' Catholic Church had all 'been of no avail'. Being

a cremationist in Luxembourg was difficult, according to Knaf, especially as:

> ... the Catholic dailies and periodicals that are read by eighty percent of the population lead continually fierce attacks on us, styling us hell-hounds; if we remember that the Roman Catholic Church keeps people in awe of herself until their death-bed and never misses an opportunity of threatening with hell the members of our Society or people who are inclined to follow our steps; if we remember further that our Government, town councils and even private enterprises keep our members at arm's length, this under pressure of the Catholic clergy ... (Knaf, 1961: 13)

Indeed, for Knaf, being a cremationist in Luxembourg was 'only short of social suicide'. There were also practical problems stemming from cremation's illegal status. Anyone from Luxembourg who opted to be cremated had to be transported to France for cremation in Strasbourg. With the ashes returning to Luxembourg, this was a 300-mile round-trip, entailing considerable expense and a great deal of form-filling at customs on both sides of the border. In addition, *Flamma* had still not reappeared and the only widespread propaganda was the occasional pro-cremation article appearing in a newspaper once a year or so.

Nevertheless, Knaf retained some hope, taking solace in the fact that, despite the lack of a crematorium, there was still 'quite a number of cremationists' of 'every class of people' in Luxembourg. The society's 1000-plus membership meant that there were three cremationists per 1000 of Luxembourg's population. Having performed 698 cremations to date, the movement had, in Knaf's opinion, 'greatly contributed to make cremation known and in general has met with no disapproval from the public at large' (Knaf, 1961: 13). The average 25 cremations per year represented 'steady progress', when compared with 12 in 1932, and had made 'some impression on the public'. Some progress had been made in getting cremation adopted by the working classes. Before 1920 almost everyone interested in cremation was wealthy, whereas 40 years later, although 65 per cent of cremationists were drawn from 'wealthy circles', the remaining 35 per cent were from 'less prosperous groups'. The cremation society remained prosperous and active, maintaining contact with the authorities, keeping the issue alive in parliament through cremationist deputies and using propaganda in an attempt to make cremation more familiar to the populace. The aim was to gain more members and thus 'better oppose the foolish misconceptions of our authorities'. The success of British cremationists, coupled with the fact that they were helping their fellow cremationists abroad through the ICF, was an 'incentive to those under-developed countries; there the cremationists feel that they are not isolated and that they have a full share in common affairs, whatever their position may be in their own country' (Knaf, 1961: 15).

In 1960 Luxembourg became more important within the ICF, as Knaf was elected its vice-president as a representative of a Latin country. The ICF then began to take the problems facing Luxembourg and other similar countries more seriously. In 1967 the ICF general council endorsed a proposal to install a committee for the organization of cremation to help Luxembourg and other 'Latin' European countries. The committee produced a proposal for a touring cremation exhibition that would visit Belgium, Luxembourg and France. The 'underdeveloped' countries also produced a plan to make a film on cremation and, realizing it would be an expensive drain on their scant resources, requested ICF financial backing.

But things were already looking up in Luxembourg, due to the modification of the Catholic Church's stance in favour of cremation in 1963. This led to an immediate and noticeable increase in cremations – evidence of the power of the Catholic Church's influence. For more than 30 years before 1963 there had been between 17 and 28 cremations annually in Luxembourg – figures which showed no real signs of increase and which fluctuated widely from one year to the next. It was, then, hardly coincidental that 1963 marked the first time that cremations in Luxembourg exceeded 30, and, two years later, that the 43 cremations performed amounted to more than 1 per cent of total deaths for the first time. By 1969 the ICF secretary-general could note that the Luxembourg cremation rate had almost doubled in three years. Cremations continued to grow fairly steadily from 64 (1.52 per cent of deaths) in 1969 to 363 (9.04 per cent of deaths) in 1987.

However, the question of Luxembourg's own crematorium remained vexed, despite the Luxembourg government again discussing the topic in spring 1968. Hopes that these discussions would lead to permission being granted for the construction of the first crematorium appeared premature a year later, as cremationists did not approve of the new legislation under discussion. The controversial parts included the requirement for the deceased to have left a declaration for cremation that was not needed for a burial. In addition, where the cause of death was in doubt, a second medical certificate was required. Third, whilst the poor were buried at no cost, there was no subsidy envisaged if they desired cremation. Still, thanks largely to the cremation society's efforts, a new law that placed burial and cremation on an equal footing came into operation on 1 August 1972. As body disposal was deemed a local authority matter, only they could build crematoria. By 1975, 39 Luxembourg local authorities had pooled resources and prepared plans for a crematorium, which they hoped to finish building the following year.

Yet, by 1978, Luxembourg still had no crematorium: the local authorities' plan had fallen through. However, seven authorities had constructed columbaria, now that the law of 1972 permitted ashes to be deposited in them (previously they had to be buried). Five other authorities were also constructing columbaria, and there were plans to build a further 17. Cremationist member of the Luxembourg parliament, Jean Gremling, asked the Minister of the Interior a parliamentary question on the topic in 1978. The minister's response, that grants would be made by authorities wherever necessary to ensure columbaria were provided where needed, was encouraging. In addition, he had instructed the Ministry of the Interior to ensure that when a parish enlarged a cemetery, or planned to build a mortuary, a columbarium should also be included in the plans.

However, the continuing lack of a crematorium in Luxembourg meant that those wishing to be cremated received a poor return from the tax system. Some bodies were cremated in Strasbourg where the French tax system, deeming cremation a 'taxable service rendered to a private individual' charged 17 per cent value added tax. On return to Luxembourg, another 8 per cent tax had to be paid as human ashes were considered 'material processed by a foreign firm and re-imported as a finished product'. This was only partly remedied with the implementation of the single European market in 1991. However, the appearance of a crematorium in Liège, Belgium, in 1983 had given Luxembourg cremationists another possible venue for cremation.

Five years later Luxembourg still had to look to Liège or Strasbourg for cremation as 'internal dissension has so far prevented it from building its own crematorium' (*Pharos*, 54(1) 1988: 15). Finally, the 'internal dissension' was overcome, and Luxembourg finally obtained its first crematorium, in October 1995. Its appearance has had a dramatic impact on cremation rates in the Grand Duchy. In 1988 there were 389 cremations, which was over 10 per cent of deaths. However, in the years 1989–95, the trend that had seen cremations and percentages increase almost every year since 1963 altered and figures became more erratic. Thus in 1989 there were only 339 cremations, which was under 9 per cent of deaths and the 1988 figure was not exceeded again until 1993 (415 cremations representing over 10 per cent of deaths). Once the new crematorium came into operation in 1995, however, the cremation rate dramatically increased. In 1999 there were 1337 cremations constituting over 35 per cent of deaths, a quite dramatic rise on the 343 cremations and over 9 per cent rate of 1995. Ironically, the 1999 cremation percentage figure was also considerably higher than that achieved in the country that originated the problematic 1804 decree – France. **Lewis H. Mates**

See also Daubenfeld.

References

Boone, P.C., Heuer, A. and Raild, N.J. (1960), 'The Sociological Aspects of Cremation', paper given at the ICF Congress in Stockholm, CRE/D4/1960/6. CSA.

Daubenfeld, Dr Arthur (1939), 'How Cremation Began in Luxembourg', *Pharos*, 5(4): 14–15.

Knaf, Charles (1961), 'Cremation in Luxembourg', *Pharos*, 27(4): 9, 11, 13, 15.

Knaf, Charles (1969), 'Cremation in the Latin Countries of Europe', paper presented at the London ICF Congress.

'Historique du Mouvement crématiste en Luxembourg' (1968), *Flamma*, January, CRE/A/LU.

MacCOLL, EWAN

Born as Jimmie Miller, the son of Scottish parents, but changing his name to Ewan MacColl, this talented musician was born in 1915 and died in 1989. Brought up in England, devoted to folk music and radical theatre, he was a lifelong communist. For many years he sang with his partner, Peggy Seeger. One of his very popular songs, 'The Joy of Living', with its own poetic merit and power to evoke a passionate human awareness of life's joy is highlighted here as the perfect example of what I have described elsewhere as the retrospective fulfilment of identity and have contrasted with the traditional prospective or eschatological fulfilment of identity in heaven (Davies, 2002: 32; see also Davies, 2005: 118, 122). It is in looking back to earlier experience, places and relationships that the individual feels a sense of fulfilment. This became particularly important in the closing decades of the twentieth century when, as in Britain, and afterwards in other countries too, individuals took advantage of the portability of cremated remains to place them in sites of deep personal significance. This song captures one spirit of the age in a mood of hope grounded in memory and locale.

Its retrospective quality is complemented by a sense of life going on in and through the life of children. Additionally, in the third stanza, there lies a form of father's blessing upon his children: it defies description as either a secular or a religious blessing, but discloses that depth of relationship and life that marks the ultimacy of existence. MacColl described this song as his 'testament' that started out as a 'farewell to the mountains and developed into a passionate embrace of Peggy and my five children' (MacColl, 1990: 376). It is reproduced here by permission.

The Joy of Living

Farewell, you northern hills,
You mountains all, goodbye.
Moorlands and stony ridges,
Crags and peaks, goodbye.
Glyder Fach, farewell,
Cul Beig, Scafell,

Cloud-bearing Suilven.
Sun-warmed rocks and the cold
Of Bleaklow's frozen sea,
The snow and the wind and the rain
Of hills and mountains.
Days in the sun and the tempered wind
And the air like wine,
And you drink and you drink till you're drunk
On the joy of living.

Farewell to you, my love,
My time is almost done;
Lie in my arms once more
Until the darkness comes.
You filled all my days,
Held the night at bay,
Dearest companion.
Years pass by and are gone
With the speed of birds in flight.
Our life like the verse of a song
Heard in the mountains.
Give me your hand then, love, and join
Your voice with mine,
We'll sing of the hurt and the pain
And the joy of living.

Farewell to you my chicks,
Soon you must fly alone.
Flesh of my flesh, my future life.
Bone of my bone.
May your wings be strong,
May your days be long,
safe be your journey.
Each of you bears inside of you
The gift of love.
May it bring you light and warmth
And the pleasure of giving.
Eagerly savour each new day
And the taste of its mouth-
Never lose sight of the thrill
And the joy of living.

Take me to some high place
Of heather, rock and ling.
Scatter my dust and ashes,
Feed me to the wind. So that I will be
Part of all you see,
The air you are breathing.
I'll be part of the curlew's cry
And the soaring hawk,
The blue milkwort
And the sundew hung with diamonds.
I'll be riding the gentle wind

That blows through your hair,
Reminding you how we shared
In the joy of living.

Douglas J. Davies

See also Hill.

References

Davies, D.J. (2002), *Death, Ritual and Belief* (2nd rev. edn), London: Continuum.
Davies, D.J. (2005), *A Brief History of Death*, Oxford: Blackwell.
MacColl, Ewan (1990), *Journeyman: An Autobiography*, London: Sidgwick and Jackson.

MALAYA, MALAYSIA AND SINGAPORE

As in Hong Kong, certain religious and ethnic communities brought cremation to modern Malaya. By 1940 a crematorium served the needs of the Japanese Singaporean community and there was a second crematorium attached to the Chinese Taoist temple, San Pao Tung, in the northern state of Perak. Some Buddhist temples also had small crematoria for the occasional use of believers, particularly in Penang with its considerable number of Buddhists, especially wealthy women, and its powerful local Buddhist association. More were built in the later 1940s (Lien-Teh, 1949:10). Legally speaking, Malaya had no specific law on cremation. The disposal of bodily remains was regarded as a natural right, so long as the method chosen did not contravene the customs and religious beliefs of the deceased.

Dismissive of the 'primitive' methods employed at the Japanese crematorium, Dr Wu Lien-Teh, a Chinese cremationist living in Malaya, was convinced that a modern municipal crematorium was required and announced his intention to raise the money to build one somewhere in the country. By 1940 the Malay cremation movement was already 'gathering momentum', particularly in Singapore where the British Chamber of Commerce, British Association, Chinese Association and the municipal council all supported the idea of building a municipal crematorium. In fact, Lien-Teh thought that, had it not been for the outbreak of war a year earlier, there would already have been a municipal crematorium somewhere in Malaya.

After the Second World War, Lien-Teh still sought a crematorium in Ipoh, the capital of Perak State. The resident commissioner supported the idea and even promised an urban site. Lien-Teh preferred an electric cremator, since hydro-electric power was cheap and easily obtained from the Perak River power station.

Success first came, however, to another part of the colony, when the Singapore municipal council debated a proposal to build a crematorium. Despite strong Muslim opposition, the pragmatic case seemed overwhelming. The municipality spent $100 000 a year on maintaining the 2500 acres of existing burial sites. Land use was becoming an increasingly important social, political and economic issue, and the municipal health officer estimated that, at current rates, in 50 years' time the colony's population would be 4.58 million, with 2.75 million living within the municipality's boundaries. Housing was an urgent necessity and land values were rising: cremation would reduce these pressures. Moreover, both gas and electricity were available to power the cremators. Thus, on 30 July 1948, the Singapore municipal council commissioners agreed to build a new crematorium for all creeds, nationalities and races, and the considerable sum of $200 000 (£25 000) was allocated to the project. Given that not all sections of the diverse (and tax-paying) Singaporean community supported the crematorium project, Lien-Teh warned that there might be a delay before construction work would be properly underway and advised that a cremation society be formed to accelerate the process (Lien-Teh, 1949: 10–11).

Based in Perak, Lien-Teh appeared to be encouraged by the development in Singapore. On 27 March 1949 he addressed a meeting of cremationists at the Buddhist Association in Ipoh. At the end of the meeting, they decided to found the Cremation Society of Perak to operate on a purely charitable, non-profit basis to promote cremation and establish crematoria through a variety of grades of membership. Lien-Teh was elected president of this, the first cremation society in Malaya. It planned a committee to design and build an inexpensive, ferro-concrete cremator fired by wood or charcoal, and, when funds permitted, an electric crematorium would follow. Supplies of electricity were abundant, and expended largely on working the rich tin mines; gas was not easily

obtainable. In 1949 Lien-Teh addressed the British Cremation Society, noting that it had inspired the efforts in the Far East where the 'cremation movement is steadily going ahead ... and needs only systematic propaganda and extra funds to win adherents to the cause' (Lien-Teh, 1949: 11).

The Cremation Society of Perak's 'model crematorium' soon opened, in May 1950, located in a neglected temple inside a cave, complete with stalactites in picturesque surroundings at the foot of a large rocky hill 300 feet high and shaped like a lion's head (which gave its name to the temple). On the main road between Penang in the north and Singapore in the south, and four miles from the centre of Ipoh, its location was advantageous. After three months of concerted effort the charcoal-fuelled crematorium was built. It combined 'western methods with eastern appearances', including arched roof-tiles and special British-supplied cement. It was the first of its kind in Malaya. A rocky promontory became the site of a 42-foot, seven-storey pagoda. Another room was capable of providing refreshments for mourners. It was hoped that the new facilities would contribute to the beauty of the neighbourhood, revive the temple itself and, of course, help acquaint people with cremation and the work of the cremation society.

The Cremation Society of Perak soon claimed other successes, including the opening, in February 1951, of a crematorium in Kuala Lumpur. Due to a shortage of land, Chinese Buddhists of the Lotus Hill Temple had built a crematorium with a pagoda to store ashes at a cost of $20 000. In 1951 there was also a new crematorium in Penang, whose oil-fired cremator was installed and maintained by a British company. The first cremations there were the remains of 900 people executed in 1942 and discovered buried in a mass grave. In late 1950 the cremation society accepted an invitation to join the International Cremation Federation but could not attend its next congress in Copenhagen. In 1957 the ICF regarded the help it gave to the Malay cremationists as its 'first attempt at what might be called colonisation: the first attempt at spreading our boundaries beyond the fortress of Europe'.

In 1952 there were over 200 cremations in Malaya. A year later the cremation society had 42 life members and 88 ordinary members. Singapore had also decided to invest further in cremation. The government had developed a plan to build three crematoria on a 13-acre site at an estimated cost of $650 000 (£45 000) to which it had contributed $217 000 itself. It was anticipated that there would be two years of preliminary work prior to beginning actual construction. Each crematorium was to be located in a park-like setting and have its own garden of remembrance flanked on one side by a cloister. The whole site, near a reservoir, was to be landscaped with trees and lawns. The project had received widespread support throughout the diverse community, with only Muslims and Roman Catholics opposing.

However, the cremation society itself was not in great health. In 1954 it only had 12 more members than the year before (142), and there had been far fewer cremations in 1953 than in the previous year: the cremation society's Lion's Head Crematorium in Ipoh only performed 11 cremations that year, and there were around 120 elsewhere. The society complained in *Pharos* that it was 'handicapped' due to a lack of funds and called for donations to help it through 'very difficult circumstances'. Yet only a year later, it seemed that progress had picked up again as the cremation society had more than doubled its membership (taking it to 312). Cremations had also increased again: in 1954, Ipoh Crematorium performed 25 cremations and there were around 210 elsewhere.

Less than a decade later there were 20 crematoria in Malaya. Ashes, which had to be taken home, were in many cases deposited in urns in Buddhist temples. The ICF Committee for Propaganda also thought that cremation promised to make a great deal more progress in the region (ICF Committee, 1963: 20). However, if progress was to be made, it had to occur without the help of a cremation society. In 1964 the Cremation Society of Perak was disaffiliated from the ICF as it had not paid its subscription for three years. It is likely that its demise coincided with the death of Dr Wu Lien-Teh who had been its inspiration and driving force.

The development of cremation in Malaya was closely paralleled by that in Indonesia. Before 1950 cremation was little practised there, and then only by the Balinese and Indian communities. In 1951 Indonesian Buddhists recognized cremation, and the first crematorium opened in Surabaya in the same year, conducting 12 cremations. By 1967 there were seven crematoria in Indonesia, all on the island of Java (at Djakarta, Surabaya, Jogjakarta, Surakarta, Semarang, Bandung and Malang). That year, Surabaya Crematorium performed 545 of the approximate 1000 cremations carried out on the island. The key difference was that there was no cremation society in Indonesia until 1973 (although when it was created, it did not survive for long).

However, the ICF's optimism in 1963 did not appear to have been justified by subsequent developments in Malaya, which was made independent in 1957 and then became Malaysia in 1963 when it merged with Singapore and Sabah and Sarawak in north Borneo. By 1992 there were seven crematoria in Malaysia, located at Hokkien, Jahore, Kuala Lumpur, Kwantung, Wah Chai and Petaling Jaya, which had two. The discrepancy in crematorium numbers when compared to the 20 crematoria listed in 1963 is presumably because the 1992 figure was for municipal crematoria only and did not include all the private crematoria attached to temples. Some minority Malaysian populations, especially the Chinese and Indians who comprise 25 per cent and 7 per cent of the population respectively, practise cremation in present-day Malaysia. There was evidence of some level of demand for cremation in 1993 when an American cremator company announced the completion of a major project in Kuala Lumpur that involved the on-site construction of four cremators and that a second project was due to be completed in the country within two years.

At the beginning of the twenty-first century around half of the 24 million population are Malays, who are Muslim and opposed to cremation. Islam is also the national religion and, as it is government policy to strongly support it, conditions are not ideal for cremation to develop much further. Indeed, as cremation is not an option for the majority of Malaysians, other ways of coping with increasingly full cemeteries are required. The state assembly in central Selangor, where cemeteries are either full or approaching capacity, has begun to consider the 'radical' idea of burying corpses vertically (*The New Straits Times*, n.d.). Another consideration was to require housing developers to set aside one hectare of burial land for every 5000 planned residents.

Cremation has had more success in Singapore, which became independent from Malaysia in

1965. The new sovereign government implemented legislative restrictions and controls to regulate the somewhat randomly scattered Chinese burial grounds. The administration simultaneously began to promote cremation amongst the Chinese community: before 1965, only about 10 per cent of Chinese were cremated (Hui and Yeoh, 2002: 10). Learning from the failures of the previous colonial municipality's attempts to encourage cremation in the Chinese community, the government avoided direct confrontation. It provided the cremation infrastructure and persuaded the Chinese to use it through the medium of 'funeral specialists' within their own community (caretakers, priests, funeral parlour owners or geomancers). This coincided with a weakening of traditional death beliefs which paralleled the 'diminished role that regional, dialect and clan associations play in Chinese social life after independence' (Hui and Yeoh, 2002: 10). The government helped foster this development in the late 1970s by building columbaria for exhumed remains at places like Yishun and Mandai. Chinese clan associations were also allowed to build columbaria and, although cremation was encouraged, the state still provided grounds for those desiring burial, thereby ensuring that the Chinese community did not feel forced to cremate. In the early 1970s there were problems with traditional Chinese coffins being too bulky to cremate. The only available coffins were those designed for Christians whose crosses offended Chinese sensibilities. These were, however, simply replaced by more fitting symbols such as bronze 'lion head' designs.

These practical adaptations were mirrored by unanticipated changes in the practice of Chinese beliefs that facilitated the use of cremation. Again, the government revealed itself to be open to altering its rules in order to adapt. For example, in 1983, the government ended its practice of allocating niches at the Mount Vernon Crematorium and instead allowed them to be chosen freely. This came after pressure from the relatives of some deceased who were retaining ashes until they were allocated a favourable niche. The 'unfavourable' niches were located in the two lower rows of the columbarium where they were most likely to be touched by cleaners' brooms and were also most exposed to dirt. Thus most opted for the two upper rows and some also consulted geomancers in search of a favourable niche.

By the 1970s the Singaporean state had successfully promoted the use of cremation: 'Whereas in the past descendants looked after their ancestral tombs, increasingly it became their duty to take care of the ashes of their ancestors' (Hui and Yeoh, 2002: 11). In 1988 just over 68 per cent of Singaporean Chinese were cremated, contributing to the general increase in cremation at the expense of burial in Singapore since its independence. In the 1990s, 80 per cent of those whose religion did not require burial opted for cremation in one of three crematoria located at Mandai, Mount Vernon and Brighthill. Those cremated came largely from the Chinese and Indian communities which comprise over 75 per cent and around 8 per cent of the Singaporean population respectively (Muslim Malays – around 15 percent of the population – are the principal non-cremators). Yet, even then, advances were still to be made. In 2002 Singapore had a fourth crematorium, at Tse Tho Aum. A total of 11 892 cremations performed that year amounted to almost 77 per cent of Singaporean deaths. **Lewis H. Mates**

References

CSA.

Hui, Tan Boon and Brenda S.A. Yeoh (2002), 'The "Remains of the Dead": Spatial Politics of Nation-Building in Post-War Singapore', *Human Ecology Review*, 9(1): 1–13, available online at: www.humanecologyreview.org/pastissues/her9 1/91tanyeoh.pdf (accessed May 2004).

ICF Committee for Propaganda (1963), 'The World Problems of the Disposal of the Dead', paper presented at the ICF Congress, Berlin, CRE/D4/1963/3.

Lien-Teh, Dr Wu (1949), 'Cremation Among the Chinese – Past and Present', *Pharos*, 15(2): 9–11.

The New Straits Times (n.d.), 'Malaysia considers vertical graves to save space', at Ananova (news website): http://www.ananova.com/news/story/ sm_839621.html? menu=news.quirkies (accessed May 2004).

MATERIALISM AND ENLIGHTENMENT

In the materialism of the second half of the eighteenth century one can trace a precise conception of death present in the writing of its main exponents: La Mettrie, d'Holbach and Diderot. In the context of a vision of the cosmos as a necessary and living totality, and of matter as full of sensitivity and movement, death was perceived as a return to nature's womb – a return necessary to achieve new forms. This theme can be found in funerary literature, which, in France from 1797, also discussed cremation. It was not by chance that this debate took place during the last phase of the Revolution, culturally dominated by the medical–philosophical influence of *idéologie*, a legacy of eighteenth century thought – and materialist thought in particular. A significant example of this debate was the proposed law presented by the member of parliament Daubermesnil (November 1797) to the Council that contained an article in favour of cremation. Although it failed due to a lack of votes, the project was preceded by a theoretical reflection in which Daubermesnil emphasized that man is part of a material universe in eternal movement, and that fire, therefore, only accelerates the work of dissolution that nature inexorably completes.

Another interesting text is that of Cambry, who in 1799 was charged by the Department of the Seine with writing a *Rapport sur les sépultures* (*Report on Burials*) in the city of Paris. Describing the indecent state of Paris' cemeteries, Cambry hoped that the choice of being cremated would become available. His text also highlighted the materialist vision of a cosmos in eternal transformation. With cremation, Cambry stated, 'all the elements that form the human body, scattered in the air, transported by the wind, unite by analogy to the bodies and appropriated elements that participate in an eternal metamorphosis of all the universal combinations' (Cambry, 1799).

In 1800 the *Institut de France*, the highest French cultural institution, on the request of the Home Office, held a public competition entitled 'The Funeral Ceremony: which regulations to adopt in the place of burial?' Of 42 essays received, 17 expressed support for the liberalization of cremation. In many of these there was the idea of a material nature in constant transformation: such a conception, which matured in the second half of the eighteenth century, was by then common in the minds of many essay writers, even in the absence of a consciously advanced materialist position. Cremation was commonly perceived as a way of returning human remains quickly to the elements – of re-entering the inexhaustible cycle of nature.

This modest start to a debate in favour of cremation was soon exhausted. A few years later, in 1801, Napoleon signed an agreement with the Catholic Church, and in 1804, with the Saint Cloud edict, resolved the cemetery problems without having to turn to cremation. For at least 50 years there is then no trace, in Europe, of the debate about cremation that ultimately developed at the end of the eighteenth century. It is interesting, though, to point out that, before the rebirth of the cremationist project in many European countries at the end of the nineteenth century, it was again a materialist physiologist, Jacob Moleschott, who offered, in his book *Der Kreislauf des Lebens* (*The Cycle of Life*) (1852), a positive valuation of cremation in the context of a conception of the cosmos as a whole living entity. He believed that phosphorus salts, the product of decaying flesh and bones from the waste in graves, remained unproductive, and accumulated in cemeteries, instead of going back usefully to the 'cycle of life'. He wrote: 'If we could burn our dead, we would enrich our air with carbonic acid and ammoniac, and the ashes that contain that which is necessary for new harvests, for animals, for men, would transform our plains into fertile fields.' He concluded: 'Only ignorance is barbarity' (Moleschott, 1857).

Marina Sozzi

References

Cambry, Jacques (1799), *Rapport sur les sépultures, présenté à l'administration centraledu département de la Seine*, Paris: Pierre Didot.

Moleschott, Jacob (1857), *Der Kreislauf des Lebens*, Mainz: Verlag von Zabern.

MEDICINE

The medical profession and individual members of it played an enormously important role in the emergence of cremation, especially in the mid- and late nineteenth century. Closely interlinked with issues of social welfare, public hygiene and town planning, doctors voiced their opinion on the value of cremation as a mode of dealing with the dead.

Important individual entries include Pini for Italy, Price and Thompson for Great Britain, while Portugal includes the influence of Vicente Teles and Ricardo Jorge. Lien-Teh played an important role in Malaysia as did José Penna and others for Argentina. Germany, too, had its influential doctors. **Douglas J. Davies**

See also Argentina; Argentine cremation socieities; Germany; Lien-Teh; Malaya, Malaysia and Singapore; Pini; Portugal; Price; Thompson.

MEMORIALS AND MEMORIALIZATION

Memorials of, and for, the dead are one of the most enduring features of many human societies. As archaeological entries in this book show, numerous prehistoric groups sometimes entombed their dead, whether as corpses or cremated remains. Modern cremation has faced the issue of memorialization of the dead in several ways.

On way is to bury ashes in much the same way as a corpse was formerly buried, except in an appropriately small grave and with a small headstone. An alternative, depositing ashes in designated memorial gardens or lawns sometimes makes it possible to know the specific location of the remains, through the keeping of records, but the practice of scattering of ashes in such places has tended to remove the possibility of a precise point of memorial. There has been considerable debate in the USA over the virtue or (conversely) disrespect involved in pulverizing remains in order make them suitable for scattering rather than being conserved in a fixed memorial (Prothero, 2001: 147–51), and this debate has involved religious, aesthetic and financial considerations. Memorial masons and those companies or authorities that provide fixed memorials for the dead make part of their living from the money invested in such memorials – money that is lost if people simply take remains and scatter them without any lasting and formal memorial. For these people or companies the increasing popularity of cremation raises the challenge of promoting memorialization.

On the other hand, cremation has also presented alternative opportunities for business in the design of artistic and other forms of elaborate urns for cremated remains. Some companies, especially in Holland, will also turn cremated remains into memorial objects or jewellery. This is not an unusual practice since Holland has a tradition of keeping mementos of the dead – for example, locks of hair – and objects created from ashes simply replace such mementos. A major exhibition in Amsterdam in 1996 reflected such possibilities in using ashes in creative ways (Davies, 1996). Others, too, have recognized the possible options available. The North American funeral director and author Thomas Lynch, for example, refers to 'dreaming up a new scheme called 'cremorialization'" in which ashes could be, as it were, 'put to work', as some object or other. This neologism, 'cremorialization', like that of 'cremains', reflects the innovatory nature of cremation, especially in North America in the later twentieth century. Lynch, who has a sense of irony, saw the potential desire to use ashes in this way as an expression of 'the Protestant work ethic that honors work and utility' (Lynch, 1997: 101).

A more serious development in the issue of memorialization in the later twentieth century concerned the cremation of babies or even foetuses and the planning of special areas devoted to their cremated remains. This is especially important given the very sparse remains of such children. Appropriate memorials in the form of infant objects also allow bereaved parents the comfort of knowing that other people, too, have experienced such a severe loss. For the wider population, the introduction of books of remembrance at crematoria has responded to the need for a visible point on which mourners might focus their attention and memory, especially if the ashes have been scattered.

Such memorials and depositions refer, primarily, to official crematorium gardens or to cemeteries with facilities for cremated remains. Quite a different situation exists when remains are taken away from such public institutions for deposition or scattering in places of private and personal significance. In such circumstances it is the wider context of the place that is identified with the dead. As already indicated, there is a significant economic element involved in this move from professionally provided memorials to the realm of private memory, just as there are consequences of removing the dead from ongoing public recognition. The privatization of memorials expresses a privatization of life in general, and this is particularly notable in societies that developed extensive public graveyards and cemeteries over some two or more centuries. **Douglas J. Davies**

See also ashes; book of remembrance; columbaria; gardens of remembrance (UK).

References

Davies, Douglas J. (1996), 'Imagination Playing with Death: A Review of the Exhibition *Midden in het leven staan wij in de dood*', Mortality, 1(3): 323–26.

Lynch, Thomas (1997), *The Undertaking*, London: Jonathan Cape.

Prothero, Stephen (2001), *Purified by Fire: A History of Cremation in America*, Berkeley: University of California Press.

MERCURY

This heavy metal has proved problematic in modern cremation as new legislation emerged in the later twentieth century related to gaseous emissions of dangerous or hazardous substances resulting from the cremation process. **Douglas J. Davies**

See also Cremation Society of Great Britain; cremators; Switzerland.

MIASMA

Miasma is a widely used term for the vapours, gases and mists reckoned to arise from decaying bodies in overfilled graves, especially during the eighteenth and nineteenth centuries. Such vapours are exemplified in the entry on **Henrietta Pratt**, who believed that 'the Vapours arising from the graves in the Church yards of populous Cities may prove harmful to the inhabitants'. Miasmas formed part of the argument and rhetoric associated with the hygiene argument advanced for preferring cremation over burial as part of sanitary reform as the **USA** entry and its treatment of 'miasma theory' demonstrates. **Portugal** offers another example. **Douglas J. Davies**

See also Portugal; Pratt; USA.

MITFORD, JESSICA

Born on 11 September 1915 in Gloucestershire, England and dying on 23 July 1996 in Oakland, California, USA, Jessica 'Decca' Mitford was one-time investigative journalist, muckraker and author of *The American Way of Death* (1963) and *The American Way of Death Revisited* (1998). Jessica 'Decca' Mitford was born into a notorious

and aristocratic family, one of the seven children of Lord and Lady Rednesdale. One sister, Unity, was drawn to Nazism, and moved to Germany, where she became a devout follower of Adolf Hitler and another, Diana, married the British fascist, Sir Oswald Mosley. Nancy the oldest, became a novelist. Two sisters chose less controversial paths Pamela opted for a quiet country life and Deborah became the Duchess of Devonshire.

At the age of 19 Mitford eloped with Esmond Romilly, her second cousin and the nephew of Winston Churchill. Their elopement, their commitment to communism, followed by their joining the International Brigade, fighting the fascists in the Spanish Civil War, led to Mitford's estrangement from her father. When the Second World War began Romilly joined the Canadian airforce and was killed in action over the North Sea in 1941. Mitford emigrated to the USA, and two years later, married Robert Treuhaft, a radical labour lawyer. The couple, along with Mitford's daughter from her first marriage, moved to Oakland, California where they were active members of the Communist Party and devoted advocates for workers' rights and civil rights for African-Americans. Deciding that 'the only thing that requires no education and no skills is writing' Mitford established her public career, producing many books: *Lifeitselfmanship* (1956), *Daughters and Rebels* (1960), *The American Way of Death* (1963), *The Trial of Dr. Spock* (1969), *Kind and Usual Punishment: The Prison Business* (1973), the autobiography *A Fine Old Conflict* (1979), *Poison Penmanship: The Gentle Art of Muckraking* (1979), *The American Way of Birth* (1992) and *The American Way of Death Revisited* (1998).

Mitford's fame and greatest cultural impact arose out of *The American Way of Death* (1963), a lucid and scathing investigation of the modern funeral industry. In the 1950s, while representing the widows of unionized longshoremen, Treuhaft discovered that undertakers were charging his clients excessive fees, often claiming all of their death benefits. Mitford later recalled that she had no interest in the funeral industry until her husband 'starting bringing home the trade publications like *Casket* and *Sunnyside, Mortuary Management* – all those wonderful names – so I began to study them.' Once 'hooked' on them, Mitford confessed, 'I found them to be compulsive reading.'

Mitford's investigations revealed a predatory

industry where funeral directors, who she called 'Dismal Traders', reinvented the traditional funeral to exploit consumers' ignorance and grief, fleecing them through aggressive and deliberate salesmanship with inflated prices for unnecessary products and services. Besides embalming, the industry could provide caskets modified with innerspring mattresses and linings made of non-abrasive fabrics, as well as clothing for corpses, 'handmade original fashions' which included men's suits and women's negligees. A new terminology was invented: the 'undertaker' became a 'funeral director,' the 'coffin' a 'casket', and 'corpses' were transformed into 'loved ones'. Part of the industry's rationale, Mitford concluded, was that it provided 'grief therapy': the emotional comfort felt by the survivors as a result of having 'restored' the deceased. Cremation appealed to the consumer's desire for 'a simple, cheap funeral', but Mitford discovered that the funeral industry had found and invented ways to exploit this market as well: 'rental' caskets, expensive urns made of marble and semiprecious metals, and the sale of 'perpetual care for the ashes'.

The American Way of Death became an instant best-seller in the United States and was the impetus behind the launch of investigations into the funeral industry in major cities across the country. Mitford and her book were attacked by the funeral industry and politicians – one accused her of being anti-Christian, 'proCommunist and anti-American'. Mitford died in 1996 while completing work on *The American Way of Death Revisited*, an expanded and updated version of her original work. Her body was cremated. **Eric Love**

MONACO

The construction of Monaco Crematorium began in 1912. A law authorizing cremation in cosmopolitan Monaco came into being in 1914, by which time a very modern crematorium, costing 100 000 gold francs, had been completed. It was, however, not opened. This anomalous situation came to the attention of the influential English colony in the principality, which was becoming increasingly interested in cremation. It was this colony's needs, rather than an indigenous requirement for cremation facilities, that put the issue on the cremationists' agenda. By 1935 the pressure was building: 100

'distinguished members' of the 'numerous and influential' English colony, who represented several different religions, sent a letter to the Minister of State of the Principality requesting cremation facilities to be made available, not only to the Principality but to the whole Riviera. The prince's reply, through his Minister of State, came in June 1935 and was not encouraging.

Undeterred, French cremationists, meeting in Marseille, visited Monaco Crematorium and Professor Barrier of the French Cremation Federation appealed to the prince to open the crematorium. The authorities claimed that the gas supply was insufficient for the cremators, but this, cremationists argued, was simple to remedy. The French also asked the 1936 Prague International Cremation Congress to support them by passing a motion that a petition be sent to the prince. The French hoped that the prince would not be deaf to the appeal, as the crematorium in Monaco would be a service to a country that contained many 'distinguished citizens of all civilised countries'. In 1937 French cremationists made another visit to the Principality while holding a national federation conference in Nice. As before, they discovered the crematorium in perfect working order. Accompanied by eminent residents of the English colony who had been campaigning to open the crematorium for some time, Barrier made renewed overtures to the prince, which, he thought, were given added weight by support gained at the Prague Congress. Unfortunately, for reasons that were 'difficult to follow', the prince still refused to let the crematorium open. However, it then became clear that the French cremationists had not received the international support that they had expected. The Czech delegate, Mencl, had to explain to the 1937 International Cremation Congress why he had not written to the Prince of Monaco as agreed at the 1936 congress. The new executive resolved to deal with the situation.

The French did not give up; in 1938 they again contacted the Prince of Monaco about the situation. The prince responded with the oft-used 'inadequate gas supply' excuse. Not satisfied, the French got the ICF executive to write to the prince, in May 1938. This time, the prince's reply was different, and more honest; he stated that, as a Catholic, he would never let the crematorium open. However, it also now appeared that the situation was more complicated than the French had presented it. At an ICF executive committee meeting in September 1938 the assistant secretary reported that he had been to Monaco and had taken photos of the crematorium. From the evidence, the executive were 'not entirely satisfied that previous reports were entirely accurate' and agreed that, before any future communication was sent to the prince, 'every effort' be made to 'verify the facts'. In the meantime, it decided that 'no good purpose' would be served by further letters to the prince.

Some hope was rekindled when the secretary-general reported receiving, at an ICF executive meeting in May 1939, a letter from the consul of Monaco in London. The consul reported that the operation of Monaco Crematorium was regulated by a decree dated 8 July 1914. The secretary-general was requested to send a copy of the letter to Henri Ferré of France, who had been heavily involved in the situation, for his observations. Yet, this information by itself was not going to alter anything. The ICF executive then decided to try to inform prominent Monaco citizens to prevail upon the prince to 'see sense'. However, the intervention of the Second World War prevented further immediate action on the topic.

After the war, it was clear that nothing had changed. At the 1948 ICF Congress, a paper compiled by Mr Jiriaroch of Czechoslovakia on the laws relating to cremation in various countries mentioned that, along with many other countries, the decisive influence against cremation in Monaco was Catholic. However, it also noted that the only crematorium in Monaco was 'prepared for excellent services but ... it is still now waiting for somebody to provide the gas mains equal to the requirement of the plant'. At the same congress the French revealed that they had not forgotten the question, a decade after the last international congress. René Hofmann raised the issue, arguing that the crematorium had 'never functioned owing to the operation of commercial interests'. The congress passed a resolution mentioning the 'unfortunate' Monaco situation and a similar situation in Hungary, and stated its opinion that the crematoria in both countries 'should be permitted to function and ... that steps should be taken to bring this into effect as soon as possible'. Indeed, in the same year Monaco Crematorium did try to obtain a license to operate, but the Monaco authorities preferred an 'expensive extension' of the cemetery instead. Outside of the ICF, the French

Cremation Federation attempted to maintain its own pressure on the prince. Three years later it reported to the ICF Congress that it had had no success in this task: a delegate complained that 'we seem to be hitting our head against a brick wall'. However, the 'persistency' of French cremationists was confidently expected to prevail and win the 'battle' to get Monaco crematorium opened.

Almost a decade later, still nothing had changed. In fact, there was a degree of ignorance over the stagnant situation in Monaco. At the ICF Congress at Stockholm, in 1960, a Mr Boone commented that it was incorrect to say that cremation was prohibited in Monaco because an edict authorizing cremation and signed by the grandfather of the then prince existed. The crematorium was not operated, according to Boone, because of administrative and financial problems. In addition, it would now cost a great deal to get the privately-owned crematorium working again, and there remained 'strong forces' opposed to it. These forces were embodied in the prince himself who was papal legate in his principality and who would not place pressure on the firm of funeral directors that owned the crematorium to begin operating it while the Catholic Church remained opposed to cremation.

Although the Catholic Church altered its attitude to cremation only three years later, it still took another 27 years for Monaco to get its crematorium, which was finally opened by a private company in 1990. The 'unusual' case of the unused Monaco crematorium reveals two things: the power and influence of the Catholic Church, which could even prevent a crematorium operating after large expense had already been committed to bricks and mortar; and the converse relative lack of influence of the institutions of cremation advocacy, despite their concerted efforts. It also reveals that the Vatican's change of attitude often took some considerable time before it had an effect on Catholic opinion in some regions. **Lewis H. Mates**

References

CSA.

SOMOTHA website at: http://www.crematorium. mc/en/debut.htm (accessed December 2003).

MORMONISM

By the beginning of the twenty-first century, the Church of Jesus Christ of Latter Day Saints (LDS), widely known as the Mormon Church, had come to uphold burial over cremation whenever local culture made this possible. This preference is rooted in a deep concern for the body, not only as a medium through which a pre-existing spirit gains valuable experience on this earth, but also as that which will be resurrected and transformed ready for a life after death (Davies, 2000). The strong Latter-day Saint commitment to a complementarity between body and spirit does not abandon the corpse as a mere shell. Because of that, popular religious sentiment thinks of the buried body as awaiting its resurrection. Behind this Mormon perspective lies the extensive preference for burial in many communities in the USA at large.

However, Mormons have not always held out for burial over cremation, at least not theoretically and theologically. The second half of the nineteenth century, for example, was a period in which numerous Mormon thinkers were open and exploratory in their views of the world, not least because they believed God was actively engaged in revealing new ideas to humanity. The strong prophetic nature of the Church had, as one consequence, the sense that new ideas could also come in through the world beyond the Church, as well through science and technology as through philosophy or religion.

When *The Salt Lake Herald* (12 August 1886) reported the Roman Catholic news that Pope Leo XIII had instructed the faithful against 'this culpable abuse in burning the human body', it did so without any comment either supportive of cremation or in opposition to it. Indeed, the following extract from the *Deseret Evening News* of 4 February 1888 shows how open and accommodating later nineteenth-century Mormon thought could be towards cremation as a way of treating dead human bodies:

> Cremation is a matter of feeling not of religion. If science declares emphatically in favour of cremation we shall learn to resign ourselves to it. Whether the dust returns to earth by slow decay or by speedy action of fire is not of moment from the religious point of view provided we believe the 'spirit returns to God who gave it'.

What is noteworthy here is the reference to science and the high status given to it. The debate is more one of a utilitarian than a theological concern. A similar note is struck a few years later when the *Deseret Weekly* (21 September 1894) reported Sir Francis Seymour's lecture against cremation given at the British Institute of Public Health in which he argued for burial without the use of solid coffins. Once more there is no LDS judgement advanced either for or against cremation as such.

It was in the later twentieth century that Mormonism became more constrained by a conservative spirit and pressed more for burial than cremation. One contributory factor is the LDS tradition of dressing the body in the special clothing used for the temple rites, including a special apron. The thought of burning these sacred garments is quite contrary to Mormon attitudes and this, to some extent, has militated against cremation. Although Mormon opinion is content with cremation in societies in which it is the cultural norm, in contexts where the option is realistic some interesting situations emerge. In Britain, for example, where by 2004 only about 28 per cent of the public are buried, and cremation is the dominant funerary form, the strong Mormon preference and practice is for burial. **Douglas J. Davies**

Reference

Davies, Douglas J. (2000), *The Mormon Culture of Salvation*, Aldershot: Ashgate.

N

NAMIBIA

Namibia has only one crematorium, situated at the Gammams Cemetery in the capital city of Windhoek. This cemetery is one of seven cemeteries in the city, four of which have reached capacity and are maintained as memorial sites. In 1970 a report was written for the heads of department of the city of Windhoek and discussed at their meeting in May 1970: it recommended approving the construction of a crematorium; that a suitable site be investigated and plans drawn up; and that tenders be called for both the building and the incineration plant. The commissioning of the report was motivated by the limited burial space remaining within the city limits and the projected price increases for graves between 1970 and 2000, which would make graves too expensive for many to afford. The interment of ashes would take up less space and would be considerably cheaper than burial, thus benefiting the city as well as its residents. At the May meeting only two councillors opposed the motion, and the project was approved.

By 1972 the building plans had been approved and five tenders received for the provision and installation of a cremation plant. During 1972 a new chapel was added to the design of the crematorium. The design of the complex was awarded through a competition held between interested architects. The winning design was that of a local artist. Authority was also obtained from the Administrator of South West Africa (Namibia) allowing the construction of the crematorium, as required by the Ordinance for Crematoria of 1971 (Official Gazette, no. 3182, 24 June, 1971).

Construction was completed in 1975, and the installation was henceforth known as the Windhoek Crematorium. The cremation unit was manufactured by Wilhelm Ruppmann Industrieofenbau Stuttgart and installed by Brockmann and Kriess, a local firm. The first cremation took place on the 26 April 1976. During 1976 only 41 bodies were cremated, but this figure has steadily grown over the years to a figure of 277 bodies for 2001. Cremation is becoming more popular in Namibia. The running and maintenance of the crematorium falls under the cemetery section of the Parks, Recreation and Cemeteries Division, Department of Economic Development, Tourism and Recreation, City of Windhoek.

Sociological and anthropological features

Namibia's population comprises many different tribes, cultures and nationalities. Being the capital city, Windhoek is very cosmopolitan. Of this diverse population it is those of European and Eastern descent who opt for cremation over burial. The indigenous Namibian cultures have deep-rooted traditions and protocols which are followed during the mourning and burial process. Christian burial sermons have been adopted, but in most cases the treatment and burial of the body follows prescribed traditional methods. The idea of cremating a family member

is unthinkable and viewed as a display of the utmost disrespect, so is not even considered as an option. In addition, the physical gravesite is considered very important for communication with ancestors.

Trends

Baha'i and Islam are on the increase in Windhoek, and these groups bury their dead, rather than cremate them. For many, cremation is the cheaper option. Grave space in the Gammams Cemetery is expensive because of the infrastructure in place and because of its situation, close to the city centre. Graves at the new cemetery on the outskirts of the city are considerably cheaper. Namibia is a vast land with great distances between towns, so families often choose the practical approach of cremation and then transport the ashes to their hometown. More and more families are opting for cremation for this reason. With the current epidemic of HIV/AIDS-related deaths, the stigma attached and poverty, more families are abandoning or refusing to claim the bodies of relatives at the state mortuary. If no family member can be traced within three months, these bodies are declared 'paupers' and are buried at the cost of the government. As space for burials is limited in the city, the Parks, Recreation and Cemetries division is working on gaining approval from the council and government to have paupers cremated instead. This would increase the cremation statistics slightly as there are, on average, 12 pauper burials per month. As would be expected, many are very sentimental about the ashes and prefer to have them placed in the wall of remembrance or scatter them at a site of significance or beauty.

Architecture and art

Visitors to the Gammams Cemetery are led to the chapel and crematorium along a 20-metre wide, hedge-lined drive. This drive runs through the centre of the cemetery, which is densely planted with trees. Graves are not visible at all for the entire length of this 400-metre drive as they are situated behind the 2-metre tall hedges.

The chapel and crematorium at the Gammams Cemetery form a single complex. The building is mostly of rough-cast concrete, with certain walls constructed of white quartz rocks. The chapel is shaped like a giant wedge with the main door at the lowest end and the podium inside at the tall end. The ceiling rises to about six metres at the podium. The wall backing the podium is constructed of white quartz and is lit by natural light through skylights. Lighting in the rest of the chapel is subdued and provides a very peaceful ambience. When seated, none of the windows or skylights is visible, as they are angled and positioned in recesses, giving the impression of a miraculous, glorious light around the speaker. The chapel seats 140 people, and extra chairs are available on request. Next to the podium is the catafalque, which is made of carved acacia. At the press of a button by the speaker the catafalque lowers the coffin below floor level, where the coffin is removed into the adjoining crematorium building and placed into a cool-room awaiting cremation.

Large lawns, bordered by decorative shrubs and rockeries, lead from the chapel entrance round to the wall of remembrance. The gardens surrounding the chapel and crematorium are known as the gardens of remembrance. Areas are provided for the laying of flowers and wreaths. The wall of remembrance is a circular wall with niches for ash-urns and marble plaques on the inner circumference. There is a small garden in the centre for visitors to rest and contemplate in peace. Each niche has sufficient space to contain five standard urns. Many now contain more than one family member.

The chapel is now shrouded in ivy and flowering creepers frame the main door. It is surrounded by gardens. With its unfinished concrete and quartz walls, it blends very much into the surrounding nature. Immediately behind the chapel/crematorium complex there are natural open spaces and a river course. Birdlife and the sounds (or tranquillity) of nature are abundant. One of the criteria in the design of the crematorium was that the building should be clean and clinical, and this was successfully implemented. The building is well lit and ventilated. The positioning of windows gives good airflow and adequate natural light throughout the building. The cremation plant itself is extremely efficient, and residual odours or smoke are never a problem. The tall exhaust chimney is masked by plantings of tall *Cupressus sempevirens* trees.

Legal, medical and public health issues

A number of documents need completion and signatures before a cremation may take place,

according to the Cemetery and Crematorium Regulations. They are:

- Application for Cremation (Schedule A): completed by deceased's family or next of kin in applying for a cremation.
- Certificate of Medical Practitioner (Schedule B): completed by the doctor who treated the deceased during their final illness
- Confirmatory Medical Certificate (Schedule C): whereby a second doctor confirms the medical certificate
- Death Certificate: a copy of the death certificate, as issued by the Ministry of Home
- Authority to Cremate (Schedule E): signed by the legally appointed medical referee to the city of Windhoek.
- Disposal of Ashes: serving to inform the cremation operator as to who is to receive the ashes – that is, family member or undertaker – or if the ashes are to be placed directly in a niche in the wall of remembrance
- Removal/Burial Order: issued by the Ministry of Home Affairs, Department of Civic Affairs and authorizing the transportation of a corpse through an urban area for the purpose of burial (or cremation)
- Notice of Interment: required by Act 81 of 1963 for all burials/cremations and providing the grave number of each individual's burial site or the cremation number for ashes. It also contains the name and address of the undertaker involved.

In the case of an unnatural death, such as an accident or suicide, where an autopsy takes place, then the Confirmatory Medical Certificate is replaced by 'Schedule D', Certificate After Post-mortem Examination, a form with which the state mortuary releases the body for cremation.

Technical and engineering factors

The Windhoek Crematorium has cool-room facilities for the temporary storage of 12 coffins. A battery-operated forklift transfers the coffins one at a time to the insertion trolley in the committal room. The Windhoek cremator (see Figure 1) has two Weishaupt diesel burners, one for the main burning chamber and a second for maintaining the temperature in the after-chamber and for the burning of excess gases. The plant is controlled by a combination of automatic and manually operated switches and levers which control the separate burners, airflow

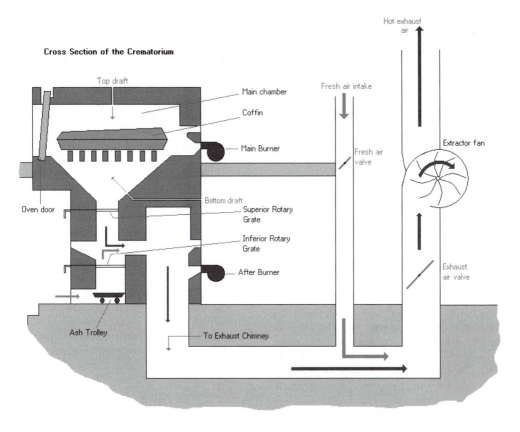

Figure 1 Cross-section of the Windhoek cremator

into the chambers and airflow out of the exhaust chimney. There are three chambers in the oven, vertically aligned. The coffin is placed into the main chamber, at the top of the system, by the insertion trolley once the temperature has reached 650 – 800°C. During the burning process the remains fall through to the superior rotary grate at the base of this chamber. With the insertion of the second coffin, the superior rotary grate is rotated, and the first remains drop down to the inferior rotary grate where the heat from the after-burner maintains the burning process and renders the remains to their final state. The temperature in the after-chamber is regulated at about 650°C, although this can sometimes climb to around 1000°C immediately after the introduction of a coffin. With the introduction of the third coffin into the main chamber, the rotary grates are again rotated and the ashes on the inferior rotary grate are deposited into a cooling pan below. All gases are sucked down through the oven chambers (except the cooling chamber), passed through a filter and out of the

exhaust chimney by an extractor fan. The temperature of the exhaust fumes averages from 250°C to 300°C.

After the ash is removed from the cooling chamber, any metal objects, such as artificial joints, orthopaedic implants and the coffin nails and screws are removed with a powerful magnet. The ash is then ground to a 2mm consistency in the cremulator and then packed into a wooden urn. The label attached to the urn has the cremation number, initials and surname of the deceased, date of birth, date of death and the death certificate number punched on to it. A cremation certificate is also issued stating the date of cremation. **Anthony J. Watkins**

NAZI CREMATION

Nazi Germany created a complicated legacy for cremation history because the Nazis used crematoria to dispose of millions of their murdered victims, and at the same time created a unified legal position for cremation in Germany.

Under the German Empire and the Weimar Republic, each German state (Prussia, Hamburg, Bavaria and so on) could formulate its own laws on burial. Consequently, in some parts of Germany it was quite difficult to be cremated. This changed under the Nazis as part of a larger process of consolidating and coordinating German society and life. In 1934 the Nazis abolished all regional variations in burial laws and placed cremation and burial on equal legal footing.

The role of crematoria in the Nazi terror regime is better known because cremation became the preferred means of disposing of all civilian victims. The methods used to murder millions of Jews were perfected in the initial murder of smaller numbers of political internees, by shooting, and of the mentally ill by gassing. The first Nazi crematoria were developed in concentration camps for political prisoners. In 1940 Dachau and Buchenwald got their first crematoria. Neither camp was a centre for massive gas-killing, but experiments in execution methods and corpse disposal were carried out there. The Topf & Söhne furnace company of Erfurt, a leading producer of crematoria apparatus, engaged in considerable experimentation to make crematoria more effective, and eventually became the main supplier of crematorium apparatus for the killing centres. Other camps were outfitted with crematoria between 1940 and 1942, including the extermination centres at Auschwitz and Majdanek in Poland. Crematoria were also used to dispose of the bodies of people killed through the 'T-4' euthanasia programme in Germany.

Jews murdered in eastern Europe were initially buried in mass graves, but Nazi officials gradually abandoned them in favour of open burning. However, the stench of mass graves and open pyres made the increased technologization of corpse disposal necessary. Gradually, bodies were disinterred for burning, and, after 1940, cremation became the primary means of disposal. By late 1941 crematoria were fully established at Auschwitz and designed to incinerate record numbers of corpses. The Auschwitz facility was greatly expanded in 1943.

Nazi practices perverted the ideals of the modern cremation movement in a number of ways. For example, modern crematoria are not supposed to emit noxious gases or smoke, but this was not the case at the killing centres.

Survivors of the camps frequently describe the stench of the crematoria. This seems to relate to a combined use of crematoria and open pyres in the camps. Although a premium was placed on rapid disposal and the future camouflaging of the genocide, in the short term, it was acceptable for the cremation process to be visible. Moreover, the crematoria were intimately connected with murder. The Auschwitz killing centres combined the gasing facility with the crematorium. Poetry – for example, Paul Celan's famous '*Death Fugue*' – exemplifies the centrality of the crematorium and its chimney as a symbol of the Holocaust: for many, the chimney was the only exit from the death camps. Finally, among the most horrific legacies of the Nazi use of crematoria was the utter disrespect for human ashes, which fulfilled the worst nightmares of cremation's earlier opponents. At Majdanek and Neuengamme ashes were used to fertilize vegetable gardens. This patent disregard of human remains, along with the incinerator approach to disposal, has caused many cremationists to label the Nazi practice 'corpse incineration' rather than 'cremation' since the Nazi practice was not reverent burial but a final act of murder and barbarism. **Tim Pursell**

See also Auschwitz; Judaism.

References

Bauche, Ulrich *et al.* (1986), *Arbeit und Vernichtung. Das Konzentrationslager Neuengamme 1938–1945*, Hamburg: VSA-Verlag.

Burleigh, Michael and Wippermann, Wolfgang (1993), *The Racial State: Germany 1933–1945*, Cambridge: Cambridge University Press.

Fischer, Norbert (1996), *Vom Gottesacker zum Krematorium: Eine Sozialgeschichte der Friedhöfe in Deutschland seit dem 18. Jahrhundert*, Cologne: Böhlau.

Pressac, Jean-Claude (1989), *Auschwitz: Technique and Operation of the Gas Chambers*, New York: Beate Klarsfeld Foundation.

Schwarz, Gudrun (1990), *Die nationalsozialistischen Lager*, Frankfurt: Campus.

Sofsky, Wolfgang (1997), *The Order of Terror: The Concentration Camp*, Princeton: Princeton University Press.

NEPAL

Cremation has long been the traditional practice for disposing of dead bodies in Nepal, influenced by the traditional Hindu–Buddhist beliefs that in order to attain future life through rebirths, the body must be destroyed after death (Ghimire, 1998: 51). Although cremation is the general disposal practice, exceptions include dead infants who are thrown into running water or buried. This is due to the belief that they lie beyond society both socially and ritually and do not need to go to the abode of ancestors (*pitriloka*), having died prior to any formal ritual binding them to it. A running-water funeral may also be given if there is no relative to perform normal funeral rites or if someone has died of a contagious disease or epidemic. In some northern areas of Nepal, among Buddhists, dead bodies are exposed in open places, reflecting traditional Tibetan practice.

Another group of Hindus who do not go through the process of cremation are the ascetics (*sanyasis*) who have overcome the social and the ritual ties. Because the fire of spiritual knowledge has already purified these ascetics, they do not require fire to sanctify their bodies nor is any further ritual performed after their burial since such ascetics have already completed these rites prior to their death, on admission to their ascetic order.

Hindus believe that, in death, the soul is separated from the body and emphasize the funeral rites in the belief that the deceased will exist as a ghost if the rites are improperly conducted. Dead bodies should be disposed of as rapidly as possible lest ghosts enter into them. It is also believed that, if the dead body is kept for a long time, it decomposes and is therefore no longer pure enough to be an offering to be made to the gods in sacrifice – for cremation is considered to be a form of sacrifice to the gods.

Certain rites, including *Vaitarni Dan*, are performed before death so that the departing soul may have an easy access to the Yamaloka. Here the *Vaitarni* means a river and, in this ritual, a cow is given as a gift to the priest in the belief that it will help the deceased to cross the river to reach to the abode of Yama, the god of death. Usually the *Vaitarni Dan* is done outside the house with the dying person lying on the purified ground. This, it is believed, helps the spirit of the deceased depart more easily.

After the death of a person, all remaining clothes are removed and the individual is covered with cloth that has not been tailored. Impure objects, animals and persons are not allowed to come in contact with the corpse, and special care is taken to ensure that the deceased will be a suitable offering to the fire god. A piece of iron or a weapon is kept with the corpse to repel evil spirits, including the spirit of the deceased (*preta*) from entering the body. In many family traditions, the *shraddha* ceremony is performed at home before the corpse is taken to the burning ghat although some do perform *shraddha* or the *pinda dan* at the cremation ground. Until the corpse is taken from the domestic vicinity no one is allowed to eat, drink or work.

The funeral procession must consist of an odd number of people, and participants are expected to be very serious in demeanour, silent, simply dressed and bareheaded. Traditionally, women do not process; however, some tribal Hindu women do so, but they return before the body is put into the fire for burning. In the procession, the head of the deceased is carried facing backwards, rather than forwards, symbolizing the south, the abode of ancestors. Those leading the procession carry the sacrificial fire in an earthen cauldron and scatter paddy mixed with red powder as the procession moves towards the cremation ground. Hindus usually take the corpse to the bank of the river for cremation although some Buddhists use a hill for the cremation site. Those using a riverbank place the body near to the water. The selected ground for cremation is first purified with the river water and then by cow dung, while the priest chants appropriate mantra to scare away demons or ghosts who are believed to be floating around the cremation ground. The main objects of the proper disposal of the corpse and the performance of all the rites and ceremonies connected with it are to free the survivors from the pollution of death and to give rest to the deceased by dismissing the soul to its place in the next world and into the cult of ancestor worship. Otherwise, the deceased continues to be *preta*, haunting its relatives and causing problems (Pandey, 1969: 236).

Since 1950, amidst these Hindu–Buddhist cremation traditions, the new emerging Christian presence in Nepal has posed a challenge to the disposal of the dead. Christians accepted the burial of the dead as a common practice in many other Christian communities and emphasized burial as normative Christian practice. Looking at burial in terms of resurrection, a simplicity of faith has led Nepalese Christians to opt for burial despite the difficulties encountered since most Christians do not own a common burial ground nor does the government make provision for it. Exactly why Nepalese Christians insist on burying is an open issue that raises questions over the potential influence of missionaries and their own traditional burial practices as well as the need to assert a Christian identity over and against the Hindu–Buddhist approach to religion, life and death. **Bal Krishna Sharma**

See also Borneo; Buddhism; Hinduism; Open-air cremation.

References

Ghimire, Beena (1998), *Hindu Death Rites*, Kathmandu: Barsha Ghimire Publications.
Pandey, Raj Bali (1969), *Hindu Samskaras*, Delhi: Motilal Banarsidass.
Parry, Jonathan P. (1994), *Death in Banaras*, Cambridge: Cambridge University Press.
Quayle, Brendan (1980), *Hindu Death and Ritual Journey*, Durham: Department of Anthropology, University of Durham.

NETHERLANDS: SOCIETIES AND LAW

In the Netherlands the Association for the Introduction of Cremation in the Netherlands (*De Vereeniging tot Invoering der Lijkenverbranding in Nederland*) sought to initiate the practice of cremation. This association, which was later to become the Royal Cremation Society 'the Facultatieve', was established by six Hague liberals in 1874, three of whom were freemasons. They believed cremation to be more hygienic than burial outside of built-up areas, which had been the rule since 1829. The association aimed to achieve a free choice for cremation by lobbying for the amendment of legislation, carrying out propaganda activities and building a crematorium. The period from 1874 to 1915 was first dominated by propaganda and promoting an amendment in the law. These efforts failed, because the case for hygiene proved insufficiently strong and because of the religious

objections concerning cremation's effect on resurrection. Another reason for the law not being amended was the legal objection that cremation would make it easier to conceal murder by poisoning.

The association eventually built the first crematorium in the Netherlands: Velsen Crematorium in 1913. The first cremation there was of former board member Dr C.J. Vaillant, on 1 April 1914. Because the Funeral Act (*Begrafeniswet*) of 1869 did not mention cremation as an option, this cremation was in fact illegal and became the subject of criminal proceedings. All parties were acquitted, however, due to the inadequacy of that same Act.

Based on the concept that labourers and other less wealthy persons did not have the option of cremation because of the expense it incurred, the Workers' Association for Cremation (*Arbeiders Vereeniging voor Lijkverbranding* – AVVL) was subsequently established in 1919. It was not until the Dutch Burial and Cremation Act (*Wet op de Lijkbezorgig*) was amended in 1955 that cremation actually became legal, and it was not until 1991 that cremation and burial were considered to be equal under the law.

Now, at the beginning of the twenty-first century, half the Dutch population opts for cremation, a situation which has been stable for quite some years. The Royal Cremation Society 'the Facultatieve' has reconsidered its idealistic objectives given now there is no longer any statutory distinction between burial and cremation since the Burial and Cremation Act of 1991 and now concentrates on providing information on making timely choices in the method of disposal of the dead. In 1990 the commercial activities of the Royal Cremation Society 'the Facultatieve' were made the responsibility of a separate organization: 'the Facultatieve Group'. **J.M.H.J. Keizer**

See also Van Lissa; Vaillant.

NEW ZEALAND

There is some evidence to suggest that the indigenous Maori practised cremation in New Zealand before the arrival of Europeans. In the colonial era, however, cremation societies were established at the end of the nineteenth century, although burial remained the exclusive form of disposal until the construction of the first crematorium in 1909. Initial acceptance of the practice was limited, however, and cremation only became the dominant method of disposal during the second half of the twentieth century, when the establishment of crematoria chapels in the 1960s and 1970s had a profound impact on the nature of funerary ritual and the funeral industry. Cremation permitted a number of final disposal options, and, as such, contributed to the development of personalized funeral rituals in New Zealand.

Maori cremation

Prehistoric Maori funeral practices were characterized by considerable diversity. Few details are known about the earliest Maori beliefs and rituals surrounding disposal, but archaeological evidence suggests that Maori followed the Polynesian practice of burying the dead in close proximity to settlements (Davidson, 1984: 173). The secondary deposition of bones in secret locations, however, became increasingly widespread in response to fears of desecration by enemies, and changing beliefs about the dangers associated with the dead (Davidson, 1984: 178). These changes may have provided the impetus for cremation. There is evidence to suggest that cremation was practised by some tribes, and that it was occasionally utilized when death occurred outside a tribal area, or where there were inadequate places for the deposition of remains (Buck, 1966: 426; Taylor, 1966: 154–56; Voykovic, 1981: 84–94). Cremation may also have been used to prevent the spread of disease. Primary and secondary burial, however, remained the dominant form of disposal (Oppenheim, 1973: 60–63), and burial remains an intrinsic element of contemporary funeral ritual (*tangi*).

Early history

European whalers, traders and missionaries began arriving in New Zealand at the end of the eighteenth century. Although early migration was limited, the European population gradually expanded, exceeding 250 000 people by the early 1870s. Communities during the nineteenth century were generally small, with minimal legislative requirements for recording disposals (Ninness, 1990). Funerals were important public and social events, and traditional religious symbols and functionaries were prevalent at burial services (Dickey, 1980: 37). Funeral reform

movements emerged in a few urban centres during the 1870s and condemned nineteenth-century mourning customs as extravagant and excessive (Cleaver, 1996: 65–75). These small groups argued for simplicity in funerary ritual and moderate funeral expenditure. Cremation was periodically discussed during this time, and the first group promoting cremation was formed in Lawrence in 1875 (Cleaver, 1996: 103–104). Other cremation societies were formed in Napier (1894), Dunedin (1900) and Auckland (1905). These associations advanced arguments for the adoption of cremation, which paralleled similar developments in Australia, Europe and North America (Nicol, 1994: 173).

Cremation was promoted as a sanitary, cost-effective, and aesthetically satisfying form of disposal. A publication by the Dunedin Cremation Society (1903), for example, emphasized that cremation was a scientific process that eliminated deadly diseases, utilized valuable land more effectively, and was generally cheaper than burial. The publication stated that it was only sentiment and tradition which motivated people to choose the 'protracted and disgusting process of putrefaction' which burial entailed (Dunedin Cremation Society, 1903:12). Cremation was also promoted as a method of disposal that precluded the possibility of being buried alive and the 'discomfort' associated with graveyard services. Feminists who considered nineteenth-century mourning customs oppressive also promoted cremation as a modern and hygienic method of disposal (Coney, 1993: 87).

As in Australia and England, there were opponents to cremation. Some noted that crimes such as poisoning would go undetected, while others believed that cremation was a reversion to pagan practices that interfered with the doctrine of resurrection. The cremationists, however, argued that doctors would take more care in certifying causes of death, and that cremation merely resolved the body into its constituent elements. These debates, and overseas disposal developments, were reported in newspapers around the country.

Twentieth-century developments

The cremation movements received limited public support. The society in Dunedin, for example, made little progress in establishing a crematorium and went into a period of decline after 1905. Although cremation was legalized by the Cemeteries Act in 1882, and municipal cemeteries were permitted to make provision for cremation (1895 Cemeteries Act Amendment), the first crematorium in New Zealand was not erected until 1909 in Karori, Wellington. This was followed by the construction of crematoria in Auckland and Dunedin. Cremation, however, was slow to gain widespread public acceptance. It was not until the 1950s and 1960s that the rate of cremation increased significantly, accounting for approximately 60 per cent of disposals by 1970 (Ninness, 1990). This development generated minimal opposition from the funeral industry. Funeral directors, striving for professional status in the 1940s and 1950s, utilized rhetoric in their trade journal that reflected the cremationists' concern with hygiene and efficiency. New Zealand funeral directors promoted cremation as a convenient and rational form of disposal that would have little impact on the provision of other services. Unlike the situation in the United States, where cremation was often promoted by the anti-traditional funeral lobby, there was little correlation between the type of funeral service and the method of disposal.

During the early twentieth century there was a shift away from home-centred death and graveyard burial services. An increasing number of people died in institutions, and funeral directors began to exert considerable influence in the funeral process. A greater number of funeral services were held in churches and small funeral director chapels, with the committal conducted at the cemetery or crematorium (Cleaver, 1996: 43–44). From the 1960s onwards, however, municipal crematoria began to build funeral chapels (FDANZ, n.d.: 5–7). This development culminated in the proliferation of single-service funerals, where the service and committal were conducted at the same venue, eliminating the need for a cortege and pallbearers. This change not only illustrated an increased degree of rationalization, but also initiated the trend towards one-stop funeral shopping and personalization. Some funeral directors realized the potential for cremation authorities to integrate vertically and include funeral directing services. A significant number of funeral directors during the 1960s and 1970s were also concerned at the time-restrictions imposed by crematoria and the subsequent abbreviation of funeral ceremonies. In response to these concerns a number of funeral directors constructed multi-facility funeral venues in the 1980s which included funeral chapels and reception lounges for refreshments after the funeral service (FDANZ, n.d.: 5–9). Some funeral directors also installed their own cremator units during this period and began to offer a wider range of disposal services.

The acceptance of crematoria and funeral director chapels was indicative of a move away from religious funeral services and towards the increasing personalization of ceremonies. Authors such as Hill (1994: 295) have noted that a significant degree of secularity was present in nineteenth-century New Zealand, evident in the levels of church attendance and acceptance of pluralism. This secularity has become particularly visible in the last 50 years. Not only has there been a significant decline in allegiance to the major Christian denominations, but there exists an increasing number of people who claim to have 'no religion' in the census statistics (approximately 25 per cent of the population). Dickey (1980) asserts that secular venues such as crematoria chapels became popular precisely because they encompassed the heterogeneous nature of private significance.

Personalization has also become conspicuous in the content of the funeral service, the increasing involvement of mourners, and the number of different funeral services being offered. Secular funeral celebrants conducting life-centered funerals have become an intrinsic part of personalization. These celebrants conduct a significant number of funerals in urban areas and attempt to construct ceremonies that reflect the individuality and personality of the deceased. Although the incineration after the service is usually witnessed only by crematorium staff or funeral directors, the final disposal of ashes has also become increasingly personalized. Cemeteries, crematoria and monumental masons have provided more memorialization options and allowed greater mourner involvement. Ashes can be scattered by crematorium staff, deposited in columbaria, or buried in cemetery ash plots with plaques or headstones. Alternatively, cremated remains can be taken by family members and buried or scattered in locations with personal significance. Burial and personal placement of ashes have superseded institutional scattering in the last two decades. As Davies

(2002: 32) suggests, this treatment represents a form of '"fulfilment" of the social person within a retrospective view of their lives'. Some funeral directors and celebrants provide ceremonies for this final treatment, but in many cases it remains a private family event.

Recent developments

The rate of cremation has remained relatively constant over the last two decades. Personal choice, cost and a concern for effective resource utilization continue to be primary reasons for the dominance of this disposal method. Cremation now constitutes approximately 70–80 per cent of disposals in urban areas, with a national average of close to 60 per cent. The last decade has witnessed intensified competition between crematoria and the establishment of low-priced cremation establishments in some cities. Over this same period, pet cremation has become increasingly popular with the recent establishment of a New Zealand Pet Crematorium Association.

There continues to be significant media interest in cremation, and a considerable degree of public misinformation about the cremation process. As documented elsewhere (for example, Nicol, 1994: 328), rumours about coffin recycling, multiple incineration, and theft of personal items are widespread in New Zealand – despite public relations campaigns by crematoria authorities and funeral directors. One aspect of cremation which is set to gain more prominence in the next decade is the environmental impact of this disposal method. Recent media reports and studies (for example, Nieschmidt and Kim, 1997) indicate that cremation may have detrimental environmental effects. In response, some companies have developed 'environmentally sustainable' burial options that will undoubtedly receive more attention in the future. **Cyril Schafer**

References

Buck, P. (1966), *The Coming of the Maori*, Wellington: Maori Purposes Fund Board.

Cleaver, P.W. (1996), 'Dealing with Death: The Pakeha Treatment of Death 1850–1910', unpublished MA thesis, University of Victoria.

Coney, S. (1993), *Standing in the Sunshine: A History of New Zealand Women Since They Won the Vote*, Auckland: Viking.

Davidson, J. (1984), *The Prehistory of New Zealand*, Auckland: Longman Paul.

Davies, Douglas J. (2002), *Death, Ritual and Belief* (2nd rev. edn), London: Continuum.

Dickey, B.R. (1980), 'Death in New Zealand as a test of the sacred', unpublished MA thesis, University of Auckland.

Dunedin Cremation Society, (1903), *Cremation versus Earth-burial*, Dunedin: Stone, Son and Co.

Griffin, G.M. and Tobin, D. (1997), *In the Midst of Life...: the Australian Response to Death*, Melbourne: Melbourne University Press.

FDANZ Inc. (n.d.), *The Last Ten Years – Update (1987–1997)*, Wellington: Funeral Directors Association of New Zealand.

Hill, M. (1994), 'Religion' in P. Spoonley, D. Pearson and I. Shirley (eds), *New Zealand Society*, Palmerston North: Dunmore Press, 292–307.

Nieschmidt, A.K. and Kim, N.D. (1997), 'Effects of Mercury Release from Amalgam Dental Restorations During Cremation on Soil Mercury levels of Three New Zealand Crematoria', *Bulletin of Environmental Contamination and Toxicology*, 58(5): 744–51.

Nicol, Robert (1994), *At the End of the Road*, St Leonards: Allen & Unwin.

Ninness, J. (1990), 'Undertakers in New Zealand 1840–1940 – Part II: The first hundred years of funeral service', *The New Zealand Funeral Director*, 52(1): 8–20.

Oppenheim, R.S. (1973), *Maori Death Customs*, Wellington: A.H. & A.W. Reed Ltd.

Taylor, A. (1966), 'Maori Burial and Cremation in the Manukau Area', *Historical Review*, 14(4): 154–56.

Voykovic, A.A. (1981), 'Nga Roimata O Hine-Nui-Te-Po. Death in Maori Life', unpublished MA. thesis, University of Otago.

NORWAY

To a considerable extent, the development of cremation in Norway may be reflected in the history of the Norwegian Cremation Society (*Norsk Kremasjons Forening*), founded on 7 February 1889 as the Norwegian Incineration Society (*Norsk Ligbrændingsforening*) until its name change in 1917. The second half of the nineteenth century witnessed great progress and development in Christiania – the Norwegian capital city, renamed Oslo in 1924 – and cremation was among the ideas from abroad considered and discussed, the impetus coming mainly from England and Germany but also from Sweden and Denmark. A group of prominent citizens took an interest in this subject, writing articles and delivering lectures on the advantages of cremation. Among these persons were: H.R. Astrup, cabinet minister and the first president of the cremation society; Dr V. Ucherman, MD; university professor Evald Rygh, mayor of Christiania; Fr. Thaulow, surgeon and director of the National Hospital; Constantin W. Talén, civil engineer and director of the municipal Tramway company; Annæus Schødt, lawyer and member of parliament; and Christian Michelsen, shipowner, member of parliament and, later, prime minister in 1905 when the Union with Sweden was dissolved. Other advocates of cremation included: Hjalmar Welhaven, well-known architect and curator of the Royal Palace; H.E. Berner, lawyer, politician and first editor of the radical newspaper *Dagbladet*; and Hans A.T. Gløersen, lawyer, master of forestry and an innovator in many fields, who also donated legacies for the benefit of cremation. Another notable spokesman for the cremation cause was Oscar Nissen, medical doctor, president of the Norwegian Labour Party and president of the Norwegian Temperance Association. As these examples make clear, supporters of cremation did not follow traditional party lines.

When first established, the Cremation Society had comparatively few members, but they were all highly qualified people, the majority coming from Christiania. A little surprising was the lack of response from the working class, and it is possible that the class difference between them and the founders of the Cremation Society was too great. The membership fee was also comparatively high. The first and most important objective of the society was to remove existing obstacles to cremation: to make it legal and to contribute to the establishing of crematoria in Norway.

In 1891 the society sent the first application to the king to permit cremation and the building of crematoria. The authorities, however, considered that new legislation was necessary to make this possible and, accordingly, the society delivered its first draft bill on cremation to the Ministry of Justice in 1892. Government, local authorities and clergy, however, adopted a rather negative attitude to the proposal. Of the six bishops in Norway at that time three had no

objections to cremation on religious or theological grounds. However, this did not mean that they were in favour of cremation. As a result of great efforts, mainly on the part of the Cremation Society, the first Act on Cremation was adopted on 11 June 1898. The supporters of cremation were not particularly satisfied with the provisions of the Act, because it raised difficulties for cremation compared to earth burial. However, the society continued its work with the legislators and this resulted in a new Act of 3 May 1913 with provisions that were more favourable to cremation.

The Act was amended in 1917 and 1961. The last amendment contained, amongst other points, a considerable enlargement of the circle of persons who might decide on the cremation of the deceased. A new act on churchyards, cremation and burial was adopted on 7 June 1996 and came into force on 1 January 1997. The Cremation Society had the opportunity to give its opinion on the proposal for the act, which is mainly a modernization of the former act; thus, there is now no longer a separate Cremation Act. The new Act allows the scattering of ashes, which was previously not allowed. The Ministry of Ecclesiastical Affairs has given further regulations concerning such scattering, which also requires permission from the county governor (*fylkesmann*). Clergymen are not obliged to officiate at ceremonies where the ashes are dispersed. Since 1917 it has been possible to lay out special burial places where the urns of persons not desiring to have their own grave are placed. Many crematoria, which usually are built next to cemeteries, also have special urn-groves close by. According to section 10 of the new Act, the municipal authorities may stipulate a fee for cremation, although this is not the case for earth burial. The Cremation Society has, however, proposed that this provision is removed. So far, only a few municipalities have introduced a cremation fee.

As soon as the Act on Cremation was passed in 1898, the society started preliminary work on the construction of a crematorium in Christiania. In the period preceding the inauguration of the crematorium, some Norwegians had been cremated abroad. The city council could not accept the society's proposal for the building of a municipal crematorium, but allocated a free site and also made a contribution of NOK10 000. Thanks to a bequest of NOK50 000 from Mr A.T.

Gløersen, the society was able to build a crematorium that was finished in 1909 and inaugurated on 24 May with Revd Jonas Dahl officiating at the service of dedication. The architect was Oscar Hoff, and it was decorated by the artist Emanuel Vigeland. However, the first crematorium in Norway already had been constructed in Bergen by the municipality. Located in the cellar of an existing mortuary chapel it was inaugurated on 7 April 1907. A cremation society had been established in Bergen in 1892, and the composer Edvard Grieg was among its members: the society was later dissolved.

To begin with, there was a certain amount of opposition to cremation in Norway, but this gradually diminished. As cremation numbers steadily increased, the board of the Norwegian Cremation Society considered it necessary to build another funeral hall with several furnaces. This new crematorium was finished in 1930. Once more, the architect was Oscar Hoff, working in cooperation with the municipal architect Harald Aars. Dean J. Maroni delivered the inaugural address, while the mayor of Oslo thanked the Cremation Society for the work done. The artistic decoration of the new crematorium was carried out by the well-known painter Alf Rolfsen, who was the winner of the competition for the work in which 16 artists took part. His murals are considered as one of the most important Norwegian decorative artworks of the period. The inauguration took place on 21 September 1937, with Bishop Dr Eivind Berggrav officiating.

After the first crematoria in Bergen and Oslo, others followed: Trondheim (1919), Drammen (1927), Kristiansund, Bergen, Tønsberg and Vestvågøy (all 1939), Borre (1940) and Stavanger (1941). After the Second World War, building recommenced in 1953 with crematoria in: Steinkjer, Tinn, Larvik, Ålesund, Halden, Tromsø, Narvik, Skedsmo, Odda, Sandefjord, Asker, Sarpsborg, Oslo (its third), Trondheim (its second), Borre, Fredrikstad, Askim, Bærum, Haugesund, Verdal, Ringerike, Kongsvinger, Gjøvik, Røros and Bodø. Thus, crematoria are now spread over practically the whole country.

In 1940 the Cremation Society transferred the crematorium in Oslo to the municipality, and all crematoria in Norway are now run by the municipalities. As a rule, Norwegian crematoria are characterized by a high standard of architecture and artistic decoration. They are often placed in landscaped gardens with places for urns, but no new columbaria are constructed. Crematoria in Norway have no reception rooms. There has been considerable development of the technical facilities and upgrading of the incinerators which now are usually placed on the ground floor rather than in the basement, as previously. Initially, furnaces were heated by coal or coke but then electricity or oil took over. Today, however, new incinerators use gas. In modern incinerators the combustion is computerized. By 2002 one crematorium, at Hamar, was also equipped with a mercury-filter device with others waiting for further regulations to be adopted by the appropriate ministry. According to regulations of 10 January 1997, coffins used for cremation must be of wooden material (cardboard and plastic are not allowed). People operating the incinerators have to attend several courses and obtain a certificate.

Throughout its existence the Norwegian Cremation Society has strongly advocated cremation and the building of crematoria, distributing thousands of pamphlets and leaflets. Initially, its propaganda emphasized the sanitary and hygienic advantages of cremation, but, later, rational issues of land saving were stressed. For a long period the society gave technical advice in connection with construction of crematoria, and it has also contributed to the artistic decoration of the chapels in new crematoria. In 1921 the society established its own funeral bureau and its profits were a welcome support to the activities of the Cremation Society. The bureau was finally closed in 1997.

In the closing decades of the twentieth century society membership amounted to around 6000 at most. Work supporting the ideology of cremation no longer seems to have any appeal to young people and recruiting qualified persons to the board is also problematic. The society, of course, underlines the advantages of cremation particularly in relation to the environment, and cremation is generally accepted as an aesthetic and rational way of disposing of the dead. On the whole, the authorities and the public have a good understanding of cremation; indeed, it has become customary and is accepted by the majority of the population. Similarly, the Church no longer objects to cremation. On the religious front, the Cremation Society has always sought to be neutral. In 1966 the Norwegian Association for Churchyard Care (*Norsk forening for kirkegårdskultur*) was established to promote landscape gardening and architecture related to cemeteries. Since 1993 this association has also dealt with technical questions concerning cremation.

By 2002 the cremation rate for Norway as a whole was 32 per cent (total number of cremations 14 154). In Oslo the rate was 66 per cent. In central Norway in cities with a crematorium the rate varies from around 40 to 70 per cent. The lowest rate in a place with a crematorium was in Vestvågøy in Lofoten – 4 per cent in 2002. By 2002 some 38 crematoria were in operation. Tromsø Crematorium was destroyed by fire in 1994 and will hopefully soon be rebuilt. Even though there is more or less one crematorium per 100 000 inhabitants, the distance to the nearest crematorium is probably the greatest impediment to cremation. People want to have the funeral and connected procedures to take place where the deceased lived and not have to send the body long distances to be cremated. In some parts of western and northern Norway the cremation rate is, relatively speaking, very low even in places with a crematorium. This might be explained by religious, sociological or cultural attitudes in the local population.

After the Second World War the Norwegian Cremation Society joined the International Cremation Federation and in 1954 the ICF held its congress in Oslo. There society also cooperated with cremation societies in other Nordic countries. The Norwegian Cremation Society was dissolved at its general assembly on 29 April 2003. At the same meeting it was decided to establish the Norwegian Cremation Foundation which was to work for the benefit of cremation in Norway. The first meeting of the foundation was held on 6 November 2003, and Mrs Ellen Akre–Aas, public trustee of Oslo, was elected president.

The following list of presidents in the Norwegian Cremation Society since its establishment in 1889 to its dissolution in 2003 gives an idea of their social position:

H.R. Astrup	Cabinet minister	1889–1891
H.E. Berner	Editor	1891–1909
Hans Daae	Colonel	1910
J. Schøning	Head postmaster in Christiania	1911–1917
Hans Daae	Colonel	1918–1926
K.V. Hammer	Economist and archivist	1927
Hans Hurum	Merchant	1927–1930
Herman Krag	Merchant	1930–1931
Hans Hurum	Merchant	1932–1934
L.J. Moltke Hansen	Director of 'Kredit Foreningen for Norge'	1934–1946
Ludvig Hansen	Director of the church and cemetery administration in Oslo	1946–1956
Erling Rikheim Sr.	Judge of the court of appeal	1956–1960
Johan Schwingel	Director of the church and cemetery administration in Oslo	1960–1972
Erling Rikheim Jr.	Attorney	1972–1983
Per Cederblad	Director of the church and cemetery administration in Oslo	1983–1998
Erling Rikheim Jr.	Attorney	1998–2003

Erling Rikheim

See also humanism for a specific Norwegian case.

O

OBJECT CREMATION

In modern cremation, care is taken not to place objects within or on a coffin if their combustion would involve the production of prohibited gases. In the past, and in many societies, various objects have, however, played a direct or indirect part in human cremation. A notable direct example was the Viking custom of burning a ship along with a high-status human being, as described under **Viking Sweden**. More indirectly, wax models of the dead person could be cremated if the human body was inaccessible, as the entry on the **Romans** shows. The Romans also burned various other objects reflecting the identity and status of the dead. From a different perspective, the entry on **Gypsies** describes how the possessions of the dead may need to be burned after a death, even though the cremation of the dead is definitely not entertained. Although, this case is one of simply burning possessions rather than cremating them, the use of fire is important here in removing objects that might, otherwise, continue to express something of the life and influence of the deceased person. In Gypsy thought funeral rites involve a clear rite of separation of the dead from the living, and this also involves the deceased's possessions if the death was one regarded as incurring a sense of impurity.

One of the most direct cases of object cremation is found in the entry on **object cremation** under **Japan**, which describes the formal cremation of objects possessing direct relationships with individuals, but burned while those people are still alive. This ritual framing of objects slightly parallels the treatment of old and well-used collections of sacred scripture in Judaism where Torah scrolls are, in a sense, entombed. Orthodox Judaism vigorously avoids cremation, whether of humans or of scripture, but did use fire as a means of making certain sacrificial offerings. These cases show that care needs to be taken when interpreting the relationship between objects and their burning with fire. **Douglas J. Davies**

See also Gypsies; impurity and purity; Japan – object cremation; Romans; Viking Sweden.

OPEN-AIR CREMATION (UK)

In England, since the passing of the Cremation Act in 1902, two sets of open-air cremations have been officially permitted. The first took place along the south coast during the First World War and was of Indian soldiers who had been wounded in France and died of their wounds in hospitals in Brighton, Netley and Brockenhurst. The second set consisted of just three cremations, in 1934, 1935 and 1937, which all took place in a field on the bank of the Basingstoke Canal adjoining Woking Crematorium. The first cremation was of the Rani, the head of the first Nepalese Legation in London; the other two were of the legation's members of staff.

Although it could be argued that such open-air cremations did not, and do not, contravene the Cremation Act and Cremation Regulations, anyone conducting an open-air cremation today would face court prosecution: it would probably be argued that the Act and Regulations require any burning of human remains to take place in a building fitted with appliances for the burning of such. The Home Office certainly thought that the cremations of the Indian soldiers in 1915 were unlawful but nevertheless allowed them to go ahead. The legality of the cremations in the 1930s was squared by accepting that a funeral pyre was itself a building fitted with appliances for the burning of human remains. Both in 1915 and the 1930s, political considerations determined the flouting, or bending, of the law. In 1915 it was important to counter anti-British propaganda in India by catering for the social and cultural needs of soldiers who had, in effect, been dragooned into a war far away from home. In 1934 Nepal was a very isolated and enclosed country. It had a titular monarchy and a dynastic prime ministership. The Nepalese Legation had just been established and at its head was the Nepalese prime minister's son. Failure to secure that the Rani was cremated in accordance with the rituals of Nepalese Hinduism would have had disastrous consequences for his standing and that of his family in Nepal, and consequently every effort was made to accommodate his wishes. In the aftermath of these cremations, the Nepalese came close to establishing a permanent facility for open-air cremations at Woking. **Stephen White**

References

White, Stephen (1997), 'Hindu Cremations in Britain', in Peter C. Jupp and Glennys Howarth (eds), *The Changing Face of Death*, London: Macmillan Press, 135–48.

White, Stephen (1992), 'An End to D-I-Y Cremation?', *Medicine, Science and the Law*, 33: 151–59.

PENNA, JOSE

Dr José Penna (1855–1919), one of the most important Latin American hygienists of his day, was born in Bahía Blanca, a seaside town in Buenos Aires province in 1855, son of Colonel Juan Penna, an Italian officer and freemason (José joined his father's masonic lodge in 1897). He completed secondary studies in the National School of Buenos Aires whilst working concurrently in a smithy (Lappas, 2000: 338). In 1873 he joined Buenos Aires University Faculty of Medicine, concluding his studies six years later with a thesis including results of experiments with dogs. While in medical school he met several future cremationists.

Penna began a rural medical practice in Cañuelas (in Buenos Aires province), and was there until his wife died of a cerebral haemorrhage at the age of 25. Returning to Buenos Aires in May 1882, he gained, on request, a stand-in post as professor of Internal Pathology. When the Hospital San Roque stopped being used as a quarantine, Penna inaugurated, on 23 December 1882, the *Casa de Aislamiento* (literally 'House of Isolation'). The new establishment soon began receiving Buenos Aires citizens suffering from smallpox, yellow fever, cholera and other infectious diseases. Although the building was small and rapidly became overcrowded, Penna's dedication to his patients and his determination to eradicate epidemics meant that his workplace virtually became his home. His hard work, stoicism and obvious preparedness to risk his life for others drew him praise from later Argentine cremationists.

Almost two years to the day after the *Casa de Aislamiento* was inaugurated, Penna helped make cremation history by performing, on 26 December 1884, the first cremation in modern Argentina, that of yellow-fever victim, Pedro Doime. The cremation began in the *Casa de Aislamiento* at 10.10 p.m. and, despite the substandard conditions and hastily improvised cremator, was completed in about an hour. In April 1886 Penna part-sponsored a new cremation by-law and went on to implement the cremation of victims of the cholera epidemic of 1886–87. Three years later he published what José Mendoza deemed 'a work of great historical merit', *La Cremación en America y Particularmente en la Argentina*, in which he described his experiments in cremation and examined in detail the historic cemeteries of Patagonia. He continued to oversee cremations when the new crematorium in *Chacarita* began operating on 13 November 1903 and then supervised the renovation of its cremators in 1911. Penna remained a cremation propagandist. In 1904 he gave a presentation on cremation at the second Latin American Medical Congress in Buenos Aires and published *La Cremación de Cadáveres* (FDR, 1928: 92; Mendoza, 1923: 18; Baca, 1928: 8).

Although, as Dr Julio Iribarne claimed, Penna's greatest project as a hygienist was cremation, he was far more than a cremationist, founding, with fellow cremationist Emilio Coni, the Argentine Medical Association (*Asociación Médica Argentina*). In 1893 he joined the National Academy of Medicine and, in the same year, his project for a new hospital for sufferers of contagious diseases was approved. Though still not finished by 1910, the institution that later became the Hospital Muñiz had formed close links with the Faculty of Medical Sciences and had been used as a location for students' practical work.

A keen educator, who adopted an intense, methodical and persevering attitude towards education, in 1893 Penna presented an internal pathology studies programme to the Faculty of Medical Sciences that incorporated 30 topics on infectious illnesses. In 1900 he was appointed to the Epidemiological Professorship of Medicine. Although Penna did not travel abroad to further his knowledge, he still had an effect beyond the Argentine borders. An innovation that he introduced for treating bubonic plague and tetanus, involving the administering of high doses of serum, was employed in France during the First World War.

A national deputy between 1910 and 1914, Penna also became the president of the National Department of Hygiene in 1911. There he continued his predecessor's work in bacteriological investigation with the creation of a new laboratory. He also reorganized the department and enacted measures against malaria, the lessons of which were shared, transmitted and developed until the disease was finally eradicated in Argentina in 1949. In the national assembly he supported several government bills related to public health and promoted the creation of the Demographic Office, the Bacteriological Institute, the Office of Sanitary Engineering, the Hospitals Alvarez and Piñero and provincial sanitary stations. He also reorganized the river and maritime sanitary services and maintained an insistence on the need to apply the law of obligatory vaccination. On returning to academia, Penna was appointed president of the Faculty of Medicine, 1916–17.

In addition to his works on cremation, Penna wrote several important books, as both a scientist and a historian of medicine. In 1893 he published *El Rol de las Epidemias en la Despoblación de América* (*The Role of Epidemics in the Depopulation of America*). He also wrote works on the history of cholera, yellow fever, bubonic plague, typhoid and smallpox. However, his most important work (with Horacio Madero) was *La Administración Sanitaria y Asistencia Publica de la Ciudad de Buenos Aires* (*Sanitary Administration and Public Assistance in the City of Buenos Aires*), published in 1910 (Jankilevich, 2002). Penna had, according to cremationist Dr Eliseo Cantón, one of the most 'robust and fecund minds' in Latin America. His work on various diseases was of 'transcendental importance' and sufficient to immortalize him.

Though an important cremation pioneer, Penna failed to establish a lasting cremation society in his lifetime. According to Eduardo Baca, shortly before his death Penna was attempting to establish a cremation society, and it is likely that this helped stimulate the eventual formation of the Argentine Cremation Association, three years later. Penna died on 29 March 1919, aged 63, and his subsequent cremation helped make him even more of a hero in Argentine cremationist circles. José Perez Mendoza, a prominent cremationist in the 1920s, claimed that Penna's cremation had a wide resonance with the public, as he was so famous. The daily newspapers gave the event a great deal of coverage and one of them even reproduced a photo in which his ashes could be seen on a table being readied for packing into an urn (Mendoza, 1923: 18–19). Penna remained an inspiration to Argentine cremationists, which was apparent when they placed a memorial plaque to him, officially inaugurated on 22 November 1924, in *Chacarita* crematorium. The post-war generation of cremationists also regarded Penna as inspirational. In 1960 the new Argentine cremation society's first news-sheet carried a picture of Penna on the front and a hagiography inside. A year earlier the cremation society's president called Penna 'the most outstanding cremation advocate in Argentina' (LAPC, 1959: 9). **Lewis H. Mates**

References

Baca, Eduardo J. (1928), *Estadística de la Cremación de Cadáveres Humanos en la Cuidad de Buenos Aires, 1884–1927*, Buenos Aires: Ferrari Hnos., CRE/C/AG/1928/1.

'F.D.R.' (1928), 'Para la Historia de la Cremación en la Republica Argentina, La Primera Sociedad Argentina de Cremación', *Boletín de la Asociación Argentina de Cremación*, 12: 91–93.

Jankilevich, Angel (2002), 'Héroes de la Salud Pública en la Argentina', *Hospital y Comunidad*, 5: 3–4 available at: http://www.aadhhos.org.ar /HyC/04/ HyC04.htm.

Lappas, Alcibíades (2000), *La Masonería Argentina a Través de sus Hombres*, 3rd edn, Buenos Aires: Alcibíades Lappas.

LAPC (Liga Argentina pro Cremación) (1959), *Memoria: Ejercicio Mayo 1958 a Mayo 1959*, Buenos Aires: Liga Argentina pro Cremación, CRE/C/AG/1959/1.

Mendoza, José Perez (1923), *Sobre Cremación*, Buenos Aires: Ferrari Hnos., CRE/C/AG/1923/2.

PETS

The cremation of pet animals became increasingly common in some societies in the twentieth century, as evidenced by the account of the New Zealand Pet Crematorium Association in the **New Zealand** entry. By the beginning of the twenty-first century in England, too, specific pet crematoria existed in many parts of the country. Their availability is widely represented on the Internet, and various companies provide what is described as a full service for the owner who is sometimes described in terms analogous to human bereavement. It is often possible for a pet to be cremated and for their remains to be treated in many of the ways resembling the treatment of human remains (Davies, 2002: 182–95. Lee and Lewis, 1992). In Tokyo a mobile crematorium service has been created to cope with home visits for dead pets (*Funeralis*, April 1990). **Douglas J. Davies**

References

Davies, D.J. (2002), *Death, Ritual and Belief* (2nd rev. edn), London: Continuum.

Funeralis. Official Publication of the HT Group, Durbanville, South Africa.

Lee, Laura and Lewis, Martyn (1992), *Absent Friend: Coping with the Loss of a Treasured Pet*, High Wycombe: Henston.

PHAROS INTERNATIONAL

Pharos International is the official journal of the Cremation Society of Great Britain and the International Cremation Federation, and is published quarterly. First published in 1934 as *Pharos: Quarterly Journal of the Federation of Cremation Authorities*, in 1937 it became the *Journal of the Cremation Society and the Federation of Cremation Authorities in Great Britain*. In 1950 the references to the society and federation in its title were replaced by the *Official Journal of the Cremation Movement* and in 1964 it became the *Journal of the Society and the International Cremation Federation*. **Stephen White**

PHOENIX

The mythical phoenix has, occasionally, served as a motif in the world of modern cremation. *Phoenix* was, for example, taken as the title of the journal of the Cremation Society of Vienna as documented in the entries, **Austrian Cremation Societies** and **Siedek**.

In literature, the phoenix is an emblem of the nature of death, immortality and resurrection (Head and Cranston, 1977: 17–20). This sacred bird of ancient Greek and Egyptian mythology is associated with the Egyptian *benu* symbolizing the sun-god Re. In Greek, 'phoenix' denotes a purple hue (Van Den Broek, 1972: 52) describing its golden body with red plumage, resembling an eagle. (Herodotus, 1988: 2.73) Whilst there are variations amongst the mythical phoenix, there are similarities between them: first, the bird lives a long time, but shows itself before its death;

second, its death brings new life; and, third, it is a bird of the sun.

There are two principal versions of the myth. The more common holds the phoenix as sitting in an aromatic nest when it is consumed by flames ignited by the sun. Then, as it burns, a new phoenix is produced. The less common tradition saw the phoenix as dead and decomposing in its aromatic nest. A new bird, regenerating from a worm, would then fly to Heliopolis in Egypt, carrying the decayed phoenix, and would then leave it on the altar of the sun-god.

Similarly, Clement of Rome describes an Arabian phoenix that builds a nest of frankincense and myrrh. When dead, a regenerated worm survives on the 'juices of the dead bird'. The worm transforms into a phoenix to carry the bones of its father to the altar of the sun in Heliopolis where the priests find that the five hundredth year was completed since the last phoenix arrived (Clement, 1912: ch. 25). Tacitus described a phoenix making a nest, shedding procreative substance over it. When it dies, a young phoenix is created, and it takes the body of its dead father to the altar of the sun to burn him there. (Tacitus, 1943: 6.28). Herodotus recorded that the phoenix comes every 500 years carrying an embalmed egg of its father, which is buried in the temple of the sun. (Herodotus, 1988: 2.73). Pliny the Elder found that when the kings of Egypt dedicated monoliths to the sun gods, the monoliths were carried by the Phoenix to Heliopolis. (Pliny, 1968: 36.67).

As a bird of the sun, the image of renewal could be the origin for the doctrine of regeneration. Clement epitomizes the influence of the emblem on the faith in resurrection by the phoenix supporting God who is the 'maker of all things to raise up again those who have piously served Him'. (Clement, 1912: ch. 26). The concept of an embodied regeneration of the phoenix is developed to represent empire, metempsychosis, and Christ throughout the Classical and Middle Ages. Thus 'the phoenix fulfilled an important function with respect to the meaning of human existence' (Van Den Broek, 1972: 9). **Hei Jean Ahn**

References

Clement of Rome (1912), *Apostolic Fathers, Volume*

1: *Clement*, The Loeb Classical Library, Cambridge, MA: Harvard University Press.

Davies, Penelope J.E. (2000), 'The Phoenix and the Flames: Death, Rebirth and the Imperial Landscape of Rome', *Mortality*, 5(3): 237–58.

Head, Joseph and Cranston, S.L. (1977), *Reincarnation: The Phoenix Fire Mystery*, New York: Julian Press/Crown Publishers.

Herodotus (1988), *The Histories*, The Loeb Classical Library, Cambridge, MA: Harvard University Press.

Pliny the Elder (1968), *Natural History*, The Loeb Classical Library, Cambridge, MA: Harvard University Press.

Tacitus (1943), *The Annals*, The Loeb Classical Library, Cambridge, MA: Harvard University Press.

Van Den Broek, V. (1972), *The Myth of the Phoenix According to Classical and Early Christian Traditions*, Leiden: E.J. Brill.

PINI, GAETANO

Gaetano Pini was born in Livorno on 1 April 1846 and studied first in Pisa and later in Napoli, where he graduated in medicine and surgery. During the Third War of Independence he enlisted voluntarily and fought alongside Garibaldi. In 1870 his *risorgimentale* (resurgent) experience ended, and he received an offer from the Milanese editor Vallardi to direct the *Italian Medical Encyclopaedia* (*Enciclopedia Medica Italiana*). The move to Milan represented a real turning point in the life of the Livornese doctor. The propagandist's intense activity as editor-in-chief of the *Encyclopaedia* and also of the *Dictionary of Medical Sciences* (*Dizionario delle Scienze Mediche*) and the *Universal Annals of Medicine* (*Annali Universali di Medicina*) brought him into contact with the dynamic atmosphere of Milanese cultural and scientific life, enabling him to carry out three projects of outstanding interest: the Rachitic Institute (*Istituto dei Rachitici*), the Hygiene Society (*Società d'Igiene*, founded in 1878) and the Cremation Society (*Società di Cremazione*). Though the cremation association project, Pini was able to bring a national perspective to his hygienic and positivist battles. He also benefited from the contacts and relationships developed within masonic lodges, all of which were fundamental for the creation of the Milanese Cremation Society.

The debate, in which Gaetano Pini participated from the start, and which led to the constitution of the Milanese Cremation Society, originated largely with the birth of the Italian Unitarian state. The basic pillars of the project, born and bred in a period dominated by positivism, were doctors and liberals, Milanese thinkers and masons. The debate developed along three very different lines: hygiene, medical–legal and moral. The debate, first, and the cremation society, later, were important elements in the socio-cultural panorama of post-Unitarian Italy and constituted an integral and important part in the complex modernization process of Italian society.

In the secular and rationalist world anticipated by Pini, cremation represented the final, and only, way of dealing with the dead. In the debate about cremation developed in medical and hygiene journals, and from 1875 in freemason publications, Pini put forward arguments on the pollution of the earth and atmosphere and on problems concerning legal medicine. For example, in response to the objection in that cremation was an obstacle to investigating the causes of suspicious deaths, he advocated stricter controls on the assessment of the causes of individual death which, in turn, led to improvements in the knowledge of human pathologies. The themes of the cremationist debate originated in the context of the need for improvement in hygienic and sanitary conditions, which started to be addressed scientifically and institutionally after the creation of the department of hygiene and specialized research institutes. In this context, Pini, being the best possible organizer, was nominated secretary of the Hygiene Society, where he had the chance to deepen his bio-medical interest and become involved in different social issues: hygiene in school buildings, child labour, control of prostitution, death in the army, drinking-water quality and improvement of the Milanese canals. By 1875 (the year of the foundation of the first cremation society and the first authorized cremation in the Italian state, both in Milan) Pini had become the organizational fulcrum, as well as the spokesman, of the Italian cremation associations. The constitution of a League of the 24 cremation societies that existed in Italy in 1882 was influenced by Pini, and represented an important stage in the history of the Italian cremationist movement. It decreed future consolidation and helped to coordinate both pressure on legislative bodies and the promotional activities aimed at influencing public opinion.

The effects of greater coordination, the creation of new societies affiliated to the League, and, most importantly, the construction of new crematoria, did not take long to emerge. In only four years, in fact, and coinciding with the second Congress in Florence 1886, the central committee of the League could proudly state that in Italy 36 associations were active and 14 crematoria were in operation. This was the last public act of Gaetano Pini, who died in Milan in 1887. **Marco Novarino**

See also freemasonry in Italy; Italy.

POLITICS

Cremation first came to the attention of the modern occidental world at the end of the eighteenth century when French revolutionaries tried to 'de-Christianize funeral rites by promoting cremation' (Prothero, 2001: 9). Thus, from the outset, cremation was indelibly tainted by those who had chosen it as a weapon in their political struggle to undermine the power of Christianity as embodied by the institution of the Catholic Church. Although the consequent political reaction in France caused the cremation issue to recede, it was, nevertheless, taken up in the later nineteenth century by those whose motives were, in many ways, similar those of the French Jacobins of the previous century. Many nineteenth-century cremationists wished to challenge the established authorities – particularly those whose power was based on religion – and, most importantly, the Catholic Church. This became explicit when, in direct opposition to the Vatican Council inaugurated in Rome, freemasons held an International Congress in Naples on 8 December 1869. The Congress, which aimed at dealing a propaganda blow against the Vatican Council, discussed practical means of countering the Church's influence, including non-confessional burial. There was also discussion of an attempt to revive the cremation of corpses, and this featured prominently in the congress's 'anti-ecclesiastical declaration'. Like the French revolutionaries before them, freemasons had given cremation a firm dogmatic significance: a person who was

pro-cremation was regarded an ally of freemasonry in the political struggle against the Catholic Church. Incidentally, an international congress of medical experts met in the same year in Florence. It deemed burial unhygienic and advocated cremation 'in the name of public health and of civilisation' (Prothero 2001: 9). Together, these paths of masonry and medicine run through many sections of this *Encyclopedia*, and, as many doctors were also freemasons, they are often indistinguishable from each other.

The actual level of masonic involvement in cremation advocacy varied considerably and depended, naturally, on the strength of the organization and the priorities of its adherents in any given country. Involvement varied from Argentina, where almost all the important first-generation cremationists and many who followed were freemasons, to Switzerland where there was very little masonic involvement. Britain and Sweden were other examples where masonic influence, as such, was low or non-existent, freemasons being generally more prominently involved in Catholic countries such as France and Italy. Others contesting the influence of the Catholic Church, such as freethinkers, also supported cremation from the nineteenth century onwards.

Some more overtly left-wing individuals became cremationists, although sometimes, as with Argentine cremation advocate and militant socialist Dr José Ingenieros, they were also freemasons or freethinkers. In Argentina, Ingenieros' political convictions were not unusual within cremationist circles. There were also more revolutionary elements involved in cremation advocacy. In 1871 France again became the arena for cremation being linked to revolution. This time, the anti-government uprising that became the short-lived Paris Commune used cremation to dispose of its dead, only two years after the Naples masonic conference.

Anarchism also provided good conditions for support for cremation. In 1972 Robert Hazemann noted that, until 1914, there was 'very little progress [regarding cremation] south of the Pyrenees and the Alps, apart from Italy and Spain, two countries which have had a certain anarchist tradition' (Hazemann, 1972: 3). Some well-known anarchists, such as Bartolomeo Sacco and Nicolas Vanzetti, chose cremation. Framed for murder and executed in 1927 by the

American state of Massachusetts they requested that their bodies be cremated and their ashes divided into two parts, one for the family in Italy and the other to rest in a Boston columbarium. Argentine cremationists gave them and other revolutionaries who had been cremated after their executions, notably the Swedish-American Joe Hill and Spaniard Francisco Ferrer, favourable coverage in their bulletins. Where communist regimes emerged, namely in Russia in 1917 and China in 1949, cremation was advocated by the authorities, although this did not necessarily meet with immediate success. Lenin's anticipated cremation in Russia was expected to be a good example to the populace, but his body was eventually preserved and placed on show in Red Square instead. Still, this did not prevent Argentine cremationists, for example, from praising the Bolsheviks' attempts at advancing cremation and their wider political project.

As well as being an ideological weapon against the influence of the Church, cremation had other attractions for 'progressives', a term adopted as embracing liberals, freemasons and freethinkers through to socialists and anarchists. A real concern for the plight of the poor motivated many cremationists, as shown at the 1936 Prague International Cremation Congress, when a Czech delegate argued that 'poor people, who during their lifetime had been the prey of human selfishness, should be honoured after death by being cremated' (*Report*, 1936: 42). Of course, this kind of sentiment was not confined to the anti-clerical left. Slightly more explicit was a quote that Argentine cremationists were fond of carrying in their journal in the 1920s, to the effect that cremation provided the 'purifying fire' that 'vanishes the abominable privileges of class'. Certainly the cheapness of cremation when compared to burial in most countries also made it attractive to those on the left, as did the fact that fewer workers would have to live next to stinking and unhygienic cemeteries. Cremation, like death, was regarded by some 'progressives' as a social 'leveller'. The cremation movement also offered an opportunity to forge international cooperation which must have appealed to all 'progressives'. At the 1937 London International Cremation Congress, the chairperson's welcome included a reference to bringing the representatives of different countries together, which would help promote peace. Given these considerations it was, perhaps, natural for

working-class cremationist groups to emerge. In Austria, a handful of socialists formed a workers' branch of the Austrian Cremation Society in 1904. This had far more explicitly left-wing politics than its parent organization, which it eventually outgrew and from which it became independent in October 1922. By the time it was dissolved by the Austrian state in 1934, it had a massive membership in excess of 160 000. In the Netherlands, the Workers' Association for Cremation was established by a trade unionist called Andries de Rosa in 1919. Like its Austrian counterpart, it was regarded as 'socialist', although it differed in that it was born separate from the main Dutch Cremation Society but later joined it, although a planned complete merger between the two failed due to political differences. However, these examples were the exception, and working-class support of cremation tended to be confined to those who were also situated and active on the political left.

From the outset, the cremation movement sought to distance itself from 'politics', despite the fact that many advocates were 'progressives' and almost certainly involved precisely because of their political attitudes. Thus, at the first International Cremation Congress in Dresden, Germany, in June 1876 the last of the 'six great principles' of cremation was that 'the sacred feelings of each family should be respected such as the request of civil and religious ceremonies'. (The first five principles concerned the practicalities of cremation.) This was disingenuous, at least so far as organizations like the freemasons were concerned, for their true motivations had been openly expressed a mere seven years earlier at their Naples congress. The emphasis placed on the practical application of cremation rather than its religious and philosophical implications must have been, at least in part, a tactic to obviate a degree of the opposition that inevitably would come from institutions such as the Catholic Church. The tactic clearly failed, as the Catholic Church came out strongly against cremation in 1886 and maintained this opposition until 1963.

Still, despite this obvious failure, the 'non-political' mantra of the cremation movement was to be oft repeated. At the Prague International Cremation Conference in 1936, a German delegate, discussing the development of cremation in different countries, argued that cremation was not political, but 'purely technical'. He complained that cremationist activities had suffered in some countries due to 'artificially aroused nationalism and the race question', and this despite 'the old motto "no religion and no politics in the cremation movement"' (*Report*, 1936: 39). *Pharos* made a similar complaint at around the same time: in the early days of the cremation society, 'enemies sought to prejudice people against us by saying cremation was against Christianity and its practitioners were atheists and political revolutionaries… a famous Victorian preacher said, "A lie is half way round the world before the truth has got its boots on"' (*Pharos*, 5(2), 1939: 7). According to some cremationists, despite the involvement of politically committed individuals, historically the cremation movement had remained 'non-political'. This was the view taken by Austrian cremationist Dr F. Michelfelt who delivered a paper on Roman Catholic Canon Law at the 1954 ICF Congress. Michelfelt admitted that, at the beginning, the cremation movement was mainly led by freemasons, freethinkers and opponents of the Catholic Church who tried to use cremation for their own ends. Curiously, he still maintained, however, that their purpose remained 'neither religious nor political'. This was echoed by Robert Hazemann, another delegate at the same congress, who, whilst recognizing where cremationist support had come from politically, made a similar point, asserting that 'there were no politics in our movement' but, generally speaking, in the past 'people of conservative views were on the whole against cremation' whereas those who were 'more or less on the left were in favour of it' (*Report*, 1954: 11).

The key, though, was not how the cremation movement 'officially' regarded itself, but how it was actually viewed from the outside by the institutions it was attempting to persuade, and some cremationists showed that they were clear on this question. Addressing the 1951 ICF Congress on 'The Church and Cremation', a Danish delegate drew a parallel between the Church's attitude to the labour movement and its attitude to the cremation movement. He argued that both movements represented social progress and were therefore resisted by conservatism as embodied in the Church hierarchy. He did not comment on the fact that there was a certain crossover in personnel between both movements, which must also have been noticed by the Church. There were at least two other unmentioned aspects of the cremation movement that made it comparable with the labour movement. First, it was very aware of its own history (though, and again like the labour movement, the lessons drawn from this history varied greatly) and, second, it was highly internationalist-minded (at least in respect of Western societies). Yet, in fairness to Michelfelt and Hazemann, it seems that the movement they were addressing in the 1950s was one that was undergoing significant change. Although anti-clericalism characterized large sections of the European cremation movement before 1939, this seems to have begun to change in the aftermath of the Second World War. Indeed, Robert Hazemann himself, on remarking that pro- and anti-cremation sentiment broadly corresponded to political affiliation, (those with left-wing political views being generally pro-cremation), added that this generalization 'was true before the war but not after the war' (*Report*, 1954: 11). Others, such as French cremationist Dr Godard in an interview with *Le Monde* in 1984, noted the same change: before 1939, he argued:

> The 'family' of cremationists at that time was made up largely of free thinkers, rather anti-clerical … The battle changed progressively. Having become outdated, anti-clericalism gave way to the public health argument, to avoid the risk of epidemics. Then, this risk having diminished, another argument was put forward; lack of space (*Pharos*, 50(2), 1984: 71).

Unlike their pre-war counterparts those who professed the 'non-political' nature of the cremation movement after 1945 were not being disingenuous, as people with more conservative views were increasingly coming to support cremation and its anti-clericalism was becoming a thing of the past.

Curiously, given his comments in 1954 and the fact that the cremation movement was broadening out politically in some countries, Hazemann was more overtly 'political' in a paper he gave at the 1957 ICF Congress. Discussing Catholic countries and opposition to cremation, Hazemann identified three types, or groups, of thinking on the situation: 'communist', 'socialist' and 'Christian democrat'. These three positions, according to Hazemann, formed two blocks, an extreme left and, more often, a coalition composed of Christian democrats and socialists. Hazemann was critical of the policy followed by those in the coalitions as the 'leftish elements have been the prisoners of clerical elements. Thus arises the incomprehensible situation of a [progressive] government which retreats on the subject [of cremation]' (*Report*, 1957: 46).

There was similar criticism of the political left in 1960 when a delegate thought it 'remarkable' that many labour movement leaders seemed 'indifferent to cremation', particularly given its cheapness and despite the fact that many personally supported it. These comments imply that cremationists still saw their natural constituency as drawn from the political left and were disappointed when the left-wing governments did not use their power to promote cremation. And this was regardless of the political changes occurring within the ranks of cremationists themselves.

Another aspect of the 'political' struggle here was that the Catholic Church, as well as having immense political influence itself, often enjoyed the support of Catholic political parties. Thus, in Belgium, for example, there was fierce opposition to cremation both from the Catholic Church and the parties overtly aligned to it. In his 1957 paper Hazemann touched on another aspect of the post-1945 change in the political complexion of the cremation movement when he remarked that 'the extreme left has painful recollections of cremation, for people were cremated alive during the war'. Thus, as more conservative elements were beginning to support cremation, so those from the political tradition that originally supported it had begun to reject it. However, even before 1945, cremation advocacy was by no means limited to the progressive elements of Western society, as some on the extreme right also favoured it. In 1933 the American cremationist Hugo Erichsen remarked that the new Hitler-led government in Germany favoured cremation and would introduce the long-awaited national German cremation law, which it subsequently did. The following year Erichsen noted that Germany had almost half of the 234 crematoria in Europe and that its 8 per cent cremation rate was second only to that of the Swiss (12 per cent). He also added that in Italy, Mussolini was not opposed to cremation (CANA, 1933: 39). Of course, the Nazi attachment to cremation reached its terrible

apogee with its application in concentration camps to dispose of the regime's victims. This was the most extreme example of cremation being advocated and supported by 'non-progressives' and employed for anti-progressive ends.

Not all cremationists in non-fascist countries were progressives who abhorred fascism. For example, at least one American cremationist involved in the Cremation Association of North America (CANA) appeared to be favourably disposed to the 1930s European fascist regimes. In a talk on 'Observations on Europe', Ray Brennan first discussed the 'labor difficulties' and widespread strikes in the United States. He then mentioned the feeling of a 'war atmosphere' in much of Europe and followed this with comments on Mussolini's great oratorical abilities and intelligence. After commenting on communism in Europe, Brennan returned to strikes at home and emphasized the need to instil the idea in cremation workers that they were 'all capitalists' and that they could all 'rise up the ladder' in their work. He argued that those in the cremation businesses needed to use ideas from Europe in order to achieve this and thereby 'stave off this leftist uprising and keep our businesses intact in a clean American way' (CANA, 1937: 40–44). The European ideas he was referring to were fascist ones. In the post-war world of Cold War antagonism to the Soviet bloc, CANA spent some time discussing international questions that appeared to have nothing to do with cremation. At the 1953 CANA annual convention, for example, Charles Howard spoke on 'Facing Soviet Russia' and Christian Science advocate Gordon Walker addressed the convention on 'Communist Aims in Russia'.

These observations on CANA indicate how it was somewhat exceptional in the cremation movement: it was composed almost entirely of businessmen who sought profits in cremation and who were largely uninterested in the progressive aspects of the practice. The one obvious exception to this was Hugo Erichsen, who regularly delivered papers to annual conventions on international developments in the cremation movement. Apart from him, no one showed much interest in the evangelistic aspect of cremation, and it is somewhat ironic that evidence of an interest in wider international questions emerged only after Erichsen had died and because the Cold War was in full swing.

In contrast to Nazi Germany, the behaviour of other European authoritarian regimes tended to emphasize the 'progressive' nature of cremation advocacy. The tentative moves towards using cremation begun by Portugal ended when an authoritarian regime took power in 1938, cremation only became a possibility again when the regime ended in 1976. A very similar situation occurred in Spain, where the Second Republic began to consider implementing cremation only for the Franco regime to prevent it. Again, cremation only had a real chance when the Franco regime was ended. Of course, both these countries had a very strong Roman Catholic tradition, and it is unlikely that cremation would have made significant advances. But at least cremation would have been an option for those who desired it, as, for example, in Argentina.

The modern cremation movement was inspired by events in revolutionary France and could not help but be regarded as 'political'. Cremation was later explicitly stated as a means to combat the Catholic Church by freemasons, and the movement's consequent attempts to claim its 'non-political' credentials, in order, presumably, to avoid drawing the Catholic Church's direct fire, rang hollow and predictably failed to convince. In this sense freemasons, by being so open about their intentions for cremation from the outset, at the very least ensured that the Catholic Church would come out as an even stronger opponent of cremation in the short and medium term. However, the cremation movement was a diverse one and differed considerably from country to country. It appeared most 'political' where opinions on the topic were most polarized, and where freemasons were strong and actively involved. These were also the places where the Catholic Church was often the strongest. Arguably, Britain was the key example of a country where the 'non-political' label could best be applied from the outset: though clearly informed by 'progressive' ideas, early cremationists were respectable middle-class individuals who could bring their influence to bear on government policy with relative ease. Of course, there were radicals involved in Britain too, such as ex-militant Chartist William Price, but they were the exception rather than the rule. From relatively early on, politicians from the political right, such as Conservative Bonar Law, chose cremation, and even Winston Churchill supported it (although he was eventually buried, much to the chagrin of the British Cremation Society). Thus *Pharos*'s claim in 1937 that cremationists were from 'almost all schools of political and religious thought' rung fairly true in Britain, at least. This relatively unpolarized attitude towards cremation, again probably due to the Catholic Church's relative lack of influence in Britain, must partly explain the British Cremation Society's success. But Britain was relatively exceptional in this sense, and it was not surprising that the Catholic Church only changed its mind on cremation in the context of a post-war European cremation movement that was far less tinged with anti-clericalism than it had been before 1939. **Lewis H. Mates**

See also Argentine cremations; Austrian cremation societies; CANA; freemasonry in Italy; Nazi cremations.

References

Boone, P.C., Heuer, A. and Raild, N.J. (1960), 'The Sociological Aspects of Cremation', paper given at the ICF Congress in Stockholm, CRE/D4/1960/6.

CANA (1924–54), Reports of CANA Annual Conventions, CRE/A/US4.

CSA.

Hazemann, Robert (1972), 'The Social and Cultural Aspect of Cremation', paper presented at the Grenoble ICF Congress.

ICF Committee for Propaganda (1963), 'The World Problems of the Disposal of the Dead', paper presented at the ICF Congress, Berlin, CRE/D4/1963/3.

Jupp, Peter (1999), 'History of the Cremation Movement in Great Britain: the First 125 Years', *Pharos*, 65(1): 18–25.

Prothero, Stephen (2001), *Purified by Fire. A History of Cremation in America*. Berkeley University of California Press.

Report of the International Cremation Congress in Prague (1936), CRE/D4/1936/3.

Report of the ICF Triennial Congress at Oslo (1954), CRE/D4/1954/2.

Report of the ICF Triennial Congress at Zurich (1957), CRE/D4/1957/2.

POLLUTION PREVENTION AND CONTROL ACT 1999 (UK)

Since its inception in the nineteenth century, cremation in the UK had been regulated primarily for the purposes of protecting individual welfare and public health. However, its inclusion in the regime of Local Air Pollution Control under Part I of the Environmental Protection Act 1990 shifted the regulatory focus, at least in part, into more mainstream environmental law. Bringing cremation into the Local Air Pollution Control (LAAPC) regime was significant in that polluting emissions from the process are now subject to control not only as a potential threat to human health but also as a potential threat to the environment in their own right.

The part of the Environmental Protection Act that governs cremation is currently being replaced by a new system of Integrated Pollution Prevention and Control (IPPC) adopted under the Pollution Prevention and Control Act 1999 pursuant to new obligations in European law. Under the new system, cremation will be governed by the Local Air Pollution Prevention and Control regime (LAPPC). The introduction of the new regime has been phased and, after a delay on the initial implementation timetable, is now in place for cremation. The law relating to pollution control for cremation is to be found principally in the Pollution Prevention and Control (England and Wales) Regulations 2000, SI 2000, No.1973, specifically in Schedule 1 at Chapter 5.1 'Disposal of Waste by Incineration'. The control regime treats emissions from crematoria in much the same way as emissions from any other small-scale incineration plant. So far as cremation is concerned, the change in legislative regime is unlikely to make much difference in the foreseeable future. Emissions from crematoria into the air will continue to be monitored and controlled by local authorities. The main difference is that the guidance that provides the context for the regulatory system will eventually be supplied by the European Commission's IPPC Bureau rather than the Department of the Environment, Food and Rural Affairs (DEFRA). **Karen Morrow**

PORTE-COCHERE

Designed to be a porch large enough for wheeled vehicles to pass through, the porte-cochère has become an essential feature of crematoria worldwide, playing, as it does, both a functional and a symbolic role. It enables the coffin to be removed from the hearse with dignity, while at the same time offering protection from capricious climates to those alighting from vehicles. The porte-cochère holds a symbolic significance in affording an architectural expression to the threshold to another state. Furthermore, in British crematoria, where people are brought in through this entrance, but exit from another, the porte-cochère is invested with a special importance. Bearing this in mind, architects have traditionally afforded careful consideration to the proportions and visual impact of this feature. Solutions range from cantilevered canopies, to columned porticos employing a variety of treatments. A colonnade is sometimes arranged to run along the front of the crematorium, allowing mourners to descend simultaneously with the funeral staff alighting under the porte-cochère.

Current recommendations, first issued to architects of British crematoria by the British Government's Department of the Environment in 1978, stipulate that the minimum length necessary for a porte-cochère is about 5.5 metres with a clear height of at least three metres. The road between the kerb of the entrance to the chapel and the outer walls or columns of the porte-cochère ought not to be less than 2.7 metres. The outer wall or columns should always be based on a kerb wide enough to allow car doors to swing clear (Arber, 2001: 84). It was suggested in 1950 that the porte-cochère might become 'one of the individual features distinctive to crematoria, not always required in ecclesiastical buildings' (Orr, 1950: 3). Architects have certainly risen to the challenge, providing a wide variety of interpretations worldwide. **Hilary Grainger**

See also architecture.

References

Arber, R.N. (ed.) (2001), *Directory of Crematoria*, Maidstone: Cremation Society of Great Britain, 83–86.

Dahl, J.L. Seaton (1945), 'The Ideal Crematorium', in P.M. Jones, (ed.), *Cremation in Britain*, London: Pharos.

Orr, H.R.W. (1950), 'Crematorium Architecture', *Pharos*, 16(4): 2–5.

PORTUGAL

The first attempts at introducing cremation in Portugal must be set in the context of the changing status of public cemeteries that began in the mid-1830s, with the new liberal regime and the influence of Romanticism. Romanticist cemeteries offered the newly emerging Portuguese bourgeoisie an opportunity to express their social status through the erection of magnificent mausoleums. In the 1840s, for example, many of these tombs included cinerary urn motifs but since, at that time, cremation was not possible nor even desired in Portugal the use of such motifs on sepulchral monuments was merely metaphoric. In fact, these urns were copies taken from ancient Roman tombs, and their use was intended to mimic a classical aesthetic. Moreover, in funeral speeches as well as in epitaphs, the word corpse (*corpo, cadáver*) was regularly replaced by ashes (*cinzas*). This, too, was just a metaphor, possibly related to a repugnance towards the odour of putrefaction – a response that became quite generalized during the Romantic period. The horror of this smell, often identified with miasma, was a consequence of a new way of seeing death as a melancholic loss. Macabre connotations, so emphasized in the Baroque period, almost disappeared as Romanticist tombs, surrounded with aromatic trees and bushes, came to be viewed as beautiful and with no reference whatsoever to the putrefaction of corpses. Much of the repugnance towards miasma had its root in medical ideas popularized in urban areas from the later eighteenth century. Indeed, it is not difficult to understand why the first favourable voices supporting cremation in Portugal came from some radical doctors. Their medical views were not intended as any kind of de-Christianization of cemeteries.

This real motivation was obvious, for example, in an article by 'S.H.' published in the journal *O Instituto* at Coimbra in 1857. ('S.H.' was probably the Marquis of Sousa Holstein, son of the Duke of Palmela). The article traces a highly negative panorama of Portuguese cemeteries, arguing that any form of inhumation was poisonous for the living, even in remote areas and when apparently fulfilling hygienic standards. The only alternative was the generalized burning of corpses and the closure of Portuguese cemeteries. The author 'S.H.' was,

himself, inspired by A. Bonneau's article recently published in the journal *Presse Littéraire*. The 'S.H.' article alleged that, in some Portuguese towns and in most rural districts, the existing cemeteries were inadequate, with many not functioning according to the law. This was true. Even Lisbon metropolitan cemeteries were criticized by 'S.H.', despite their location inside ancient farms and outside the city. The author also referred to the British cemetery of Lisbon as possessing even more defects. All Portuguese rural cemeteries were seen as in an even worse condition as regards miasma. The 'S.H.' article reflected an extreme belief in the fatal consequences of miasmas, especially when carried by the wind into the city. Similarly, rainwater from cemeteries could harmfully infiltrate the wells and city water conduits. 'S.H.' was motivated by medical beliefs. He argued that cremation technology was already available and was fairly cheap. As for religion, he suggested that a chapel for religious services should exist beside each crematorium. Ashes should be enclosed in urns and delivered to the family or buried next to each crematorium. Family columbaria could also be built as sanctuaries of reverence towards the ashes of one's ancestors. These monuments, he proposed, should have a bust of the deceased on the top of each urn, to prevent a crisis in the craft of applying fine art to tomb design.

Despite the early date of this article, cremation had been proposed in 1800, half a century earlier, albeit somewhat timidly, by the doctor and professor Vicente Teles. Even then, cremation was seen as a solution to the dangers of miasmas. However, Teles probably knew that establishing cremation in Portugal was, at that time, socially unacceptable, especially given the population's deep religious beliefs that would change only slowly. Even after 1857, the 'S.H.' article had no direct impact on advancing cremation. The general view was that the article was exaggerated and radical, written by a putrefaction phobic. It could not be taken as representative of Portuguese public opinion, even amongst doctors and in urban areas. Portuguese society was not yet prepared to cremation.

It was not until the 1870s that some Portuguese doctors and politicians began to discuss the issue of cremation more overtly. In 1876 Lisbon municipality proposed an enlargement of the metropolitan Prazeres Cemetery, and the municipality's vice-president suggested the erection of catacombs to enable the transfer of bones from ancient graves. Seeing his opportunity, the Marquis of Sousa Holstein, adopting the ideas behind his 1857 argument, publicly proposed the burning of all corpses as an alternative solution to the enlargement of Lisbon's cemeteries. In December 1879 a report, commissioned by Lisbon municipality and directed by Téofila Ferreira, suggested radical ideas for controlling the growth of cemeteries and making death more hygienic. This report, published in 1880, presented several solutions to the problems facing Lisbon cemeteries, which involved a new necropolis outside the city. Whilst it proposed retaining the older metropolitan cemeteries, these would be only for inhumations in existing private vaults and chapels. One of the commission's aims had been to end the existing practice of using communal graves and to give everyone the right to an individual grave, and it proposed to resolve the problem of finding space by creating the new necropolis and building a crematorium. In the new metropolitan cemetery, all temporary graves would be exhumed after five years, and the bones transferred to catacombs. If the bones were not requested by the relatives they would be cremated. A direct cremation of corpses right after the death should also be possible, but only as an option for those who wanted it. This report showed the obvious inspiration of Haussmann's ideas for a new necropolis in Paris, located far from the city and served by railway, where all the corpses should be cremated. Reference was also made to similar proposed developments in Berlin and Rio de Janeiro.

On 12 September 1880 there were Portuguese delegates present at the special session of the International Hygiene Congress in Milan, who both witnessed experiments in cremation and established an International Commission on the topic, passing resolutions calling for cremation to be made optional in the laws of all countries. Nevertheless, neither the 1879 report conclusions nor these 1880 international resolutions were applied in Portugal – even in Lisbon. No new metropolitan necropolis was established in this city; instead, the existing cemeteries were enlarged and catacombs were built. Cremation in the cemeteries of Lisbon remained postponed for many years. However, if it had been implemented in the 1880s, cremation would have probably met with complete disinterest.

Meanwhile, in Europe, several doctors looked into the matter of miasmas from a more scientific perspective, the eminent doctor Ricardo Jorge being Portugal's chief researcher. Analysing air and water at cemeteries in Lisbon and Oporto, he concluded that miasmas were not as harmful as the Romanticist view implied. For Ricardo Jorge, the air around a cemetery was as pure as in any other place and the deep waters of their subsoils were harmless so long as land was chosen well and other sanitary prescriptions observed. His conclusions took a considerable time to spread, especially amongst politicians but, with the progressive demystification of the danger of miasma, some cremationist proposals that were based exclusively on medical axioms were temporarily abandoned. By the close of the nineteenth century cremation had become more and more an ideological matter. In addition to some doctors, some freemasons and republicans (almost all of whom were also freemasons and who had begun to undermine the monarchy during the same period) also came to favour cremation, with those of a positivist outlook envisaging it, in particular, as a public service. However, most of their discussions on cremation remained theoretical and restricted to small coteries.

Cremation only became possible in Portugal in the aftermath of the republican revolution which culminated on 10 October 1910 when progressive republicans took political power and ended the monarchy. In the following two years, a great deal changed in Portuguese cemeteries. One aspect of such change were plans to construct a crematorium in one of the Lisbon metropolitan cemeteries – Alto de São João. Work began and some tombs had to be moved in order to make space for the rather visible location of the crematorium in the cemetery – immediately after the entrance, facing the north side of the main avenue. By 1912 the more radical republicans wanted to de-Christianize the cemeteries and open mortuary chapels to all creeds. However, even in Lisbon, the vast majority of the population was opposed to this, and the republicans were unable to proceed with their plans. Before the crematorium in Alto de São João cemetery could be completed the initial revolutionary fervour faded and construction work subsequently became intermittent taking many years. Indeed, it was not until 1925 that Alto de São João Crematorium was officially opened, at the insistence of some republicans and freemasons who gathered in a congress in 1924 and passed a resolution supporting cremation. The crematorium was designed as a Neo-Romanesque chapel but with no explicit Christian symbols – decorated only tile panels by Carlos Botelho, representing cremation in antiquity. A small iron rail, in Art Nouveau style, marks the place where relatives and friends see the coffin for the last time, before it enters the crematorium furnace. Alfredo Guisado, himself a freemason and a member of the municipality, also promoted important ideological improvements in the cemetery of Alto de São João, including the erection of several monuments dedicated to great Portuguese republican figures.

The first corpse was cremated in Alto de São João Crematorium on 28 November 1925. Yet, in the 11 years between 1925 and 1936 there were only 21 voluntary cremations in Portugal, and most of these were of foreigners who had died in the country. The truth was that the first crematorium in Portugal was established by, and for, a very small group of people and this explains why there were no crematoria built in other Portuguese cemeteries during the following decades. Very few wanted to be cremated, and those who did lived almost exclusively in Lisbon, the most open-minded and cosmopolitan Portuguese city.

Alto de São João Crematorium was closed after 1936 due to the consolidation of the dictatorial regime, the Estado Novo. It did not re-open again until 1985, although the British cremator company Dowson & Mason had received earlier enquiries from Portugal (immediately after the dictatorial regime was brought down by a coup d'état). Between 1936 and 1985 only three corpses were cremated in Alto de São João: exception was made as all three were foreigners.

Table 1 gives the official statistics of numbers cremated in Alto do São João Crematorium between 1985 and 1987 and 1994 and 1996.

Table 1 Cremations at Alto de Sãu João Crematorium, 1985–87 and 1994–96

Year	Number of cremations	Foreigners as % of total cremations
1985	18 (including 10 foreigners).	56
1986	67 (including 41 foreigners).	61
1987	119 (including 66 foreigners).	55
1994	598 (including 107 foreigners).	18
1995	744 (including 135 foreigners).	18
1996	792 (including 99 foreingers).	13

As can be clearly seen from the table, foreigners comprised the majority of cremations in the early years, but by 1996 Portuguese cremations far outnumbered those of foreigners. It should be noted that cremations of bone remains in Alto de São João Crematorium showed an increase similar to that of corpse cremation, although the numbers were slightly lower until 1996. That year, over 7 per cent of deaths in Lisbon resulted in cremations.

In December 1995 official permission was granted to open a new crematorium in the Prado do Repouso Cemetery, in the city of Oporto – the largest city in northern Portugal. This crematorium was designed a couple of years earlier by the architect Manuel da Silva Lessa and built in an extremely separate and isolated area of the cemetery. A special garden was created around it, featuring a contemporary sculptural work by Armando Alves. In 1996, 53 cremations took place here. The number of cremations increased in subsequent years: 66 in 1997; 83 in 1998; 156 in 1999; 162 in 2000; 240 in 2001; 306 in 2002 and 394 in 2003. The statistics tells us also that, initially, many of those cremated in Oporto were Hindu immigrants from India. Portuguese are now also being cremated there, although cremation clearly still accounts for a very small proportion of the total deaths. In Lisbon cremation is more popular: in 2002 over 23 per cent of deaths in the city resulted in cremations. This city even has a second crematorium, built in the new

Carnide Cemetery, which opened in the mid-1990s.

We should mention that these three major crematoria in Portugal – two in Lisbon and one in Oporto – are also receiving corpses from other regions where there are no crematoria. This is presumably also the case for Portugal's fourth crematorium, officially approved in 2000 and built in the small town of Ferreira do Alentejo (in southern Portugal). The municipality did not provide clear information about the reasons behind the construction of this crematorium – the first to function outside the metropolitan areas of Lisbon and Oporto. However, an undated statistic for cremations there was provided: 145 Portuguese, 65 Germans, 51 British, 31 Irish, 16 Dutch, 11 Swiss, 9 French, 7 Ukrainians, 6 Americans and some other nationalities are represented, including a few Africans. Overall, foreigners still represent the majority in these figures. Presumably, most of these cremations did not come from the small town of Ferreira do Alentejo, but originated in the Alentejo and Algarve holiday districts. Nevertheless, cremation in Portugal is increasingly gaining a degree of acceptance, and a few other crematoria are now planned.

In the town of São João da Madeira (near Oporto), construction of a crematorium was begun in 1982 – following a request by some families – but was never completed. Today, the municipality is now considering finishing the work, since some of its citizens are being cremated in Oporto. In the city of Guarda (in north-eastern Portugal), a crematorium was planned by the architect who designed its new cemetery. However, the crematorium was not built as, taking into account the number of possible users, it was considered too expensive. The municipality now claims that, in order to be an affordable investment, the Catholic Church in this city should promote cremation within the religious community or, at least, publicly state its acceptance. This deep concern to inform the population about the Catholic Church's toleration of cremation was common to almost all Portuguese crematoria projects in the late twentieth and early twenty-first centuries. In the 1990s, for example, leaflets were published and distributed in the major cemeteries of Lisbon and Oporto, all including official statements by local leaders of the Catholic Church (as requested by the two municipalities) saying that cremation was perfectly acceptable.

In conclusion, cremation in Portugal is increasing, especially in urban areas, where religious prejudices and traditions are becoming less deep-rooted. Crematoria are now usually considered in plans for new urban cemeteries or reforms for existing ones, such as in the city of Coimbra or in the Oporto suburb of Matosinhos. There is also a plan for a crematorium to serve several towns of the Leiria district. A site at the very new necropolis in the city of Bragança (in north-eastern Portugal) is already reserved for the building of a crematorium, when it becomes necessary. There is a similar situation in Faro (the main city in the Algarve), where the new necropolis will open in late 2004, with the crematorium scheduled for a future phase of works. **Francisco Queiroz**

References

Costa, Felícia (1997), *Fogo e Imortalidade*, Lisbon: Câmara Municipal de Lisboa.

Catroga, Fernando (1999), *O céu da memória – cemitério romântico e culto cívico dos mortos*, Coimbra: Minerva.

Ferreira, Teófilo, Camara, Joaquim J.R. and Namorado, Joaquim A.O. (1880), *Os cemiterios em Lisboa – parecer apresentado à Câmara Municipal de Lisboa*, Lisbon: Typographia Portugueza.

Jorge, Ricardo (1885), *Hygiene social aplicada à nação portugueza*, Oporto: Liv. Civilização.

Queiroz, Francisco (2002), 'Os cemitérios do Porto e a arte funerária oitocentista em Portugal – consolidação da vivência romântica na perpetuação da memória', unpublished PhD thesis, Universidade do Porto, Vol.1, Tome II: 390–96.

'S.H.' [Sousa Holstein] (1857), 'Inconvenientes dos cemitérios – sua substituição pela ustão dos cadaveres', *O Instituto* (Coimbra), V: 175.

Teles, Vicente C.S. Silva (1800), *Memoria sobre os prejuízos causados pelas sepulturas dos cadaveres nos templos e methodos de os prevenir*, Lisbon: Officina da Casa Literária do Arco do Cego.

POSTMORTEM EXAMINATION

The move to establish cremation has, in most countries in the nineteenth and twentieth centuries, raised legal issues over the proper registration of death and the cause of death. A key concern lay with the potential use of cremation to remove the evidence of murder, as by poisoning, by the elimination of the corpse and any subsequent possibility of exhumation for legal reasons. **Douglas J. Davies**

See also Brodrick Committee (for the UK); Certificates and Medical Forms (UK); Law; Germany; Namibia.

PRATT, HONORETTA

Honoretta, Honora or Heneretay Pratt was frequently cited in histories of cremation as a forerunner of cremation on account of hers in 1769. She was born on 29 September 1679 to a father, Sir John Brooks, who had been knighted for his father's services to the Royalist cause in the English Civil War, and to a mother who was the daughter of Sir Hardress Waller, the regicide who signed the death warrant for, and helped arrange the execution of, King Charles I. Through her mother she was related to the Earls of Shelburne. She married John Pratt and went to live in Ireland, where he became deputy vice-treasurer and, then, constable of Dublin Castle. In 1725 he was imprisoned after large discrepancies were discovered in the accounts for which he was responsible. After his imprisonment, he retired to his property at Cabra Castle. Pratt's older brother, Benjamin, had been provost of Trinity College, Dublin, and both had been friends of Jonathan Swift.

In *The Toast* William King described Pratt, before his downfall, as 'a husband without a wife', and certainly after 1725, if not before, Honoretta returned to live in England. From 1710 onwards she features in the correspondence and papers of Swift. By 1735 she had taken up permanent residence in the London house of Lord Shelburne and was spending a great deal of time in the company of Katherine Darnley, the illegitimate daughter of James II and dowager Duchess of Buckingham. She was with the duchess's son, the Duke of Buckingham, when he died in Rome in 1735. The death of the duchess in 1743 could have been a difficult time for her because of the duchess's surprising appointment of Sir Robert Walpole and Lord Hervey, arch Whigs, as her executors. This put into their hands papers which must have revealed at least some of the duchess's treasonable activities on behalf of her brother, the Old Pretender, and Honoretta was probably privy to some of these.

She survived, however, until 1769, when she died a very wealthy woman through the liberality of the duchess and an annuity under the will of the Earl of Shelburne. In her will she asked that 'my Body be burnt upon the place where my late dear niece Ann Place lies buried'. Whether – and, if so, how – her wishes were carried out, contemporary accounts do not agree; but, if they were carried out, it is almost certain that it was by a chemical cremation using unslacked lime. In the 'new' burial ground of St George's, Hanover Square, which been opened in 1764, there used to be a memorial stone to her which bore the inscription:

> This worthy woman believing that the Vapours arising from the graves in the Church yards of populous Cities may prove harmful to the inhabitants and resolving to extend to future times as far as she was able that Charity and benevolence which distinguished her thro life ordered that her body should be burnt in hope that others would follow the example a thing too hastily censured by those who did not enquire her motives.

It is not known for sure when the stone was erected, but the negative of a photograph of the stone in the possession of the Cremation Society of Great Britain bears the legend 'the inscription was revived by a kinsman in 1810'. In 1910 the Cremation Society had the stone cleaned. The last record of the stone is in the lists of monuments in the Public Record Office and Westminster City Archives which were compiled when the burial ground was developed under the St George Hanover Square Burial Ground Act 1964. These give no clue as to what became of the stone. **Stephen White**

References

White, Stephen, (2001), 'Honretta Pratt: Cremated 1769?', *Pharos International*, 67(1): 12–17.
Annual Register, 1769: 133.
Gentleman's Magazine, 39, 1769: 461.
Gentleman's Magazine, 49, 1779: 256.
St. James' Chronicle 26–28 September, 1769: 3d.
Middlesex Journal, 26–28 September, 1769: 3c.

PREMATURE BURIAL

The fear of waking up inside a coffin under six

feet of earth has been with humanity ever since coffin burials became common in the sixteenth and seventeenth centuries. In 1743 the French physician Jean-Jacques Bruhier translated a Latin thesis about apparent death, with some evocative additions of his own. His book arrived just at the right time, when people began to doubt the traditional Christian dogma about life and death, and to speak of a process of dying that might not be irreversible. It became an international bestseller and triggered a pan-European fear of being buried alive. People placed notes in their wills requesting that their bodies should be kept above ground for two or three days, or that an artery should be cut before they were buried. In Germany, Bruhier's notions of putrefaction as the only certain sign of death were taken to their logical extreme, and waiting mortuaries were erected all over the German states. In these remarkable establishments, corpses were incubated in a warm, humid atmosphere until they were rotten and bloated. Only then could these corpses be buried, since waking up in a coffin was considered the most dreadful fate that could happen to a human being, and the aim was to prevent premature burials at any cost.

The books by Bruhier and other anti-premature burial propagandists contain many horrible stories of people either being buried alive or narrowly escaping this dire fate. Some of them were old folk legends, like the tale of the lady buried with a valuable ring on her finger. She was disinterred by a greedy verger who tried to cut off her finger to steal the ring; in this moral tale, the prematurely buried lady awoke with a piercing scream, and the thieving menial fell dead on the spot. There are also many accounts of corpses and skeletons found in strange, contorted positions, indicating that they had been buried alive. But while much was made, for example, of a corpse found turned on its side, this could simply be the result of the coffin being tilted when lowered into the grave. A contorted face or drawn-up hands could be results of natural postmortem changes, as could a burst coffin caused by the build-up of intestinal gases. The old reports of prematurely buried people gnawing or even eating their own fingers in their agony were probably misinterpretations of rodents having fed off the corpse. Still, there have been some *bona fide* cases, mainly during cholera epidemics, of people mistakenly declared dead, put in a coffin and buried, who have

knocked on the coffin lid or otherwise been found to be alive. Thus, as discussed in detail in my book *Buried Alive*, the fear of being buried alive, though vastly exaggerated, was not entirely unfounded.

After the discovery of the stethoscope, and the value of using heartbeat (auscultation) as a sign of death, the European fear of premature burial gradually abated from the 1840s onward. The last German waiting mortuaries were closed in the 1890s. Nevertheless, the London Society for the Prevention of Premature Burials was active as late as the 1910s, and there was also organized anti-premature agitation from various American quacks and spiritualists. The growing practice of embalming and cremation in the late nineteenth century effectively served to deter the fear of being buried alive. The American morticians were right to claim that a corpse that had passed through their embalming workshop would never wake up again. Cremation was another solution for people fearful of being buried alive and, doubtless, served to increase its popularity. Still, there was the old story of the horrific, muffled scream coming from the coffin as it went into the crematorium oven. **Jan Bondeson**

References

Bondeson, Jan (2001), *Buried Alive*, New York and London: WW Norton.

Bruhier, J-J. (1746–49), *Dissertation sur l'incertitude des signes de la mort*, vols 1–2, Paris.

PRICE, DR WILLIAM

The doctor Dr William Price, who was prosecuted and acquitted for cremating his infant child in 1884 is commonly, if not wholly accurately, said to have 'legalized' cremation in England and Wales. What his action in fact did was to break the deadlock between the Cremation Society of England, which wanted to press ahead with cremations at its crematorium at Woking, and the Home Office, which had threatened to prosecute the society if it did so. The Cremation Society had been given legal advice that cremation was not in itself unlawful and that, consequently, cremations could be carried out without breaking any law. The direction given to the jury by the judge, James Fitzjames Stephen, at Price's trial vindicated that opinion.

William Price was born in 1800 in Rudry, Glamorgan. His early years were passed in increasing poverty as his father, an Anglican clergyman, descended into insanity. In Rudry, he was affected by his acquaintance with industrial hardship and with the romance of the Celtic associations of the surrounding countryside. In 1814 he was apprenticed to a local surgeon-apothecary and in 1820 moved to London where he studied under some of the most eminent practitioners of their day: the surgeon Sir William Blizzard at the London Hospital in Whitechapel, the surgeon John Abernethy, the physician Richard Powell and the obstetrician, Robert Gooch. At the age of 21 he became a licentiate of the Society of Apothecaries and, a month later, the youngest-ever member of the Royal College of Surgeons. At this point he returned to the Llantrisant area of Glamorgan to set up a doctor's practice, and, apart from a few sojourns abroad – the most notable being in France in 1839 whither he fled, dressed as woman, in the wake of the Chartist riot at Newport – he remained there for the rest of his life.

Shortly after qualifying as a surgeon, he was elected by the workforce of the Ynysyngharad chain works in Pontypridd to be their doctor, a position he retained for more than 20 years. He was a radical, an individualist, and a Welsh cultural nationalist. He espoused Chartism of the physical, as opposed to moral, force variety. 'You shall not put a sword in my hand and a rope round my neck,' he memorably quoted himself as having said when recounting his part in the Newport uprising some 50 years earlier: 'If I take a sword in my hand I shall use it, and no one shall take it from me but at the cost of my life'. Price vehemently opposed vaccination, which had killed an infant brother of his. He had an entirely realistic appreciation of the hazards of surgery, which led to his relying on what might today be called alternative medicine. He also founded the first, albeit short-lived, cooperative society in Wales.

After the failure of Chartism, his individualism led him to espouse causes and champion views in a way that made him appear eccentric. There can be no doubt of the sincerity of his opinions, which he maintained virtually unchanged, and broadcast with vigour, throughout his life: his rhetoric was praised by Lady Charlotte Guest. There was also about Price, however, something of the showman and prankster. He was probably protected to some extent by the Crawshay family to which he seems to have acted a family doctor. He was also a personal friend of William Crawshay, the owner of the Cyfartha ironworks in Merthyr Tydfil, who was succeeded as owner by Robert, who was married to Rose Mary Crawshay, one of the original signatories of the Declaration of 1874 which led to the foundation of the Cremation Society of Great Britain: Price must have been at least acquainted with her. Francis Crawshay, Robert's stepbrother, and owner of the Treforest tin-plate works shared in Price's romantic notions of Welsh history.

Some have suggested that Price's increasing eccentricity was a symptom of a hereditary insanity, and certainly some aspects of his behaviour were very similar to those of his father. However, whether or not he suffered from any mental illness in the later part of his life, it is unlikely that it could have been inherited from his father if, as has been claimed, his father's disorder was caused by injuries received from a fall from a horse. On his first visit to France, Price claimed to have discovered, on a stone in the Louvre, a text written in hieroglyphics used by the ancient Druids, which only he could decipher and which validated his claim to be the Archdruid Morgannwg. He said that it had taken him 20 years to decipher the text and he published it as *Gwyllis yn Nayd* (*The Will of my Father*) in 1871. It was written in a form of Welsh that even contemporary Welsh speakers would have had some difficulty comprehending and, when translated into English, would have been opaque to all but those most deeply steeped in legendary Welsh literature and, perhaps, not even accessible to them. Possibly, it loses something in translation. Price also contended that Homer was born in a hamlet near Caerphilly and was the architect of Caerphilly Castle.

Price was a believer in the equality of the sexes, female emancipation and free love. He never married. In his forties he fathered three children with different mothers. Between 1882 and 1886 he fathered three more with his housekeeper. Two he called Iesu Grist, the Welsh for Jesus Christ, and it was the death and cremation of the first of these that led to his prosecution in 1884 at Glamorgan Assizes in Cardiff. The child had died, and Price's attempt to cremate his body in a barrel of petrol at

Caerlan, his farm high on a hillside at Llantrisant, had been halted by the local policeman who managed to extricate the corpse from the barrel with a stick. At the Assizes Price was charged with one offence of cremating, rather than burying, the body of his child, thereby causing a common nuisance, and another of cremating a body with intent to prevent the holding of an inquest. The prosecution contended that, since everyone, with certain exceptions, had a right to Christian burial, anyone who had the obligation of disposing of a dead body, or who undertook to dispose of it, could do so lawfully only by burying it: to cremate it was therefore illegal even if no nuisance were caused. The judge, Fitzjames Stephen, after a close analysis of both the legal and canonical authorities, rejected this contention and ruled, in effect, that any manner of dealing with a dead body was lawful so long as it did not cause a public nuisance or obstruct the coroner in the execution of his duty or outrage public decency. When it was finally left to the jury to decide whether Price had conducted his cremation in such a way as to cross these lines, they were unable to agree and the proceedings moved on to the next charge. The jury, after some prevarication, acquitted Price of this. The following morning, when the court reassembled to retry the first charge, the prosecution announced that it would be offering no evidence and Price was therefore acquitted. He completed the cremation of his son the same day.

By the time Price died in 1893 another crematorium had been opened in Manchester, and Cardiff itself had a small one on Flat Holm, the cholera quarantine island in the Bristol Channel. In accordance with the wishes expressed in his will, Price was cremated on a semi-open furnace on the spot where he had cremated Iesu Grist. He had marked it out previously with a staff topped by a crescent moon, now in the Welsh Folk Museum at St Fagan's. Tickets were printed for admission to the environs of the pyre, and estimates of the crowd attending the cremation ranged from 6000 to 20 000. Memorabilia of the cremations of Price and his son, such as the tickets for admission to his own and the medallions he had struck on the occasion of his son's, were finally dispersed in 1986 at an executor's sale of the estate of his daughter, Penelopen, who never married.

Price is commemorated in Llantrisant by a statue in the town centre and a plaque on the gatepost of the building where his house once stood, by a display at the Welsh Folk Museum at St Fagan's, and stained glass windows at in the north chapel of Glyntaff Crematorium, Pontypridd. **Stephen White**

References

Ap Nicholas, Islwyn (1940), *Dr William Price: A Welsh Heretic*, London: Foyles' Welsh Co. Ltd.

Bracegirdle, Cyril (1997), *Dr William Price – Saint or Sinner?*, Llanurst: Gwasg Carreg Gwalch.

Cule, John (1960), 'Dr William Price (1800–1893) of Llantrisant: A Study of an Eccentric. A Biography of a Pioneer of Cremation', unpublished MD thesis, University of Cambridge.

Davies, Brian (1980), 'Empire and Identity: The 'Case' of Dr William Price', in David Smith (ed.), *A People and a Proletariat: Essays in the History of Wales 1780–1980*, London: Pluto Press, 72–93.

Guy, John (1989), 'The Rudry Radical: Dr William Price of Ty'Nycoedcae', commemorative lecture delivered at Rudry to the Caerphilly Local History Society.

R v. Price (1884) 12 QBD 247; 15 Cox CC 389.

Richards, Haydn (1993), *Sacred Fire*, Port Talbot: Alun Books. (A novel.)

White, Stephen (2002), 'A Burial Ahead of its Time? The Crookenden Burial Case and the Sanctioning of Cremation in England and Wales', *Mortality*, 7(2): 171–90. Also, in a slightly different version, in T.G. Watkin (ed.) (2002), *The Trial of Dic Penderyn and Other Essays*, Welsh Legal History Society, 2: 151–79.

Q

QUAKERS (RELIGIOUS SOCIETY OF FRIENDS)

The Religious Society of Friends, despite amassing voluminous writings on faith and practice, has very little to say about death or the afterlife. Their central belief in the imminence of God – 'the Light of Christ Within' or 'that of God in everyone' in current usage – underlies Quaker disinterest in such matters. From the beginning of the movement, burial, however, was a contentious matter. Quakerism was born into the social, political and religious turmoil of the English Civil War. Quakers, like many other contemporary sects, railed against the established Church and were excluded from its rites, including burial. This principle of exclusion from mainstream religion necessitated, at a practical level, burial practices which were specifically Quaker. The establishment of Quaker burial grounds was a pressing concern from the outset. Their testimony to plain living led to a series of prescriptions regarding the rituals of death and burial. Gift-giving was proscribed, as was the holding of wakes; for over a century gravestones were expected to be as simple as possible, with only the names and dates of birth and death inscribed thereon. It is probable that the rise in the popularity of cremation among the general population in Britain found favour among Friends for these reasons.

Quaker literature (especially in the seventeenth and eighteenth centuries) has dealt substantially with practices of burial but rarely, if ever, touches on the practice of cremation. Although there are no specifically formal Quaker records concerning the disposal of Friends' bodies it is apparent from informal records that Quaker practice has closely mirrored (British) national trends. Since the 1960s Friends have displayed an increased awareness of environmental issues, which is likely to have increased the rate of cremation among them. In other parts of the world where Quakerism flourishes – in Kenya and the USA for instance – despite the variations in the form of Quaker faith and practice, preferences for cremation or burial are again likely to reflect the ambient social climate. Quakers throughout the world have never been much excited about the threshold of death. **Peter Collins**

R

RADEMAKER, L.A.

L.A. Rademaker, in the Netherlands, encountered cremation through his professional position as editor of *Het Vaderland* (*the Homeland*) in the early twentieth century. In his 1915 report, he noted that horror stories of cremation were incorrect and he set about writing an objective description of all aspects of cremation (Cappers, 1999: 150). Rademaker was a great advocate of cremation but was not entirely satisfied with the location of the columbarium on the site of Velsen Crematorium.

He believed it should be built on a hill, in the full light and sun. There were many reactions to Rademaker's 'propaganda', both positive and negative. It even led to a dispute between him and the Jesuit H. Bolsius, whose opinions were diametrically opposed to those of Rademaker.

In 1921 Rademaker was involved in the possible merger of the Association for Cremation 'the Facultatieve' (*Vereniging voor Lijkverbranding*) and the Workers' Association for Cremation (AVVL), as a commission and board member of the Hague department of 'the Facultatieve'. He was able to gain permission to make a film on the subject of cremation in 1923. Claiming that only the technical side of cremation would be depicted, he gained the approval of the other board members.

From 1930 onwards, Rademaker gave an increasing number of lectures on various aspects of cremation. He was always a great instigator of ideas during his career at the Association. He also wished to establish a Christian Association for cremation, for example, and a national day for commemoration of cremated persons. Rademaker had been a member of the board since 1928 and chief editor of the magazine of the association of Messages and Communiqués (*Berichten en Mededelingen*), until stepping down in 1946 and being made an honorary member of 'the Facultatieve' in 1947. **J.M.H.J. Keizer**

See also Netherlands: societies and law.

Reference

Cappers, Wim (1999), *Vuurproef voor een grondrecht*, Zutphen: Walburg Pers.

REMAINS

The remains resulting from cremation are treated in a variety of ways from society to society. Sometimes they are crushed, and sometimes simply gathered and placed in urns. **Douglas J. Davies**

See archaeology – Bronze Age; ashes; cineraria; cremains; cremulation; eternal reefs; fountain dispersal (Budapest); identity, memorials and memorialization; South Africa; Sweden; urns; Viking Sweden.

RESURRECTION

The Christian idea of resurrection has played a significant part in debates on cremation with its apparently destructive treatment of the body. Here one account deals with the broader background issues and another on the more specific focus of the resurrection of the body. Other entries also address these themes, such as **Catholic Church**.

RESURRECTION AND CHRISTIAN THOUGHT

Christian modes of burial were taken over from the Jews, but interpretations of death were directly modelled on beliefs about Jesus because earliest Christian testimony affirmed that he 'was raised from the dead'. Narratives told of his tomb being empty and described him appearing in bodily form to his disciples on several occasions. The subsequent belief in the resurrection of Jesus came to be pivotal for Christians whose hope for a life after death is based on the earliest Christians' experience of the resurrection of Jesus. These beliefs are relevant for modern cremation in three ways.

First, with the Christianization of Europe, burial became the dominant mode of disposal. Because the doctrine of bodily resurrection had been held in Europe and in the Mediterranean basin for nearly 2000 years those challenging burial were challenging long-established Christian tradition and authority. Second, the Church exercised a theoretical and practical custodianship of the bodies of Christian dead until the promised Day of Resurrection at the end of time. This set a complex framework of ethical sanctions around death and beliefs about disposal. In the modern era, therefore, cremation would come to be associated with secular movements, anti-Catholic funeral reform, and challenges to understandings of the human self. Third, the Church's position had been buttressed through its management and ownership of local burial grounds, and burial practices largely supported social class structures. Accordingly, cremation became perceived as the democratic mode of disposal that could serve as an instrument of social change, especially under left-wing governments.

In Europe before 1000 AD, cremation was practised by Vikings and by certain pagan groups.

Christians periodically used it used as a punishment for heretics and witches. Cremation thus acquired an anti-Christian reputation. Although it has sometimes been adopted as a deliberately secular and political gesture, it could not be widely promoted as an alternative to burial until modern times when alternative ideas about the role of the Church in society, doctrines about life after death and the secularization of the ownership and provision of burial grounds became promoted and accepted.

The New Testament

The starting point for Christian debates on the mode of disposal is the resurrection of Jesus and his appearances to his disciples. The disciples' accounts range from the physicalist – that he bore visible wounds of his crucifixion, to transformationist – that he could walk through doors. Nevertheless, Christian convictions rapidly formed around an expectation that, because Christ had been physically raised from the dead, those who believed in him would also be physically raised. 'Christ is the first-fruits of a whole harvest of the dead,' wrote St Paul in a key document, 1 Corinthians 15:20.

Paul's dominant metaphor in 1 Corinthians 15 is that of the seed. Sown as a natural body, the corpse will rise again as 'a spiritual body', a metaphor which carries ideas both of continuity and change. Paul's insistence on the resurrection of dead Christians is underlined by his statement, 'If Christ did not rise, then neither are the dead raised' (1 Corinthians: 16). Thus, for the first great Christian apologist, the concept of the resurrection of the body means both restoration and redemption of the person as a psychosomatic unit. It should be noted, however, that whilst Paul's seed metaphor remained the key New Testament metaphor for resurrection, it contrasts with his statement that the resurrection of Christians begins with their baptism (Romans 6). Meanwhile, and at intervals thereafter, Paul's belief in the psychosomatic unity of the person has regularly been challenged by views of the body as distinct from, and inferior to, the soul. In the modern era this has taken an additional form – among some Christians as well as non-believers – in which the body can be regarded as unnecessary for a future life after death.

Over the first two centuries AD, when the first Christian creeds were formulated, the Pauline assertion about the resurrection of the dead was transformed. Whilst for Paul the 'body' stood for a psychosomatic unity (following Jewish tradition), an emphasis on the resurrection of the flesh gained ground. J.G. Davies advanced four reasons for this. First, the first resurrection accounts had emphasized Jesus' physicality. Second, millennial beliefs arose in the second century, based on the Revelation of St John 20, which predicted the participation of the righteous dead in the 1000-year reign of the Messiah on earth – which meant that the righteous dead must therefore be physically raised on earth. Third, when Christian doctrines were challenged by Gnosticism, which stressed a body–soul dichotomy, claiming the flesh as evil and the soul as the core of personal identity, the Christians' doctrine of a physical resurrection became an appropriate weapon, stressing the potential goodness of the body and its future role. Fourth, as the Christian Church spread through societies of Greek culture, it encountered and gradually accepted a belief in the immortality of the soul. This set up an enduring tension between resurrection and immortality that was never resolved. Unwilling to relinquish the tradition about the resurrection of the body, the Church stressed this to help maintain a balance.

Patristic and medieval formulations

While Christian thought about the resurrection of the body never entirely abandoned the Pauline metaphor of the seed, in subsequent developments it proved not to be the dominant metaphor. The Christian Fathers sought metaphors to illustrate how, by the power of God, personal identity could survive death or be revived after it. The works of three Fathers of the Church exemplify this.

Irenaeus, in the second century AD, defended a material concept of the resurrection of the body against opponents arguing for a more spiritual understanding: 'The particles of our flesh – nourished by the eucharistic bread which was literally the flesh of Christ – would be reassembled by God so that no detail of bodily structure was lost' (Bynum, 1995: 59). From the second to the fourteenth centuries Christian doctrine, preaching and miracle-stories insisted on the resurrection of exactly the material parts of the body that had been laid in its grave (Bynum, 1995: 8). Origen, in the third century, sought to steer a middle course between the

Gnostics for whom there was no future for the body and those who favoured the reanimation of dead flesh. He employed the seed metaphor, stressing transformation over continuity, observing that, as humans regularly ate and excreted, so their bodies were not always the same. Bodies would not be reassembled with parts or organs entire. In heaven humans would have a spiritual and luminous body, without signs of age or gender. Augustine dictated the shape of Christian orthodoxy from the fifth until the twelfth century. He discarded the 'seed' metaphor, preferring the 'reassembled statue' wherein all particles would be reassembled. Bodily resurrection would be the restoration both of bodily material and bodily wholeness, and the cult of relics will have formed part of the context for his arguments. Resisting the problems raised by cannibalism, Augustine denied that eating and excretion processed the body (Bynum, 1995: 103). People would be raised aged around 30, with physical signs of gender and perhaps revealing scars. Augustine's stress on the yearning of the separated soul for reunion with the body had important effects for the medieval notion of flesh as essential for personhood. Yet he also argued that the mode of disposal – whether burial, cremation or exposure – would neither affect nor constrain God's power in resurrecting human beings. In *How to help the dead* he stressed concern for corpses as a natural and pious instinct; neither destruction, nor digestion, nor dissolution could finally affect the body's future resurrection. He stressed the return of every scrap of the body when it was being reforged at the end of time.

Thomas Aquinas of the thirteenth century dominated Catholic theology after Augustine. He rejected the metaphor of the seed on different grounds, holding that resurrection was not a natural process but a supernatural one. Like Origen, he came under some criticism for privileging personal identity over physical continuity. The resurrected body would be identical with the old, numerically and specifically but not qualitatively: it would be raised with a new quality of glory. Aquinas reinterpreted 1 Corinthians 15: 35, proposing that the two questions come from different opponents and concluding that the seed metaphor is the answer to the second question – that is, it illustrates the nature of the risen body but not its cause. Resurrection is the opposite of generation: bodies return by divine, and not natural, power. Bodies are not like clothes, taken off at death and put on again at resurrection. Immortality is an add-on. In the dead body there is no indication, power or inclination; and the soul does not yearn for the body.

Until the modern era no mainstream theologian, whatever their solution to the problems of personal identity in the resurrected life, denied the doctrine of the resurrection of the body. Under normal circumstances, God would reassemble and reanimate the same material particles out of which bodies had been once composed. Down to at least the seventeenth century, sermons, hymns and funeral customs offered Christians the hope of resurrection in terms of reunited fragments. The doctrine of the resurrection of the body survived the separation of the Western and Eastern Churches in the tenth century. It survived the Reformation; indeed, for Protestant reformers, the sovereignty of God over the dead was reinforced. Once prayers for the dead had been outlawed, no earthly influence could be brought to bear on their destiny. Their future was entirely in God's hands.

Furthermore, as death was the point at which all human influence over the dead ceased, funeral rituals could have no effect on them. As the English 1552 *Book of Common Prayer* instructed, the dead could only be committed, not commended. Funerals could benefit only the living; Calvinist liturgies particularly emphasized this point. Funeral rituals, therefore, unable to influence the postmortem destiny of the dead, took on a new emphasis, that of the earthly status of the survivor. In retrospect, this disjunction laid preconditions for the late twentieth century. In a society where death is seen as a natural, not supernatural, event and where there is neither belief in God nor in life after death, funeral rituals concentrate on benefiting the survivors, celebrating, in Davies' (2002) phrase, 'retrospective' rather than 'prospective' fulfilments of human identity. In the meantime, the secularizing tendencies of modernization brought about a complex of circumstances which seriously reduced popular belief in the resurrection of the body.

Attitudes to the resurrection in the modern era

In the UK the established status of the majority Anglican Church and the quasi-established character of the Church of Scotland helped to undergird the doctrine of the resurrection of the body. The key factor was their near-monopoly in the ownership of burial grounds. In the late eighteenth and early nineteenth centuries, the emergence of the first secular burial grounds began to awaken people to alternatives. Free Churchmen were often among the promoters of commercial burial grounds after 1820.

In the mid-nineteenth century the established Church's monopoly was weakened by two secularizing developments in the ownership of burial grounds and in attitudes to the corpse. In conditions of rapid industrialization and accompanying urbanization, the churches failed to extend their burial grounds, contributing to the scandalous use and re-use of the restricted and congested urban burial grounds. Body-snatchers raided burial grounds for medical specimens. Such scandals helped mould a new perspective on corpses, particularly as a public health issue. The decaying corpses in graveyards were believed to exude miasmas which were injurious to health. Corpses and burial grounds thus came to be seen not so much as a collection of bodies awaiting a supernatural future but as actively endangering the health of the living. Reformers such as Dr George Alfred Walker pointed out that the Church of England condoned practices which disturbed the bodies of the dead in ways inconsistent with their beliefs about respect for the corpse awaiting Christian resurrection. Concerns for public health lay behind the new burial laws of the 1850s. This legislation closed churchyards in towns of over 5000 inhabitants and established cemeteries under the control of secular and elected local government authorities, for which the theological or religious interpretation of the corpse was beyond their remit. When churchyards gave way to cemeteries, the Church lost not only its monopoly on ownership of burial grounds, but also its authority in the interpretation of death.

About the same time, doctrines of the afterlife – in particular, those of salvation, judgement and hell – were also becoming subject to intellectual reformulation. The loss of the churches' control over burial grounds weakened their capacity to symbolize their after-death doctrines through their practical and symbolic custodianship of the dead in their churchyards. A moral component was also involved in that the Church acted as a gatekeeper for those who had died. As long as the Church taught – and people believed – that the dead lay awaiting a general resurrection, in which bodies and souls would be reunited to face God's judgement, the Church could continue to signal its belief that there were moral tests or qualifications about entering the future life.

From the 1840s onwards, the new secular movement in the UK began to push for doctrines of the immortality of the soul as opposed to that of the resurrection of the body. They sought to stress that, if there were a life after death, there was nothing either supernatural or moral about it. This found further expression in the Spiritualist movement, which emerged in the mid-nineteenth century and peaked in the inter-war years of the twentieth century. After 1945 the continuing decline of the Church's influence on forming people's beliefs made space for beliefs in reincarnation and interest in near-death experiences, which also offered concepts of life after death free from traditional Christian interpretations and free from the claims or authority of the Church. Postmodern interpretations of death have all stressed the autonomy of the individual and the wide range of choices about beliefs in this life and the next, all of which are to be counted as valid.

The period of modern cremation

The rise of cremation as an alternative to burial thus emerged in the secularizing contexts of the mid-nineteenth century and contributed thereafter to the secularization of attitudes to the body and to postmortem identity. The public health perspective on the disposal of the dead had been established in the 1840s. It went a stage further when cremation was proposed. From the 1840s medical conferences had begun to discuss the beneficial advantages of cremation for public health, to which the costs of traditional earth burials and the shortage of land for housing, leisure and food production came to be added. Thus both the corpse and the burial ground came to be viewed from perspectives of health and economy. Sir Henry Thompson employed arguments like these to establish the Cremation Society of Great Britain in 1874. His arguments relied on secular perspectives of dead bodies and their treatment and thus sidelined the traditional religious interpretations about the disposal of the dead.

In 1884 cremation was permitted in the

Regina v. *Price* case and officially approved by the Cremation Act 1902. However, it attracted little popularity all the while it was only promoted by liberal- and secular-minded people and as part of the late Victorian shift towards simpler and less expensive funerals. Belief in the resurrection of the body was still widespread and was sufficient for conservative and traditionally-minded people to stand aloof from cremation.

Although the forces that led to the growth of cremation are complex, the experience of the First World War undoubtedly affected both popular and doctrinal attitudes and practices about death, including those relating to the resurrection of the body. Before the war, many theologians had already diluted their doctrines of hell. After 1914 the experience of modern warfare and the pastoral pressures of mass bereavement meant that both clergy and theologians reduced their traditional emphases on doctrines of judgement. Many clergy made accommodation for the needs of bereaved people by jettisoning Protestant principles forbidding prayers for the dead. This was correlated with the increasing resort to Spiritualism. Beliefs about the resurrection of the body were also challenged. Among soldiers there was widespread cynicism about, and abandonment of, beliefs in the resurrection of the body. Soldiers on active service became familiar with horribly disfigured or fragmented corpses that – in ways not yet analysed – contributed to their discarding traditional or lingering beliefs in the resurrection of the dead.

After 1918 Protestant theologians caught up with, or were forced to acknowledge, the shifts in popular belief. In the early 1920s there were two heresy trials in the UK, involving senior figures, Hugh Major, an Anglican, and Leslie Weatherhead, a Methodist. Both were accused of denying traditional doctrines of the resurrection of the body. Each was acquitted, but the public debate which the trials provoked revealed that many people had already discarded the resurrection of the body as a necessary component of Christian orthodoxy. The Cremation Society of Great Britain grasped the publicity potential of this shift in public opinion, emphasizing that cremation was not an intrinsic barrier to the postmortem fulfilment of Christian identity. Bishop Gore of Oxford pronounced in favour of cremation in 1924.

During the 1939–45 war, the decline of

traditional resurrection beliefs in the Church was revealed in the debates in the Convocation of Canterbury on appropriate liturgies for cremation services. These focused on the implications of the choice of cremation for the authority of the Church; for the convenience of bereaved families; for the public use of churchyards and their maintenance costs; and upon the precise moment in the funeral service when the body could be said to have been 'committed'. The debate almost entirely ignored the effects that cremation might have upon the postmortem prospects for the dead. Cremation supporters in the Lower House of Convocation pressed for cremation to be regarded as a prelude for the burial of the ashes in consecrated ground. Bishops (the Upper House) recommended that cremation be regarded as an alternative to burial. The Convocation's conclusion in 1944 was that 'Cremation had no theological significance'.

This was a huge fillip for the British cremation movement. It was encouraged even more when, shortly after, the Archbishop of Canterbury, William Temple, died and was cremated. No one in the Convocation debates had mentioned the judgement of Augustine that disposal rituals have no effect upon the destiny of the dead. Yet, in retrospect, the Convocation's decision was a strange one for a Church which had, for nearly 2000 years, practised the burial of the human body in expectation of its resurrection to face processes of judgement, purgation and, finally, eternal life with God. The decline of this traditional belief awaits rigorous and systematic study. It was as if the traditional doctrine of the resurrection of the body had been abandoned by popular consensus, even though that consensus had never officially been tested.

Given the shift from burial to cremation within the quarter-century following 1944, the reticence of the churches to address the theological implications of cremation has been striking, in retrospect. Christians have never said that burial was 'without theological significance'. For Christians, the hope and the future of humankind rests on belief in Jesus' resurrection and on his triumph over evil and death. Yet although a familiar choice of Bible reading at funerals is 'Christ's resurrection is the first-fruits of a whole harvest of the dead' (1 Corinthians 15:20), there is little awareness of the dissonance of this passage in a crematorium context. Neither has the truncation of the funeral liturgy been

addressed – a truncation effected by the cremation process (Lampard, 1993). Here the words committing the body are spoken some minutes or hours before its committal to the flames, and which the mourners will not expect to witness.

It has been proposed that the popularity of cremation has itself contributed to the continuing decline of traditional beliefs in the resurrection of the body. Davies has pointed out that the implicit message of cremation is that the body after death is finished and has no future role to play: 'What cremation allows to come to the forefront is the otherwise strongly implicit belief in a human soul which leaves the body after death and continues into another dimension' (Davies, 1990: 31). This could imply on the one hand that the decline in resurrection beliefs has removed formerly widespread underpinning of burial customs, and thus eased the adoption of cremation. On the other hand, the popularity of cremation which has been traced to changes in family structure and to geographical and social mobility (Jupp, 1993a) has contributed to a continuing decline in resurrection beliefs, themselves formerly underpinned by traditional burial practices in burial grounds owned by the churches.

A rearguard respect is still paid to traditional resurrection beliefs by at least two Christian denominations in the UK. First, whilst only a minority claiming affiliation to a selection of the major denominations believes in the resurrection of the body, the Roman Catholic Church has the largest percentage – 18 per cent (Davies and Shaw, 1995). Second, the Church in Wales insists on the burial of cremated ashes. Church in Wales clergy are forbidden both to participate in, and permit, the scattering of ashes. Underlying this ruling is a conviction that the integrity of the body has a doctrinal significance. This is consistent with the traditional doctrine of the resurrection of the body, symbolized by the return to the earth of all the human remains, even when they have first been cremated (Denison, 1999).

Two new trends give contrary signals as to whether the doctrine will ever be revived. First, a handful of Anglican dioceses is currently considering the introduction of 'green' or 'woodland' burial sites. Yet their strategy documents do not include beliefs in the resurrection of the body: environmental concerns come before theological. Second, the UK Home Office is debating proposals for the re-use of old graves. Whilst some official church organizations support these moves, Home Office supporting documents do not list any arguments about the awareness or relevance of resurrection beliefs.

The failure of the churches in the second half of the twentieth century to think through the interrelationship between modes of disposal, personal identity after death, pastoral care of the bereaved and the role and significance of churchyards, is considerable. The churches' ability to act is affected, both practically and politically, by their refusal either to own crematoria or to extend, in any large measure, their burial grounds. If the churches owned crematoria, they would be forced to work out theologies and liturgies of cremation that were of a piece with traditional Christian doctrines and also satisfy more of the needs and demands of people facing death or preparing funerals. **Peter Jupp**

See also Catholic Church.

References

Augustine, St (n.d.), *Augustine* trans. M. Allies, London: Burns & Oates.

Brown, Peter (1981), *The Cult of the Dead*, London: SCM Press.

Bynum, Caroline W. (1995), *The Resurrection of the Body in Western Christianity, 200–1336*, New York: Columbia University Press.

Chadwick, Owen (1974), *The Secularisation of the European Mind in the Nineteenth Century*, Cambridge: Cambridge University Press.

Davies, Douglas J. (1990), *Cremation Today and Tomorrow*, Nottingham: Grove Books.

Davies, Douglas J. (2002), *Death, Ritual and Belief* (2nd rev. edn), London: Continuum.

Davies, Douglas J. and Shaw, Alastair (1995), *Re-using Old Graves: A Report on British Attitudes*, Crayford: Shaw & Sons.

Denison, Keith (1999), 'The Theology and Liturgy of Funerals: A View from the Church in Wales, *Mortality*, 4(1): 63–74.

Jupp, Peter (1993a), 'Cremation or Burial? Contemporary Choice in City and Village', in David Clark (ed.), *The Sociology of Death*, Oxford: Blackwell.

Jupp, Peter (1993b), 'The Development of Cremation in England, 1820–1990: A Sociological Account', unpublished PhD thesis, University of London.

Jupp, Peter and Rogers, Tony (eds) (1997), *Interpreting Death: Christian Theology and Pastoral Practice*, London: Cassell.

Lampard, John (1993), 'Theology in Ashes – The Failure of the Churches to Think Theologically about Cremation', in *Bereavement and Belief*, London: The Churches' Group on Funeral Services at Cemeteries and Crematoria.

Prothero, Stephen (2001), *Purified by Fire: A History of Cremation in America*, Berkeley: University of California Press.

Rowell, D. Geoffrey (1974), *Hell and The Victorians, A Study of the Nineteenth Century Theological Controversies Concerning Eternal Punishment and the Future Life*, Oxford: Oxford University Press.

Rowell, D. Geoffrey (1977), *The Liturgy of Christian Burial*, London: SPCK/Alcuin Club.

RESURRECTION OF THE BODY

In the second century, Tertullian's *De Resurrectione Carnis* (*The Resurrection of the Dead*, 210 AD), articulated the doctrine of resurrection generally embraced by the Christian tradition to present times: '... the flesh shall rise again: certainly of every man, certainly the same flesh, and certainly in its entirety'. In *De Carne Christi* he goes further: what is raised is 'flesh, suffused with blood, built up with bones, interwoven with nerves, entwined with veins ... undoubtedly human'. Resurrection of the body means, literally, the body's return to life after dying by God's intervention. Only the select or those 'saved' by God's grace are resurrected, conditional on the individual's obedience to God's will and baptism. More than Tertullian's teachings, the resurrection of Jesus of Nazareth, three days after his crucifixion and death, established the foundations of the Christian faith. According to Paul (1 Corinthians 15: 13–18), 'For if the dead are not raised, then Christ has not been raised. If Christ has not been raised, your faith is futile and you are still in your sins'. Luke's Gospel tells of Jesus, after the resurrection, appearing to his disciples. Responding to their terror, believing him to be a ghost at first, he said: 'Look at my hands and my feet; see that it is I myself. Touch me and see; for a ghost does not have flesh and bones as you see that I have' (Luke 24: 39–40). Noticing the disbelief among them

Jesus asked the disciples if they had any food; he took a piece of broiled fish and ate it in their presence. This simple act proved that he was flesh and bone, human – not an apparition or disembodied soul.

Furthermore, Christian doctrine tells its followers that Jesus will return to earth to resurrect humanity, restoring the bodies lost at death, in preparation for the Final Judgement. In this scheme the body is reconstituted regardless of its condition, even if it has reduced, through natural decomposition (oxidation) or artificial means like cremation, to dust and bone. Christian tradition states that the reassembled body will be incorruptible: free from weakness, disease, and pain. Again, from 1 Corinthians 15: 51–55: 'We will not all die, but we will all be changed, in a moment, in the twinkling of an eye, at the last trumpet ... the dead will be raised imperishable [for] this body must be put on imperishability, and this mortal body must be put on immortality.'

When cremation returned as a reform movement during the last quarter of the nineteenth century its religious opponents based their objections on Christian principles: cremation annihilated the body when Christian tradition, anticipating the resurrection, favoured that it be protected and preserved, as much as possible, by earth burial. The problem was that this stance implied something rather un-Christian: that cremation might frustrate the Divine will; the process leaving the body in a state beyond God's ability to reconstitute and revive it. Did cremation threaten resurrection? Advocates of cremation exploited this question. Louis Windmuller, writing in the *North American Review* (1898), argued: 'God, doubtless, has the power to collect not only bones but the very atoms which compose our mortal frames, whether they consist of ashes into which a Gorini furnace had converted them in an hour ...] or whether they had gradually been turned by decomposition into a heap of dust.' The Catholic Church banned cremation in 1886 in Canon 1203 of the *Corpus Juris Cononici* – 'The bodies of the faithful must be buried; their cremation is forbidden' – denouncing cremation as an affront to the doctrine of resurrection. Under this pronouncement cremated remains were banned from the funeral mass and priests were forbidden from attending crematories or conducting services there. The cremation ban was finally lifted in 1963. **Eric Love**

See also Catholic Church.

References

Bynum, Caroline Walker (1995), *The Resurrection of the Body in Western Christianity, 200–1336*, New York: Columbia University Press.

Pagels, Elaine (1989), *The Gnostic Gospels*, New York: Random House.

Prothero, Stephen (2000), *Purified by Fire: A History of Cremation in America*, Berkeley: University of California Press.

Tertullian (1956), *De carne Christi: Tertullian's Treatise on the Incarnation*, ed. Ernest Evans, London: SPCK.

Tertullian (1960), *De resurrectione carnis liber: Tertullians' Treatise on the Resurrection*, ed. Ernest Evans, London: SPCK.

Windmuller, Louis (1898), 'Graveyards as a Menace to the Commonweal', *North American Review*, 167, August.

RITES OF PASSAGE

The expression 'rites of passage' was developed in 1909 by the anthropologist Arnold van Gennep (1873 – 1957). It is ironic that, in his lifetime, he was not accepted into one significant group of anthropologists –indeed, his treatment has been described as 'an academic disgrace' (Van Gennep, 1967: xi) – but that, much later, his idea of rites of passage gained tremendous currency, even to the point of inappropriate use. Van Gennep focused on social life and on the way in which individuals passed from one social status to another, – say, from being a boy to a man, from a single woman to a wife or, indeed, from being alive to being dead. He thought of 'society' as the environment in which we live and that, as it were, looked after us.

Among the dominant French group of sociologists of his day, the one that kept him marginal, it was fashionable to almost personify 'society', to speak of it as an agent, as something that operated and achieved things. Van Gennep shared that view and spoke of society as almost taking individuals by the hand and conducting them from one status to another. His preferred image was of society as a house with an individual being conducted from one room to another. Central to that image was the threshold of each room and the spaces or passages between rooms. The Latin word for threshold was *limen* and he used this in constructing the threefold form of rites of passage (Van Gennep, 1960). These comprised the pre-liminal, the liminal and the post-liminal phases. In the pre-liminal phase a rite would separate someone from their pre-existing status. This might involve a celebration or some event indicating that a change was now going to take place. After this, there followed the liminal period of separation from the ordinary ongoing life of society. In rituals of initiation, for example, boys or girls might be taught the rules and customs of their society, along with the duties their new status would demand of them. Often people learned to bond with those undergoing a liminal stage with them as Victor Turner explained in his important study of liminality (1969). Then, when all was accomplished, in the post-liminal phase, these individuals would be brought into mainstream society and reincorporated into it, as those possessing a new status. To focus on the *limen* and liminality is, generally speaking, simpler than Van Gennep's other, French terms of *séparation, marge* and *aggregation*.

One often ignored point is that, depending on the overall purpose of any one such set of rites of passage, Van Gennep thought that one of these three elements (separation–liminal apartness–integration) would be emphasized over and above the others. In a marriage, for example, rites might stress the separation of a girl from her family as she now becomes a wife and daughter-in-law in the family of her husband. When it came to funerals Van Gennep emphasized the transitional element, a point that stresses the way in which the dead are passing from the realm of the living to some other world. For the greater part of human history people have believed, as the great majority still do believe, that the dead pass from this life into another domain, and funeral rites have served to accomplish that transition. Important questions arise where no such belief exists.

When developing Van Gennep's scheme it is worth observing that there are often several different groups involved in a funeral ritual, and some of these have a different interest and investment in what is going on. This becomes particularly important, for example, in societies where not all believe in an afterlife. Indeed, in many contemporary western European-style societies a majority may not so believe. In the case of the wedding mentioned above, for example, some see the event as focusing on the separation of girl from her original family whereas others may focus on her incorporation into her new family of in-laws. The same applies to death rites: a Christian priest, for example, may focus on the transition of the dead from this world to the next whereas others might see the funeral primarily in terms of the separation of the dead from the living and the living from the dead. It may even be that, so far as individual memory and lifestyle are concerned, the dead pass into memory in a kind of constant liminality. They are neither dead and gone nor present in the flesh but are retained as part of daily memory. This is made practically possible, in one sense, if a person retains the deceased's ashes in the house and, for example, talks and relates to them as a kind of influential presence.

This particular aspect of separation and retention is made more acute by modern cremation than was the case with burial and may explain why concern is sometimes expressed over just what form the rite should take at a crematorium. Unlike burial that, by custom, has involved the relatively simple task of lowering a coffin into the grave, cremation often offers a variety of options. Since the directly equivalent rite of actually placing the coffin into the cremator is very seldom witnessed, the focus falls on what happens in the chapel or ceremonies' room. Should the coffin, for example, be simply left on the catafalque and the people depart? Should it be simply surrounded by a drawn curtain or gates and left there while the family leave? Or should it be removed by some descending mechanism, conveyor system or the like? On these questions opinions vary, and the thoughts and feelings of the bereaved are often taken into account. In terms of Christian liturgy, for example, a question emerges over the difference between the commending of the deceased person to God and the actual committal of the body for cremation. Sheppy, for example, argues for replacing each by the notion of 'release' (1997: 49). The additional question of cremated remains and what precisely is done with them in relation to the deceased person and the preceding funeral service is also significant, and most Churches have given relatively little attention to dealing with the problem, Jupp and Rogers' (1997) collection of theological material being the exception here. In terms of the anthropology of rites of passage, however, the question arises as to when, and if, any separation occurs at all. Is it perhaps the entire event at the crematorium that is the separation and not any single part of the ceremony? Might this explain some people's attitudes to crematoria as being different from attitudes to churches? Churches, for example, serve as the arena for numerous rites of passage associated with birth, marriage and death and cannot be totally identified with any one of them.

But, with cremation, the issue of rites of passage is made more complex because of the subsequent question of the ashes. As we see in the entry on Robert **Hertz**, another anthropologist of the same time and general thought-world as Van Gennep, cremation is seldom a single event. It is followed by the remains and by what happens to them. There is a sense in which, for example, it is the remains that provide the option for the post-liminal rite – for incorporation into a new status. In terms of traditional Christianity, for example, the burial of remains, analogous with the burial of the body, marks the postmortem identity of the dead as those 'awaiting the resurrection'. A great deal of confusion came to exist in the mid- and later twentieth century in some countries – and certainly in England – when priests were involved in the actual crematorium service connected with the body and coffin but not with the cremated remains. In symbolic terms the crematorium service was directly equated with the burial service with the question of ashes left very much open and uncertain. This became increasingly the case when family members took the ashes and engaged in the private placing of them.

Strictly speaking, Van Gennep's rites of passage were social rites with a public focus. What, then, of the privatized acts of bereaved families or individuals? In one sense, Van Gennep's notion of rites of passage no longer applies and we are confronted by new, personal, invented acts. Even so, some aspects of the dynamics of Van Gennep's scheme may still be useful. Some of the issues involved in this are discussed in the entry on **ashes–remains**, on **identity**, and especially in **Christianity–Fire** where the idea of types of fulfilment of identity is explored. For there is an important sense in which Van Gennep's concern over status needs to be developed in terms of personal and interpersonal identity. In a private

rite with ashes a family may well mark the transition of the dead into a place that he or she once loved and/or, in so doing, also finally mark a separation from that person.

However, there is another topic in relation to which the idea of rites of passage is problematic – that concerning the memory of the survivors. Van Gennep's focus was largely on 'society', its members and their status. It was not on individuals and their personal concerns, and yet it is precisely that individual focus that is significant in many contemporary societies with their emphasis on individualism, personal choice and fulfilment. In that connection memory becomes important, for the dead seldom ultimately and finally 'depart' through some neat rite; they always help compose part of the identity, memory, dreams and thoughts of the living. It is precisely within that framework of identity and close relationship that the private use or disposal of cremated remains becomes significant. Here the focus falls not only, and perhaps not primarily, on changes in social status, but on personal memory and the location or relocation of the dead within the identity of the living.

One of the major theoretical criticisms leveled against Van Gennep's rites of passage came from the anthropologist Maurice Bloch and his important study of ritual called *Prey into Hunter* (1992). Bloch was also interested in changes that affected individuals as members of a society and was especially concerned with the way in which the everyday world that ended in death was, in a symbolic sense, overcome through special rites that yielded a new power and energy to people. There was, ultimately, a conquest of death and a gaining of a new sense of life. These are complex issues, one aspect of which involves violence and is addressed in the entry on **dignity and violence**; but here we remain with one feature of modern cremation that lies in a sense of the conquest of death, not in the traditional religious sense of hope for an eternal future, but in a reappraisal of, and engagement with, memory. The combination of memory and hope is complex, not least in relation to fear. Fear was an important issue for Van Gennep as it related not only to the changes brought about by death and to the new frontiers that needed to be crossed by both the dead person and mourners, but also to a defensive attitude towards the dead. He spoke of these as 'magico-religious aspects', although many might now wish to approach them as psychological, or indeed as religious, aspects, but still involving the potential for fear and anxiety. Even so, ashes may be one symbol in and through which individuals can 'see through' or find their way past the dead corpse and gain a new perspective, offering new possibilities of hope for the future. Hope may take many forms and is an extremely important factor especially when it is directed towards ideas of the ongoing life of families and society as Bloch and Parry (1982) showed. What will be obvious, even in this brief discussion, is that the issue of rites of passage is complex and, although it is of serious importance for cremation, is no simple formula that can be applied easily to any number of human activities. **Douglas J. Davies**

See also ashes – remains; Christianity – fire; dignity and violence; Hertz; identity.

References

Bloch, Maurice (1992), *Prey into Hunter*, Cambridge: Cambridge University Press.

Bloch, Maurice and Parry, Jonathan (1982), *Death and the Regeneration of Life*, Cambridge: Cambridge University Press.

Jupp, Peter and Rogers, T. (1997), *Interpreting Death*, London: Cassell.

Sheppy, Paul (1997), 'Towards a Theology of Transition', in Peter C. Jupp and Tony Rogers (eds), *Interpreting Death: Christian Theology and Pastoral Practice*, London: Cassell, 42–55.

Turner, Victor (1969), *The Ritual Process*, London: Routledge and Kegan Paul.

Van Gennep, Arnold (1960), *The Rites of Passage*, London: Routledge & Kegan Paul. First published 1909.

Van Gennep, Arnold (1967), *The Semi-Scholars*, trans. and ed. Rodney Needham, London: Routledge & Kegan Paul. First published 1911.

RITUAL AND SYMBOLISM

Human life is organized in and through societies that, over time, develop their own ways of understanding existence. Ritual and symbolism play a large part in this process of meaning-making and are particularly important as far as cremation itself is concerned since it, too, usually takes a ritual form. Here we consider key elements of ritual and symbolism: other related entries deal with **ashes** and **corpse symbolism**.

Ritual is a pattern of behaviour that carries symbolic significance and often utilizes symbolic objects. In its public form, specially delegated or trained individuals perform actions that tend to become traditional and repeated in subsequent ritual events. They may use particular objects or speak particular words that, in the context of the ritual, assume a distinctive significance. Words, objects and actions become powerful in ritual, and much of that power comes from the symbolic significance with which they are invested. People generally accept that there are particular times, periods or events that stand apart from the ordinary incidents of everyday life. These times allow the underlying values and beliefs of a society and its individual members to come to a sharper focus than they do during the business of daily existence. The recollection of prime values is closely related to their renewed expression in the rite; sometimes this involves issues of ritual purity and impurity as a separate entry indicates. Abstract levels of thought are brought into close relationship with people's emotional energies through ritual words and actions. In this sense, a symbol can be thought of as a combination of, on the one hand, social values, philosophical or religious thought and, on the other, the emotional experience and practical way of life of people (Rappaport, 1999: 405).

An elementary behaviour

In the Introduction and the entry on **fire** cremation is approached as an elementary form of human behaviour in which fire is used to deal with death. To speak of cremation as an elementary form is to describe an irreducible scheme of behaviour widespread in human societies. There is something basic and fundamental about it. Just as earth and corpse combine in land burial, or water and corpse in sea burial, so fire and the dead unite in cremation. Similarly, in those cultures where bodies are exposed so that wild creatures may devour the flesh, the corpse is brought into relationship with what might be described as a non-social entity. In cremation, then, corpse and fire provide an elementary form of behaviour within which fundamental aspects of human thought and feeling are brought together. It is in this sense of uniting basic aspects of existence that we speak of cremation as an elementary form of behaviour.

The availability of ritual is especially important at times of death and bereavement when people are likely to question the meaning of their life and of the lives of those they have lost, and when they are at the greatest need of support from other members of their society. Thought and feeling come together in the ritual action of funerals and, even when the emotion of the day overwhelms central participants they can, later, look back on what happened and, at future funerals, when they are present as less central participants, they can reflect on the significance of what takes place. Human beings are, in a very deep sense, ritual creatures and the need to 'do something' at times of stress and crisis cannot be overemphasized. Indeed, the need to do something can be more important than extensive abstract explanations of the 'meaning of life' and the like. Thought alone seldom suffices so that, for example, René Descartes' famous philosophical statement, 'I think therefore I am', is seldom true for ordinary people for whom existence is based as much in action as in thought. It is action and not philosophical talk alone that brings a sense of relief, joy and completion to human experience. This is not to say that ideas and the words that express them in ritual are not important, but is to emphasize the power of the ritual context of action: words and actions, along with the buildings hosting funeral rites or the locations where memorials are placed, can all serve as a form of 'words against death' (Davies, 2002: 7)

Forms of ritual, and the symbolism that they express, undergo transformation with time, and it is not always accurate to agree with the popular idea that funeral rites are amongst the most extremely conservative and unchanging aspects of social practice. Many of the entries in this Encyclopedia bear witness to the dramatic changes in funeral custom that have come about in many societies, most especially with the adoption of cremation as in Japan or, occasionally, as in the case of Christians in Nepal, where cremation was rejected for burial. Amongst the most significant changes effected by cremation concerns cremated remains and the way in which they may function as a symbol. If we follow one widespread definition of a symbol as something that participates in that which it represents, we will find particularly interesting issues emerging over the idea of the corpse as the symbol of the 'person' it once was and, second, the question of how the ashes may be a symbol of the deceased. **Douglas J. Davies**

See also ashes – remains; corpse symbolism; fire – cosmos and chaos; impurity and purity.

References

Davies, Douglas J. (2002), *Death, Ritual and Belief* (2nd rev. edn), London: Continuum.

Rappaport, Roy A. (1999), *Ritual and Religion in the Making of Humanity*, Cambridge: Cambridge University Press.

ROBINSON, WILLIAM

William Robinson (1838–1935) was an established authority on garden design before joining the Cremation Society of England. Best known for *The English Flower Garden and Home Grounds*, published in 1883 and appearing in 15 different editions and nine reprints during his lifetime, Robinson also produced *The Garden* and *Gardening Illustrated* magazines. Inspired by cemetery reformer and landscape designer J.C. Loudon, to whom he dedicated his first issue of *The Garden*, Robinson advocated a 'natural' garden with wide, sweeping lawns, shapely rose and shrub beds and hardy, herbaceous borders.

His most significant contribution to the cremation movement first appeared in 1880: *God's Acre Beautiful; Or, the Cemeteries of the Future*, an aesthetic foray into the possibilities of urns as artistic objects surrounded by a permanent living memorial. He later published *Cremation, and Urn Burial; Or, the Cemeteries of the Future*, a similar work. Beyond its aesthetic contribution, the first book defended cremation as a sanitary necessity, especially in an appendix meant to contrast his envisioned ideal with disclosures of the worst cemetery abuses. Robinson finally gained the opportunity to put his ideas into practice when he designed the original layout for the gardens of London's Golders Green Crematorium. In recognition of his contributions, the Cremation Society made Robinson a vice-president. By the 1930s, long-time acquaintance and society member Dr Herbert T. Herring was taking a primary interest in overseeing the landscape at Golders Green, an interest ultimately transferred to H.D.E. Carter,

son of the Golders Green superintendent who had assisted Robinson's early landscaping efforts.
Lisa Kazmier

See also Golders Green Crematorium.

References

Grainger, Hilary (2002), 'The Development of the Gardens at Golders Green Crematorium', in Peter C. Jupp and Hilary Grainger (eds), *Golders Green Crematorium 1902–2002: A London Centenary in Context*, London: The London Cremation Company, 49–57.

Helmreich, Anne (2002), *The English Garden and National Identity: The Competing Styles of Garden Design, 1870–1914*, Cambridge: Cambridge University Press.

Robinson, William (1880), *God's Acre Beautiful; Or, the Cemeteries of the Future*, London: The Garden Office.

Robinson, William (1998), *The English Flower Garden and Home Grounds*, London: Bloomsbury.

Transactions of the Cremation Society (1903), Vol. 16, 28. See also Grainger (2002) above.

ROMANIA

At the 1936 International Cremation Congress in Prague the Romanians were regarded as the pioneers of cremation in south-eastern Europe. Romania's status was secured by virtue of the fact that it possessed a crematorium, unlike Yugoslavia, Bulgaria, Hungary or Greece. But cremation was still only in its early infancy in Romania. In 1935 Bucharest Crematorium was responsible for the disposal of 0.19 per cent of the country's dead, placing it just behind France (0.2 per cent) and Luxembourg (0.64 per cent) at the bottom of the European league table of cremating countries. Bucharest Crematorium, built at the expense of the Romanian Cremation Society (called 'Cenusa' – literally 'ashes, cinders, mortal/earthly remains'), did not begin operating until February 1928 and cremated a total of 262 corpses that year. This figure rose to 602 in 1934. *Cenusa* itself had only been in existence since 1923.

Although the Yugoslavs appeared to contribute more to the 1936 Cremation Congress, the Romanians were evident too, when M. Popovici of Cenusa spoke on 'The Duty of the Municipalities to Assist Cremation Societies'.

Popovici outlined problems that were hindering the Romanian cremationists' work. First, there were popular misconceptions about the society. When Cenusa was first established, the idea inexplicably spread that it wanted to 'buy' people who were still living but who intended to be cremated, and that it would pay them varying amounts commensurate with their social status. Apparently, Cenusa received many enquiries from people of different social classes attempting to sell their corpses! A more widely held belief was that Cenusa was a charity and that therefore all its services were free. The truth was that the society was a non-profit-making organization. Although it charged for cremations, its directors were not paid and all income went back into maintaining, improving and expanding the cremation facilities that it had established.

The main and most worrying problem for Popovici, however, was the sluggishness of the society's growth. After 14 years of existence its membership had barely reached 1000. This was despite the facts that Cenusa was 'recognized as one of the most humanitarian institutions, of immeasurable social, hygienic and economic advantage to the municipality of Bucharest, that membership fees were low and that the practical benefits of membership were considerable. A member of one year's standing or more who died had most of their funeral expenses met by the society (including the costs of the coffin, hearse, chapel, mortuary and cremation itself, but not the clergyman's fee nor the cost of a columbarium niche). Even for non-members, a cremation was far cheaper than the most modest of burials. According to Popovici, Cenusa offered other 'advantages of an economic, hygienic, and social character', which involved 'unexcelled cleanliness' in a crematorium that was staffed by people distinguished by their 'humane and civilised behaviour' (*Report*, 1936: 54). Given all this, Popovici was at a loss to explain why the society had only made 'quite minimal' progress.

In reality, Popovici, though understandably frustrated by the lack of tangible signs of the success of Cenusa's efforts, was understating the real progress that Romanian cremationists had achieved. In comparison with other Balkan states, Romania at least had a functioning crematorium, and this had been achieved only five years after the foundation of Cenusa. Most remarkably, the crematorium had been built by the society itself rather than by the municipality, as happened elsewhere. The Serbian Cremation Society, 'Oganj', in contrast, had been sporadically active since 1904 and yet was, in 1936, still almost 30 years away from achieving its goal of a crematorium in Belgrade. In addition, Bucharest Crematorium was the first to be built in south-eastern Europe by four years and the first to be operational in the region by 24 years (the next was Debrecen Crematorium in Hungary, built in 1932 and finally opened in 1951). Romania was the only eastern European country bar Russia that had a crematorium before the Second World War.

In terms of membership Cenusa was on a par with that of all the Yugoslav cremation societies together, and Belgrade's Society had been in existence for very much longer. The Argentine Cremation Association's (AAC's) membership peaked in the late 1920s at less than 500, and Hungary did not even have a cremation society. Only the French Federation's membership was superior, more than three times greater, in fact, but, given the long tradition of cremation advocacy in that country, and the larger population, this was to be expected. Of course, there was a long way to go for cremation in Romania, but this should not obscure the achievements of Cenusa in a relatively short space of time.

Reading between the lines of Popovici's speech, another mitigating circumstance for Romanian cremationists, was that they had failed to gain significant support from the municipality for their project. The municipality was avoiding the issue for 'political–religious reasons', but it remained, argued Popovici, their 'moral duty' to support the 'useful' cremation societies 'in every way and to do their best to popularise them' (Report, 1936: 54). Again, in contrast to Hungary and later Yugoslavia, Romanian cremationists had been forced to act independently and establish a crematorium using their own finances, an unusual and therefore considerable and noteworthy achievement. Recognition that cremation 'causes a real revolution among the religious population' implies that religious opposition had been strong in Romania, outside, as well as inside, the municipalities.

Another obstacle in the way of advancement of cremation in Romania in the inter-war period was the considerable financial demands that building and running the crematorium had placed on Cenusa. In order to maintain an income and keep the crematorium running, Cenusa was somewhat reliant on performing the 'administrative cremations' of, for example, body parts from anatomical institutes, which paid well for the service. A Czech delegate at the 1936 Congress, Mencl, argued that these kinds of cremation repelled others from using the crematorium as it was regarded as a service for the disposal of refuse rather than a place for respectable people to take their dead. Popovici responded that the payments it received for the 'administrative cremation' service were vital to balancing the crematorium's budget and that, at least for the foreseeable future, it was impossible to survive without them. One positive aspect for Mencl was that at least Bucharest Crematorium performed far fewer such specialist cremations than did, for example, the Russian crematoria.

A positive development in this period was the society's establishment of a journal, *Flacâra Sacra* (*Sacred Flame*), in 1934. An eight-page monthly, *Flacâra Sacra* contained reports on the indigenous movement and a good deal of material on the cremation movements in Germany, Malaysia, Czechoslovakia, Britain, France, Yugoslavia, Austria and elsewhere. In 1937, although Popovici could not attend the London International Cremation Congress, Cenusa was apparently on an 'upward grade', and religious opposition to cremation and support for earth burial were gradually being overcome. That year had also seen 184 new members recruited: the society could now muster 1006 members. Nevertheless, international cooperation was apparently not high on Cenusa's agenda as it did not join the International Cremation Federation (ICF) when it was established in 1938.

As with most of the rest of continental Europe, the Second World War caused Romanian cremationists many problems. A cremator that had been ordered and paid for before the war was not delivered before its outbreak. Air raids did a considerable amount of damage to Bucharest Crematorium, and this placed Cenusa in financial difficulties in the immediate post-war period, making the later 1940s a 'period of great difficulty'. The crematorium required a new cremator even more desperately now, and it still had not received the one it had paid for in 1938. Although there remained much to be done from both 'technical' and 'moral' standpoints, conditions were at least improving. An important change was that the Orthodox Church was no longer quite so antagonistic towards cremation, although the tradition of earth burial, of course, remained strong. Hope was also drawn from the increase in cremations, which continued despite damage to the crematorium. In 1945 there were 600 cremations, almost three times as many as in 1944 (225), although this figure still had some way to go to surpass the highest pre-war figures. Another encouraging sign was that corpses for cremation were being brought from the provinces to the capital in increasing numbers.

The contact established in late 1946 between the ICF and Romanian cremationists was the last to occur for many years. There was a lack of communication between the ICF and several Eastern Bloc countries in the post-war period, including Poland, East Germany and the USSR, although Romania seemed especially uncommunicative. This lack of communication was evident in 1983, when the Dutch cremationist J.J. Visman announced that he could not obtain cremation figures from Romania – as well as from East Germany and the USSR. By late 1987 it was clear that the Ceausescu regime's problems were doing considerable harm to the cause of cremation in Romania. A power crisis meant that low gas pressure was insufficient to allow the full cremation of corpses. Groups opposing the regime claimed that it was dealing with the problem by giving some ashes to relatives and secretly burying the rest of the half-cremated bodies in mass burials. This did not apply to the corpses of the wealthy and powerful, which the authorities retained until the gas pressure was high enough for a complete cremation.

After the rapid inter-war advance, the progress of cremation in the post-war world seems to have been very slow in Romania, in contrast to countries such as Hungary and Yugoslavia which made more progress after 1945 than they had before. In fact, Romania did not get a second crematorium until after the fall of the Ceausescu regime and this, operating in Bucharest by 1993, seemed to have little effect on cremation figures. In 1999, 1172 cremations were performed in Romania, representing only about 12 per cent of deaths in Bucharest. After being so advanced in comparison with other south-eastern European countries, Romania came to be one of the least developed in terms of its cremation rate. In contrast, Bulgaria, which only got its first crematorium in 2001, carried out almost five times as many cremations as Romania in 2002 (5254 or almost 5 per cent of deaths). By now, Romania had long ceded its leadership position in respect of cremation. By 1999, Hungary and Slovenia were cremating a third or more of their dead and had become the trailblazers in the former Eastern Bloc. **Lewis H. Mates**

References

CSA.

Flacâra Sacra (1937–1939), CRE/AO/RO.

Report of the International Cremation Congress in Prague (1936), CRE/D4/1936/3.

Visman, J.J. (1983), 'Twenty-five Years of Cremation in Europe', *Pharos*, 49(1): 36–38.

ROMANS

The Romans believed that their earliest burial practice was inhumation (Cicero, *Leg.* 2.56; Lucretius 6.1279; *Pliny, HN* 7.187). No extant Roman source discusses the origin of cremation, but it was assumed to have been in use by the supposed date of the codification of Roman Law in the XII Tables (451/0 BC), whose provisions treated both cremation and inhumation as current. In fact, archaeological evidence shows that cremation was being used at Rome several centuries earlier and that the Etruscans also practised both rites. The pre-existence of inhumation was the explanation for the custom recorded in the first century BC of inhuming a bone from a body which was to be cremated (Cicero, *Leg.* 2.55; Varro, *de LL* 5.23).

Cremation was the standard rite between the fourth century BC and the first century AD in Rome, Italy and the western Roman Empire, where it was the native practice in most areas that came under Roman control. Exceptions to the norm excited comment: for example, the use of inhumation by the Cornelii family until the dictator Sulla requested that his remains should be cremated so that his enemies could not desecrate them (Cicero, *Leg.* 2.57) and the embalming of Nero's wife Poppaea 'in the manner of foreign kings' (Tacitus, *Ann.* 16.6). Cremation was 'the Roman custom' for everyone except babies, although it did not predominate in the eastern Roman Empire.

A drastic change took place during the second century AD. At the beginning of the century, cremation was completely dominant in Italy; by the end of the century inhumation had almost entirely replaced it. The practical consequences can be seen at burial sites such as Isola Sacra (Ostia), where tombs that were built for cremation burials had to be adapted to take inhumations. This was probably the most drastic change in a society's burial rites until the late twentieth century, yet it is totally unremarked upon in Roman literature and is known only from archaeological evidence. The reasons have been much discussed, without any wholly satisfactory explanation. The influence of Christianity and Judaism, which had theological objections to cremation, is unlikely to have been strong enough at the relevant date. Oriental mystery cults such as those of Isis and Mithras may have had more effect in changing people's attitudes to the remains of the dead, but there is nothing to link them directly with rejecting cremation. The greater accessibility of marble sarcophagi became an incentive to use inhumation. The reign of Hadrian introduced a higher evaluation of Greek culture, and more positions of influence were occupied by people from the East for whom cremation was not a native practice. All these factors must have contributed to a change of fashion, but it should be noted that cremation remained the normal rite for emperors in the third century, well after the rest of society had abandoned it. A freedman of the Emperor Domitian who inhumed his wife in the late first century AD 'could not bear the smoking pyre and the shouting of cremation' (Statius, *Silv.* 5.1.226–27), and a general change in sentiment along these lines must have taken place during the following century.

The cremations of emperors became events of national significance which developed differently from other funerals (Arce, 1988). The size of the pyre became the main feature: coins and literature from the second and early third centuries AD show pyres of three or four tiers, with the body placed in an opening on the second tier. The outside could be decorated with drapery, carvings and paintings. Horsemen performed manoeuvres around the pyre. If it was not possible to cremate the corpse itself at Rome, a wax model was cremated instead, as was the case for Septimius Severus who died at York in 211. During the cremation, an eagle was released from a cage on top of the pyre to signify the emperor's soul being carried up to the gods

(Herodian, 4.2.11); burning off the human body evidently came to be seen as part of the deification process, as in the myth of Hercules.

The basic procedure followed for other cremations can be reconstructed from archaeological and literary evidence, although there must have been variations according to place and time. The pyre had to be built outside city boundaries. A site which was regularly used for pyres was called an *ustrinum* or *ustrina* (some tombs for multiple use at Ostia had their own one built into their structure); one where a pyre was built over or in a pit which then formed the grave was called a *bustum* (Servius, *In Aen.* 3.22, 11.201). *Busta* were unusual at Rome and Ostia, but common in northern Italy, along the northern frontier, and in south-eastern Gaul, especially in the first century AD.

The pyre was normally built in the open, probably over a shallow pit to help the circulation of air (McKinley, 1997: 132). It was constructed with layers of logs, each layer being laid at right-angles to the previous one (Vitruvius, 2.9.15; Seneca, *Herc.Oet.* 1637), as shown in the two surviving depictions of an ordinary (as opposed to imperial) pyre in Roman art. The funerary worker called an *ustor*, mentioned with derision in Roman literature (Catullus, 59.5; Lucan, 8.738), probably specialized in building and supervising pyres. The body, dressed in its best clothes and lying on a decorated couch or wooden bier, was laid on top of the pyre, so the minimum dimensions would be determined by the size of the body, but it is likely that the size of the pyre was a status symbol, in keeping with other ways in which cremation could become a form of conspicuous consumption. The type of wood used seems to have depended on what was available locally; papyrus and incense could be added to help combustion. It was important for a pyre to be built for one individual, unless two closely connected people were cremated together (Lucan, 5.281-2; Herodian, 4.6.1). Being cremated on a pyre intended for someone else was regarded as highly undesirable, but it is likely that mass cremation was used for the bodies of the very poor in Rome and other large cities during the first century AD, and in emergencies such as outbreaks of plague (Lucretius, 6.1282–86; Martial, 8.75.10). Incomplete cremation was another outcome to be deplored, being regarded as an insult to the deceased and, in some people's eyes, not enabling the soul to reach the afterlife; it also failed to reduce the remains to a convenient size for burial (Noy, 2000a).

The pyre was lit with a torch after a final *conclamatio*, the calling of the deceased's name (Servius, *In Aen*. 6.218). The lighting was done, where possible, by a close relative such as a spouse or parent. Modern reconstructions show that the body should remain in place on top as the pyre burned down (McKinley, 1997: 134); foot bones are sometimes less well cremated than the rest of the body because they were away from the centre of the fire. Pyre-goods might be thrown on to the burning pyre, if they had not been placed there before lighting. The Romans regarded the ostentatious burning of large objects as a Gaulish custom (Caesar, *B.G*. 6.19.4; Pomponius Mela, 3.19), but objects burnt on Roman pyres include weapons, jewellery, clothing, ceramics (sometimes ritually broken first), gaming counters and food (animal bones may also come from pyre-side sacrifices) – status and local custom were probably the governing factors. There are occasional references to mourners throwing themselves on to a pyre due to excessive grief (Pliny, *HN* 7.122, 7.186) or killing themselves beside the pyre (Tacitus, *Ann*. 14.9.2; Suetonius, *Otho* 12), and to corpses apparently returning to life on the pyre, when it was too late to save them (Pliny, *HN* 7.173; Valerius Maximus, 1.8.12-13).

A complete cremation by Roman methods would take up to eight hours, and the pyre was normally lit early in the morning (Asconius, *Mil*. p. 28) rather than being left to burn overnight. Staying by the pyre until the end was therefore a sign of devotion to the deceased, but gifts given 'at the pyre' (Seneca, *Brev.Vit*. 10.5; ILS 7212) may have been distributed when the cremation was completed, as an incentive for mourners to stay. Eventually the fire was quenched with water or wine (Statius, *Silv*. 2.6.85-93; *Theb*. 6.235–36), symbolizing the end of the cremation. This would also help the fragmentation of the bones which the heat and the collapse of the pyre had already caused; there is some debate about whether further manual crushing of the bones was normal. The remains had to be removed from the pyre for final burial (except for a *bustum*), and particularly grief-stricken mourners are described as climbing into the ashes while they are still hot, or 'embracing the pyre' (Statius,

Silv. 2.1.24, 3.3.9); witches were also supposed to collect remains which were still warm (Ovid, *Her*. 6.89–90; Lucan, 6.533–37; Apuleius, *Met*. 2.20). The normal procedure was probably to allow the remains to cool overnight, and then to return the next day (Servius, *in Aen*. 11.210). The extent to which fragments of human bone were sorted from other pyre debris (which might include animal bones) varied greatly, but washing them with water, wine or even milk seems to have been common (Petronius, *Sat*. 77; Tibullus, 3.2.17–22). The collection of the remains (*ossilegium*, a term only found in late Latin) might be done by the family or by professionals (Sidonius, *Ep*. 3.13.5), and the proportion which was collected was also very variable – anything from the whole skeleton to just a symbolic handful of bones.

The cremated bones gathered from the pyre were placed in a grave. This was very important; disposing of them by other means, such as throwing them in a river, scattering or abandoning them, was a deliberate desecration (Cicero, *Leg*. 2.56; Tertullian, *De Anima* 33; Lactantius, *De Mort. Pers*. 21.11). The remains might be placed directly in the ground, perhaps being wrapped in a cloth first, but were more likely to be put in some sort of container, ranging from a used or defective pot to an elaborately carved marble cinerarium (ash container). The portability of cremated remains meant that there could be a great distance between the site of cremation and the final place of burial, and the ashes of some people who died overseas were eventually interred at Rome (Ovid, *Tr*. 3.3.65).

Cremation had several purposes for the Romans. The basic practical one was to render the corpse inert as quickly as possible (probably within two days of death in most cases – cremation on the day of the death seems to have been regarded as excessively hasty (Tacitus, *Ann*. 13.17, 14.9)) as there were only limited means for preventing putrefaction. It also made the remains more convenient for final disposal, and prevented any outrage being perpetrated on a still-recognizable corpse (Lucan, 8.764–67; Suetonius, *Nero* 49). At the same time, cremation provided an opportunity for ostentatious display, particularly in the size of the pyre, the nature of the goods burnt on it and the behaviour of the people around it. **David Noy**

References

Arce, J. (1988), *Funus Imperatorum: los Funerales de los Emperadores Romanos*, Madrid: Alianza.

McKinley, J. (1997), 'Bronze Age "Barrows" and Funerary Rites and Rituals of Cremation', *Proceedings of the Prehistoric Society*, 63: 129–45.

Noy, D. (2000a), '"Half-burnt on an Emergency Pyre": Roman Cremations Which Went Wrong', *Greece & Rome*, 47: 186–96.

Noy, D. (2000b), 'Building a Roman Funeral Pyre', *Antichthon*, 34: 30–45.

RUSSIA AND THE USSR

The case of cremation in the former USSR and in contemporary Russia is of interest because of the way in which this ritual practice of funerary rites could be used as a means of ideological expression, not unlike the role it played in Italy, although in that case it was related to freemasonry, freethinking and the Roman Catholic Church whereas in the USSR it was related to communism and the Russian Orthodox Church. To express something of this complexity we present two overlapping descriptions of the Russian–USSR case shaded with differing emphases. **Douglas J. Davies**

BACKGROUND AND CHANGE

In Tsarist Russia cremation met with great hostility and resistance from the Russian Orthodox Church which, crucially, spoke against it whenever the case was advanced in parliament. The advantages of cremation from economic, social and aesthetic perspectives, and the issues of introducing 'burial by fire' and the building of crematoria were frequently raised in government from the 1880s onwards. After the communist revolution in 1917 and the banning of the Church and religious practices by Lenin, cremation was given a second chance with the passing of a bill that legalized the practice and ordered the building of crematoria around the country. Bolshevik leaders were expecting a rise in deaths due to epidemics and casualties in the civil war and, accordingly, a special committee was set up to deal with the development of mortuaries and crematoria to cope with this. In 1919 the government ordered the building of the first experimental crematorium in Leningrad. However, the programme was delayed due to economic problems. In the following year, the old sauna building in western Leningrad was converted into a crematorium and on 14 December 1920 the first official cremation in Russia and the USSR took place. However, serious technical problems and high maintenance costs forced the crematorium to close down after only a few months of operation, after performing a total of 379 cremations. Of these, only 16 bodies were burned in accordance with the deceased's wishes, demonstrating that cremation was still a novel and unpopular practice.

Being unwilling to give up its efforts at making cremation 'an all-people's burial choice' the government launched a large propaganda campaign aimed at familiarizing people with cremation. Numerous exhibitions were opened in the latter part of the 1920s, both in Leningrad and Moscow, showing the advantages of 'burial by fire' and introducing it as a standard for cultural and scientific progress as accepted in many other developed societies. 'Side by side with the car, tractor and electrification – make way for cremation!' is an example of a slogan that the authorities used to try to persuade the masses to accept cremation as a beneficial scientific development. In the same period, the first Moscow crematorium was opened in 1927 on the site of Donskoi Monastery and, before the Second World War, another was built in the eastern Ukraine in Kharkov. However, Russian crematoria differed in certain technical respects from their Western counterparts: the cremation furnaces were larger due to the traditionally larger coffins, and no seating was provided in the ceremonial halls because of the Russian custom of standing around a coffin. The first official statistics of cremations that were issued annually in the 1930s showed constant increases, starting with 8379 cremations in 1931 and reaching 12 000 by 1938. The authorities set an example for the population by cremating most senior members of the Soviet Party, famous scientists and other important citizens such as Feliks Dzerzhinsky (1927), Joseph Stalin (1961), Soviet Minister of Defence Marshall Malinovsky (1967) and the first man in space Yuri Gagarin (1967), whose ashes were placed in the Kremlin wall.

The 1970s witnessed a great rise in the number of crematoria built around the major cities of the Soviet Union partly due to the increase in population and shortage of land for burials in rapidly developing multi-million population cities. Nikolo-Archangelski Crematorium, which became the largest in Europe, was built in 1973 in Moscow occupying 2 100 000 square metres. Of 3 million deaths per year, only 22 per cent resulted in cremation but, with the increase in crematoria to eight in six major cities, the official statistics showed a cremation rate of around 40 per cent by the mid-1980s.

With the collapse of the Soviet Union in 1991, freedom of religious beliefs and practices was re-established, allowing people to choose the fate of their corpse. More crematoria were opened in the Commonwealth of Independent States (CIS), European parts of Russia and even Siberia, with some being privately run. By the beginning of the twenty-first century, the two largest Russian cities of Moscow and St Petersburg, with populations of over 11 and 6 million respectively, have the highest cremation in the country with approximately 57 per cent and 63 per cent respectively, significantly higher than the national average of 35 per cent. **Dmitri Gorokhov**

RUSSIAN AND SOVIET UNION TRANSITIONS

The Russian Orthodox Church was always deeply hostile to cremation because of its belief in the resurrection of the body, so the idea found few supporters in Russia before the Bolshevik Revolution of 1917, although it was discussed in St Petersburg in the 1890s. However, the Bolshevik leaders, especially Lenin and Trotsky, strongly favoured the use of cremation on scientific and hygienic grounds. A decree of 7 December 1918 legalized the practice of cremation, but at this time the requisite technology did not exist in Russia, despite some experiments in Petrograd during the civil war, prompted by the great loss of life. When Lenin died in January 1924, Stalin and Kalinin, seeing the propaganda value of a link with Russian tradition, favoured the preservation of Lenin's corpse by embalming and its display in a crypt, which was carried out despite the wishes of Lenin's relatives and senior colleagues such as Trotsky. It was not until October 1927 that the first crematorium was opened in Moscow (on land confiscated from the Donskoi Monastery) and the Society for the Dissemination of the Idea

of Cremation (ORRIK) was founded. From this point onwards, senior Bolshevik leaders were cremated and their ashes placed in the Kremlin wall (except Stalin who, like Lenin, was embalmed, until his body was cremated in 1961). But, even then, the practice developed slowly, and it was only in the mid-1930s that a programme was initiated to build crematoria in other major cities (such as Kharkov in Ukraine in 1935). One of the motivations for this programme was the extensive destruction of churches and village communities which had occurred during the anti-religious and agricultural collectivization campaigns of 1929–33.

The unprecedented rate of urbanization also created huge problems, one of which was the disposal of the dead, and state cemeteries, as well as crematoria, were to meet this need. During the Second World War further destruction of churches and cemeteries occurred, although some rebuilding took place in the rather more tolerant (for Orthodoxy) atmosphere of the later Stalin years. But Khrushchev resumed the attack on the churches in his campaigns of the late 1950s and early 1960s, resulting in the destruction of large numbers of churches and a renewed drive to build bigger and 'better' crematoria (such as the excessively propagandistic one built in Kiev in the 1970s and now abandoned) and to extend the practice of cremation amongst a rather reluctant population, who not only saw cremation as repulsive and un-Russian (even for non-believers) but also viewed the furnaces as uncomfortably reminiscent of Nazi death-camps (one reason why British, rather than German, technology was mainly used). As part of the drive to create secular Soviet rituals as a substitute for religious practices, started by Khrushchev but fully developed under Brezhnev in the 1970s, funeral ceremonies were introduced in the major crematoria (such as in Leningrad), and, by the 1980s, cremation was the cheapest and only realistic option for many inhabitants of the large Russian cities.

The freedom of religious association and ending of anti-religious activity introduced by Gorbachev, as well as the subsequent collapse of the Soviet system and the USSR in 1991, produced a great revival in the influence of the Russian Orthodox Church and the restoration of its infrastructure. This led, in turn, to a revival in the practice of burial, especially for the new rich. However, burial remains an expensive option, and cremation, despite its unpopularity, is the only practical choice for much of the impoverished and largely secularized urban population. **Christopher Binns**

References

Binns, C. (1980–81), 'The Changing Face of Power: Revolution and Accommodation in the Soviet Ceremonial System', Part 1 *Man* (NS), 14 (1980): 585–606 and Part II *Man* (NS), 15 (1981): 170–87.

Lane, C. (1981), *The Rites of Rulers: Ritual in Industrial Society – The Soviet Case*, Cambridge: Cambridge University Press.

Merridale, C. (2000), *Night of Stone: Death and Memory in Russia*, London: Granta.

S

SATI

Sati (or Sutee as it was termed in the nineteenth century) is the traditional Hindu public practice of a widow immolating herself on her husband's pyre. It has always been an element in the Indo-Western encounter and an ingredient in the European perception of India. *Sati* has been a cause of controversy for at least a millennium, both among Westerners who ruled India, and among Hindu rulers, thinkers and social reformers. It is considered a custom by some, a ritual by others. It has always been prevalent among certain sections of Indian society.

The word Sati (literally 'good', 'devout', 'true') today has three meanings: the act, the rite and the person who, by performing the ritual, becomes a part of the Goddess Sati. In honour and in memory of these brave and devout women were erected *vira-kalas*, hero-stones that are still worshipped. Many of these stones claim that the wife has committed Sati out of tremendous love for her husband, so that they can be together after death. Even at the beginning of the twenty-first century some Hindu women still believe in this. A large number of Sati were committed just after the Second World War among the Mughals in Rajasthan, when the women may have died to protect their honour from the invading enemies,

after their men had perished in the battlefield. Sati was performed mainly in this region, and in Bengal, by the Kshatrya social groups. Although it was originally forbidden to Brahmanas, when it was allowed it led to curious changes in the rules of concremation for Brahmana widows, because of the exegetical effort to overcome the original ban. Women from lower castes also performed Sati. Kumar (1992) explains this, arguing that the women's self-immolation enabled their families to become highly respected, and increased the possibility of intermarriage.

The origins of Sati are complex – an intermingling of religious, social and psychological factors. Even today, according to the normative view, a woman's path to heaven is through her character and her devotion to her husband. It is thought that a woman's life serves no purpose after the death of her husband. Widows have to wear white saris and, if they are allowed to live with their marital or natal relatives, they are treated as unpaid servants. They are also seen by the rest of population as having the power to put curses on others. At present, most widows prefer to dedicate their lives to God, and many of them, especially from Bengal, go to live in Varanasi (Banaras), where they work in temples and social institutions. Traditionally, the life of a widow was so bad (and continues to be so to this day in India) that the women may have preferred death to humiliation, while women who performed Sati were glorified to excess. In Bengal, a system called *Däyabhaga* prevailed, entitling a woman equal property along with male relatives of the departed husband. This may be the reason for the Sati system being more common in that region – because the widow was forced to commit Sati.

Sati can also be seen as a case of the survival and revival of a more universal practice. The immolation of widows can be found in Greek, Scandinavian, Gallic and Thracian myths and rites. Over time, there has been opposition in India to the practice of Sati. In the Kerala tradition, Shankara is credited with the abolition of Sati (Kane, 1973, II:I: 506). Tantrics also denounced Sati. Albuquerque abolished it in Goa in 1510 AD, and Akbar and Maratha chiefs fought against it, too. Rajaram Mohan Roy, through his organization Brahmo Samaj, also fought to eliminate Sati, resulting in its being banned by the British government in 1829 (Sharma, 1988:

x). Although the practice has decreased since then, it has never entirely ceased, and actually increased during the 1980s. There was a Sati reported in Rajasthan in 1987, which caused considerable controversy and social turmoil. This case provoked new legislation that outlawed not only the practice itself, but also its encouragement and glorification. **Mariana Caixeiro**

References

Duboi, Abbé J.A. (1959), *Hindu Manners, Customs and Ceremonies*, Oxford: Clarendon Press.

Hawley, J.S. (ed.) (1994), *Sati: The Blessing and The Curse*, Oxford: Oxford University Press.

Kane, P.V. (1973), *History of Dharmashastra*, Poona: Bhandakar Oriental Research Institute. First published 1941.

Kumar, R. (1992), 'Gender, Politics and Identity at Times of Crisis: The Agitations Around Sati Data in India'. *Discussion Paper (309–August)*, Sussex: Institute of Development Studies.

Penzer, N.M. (ed.) (1925), *The Ocean of Story, Vol. IV*, London: Chas. J. Sawyer.

Sharma, A. (1988), *Sati. Historical and Phenomenological Essays*, Varanasi, Motilal Banarsidass.

SCHULTE, JULIUS

Julius Schulte, the Austrian architect was born in Steyermühl, (Upper Austria) on 14 May 1881 and died in Linz on 11 August 1928. The son of a director of an industrial plant, he studied architecture between 1899 and 1905 at Vienna's Technische Hochschule and then with Friedrich Ohmann at the Akademie and his private studio between 1905 and 1908. In 1909 he was an architect with the building department of the city council of Linz; then, from 1921, a freelance architect in Linz before becoming a professor at the Technische Hochschule in Graz in 1926.

Schulte is considered to be one of the most significant architects of Upper Austria. He was architect of Linz Crematorium (1925–29), the first of its kind to be erected in Upper Austria. He designed the conversion of the Stadtwäldchen (municipal woods) into an urn grove, a gate, a gatekeeper's house and a ceremonial hall with a cremation installation located directly below it. Because Schulte died in 1928, the construction project was carried out and completed by his pupils, Hans Arndt and Paul Theer who expanded Schulte's design for the *Aschengarten* ('ash garden') with a well-integrated portrait gallery. Schulte's project for Linz crematorium was based on the concentric effect of the circular ground-plan. Built about ten years prior to the world-renowned Swedish model by Gunnar Asplund in Stockholm, it exhibits a unique union of expressionistic and economical elements.

Schulte's development as an architect was marked by his divergence from the national Romanticism of the time; he tended towards a Baroque-bourgeois tradition that can be seen as a kind of patriotism. His style changed with the fall of the Habsburg Monarchy and the founding of the Republic and came to be characterized by the use of expressionistic elements. With the help of his differentiating perspective, he had the gift of building technical projects in an indicative and symbolic way while always retaining the relationship to the original task. The economical tendencies of the times were expressed in his later buildings by a special emphasis on basic geometric shapes. His works are characterized by how well they fit into the topographical and town-planning situation at hand. His buildings, always of a high quality and sometimes enriched with distinct physiognomical elements, usually dominate their surroundings. His principal works include: the Reformed church, St Veit an der Glan/Kärnten (1909–12); the fire brigade training school building (the former Permanganatfabrik) industrial plant, Linz (1919); the Römerbergsiedlung, housing estate, Linz (1923–28); the bridge leading over the Traunfall, Steyermühl (1924); the water tower of the brewery at Gmunden (1925): the Beurle family home, Linz (1926–27); the Ebensee school building (1927); Linz Crematorium (1925–29). **Bruno Maldoner**

References

Arndt, H. and Theer, P. (1933), *Julius Schulte und seine Schüler*, Innsbruck: Wagner.

Achleitner, F. (1980), *Österreichische Architektur im 20. Jahrhundert*, Vol. 1, Salzburg and Vienna: Residenz Verlag.

Achleitner, F. (1983), *Österreichische Architektur im 20. Jahrhundert*, Vol. 2, Salzburg and Vienna: Residenz Verlag.

SCHUMACHER, FRITZ

Although relatively unknown today, the German Fritz Schumacher was counted as one of his generation's most innovative architects, particularly in the areas of religious architecture and urban planning. In addition to designing two of the most widely admired crematoria in Germany, Schumacher was an active supporter of the cremation movement. His architectural writings include a treatise on the design of crematoria – a field in which he was recognized as an expert.

Born into a diplomatic family in Bremen in 1869, Schumacher's early years were spent in Bogotá, Colombia and New York. After studying in Munich and Berlin, in 1901 Schumacher became a professor for interior design at the technical university in Dresden. He first made a name for himself at the 1906 exhibition of arts and crafts held at Dresden. A model interior for a Protestant church was widely admired by the public, churchmen and leading architectural critics. Schumacher was also selected to design an important new crematorium complex for Dresden. From 1909 Schumacher's activity focused on Hamburg where he became a director of construction (*Baudirektor*). There he became deeply interested in urban planning and the place of cemeteries, helping to redesign them and also designing Hamburg's second crematorium in the Ohlsdorfer Cemetery. Hamburg had been a pioneer in legalizing and introducing cremation in Germany, and had possessed a crematorium since 1892, but in the 1920s a new one was called for. Once again, Schumacher's architecture was ground-breaking. Whereas his luxurious Dresden crematorium epitomized the monumental tendencies of architecture prior to the First World War, his Hamburg crematorium epitomizes the abstracting qualities of Weimar architecture. The Ohlsdorfer Crematorium went into operation in 1933, the same year in which Schumacher retired. **Tim Pursell**

References

Frank, Hartmut (ed.) (1994), *Fritz Schumacher, Reformkultur und Moderne*, Stuttgart: Hatje.

Kayser, Werner (1984), *Fritz Schumacher: Architekt und Städtebaue*, Frankfurt: H. Christians.

Schumacher, Fritz (1935), *Stufen des Lebens*, Stuttgart and Berlin: Deutsche Verlags-Anstalt.

Schumacher, Fritz (1935), *Strömungen in deutscher Baukunst seit 1800*, Leipzig: C.A. Seemann.

Schumacher, Fritz (1939), *Die Feuerbestattung*, Leipzig: J.M. Gebhardt's Verlag.

SECONDARY BURIAL

Cremated remains have often been accorded a burial or entombment as a secondary rite, or secondary burial, following the initial cremation process. See the material on Robert Hertz as the key anthropological interpreter of such practices. **Douglas J. Davies**

SECULARIZATION AND SECULARISM

In sociological terms, secularization refers to a process by which religious institutions lose control over, and direct influence on, the formal organization of a society. A corresponding emphasis is placed on the sense of human control over social life and its many ventures. Secularism, by contrast refers to a direct ideological position that actively works for the removal of such religious influence. It is useful to note this distinction between secularization as a social process brought about by many factors and secularism as a concrete ideology explicitly pursued by individuals or groups.

Both the process of secularization and the ideology of secularism may be observed in the history of the development of cremation in modern societies. The entries on **freemasonry in Italy** and **Italy–secularization** offer good examples of the way in which Freemasonry in some, but not all, European countries was an active force of secularism, while the **materialism and enlightenment** entry describes the wider cultural background of some European secularism. Indeed, cremation came to be one of the major vehicles through which a secularist ideology could be pursued against the formal structure and operation of the Catholic Church. However, in Britain, that was not the case, and cremation emerged as one aspect of the scientific and social welfare and sanitary reforms of the later nineteenth century. Together, those reforms, along with the growth in scientific and rational modes of controlling many aspects of life, including illness, tended to foster the process of secularization.

Some sociologists argue that although secularisation leads to a reduction in the public influence of religion that does not mean that religion is not important for the private aspects of people's lives. Here, cremation becomes one interesting test case of that theory for, although the great majority of people still avail themselves of religious funerals in that clergy act as officiants, many of these events include increasing amounts of material that is not traditionally religious but reflects the music or favourite readings of the deceased or their family and friends. At the same time, however, there is a small, but growing, trend for funerals to be led not by clergy but by specialist officiants capable of providing a religious, secular or mixed form of rite. The entry on **New Zealand** describes the significant part played by such ritual leaders in that country, and something similar could also be said for Australia. The fact that crematoria are not owned by churches in these countries makes it relatively easy for them to be a place of secular or mixed activity.

The very architecture of crematoria also plays its part in the possibility of fostering either a general secularization or an active secularism as in some earlier Italian cremation 'temples'. In the USA, by contrast, there is a very much higher level of active religious participation in public religion and burial has, until the later twentieth century, been the predominant form of funeral and has taken a clear religious form. Cremation has often been a marginal activity and crematoria of the European variety with large chapels and ceremony rooms have not been as evident. **Douglas J. Davies**

See also architecture – Italian; freemasonry in Italy; Italy – secularization; materialism and enlightenment; New Zealand; USA.

SHELLEY, PERCY BYSSHE

Percy Bysshe Shelley, the English poet, was cremated at Viareggio on the shore of the Gulf of Spezzia on 16 August 1822. Shelley had been living in Italy since his exile from England in 1818. In the summer of 1822, he and Mary Shelley and their friends, Jane and Edward Williams, were living in the Casa Magni at San Terenzo, near Lerici. At the beginning of July, Shelley and Edward Williams sailed across to Leghorn to go to Pisa to welcome Leigh Hunt, who had come from England to collaborate with Shelley and Byron on the founding of a new

paper, *The Liberal*. During their return on 8 July their yacht was overtaken by a storm and either swamped or, accidentally or deliberately, rammed by a *felucca*. On 17 July Williams's body was found washed up near the mouth of the Serchio in Tuscany. The next day, Shelley's was found on the shore three miles north of Viareggio and that of Charles Vivian, their crew, even further north near Massa.

The quarantine laws of the Florentine and Lucchese governments were very strict. Vivian's body was burnt there and then, and his ashes buried on the spot. Williams's body was buried before it could be positively identified. Shelley's was identified and then buried in quicklime. None of those closest to Shelley and Williams, however, wanted their bodies to remain where they had been buried. It was eventually decided that Shelley's would be buried in the Protestant cemetery in Rome where his son and Keats were buried. When the commander of the fort at the mouth of Serchio, strictly applying the quarantine laws, refused to allow the exhumation, the solution of cremating the bodies and transporting the ashes was hit upon. Williams's cremation took place on 15 August; Shelley's the next day. As far as one can tell from surviving accounts, the furnace for the cremations was made at Leghorn and consisted of an iron container about five feet long by two feet wide by two feet deep with a grill base, mounted on legs two feet high. What was left of the bodies fell apart as they were placed in the container. Wood was piled under and over it and ignited. Both cremations took about five hours. They were stage-managed by Edward Trelawny, 'the personification', as Byron put it after their first meeting, 'of my Corsair'.

Williams's ashes minus his jawbone, which Trelawny retained, were finally buried with Jane Williams and Thomas Hogg, her second husband, in Kensall Green in 1884. The old Protestant cemetery at Rome being closed, Shelley's ashes were buried in the new one on 21 January 1823, but when Trelawny arrived in Rome he did not like the location of the grave. He purchased a plot where he had two adjacent tombs constructed. To one of these he transferred Shelley's ashes.

Trelawny wrote at least six accounts of the cremations during his lifetime. In his first published account in 1858, he made changes both for dramatic effect and in response to the rise in Shelley's reputation in the intervening years. The emphasis, which in the earlier accounts he had tended to place on Williams' cremation as it was the first to take place, was shifted more to Shelley's cremation, and details of the cremations were transposed from one account to the other. Commentators thought that Trelawny's account of the cremations did the cremation cause no good at all, and opinion was no different when he republished it in 1878, four years after the foundation of the Cremation Society of England, as *Records of Shelley, Byron and the Author*. One of the main changes Trelawny made in the *Records* resulted from his attempt to defend the most incredible part of his earlier account – namely the resistance of Shelley's heart to the fire and Trelawny's snatching it from the flames. Whether or not the heart was in fact preserved, Mary Shelley and Leigh Hunt argued over the possession of what both believed to be the heart; and, if the heart was preserved, it was probably eventually interred in the grave, or even in the coffin, of Sir Percy Shelley, Shelley's son, in the churchyard of St Peter's Bournemouth, in 1889. Other alleged remnants of the cremation, ashes and fragments of bone, were being exhibited around London in the 1870s. The British Museum has a thick red leather-bound volume containing the manuscript of Mary Shelley's long letter to Maria Gisborne about Shelley's death. Inset into the back cover of this volume and covered with glass are, allegedly, fragments of Shelley's skull and some of his ashes once in the possession of Trelawny.

Neither of the best-known depictions of Shelley's cremation, W. Howitt's *Homes and Haunts of the British Poets* (1846) and Fournier's painting, *Funérailles de Shelley* came close to an accurate portrayal of the event. In 1878 Gerome was working on a painting of it, which he never finished.

When Trelawny died in 1881, he was cremated at Gotha and his ashes were placed in the tomb adjacent to Shelley's in Rome. **Stephen White**

See also art; Frankenstein.

References

Biagi, Guido (1898), *The Last Days of Percy Bysshe Shelley. New Details from Unpublished Documents*, London: T. Fisher Unwin.

Gay, H. Nelson (1913), 'The Protestant Burial-Ground in Rome: A Historical Sketch' (with Unpublished Documents regarding the Graves of Keats and Shelley)', *Bulletin and Review of the Keats-Shelley Memorial*, 2: 33–59.

Marchand, Leslie (1952), 'Trelawny on the Death of Shelley (A Re-examination of the Evidence in the Light of Two Unpublished Autograph Manuscripts in the Keats-Shelley Memorial', *Keats-Shelley Memorial Bulletin*, 4: 9–34.

Marchand, Leslie (1955), 'A Note on the Burning of Shelley's Body', *Keats-Shelley Memorial Bulletin*, 6: 1–3.

Trelawny, Edward John (1858), *Recollections of the Last Days of Shelley and Byron*, London: E. Maxon.

Trelawny, Edward John (1878), *Records of Shelley, Byron and the Author*, London: Basil Montagu Pickering.

White, Stephen (1989), 'The Call-Shelley Agreement about Shelley's and Trelawny's Graves', *Keats-Shelley Review*, 4: 95–100.

SIEDEK, OSKAR

Oskar Siedek (1853–1934), being a proponent of the Austrian Society of Cremation 'Die Flamme' ('The Flame') and its chairman for many years, is said to have paved the way for modern cremation in Austria. One of his most important achievements was his commitment to constructing the first crematorium in the territory of the Austro-Hungarian Monarchy, which was built in Liberec (Czech Republic) in 1914 and was set in operation in 1918.

Siedek was born on 24 May 1853 in Napajedla (Czech Republic) and was the son of the director of a sugar factory. He attended high school in Vienna, received commercial training in Dresden and returned to Vienna where he started to work in a sugar factory, later becoming a bank official (*Creditanstalt*) until his retirement. Early 1885, when Siedek became fascinated by the model of a cremator that was exhibited in the window of a branch shop of Siemens in Vienna, is usually referred to as the beginning of cremation in Austria. It is said that it was then that Siedek decided to found a society for the advancement of cremation.

In April 1885 the foundation assembly of the Austrian Cremation Society 'Die Flamme' was held. Siedek presided over the society from 1904 until his death in 1934 and also did great service for the international movement of cremation. In 1886 he was co-founder and, subsequently, president of the Association of German-Speaking Societies of Cremation. Apart from that, he worked in the editorial office of the journal *Phoenix. Blätter für facultative Feuerbestattung.* In total, some 28 societies and associations of cremation at home and abroad admitted him as an honorary member. Apart from his ambitious advocacy for cremation Siedek also was an active member of the Old Catholic Church where he acted as a synodal councillor. He died on 12 April 1934 at the age of 81, and his body was cremated in Vienna. **Christian Stadelmann**

See also Austria.

Reference

Österreichisches Biographisches Lexikon 1815–1950 ed. Österreichische Akademie der Wissenschften H, Vol. 12 (56th part) 2003, 230f.

SIEMENS, FRIEDERICH

Friedrich Siemens, a German engineer, designed one of the first cremators. His first cremator, presented at the world exhibition in Vienna in 1873, was not actually intended for cremation and did not have the required effect. He subsequently developed a hot-air cremator, which worked much better. A large group of experts and journalists attended the tests, which were mainly carried out on dead horses. They were successful, as the carcasses were quickly and fully incinerated. Moreover, tests showed that no hazardous substances were emitted from the chimney.

On 9 October 1874, the first cremation of a dead body took place in a Siemens cremator. Unfortunately, it did not progress as planned, due to the member of the clergy not turning up. Siemens therefore requested that those present 'bare their heads and offer prayer in private'.

During the first European Congress of the Fellowship of Cremation in Dresden, engineer R. Scheider gave a lecture on Friedrich Siemens' cremators. More lectures were to follow, including several in the Netherlands. On 10 December 1878, the crematorium in Gotha, Germany, commissioned the first Siemens cremator. Friedrich Siemens was followed by a number of apprentices, many of whom continually improved their 'master's' original cremator model. In 1884 Siemens was appointed an honorary member of the Royal Cremation Society 'the Facultatieve' *Koninklijke Vereniging voor Facultatieve Crematie* in the Netherlands. **J.M.H.J. Keizer**

SOUL

The formerly widespread practice of cremation in Europe gradually ceased with the spread of Christianity and in particular with the consequential belief in resurrection of the body understood as entailing the restoration to life of the buried corpse. There was no necessary connection between choosing burial and believing in resurrection because God had the power to locate the particles of the former body no matter how widely they had been dispersed. But Christian sentiment certainly did associate believing in bodily resurrection with repugnance towards cremating the body. However during the nineteenth and twentieth centuries it became increasingly common for Christians to 'spiritualize' their belief in the resurrection of the body so that it was no longer associated with any expectation that they would get their old bodies back. This change in understanding played a crucial role in the re-establishment of the practice of cremation in the mid-nineteenth century and in its widespread popularity in the second part of the twentieth. This was not, of course, an issue for those among the pioneers of the restoration of cremation who rejected any kind of belief in a future life, but it was certainly an important factor in enabling the practice of cremation to spread through the Christian community.

However, belief that human personality can survive not only bodily death but also the complete destruction of the body through cremation depends on the validity of some concept of the soul. This is fully accepted in *The Catechism of the Catholic Church* (1994: 83 and 227) and its affirmation that the soul 'is immortal: it does not perish when it separates from the body at death'. In death 'the human body decays and the soul goes to meet God, while awaiting its reunion with its glorified body'. Protestant theologians are less clear. There is a strong tendency among them to prefer the language of resurrection to the language of immortality. On the other hand there is an overwhelming consensus that there could be no physical continuity between our present embodiment and our future 'spiritual bodies'. Instead, what would ensure continuity would be 'our personality', 'the essential part of what we are', 'the vital principle of our being' or 'our moral and intellectual qualities'. Such phrases are used in preference to the word 'soul' although they are actually the meanings given to the word 'soul' in the *Concise Oxford Dictionary* (Badham, 1976: 86).

Two reports by the Church of England Doctrine Commission (1938: 207; 1996: 191–92, 10–11) help to clarify the situation. According to the earlier report, Christians should reject 'literalistic belief in a future resuscitation of the actual physical frame laid in the tomb...none the less in the life of the world to come the soul or spirit will still have its appropriate organ of expression and activity'. The later report states that '[i]t is not to be supposed that the material of the resurrected body is the same as that of the old'. It suggests that the idea of the soul should be redefined as the 'complex information bearing pattern of what we are' and it affirms that 'that pattern can surely be considered the carrier of memories and personality'.

Douglas Davies (1997) has shown that, in popular belief, the immortality of the soul has almost totally replaced belief in the resurrection of the body as an expression of Christian hope. In television documentaries, popular books and student debates there remains considerable public interest in discussions about the soul whereas belief in the resurrection of the body attracts no attention. The only exception to this is in relation to Jesus Christ whose resurrection is seen as wholly unique and as having nothing whatever to do with what Christians might themselves expect (Badham, 1998: 2 and 121).

Richard Swinburne (1986: 1–2) argues that 'though the mental life of thought, sensation and purpose may be caused by physico-chemical events in the brain, it is quite different from those events'. He believes that conscious experiences are themselves causally efficacious and that the 'the human soul' can acquire independence of the brain. Keith Ward (1985: 149–50) likewise believes that, although the soul depends on the brain, it need not always depend on the brain any more than our present lives still depend on the womb which sheltered us before birth. This understanding of the soul as an emergent property means that one can fully accept everything that modern science teaches concerning the dependence of mental events on brain processes while at the same time being open to the possibility that the soul might nonetheless be able to survive the death of the body. Many believe that near-death experiences may be relevant here, since some people who were resuscitated from near the brink of death are convinced that when their hearts stopped beating they left their bodies and watched the resuscitation process from above. They often believe that if they had not been 'brought back' they would have gone on to new life (Badham and Ballard, 1996).

Such discussions of the soul are almost certainly a factor in the growing popularity of cremation. The remains of the physical body are no longer seen as being in any way relevant to the possibility that human personality might survive bodily death. Hence the total destruction of the corpse through cremation poses no threat, but might indeed be thought to clarify the view that the soul has been released to new life. **Paul Badham**

See also early modern western Europe.

References

Badham, P. (1976), *Christian Beliefs about Life After Death*, London: Macmillan.

Badham, P. (1998), *The Contemporary Challenge of Modernist Theology*, Cardiff: University of Wales Press.

Badham, P. and Ballard, P. (1996), *Facing Death*, Cardiff: University of Wales Press.

Catholic Church (1994), T*he Catechism of the Catholic Church*, London: Chapman.

Church of England (1938), *The Report of the Commission on Doctrine Appointed by the Archbishops of Canterbury and York in 1922*, London: SPK.

Church of England Doctrine Commission (1996), *The Mystery of Salvation*, London: Church House Publishing.

Davies, Douglas, J. (1997), 'Theologies of Disposal', in P.C. Jupp and T. Rogers (eds), *Interpreting Death: Christian Theology and Pastoral Practice*, London: Cassell.

Swinburne, R. (1986), *The Evolution of the Soul*, Oxford: Clarendon Press.

Ward, K. (1985), *The Battle for the Soul*, London: Hodder.

SOUTH AFRICA

To understand the development of cremation in South Africa one has first to appreciate the tribal nature of its heterogeneous population that, as the twenty-first century begins, is made up of the major tribes as shown in this Table.

Description	Millions	%
English-speaking whites	2	5
Afrikaans-speaking whites	3	7
Coloured	3	7
Xhosa blacks	10	24
Zulu blacks	8	20
Continentals & orientals	1	2
Other black tribes	14	34
Total	41	100

It is also important to know that, as the present century begins, 40 per cent of the total population lives in eight major metropolitan areas, over 50 per cent of the population is aged under 21, and an estimated 30 per cent of the population is HIV positive. Each major segment of the population has its own funeral customs and beliefs about the afterlife. For blacks, communication with ancestral spirits is very important; hence cremation remains a taboo, as it is believed that cremation will cause the spirit to become lost. It is also taboo to bury more than one body in a grave, as the upper body may suffocate the lower. A finite place of burial is essential, and the amount spent on the funeral is seen as an investment to ensure that ancestral spirits remain favourably disposed towards the living. That leaves a potential cremation market of only 21 per cent of the population. From this must be excluded the Roman Catholic continentals who are very traditional, and Muslims, which leaves a potential market of about 12 per cent, and from this must be excluded those who live distant from a crematorium, and those very traditional Afrikaans whites who view cremation as anti-biblical. This means that, out of 41 million people, the true market for cremation is probably only 4 million. Given a death rate of about 8.5 per 1000, the annual market should be approximately 35 000. The actual cremation figure for 2000 was 31 836. Another limiting factor to growth in this market is that many of the English-speaking whites and coloureds have, in recent years, left the country and emigrated to safer climes, taking elderly parents with them. The development and history of cremation in South Africa therefore has to be seen against the demographics of the country.

The pioneering years: 1900–45

The first furnace, as opposed to open-pyre type of crematorium, was built in South Africa in 1918 by the municipality of Johannesburg, specifically for the use of the large Hindu population in the area. The crematorium has a ceremonial hall for the observance of religious rites, and there are a number of large trees nearby for affixing nameplates, removed from the coffins before cremation – part of the Hindu ritual. The ceremonial hall is totally enclosed, itself unusual for a Hindu crematorium, but – in accordance with custom – there are no chairs but only standing room, in this case for about 200 people. No memorialization options are provided. This crematorium is still operative, and is still owned by the local authority. One single Dowson & Mason cremation unit of 1970s design is used.

The second crematorium was built in Durban in 1926, by the S.A. Crematorium Company, a private company which leased an area within the municipal Stellawood Cemetery. When it was built, it had coke-fired cremators, later replaced with South African-manufactured gas-fired Sinderator cremators, which in turn were replaced with two Dowson & Mason units, which were ultimately replaced with two ALL cremators from the USA. Unfortunately, a fire destroyed most of the building housing the cremators, and, when it was rebuilt, two South African-designed gas-fired Macroburn units were installed. Durban is a very English city with many direct descendants from the UK making for a very high level of cremation of English-speaking whites. For nearly 40 years, Durban Crematorium was the only privately-owned crematorium in the country. In 1969, however, the crematorium was acquired by the HT Group (Pty) Ltd. The original owners were very keen to promote cremation and published a booklet entitled *The Advantage of Cremation* which was widely distributed. There is a chapel seating about 150 people with niches, spaces for wall plaques and ash graves available, although space is at a premium.

The third crematorium was built in 1932, in the major metropolitan area of Johannesburg by the Johannesburg municipality. The municipality was not very keen on running the crematorium and, soon after it was opened, they offered it for sale; however, there were no buyers, and the municipality continues to run it to this day. In 1936 the chapel was enlarged to accommodate 120 people, and there is an underground crypt for ash-urns, but usage has fallen off and the crematorium is now little used for funeral services and is only just functional. The first cremator was coke-fired with a locally-built gas unit added in 1936. In 1939 the coke unit was replaced with two imported gas units. By 1982 there were two single 1970s-design Dowson & Mason units, and one double South African-designed Sinderator unit. The two singles were later converted to a Dowson & Mason twin-reflux unit. These were all replaced by new units in the 1980s.

The fourth crematorium was opened in 1934 in Cape Town's Maitland Road Cemetery, and was built and managed by the Board of Trustees of the Cape Peninsula Cemeteries. In 1970 the control of the public cemeteries, including the crematorium, passed to the Divisional Council of the Cape. This local authority was very active in promoting the concept of cremation, particularly amongst the coloured people, and organized information brochures and regular open days to educate church leaders on its merits. This policy resulted in the numbers of cremations rising from an annual figure of 2000 in 1978 to over 6000 in 1986. The author wrote a pamphlet entitled *Thirty Questions and Answers about Cremation* which was subsequently published in *Resurgam*, and was later adopted by all the UK crematoria, as well as those in Australasia and the USA.

The local authority continued to manage the crematorium until it was privatized in 1999, when the HT Group (Pty) Ltd acquired the lease. There is a chapel seating 150 people, with ancillary facilities of niches, wall spaces for plaques and a book of remembrance. Interestingly, the chapel is the most used crematorium chapel in the country, mainly because the coloured people usually have a double service (first at home, and then at the place of disposition), preferably on a Saturday morning when all can attend. The cremators were originally two oil-fired units, with a further two added in 1942. In 1973 two reflux Dowson & Mason units were installed, with a further two doubles added in 1992, also of 1970s design.

The fifth, and final, crematorium to be built in this pioneering stage was that at Brakpan, built in 1945 by the municipality on the borders of its cemetery. The muncipality continued to manage it until it was privatized in 1988 and acquired by the HT Group (Pty) Ltd. The crematorium has a chapel seating 100 people, and niches, walls for plaques and a book of remembrance are all available. The cremators were originally coal-fired, and after various overhauls, an ALL Model 2000 was installed in 1990.

This pioneering stage of cremation was characterized by large investments in major metropolitan areas, designed to cater primarily for the English-speaking white market consisting largely of entrepreneurs in the blossoming South African economy, and not for the Afrikaans whites who, at this stage, were blue-collar workers who would soon become the bureaucrats. The only other concession was for the Hindu population in Johannesburg. In Durban, Pretoria and Cape Town, the Hindus made use of the open-pyre method of cremation.

One observation that must be made is the minimal usage (2 per cent) of the book of remembrance concept in South Africa. This is due, in part, to the low usage (approximately 8 per cent) of crematorium chapels; crematoriums have become increasingly purely functional with no funeral ceremony being held there. Thus, a very high percentage (around 92 per cent) of funeral ceremonies are held at other localities rather than the crematorium itself.

The growth years: 1946–65

This period represents steady growth in the provision of cremation facilities, with crematoria being constructed by local authorities in Pietermaritzburg (1951), Port Elizabeth (1953), Pretoria (1957), East London (1959) and Krugersdorp (1961). The Clare Estate Hindu Cemetery and Crematorium Committee was forced to close its open-pyre facility in Durban and build a conventional furnace crematorium, which was opened in 1964. In 1965 the HT Group (Pty) Ltd built a crematorium in Bloemfontein's municipal cemetery. Pietermaritzburg installed electrically-fired Barnes Birlec units; Port Elizabeth and East London had Gibbons Askham diesel-fired units; and Pretoria opted for coal-fired units. Over the years, most were converted to Dowson & Mason units. Krugersdorp and Port Elizabeth have both subsequently been taken over by the HT Group (Pty) Ltd, in 1987 and 1997 respectively. By the end of this phase of development, there were cremation facilities in all the major metropolitan areas, with some areas even having choices. However, the market remained almost entirely restricted to Hindus and English-speaking whites.

The steady years: 1966–90

This period saw only six new crematoria open for business. Three were built by local authorities: Tongaat in 1973, Vanderbijlpark in 1981, and a second facility in Pietermaritzburg in 1987. Three were built by various Hindu trusts: Verulam in 1985, Lenasia in 1985 and Newcastle in 1989. Of the six, only Vanderbijlpark was not built for the Hindu community. These new facilities were built not so much to meet increasing demand for cremation, but to prevent further pollution of the environment by traditional open-pyre cremation. During this period Dowson & Mason's position as provider of cremators changed when four of the six new crematoria opted for locally-designed cremators. Vanderbijlpark Crematorium was acquired by the HT Group (Pty) Ltd in 1988.

The hectic years: 1991–2001

This ten-year period saw a rash of small cremation facilities being established, almost entirely by private enterprise, and mostly in non-traditional cremation areas. Facilities were established in George (1991) within municipal grounds and Ladysmith (1991), both of which are unique in that the cremators were built by people with no knowledge of the human cremation process and with no input from recognized authorities on the subject. These were followed by Pietersburg (1991), which was also a first in that the cremator was erected within the grounds of a funeral home in the city centre, using an ALL 2000 unit. Malmesbury (1991) was the next to follow, and this, too, was unique in that there are no public facilities at all. The owners collect bodies from surrounding funeral directors, and return the cremated remains direct to them. The facility is located in an industrial area about 60 kilometres from Cape Town. Of the ten crematoria opened during this period, only one was built by a local authority; the rest were all constructed by private enterprise. They are: Worcester (1993), Port Shepstone (1993), Durban Chatsworth (1996), Eshowe (1997), Kempton

Park (1997), Klerksdorp (1997), Nelspruit (1997), Johannesburg Fourways (2000), Despatch (1999) and Middelburg (2000). Worcester Crematorium operated in a similar manner to Malmesbury, in that it, too, had no public facilities, the dead being transported in special vehicles from Cape Town (about 90 kilometres away) and the cremated remains being returned the next day. The reason for this mode of operation was that Cape Town Crematorium belonged to the local authority which was determined to retain its monopoly and consequently refused any application from a private entrepreneur to build a competitive facility within its area of jurisdiction. A major firm of funeral directors then built a crematorium at Worcester and transported their own cremation clients there for cremation. An entrepreneur had built Malmesbury Crematorium for the same reason two years earlier.

Legislation

The legislation governing cremation in South Africa is virtually identical to that used in the UK (from which it was derived). There are the same requirements of a declaration under oath by the applicant for cremation, a form to be signed by the attending doctor; a form signed by the confirmatory doctor and, finally, the authority signed by the medical referee. One problem that has never been resolved is that some of the provincial authorities use different questions with different form numbering, making life difficult for funeral directors. Everyone is convinced that the confirmatory form provides no safeguard at all, but fees are changed for completing the form, so the medical profession fights against its abolition. Some of the private crematorium operators use their own forms incorporating the legal questions, but adding many more, based on US legal precedents against crematorium operators. The National Funeral Directors' Association in South Africa has produced a model set of forms for use by its members. There is, regrettably, no association representing cemetery and crematorium operators.

Memorialization

Memorialization plays a very low-key part in the cremation process in South Africa, in so far as it affects crematoria. Today, many churches and other organizations provide some form of memorialization and, given the comparatively low usage of crematoria chapels, few people feel any need to return to a crematorium if, indeed, they were ever there in the first place. Whilst many of the older crematoria provided niches, wall space for plaques and a book of remembrance, demand has remained consistently low. Certainly in Cape Town, some 37 per cent of those choosing cremation will scatter the remains; 15 per cent will bury them in a garden of remembrance (not necessarily at a crematorium); 1 per cent will use a wall niche somewhere; 4 per cent will let their families decide; and 13 per cent will bury them somewhere. There is no legal impediment to the disposition of cremated remains within South Africa, and many just bury remains in their gardens, or in some place close to their hearts, such as along the coastline, or in a nature reserve.

The future

None of us has the ability to gaze into the crystal ball and see the future, but I cannot help but wonder how the AIDS pandemic will be handled in the future. According to the medical experts, we know very little about the virus and about how long it survives after the death of the person, and what effect there is on the surrounding earth or water supplies and so on. All we do know for certain is that heat destroys it. Whether the South African authorities will make cremation mandatory for AIDS victims remains to be seen. This would be a bold step given the black concept of the afterlife and the need to consult ancestral spirits. If this does not happen, the growth in cremation will slow down, as the largest users, namely English-speaking whites, are emigrating in ever-increasing numbers. Without doubt, no more cremators will be imported into to the country if the exchange rate remains strongly disadvantageous, and the market is not large enough to sustain a local manufacturer, although, hopefully, an overseas manufacturer will see the benefit of manufacturing in South Africa for export overseas.

Selected statistics

In 1954 there were six crematoria, conducting 2635 cremations. By 1970 ten crematoria conducted 7708 cremations. This had increased by 1980, to 11 facilities cremating 12 163 people. The year 1991 saw 18 crematoria perform 22 377 cremations, and, by 2000, 31 crematoria

conducted 31 836 cremations. The really interesting statistic is that in Cape Town in 1970, only 25 out of 1410 persons cremated were other than white (1.7 per cent). This had increased by 1983 to 1054 out of 4052 (26 per cent): that was the last year when separate statistics were available by race. This shows what can be achieved by a sound marketing policy.

Attitude change

The attitudes of different population groups towards cremation have changed over the years and can be summarized as follows. With blacks, as in the USA and other parts of the world, traditional burial is the preferred method of disposition. Amongst South Africa's black population, the need to consult the ancestral spirits is too high to ignore for the sake of expediency. Some blacks have opted for cremation, but in such small numbers that it is statistically irrelevant. No one believes that this will ever change in the future. A high percentage of English-speaking whites, with their British cultural background, opt for cremation – probably around 85 per cent. They tend to be the entrepreneurs living in the large metropolitan areas, with high incomes and high mobility. As many have already left the country for safer climes, taking their elderly parents with them, in the long term there will be no growth in cremation from this segment of the population. Afrikaans-speaking whites owned a Calvinistic background with church-teaching that cremation was the way of the heathen and was anti-Biblical. However, as in many areas of life, they have had to rethink their principles, and more and more are opting for cremation, particularly those in the metropolitan areas. They were the bureaucrats of the country with a 'guaranteed' income and much certainty for the future. With the advent of black majority rule, that security has gone, and this segment is now having to adjust to the uncertainties of capitalism, hence there has been a significant downsizing of funerals, and a switch to cremation. This has been helped by the rapid increase in facilities outside metropolitan areas. Coloured people have traditionally opted for earth burial, but in recent years (since approximately 1981), they have rapidly increased in adopting cremation as their churches have seen the benefits and encouraged a more sensible approach towards funeral expenditure. Many of the coloured churches have burial societies, which the church administers on behalf of its adherents, and they contract with funeral companies to provide services at a fixed price with a fixed specification. They obviously therefore look for ways of keeping funeral costs down. This should be an obvious growth point for cremation, particularly in areas where burial has been the norm. However, many coloureds are converting to Islam, and burial is the prescribed method of disposition for them.

Whilst many folk believe that the funeral profession in its broadest context is very traditional, stable and predictable, the development of cremation in South Africa proves just the opposite. It is a constantly changing scenario, with all sorts of extraneous events affecting the domestic market. Probably the most significant developments over recent years has been the number of private entrepreneurs coming into the cremation market, coupled with the move towards purely functional facilities without provision for any funeral ceremonies or memorialization. Of the 32 crematoria in 2001 only ten belonged to local authorities (the remaining 22 belonging to private enterprise). The future growth does, however, look limited, unless deaths resulting from AIDS are required to be cremated. **Chris J. Molyneux**

SPAIN

Cremation was one of the preferred methods of corpse disposal for the first cultures known in the Iberian peninsula, the Megalithic and Iberian. Some of the most important and impressive archaeological discoveries are the Lady of Elche and the Lady of Baza, two realistic cinerary urns with small-sized apertures at the back of the sculptures prepared for the ashes of someone reckoned to be a member of an Iberian urban elite.

Although the Romans used both inhumation and cremation, the rise of Christianity halted the practice because it was identified with paganism. Of course, it was a generalized phenomenon across Europe, but the Muslim invasion of 711 CE created a distinct society in which cremation would came to have a different social meaning. The three peoples of the Book – Muslims, Jews and Christians – historically forbade cremation as a method of corpse disposal (with Muslim and Orthodox Jews continuing to do so) and, although there were exceptions, the three

communities lived in peace, with the community of the living being reflected in the community of the dead as each possessed its own funerary space. This tolerance started to vanish from the pogroms of 1391 onwards, and disappeared totally after the unification of Spain.

This process of unification converted multicultural Spain into a country that had no space for non-Christians and later, non-Catholic, communities, and this change was reflected again in the funerary space and in rituals. The Edict of the Expulsion of the Jews of 1492 forced those Jews who did not take the path of exile to convert to Christianity, and the same happened with the Moorish communities albeit under a longer, less defined process. Finally, all of Spain's inhabitants were considered formally Christians, and the only permitted funerary spaces were Christian, too. Forced conversions obviously produced some people who simulated adherence to Christianity while privately maintaining the practice of their old faith. The consequence of this was that crypto-Jews who were discovered or denounced and who did not repent of their 'mistakes' were defined as unable to remain within either the community of the living or of the dead: they were sentenced to death by fire and their ashes were scattered – the worst penalty for an individual of that time irrespective of whether they were Christian, Moor or Jew.

This was the only practice of cremation in Spain, which was applied to sincere Christians only under the most exceptional circumstances, such as for rebellion against the Crown or the unique case of witchery which ended in a death penalty by fire. Because of this, when the crypto-Jewish community was finally extinguished in the last third of the seventeenth century, cremation ceased since it was the worst imaginable penalty and an affront to human dignity. Cremation for Christians was inconceivable, and this stigma constituted a basic reason for the delay in the introduction of modern cremation in Spain. The other reason was the attitude of the Catholic Church.

This negative value was so deeply rooted within Spanish culture that cremation did not even become a vehicle for anti-clerical activists for fighting their battles against the Catholic Church: their only triumph in this funerary area lay in the establishment of distinct civil and Protestant cemeteries. Until recently, the Catholic Church identified cremation as 'a practice of the enemies of the Church' precisely because Protestant Churches permitted it and because it was also identified with the foreign practice of freemasonry, although there is no record that cremation occupied a significant place in Spanish masonic agendas. The dark version of cremation is also absent: in the worst moments of the carnage of the Civil War, the fascist regime did not cremate the bodies of *desaparecidos* (missing people); rather they were buried in common graves of up to 2500 people, which only began to be excavated in 2000. Although, as the Nazis sadly demonstrated, cremation is far more efficient than burial when dealing with huge numbers of bodies, the aversion to cremation was so extreme that death squads never used it as a disposal method.

Until the year 2002 cremation was not treated as equivalent to burial by the Catholic Church, as evidenced by its prohibition of placing ashes inside a church. This year marked, however, a totally revolutionary initiative towards the inhumation of ashes in the vaults of concrete churches including St Barbara, itself the important resting place of the Bourbon King Ferdinand VI. This initiative is somewhat reminiscent of the situation existing prior to the creation of cemeteries separate from churchyards: it also involves a new or returned source of income for the parishes. Although the Second Vatican Council (Vatican II) initially authorized cremation in 1963, both the dark precedent of cremation as a punishment, and the fact that Jesus Christ had been buried prior to his resurrection, fostered the low value of cremation in the view of the Spanish Catholic Church.

Traditionally, cremation had no connection with religious identity. From 1939 to 1975 the dictatorship was defined as a national Catholic regime and, because of that, cremation was inconceivable in the first decades of Franco's government whose obsession with 'judeomasonic conspiracy' is very illustrative of this point. Despite the Catholic Church's acceptance of cremation in 1963, its practice was so contrary to Catholic aesthetics and custom that the first Spanish cremation only took place in 1973, ten years later. Only when the evolution towards social secularization was completed in the last decade of the twentieth century did cremation begin to achieve any significance and acceptance as a method of corpse disposal.

Cremation as a legal and permitted practice began in 1973 in Madrid, although there were a couple of cremations conducted, with Hindu rites,

in a public cemetery some years earlier. In the first ten years after legalization, cremation was practised mainly by foreign citizens, especially British and German tourists. It continued to be stigmatized as 'heretical or improper' by the majority of the population. Although nowadays there are locations in which cremation percentages are higher than in Madrid because of the significant presence of Europeans (for example, Malaga and Costa del Sol), Madrid is a good example of the rise of cremation as a practice. Table 1 and Figure 1 show the cremation statistics between 1973 and 2001 in tabular and graphical form.

Table 1   Cremation statistics, 1973–2001

Year	% of cremations
1973	0.17
1974	0.26
1975	0.42
1976	0.64
1977	0.78
1978	0.97
1979	1.08
1980	1.19
1981	1.22
1982	1.28
1983	1.90
1984	2.29
1985	4.03
1986	5.35
1987	5.96
1988	6.46
1989	8.70
1990	10.70
1991	12.73
1992	15.68
1993	16.37
1994	17.94
1995	18.68
1996	18.45
1997	20.26
1998	19.49
1999	21.21
2000	22.14
2001	23.32

Source: Empresa Mixta de Servicios Funerarios de Madrid, SA.

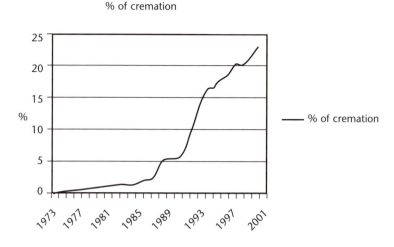

% of cremation

Figure 1   Rise in cremation rate, 1973–2001

As we can see, 1989–91 marks a period when cremation took an increasing importance. This is when the intermediate model of funerary services – with wakes celebrated in non-dedicated locations in hospitals or family homes – evolved into a consolidated funerary service that took (and takes) place in an specific location called a *tanatorio* (thanatorium), which offers a complete range of funerary services by dedicated personnel. This new funerary service also covered cremations since the company managed all the public cemeteries and the only crematorium until 1997, when a new, privately-owned crematorium was inaugurated outside the city. This evolution towards funerary modernity brought with it cremation as a standard choice.

Hygiene, but not hygienism, is also an important factor in understanding both the delay and then the rapid acceptance of cremation. Although new cemeteries developed at the same time as in the rest of Europe, no further steps were taken in terms of the potential hazards of putrefaction. The Spanish population took some 21 years (1787–1808) to respect a Royal Act over new cemeteries, and almost half a century more to accept the idea completely: cremation was totally beyond popular consideration. Wakes continued to be held at home with no special safety measures in respect of the corpse and, until the last quarter of the twentieth century, the hygienic aspect of cremation was not entertained. Only when wakes were removed from homes to *tanatoria* and when health hazards were culturally related to the presence of

corpses inside a family home did the hygienic rationale of cremation come to be appreciated. This paralleled the beginning of the diminishment of importance, to the population, of links with cemeteries and a renewed emphasis on hygiene. As testimony to this disposal in common graves reserved for the poorest people was replaced by cremation. However, as cremation was increasing and as there remained considerable usable burial space in the new cemeteries (Madrid, for example, has enough burial space to last beyond the beginning of the twenty-second century), cremation is not needed on the grounds of land availability. Nevertheless, burial space is increasingly being regarded as a waste of space and those who were previously destined to common burial are now placed in temporary graves and their remains cremated if no relative claims them. In the twentieth century, a common grave was so stigmatizing that the majority of the urban population paid for so-called 'burial assurance' which provided a 'society burial', a permanent burial shared with other members of the burial society who died on the same day. These permanent burials were abandoned in the 1980s; since then, society burials have been temporary, for ten years, after which a good percentage of the remains are cremated. Similarly, cremation is also positively valued for ending the problem of space in family vaults. Economics is also an integral part of the set of positive, explicit cultural values about cremation. Whereas Spanish society in the first half of the twentieth century saw funerary costs as a sound family investment that has quite changed in the early twenty-first century with cremation being seen as not involving a waste of money. Although the difference in cost is not in fact great, the saving of money is still often offered as the explicit reason for preferring cremation.

Cremation has also started to change funerary uses and customs. More than half of cremated remains are removed from the crematorium and scattered elsewhere, contributing to the decrease of importance of customs related to periodical visits to family graves. Scattering removes the possibility of any special ceremony or rite associated with a place. Cremation has powerfully contributed to the change of the funerary ritual from a ritual extended in time to one concentrated in a few days.

Interestingly, although cremation is now very positively viewed and increasingly adopted, people reject crematoria themselves when public or private agencies seek to establish one close to their homes. On different occasions between 1997 and 2002 residents have prevented the opening of a new crematorium, alleging that it constitutes a health hazard. This apparent contradiction illustrates rather clearly the importance of hygiene – albeit from a symbolic rather than scientific perspective – as a factor involved in the acceptance of cremation.

The disposal of cremated remains from 1986 to 2001 show the following approximate percentages:

- Family custody   62.43%
- Perpetual grave   5.88%
- Mausoleum   1.00%
- Columbarium   22.8%
- Shared deposition site 7.33%

Family custody describes private disposal by the families outside cemeteries which, as in other parts of Europe, indicates a definitive departure from previous burial practices that concentrated corpses in a community of the dead – a necropolis – more or less paralleling the city of the living. Instead, remains are scattered or deposited in locations not related to death and totally defined by the desires of the deceased or their family. What was once the greatest punishment for pre-modern Spaniards – cremation and the scattering of ashes – is today favoured as a final destiny even by leading figures such as intellectuals or artists. Maybe the only

significant difference is that, until 2000, there were no garden areas within cemeteries in which families could scatter ashes.

It seems that the tendency towards cremation will increase in the future. In Madrid a massive new cemetery was built in 1973 to cope with the massive wave of immigrants from the countryside, but the surprising acceptance of cremation now makes it look as though disposable cemetery space will be available for well over a century of constant use. As yet relatively unstudied, cremation remains a significant factor in the evolution of a society previously quite centred on death rituals and culture to a society in which death culture is now under a strong taboo. **Juan L. Chulilla**

SPONTANEOUS HUMAN COMBUSTION

Spontaneous human combustion refers to the phenomenon of a person's body, or body part, being destroyed by heat in the absence of any external heat source. The term has been used to refer to either or both of the initial ignition of the body and its continuing combustion thereafter, although some investigators reserve the term 'spontaneous human combustion' for the former and use the term 'preternatural combustion' for the latter. Victims, alleged to have died as a result of spontaneous human combustion, are typically found where they have fallen with their torso, including its bones, totally destroyed but with their extremities, particularly their legs, not wholly consumed and with their immediate environs, whether indoors or out, showing very little, if any, sign of burning. The earliest reported case, an alcoholic pauper in Paris, comes from the seventeenth century and an explanation much favoured from then, and enthusiastically advanced by the temperance movement in the nineteenth century, connected the phenomenon with a body's suffusion with alcohol. Novelists, the best known being Dickens in *Bleak House*, have woven death by spontaneous combustion into their narratives.

Though widely credited, the phenomenon has always had its doubters. A crucial, and well-publicized, test of it was occasioned by the death of the Countess von Görlitz in Darmstadt in 1847. Her footman, Stauff, was tried for her murder and looked to be on the verge of being cleared by doctors attributing the death to spontaneous combustion when the court appointed two chemists, von Libieg and Bischoff, to test their conclusions. The result was that Stauff was convicted and afterwards confessed.

The suggestion that a body could spontaneously ignite and burn, as if from within, has always been controversial. What needs to be explained is:

1   How could such an ignition take place?
2   How could such combustion be sustained?
3   How could a fire intense enough to reduce bones to ash or dust (which modern cremators operating at temperatures about 800°C do not totally succeed in doing) leave such insubstantial marks on its immediate environs?
4   Why do the legs and feet tend not to be totally destroyed?

Verification of the existence and mechanism of spontaneous human combustion has been hindered by the fact that scientists and judicial officers called to investigate fires have tended to believe it to be extremely rare, if not impossible. Thus observed instances of it taking place – if instances they be – are not likely to be recognized as such by their observers, who, in any case, would not remain observers for long because they would extinguish the fire.

In 1991 the body of a murdered woman was found in woods in Oregon. She was lying on a deep layer of dead leaves and burning with a very low flame. Her torso was almost completely destroyed. She was photographed. The incident gave credence to the 'wick effect' explanation of spontaneous human combustion, advanced as early as 1830 by Dupuytren: a clothed body can burn like a candle with an external wick. If the initial combustion of the person's clothes is allowed to continue long enough to begin to liquefy their body fat, the fat seeps into the clothing and the clothing performs like a wick drawing its fuel from the body. The body burns slowly with a low flame and the low flame explains why the environs remain relatively unscathed. The survival of the legs is explained by their being less adipose than other parts of the body and, perhaps, to their being relatively unclothed. An experiment with a pig clothed in a blanket in an enclosed room reproduced this effect. The pig burned for more than six hours with a flame less than 1½ feet high and reached a heat of 812.7°C. Little harm was done to its

immediate surroundings, but a television screen standing high up in the room melted (a type of phenomenon also sometimes observed in cases of possible spontaneous combustion). When the experiment was stopped, the pig's bones had become friable. One hypothetical explanation for this type of combustion breaking down the bones when cremation does not is (a) the lengthier combustion, (b) the relatively varying temperatures during the combustion as opposed to those during cremation, which (c) in combination release the marrow inside the bone as fuel for the fire, thus creating intense heat inside the bone.

The wick effect is now the most favoured explanation amongst forensic scientists for the sustained burning, but they do not allow that the initial ignition is possible without an external source of heat – perhaps a dropped match, or a person falling into a fire. If the question 'Why did the victim not extinguish the fire at the start?' is asked, the answer is that they must have been disabled in some way, either drunk, unconscious, suffering a stroke or heart attack, or, perhaps, asleep. Nevertheless there are still those who believe that, in some of these cases, the body has ignited spontaneously, while admitting that no proven explanation of how this could happen has yet been given. The most ardent advocate of this, perhaps, is John Heymer, a former Welsh coroner's officer. Others believe spontaneous human combustion to be a paranormal phenomenon, some being sustained in their views by surprising coincidences associated with alleged examples, such as that of two very young victims who simultaneously burst into flames in different houses in 1899 in Sowerby Bridge, West Yorkshire: they were sisters and were both being attended by a doctor named Wellburn. **Stephen White**

References

Adelson, Lester (1951), 'Spontaneous Human Combustion and Preternatural Combustibility', *Journal of Criminal Law, Criminology and Police Science*, 42(6): 793–809.

Arnold, Larry (1996), *ABLAZE! The Mysterious Fires of Spontaneous Human Combustion*, New York: M. Evans.

De Haan, J.D. and Nurbakhsh, Said (2001), 'Sustained Combustion of an Animal Carcass and its Implications for the Consumption of

Human Bodies in Fire', *Journal of Forensic Science*, 46(5): 1076–81.

De Moulin, D. (1975), 'Spontaneous Combustion: An Odd Chapter in the History of Burns', *Archivum Chirurgicum Neerlandicum*, XXVII-IV: 223–27.

Dupuytren, M. (1830), 'Leçon sur la Combustion Dite Spontanée', *La Lancette Française*, 2(97): 385–86.

Gee, D.J. (1965), 'A Case of 'Spontaneous Combustion'', *Medicine, Science and the Law*, 5: 37–38.

Harrison, Michael (1976), *Fire from Heaven or How Safe are You from Burning?*, London: Sidgwick and Jackson.

Heymer, John (1996), *The Entrancing Flame*, New York: Little Brown.

Randles, Jenny and Hough, Peter (1992), *Spontaneous Human Combustion*, London: Robert Hale Ltd.

Tardieu, Ambrose (1852), 'Observations on Combustion of the Human Body Taking Place Spontaneously, in Reference to the Murder of the Countess of Görlitz , on the 13 June 1847', *Edinburgh Medical and Surgical Journal*, 78: 95–136.

STEPHEN, JAMES FITZJAMES

The judge at the trial of William Price in 1884 whose ruling that cremation was not itself unlawful gave the Cremation Society of England the assurance for which it had been waiting since 1879 that cremations carried out at its crematorium at Woking would not bring prosecutions in their wake. Price was acquitted in February 1884, and the first cremation at Woking took place in March 1885. Stephen was born in 1829 into an extremely fecund family: its male members populated the governments and legal systems of Britain, Australia and New Zealand; Stephen's brother was Leslie Stephen, who was among other things, founder of the *Dictionary of National Biography*, member of the Bloomsbury circle and father of Virginia Woolf. His father was James Stephen, who in 1836 became Under-Secretary at the Colonial Office, where his industry, earnestness and reluctance to delegate earned him the soubriquets of 'King Stephen', 'Mr Over-Secretary' or 'Mr Mother-Country'.

Educated first at Eton, which he detested, then at King's College, London, and then Cambridge, where he was an active member of the exclusive and semi-secret 'Cambridge Conversazione Society', better known as 'The Apostles', James Fitzjames Stephen started his career as a barrister. Almost simultaneously, however, he took up the higher journalism. In 1855 he joined the staff of the newly formed *Saturday Review* and in 1865 he moved to the newly established *Pall Mall Gazette*. He was a prolific journalist. In the first ten years of the *Saturday Review* he is said to have contributed over 300 articles, and between 1865 and 1869 he produced over 800 leading articles and 200 notes for the *Gazette*. These were in addition to occasional contributions to other journals such as *Fraser's Magazine*, the *Cornhill Magazine* and the *Edinburgh Review*. Apart from law, he wrote about political theory, philosophy, ethics, religion, culture and literary criticism, although his canons of the latter were somewhat Gradgrind-like. Stephen's father had been a member of the Protestant and Evangelical Clapham Sect, centred around William Wilberforce, and through the marriages contracted by the Stephens, Stephen became part of the web of the Victorian intelligentsia that included the Thackerays, Arnolds, Stracheys, Trevelyans and Macaulays. In 1869 he went to India as legal member of the Vice-Regal Council, a position previously occupied by Macaulay, whom he admired and with whose family his had been connected in the Clapham Sect, and Sir Henry Maine, who had taught him at Cambridge and who had introduced him to 'the Apostles'. In 1865 he been engaged in the defence of the authors of *Essays and Reviews* and he would probably have represented Charles Voysey – later to become a founder member of the Cremation Society – at his trial for heresy had he not left for India: as it was, a large part of the defence Voysey made on his own behalf was initially drafted by Stephen.

India was a watershed for Stephen. While returning from India, he wrote the book for which he is generally best known, *Liberty, Fraternity and Equality*, a critique of John Stuart Mill's *On Liberty*. Some measure of the effect of India on Stephen's views can be gauged by comparing this work with the fulsome review he wrote for the *Saturday Review* of Mill's book when it first appeared in 1859. Almost the only criticism he then made of Mill was to upbraid him for holding a deeply pessimistic view of the English character similar to that which Stephen himself was to adopt in his later years. Stephen correctly perceived, and espoused, the strains of authoritarianism in Benthamite utilitarianism, and his complaint against *On Liberty* in 1872 was that it undesirably deviated from the strict Benthamite position. Despite standing twice as a Liberal candidate for parliament, on the second occasion, in 1873, having been virtually promised the solicitor-generalship, Stephen could not be a totally convincing Liberal candidate. He came to despair of democracy and eventually, in 1886, seceded from the Liberals over Irish Home Rule.

Stephen had returned from India a fervent advocate of the codification of the law and of the criminal law in particular. Although he had previously stressed how the effectiveness of the criminal law rested on other social and moral influences, after India he came to stress the importance of the criminal law as a buttress of morality when the influence of religion was declining: he had long lost his faith in Christianity but doubted the capacity of the newly enfranchised to exercise the self-restraint that was necessary to the smooth functioning of civil society. It is against this background that his writings on criminal law, culminating in his magisterial three-volume work *A History of the Criminal Law of England*, and his tireless work for codifying the criminal law must be seen. The closest he came to success was in 1880 when a Criminal Code Bill, which was essentially his work, was lost in the turmoil of Irish politics. He had more success overseas where several British colonies adopted criminal codes based on his model.

In 1879 Stephen was made a judge. His view on the proper role of the criminal law was to affect most decidedly the ruling he made at the trial of William Price. With his background of involvement in religious cases such as the *Essays and Reviews* litigation, his familiarity with current political and ethical thought, and his unsurpassed knowledge of the development of criminal law, there was hardly a judge better equipped to preside over Price's trial. All these influences can be seen in his charge to the grand jury in which he argues that neither in the legal precedents nor in canonical writings is there anything that outlaws cremation as such.

Although Stephen is often thought of as an arch conservative, intolerant of diversity, he was very much opposed to judges extending the scope of criminal law through judicial law-making. For them to do this was to undermine the certainty of the criminal law without which its effectiveness would be much diminished. Similarly, he did not want *any* respect in which the criminal law might be held to be diluted by its being used to crush opinion. These views were manifested in another trial at the Glamorgan Assizes in 1887 after a deceased local politician had been scurrilously traduced in a local newspaper: Stephen ruled that it was not an offence (of criminal libel) to defame the dead. They are apparent, too, in the assistance he gave the National Secular Society and others in their attempts to get the laws against blasphemy repealed. This strain in his thought can be illustrated by several passages in his charge to grand and petty juries:

> I do think, however, that it can be said that every practice which startles and jars upon the religious sentiments of the majority of the population is for that reason a misdemeanour at common law ... the great leading rule of criminal law is that nothing is a crime unless it is plainly forbidden by law .... For my part I entertain the strongest opinion that it is not the duty of judges to invent new crimes .... There were some people in the world who took offence at their neighbours doing anything which they did not like themselves, or which was not according to their own habits and practice, and there were many persons who were extremely indignant as soon as they heard that anyone had political or religious opinions with which they did not agree, or were addicted to habits and ways of life which were considered absurd or wrong. That was a habit that was not to be commended, and which the law of this country did not protect....

It is clear that Stephen was relieved that he was able to give the ruling he did in the Price trial: Price was a very experienced litigant, and Stephen enjoyed Price's conduct of his own defence. The outcome of the trial might have been very different if Justice Kay, who tried the case of *Williams* v. *Williams*, had presided. He had refused Eliza Williams's claim against Henry Crookenden's executors for having carried out his wishes to be cremated. Several reports of the case, though not the official one, have Justice Kay saying that cremation was illegal (see White, 2002). Growing signs of incapacity towards the end of the 1890s eventually forced Stephen's retirement from the bench in 1891. He died in 1894. **Stephen White**

See also Cremation Society of Great Britain; Price.

References

Colaiaco, James A. (1983), *James Fitzzjames Stephen and the Crisis of Victorian Thought*, London: Macmillan Press.

Hostettler, John (1995), *Politics and Law in the Life of Sir James Fitzjames Stephen*, Chichester: Barry Rose Law Publishers Ltd.

Smith, K.J.M. (1988), *James Fitzjames Stephen: Portrait of a Victorian Rationalist*, Cambridge: Cambridge University Press.

Stephen, Leslie (1895), *The Life of Sir James Fitzjames Stephen*, London: Smith, Elder & Co.

Radzinowicz, Leon (1957), *Sir James Fitzjames Stephen 1829–1894 and his Contribution of the Development of Criminal Law*, London: Bernard Quaritch.

Stephen, Sir James (1892), *Horae Sabbaticae: Reprints of Articles Contributed to The Saturday Review. First, Second and Third Series*, London: Macmillan & Co.

R v. Ensor (1887), 3 TLR 366.

R v. Price (1884), 12 QBD 247; 15 Cox CC 389.

White, Stephen (2002), 'A Burial Ahead of its Time? The Crookenden Burial Case and the Sanctioning of Cremation in England and Wales', *Mortality*, 7(2): 171–90. Also, in a slightly different version, in T.G. Watkin (ed.) (2002), *The Trial of Dic Penderyn and Other Essays*, Welsh Legal History Society, 2: 151–79.

Williams v. Williams (1882), 20 Ch.D 659; 51 LJ 385, 46 LT 275, 46 JP 726, 15 Cox CC 39.

STOCKHOLM WOODLAND CREMATORIUM

The crematorium in the Woodland Cemetery at Enskede outside Stockholm (1935–1940), arguably the most well known and most admired of all twentieth-century crematoria, was designed by Erik Gunnar Asplund (1885–1940), shortly before he died. Asplund emerged as the outstanding architect in Sweden and, after Alvar

Aalto (1898–1979) and Eliel Saarinen (1873–1950), in the other Nordic countries, too.

It is important to acknowledge from the outset that cremation was an accepted practice in Sweden by the 1930s. One of the first crematoria was built in Sweden, in 1889, in the Eastern Cemetery in Gothenburg, to the design of Hans Hedlund. Swedes encouraging cremation fostered a climate which encouraged the siting of crematoria near centres of population. While it was widely acknowledged that Scandinavian countries were distinguishing themselves in the design of good modern buildings with social purpose during the 1930s, it was also felt by architectural commentators, including Howard Robertson, that Sweden, in particular, was responsible for some of the most sensitive designs for crematoria. In many Swedish towns the crematorium is one of the most thoughtfully designed of all the public buildings. Quality and enlightenment were key concepts in a country that exhibited a serious sense of social values. These were nowhere more eloquently expressed than in crematoria.

Asplund's Woodland Cemetery and Crematorium is undoubtedly the most celebrated example. Franco Borsi's description invokes its achievement:

> Asplund succeeded in combining the blood-curdling yet romantic howl of the wind in the virgin forest and over the great meadows, a rarefied classicism with marble cross and open portico, and the aggressive functionality of the crematorium, where even the mouths of the furnaces are exactly shaped to fit a coffin. Thus he succeeds in giving to each part, each functional element, not only its own shape, but also its own essential symbolic form, so that nature is nature, the cross is cross without a base or any other architecture but itself, meadow is meadow, the wood is wood, and everything in the austere solemnity of the place exudes an impression of finality and proclaims indeed a final symbolic message. (Borsi, 1987: 137).

A better understanding of Asplund's achievement can be reached through the identification of some of the sources and influences that achieved synthesis and resolution at the Woodland Crematorium. In 1915 Asplund won the competition for the Woodland Cemetery with his contemporary Sigurd Lewerentz, with whom he helped to found the Separatist Free School of Architecture in Stockholm in 1910, which aligned itself with the 'national realist' tendency. The Cemetery was a commission that would occupy them for nearly the next 25 years. Early proposals showed an informal and romantic arrangement in a pine forest, but these were replaced by Lewerentz's later design that involved a more formal solution, including a classical propylaeum placed on a central axis and a necropolis. Sketches include a large stone cross seen against the sky. 'But the whole was also guided by underlying mythical themes to do with the transition from life to death, the procession of burial and redemption and the transubstantiation of natural elements such as water and light. There were echoes too of Nordic burial mounds, and of Christ's route to Calvary' (Curtis, 1996: 145).

Asplund designed the Woodland Chapel between 1918 and 1920. Placed on the cross-axis of the cemetery, it combines the aesthetic of a temple with that of a Nordic hut. It nestles between conifer trees, the trunks of which find an echo in the slender wooden Doric columns of the portico. The austerity of the interior is mitigated by the lighting fixtures and columns. The rustic, textured roof forms a triangular shape, which not only reflected indigenous Scandinavian architecture, but also 'inevitably recalled the image of a schematic classical pediment, and so touched off a string of primitivist associations concerning the possible origins of classical elements in the forms of huts or even the forms of nature' (Curtis, 1996:145). Many aspects of the chapel presaged the design of the crematorium.

At the Woodland Crematorium, Asplund created what has justifiably been described as the most perfect example of genuine twentieth-century monumental and religious architecture in existence. It comprises three chapels – one large, two small – the crematorium and the columbarium. The extraordinary impact of the crematorium owes as much to its inspirational setting as its architectural configuration. Furthermore, it is clear that Asplund had orchestrated carefully the relationship between architecture and landscape. On entering the cemetery the visitor is compelled to mount the gentle, silent slope towards the grey granite cross which stands dramatically against the sky. The approach is contrived almost as a 'solemn ascent, a latter-day Sacred Way or even Hill of Calvary' (Curtis, 1996: 340). The configuration of the chapel and the cross draw attention to the harmony between structure and background, between building and nature. The approach towards the crematorium continues this ascent, past the burial plaques, the cross, then the small chapels, and into the covered court in front of the main chapel (Kidder-Smith 1962: 213). This main entrance consists of a low rectangular classical portico, forming a porte-cochère or loggia, with plain posts and lintels. Its simple monumentality, derived from Greek architecture, results from a reposeful balance between vertical and horizontal elements. The loggia frames views to a wood to the south, and a small hill, where the sun sets, to the west.

The crematorium itself is constructed from a concrete frame, clad in stone, but the execution is very precise and adds to the purity of the whole. The pristine, smooth exterior surfaces, where decoration has been proscribed, the enclosure of volumes rather than the creation of masses and the general regularity, as opposed to axial symmetry, are all hallmarks of modernism. They are, however, combined inextricably with a deep appreciation and feeling for classicism.

Beyond the sculpture by Joel Lundqvist, which reaches heavenwards through the open courtyard, symbolizing the release of the soul, lies the main chapel, which can accommodate 300. This can be separated from the courtyard by the lowering of a bronze and glass door into the ground. When this massive gate is removed, a new and moving relationship is created between interior and exterior space, allowing hundreds to attend services. The cremation facilities are situated behind the complex and reached by a road at the rear. The underside of the roof is constructed in timber to allow the rain to run away on the gently sloping floor beneath.

Generations of architects have admired this crematorium, in the way that others have venerated Le Corbusier's church, Notre Dame du Haut at Ronchamp (1950–54). The buildings share many qualities, in the sense that both offered solutions which differed radically from the accepted norm. Both structures exploited the relationship between architecture and nature, between symbolism and 'place'. At Woodland Crematorium Asplund recognized the importance of creating an environment suitable for the intense personal and psychological experience of the transition from life to death and from death to the paradise promised to believers. Here the singular function of the crematorium is outweighed by the spiritual and symbolic language of the architecture and setting. Asplund's understanding of the cathartic role that nature might play in this process has been inspirational. The presence and careful framing of the wider landscape beyond the buildings allow for a more collective response to the shared human experiences of loss and memory and the assumption of the individual into a greater natural scheme.

Many architects, particularly in the post-war period, have recognized the pre-eminent importance of the siting and settings of crematoria, which goes some way to explain the iconic status now enjoyed by the Woodland Crematorium. **Hilary Grainger**

See also Asplund; Lewerentz; Sweden – Skogskyrkogården (Woodland Cemetery).

References

Borsi, Franco (1987), *The Monumental Era: European Architecture and Design 1929–1939*, New York: Rizzol.

Curtis, W.J.R. (1996), *Modern Architecture Since 1900* (3rd edn), London: Phaidon.

Kidder-Smith, G.E. (1962), *The New Architecture of Europe*, London: Pelican.

SURINAME

Like other Caribbean countries Suriname is characterized by a multi-ethnic society whose heterogeneity is, among many others, reflected in perceptions and practices concerning death and disposal. Cremation is common practice among the Hindustani (East-Indians), who form about 40 per cent of the population and who follow their forefathers in India by preferring to cremate their deceased relatives in the open air. However, until the 1960s Dutch colonial assimilation policy and a dominant Creole culture, both strongly based on Christian principles, obstructed any other form of disposal than burial. The Christian symbolism of the resurrection of the body was, in particular, not felt to go with the practice of cremation. In 1969 funerary statutes were changed in favour of the Hindustani, which allowed them to cremate their dead bodies in the open air and, today, cremation is mainly practised by this community.

Ancestors against cremation

The descendants of the African slaves, Creoles and Maroons, who form another 40 per cent of the population, still have serious objections to cremation. Many perceive the overt burning of the body as disgusting or barbaric and use the word 'barbecue' when they refer to cremation. Although cemeteries are overfull and sometimes in a neglected condition, most of the African-Surinamese people do not consider cremation as an alternative to burial. The opening of a 'modern closed crematorium' in the mid-1990s in the capital city did not really alter this general aversion. Even a careful promotion of cremation by some undertakers, expressed in terms of relatively low costs, does not convince the majority of the African-Surinamese population despite their experience of economic recession and increasing poverty. Cremation only gains popularity among higher-class Creoles and the so-called 'mixed' people, whereas the middle- and working-class Creoles and Maroons hold on to their burial tradition. This persistence is not only rooted in Christian motives. On the contrary, biblical arguments are put forward more by representatives of the clergy than by the laypeople. The latter profess Christianity, but are as much dedicated to the popular African-Surinamese religion called Winti. A generally shared belief and experience in Winti is the unremitting intertwinement of the world of the living and the world of the dead, and it is in this belief that another, even stronger, argument against cremation can be found.

In the Winti world-view death implies a continuation of life in another form, in which contacts between the living and the deceased or their spirits are still possible and often necessary. A rich ancestral cult exemplifies the strong bonds between the living and the dead. Ancestral spirits, the *kabra* or *kaaba*, play an important role in family ceremonies and in case of feud, illness, misfortune or other difficulties these spirits are consulted to find the cause of the problem. *Kabra* are still part of the family and its fortunes. As a result, the African-Surinamese life-world does not only imply the living but also the dead. Although the ancestors continue to exist only in spiritual form, the burning of the body is considered offensive towards deceased relatives and future bonds with them. Cremation will harm the relation with the ancestors-to-be and this, in turn, would affect success in daily life. Besides, the grave as a physical place is frequently used to contact spirits of the dead. And for those who find other ways to communicate, the grave is at least a safe place to entrust their dead relatives. As remains are (said to be) used to practise *wisi* ('black magic'), numerous African-Surinamese fear that ashes, in particular, will be misused to 'do bad things'. A solid grave will protect against these practices and continues to be the chosen resting place – just like the mourning song below prescribes:

> *Tamara nanga beifi*
> *Wi e hari dedebro*
> *Wi heri skin kon steifi*
> *Na grebi a musu go*

> Tomorrow with a shiver
> We heave our last sigh
> Our whole body will stiffen
> To the grave, there is its side

Yon van der Pijl

SWEDEN

The three entries that follow provide basic information on cremation in Sweden and are an introduction to separate, detailed, entries on Swedish architects (**Asplund, Lewerentz**), cemeteries (**Stockholm Woodland Crematorium**), and late twentieth-century use of cremated remains (**Ashes–Sweden**). **Douglas J. Davies**

BACKGROUND AND HISTORY

While, in the seventeenth century, all burials took place in town cemeteries, these soon became overcrowded and led to sanitary and health problems when rapid urbanization took place. Five years after its founding, the Swedish Cremation Society inaugurated the first Swedish crematorium, at Hagalund (*Haga krematoriet*) in Solna, just outside Stockholm. The first cremation took place there on 15 October 1887. Prior to this, corpses had to be sent to Gothia for cremation, which was very expensive. The crematorium itself was financed by private

donations and designed by the architect Professor Magnus Isaeus and its cremator was constructed by Brigadier-General Gustav Klingenstierna, the first director of the Swedish Cremation Society. (His system of cremator design is detailed in the second entry under **cremators**.) The crematorium was a temporary building and, in 1909, a new crematorium (*Norra krematoriet*), with the first Swedish columbarium was designed by the architect Gustav Lindgren. It was used as a crematorium until February 1989 and witnessed a total of 94 838 cremations over its 80 years. The restored building was reopened in 2002 but only as a chapel and columbarium.

The Swedish Cremation Society did not originally inform the authorities that it existed and that it had built a crematorium. Accordingly, the Swedish Lutheran Church felt ignored and demanded that cremation be prohibited, but was unsuccessful in its demands. In 1888 cremation was legalized, but the new law ensured that no cremation could take place before a postmortem had been conducted. This law existed for 29 years and was a hindrance to the propagation of cremation in Sweden. It took even longer before cremation achieved equality with burial – in fact, until another law of 1957. When the new funeral tax was introduced, cremation came to be equal with burial in every sense.

The second crematorium was built in Gothenburg in 1890. The following Swedish crematoria, with their dates of construction are listed in some detail to give a sense of the pace of development of the movement across the country: Stockholm (1882); Gothenburg (1890); Örebro (1922); Helsingborg (1928); Luleå (1930), Vänersborg (1931), Malmö (1932), Sundsvall (1932), Kiruna (1933), Eskilstuna (1934), Sandviken (1935), Kramfors (1935), Kalmar (1935), Fagersta (1936), Vetlanda 1936), Linköping (1936), Karlshamn (1937), Trelleborg (1937), Falun (1938), Karlstad (1938), Norrköping (1938), Lidköping (1939), Katrineholm (1940), Halmstad (1941), Kristianstad (1942), Växjö (1943), Borås (1944), Karlskoga (1948), Östersund (1952), Umeå (1952), Västerås (1953), Mora (1954), Ystad (1956), Trollhättan (1956), Kristinehamn (1956), Motala (1956), Ängelholm (1956), Höganäs (1957), Ludvika (1958), Värnamo (1958), Huskvarna (1958), Jönköping (1958), Lund (1960), Bollnäs (1960), Gävle (1960), Landskrona (1961), Skellefteå (1961), Huddinge (1961), Nässjö (1962), Skövde (1962),

Oskarshamn (1963), Filipstad (1964), Uppsala (1965), Nynäshamn (1965), Alingsås (1966), Nyköping (1967), Visby (1967), Ronneby (1967), Sollentuna (1969), Varberg (1969), Nacka (1970), Enköping (1970), Arvika (1972), Karlskrona (1981), Mariestad (1982), Tranås (1982) and Gällivare (1988).

At nearly all of these crematoria, the cremators have been rebuilt or replaced by newer and modern ones and, by the end of the twentieth century, Borlänge, Avesta, Södertälje and Eslöv had been closed down completely. All the Swedish crematoria are owned by the Swedish Church except the two in Stockholm and one in Tranås, which are owned by local municipalities. Swedish citizens pay a special funeral fee or tax every year, and this covers the final cost of cremation. In 1936 the Swedish cremation rate was approximately 5 per cent, in 1956 some 22 per cent and in 1979 it was 50 per cent. By 2002 it had reached practically 70 per cent and by 2003 some 72 per cent.

Swedish cremation institutions

The European interest in cremation prompted a group of idealistic, well-educated Swedes to found the Swedish Cremation Society on 31 May 1882, to promote cremation and secure its legalization for those desiring it. Per Lindell, an engineer, was the society's founder and first director, Brigadier-general Gustav Klingenstierna its first chairman while the universally known Alfred Nobel was also a member. Five years after its establishment, the society inaugurated the first Swedish crematorium, which it owned until 1973 when the city of Stockholm bought it. In 1888 it achieved the aim of having cremation legalized in Sweden. However, to be cremated, one had to prove membership of the cremation society so that, from the outset, members were private citizens desirous of demonstrating their wish for cremation after death. In 1957 the society's statutes changed to permit cemetery and crematorium authorities to gain membership.

The society was reorganized in 1983 and changed its name to the Swedish Federation of Cemeteries and Crematoria Association. It has become a professional service and trade organization for Swedish cemetery and crematoria owners, taking care of its members' interests, representing and defending them in relation to the authorities and specializing in technical, educational and environmental

subjects. Its main task is to cover the sector, to administer professional training and service, to convey information and to represent its members internationally. Now nearly every crematorium is a voluntary member of the Swedish Federation, which produces the journal *Kyrkogården*, founded in 1929, and holds national conferences. It has its own technical advisers and an education department providing a three step-education for crematoria employees. The country is divided into five districts with federation advisers commissioned to foster contact with member organizations, to advise, help and promote information in matters concerning funeral systems and activities.

In 1987 the federation initiated a Research Foundation for Crematoria Techniques to promote research and to improve environmental and work contexts, filtering of gas emissions, treatment of ash processing and construction design. The federation is a member of both the Nordic Forum on Cemetery and Crematoria Subjects and the International Cremation Federation. All Nordic cemetery and cremation associations are members of the Nordic Forum, which arranges a conference and general council every fourth year. The general council appoints an executive committee consisting of one representative from every Nordic country. Since 1997 the president has been recruited from the Swedish Federation. **Ulf Lagerström**

See also cremators – Siemens, Scheider and Klingenstierna cremators.

CREMATED REMAINS

Early cremations in Sweden – from the 1880s onwards – were, without exception followed by the interment of permanent urns in existing family graves or in individual graves at the cemeteries. Fairly soon, specific areas of the cemeteries were designated for the burial of individual urns. During the 1920s and 1930s the cremation movement encouraged the construction of special columbaria in churches and crematoria, and the provision of special constructions in the cemeteries where urns could be immured. This, however, became a feature only of major cities. Thus, in Stockholm there are six churches that have a columbarium. New columbaria are no longer built.

It was only in 1958 that the desire expressed

by supporters of the cremation movement for completely anonymous burials in a garden of remembrance was answered. The scattering of ashes is now practised on a large scale within a particular area of Skogskyrkogården Cemetery (the Woodland Cemetry) in Stockholm and also in other larger cemeteries. However, the most common practice is to inter ashes in a perishable urn within a clearly marked and designated area within a cemetery. Relatives of the deceased are not expected to be present when the ashes are scattered or interred. In 1995 about 60 per cent of all Church of Sweden parishes stated that a garden of remembrance was available. In the year 2000 not quite 40 per cent of all those cremated were interred in a garden of remembrance. In some places, including a number of towns in southern Sweden, the majority – up to two-thirds – of the cremated remains are given an anonymous burial place, whereas the figure in the traditionally religious city of Gothenburg was less than a third.

Following an application, the county council may grant permission for cremated remains to be scattered on water or on non-cultivated large open areas. Applications are normally granted and, during the late 1990s, this practice increased somewhat. In the year 2000 the remains of 1 per cent of deceased people – some 1000 ash remains – were scattered somewhere other than in a cemetery. In such cases, scattering on the sea or on one of the large lakes is the most common, but ashes are also scattered over land, particularly in the mountains. Swedish legislation on funerals states that ashes must be interred or scattered within one year following the death. Keeping the ashes of a deceased person at home is not permitted. **Göran Gustafsson**

See also ashes – Sweden.

SKOGSKYRKOGÅRDEN (WOODLAND CEMETERY)

When it became apparent at the beginning of the twentieth century that Stockholm's burial grounds must be expanded, an international competition was initiated to ensure the dignity, artistic quality and harmony of the buildings, planting and landscape of a new cemetery – Skogskyrkogården, the Woodland Cemetery. Three prizes were distributed, all awarded to Swedish participants, with the first prize going to

the architects Erik Gunnar Asplund and Sigurd Lewerentz, and their proposal was, in the main, recommended by the jury for implementation.

A small part of the cemetery and the first chapel, the Woodland Chapel, designed by Asplund, were completed in 1920. The plastered wooden chapel with its whitewashed walls and black roof is adorned by Carl Milles' sculpture 'The Angel of Death', iron gates designed by Asplund and an altar painting by Gunnar Torhamn. When an increasing number of cremations in the 1930s made new facilities necessary, Asplund was commissioned to create a new crematorium at the Skogskyrkogården/Woodland Cemetery. His plan comprised three burial chapels with a common technical area. A piece of sculpture by Joel Lundqvist called 'The Resurrection' was erected in the monument hall in front of the largest chapel. A place for outdoor funeral ceremonies was arranged in conjunction with this hall. In order to permit simultaneous ceremonies in all three chapels, the architect ensured privacy by arranging gardens and waiting rooms between them. By varying the height of the buildings, he emphasized the gentle slope down to the adjacent open-air columbarium and the main entrance of the cemetery. The interior of the chapels is conceived in such a way that the catafalque and the coffin constitute the focal point. Instead of placing flowers around the coffin, they may be placed between the catafalque and the walls. Wreaths may either be hung on special stands that can be pulled out of the floor or on the side walls.

A lily pond lies between the largest chapel, called the Chapel of the Holy Cross, and the area for outdoor ceremonies. A small graveyard with a columbarium is located on the northern side of the chapels. The urns are kept either in niches in the walls or in graves. The Chapel of the Holy Cross is adorned by Sven Erixson's fresco 'Life-Death-Life', and the Chapel of Hope by Otte Sköld's wall mosaic in marble. In the third chapel, the Chapel of Faith, the wall behind the altar is decorated with a stucco relief created by Ivar Johnsson. The crucifix in the Chapel of the Holy Cross bears a gilded silver figure of Christ by John Lundqvist. The enamel crucifix in the Chapel of Hope is a work by Otte Sköld while the onyx altar crucifix in the Chapel of Faith was created by Ivar Johnsson. The chapel doors are decorated with bronze reliefs executed after sketches by the sculptor Bror Hjort. The architect's imposing granite cross on the lawn outside the chapels is a gift from an anonymous donor. Erik Gunnar Asplund died in 1940. He rests beside the Chapel of Faith under a simple epitaph bearing the words, 'His work lives'.

In December 1994 the Woodland Cemetery was inscribed on UNESCO's World Heritage List with this affirmation:

> Skogskyrkogården (The Woodland Cemetery) is an outstandingly successful example of a designed cultural landscape which blends landform and natural vegetation with architectural features to create a landscape that is ideally suited to its purpose as a cemetery. The creation of Asplund and Lewerentz at Skogskyrkogården/the Woodland Cemetery established a new form of cemetery that has exerted a profound influence on cemetery design throughout the world.

In May 1995 the Fondazione Benetton Studi Ricerche dedicated the Premio Internazionale Carlo Scarpa per il Giardino to the Woodland Cemetery. **Börje Olsson**

SWITZERLAND

The Swiss cremation movement was led by a single person – a man who pleaded his ideas with great commitment and devotion, the Zurich merchant Johann Jakob Wegmann--Ercolani. Three experiences confirmed him in his selfless mission. Towards the middle of the nineteenth century he visited Pompeii, the ancient city buried under the ashes of Mount Vesuvius where he saw columbaria, small monuments with urns containing ashes. These prompted him to reflect on whether cremation might not also have many advantages as a modern method of disposing of the dead. Then, in February 1861, a day after the defeat of King Francis of Naples and Sicily, he arrived in Gaeta. He stepped on to an earth bank which, judging from the stench of decomposing bodies, was a temporary burial ground for humans and horses: covered by only a thin layer of earth, the smell from the half-decayed corpses was nauseous. One of his friends, a defender of the city, proposed to a council of war that the dead soldiers and animals should be burned – to no avail! It was felt that such an action would be deeply anti-religious. And yet there were no

misgivings of this nature when thousands more subsequently succumbed to typhoid fever. The third experience related to the fact that bodies interred at a cemetery in Zurich had not decomposed, but had turned to wax making God's acre no longer fit for use; at the cost of great sacrifices, a new plot had to be created.

In 1874 Wegmann-Ercolani published a written statement of his views on cremation and, together with friends, called meetings in Zurich attended by many people. Speakers from all walks of life expressed their favourable opinion of cremation from every perspective – religious, scientific, sanitary and even aesthetic. Professor Albert Heim, researcher from the Swiss Alps, spoke, even then, of the risk of contaminated springs and groundwater and pointed out the increasing difficulty of providing suitable soil (that is, one which promotes decomposition) for cemeteries.

The great interest generated by these events prompted the founding of a cremation association, which soon attracted many famous people, such as Gottfried Keller. After settling a number of legal difficulties and having received a gift of land from the city of Zurich in the new Sihlfeld Cemetery, Switzerland's first crematorium was inaugurated on 15 June 1889. It was so successful that the city council subsequently decided to contribute 30 Swiss francs to each cremation so long as a grave would not be required for the ash-urn. In December 1899 the Cremation Association of Zurich transferred ownership of the crematorium to the municipal council at no cost and promised a 50 000-franc contribution to the construction of a new, bigger and finer facility. In September 1912 voters approved a loan of over 500 000 Swiss francs, and the new crematorium was opened in March 1915. The city had already committed itself to free cremation for deceased residents at the turn of the century.

Zurich blazed a trail, with Basle following in 1898 and Geneva in 1902. Both the latter cities are also capitals of Protestant cantons where there were no religious difficulties to overcome. The state – that is, the city – even assumed the role of building-owner, something that would not have been conceivable in certain other locations. Encouraged by these cities, residents elsewhere also set up cremation associations aimed at constructing and operating crematoria. Nevertheless, there were still prejudices and obstacles to be overcome in Switzerland, even in Protestant cantons. Objections from the Catholic Church were particularly vociferous. In cantons with a Catholic majority, legal hurdles were often placed in the way of cremation because there was no legislation on funeral ceremonies at the national level, this being a matter for the cantons. The new Swiss constitution simply stipulates that human dignity must be respected. In St Gallen canton voters rejected cremation in two referenda held in 1892 and 1899, thereby blocking the construction of a crematorium. There was much opposition in central Switzerland, too, with supporters of the cremation movement having to defend their rights before the Swiss Federal Supreme Court. Despite all religious and legal obstacles, however, cremation has made significant progress in Switzerland and is likely to become even more acceptable now that the Catholic Church has substantially revised its position on this subject.

Today there are 27 crematoria in Switzerland, located throughout the country. A new crematorium is currently under construction in Winterthur near Zurich. Another one has been built in Locarno, Tessin. Twelve crematoria are publicly owned, one belongs to a foundation, the others belong to cooperatives. In Switzerland there are over 60 000 cremations per year. In the cities the cremation rate is 70–80 per cent. In rural areas the rate of cremations is still growing, although for Jews and Muslims inhumation remains a religious imperative. After the process of cremation the ashes are placed in an urn which is then set into a single or family grave or a niche in a cemetery. In several cantons, families are allowed to take the urn home. Then they are free to do as they wish: scatter the ashes into a river or in a forest or strew the ashes over the mountains.

In 1986 the Federal Ordinance on Clean Air was enacted. This not only defined emission standards but also set maximum levels for emissions. At that time, the new emission standards for mercury posed a particularly difficult technical problem because, until recently there were no adequate means for filtering mercury from waste gas emissions. Once this technology had been developed, it was integrated into the Clean Air Ordinance in 1998 and, nowadays, the installation of suitable waste gas treatment devices is compulsory and considered as standard. Today, 24 crematoria are run on electricity and three on gas. In Aarau,

Basel, Lugano and Zurich filters have been installed, so that the present Clean Air Regulations on treatment of waste gas emissions, in particular mercury, can be dealt with.
Marianne Herold

T

TAX

Church taxes in some countries have contributed their part in the development of cremation as the entry on **Sweden** shows for a funeral tax.
Douglas J. Davies

TELOPHASE SOCIETY (USA)

The Telophase Society was the pioneering company in inexpensive, direct cremation services and a major contributor to the contemporary cremation boom in the United States. It was founded in 1971 by Thomas B. Weber, a biochemist, and its curious name refers to the last stage in cell division. Like memorial societies, which were springing up across the country during the heyday of the counterculture, Weber's organization charged a membership fee and marketed itself as a society. But the Telophase Society was actually a for-profit business, and a successful one at that.

Weber's company offered no-frills cremations and sold its service directly to cost-conscious and environmentally-concerned consumers. It kept its overheads low by operating out of a modest storefront, and for its first few years of operation it did not even own a crematory. The company did not offer funerals or memorial services, caskets or flowers. Its one and only offering was direct cremation. For a fee that began at $250 (roughly the social security death benefit at the time), Weber would obtain a death certificate, pick up a corpse, bring it to a crematory, and deliver or scatter the remains. Though disparaged by funeral directors as a 'bake and shake' and 'burn and scatter' outfit, the Telophase Society was tremendously successful, spawning a variety of imitators. The most notable was the Neptune Society, established in 1977 in San Francisco by Dr Charles Denning. Unlike the Telophase Society, the Neptune Society offered a variety of services in addition to simple cremation and scattering. In fact, 'Colonel Cinders', as Denning was called, was renowned for throwing lavish 'fun funerals' on his 100-foot yacht. In the mid-1980s, Denning claimed that the Neptune Society handled more corpses than any other business in California, including the massive Forest Lawn Memorial Park outside Los Angeles.

The Telophase Society faced a series of legislative, regulatory, and public relations hurdles put up by funeral directors, cemetery operators and their friends in the California state legislature, but it prospered nonetheless, expanding beyond San Diego to other locations in California. In the process, it proved that there was considerable demand for an inexpensive option to the embalm-and-bury regime.

Over time both the Telophase Society and the Neptune Society began to offer many of the services available at most crematories. In 1997, Stewart Enterprises, a multinational funeral home and cemetery firm, acquired the California operations of both the Telophase Society and the Neptune Society, which by that time claimed over 100 000 members. **Stephen Prothero**

'THE ASHES'

'The Ashes' is both the name of the series of cricket matches, played at Test match level, between England and Australia and the name of the trophy for which the sides compete. On 29 August 1882, at 3.45 pm, England had begun their second innings against an Australian touring team needing only 85 runs to win. Their second wicket fell with 50 runs scored. Their remaining eight wickets fell within the hour for the addition of only 27 runs. Not only was this a spectacular defeat for the English, it was also the first occasion on which they had been beaten by the Australians at home. Shortly afterwards, an obituary appeared in *The Sporting Times* (the representation here is not a facsimile):

In Affectionate Remembrance
OF

ENGLISH CRICKET,

WHICH DIED AT THE OVAL
ON

29th AUGUST, 1882,

Deeply lamented by a large circle of sorrowing
friends and acquaintances

R.I.P.

N.B.—The body will be cremated and the
ashes taken to Australia.

The obituary appeared at a time when the Cremation Society of England and the Home Office were deadlocked over the society's desire to use its crematorium at Woking to cremate human bodies: the Home Office had told the society that, if it went ahead before legislation regulating cremation was passed, anyone involved would be prosecuted. (The deadlock was not broken until William Price was prosecuted and then acquitted for cremating his son in 1884.) The author of the obituary was 'Bloobs', the editor of *The Sporting Times* – in fact, Reginald Shirley Brooks, eldest son of the Shirley Brooks who had proposed the establishment of the Cremation Society in 1874. Cremation was the butt of many, usually very unwitty, jokes, and the obituary was at least as much a joke about cremation as about English cricket. When Ivo Bligh (later Lord Darnley) led an English team to Australia towards the end of 1882, his mission allegedly was described as being 'to recover the ashes'. In the museum at Lord's Cricket Ground in England is a small urn containing what has variously been described as:

(a) the remains of King Cole, a member of an Aborginal team who died during its tour of England in 1868;

(b) the incinerated product of the leather case of a cricket ball which had been thrashed from its core during an informal cricket match towards the end of 1882, involving the visiting English team and members of the household of their host, Sir William Clarke, at Rupertswood, Victoria, and presented to Bligh by Clarke;

(c) a bail, or the veil of a lady, who burned it (whether bail or veil) and presented it to the victorious English team around the beginning of February 1883; or

(d) the ashes from a fire placed in the urn by a butler or chambermaid after the chambermaid had accidentally spilled the original contents of the urn and then disposed of them. The lady was Florence Morphy, later Countess Darnley. The butler and chambermaid worked for Lord Darnley.

After Lord Darnley's death in 1927 the urn and its contents, whatever they may be, became the property of the Marylebone Cricket Club. It is the trophy for which the English (and Welsh) and Australian teams compete, although, whichever side triumphs, the MCC has never yet allowed the urn to return to Australia. **Stephen White**

References

Green, Stephen (1982), 'Centenary Reflections', *The Cricketer*, 63(9): 37.

Twigg, John (1987), 'New Light on the Ashes', *International Journal of the History of Sport*, 4(2): 231–36.

White, Stephen (1990), 'A Burning Issue', *New Law Journal*, 140: 1145, 1157. Reprinted as 'Cricket and Cremation', *Pharos International*, 565(4): 134–35.

Willis, Ronald (1982), 'A Spark in The Ashes', *The Cricketer*, 63(8): 31.

Willis, Ronald (1982), *Cricket's Biggest Mystery: The Ashes*, Guildford: Lutterworth Press.

THOMPSON, SIR HENRY

Many consider Sir Henry Thompson (1820–1904) the father of the cremation movement, at least in Britain. Knighted by Queen Victoria in 1867 for his successful operation on Leopold I of Belgium, the Royal College of Surgeons' member first drew attention to cremation by publishing 'The Treatment of the Body after Death' in the January 1874 issue of the journal *Contemporary Review*. Thompson's own interest in the subject rested chiefly upon his favourable impressions of Lodovico Brunetti's Vienna exhibition in 1873. He applied great enthusiasm to the cause, by launching the Cremation Society of England in 1874 and serving as its first president until his death 30 years later. During that time, the society managed to build and open its Woking crematorium and propagate the society's vision well enough to secure passage of the Cremation Act of 1902. The Act gave the Home Office the responsibility for regulating cremation procedures against undetected homicides, and the first regulations essentially duplicated the precautions that Thompson had created. Thompson also guided the founding of a separate venture, the London Cremation Company Ltd, which opened its Golders Green facility in 1902.

Long before that, he was well known for his ability to surprise the Victorian upper classes, having joined a group agitating to open cultural facilities on Sunday and having, anonymously at first, proposed to test the efficacy of prayer in a hospital experiment. By the time Thompson became a baronet in 1899, he could claim laurels as an artist, an advocate of geriatric health, an astronomer, a novelist and a motorcar enthusiast.

London society, though, best knew Thompson for his formal dinners, as he gave over 300 'octaves' which included the best and brightest of men from a wide array of fields. The son of a Baptist grocer, Thompson rose to being worth over £200 000 when he died. He always remained, as the *Lancet* eulogized him, a 'many sided brilliant man', but his unassailable respectability and recognized authority lent cremation the kind of leverage it needed to defend itself against early detractors. His many interests also ensured that the early membership of the Cremation Society included writers, artists, aristocratic philanthropists and religious men, as well as scientists and physicians, an important boost to building a reform movement. **Lisa Kazmier**

References

British Medical Journal, 23 April 1904: 991–93.

The Times, 19 April 1904.

Concise Dictionary of National Biography: From Its Earliest Times to 1985 (1992), Vol. 3, Oxford: Oxford University Press: 2963.

Cope, Zachary (1951), *The Versatile Victorian, Being the Life of Sir Henry Thompson, 1820–1904*, London: Harvey & Blythe.

Sala, (Mrs) George Augustus (1892), *Famous People I Have Met*, London: James R. Osgood McIlvaine & Co., 75–86.

Thompson, Henry (1874), 'The Treatment of the Body after Death', *Contemporary Review*, 23: 319–28.

Thompson, Henry (1888), 'The Progress of Cremation', *Nineteenth Century*, 23: 1-17.

TIBET

In Buddhist Tibet cremation is one of a variety of funerary practices that are generally ranked in terms of social and religious status. Embalmment and cremation are usually seen as the purest and most desirable forms, along with (in Central Tibet) 'sky-burial' – the ritual dismemberment and feeding of the corpse to vultures. By contrast, burial in the ground or water is seen as either of low status or as the result of dire circumstances.

In each case, the status of the funeral is related to deeply held cosmological ideas that separate death moving 'upwards' (in flames, the sky or embalmment in reliquary monuments called *chorten*) from death moving 'downwards' (into the ground or the water). These images are in turn linked to Tibetan understandings of the bodily movement of the consciousness (*namshey*) at death: either up out of the body through the 'aperture of Brahma' at the top of the cranium, and thence to 'higher rebirth', or downwards through other bodily orifices, to lower rebirths – as animals, ghosts or hell-beings. Tibetan religious history also speaks of a final, ultimate demise, in which the deceased spontaneously dissolves into a 'rainbow-body', a prelude to final spiritual enlightenment and sign of the deceased's total renunciation even of the illusory reality of physical form.

Tibetan Buddhist funerary rites are often highly elaborate, lasting between three days and a week. The spirit of the deceased is summoned by ritual practitioners in order to receive tantric initiations, which empower it with the status of the divine Buddha that was at the heart of the deceased's spiritual practice during life. In a rite called *zhinsre* ('the burning of alms'), the corpse is then cremated, along with high-status food and drink, which combine to act as an offering to the evoked Buddha.

Within the Tibetan understanding of the process of death – in which the consciousness of the dead is guided on a lengthy and perilous journey away from his present life and towards his next rebirth – several progressive 'cremations' are often required. As the spirit of the dead is periodically recalled to hear recitation of the *Bardo Thodol*, or the 'Book of the Dead', by the living, many Tibetan traditions seek to 're-embody' his momentarily present consciousness in various earthly simulacra – first, a straw dummy wearing his clothes, then often a pot – which are marked at first by the name and full details of the deceased, then simply by his name, and then, finally, simply the first syllable of his name. Each of these is burned in turn in order to gradually relinquish the deceased's attachment to the world he has left. In these cases, the external burning of the body and its symbols is often associated with the meditative tantric practice of *tummo*, or 'inner fire', a yogic discipline that is seen as a prelude to the attainment of spiritual enlightenment.

As a result, the cremated remains are often treated as a source of religious blessing (*chinlab*). In everyday cases, the ashes are pressed into *tsa-tsa* – moulded images of Buddhas –- that are either placed inside *chorten* or in high, clean

places beyond the limits of habitation, in order to represent the dead's renunciation of worldly life. By contrast, the cremated remains of high religious virtuosi (and, in certain cases, royal persons) are carefully searched for signs of miraculous manifestations – such as small images of deities, hardened bones 'engraved' with religious symbols by decades of meditative practice, and *ring-srel*, (small pearl-like spheres) – which are kept as religious relics.

The details of Tibetan funerary practices reflect a deep underlying duality in the Mahayana Buddhism of the region, seeking as it does both to promote a world-departing renunciation amongst the worldly, and yet also to retain the compassionate blessing of the departing religious in the form of sacred relics. **Martin A. Mills**

References

Corlin, C. (1988), 'The Journey Through The Bardo', in C. Corlin, S. Cederroth and J. Linstrom (eds), *On The Meaning Of Death*, Uppsala: Uppsala University Press.

Fremantle, F. and Trungpa, C. (1987), *The Tibetan Book of the Dead*, London: Shambala. First published in 1975.

Martin, D. (1992), 'Crystals and Images from Bodies, Hearts and Tongues from Fire: Points of Relic Controversy in Tibetan History', in S. Ihara and Z. Yamaguchi (eds), *Tibetan Studies: Proceedings from the 5th Seminar of the International Association for Tibetan Studies, Narita (Japan) 1989*, Narita: Naritasan Shinshoji.

TYPHOID

Typhoid as a serious illness, often resulting in epidemics, led to relatively large numbers of deaths and to the question of cremation, even in societies that only favoured or normally practised burial. **Douglas J. Davies**

See also cholera and typhoid.

U

UNDERTAKERS AND EARLY CREMATIONS (UK)

Undertakers made an important contribution to

the early cremations at Woking, England's first crematorium. As with burial, they provided a coffin and transport and negotiated between all those involved, but cremation created new challenges. Three London firms were principally involved in the early years (1885–95): William Garstin of Wigmore Street (also trading as The Funeral Company in Blackfriars Road); Halford L. Mills of Paddington (also trading as the Reformed Funeral Company); and the London Necropolis Company of Westminster Bridge Road (owners of Brookwood Cemetery, near Woking). Garstin had been responsible for the repatriation of Lady Dilke to Dresden for cremation in 1874, and the Cremation Society of England endorsed Garstin's services in promotional literature; the Society's Founder and President, Sir Henry Thompson, did likewise in his first edition of *Modern Cremation* (1889). The Funeral Company arranged the cremation of Jeanette Pickersgill on 25 March 1885. Garstin's were responsible for the second cremation in October 1885, but not the third in December. They arranged seven of the ten cremations the following year, nine of the 13 in 1887, and 13 out of 28 in 1888. The majority of cremations were from the London area, and the coffin was either brought by horse-drawn hearse or by the train from Waterloo station to Woking. Horse-drawn transport provided by a Woking-based carriage master was used for the two-mile journey to the crematorium. Undertaking firms from other parts of the country also brought funerals direct to Woking Crematorium.

Halford Mills, who only arranged a modest numbers of cremations, was irritated that the society preferred to use Garstin's. In 1891 the industry was made aware of the relationship through the pages of *Undertakers' Journal* which Mills owned; a change in recommendation occurred between Garstin and the society as the London Necropolis Company became the leading firm for managing cremation funerals. In *Modern Cremation* Thompson quoted a 'Schedule of Expenses' for cremations. In 1889 a pine coffin, delivery to the residence and attendance of staff, transport to the crematory (from within a four-mile radius of Charing Cross), hearse, driver and bearers could be provided for £8 l0s. The society's cremation fee was £6 (Thompson, 1889: 78–79). Garstin's records indicate that these costs were frequently exceeded, thus defeating one of the society's objectives of providing an economic alternative to burial.

The London Necropolis Company had arranged one cremation out of the 13 in 1887, but by 1892 this had increased to over one-quarter of all cremations. Its undertaking service was based at the firm's private station in Westminster Bridge Road which ran funeral trains to Brookwood Cemetery (Clarke, 2004). Company minutes indicate that the company gave a favourable discount to the society for endorsing its services. As more cremations arrived from outside the metropolitan area managed by other funeral directors, the dominance of the London Necropolis Company gradually diminished.

Although undertakers always transported the body to Woking Crematorium in a coffin, some bodies were cremated solely in a shroud; the coffin then being used to contain the casket of ashes for earth burial. Writing in *Modern Cremation* Thompson advocated the envelopment of the shrouded body in a long narrow sheet which was then lifted out of the coffin; Halford Mills supplied woollen envelopes for the same purpose, but this practice had ceased by the end of 1888 with the society insisting on the body remaining in a coffin. Undertakers' records indicate that elm and oak were used for the construction of cremation coffins. Although the Cremation Society provided a small range of urns, undertaking firms constructed wooden caskets for ash burial. Relatives would often wait at the crematorium or adjourn for refreshments while the cremation took place, before collecting the ashes for return to London. **Brian Parsons**

See also New Zealand.

References

Clarke, J.M. (2004), *London's Necropolis*, Stroud: Sutton Publishing.

Thompson, H. (1889), *Modern Cremation: Its History and Practice, with Information Relating to the Recently Improved Arrangements Made by the Cremation Society of England*, London: Kegan Paul, Trench, & Co Ltd.

URNS

CHINESE

Containers for cremated remains vary in China according to regional custom. Round porcelain jars are found mostly in south China, such as in

Guangdong and Fujian provinces, while in eastern, northern and most other parts of China wooden boxes are used. Following the tradition that coffins are mostly made of wood, these boxes, too, are usually produced from high-quality timber, such as *nanmao*, which is widely distributed in China and includes black, fragrant, coloured and golden varieties with golden *nanmao* being the rarest. *Nanmao* was, traditionally, the first choice for coffins while *padauk* was used mostly for furniture. In the case of the boxes, these woods are sometimes combined with other materials, such as copper, porcelains, jades, crystals, alloys, glasses and plastics. They also involve many craftwork skills, varying by region, including lacquerware in Fujian, Dongyang woodcarving in Zhejiang, cloisonné techniques in Beijing and Suzhou *padauk* carpentry in Jiangsu. The resulting objects are very beautiful, some in the shape of pavilions, halls or cabinets, some like coffins but most are hexahedrons carrying portraits of the deceased and other meaningful pictures on each face. Because cremated remains are not ground in China, the containers need to be fairly large to hold all of the pieces. **Zhu Jinlong**

HISTORY

The earliest established use of urns for the containment of ashes dates back to the Bronze Age. The early British buried their dead or cremated them and then buried the ashes in urns, in round barrows. Of the many Bronze Age urns no two are exactly the same. Cinerary urns varied in height from six inches to three feet, and the most common shape resembled that of an ordinary garden flower pot with a deep rim at the top, probably to give the vessel greater strength. Decorations varied with combinations of straight and curved lines, zigzag or herringbone patterns, indents and similar simple markings.

The design, quality and materials of Roman urns tended to be dictated by the wealth and taste of the deceased. Some were costly, being made of silver or gold, others were made in bronze, marble, glass or merely baked clay.

With the nineteenth-century revival of cremation came the introduction of columbaria, designed either as part of the crematorium building or arranged alongside. The wall niches varied in accordance with the size and shape of the urns to be housed within. As the twentieth

century progressed, urn design developed accordingly, and they were produced in all shapes, sizes and materials. Urns most often take the form of traditional classical vessels designed in a variety of different materials including wood, metal, terracotta, marble and stone. The introduction of plastics allowed the production of durable urns, which can be buried or used as temporary containers before scattering takes place or for transportation. American companies in particular specialize in 'novelty' urns such as miniature golf bags. Late twentieth-century trends suggest that, as religious belief wanes, the scattering and burial of ashes often takes place in locations far from crematoria grounds or cemeteries, reducing the need for elaborate urn designs. **Hilary Grainger**

See also Argentina; ashes – remains cineraria; Sweden.

USA

The following contributions document and interpret the emergence of modern cremation in the USA in a strongly complementary fashion. Robert Habenstein sets the historical scene through his 'Cremation Reform and the Sanitation Movement in the Nineteenth Century' before providing types of groups that fostered the cremation idea and its implementation in his 'Forms and Movements'. Stephen Prothero then accounts for changes in cultural attitudes towards cremation rites, practice and memorialization in his 'The Twentieth Century: The First 50 Years'. **Douglas J. Davies**

CREMATION REFORM AND THE SANITATION MOVEMENT IN THE NINETEENTH CENTURY

Cremation has presented itself in various sequences and places throughout the history of Western civilization. Whether among the pre-Christian Greeks, Romans or pagans in northern Europe, three related characteristics were important: cremation was practised among people of wealth and high status; burning of valuable objects underscored the importance of the deceased; and, primarily, the flames would serve to transport the body's spirit to the gods above (Eassie, 1875; Ellis, 1943; Erichsen, 1887).

Hebrews rejected cremation as did most Christians. A few early Christians, however, would practise cremation but by the fourth century it had not only been given up but had been prohibited by Constantine the Great (274–337 AD). Nevertheless, for the next 150 years or more, intermittent plagues and epidemics of contagious diseases rapidly killed thousands of people, forcing populations to use pit burials into which a large number of bodies were dumped. These acts of desperation, as during the fourteenth-century Black Death epidemic, caused by rats bearing deadly plague-carrying lice and fleas, left little or no time for ceremony (Puckle, 1926). In America, where land was more available, burial of several bodies in one grave during a plague might still take place to save time, but cremation was a long way off. Nonetheless, crowded, water-soaked old urban cemeteries were suspect and were roundly condemned in the nineteenth century by sanitationists and many plague-conscious physicians.

New philosophies and social reform

The eighteenth-century period of Enlightenment affected religious and philosophical thought in England, Scotland, France and America. While the dignity of man might be the point of departure for new, liberal thinking in these countries, the Wesleyan movement would carry religion specifically to the common man. John Wesley (1703–91), in developing Methodism, sought out persons high enough in society to lead the type of social reform that would hopefully ameliorate conditions of the poor and desolate. Among the clergy in New England who moved toward ethical philosophy was William E. Channing (1787–1842) a prominent Unitarian clergyman of Massachusetts who preached against a Calvinism that emphasized man's total depravity. Instead, Channing embraced a confidence in all aspects of the human character: intellectual, moral, and spiritual. His thought led the way to social reform (Cooke, 1902). Others followed, incorporating what in England had become a civic reform approach developed early on by Sir Edwin Chadwick (1800–90), disciple of Jeremy Bentham and sometimes referred to as 'the first bureaucrat of modern England'. Chadwick was appointed to the first sanitary commission in 1839, and his report became the textbook of sanitation throughout the remainder of the century.

Immigration and the growth of American cities

From the mid-nineteenth century until shortly after the First World War, 35 million emigrants left Europe for American shores. As many as one-third of these returned, most of whom had failed to find their fortunes. Earlier immigrants were English and Scots-Irish. Later, the Irish, suffering from the potato famine, came in great numbers, particularly during the 'great famine' of mid-century. Germans came early and late, and the Polish, along with other middle eastern Europeans, were numerically the largest group of newcomers after the mid-century, along with the Jews fleeing Russian pogroms. Also the 1849 Gold Rush and the building of the transcontinental railroad brought many people to California, including Asians (Mindel, Habenstein and Wright, 1998). Urban growth in the nineteenth century moved steadily upwards: 5.33 million lived in cities of 8000 population or more in 1800, 23 million at the mid-century, and nearly 63 million by 1890. Unfortunately, the rapid growth of the cities led to overcrowding, poverty, the rise of slums, unemployment, class antagonism and difficulty in maintaining city management (Weber, 1899).

Urban health and welfare sanitation

In major cities the extremes of wealth and poverty became visible, with labourers crowded into ethnic enclaves in factory districts along with new immigrants. It was here that public health problems – with an emphasis on sanitation – increased alongside population growth in general. Again, it was in New England that the necessity of civic organization and administration of cities was brought before the professional and laypeople as a matter of achieving a tolerable or better existence for all. In the later half of the nineteenth century such efforts increased to the point of becoming a social movement so that sanitation and public health became a foremost concern. In cities, public health organization advanced more rapidly than at the level of the state and federal divisions of the American government. State boards of health were slow in developing, but all states had established them between 1855 and 1909. The public health reform movement formally got underway in 1850 with the *Report of the Massachusetts Sanitary Commission* which drew its inspiration from the excellent sanitation work of Sir Edward Chadwick in 1843. The author was Lemuel Shattuck, a statistician who had a lay interest in the problem of sanitation and public health. Shattuck stated clearly that the health of the individual is a community matter, and its protection is the duty of public authority and administration. Yet, probably the most signal contribution to the field of public health in the nineteenth century was made through the efforts of the Sanitary Commission during the Civil War organized by Dr Henry Bellows, the Unitarian minister of All Souls Church in New York City. Boards of health, as well as citizen sanitation committees, had also appeared in many large cities attracting physicians, attorneys, social scientists and civic-minded businessmen. In all these groups, cremation was looked upon favourably from a sanitation perspective. A national health service came even later. Despite the fact that John Adams, America's second president, began his annual message to Congress on 8 December 1789 with reference to the yellow fever epidemic of 1783 and urging federal laws through quarantine legislation, they were not enacted by the US Congress until 1893 (and amended in 1901). By then, the US Public Health services had been created and had begun a slow accretion of power that increased more rapidly in the early years of the twentieth century.

Bacteriology, earth burial and cremation

As these sanitation movements were growing, the medical world was undergoing an enormous forward movement. The advance and elaboration of the theory of disease was signalled by the work of Louis Pasteur (1822–95) in France, Robert Koch (1843–1910) in Germany, and Joseph Lister (1827–1912) working in Scotland. In late nineteenth-century America, it was thought that the earth generated diseases in the decaying body. Consequently, the growing sanitation movement proposed that cremation should be substituted for earth burial. But in the face of the rising germ theory these convictions were put aside.

Physicians who were inclined towards cremation had been publishing papers emphasizing the 'flame' rather than the 'grave' with its dangerous filth as more than merely a sanitary act but as a necessity to forestall a dozen deadly diseases. The new germ theory turned attention to the causation and successful control of the groups of insect-borne diseases such as malaria, yellow fever and trypanosome disease and typhus as understood through the new science of bacteriology. Before the nineteenth century ended, the medical world ceased to support cremation theory based on putrefaction and turned to immunization as the new path to freedom from, or control of, contagious disease. Lister's germicides, for one thing, were the answer to the startling discovery of finding poisonous germs nearly everywhere.

Cremation, embalming and funeral directing

Those who felt cremation and sanitation were necessarily paired stood to be somewhat dismayed by a quietly growing method of preparing the dead body through the use of chemicals – that is, by embalming (Habenstein and Lamers, 1962). If the body were either to contain germs or to generate poisonous fluids in the earth, to replace its blood with strong chemicals, such as arsenic, would not only preserve the body but would make it germ-free.

A historic epoch in America's path through the nineteenth century was its greatest tragedy – an internecine war between northern and southern states. Much of the American Civil War was fought in the south-east and middle eastern states of the country. In battle after battle, thousands of young men were shot at close range. When battles were over and the troops withdrew, the dead were officially identified and would generally be buried on the spot. However, parents, relatives, or mobile undertakers could take dead bodies to undertakers' parlours to embalm them and ship them home. Embalming was not in vogue in American society but was useful to people who had lost their loved ones in a bloody war and wanted to bring their bodies home.

After the Civil War embalming did not become immediately widely employed, but it would soon be popularized by funeral directors who had first stressed its use for sanitation purposes. Soon, however, changing from coffins that merely boxed the dead to caskets that openly displayed the embalmed body, funeral directors presented a natural visage by virtue of their cosmetic skills. The body could then be displayed for a few or many days before burial took place. Cremation would in no way be a necessity and, once embalmed with germ-killing chemicals, the body could not be a threat to the public after burial. At the close of the nineteenth century in America, mainly because of the new application of germ theory to control germs and the use of embalming to take away the fear of the dead buried body, the strong arguments for cremation were no longer compelling. Through various points of view and group efforts, cremation would offer an alternative that had its own cultural appeal. As urban dominance increased cremalists, cemetarians, funeral directors, and sanitarians would find themselves more and more involved with one another. In any event in the twentieth century a new growth in cremation was in the offing. **Robert W. Habenstein**

References

Cooke, George W. (1902), *Unitarianism in America*, Boston, MA: American Unitarian Association.

Eassie, William (1875), *Cremation of the Dead: Its History and Bearings upon Public Health*, London: Smith, Elder & Co.

Ellis, Hilda R. (1943), *The Road to Hell: A Study of the Conception of the Dead in Old Norse Literature*, Cambridge and London: University of London Press.

Erichsen, Hugo (1887), *The Cremation of the Dead*, Detroit, MI: D.O. Haynes & Co.

Habenstein, Robert W. and Lamers, William M. (1962), *The History of American Funeral Directing*, Milwaukee, WI: National Funeral Directors Association.

Lewis, R.A. (1952), *Edwin Chadwick and the Public Health Movement, 1832–1854*, London: Longmans, Green and Co.

Mindel, Charles H., Habenstein, Robert W. and Wright, Roosevelt, Jr (1998), *Ethnic Families in America*, Upper Saddle River, NJ: Prentice Hall.

Puckle, Bertram S. (1926), *Funeral Customs: Their Origin and Development*, New York: Frederick A. Stokes Co.

Weber, Adna (1889), *The Growth of Cities*, New York: Columbia University Studies.

FORMS AND MOVEMENTS

Following the manorial-centered Middle Ages with its slow economic growth, its population held relatively stable mostly by wars, famines, epidemics and low-level agricultural technology, a new era in the form of a maritime-centred mercantilism provided a more vibrant and richer society to western Europeans. Ideas and ideologies changed as world explorers brought home their rough-handed anthropologies. The rationalists of the eighteenth century moved towards a wider world and ways of understanding and possibly controlling its adversities. Nothing was so adverse as disease or more crushing than sudden death. In the nineteenth century, rational minds, broadened by shared information and exploring the scientific nature of things, turned towards causation and control. Cremation, once connecting flames to the spirit world, was examined by science-oriented, enquiring minds. A few of these could be found almost anywhere in Western countries. Some would put a final point to their beliefs, becoming exemplars through their own cremation.

Rational exemplars and leaders

The best-known exemplar of cremation in America comes from the activity of Dr Francis Julius LeMoyne, son of French Huguenot and Irish immigrant parents and a prominent physician of Washington, Pennsylvania. In 1876 Dr LeMoyne, known for his vigorous social reformist views, erected on his property in his home town America's first crematory. It was constructed for what he considered a better way of disposing of the dead, including his own body and those of his friends. Some years later, the first modern cremation was performed at his crematory, organized primarily by Theosophist Colonel Henry S. Alcott (cf. Prothero, 2001). Baron de Palm, an elderly freemason, was given a Theosophic funeral in the New York Masonic Hall and his body taken to LeMoyne's crematory. The second cremation took place in 1878, when the remains of Mrs Ben Pitman, wife of a well-known Cincinnati stenographer, was, in contemporary parlance, 'given to the flames'. The following year LeMoyne himself was cremated there. Forty other private cremations followed and, after 1886, the crematory was closed down. Meanwhile others had appeared in the north-east quadrant of the United States as general sanitation reform spread through the more populated states (Erichsen, 1887).

Leaders in the early years were drawn from four groups led by medical people such as Dr Samuel Gross; Dr M.L. Davis, an energetic sanitation reformer and designer of a highly workable cremation furnace; Dr James F.A. Adams, respected author of medical tracts on cremation and burial; and Dr W.H. Curtis who, in 1892, wrote a 14 000-word report on cremation to the American Public Health Association. Doctors were sought for, and served in, fledgling cremation societies and associations. Dr William Porter, president of the Tri-State Medical Society, wrote in the *New England Medical Monthly* that bodies of those dying of typhoid fever would, in his judgement, be better cremated. Most of the medical world agreed (Habenstein, 1949). Others who were strongly in favour of cremation were found in the sanitation branches of city and state governments and in liberal religious groups such as Unitarians, Universalists and Episcopalians who participated in the cremation movement on a social–philosophical basis.

'Ladies that saved the cities'

Women strongly in support of cremation were in the women's club movement, including those who earlier had participated in the sanitation committee that was active as a civilian body during the Civil War. Many women became national figures, such as: Julia Ward Howe, who lectured on reform as women's work as well as men's; Margaret Fuller, writer and poet; and Elizabeth Cady Stanton, abolitionist and advocate of women's rights. These are but a few of the women who helped change the character of nineteenth-century American life (Croly, 1897). Well-known people not only expressed their views on cremation in speaking and writing, but they carried the argument by example, and their leadership activities were published in many outlets: journals, magazines, newspapers and in serious works by professionals.

Types of early association and society

From a formal standpoint, the various cremation societies reveal commonalities in organization, membership, officers and trustees, as well as a complex of leadership–follower relations, diversely defined roles and a rationale. The aims and goals might be somewhat different. Four types appear when one asks what the organizations were trying to accomplish (for elaboration see Habenstein, 1949).

The reform-oriented society

This type of cremation society sought to induce a reform in nineteenth-century burial practices by means of argument based on rational and ethical appendages supported by discoveries in medical science, all reflecting the pressure of humanitarian principles. Reform was the objective, propaganda the method to be used, and the society the instrument of distributing such propaganda. It was felt that religion should not concern itself about cremation because Christians had, in ancient times, been both buried and cremated. Cremation was rational, decent, clean and economical and thus to be preferred by all intellectually-minded people. Arguments cited abuses of intramural burial, proposing that such burials constituted a menace to the living. Existing mortuaries were attacked directly for their lack of social conscience and their outrageous expense. Outstanding examples of this kind of society are the New England Society, the Lancaster (Pennsylvania) Cremation and Funeral Reform Society, and the Cremation Society of Southern California.

The cremation service-oriented society

This type of society may be viewed as the usual, but not invariable, outgrowth of the first type. The society might, however, divide into two differently functioning units – one continuing to propagandize and the other focusing on the erection and operation of a crematory. However, it was soon found that crematories are investments, and without philanthropic intervention must pay their own way. Local resistance to the proposed locations often made the cemetery the only available site for the proposed crematory. Consequently, the society that owned and operated a crematory found itself competing with funeral directors and cemetery managers but was forced to operate within the system of ethics of the mortuary profession. Such a society then had to float precariously in choppy seas of business, temper its arguments, maintain an 'ethical' relationship with other mortuary professions, and seek to develop a market sufficient to maintain its crematory. This would mean that the argument for cremation as a cheaper form of burial had to be played down, along with any claim that the cremation society with a crematory could be practising 'burial reform'. Meetings of the members of the societies that operated crematories turned towards operation and management and emphasized their delivery of service. Examples of this group include the Massachusetts Cremation Society, the Buffalo Cremation Company and the Davenport Cremation Society.

The cremation assurance-oriented society

This type of cremation society might be associated with the activities of German ethnic and national groups in America. Their highest legitimization for cremation practice was found at the level of ancient Germanic and Scandinavian pagan mythology with an appeal to literary imagery replete with mythical allusions to soaring flames, Valhalla, fire burial and other similar images. Relations amongst members were characterized by a spirit of mutual aid and fraternal benevolence but always with the proviso that the society was structured as a sound business proposition. It follows that the rationale for cremation contained arguments at two levels of appeal: one mythical–poetic and the other practical–utilitarian. Examples of such cremation assurance societies include the San Francisco, the Philadelphia and the St Louis Cremation Societies, along with the Michigan Cremation Association and the Benevolent Society for Propagation of Cremation in the United States.

The cremation business-oriented society

This late nineteenth-century type of society represented the grouping together of a number of persons who created a set of services to be offered to the public at large for money. A crematory was always erected immediately. The relationship among the members was that of business associates, developing from joint-stock-issuing operations. The relationship with the public might be regarded as tending towards the impersonal. Advertising and the maintenance of 'public relations' became the acceptable way of furthering the cremation movement. The number of cremations performed in a year became a business secret and was divulged with only the greatest reluctance, if at all. The cremation business association provided little more for its personnel than a set of impersonal, functionally organized relationships oriented towards the acquisition of economic goods of immediate utility. By the end of the nineteenth century societies of this sort had evolved rapidly into 'service-business' associations connected with cemeteries and funeral homes.

Reform versus business society

By the end of the nineteenth century – starting from LeMoyne's first crematory in 1876 – the number of cremations amounted to 13 381, and the number of active crematories had increased to 24. For various reasons, four others had not continued. Of those active, five were located in New York; California and Pennsylvania had four each, and Massachusetts had two. The other 16 were distributed throughout the upper eastern and central quadrants of the United States. Interestingly, by the end of the century, while a few crematories were operated by municipalities, many funeral directors were either establishing crematories or arranging 'cremation services' that would often end in established cemeteries.

Dr Erichsen's life dedication

Dr Hugo Erichsen, it might be said, represented cremation as a social reform, as Dr LeMoyne had adopted cremation as a personal belief. For many years Erichsen practised medicine in Detroit, Michigan, and devoted all his spare time to advancing the cause of cremation by publishing books – most importantly *Cremation of the Dead* in 1877 – and innumerable pamphlets, giving speeches, and organizing cremation societies at the state and national levels. It was Dr Erichsen who called all cremationists and others associated with cremation to the organizing of a national association, the first meeting to be in 1913 in his home city, Detroit, Michigan. The response was somewhat surprising, since those he expected and wished for most – the cremation reformists – did not appear, except for one representative of the Massachusetts Cremation Society. There were no philosophical groups represented, no other associations nor anyone representing the public and municipalities. With one exception – Annie Hall, a women's rights protester – there was no voice for cremation as a social sanitation reform.

Dr Erichsen, as first president of the newly formed Cremation Society of America, found it possible to set up the formal structures of an association but was crestfallen to find the practicalities of it were totally pointed towards trade organization activities. Despite his second year as president of the new Cremation Association of America he was unable to attract

members to any reform activities. Dr Erichsen would spend many years on the 'outside' of the association, still writing, speaking and giving suggestions to tradesmen who were mainly uninterested. All in all, he spent 50 years on what would be futile efforts to create a professional association widely interested in public needs. He might have realized this from the 1913 meeting in which only business-oriented subjects were discussed and when crematory operators and mausoleum managers would talk only about high rental charges. The rather light representation of funeral directors would, however, change as they came to see that cremation could be reasonably remunerative, particularly if it included the sale of urns for the deceased's ashes. So it was that the simplicity of later nineteenth-century cremations gave way to increasingly more complex forms as the new century lost much of the inclination for social reform, moving towards economy on the one hand and individuality primed with fashion verging towards idiosyncrasy on the other.
Robert W. Habenstein

References

Croly, Jennie C. (1897), *The History of the Women's Club Movement in America*, New York: Henry G. Allen.

Erichsen, Hugo (1887), *The Cremation of the Dead*, Detroit, MI: D.O. Haynes & Co.

Habenstein, Robert W. (1949), *A Sociological Study of the Cremation Movement in the United States* University of Chicago: University of Michigan Dissertation Services, Bell and Howell Co., Ann Arbor, MI 48106-1346.

Lange, Louis (1903), *Church Women and Cremation*, New York: United States Cremation Co.

Prothero, Stephen (2001), *Purified by Fire: A History of Cremation in America*, Berkeley: University of California Press.

Organizations
Cremation Association of North America, Chicago, Illinois, USA.

National Funeral Directors Association, Milwaukee, Wisconsin, USA.

THE TWENTIETH CENTURY: THE FIRST FIFTY YEARS

During the first half of the twentieth century, American cremationists shifted their collective attention from debating cremation to building and running crematories. By the turn of the century, the United States witnessed 1000 cremations annually, so individual cremations were no longer notorious, nor even noteworthy. The great cremation versus burial debate of the late nineteenth century came to a close with no clear resolution, except perhaps that the disposition of the dead would be a matter of individual preference rather than social fiat. As if to indicate that the period of argument had ended, the three main pro-cremation monthlies of the nineteenth century – *Modern Crematist, The Urn* and *The Columbarium* – all ceased publishing by the late 1890s. What the *New York World* had dubbed 'this curious controversy between the sextons and the stokers' was over, and a new phase in US cremation history had begun.

During this 'bricks-and-mortar' phase, control over the cremation movement shifted from non-profit societies to for-profit businesses, and from crusading social reformers to pragmatic businessmen. In 1913 in Detroit, a cadre of these businessmen formed the first trade association devoted to the cause: the Cremation Association of America (CAA). Loosely modelled on the National Funeral Directors Association, the CAA (now the Cremation Association of North America) was the brainchild of Dr Hugo Erichsen, who began his career as a crusading cremationist and ended it as the head of a burgeoning trade association. CAA members focused primarily on designing, building and operating crematories. In 1900 there were 25 crematories up and running in the United States – four in California and the rest in the north-east and the mid-west. By 1919 that figure had jumped to 70, including 18 in California, but there was not even a single crematory operating in the south. Over the next two decades, investors built crematories at a rate of about six per year, and the cremation option became available to every region in the country. By 1950, US crematories were conducting about 300 000 cremations per year, and the cremation rate – the ratio of cremations to deaths – had risen to approximately 4 per cent. During this era, crematory operators also worked hard at beautifying their facilities.

Throughout the nineteenth century, public health had been the main reason to cremate. The sanitary argument for cremation was rooted in the old miasma theory of disease, which postulated that infectious diseases were spread by noxious gases – miasma – emitted from decaying organic matter, including graveyard corpses. As germ theory gained acceptance around the turn of the century, however, the old public health argument for cremation faded away. As early as 1895, an article in the *Journal of the American Medical Association* observed 'a growing feeling that the dangers apprehended from cemeteries have been considerably overestimated'. By 1917 *Park and Cemetery* reported 'that there is no reason to apprehend danger of contamination of the water or air by the modern cemetery'.

Stripped of its old justification in public health, cremation became a rebellion in search of a cause. Cremationists found that cause in aesthetics. Whereas in the past they had argued that cremation was more healthy than burial, now they said that it was more beautiful. In order to make good on that claim, crematory operators built new crematories far more elegant than the merely functional, and often ugly, first-generation facilities. They also renovated existing crematories, festooning them with flowers, plants, Oriental rugs and arts-and-crafts furniture. Some even used songbirds. The Gardner Earl Memorial Crematory in Troy, New York, included an elaborate mosaic floor, an onyx altar, carved bronze doors, and five Tiffany stained-glass windows. Cremationists also moved columbariums up from basements, bathing them in light and, in some cases, opening them out to spectacular gardens. In 1934 the venerable Mount Auburn Cemetery outside Boston retrofitted the first floor of its crematory chapel for columbarium niches.

In the 1930s *Reader's Digest* helped popularize this new aesthetic argument for cremation when it published an essay called 'Light, Like the Sun,' an autobiographical account of Frances Newton's conversion to the cremation cause. Newton's father was getting old, so she went to her local cemetery to find a burial plot. But the day was cold and wet and the cemetery expensive and overcrowded – 'a monstrous blight upon the land' (cited in Prothero, 2001: 156). While at the cemetery, Newton met a young man who steered her towards cremation. As he explained the procedure to her in a beautiful crematory chapel, Newton began to associate cremation not with hell but with the sun, not with punishment but with freedom. Cremation, she decided, was the way to go.

As cremationists came up with new arguments for their practice, they also experimented with new cremation rites. In the early years of the American cremation movement, cremations were almost always witnessed and ritualized, and crematory rites were modelled on the traditional graveside committal service. Most early US crematories had only one floor, typically divided into two main rooms. At the height of the service, officiants would push the casket from the chapel room to the retort room. Over time, more and more crematories moved their furnaces into the basement and built trap doors in their chapels, providing for a more dramatic exit for the corpse, down through the floor rather than out through a door. As the century wore on, however, the crematory was gradually secularized. Ritualization moved away from the crematory to churches, cemeteries and scattering sites. Rather than remembering the dead at the time of the cremation, many families memorialized deceased family members after cremation. Not until late in the twentieth century would the tradition of ritualization at the crematory return to the US scene in force. Crematory operators also experimented with new cremation technologies. The US Patent Office certified dozens of new cremation-related patents in the first half of the twentieth century. A portable crematory called 'Hygienic Wagon and Portable Furnace' received a patent in 1907. Other inventors received patents for a variety of urn designs, including one with a slot for a photograph of the deceased. Crematory operators also experimented with a variety of furnace designs, fuels and burners. Indirectly-fired oil-burning furnaces eventually emerged as the favourites, because they were both more economical than the alternatives and produced less smoke than wood, coke, coal or electricity.

Cremationists also settled on what came to be known as 'the memorial idea'. In the nineteenth century, many pioneering cremationists had seen cremation as an alternative not only to burial, but also to memorialization. To choose cremation was to scatter the ashes to the winds. To go into the cremation business was to tackle the undertakers and the cemetery operators head-on. Over time, however, crematory operators accommodated themselves to the funeral industry. Especially in the 1920s and 1930s, cremationists began to speak about a single 'memorializing movement' that would 'unite in one craft' not only crematory operators, funeral directors and cemetery superintendents but also casket-makers, funerary florists and mausoleum operators. Advocates began to refer to cremation not as final disposition but as 'a preparation for memorialization'. On the West Coast, that often meant depositing inurned ashes within a columbarium, while on the East Coast that typically meant burying them in a cemetery. Walter B. Londelius, the superintendent at Forest Lawn Memorial Park in Glendale, California, argued in the late 1920s for 'the memorial idea'. After cremation, he argued, the postmortem ritualization was only one-third complete, since 'cremation, niche and urn' were to him three inseparable features of what he called 'urn interment' (Londelius, 1928: 26–27). In 1929 Henry Adams of Forest Hills Cemetery outside Boston began speaking about cremation as 'preparation of the body for the ground'. Soon cremationists were speaking more broadly of 'cremation as a preparation for memorialization' (Adams, 1935: 33). Moreover, the most common site for a crematory became the cemetery.

Cremationists also made peace with Christianity in this bricks-and-mortar period. During the late nineteenth century, many key cremationists were unconventional religious folk – freethinkers, agnostics or Theosophists. For them, cremation was not just an alternative to burial; it was an alternative to Christianity. As the new pragmatic spirit took hold, however, cremationists made peace with the Church. Crematory operators now referred to their service in explicitly theological terms – as 'a last baptism by incandescent heat'. They also outfitted their crematories with chapels, complete with organs and pews and lecterns, to evoke the sacredness of a church. The 1963 decision by the Roman Catholic Church to lift its 1886 ban on cremation was in part a response to these efforts to Christianize cremation. Cremation rates did not rise dramatically during the first half of the twentieth century, in part because religious opposition remained strong. In the late 1930s and early 1940s, Catholic periodicals such as *Ave Maria, Sign, America, Catholic Digest* and *Catholic Mind* all denounced the practice as an abomination. Nonetheless, cremation made significant headway during this quiet period. Cremationists settled on new technologies and new arguments for their cause. They also built

hundreds of new crematories from coast to coast. That infrastructure provided a firm foundation for the cremation boom of the 1960s and beyond. **Stephen Prothero**

References

Adams, Henry S. (1935), 'Cremation Problems in the East', *Report of the Proceedings of the Annual Convention of the Cremation Association of America*.

Landelius, Walter B. (1928), 'Cremation and Modern Crematory Construction', *Association of American Cemetery Superintendents Proceedings*.

Newton, Frances (n.d.), 'Light, Like the Sun', available at: http: //funerals.org/faq/light.htm (accessed February 2005).

Prothero, Stephen (2001), *Purified by Fire*, Berkeley: University of California Press.

V

VAILLANT, C.J.

Dr C.J. Vaillant was the first person to be cremated in the Netherlands, on 1 April 1914 in Velsen Crematorium. Vaillant studied medicine at Leiden and, following a period in Paris, became a general practitioner of medicine in Schiedam where he developed a flourishing practice in which he also paid attention to the poor. Vaillant was one of the original founders of the Association for Cremation 'die Facultatieve' (*Vereeniging voor Lijkverbranding*) and became a correspondent for the Schiedam region during its early years. Vaillant was a very valuable member of the association, fighting for legalisation of facultative cremation and, as a doctor, striving to do as much research as possible into the medical aspects of cremation and burial. He had clearly indicated his desire to be cremated and hoped this could take place in the Netherlands.

At the time of his death, the first cremator had just been approved, so Vaillant could indeed be cremated in the Netherlands. There were negotiations with the government and the police prior to the cremation, in order to ensure that it would take place without disturbance as the practice was still in fact against the law. The government gave their guarantee but a police officer was, nevertheless, present in the background. It was also agreed that criminal proceedings would be initiated after the cremation, so that the association would be taken to court. The cremation was attended by many people and progressed quietly.

Afterwards, the court took a long time to pass judgement but, in the end, the board members of the association were all acquitted. This was a breakthrough for subsequent cremations. In the event, therefore, Dr Vaillant's wish to be cremated and his prominent membership of the association laid the foundations for modern-day cremation. **J.M.H.J. Keizer**

See also Netherlands: societies and law.

VAMPIRES

In Europe, for many centuries, certain people were thought likely to return after death and cause trouble for the living. These were often people who had been troublesome during their lives – such as alcoholics and suspected witches – or had died 'before their time'. Executed criminals, by meeting both these criteria, became strong candidates for revenant status. It should be noted that such people were never believed to return in their corporeal form but always as spirits, although it is probably too late to correct that image as presented in films about vampires. But the way to hasten the spirit off to the afterworld was to 'kill' the corpse of the supposed vampire a second time.

Vampirism was a standard explanation for epidemics in much of Europe, and since epidemics were not uncommon, literate outsiders occasionally had the opportunity to observe exhumations of supposed vampires and write detailed accounts of them. This is why we now have substantial knowledge of what caused people to suppose that the dead came out of their graves – but as spirits – and attacked the living. One of the best of these accounts, known as *Visum et Repertum*, was written in the early 1730s and signed by five people, three of them medical officers.

Oddly, there is nothing in the medical facts in the account that will not stand up to examination. The writer – one of the medical officers – gave a detailed description of the bodies, some of which were even dissected, and reported several things that seemed puzzling, such as the presence of liquid blood. We now know this to be normal for corpses in certain circumstances. When the blood was at the lips (caused when bloating forced blood from the lungs out through the mouth) it was assumed that the deceased had been occupying his time after death by sucking the blood of the living.

We all know how you kill such a corpse – with a stake. But this was just one of many ways of killing a vampire, and the only one that found success in Hollywood. But, in reality, bodies were decapitated, cut into pieces, the heart removed – any method that would kill the living might also be used to kill the dead. The most common method – and the one used in our eighteenth-century account – was to ensure a really thorough cremation of the body. In fact, those bodies were first decapitated, then burned, and finally thrown into a river. Indeed, cremation was often the method of last resort. According to an account from Wendic folklore:

> In order to free themselves from this plague the people dug the body up, drove a consecrated nail into its head and a stake through its heart. Nonetheless, that did not help: the murdered man came back each night (that is, in nightmares). Then they decided to dig up the corpse once again –- it had been buried again – and they burned it at the Branitz pool and strewed the ashes into all the winds. (Veckenstedt, 1883 in Barber, 1988: 71–72)

This leads us to ponder the whole point of cremation. We might assume that people cremate in order to get rid of dead bodies, but in fact it is extremely difficult to get rid of a body by burning: being largely composed of water, it takes a huge amount of fuel to complete combustion. A seventeenth-century account describes a supposed vampire being cremated with about 21 cubic metres of wood (Klapper, 1909: 77). In modern cremations, if oil is used to heat a furnace, and if the furnace has to be heated for each cremation, the average oil consumption 'may be as high as 24 gallons' (Polson, Brittain and Marshall, 1953: 119). Because bodies are difficult to burn, various accelerants, such as pitch and animal fat, have often been added to a wood fire used for cremation.

So in the past, before the use of modern cremation furnaces, which create intense heat and recirculate it, cremations often merely turned the body into charred flesh and bone, which then had to be disposed of. The messiness of disposal caused people to come up with the idea of cremating the body at or in the grave, so that it did not have to be moved there from where it had been burned. Both the Greeks and the Romans did this.

It is important to note that one cannot cremate a body effectively by simply tossing it on to a fire: because combustion can take place only where oxygen is available, the body cannot burn at all where it is touching either the ground or solid fuel – it could not do so even if it were itself combustible. Evans illustrates this issue with an analogy: 'The individual pages of a book blaze readily, but the closed book hardly burns at all' (Evans, 1963: 86). So we can hardly be surprised that so many 'partial cremations' are reported. For cremation to be more or less complete, the family of the deceased has to have at its disposal considerable time and fuel, and the corpse has to be kept away from the ground, on some kind of platform that allows oxygen to circulate. All of this makes cremation expensive, so it is common for it to be used only for high-status people, while low-status people do the actual work (Schlenther, 1960: 39, 40).

A purely practical person, watching a cremation, might wonder why remains that are to be buried should first be cremated. In fact, we need to look at cremation not from our point of view but from that of the people who invented it. And those people clearly saw the changes in the body after death as evidence of a sort of continued life (Barber, 1988). Worldwide, 'real' death is thought to begin when the body stops changing. That is the proof that the body's servo-mechanism, the spirit, has departed for the afterworld. It is common for a buried body to be dug up after some years to determine whether or not it has ceased changing. If it has, this is taken for proof that the body's spirit has departed and the deceased is at peace. This process can be hastened by cremation, which reduces the body, if not to cinders, at least to something that no longer undergoes change. But, of course, this does not explain partial cremations, which often merely scorch the corpse.

If the real issue is the safe removal of the body's spirit, we will do well to investigate that spirit to determine why fire is an effective means of routing it from the body. Our best clue is that the spirit is an insubstantial copy of the body – the same form without the substance. Indeed, some scholars have suggested that the spirit is an interpretation of the dream-image (Wiedemann, 1909: 34; Tylor, 1871: i, 450) and others that it is an explanation of reflections (Harva, 1938: 349), since the spirit world is often taken for a reversed version of our own world. Both dream and reflection are insubstantial versions of the physical body. But although the reversed quality of the spirit world explains why it was common to bury the potentially restless dead in a position opposite to that of less threatening corpses – say, prone instead of supine – and even why reflections in either water or crystal are commonly used to consult the spirits, both theories leave us helpless to explain why the mere presence of fire would drive out spirits.

To understand this we need to realize that we have divided up what was once seen as a whole (Barber and Barber, 2004: ch. 15). The spirit world was clearly compounded not out of a single insubstantial version of the physical body but out of all of them, which were taken as different manifestations of a single entity. In other words, the dream-image and the reflection were not seen as different phenomena at all, merely as different versions of the same phenomenon. And whilst neither of these explains why fire drives out spirits, a third insubstantial double, the shadow, does this rather well (at night you can see the shadow being driven out of your body by a fire) and it, too, is viewed merely as one manifestation of the spirit world. This is why, historically, it has been so common for one word to refer to all the different insubstantial 'doubles' that physical bodies seem to have. We think of the Greek *skiá* as the word for shadow, but Liddell and Scott's Greek-English Lexicon also offers: 'reflection, image; shade of one dead, phantom'.

Once we understand that these different phenomena were once viewed as a single entity, we can see why they had a significance we now find hard to understand. In India it was taboo for an Untouchable to allow his shadow to fall on a Brahman. This is difficult to make sense of as long as you see the shadow as merely a meaningless optical phenomenon. But if you see it as something that appears purposefully in dreams, exits the body and enters water at will, and acts as a kind of servo-mechanism for the body (the evidence for which is that its temporary absence is manifested in sleep, its permanent absence in death) then its contact can be seen as very problematic indeed. Moreover, it suddenly makes sense for someone to ensure the absence of spirits at night by carrying a candle through all the rooms of the house, as Crooke reported from India (Crooke, 1926: 206). Similarly, it makes sense to touch fire to the corpse to drive the spirit out, even if the fire does not completely dispose of the body.

Now we can also see why, throughout Europe, mirrors were turned to the wall in the presence of death: the mirror might keep the spirit from departing to wherever spirits go. Similarly, standing water, itself a reflector, in the house was often poured out. Likewise, a container of water might be left at the graveside, with the expectation that the spirit might enter it and, when the water was later poured out, be freed to leave peacefully without disturbing the living. Cremation appears to be one of many methods used to ensure that the spirits – especially those of people apt to cause trouble after death – are nicely separated from the corpse and encouraged to move along. **Paul Barber**

References

Barber, E.W. and Barber, Paul T. (2004), *When They Severed Earth from Sky: How the Human Mind Shapes Myth*, Princeton, NJ: Princeton University Press.

Barber, Paul T. (1988), *Vampires, Burial, and Death: Folklore and Reality*. New Haven, CT: Yale University Press.

Crooke, William (1926), *Religion and Folklore of Northern India*, Oxford: Oxford University Press.

Evans, W.E.D. (1963), *The Chemistry of Death*, Springfield, IL: Charles C. Thomas.

Harva, Uno (1938), *Die religiösen Vorstellungen der altäischen Völker (FF Communications No. 125)*, Helsinki: Söderström.

Klapper, Joseph (1909), 'Die schlesischen Geschichten von den schädigenden Toten', *Mitteilungen der schlesischen Gesellschaft für Volkskunde*, 11: 58–93.

Polson, C.J., Brittain, R.P. and Marshall, T.K. (1953), *The Disposal of the Dead*, New York: Philosophical Library.

Schlenther, Ursula (1960), *Brandbestattung und Seelenglauben*, Berlin: Deutscher Verlag der Wissenschaften.

Tylor, Edward (1871), *Primitive Culture*, London: John Murray.

Wiedemann, A. (1900), *Die Toten und ihre Reiche*, Leipzig: J.C. Hinrichs'sche Buchhandlung.

VAN LISSA, P.K.

The Hague-based medical doctor Van Lissa became a member of the board of the Association for Cremation (*Vereniging voor Lijkverbranding*) in 1891, and took over its propaganda activities in 1904. At the request of *Vivat's Illustrated Encyclopaedia*, he wrote an article on cremation that was widely praised. His oral propaganda was equally successful; his lectures were well attended and successfully recruited new members. Van Lissa continued to lobby for amendment of the law in the Netherlands (as many people preferred to have their cremation carried out abroad where it was 'cheaper and less complicated'), and pursued the idea of constructing a crematorium in the Netherlands. Following lengthy consultations within the Association for Cremation, the decision was taken in 1908 to build a crematorium on the site of Westerveld Cemetery. Building commenced on 13 February 1912, and the crematorium opened on 27 September 1913. A large group of journalists was given a guided tour by Van Lissa. He also organized the first cremation in Velsen Crematorium on 1 April 1914, that of Dr C. J. Vaillant, a founding member of the Association for Cremation. Since cremation was still against the law in the Netherlands, Van Lissa was brought to trial. After a long wait, due to the First World War, he was acquitted. Fierce discussions followed and negotiations began on the legalization of cremation. The cremations that ensued were organized by Van Lissa, who was also responsible for the operation of the crematorium. Following his part in problems surrounding the construction of a second cremator and a second columbarium, Van Lissa retired from the association in 1924. Despite the necessary disquiet during the board change, he was thanked by all involved. **J.M.H.J. Keizer**

See also Netherlands: societies and law; Vaillant.

VIENNA CREMATORIUM

The first crematorium to be built in the Austro-Hungarian Empire was at Liberec (German: 'Reichenberg', today on Czech territory) during the First World War. Much political conflict was involved in its planning, and the first cremation was not conducted until 31 October 1918 – three days after the Czechoslovakian Republic had been proclaimed. The new Social Democratic town administration of Vienna tried to remedy the non-availability of cremation when, on 1 April 1921, it decided to advertise the project of a new crematorium as a public competition. Despite the judge's decision, it was the plan of architect Clemens Holzmeister (1886–1983) that was finally accepted and implemented. This, his first monumental structure, brought him international recognition.

The crematorium was built in Wien-Simmering, close to the great Central Cemetery on the site of the former Neugebaeude Castle. The architectural concept underlying this oriental-looking building was taken from the former sixteenth-century castle itself. The crematorium's opening attracted some severe political opposition. The Christian Democrat minister for social administration, Richard Schmitz (1885–1954), tried to prevent the opening by prohibiting all cremation in Austria, but Social Democrat mayor of Vienna, Jakob Reumann (1853–1929), opened the crematorium anyway. Despite the lawsuit that followed, itself heatedly discussed in the daily press, the first cremation took place on 17 January 1923. One year later, on 21 January 1924, the Constitutional Court legalized cremation in Austria. It was, however, only after 1945 that cremation slowly gained general social acceptance. This acceptance was assisted when, finally, the Catholic Church admitted cremation as an alternative to burial in 1963. This change of attitude was reflected in the addition, in Wien-Simmering Crematorium, of three altar crucifixes that were consecrated according to Roman Catholic rite. **Christian Stadelmann**

See also Holzmeister.

References

Georgeacopol-Winischhofer, Ute, Wehdorn, Armine and Wehdorn, Manfred (1998), *75 Jahre Feuerhalle der Stadt Wien*, Wien: Stadt Wien, Magistratsabteilung 43, Städtische Bestattung.

VIKING SWEDEN

During Sweden's Viking Age from 800–1050 AD, the most common form of funeral was cremation, a custom extending from before the Viking Age. The oldest cremations in Sweden are dated to approximately 7000 BC (Larsson, 1988), but are very scarce. Not until the Bronze Age, around 1000 BC, did the custom of cremation become fully accepted, and by the beginning of the Iron Age, 500 BC, the vast majority of funerals were cremations. Inhumations did occur during the Bronze and Iron Ages although they varied in number in different areas of the country. When Christianity was introduced around 1050 AD cremation disappeared, not to be reintroduced until the end of the nineteenth century.

This means that Viking Age cremations marked the end of a very long tradition during which details of the custom naturally changed overtime. In the oldest cremations only human bones are found, while the more recent also contain cremated animals sacrificed to the gods or to the deceased, either having been cremated on the pyre together with the human being, or perhaps on separate pyres. During the Bronze Age and Early Iron Age the bones were carefully collected from the pyres, leaving the soot and charcoal behind, and then buried. This way of handling the bones creates what is called clean cremated bones. Over time, humus acids colour the bones brownish, just as with uncremated skeletons. Late Iron Age cremations differ from this, with funeral layers of mixed bones, soot and charcoal and bone fragments of grey or even black colour. The bones were normally crushed after the cremation, and the most usual fragment size varies between 0.5cm and 2cm. There are a few exceptions where large fragments of human skeletons have been found and where it is most probable that the bones have not been crushed (Sigvallius, 1994). In some cremations hammer stones have been found which might also have been used in other rituals for crushing bones (Kaliff, 1992). During the Viking Age itself, the deliberate crushing of cremated bones was not taken as far as in earlier days, for the fragment size is normally somewhat larger. In this way, cremations in Sweden apparently differ from cremations on the Continent and in Britain, where the cremated bones were not deliberately crushed (McKinley, 1993).

The custom of crushing the bones has probably been combined with further ritual – for example, scattering the bones on areas other than in the burial mound. Most cremations contain far too few bone fragments (Holck, 1996), implying that not all the bone material was transferred from the pyre to the grave, which are usually situated in two different locations. Traces of funeral pyres, where repeated cremation has taken place, followed by cleaning of the surface, have been found in middle Sweden (Kaliff, 1997). In cremations from the Bronze Age and Early Iron Age, bone fragments are often found collected in urns or other containers, whereas burials from the Late Iron Age normally contain layers of bone, soot, charcoal and artefacts. In many, but not all, Late Iron Age graves there are urns containing some larger fragments of bone than in the surrounding cremation layer: these often turn out to be the bones of horses and, in some of these urns, there is no trace of human remains. In Early Iron Age burials, where the bones have been scattered in small concentrations all over the grave monument, it is often difficult to decide whether there is one or more funerals represented in the monument. In the Bronze Age and in the first part of the Early Iron Age there are hardly any animal bones found in cremations, but in the Late Iron Age the number of different species increases. In the earliest cremations, bear claws and bones from sheep or goats are the most common. The bear claws are remains of hides used as gifts or bedding for the deceased. As regards sheep and goats, the most common finds are fragments from the feet and head. They can hardly be regarded as remains of hides, but are more likely to be symbolic offerings.

In the Migration period, 350–550 AD, the number of animals in graves increases. Until this point, fragments from sheep or goats are the most common finds, but during this period there is a greater incidence of fragments from other species and a larger number of individual animals. At the end of the period the dog is the most common animal in the cremations, and they almost always prove to be complete dogs, rather than hides or parts of the animals. Many other animals become increasingly common in the graves: horses, pigs, cattle, cats, chicken, geese, birds of prey, waders and fish. The peak of the tradition is reached during the period before the Viking Age, namely the Vendel period, 550–800 AD. This is the period when really large numbers of animals of different species are sacrificed on funeral pyres. At the end of the Viking Age there is a decline in the custom: the number of animals decreases. At the same time, during all these hundreds of years when animals where sacrificed in the flames at funerals, there

still are graves totally devoid of animals (Sigvallius, 1994).

Boats in graves

The oldest written source about Viking Age cremations comes from the Arabian explorer Ibn Fadlan. In the year 932 AD he witnessed a cremation of a Viking chieftain on the shores of Volga. The Viking was cremated in a ship and the description of the procedure is detailed (Birkeland, 1954). While it can be risky to place too much trust in written sources of such antiquity, especially when only one is known, it is probable that this description is fairly accurate since the animal sacrifices mentioned by Fadlan are precisely of those whose remains are found in cremations. According to Fadlan's description, the chieftain was cremated in a ship. Often, when Viking ships are discussed, we think of large seafaring vessels, with crews of many men that could sail over the seas to trade and to rob. But far from all Viking Age craft were large ships; many different kinds of boat have existed, from large seafaring vessels to small skiffs (Greenhill, 1993). The funerals where we can be certain to have found boats of any kind are rather few, totalling around 400 from Sweden, Norway and Denmark (Müller-Wille, 1970). These funerals are not all from the Viking Age; on Bornholm, for example, boats in graves are known from the Early Iron Age, 100–300 AD (Nylén and Schönbäck, 1994). The peak of the tradition with boats in graves was reached during the Vendel Period. Some of these graves are not cremations, but inhumations where the wooden construction of the boat (or at least rivets and nails lying in the form of a ship) is preserved. This is something that never happens in cremations where all organic artefacts are consumed by the flames and the rest is mixed in a fairly small area. Still, most funerals from the Iron Age are cremations. To find a small boat, or even a large vessel, in a cremation where the boat was placed on the pyre, is not as easy as to find remains of sacrificed objects or animals since the fire consumes the wooden construction, rendering the remains of the boats both scarce and difficult to interpret.

Many Viking Age, and older, cremations contain larger or smaller amounts of rivets and nails, probably the remains of some kind of boat, small or large. It is relatively easy to argue that a cremation contains traces of boats if large numbers of rivets and nails are found, and even easier if they are found in a positions that reveal the shape of the boat. This does not, however, give a fair picture of the occurrence of boats in graves. Not all boat constructions contained rivets and nails; some were built with wooden nails and some sewed together with ropes (Greenhill, 1993). From such boats nothing would be left after cremation. Neither does the position of the rivets and nails in cremations tell us anything about whether or not a boat was cremated since the burial mounds were not normally constructed on the spot where the pyre once was. As the ashes were shovelled up on to the mound, the rivets and nails followed and the shape of a boat is gone forever. This means that many more burial mounds than the obvious ones most probably contained boats. It was not only chieftains who were buried, inhumed or cremated with some sort of boat. Many graves containing remains of boats are those of quite ordinary people. There is, however, a striking difference between the graves where the remains of boats, in the form of rivets and nails, are found, and graves without artefacts of this kind. In the former types of cremation the boat remains are accompanied by a larger number of animals, in terms of both individuals and different species, and also a larger number of different kinds of other artefacts, than in the graves containing no rivets or nails.

There can, of course, be different explanations for this – one concerning different religious practices and another concerning social difference. Whichever explanation is chosen, it is obvious that boats in graves are common during at least the Vendel Period and Viking Age. It is not a custom reserved solely for the highest social groups, but applies to a large part of the population, with the possible exception of the poorest. The graves of ordinary people do not contain seafaring vessels but, perhaps, smaller boats and even dried-up or wrecked skiffs (Arbman, 1940). Here, then, is a custom with a very long tradition, dating back at least to the Bronze Age a couple of thousand years earlier, even if the meaning of the custom changed during the passing of time. (Almgren, 1927; Varenius, 1992). **Berit Sigvallius**

References

Almgren, O. (1927), *Hällristningar och kultbruk*, KVHAA.

Arbman, H. von (1940), *Die Gräber*, Uppsala: Almqvist & Wiksell.

Birkeland, H. (1954), 'Nordens historie i middelalderen etter arabiske kilder', *Skrifter utgivna av det Norske Videnskapsakademi*, i Oslo. 2 Bind. Oslo.

Greenhill, B. (1993), 'The Place of the Årby Boat in the Boatbuilding Traditions of Northern Europe – a Suggestion', in C.O. Cederlund (ed.), *The Årby Boat*, Statens historiska museum.

Holck, P. (1996), 'Cremated Bones. A Medical-Anthropological Study of an Archaeological Material on Cremation Burials' (2nd rev. edn), *Antropologiske skrifter*, no. 1b, Oslo: Anatomical Institute, University of Oslo.

Kaliff, A. (1992), 'Brandgravskick och föreställningsvärld. En religionsarkeologisk diskussion', *Societas Archaeologica Upsaliensis*.

Kaliff, A. (1997), *Grave and Cultic Place. Eschatological Conceptions During the Late Bronze Age and Early Iron Age in Östergötland*, Department of Archaeology, Uppsala: University of Uppsala.

Larsson, L. (1988), *The Skateholm Project. I. Man and Environment*, Kungliga Humanistiska Vetenskapssamfundet i Lund LXXIX.

McKinley, J. (1993), 'Cremated Bone', in 'Sancton I Anglo-Saxon Cemetery. Excavations Carried Out Between 1976 and 1980', ed. J. Timby, *Archaeological Journal*, 150, The Royal Archaeological Institute.

Müller-Wille, M. (1970), 'Bestattung im Boot. Studien zu einer nordeuropäischen Grabsitte', *Offa*, Band 25/26 – 1968/1969.

Nylén, E. and Schönbäck, B. (1994), 'Tuna i Badelunda. Guld Kvinnor Båtar', *Västerås kulturnämnds skriftserie*, 27.

Sigvallius, B. (1994), 'Funeral Pyres. Iron Age Cremations from North Spånga', *Thesis and Papers in Osteology*, I, University of Stockholm.

Sigvallius, B. (1997), 'Brandgravar med nitar och spikar', in A. Åkerlund, S. Bergh, J. Nordbladh and J. Taffinder (eds), *Till Gunborg, Arkeologiska*, SAR. Stockholm Archaeological Reports, No.33, University of Stockholm.

Varenius, B. (1992), 'Det Nordiska skeppet. Teknologi och samhällsstrategi i vikingatid och medeltid', *Stockholm Studies in Archaeology*, 10.

W

WAR

For millennia, cremation has had a complex relationship with warfare, given the large numbers of corpses resulting from battle, concentrated in a small area and requiring rapid disposal to preclude disease. Lucan, in his *Pharsalia*, gave an account of Pompey's army at Durazzo which, failing to bury the bodies of horses killed in battle, was destroyed by the ensuing epidemics; a similar fate befell Constantine the Great's army (Erichsen, 1942: 31). Even those who ordinarily shunned cremation occasionally regarded it as a solution to the disposal of the dead resulting from war or pestilence. In Greece, by 480 BC cremation was largely employed only after battles and for Athenian plague victims. In Israel in early Christian times, there were examples of corpses cremated during war or plague despite burial being the normal practice (Riquet, 1972: 2). The early Catholic Church also adopted this position. Pope Innocent I (401–417) maintained the Church's opposition to cremation but allowed for dispensation to be given in exceptional cases such as epidemics or war, and the Church maintained this attitude through the centuries. Thus, Christian peoples did, on occasion, employ cremation as a means of disposal in these extreme circumstances. For example, in 1431, during the Hundred Years' War, the French piled up the dead outside Paris and burnt them on a huge pyre. This was, incidentally, the same year that the French leader, Joan of Arc, was burned at the stake.

Examples of the use of cremation during wartime in the nineteenth century include the Battle of Waterloo on 18 June 1815, when some 4000 corpses were reduced to ash on the battlefield on funeral pyres of resinous wood. In Spain, monarchist Carlist troops cremated many dead after the battle of Cuenca in 1874. Latin American armies also occasionally practised cremation as at the Battle of Rivas, Nicaragua, on 28 June 1855 between government troops and 'Walker's filibusters'; the latter's commander, 12 officers and 100 men were all cremated. Cremation was employed by Charlone's forces during campaigns against the indigenous Indians at Bahía Blanca in the late 1850s and also in the war between Argentina and Paraguay, 1864–70.

The Crimean War (1854–56) aided the cause of cremation in another way. The need for advanced armaments led Sir Henry Bessemer to design a process that produced new types of steel that were capable of withstanding higher temperatures, thereby increasing cannon firepower. In peacetime, these new steels also allowed the development of cremators that could withstand the high temperatures necessary for the rapid cremation of corpses (Jupp, 1999: 19). During the Franco-Prussian War (1870–71), the Prussian army used portable cremators (*La Vanguardia*, 1919). That conflict also provoked the uprising that created the Paris Commune, which also cremated some of its dead. A form of cremation was also eventually required for one of the conflicts' battlefield mass burial sites. After the battle of Sedan in 1870 more than 40 000 animals and humans were superficially buried in shallow mass graves until local Belgian villagers began to suffer from epidemics of diseases. In 1872 the Belgian government acted by sending in Colonel Creteur to deal with the problem. The mass graves were exposed by the application of chloride of lime, and dilute muriatic acid was poured over them. This process laid bare the top layers of corpses, and large quantities of coal tar were poured over them, soaking down through the layers of corpses. More lime was applied and then bundles of kerosene-soaked hay were thrown on to the grave-pits and set alight. Creteur estimated that 200–300 bodies were consumed in 50–60 minutes. The remaining mass, consisting largely of calcined bones, was about a quarter of the original contents and, when reburied, this semi-cremated burial caused no further trouble to the local inhabitants (Erichsen, 1942: 31).

The horrors of wartime burial convinced some to become advocates of cremation. One such convert was Johann Peter Trusen, a Prussian regimental doctor, who argued for compulsory cremation on the battlefield after having experienced the dangers of diseases arising from unsatisfactorily buried soldiers' bodies in the 1850s. Similarly, the Swiss father of cremation, Jakob Wegmann--Ercolani, came to support the practice partly due to his experiences of the horrors of buried battlefield dead in Italy in 1861. Cremationists naturally used such examples to advance their agenda. In 1867, at an international congress in Paris on soldiers during wartime, two Italians spoke in favour of the use of cremation. At the 1880 International Hygiene Congress, the second part of a motion passed by delegates at a session on cremation requested governments that accepted the Sanitary Convention of Geneva to add an article stating that their armies would be provided with portable cremators for the disposal of their battlefield dead.

However, cremation was not always employed, even at times of war. For example, during the American Civil War (1861–65), most of those killed were buried on the battlefields. Relatives who wanted to bring the bodies of their loved ones home had them embalmed for the journey, and cremation was therefore unnecessary. In 1861 a proposal to cremate the buried semi-decayed bodies of those killed at the Italian city of Gaeta was rejected by a council of war for religious reasons. Despite the obvious utility of cremation in wartime, and the implication that it could improve sanitary standards in cities if employed for the disposal of all corpses, the ancient distinction between using cremation in extreme circumstances, but not in the course of everyday life, appeared to remain. Thus in 1874, after the experience of cremation in the Franco-Prussian war, a British journalist wrote: 'Where needed, as on the battlefield or in the plague-stricken city, cremation may be properly resorted to as a sanitary agent' (Newspaper cuttings, 1874: 7–8). Nevertheless, he argued that even London possessed space for cemeteries outside the city, and therefore that cremation was not needed under normal circumstances.

The Great War, 1914–18

The twentieth century's two massive wars had widespread repercussions for the development of cremation. Despite its incredibly high numbers of casualties, The Great War witnessed very little actual use of cremation, most bodies being buried on or near the battlefield (Erichsen, 1942: 32). The bodies of US troops were buried in temporary cemeteries as they could not be shipped back while hostilities were ongoing. At the end of the war, the families of American dead chose to either have their relatives buried in a permanent overseas cemetery or shipped home, with 60 per cent (representing 47 000 corposes) requesting the latter option. In order to safely transport the corpses, the army's quartermaster corps chemically treated them, wrapped them in

blankets and placed them in hermetically sealed caskets, which were in turn placed in protective containers for shipping home (Sledge, 2003). The US army went to considerable trouble to transport these corpses when cremation would have made the whole process far quicker, cheaper and easier.

In Russia the Bolshevik regime adopted cremation during the civil war following their accession to power in 1917, although for numerous reasons little initially came of this. Inter-war cremationists lamented the fact that cremation had not been used during the Great War. At the 1936 International Cremation Congress in Prague, a Yugoslav delegate noted that during the war, although many had seen the necessity of mobile war cremators, they had not been used and that, as a consequence, soldiers' bones still lay scattered around some battlefields. At the same congress another delegate noted that many in the Great War had been killed far from their kin and that it would have been far better if they could have been cremated and returned home to their relatives, but that this only occurred occasionally.

The Great War also brought many problems for domestic cremation projects, in that it disrupted the work of cremation societies. Some, like the French society, had members killed in battle; the Yugoslavs had their work interrupted by the Balkan Wars (1912–13) as well. The Great War caused a dramatic increase in the cost of building materials and projects that had already been established, such as the construction of Vienna Crematorium, were postponed. Post-war inflation also reduced the purchasing power of cremation societies, limiting their ability to pay for both crematoria and propaganda. The Great War also had many wider effects, both favouring and hindering the development of cremation. On the negative side, cremationist Robert Hazemann claimed that, in France, the Catholic Church had taken 'a step forward' into the political arena during the Great War, 'for every war means a retreat for reason and an advance of the forces of emotionalism and superstition'. Given the Church's staunch opposition to cremation, this was bad news for cremationists. Nevertheless, context remained important and, for example, the close of the war effected a swing to the left in internal Finnish politics, making the climate more favourable to cremation, although an actual crematorium there still took more than 40 more years to emerge.

E.S. Turner claimed that, in Britain, the 'cataclysm' of the war, a traumatic experience for all those involved, changed social customs and none more than the attitude to death and mourning. There was a consequent dilution and diminution of previous customs of mourning, funerals became simpler, memorials placed on graves less elaborate and so forth. Thus the 'seedbed' was prepared for the dramatic growth in cremation after 1945 (Turner, 1972: 2). Peter Jupp agreed with this assessment, pointing out that arrangements for the public mourning of the war dead '[P]aradoxically ... was to make ordinary grief, on the other 364 days of the year, less conspicuous' and that war graves 'only threw into prominence the difficulties of maintaining older cemeteries, many of them 70 years old' (Jupp, 1999: 21; 1990: 17–18). Yet, as Jupp pointed out, the British cremation rate still remained low in the inter-war years.

The Second World War, 1939–45

The Second World War had numerous effects on the development of cremation, although, once more, it was not employed on the field of combat. As Hugo Erichsen articulated in 1942, in the 'mass slaughter' of modern warfare, the use of mobile crematoria on the battlefield was 'entirely out of the question'. Erichsen concluded that either mass burial or, more preferably from a sanitary point of view, the kind of mass cremation performed by Creteur in 1872 should be employed (Erichsen, 1942: 32). The USA, for example, largely repeated previous practice but with four times as many corpses to transport than after the Great War, and often from more distant places (Sledge, 2003). Again, cremation would have solved many logistical problems. The saturation bombing raids carried out by all the main protagonists in the Second World War brought death to civilians on an unprecedented scale, and yet cremation was still not widely employed to deal with these casualties. Thus, for example, after one of the most devastating raids, that of the Allied incendiary attacks on Dresden in February 1945, only a very small proportion were cremated, the vast majority instead being buried in mass graves. In Britain, local authorities were asked to proceed on the matter of disposal of civilian casualties without real guidance from central government and, again, cremation was not widely employed (Bullett, 1984: 25, 27).

With regard to the cremation movement, communication between cremation societies that had only recently been formally established in the form of the International Cremation Federation (ICF) was made increasingly difficult or impossible. Naturally, the ICF had to abandon efforts to place pressure on the Hungarian government to open Debrecen Crematorium and the Prince of Monaco to allow the opening of the unused crematorium there. The ICF maintained as much correspondence as it could with neutral countries and the British Commonwealth, but occupied countries were another matter. French cremationists, for example, could only communicate with the international movement via their Swedish counterparts. Indeed, the French could not even communicate properly with their comrades who happened to be resident in the German-occupied zone. Thus the French Federation was unable to hold a national congress during wartime.

Cremation projects often had to be put on hold, including a planned extension to gardens at Golders Green in England, the new French crematorium at Chambéry and Belgrade's crematorium. Romanian cremationists never received a cremator that they had ordered and paid for before the war broke out. Lack of fuel in many countries during the war led to the closing down of crematoria. In France, of six crematoria, only Paris was in operation after 1943. Bombing, too, caused extensive damage to crematoria and cremationist facilities in many countries. In France, for example, the headquarters of Strasbourg Cremation Society was bombed, although its crematoria remained intact. Romanian cremationists were not so lucky and the air-raid damage to Bucharest Crematorium, owned by Cenusa, placed it in serious financial difficulties after the war. The 1945 bombings also damaged or destroyed 70 per cent of Tokyo's crematoria. Some cremation societies were disbanded, including several in France. Others, such as Luxembourg Cremation Society, lost out to the occupying Nazi administration, with its cremation joint stock company being dissolved and its funds confiscated. The Luxembourg cremationist paper, *Flamma*, was terminated in 1941 as it was compelled to carry German propaganda. The Yugoslav cremation societies suffered badly, being outlawed by occupying forces, having their property confiscated and their offices and records almost entirely destroyed. These events had the consequence of reducing cremation society memberships in these countries. Important cremationists also suffered. Some French, Luxembourg and Yugoslav cremationists were deported and imprisoned and others, like the president of Nice Cremation Society and the secretary of the Plamen Society, were killed.

Although most ICF activities 'automatically closed down' during the war, the organization could have suffered further. Immediately before the German invasion of Holland, the German Cremation Association attempted to compel the transfer of the ICF secretariat and funds to The Hague. This move was resisted and, instead, ICF funds were invested in the British Post Office. This way, ICF records were maintained and funds retained: it lost only some £93, the dues paid by the German Cremation Association into an ICF account in a German bank in 1939. Financial problems did arise, however, with the dramatic post-war inflation. In 1957 the treasurer reported that the ICF was having problems as it was operating on a pre-war budget and the extensive price rises since the end of the war had not been taken into account. A devaluation of the French franc meant that money donated before the war for crematorium projects there lost much of its value.

In at least one country, war conditions momentarily advanced cremation in legal terms. In Sweden, a legal amendment in 1943 allowed for the cremation of people who died as a consequence of the war or due to infectious diseases. In countries that were not directly bombed, there were some advances, as in Canada where a crematorium was built at New Denver for the Japanese population, evacuated from British Columbia's coastal areas. Numbers of cremations in Canada continued to rise steadily in the war years, although at a slower rate than before 1939. Japanese influence worked in both directions elsewhere. In the Far East, Japan was the invading imperial power. Shintoism required that all Japanese dead should be cremated and the ashes returned to their families, even during wartime (Lien-Teh, 1949:11). Thus, the Japanese army helped advance cremation in Hong Kong when it built a crematorium there for its war dead. The cremators it used were employed elsewhere in Hong Kong until as late as 1979, although this wartime crematorium was not the first built in the colony (Lee, 1988). In Malaya Dr Wu Lien-Teh blamed the disruption caused by

the war and the threat of Japanese invasion for the fact that a municipal crematorium did not already exist in there. Japan had been in armed conflict with China for some years before 1939. At the outbreak of the Sino-Japanese war, the Chinese army practised cremation for a while but it proved to be too slow and expensive (Erichsen, 1942: 32).

Territorial and geopolitical changes at the end of the conflict brought about advances and created new obstacles. Roman Catholic Poland, where the pre-war government had prohibited cremation, gained territory that included several crematoria from eastern Germany. However, the wider political changes that swept eastern Europe in the immediate aftermath of the Second World War were not so favourable to international cooperation over the development of cremation, at least within Europe. The Czechs, important within the ICF before 1939, were unable to attend the first post-war ICF congress at The Hague as they had not succeeded in getting permission to enter Holland. The Yugoslavs were also not in attendance, and the Poles, though gaining all the eastern German crematoria, remained uncommunicative with the ICF for decades. The Russians did not reply to the ICF invitation and the Romanians, though in touch in 1946, were particularly uncommunicative after then. The developing Cold War meant that the ICF would have only tenuous links with very few Eastern Bloc countries, mainly Czechoslovakia and Yugoslavia, until after the fall of the Berlin Wall in 1989. Yet, despite this lack of communication, the new communist regimes of eastern Europe offered the potential, at least, of fostering greater progress towards cremation than had occurred under the pre-war governments.

A shorter-term problem was the understandable absence of German cremationists, as the ICF executive had, in 1948, 'not seen our way to receive that country'. Before 1939 Germany had been in the vanguard of cremation in Europe. Now split into two and reduced in territorial size, Germany's absence from the ICF was not as important as it might have been because cremation had lost much of its popularity there. Still, this decline of the 'legitimate' use of cremation in Germany after 1945 was a blow to the cremation movement's development, as was the fact that its 'illegitimate' use in German-occupied territories during the

Holocaust led to the practice being regarded with revulsion by many both within and outside the country. These were indirect effects of the war, in that the conflict threw up circumstances that allowed these awful events to happen. During his presidential address to the 1948 ICF Congress at The Hague, Dr P.H. Van Roojen noted that the war had temporarily paralysed the international movement. However, he went on say: 'Happily, the idea of cremation won ground in several countries during the war, with the consequence that the movement has come out much stronger ultimately' (*Report*, 1948). Cremation had apparently made 'great progress' in countries that had remained 'free from domination' during the war. Clearly some progress had been made in countries like Britain that had not been invaded. One element related to the war that gave further impetus to cremation was the fact that, due to enemy bombing, many people required rehousing. This supported the cremationist argument that land should be used for housing rather than cemeteries.

An important long-term effect of the Second World War was that it altered popular attitudes to death, thereby boosting the popularity of cremation. French cremationists noted that, after the Second World War, those who favoured cremation now included 'people of conservative views' who had been 'on the whole against cremation' before 1939. This was echoed by another French cremationist, Dr Godard, in 1984. In 1954 Dr C.F. White claimed that, in Britain, the war had been a stimulus to cremation because many knew people who had no known grave and there 'had been less emotion about death and they had concentrated their thoughts less on the physical body and more on the personality of the deceased' (cited in Jupp, 1999: 22). Peter Jupp argued that, in Britain, cremation as the basis of 'a municipal solution to the urban problem of the disposal of the dead was laid well before 1939'. In Britain the cremation rate doubled from almost 4 per cent to just under 8 per cent during wartime, the war having a 'popularising effect' on cremation (Jupp, 1999: 22). The Cremation Society of Great Britain, in the context of heavy civilian casualties caused by air raids, approached the Home Secretary and was able to further cremation by helping to make it a choice that was more available to the public. The war conditions also helped reveal the problems with the complex legislation that had

developed regarding the disposal of the dead and the need for its simplification. As in the Great War, but on a far larger scale becaus of the civilian casualties, the Second World War also altered popular attitudes to death in a way that was favourable to cremation. The widespread bombing helped split up established poor communities where there was a social stigma attached to inexpensive funerals and thereby allowed the poor to opt for cheaper funerals without losing face. The demands of post-war economizing also made cremation more attractive to local authorities (Jupp, 1990: 19, 23–24).

Cremationists in countries not directly involved in the conflict had differing ideas of its effects. Argentine cremationists in the 1950s, though arguing that the Second World War had increased social progress in the world, did not think that it had had any effect in their country. In fact, for unknown reasons, they argued that conditions in their country had regressed during this period. The only indication from cremationists that the war had altered attitudes within key institutions that had previously opposed cremation came from the Romanians. They claimed in 1946 that the Orthodox Church there had slightly softened its attitude against cremation, but the extent to which this was a direct consequence of the war was unclear. In summary, it is clear the Second World War had many and diverse effects, of short-, medium- and long-term consequences both favouring and militating against cremation. On balance, it seems that many, but not all, short-term effects were to cremation's detriment, but that the longer-term changes in social attitudes engendered or furthered by the war, broadly acted as a spur to the acceptance of cremation.

Nuclear and conventional war, 1945–2004

The final months of the Second World War heralded the beginning of a new age in warfare as the Allied use of atomic 'H' bombs on the Japanese cities of Hiroshima and Nagasaki brought the horror of a new type of 'instant cremation' to the unfortunates near the epicentre of the blasts. Hiroshima was the target for the first atomic bomb, 'Little Boy', on 6 August 1945. Approximately 70 000 people were killed and another 80 000 injured and three-quarters of the city's buildings were destroyed or severely damaged. Three days later Nagasaki suffered 30 000 deaths and another 45 000 injured and over a third of the city was destroyed by the second atomic device. As Alan Bullett said: 'nuclear war brings a new dimension to horror on an unprecedented scale' (Bullett, 1984: 25). It was this scale, the high number of deaths caused, that would provide a serious logistical problem for the survivors. The longer the dead remained undisposed of, the greater the health risks for the living.

In 1984, using Home Office figures, Alan Bullett estimated the numbers of dead requiring disposal from two different sized nuclear devices being detonated on urban areas, although he pointed out that a full-scale nuclear attack could kill 60 per cent of a country's population. Almost 12 000 people in the immediate vicinity of a detonated 150 KT device would leave no trace of their bodies. There would be instant death up to a radius of 1.6 miles from the epicentre of the blast leaving a total of around 53 000 bodies requiring rapid disposal. A one-MT device, however, would kill around 200 000 people over an area of 35 square miles. The first period after a strike would be one of 'utter shock and dislocation', and it would be very difficult to dispose of the dead. A second period of lower, but sustained, levels of deaths from injuries and radiation sickness would then ensue (Bullett, 1984: 27). Ostensibly, mass cremation would be a useful and rapid means of disposal of these casualties. Bullett argued that, in the immediate aftermath of an attack, cremation could not be employed, but that disposal of bodies by some form of burning had to be considered. Some idea of the kind of cremation that could be practised in such circumstances was given by the mass outdoor cremations of farm animals killed by diseases such as foot-and-mouth. The same method could, Bullett argued, be used for the disposal of large numbers of bodies killed during conventional warfare. However, in nuclear war, fuel was likely to be irreplaceable for some time and could therefore only be used for highest-priority activities such as transportation of food or medical supplies. Even straw and kindling wood that could be used on open-air mass pyres would be necessary for heating, and old tyres – a feature of the open-air animal cremations in Britain in 2001 – would probably be required for vehicles. Bullett was clear that mass burial would be the only option in the circumstances of a

nuclear attack, but underlined that there was a need, first, to identify good mass burial sites that would not require the moving of bodies over long distances and would not affect underground water supplies or pose other environmental risks. As in the Second World War, central government had delegated the disposal of bodies in the event of a nuclear attack to the local authorities and had provided few guidelines. Bullett believed strongly that cremationists had an important role to play in terms of using their experience to advise local authorities about any method of disposal that was employed in these circumstances (Bullett, 1984: 27–28).

In January 2001, documents released from the National Record Office revealed that many years before Bullett's study, the Scottish authorities had come to the same conclusion. In response to a parliamentary question in 1961 from an MP who wanted to know about the designated burial officer for Western Scotland, civil servants from the Scottish Office conducted research on the likely consequences of a nuclear attack on Scotland. Their report in 1970 predicted that a nuclear attack on Scotland could kill 1 million people. The Scottish Office and local authorities drew up contingency plans that dealt with ways of disposing of the dead. Cremation, it was argued, would use too much fuel and the sinking of corpses in hulks of ships at sea would require too much handling. The one solution was mass burial pits dug by the 'unemployed'.

In recent years, the grisly spectre of an 'instantaneous cremation' suffered by the victims of nuclear weapons was evident in US soldier Selina Perez's description of dead Iraqi soldiers as 'crispy critters'. The victims of depleted uranium warheads during the first Gulf War, the Iraqi's bodies had, according to Patricia Axelrod, been 'burned to near-cremation':

> These were people whose blood had boiled and evaporated. Their uniforms burned away with their skin down to naked, blackened bones, leaving vacantly staring charcoaled skeletons brittle enough to break up into skull, torso, legs, arms, and ashes. Calling them 'crispy critters' was Perez's way of dealing with the horror of disposing of the radiated remains of death by depleted uranium (DU) in the Persian Gulf. (Axelrod, 1999).

The second Gulf War, begun in 2003, again

revealed that cremation was still not regarded as a useful means of corpse disposal, even if the corpses in question were infected with chemical agents. Apparently anticipating (wrongly, as it turned out) that the Iraqi regime might use some of the chemical and biological weapons that Western powers had supplied it with, elaborate measures were planned to deal with contaminated corpses of war dead. The military ruled out the use of mass burial, but there was the option of temporary interment if the remains could not be completely cleansed. However, the military planners noted that some countries might raise objections to such burials on their territory and, even if corpses were not contaminated, temporary interment was regarded as a 'last-case scenario', necessitating high-level approval. Cremation appeared to be an ideal option, as it could be carried out relatively rapidly without exposing troops to possible contamination. However, the planners thought that 'some Americans may consider cremation to be repugnant or against religious beliefs', and this public opposition was the main reason why cremation was not favoured among the military (Sledge, 2003). Curiously, only a few days earlier, the *Chicago Tribune* reported that the Pentagon *was* 'considering cremating the remains of any US troops killed by biological or chemical attacks in Iraq rather than bringing them home for burial' (*Chicago Tribune*, 2003).

Instead, as in the past, the favoured option was to use a containment system. That such an elaborate, time-consuming and expensive procedure was chosen over cremation for the disposal of those killed by chemical or biological attacks is a testament to the perceived strength of opposition to cremation by much of American society, despite the current 28 per cent cremation rate in the country. This, perhaps, reflects Marvin's and Ingle's theory that the United States values its military dead because they are a kind of sacrifice that helps bind the nation together under a single president and flag – a flag that is always a paramount symbol in covering the containers of the dead (Marvin and Ingle, 1999).

War once provided an 'extreme' occasion when cremation could be used by peoples who did not ordinarily employ the practice. Now, paradoxically, although cremation is a more common practice in everyday occidental life than at any time over the last two millennia, its use in wartime seems even less probable. The

only kind of cremation likely to be employed on the modern battlefield – which can include the civilian populations of towns and cities – is the 'instantaneous' type that occurs when nuclear warheads, depleted uranium shells or similar weapons are used on human beings. **Lewis H. Mates**

Note: Material from numerous other entries in this *Encyclopedia* has been incorporated into the above account.

References

Axelrod, Patricia (1999), 'The Gulf War: Depleted Uranium', from 'Secrets and Lies' in *The Boston Phoenix*, 7–14 October, available at: http://www.geocities.com/iraqinfo/index.html?page=/iraqinfo/gulfwar/du.html (accessed May 2004).

Bullett, Alan W. (1984), 'Disposal of the Dead in War – A Review of the Problems', *Pharos*, 50(1): 25–33.

Chicago Tribune (7 February 2003), 'Cremation Eyed for Bio-war Dead' available at: http://www.chicagotribune.com/news/nationworld/chi-0302070411feb07,1,3039873. story (accessed May 2004).

CSA.

Erichsen, Dr Hugo (1942), 'Cremation on the Battlefield', CANA Annual Convention Report: 31–33.

ICF Committee for Propaganda (1963), 'The World Problems of the Disposal of the Dead', paper presented to the ICF Congress at Berlin, CRE/D4/1963/3.

Jupp, Peter (1990), *From Dust to Ashes: The Replacement of Burial by Cremation in England 1840–1967*, London: The Congregational Lecture, London School of Economics.

Jupp, Peter (1999), 'History of the Cremation Movement in Great Britain: the First 125 Years', *Pharos*, 65(1): 18–25.

Kazmier, Lisa (2001), 'A Symbolic Space: Rural Myth, the Great War and the Growth of Cremation', *Pharos*, 67(3): 3–6, 8–9.

La Vanguardia (1 January 1919), article reproduced in *Boletín de la Asociación Argentina de Cremación*, 10 December 1926: 14–15.

Lee, John Sheung-yee (1988), 'Cremation in Hong Kong – Part I', *Pharos*, 54(2): 56–59.

Lien-Teh, Dr Wu (1949), 'Cremation Among the Chinese – Past and Present', *Pharos*, 15(2): 9–11.

Marvin, Carolyn and Ingle, David W. (1988), *Blood Sacrifice and the Nation*, Cambridge: Cambridge University Press.

Newspaper cuttings (1874), CRE/H1.

Pinaud, Fr. (2004), 'Is Cremation Allowed?' available at: http://www.catholicapologetics.info/cremat.htm (accessed May 2004).

Report of the ICF Congress at The Hague (1948), CRE/D4/1948/1.

Riquet, Michel (1972), 'The Catholic Church and the Cremation of Corpses', paper presented at the Grenoble ICF Congress 6–8 June.

Sein, Dr Andres S. (1936), *Crematorio de Buenos Aires – Ordenanzas y Decretos Reglamentarios Sobre la Incineración de Cadaveres Humanos, Vigentes en la Capital Federal cuyo Cumplimento se Observa en el Crematorio de Buenos Aires*, Buenos Aires: Eduardo Ghio, CRE/F/AG/2.

Sledge, Mike (16 February 2003), 'U.S. Military Ponders Options for Handling War Dead', in *Dallas Morning News* available at: http://www.aiipowmia.com/inter23/in021603ward ead.html (accessed May 2004).

Turner, E.S. (1972), 'An Evaluation of Factors Leading to the Progressive Adoption of Cremation in the UK', paper presented at the Grenoble ICF Congress, 6–8 June, CRE/D4/1972/14.

WESTMINSTER ABBEY

Westminster Abbey had long been a place of burial but, by the end of the nineteenth century, it was practically full. The Dean and Chapter therefore decided in March 1908 to restrict burials to cremated remains alone. In fact, another burial of a corpse (possibly more than one) took place afterwards, the last being in 1920 with the Unknown Warrior. The first known interment of ashes was probably those of Sir Henry Irving in October 1905. The decision to accept only cremations was taken apparently on pragmatic grounds: 'in view of the very limited space now available for interments within the Abbey Church, and of the close proximity of the dwelling houses in the Cloisters ... the Dean and Chapter agree that the time has now arrived when it is most desirable to secure, if possible [*sic*: it is unclear why this caveat was entered and what it means], the cremation of bodies before interment in the Abbey Church and Cloisters' (Act of Chapter, 2 March 1908). This was the position maintained until 1989 when the

Chapter determined that there would be no more burials of ashes of people without Abbey connections in the Abbey. When it was realized that there had been interments of ashes, the Chapter resolved that ashes might be buried in the Abbey at the discretion of the Dean. The last interment of ashes of someone not directly connected with the Abbey was Sir Laurence Olivier in 1991. Since 1905 there have been just over 100 burials of cremated remains (except the Unknown Warrior), among them Thomas Hardy (without his heart), Rudyard Kipling, Neville Chamberlain, Sidney and Beatrice Webb, Ernest Bevin, Gilbert Murray, Ralph Vaughan Williams, Sybil Thorndike and Laurence Olivier. There is one immurement – Canon Sebastian Charles in the South Choir Aisle. **Wesley Carr**

WIDLAR, ANTON

Anton Widlar (1870–1917) is always referred to as the initiator of the Labour Cremation Society 'Die Flamme'. The first meeting of this society was intended to be as a branch of the Austrian Cremation Society 'Die Flamme' and was convened by Widlar on 19 April 1904 in the Favoriten district of Vienna. Widlar and his supporters felt that there was a need to found this new society because, although the parent society had several working-class members at that time, cremation still was not sufficiently well advertised among working men and women. Their belief that the idea of cremation perfectly suited the political concept of social democracy, and therefore should be integrated into its cultural policy, proved to be correct. After some difficulties during the first few years, the Labour Cremation Society soon recorded a larger membership than its parent society. The principal activists of the Labour Cremation Society were to be Andreas Masser and Ludwig Eichbaum.

Anton Widlar was born in Vienna in 1870. He worked as a china painter, forming a career within the Vienna workers' movement that was exemplary for those days. Nevertheless, he never became a leading figure within the Social Democratic organizational structure, and was generally known as a 'quiet person'. Having been politically trained in a society for workers' education, Widlar became an active member of the district administration in Favoriten – an extensive district of Vienna almost solely inhabited by a labour population. Widlar changed to working in the book-keeping department of the expanding *Arbeiter-Zeitung* and in the administration of the *Arbeiterinnen-Zeitung*. His name is mentioned here and there among the delegation of a Social Democratic party congress, on the list of a committee for a local board or in the management of a workers' health insurance scheme. The little status he gained from his work for the cause of cremation came after his death from pneumonia on 25 January 1917 at the age of 47 when his body was transported to, and cremated at, the nearest crematorium at that time: Zittau in East Germany. This was quite remarkable as the activity of the Labour Cremation Society was then primarily of an idealistic nature since its members in general could not afford the high transportation costs. Vienna Crematorium was not to be opened until 1923. **Christian Stadelmann**

See also Austrian cremation societies – Labour Cremation Society 'Die Flamme'.

References

Arbeiter-Zeitung, 26 January 1917.

Michelfeit, Franz (1954), *50 Jahre Arbeiterfeuerbestattung in Österreich*, Wien: Vereinder Freunde der Feuerbestattung 'Die Flamme'.

WOMEN

The distinctive place of women in the emergence, fostering and use of cremation is observed in the Introduction and in entries on **Dilke**, **gender** and the **USA**. **Douglas J. Davies**

Z

ZIMBABWE (RHODESIA)

The ancient sub-Saharan tradition of burial meant that cremation was not practised by the majority native population of Rhodesia, nor, indeed, by that of any part of Southern Africa (a vast area including the Roman Catholic former Portuguese colonies of Mozambique and Angola). Cremation was introduced into Southern Africa

in modern times when, in the nineteenth century, Indians came to work on the sugarcane plantations in Natal, South Africa. By the mid-twentieth century there were small communities of Indians in all the larger towns in Rhodesia, as well as in Malawi, Zambia and, of course, South Africa itself. As Hindus, these people brought their custom of cremation, normally performed on an open, wood-fuelled pyre, with them. Very few were not cremated. There was evidence before the Second World War that Europeans also wanted access to cremation as, in 1938, a congress of the Federation of Women's Institutes in Gwelo passed a resolution stating that the practice should be made possible in the country.

The situation in Bulawayo, Rhodesia, was, according to Dr Alan Dods (1968), typical of that of the larger towns in Southern Africa. In the municipal cemetery a basic open-air construction with a corrugated-iron roof served for Hindu wood-pyre cremations. Though initially used solely by Hindus, increasing requests to use the facilities were being made by Europeans after 1945. This was despite the fact that the process was a long one, especially for Hindus who were obliged to wait for between four and five hours until the corpse was reduced to ashes. In 1954 external developments triggered action. A new railway bridge with a commanding view over the cremation facilities abruptly removed any possibility of privacy for ceremonies held there. A visit of a British cremationist at around the same time sparked Dods' interest in cremation. Those concerned by the plight of the cremation facilities wrote to Bulawayo's town clerk asking that fencing be erected to restore their privacy and preclude any public outcry. This act, which was successful due to the town clerk's helpful attitude, was the first element of what, some four years later, would become the Cremation Society of Rhodesia.

In 1956, before the cremation society was firmly established, the first 'Western' crematorium in Rhodesia was built 300 miles to the north-east of Bulawayo in the capital, Salisbury (now Harare). As with Bulawayo, before this development Hindus had had their own cremating facilities. Salisbury municipality was responsible for building a 'fine' crematorium, which was located in a tranquil woodland landscape seven miles from the city centre. It took another two years before, on 14 April 1958, a handful of people met in Bulawayo City Hall to discuss forming a cremation society. Subsequently, at a public meeting chaired by Bulawayo's mayor on 5 September 1958, the Cremation Society of Matabeleland (the area around Bulawayo) was founded. It aimed to encourage the Bulawayo municipality to build a crematorium and to promote cremation by means of propaganda. It also wanted to join the International Cremation Federation (ICF) and avail itself of the experience and propaganda of other member countries.

Four years later the society secured its main goal when, in 1962, Bulawayo municipality built a crematorium near the city centre. The British company Dowson & Mason supplied the hardware for the committal, cremator and fan rooms. The cremator itself was oil-fired. In discussion with the city council's public health committee, it was decided that there should be no columbarium in the garden of remembrance, and that the only form of memorial should be a book of remembrance. The influence of British practices was clear in both this and in the decision over the mode of ash disposal, it being noted that, in England at that time, some 95 per cent of ashes were scattered. One unnamed religious sect wanted to inter ashes, so the cremation society suggested that a part of cemetery be used for the burial of ashes and urns. This allowed the garden of remembrance, which surrounded the crematorium, to remain free of memorials.

By 1961 the Cremation Society of Matabeleland had begun to produce its own newsletter. It had joined the ICF, received much help from the Cremation Society of Great Britain, and *Pharos* was widely circulated amongst the membership. Some members had asked whether, now that the crematorium was in existence, a cremation society was still necessary. Dods was positive that it was, as in countries without cremation societies cremation numbers remained static, whereas they increased in countries where there was an active cremation society.

Three years later, on 10 June 1965, an adjacent crematorium chapel was formally opened in Bulawayo. With the new building, the original entrance to the crematorium now formed an alcove containing a catafalque. The cremator chimney became less prominent as it now formed the buttress in the gable end of the chapel. The chapel's opening ceremony was an important event, with leaders of the Protestant Christian Churches, Hindus and 'Reformed Jews' all reading out short relevant passages from their respective scriptures. To make it suitable for the use of the Hindu community the crematorium possessed no religious symbols. Another advantage was the stream that ran through the crematorium grounds – particularly good for Hindus, who traditionally scatter ashes on running water.

With regard to the disposal of ashes, in 1974 around 50 per cent were scattered, another 25 per cent were placed in columbaria, 15 per cent were buried and the remaining 10 per cent taken elsewhere.

The cremation society's membership in its first year was only 17. It was thought that this figure would not appreciably increase unless there were tangible benefits to membership. The skilful persuasion of the society's chairman, Mr Verity Amm, subsequently managed to convince Bulawayo funeral directors to agree an almost 40 per cent reduction in the cremation charge for society members, as well as a 50 per cent discount in transportation costs for corpses that had to be carried some distance to the crematorium. Although these considerable benefits were well advertised in the national press, there was a smaller than anticipated growth in membership in the first decade. By 1968 the membership of the only active cremation society in Southern Africa was 111. At that time around 15 per cent of the members were based in Salisbury and other Rhodesian towns. The society therefore changed its name, at a special meeting on 6 February 1968, to the Cremation Society of Rhodesia. It then began to amend its constitution to enable branches to be established elsewhere. In addition to internal restructuring, and in an attempt to widen its influence, the society that year also produced a landscape plan for Bulawayo Crematorium, since the existing garden was regarded as 'too formal' (Dods, 1968: 68). It also encouraged local churches to inaugurate gardens of remembrance in their churchyards and, in dialogue with florists and funeral directors, sought to change the somewhat bizarre requirement in Bulawayo that all floral tributes should be cellophane-wrapped.

In less than a decade there was a significant increase in the percentages of Europeans and Asians cremated in Rhodesia. In 1958, 21 per cent of these groups were cremated; by 1967 this figure had risen to almost 44 per cent. This success was obvious at Salisbury where, only 12 years after it was built, the columbarium already required extending and the space on the paths through the garden of remembrance allocated to plaque-memorials was almost exhausted. However, success had come at a price: the beautiful wooded countryside leading up to the crematorium became the new municipal cemetery covered by stone memorials. Dods thought that the cremation society needed to establish an active branch in Salisbury to protect the crematorium by persuading the municipality to stop the erection of further memorials and install a book of remembrance instead.

A final and, given the potential, vital task for the cremation society in 1968 was to approach Bulawayo municipality with regard to the use of the crematorium by Africans. Although rural Africans were still very much opposed to cremation, it appeared that, as in South Africa, urban Africans were 'adopting the white man's ways very rapidly' (Dods, 1968: 68). In 1968 Bulawayo's population comprised 55 000 Asians and Europeans and 155 000 Africans. The increasing movement of Africans from the kraals, where, incidentally, land for burial was plentiful, into urban areas was a relatively new phenomenon. Dods and his wife were 'personally aware of educated Africans who have expressed a wish to be cremated, but have regarded the crematorium as a preserve of the European' (Dods, 1968: 69). Recently, he had spoken on cremation to the older and well-educated pupils of an Anglican African secondary school, and only a handful had heard of cremation. Some pupils had expressed the traditional fear of possibly angering the spirits of the dead and incurring their wrath by cremating their body. Dods countered this by noting that cremations were only performed on those who had expressed the desire to have their bodies disposed of in that way. He thought that, if the opinions he heard at the school were typical, then cremation would slowly gain acceptance amongst the African population. He was optimistic about the prospects of cremation in Rhodesia, saying that it was rapidly advancing there, certainly in comparison with South Africa. This was a slightly curious claim, given that South Africa got its first 'Western' crematorium in 1918 and had nine by 1961.

The following decade did not, however, justify Dods' optimism. Although the cremation figures hit over 55 per cent in 1970, this percentage did not change much throughout the decade. Moreover, the figures only referred to the Asian and European populations of the two main cities, and were thus quite unrepresentative of the entire population. Worse still, by 1978 the Rhodesian Cremation Society only had 142 members, 14 less than it had in 1972.

The 1980s did, however, see some positive developments. The first was the presence of a Zimbabwean (as opposed to Rhodesian) delegate at the Cremation Society of Great Britain's annual conference. Mr Hodza, who was the curator of cemeteries and crematoria in Harare, was the first-ever delegate from the country at this event. The second was the announcement, in 1986, that a new crematorium in Bulawayo would be operational by that July. Yet, at the same time, the cremation rate amongst the European and Asian communities dropped considerably; cremation numbers declined while the numbers of deaths rose quite considerably. Thus, in 1983 the two Zimbabwean crematoria performed 1183 cremations (220 less than in 1979) out of 7819 deaths, a rate of only 15 per cent. (Bulawayo performed 386 cremations out of 3117 deaths, a rate of 13 per cent, while Harare (formerly Salisbury) performed 797 cremations out of 4,702 deaths, a rate of 17 per cent). The cremation society also appeared to have gone into stasis and was finally replaced by the Harare Department of Works as a source for statistics from the country in *Pharos* in 1991. That year, Harare Crematorium performed just 686 cremations, a cremation rate of just under 10 per cent. By the end of the 1980s the cremation rate in Harare, with 772 cremations out of 11 414 deaths, was down to under 7 per cent. The peak year for numbers of cremations was 1979. This was also the last year of white rule of the country, and suggests that, despite Dods' optimism, cremation had remained an almost exclusively white European and Hindu ritual.

In recent times, cremation in Zimbabwe has been beset by more problems. In January 2003 there were the first indications of serious problems for the country's cremation services engendered by the economic crisis. A foreign currency shortage led to an acute lack of liquefied petroleum gas, used to fire the cremators. This prevented the operation of Harare city council's crematorium at Warren Hills Cemetery in the Warren Park high-density suburb. Corpses were consequently piling up at the city's funeral parlours, and in the midsummer heat their prolonged storage was proving difficult. There were cases of Zimbabweans who had emigrated, returning to their country for the funerals of relatives and only then finding out that the cremations could not be performed. Many had to return to their new countries without having cremated their relatives. The city council's supplier, Mobil, could not secure the necessary fuel as it did not have the foreign currency to import it from South Africa. According to a council representative, the crematorium was in working order and the council could buy the foreign currency, if it was made available. However, the diesel-fired crematorium in Bulawayo was still operational. Located in West Park Cemetery, it remained the only crematorium in the city. By summer 2003 the situation had worsened and was now regarded as Zimbabwe's 'worst political and economic crisis since independence in 1980' (Shaw, 2003). Massive inflation and a continued shortage of hard currency had stoked unemployment and led to shortages of fuel, medicine and food, crippling both private industry and the municipalities, which were finding it increasingly difficult to provide basic services. In June, Harare city council's supply of gas for the cremators in the only municipal crematorium in the town once again ran out. Apparently, this shortage had recently worsened when Noczim (the National Oil Company of Zimbabwe), which had been responsible for importing the gas, was wound up following the deregulation of the oil industry. Private funeral homes quickly accumulated almost 100 corpses that were designated for cremation. An option taken by some relatives was to transport the corpses to Bulawayo Crematorium, which was still operating.

This was only a partial solution as Bulawayo's by-laws made it difficult to cremate non-residents. Although diesel was also in increasingly short supply, Bulawayo still had no fuel problem by the end of August. However, it was so swamped with corpses by this point that the authorities there had refused to accept any more from the capital. Another possible solution in Harare was to use the small Hindu crematorium at Pioneer Cemetery in Mbare, which was used by the majority of the small Hindu community in the city. In accordance with Hindu tradition the crematorium was wood-fired and could therefore be operated in the fuel crisis, but the Hindu community leaders still had to make a decision on whether to lift the religious requirements of cremation there. By the end of the August there were still over 100 corpses in mortuaries awaiting cremation. Some of the corpses that had been waiting there for more than a month had begun to decompose.

The problems for cremation remained confined largely to the Zimbabwean communities of Indian and European descent and were only one aspect of the larger problem of the disposal of Harare's dead. The majority of the rural poor could still follow the African tradition of burying their dead on family plots in the countryside, but this option was not open to all urban-dwellers. By early August, Harare Central Hospital morgue was holding over three times its capacity of corpses, whose relatives could not afford to bury. By late August, in some of the public mortuaries, corpses had to be stacked on the trays, and some were even piled up on the floors. The situation was further exacerbated not only by the small size of most mortuaries but also by the AIDS epidemic which was killing at least 3800 people per week. Due to the economic crisis, a normal urban burial – even at the black market rate which was about a third of the 'official' rate – was still far beyond the financial reach of the average Zimbabwean. Yet even an 'official' rate burial was about half the price of a cremation, due to the high cost of imported gas.

As in many cities in the developed world, other pressures seem to be pushing Harare towards cremation. In 1999, six of Harare's seven cemeteries were full, and the expanding city was running out of residential space. But even if cremation were to be made more easily available and much cheaper than burial, it seems unlikely that many more poor black Zimbabweans will opt for it in the near future. This is largely due to the continued strength of the burial tradition. In 1999 even the crematorium attendants did not wish to be cremated, preferring instead burial with their clans in the countryside. As Professor Gordon Chavunduka (a sociologist formerly of the University of Zimbabwe) explained, cremation

> ... is totally against cultural traditions ....
> The philosophy of death in Shona [local African] society says it takes about a year for a spirit to leave the body and join the

spirits of the ancestors.... If the body is cremated, that spirit would be blocked. Although it would remain alive, it would be angered that traditional burial rites had not been followed properly and could return to punish the family and community. (Bartlett, 1999).

The strength of this belief can be illustrated by what happened after a white golfer had his cremated ashes scattered around the green of his club's ninth hole, the site of his only 'hole-in-one'. Black golf club members who dropped shots on the ninth green began to blame the spirit of their former fellow club member. Groundsmen were also perturbed by what had happened – so much so, in fact, that what remained of the ashes were soon swept into 'the rough'.

The last cremation figures from Zimbabwe show that in 2000 there were 840 cremations out of 11 623 deaths in Harare, a cremation rate of just over 7 per cent. Given the combination of economic problems and the strength of traditional customs, this rate has very little prospect of increasing in the near future. And this is despite the fact that cremation offers Harare, at least, one way of dealing with some of the problems of corpse disposal that beset all large cities. **Lewis H. Mates**

References

Bartlett, Lawrence (1999), 'Zimbabwe-AIDS: Cremation a Burning Issue in Zimbabwe as AIDS Toll Rises', Agence France-Presse, 29 August, available at: http://www.aegis.com/news/afp/1999/AF990835.html (accessed May 2004).

Chimhete, Caiphas (2003), 'Corpses Pile-up. Cremation Backlog as Petroleum Gas Runs Out', *Zim Standard*, 25 August, available at: http://www.zimbabwesituation.com/aug25_2003.html#link7 (accessed May 2004).

Czujko, Richard (2004), 'No Use Complainin': From a Zimbabwe Diary', available at http://www.gowanusbooks.com/zimbabwe-diary.html (accessed May 2004).

Dods, Dr Alan S. (1968), 'Cremation in Rhodesia and Southern Africa', an address to the British Cremation Society's annual conference, reproduced in *Pharos*, 34(3): 67–69.

Mail and Guardian (30 August 2003), message posted on the 'online policy forum', located at: http://forum.mg.co.za/showflat.php?Cat=0&Bo

ard=talkb&Number= 86291 &page=0&view= collapsed&sb=7&o=&fpart=3 (accessed May 2004).

Pharos, 1934– present day, CRE/A/UK/19.

Shaw, Angus (2003), 'Cadavers Pile Up at Zimbabwe Hospital', Associated Press, 2 August, available at: http://www.aegis.com/news/ap/2003/AP030814.html (accessed May 2004).

Sunday Times (South Africa) (12 January 2003), 'Bodies Pile Up at Harare Mortuaries', available at: http://www.suntimes.co.za/2003/01/12/news/africa/africa07. asp (accessed May 2004).

The Daily News (8 January 2003), 'Fuel Shortage Hits the Dead', located at: www.zic.com.au/updates/2003/14january2003.htm. (Accessed: May 2004).

ZOROASTRIANISM

Zoroastrianism is a religious tradition founded on a theological dualism between good and evil. The physical world has been created by the good Ahura Mazda (Ohrmazd) in order to provide a battleground in which to defeat the forces of evil ruled by Angra Mainyu (Ahriman). The role of a Zoroastrian is to worship good and to actively fight and destroy all evil by prayer, ritual and the application of the Zoroastrian belief of 'right thoughts, right words, right actions'. This dualism exists at all theological levels. Ohrmazd creates all good creatures in the world and Ahriman counter-creates all evil creatures. The basic tenet in Zoroastrian texts is that anything that is beneficial is good and anything that has the capacity to harm is evil.

Zoroastrianism is fundamentally an apotropaic religion – one that seeks to turn away evil. Its religious texts are dominated by instructions on how to ward off evil by maintaining a state of physical and mental purity. All forms of pollution are the direct result of the presence of evil, and the greatest indication of this is when an individual dies. Death is a victory for Ahriman and the corpse itself is literally surrounded by demons (Denkard, 6: 52 in Shaked 1979). Therefore, a corpse is the most dangerous source of pollution which must be contained by prayers and rituals of protection. It must also be disposed of in a way that presents the least danger.

The physical elements of the world (earth, air [the sky], fire and water) are also sacred to Zoroastrians as they are representations of the

Amesha Spentas (the Bounteous Immortals) who are 'Ohrmazd's assistants'. The elements provide the point of contact between a Zoroastrian and Ohrmazd, and each Amesha Spenta is identified with, and represented by, a particular element. Ohrmazd himself is identified with fire, and hence the name 'fire temple' is given to a Zoroastrian building of worship. For Zoroastrians, fire provides the focus on which to express the worship of God in a similar manner to the role of the cross in Christianity. However, this means that it is crucial to Zoroastrian doctrine that the physical elements are not polluted by dead matter (*nasa*). The prescribed method of disposal of the dead in Zoroastrianism is by exposure to wild birds and animals and the 'purifying rays of the sun', initially on rock in uninhabited places and later in special stone buildings called 'towers of silence' (*dakhmas*). However, Zoroastrians have, at certain times, buried their dead. This practice has been justified by the use of stone-lined tombs or by utilizing rock-cut caves.

In modern times, as Zoroastrians have migrated, their diaspora communities have had to adopt the funerary practices of their host countries. In the West, the prescribed methods of disposal of the dead are burial and cremation. Zoroastrians have adapted both these methods of disposal in order to maintain their doctrinal beliefs. Zoroastrian burial procedures have entailed little adaptation in the West – they primarily involve the use of brick-lined graves. For cremation, however, Zoroastrians have had to adopt a more reasoned approach to equate the practice with their scriptures. Fire cannot be polluted, and by its very nature a cremation should involve fire. However, Zoroastrians interpret the action of a cremator as a generator of intense heat. In those modern cremators where this heat is generated by electricity rather than by a 'physical' fire the sacred element is not polluted by contact with the body, rather it is replaced by electricity, and the heat released is responsible for 'touching' and thereby burning the dead. This emphasis on electricity and the 'science' of cremation is a recurring theme within the Zoroastrian communities in India and the Western diaspora. So, for example, in 1938, the president of the British Zoroastrian Association argued that, from a scientific point of view, fire 'can never be defiled for it consumed all impurities but ultimately retains its integrity and

remains pure by itself' (Hinnells, 1996:136). In more recent times, the Zoroastrian community magazine *Parsiana* has carried arguments for and against the use of cremation. Proponents of this means of disposal emphasize the use of electricity and heat (for example, *Parsiana*, 1984: 11), whereas the more traditional elements continue to argue that cremation involves fire and therefore involves pollution (*Parsiana*, 1989: 11).
Alan Schofield

References

Boyce, M. (1984), *Textual Sources for the Study of Zoroastrianism*, Manchester: Manchester University Press.

Boyce, M. (1987), *Zoroastrians, Their Religious Beliefs and Practices*, London: Routledge & Keegan Paul.

Choksy, J.K. (1989), *Purity and Pollution in Zoroastrianism*, Austin: University of Texas Press.

Hinnells, J. (1996), *Zoroastrians in Britain*, Oxford: Oxford University Press.

Parsiana (1984), 7(4).

Parsiana (1989), 11(10).

Shaked, S. (1979), *The Wisdom of the Sasanian Sages (Denkard IV)*, Persian Heritage Series, No. 34, Boulder, CO: Westview Press.

Williams, A. (1989), 'The Body and the Boundaries of Zoroastrian Spirituality', *Religion*, 19: 225–39.

CREMATION STATISTICS

GENERAL NOTES

Most cremation statistics are taken from *Pharos*. Others come from a report on international cremation in the 1948 ICF Congress report, reports by Hugo Erichsen to CANA conventions in 1932, 1933 and 1934 and *Flacâra Sacra* (a Romanian cremationist newsletter), all located in the Cremation Society Archive. Finally, some are taken from the entries of contributors. The gaps in the statistics are due to the fact that they are often not collected by the government; sometimes cremation societies can collect them, but this task can also prove difficult. Thus, for example, the Australian Cemeteries and Crematoria Association cannot get hold of accurate statistics for recent years and has failed, as yet, to get the government to undertake this task. Pre-1938 comprehensive figures for New Zealand are equally impossible to find, as some of the local councils of the period kept confusing and incomplete records.

In the tables:

- The figure in brackets represents cremations as a percentage of total deaths.
- 'N/A' means that the figures are unavailable.
- Blank spaces between sets of figures also mean that the figures are unavailable.
- 'Est' means that a figure is an estimate.
- 'X' means that the country's figures appear in five-yearly totals.
- An asterisk set against a country indicates that the relevant note below is applicable.

NOTES ON SPECIFIC COUNTRIES

ARGENTINA

The figures 1980–1999, kindly provided by the municipal authorities, refer to Buenos Aires city crematorium only. The 1999–2001 figures are approximations only.

AUSTRALIA

The statistics for 1924 and before refer to Adelaide Crematorium, which was the only modern crematorium operating in Australia between 1903 and 1924. At Melbourne's Springvale Necropolis, 196 cremations were conducted between 1905 and 1933, in basic furnaces constructed within the cemetery grounds. A modern purpose-built crematorium was not opened at Springvale until 1936. There were also periodic open-air funeral pyre cremations conducted in various locations in Australia after the first such cremation in Victoria in 1890. The figures for 1936 have been kindly supplied by Robert Nicol. Some of them are reproduced from his book, *This Grave and Burning Question. A Centenary History of Cremation in Australia* (Adelaide: Adelaide Cemeteries Authority, 2003). Due partly to the expansion of cremation facilities, recent figures have proved impossible for Australian cremationists to collect.

BRAZIL

The figures refer to Saõ Paulo only.

CHINA

The 1924–29 and 1932 figures relate only to Shanghai Crematorium, which was used solely by foreigners.

CUBA

The figures are for Havana City only.

CZECHOSLOVAKIA

A note with the 1982 figures in *Pharos* (49(3) 1983: 109) states that the figures are those from the Czech Cremation Society based in Prague and not from the Slovakian Cremation Society. It is unclear to which other Czechoslovakia cremation figures this applied.

CZECH REPUBLIC

The 1991 figures are based on estimates.

GERMANY

The figures from 1951 to 1992 refer to West Germany only.

GHANA

One cremation pyre was built in 1993. By 1995 four open-air pyre cremators were operational.

HONG KONG

The 1931–32 figures relate only to the European crematorium, built in 1899.

ITALY

The pre-1965 figures are incomplete. Those for the period 1876–1929 were kindly supplied by Fulvio Conti. The 1988–2002 figures are taken from the Italian Cremation Federation website at: www.cremazione.it.

LUXEMBOURG

Cremations took place abroad, mostly in Strasbourg, until 1995.

MAURITIUS

The cremation rates recorded here are an average cremation rate of four different districts in the country.

NAMIBIA

The statistics only cover white Africans, as black Africans generally do not cremate.

PORTUGAL

From 1995 onwards the figures refer to Lisbon Crematorium and Lisbon deaths only.

ROMANIA

The 1998–99 figures refer to Bucharest only.

SLOVENIA

The figures from 1998 refer only to cremations at Ljubljana crematorium and not the new Maribor facility, so the total percentage cremated is higher than the figure given in the table.

SOUTH AFRICA

All cremations as percentage of deaths are estimates as many deaths are never registered in the country. There were only two crematoria operating before 1933, and they were used at a low level in the early years.

SPAIN

The figures for 1988–96 denote the approximate numbers of cremations.

TRINIDAD AND TOBAGO

The 1994 figure includes 2000 Hindu cremations. Other figures given exclude this approximate annual figure.

USA AND CANADA

The statistics were measured by CANA in five-year periods from 1914–58, so the figures given cover the periods 1914–18, 1919–23, 1924–28, 1929–33, 1934–38, 1939–43, 1944–48 and 1949–53. Statistics for 1953–57 are unavailable for both the USA and Canada. From 1958 they are recorded annually. These figures have been taken from the CANA website at: http://www.cremationassociation.org. The Canada figures up until 1932 are for cremations performed at Mount Royal Crematorium, Montreal, only. The total Canadian cremation figures for 1913–32 are therefore higher than those recorded here.

ZIMBABWE (FORMERLY RHODESIA)

Statistics before 1979 refer to white Europeans and Asians only as black Zimbabweans do not normally cremate. Before 1956 the statistics refer to open-air pyre cremations, as there was no Western crematorium. The 1981–82 figures are total cremations, but the cremation percentage given is only that of Bulawayo. The 1983 figures refer to the whole country. The 1984–87 figures cover only Harare and refer only to the 'European community'.

	1876	1877	1878	1879	1880
Argentina*					
Australia*					
Austria					
Belgium					
Brazil*					
Bulgaria					
Canada*					
China*					
Columbia					
Cuba*					
Czechoslovakia*					
Czech Republic*					
Denmark					
Finland					
France					
Germany*			1 (N/A)	17 (0.001)	16 (0.001)
Ghana*					
Haiti					
Hong Kong*					
Hungary					
Iceland					
Ireland (Eire)					
Italy*	2 (N/A)	14 (N/A)	17 (N/A)	17 (N/A)	45 (N/A)
Japan					
Latvia					
Luxembourg*					
Mauritius*					
Namibia*					
Netherlands					
New Zealand					
Norway					
Portugal*					
Romania*					
Singapore					
Slovak Republic					
Slovenia*					
South Africa*					
South Korea					
Spain*					
Sweden					
Switzerland					
Trinidad and Tobago*					
United Kingdom					
USA*					
USSR/Russia					
Yugoslavia					
Zimbabwe (Rhodesia)*					

	1881	1882	1883	1884	1885
Argentina*					
Australia*					
Austria					
Belgium					
Brazil*					
Bulgaria					
Canada*					
China*					
Columbia					
Cuba*					
Czechoslovakia*					
Czech Republic*					
Denmark					
Finland					
France					
Germany*	33 (0.003)	33 (0.003)	46 (0.004)	69 (0.006)	76 (0.006)
Ghana*					
Haiti					
Hong Kong*					
Hungary					
Iceland					
Ireland (Eire)					
Italy*	75 (N/A)	69 (N/A)	70 (N/A)	116 (N/A)	155 (N/A)
Japan					
Latvia					
Luxembourg*					
Mauritius*					
Namibia*					
Netherlands					
New Zealand					
Norway					
Portugal*					
Romania*					
Singapore					
Slovak Republic					
Slovenia*					
South Africa*					
South Korea					
Spain*					
Sweden					
Switzerland					
Trinidad and Tobago*					
United Kingdom					3 (N/A)
USA*					
USSR/Russia					
Yugoslavia					
Zimbabwe (Rhodesia)*					

	1886	1887	1888	1889	1890	1891
				49 (N/A)	121 (N/A)	134 (N/A)
	95 (0.008)	110 (0.01)	95 (0.008)	128 (0.01)	111 (0.009)	165 (0.01)
	175 (N/A)	167 (N/A)	214 (N/A)	283 (N/A)	248 (N/A)	220 (N/A)
		13 (0.02)	23 (0.03)	46 (0.06)	38 (0.05)	57 (0.07)
				21 (0.04)	32 (0.05)	39 (0.06)
	10 (0.002)	13 (0.002)	28 (0.005)	46 (0.008)	54 (0.008)	99 (0.01)

	1892	1893	1894	1895	1896
Argentina*					
Australia*					
Austria					
Belgium					
Brazil*					
Bulgaria					
Canada*					
China*					
Columbia					
Cuba*					
Czechoslovakia*					
Czech Republic*					
Denmark		4 (0.009)	15 (0.04)	18 (0.05)	21 (0.06)
Finland					
France	159 (N/A)	189 (N/A)	216 (N/A)	187 (N/A)	200 (N/A)
Germany*	221 (0.02)	256 (0.02)	267 (0.02)	263 (0.02)	312 (0.03)
Ghana*					
Haiti					
Hong Kong*					
Hungary					
Iceland					
Ireland (Eire)					
Italy*	248 (N/A)	237 (N/A)	216 (N/A)	213 (N/A)	225 (N/A)
Japan					
Latvia					
Luxembourg*					
Mauritius*					
Namibia*					
Netherlands					
New Zealand					
Norway					
Portugal*					
Romania*					
Singapore					
Slovak Republic					
Slovenia*					
South Africa*					
South Korea					
Spain*					
Sweden	52 (0.06)	63 (0.08)	49 (0.06)	34 (0.05)	61 (0.08)
Switzerland	39 (0.07)	41 (0.07)	40 (0.06)	44 (0.07)	64 (0.11)
Trinidad and Tobago*					
United Kingdom	107 (0.02)	131 (0.02)	125 (0.02)	208 (0.03)	201 (0.03)
USA*					
USSR/Russia					
Yugoslavia					
Zimbabwe (Rhodesia)*					

	1897	1898	1899	1900	1901	1902
						3 (N/A)
	14 (0.04)	18 (0.05)	28 (0.08)	28 (0.07)	34 (0.09)	44 (0.12)
	210 (N/A)	231 (N/A)	246 (0.03)	301 (0.04)	307 (0.04)	305 (0.04)
	374 (0.03)	424 (0.04)	515 (0.04)	636 (0.05)	692 (0.06)	861 (0.08)
	233 (N/A)	236 (N/A)	263 (N/A)	263 (N/A)	184 (N/A)	215 (N/A)
	70 (0.09)	73 (0.10)	72 (0.08)	70 (0.08)	62 (0.07)	66 (0.08)
	69 (0.12)	99 (0.17)	95 (0.16)	136 (0.21)	144 (0.24)	217 (0.38)
	250 (0.04)	341 (0.05)	367 (0.06)	444 (0.07)	445 (0.07)	444 (0.08)

	1903	1904	1905	1906	1907
Argentina*		2 (N/A)	1 (N/A)	6 (N/A)	3 (N/A)
Australia*	3 (0.006)	2 (N/A)	1 (N/A)	4 (N/A)	6 (N/A)
Austria					
Belgium					
Brazil*					
Bulgaria					
Canada*	6 (N/A)	16 (N/A)	19 (N/A)	19 (N/A)	27 (N/A)
China*					
Columbia					
Cuba*					
Czechoslovakia*					
Czech Republic*					
Denmark	51 (0.14)	47 (0.13)	73 (0.19)	77 (0.29)	75 (0.20)
Finland					
France	315 (0.04)	359 (0.05)	345 (0.04)	365 (0.05)	474 (0.06)
Germany*	1 074 (0.09)	1 381 (0.12)	1 768 (0.15)	2 054 (0.18)	2 977 (0.27)
Ghana*					
Haiti					
Hong Kong*					
Hungary					
Iceland					
Ireland (Eire)					
Italy*	195 (N/A0	212 (N/A)	308 (N/A)	307 (N/A)	345 (N/A)
Japan					
Latvia					
Luxembourg*					
Mauritius*					
Namibia*					
Netherlands					
New Zealand					
Norway					13 (0.04)
Portugal*					
Romania*					
Singapore					
Slovak Republic					
Slovenia*					
South Africa*					
South Korea					
Spain*					
Sweden	66 (0.08)	67 (0.08)	85 (0.10)	70 (0.09)	87 (0.11)
Switzerland	280 (0.47)	374 (0.61)	479 (0.76)	526 (0.89)	719 (1.21)
Trinidad and Tobago*					
United Kingdom	475 (0.08)	569 (0.09)	604 (0.10)	743 (0.12)	705 (0.12)
USA*					
USSR/Russia					
Yugoslavia					
Zimbabwe (Rhodesia)*					

	1908	1909	1910	1911	1912	1913
	2 (N/A)	2 (N/A)	3 (N/A)	1 (N/A)	X	0 (0)
	9 (N/A)	6 (N/A)	8 (N/A)	8 (N/A)	3 (0.005)	10 (0.02)
	52 (N/A)	88 (N/A)	97 (N/A)	74 (N/A)	71 (N/A)	64 (N/A)
	102 (0.26)	105 (0.29)	127 (0.36)	138 (0.37)	165 (0.45)	203 (0.57)
	433 (0.06)	425 (0.06)	502 (0.07)	513 (0.07)	547 (0.08)	656 (0.09)
	4050 (0.36)	4779 (0.44)	6084 (0.58)	7555 (0.67)	8858 (0.86)	10168 (1.01)
	312 (N/A)	431 (N/A)	391 (N/A)	393 (N/A)	409 (N/A)	461 (N/A)
	23 (0.07)	49 (0.15)	91 (0.28)	121 (0.38)	143 (0.44)	208 (0.64)
	87 (0.11)	81 (0.11)	96 (0.12)	65 (0.09)	91 (0.11)	97 (0.13)
	750 (1.30)	914 (1.54)	1211 (2.14)	1410 (2.37)	1587 (2.93)	1818 (3.28)
	795 (0.13)	855 (0.14)	840 (0.15)	1023 (0.17)	1134 (0.20)	1188 (0.21)

	1914	1915	1916	1917	1918
Argentina*	5 (N/A)	5 (0.004)	6 (N/A)	1 (N/A)	5 (N/A)
Australia*	6 (0.01)	11 (0.02)	8 (0.01)	14 (0.03)	13 (0.03)
Austria					
Belgium					
Brazil*					
Bulgaria					
Canada*	77 (N/A)	62 (N/A)	62 (N/A)	69 (N/A)	109 (N/A)
China*					
Columbia					
Cuba*					
Czechoslovakia*					83 (0.04)
Czech Republic*					
Denmark	230 (0.64)	249 (0.67)	311 (0.79)	348 (0.89)	360 (0.92)
Finland					
France	689 (0.08)	647 (0.07)	582 (0.07)	553 (0.08)	536 (0.06)
Germany*	11 138 (0.86)	10 650 (0.73)	11 463 (0.88)	13 942 (1.04)	15 873 (0.98)
Ghana*					
Haiti					
Hong Kong*					
Hungary					
Iceland					
Ireland (Eire)					
Italy*	451 (N/A)	375 (N/A)	382 (N/A)	379 (N/A)	520 (N/A)
Japan					
Latvia					
Luxembourg*					
Mauritius*					
Namibia*					
Netherlands	1 (0.001)	46 (0.06)	90 (0.11)	98 (0.11)	135 (0.12)
New Zealand					
Norway	263 (0.79)	279 (0.83)	331 (0.95)	360 (1.04)	503 (1.14)
Portugal*					
Romania*					
Singapore					
Slovak Republic					
Slovenia*					
South Africa*					
South Korea					
Spain*					
Sweden	123 (0.16)	115 (0.14)	137 (0.18)	126 (0.16)	173 (0.17)
Switzerland	2 019 (3.76)	2 161 (4.19)	2 357 (4.66)	2 182 (4.09)	1 243 (1.66)
Trinidad and Tobago*					
United Kingdom	1 279 (0.27)	1 410 (0.22)	1 366 (0.24)	1 509 (0.27)	1 795 (0.26)
USA*		X	X	X	6 5571 (N/A)
USSR/Russia					
Yugoslavia					
Zimbabwe (Rhodesia)*					

1919	1920	1921	1922	1923	1924
6 (N.A)	15 (N/A)	9 (N/A)	8 (N/A)	28 (N/A)	88 (0.06)
18 (0.03)	11 (0.02)	21 (0.03)	21 (0.04)	25 (0.04)	28 (0.05)
				835 (N/A)	1 424 (N/A)
74 (N/A)	118 (N/A)	98 (N/A)	141 (N/A)	152 (N/A)	167 (N/A)
					10 (N/A)
670 (0.38)	657 (0.37)	769 (0.48)	1833 (1.12)	2038 (1.43)	2543 (1.75)
455 (1.15)	555 (1.39)	595 (1.64)	740 (1.88)	788 (2.08)	879 (2.31)
595 (0.09)	560 (0.08)	551 (0.08)	560 (0.08)	647 (0.10)	690 (0.10)
15 905 (1.63)	16 855 (1.81)	19 507 (2.27)	26 914 (3.02)	33 480 (3.86)	33 523 (4.37)
558 (N/A)	610 (N/A)	497 (N/A)	568 (N/A)	531 (N/A)	530 (N/A)
162 (0.18)	177 (0.22)	196 (0.25)	186 (0.23)	218 (0.31)	256 (0.36)
458 (1.28)	537 (1.60)	583 (1.90)	665 (2.05)	788 (2.50)	805 (2.61)
193 (0.23)	168 (0.22)	185 (0.25)	214 (0.28)	244 (0.36)	324 (0.45)
2 128 (3.87)	2 315 (4.13)	2 305 (4.65)	2 611 (5.19)	2 951 (6.42)	3 341 (6.82)
2 031 (0.35)	1 796 (0.34)	1 922 (0.37)	2 009 (0.36)	1 988 (0.39)	2 395 (0.44)
X	X	X	X	7 247 (N/A)	X

	1925	1926	1927	1928	1929
Argentina*	125 (0.08)	186 (0.09)	215 (0.1)	271 (0.14)	278 (0.19)
Australia*	81 (0.15)	157 (028)	336 (0.58)	507 (0.85)	738 (1.21)
Austria	1 880 (N/A)	2 391 (N/A)	2 965 (N/A)	3 247 (N/A)	3 568 (N/A)
Belgium					
Brazil*					
Bulgaria					
Canada*	219 (N/A)	246 (N/A)	251 (N/A)	352 (N/A)	354 (N/A)
China*	26 (N/A)	30 (N/A)	36 (N/A)	35 (N/A)	27 (N/A)
Columbia					
Cuba*					
Czechoslovakia*	3 045 (2.09)	3 363 (2.30)	3 757 (2.42)	4 090 (2.78)	4 740 (3.05)
Czech Republic*					
Denmark	976 (2.63)	1 223 (3.21)	1 262 (3.14)	1 385 (3.60)	1 570 (3.98)
Finland		64 (N/A)	105 (N/A)	171 (N/A)	210 (N/A)
France	834 (0.12)	873 (0.12)	849 (0.12)	976 (0.14)	1 118 (0.15)
Germany*	36 107 (4.79)	40 065 (5.39)	45 758 (5.98)	48 385 (6.47)	56 794 (6.97)
Ghana*					
Haiti					
Hong Kong*					
Hungary					
Iceland					
Ireland (Eire)					
Italy*	517 (N/A)	508 (N/A)	441 (N/A)	462 (N/A)	463 (N/A)
Japan					
Latvia					
Luxembourg*					
Mauritius*					
Namibia*					
Netherlands	262 (0.36)	318 (0.43)	352 (0.45)	406 (0.55)	450 (0.54)
New Zealand					
Norway	816 (2.68)	875 (2.92)	934 (3.00)	1063 (3.51)	1171 (3.66)
Portugal*	2 (N/A)	1 (N/A)			
Romania*				186 (N/A)	318 (N/A)
Singapore					
Slovak Republic					
Slovenia*					
South Africa*					
South Korea					
Spain*					
Sweden	343 (0.48)	450 (0.63)	455 (0.59)	588 (0.80)	800 (1.07)
Switzerland	3 619 (7.56)	3 670 (7.90)	4 228 (8.59)	4 528 (9.32)	5 029 (9.97)
Trinidad and Tobago*					
United Kingdom	2 701 (0.50)	2 877 (0.56)	3 265 (0.59)	3 436 (0.65)	4 341 (0.72)
USA*	X	X	X	101 467 (N/A)	X
USSR/Russia			226 (N/A)	4 025 (N/A)	5 208 (N/A)
Yugoslavia					
Zimbabwe (Rhodesia)*					

	1930	1931	1932	1933	1934	1935
	322 (0.22)	359 (0.25)	347 (0.25)	435 (0.32)	425 (0.3)	426 (0.26)
	878 (1.59)	1107 (1.96)	1333 (2.35)	1780 (3.01)	1742 (2.70)	3403 (5.35)
	3566 (N/A)	4073 (N/A)	3969 (N/A)	3849 (N/A)	3083 (4)	3116 (N/A)
				29 (N/A)	44 (N/A)	75 (N/A)
	334 (N/A)	353 (N/A)	407 (N/A)	3044 (0.55)	X	X
			69 (N/A)			
	4725 (3.32)	4907 (3.40)	5451 (3.81)	5293 (3.76)	5276 (3.88)	5692 (4.04)
	1694 (4.44)	2148 (5.29)	2522 (6.35)	2702 (7.06)	2942 (7.73)	3306 (8.10)
	211 (N/A)	206 (N/A)	286 (N/A)	292 (N/A)	280 (N/A)	304 (N/A)
	1146 (0.18)	1245 (0.18)	1202 (0.18)	1276 (0.18)	1210 (0.19)	1330 (0.20)
	53979 (7.51)	59119 (N/A)	60266 (8.05)	63674 (8.63)	62262 (8.62)	70062 (8.59)
		44 (N/A)	60 (N/A)			
			433 (N/A)	405 (N/A)	406 (N/A)	426 (N/A)
			N/A (0.4)	N/A (0.56)	22 (0.62)	N/A (0.64)
	505 (0.70)	555 (0.72)	636 (0.87)	636 (0.88)	668 (0.95)	747 (1.01)
	1185 (4.00)	1418 (4.62)	1574 (5.22)	1618 (5.60)	1681 (5.93)	1884 (4.56)
				1 (N/A)	4 (N/A)	8 (0.001)
	382 (0.14)	524 (0.21)	470 (0.15)	602 (0.22)	580 (0.20)	468 (0.15)
				93 (N/A)	123 (N/A)	125 (N/A)
	1010 (1.41)	1310 (1.70)	1522 (2.13)	1910 (2.74)	2309 (3.30)	2879 (3.95)
	4883 (10.40)	5665 (11.46)	6036 (12.09)	6075 (12.88)	6052 (12.93)	6397 (12.73)
	4533 (0.87)	5195 (0.93)	6315 (1.14)	7471 (1.33)	8337 (1.54)	9614 (1.77)
	X	X	X	142346 (N/A)	X	X
	6328 (N/A)	8379 (N/A)	9056 (N/A)	9042 (N/A)	12152 (N/A)	12083 (N/A

	1936	1937	1938	1939	1940
Argentina*	422 (0.26)	479 (0.3)	510 (0.32)		
Australia*	4 099 (6.27)	5 132 (7.96)	6 242 (9.39)	6 742 (9.75)	7 730 (11.30)
Austria	3 012 (N/A)	3 321 (N/A)	N/A (N/A)	4 637 (4.56)	4 526 (4.55)
Belgium	78 (N/A)	94 (N/A)	98 (N/A)	120 (N/A)	96 (N/A)
Brazil*					
Bulgaria					
Canada*	X	X	4 160 (0.75)	X	X
China*					
Columbia					
Cuba*					
Czechoslovakia*	5 881 (4.23)	6 369 (4.56)	6 953 (4.86)	7 059 (4.8)	7 700 (5.01)
Czech Republic*					
Denmark	3 460 (8.46)	3 893 (9.63)	4 031 (10.32)	4 343 (11.3)	4 756 (11.9)
Finland	315 (N/A)	290 (N/A)	332 (N/A)	312 (0.58)	352 (0.48)
France	1 267 (0.19)	1 257 (0.20)	1 340 (0.21)	1 195 (0.19)	1 117 (0.15)
Germany*	76 624 (9.63)	80 407 (10.12)			
Ghana*					
Haiti					
Hong Kong*					
Hungary					
Iceland					
Ireland (Eire)					
Italy*	417 (N/A)	408 (N/A)	470 (N/A)	388 (N/A)	
Japan					
Latvia					
Luxembourg*	N/A (0.75)	18 (0.5)			20 (N/A)
Mauritius*					
Namibia*					
Netherlands	791 (1.07)	890 (1.18)	870 (1.17)	976 (1.28)	1 061 (1.21)
New Zealand				1 062 (6.67)	1 191 (7.50)
Norway	1 963 (6.52)	2 201 (7.28)	2 282 (7.81)	2 498 (8.36)	2 739 (8.55)
Portugal*	6 (N/A)				
Romania*	369 (0.13)	581 (0.20)	229 (0.08)	216 (0.08)	
Singapore					
Slovak Republic					
Slovenia*					
South Africa*	141 (N/A)	157 (N/A)	200 (N/A)	202 (N/A)	243 (N/A)
South Korea					
Spain*					
Sweden	3 391 (4.53)	3 942 (5.23)	4 434 (6.10)	4 732 (6.5)	5 224 (7.2)
Switzerland	6 456 (13.55)	6 581 (13.92)	6 791 (13.98)	7 238 (14.63)	7 309 (14.40)
Trinidad and Tobago*					
United Kingdom	11 289 (2.01)	14 129 (2.44)	16 312 (3.01)	19 813 (3.51)	25 175 (3.84)
USA*	X	X	182 054 (2.56)	X	X
USSR/Russia			12 000 approx.		
Yugoslavia					
Zimbabwe (Rhodesia)*					

1941	1942	1943	1944	1945	1946
8 760 (12.31)	9 605 (12.77)	10 763 (14.45)	10 948 (15.73)	11 459 (16.31)	12 723 (17.04)
4 645 (4.93)	4 463 (4.93)	4 632 (4.91)	6 024 (5.49)	2 127 (1.22)	3 147 (3.33)
94 (N/A)	110 (N/A)	100 (N/A)	107 (N/A)	104 (N/A)	124 (N/A)
X	X	6 319 (1.08)	X	X	X
8 563 (5.63)	10 235 (6.68)	10 379 (6.74)	13 572 (8.4)	15 004 (8.11)	10 130 (7.53)
4 714 (11.9)	4 929 (13.1)	5 212 (13.7)	5 853 (14.2)	6 646 (15.7)	6 582 (15.6)
379 (0.51)	339 (0.6)	335 (0.67)	338 (0.49)	416 (0.82)	604 (1.31)
1 107 (0.16)	1 104 (0.16)	1 162 (0.18)	352 (0.04)	445 (0.07)	744 (0.14)
21 (N/A)	21 (N/A)	10 (N/A)	19 (N/A)		
1 067 (1.19)	1 244 (1.44)	1 223 (1.33)	1 074 (0.99)	592 (0.42)	1 549 (1.93)
1 533 (8.99)	1 845 (10.18)	1 835 (10.72)	2 142 (12.56)		
2 742 (8.7)	2 779 (8.7)	2 901 (9.2)	3 266 (10.0)	3 677 (12.6)	3 545 (12.4)
261 (N/A)	278 (N/A)	350 (N/A)			
5 291 (7.4)	5 266 (8.2)	5 936 (9.0)	7 115 (10.0)	7 796 (10.9)	8 342 (11.85)
6 805 (14.38)	7 022 (14.96)	7 056 (14.88)	8 066 (15.41)	8 025 (15.72)	8 431 (16.77)
26 221 (4.31)	28 528 (5.23)	34 259 (6.04)	39 016 (7.0)	42 963 (7.8)	50 160 (8.9)
X	X	226 227 (3.21)	X	X	X

	1947	*1948*	*1949*	*1950*	*1951*
Argentina*					
Australia*	13 137 (18.13)				N/A (23.12)
Austria	3 568 (3.96)	3 333 (4.05)	N/A (4.25)	3 943 (4.63)	4 297 (4.86)
Belgium	117 (N/A)	211 (N/A)	172 (N/A)	144 (N/A)	150 (N/A)
Brazil*					
Bulgaria					
Canada*	X	8 375 (1.39)	X	X	X
China*					
Columbia					
Cuba*					
Czechoslovakia*	9 568 (9.08)	9 902 (10.1)	11 201 (10.71)	11 937 (11.6)	13 248 (12.05)
Czech Republic*					
Denmark	6 603 (15.4)	6 407 (17.7)	6 974 (18.4)	7 504 (19.5)	8 016 (20)
Finland	612 (1.29)	797 (1.81)	881 (2.0)	916 (2.0)	994 (2.4)
France	813 (0.15)	858 (0.17)	933 (0.16)	900 (0.17)	963 (0.17)
Germany*					43 800 (8.2)
Ghana*					
Haiti					
Hong Kong*					
Hungary					
Iceland					
Ireland (Eire)					
Italy*	349 (N/A)				
Japan					
Latvia					
Luxembourg*	18 (N/A)		18 (0.52)	28 (0.81)	17 (0.48)
Mauritius*					
Namibia*					
Netherlands	1 224 (1.57)	1 327 (1.83)	1 581 (1.95)	1 520 (2.01)	1 671 (2.16)
New Zealand	2 462 (15.15)	2 683 (15.52)	2 845 (16.19)	3 165 (17.50)	
Norway	3 790 (13.0)	3 691 (13.2)	4 049 (14.2)	4 422 (15.2)	4 779 (15.2)
Portugal*					
Romania*					
Singapore					
Slovak Republic					
Slovenia*					
South Africa*					
South Korea					
Spain*					
Sweden	8 970 (12.2)	9 494 (14.0)	10 076 (14.5)	10 697 (15.3)	11 185 (16.0)
Switzerland	8 803 (17.13)	8 852 (17.0)	8 887 (17.97)	9 021 (19.04)	9 634 (19.28)
Trinidad and Tobago*					
United Kingdom	61 160 (10.48)	64 290 (12.12)	79 607 (13.88)	89 557 (15.59)	107 161 (17.42)
USA*	X	264 002 (3.72)	X	X	X
USSR/Russia					
Yugoslavia					
Zimbabwe (Rhodesia)*					

	1952	1953	1954	1955	1956	1957
					532 (0.32)	562 (0.31)
	N/A (24.39)	N/A (25.68)	N/A (25.5)	N/A (26.62)	N/A (28.03)	N/A (29.53)
	4 418 (5.37)	4 327 (5.22)	4 584 (5.45)	4 524 (5.36)	4 823 (5.58)	5 045 (5.69)
	144 (N/A)	147 (N/A)	163 (N/A)	166 (N/A)	161 (N/A)	156 (N/A)
	X	12 225 (1.94)	X	X	X	X
	13 880 (14.25)	16 320 (16.51)	17 414 (17.50)	18 311 (19.63)	20 166 (16.96)	22 564 (16.96)
	8 728 (22.2)	8 963 (22.7)	9 460 (23.8)	9 790 (25.3)	10 269 (25.9)	11 436 (27.6)
	1 063 (2.7)	1 066 (2.6)	1 255 (3.3)	1 391 (3.5)	1 465 (3.78)	1 577 (3.87)
	912 (0.17)	933 (0.17)	956 (0.17)	953 (0.17)	1044 (0.19)	995 (0.19)
	47 200 (8.8)	50 800 (8.9)	52 414 (9.6)	54 904 (9.6)	58 463 (9.9)	61 744 (10.06)
	18 (0.5)	22 (0.6)	15 (0.4)	21 (0.6)	23 (0.6)	24 (0.63)
	1 818 (2.33)	2 024 (2.51)	2 218 (2.88)	2 457 (3.02)	2 547 (3.01)	2 584 (3.13)
	3 876 (20.51)	3 887 (21.18)	4 295 (22.75)	4 528 (23.55)	4 814 (24.44)	5 178 (24.82)
	N/A (15.3)	N/A (16.2)	4 779 (16.7)	5 070 (18.0)	5 375 (18.2)	5 494 (18.25)
	2 263 (N/A)	2 435 (N/A)	2 635 (N/A)	2 770 (N/A)	2 989 (N/A)	2 997 (N/A)
				N/A (6)		
	11 686 (17.1)	12 772 (18.4)	13 364 (19.4)	14 101 (20.6)	15 609 (22.3)	16 838 (23.1)
	9 501 (19.95)	10 120 (20.36)	11 537 (21.0)	10 693 (23.0)	11 183 (21.68)	11 676 (22.86)
	107699 (19.27)	111728 (19.86)	125521 (22.29)	141353 (24.37)	153238 (26.27)	163358 (28.36)
	X	299202 (4.05)	X	X	X	X
		36 (N/A)	27 (N/A)	27 (N/A)	63 (N/A)	213 (N/A)

	1958	1959	1960	1961	1962
Argentina*	587 (0.35)	596 (0.34)			622 (0.34)
Australia*	N/A (29.25)	N/A (30)	N/A (31.37)	N/A (32.1)	N/A (32.7)
Austria	4 954 (5.68)	5 102 (5.83)	5 400 (6.05)	5 312 (6.23)	5 715 (6.31)
Belgium	178 (N/A)	168 (N/A)	204 (N/A)	203 (N/A)	244 (N/A)
Brazil*					
Bulgaria					
Canada*	3 724 (2.75)	4 096 (2.93)	4 537 (3.25)	4 891 (3.47)	5 138 (3.58)
China*					
Columbia					
Cuba*					
Czechoslovakia*	24 240 (19.29)	28 021 (21.72)	30 402 (24.26)	33 191 (26.33)	39 062 (28.2)
Czech Republic*					
Denmark	11 922 (28.6)	12 214 (28.98)	13 113 (30)	13 329 (30.85)	14 729 (32.4)
Finland	1 658 (4.28)	1 700 (4.37)	1 797 (4.5)	1 680 (4.16)	1 794 (4.2)
France	991 (0.20)	986 (0.19)	1 054 (0.20)	953 (0.18)	1 131 (0.21)
Germany*	61 447 (10.3)	61 616 (10.18)	66 952 (10.41)	66 079 (10.53)	68 742 (10.62)
Ghana*					
Haiti					
Hong Kong*					
Hungary					
Iceland	41 (3.52)	40 (3.22)	54 (4.63)	42 (3.37)	44 (3.56)
Ireland (Eire)					
Italy*					
Japan					
Latvia					
Luxembourg*	16 (0.46)	24 (0.66)	26 (0.7)	25 (0.7)	24 (0.59)
Mauritius*					
Namibia*					
Netherlands	2 854 (3.39)	3 096 (3.61)	3 501 (4.0)	3 940 (4.48)	4 428 (4.71)
New Zealand	5 261 (25.69)	5 860 (27.74)	5 905 (28.26)	6 515 (29.45)	6 818 (30.88)
Norway	5 968 (19.06)	6 068 (19.21)	6 446 (20)	6 675 (20.28)	7 267 (21.41)
Portugal*					
Romania*					
Singapore					
Slovak Republic					
Slovenia*					
South Africa*	3 160 (N/A)	3 432 (N/A)	3 604 (N/A)	3 863 (N/A)	4 059 (N/A)
South Korea					
Spain*					
Sweden	17 037 (24.0)	17 701 (25.0)	19 925 (26.6)	20 156 (27.3)	21 710 (28.3)
Switzerland	11 611 (23.56)	11 863 (24.0)	12 417 (24.12)	12 472 (24.13)	13 569 (24.68)
Trinidad and Tobago*					
United Kingdom	180075 (30.58)	190819 (32.30)	204034 (34.71)	224464 (36.46)	240589 (38.7)
USA*	58 760 (3.57)	59 376 (3.58)	60 987 (3.56)	61 595 (3.62)	63 435 (3.61)
USSR/Russia					
Yugoslavia					
Zimbabwe (Rhodesia)*	270 (20.23)	315 (24.98)	415 (28.07)	465 (33.9)	486 (35.0)

1963	1964	1965	1966	1967	1968
728 (0.39)	757 (0.39)	787 (0.4)	905 (0.47)	923 (0.46)	938 (0.44)
N/A (34.4)	N/A (36.5)	35 561 (35.7)	38 225 (36.8)	38 281 (37.3)	39 237 (35.8)
5 826 (6.41)	5 923 (6.68)	6 533 (6.93)	6 707 (7.37)	7 289 (7.67)	7 656 (8.00)
211 (N/A)	219 (N/A)	282 (N/A)	290 (N/A)	311 (N./A)	373 (N/A)
5 792 (3.93)	6 382 (4.37)	6 906 (4.64)	7 388 (4.93)	7 991 (5.32)	8 081 (5.27)
40 382 (30.38)	43 513 (32.37)	45 800 (32.5)	48 173 (33.9)	51 997 (34.0)	55 014 (34.0)
15 311 (33.4)	15 747 (33.6)	16 521 (34.5)	17 465 (35.4)	17 472 (36.1)	17 935 (37.9)
1 777 (4.2)	1 811 (4.3)	1 831 (4.1)	1 930 (4.4)	2 269 (5.1)	2 445 (5.4)
1 193 (0.21)	1 199 (0.23)	1 225 (0.22)	1 307 (0.25)	1 431 (0.26)	1 513 (0.27)
73 158 (10.87)	72 273 (11.23)	N/A (11.54)	N/A (11.22)	N/A (12.04)	N/A (12.59)
		3 339 (N.A)			
			58 (4.17)	63 (4.55)	61 (4.39)
		716 (N/A)	797 (N/A)	799 (N/A)	877 (0.17)
31 (0.78)	35 (0.89)	43 (1.04)	46 (1.11)	51 (1.22)	71 (1.73)
4 941 (5.16)	5 450 (5.83)	6 349 (6.48)	7 474 (7.44)	8 151 (8.17)	10 177 (9.7)
6 729 (30.02)	7 559 (33.07)	7 698 (34.68)	8 349 (35.11)	8 413 (36.57)	9 122 (37.29)
7 780 (21.11)	7 640 (21.31)	7 734 (22.9)	8 509 (23.63)	8 601 (23.89)	9 246 (24.85)
4 769 (N/A)	4 265 (N/A)				
22 787 (29.8)	23 807 (31.1)	24 870 (31.8)	26 202 (33.4)	27 898 (35.0)	29 971 (36.3)
14 276 (25.05)	14 086 (26.34)	15 263 (27.58)	15 841 (28.83)	16 338 (29.62)	17 778 (31.03)
261 340 (41.0)	255 613 (43.2)	271 130 (44.4)	294 134 (46.89)	194 284 (48.58)	327 917 (51.22)
67 330 (3.71)	67 658 (3.76)	70 796 (3.87)	73 339 (3.94)	77 375 (4.18)	83 977 (4.35)
				215 (5.32)	263 (6.23)
567 (37.8)	542 (39.1)	579 (39.3)	674 (45.94)	684 (47.66)	799 (47.2)

	1969	*1970*	*1971*	*1972*	*1973*
Argentina*	1 081 (0.49)	1 231 (0.55)	1 231 (0.55)	1 311 (0.59)	1 382 (0.6)
Australia*	41 343 (38.67)	10 831 (N/A)	10 506 (36.4)	43 315 (37.6)	44 213 (40.2)
Austria	8 132 (9.4)	8 893 (8.9)	8 600 (8.9)	8 938 (9.3)	9 609 (10.4)
Belgium	383 (N/A)	465 (0.391)	460 (0.387)	774 (0.663)	1 072 (0.903)
Brazil*					
Bulgaria					
Canada*	8 408 (5.44)	9 188 (5.89)	9 406 (5.98)	11 717 (7.21)	15 880 (9.68)
China*					
Columbia					
Cuba*					
Czechoslovakia*	N/A (37)	64 004 (39.0)	63 970 (39.0)	64 481 (40.0)	69 901 (41.7)
Czech Republic*					
Denmark	18 901 (39.4)	19 843 (41.0)	20 522 (42.1)	21 818 (43.3)	22 813 (45.07)
Finland	2 738 (5.9)	2 833 (6.3)	2 959 (6.4)	3 010 (6.8)	3 098 (7.2)
France	1 600 (0.28)	1 755 (0.33)	1 800 (0.33)	1 949 (0.36)	2 139 (0.38)
Germany*	N/A (12.56)	N/A (13.93)	N/A (13.8)	N/A (14.55)	N/A (15)
Ghana*					
Haiti					
Hong Kong*					
Hungary					N/A (12)	N/A (13.1)
Iceland			70 (4.66)	96 (6.63)	70 (4.75)
Ireland (Eire)					
Italy*	994 (0.19)	1 051 (N/A)	1 080 (N/A)	1 227 (N/A)	18 730 (N/A)
Japan					
Latvia					
Luxembourg*	64 (1.52)	71 (1.7)	80 (1.8)	92 (2.08)	105 (2.57)
Mauritius*					
Namibia*					
Netherlands	12 468 (11.6)	14 949 (13.64)	17 942 (16.28)	21 519 (18.97)	24 288 (21.94)
New Zealand	9300 app. (38.5)	9 892 (39.82)	9990 app. (41.12)	10230app.(42.09)	
Norway	9 605 (25.21)	9 936 (26.55)	9 832 (25.31)	10 251 (26.13)	10 435 (26.15)
Portugal*					
Romania*					
Singapore					
Slovak Republic					
Slovenia*					
South Africa*		3 160 (N/A)	3 432 (N/A)	3 604 (N/A)	3 863 (N/A)
South Korea		N/A (11)			
Spain*					
Sweden	31 872 (38.3)	32 182 (40.3)	33 136 (40.0)	35 051 (41.06)	36 395 (42.6)
Switzerland	18 778 (32.51)	19 547 (34.2)	20 626 (35.7)	21 004 (37.24)	37 984 (39.4)
Trinidad and Tobago*					
United Kingdom	339096 (53.2)	353891 (55.65)	354996 (56.07)	375 773 (57.3)	384144 (59.34)
USA*	85 683 (4.46)	88 096 (4.59)	92 251 (4.78)	97 067 (4.94)	112 298 (5.69)
USSR/Russia					
Yugoslavia	381 (8.93)	464(10.0)		N/A (11.5)	660 (N/A)
Zimbabwe (Rhodesia)*	N/A (50)	895 (52.82)	1 000 (55.35)	1 229 (61.4)	1 225 (58.6)

1974	1975	1976	1977	1978	1979
858 (0.37)		1 748 (0.72)	1 920 (0.82)	2 210 (0.96)	
	47 976 (44)	50 587 (44.9)	48 407 (44.49)	49 858 (45.98)	49 284 (46.24)
10 137 (10.82)	11 168 (11.62)	11 271 (11.85)	11 312 (12.25)	11 860 (12.53)	91 250 (12.66)
1 528 (1.322)	2 006 (1.68)	2 663 (2.24)	3 275 (2.91)	4 200 (3.6)	5 287 (4.7)
17 415 (10.44)	20 694 (12.36)	22 615 (13.23)	24 713 (14.75)	28 456 (16.64)	30 274 (17.75)
72 200 (42.2)	75 869 (45.0)	77 503 (45.6)	78 384 (48.5)	79 931 (66)	88 559 (69.7)
23 921 (46.03)	24 738 (48.5)	27 074 (50.1)	25 977 (51.3)	27 926 (52.8)	30 003 (54.8)
3 600 (8.03)	3 811 (8.65)	4 059 (9.1)	4 274 (9.6)	4 289 (9.8)	4 445 (10.2)
2 415 (0.44)	2 338 (0.42)	2 833 (0.51)	3 676 (0.65)	4 287 (0.79)	4 975 (0.92)
N/A (15.8)	N/A (16.3)	N/A (16.8)	N/A (17.2)	N/A (17.2)	126 019 (17.7)
N/A (11.4)	16 577 (12.7)	18 096 (12.7)	18 897 (13.7)	20 541 (14.7)	20 882 (15.21)
87 (5.82)	75 (5.31)	72 (5.36)	115 (8.01)	86 (5.84)	83 (5.60)
21 110 (N/A)	1 429 (N/A)		1 729 (N/A)	1 661 (N/A)	1 875 (N/A)
626 159 (N/A)		N/A (87)	707 816 (88.0)	696 286 (89.0)	710 314 (90.0)
96 (2.21)	132 (3.02)	145 (3.22)	143 (3.98)	168 (4.0)	163 (4.09)
26 574 (24.5)	29 863 (26.26)	32 173 (18.18)	33 435 (30.48)	36 304 (31.91)	37 754 (33.48)
11 286 (44.68)	11 244 (44.77)	11690app.(45.91)	12 212 (47.03)	12 107 (49.08)	12 573 (49.48)
10 669 (27.16)	10 980 (27.81)	11 335 (28.4)	11 423 (28.8)	11 641 (28.9)	12 201 (29.7)
4 059 (N/A)	4 769 (N/A)	4 265 (N./A)			954 (5.26)
37 984 (44.1)	39 540 (44.9)	41 896 (46.2)	42 305 (48.0)	43 567 (48.6)	45 439 (50.0)
23 180 (41.31)	23 850 (42.64)	24 785 (43.25)	25 096 (45.38)	26 653 (46.18)	27 110 (47.07)
389 213 (59.05)	395 032 (61.43)	413 712 (62.32)	405 729 (63.62)	416 115 (63.92)	414 156 (64.85)
119 480 (6.18)	123 918 (6.55)	140 052 (7.33)	145 435 (7.66)	165 182 (8.58)	179 393 (9.42)
788 (17.2)	881 (18.1)				
1 295 (61.75)	1 308 (68.37)	1 334 (50.2)			1 403 (N/A)

	1980	1981	1982	1983	1984
Argentina*	2 436 (6.6)	2 378 (6.9)	2 668 (7.6)	2 962 (8.1)	2 840 (7.5)
Australia*	50 523 (46.46)	51 462 (47.21)	53 811 (46.89)	52 541 (N/A)	55 459 (49.98)
Austria	11 530 (12.47)	12 206 (13.16)	12 218 (13.38)	12 397 (13.33)	12 013 (13.57)
Belgium	5 287 (5.4)	7 170 (6.47)	8 194 (7.25)	10 400 (9.3)	11 369 (10.37)
Brazil*					
Bulgaria					
Canada*	32 423 (18.85)	34 884 (20.16)	37 222 (20.26)	41 887 (22.76)	44 630 (24.06)
China*					
Columbia					
Cuba*					
Czechoslovakia*	86 646 (64.4)	88 500 (68.31)	90 202 (69.35)		
Czech Republic*					
Denmark	30 003 (56.4)	33 021 (58.5)	33 033 (59.6)	34 494 (60.3)	34 811 (69.92)
Finland	4 508 (10.1)	4 677 (10.5)	4 635 (10.7)	4 828 (10.07)	5 201 (11.53)
France	5 640 (1.04)	6 798 (1.20)	8 205 (1.53)	10 247 (1.82)	11 812 (2.11)
Germany*	131 333 (18.4)	135 195 (18.7)	137 199 (19.2)	139 370 (19.4)	138 339 (19.87)
Ghana*					
Haiti					
Hong Kong*					
Hungary	19 948 (13.8)	22 153 (15.33)	22 156 (15.58)	20 150 (13.54)	24 129 (16.53)
Iceland	96 (6.24)	123 (7.43)	113 (7.14)	121 (7.32)	191 (12.05)
Ireland (Eire)			218 (N/A)	350 (N/A)	378 (1.18)
Italy*	2 230 (N/A)	2 298 (N/A)	2 510 (N/A)	2 776 (N/A)	2 958 (0.52)
Japan	737 248 (91.1)		738 316 (92.64)	765 740 (93.4)	
Latvia					
Luxembourg*	200 (4.86)	248 (6.04)	210 (5.08)	271 (6.47)	292 (7.17)
Mauritius*					
Namibia*					
Netherlands	39 947 (34.96)	41 942 (36.31)	44 002 (37.53)	45 008 (38.22)	46 511 (38.83)
New Zealand	13 450 (50.42)	13 038 (52.0)	13 330 (52.2)	13 647 (52.51)	13 306 (52.43)
Norway	12 370 (30.2)	12 618 (30.4)	12 294 (29.9)	12 368 (29.83)	12 560 (29.63)
Portugal*					
Romania*					
Singapore					
Slovak Republic					
Slovenia*	1 200 (6.38)	1 410 (7.53)	1 616 (8.23)	2 017 (9.74)	2 384 (11.79)
South Africa*					
South Korea		N/A (14)			
Spain*					
Sweden	47 130 (51.4)	48 286 (52.5)	48 930 (54.0)	49 426 (55.05)	49 866 (55.12)
Switzerland	28 561 (48.41)	29 422 (49.23)	29 627 (50.04)	30 915 (51.27)	30 447 (51.77)
Trinidad and Tobago*					
United Kingdom	420 717 (64.48)	421 597 (65.64)	430 453 (66.54)	431 531 (67.1)	421 571 (67.0)
USA*	193 343 (9.74)	217 770 (10.96)	232 789 (11.73)	249 182 (12.4)	266 441 (13.02)
USSR/Russia					
Yugoslavia					
Zimbabwe (Rhodesia)*		1 247 (12.71)	1 179 (13.36)	1 183 (15.1)	789 (10.29)

1985	1986	1987	1988	1989	1990
3 309 (9.5)	3 277 (9.6)	3 830 (11)	3 984 (10.07)	4 258 (12.4)	5 391 (14.9)
56 506 (47.9)	55 892 (48.6)	56 995 (N/A)		59 438 (47.85)	56 657 (47.2)
12 517 (14.07)				N/A (14.84)	12 886 (15.53)
13 271 (11.98)	14 433 (13.06)	15 170 (14.36)	15 691 (15.18)	18 484 (17.01)	20 873 (19.9)
49 216 (25.84)	54 482 (27.94)	53 867 (27.34)	57 568 (30.85)	60 087 (30.74)	62 797 (32.53)
	99 269 (53.54)	97 739 (54.6)	97 630 (54.78)		101 436 (55.22)
36 705 (62.85)	36 805 (63.3)	37 652 (64.7)	38 597 (65.4)	39 258 (66.1)	40 979 (67.2)
5 670 (11.76)	5 604 (11.89)	6 363 (13.2)	6 589 (13.4)	6 716 (13.7)	7 606 (15.2)
14 565 (2.64)	17 365 (3.15)	20 306 (3.86)	24 435 (4.66)	28 592 (5.40)	33 752 (6.14)
N/A (20.54)				159 750 (23.1)	169 318 (23.9)
26 787 (18.7)	27 353 (18.69)	29 209 (20.5)	29 011 (20.87)	30 409 (21.59)	31 609 (22.1)
116 (7.02)	100 (6.26)	124 (7.2)	134 (7.4)	121 (7.1)	126 (7.2)
559 (1.68)	508 (N/A)	609 (1.95)	627 (1.98)	754 (2.42)	803 (2.52)
3 049 (0.5)	3 375 (0.61)	3 626 (N/A)	3 650 (0.7)	4 350 (0.8)	5 200 (1.0)
770228 (93.78)	787350 (94.52)	792824 (95.7)	837185 (96.19)	832530 (96.65)	867608 (97.1)
299 (7.59)	333 (8.38)	363 (9.04)	389 (10.13)	339 (8.5)	350 (9.27)
49 163 (40.15)	50 416 (40.24)	51 317 (41.99)	53 309 (42.95)	56 063 (43.49)	57 138 (44.36)
14 724 (53.58)	14 604 (54.00)	14 890 (53.99)	14 964 (54.6)	15 039 (54.9)	15 120 (56.2)
18 (0.02)	67 (0.07)	119 (0.12)			
					3 148 (N/A)
2 968 (14.95)	3 168 (16.25)	3 771 (19.01)	4 045 (21.15)	4 290 (22.98)	4 684 (25.24)
				N/A (8)	21 705 (N/A)
			5 000 (1.7)		8 500 (2.83)
52 828 (56.21)	53 307 (57.2)	54 602 (58.6)	56 366 (58.3)	56 195 (61.1)	58 093 (61.1)
31 674 (53.41)	32 678 (53.41)	32 719 (54.98)	33 699 (56.45)	34 571 (58.78)	37 513 (58.85)
				1 500 (18.75)	
443687 (67.77)	440997 (68.78)	431954 (69.05)	436850 (69.31)	437654 (67.8)	438066 (69.81)
289091 (13.87)	300587 (14.32)	323371 (15.21)	332183 (15.31)	352370 (16.36)	367975 (17.2)
725 (18.13)	723 (28.35)	706 (N/A)		N/A (14.37)	655 (11.48)

	1991	1992	1993	1994	1995
Argentina*	5 774 (16.6)	5 477 (16)	5 493 (16.1)	5 680 (16.8)	6 440 (20.2)
Australia*	61 631 (51.53)	57 459 (47.57)	57 104 (46.96)		67 500 (53.67)
Austria	13 079 (15.68)	12 841 (15.44)	12 662 (15.34)	12 976 (16.08)	13 171 (16.23)
Belgium	21 804 (20.61)	24 106 (22.8)	26 794 (24.77)	27 720 (26.43)	29 066 (27.43)
Brazil*			2 164 (3.4)	2 411 (3.2)	2 846 (3.85)
Bulgaria					
Canada*	66 087 (33.89)	64 557 (34.86)	70 017 (36.17)	75 489 (38.45)	79 206 (37.62)
China*	2 156 000 (34)	2450000 (36.4)			2630000 (33.2)
Columbia			42 490 (16.76)	43 682 (20.34)	48 812 (28.73)
Cuba*					
Czechoslovakia*					
Czech Republic*	93 175 (53.0)	89 054 (87.6)	87 309 (73.7)	86 695 (73.9)	85 494 (72.5)
Denmark	40 666 (68.4)	41 474 (68.2)	43 189 (68.6)	42 763 (69.9)	43 857 (69.38)
Finland	7 846 (15.9)	8 121 (16.4)	8 986 (17.6)	9 163 (19.2)	9 774 (19.8)
France	37 645 (7.17)	42 953 (8.24)	49 743 (9.39)	55 400 (10.65)	62 212 (11.76)
Germany*	188 116 (26.7)	191 759 (27.6)	292 034 (32.5)	317 517 (35.9)	316 524 (35.78)
Ghana*			1 (N/A)		150 (1.88)
Haiti					
Hong Kong*			21 862 (75.8)	21 454 (74.2)	22 585 (75.85)
Hungary	31 186 (21.27)	34 306 (23.3)	36 544 (24.61)	36 973 (24.85)	37 797 (26.14)
Iceland	115 (6.4)	144 (8.2)	169 (9.6)	173 (10.1)	171 (8.9)
Ireland (Eire)	835 (N/A)	907 (N/A)	945 (2.99)	1 061 (3.46)	1 179 (3.74)
Italy*	6 280 (1.1)	7 471 (N/A)	8 800 (1.6)	10 561 (1.9)	14 602 (2.6)
Japan	876246 (97.43)	903978 (97.64)	923093 (97.86)	922267 (98.31)	963540 (98.55)
Latvia					
Luxembourg*	326 (8.51)	371 (9.5)	415 (10.6)	384 (10.1)	343 (9.03)
Mauritius*					
Namibia*	148 (N/A)	143 (N/A)	150 (N/A)		147 (11.58)
Netherlands	58 786 (45.28)	60 118 (46.29)	64 520 (46.83)	64 505 (48.39)	63 237 (46.61)
New Zealand	15 198 (57.76)	15 295 (57.2)	15 562 (57.01)	15 702 (57.95)	15 896 (57.8)
Norway					13 669 (30.0)
Portugal*	401 (0.38)	440 (0.43)	744 (0.72)	1008 (1.01)	743 (6.95)
Romania*					
Singapore					
Slovak Republic			N/A (75.16)		7 079 (13.44)
Slovenia*	5 300 (27.43)	5 552 (28.72)	5 957 (29.77)	5 994 (30.96)	6 601 (34.80)
South Africa*	22 377 (N/A)	25 186 (N/A)	24 315 (N/A)	26 480 (N/A)	26 431 (9)
South Korea	N/A (18)			N/A (20)	
Spain*		14 000 (4.66)	14 000 (4.51)	15 000 (4.8)	18 000 (5.25)
Sweden	59 607 (62.7)	60 385 (63.8)	61 237 (63.2)	60 221 (65.6)	60 824 (64.74)
Switzerland	37 405 (59.72)	37 939 (61.19)	39 345 (62.94)	40 084 (64.84)	41 369 (65.26)
Trinidad and Tobago*		584 (N/A)	637 (N/A)	2 850 (33.63)	
United Kingdom	441108 (69.53)	437000 (69.24)	453045 (70.08)	434223 (72.14)	445574 (70.07)
USA*	400 465 (18.5)	415966 (19.11)	448532 (19.78)	470915 (20.6)	488224 (21.14)
USSR/Russia	N/A (34.62)				
Yugoslavia					
Zimbabwe (Rhodesia)*	686 (9.67)	705 (8.18)			669 (11.47)

1996	1997	1998	1999	2000	2001
6 232 (20.4)	6 776 (22.2)	7 063 (22.9)	7 834 (25.4)	14 652 (N/A)	16 632 (7.53)
68 208 (54)	69 800 (54.07)				
13 720 (16.98)	14 006 (17.63)	14 139 (18.05)	16 155 (20.66)	16 663 (21.99)	16 048 (21.46)
29 121 (27.65)	30 580 (29.35)	32 389 (30.97)	33 831 (29.63)	35 798 (33.98)	36 678 (35.17)
					4 970 (4.31)
81 960 (39.45)	85 196 (40.69)	90 200 (32.85)	101 454 (46.15)	106 747 (47.7)	108 436 (48.5)
2830000 (35.2)	2950000 (27.25)	3200000 (39.6)	3363000 (41.52)	3737000 (46)	3781000 (47.3)
				69 (0.38)	89 (0.47)
85 650 (75.93)	85 943 (76.23)	83 412 (76.16)	83 902 (76.44)	82 772 (75.94)	81 940 (76.04)
43 377 (71.01)	42 722 (71.27)	41 660 (71.11)	42 299 (70.76)	41 651 (71.78)	41 707 (71.3)
10 823 (22.0)	10 997 (22.4)	11 834 (24.02)	12 466 (25.26)	13 037 (26.42)	13 391 (27.58)
68 317 (12.73)	73 025 (13.73)	80 534 (24.02)	87 010 (16.70)	93 412 (17.42)	100238 (18.91)
333373 (37.76)	338414 (39.7)	332914 (39.1)	338469 (40.1)		
200 (2.0)	210 (2.08)	250 (2.08)	250 (1.67)	300 (1.76)	334 (1.78)
		239 (N/A)	249 (N/A)	268 (N/A)	245 (N/A)
23 204 (72.4)	24 077 (75.06)	25 842 (78.5)	26 146 (78.31)	27 113 (79.76)	26 893 (80.75)
38 690 (27.01)	38 739 (27.77)	37 522 (26.57)	42 513 (29.58)	44 714 (33)	43 784 (33.68)
208 (11.07)	205 (11.12)	232 (12.74)	251 (13.2)	212 (11.63)	234 (13.6)
1 236 (2.92)	1 283 (4.06)	1 460 (4.56)	1 634 (5.2)	1 759 (5.5)	1 728 est. (5.8)
16 500 (3.0)	20 681 (3.8)	23 613 (4.3)	27 200 (4.9)	29 559 (5.28)	34 758 (6.3)
938877 (98.7)	967061 (98.8)	1015057 (98.42)	1017917 (99.31)	999 255 (99.41)	1028615 (99.53)
				1 127 (11.03)	1 297 (12.39
		1 259 (32.37)	133 7 (35.25)		
					640 (9.5)
178 (13.66)	204 (15.44)	190 (N/A)	222 (N/A)	231 (N/A)	217 (N/A)
65 014 (47.26)	64 997 (47.76)	66 322 (48.24)	67 569 (48.1)	68 700 (48.89)	69 039 (49.22)
15 941 (57.98)	14 886 (55.46)	16 016 (57.41)	16 248 (58.31)		16 848 (60.29)
13 876 (31.0)	10 879 (31.0)	13 620 (31.0)	14 182 (31.42)	14 039 (31.75)	14 144 (32.03)
792 (7.19)	846 (8.53)	1 041 (11.03)	1 385 (14.46)	1 544 (16.43)	1 765 (19.58)
		1 137 (11.37)	1 172 (11.72)		
					11 421 (75.55)
6 097 (11.9)	6 951 (13.34)				
6 678 (36.94)	7 426 (39.23)	6 963 (36.57)	6 726 (35.62)	7 085 (38.17)	7 823 (42.41)
26 658 (9)	28 520 (8)	29 291 (9)	29 799 (7)	31 836 (7)	33 427 (6)
			N/A (30)		
20 000 (5.92)	31 634 (9.59)	35 995 (10.91)	43 048 (13.04)	48 689 (13.69)	53 694 (15.0)
61 734 (65.65)	62 953 (67.49)	63 273 (67.84)	648 179 (68.42)	64 867 (69.54)	65 223 (69.57)
40 773 (65.09)	42 304 (67.32)	41 746 (67.97)	42 891 (70.68)	45 104 (72.17)	45 681 (75.51)
		261 (2.9)	367 (4.08)	365 (4.01)	
445934 (71.28)	446305 (72.02)	439145 (71.42)	444169 (69.86)	437609 (71.50)	427944 (70.64)
492434 (21.31)	541602 (23.6)	553364 (23.75)	595617 (23.75)	630800 (25.39)	650776 (26.9)
747 (10.97)	709 (8.39)	717 (6.65)	772 (6.76)	840 (7.22)	

	2002
Argentina*	34 320 (13.73)
Australia*	
Austria	17 059 (22.63)
Belgium	39 659 (37.26)
Brazil*	
Bulgaria	5 254 (4.67)
Canada*	
China*	4152000 (50.6)
Columbia	
Cuba*	
Czechoslovakia*	
Czech Republic*	83 406 (77.05)
Denmark	42 539 (72.36)
Finland	14 354 (29.05)
France	109950 (20.38)
Germany*	
Ghana*	360 (1.87)
Haiti	196 (N/A)
Hong Kong*	28 436 (82.87)
Hungary	47 199 (35.57)
Iceland	274 (15.06)
Ireland (Eire)	1880 est. (6.41)
Italy*	38 691 (6.91
Japan	
Latvia	
Luxembourg*	
Mauritius*	N/A (8.5)
Namibia*	226 (N/A)
Netherlands	70 951 (49.61)
New Zealand	16 811 (60.38)
Norway	14 224 (31.81)
Portugal*	2 007 (23.18)
Romania*	
Singapore	11 892 (76.6)
Slovak Republic	
Slovenia*	8 969 (48.14)
South Africa*	34 901 (6)
South Korea	104 000 (42)
Spain*	59 993 (16.9)
Sweden	66 503 (70.0)
Switzerland	46 419 (75.15)
Trinidad and Tobago*	
United Kingdom	437124 (71.89)
USA*	676890 (27.78)
USSR/Russia	N/A (35)
Yugoslavia	
Zimbabwe (Rhodesia)*	

A CHRONOLOGY OF CREMATION

Drawn from the *Encyclopedia* entries, this information provides a broad impression of the practice of cremation across the globe and throughout the millennia. Cremation rates are only mentioned here if they do not feature in the full table of cremation figures.

BC

8000	China – cremation occurs in the New Stone Age.
7000	Sweden – cremation is occurring from approximately this time.
4000	Britain – cremation occurs from the Early Neolithic period (4000–3000 BC) to the early (Pagan) Saxon period (410–650 AD).
2300	Britain – cremation occurs alongside inhumation during the Early Bronze Age (2300–1500 BC). Cremation predominates in Middle Bronze Age (1500–1100 BC). Cremation decreases in Late Bronze Age (1100–700 BC)
1400–1150	Greece – cremation becomes more common after this time, in the Postpalatial period.
1050	Greece – some communities adopt cremation as a common, but not universal, rite in the Early Iron Age.
1000	Sweden – the custom of cremation becomes fully accepted in the Bronze Age.
700	Greece – after approximately this time, cremation is still practised largely where it had been from the Early Iron Age, but does not spread widely.
500	Sweden – the vast majority of funerals are cremations at the beginning of the Iron Age.
480	Greece – by the end of the Archaic period, cremation has receded and inhumation is dominant throughout Greece.
400	Cremation is standard until the first century AD in Rome, Italy and the western Roman Empire.

AD

43	Britain – cremation predominates in the early Roman period (43–150 AD).
c. 210	Tertullian's *De Resurrectione Carnis* articulates the doctrine of resurrection within the Christian tradition..
211	Rome – a wax model of Septimius Severus is cremated instead of his body; he died in York, Britain.
250	Britain – cremation predominates in parts of the northern frontier zones (adjacent to Hadrian's Wall) in the late Roman period (250–410 AD).
313	The Roman Emperor Constantine (274–337) is converted to Christianity. He later prohibits cremation.
410	Britain – cremation predominates in the northern and eastern areas of Saxon occupation (Yorkshire, Lincolnshire and East Anglia) in the early Saxon period.

618	China – by the Tang Dynasty (618–907), cremation is becoming more popular, being adopted by Han people in remote areas and Buddhists in middle China.
676	Korea – in the Unified Silla period (676–935) Buddhist cremation peaks in popularity.
700	Japan – Buddhist priest Dôshô cremated, although cremation was practised in Japan well before this time.
	Britain – a few Norse cremations occur from the eighth to tenth centuries AD.
800	Sweden – cremation is the most common funeral during the Viking Age (to 1050 AD).
918	Korea – during the Goryeo Dynasty (918–1392), cremation remains widespread.
932	The cremation takes place of a Viking chieftain on the shores of the Volga, as recorded in the oldest written source about Viking Age cremations.
960	China – cremation peaks in popularity during the Song, Liao and Kin, Dynasties (960–1279).
1050	Sweden – Christianity is introduced and cremation disappears.
1185	Japan – by the end of the Heian period (794–1185) cremation was 'closely tied to Buddhist belief and ritual'.
1262	Japan – Shinran, founder of the Jôdô Shinshû (True Pure Land) school of Buddhism is cremated, the practice being especially popular among his adherents.
1279	China – cremation is in vogue in a large area during the Yuan Dynasty (1279–1368).
1300	Pope Boniface VIII announces the *ipso facto* excommunication of anyone who boiled a corpse to separate the flesh from the bones (for transportation purposes).
1368	China – the beginning the Ming Dynasty (1368–1644), which, in the third year of the Hongwu regime, bans cremation.
1392	Korea – the increasing influence of Confucianism during the Joseon Dynasty (1392–1910) sees cremation gradually abandoned in favour of burial.
1401	England – burning at the stake becomes the punishment for heresy.
1431	France – in Rouen, Joan of Arc is burned at the stake; in Paris, the French burn their dead on a huge pyre.
1510	India – Albuquerque seeks to abolish *Sati* in Goa.
1543	Andreas Vesalius publishes *De humani corporis fabrica*.
1556	Britain – Thomas Cranmer is burned as a heretic in Oxford.
1562	France – Languedoc, burned 6 per cent of its suspected heretics from 1500.
1593	France – Trier, 368 men and women are burned for sorcery from 1587.
1603	Japan – by the Tokugawa period (1603–1868), 'Buddhist priests were entrenched as funerary specialists' though funeral rites were not uniform across the country.
1605	Britain – Guy Fawkes apprehended and executed for treason.
1642	France – Paris, Theophraste Renaudot advocates cremation at a conference on the decay of the human body.
1644	China – the Qing Dynasty (1644–1911) maintains the illegal status of cremation (except for the poor) which disappears apart from in some localized economically developed areas.

1654	Japan – Emperor Gokômyô is buried, signifying the imperial court's abandonment of cremation after practising it for centuries.
1658	Britain – Sir Thomas Browne publishes *Hydriotaphia. Urne-Buriall. Or, A Brief Discourse of the Sepulchrall Urnes lately found in Norfolk.*
1666	Britain – The Great Fire of London occurs.
1726	England – the last definite English live burning takes place.
1727	Scotland – the last witch is burned.
1743	French physician Jean-Jacques Bruhier translates a Latin thesis about apparent death.
1769	Wolfgang Von Goethe writes 'Apparent Death' (*c.* 1769).
	Britain – Honoretta Pratt is cremated.
1786	Britain – London, 20 000 said to have attended a punishment burning.
1789	England – Parliament abolishes burning as a punishment.
1797	France – Daubermesnil proposes a law on cremation.
1799	France – Paris, Cambry's *Report on Burials* supports cremation.
1800	France – 17 of the 42 essays submitted to an Institut de France competition on burial regulations support the liberalization of cremation.
	Portugal – doctor and professor, Vicente Teles, proposes cremation.
1801	France – Napoleon signs an agreement with the Catholic Church.
1804	France – Napoleon Bonaparte imposes the Saint Cloud Edict.
1815	Belgium – 4000 corpses are cremated after the Battle of Waterloo.
1818	Britain – Mary Wollstonecroft Shelley publishes *Frankenstein*.
1822	Italy – English poet Percy Bysshe Shelley is cremated on the shore of the Gulf of Spezzia.
1830	France – Dupuytren advances the 'wick effect' theory of spontaneous human combustion in *La Lancette Française*.
1840	Britain – cremation suggested on public health grounds during a cholera epidemic.
1844	USA – Edgar Allen Poe publishes his poem, 'The Premature Burial'.
1852	Jacob Moleschott supports cremation in *The Cycle of Life*.
1854	Britain – Sir Henry Bessemer develops his steel process due to the needs of the Crimean War (1854–6).
1855	Germany – Prussian regimental doctor Johann Peter Trusen calls for obligatory cremation for soldiers killed in battle.
	Nicaragua – over 100 dead are cremated after the Battle of Rivas.
1857	Italy – Ferdinando Coletti becomes the first to open debate in the country with a memoir on the incineration of corpses read at Padua Academy of Sciences, Letters and Arts.
	Portugal – 'S.H.' publishes a pro-cremation article in *O Instituto* at Coimbra.
1861	Italy – In Gaeta, a proposal to cremate the contents of a temporary war burial ground is vetoed for religious reasons.

1863	Australia – in Sydney, Dr John Le Gay Brereton presents the earliest documented pro-cremation talk in the country.
1865	Latin America – the Paraguayan War (1865–1870) sees some rudimentary cremation.
1866	Italy – Dr Vincenzo Giro publishes *Observations on the Incineration of Corpses in* the *Gazzetta Medica Italiana*.
1867	Argentina – cholera victims are cremated at Pergamino, Buenos Aires Province.
	France – In Paris, Friedrich Siemens' regenerative gas burner receives a special award at the International Technological (World) Exposition. An international Congress on soldiers wounded in war is held where two Italians support cremation. Dr Jules Guerin publishes a pro-cremation article in *La Gazette Médicale de Paris*.
	Italy – Professor Giovanni Du Jardin supports cremation in the Genoese newspaper *La Salute*. Member of Parliament Salvatore Morelli proposes the replacement of cemeteries by 'cremation temples'.
1869	Italy – the second International Congress of Medical Sciences, is held, in Florence and is addressed by Drs Castiglioni and Coletti. The International Freemason Congress is held in Naples (in direct opposition to the Vatican Council inaugurated in Rome).
1870	Italy – an Indian prince, who died in Florence is cremated on a wood-pyre.
	The Prussian army uses portable cremators during the Franco-Prussian war (1870–71).
1872	Italy – cremation experiments conducted by Professors Polli, Clericetti and Gorini.
	Belgium – Colonel Creteur 'cremates' the poorly buried corpses of those killed during the battle of Sedan (1870).
1873	Austria – Italian Lodovico Brunetti's cremator system features at the Vienna World's Fair.
	Australia – Melbourne 1873, Dr James Neild speaks to the Royal Society of Victoria 'On the Advantages of Burning the Dead'.
	Japan – the new Meiji state (1868–1912) outlaws cremation.
	Italy – Senator Maggiorani supports cremation in parliament.
1874	Germany – in Dresden, the first experimental cremation performed on the corpse of Briton, Lady Dilke, in a Siemens cremator. An International Cremation Congress is also held there.
	Switzerland – a cremation society is formed.
	Netherlands – the Association for Cremation 'die Facultatieve' is founded.
	Britain – Sir Henry Thompson publishes 'The Treatment of the Body after Death' in *Contemporary Review* and the Cremation Society of Great Britain is formed.
	Austria – Vienna, the first cremation society is founded. Vienna City Council rejects a motion to introduce optional cremation.
	Australia – the South Australian Minister of Justice reads part of Thompson's pro-cremation article in a parliamentary debate on a new public cemetery in Adelaide.
	Italy – the masonic Grande Lodge of Italy constituent assembly commits itself to greater promotion of cremation.
	Belgium – the Commune of Brussels discusses setting land apart for a crematorium in a new cemetery.

France – a parliamentary bill to allow the Paris municipality to cremate fails.

Spain – Carlist troops cremate dead after the battle of Cuenca.

1875 Italy – the first Italian Cremation Society is founded in Milan, and cremation is authorized.

Britain – Sir Francis Seymour Haden proposes in letters to *The Times* what becomes known as the 'Earth to Earth' system. William Eassie publishes *Cremation of the Dead.*

Japan – the cremation prohibition is repealed.

New Zealand – the country's first cremation society is formed in Lawrence.

Serbia and Croatia – Dr Jovan Jovanovié-Zmaj publishes an article on cremation in a popular Serbian magazine. Professor Fran Gundrum Oreovièanin advocates cremation in Croatia.

1876 Italy – Milan, the body of Alberto Keller is the first to be cremated in Italy in the first modern crematorium in the world.

USA – Francis Julius LeMoyne performs the first modern cremation in the USA, but his cremator is then shut down until 1878.

Germany – the first European Cremation Congress is held in Dresden.

Portugal – in Lisbon, the Marquis of Sousa Holstein publicly proposes cremation as an alternative to cemetery enlargement.

Argentina – Juan A. Kelly writes a pro-cremation thesis.

1877 Italy – Lodi Crematorium is inaugurated.

USA – Hugo Erichsen publishes *Cremation of the Dead.*

1878 Germany – Gotha crematorium opens, the first in Germany.

USA – LeMoyne performs the second cremation in the country.

1879 Argentina – Argentine Scientific Society conference supports cremation.

Germany – the first modern cremation is performed at Gotha.

USA – LeMoyne is cremated in his own furnace – the only operable cremator in the country.

Britain – the bishop of Rochester refuses the Cremation Society of England permission to build a crematorium in a private cemetery at New Southgate, north London.

1880 Britain – William Robinson publishes *God's Acre Beautiful; Or, The Cemeteries of the Future.*

Italy – the International Hygiene Congress at Turin holds a special session in Milan on cremation.

Portugal – a report published by Lisbon municipality proposes the implementation of cremation.

France – the Society for the Propagation of Cremation established in Paris.

1881 Germany – Briton Edward Trelawny, friend of Shelley, is cremated at Gotha Crematorium.

Italy – Milan, Coletti is cremated. The Cremation Society of Padua takes his name.

Denmark – an Association of Cremation is founded.

1882   Italy – A league of 24 Italian cremation societies with 6000 members is formed and holds its first congress in Modena. Turin's masonic lodges form a temporary committee to promote a crematorium in Turin.

New Zealand – cremation is legalized by the Cemeteries Act.

Sweden – a cremation society is established.

Belgium – a cremation society is founded, but the Minister of Interior declares cremation illegal.

Britain – two of the three 'Hanham cremations' take place. The Home Office does not interfere, but Charles Cameron's cremation bill fails in parliament.

The body of English cricket is 'cremated', and 'the Ashes' sent to Australia.

1883   Italy – a controversy arises over the decision not to cremate the corpse of General Garibaldi, the Grand Master of the Grand Lodge of Italy. Ariodante Fabretti is elected president of the newly constituted Turin Cremation Society. The 'cremation temples' of Cremona, Rome, Varese and Brescia are built.

1884   Britain – William Price is acquitted for cremating his son Iesu Grist (Jesus Christ), and Justice James Fitzjames Stephen declares that cremation is not illegal.

Argentina – the first cremation in modern Argentina is performed in an improvised cremator.

The Vatican advises against cremation.

Italy – in Milan, Gaetano Pini publishes *Cremation in Italy and Abroad From 1774 to the Present Day*.

1885   Austria – in Vienna, Oskar Siedek founds the Austrian Cremeation Society 'Die Flamme'.

Britain – the first cremation takes place in Woking Crematorium.

Italy – the second Congress of Italian Cremation Societies is held in Florence.

1886   Italy – 14 crematoria and 36 cremation societies exist with 668 cremations performed since 1876.

Germany – the Association of German-speaking Organizations to Reform.

Funeral Matters and Cremations is founded in Gotha.

The Catholic Church bans cremation.

Australia – New South Wales cremation bill is passed by the Upper House but ultimately fails in the Lower House.

Denmark – the first cremation is held in Nylandsvej Crematorium in the Frederiksberg municipality of Copenhagen. The authorities then immediately close it down.

Argentina – the cremation of cholera victims begins. Buenos Aires municipality then passes a cremation by-law and several short-term crematoria are constructed.

1887   Sweden – the first modern Swedish cremation is performed at Hagalund, Solna, just outside Stockholm.

Finland – the first public presentation of the idea of cremation takes place.

USA – LeMoyne's cremator is closed down.

Australia – Adelaide, John Mildred Creed addresses the first Intercolonial Medical Congress meeting on cremation.

France – the Senate ratifies a cremation law, effective from 1889.

Serbia – Dr Jovan Jovanovié-Zmaj publishes an article about the contemporary European cremation movement.

1888	Italy – cremation cited for the first time in law. Turin 'cremation temple' is built.

Sweden – cremation is legalized, but the law becomes a hindrance.

Denmark – Royal and Municipal Court judges declare cremation illegal.

1889   Norway – a cremation society is founded.

Finland – a cremation association is formed in Helsinki.

Switzerland – the first Swiss crematorium is inaugurated in Zurich.

France – the first modern cremation in the country is performed at Père-Lachaise, Paris.

Australia – a New South Wales Cremation Society is established.

1890   Australia – Adelaide, Dr Robert Wylde calls for the founding of a cremation society in South Australia.

Sweden – Gothenburg, the second Swedish crematorium, becomes operational.

Germany – Berlin hosts an International Cremation Congress.

1891   Germany – Heidelberg Crematorium opens, the country's second.

Australia – the new Cremation Society of South Australia secures Australia's first cremation legislation.

Denmark – the Supreme Court confirms that cremation is prohibited.

1892   Italy – cremation receives detailed legal regulation for the first time.

Germany – Hamburg crematorium opens, the country's third.

USA – Dr. W.H. Curtis writes a report on cremation to the American Public Health Association.

Australia – Victoria, a Royal Society committee to investigate cremation reports strongly in its favour. The Cremation Society of Victoria is formed.

Norway – the Cremation Society delivers its first draft cremation bill to the Ministry of Justice. Bergen Cremation Society is established.

Britain – Manchester crematorium opens, the second in Britain.

Denmark – cremation is legalized in the first cremation law.

1893   Britain – the House of Commons Select Committee on Death Certification is established.

Denmark – the first legal cremations occur after the reopening of Nylandsvej crematorium.

1894   Hungary – Budapest hosts the Eighth International Congress on Hygiene, the sixth Federation of German-Language Cremation Societies Conference and an International Cremation Congress.

New Zealand – the Napier Cremation Society formed.

USA – the Central Conference of American Rabbis 'decides that no ritual associated with burial should be withheld in the case of cremation, and that ashes could unquestionably be buried in Jewish cemeteries'.

Britain – the first Act of Parliament concerning cremation, the Cardiff Corporation Act, is passed.

Italy – Ariodante Fabretti is cremated at Turin.

1895   Australia – the first cremation of a European, takes place on a log pyre, in Melbourne. Two Indians are also cremated.

New Zealand – the Cemeteries Act Amendment allows municipal cemeteries to make provision for cremation.

1896   Italy – Milan crematorium's cremation system is improved by Paolo Gorini.

1897   Italy – the Genoese Cremation Society founded.

Australia – Dr Gregory Sprott tells the Royal Society of Tasmania that cremation is inevitable.

1898   Norway – the first Cremation Act is adopted.

1899   'Czech lands'- the Association for Cremation is founded.

France – Rouen, the country's second crematorium opens.

Hong Kong – a 'Western' crematorium for Europeans is opened.

1900   USA – there are 24 crematoria in existence with 13 381 cremations performed since 1876.

New Zealand – Dunedin cremation society is formed.

Britain – the London Cremation Company is established.

1901   Britain – Kingston-upon-Hull, the first British municipal crematorium opens.

Denmark – poet Sophus Schandorph is cremated.

1902   Britain – the Cremation Act is passed. The London Cremation Company opens its Golders Green crematorium, the seventh in Britain and London's first crematorium.

Denmark – Minister Viggo Hørup is cremated. The National Cremation Association, the second Danish cremation society, is founded.

Canada – Mount Royal Crematorium opens in Montreal. The Quebec parliament approves the necessary legislation but places restrictions on the facility.

1903   Australia – the Cremation Bill finally passes through the Victoria Parliament after failures in 1895, 1898 and 1899–1900. In Adelaide the first human cremation in a purpose-built modern crematorium in Australia takes place.

Britain – the first set of Cremation Regulations is introduced.

Argentina – 'Chacarita' crematorium opens in Buenos Aires but a new cremation by-law complicates matters.

France – the country's third crematorium opens in Reims.

1904   Austria – the Labour Branch Society for Cremation 'Die Flamme' is founded.

Germany – Hamburg, Orthodox authority Rabbi Meir Lerner issues a 'widely cited denunciation of cremation'.

Britain – 13 crematoria are operational. Architect Albert Chambers Freeman publishes *Crematoria in Great Britain and Abroad*.

Serbia – Belgrade, a cremation society is founded in Belgrade.

Hungary – the government refuses to approve the cremation society's statutes thereby ensuring that it cannot exist legally.

Luxembourg – Dr Arthur Daubenfeld establishes a cremation society.

1905   Australia – In the state of Victoria the first cremation under the 1903 Cremation Act is carried out in primitive facilities.

Tasmania – the Cremation Act 1905 is passed and two open-air cremations are performed.

New Zealand – Auckland cremation society is formed.

1906   Germany – the Kingdom of Saxony legalizes cremation.

Belgium – a new cremation society, the Belgian Society for the Propagation of Cremation, is established.

1907   Norway – the first crematorium in Norway is inaugurated in Bergen and the first modern cremation conducted.

USA – 'Hygienic Wagon and Portable Furnace' is patented.

1908   Australia – Cremation Society of New South Wales is founded.

1909   Italy – 31 crematoria are operating and 6404 cremations have been performed since 1876.

Austria – the Administrative Court rejects the construction of Graz Crematorium.

New Zealand – the first crematorium is erected in Karori, Wellington.

Norway – the second Norwegian crematorium is inaugurated in Christiana (Oslo).

1910   Germany – 20 crematoria are functioning.

Belgium – Brussels hosts an International Cremation Congress.

1911   Germany – Dresden Crematorium opens; the 'world's most lavish' city hosts the International Cremation Congress.

Italy – an International Cremation Congress is held in Turin during the International Exposition of Industry and Labour.

China – Dr Wu Lien-Teh uses cremation to control an outbreak of the pneumonic plague in the city of Harbin, Manchuria.

1912   Greece – the country's first debate over cremation takes place.

Australia – Cremation Society of Tasmania is formed. A formal cremation campaign is launched in Queensland.

Luxembourg – first cremation of a cremation society member takes place in Mayence (Germany).

1913   USA – In Detroit, the Cremation Association of America (CAA) – later to become the

Cremation Association of North America (CANA) in 1975 – is formed. Fifty-two crematoria perform 10 119 cremations that year.

Germany – Social-democratic politician August Bebel is cremated – an event that is later considered a 'watershed'.

Norway – a new, more favourable Cremation Act is passed.

Canada – the second Canadian crematorium is opened in Vancouver.

1914	Netherlands – the first modern cremation takes place in the first Dutch crematorium at Velsen.

Sweden – the Baltic Exposition held at Malmö exhibits a cremation room.

Denmark – the two Danish cremation associations merge to form the Danish Cremation Association.

Italy – Milan hosts an International Cremation Congress.

Monaco – a crematorium is built but never permitted to operate by the Catholic Prince.

1915   Australia – the Brisbane Cremation Association is established.

Britain – open-air cremation of Indian soldiers who had died of war-wounds.

USA – Revolutionary trade unionist Joe Hill is cremated.

Iceland – the Icelandic Parliament (*Alþingi*) passes a law on cremation.

1916   Germany – Gotha hosts an International Cremation Congress.

Luxembourg – a joint stock company to construct a crematorium is established.

1917   The Code of Canon Law (1203) restates the Vatican's stance on cremation.

1918   The Great War (1914–18) ends. Although cremation was little used on the battlefield, the war has many far-reaching effects on the acceptance of cremation in Britain.

Russia – a decree legalizes cremation.

South Africa – the first furnace (rather than 'open-pyre' crematoria) is built by the municipality of Johannesburg.

Czechoslovakia – Liberec Crematorium is finally operational, after the initial decision to build it was taken in 1898 and the building's construction was completed in 1915.

1919   Czechoslovakia – the national parliament approves a cremation law, and the first cremation is performed at Liberec.

Netherlands – the Workers' Association for Cremation established.

USA – Seventy crematoria are in existence.

Norway – the third crematorium in Norway opens in Trondheim.

1920   Sweden – Stockholm Woodland Cemetery is completed.

Russia – an experimental crematorium is built in Leningrad, and the first official cremation in Russia takes place.

1922   Argentina – the Argentine Cremation Association is established. Buenos Aires. A new cremation by-law passes unanimously and unmodified.

1923   Austria – the first modern cremation is performed in Wien-Simmering Crematorium in Vienna.

Australia – New South Wales cremationists reorganize and form the Cremation Society of Australia.

Romania – a cremation society is formed.

1924   Russia – a cremation exhibition is held in Moscow. Lenin is embalmed rather than cremated.

Australia – a new Cremation Society of Victoria is established.

Britain – the Federation of British Cremation Authorities is formed. There are 16 operational crematoria.

Austria – the Constitutional Court, after a second examination of the issue, confirms the lawfulness of cremation.

1925   Austria – the insurance-based Austrian People's Cremation Society is founded.

Australia – a modern crematorium built in Rookwood Cemetery is immediately successful.

Italy – Lugano hosts an International Cremation Congress.

Portugal – the first cremation occurs at Alto de Saõ João Crematorium, Lisbon.

1926   Finland – the first modern cremation is performed.

South Africa – the country's second crematorium is built in Durban.

1927   Russia – the first crematorium is opened in Moscow and the first modern cremation performed. Senior Bolshevik leaders are cremated (except Stalin initially). The Society for the Dissemination of the Idea of Cremation is founded.

Poland – the first modern cremation is performed.

Australia – Melbourne opens a modern crematorium.

China – the first crematoria are opened in Shanghai and Dalian.

1928   Argentina – Buenos Aires municipality unanimously allows the deposit of ashes in churches.

Scotland – a separate set of Cremation Regulations is approved.

Romania – Bucharest, the country's first crematorium opens and functions.

1929   Italy – the Agreement (*Concordato*) between the fascist regime and the Catholic Church is signed.

1930   England and Wales – 21 crematoria are operating.

Germany – 102 crematoria are operating.

Korea – a crematorium is built in Seoul.

Belgium – a crematorium is constructed in Uccle, south of Brussels, but is not opened.

Iceland – Reykjavík municipality selects a committee to formulate suggestions for a crematorium.

France – the French Cremation Federation is formed.

1931   Slovenia – Maribor, the second Yugoslavian cremation society is established.

Hungary – a crematorium is built in Debrecen, but is not permitted to operate.

1932   Belgium – the first cremation law passed, and first modern cremation in Belgium takes place.

            South Africa – the country's third crematorium is built in Johannesburg.

            Serbia and Croatia – Belgrade city council allocates land to the cremation society to build a crematorium. A new Zagreb cremation society is established.

            Britain – Frederick George Marshall introduces the idea of a Book of Remembrance to the Cremation Society.

1933   Britain – the Cremation Society forms the Council for the Disposal of the Dead.

            Canada – the third Canadian crematorium is opened in Toronto.

1934   Austria – the new authoritarian clerical-conservative regime dissolves the Labour Cremation Society and confiscates its assets.

            Germany – the Nazis introduce a single national cremation law placing cremation on an equal footing with burial.

            Britain – *Pharos* is first published.

            Iceland – the Society for Cremation is founded.

1935   Scotland – new Cremation Regulations are introduced.

1936   Italy – the Italian Federation for Cremation succeeds in organizing its national congress in Turin.

            Portugal – Alto de Saõ João Crematorium in Lisbon is closed by the dictatorial regime, the Estado Novo.

            Czechoslovakia – Prague hosts an International Cremation Congress.

            Latin America – cremation is legalized in many countries but this does not lead to the immediate establishment of crematoria.

1937   Hong Kong – the Hindu and Japanese communities open crematoria.

1938   Britain – the first Book of Remembrance is installed at Woking Crematorium. London hosts the International Cremation Congress that forms the ICF.

            Austria – the Nazis integrate the cremation society into the Ostmärkische Feuerbestattung.

            Rhodesia – the Federation of Women's Institutes calls for cremation to be made possible in the country.

1939   Britain – Princess Louise (daughter of Queen Victoria), and Sigmund Freud are cremated at Golders Green Crematorium. Fifty-eight crematoria are operating.

            Yugoslavia – a cremation federation is formed.

1940   The Nazis fit Dachau and Buchenwald concentration camps with their first crematoria and others follow in Auschwitz and Majdanek (Poland) before 1942. Cremation becomes the primary means of corpse disposal in the camps.

1943   Greece – the first legal ban on cremation ban is issued.

            Austria – The Nazis greatly expand the Auschwitz cremation facility.

1944   Britain – the Church of England Convocation of Canterbury publishes a report on cremation issues.

1945	Germany – by late January concentration camp crematoria are destroyed. Dresden is target of heaviest aerial bombardment in the Second World War.
	Japan – Hiroshima and Nagasaki are the targets for the first atomic bombs.
	The Second World War (1939–45) ends. The war has numerous significant effects on cremation, although, once more, it is not employed on the field of combat.
	Austria – the Austrian Cremation Society 'Die Flamme' is re-established.
	Britain – the Federation of British Cremation Authorities first publishes its Code of Cremation Practice.
1946	Greece – a cremation association is formed.
1948	Northern Ireland – the Belfast Corporation (General Powers) Act is passed, empowering Belfast Corporation to build a crematorium.
	Iceland – a crematorium built at Fossvogur Church, Reykjavik, and the first modern cremation in Iceland takes place.
	Netherlands – The Hague hosts an ICF Triennial Congress.
	Venezuela – cremation becomes accepted in law but this does not stimulate its development.
1949	Malaya – Ipoh, the Cremation Society of Perak is formed, but is short-lived.
1950	Ghana – Cape Coast, first crematorium is established.
	China – the Haihui Temple crematorium set up in Shanghai with governmental approval.
	Malaya – the Cremation Society of Perak's 'model crematorium' opens in Ipoh.
1951	Britain – the government's Interdepartmental Committee on Cremation completes its work. There are 59 crematoria in operation.
	Denmark – Copenhagen hosts an ICF Triennial Congress.
	Hungary – Debrecen Crematorium is permitted to operate, 20 years after it was built.
	Malaya – a crematorium is opened in Penang and another one by Buddhists in Kuala Lumpur.
	Indonesia – Buddhists open the first crematorium in Surabaya.
1952	Britain – a second Cremation Act is passed.
1954	Norway – Oslo hosts an ICF Triennial Congress.
1955	Netherlands – the Burial and Cremation Act is amended to make cremation legal for the first time.
1956	Britain – Dr. M.R.R. Davies publishes *The Law of Burial, Cremation and Exhumation*.
	China – A Communist Party Central Committee working conference produces a 'proposal for cremations'.
	Argentina – the Argentine Pro-Cremation League is established.
	Rhodesia – country's first 'Western' Cremation opens in Salisbury (now Harare).
1957	Sweden – cremation achieves legal equality with burial.

	Switzerland – Zurich, hosts an ICF Triennial Congress.
1958	China – Babaoshan crematorium opens in Beijing.
	Rhodesia – the Cremation Society of Matabeleland is founded in Bulawayo.
1960	Greece – the Orthodox Church condemns cremation.
	Britain – after this date it was 'much less likely for crematoria to be established in existing cemeteries'.
	Sweden – Stockholm hosts an ICF Triennial Congress.
1961	The ICF asks Pope John XXIII to repeal the Catholic ban on cremation.
	Britain – there are 161 crematoria in operation.
	Northern Ireland – the first crematorium on the island is opened in Belfast.
1962	Rhodesia – the country's second 'Western' crematorium opens in Bulawayo.
	Hong Kong – the first 'full-sized' public crematorium opens at Sai Wan (later known as Cape Collinson).
1963	The Vatican lifts penalties attached to cremation but reiterates Church's traditional position of favouring burial.
	USA – Jessica Mitford publishes *The American Way of Death*.
1964	Finland – the second and third crematoria open in Karjaa and Espoo.
	Yugoslavia – the country's first crematorium opens in Belgrade.
1965	Britain – the Brodrick Committee is established (and reports in 1971). Cardinal Heenan sends a representative to the Cremation Society Conference.
1966	Austria – the Archbishop of Vienna officially visits Wien-Simmering Crematorium.
1967	Guatemala – a short-lived National Cremationist Association is launched.
	Indonesia – there are seven crematoria in operation, all on the island of Java.
1968	Hungary – the country's second crematorium is opened in Budapest.
1969	Suriname – a legal change allows Hindus to use open-air crematoria.
1970	New Zealand – approximately 60 per cent of deaths are followed by cremation.
1971	USA – the Telophase Society is founded by biochemist Thomas B. Weber.
	France – in Toulouse, the country's first new crematorium in 50 years opens.
1972	Greece – the Orthodox Church condemns cremation again.
	France – Grenoble hosts an ICF Triennial Congress.
	Luxembourg – a new law places burial and cremation on an equal footing.
1973	Spain – the first modern cremation is performed.
	Russia – the Nikolo-Archangelski Crematorium, which becomes the largest in Europe, opens in Moscow.
	Indonesia – a short-lived cremation society is founded.
1974	Argentina – Mendoza, the country's second crematorium is established, 78 years after the first.

1975	Denmark – a law guarantees the individual the freedom to choose the manner of their body's disposal.
	Colombia – the first interest in cremation begins.
1976	China – Mr Zhou Enlai, the first premier of New China, is cremated.
1977	USA – the Neptune Society is established by Dr. Charles Denning in San Francisco.
1978	France – the first 'truly modern' crematorium opens in Mulhouse, marking the beginning of 'modern cremation' in France.
	Yugoslavia – Ljubljana crematorium opens.
1979	Hong Kong – Diamond Hill crematorium facilities are upgraded and a new crematorium at Kwai Chung is built.
1980	China – 1183 crematoria are operational.
	France – ten crematoria are in operation.
1982	Eire – Glasnevin Crematorium is opened in Dublin, the first in Eire.
	Colombia – a crematorium opens in Bogotà.
1983	Sweden – the Cremation Society is reorganised and changes its name to the Swedish Federation of Cemeteries and Crematoria Association.
	Denmark – the Association of Danish Crematoria is founded.
	Yugoslavia – a new crematorium replaces the temporary facilities in Belgrade.
	Brazil – the country opens its first crematorium in Saū Paulo.
1984	Mexico – in Mexico City, the municipal authorities announce cremation to be the solution to disposal problems.
1985	Northern Ireland – councils are empowered to establish crematoria.
	Portugal – Alto de Saõ João crematorium in Lisbon is re-opened.
	China – the State Council produces the first administrative regulation of funerals.
	Hungary – the country's third crematorium opens in Szeged.
1986	Ghana – a Cremation Society is formed.
1987	Sweden – the Federation initiates a Research Foundation for Crematoria Techniques.
	Italy – cremation is made equal to burial in the law and becomes a free public service paid for by municipalities.
1988	Latin America – cremation begins to become more popular in several countries.
1989	India – an electric crematorium is inaugurated in Banaras (Varanasi).
1990	Britain – the Environmental Protection Act is passed.
	Monaco – a crematorium is finally opened.
1991	Depleted uranium is used in the First Gulf war.
	Netherlands – cremation and burial are considered legally equal for the first time.
	Austria – the Wiener Verein society becomes a limited company.
	Brazil – the country's second crematorium opens in Rio.

1992	Italy – the Turin Cremation Society creates the Ariodante Fabretti Study Centre.
1993	France – a new cremation law is passed.
	Mexico – the short-lived National Association of Cremationists is formed.
	Romania – the country's second crematorium opens in Bucharest.
1994	USA – Celestis is incorporated.
	El Salvador – the first crematorium starts operating.
1995	Germany – Gotha has a 90 per cent cremation rate.
	Venezuela – the country's first crematorium begins operating.
	Luxembourg – the country's first crematorium opens.
1996	Portugal – a crematorium is opened in the Prado do Repouso Cemetery, Oporto.
	Guatemala – the first crematorium begins operating.
1997	Britain – F.G. Marshall Ltd introduces the 'Visual Reference System' for Books of Remembrance.
	USA – The first Celestis service is launched.
1998	USA – Jessica Mitford's *The American Way of Death Revisited* is published posthumously.
	Italy – 37 crematoria are operational.
	Slovenia – the second Slovenian crematorium opens in Maribor.
	Peru – the country's third crematorium opens in Cuzco.
1999	USA – Celestis sends cremains to the Moon's surface.
	Britain – the Pollution Prevention and Control Act is passed.
	Italy – the Ariodante Fabretti Study Centre becomes a Foundation.
2000	Britain – a review of the law relating to Death Certification is, instituted as a result of the conviction of Dr Harold Shipman for the murder of numerous patients.
	Portugal – the fourth crematorium is officially approved in Ferreira do Alentejo (in the south).
	Eire – Mount Jerome Crematorium is opened in Dublin, the second in Eire.
	Ecuador – the first two crematoria are built, in Quito and Cuenca.
2001	Britain – the total of 18 210 028 cremations performed in the country is estimated to have saved well over 12 000 acres. It is revealed that the Scottish authorities had concluded that cremation could not be used to deal with the mass deaths caused by a nuclear strike.
	South Korea – revised legislation on funeral policy boosts cremation.
	Eire – Newlands Cross Crematorium is opened in Dublin, the third in Eire.
	Bulgaria – the country's first crematorium opens.
2002	Italy – over 40 cremation societies are in existence with more than 160 000 members in the Italian Federation.
	South Korea – 45 crematoria are operational.

China – 1500 crematoria ('funeral rooms') are in operation.

Ghana – 14 cremations take place between January and 30 August – only one is a Ghanaian. An opinion poll reveals an almost 100 per cent aversion to cremation among Christian leaders in Accra.

Kenya – the cremation of Mary Nyambura Kuria sparks controversy.

Spain – cremation is now treated as equivalent to burial by the Catholic Church.

2003   USA – the military authorities rule out the use of cremation to dispose of corpses contaminated by chemical or biological agents during the second Gulf War.

Zimbabwe – an economic crisis causes the cremation services serious problems.

CREMATION SOCIETY ARCHIVE SOURCES

The following sources have been used extensively throughout the *Encyclopedia*; they belong to the Archive of the British Cremation Society lodged at the library of Durham University, England.

JOURNALS AND NEWSLETTERS

Boletín de la Asociación Argentina de Cremación (*Bulletin of the Argentine Cremation Association*) nos 1–7, 9–12, CRE/A/AG/1.
Flacâra Sacra, newsletter of the Romanian Censua Cremation Society, CRE/AO/RO.
Oganj, newspaper of the Oganj Cremation Society of Belgrade, CRE/AO/AU.
Pharos, 1934–present day, CRE/A/UK/19.

MATERIAL FROM VARIOUS NATIONAL CREMATION SOCIETIES

USA and Canada: CANA Annual Convention Reports 1924–1954, CRE/A/US4.
France: Documents (1993), 'Documents Pour l'Histoire de la Cremation'. L'Association Crématiste de Strasbourg: Strasbourg, B/FR/4.

REPORTS OF INTERNATIONAL CREMATION CONGRESSES

1936, Prague, CRE/D4/1936/3.
1937, London, CRE/D4/1937/1.

REPORTS OF ICF TRIENNIAL CONGRESSES

1948, The Hague, CRE/D4/1948/1.
1951, Copenhagen, CRE/D4/1951/2.
1954, Oslo, CRE/D4/1954/2.
1957, Zurich, CRE/D4/1957/2.
1960, Stockholm, CRE/D4/1960/1.

OTHER ICF MATERIAL

ICF Bulletins, CRE/D3, 1961–1972.
ICF Annual Reports, CRE/D2, 1938, 1951–1976.
Programme of the 1972 ICF Congress at Grenoble, CRE/D4/1972/3.
Report of the Working Session at ICF Congress, London 29 May 1969, typescript, CRE/D4/1969/9.
Secretary General's Report to 1969 ICF Congress, London, CRE/D4/1969/1.

BRITISH CREMATION SOCIETY ARCHIVES

Correspondence, CRE/P/2.
Newspaper cuttings, CRE/H/1, from 1874.

SELECT BIBLIOGRAPHY

Ariès, P. (1977), *The Hour of Our Death*, London: Penguin.

Augé, Marc (1995), *Non-places: Introduction to an Anthropology of Super-modernity*, trans. John Howe, London: Verso.

Augustine, St (1945), *The City of God*, Vol. 2, ed. R.V.G. Tasker, London: J.M. Dent and Son.

Aztecs (2002), London: Royal Academy of Arts.

Basevi, W.H.F. (1920), *The Burial of the Dead*, London: Routledge and Sons.

Bloch, Maurice (1992), *Prey into Hunter*, Cambridge: Cambridge University Press.

Bloch, Maurice and Parry, Jonathan (1982), *Death and the Regeneration of Life*, Cambridge: Cambridge University Press.

Browne, Sir Thomas (1893), *Hydriotaphia Urn Burial; With an Account of Some Urns Found at Brampton in Norfolk*, with introduction and notes by Sir John Evans, London: Charles Whittingham and Co. at the Chiswick Press.

Buber, Martin (1958) *I and Thou* (2nd rev. edn), trans. Ronald Gregor Smith, Edinburgh: T. & T. Clark.

Burkert, Walter (1983), *Homo Necans: The Anthropology of Ancient Greek Sacrificial Ritual and Myth*, trans. Peter Bing, Berkeley: University of California Press.

Campbell, Joseph (1959), *The Masks of God: Primitive Mythology*. London: Souvenir Press.

Cappers, Wim (1999), *Vuurproef voor een grondrecht*, Zutphen: Walburg Pers.

Catholic Church (1994), *Catechism of the Catholic Church*, London: Chapman.

Chagnon, N.A. (1992), *Yanomamo*, New York: Harcourt Brace College Publishers.

Chardin, Teilhard de (1970), *Hymn of the Universe*. London: Collins (Fontana).

Church of England (1938), *The Report of the Commission on Doctrine Appointed by the Archbishop of Canterbury and York in 1922*. London: SPCK.

Church of England Doctrine Commission (1996), *The Mystery of Salvation*, London: Church House Publishing.

Cicero (1972), *The Nature of the Gods*, trans. Horace C.P. McGregor, intro. J.M. Ross, Harmondsworth: Penguin. First published 1944.

Cobb, J.S. (1901) *A Quarter-Century of Cremation in North America*, Boston, MA: Knight and Millet.

Curl, J. Stevens, (2001), *The Victorian Celebration of Death*, Stroud: Sutton.

Daly, Brian E. (1991), *The Hope of the Early Church: A Handbook of Patristic Eschatology*, Cambridge: Cambridge University Press.

Dante, Alighieri (1955), *The Divine Comedy – 2 Purgatory*, trans. Dorothy L. Sayers, London: Penguin Books.

Davies, Douglas J. (1990), *Cremation Today and Tomorrow*, Nottingham: Alcuin/GROW Books.

Davies, Douglas J. (1995), *British Crematoria in Public Profile*, London: The Cremation Society of Great Britain.

Davies, Douglas J. (1996), 'The Sacred Crematorium', *Mortality*, 1(1): 83–94.

Davies, Douglas J. (1997), 'Theologies of Disposal', in P.C. Jupp and T. Rogers (eds), *Interpreting Death: Christian Theology and Pastoral Practice*, London: Cassell.

Davies, Douglas J. (2000a), 'Robert Hertz: The Social Triumph over Death', *Mortality*, 5(1): 97–102.

Davies, Douglas J. (2000b), *The Mormon Culture of Salvation*, Aldershot: Ashgate.

Davies, Douglas J. (2002), *Death, Ritual and Belief* (2nd rev. edn), London: Continuum.

Davies, Douglas J. (2005), *A Brief History of Death*, Oxford: Blackwell.

Davies, Douglas J. and Guest, Mathew (1999), 'Disposal of Cremated Remains', *Pharos*, Spring: 26–30.

Davies Douglas J. and Shaw, Alister (1995), *Reusing Old Graves: A Report on Popular British Attitudes*, Crayford: Shaw and Sons.

Denziger, Heinrich (ed.) (1967), *Enchiridion symbolorum definitionum et declarationum de rebus fidei et morum / quod primum edidit Henricus Denzinger; et quod funditus retractavit auxit notulis ornavit Adolfus Schonmetzer. Editio 34 emendata*, Freiburg : Herder.

Eassie, William (1875), *Cremation of the Dead: Its History and Bearings upon Public Health*, London: Smith, Elder & Co.

Eggers, Dave (2000), *A Heartbreaking Work of Staggering Genius*, New York: Simon and Schuster.

Eliade, Mircea (1960), *Myths, Dreams and Mysteries*, London: Collins, Fontana Library.

Eliade, Mircea (1979), *A History of Religious Ideas*, Vol. 1, London: Collins.

Erichsen, Hugo (1887), *The Cremation of the Dead*, Detroit, Mich: D.O. Haynes and Co.

Evans, W.E.D. (1963), *The Chemistry of Death*, Springfield, ILL: Charles C. Thomas Publisher.

Fraser, James W. (1965), *Cremation: Is it Christian?*, Neptune, NJ: Loizeau Brothers.

Frazer, James G. (1930), *Myths of the Origin of Fire*, London: Macmillan.

Georgeacopol-Winischhofer, U., Wehdorn A. and Wehdorn, M. (1997), *75 Jahre Feuerhalle der Stadt Wien*, Vienna: Stadt Wien, Magistratsabteilung 43 Städtische Bestattung.

Girard, René (1986), *The Scapegoat*, Baltimore, MD: John Hopkins University Press.

Gittings, C. (1984), *Death, Burial and the Individual*, London: Routledge.

Hertz, R. (1960), *Death and the Right Hand*, trans. Rodney and Claudia Needham, London: Cohen & West. First published 1907.

Hocart, A.M. (1973) *The Life-Giving Myth and Other Essays*, intro. Rodney Needham, London: Tavistock Publications with Methuen and Co. Ltd. First published 1952.

Homer (1972), *The Odyssey*, trans. E.V. Rieu, Harmondsworth: Penguin.

Howarth, Glennys (1996), *Last Rites: The Work of the Modern Funeral Director*, Amityville, NY: Baywood Publishing Company, Inc.

Inge, John (2003), *A Christian Theology of Place*, Aldershot: Ashgate.

Irion, Paul C. (1968), *Cremation*, Philadelphia: Fortress Press.

James, M.R. (1953), *The Apocryphal New Testament*, Oxford: Clarendon Press.

Jones, Lindsay (2000), *The Hermeneutics of Sacred Architecture, Vol. 1: Monumental Occasions*, Cambridge, MA: Harvard Center for the Study of World Religions.

Jung, C.G. (1993), *Psychology and Alchemy* (2nd edn), trans. R.F.C. Hull, London: Routledge. First published 1944.

Jupp, Peter (1990), *From Dust to Ashes: The Teplacement of Burial by Cremation in England 1840–1967*, London: Congregational Memorial Hall Trust.

Jupp, P. and Rogers, T. (1997), *Interpreting Death*, London: Cassell.

Knipe, David M. (1975), *In the Image of Fire, Vedic Experiences of Heat*, Delhi: Motilal Banarsidass.

Lahtinen, Tuomo (1989), *Kremering in Finland*, Åbo: Åbo Akademi.

Kübler-Ross, Elisabeth (1970), *On Death and Dying*, London: Tavistock.

Levenson, J.D. (1993), *The Death and Resurrection of the Beloved Son: The Transformation of Child Sacrifice in Judaism and Christianity*, New Haven, CT: Yale University Press.

Lévi-Strauss, Claude (1970), *The Raw and the Cooked*, London: Jonathan Cape.

Lincoln, Bruce (1991), *Death, War and Sacrifice, Studies in Ideology and Practice*, Chicago: Chicago University Press.

Litten, J. (1991), T*he English Way of Death: The Common Funeral since 1450*, London: Robert Hale.

Lynch, Thomas (1997), *The Undertaking*, London: Jonathan Cape.

Malinowski, Bronislaw (1974), *Magic, Science and Religion and Other Essays*, London: Souvenir Press. First published 1948.

Marett, R.R. (1933), *Sacraments of Simple Folk*, Oxford: Clarendon Press.

Nicol, Robert (1994), *At the End of the Road*, St Leonards: Allen & Unwin.

Nicol, Robert (2003), *The Grave or Burning Question. A Centenary History of Cremation in Australia*, Adelaide: Adelaide Cemeteries Authority.

Nigosian, S.A. (1993), *The Zoroastrian Faith*, Montreal and Kingston: McGill-Queen's University Press.

Nygren, Anders (1982), *Agape and Eros*, trans. Philip S. Watson, London: SPCK.

Parry, J.P. (1994), *Death in Banaras*, Cambridge: Cambridge University Press.

Polson, C.J., Brittain, R.P. and Marshall, T.K. (1953), *The Disposal of the Dead*, New York: Philosophical Library.

Prothero, Stephen. (2001), *Purified by Fire: A History of Cremation in America*, Berkeley: University of California Press.

Raglan, Lord (1964), *The Temple and the House*, London: Routledge and Kegan Paul.

Rappaport, Roy A. (1999), *Ritual and Religion in the Making of Humanity*, Cambridge: Cambridge University Press.

Richardson, R. (1987), *Death, Dissection and the Destitute*, London: Routledge and Kegan Paul.

Robinson, W. (1880), *God's Acre Beautiful; Or, the Cemeteries of the Future*, London: John Murray.

Robinson, W. (1889), *Cremation and Urn-burial; Or, the Cemeteries of the Future*, London: Cassell.

Smale, David A. (2002), *Davies' Law of Burial, Cremation and Exhumation* (7th edn), Crayford: Shaw and Sons.

Snodgrass, Adrian (1992), *The Symbolism of the Stupa*, Delhi: Motilal Banarsidass.

Thomas, Keith (1973), *Religion and the Decline of Magic*, Harmondsworth: Penguin Books.

Thompson, Henry (1874), 'The Treatment of the Body after Death', *Contemporary Review*, 23: 319–28.

Turner, Harold W. (1979), *From Temple to Meeting House: The Phenomenology and Theology of Places of Worship*, The Hague: Mouton.

Turner, Victor (1969), *The Ritual Process*, London: Routledge and Kegan Paul.

Van Gennep, Arnold (1960), *The Rites of Passage*, London: Routledge & Kegan Paul. First published 1909.

Van Gennep, Arnold (1967), *The Semi-Scholars*, trans. and ed. Rodney Needham, London: Routledge & Kegan Paul. First published 1911.

Watson, William (1909), *New Poems*, London: John Lane, The Bodley Head.

Weber, Frederick Parkes (1918), *Aspects of Death and Correlated Aspects of Life in Art, Epigram and Poetry*, London: T. Fisher Unwin.

Winter, Henning (2001), *Die Architectur der Krematorien im Deutschen Reich 1878–1918*, Kasseler Studien zur Sepulkralkultur, Bd. 10. Dettelbach: Verlag J. H. Roell.

Winter, J. (1995), *Sites of Memory, Sites of Mourning*, Cambridge: Cambridge University Press.

INDEX